To Father
love from John
Christmas 1992.

D1437304

THE VIEW FROM NO.11

Also by Nigel Lawson
(with Jock Bruce-Gardyne) *The Power Game*

NIGEL LAWSON

THE VIEW FROM No. 11

MEMOIRS OF A TORY RADICAL

BANTAM PRESS

LONDON · NEW YORK · TORONTO · SYDNEY · AUCKLAND

TRANSWORLD PUBLISHERS LTD
61-63 Uxbridge Road, London W5 5SA

TRANSWORLD PUBLISHERS (AUSTRALIA) PTY LTD
15-25 Helles Avenue, Moorebank, NSW 2170

TRANSWORLD PUBLISHERS (NZ) LTD
3 William Pickering Drive, Albany, Auckland

Published 1992 by Bantam Press
a division of Transworld Publishers Ltd
Copyright © Nigel Lawson 1992

A catalogue record for this book is available from the British Library

ISBN 0593 022181

Typeset in 10/12pt Times by
Chippendale Type Ltd, Otley, West Yorkshire.
Printed in Great Britain by
Mackays of Chatham Plc, Chatham, Kent

To my children

CONTENTS

CONTENTS

CHAPTER 8: THE BLACK ART OF MONETARY CONTROL

CHAPTER 9: 1981 – A TIGHT AND CONTROVERSIAL BUDGET

CHAPTER 10: 'THERE IS NO ALTERNATIVE'

PART TWO: CABINET MINISTER

CHAPTER 11: ON BECOMING A SECRETARY OF STATE

CONTENTS

CHAPTER 19: PRIVATIZATION – 2: THE BIRTH OF POPULAR CHAPITALISM

CHAPTER 20: PRIVATIZATION – 3: THE PROGRAMME REACHES A CLIMAX

PART THREE: THE VIEW FROM NUMBER ELEVEN

CHAPTER 21: BECOMING CHANCELLOR

CHAPTER 22: ALL THE CHANCELLOR'S MEN

CONTENTS

CHAPTER 27: AN AGENDA FOR TAX REFORM

CHAPTER 28: 1984 – MY FIRST BUDGET

CHAPTER 29: 1985 – PROTESTS AND PENSIONS

CHAPTER 30: 1986 – PRINCIPLES AND A PENNY OFF

CONTENTS

CHAPTER 35: TRADE UNIONS AND THE LABOUR MARKET

CHAPTER 36: THE MYTH OF A MONETARIST GOLDEN AGE

CHAPTER 37: THE STERLING CRISIS OF 1984–85

CHAPTER 38: 'JUDGE AND JURY'

CHAPTER 39: ENTER THE ERM

CONTENTS

CHAPTER 44: . . . TO THE LOUVRE

PART FOUR: POLICIES AND PEOPLE

CHAPTER 45: THE STORY OF THE POLL TAX – 1

CHAPTER 46: THE STORY OF THE POLL TAX – 2

CHAPTER 47: REFORMING SOCIAL SECURITY

CHAPTER 48 REFORMING EDUCATION

CONTENTS

CHAPTER 54: A SURFEIT OF RESIGNATIONS

CHAPTER 55: 1987 – A PRE-ELECTION BUDGET

CHAPTER 56: AN ELECTION WON ON THE ECONOMY

CHAPTER 57: POLITICS AFTER THE POLLS

CHAPTER 58: PUBLIC SPENDING REVISITED

CONTENTS

CONTENTS

CONTENTS

PART SIX: ANNEXES

LIST OF ILLUSTRATIONS

LIST OF ILLUSTRATIONS

FOREWORD

THIS IS NOT AN autobiography, but a ministerial, and in particular a Chancellorial, memoir. In other words, it excludes all that is most important in life. But politics and political office do matter, particularly when they are about more than office for its own sake. That was certainly the case with the Thatcher era, and with my part in it.

If this book is not an autobiography, neither is it an essay in the higher economic scholasticism. Although I have been heavily involved in economic policy and have sought to come to terms with rival economic ideas, I have done so as a politician rather than as an economist. But no account either of the Conservative Government of the 1980s or of the work of a modern Chancellor of the Exchequer can make sense without an explanation of the economic thinking that lay behind so many of the key decisions that were taken. I have sought to provide this in as plain English as the subject matter permits, with a few charts and tables and a glossary to ease the reader's path.

When I started this book I drafted it in strict chronological order, describing the events of 1979–89 as they happened. This certainly conveyed the reality of a Minister's, and in particular a Chancellor's life, with so many different problems and issues jostling to be addressed at one and the same time. But it soon became clear that this real-life treatment would make the story all but incomprehensible. I have therefore compromised between the chronological approach and dealing with one subject at a time. As a result, some of the key conclusions emerge early on in the book. I have, however, liberally sprinkled dates to enable the reader to follow what was happening when.

Although the book is an account of the period, and of my part in it, as I saw it and see it, and in that sense is inevitably subjective, I have sought to be both accurate and fair. Should any inaccuracies have none the less inadvertently crept in – for I did not keep a diary – I apologize; but I would be surprised if they alter the account in any material way.

One point, however, needs to be made clear at the outset. The book was virtually completed before the turmoil in the foreign markets of mid-September 1992, which led to the departure of sterling from the European exchange rate mechanism. My long-suffering publisher has kindly allowed me to insert a very brief comment on that sorry event in the final chapter of the book; but that is all – except to add that nothing that has happened has caused me to resile from the view I took of the ERM as Chancellor.

Many readers may be particularly interested in the dramatic events leading up to my resignation as Chancellor in October 1989, recounted in part four of the book. But I would direct the reader's attention to the first three parts, which are intended to shed some light on the working of British government. Most books about how decisions are taken in government tend to be written by academics or journalists: indeed, as a journalist many years ago, I co-wrote one myself. This, book gives the view from the inside. A further reason for directing readers to the first three parts is that many of the central policies of the Thatcher era were formulated at a very early stage, and remained in place thereafter. Thus some of the main discussion of the issues, and even of personalities, occurs in these parts.

Lastly, the most obvious characteristic of this book is that it is a very long one. In one of his novels, Disraeli writes 'Read no history: nothing but biography, for that is life without theory'. This book is long, at least in part, because it contains something of all three. I have sought to make this tolerable to the modern reader by providing an unusually detailed table of contents. This should be treated, not as a table d'hôte, but more as an à la carte menu; enabling the reader to choose those dishes he or she likes, and to omit those he or she finds indigestible. I hope, however, that most will sample most.

ACKNOWLEDGEMENTS

FIRST AND FOREMOST, I must thank my wife, Thérèse, who saw far too little of me during our time at Number 11 and far too much of me while I was at home writing this book, and who has given me so much support – often against her better judgement.

I am most grateful to my indefatigable research assistant, Dominic Hobson, whose diligence in going through the published literature on the period and marrying it with my own recollections was of particular help to me.

I must also thank Samuel Brittan, a good friend since our days at *The Financial Times* together three dozen years ago, during which time we seem to have been engaged in almost continuous conversation about many of the issues discussed in this book, and much else besides. I have benefited greatly both from his suggestions about the structure of the book and from his constructive criticisms of the various drafts, of which he kindly read every word. He must not, however, be assumed to share any of the views expressed. Some others read parts of the book in draft; and, in the midst of their busy lives, let me have their comments: I thank them, too.

I must also thank my publisher, Mark Barty-King, for his forebearance in receiving a book far longer and thus later than he had expected, and to his assistant, Jennie Bull, who worked so heroically on it. I am greatly indebted to Jacqui Etheridge, who impeccably typed the final draft, cheerfully working at all hours to complete the job; while Anne Shotts efficiently typed some early drafts, often at very short notice. Mandy Bentley and Buffy Gaydon also helped out with the typing.

I am grateful, too, to the admirable staff of the House of Commons library, who so diligently answered all my queries, and equally to *The Financial Times* library, in particular its head, Mary Batten, for providing Dominic Hobson with access to its facilities and much patience and help. Christopher Flood provided up-to-date numerical data, while David Snaddon and Peter Cheek went out of their way to help with research and checking. The paper's graphics department, in particular Christopher Walker, very kindly provided most of the charts and tables on a freelance basis.

I must thank the Treasury, my home from home for so many years, for taking so much trouble to find almost all the key papers of the period for which I asked them, and for making a room available to me in which to re-read them; and Mr William Keegan, whose book about me I cannot entirely endorse, but which contains references, especially in relation to the early years, which saved me considerable trouble.

Finally, my thanks are due to my son, Tom, for his patience in teaching me how to use a word-processor.

Newnham, 1992

PART ONE

——

Foundations

CHAPTER 1

FORMATIVE YEARS

Beginnings · Early Beliefs · Economic Evolution

Beginnings

BY WAY OF VERY brief personal background, I was born on 11 March 1932 into a comfortable Hampstead household, complete with nanny, cook and parlourmaid. My father was a tea merchant, the proprietor of a small but successful firm in the City of London and my mother's father was the wealthy senior partner of a firm of stockbrokers. My family was not an especially political one. When the war ended I was sent to Westminster School, where my father had been educated. Unlike many public schools, Westminster is a worldly place. My main intellectual interest then was mathematics, in which I won a scholarship to Christ Church, Oxford, in 1951. I had intended to read law, but was dissuaded by a distinguished former Law Officer, Sir John Simon, who advised me that the study of law at Oxford was a poor preparation for the bar, which at that time I was contemplating as a future career. So, like many others, I read Philosophy, Politics and Economics (PPE), specializing in philosophy, partly because of a natural affinity between mathematics and philosophy.

Oxford philosophy was much influenced at the time by the school of Linguistic Analysis, and I became fascinated by it. It was in many ways an arid school, being concerned solely with the logical elucidation of every proposition. But it trained its practitioners to think clearly and identify nonsense, however dressed up, which was not a bad training for politics. Philosophy satisfied my taste for theory: my interest in economics lay in its practical application to policy. Economic policies cannot be chosen just by references to the eternal verities. Too much depends on the circumstances of time and place. Moreover, if there are any such verities, they are probably of the non-technical, uncomfortable kind listed in Kipling's *The Gods of the Copybook Headings.**

My extra-mural interests were not primarily political. Much has been made of a taste for poker, but it is an interest shared by many undergraduates and I have not played since I left Oxford. I acted, without great distinction, fenced, skied (for the University second six) and went to a large number of parties. I never spoke at the Oxford Union, nor did I bother to join the University Conservative Association. This was mainly because my contemporaries in the acting set were rather more amusing than those in the political set. I did join a somewhat decadent high Tory dining club, the Chatham, where a large amount of mulled claret was consumed and the invited speakers tended to be Tory mavericks like Leo Amery, Bob Boothby and 'Hinch' Hinchingbrooke. My only serious political involvement was with the Strasbourg Club, which was devoted to the then unfashionable cause of European union, and of which I became president.

After (somewhat to my surprise) getting a first, and two years' national service with the Navy, where I was lucky enough to be given my own command (a motor torpedo-boat), in the summer of 1956 I joined the staff of the *Financial Times,* where my contemporaries included Andrew Shonfield, William Rees-Mogg, Michael Shanks, Samuel Brittan and Jock Bruce-Gardyne. The choice was wholly fortuitous. Having been rejected by the Foreign Office, I thought of journalism as an alternative way of becoming involved in public affairs. The *FT* was at that time the only national newspaper which did not insist on preliminary apprenticeship in the provinces, and took untrained graduates straight from Oxford or Cambridge.

I stayed there a little over four years, as feature writer, industrial reporter, oil correspondent, features editor, and finally chief writer of the Lex column, and learned a great deal, under the remarkable editorship of Gordon Newton, before leaving to become the first City Editor of the newly formed *Sunday Telegraph.* I always endeavoured in my columns to discuss economics in a manner intelligible to the layman. Although I probably failed more often than not, it was mainly for this reason that Oliver Poole, the chairman of *The Financial Times*

---

*For instance:
  In the Carboniferous Epoch, we were promised Abundance for all,
  By robbing selected Peter to pay for collective Paul;
  But, though we had plenty of Money, there was nothing Money could buy,
  And the Gods of the Copybook Headings said: 'If you don't work you die'.

and joint chairman of the Conservative Party, offered me in 1963 a post in the office of the Prime Minister, Harold Macmillan, to help him with his political speeches.

Macmillan resigned almost immediately on health grounds. I stayed on throughout the premiership of Sir Alec Douglas-Home, who claimed to understand economics only by using matchsticks. This was a characteristically modest assessment of his talents, and I came to admire Alec enormously. Working for the Prime Minister allowed me a unique glimpse of politics and government from the centre. After some seven years as a critical observer of the nation's economic management, proximity to the exercise of power sharpened the urge to test my criticisms in practice. I felt I ought to get out on the field and play.

Not wishing to be a backroom boy, however eminent, I declined the Directorship of the Conservative Research Department after the 1964 General Election and at the end of 1965 I was appointed editor of the *Spectator* in succession to Iain Macleod, where I stayed for the next four and a half years. I was sacked by the then proprietor, who wished to control editorial policy himself, while I was away contesting (unsuccessfully) the then Labour seat of Eton and Slough in the 1970 general election. I was selected in 1972 as prospective Conservative candidate for Blaby in Leicestershire, a new and very much more promising constituency in the heart of England, between Leicester and Rugby. Confident of electoral success, I took up a research fellowship at Nuffield College, Oxford later that year. I completed there much of my share of the work which culminated in the book I published with my old friend Jock Bruce-Gardyne in 1976, *The Power Game*. It examined four major political decisions and among its conclusions was the proposition that 'So often it is pure hazard which tips the scale of decision in the end'. I was eventually elected Member of Parliament for Blaby in February 1974, on the eve of my forty-second birthday.

Early Beliefs

Although my parliamentary career started late, my political recollections go back to the immediate post-war years. I suppose nowadays nobody of any significance calls himself or herself a socialist, except between consenting adults in private, without at least a twinge of embarrassment. That was decidedly not the case when my political views were formed. The Attlee Labour Government that had swept into office with a landslide majority in 1945 was proud to call itself socialist, and determined to build a new socialist Jerusalem in Britain. After all, had not the war been won thanks to an unprecedented co-ordination of national activity by State planning and State control? Surely this formula would prove just as triumphant in winning the peace – particularly since the old hierarchical

5

order had been swept aside by a new spirit of egalitarianism symbolized by the ration book and the queue.

For Churchill's Conservatives, the war had not been about that at all. It was a victory not for State planning and State control, but for the forces of freedom; and the spirit that had welded the nation together had been not egalitarianism but patriotism. It was to this interpretation that I was instinctively attracted, but I watched with interest how the new Labour Government – the first peacetime government of which I was politically conscious – set about its task.

The experience confirmed all my prejudices. For a country that felt it had won the war, the economic failure of the Attlee years was a national humiliation. But the failure was more than just economic. It seemed to me that in every respect the socialism the Labour Government was seeking to put into practice went against the grain of human nature – not least its Utopian disregard of original sin or of what Anthony Quinton has called 'man's moral and intellectual imperfection'.

Anyone imbued with a sense of this imperfection was no more likely to be attracted by the anarcho-capitalism later to be fashionable in some extreme free-market circles, especially in the United States, in the 1970s and '80s, than by post-war ideas of reconstructing society from Whitehall. But the latter have been the practical threat during my adult lifetime. Both are types of Utopianism which overlook the dependence of political, personal and economic freedom alike on the tradition of an ordered and orderly society. As Edmund Burke said to the voters of Bristol, liberty 'not only exists along with order and virtue but . . . cannot exist at all without them'.

Order in turn is dependent on a very unfashionable virtue, the recognition of duly constituted authority, order, rank and precedence. It is, of course, an error to attribute to a dramatist the words of his characters. But Shakespeare was clearly preoccupied with the problems of legitimate authority and the need for it. He had no illusions about the imperfections of those all too often likely to be at the top – 'a cur's obeyed in office'. Nor was he lacking in sympathy for those at the bottom: for instance, Lear's reference to 'poor naked wretches' with 'houseless heads and unfed sides'. But to destroy authority does not increase compassion and understanding. In the words of Ulysses in *Troilus and Cressida:*

> Take but degree away, untune that string
> And hark! what discord follows; each thing meets
> In mere oppugnancy.

Many modern political thinkers have queried whether this essentially pre-capitalist ordered structure is in fact compatible with capitalism. The Austrian-American economist and sociologist, Joseph Schumpeter, writing in the early 1940s, emphasized the paradox that:

> Capitalism creates a critical frame of mind which, after having destroyed the moral authority of so many other institutions, in the end turns against its own; the bourgeois finds to his amazement that a rationalist attitude does not stop at the credentials of kings and popes but goes on to attack private property and the whole scheme of bourgeois values . . . From the fact that criticism of the capitalist order proceeds from a critical attitude of mind, i.e. from an attitude which spurns allegiance of extra-rational values, it does not follow that rational refutation will be accepted. Such refutation may wear the rational garb of attack, but can never reach the extra-rational driving power and that always lurks behind it. Capitalist rationality does not do away with sub- or super-rational impulses. It merely makes them get out of hand by removing the restraint of sacred or semi-sacred tradition.

Schumpeter believed that capitalism would be destroyed by its cultural and political – not its alleged economic – contradictions. Similar fears have been expressed more recently by American writers such as Irving Kristol and Daniel Bell.

The outcome has often seemed a pretty close-run thing. But in the end Schumpeter underestimated the ordinary wage and salary earner, who has been better able to see through Utopian pretensions than many so-called intellectuals. (The post-war years have also seen the rise of a conspicuously successful form of capitalism in Japan and in the newer industrial countries of the Far East, which owes little to Western rationalism or extreme individualism.)

But the most striking practical victory of capitalism, which Schumpeter, who died in 1950, could hardly have foreseen, was the disintegration of the collectivized economies of the former Soviet Union and Eastern and Central Europe – a rare example of an historical experiment testing a theory to destruction. Post-Communist rulers have, with varying degrees of success, tried to pick up the pieces after the disintegration of a socialism which lacked both liberty and order and which was held together in its last years only by cynicism and corruption.

I cannot of course claim to have foreseen these momentous events in observing post-war England. But my instinctive suspicion of creeping socialism was reinforced by all I saw of the Labour Government of 1945–51. Yet despite the fact that, within little more than six years, the Attlee Government had been voted out of office, battered by economic failure and exhausted of ideas, it proved to have set the political agenda for the next quarter of a century. It may have been defeated at the polls, but it had captured the moral high ground. The two key principles for which it stood, big interventionist government and the drive towards equality, remained effectively unchallenged for more than a generation.

There is another aspect of the post-war consensus about which I have always had misgivings – the downgrading of nationalism. As early as 1967 I wrote in a *Spectator* series, 'A Tract for The Tories':

> Today 'nationalism' is out of fashion among the opinion-formers. Thanks to a superficial misreading of history, it is accused of having been responsible for two world wars and has widely come to be regarded as a political sin of the first magnitude, fortunately found only in such antiquated and obsolete figures as General de Gaulle. In fact the real danger comes from ideologies not nationalism; for while a nation may properly respect the nationhood of others, an ideology knows no frontiers . . .
>
> Once [the Tories] lose their claim to be, in the fullest sense, the 'national party', they are left, as they are in danger of being left today, either as the party of the 'individual' - a noble but to most people an austere and forbidding creed – or else as the party of the middle classes, which condemns them to a permanent minority.

All this had to change. It is to Margaret Thatcher's great credit that she, at last, successfully challenged this debilitating post-war consensus. True, by 1979 the tide of ideas was flowing her way. But tides still have to be caught.

Economic Evolution

If my political perspective was formed early on, my approach to economic policy, at least in one important respect, took longer to evolve. While always a firm believer in the market economy and the enterprise culture, it took some time for me to recognize that this needed to be set within a firm framework of financial discipline if inflation was to be suppressed. This was partly because I had been brought up as a Keynesian (my economics tutor at Oxford had been Keynes's pupil and biographer, Roy Harrod), and the Keynes of the *General Theory* displayed, to say the least, a distinctly cavalier attitude to inflation. But it also stemmed from the fact that during the 1950s and the 1960s Britain's inflation rate averaged a shade under 4 per cent, and except at the very end of that period showed no sign of acceleration. When it rose above 5 per cent in 1969, it was the first time that this had occurred for fourteen years.

For some time, therefore, I wrongly took relatively low and non-accelerating inflation for granted. Ironically, in the light of subsequent events, I failed to appreciate the importance of the discipline that was being exerted by the Bretton Woods fixed exchange-rate system. But when inflation did start to take off at the end of the 1960s and the early 1970s, my perspective quickly changed. It was clear to me that the overriding object of macroeconomic policy must be the suppression of inflation. Moreover, unlike the conventional wisdom of the time – embraced by pretty well the entire economic establishment and even (then) by Margaret Thatcher – I was equally clear that incomes policy, of which I had been publicly and consistently critical right from the start, was no solution.

So by the time I entered the House of Commons in 1974, the views I had arrived at, and which I continue to hold today, could be summarized in terms of two interconnected reversals of the post-war conventional wisdom. The first is the conviction that the recipe for economic success is the greatest practicable market freedom within an overall framework of firm financial discipline – precisely how that discipline is best applied being essentially a second-order question, though important, and one which was to prove surprisingly explosive. This is in stark contrast to the approach that culminated in the débâcle of the 1970s, in which an ever-increasing erosion of market freedom was accompanied by the progressive abandonment of financial discipline.

The second reversal is that which I made the theme of my Mais lecture as Chancellor in 1984. That is to say, instead of seeking to use macroeconomic (i.e. fiscal and monetary) policy to promote growth and microeconomic policy (of which incomes policy was a key component) to suppress inflation, the Government should direct macroeconomic policy to the suppression of inflation and rely on microeconomic (or supply-side) policy, such as tax and labour market reform, to provide the conditions favourable to improved performance in terms of growth and employment.

Of course, there is more to it than that, as will become apparent later on. But that was, and is, the essence of it.

CHAPTER 2

MEMBER OF PARLIAMENT

*New Boy · Prime Minister's Questions
Advent of Margaret Thatcher · Opposition Whip
Preparation for Office*

New Boy

THE GENERAL ELECTION OF February 1974, which brought me into the House of Commons as Member of Parliament for Blaby with a comfortable 12,000-plus majority, also ushered in a Labour Government with no overall majority. It was obvious that Harold Wilson, once again (somewhat to his surprise) Prime Minister, would soon call another election, in an attempt to repeat his success of the 1960s, when after scraping in very narrowly after thirteen years of Tory Government in October 1964 he dissolved Parliament and won by a landslide in March 1966.

Having drafted, with some misgivings, the Tory manifesto for the February election, I was asked, along with my old friend Douglas Hurd (who had entered the House with me) and one or two others, to help Ted Heath to cobble together a platform to avert this disaster. The outcome was a somewhat bizarre manifesto, but the main objective was achieved. A re-run of 1966 was averted. Labour won the October 1974 election with an overall majority so narrow that they were constantly fighting for survival and, with the normal attrition of by-election defeats, were eventually forced to call an election at a time not of their choosing, having been defeated on a 'no confidence' motion on the floor of the House of Commons in March 1979 – the first time this had happened for over half a century.

Losing manifestos have only one home: the scrapheap. But that of October 1974 was to prove an unfortunate exception. Ted had put his former Education Secretary, Margaret Thatcher, in charge of housing policy, with a policy group, of whom I was one, to assist her. This was my first experience of working with Margaret, and I was impressed by her vigour and energy. While almost all her former Cabinet colleagues – the great exception being her economic mentor, Keith Joseph – were demoralized by ejection from office, she went to work with a will. As a result, of the few specific pledges in the manifesto, hers stood out. The centrepiece was an undertaking, first to reduce the rates by transferring the cost of teachers' pay to the central exchequer, and subsequently to abolish domestic rates altogether, 'replacing them by taxes related to people's ability to pay'.

The abolition of domestic rates was highly controversial within the party, both within the policy group and at the wider back-bench meeting subsequently convened, not least because no-one had the slightest idea what the replacement tax would be. But at least it was fully, indeed passionately, discussed, and – subject to what the alternative might prove to be – probably secured majority support. That could not be said about the second major pledge in the housing field. This was inserted by Margaret at the last moment, though clearly with Ted's approval. To my horror, I discovered that we had pledged ourselves to reduce mortgage rates, then 11 per cent, to 9½ per cent forthwith, and to cap them at that level in perpetuity.

Unlike the pledge to abolish domestic rates, which was to rise from its grave to haunt the Tory Government years later, the economic nonsense of a 9½ per cent mortgage cap was well and truly destined for the scrapheap. Indeed, during the entire eleven-and-a-half-year Thatcher premiership, the mortgage rate only once went as low as 9½ per cent, and then for only three months. But it did provide an early demonstration of Margaret's devotion to the cause of the home-buyer, irrespective of the economic consequences; and, as a result, her antipathy to high interest rates. Her detestation of inflation was genuine enough; but while willing the end, she was repeatedly reluctant to embrace the means.

But to come back to my own story: I had entered the House of Commons rather later and rather better known than most new Members. This meant, to those on the Labour benches, and some on the Conservative benches, too, that I needed to be taken down a peg. I was soon made aware that the House of Commons is like a school, in which the new boys are expected to show all the humility of new boys, irrespective of whether or not they have achieved anything before passing through its portals.

Prime Minister's Questions

In other words, I had to establish myself in parliamentary terms from scratch. It clearly made sense to specialize in economic policy, but I felt I needed to do more than that. The obvious answer was to specialize in Prime Minister's questions, too. As radio listeners were subsequently to discover, this plays, somewhat noisily, to a packed House for a quarter of an hour every Tuesday and Thursday. For a new Opposition back-bencher, the opportunity to practise his parliamentary skills by asking awkward questions of the Prime Minister of the day had obvious attractions, even if with a Prime Minister as experienced as Harold Wilson it was something of a high-risk occupation. Fortunately, I had been studying Wilson closely for over ten years, first as special assistant to the then Prime Minister, Alec Home, in 1963–64, when Wilson was Leader of the Opposition, and subsequently as a journalist, during his first premiership.

As a result, I had come to understand him rather better than most Tory Members and to know his weaknesses, which enabled me (according to Wilson's own later account) to become his most effective questioner on the Tory side, though he suffered even more at the hands of his own Labour colleague, the defiantly left-wing mining MP, Dennis Skinner, with whom I established an unprincipled informal collaboration. When Wilson surprisingly resigned in March 1976 I found his successor, Jim Callaghan, very much harder to deal with, and rather lost interest in this particular art-form. But by then I had already established a parliamentary reputation of sorts.

There are some who affect to believe that Prime Minister's questions are little more than a silly game, and nothing to do with the serious business of politics, let alone statesmanship. Certainly, the questioning does not even pretend to be a search for information. But what it does provide is a continuous public examination of the character and competence of the Prime Minister of the day; and I have never known a Prime Minister who did not take it very seriously indeed.

Specializing in economic policy meant a number of things. I spoke in economic debates and in particular Budget debates (I had made my maiden speech appropriately enough on All Fools' Day 1974, during Denis Healey's first Budget debate). I got myself on to the standing committee on successive Finance Bills, where the Bill that enacts the Budget is subjected to clause-by-clause, line-by-line scrutiny. I became a member (in the place of my dear friend Jock Bruce-Gardyne, who sadly lost his seat to a Scottish Nationalist in the second 1974 election) of the then General Sub-Committee of the Expenditure Committee, the precursor of today's Select Committee on the Treasury and Civil Service. I also joined the *ad hoc* select committee set up by the Labour

Government under the chairmanship of Douglas Jay to recommend the form that the Wealth Tax to which they were committed should take; an exercise which the Tory members of the committee, well led by Maurice Macmillan, were eventually and with no little elegance to abort.

After the October 1974 election Ted Heath made the somewhat bizarre decision effectively to split the position of Shadow Chancellor in two, giving the job of the front legs of the pantomime horse to Robert Carr and that of the back legs to Margaret Thatcher. Her principal remit was to lead the assault on Labour's promised second 1974 Budget, the main purpose of which was to introduce a swingeing attack on inherited wealth (including family businesses) in the shape of the Capital Transfer Tax. The battle was effectively joined at the committee stage, where I found myself working with her once again, and got to know her rather better. It was an exercise in which the ability to master detail she had acquired as a lawyer stood her in good stead.

Interestingly, of the fifteen Tories on the standing committee of that Finance Bill, no fewer than nine were to become Cabinet Ministers during the Thatcher years: apart from Margaret herself, there were David Howell, Norman Lamont, John MacGregor, Tony Newton, Cecil Parkinson, Peter Rees, Nicholas Ridley and myself. We were an effective team. It was, indeed, in the middle of that committee stage that Margaret was elected Leader of the Conservative Party. And happily, as Chancellor under her premiership, I was able to transform the economically and socially damaging Capital Transfer Tax into a broadly acceptable Inheritance Tax.

When Margaret Thatcher defeated Ted to become leader in February 1975 it was more a rejection of Ted – on personal and political grounds alike – than a positive endorsement of her, at least so far as the majority of her parliamentary colleagues were concerned. As one of the few, at that time, who broadly shared her political and (in particular) economic thinking, I was greatly relieved. The Conservative Party badly needed a new approach, and she clearly meant to provide it. Owing largely to her background, perhaps, Margaret was thankfully free of that middle-class guilt that had made most leading politicians, of both parties, who had received expensive private educations, ashamed of quality, embarrassed by capital and tolerant of the excesses of organized labour.

Advent of Margaret Thatcher

Margaret instinctively realized the need to regain the moral as well as the practical initiative from collectivism. In this she was strongly fortified by the writings of the economist and philosopher Friedrich Hayek. Although Hayek's popularity was largely confined to non-mainstream bodies like the robustly free-market Institute of Economic Affairs, his warnings conformed very closely to recent British experience. He had given advance notice of the evils of socialism and central planning in *The Road to Serfdom*, a book first published in Britain in March 1944 and dedicated ironically to 'the socialists of all parties'. Hayek's development of the concept of a spontaneous natural order provided a strong philosophical underpinning for the market, not least by demonstrating that our understanding of the nature of society and the economy is too partial to admit economic management by the state.

Economic planning was both impossible and unnecessary. Individual agents acting on incomplete information could none the less operate a market economy by means of the price mechanism. This was a much more efficient means of transmitting consumer wants and needs than the vast bureaucracies of Whitehall and the nationalized industries, as I had argued for nearly twenty years. Above all, Hayek also opened up for the first time since the war the possibility of a morally superior political conception to that of socialism, by elevating private actions above public direction and dismissing 'social justice' as both vague and arbitrary. These were all ideas which, like Margaret Thatcher, I had nursed, without much articulation, since I had left Oxford; and they fitted naturally with my subsequent realization that the fundamental defect of the British economy was not a shortage of demand but a failure of supply.

At a more down-to-earth level, Margaret was unusual, for a Tory leader, in actually warming to the Conservative Party – that is to say, the party in the country, rather than its Members of Parliament. Certainly, that had not occurred for many years. Harold Macmillan had a contempt for the party, Alec Home tolerated it, Ted Heath loathed it. Margaret genuinely liked it. She felt a communion with it, one which later expanded to embrace the silent majority of the British people as a whole. What was initially an unusual and rather endearing trait was eventually to become part of the hubris that led to her nemesis.

After a little while I had the good fortune to be asked by her to be part of a small team of back-benchers – known to the Press subsequently as the 'Gang of Four' – who joined her each Tuesday and Thursday to discuss the best line of attack and the best form of words for her to use during Prime Minister's questions. The other members of the team were Norman Tebbit, Geoffrey Pattie and George Gardiner. Norman, whose populist manner and street-fighter approach to parliamentary debate concealed from most observers at the time his shrewd political judgement, was particularly good at this. He, Margaret and I, while all quite different personalities, had a very similar approach to both politics and policies, and cemented an alliance that was to last well into our time as Cabinet colleagues.

Opposition Whip

As it happened, I did not remain on the back benches for too long, though the manner of my leaving them was somewhat astonishing. In November 1976 the Chief Whip, Humphrey Atkins, invited me to join the Opposition Whips' Office. A more unlikely Whip would have been hard to imagine – even though my only two rebellions had been in Ted's time, when I had voted against government financial assistance to the Chrysler motor car company and against the Healey mini-Budget of July 1974 which *inter alia* reduced the rate of VAT from 10 per cent to 8 per cent, when in each case the official Opposition line had been to abstain. In the Conservative Party at any rate, any new nominee for the Whips' Office requires the endorsement of all the existing Whips: a single blackball excludes. I am not sure which was the more surprising: to have been suggested in the first place, or to have been universally accepted. In any event, having established that, as an Opposition Whip, I would still be free to speak in the House, I accepted.

During my year in the Whips' Office, I was able to learn a fair amount about parliamentary tactics and procedure, and perhaps even more important, about my parliamentary colleagues. But my main achievement as a Whip was of a somewhat freelance nature. From the moment I first entered Parliament in 1974, in Finance Bill after Finance Bill, I had been campaigning for the indexation of the tax system in general, and of the personal allowances in particular, so as to prevent the system from being insidiously subverted by inflation without parliamentary approval of any kind.

Following the 1977 Budget, I became the Opposition Whip on the standing committee on the Finance Bill. Astonishingly, the Government had carelessly included among the Labour back-benchers on the Committee two – Jeff Rooker (who understood what he was doing) and Audrey Wise (who may not have done) – who were sympathetic to the indexation of personal allowances, as a means of preventing those on low incomes from being dragged into the tax net simply by virtue of inflation. As soon as I discovered that, I arranged with Rooker to co-ordinate tactics.

I also went to see Geoffrey Howe, whom Margaret had made Shadow Chancellor, to let him know that there was a real chance of inflicting a serious defeat on the Government and getting the principle of the indexation of the tax system on to the statute-book. He was initially more attracted to the former than the latter, fearing it might tie his hands as Chancellor – though he could also see that, for a party pledged to reduce the burden of income tax, preventing inflation from increasing it by stealth made sense.

In practice, of course, there was (rightly) no way in which a future

Chancellor's hands could be completely tied, since he had the unfettered right to propose each year whatever level of allowances he saw fit; but I suggested that this could be made clearer by amending the Rooker-Wise 'automatic' indexation amendments to provide an explicit procedure for the Government to seek parliamentary approval to override the indexation provisions in any given year. This satisfied him, and he suggested we should forthwith see Margaret, who he feared would be difficult to persuade, given her general prejudice against indexation of all kinds.

Happily, she eventually agreed to the course I proposed; and by some careful manoeuvring I was able to secure the Government's defeat in committee by a majority of one. Rather than risk the humiliation of a further defeat on the floor of the House, the Government conceded without a fight at the Report stage, the final stage of the Bill; and the indexation of the personal tax allowances thus reached the statute-book. One of our first acts in Government was to tidy up and extend this legislative innovation.

The following November, after an eventful year as a Whip, I was asked by Margaret to become an Opposition Treasury spokesman, under Geoffrey Howe. He remained a close friend and colleague for the rest of my relatively short time in Opposition and considerably longer time in Government.

A fine mind, intellectual conviction, courage, integrity, tenacity, resilience, great courtesy allied to almost ruthless ambition, more than made up for a somewhat colourless public personality (although he was far from colourless in private) and lack-lustre parliamentary performances. Although in no sense an economist, his experience of trying to implement the absurdities of a statutory prices and incomes policy as Minister for Consumer Affairs in the Heath cabinet, coupled with his liberal principles in the true sense of the word, meant that there was a ready meeting of minds. Very much a lawyer, he is a glutton both for work and for detail, and needs remarkably little sleep.

This is something he shares with Margaret; but in other respects they could scarcely be more different. For him politics is about being reasonable, and persuasion a matter of patient education. My manner, too, is very different from Geoffrey's, but I never felt his to be a sign of weakness, as she clearly did. Curiously, in the light of subsequent events, our only significant policy difference was over Europe, where the drift towards a United States of Europe was something that I viewed with deep foreboding, but which Geoffrey manifestly did not.

Preparation for Office

As a Shadow Treasury spokesman, I inevitably became more deeply involved in the preparations we made for office, which Margaret had initiated as soon as she had become Leader in 1975. For me, this meant chiefly the unprecedentedly detailed and thorough work we did to identify the scope for public expenditure savings. This was something that had been unwisely neglected during our previous period of Opposition in the 'sixties, as a result of which, when the Heath Government took office in 1970, nothing at all was done in that vital first hundred days, and when it did get round to it, it did too little.

By contrast, between 1975 and 1979, not only did a Shadow Treasury team, ably assisted by the Conservative Research Department, and in particular by Adam Ridley, who had been a member of the Central Policy Review Staff (CPRS: the so-called think-tank) during the Heath Government, scrutinize every Government spending programme, but a Shadow public expenditure round was then conducted with the various Shadow spending Ministers. I myself chose to concentrate on housing where, unlike many other areas of public expenditure, there is a flourishing private sector alternative to public provision, to which more and more people aspire; and with the invaluable assistance of Mark Boleat, now Director General of the Building Societies Association, I was able to produce a paper identifying very substantial savings indeed.

On the tax side, in which I was also involved, rather less preparation was done, since the principal difficulty was not so much identifying the course we wished to steer but securing the public expenditure savings which would enable us to embark on it. Nevertheless, the little we did do was done with meticulous thoroughness, thanks largely to Arthur Cockfield, the former Inland Revenue official (he claimed to have been the inventor of PAYE – Pay As You Earn) who had been tax adviser to the then Chancellor, Tony Barber, during most of the Heath Government and was recalled by Margaret for the purpose. We looked into the theoretically attractive idea of a wholesale switch from an income tax to an expenditure tax system, and had a long session with Professor James Meade, its foremost exponent, but (in my view rightly) shrank from the upheaval and practical problems that would have been involved.

Looking back, however, while we were right to concentrate on the public expenditure side, where the political battle is toughest, we should perhaps have done more work than we did on tax reform. But that said, the programme of tax reform we did in the event carry out was no small achievement.

A bigger error, in hindsight, was to do so little work in Opposition on the conduct of monetary policy – not least because this was where the official Treasury was weakest and the Bank of England was little better. That monetary policy was the weapon with which we would slay the dragon of inflation was not in doubt. Lingering dissensions within the Conservative Party discouraged too obvious and explicit attention to monetary strategy and tactics, as well as an anxiety to avoid giving hostages to fortune. We also assumed too readily that the task was essentially one of applying with conviction the approach that a reluctant Labour Government had had forced upon it by the International Monetary Fund (IMF). When it all turned out to be much more complicated than that, far too much time had to be spent in Government in hacking a path through the jungle. Maybe even if we had done the work, we would not have emerged with the right answer. But it would have been less difficult, and certainly far less damaging, to have addressed the key issues far more thoroughly than we did, and reached a measure of agreement on them, in the relative tranquillity of Opposition.

Alongside the official preparations for Government, there was the parallel and highly secret 'Stepping Stones' exercise, conducted under the aegis of Keith Joseph at the Centre for Policy Studies. The convenor of this work, in which I was also among those involved, was John Hoskyns, a former army officer turned computer expert, who was fired by a determination to save Britain from seemingly inexorable decline. He had offered his services to Keith after losing faith in Harold Wilson, and was to become the first head of Margaret Thatcher's Number 10 Policy Unit before resigning in despair. His insistence on a coherent long-term strategy, his freshness of approach and his readiness to think the unthinkable were invigorating, though perhaps at times removed from political reality. I cannot recall the 'Stepping Stones' papers having much practical influence in Government except in so far as they helped to maintain the momentum for a radical reform of trade union law.

I made the most of my period in Opposition, the first five years of my time in the House of Commons, learned a great deal and contributed what I could. But it was a dismal and depressing experience to live through the failures of the 'seventies, in one sense so close to the centre of events, yet wholly unable to influence them. The cliff-hanging one-vote defeat of the Labour Government on a confidence motion on Wednesday, 28 March 1979 came as a blessed deliverance.

Only one thing remained to be done before Parliament was dissolved for the election which we were widely expected to win. Denis Healey had prepared a Budget for the following Tuesday, 3 April. This could no longer be delivered. Instead, a very brief Finance Bill had to be introduced to enable those taxes that have to be enacted by Parliament afresh each year, notably income tax, to continue in being until the first Budget of the new Parliament, after the general election.

Geoffrey and I met Denis Healey and his Chief Secretary, Joel Barnett, in the Chancellor's room in the House of Commons, to agree the contents of his holding Bill. There was only one minor point of contention. Should the personal allowances remain unchanged in money terms, as would hitherto have been correct, or should they – following the enactment of 'Rooker-Wise' – be indexed? Hoist by my own petard, Geoffrey and I were obliged to compromise: the Bill *would* index the allowances, but the extra money would not reach the voters' pockets until after the election on 3 May. In fact, it is unlikely in the extreme that the Inland Revenue could have beaten the 3 May deadline even if we had not made this stipulation. In any event, it was Labour's last throw: the general election of May 1979 produced an overall Conservative majority of forty-four and the start of my ten years as a Minister in the Thatcher Government.

Almost fifteen years after I had first resolved to 'get out on the field and play' I was at last about to do so. But outside the small world of parliamentary politics there was no great sense that the whole nature of the game was about to change. Jim Callaghan's warning during the election that a Thatcher Government was 'too big a gamble for the country to take' was dismissed by most commentators as routine electioneering, but he understood very well that the moral and intellectual tide was against him. On the eve of the election he confessed to his political adviser, Bernard Donoughue, that the Attleeite settlement that had dominated politics since the war had probably run its course:

> You know there are times, perhaps once every thirty years, when there is a change in politics. It then does not matter what you say or what you do. There is a shift in what the public wants and what it approves of. I suspect there is now such a sea change – and it is for Mrs Thatcher.

CHAPTER 3

PRESENT AT THE CREATION

*A New Course · Financial Secretary
Helpers and Advisers · The 1979 Inheritance
The Underlying Malaise*

A New Course

IT IS DIFFICULT TO convey the excitement of those first few weeks in office – the most exciting of my political life. It is a thrill for any politician to become a Minister for the first time – certainly a Treasury Minister. It is a particular thrill to do so at the start of a new government, with a comfortable majority in the House of Commons.

Of course, the Private Office's deft organization of the mundane details of one's personal routine, the car and the driver, the politeness and deference, are all very agreeable. And at the Treasury, in particular, the standard of the (usually prompt) submissions in response to any ministerial query is impressively high. But the real sense of excitement came from being part of a team that had come to office determined to set an entirely new course for the economy and indeed for the country. This was no slogan: we meant it, and we had been preparing for it with exceptional thoroughness.

Even the traditionally cynical Civil Service was quick to recognize that something genuinely new was happening. I recall David Hancock, then a particularly able Treasury official, and subsequently Permanent Secretary to the Department of Education and Science, writing to me in August 1980, referring to us as 'what seems to me to be the most radical government we have had since the war – radical in the sense of making a break with what has gone immediately before'. And in a book published in 1982, Leo Pliatzky, a former Second Permanent Secretary to the Treasury and Permanent Secretary to the Department of Trade, wrote that,

> The Conservative Government elected in May 1979 was more than just another change of Government; in terms of political and economic philosophy it was a revolution.

I also recall his expressing, in an earlier radio interview, astonishment – not to say shock and horror – for a different reason: he complained that economic policy was being determined by Ministers (instead of, presumably, by Treasury officials). Although the voluble and innovative Pliatzky was not a typical Civil Servant, in both cases he accurately reflected the Whitehall view of the new Government.

Financial Secretary

But all that lay a little way ahead when the telephone rang at my home in my Leicestershire constituency on the morning of Saturday, 5 May 1979, two days after the election. It was Number 10 on the line: the Prime Minister wished to speak to me. I warmly congratulated her on her splendid victory and then she got down to the matter in hand. 'I want you to go to the Treasury,' she said. 'I have made Geoffrey Chancellor and John Biffen Chief Secretary. I would like you to be . . . ' there followed a disconcerting pause, which I broke by suggesting 'Financial Secretary?' 'Yes, that's right,' she replied.

I was greatly relieved. I had been a front-bench Opposition spokesman for only the previous eighteen months. She could easily have given me something less. Financial Secretary to the Treasury, the number three job in the most powerful Government Department, both of whose top two jobs are of Cabinet rank, was the most I had hoped for.

Geoffrey Howe had, of course, been Margaret's shadow Chancellor in Opposition and he and I had worked closely together in preparing for Government. John Biffen was a somewhat surprising choice as Chief Secretary: I had expected the job to go to John Nott, who had been a Minister of State at the Treasury in Ted Heath's Government, and had made no secret of wanting it. Instead, Nott became Secretary of State for Trade. Later, his frustrated ambition for the Chancellorship soured his relations with Geoffrey Howe and ultimately led him to quit politics altogether in favour of a very successful and lucrative stint as chairman of the merchant bankers, Lazards.

The job of Chief Secretary, invented by Harold Macmillan in the early 'sixties to relieve the Chancellor of what had become an unbearable load, is to ensure that public expenditure is kept under control. It requires unceasing vigilance to that end, and an ability and appetite to master detail.

That was not John Biffen's forte, and his was not to prove a successful appointment. But John was then quite close to Margaret, thanks largely to his record of opposition to Ted Heath, and at that time she may not have had the fullest understanding of the role of Chief Secretary.

Geoffrey's first and simplest task was the allocation of duties among his ministerial team. John Biffen's responsibility – public expenditure – went automatically with the job of Chief Secretary, so what this meant was the allocation of the rest between myself and the two Treasury Ministers of State, Peter Rees in the Commons and Arthur Cockfield in the Lords. Normally, the Financial Secretary's main responsibility is those taxes that are collected by the Inland Revenue – generally speaking, direct taxation – and the Department of Inland Revenue itself; but although taxation interested me greatly, it was clear that with two eminent tax experts as his two Ministers of State, they had a far better claim to deal with taxation than I did. Fortunately, Geoffrey had a collegiate approach to Budget-making, which I sought to emulate when I became Chancellor: so I was able to be involved in tax when it mattered most, while avoiding the chore of having to approve and sign the replies to the huge volume of MPs' letters on constituents' tax complaints that the Chancellor of the Exchequer receives.

More important, I was able to secure the portfolio of other duties I most wanted. These included in particular monetary policy – at the very heart of our new economic approach – with which went the banks, the building societies, the Department of National Savings and exchange control, whose abolition I had advocated in the last article I had written before the election; privatization (then known, quaintly, as 'disposal of assets'), a brand new responsibility on which I was particularly keen, and which has remained in the Financial Secretary's bailiwick ever since; and the European Community Budget.

I also found myself for the first time appointed to a Cabinet committee, although it had no policy role. This was the rather curious 'L', or legislation, committee, which vets the Bills being introduced to Parliament for any obvious political or administrative blunders. By tradition, the Financial Secretary is the Treasury representative on the 'L' committee, making him the only Minister outside the Cabinet to serve in his own right on any of the main Cabinet committees. But these accoutrements of power were much less important than the sense of purpose we brought to the Treasury. Our discussions in Opposition had instilled in us a determination to set a new course for the economy and country. Our policies aimed at a conscious break, not merely with the outgoing Labour Government, but with the entire post-war political consensus which had manifestly failed.

Financial Secretary had been the post from which Enoch Powell, accompanied by Nigel Birch as Economic Secretary, had persuaded the then Chancellor, Peter Thorneycroft, to resign in 1957, along with them, in protest against the increase in public expenditure on which the Macmillan cabinet had insisted. But its importance has varied over the years.

My responsibility for monetary policy was something I took particularly seriously, and I inaugurated a system of monthly meetings to assess the state of play with officials from the Treasury and Bank of England under my chairmanship. The position of the Bank in those days was somewhat paradoxical. While it regarded monetary policy as very much part of its own bailiwick, not to be usurped, it believed in it far less than the new Government did. The Deputy Governor, Kit McMahon, who was by training a professional economist, was an unreconstructed neo-Keynesian; and even the Governor, Gordon Richardson, impressively leonine in appearance, believed that his main job was to warn the Government of the day to curb its Budget deficit and to encourage it to be firm on pay.

Another very different perspective arose from my appointment as Britain's 'Budget Minister' (for that was what, in Community parlance, my devolved responsibility for the European Community Budget – which had previously lain with Joel Barnett – was called). This involved regular trips to Brussels to attend meetings of the Budget Council (the Council of Budget Ministers) and haggle interminably over the minutiae of the Community Budget, visits which gave me an early insight into the reality of EC membership: the cumbersome and jargon-ridden nature of its proceedings, the self-conscious moral authority of the Commission, and above all the intensity and dominance of the Franco-German axis, which our Labour predecessors had ineffectually tried to counter by developing a high-spending alliance with the Italians.

Somewhat embarrassingly, Geoffrey also asked me to assist John Biffen with public expenditure control. This was ostensibly because I had been heavily involved in the work we had done on this in Opposition, but it also reflected Geoffrey's doubts about John. Understandably, spending Ministers were less than overjoyed, when they came to negotiate their spending programmes bilaterally with the Chief Secretary, to find me sitting alongside him, asking the awkward questions he had refrained from posing.

All in all, it gave me an exceptionally heavy burden for a non-Cabinet Minister; but apart from the public spending chore, it was what I wanted; and fortunately I am physically robust.

I was rather less fortunate with my room, having been automatically allocated that of my Labour predecessor, Bob Sheldon. But I discovered too late that the charming oak-panelled sanctuary traditionally occupied by the Financial Secretary had been allowed by Sheldon to pass to the Minister of State, and had accordingly been allocated to Peter Rees.

PRESENT AT THE CREATION

The room which I had inherited was in every way inferior, other than size. I decided to civilize it as best I could by acquiring some pictures from the Government Picture Collection, run by the admirable Wendy Baron. This was easier said than done: first pick went to our Embassies abroad, with Ministers having to make do with what was left; and the Financial Secretary quite properly had to wait until the Cabinet had made its choice. Eventually I managed to secure an imposing portrait of an undistinguished but long-serving eighteenth-century Chancellor of the Exchequer, Henry Pelham, resplendent in his gold and black Chancellorial robe, and an Ernest Proctor nude entitled 'The Judgement of Paris' to cheer things up a little.

Helpers and Advisers

My Private Office, headed by a brisk and competent young official in her mid-twenties, Paula Diggle, was perfectly acceptable. But knowing the critical importance of the Private Office in a Minister's life, I was determined to choose the ablest Treasury HEO(A) – the Civil Service grade below Principal, which was all the Financial Secretary was permitted – that I could find to replace Paula when her stint expired in a few months' time. Her two successors, first Stephen Locke and then David Willetts, were both excellent. Securing David was quite a battle. He had worked for me for a short time in Opposition, in 1978, before he joined the Treasury, and the machine took the view that this made the appointment politically suspect and therefore unsuitable. Douglas Wass, the Permanent Secretary, went so far as to offer David the job of his own private secretary, instead. But I stuck to my guns, Geoffrey declined to overrule me and the mandarinate had to concede. Any Minister – and particularly any Cabinet Minister – who does not insist on a principal private secretary of his own choice, rather than that of the Permanent Secretary, whose criteria (often described as 'career development') may be different, is most unwise.

As a brand new Minister, I soon felt a Parliamentary Private Secretary (PPS) would be helpful to keep me fully in touch with feeling on the back-benches. He would also be able to help me with my pairing problem. This had rapidly become a major headache. My regular pair had lost his seat in the general election – the one Conservative victory I had viewed with some anguish – and there was no chance of finding a new one. Fortunately, Bob Boscawen, who had been made a Whip, and therefore had no real need for a pair, very kindly offered me his, the old-style Yorkshire ex-miner Eddie Wainwright, who had represented Dearne Valley for the past twenty years. But Eddie, though personally friendly, proved strangely unwilling to pair with me when I needed him most. It soon turned out that he was being heavily leaned on by the Labour

Whips, who had decided to make life as difficult for me as they possibly could; and Eddie, most of whose energies were devoted to battling against Arthur Scargill, who was trying to wrest his Dearne Valley seat from him, felt he could scarcely fight his own Whips as well.

To make matters worse, in those early days Ministers outside the Cabinet were not permitted to have a PPS. Eventually, however, it was decided that I could share one with Peter Rees. We had some difficulty in agreeing on a suitable candidate, and eventually settled on Ray Whitney, the member for High Wycombe: but he abandoned the post fairly quickly, pleading a desire to speak with greater freedom from the back-benches. We replaced him with Mark Lennox-Boyd, who stayed with me throughout my time as Energy Secretary and the earlier part of my Chancellorship, too. Mark was a gentle, likeable, politically sensitive son of a former Colonial Secretary, with no firm political views of his own: altogether a most suitable PPS.

A number of special advisers, explicitly political appointees recruited as temporary Civil Servants, were also part of the team. Adam Ridley, the economic supremo of the Conservative Research Department between 1974 and 1979, had thought that his work in Opposition would guarantee him a slot as head of the political staff at Number 10. He duly reported there the day after the election, only to find that Margaret had appointed John Hoskyns. Somewhat aggrieved, he became special adviser to Geoffrey Howe instead. Because it had two Cabinet Ministers, and its responsibilities were so wide-ranging, the Treasury was permitted two additional special advisers. Peter Cropper, the Research Department's tax expert, was technically appointed adviser to John Biffen, and George Cardona, who had advised the Shadow Treasury team on public expenditure, technically became adviser to me (even though I was not a Cabinet Minister). In fact these labels meant little. The three special advisers formed a team responsible to the Chancellor, and other Treasury Ministers used whatever time could be spared.

Special advisers were a Labour innovation to which Margaret Thatcher acceded only slowly, although eventually every Cabinet Minister ended up with at least one. As political appointees they were clearly *parti pris*, and were therefore treated initially by the Whitehall machine with the gravest suspicion. There had been some bad experiences under Labour and some Departments remain highly resistant to special advisers to this day. That was not the case at the Treasury, where it was rapidly realized that they were an extremely useful adjunct to the official machine, enabling officials to test the political reaction to proposals below ministerial level.

The official Treasury is a very fine institution indeed. I remember being at a cocktail party with Leo Pliatzky very early on, when he said he was sure I was enjoying the Treasury. 'They are the praetorian guard', he said. A good phrase, true, and how they see themselves. I had known the Treasury for a long time so its denizens' generally very high quality of intellect and pride in their job (despite the policy demoralization in the closing period of the outgoing Labour Government) was no surprise to me. It was a real pleasure to work with them.

Nevertheless it was clear that our policies did not commend themselves to more than a very small number of Treasury officials. The official Treasury recognized that the old policies had failed – indeed, they were almost shell-shocked by the scale of that failure, whose nadir had been the sterling crisis of 1976, when the UK had had to be humiliatingly bailed out by the IMF. Pliatzky, the senior Treasury official in charge of public expenditure in 1976, later wrote of that episode that it was 'difficult to express what an anxious and worrying time that was'. However, they had little faith in any alternative. They welcomed our determination to curb public expenditure: economic fashions come and go, but the one constant belief at the heart of the Treasury, which governs its thinking on much else too, is its mission to stand firm against the desire of politicians of all parties and the whole of the rest of Whitehall to devise new ways of increasing Government spending. But monetarism was seen by most of them, not least by the Permanent Secretary, Douglas Wass, as at best an intellectually interesting variety of mumbo-jumbo to which lip service probably had to be paid to appease the financial markets.

In principle they welcomed a government that knew its mind, after the drift and ultimately the death-wish of the outgoing administration: but like the commentators in the Press, they had little doubt that we would abandon the policies on which we had embarked, not least the rejection of incomes policy, before very long. The only argument was whether the U-turn would occur in six months' time or whether it would take as long as a year for the Thatcher Government to introduce an incomes policy.

The indispensable element of the revolution which so astonished Whitehall was Margaret Thatcher herself. She had set out from the very beginning as a Prime Minister who knew her own mind, and led from the front from the word go. But in those days she had no Number 10 bunker to envelop her, nor did she yet feel wholly self-sufficient. She considered the Treasury to be *her* Department. Of her four predecessors as Tory Leader and Prime Minister, Eden was a Foreign Office man through and through, Macmillan deeply distrusted the Treasury, which he regarded as deflationary and responsible for the depression of the 'thirties, Douglas-Home was in the Eden mould, and Heath sought (improbably) to model himself on Macmillan.

But at a time when most of the Party and indeed most of her Cabinet were still 'wet', it was the Treasury that Margaret ensured was 100 per cent 'dry' and on whose support she relied. (The terms 'wet' and to a lesser extent 'dry' were important defining terms in those days. The term 'wet' was originally coined by Margaret Thatcher for those Tories who had no stomach for the fight ahead, but was later self-consciously endorsed by the paternalist wing of the party. The word 'dry' came more slowly and hesitantly into circulation to indicate the opposite of 'wet'.) Partly for that reason, partly thanks to the relationship forged in Opposition, she frequently asked me to see her about something that had cropped up, and very occasionally I would take the initiative and seek a meeting. All this was distinctly unusual for a Minister who was not even in the Cabinet. But the relationship, although close, had no social dimension to it. There may have been some rare exceptions, but in general that was not her style.

The 1979 Inheritance

During any election, officials prepare briefs to cater for the possibility of the incumbent government being defeated, binding them in red if the Opposition is Labour and blue if it is Conservative. The blue plastic folder which greeted Treasury Ministers in May 1979 confirmed in much greater detail the rather gloomy assumptions we had made in Opposition. The main difference was that the prospect for inflation was far worse than we had expected. Nevertheless the new Conservative Government, unlike some preceding incoming administrations, made little play with the misfortunes of its inheritance. An over-emphasis on how bad things are only weakens external and internal confidence, to no good purpose. Even from a partisan point of view it is a pointless tactic. For once an election has been won, there is little gain to be had from gloating over the other party's misfortunes. But the main reason for the lack of speeches on the horrors of the 1979 inheritance was simply that we were so busy with our own agenda that we had little time for such exercises. The economic sickness we set out to cure went far deeper than the state of the conjuncture in May 1979.

Nevertheless a short retrospect on the economy as it was in the spring of 1979 should help to put the policies of the new government in perspective. The most uncontroversial fact about 1979 is that it was a peak year of a business cycle, like 1973 before it and 1988 or 1989 after it. Another indisputable feature is that, for all Labour's rhetorical emphasis on manufacturing, manufacturing output had in fact fallen in absolute terms, since its 1973 peak. It did not regain and overtake that earlier level until 1987, during my own period as Chancellor. It is not unduly partisan to suggest that the 1979 boom was disappointingly weak from an output point of view, while severe in the degree of inflationary pressure it piled on a fragile economy with high inflationary expectations.

This pessimistic diagnosis was subsequently reinforced by the Treasury's analysis of the slow-down in the underlying trend of output.*

The Labour Government had been forced to curb monetary growth and public sector borrowing and spending as a result of the sterling crisis which culminated in the IMF loan of 1976. Partly as a result of that squeeze, and partly because of a temporary dampener imposed by pay ceilings, average annual headline inflation had fallen from 24.2 per cent in 1975 to 8.3 per cent in 1978. But the respite was short-lived, and by April 1979 the annual increase in the retail price index (RPI) was back in double figures and clearly accelerating. In the latest six months the annualized rate was already 12.3 per cent (excluding seasonal foodstuffs). The increase in the oil price, following the deposition of the Shah of Iran, was about to push up the headline inflation rate still further. As Alec Cairncross, a former Chief Economic Adviser to the Government, has subsequently written,

> There were those in America, Germany and elsewhere who hoped that a changed Britain would emerge, phoenix-like, from the [1976] crisis, free from past illusions and able to hold to a steady line of policy . . . But there was little change of heart in the Labour Party. The Prime Minister might denounce public spending as a way of coping with depression, but he was prepared to back a PSBR [public sector borrowing requirement] of not less than £9 billion. The Chancellor had every intention of restoring the cuts when it seemed safe to do so and the PSBR was back above £9 billion by 1978–79, Labour's last year in power.

Denis Healey, the Labour Chancellor, had indeed taken the opportunity of sterling's recovery following the IMF agreement to boost public sector spending and borrowing once again. Between 1977–78 and 1978–79 the public sector borrowing requirement rose from £5.4 billion to £9.3 billion, that is to say from 3½ to 5¼ per cent of GDP, despite the economic upturn, which should have led to public sector borrowing falling as a share of GDP. A further increase to £10 billion or £11 billion (over 6 per cent of GDP) was forecast by Treasury officials for the financial year 1979–80 – equivalent in 1992 terms to a PSBR of getting on for £40 billion at the peak of the economic cycle.

As Andrew Britton records in his authoritative account of the period, 'The possibility of an early general election was given increasing weight in the conduct of economic policy . . . The most difficult problem was the negotiation of an acceptable deal with the trade unions on pay and

---

*The Treasury has estimated that the trend growth of non-North Sea output fell from 2¾ per cent per annum in 1964–73 to only ½ per cent per annum in 1973–79 before recovering to around its earlier rate in 1979–89.

prices.' Pay policy had already been in deep trouble from the start of the so-called Phase Three in July 1977. The White Paper of 1978 called for a 5 per cent pay norm (in a year when inflation was running at 8 per cent) which was bound to be widely disregarded, and duly was, with a nine weeks' strike at Ford Motors in the autumn ending with a much-publicized 17 per cent pay rise. By the time we took office in the spring of 1979, earnings in manufacturing were rising at an annual rate of 13 per cent and in the whole economy by 15 per cent. The Labour Government still attempted to impose modified versions of its norm on the public sector. Strikes against these attempts led to the notorious 'winter of discontent', when the dead were left unburied, and the final crumbling of the Government.

The outgoing Labour Government did take one other decision, albeit a negative one, whose fateful importance was not widely recognized at the time: not to join the Exchange Rate Mechanism (ERM) of the European Monetary System (EMS). This duly came into being, with the participation of all the member states of the European Community except Britain, in March 1979, two months before Labour left office.

The Underlying Malaise

What worried me more than the 1979 conjuncture was the long-term decline of the British economy, and the climate of defeatism this engendered. This had its origins well before the 1974–79 Labour Government, but the debility reached an acute stage during its period in office.

For the Western world as a whole, the post-war golden age had finally come to an end after the first oil price explosion of 1973–74, triggered off by the Yom Kippur War between Israel and Egypt. Even during the golden age there had been growing concern in Britain as our growth rate, although not greatly different from that of the United States, lagged well behind that of the rest of Europe and Japan. Over the six years from the cyclical peak of 1973 to that of 1979, which as it happens broadly corresponded with Labour's period of office, the British economy all but stopped growing altogether. Excluding North Sea Oil, to provide a true measure of underlying performance, the average annual rate of growth over that period was a half of one per cent.

However, if the deterioration in Britain's growth performance was bad enough, the deterioration on the inflation front was even worse. The average annual rate of inflation had risen, seemingly inexorably, from 3½ per cent under the Conservative governments of 1951 to 1964, to 4½ per cent under the first Wilson administration, to 9 per cent under Heath and to 15½ per cent under the Labour government of 1974 to 1979. By the time Margaret Thatcher became Prime Minister, the British economy was trapped in the cycle of low growth and high inflation which economists called 'stagflation'; and mainstream Keynesianism was intellectually and politically bankrupt of solutions to it.

Even the normally staid Bank of England, in its March 1978 *Bulletin*, gave way to a despair that was rapidly becoming endemic:

> The United Kingdom has long been a country where productivity grew relatively slowly; but . . . the United Kingdom's performance has in the last five years become even poorer . . . If the will were there, productivity could clearly be transformed. The consequences of failing to arrest this country's industrial decline are likely to become more pressing and obvious as time goes on. Now condemned to very slow growth, we might later even have to accept, if present trends continue, declines in real living standards.

Trade union power, which had been greatly enhanced by the war, was entrenched in the 'sixties and 'seventies both by legislation and by the involvement of trade union leaders in economic planning and incomes policies. Profits, not surprisingly, sank. The real rate of return on capital invested in British industry (excluding the North Sea) declined according to official estimates from an average of 10 per cent during the period 1964–73 to an average of 5½ per cent during the period 1973-79. 'Profit' had become a dirty word, and 'capitalist' a term of abuse, as income tax rose under Labour to a top rate of 83 per cent on earned income and 98 per cent on investment income. Management, ground between the upper and nether millstones of government interference and trade union power, had all but ceased to manage. Instead, the energetic ones tramped the corridors of Whitehall in search of subsidies, and the less energetic took to the golf course.

But it went deeper than that. The 'winter of discontent' in 1978–79, had shown the ugly face of trade unionism and raised, once again, the question first asked during the miners' strike of 1974: had Britain become ungovernable? Indeed Labour Ministers had secured considerable high-level American support in the 'seventies by warning that the election of a Conservative Government would lead to uncontrollable civil unrest and the risk of a far-left government rising to power on its back.

By 1979 Britain was pitied abroad and mired in an all-pervasive defeatism at home. This was the culmination of trends that had begun long before the Labour Government of 1974–79, but which by the end of that period had become pathological. That was what we set out to reverse.

CHAPTER 4

RESTORING INCENTIVES AND REMOVING EXCHANGE CONTROL

An Early Budget · Khomeini and Clegg
The New Fiscal Strategy · Tax Reform: The First Steps
The Attack on Public Spending · Currency Freedom at Last
Abolition in Retrospect · An EC Sequel

An Early Budget

MARGARET THATCHER AND HER economic team decided in Opposition that if there were a May election in 1979, there would be a new Budget on 12 June, Arthur Cockfield having demonstrated that this was the earliest practicable date. Geoffrey Howe informed Treasury officials of the plan as soon as we took office.

We were determined not to repeat the mistake of the Heath Government, which had come into office in June 1970, but did nothing on the economic front until October of that year, when it announced an inadequate public expenditure package for the following financial year. There was no Budget until April 1971, by which time the Government was already being driven by events and felt the need to respond to the surge in unemployment. We decided in Opposition that we would introduce a Budget as soon as we possibly could and that it would contain both the main tax changes we had prepared and a major assault on public spending – *starting with the year in progress.*

We also resolved that our first Budget should make a decisive start to the process of reducing the deficit, and to do so entirely by cutting government spending. A quick start was made possible by the detailed work we had done in Opposition. Plans for public spending cuts had been agreed with Shadow Ministers in the summer of 1978 when the election had looked likely that autumn; and these plans were updated by the Shadow Treasury team in time for the actual election of May 1979.

We had come to office at a time when the UK economic cycle had peaked and was about to turn down – as for that matter was the world economy – and it would have been much easier to have deferred our attack on the deficit (and indeed on inflation via higher interest rates). But we consciously decided to press ahead, because deferment can become a way of life. Had the necessary action been postponed, the momentum would have been lost and, so, too, much of the new Government's credibility (or rather, the credibility it was seeking to build).

Right from the start, too, we attached the first importance to specific tax measures. For we were engaged not only in the battle against inflation, but also, and in parallel, on supply-side* measures to improve economic performance. We were clear that a significant reduction in income tax was needed to restore incentives. But given the Budget constraint, this inevitably meant a large increase in Value Added Tax (VAT), and hence in the Retail Prices Index (RPI), at a time when UK inflation was already soaring and sharply rising oil prices were about to have a further adverse effect on the RPI. Again, it would have been much easier to have deferred the tax switch; but if we had not made it then it would never have happened at all, and we had decided that it must. We could console ourselves that we were paying a short-term price for a lasting gain: in the longer run, you no more cause inflation by raising indirect taxes than you cure it by providing subsidies.

In short, in the macroeconomic and microeconomic fields alike, we made a conscious decision to forge ahead without delay despite the unpropitious nature of the conjuncture. In retrospect I still believe that this decision was absolutely right and of the first importance.

Khomeini and Clegg

We came to office at a bad time in many ways. On top of the underlying rise in inflation, there was superimposed a new world oil price explosion. This had been triggered by events in Iran, culminating in the deposition and exile of the Shah on 9 February 1979. The price increase came in three surges: in the winter of 1978–79, in the summer of 1979, and (following the outbreak of the Iran–Iraq war) in the closing months of that year. The spot price of Saudi Arabian light oil peaked at a record high of $41 a

---

*The term 'supply-side' was invented by economists long before we came to office as a deliberate contrast to the emphasis on regulating demand which had dominated so much of post-war economic policy. The expression was used by left-wing economists who believed intervention and government support would improve performance, as well as free-market ones who rested their hopes on improving the performance of markets. Margaret Thatcher hated the expression 'supply-side', but neither she nor anyone else came up with anything better.

barrel at the end of 1979 – some three times its level at the beginning of 1978 – largely, it must be said, as a result of panic stockpiling rather than because of any significant reduction of supply.

The annual inflation rate in the Group of Seven main industrial countries rose by five percentage points between 1978 and 1980, more or less in line with the Organization for Economic Co-operation and Development's (OECD) ready-reckoner estimates of the oil price impact. But the effect of a large oil price rise is not only to add to recorded inflation, but to bring recession as well. For while the spending power in the oil-consuming countries falls, the oil producers – many of them underpopulated desert sheikhdoms – cannot, initially, spend their additional resources. There is no way in which both these evils can be fought simultaneously: the government of the day has to choose. The UK response to the first oil shock, in 1973, had been to seek to avert the recession. Our response to the second oil shock, in 1979, was to refuse to accommodate the rise in inflation. This in itself was a decision of crucial importance, and highly controversial at the time.

As if that were not enough, we had another purely domestic shock effect with which to contend: namely the Clegg wage awards. After the 1978–79 'winter of discontent' the outgoing Labour Government had, in March 1979, set up a Commission on Pay Comparability under the chairmanship of Professor Hugh Clegg of Warwick University to investigate relative rates of pay in the public and private sectors and to make recommendations. It undertook to honour the Clegg recommendations, come what may.

Unfortunately, in the heat of the election campaign, Margaret Thatcher felt electorally obliged to match this pledge. She did so on the advice of Jim Prior, the Shadow Employment spokesman, and Peter Thorneycroft, the Party Chairman, who was wrongly believed to be an economic 'dry'*, and against the more cautious counsel of Geoffrey Howe and myself. Clegg reported in August 1979, recommending staged pay increases for public sector employees of up to 26 per cent. This not only added considerably to public expenditure, but contributed to the rapid rise of earnings in the whole economy, which peaked at over 20 per cent in 1980.

The New Fiscal Strategy

Despite this discouraging background we decided to press on with our radical fiscal plans. For if we had waited for a good moment to make them, the opportunity would have slipped from our grasp.

The overall framework was determined by our decision to make a

---

*Peter Thorneycroft owed this reputation to his courageous resignation as Chancellor at the beginning of 1958 after a clash with Harold Macmillan on public expenditure. The episode gave a false impression, however, of his degree of commitment to our sound money approach.

significant start on cutting the PSBR (the Budget deficit). Our aim was to reduce from £9¼ billion, or 5¼ per cent of GDP, in Labour's last year, 1978–79, to £8¼ billion or 4½ per cent of GDP in 1979–80. The 1979–80 outlook, however, was for a PSBR of some £10 billion to £11 billion, depending on the economic assumptions made. Unreconstructed Keynesians might have argued that, on the contrary, the situation called for a stimulus and an even higher PSBR. But right from the beginning we had set our face against this sort of fine-tuning. As for simply allowing the PSBR to rise as a result of the lower tax revenues and higher spending (on unemployment benefit and the like) caused by the recession, without any deliberate stimulus: this would have been perfectly acceptable had the PSBR not been far too high to start with.

We thus had a gap of up to £3 billion to bridge, even without taking account of our own tax measures. As our income tax reductions would cost around £4 billion, we had a sum of nearly £7 billion to find. Clearly we had to curb public spending. The expenditure position we inherited was unacceptable both in its absolute level and also in the growth which was planned. It is always difficult to cut public expenditure once the financial year is under way – Joel Barnett, Labour's Chief Secretary, had declared it to be impossible – and by the time we took office the year was already several weeks old. But it had to be done.

As a signal, within days of taking office, Margaret Thatcher appointed Derek Rayner of Marks & Spencer to head an Efficiency Unit within the Cabinet Office. Incoming Conservative Governments usually tend to be overoptimistic about the scope for 'eliminating waste' – a pledge which is always more popular than specific spending cuts. Such elimination was always likely to have only a marginal impact on the spending totals, although perhaps rather more impact on the psychological climate.

But our main hope of making an early dent in public expenditure was an emergency squeeze on cash limits, starting in the current (1979–80) financial year. Initially Anthony Rawlinson, Treasury Second Secretary in charge of public expenditure, recommended a cut in cash limits of 1½ per cent. This proposal went up via John Biffen and Geoffrey to Margaret, who rightly dismissed it out of hand as inadequate. Eventually we ended up with overall reductions of 3 per cent in manpower budgets, expected to save over £1 billion.

Geoffrey also managed to find over £1½ billion of specific economies by trimming the plans of the nationalized industries, by cutting so-called 'industrial support' and a whole rag bag of other measures. In addition, a target of £1 billion was set for 'asset disposals'. The largest contribution was to come from a sale in the Government's shareholding in British Petroleum, a measure to which Labour could hardly object very strongly as it had already resorted to it in 1977.

In total our public expenditure cuts would save £4 billion in the fiscal year that had just started. This was a good deal less than required to finance our income tax changes and make a start in reducing public borrowing. So the centrepiece of the Budget had to be a massive switch from direct to indirect taxes. In the event our tax changes were broadly neutral. (They brought in £½ billion in a full year but actually cost £1 billion in 1979–80.) Our intention was to start the process of cutting the PSBR below what Denis Healey had planned, although in the event it overshot to very nearly £10 billion.

Tax Reform: The First Steps

We resolved on the switch to indirect tax at the first ministerial meeting I ever attended, called by Geoffrey Howe on the morning of 9 May to discuss Budget strategy. The new Government had inherited from Labour two rates of VAT: a higher rate of 12½ per cent charged on so-called luxury items like petrol, boats and caravans and a lower rate of 8 per cent on everything else. We consolidated them into a single rate of 15 per cent, where it was to remain for over a decade.

In 1979 the near doubling of VAT to 15 per cent was a contentious decision. It added 3½ to 4 per cent to the RPI at a time when inflation was resurgent, oil prices were rising and the workforce, which had become accustomed to link its annual pay increases to headline inflation, was chafing under the frustration of four years of incomes restraint. Not only the Labour Party, but even a number of economically sympathetic commentators, such as the London Business School and Samuel Brittan in the *Financial Times,* argued that the increased rate would fuel inflationary expectations, give a fillip to the gathering wage explosion and increase the unemployment cost of reducing inflation.

Margaret Thatcher herself was at first fearful of the 15 per cent VAT rate, even though the manifesto had clearly promised a switch from income tax to VAT, partly because it was a bigger switch than she had in mind and partly because of the initial RPI effect. (Throughout her time she was acutely sensitive to any administrative decisions that affected the RPI, although this was not enough to deter her from the Poll Tax.) But Geoffrey persuaded her that if we did not grasp this nettle in the first Budget it would never be grasped at all.

There was some discussion of the shape of our income tax cuts. Geoffrey Howe, Arthur Cockfield and I had agreed in Opposition that the first Budget should raise VAT to 15 per cent to finance the cut in the top rate of income tax from 83 per cent to 60 per cent, plus either a dramatic cut in the 33 per cent basic rate or a smaller, but still sizeable cut to 30 per cent (at which it had stood under the Heath Government) plus a worthwhile real increase in the personal allowances. Geoffrey eventually opted for the latter course. In addition, the threshold for the Investment Income Surcharge, the 10–15 per cent additional income tax payable on income from savings, which penalized many older people in particular, was raised almost threefold. The cut in the top rate of income tax was massive, but did no more than bring the UK rate into line with the European average.

Contrary to popular mythology, Geoffrey Howe did not pledge the Government to a 25 per cent basic rate of income tax, but set it out more as an aspiration: 'Our long-term aim should surely be to reduce the basic rate of income tax to no more than 25 per cent.' It was to take nine years before I, as his successor, was able to realize this aspiration.

The pressure of time meant that all the more detailed tax changes we had in mind had to be left until the 1980 Budget. But we had nevertheless succeeded in producing a substantial Budget in forty days and forty nights. It was rapturously received by our supporters on the back benches. The Opposition was still too demoralized by its election defeat to mount any serious attack on it, even though the change in the method of uprating pensions (described below) and the higher rate tax cuts were both anathema to Labour.

But despite the 1979 Budget's huge success, Geoffrey Howe was to do little more on the tax reform front. This was partly because he tended to be a 'small print' man on tax matters: it was he who set up the Keith Committee on the administration of the tax system. It was also partly because he instinctively favoured a consultative approach, which in our system at least, given the strength of vested interests, makes radical tax reform more difficult, if not impossible. Geoffrey did, however, publish Green Papers on the taxation of husband and wife, where his wife Elspeth played a part in persuading him to focus on the issue, and on company taxation, where Arthur Cockfield was the prime mover.

The Attack on Public Spending

The most controversial decision announced in the 1979 Budget was the repeal of the Labour Government's legislatively enshrined formula for uprating pensions. Under this formula they were increased each year in line with prices or earnings, whichever rose faster. We decided to switch to straightforward indexation in line with prices.

As earnings normally rise faster than prices, Labour's commitment was an expensive one, which it then did its best to evade. In 1976, when, following a steep rise, inflation was expected to fall, Labour changed from an historic to a forecast basis for annual upratings, saving a huge sum of money by somewhat shabby means. It then saved further sums by consistently under-forecasting inflation and earnings increases.

The very large 19½ per cent increase in pensions announced by Geoffrey in his 1979 Budget, together with 17½ per cent increases in other benefits, was designed to compensate for Labour's most recent under-forecast and to soften the blow of the change in the form of indexation. But even in the new form the forecast basis was manifestly still unsatisfactory, and we eventually and rightly switched back to the historic basis. The politically brave decision to change the pensions formula was a critical part of regaining control of public expenditure – and evidence, too, of a government that took the long view rather than seeking merely short-term expedients.

As soon as the Budget was out of the way, we started work on further reductions in public expenditure, with John Biffen conducting our first annual public expenditure round. His habit of concluding bilateral discussions with spending Ministers by proposing that they split the difference soon became rather too well known for the Treasury's comfort. The outcome, the Public Expenditure White Paper of November 1979, containing the new plans for the year ahead, 1980–81, was probably more important for its sentiments than its contents. Its opening sentence – 'Public expenditure is at the heart of Britain's present economic difficulties' – caused some consternation among officials accustomed to less robust prose in government publications. It aimed to stabilize public spending by a mixture of higher prescription charges, savings in transport, housing and education expenditure, and by additional 'asset disposals'. It was disappointing to find that, with social security spending rising as unemployment rose sharply, cuts of £3½ billion merely left overall public spending unchanged. The White Paper's stated goal of reducing public expenditure as a proportion of GDP proved impossible to achieve in recession. But at least it did establish a certain austere flavour. In the summer of 1979 I minuted Geoffrey Howe:

> To plan public expenditure before the required growth is available to support it would ensure that, in the event, growth of output does not take place. Public expenditure cannot any longer be allowed to precede, and thus prevent, growth in the private sector.

Or as Geoffrey had put it more succinctly in his Budget speech, 'Finance must determine expenditure, not expenditure finance.' As soon as the ink was dry on the interim White Paper of November 1979, we conducted a thorough review of Government spending over a three-year period. The results were set out in our second and fuller public expenditure White Paper, experimentally published on Budget Day, 26 March 1980. This expressed the Government's hope 'not merely to halt the growth of public expenditure but progressively to reduce it' by 4 per cent in volume terms over the four years to 1983–84. The main reductions shown in the inherited programmes were in subventions to nationalized and private industries, in housing and in education. There were also further tentative gestures toward privatization. While this overall hope was, of course, never realized, had we not started with the determination to make actual cuts, we might never have succeeded in the more modest but virtually unprecedented aim of reducing public spending as a proportion of the national income.

Currency Freedom at Last

The 1979 Budget had contained an important relaxation of exchange control. I had long been convinced that exchange control should be abolished altogether and had already urged (with the due caution proper to my new responsibilities) 'a substantial relaxation of exchange control' in my 'maiden speech' as an Opposition Treasury spokesman on 10 November 1977.

The context at that time was the prospect of a substantial improvement in the oil sector of Britain's overseas trade balance, which inevitably had implications for the rest of the balance of payments. What is often overlooked is that the one certainty about the overall balance of payments is that, like the balance sheet of a company, it has to balance: it is what is known as an accounting identity. If one sector of the current account, in this case oil, shows a sharp improvement, there will either have to be an offsetting deterioration in the rest of the current account, which is largely composed of trade in manufactured goods – the mechanism by which this occurs would normally be a rise in the exchange rate – or else an offsetting deterioration in the capital account, which could be brought about by an outflow of capital. It was clear that a relaxation of exchange control might help create such an outflow; while in the longer term the capital invested overseas would yield a useful stream of foreign exchange in the years ahead as North Sea oil gradually ran out.

I had another opportunity to return to the charge in a column I had been writing every fortnight for the now defunct *Financial Weekly*, alternating with Harold Wilson for political balance, for some months in 1978–79. Exchange control was the subject of the last column I was to contribute, which appeared on 20 April 1979 in the middle of the election campaign and which argued the case for exchange control abolition. There was no mention whatever of the subject in the manifesto and I was anxious to put down a clear marker before we took office. I cleared the principle with an apprehensive but fundamentally sympathetic Geoffrey Howe – then Shadow Chancellor. Howe himself agreed about the desirability of abolition but did not yet share my view about doing it as soon as possible. Nor had Margaret been squared.

At that time Britain operated the most restrictive exchange control regime of any major industrialized country. It had been imposed as a temporary measure at the outbreak of the Second World War in 1939, and maintained ever since. People had lived with exchange control for so long that it was not in any real sense an issue: it was a fact of life; and there was considerable nervousness that any raising of the topic by the Conservative Opposition might lead to a run on the pound for which the Tories might be blamed.

Nevertheless, when we came to office it was very clear that officials, irrespective of their own views, expected us to abolish exchange control. This was partly because they attached more authority to my *Financial Weekly* article than it deserved, but even more because most of the top people at the Bank of England – especially those responsible for administering exchange control – actively wanted to see it go, with the support of some, although not a majority, of the official Treasury. Against this background and in the knowledge of my views, Geoffrey Howe asked me to look at the pros and cons of exchange control abolition, and the timescale, assisted by a team of Treasury and Bank officials. Douglas Dawkins, the then head of exchange control at Threadneedle Street, led the Bank side and David Hancock was the senior Treasury official. I had no doubt that, with sterling buoyed up by a combination of its petro-currency status and growing international confidence in the sound monetary policies of the new Government, early and complete abolition was not only achievable but economically necessary.

Abolition was none the less a radical and highly controversial step. It was impossible to predict the scale of the capital outflow which might result; but the pent-up demand for overseas portfolio investment in particular suggested it would be large. Labour, after all, had insisted on retaining exchange controls in the expectation that without them capital would flee the ramshackle British economy. Abolition was bound to be a leap in the dark. Fortunately, perhaps, neither I nor the Treasury or Bank officials concerned focused our attention at the time on the important practical consequences abolition was to have for the conduct of monetary policy.

Geoffrey Howe, for understandable reasons, favoured a cautious, step-by-step approach. In particular, he – and I – saw the first step, taken in the Budget in June, as dipping a toe into the water to test the temperature and see how the financial markets reacted. Hence the limited nature of the relaxation package announced in the Budget. It was confined to companies investing abroad and individuals travelling and living in foreign countries. Geoffrey announced the automatic clearance of any direct foreign investments of up to £5 million. He also raised the travel allowance and restored the use of sterling finance for third country trade, which Labour had halted amid the sterling crisis of 1976. But we left the controls on overseas portfolio investment more or less untouched.

The reaction to the Budget relaxations caused no problems and the following month Geoffrey accepted a recommendation of mine to make a modest start on the portfolio side. Accordingly we freed institutions to invest in securities which were either denominated in a European Community currency or issued by supranational organizations like the World Bank. All remaining restrictions on foreign direct investment were axed at the same time.

Finally, on 4 October 1979 I minuted Geoffrey Howe, arguing that we should now move to complete abolition. After careful analysis, I and my Bank/Treasury team were satisfied that there was no coherent halfway house. Conditions in the currency markets could scarcely have been more propitious. 'I do not believe that the abolition of controls will make a fundamental difference to the exchange rate,' I wrote in my minute. The strength of the pound owed far more to the oil factor and to the soundness of our policies than to exchange controls.

After taking him through our report in painstaking detail, I persuaded him – somewhat nervously – to agree. Once he was convinced, he in turn persuaded an even more hesitant Margaret Thatcher.

Much later on in a lecture in 1991, he himself subsequently described the process in these terms:

> First, the ending of Exchange Control. I count this one of the most important achievements of my Chancellorship – and certainly the most fraught with worry . . . It still stands as the only economic decision of my life that caused me to lose a night's sleep. But it was right.

When the decision was put to Cabinet (at the eleventh hour, to ensure secrecy), Ministers were taken completely by surprise; but the only open opponent was Michael Heseltine, then the Environment Secretary, who argued that people would abuse their unaccustomed freedom, and buy villas in the south of France rather than invest in productive assets at home. Geoffrey made his historic announcement to the House of Commons on 23 October. Even the day before, the dollar premium (at which the limited pool of foreign exchange for portfolio investment changed hands) was still around 20 per cent: a remarkable tribute to our success in avoiding any hint of a leak. The whole exercise, as Hancock remarked to me at the end of it, was a perfect example of how Ministers and officials ought to work together. The Bank of England had a special tie designed, in which the Bank's traditional Britannia emblem was flanked with the laconic inscription 'EC 1939–1979'. Geoffrey and I were each presented with one, and as Chancellor I always made a point of wearing mine on Budget Day.

Twenty-five Treasury officials and an entire Bank of England department employing 750 people, costing £14½ million a year, were no longer required. Some took early retirement and others were redeployed, most finding jobs in the City through the good offices of the Bank. The

Labour Party was predictably hostile to the decision, Denis Healey calling it 'reckless, precipitate and doctrinaire'. The Liberals, on the other hand, endorsed the decision warmly. Enoch Powell, then sitting as an Ulster Unionist, simply said 'Is the Chancellor aware that I envy him the opportunity and privilege of announcing a step that will strengthen the economy of this country and help to restore our national pride and confidence in our currency?' So did I.

A more considered if markedly less orthodox Labour reaction was given in the House of Lords on 17 November, by Harold Lever, the millionaire financial expert who had been a member of the Wilson and Callaghan cabinets. Lever welcomed 'the end of this exchange control, which has served no useful purpose, and the abolition of which could be a considerable encouragement to a great trading, insurance and banking nation like our own' and which was 'not even a useful machinery for protection against a run on sterling'.

Abolition in Retrospect

By October 1979, the pound was rising strongly under the influence of oil, 'the Thatcher factor', and our relatively tight monetary policies. And in the short run, my hunch that the relaxation of exchange controls would not lead to any softening of the exchange rate was quickly proved correct. The Bank of England estimated that the relaxation of exchange controls led to an outflow of £1 billion in the third quarter of 1979, and around the same in the fourth quarter, much of it representing no more than the early repayment of outstanding liabilities. The pound scarcely paused at all. Indeed, between 1979 and 1981 the strength of sterling subjected the British economy to a tight financial squeeze of astonishing power and effectiveness. At the same time, the consequent capital outflow led to a significant rise in the UK's net stock of overseas assets – although the official statistics in this area are, regrettably, almost worthless.

From a wider perspective it is hardly possible to overstate the critical importance of our decision. Politically it was the first significant increase of market liberalization undertaken by the Thatcher Government. It marked the start of a process of deregulation which has embraced the world in general and the European Community in particular. Industrially, by enabling UK firms to invest where they liked, it ensured that investment in the UK would yield a worthwhile return – the economy had to compete. Without it the City would have been hard put to remain a world-class financial centre.

Abolition also greatly affected the practical conduct of monetary policy, making direct controls on UK lending institutions – even if desired – largely ineffectual. In addition, as part of a worldwide move (in which it played an influential role) towards freedom of capital movements, it

41

changed the entire international financial and economic environment in ways that I discuss in a later chapter. Finally, it was an important blow for freedom – not least so far as the notorious foreign travel allowance was concerned. I well remember, in the immediate aftermath of abolition, how difficult people found it to grasp that they could go into a bank and acquire as much foreign exchange as they liked, and without having to have their passport stamped with the amount entered. Some people even missed the experience as an essential ingredient of a foreign holiday.

The abolition of exchange control in 1979 was also another nail in the coffin of those who believe that major changes should be made only on a bipartisan basis; that is to say, only when there is a consensus. On that basis we would still have had exchange control today. As it was, by defying the consensus, we not only brought about an important and successful change, but moved the consensus, in due course, too. Coupled with the highly controversial tax and public spending changes announced in the Budget earlier in 1979, it constituted the most radical first year of any new Government within living memory; and no praise is too high for Geoffrey Howe's courage and determination in seeing it through.

An EC Sequel

The announcement of 23 October 1979 left only one piece of unfinished business, which I was able to clear up nearly eight years later. The legislation implementing exchange control, codified in the 1947 Exchange Control Act, remained on the statute-book, even though we had no intention of using it. Treasury officials were in favour of retaining the legislation, in case we (or, more plausibly, a Labour Government) ever wished to reimpose controls. I attached little importance to considerations of that kind, but was nevertheless forced to abandon plans to repeal the legislation (in addition to abolishing the regulations and practical arrangements made under it) when it emerged that we were obliged under a European Community Directive of 21 March 1972 to maintain reserve powers to impose exchange controls.

The Directive required Member States to have on the statute-book powers to control capital flows in either direction, but these were meant to be used in emergencies and on the basis of EC agreement. Our pre-1979 practice of permanently operating rigorous exchange control was in clear violation of this, and we had had a succession of temporary waivers from complying with the free capital movement articles of the Rome Treaty. So, too, of course, had many other EC countries.

Nevertheless the Directive did prevent us from repealing the Exchange Control Act, as Geoffrey Howe noted in a written answer on 16 May 1980. The position was, however, very unsatisfactory. As long as the legislation was on the statute-book, there was always the fear in the markets that it might be used. It was not until the late summer of 1986, in the margin of an informal EC Finance Ministers' meeting at Gleneagles, that I was able to negotiate a private deal with Jacques Delors, the President of the European Commission, that would enable me to repeal the legislation. Delors was seeking to bring the 1972 Directive up to date, as he saw it, in the light of the Single Market programme; but this still meant a Directive setting out the (less frequent) circumstances in which exchange controls could be invoked: he did not initially envisage complete abolition.

Essentially, what I agreed with Delors was that we would repeal the 1947 Act, notwithstanding the 1972 Directive, but that in return I undertook that we would do whatever was necessary to comply with the new Directive once it was agreed. If the worst came to the worst, I was pretty confident that I could block any undesirable Directive. In the event, what was agreed, in 1988, was the Freedom of Capital Movements Directive. This was a highly satisfactory outcome, as it committed major member states to the abolition of all exchange controls within two years. My private deal with Delors was never made public for fear of embarrassing both parties, but I was glad as Chancellor to be able to complete the unfinished business I had left as Financial Secretary. Official Treasury anxieties about surrendering powers that might be needed by a future Government were fortuitously much alleviated by a speech shortly afterwards by Roy Hattersley, then Shadow Chancellor, indicating that a future Labour Government would not reimpose exchange controls *per se,* but would endeavour in some way to direct portfolio investment. When I announced the repeal measure in my 1987 Budget, Labour did not even bother to debate it.

———

CHAPTER 5

BLOOD, TOIL, TEARS AND SWEAT

*The Coming of Monetarism · The Honeymoon Ends
Pay Freeze Rejected · Forecasts – a Self-inflicted Wound
Search for a Treasury Guru · 1980 Budget: An Enterprise Package
A Two-sided Budget?*

The Coming of Monetarism

THE 1979 BUDGET WAS important not only as a tax-reforming Budget. It was also the first major statement of the new Government's economic policy. This became known by the single word 'monetarism', although in fact that was only part of the story. The core of monetarism, as its name suggests, is the proposition that inflation is a monetary phenomenon. Rapid and continuous inflation is not due to excessive pay settlements, world commodity price movements or disappointing productivity trends. All these things may precipitate an initial upward movement of prices and pay; and they may increase the unemployment cost of curbing inflation. But prices and wages cannot carry on chasing each other ever upwards unless a sufficiently easy money policy accommodates the process.

The process linking money and inflation has never been better described than by the great eighteenth-century Scottish philosopher and political economist David Hume, who wrote as long ago as 1752:

> Though the high price of commodities be a necessary consequence of the increase of gold and silver, yet it follows not immediately upon that increase; but some time is required before the money circulates through the whole state, and makes its effects be felt on all ranks of people. At first, no alteration is perceived; by degrees the price rises, first of one commodity, then of another, then of another; till the whole at last reaches a just proportion with a new quantity of specie which is

in the kingdom. In my opinion, it is only in this interval or intermediate situation, between the acquisition of money and rise of prices, that the increasing quantity of gold and silver is favourable to industry.

The setting of an annual target for the growth of the money supply had already been inaugurated by Denis Healey, Chancellor in the previous Labour Government, essentially to propitiate the IMF and the financial markets. The definition of money the Treasury had then chosen was £M3, pronounced Sterling M-three (roughly speaking, cash plus bank deposits of all kinds). But simply to continue with 'unbelieving monetarism' à la Healey was clearly out of the question. Some degree of shock treatment was essential if inflationary expectations were to be wrenched down.

This was implicit – although I was never quite sure how far Geoffrey recognized this – in our decision to announce in the 1979 Budget a slight reduction in the £M3 target we had inherited, despite the fact that inflation was rising and that we had raised nominal GDP still further through the increase in VAT. This made the £M3 target very tough indeed, implying an actual fall in the real money supply (i.e. after allowing for inflation). Indeed, had we raised interest rates sufficiently to stand a chance of hitting that target – which would have meant raising them by much more than we did: perhaps by as much as Paul Volcker, the Chairman of the Federal Reserve Board, subsequently raised rates in the US – the shock would have been even greater than that which British industry did in fact suffer.

None the less, we took the new £M3 target seriously. It was in order to try to meet it that Geoffrey had announced in his 1979 Budget speech an increase in interest rates from the 12 per cent we had inherited in May 1979 to 14 per cent – the highest they had been since the sterling crisis of 1976, when the Labour Government had been obliged to seek assistance from the IMF. But this time we were doing it when sterling was strong and rising.

Douglas Wass, the Treasury Permanent Secretary, was keen to demonstrate that he could give effective backing to a policy that he did not at heart support. For he was above all anxious to prevent the politicization of the higher Civil Service. Indeed, like other 'unbelieving monetarists', he was sometimes more unyielding in his advice than our genuine intellectual supporters, no doubt for the best of motives. In July 1979, he gave a valid warning in a memorandum to Geoffrey Howe, of the dangers of a backlash against policies which were 'relatively strange to a British audience' and whose long-term nature was not understood. Geoffrey responded with a public relations exercise which had some limited success.

BLOOD, TOIL, TEARS AND SWEAT

The Honeymoon Ends

But the battle had only just begun. I minuted Geoffrey at the end of August 1979:

> Now that the (hundred day?) honeymoon is over, and at least until the fruits of our policies show up (which will not be for some time yet), they will attack us whatever we do; for 'primitive monetarism' if we continue on our present course and for weakness, U-turns and general Heath/Barber recidivism if we do not. There is no way in which we can avoid being attacked, whatever we do: we must be guided by the reflection that it is better to be attacked for the right policies than the wrong ones and concentrate on getting our own message across, *for which purpose incidentally, 'primitive' language is essential: nothing else will be understood.* [Italics added.]

After approving the emphasis on the need to adjust expectations to reality and the disaster that would follow any change of course, I argued the need for,

> a third note that really must be struck along with the other two, a note of confidence and above all of hope; the message that there is indeed light at the end of the tunnel. This is absolutely vital, not least if we are to maintain a reasonable degree of business confidence over the difficult eighteen months that lie ahead. But of course it goes wider than that. Churchill may have told the British people that he had nothing to offer them but blood, toil, tears and sweat; but that was not strictly true. There was something else he offered them: the promise of victory – and that was why they followed him.

Striking this note was not made any easier, however, by the fact that by early November 1979 £M3 was growing at an annualized rate of 14 per cent, well above the top of our target range, despite the cosmetic improvement created by the so-called 'corset' (explained in Chapter 8). Confidence in the financial markets was fragile, making it a constant struggle to sell sufficient gilt-edged stock to finance the Budget deficit outside the banking system; and the deficit itself was running above forecast.

Accordingly, Geoffrey announced on 15 November a package of measures designed to rein back both the Budget deficit and monetary growth. The collection of Petroleum Revenue Tax was advanced two months, which the oil industry could well afford with North Sea production and prices both at record heights. To enable the Bank of England to sell sufficient gilts to finance the burgeoning PSBR, the Bank of England's Minimum Lending Rate was raised by three percentage points to 17 per cent, the biggest single interest rate increase ever announced, which took nominal short-term rates to an all-time record level.

Excuses could have been found for avoiding such an unpopular package. In particular, as indeed was soon to occur, we could have pointed to the rise in the exchange rate as evidence of an effective policy tightening.* But it was time for primitive signals. Whatever our hopes for the future, underlying inflation – and not just the RPI – was still rising. The labour market was still very tight – unemployment, which normally lags the economic cycle, continued to fall until the last quarter of 1979 – and over the winter of 1979–80 there were long and bitter strikes in the steel and engineering industries. We thus had to demonstrate in the clearest possible way our commitment to the monetary approach to inflation and a degree of obstinacy in its pursuit. However, a gesture to the anxieties aroused by high interest rates – not least on Margaret's part – was the announcement by Geoffrey on the same day of his intention to publish a Green Paper on methods of monetary control.

Pay Freeze Rejected

The honeymoon was indeed over. By the late summer of 1979 the economy had passed its peak, even though the recession proper did not begin until 1980. Inflation measured by the RPI seemed to be moving inexorably upwards, boosted by the impact of rising oil prices, the pay explosion and our switch from income tax to VAT. Meanwhile businessmen were beginning to complain of the triple squeeze from high interest rates, rising pay costs and a rising exchange rate. Above all, there was a widespread lack of understanding, even among the business community, of the extent of our break with the old consensus, while press commentators were free with predictions of an imminent 'U-turn'.

There were recurrent rumours about the reimposition of pay policy. Margaret Thatcher was somewhat abivalent and, unlike me, had supported the idea of an incomes policy in the past. In his autobiography, Garret Fitzgerald, a reliable witness, recalls a conversation he had with her at a Bilderberg meeting in Turkey in 1975, when she was Leader of the Opposition and he was Ireland's Foreign Minister. She had learned a good deal from the discussions, she told him, 'for example the inadequacy of the money supply approach, because so much had to be done by way of supportive action to make the money supply work. If inflation were very high an incomes policy was necessary, but there should be a statutory policy only for a very short time'.

Thankfully, on this occasion she rejected the idea, but others did not. Jim Prior, the Employment Secretary, was arguing in Cabinet for a

---

*Moreover, contrary to what our critics allege, we were well aware of the deficiencies of £M3 or any other specific indicator of monetary conditions, and we pointed out at the time the elements of distress borrowing in the growth of credit and money.

public sector pay norm, an idea which in May 1980 gained the support of John Hoskyns, the head of the Number 10 Policy Unit. I derided the proposal in a minute to Geoffrey as a 'well trodden route to disaster', divorcing pay from market conditions and politicizing the wage-bargaining process. The only practical effect of this climate was to make the unions determined to secure the largest possible pay settlements before any clampdown occurred.

Although we had decided to take on the chin the short-term effect on the RPI of the Budget switch from income tax (which does not feature in the index) to VAT (which of course does), it seemed worth trying to mitigate the effect on inflationary expectations. While still in Opposition, I had floated the idea of a 'cost of living index' which would remain unaffected by changes in the balance between direct and indirect taxation and had circulated a paper by a bright young economist, Douglas McWilliams (later to become chief economic adviser to the Confederation of British Industry) outlining an index of this kind. Since a switch from direct to indirect taxation was part of the platform on which we had been elected, Geoffrey gave me the go-ahead to produce such an index once we were in Government.

The Central Statistical Office (CSO) was initially rather suspicious of my project. But once I had satisfied its top officials that I wanted it done on a proper statistical basis, they co-operated unreservedly. They did insist, however, that it should be given the colourless title 'Tax and Prices Index' (TPI) rather than 'Cost of Living Index' which I had preferred. A new index was produced by a small Treasury and CSO team under my chairmanship and launched on 17 August 1979. It came out on the day of publication of the July RPI, which showed a 4.3 per cent rise in a single month, largely due to the Budget changes.

The TPI, which continues to be published, produced moderately useful material for speeches, but it never really caught on. When I returned to the Treasury in 1983, it seemed to me more important to try to focus attention on the underlying RPI, that is the RPI excluding mortgage interest payments, which most other countries rightly exclude from their consumer price indexes. (The TPI incidentally does include such payments.)

Forecasts – A Self-inflicted Wound

Many of our problems were the inevitable side-effects of attempting a radical change of course during a difficult world and domestic economic conjuncture, and against the background of a public and a party that had not been fully prepared for the change. But there was one self-inflicted wound: the obligation to publish short-term economic forecasts at Budget time and in the autumn. This was a statutory requirement under the 1975

Industry Act, thanks to an amendment moved by a Labour member, Dr Jeremy Bray. Ironically, the Bray Amendment was carried against the wishes of the then Labour Government only by the support of the Conservative Opposition when we were still too depressed by the successive election defeats of 1974 to pass up the chance of defeating the Government. It was a pyrrhic victory.

As soon as we took office, I urged Geoffrey Howe to repeal the Industry Act in its entirety, or failing that, at least the Bray Amendment itself and the obligation to maintain, and publish the results of, a computer model of the economy. By 1979 there were a number of reputable alternative models in the academic world and the private sector whose results the Treasury could have assessed. Professor Alan Budd of the London Business School (LBS), had in 1977 floated the idea of the Treasury using and assessing a variety of forecasts by outside bodies. He pointed out *en passant* that the Treasury spent twice as much on forecasting as the LBS and the National Institute of Economic and Social Research put together; so there was plenty of scope for budgetary and staff economies as well.

In a minute to Geoffrey sent in June 1979, I pointed out that the US Treasury made no economic forecasts of its own and relied entirely on outside forecasters (including those of the Federal Reserve). But my main argument against the Treasury forecasts was the political burden they imposed. Because they enjoyed the *imprimatur* of the Treasury they were, as I wrote to Geoffrey at the time, 'invested by the outside world with a spurious authority, not to mention the status of deliberate policy choices'. I warned that it would be impossible simply to cease *publishing* the forecasts while continuing to make them. 'So long as forecasts of this kind are made by the Treasury, they will leak and we shall be accused of suppression and worse if we do not publish them.'

The argument that Treasury officials successfully used to defeat my proposal was that, once Parliament had been provided with so-called information, that information could not be withdrawn. Behind this rare passion by Treasury officials for Parliamentary rights was a deep in-house commitment not merely to the Treasury forecasts, but to the Treasury model as a central tool of analysis and policy evaluation.* A further political embarrassment was the systematic leaking of the forecasts by a hostile insider to a journalist on *The Times* . We never found out who he was, but he became known inside the Treasury as 'Deep Throat'. The leaks purported to show that Ministers were so embarrassed by the Treasury model's forecasts that they were 'fiddling

---

*It might strictly speaking have been possible to keep some much smaller version of the Treasury model in being for the purposes of policy simulation without the commitment to the forecasts, although I was not keen even on that.

with the figures' to avoid their implications.

I am not ashamed of having taken steps to prevent nonsensical forecasts from being published. Inevitably forecasts are attributed by Opposition and commentators alike to 'the Chancellor' and there is a limit to how far Chancellors can distance themselves from the forecasts published in their name – as I know from my later efforts to do so. The Treasury and other mainstream forecasters are fond of boasting that their predictions are not mechanical extrapolations of a model (which would in any case be difficult to make in view of the number of 'exogenous' assumptions required to crank up the whole model) but require the exercise of judgement in which Ministers have every right to take part.

The initial forecast the Treasury prepared over the New Year for the 1980 Budget was unbelievably gloomy. On closer investigation I found that the Treasury forecasters were predicting the worst economic downturn since the Great Slump of 1929–31. Yet they expected no fall in inflation at all. This was clearly absurd and underlined the inadequacies of the model. I minuted Geoffrey in February 1980 that it would be both ridiculous and dangerous to publish such a forecast:

> Even if we do believe the forecast (which I do not) it would be folly to publish it in anything like the present form. This would have a very serious impact indeed on expectations which are crucial to policy. In addition it could well cause so much political opposition to the policy – not merely among the official Opposition – as to force its abandonment (and/or perhaps a lurch into full-scale protectionism). To run such risks merely for the sake of a forecast whose margins of error are known to be very large indeed would be absurd.

We eventually published a more realistic forecast at the time of the Budget which included a more moderate decline in output but also a fall in inflation. Events roughly corresponded with this outcome, although inflation fell faster than we predicted; so, if anything, the changes we insisted upon did not go far enough.*

Denis Healey used to claim that he wanted to be to the forecasters what the Boston strangler was to door-to-door salesmen. I wholeheartedly

---

*The Treasury economists were originally forecasting in the run-up to the 1980 Budget a savage recession in 1980 with a 6½ per cent fall in GDP, but no change in inflation: a singularly unlikely conjunction. Largely at my insistence we published instead in the Budget Red Book a GDP fall in 1980 of 2½ per cent (severe enough in all conscience) and a gradual fall in RPI inflation from a prevailing 19 per cent to 13½ per cent in the second quarter of 1981. The outcome was a fall in GDP of 2 per cent and (more important) a faster fall in inflation to 11½ per cent in the second quarter of 1981.

shared the sentiments but neither of us succeeded in acting on them. Perhaps I should have returned to the charge when I became Chancellor in 1983. But I was lulled by a period of years when the forecasting record was pretty good, as it tends to be when the economy is expanding at trend rates or slightly below them. It is at crucial turning points that the models let us down. The problem was not just one of poor forecasts of the future – of which I was in any event invariably sceptical – but also of poor statistics, which gave a misleading impression of the present and recent past. I did, belatedly, take the opportunity to strengthen the CSO and bring it within the Chancellor's sphere of responsibility shortly before my resignation in 1989, with what result it is too soon to say. However, there was no sign of Alan Budd, when he became Chief Economic Adviser in 1991, taking up his earlier proposal to privatize the forecasts.

Search for a Treasury Guru

By a stroke of good fortune the post of Chief Economic Adviser to the Treasury (who was also Head of the Government Economic Service, and thus theoretically responsible for all the economists throughout Whitehall) fell vacant at the end of 1979. Fred Atkinson, who was due to retire, was an amiable and shrewd, if laid-back, economist, who was curious about our new approach, but knew that he was not the person to take the Treasury into a new era.

My own view was that the job could be done effectively only by somebody who sympathized with the new beginning initiated after the election, but who understood more mainstream ways of thinking and could command the respect of Treasury economists. Well before the 1979 election I had come to the conclusion that the best bet was probably Terry Burns, the young Director of the Centre for Economic Forecasting at the London Business School, and had invited him to lunch at the Garrick Club to sound him out. He was clearly both sympathetic to our thinking and interested in the job. He was also already a member of the Treasury's Academic Panel. After much discussion and consultation, Geoffrey Howe accepted my strong recommendation that he should be appointed. Terry was only thirty-six when he arrived at the Treasury in early 1980 and his appointment was greeted with the rave notices that the British reserve for the very young and the very old. The appointment proved a great success, tarnished only by his failures in the forecasting area in the late 1980s and early 1990s – the very area, ironically, where he had originally made his academic reputation. He subsequently rose (well after my resignation as Chancellor) to be Permanent Secretary to the Treasury.

Burns was soon forgotten by the media in the flurry of excitement created by Margaret Thatcher's decision to appoint Alan Walters as her personal economic adviser at the beginning of 1981. Outsiders never really understood the difference between the Burns and Walters posts. Burns was a very senior Treasury official, whereas Walters was a freely floating personal Number 10 adviser. Walters' declared view was that it was best for an adviser in either position not to stay too long – he suggested not more than four years. Regrettably, he did not see fit to follow his own advice when he returned to Number 10 in 1989.

1980 Budget: An Enterprise Package

The Budget of 26 March 1980 was not intended to be particularly memorable or imaginative in the macro sphere. Its one measure of genuine tax reform was the simplification produced by abolishing the 25 per cent lower rate tax band on the first £750 of taxable income, which Denis Healey had introduced in 1978 at the behest of the TUC. Ironically, this reform was to be unwisely reversed by Norman Lamont in his pre-election Budget of 1992.

But despite its lack of drama and its overall neutrality, the Budget contained not only the launch of the Medium Term Financial Strategy (MTFS), discussed at length in Chapter 7, and whose importance dwarfed the rest of the Budget, but also the rather more popular and comprehensible 'Enterprise Package'. The latter comprised a series of small business initiatives we had first outlined in *The Right Approach to the Economy* in 1977. Corporation Tax, Capital Gains Tax and Capital Transfer Tax were reduced for small businessmen. There was also a venture capital scheme which allowed investors in business start-ups to offset any losses against income tax.

The most eye-catching innovation, however, was the establishment of six experimental 'Enterprise Zones' in run-down inner-city areas. The idea had been personally pioneered by Geoffrey in a speech on the Isle of Dogs in 1978 as part of a wide-ranging programme to 'increase the wealth-creating vitality of our economy'. Investment there was freed of all capital and income taxes, business rates and industrial levies, although Geoffrey had to water down his original aim of making them into miniature Hong Kongs, free of all planning restrictions. The enterprise package was itself only part of the new Government's barrage of measures designed to roll back the frontiers of the State and improve the functioning of the market economy. We had, by the time of the 1980 Budget, not only abolished exchange control, as described in the previous chapter: we had also abolished all forms of pay controls, price controls, and dividend controls, all of which had been in operation, under governments of both parties, for most of the previous decade; while preparations for the first privatizations were already well underway. It all added up to a coherent and far-reaching programme of deregulation, whose magnitude and importance was not, in those early days, clearly recognized.

A Two-sided Budget?

The MTFS introduced for the first time a framework in which public expenditure and taxation were brought together – a badly needed innovation. This was reinforced in 1980 by bringing the Budget forward from April to March (where it has remained ever since) and delaying the publication of the Public Expenditure White Paper until Budget day. This had the merit of showing the public, and the spending Ministers, that taxation was needed to pay for expenditure and that changes on one side of the accounts led to changes in another.

Nevertheless the experiment was not repeated for the remainder of the Thatcher years. Jim Callaghan, then Leader of the Opposition, complained through the 'usual channels' (parliamentary jargon for the Government and Opposition Chief Whips) that Parliament was being given too much information to digest in one day, a complaint echoed by the media. However, in March 1992 Norman Lamont, Chancellor in the John Major administration, was to return to the charge, publishing a White Paper proposing that in future publication of the government's public expenditure and tax plans would be brought together in a single 'two-sided' Budget in December, starting in December 1993.

While it clearly makes sense conceptually, in addition to the difficulty for the House of Commons in absorbing so much complex information at the same time, which was the 1980 complaint, the proposal suffers from two practical disadvantages. The first is the need to determine an appropriate PSBR for the year ahead, and to frame a Budget consistent with this, four months before the start of the new financial year, at a time when the margin of uncertainty over the outcome of the PSBR for the current year remains enormous.

The second, and probably in practice the more serious if the Budget is seen, as it should be, as an opportunity for supply-side reform rather than fiscal fine tuning, is the immense burden of work the new system will impose on the Chancellor of the day and his top officials during the three-month period between his return (however refreshed) from his summer holiday in September and his Budget in December, when all the key decisions on both public expenditure and taxation will be concentrated. This is a problem that other countries avoid by having two different government departments, headed by two different Ministers, responsible for the two sides of the Budget. Thus although the intention is laudable, it is by no means obvious that the outcome of the proposed reform will be better decision-making.

I had myself been thinking about this problem since I sat as the statutory Conservative on the 'Armstrong Committee' on budgetary reform, set up by the Institute for Fiscal Studies in 1978, which I had to leave at an early stage when I joined the Government in May 1979. The Committee, which reported in July 1980, favoured not merely publishing the Government's tax proposals in the autumn, side by side with its expenditure plans, but doing so in an explicitly tentative form, as a basis for public discussion and debate before the real Budget was presented in the spring. It was also proposed that, as a background to the discussion and debate, the Government should, at the same time, publish its initial economic assessment for the following financial year. The Committee described its proposed innovation as a 'Green Budget'.

A Green Budget would clearly have met the Callaghan objection, but in every other way it would have been a disastrous route to take and we rightly gave it no house room. Publication of a Green Budget would provide a field day to every expenditure pressure group, every single-issue lobbyist, and every vested interest. It would bring about an enormous deterioration in the quality of Budget-making, both on the public spending and on the tax side. It would in practice make our system much more like that of the US, which would not be a change for the better. This was also the view of Jim Baker (the US Treasury Secretary who later went on to become President Bush's Secretary of State) with whom I compared notes. One piece of evidence that he was right was the chronic US fiscal deficit of the 1980s and beyond; another that the US tax system is far more seriously riddled with special interest breaks than the British one. The 1992 White Paper wisely steered well clear of a Green Budget.

CHAPTER 6

STERLING AND RECESSION, 1979–81

The Sharp End · Obstinacy and Bare Knuckles
Sterling Climbs in Earnest · Treasury Devaluationists
A Retrospect on Sterling · Thatcherism in Zurich

The Sharp End

TO BUSINESS AND INDUSTRY what mattered at this time was the fact that the economy was in recession and that they were being crucified by a sharply rising exchange rate. Moreover the general gloom was deepened by an unprecedentedly sharp rise in unemployment. For if the severity of the squeeze in output was fully foreseen by the Government, the size of the accompanying rise in unemployment came as a shock. Whereas employers had reacted to previous recessions by holding on to labour as long as possible, the squeeze of the early 1980s led to a blitz on overmanning. The long-standing relationship between output and jobs, used in Treasury forecasting, was shattered (as most forecasts and relationships tend to be when they are really needed by policy-makers).

The total loss of output between the cyclical peak in the second quarter of 1979 and the recession low point in the first quarter of 1981 was 5½ per cent. Employment, however, fell from its peak of 23.1 million in the fourth quarter of 1979 to a low point of 21 million in the first quarter of 1983, a drop of nearly 10 per cent. The rise in recorded unemployment was even greater. It more than doubled in 1980 and 1981, to reach 2⅓ million at the end of 1981, and then continued to climb, at a slower pace, for the best part of the next five years. The manpower squeeze was especially severe in manufacturing, where more than 2 million jobs, corresponding to 14 per cent of total employment, were lost.

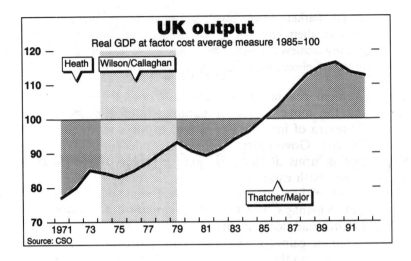

UK output

Real GDP at factor cost average measure 1985=100

Heath

Wilson/Callaghan

Thatcher/Major

Source: CSO

The human and political costs were obviously large. It was not simply a matter of the numbers unemployed, but who the unemployed were and the length of time they spent in the dole queue. The shake-out went far beyond the sort of people who are always in and out of work, as well-established workers who had been earning good wages found themselves unemployed for the first time in their lives. Large numbers of school-leavers – of whom, for demographic reasons, there were an unusually high and rising number – found it impossible to get the sort of job they had expected and difficult to find work of any kind. This, inevitably, caused anxiety not merely to them but to their parents; and cast a blight, too, on the parents of those who were about to become school-leavers, who worried whether there would be a job for Johnny to go to. And as time passed, the hitherto largely unknown spectre of long-term unemployment, that most debilitating of conditions, began to loom large, as the average duration of unemployment steadily increased.

The other side of the story, however, was a long overdue and badly needed onslaught on decades of overmanning, which paved the way for a remarkable improvement in productivity, especially in manufacturing. There was both an immediate recession spurt and a longer-term improvement. Partly as a result, the annual increase in unit wage costs plunged from 22 per cent in 1980 to 9 per cent in 1982 and 4 per cent in 1983. As Professor Geoffrey Maynard put it in a book which deserves to be better known:

> By refusing to accommodate rising costs and poor productivity with exchange rate depreciation, macro-policy imposed pressure on industry to raise productivity, lower costs and generally move its

product up market. Many firms, whose managements were often vociferous in their criticism of government exchange rate policy, subsequently achieved productivity improvements and product up-grading to an unprecedented extent.

The management revolution was due not only to the exchange rate squeeze and the move to higher nominal interest rates, but also to the end of the era of incomes policy and to the widespread impression that the Thatcher Government, unlike its predecessors, would not bail out loss-making firms at the first political outcry – or indeed at all. The policy thus both established the Government's counter-inflationary credentials and at the same time reinforced management's newly redis-covered right to manage. The squeeze was relaxed only when there were clear signs that it had done its job.

I believe that we gained far more than we lost in microeconomic terms – i.e. quite apart from the beneficial effects for inflation – from the higher exchange rate. Of course, there were real costs as well as benefits. But as I have already indicated, a shock *was* needed if attitudes were to change. Overall, so far from losing our industrial base, our industrial base emerged from the fire more productive, more efficient, more competitive in the best sense, and very much better managed. This was the so-called 'leaner and fitter' effect – even though I was hardly the person to use at least the first part of that metaphor.

The unfinished task was to create the conditions in which the produc-tivity improvements could be reflected in greater total output, as well as higher output per head. In any case, once the cultural change had been largely secured, the case for continuing the shock treatment was very much weaker. Hence the relaxation of the squeeze in the course of 1981 and the shift to what Geoffrey Howe called in October 1982 (when I was no longer in the Treasury) 'flexibility without laxity'.

Obstinacy and Bare Knuckles

A good deal of obstinacy was needed to persevere with our chosen course. Many Press commentators could scarcely contain their impatience to see a U-turn. Industrialists could not, of course, be expected to enjoy what was happening. I remember travelling the country as Financial Secretary and addressing meetings of businessmen, sometimes on governmental and sometimes on Conservative Party occasions, and receiving an almost universally hostile reception when it came to the questioning. The main theme was invariably how the Government was crucify-ing British industry with the high exchange rate and how it clearly did not understand the consequences. This experience, incidentally, was probably the origin of the myth that the Thatcher Government generally, and I in particular, were hostile to manufacturing industry and considered it of little importance.

Not only was the honeymoon with business well and truly over, but for a time divorce was in the air. Maurice Hodgson, the Chairman of ICI, visited Margaret in October 1980 to warn her that the company would make a third quarter loss for the first time in its history; and Michael Edwardes, the Chairman of British Leyland (subsequently to change its name to Rover Group), proclaimed that if the Government 'cannot find a way of living with North Sea oil, then I say: leave the bloody stuff in the ground'. This phase culminated in a widely publicized attack on the Government at the CBI's annual conference in November 1980, which passed a motion critical of Government policy on interest rates, on exchange rates and on public spending. It was there that Terence Beckett, the newly installed Director-General, hit the headlines by declaring:

> We have got to take the gloves off and have a bare knuckle fight [with the Government] because we have to have an effective and prosperous industry . . . Our short-term needs are clear. We have got to have a lower pound, lower interest rates and a reduction in the National Insurance surcharge.

All this was too much for five of the CBI's most substantial member companies, which promptly resigned from the organization. At a subsequent Number 10 meeting between Margaret and a somewhat chastened Terry Beckett, the CBI Director-General explained that industry loved her after all.

The complaints from industry about the strength of sterling were all the more strident because the discipline was not one to which they had been accustomed. For most of post-war history, the movement of sterling had been persistently and unequivocally downwards. Indeed British policymakers, viewing the periodic struggles of German Governments to keep down a rising Deutschmark were inclined to react in terms of the New York Jewish idiom, 'I should have such problems'.

The first intimation that such problems could occur even in Britain came after the Labour Government's deal with the IMF in 1976. The resulting return of confidence led in the following year to the unfamiliar spectacle of a strengthening pound. Sterling's movements at this time are best tracked by means of the so-called sterling index, which is a trade weighted average of the exchange rate against various currencies. (The sterling D-Mark rate came into its own rather later.) The 1977 upsurge was not in retrospect that large and the pound regained little more than half the ground lost in the 1976 crisis. But the rise was enough to alarm the Treasury's Permanent Secretary, Douglas Wass, who was a strong believer in a 'competitive' pound.

The authorities used both intervention and lower interest rates to stem the rise. MLR was slashed dramatically, from 14 per cent at the beginning of 1977 to 5 per cent in October of that year. After that Denis Healey, acting on Gordon Richardson's advice, uncapped the pound – the only time (according to his memoirs) that he overruled Wass. The Labour Government's worries about a rising pound were, however, all too short-lived. MLR had to be increased several times in the course of 1978 to prevent sterling falling too far, and again in January 1979.

Sterling Climbs in Earnest

It was only after that, that the pound began its more dramatic rise. By election day, 3 May 1979, sterling was still below where it had been before Labour's crisis negotiations with the IMF. After the Conservative victory, sterling began to take off, with only a temporary relapse in the closing months of 1979 when Paul Volcker's arrival at the Fed led to the imposition of a fierce monetary squeeze in the US.

By the end of January 1981 the pound was more than 20 per cent higher than it had stood on election day. Many commentators prefer to look at estimates of the real exchange rate, i.e. taking into account inflation, which at that time was significantly higher in Britain than in major competitor countries. On the basis of relative producer prices, the real appreciation of sterling at its peak was some 30 per cent. (A real appreciation of nearly 50 per cent can be obtained on the basis of IMF unit labour costs, but the realism of that particular index is open to question.)

Our decision to do nothing to prevent the pound's rise, despite the complaints of businessmen, was a deliberate one. At the end of August 1979, to the astonishment of Treasury officials, I wrote to Geoffrey Howe:

> So far from wishing to do anything to lower the exchange rate, I believe that the strong pound is the biggest thing we have going for us. Not only is it an integral part of our anti-inflation policy, but any attempt to weaken it would quickly lead to a very serious loss of confidence in our resolve to stick to that policy. We *must* have expectations working for us and not against us: that is fundamental. Thus it is even, I believe, unwise to *hint* that we are unhappy at the strength of the pound.

Not wishing to appear too outrageous, I added that 'a rapidly and inexorably rising pound would be another matter, but that is neither the reality nor the prospect.' Like almost everyone else, I failed to see how far the pound would eventually rise and how long its strength would persist.

Anyone who can explain why the exchange rate moves as it does under a floating regime would be able to predict future movements and thus become a multi-millionaire, which I am not. Nor, incidentally, are those who claim to have a simple monetarist explanation of exchange rate behaviour. But looking back, not entirely with hindsight, on the huge rise of sterling in 1979–80, three factors almost certainly played a part:

1. *The Thatcher Effect*: by this I mean financial market confidence in the new Government with its stern new approach.

2. *The Oil Effect*: in other words the belated recognition of sterling as a petro-currency at a time when oil prices were rising sharply, following the Iranian Revolution and the outbreak of the Iran–Iraq war.

3. *The Carter Effect*: this last is often forgotten in the UK; but the Carter Presidency, especially towards the end, forfeited the confidence of the world's financial markets with disastrous consequences for the dollar. When Ronald Reagan was elected in November 1980, and inaugurated the following February, the market's attitude to the dollar changed completely.

While we were in no doubt about the policy that we wished to pursue, we were in two minds over the pace at which it was sensible to seek to squeeze inflation out of the system. Geoffrey's instinct was for a policy of gradualism, and the MTFS explicitly charted a gradualist path. But the big question was the severity of the first step. I was conscious that while too great a shock could cause unnecessary dislocation to the economy, it was also true that too gradualist a start would do nothing to change expectations – which was urgently needed – and would dissipate much of the benefit of having a new Government in place plotting a new course for the economy.

Treasury Devaluationists

One problem I had not fully expected, and which was not easy to deal with, was the devaluationist tendency of some senior Treasury officials and economists. My relations with Treasury officials were good, if only because they felt they could obtain from me some clarification of the weird doctrines which the new Government was embracing; although they thought I was mad to welcome the high exchange rate, even to the extent it had reached in the summer of 1979. But common sense eventually prevailed as it tends to do, and it increasingly came to be accepted that the high exchange rate was squeezing inflation out of the economy. We remained uncertain about the extent to which we should seek to rein back the growth of £M3, and its unexpectedly rapid expansion was never tolerated explicitly, for fear of upsetting the financial markets. But the reality was different from the rhetoric, and despite the £M3 numbers, as sterling soared, interest rates were reduced to 16 per cent in July 1980 and 14 per cent in November 1980. These fully justified reductions occurred, incidentally, before the arrival of Alan Walters to preach the low interest rate gospel.

The Treasury's devaluationist tendency at that time stemmed largely, I suspect, from the failures of the 1960s, when the 'establishment', and notably the then Prime Minister, Harold Wilson, equated devaluation or any mention of it, with treachery of the deepest hue – while simultaneously pursuing a domestic economic policy that was incompatible with the maintenance of the external value of the pound. The ensuing disaster led a number of senior Treasury officials to overreact and come to believe (as the foreign exchange market long had) that a falling pound was an inescapable fact of life and they had better learn to live with it. This was not a view shared, incidentally, by the Bank – with the conspicuous exception of its then Deputy Governor, Kit McMahon.

Happily, this strand in the collective wisdom of the official Treasury became steadily less pronounced as the years passed; and was wholly absent by the late 1980s. The main home of the sinking currency school nowadays is the United States, especially the East Coast intellectual establishment, Republican as well as Democrat. But it was very much present on Great George Street when I was Financial Secretary. Its most vigorous manifestation occurred in the autumn of 1980 when Douglas Wass persuaded Geoffrey to allow him to set up, under his own direction, a Treasury working group on 'competitiveness' which was official Treasury code for devaluation. On 1 December, the Working Group submitted its report and Geoffrey in due course passed it to me for comment.

It would have been rather more impressive if the group had openly embraced devaluation instead of insinuating it. Because it employed the techniques of the Circumlocution Office, the report professed to be concerned about some future downward pressure on sterling which a poor trade performance would cause. As I wrote in my comments to Geoffrey, 'the innocent reader might be pardoned for thinking that if the lack of competitiveness leads – via poor trade performance – to a lower exchange rate there is no need for artificial measures to achieve this all too familiar end; whereas if it does not there is equally little point in seeking to induce it.' I went on to add,

> Who can seriously doubt that, in real life, the better German domestic performance – both in terms of inflation, which affects the level of wage settlements, and in terms of the real yardstick of productivity progress – is in no meaningful sense cancelled out by the . . . appreciation of the exchange rate . . . ? Take two countries each with precisely static competitiveness in the economist's sense. But one has achieved this via stable prices (and wages), high productivity growth and a rising exchange rate, whereas the other has achieved it via rapid inflation (and a wage explosion), declining productivity and a falling exchange rate. Is it seriously suggested that there is nothing to choose between them? Everyone knows that in the real

world an improvement in competitiveness due to a rise in productivity is infinitely to be preferred to a statistically equivalent rise in
competitiveness produced by a fall in the exchange rate.

Although it offered no specific policy prescriptions, the Treasury Paper
was excessively pessimistic in tone. It was clearly designed to justify
an immediate and significant devaluation of sterling. But this was not
advocated directly. Indeed it was not at all clear what Wass and his
group were advocating in practice unless it was a relaxation of the
battle against inflation, which would have been disastrous. Of course,
the official Treasury, *ceteris paribus*, always tend to favour low interest
rates, low public expenditure, low government deficits and high taxes –
i.e. a tight fiscal stance but not too tight a monetary policy; this combines
its austere conviction that investment is serious but consumption is
frivolous, with its mission to curb public spending. The Treasury never
again came as near to open advocacy of devaluation as in its 1980 report.
But the tendency did not disappear overnight.

It is easy to forget that in 1980 we were emerging from a decade of
negative real interest rates, which was clearly a fraud on the savers –
who felt it bitterly – and incompatible with the survival of a capitalist
system. The move to adequate positive real interest rates was a gradual
one. Measured in the conventional way, short-term real rates were only
barely positive on average in the three years 1979–81, inclusive. They
became significantly positive only when inflation started to fall sharply
in 1982 and interest rates were lowered much more gradually.* Even so,
real interest rates never reached as high as 4 per cent during the whole
of Geoffrey Howe's Chancellorship.

A Retrospect on Sterling

The question is whether, with hindsight, there was a preferable alternative to the policy we pursued; an alternative that would have squeezed
inflation out of the system without the high exchange rate which put
such pressure on the internationally traded sector of the economy and
on manufacturing in particular.

Excessive pay increases played a large part in the employment squeeze.
Private sector expectations took some time to adjust to the new climate,
quite apart from the knock-on effects of Clegg, VAT and oil prices
already mentioned. It is easy to say that the sterling overshoot was
deeply damaging; and certainly it seems to sit awkwardly with my later
advocacy of the ERM as a desirable measure of exchange rate stability.

---

*Measuring real interest rates as the three-month inter-bank rate deflated by the RPI
exclusive of mortgage interest payments.

But in the early 1980s, after the false trails that had led to the débâcle of the previous decades, some degree of shock treatment was needed, and the exchange rate provided it. Moreover inflation generally in the Group of Seven was too high and too variable to make exchange rate stability a credible objective at that time.

The rise in the pound can be divided into two phases. There was the surge from the beginning of 1979 to the autumn of 1980. Although this was neither planned nor intended, we were able to use it to achieve both our counter-inflationary objectives and the necessary improvement in industrial efficiency. Then there was the further rise to the peak at the end of 1980 and the beginning of 1981. This was a clear example of over-shooting and is the type of counterproductive movement which should ideally be combated either by a system of international exchange rate management or in a regional system like the exchange rate mechanism of the EMS. If either such system had been in working order, it might have been possible to maintain existing interest rates while using co-ordinated international intervention to offset currency overshooting. But no such international system existed, while the ERM had been established for only a year, and sterling was in any case not part of it.

It was, of course, right to reduce interest rates as clear evidence arrived of progress in reducing inflation and, as far as the international position – which was dominated by the Fed's tight money drive – allowed. But Alan Walters' attempt, with the enthusiastic support of Margaret Thatcher, to hurry the process by using the 1981 Budget to reduce interest rates, was not in those terms a great success. Base rates, which stood at 14 per cent on the eve of that Budget, were cut to 12 per cent in its wake. That was just below the rate of inflation, then 12¾ per cent. Within six months MLR had to be jacked up to 14 per cent to fight off the downward pressure on the pound; and by the beginning of October it was up to 16 per cent. It was not until the end of February 1982 that it came below 14 per cent again and not until July of that year that it was back to 12 per cent – by which time inflation was down to 8½ per cent and falling fast.

Thatcherism in Zurich

As Financial Secretary, I was inevitably deeply concerned with these monetary issues. I was also well aware of the need to provide some answer to the angry clamour of businessmen and their supporters in the Press and elsewhere for a lower exchange rate, without admitting too explicitly that we were relying on the high exchange rate to squeeze inflation out of the system. My major speech to the Zurich Society of Economics on 14 January 1981, has to be seen against this political background. At the same time, I was concerned that the word 'monetarism' – even when correctly used and not treated simply as a hate word – was an inadequate description of the Government's policy. Indeed it was Keith Joseph, Margaret Thatcher's economic mentor and the John the Baptist of monetarism within the Conservative Party, who had entitled his 1976 Stockton lecture 'Monetarism is not enough'. He pointed out there the need for it to be accompanied by measures that would improve economic performance by the encouragement of enterprise at all levels. This became the party line, reflected in the 1979 manifesto and in numerous speeches.

I spent some time trying to make the twin strands more explicit and coherent. One reason for the confusion was that the anti-inflation macro policy produced results sooner than the enterprise-inducing micro policy did; but the misunderstandings went deeper still. It was largely to clear up this confusion that I entitled my Zurich speech 'Thatcherism in Practice'. This was, so far as I was aware at the time, the first ever use of the term 'Thatcherism' to describe our policies. (I later discovered that it had been used by the recherché, and now defunct, publication *Marxism Today* before we had even taken office in 1979, but no-one had taken any notice.)

The speech caused something of a stir. Michael Foot, then Leader of the Opposition, seized on my admission that we had 'so far, on balance, *increased* the real burden of taxation overall'. But in general it was well received, both by the more serious commentators, as the first detailed and coherent account of the Government's economic policy, and by Margaret Thatcher. I have to confess, however, that I gave an advance copy of the speech to Geoffrey very late in the day, giving him little practical opportunity to suggest any changes.

'Thatcherism' is, I believe, a useful term, and certainly was at the time. No other modern Prime Minister has given his or her name to a particular constellation of policies and values. However it needs to be used with care. The wrong definition is 'whatever Margaret Thatcher herself at any time did or said'. The right definition involves a mixture of free markets, financial discipline, firm control over public expenditure, tax cuts, nationalism, 'Victorian values' (of the Samuel Smiles self-help variety), privatization and a dash of populism.

A subsequent formulation of the Government's supply-side policy objective which I was to use frequently and which was also much used by Margaret was the recreation of the 'enterprise culture' in the UK. The model in this case was the United States – although that country had in turn derived it from the vigorous enterprise culture of Victorian England and Scotland, and developed it further. As far as I know the 'enterprise culture' was my coinage and the 'dependency culture' was Margaret Thatcher's.

Be that as it may, the point here was that we were seeking not simply to remove various controls and impositions, but by so doing to change the entire culture of a nation from anti-profits, anti-business, government-dependent lassitude and defeatism, to a pro-profit, pro-business, robustly independent vigour and optimism. I was later to be castigated for creating a climate of excessive optimism. There may be some truth in this – corrections tend to overshoot – but correction in this direction was badly needed. I remain in no doubt that a necessary precondition of economic success is a fundamental business optimism based on self-belief and the will to succeed. Defeatism, the characteristic of pre-Thatcher Britain, is invariably self-fulfilling.

The Zurich speech was also highlighted by the British press because of its hint that the forthcoming Budget might have to be a tough one. In fact, much of the speech – inevitably, in view of the supposedly expert audience – was devoted to explaining in some detail why British monetary policy remained tight despite the misfortunes of our headline monetary target. More important was my declaration that 'to have abandoned the fight against inflation on the grounds that the world recession and the transformation of sterling into a petro-currency provided sufficient problems to be getting on with, would have been a dereliction of duty which we had no intention of committing.' But the most important contribution of the speech was putting the monetary exposition side by side with an account of the deeper cultural changes we were trying to encourage.

CHAPTER 7

THE MEDIUM TERM FINANCIAL STRATEGY

The Origins · What It Said and Why
Borrowing Targets · The Abiding Legacy
A Personal Postscript

The Origins

LOOKING BACK ON THESE events from the perspective of the early 1990s, Geoffrey Howe generously told the Institute for Fiscal Studies:

> There emerged the rigorous discipline of the Medium Term Financial Strategy, and for that we owe a great deal to the clear-sighted tenacity of its chief draftsman, Nigel Lawson. The MTFS, too, was not instantly applauded by the Bank of England nor in Number 10, where the then incumbent had little enthusiasm for what she described as 'graph paper economics'. I have no doubt, in retrospect, about the overriding need for such a device.

During our period in Opposition, I had developed the idea of a stabilization programme extending several years ahead to replace the short-term and unbelieving monetarism of Denis Healey. I set out my thinking in a *Times* article published on 14 September 1978 in the following terms:

> The time has come for a wholly new approach to economic policy in Britain. The overriding need is for a long-term stabilisation programme to defeat inflation, recreate business confidence and provide a favourable climate for economic growth. At the head of such a programme must lie a firm commitment to a steady and gradual reduction in the rate of growth of the money supply, until it is consistent with our best

guess at a potentially sustainable rate of economic growth. Only in this way can inflation be wrung out of the system. But this alone is not enough . . . An equally important part of a long term stabilisation plan has to be a reduction in the present Budget deficit . . . Indeed, something akin . . . to the old balanced Budget discipline needs to be restored: the secret of practical economic success, as overseas experience confirms, is the acceptance of known rules. Rules rule: OK?

I wrote this article when I did because, like everyone else, I expected an election in the autumn of 1978. (Indeed the Liberals had left the Lib-Lab Pact in the summer of that year on that clear understanding.) I was therefore anxious to put the idea into circulation before the campaign began. As luck would have it, the article appeared in print just after Jim Callaghan had announced the postponement of the election until 1979. The piece still achieved its purpose. Geoffrey Howe, then shadow Chancellor, was impressed by the argument and in particular the sentence 'Rules rule: OK?'

But neither he nor I had any time to address ourselves to the MTFS until the June 1979 Budget was out of the way. I then suggested to him that we should have a stabilization plan along the lines of my *Times* piece. Geoffrey agreed and asked me to work it out with the help of Peter Middleton, then an Under Secretary and the closest approximation to a monetarist the official Treasury could produce, and Adam Ridley, Geoffrey Howe's own senior political adviser who had earlier been a Treasury official. We set to work, and the result was the Medium Term Financial Strategy.

I had hoped the MTFS would be introduced at the time of the November 1979 interim Public Expenditure White Paper. This would have been possible as the main outlines had already been worked out within the Treasury by then. But because of internal opposition we had to be content with a Treasury Seminar attended by outside experts, including Terry Burns who argued forcefully in favour of the idea.

John Biffen, the Chief Secretary, was characteristically opposed to the whole concept, believing that governments should never impale themselves on hooks in this way, since it reduced their room for manoeuvre as circumstances changed. That of course was the point of the whole exercise. The MTFS was intended to be a self-imposed constraint on economic policy-making, just as the Gold Standard and the Bretton Woods system of exchange rates had been in the past, and the ERM came to be for most European Community countries in the 1980s.

John felt so strongly about it, however, that he wrote personally to Margaret setting out his objections to the MTFS, which understandably annoyed Geoffrey when he got to hear of it. Douglas Wass, too, was unenthusiastic about the MTFS and sought to neuter it.

THE MEDIUM TERM FINANCIAL STRATEGY

What It Said and Why

The actual text of the first MTFS in the 1980 Red Book is still worth reading, as it is often misrepresented even in academic commentaries. It started off with the Government's determination to 'bring down the rate of inflation and to create conditions for a sustainable growth of output and employment'. To that end it would 'progressively reduce the growth of the money stock' and 'pursue the policies necessary to achieve this aim'. It established a target range of 7–11 per cent growth for £M3 for 1980–81 and set out a path, declining by 1 per cent each year to reach a range of 4–8 per cent by 1983–84. The precise targets for the intervening years would be decided at the time. Right underneath the first table, and at the very beginning of the whole section was a crucial footnote which read: 'The way in which the money supply is defined for target purposes may need to be adjusted from time to time as circumstances change.' But it suited our critics to pretend it was not there. There followed Paragraph 3, which enunciated the central doctrine:

> Control of the money supply will over a period of years reduce the rate of inflation. The speed with which inflation falls will depend crucially on expectations both within the UK and overseas. It is to provide a firm basis for those expectations that the Government has announced its firm commitment to a progressive reduction in money supply growth. Public expenditure plans and tax policies and interest rates will be adjusted as necessary to achieve the objective. At the same time, the Government will continue to pursue policies to strengthen the supply side of the economy by tax and other incentives, and by improving the working of the market mechanism.

The document also set out the Government's intention of making a substantial reduction over the medium term in the PSBR as a percentage of GDP. It added that the relationship between the PSBR and the growth of the money supply was not simple, being affected by the economic cycle, the rate of inflation, the structure of taxation, public spending and much else.

In the early years, and especially when the MTFS was first launched, press and political attention was focused chiefly on the 'implied fiscal adjustment' line in the key table. This was Treasury jargon for tax cuts, and was the difference between projected revenue and expenditure after allowing for stated public borrowing objectives. Our 1980 projections suggested that, despite the tough times we were going through, there would be scope for tax cuts in the last two years of the parliament, 1982–83 and 1983–84, as indeed there proved to be. The Press saw this as the central purpose of the MTFS: to keep the potentially mutinous troops – especially in the House of Commons – quiescent with a promise of jam tomorrow. And it probably did serve that useful purpose at that time. This was not, however, what the MTFS was really about.

I do not, of course, claim intellectual paternity of the idea of a medium-term financial strategy. Several economists (including Terry Burns and Alan Budd in the October 1977 London Business School Economic Outlook) had suggested something similar. But I was responsible both for introducing the idea into the political arena and for getting it past the watering-down instincts of permanent officials.

It is sometimes suggested that the MTFS came too late to influence the disastrous 1980 wage round. This is to misunderstand what was realistic. We were generally anxious about the trend of wage settlements in the winter of 1979–80; but there was little we could do to restrain pay until the explosion following the inevitable breakdown of the Labour Government's pay policy and the Clegg awards had spent itself. Our long-term aim was decentralized wage bargaining which took account of local market forces, productivity, regional differentials, job security and profitability. Obviously we hoped that our medium-term plans would affect expectations, as any credible policy must and should. But the role of the technical economic theory known as 'rational expectations' was much exaggerated by the critics. (In later years it began to influence parts of the Treasury model under the revised form of 'consistent expectations' but it was scarcely known by either Ministers or officials in the crucial formative period.)

The purpose of the MTFS was to confirm and consolidate the complete change of direction on which we had embarked. In the first place it was explicitly medium term. So far from believing that there was any short-term mechanical link between financial policy and inflation, we were sure that a financial approach would work only if we persisted in it year in, year out; and that progress would not be in a straight line. In the second place, we wanted to signal a shift from a real to a nominal framework for macroeconomic policy. This sounds something of a mouthful. But at the time I tried to spell out its meaning in simple terms in my 1980 lecture, *The New Conservatism**:

> The distinctive feature of our medium-term financial strategy, which differentiates it from the so-called national plans of other times and other places, is that it is confined to charting a course for those variables – notably the quantity of money – which are and must be within the power of governments to control. By contrast, governments cannot create economic growth. All the instruments which were supposed to do this have succeeded only in damaging

*See Annexe 1 for full text.

the economy and have ultimately broken in the hands of the governments that sought to use them.

So far as inflation was concerned, the twofold error of previous Governments had been the commitment to full employment, come what may, and the false teaching of the neo-Keynesian economic establishment that the route to full employment was ever more monetary (and fiscal) expansion. Too many monetarists spoiled their case by making it all sound much too easy and by failing to recognize the political realities. They tended to treat monetary growth as if it were an autonomous prime cause of inflation, as if Governments foolishly over-expanded the money supply simply out of ignorance or sheer perversity. This was, of course, nonsense. Previous Governments may have lacked backbone, and held a self-defeatingly limited idea of the range of the politically possible. But their actions, however mistaken, were the result of political pressures rather than caprice. An important part of the point of the MTFS was to commit the Government to resisting such pressures in the future.

Borrowing Targets

Most political discussion concentrated, not on the arcana of monetarism, but on the more widely comprehensible figures in the MTFS showing a declining path for public sector borrowing up to 1983–84. The object of this was threefold. First, it was a way of bringing expenditure and revenue together. Second, it was important that the PSBR objective for the coming year should not stand alone, but should be seen as part of a medium-term programme for reducing it to a low proportion of GDP. Third, it was believed at the time that a declining PSBR would enable our monetary objectives to be reached without 'excessive reliance on high interest rates'. Or as I put it to the *Financial Times* Euromarkets Conference in January 1980:

> Too high a PSBR requires either that the Government borrows heavily from the banks, which adds directly to the money supply; or, failing this, that it borrows from individuals and institutions, but at ever-increasing rates of interest which place an unacceptable squeeze on the private sector.

Later I became sceptical of the link between Budget deficits and interest rates in a world of free capital movements. Even in 1980, I had my doubts about how strong the link really was. But in so far as a link existed, it could only be in the direction the Treasury alleged.

Getting the Government to commit itself to declining deficits was not only a way of disciplining Chancellors – of putting them on a hook; it was also a way of disciplining the Cabinet in its capacity as a bevy of spending Ministers. Moreover the promise of low interest rates if the MTFS were followed was an important *ad feminam* argument to persuade Margaret (and subsequently Cabinet colleagues) to accept the MTFS. Although initially highly sceptical, Margaret was brought round by Geoffrey by the argument that the MTFS would be (a) a powerful weapon against spending Ministers and (b) an influence for lower interest rates. Her opposition turned out to be not nearly as deep-seated as that of the Bank of England, which wanted to retain complete and unfettered discretion over monetary policy.

A number of senior Treasury officials were worried by the apparently smooth declining path of the PSBR in the Strategy. They feared that we were so anti-Keynesian that we failed to realize that Government borrowing could not decline in a recession. In the end, the Red Book made it very clear that the smooth path was illustrative. I pointed out in a well-reported speech in January 1980, even before the MTFS was launched, that the actual path of decline was likely to be 'stepped', falling in normal years and remaining level in recession years.

In further speeches then, and subsequently as Chancellor, I consistently drew a distinction between the effect of the business cycle on the PSBR, which should not be a cause for alarm or for action of any kind, and the activist use of the PSBR in an attempt to dampen the cycle, which should be firmly eschewed. The conceptual distinction could not be clearer; yet it is something the Treasury Select Committee and many others never seemed to understand, despite my many attempts to explain it. The original discipline of a declining PSBR, and the subsequent discipline of a balanced Budget, which I introduced as Chancellor, have both to be understood over the economic cycle as a whole. This is sometimes described as 'allowing the automatic stabilizers to come into play'; but never by me. For the description begs the whole question of whether fiscal surpluses and deficits have any serious capacity to stabilize or destabilize the economy in the first place. In my opinion they do not – indeed if they did the 1981 Budget would most certainly have been seriously destabilizing, as the notorious 364 economists wrongly predicted.

The true consideration has nothing whatever to do with short-term 'stabilization'. It is that tax policy needs to be seen in a medium-term, not to say long-term, supply-side context. In other words, taxes should be changed (reduced or reformed or both) in order to improve economic performance. Unnecessary fluctuations in tax levels are inimical to economic performance and undermine any benefits of reduction or reform by casting doubt on the durability of the change. By the same token, taxes should be reduced only if the reduction can be sustained – which means that they need to be justified not by the vagaries of the economic cycle, but by the underlying level and trend of Government spending.

Tax changes should be made only if they are for the better, and if they are for the better they should not be undone. In other words, once the position has been reached where the long-term fiscal objective – in my view a balanced Budget when the economy is growing at its sustainable trend rate – has been attained, then the revenue shortfall that occurs as a result of a recession should neither be made good by tax increases nor augmented by 'Keynesian' tax reductions designed (vainly) to counter the recession. Precisely the same applies, in reverse, to the revenue surplus that occurs as a result of a boom.

The Abiding Legacy

'The best laid schemes o'mice an' men/Gang aft a-gley.' The MTFS was not fulfilled in any literal sense, at least not on the monetary side. The liberalization of financial markets which we had ourselves launched changed the meaning of the monetary aggregates and made them much more difficult to predict and control. The original 1980–81 monetary target was heavily overshot. So, less heavily, was that for 1981–82; and the objectives for the subsequent two years were met only after the targets had been raised, and then by somewhat artificial means (the technique known as 'overfunding'). The target definitions of money were also changed in subsequent years.

Nevertheless, in terms of its fundamental aims, the MTFS succeeded. I remember a meeting I had with senior Treasury officials shortly before the 1980 Budget, when we were finalizing the MTFS for publication. One of them asked me if I cared to write down what I thought inflation would come down to over the period. Never one to resist a challenge, I scribbled down an illustrative path, culminating in 5 per cent in the final year (1983–84). Inflation at the time of our discussion stood at virtually 20 per cent. With the exception of Terry Burns, they all thought I had taken leave of my senses, although of course they did not put it quite so bluntly. In fact, inflation turned out to be slightly below 5 per cent in 1983–84.

There can be no doubt that the MTFS came to play a central role in the Government's economic policy. We could not have kept the show on the road, particularly in the early days, when the majority of the Cabinet were 'wets', without it. In particular the controversially tight 1981 Budget, discussed in Chapter 9, would never have been introduced had it not been for the MTFS. Even a highly critical witness such as Christopher Allsopp (a Bank of England economist at the time) conceded in a 1991 post mortem:

There appears to be a widespread agreement that macroeconomic policy should concentrate on providing a stable and stabilising nominal environment which is conducive to the control of inflation and within which supply-side improvements are most likely to be successful. This, it may be argued, is the abiding legacy of the medium-term financial strategy.

The fiscal side of the MTFS wore better than the monetary side. Until the late 1980s, the Government came as close to fulfilling its forward objectives for the PSBR as can be expected in an uncertain world. After that the departures from target were initially in the favourable direction of Budget surplus and debt repayment, with some erring in the opposite direction in the early 1990s.

A Personal Postscript

In the New Year's Honours list for 1981 I was made a Privy Councillor. This is the most parliamentary of all honours, enabling the recipient to graduate from being an honourable Member to a Right honourable Member. It comes automatically on promotion to the Cabinet: for Ministers outside the Cabinet it is rather more selective. I went on 18 February 1981 to Buckingham Palace to be sworn in by the Queen. The ceremony is as brief as it is bizarre, requiring the recipient to progress to the monarch by a complex mixture of bowing, walking, and kneeling at specified intervals. The procedure is so complicated that the Clerk of the Council, then Sir Neville Leigh, was in the habit of arranging a rehearsal beforehand.

However, it soon became clear that my Privy Councillorship was a consolation prize. For on 5 January 1981, Margaret Thatcher announced her first Cabinet reshuffle, in which John Biffen was moved from being Chief Secretary to Secretary of State for Trade. The need for a new Chief Secretary was not in dispute; but it came as a great blow to me that Leon Brittan – hitherto a young Minister of State at the Home Office with no previous experience of economics or finance – was brought in and promoted to the job above my head. The first I heard of the news was when I received a telephone call in my constituency just before the public announcement was made. Geoffrey Howe was not even in town when I returned to London the following day, having an urgent appointment in Ireland.

Although Leon was a close friend of Geoffrey (and Elspeth) Howe, who was very glad to have him at the Treasury, the main sponsor of his promotion was undoubtedly Willie Whitelaw, who was not only Home Secretary but effectively deputy Prime Minister and for whose political feel Margaret had at that time considerable respect. Willie was at that time determined both to advance his protégé at the Home Office and to block my path to the Cabinet. Subsequently, Willie and I were to become close colleagues and good friends; but that was not the case then, when I underestimated him and he distrusted me.

No-one, of course, has any pre-emptive right to any particular job. But having worked round the clock for the best part of two years, I did not rush back to full-time office duties in the first working week of the New Year, an indulgence which was described by some as 'sulking', although in fact I was determined not to sulk, and simply needed a few days to get over it. Instead, I took an early opportunity of letting Margaret know directly of my disappointment.

No doubt sensing how I might be feeling, she kindly invited Thérèse and myself to Sunday lunch at Chequers on 18 January. Apart, of course, from Denis, no-one else was there. It was Thérèse's first close encounter with Margaret, to whom she took an instant liking which never waned – although she was somewhat taken aback when, very early on in the proceedings, Margaret cautioned her to be very careful never to repeat anything from the privileged conversations she was about to hear. In fact, the conversation between Margaret and me over lunch, although friendly and moderately indiscreet – with Denis making his usual blunt interjections of the kind subsequently made familiar to a wider public through the 'Dear Bill' column in *Private Eye* – was pretty inconsequential.

After lunch she whisked me off to the small room she used as her study, leaving Denis to entertain Thérèse in their cosy, chintzy, television room. Thérèse later told me that after about a minute's politesse, he said, 'Why don't you read the newspapers, dear' and promptly fell asleep in his armchair. Meanwhile, in the course of our discussion *à deux*, Margaret assured me that she intended to put me in the Cabinet in her next reshuffle. Suddenly, there was a tremendous hullabaloo, which turned out to be a false fire alarm. Margaret and I carried on with our talk, but Thérèse was rushed by the staff to the safety of the communications room by the front door and left there on her own. She found herself in a small room full of elaborate telecommunications equipment, including the hot line to the US President. She was sorely tempted to pick it up and see what happened, but refrained.

When the time came to leave, we had first to wait on the front steps while every fire engine in Buckinghamshire screeched round the circular drive and, discovering that their arrival was unnecessary, out again. On the way home I told Thérèse what Margaret had said. I was well aware that the undertaking she had given me, although undoubtedly sincere, was vulnerable to the hazards of political life, as all such undertakings are. But I left Chequers feeling rather better than I had on arrival.

Meanwhile, Leon's move brought me some practical benefit. For as soon as he had run himself in I was able to turn over to him all the public expenditure work I had been doing, which he was fully capable of handling himself and which I should never have had to assume.

CHAPTER 8

THE BLACK ART OF
MONETARY CONTROL

Nuts and Bolts · Which 'M' to Control?
How to Control It? · The 'Corset'
The Prime Minister Blows Her Top · Monetary Evolution
Building Societies

Nuts and Bolts

REDUCING INFLATION, LIKE MOST things in life, has its price. One cost is that of a corrective recession or slow-down. The first effects of a financial squeeze are felt on output, profits and employment. The prize of lower price increases comes later. A particular cost is that of temporarily high interest rates. There is a mild paradox here. In a low inflation world, interest rates are lower than in a high inflation one. But the immediate effect of a monetary squeeze, which makes money hard to obtain, is to cause interest rates to rise still further. They subside later when the squeeze has worked through to reduce actual and expected inflation.

Enormous amounts of time and ingenuity have been spent on the search for technical gimmicks which will reduce the interest-rate cost of a monetary squeeze. This is at bottom a vain search. There are always improvements that can be made to a country's monetary system. But if inflation is to be squeezed, money has to become more difficult to borrow. And in a liberalized financial system that must mean paying a higher price for it.

There are ways of reducing the transitional costs of an anti-inflation policy. But they involve much more fundamental issues than tinkering with the mechanics of monetary control. The length and severity of both the recession and the period of high interest rates will be reduced by events or policies which lower inflationary *expectations* and by anything which increases the *credibility* of the Government's or central bank's commitment to low inflation. Since the early 1980s, an enormous mathematical literature has been generated by those two italicized terms, but it is doubtful how much it adds to the basic ideas. Achieving credibility is far more difficult than tinkering with monetary mechanics. The key is to have a good track record, which is why Germany succeeded for so long in maintaining stable prices with much lower interest rates, and less violent fluctuations in its rates, than the UK.

There was no more assiduous seeker for gimmicks which would supposedly give us tight money without high interest rates than Margaret Thatcher, who, like many others in this field although few Prime Ministers showed a surprising interest in the minutiae of monetary control, often at the expense of more fundamental truths. Undoubtedly there were problems in the monetary control system we inherited; and from the autumn of 1979 I convened a series of meetings with Treasury and Bank of England officials to study alternative methods which culminated in the Green Paper on Monetary Control, which appeared on 20 March 1980, just before the Budget.*

Which 'M' to Control?

Money is anything which can be used for settling debts. There is, of course, no hard and fast boundary between money and non-money, but a whole spectrum of assets which can be used with greater or lesser ease. The most indisputable forms of money are notes and coins – 'the readies'. These and other assets, such as current account bank balances, which are readily available, are called by economists 'narrow money'. Narrow money with the addition of those financial assets which are less readily available, and which normally earn interest, but are useful as a reserve of spending power, is known as 'broad money'.

Monetary statisticians use a system, off-putting to the uninitiated, in which the narrowest kind of money – overwhelmingly notes and coins – is known as MO. As the definition gets wider, the number after the M becomes higher. M1, for instance, comprises not only cash but current (or 'sight') accounts. £M3 consisted of notes and coins ('cash') plus *all* bank deposits. The £ symbol signified the exclusion from this of deposits denominated in foreign currencies. A still wider definition, M4, includes deposits with the building societies. There is a yet wider concept, including some easily withdrawable national savings deposits and local authority deposits, known as M5. Just to add to the

*READER'S HEALTH WARNING. What follows is an issue of passionate interest to a small number of people and mind-numbing gobbledygook to many others. The general reader can safely turn straight away to Chapter 9 without losing the thread of this book.

confusion some monetary economists prefer to call the wider aggregates 'liquidity' rather than money.

When we came to office, the main competitors for the role of monetary targets were £M3 and M1. Treasury officials were greatly attached to £M3. By an accounting identity, which the non-specialist will have to take on trust, the increase in £M3 was approximately equal to bank lending *plus* the PSBR *minus* net sales of gilt-edged securities other than sales to the banks themselves.*

Historically, the main source of large increases in the money stock thus defined has been excessive Government borrowing. In twentieth-century Britain, Governments no longer clip coins to meet their spending needs. But the main source of growth in £M3 under Denis Healey was the large PSBR, some of which was financed from the banking system rather than by the sale of gilts. Officials liked the emphasis on £M3 precisely because of its close links with the PSBR. They felt that this helped them to control public spending, which was what most concerned the Treasury. Moreover, £M3 had gained considerable cachet in most (though not all) monetarist circles for apparently having given early warning of the Heath inflation of the early 1970s, which M1 had not.

Nevertheless, we soon ran into an embarrassing paradox. We had raised interest rates sharply, the pound was rising rapidly and recession was gathering force – all signs of a severe monetary squeeze. Yet £M3 was shooting well above the target range. The increase in short-term interest rates was itself making bank deposits, which were a major component of £M3, particularly attractive to hold.

How to Control It?

Even more controversial than which monetary aggregates to target was the question of how to control them. It was a relatively straightforward matter to monitor the Budget deficit and make sure that it was financed by selling gilt-edged stock and not by borrowing directly or indirectly from the banking system.

The real problem, so far as broad was concerned, was the control of the element that corresponded to the amount of bank lending to the private sector. In nearly all the advanced industrial countries central banks operate by influencing short-term interest rates – usually three months or less – the assumption being that the higher the cost of borrowing, the less the banks will be able to lend. But this is far from a precision instrument. The demand for credit is influenced by other factors besides its cost alone, such as the expected rate of return on the

---

*More precisely: the rise or fall in £M3 equals the PSBR *less* sales of gilts outside the banks *plus* the net external inflow to the private sector *less* the increase in banks' non-deposit liabilities. The definition is taken from the Green Paper, *Monetary Control*, page 1.

investment of borrowed money, the expected capital gain on any asset acquired with borrowed money, and in general the degree of confidence that exists – none of them factors the authorities can directly control or even accurately predict. Moreover, as I have already noted, the immediate impact of higher interest rates is to make the holding of bank deposits, which form the bulk of broad money, more attractive. But despite these complications it remains the case that higher interest rates will, at the end of the day, curb the demand for credit and thus reduce the growth of broad money – and that there is no other way, in a free economy, of achieving this objective.

Pure monetarists could legitimately point out that central banks were influencing not the supply of money but the demand for it. Instead of guessing what level and pattern of interest rates could be associated with what size of money stock, could not the latter be controlled directly, leaving the rate of interest to find its own level in the market place? Unfortunately, this is easier said than done. Central bank control works because the key banks in the system – in the UK the clearing banks – are either accustomed, or compelled, to hold deposits at the central bank, equivalent to a small proportion of total deposits. These act as reserves and help to settle transactions with other banks.

The Bank of England, like other central banks, will always lend to banks which run short of these reserves. The rate which it charges for these loans will determine what the banks charge to their own borrowers, and thus the price of credit throughout the system. In order to maintain its control of short-term interest rates, the Bank takes care to ensure that, so far as possible, such a shortage always exists. (The British arrangements are complicated by the fact that the Bank of England does not lend directly to the clearing banks but via a group of small, but select financial institutions known as discount houses. This does not affect the main argument.)

The monetarist reformers wanted the Bank of England, instead of trying to influence the demand for money via interest rates, to control the supply of money more directly by setting a target for the banks' reserves with the Bank. They regarded these reserves as the 'base' of the much larger volume of bank deposits: hence the expression 'Monetary Base Control' or MBC. Although MBC enthusiasts sometimes skate over the issue, there can be no question of the Bank of England refusing to lend to the banks if they are short of reserves. For its task is to support the financial system – not to engineer its collapse – by acting as 'lender of last resort'. The MBC proposal, in its more realistic form, is that the Bank should let its lending rate to the money market rise or fall to whatever extent is required to keep bank reserves to a predetermined growth path.

The most influential UK proponent of MBC was Gordon Pepper, then a partner in the stockbroking firm of W. Greenwell. Pepper had done highly useful work in translating the rarefied concepts of monetarist academics into the actual day-to-day operations of the banking system. Then in his prime, he had established a private line to Margaret Thatcher when she was Leader of the Opposition. But like many such technical experts, he greatly exaggerated what could be achieved by institutional changes in financial mechanisms.

The secret of his appeal to Margaret Thatcher was that he had persuaded her that a given degree of monetary tightness could, through MBC, be secured at an appreciably lower level of interest rates than the UK was experiencing. Given her – by no means unique – detestation of high interest rates, a promise of sufficient monetary tightness to bring down inflation at lower interest rates had an irresistible appeal.

In fact real interest rates in 1980 were not particularly high – indeed, on the basis of headline inflation they were at times negative, decidedly so after allowing for tax. But they came as a shock compared with the rates prevailing during the financial year 1977–78, when real bank base rates averaged *minus 6½ per cent* – a ludicrous figure, which if it had persisted would soon have secured Keynes's euthanasia of the *rentier*.

Ironically, the US Federal Reserve under Paul Volcker had inaugurated a temporary experiment with a form of monetary base control in the autumn of 1979. The tight money which it embodied did succeed in bringing down US inflation quickly, but interest rates fluctuated very sharply and were often very high; the interest rate on call money reached a peak of over 20 per cent in 1981, much higher than anything seen in the UK.

MBC in the UK was advocated in two forms: with or without a mandatory requirement for the banks to maintain given reserves at the Bank of England. If mandatory reserves exceeded the amount that banks wanted to hold voluntarily, they would act as a tax on them. But the result would simply have been to redirect the lending via offshore subsidiaries outside the Bank's control. So I agreed with the Bank of England that a non-mandatory version was the only one worth considering.

There remain other problems with MBC, even if the Government is prepared to take the risk of large interest rate fluctuations. The biggest one is that the ratio of total deposits to reserves – the 'base multiplier' - may not be stable. Even slight variations in this multiplier would cause enormous variations in all the broader measures of the money stock. These unpredictable elements would have compounded the existing problem of the short-term instability of the demand for money. The Bank of England, which deeply disliked the whole idea of MBC, inevitably also raised many more technical problems connected with money market management.

Not surprisingly, the Green Paper was distinctly cool about MBC, although it did ask readers for views on whether 'the difficulties could be surmounted'. Given the problems we were experiencing with monetary control, I was personally attracted to the idea of MBC – although highly doubtful of its promise of lower interest rates for a given degree of monetary tightness. I also shared the suspicion that the Bank of England's root-and-branch opposition to MBC was at least in part because it would have meant the demise of that venerable top-hatted institution unique to the City of London, the Discount Market.

But I was in no doubt that to go to MBC would have been a leap in the dark for the authorities and the banks alike, with the risk of extraordinary interest rate volatility (as in the US), at least until the system settled down. I was also impressed by the fact that, apart from Switzerland, no country in the world had tried it out in practice; and the Swiss were before very long to drift away from it in practice in favour of loosely linking their currency to the Deutschmark. Above all I was convinced that such an experiment had a chance of success only if those responsible for its implementation wished to make it a success. Given the Bank's profound antipathy, it would all too likely have proved the disaster they predicted. Certainly the risk was too great to take.

Margaret Thatcher was deeply disappointed by this conclusion, and throughout her time in office, whenever interest rates had to rise significantly, her interest in MBC in some shape or form revived. It was encouraged from the beginning of 1981 onwards by Alan Walters, part of whose appeal to her was that he was usually in favour of lower interest rates (whether via MBC, of which he was an advocate, or by 'letting the pound find its own level' on the foreign exchange markets).

No serious advocate of MBC today believes that bank lending can be fine-tuned. The credit cycle is endemic and unpreventable: the practical question is how far it can be dampened. The early MBC enthusiasts claimed that it was a sure means of monetary control, whereas interest rates were not. To which the practical man rightly replies: 'If MBC is so superior, why is it that nobody – not even the powerful and independent German Bundesbank – uses it?' The Bundesbank's so-called 'Minimum Reserve Requirement' is *not* a means of directly controlling either bank lending or even the money stock. It is a seldom-used auxiliary means by which the Bundesbank generates the interest rate it believes necessary, as the Bundesbank itself has frequently explained.

The 1980 Green Paper is still worth reading in the 1990s, not least because it punctures some perennially topical delusions. One of these concerns the use of some kind of reserve assets ratio – which has an attraction for Labour Party advisers, who see it as a form of direct control over credit. The Green Paper makes it clear that it is not, any more than the Bundesbank's Minimum Reserve Requirement is. There was indeed a scheme by which the Bank of England could call on the banks to increase their deposits with it by a specific amount when it wanted to tighten credit, known as Special Deposits, which earned no interest. These were instituted in 1960, but they were not as effective as intended because the banks could offset a call for them by bidding for funds in the wholesale money markets. The practical point, however, is that the Bank sought to use the scheme to raise interest rates, and not to control the money stock directly.

The 'Corset'

A much more effective scheme, at least superficially, was known officially as the Supplementary Special Deposits scheme and more familiarly as 'the corset'. This imposed draconian Special Deposit requirements on banks whose interest bearing deposits – and therefore their ability to lend – exceeded prescribed levels. If it had worked effectively, banks would have had to either increase lending rates to borrowers or (as was hoped) ration their access to credit. But the scheme rapidly became cosmetic. Instead of going directly to the banks, business borrowers (often on the advice of their bankers) issued commercial bills which the banks 'accepted' (i.e. guaranteed), but which did not add to their loans or deposits. This became known as the 'bill leak'.

The abolition of exchange control made the corset into a complete mockery. A bank whose deposits were up against the corset limits could use its Paris branch to bid for sterling funds and that branch could make the loan to the UK resident. Over the ten-month period between the ending of exchange control in October 1979 and the eventual abolition of the corset in June 1980, the Euro-Sterling Market expanded from £14 billion to £23 billion. The episode is of more·than historical interest; for it illustrates the traps that lie in wait for all the clever schemes for 'soft' controls which are supposed to tighten credit without the need to raise interest rates.

Of course we should have abolished the corset much earlier. But the real problem caused by its abolition in 1980 arose from the Bank of England's inability to foresee the scale of the rise in £M3 when the corset was eventually lifted. The immediate increase was almost £3 billion, a rise of nearly 5 per cent in the month from June to July 1980. The surge continued in subsequent months, and in the year to February 1981, £M3 rose by 20 per cent, nine percentage points above the upper end of the target range. While in one sense this mattered little, since what was happening was that lending that been routed outside the UK banking system was being re-routed within it, it alarmed the financial markets and made the true monetary position impossible to discern.

The Prime Minister Blows Her Top

Nevertheless, those of us responsible for the conduct of monetary policy at the Treasury, although annoyed by the failure of Bank intelligence, were reasonably relaxed about the high money numbers, knowing that a tight monetary squeeze was being inflicted by high interest rates and a high and rising pound. Indeed on 3 July 1980, Geoffrey felt able to reduce MLR from 17 to 16 per cent.

Constitutionally the Bank was subordinate to the Treasury, and merely carried out in the financial markets the wishes of its political masters. In reality, apart from the critical issue of the level of interest rates, the Bank had considerable discretion. Yet as monetary concerns assumed greater importance in economic policy after 1975, and still more after 1979, the activities of the Bank became central to the success of Government strategy. The tension was undoubtedly exacerbated by our making it clear that the Chancellor was now in unequivocal control of monetary policy. The Bank could not be expected to like the new approach, even though it had never at that time taken monetary policy very seriously or (with the exception of one of its senior economists, Charles Goodhart) thought deeply about it. Successive Governors concentrated instead on reading stern lectures on matters outside their responsibility, such as the need to control public spending and to maintain a tight incomes policy.

One innovation I made as Financial Secretary, which persists to-day, was a monthly meeting, which I chaired, with Treasury and Bank officials to review funding policy for the coming months. It allowed my officials and me to question Bank officials and query the maturities and coupons they had selected. This brought a wide range of bank activities within the Treasury's purview to a greater extent than before. Bank officials undoubtedly found our involvement intrusive.

I have never found any incompatibility between my forthright approach to the Bank as a Treasury Minister, and my subsequent espousal of an independent but accountable Bank of England. My own view has always been that the Bank of England must either be properly subordinate to the Treasury, as the Banque de France has traditionally been to the French Finance Ministry, or independent but accountable, like the Bundesbank or the US Federal Reserve. Independence was not on the agenda in 1980 and the Bank was in any case not ready for it. It is true that our 1977 policy document, *The Right Approach to the Economy*, had stated that 'we favour a more independent role for the Bank of England'. But the word 'more' was an important qualification, and the text makes clear that what was envisaged was freedom of speech rather than freedom of action. And not even this modest proposal survived into the 1979 manifesto.

THE BLACK ART OF MONETARY CONTROL

There were other factors in the deterioration of relations between the two institutions, which together comprise 'the authorities'. Senior Treasury officials were annoyed that their Bank counterparts, to whom they did not consider themselves one whit inferior, received far higher salaries. One high-flying Treasury official, David Walker (subsequently head of the Securities and Investment Board) received a large increase in salary as a result of moving to the Bank: subsequently, a no poaching understanding was reached between the two institutions. Another source of tension was that the Deputy Governor, Kit McMahon, made no secret of his hostility to Government policy while the Governor, Gordon Richardson, had a proconsular sense of his own position.

As the Minister with special responsibility for monetary policy, I became the Ministerial contact between the Treasury and the Bank. This greatly upset Richardson, who felt that, as Governor, his relations should be exclusively with the Chancellor except when he wished to see the Prime Minister. On no account should he be required to talk to a mere Financial Secretary. My relations with him and lesser Bank officials were severely tested during the preparation of the Green Paper, not because of fundamental disagreements, but because Bank officials felt that their authority was being infringed. A low point was reached when I had to call Gordon Richardson out of the regular Thursday morning meeting of the Bank's Court to speak to him on an urgent matter. Happily, since we both left office, relations between us have much improved.

These strains were as nothing compared to Margaret Thatcher's fury at the overshoot of the monetary target following the abolition of the corset. She was not appeased by the practical evidence of the severity of the squeeze, as she felt that the Government was being brought into ridicule, and with it the credibility of its counter-inflationary strategy. Fortified by a chance meeting with the Swiss–American economist, the late Karl Brunner, on holiday, she took up once more the issue of Monetary Base Control. She called a meeting in early September 1980 when she was not amused to find that both Richardson and McMahon were abroad, and that she had to be content with giving a piece of her mind to two less senior officials – John Fforde and Eddie George. She was understandably if excessively angry that the Bank should have had so little intelligence about the size of the bill leak, and the consequent effect on the money numbers of its disappearance following the abolition of the corset.

One result of this tantrum was that she convened three seminars on monetary policy at Number 10 in the autumn of 1980 to which she invited academic economists as well as Treasury Ministers and Treasury and Bank officials. Throughout her premiership she had a fondness for seminars, which were occasionally useful, but her unfortunate habit of playing to the gallery increased as the years went by. These early seminars were already characterized by an embarrassing tendency to abuse Geoffrey Howe in front of officials, which reflected not merely her monetary unhappiness, but also her growing irritation at his manner and mode of argument.

Monetary Evolution

After all these traumas the evolutionary changes in monetary control announced by Geoffrey on 24 November 1980, were something of an anticlimax. Indeed most attention was, not surprisingly, gained by the announcement on the same day that MLR was being reduced by a further two points to 14 per cent.

Geoffrey's announcement had three parts. First, the end of the Reserve Assets Ratio requirement, which was manifestly ineffective as a means of control, was foreshadowed. Second, the Bank was to develop changes in its operations 'to allow the market a greater role in the determination of the structure of short-term interest rates'. Third, he hinted at the abolition of the compulsory Clearing Bank cash ratio. These measures were all implemented the following August. The most interesting aspect was the official explanation: 'These steps would be consistent with the gradual evolution towards a monetary base system and will help to judge how far such a system will contribute towards our medium-term monetary objectives.' An experienced Whitehall watcher would have seen that this was the thumbs down for MBC.

The details of the new Bank of England procedures that were to be announced in August 1981 included the abolition of MLR (the old Bank Rate under another name). Instead short-term lending to the money market by the Bank would be made within an undisclosed band. This band would determine base rates – the rates on which bank overdraft rates are based, the extent by which they exceed base rate depending on the bank's assessment of the creditworthiness of the borrower.

The main point of the change, particularly in the view of Treasury officials, was to depoliticize interest rate changes and thus enable them to be speedier, particularly in an upward direction, and more flexibly used. In other words, since governments had felt politically inhibited in the use of the interest rate weapon, particularly in the light of the home-buyers' vote, this inhibition could usefully be diminished if it *appeared* that the banks rather than the Government were initiating any change. The aim was admirable, which made the change difficult to resist; but I was well aware that it was more apparent than real. As the Government still initiated interest rate changes via the Bank of England, the supposed experiment was a particularly transparent smokescreen. Not surprisingly, although the system was maintained, the pretence was before long abandoned. It fooled no-one and merely made the Government look indecisive, which could sometimes be a disadvantage in the foreign exchange markets.

It would indeed be desirable to move as far as possible to depoliticize interest rates, but the only way to do this is to go the whole hog towards an independent, but accountable, central bank, with freedom to run its own day-to-day operations, including the determination of short-term interest rates.

Building Societies

One matter in which I was inescapably involved as Financial Secretary was the regulation of building societies, which was a direct responsibility of the Treasury – unlike the banks, whose prudential regulation was a statutory responsibility of the Bank of England. I was able to strike a blow for freedom almost as soon as I took office. I discovered that there were restrictive guidelines on building society lending of which I had been completely unaware. These had been introduced by Labour in 1975 and worked through the Government agreeing with the Building Societies' Association (BSA), quarter by quarter, the total figure for lending, which the BSA then allocated among its members. Needless to say the actual figure always departed from the agreed total; and the departure was ostensibly taken into account when setting the figure for the next quarter. One of the first questions officials asked of me on taking office was what guideline I wished to set for the coming quarter; and the submission suggested a figure. Instead of agreeing the figure, I asked officials what purpose the arrangement served. On being given no convincing answer, I told them I was not going to set any figure; and this little-known control duly came to an end without any public announcement. This first step in what was to become a far-reaching programme of financial deregulation, with consequences – some of them wholly unforeseen – which were to have a major impact on the course of the economy and the conduct of policy, could scarcely have been more discreet.

But I soon came to the conclusion that further building society liberalization should be put on the back burner. The societies accounted for a third of all personal liquid assets; yet they were excluded from the official definition of £M3. We could afford a relatively relaxed attitude because at the time the societies operated an interest rate cartel under which building society rates were kept below the market-clearing level and fluctuated much less than market rates. For this reason, and because the banks did not at that time make mortgage loans to any significant extent, a mortgage 'queue' had developed. As I put it in a minute to Geoffrey: 'The one form of lending that is really dramatically affected by a general rise in interest rates is lending for house purchase, since the building societies do not fully adjust, with the result that the flow of funds into and out of the societies is immediately affected.'

In the difficult circumstances of the time, I was anxious not to lose this effectiveness. The Bank, on the other hand, supported by some Treasury mandarins, was strongly in favour of early Government action to smash the building society cartel. This was partly, no doubt, on grounds of general competition policy, but also because of a feeling at the Bank that if its clients, the commercial banks, had been forced to end their cosy understandings and compete, then it was only fair that building societies should be obliged to do the same.

I successfully resisted this pressure, minuting Geoffrey Howe to the effect that, while the cartel was not something I would wish to defend, it was clear that it was gradually crumbling and would eventually disappear altogether – as indeed was to happen. Meanwhile the cartel's lingering existence was fortuitously helping us in our battle against inflation.

The choice of when to force the pace of liberalization and when to make haste slowly is always a delicate one. No 'big bang' can encompass all controls and restrictions at the same time. What we decided to do with building societies was to allow the crumbling to take place at a natural pace, as competition developed from the banks.

Meanwhile I devoted a speech in May 1980 to the Building Societies' Association annual conference warning the movement against becoming too aggressive too soon. If the societies started competing too aggressively with the banks, I told them, monetary policy would have to focus on wider aggregates which included building societies' shares and deposits. In fact, I had no desire for this to happen prematurely as it would have raised the level of interest rates required for any particular degree of monetary tightness. But my speech did foreshadow the authorities' eventual move – endorsed by most outside analysts – from tracking £M3 to tracking M4, which includes building society deposits, as the relevant measure of broad money or liquidity.

CHAPTER 9

1981 – A TIGHT AND
CONTROVERSIAL BUDGET

*Origins of the 1981 Budget · A Penchant for Company Cars
Taxing the Banks · Biting the Tax Bullet
The Fiscal Arithmetic · The Political Row
The Economic Row · Inflation Starts to Fall*

Origins of the 1981 Budget

IT WAS NOT THESE monetary conundrums but the Government's problems with the Budget deficit that lay behind the 1981 Budget, which
defiantly raised the tax burden in a recession and provoked a notorious
letter of protest to *The Times* from 364 economists. Yet its success in
turning round sentiment and as a prelude to more than eight years of
economic growth made it in retrospect seem climacteric. As a result
there has been some myth-making and attempts to claim the credit. It
is worth setting the record straight.

The Government did not set out with the deliberate intent of making
a dramatic doctrinal challenge to economic orthodoxy or to the political
faint-hearts in its own ranks. The 1981 Budget was essentially a response
to the fiscal difficulties which had emerged in the financial year 1980–81.
As that year progressed it became clear that the Budget deficit as
measured by the PSBR was running well ahead of the £6 billion target
set the previous March and embodied in the MTFS. By November 1980
it was apparent that the deficit would be at least £11½ billion; and the
eventual out-turn was £12½ billion or 5¼ per cent of GDP (equivalent to
some £30 billion in early 1990s terms).

Roughly half the overrun, which was largely on the public expenditure side, could be attributed to the recession. Although, in output terms, no deeper than forecast, it was accompanied by a much greater than expected rise in unemployment, and hence spending on social security benefits. It was also having a much more severe effect on the finances of the nationalized industries than had been predicted. But a good deal was also due to weaknesses in our system of public expenditure control, which I discuss in the next chapter.

In the circumstances it was clear that the forthcoming public spending round would need to be a very tough one. At the July 1980 Cabinet meeting on public expenditure, Geoffrey secured the agreement of Cabinet to a substantial reduction in the so-called public expenditure planning total for 1981–82. But when it came to the autumn public expenditure round of bilateral discussions between the Treasury and spending Ministers, the specific savings needed to achieve this overall reduction were not forthcoming. And even where they were, the success was short-lived. Patrick Jenkin, the Social Services Secretary, responsible for the biggest budget of all, argued that the only means by which he could find the savings demanded of him by the Treasury was by abandoning the annual uprating of pensions in line with inflation, an offer John Biffen, the Chief Secretary, gratefully accepted. The decision was subsequently overturned by Cabinet, as Patrick had no doubt expected it would be.

This was an object lesson to Treasury Ministers in a standard spending Minister's ploy: the political boomerang offer. Subsequently, when I became Chancellor, I made a point of warning each of the four Chief Secretaries that served under me about it and of the importance of securing savings that would not be too politically difficult for Cabinet to swallow – not to mention the *sine qua non* of getting Margaret fully signed up before the matter ever went to Cabinet.

The public spending round for 1981–82 was particularly hard fought. Its final resolution required no fewer than three Cabinet meetings in the first half of November 1980, the first two of them devoted to nothing else. In the end, Geoffrey had to settle for an overall reduction, achieved principally by squeezing cash limits, of only half the figure the Cabinet had agreed in July. The outcome was manifestly inadequate, especially in view of the deteriorating fiscal position for 1980–81 and, in consequence, the steadily worsening outlook for 1981–82.

The position was clearly unacceptable, on a number of levels. The private sector, hard hit by the recession and the rising exchange rate, was increasingly resentful that the public sector appeared to be getting off relatively lightly – an argument with which Treasury Ministers had considerable sympathy. Quite apart from the manifest unfairness, the public sector was felt to be 'crowding out' the private sector: the precise reverse of what the Government had entered office to bring about. The argument was that high public spending, resulting in high public borrowing, pushed up interest rates, which in turn choked off private sector investment.

In retrospect I believe we overstated that effect. Short-term interest rates, which (apart from the level of stocks) have little direct bearing on private investment anyway, are determined not by the scale of the PSBR but by the needs of the Government's anti-inflation policy. Long-term interest rates, which have a direct impact on equity yields and thus on private investment decisions, are determined by the balance of supply and demand in the capital market. As the capital market was becoming increasingly a single global market, the public borrowing of any one country – with the important exception, because of its sheer size, of the United States – had a correspondingly diminished effect.

But the crowding-out thesis was in any case only part of the story. Another consideration which carried considerable weight, not least with the official Treasury at that time, was the belief that the burden needed to be shifted from companies, hard hit by high interest rates and a high exchange rate, to individuals, who benefited from the high exchange rate – provided they were in work. Yet a further important factor was that the Government's credibility in the financial markets clearly depended greatly on the extent to which it was seen to be taking the newly published MTFS seriously. And with the wayward behaviour of £M3, it was all the more important that the fiscal side of the MTFS – the declining path for public borrowing – should be observed.

Finally, of course, it was no bad thing to demonstrate to the Cabinet colleagues and to the country alike that failure to curb public spending, on which the Government had set such store, would mean higher taxes. Thus it was that on 24 November 1980, for the first and only time, the Thatcher Government came close to introducing a mini-Budget of the kind that had characterized the Healey Chancellorship and which we had resolved to eschew. Geoffrey Howe announced a percentage point increase in employees' National Insurance Contributions from 6¾ per cent to 7¾ per cent, to take effect from 1 April 1981. It was true, of course, that National Insurance Contribution rates were, for administrative reasons, always reviewed and announced in the autumn. But on this occasion Geoffrey also announced a new Supplementary Petroleum Duty (SPD) of 20 per cent of the gross return of each field to take effect from 1 January 1981, an impost which it was felt the prosperous North Sea oil industry could well afford. Each of these measures was expected to bring in an extra £1 billion in 1981–82.

To soften the blow the Government had announced three days earlier a £245 million package to increase various employment subsidies and launch a Community Enterprise programme. Less happily, there were further increases in aid to hospitalized enterprises in the state sector, notably British Leyland and British Steel, and in the External Financing Limits of the nationalized industries generally. On 24 November itself,

MLR was reduced from 16 to 14 per cent.

While Geoffrey was announcing his measures to the House, I invited to my room at the Treasury, at his request, the chairmen of all the main oil companies operating in the North Sea, to inform them of the new impost which they would be asked to bear and why the Government felt justified in imposing it. I was flanked by a silent Hamish Gray, David Howell's number two as Minister of State for Energy, who was clearly unhappy at the tax and expected the chairmen to react angrily to it. In the end, the meeting went remarkably well, which made a favourable impression on Hamish, something that was to stand me in good stead when, less than a year later, I succeeded David Howell as Secretary of State for Energy and inherited Hamish as the most loyal of deputies.

The November measures had their expected favourable effects on financial confidence. Nevertheless the PSBR overrun continued unabated. As we embarked on the preparation for the 1981 Budget, it was clear that further increases in taxation would be required. The only question was how much, and where the burden should fall.

A Penchant for Company Cars

One area that had long seemed to me an obvious candidate was the taxation of fringe benefits, better known as 'perks', and in particular the commonest perk of all, the company car, the use of which was grossly undertaxed. As long ago as July 1979, I had minuted Geoffrey:

> The fringe benefit society and its proliferation of perks arose as the most effective way round (a) excessive marginal rates of tax and (b) the constraints of a formal incomes policy. Since we have largely eliminated (a) and are pledged to eschew (b), the need for perks (as a way of life) has disappeared and I believe we should launch a major attack on fringe benefits in next year's Finance Bill – and indeed trail it this year.

The prevalence of the company car, and the distortions and dishonesty inseparable from it, were a peculiarly British phenomenon. In the United States, where tax rates were never so high as to make remuneration in cash unattractive, and where – apart from a short-lived aberration during the Nixon Administration – incomes policies were unknown, the company car is a rarity. Largely, as a result of my minute, Geoffrey asked Peter Rees, the Minister of State, to look at this, and Peter had a series of meetings with enthusiastic Revenue officials, whose zeal was fortified by the virtual absence of the equivalent of the company car in the Civil Service and who duly advised on the most promising way ahead.

Geoffrey, however, was a great believer in consultation before legislation, and he instructed the Inland Revenue to issue a consultative paper on the subject. This eventually arrived on Margaret's desk in August 1980 with a short covering note from Geoffrey recommending immediate publication. As soon as she had read it, she exploded. Her distaste for the Inland Revenue was reinforced by the advice she received from David Wolfson, a member of the Great Universal Stores family, and the then head of the Prime Minister's Political Office, who told her that were we to act on it, no businessman would vote for us again.

Margaret told her office to summon Geoffrey to her presence instantly, but he was on holiday in France. Her office then tried to get hold of Peter Rees, but she was unwilling to wait for him to make the journey from his home in Wales. As a result I was summoned to Number 10 from my rather less distant home in Leicestershire to be the unfortunate recipient of her wrath. After she had subsided, I agreed to instruct the Revenue to defer publication of a consultative document until Geoffrey had returned from France and she had had the opportunity to discuss it with him. When she did so, he agreed to bury the paper altogether, but nevertheless persisted on the substance in his usual dogged way.

He insisted on a modest increase in the tax on perks in the 1981 Budget, largely on company cars and the petrol supplied for their use; and he froze the threshold over which benefits in kind became taxable. In law such benefits are taxable only in the hands of 'directors and higher paid employees', a formulation devised by an earlier Labour Government at the behest of the trade unions who did not want their own members' perks to be liable to tax. The definition of a higher paid employee was set afresh in each year's Finance Bill: when we took office in 1979, it was defined as those earning (including the taxable value of any perks received) in excess of £8,500 a year. We maintained the same nominal threshold, unindexed, throughout the Thatcher years, leading to a small but growing correspondence from those who, missing the point, understandably queried how somebody on well below average earnings could be classified as a 'higher paid employee'. But it fell to me, as Chancellor, to implement the significant attack on the undertaxation of the company car I had advocated in 1979.

Taxing the Banks

Meanwhile, other avenues had to be explored in the desperate circumstances in which we found ourselves in 1981. Apart from North Sea oil, there was one other sector of the economy that was doing well while business and industry in general suffered: the banks. This was largely because, in those days, the banks enjoyed a substantial 'endowment' income from money kept in current accounts on which no interest was paid. Clearly the higher the level of lending rates, the greater this endowment income became.

In the circumstances, and somewhat in conflict with our non-interventionist philosophy, we decided to ask the banks to take over the responsibility for financing a proportion of the Government's fixed rate export credit scheme. This would involve the banks in assuming a financial liability which they could well afford. But the main attraction to the Treasury was that it would 'score' as a reduction in public expenditure. Whether it ought to score in purely economic arithmetic was beside the point at a time when a Government was fighting to maintain confidence in its budgetary strategy during the worst post-war recession to date and in the face of disaffection in its own ranks.

Geoffrey accordingly asked me, as Financial Secretary with delegated responsibility for the banks, to negotiate an agreement along these lines. I duly held a meeting at my room in the Treasury with Jeremy Morse, Chairman of Lloyds Bank, in his capacity as Chairman of the Committee of London Clearing Banks, at which I argued that, in return for their acquiescence, the banks, whose reputation among the hard pressed business community was not particularly favourable, would be able to promote themselves as public spirited and patriotic citizens helping the UK exporter. But I was not so naïve as to believe that this not particularly juicy carrot would suffice without some sort of stick as well, and accordingly agreed with Geoffrey that, if all else failed, we would have to impose some sort of additional taxation on the banks.

In a series of meetings, Morse insisted that there was no way the banks could justify to their shareholders taking over the financing of fixed-rate credit to exporters. I hinted that the alternative would be some form of special tax on the banks. Morse, assuming that I was bluffing, declared that that would be the lesser evil, since the banks would not have any problems with their shareholders in that event. For good measure, however, he wrote to Margaret to complain about this threat – a singularly pointless exercise, since Margaret had no love for the banks, regarded Morse himself as a neo-Keynesian 'wet', and had been kept fully on side by Geoffrey about the work I had asked Treasury officials to do on a scheme to extract a contribution from the banks towards solving the pressing PSBR problem.

A once-for-all bank levy of 2½ per cent of the value of non-interest bearing bank deposits on the eve of the Budget was duly announced as part of the 1981 Budget on 10 March, to bring in some £400 million of additional revenue. It caused some disquiet on our own benches, notably on the grounds of retrospection. This was the least valid objection of all. For if the date on which the levy was based had been later, it would have been a simple matter for the banks to decide to pay a modest rate of interest on current accounts, even on a purely temporary basis, thus reducing the yield from the levy to zero. Happily, there was only one resignation on the issue, that of Tim Renton, at the time PPS to John

Biffen. As for the other bank chairmen, their anger at the Government was matched by their criticism of Morse for mishandling the situation on their behalf: it appeared that he had told them of the fixed-rate export credit proposal, but they had not been aware of the likely alternative.

Biting the Tax Bullet

Even with this source of revenue on top of the one percentage point increase in National Insurance contributions and the new Supplementary Petroleum Duty, the prospective PSBR gap remained a yawning one. Geoffrey believed in a collegiate approach to Budget making, holding a series of meetings with the other Treasury Ministers as well as his top Treasury, Inland Revenue and Customs and Excise officials and the special advisers present. We were determined not to reverse the income tax cuts we had introduced in 1979, but felt that VAT at 15 per cent was as high as it could go. With businesses hard hit by recession, there was no question of any increase in Corporation Tax: instead some modest reliefs were required. We were thus left with the excise duties on alcoholic drinks, tobacco, petrol and derv, all of which we decided to increase by double the amounts required to keep pace with inflation.

But as Budget meeting followed Budget meeting, it became clear that this was not enough. In an atmosphere of mounting gloom, the economist then responsible for the Treasury's short-term forecasting would give his latest estimate of the current year's PSBR and his latest forecast of the PSBR for 1981–82. Each set of figures he produced was worse than the previous one. Towards the end of February when the final Budget decisions had to be taken, the prospective PSBR for 1981–82, even taking into account the increase in National Insurance contributions, but before any Budget measures, was forecast to be £14 billion. Not only was the sheer size alarming; but it meant that the PSBR was still rising at time when the Government's policy, newly enshrined in the MTFS, was to bring it down substantially.

Meanwhile, at a meeting at Chequers in January, Geoffrey Howe had warned Margaret of the serious deterioration in the public finances and of his sombre conclusion that he would have to do whatever was necessary to get the 1981–82 PSBR down to at most some £10 billion. She was not amused. She was even less amused in February, when he informed her that the picture was even worse and that he would have to raise taxes in the forthcoming Budget by £3½ billion. She convened a meeting at Number 10, at which her new personal economic adviser, Alan Walters, who had taken office at the beginning of the year, was also present. Walters strongly supported Geoffrey's analysis, adding that, in his view, the increase in taxation should if anything be even larger – say £4 billion. Margaret responded angrily that she had not been elected to put up taxes;

but eventually and with a heavy heart agreed to a Budget that would increase taxation on the scale recommended both by her Chancellor and her economic adviser, on the clear understanding that this would permit a significant reduction in interest rates.

To bridge the gap that remained even after the substantial real increase in the excise duties, it was clear that we would have to bite the bullet and raise the burden of income tax. But we remained – rightly – determined not to reverse the 1979 cut in the basic rate. This meant acting on the personal allowances. Initially it looked as if we could meet our target by confining the increase in the allowances to half that required by the indexation formula. But as the forecasts deteriorated, it became apparent that we would not be able to increase the allowances at all for 1981–82.

As the main architect of the indexation provisions, I had no hesitation in supporting this course of action. Indeed I volunteered to take the Finance Bill clause setting aside indexation of the personal allowances through the committee stage on the floor of the House myself, which I duly did. Although Michael Foot and others called for my resignation, I had little difficulty in reminding the House that the whole purpose of my Amendment to the Rooker-Wise Amendment in 1977 (already described in Chapter 2) had been to make it clear that indexation, although the presumption, was not automatic. Under the pre-1977 system the maintenance of the existing allowances for a further year in unchanged cash terms would have required no Finance Bill legislation whatever. It was only because of the Rooker-Wise-Lawson Amendment that the Government had to come out in the open and treat the non-indexation of the allowances as a tax increase, raising £2 billion of additional revenue, and could no longer increase the tax burden by stealth.

The Fiscal Arithmetic

The overall increase in taxation on the fully indexed basis nowadays employed, although not at that time, was £4½ billion. Adding back the increase in employees' national insurance contributions, the increase was well over £5 billion or around 2 per cent of GDP, equivalent to some £12 billion in terms of the early 1990s. The projected effect was to reduce the PSBR from the then estimated 6 per cent of GDP in 1980–81 to 4¼ per cent of GDP, or £10½ billion, in 1981–82. In the event, the out-turn was considerably better, at £8½ billion. We thus more than achieved our target. If we had had more accurate forecasts, we might well have done less, and not felt it necessary to freeze the personal allowances. But this might have been a mixed blessing. For the Budget might then not have made the salutary public impact that it did, and our long-term aim of sharply reducing the Budget deficit might have taken longer to achieve.

1981 – A TIGHT AND CONTROVERSIAL BUDGET

THE 1981 BUDGET
(Figures are on an indexed basis)

	£ billion
Estimated PSBR outcome, 1980–81*	13.5
Expected PSBR, 1981–82 before Budget measures	14.5
Effect of Budget measures:	
Non-indexation of income tax allowances and thresholds	−1.9
Increase in Excise Duties above indexation	−1.2
Oil tax increases and other	−1.2
Expenditure changes	+0.3
Total impact of Budget	−4.0
Forecast PSBR, 1981–82	10.5
Actual outcome	8.6

*Final outcome 12.5

The Political Row

To introduce a tax-raising Budget on this scale in the depth of the recession was inevitably highly controversial. At the Cabinet of Tuesday, 10 March, at which Geoffrey unveiled the Budget to his colleagues, he was roundly attacked by the usual wets: Jim Prior, Peter Walker, Ian Gilmour – all of whom subsequently claimed that they had toyed with the idea of resignation. Margaret knew full well that the Cabinet would be a difficult one and had armed herself with a concession – in future there would be a pre-Budget discussion of Budget strategy in January or February of each year, and there would be a further Cabinet discussion of economic policy each July, in advance of the annual spending round. These innovations were duly implemented and no doubt Jim Prior, in particular, felt he had gained something of value. But from my own experience as Chancellor I can confirm that these concessions in no way derogated in practice from the sovereignty of the Chancellor of the day over the Budget, subject only to the need to carry the Prime Minister with him.

Among our own back-benchers, the focus of discontent was on the specific measures rather than on the economic doctrines supposedly violated by the Budget. Somewhat surprisingly they homed in on the increase in the duty on petrol. Advised by Michael Jopling, the Chief Whip, that we would have difficulty in getting the relevant Finance Bill clause through the House, we decided to offer a limited concession. We would go ahead with the petrol duty increase as proposed – we needed the money – but we would make the far less costly sacrifice of confining the increase in the duty on fuel for diesel engined road vehicles ('derv') to no more than that required to keep pace with inflation. We argued that this concession would have a directly beneficial impact on business costs. At the same time Geoffrey austerely made it clear that he would have to recoup the revenue lost by the derv concession elsewhere, which he duly did by moving an amendment to increase the tobacco duty still further, adding a further 3 pence, making an extra 17 pence in all, to a packet of twenty cigarettes. Such is the success of the anti-smoking lobby that the tobacco duty is the one tax where an increase commands more friends than enemies in the House of Commons. Thus was the back-bench rebellion against the 1981 Budget overcome, without any alteration whatever to the overall Budget arithmetic.

The Economic Row

The most memorable reaction to the 1981 Budget came not from the world of elected politicians, but from academics, in the shape of a round-robin letter signed by no fewer than 364 economists (one for every day in the year save Christmas day). Its text, published in *The Times* of 30 March 1981 read:

> We who are all present or retired members of the economic staff of British universities, are convinced that:
> There is no basis in economic theory or supporting evidence for the Government's belief that by deflating demand they will bring inflation permanently under control and thereby introduce an automatic recovery in output and employment;
> Present policies will deepen the depression, erode the industrial base of our economy and threaten its social and political stability;
> There are alternative policies;
> The time has come to reject monetarist policies and consider which alternative offers the best hope of sustained recovery.

The statement was prepared and circulated in the universities by two Cambridge economics professors, Frank Hahn and Robert Neild, on 13 March. The signatories included five former chief economic advisers to the Government – Robert Hall, Alec Cairncross, Bryan Hopkin, Kenneth Berrill, and Terry Burns' immediate predecessor, Fred Atkinson.

1981 – A TIGHT AND CONTROVERSIAL BUDGET

Their timing was exquisite. The economy embarked on a prolonged phase of vigorous growth almost from the moment the letter was published. So far from launching the economy on a self-perpetuating downward spiral, the Budget was a prelude to eight years of uninterrupted growth and left our economic critics bewildered and discredited.* It brought public borrowing back on track, and rescued the fiscal side of the MTFS. The one achievement it did not secure was the one that Margaret Thatcher and in particular Alan Walters had seen as its *raison d'être*: the 2 per cent cut in interest rates (to 12 per cent the day after the Budget). This had to be reversed within six months and interest rates were raised a further two percentage points to 16 per cent in October of the same year, to halt a run on the pound.

In the course of time the 1981 Budget came to be seen almost as a political equivalent of the Battle of Britain: the Thatcher Government's finest hour; its most widely acknowledged success and a turning point in its political fortunes. Hence the myth-making and attempts to claim the credit.

But the truth is beyond dispute. As Geoffrey was later to declare his 1991 IFS Lecture:

> There has sprung up a myth about the paternity of those difficult Budget judgements, the implication being that the 1981 Budget was somehow 'made in No. 10' against Treasury advice. Those Budget judgements were in fact fashioned by the Chancellor of the Exchequer with the help of Treasury Ministers and on the strength of Treasury advice.

Inflation Starts to Fall

What really mattered, of course, was that the policy was working. The RPI, in its customary way, moved in fits and starts. Its year on year increase reached a peak of 21.9 per cent in May 1980. It then fell sharply to 16.9 per cent in July when the VAT increase dropped out of the annual comparison, and then more gradually to 13 per cent in January 1981 and 12 per cent in April. It fluctuated around that level during the rest of 1981 before plunging decisively to 5 per cent by the end of 1982.

Other indicators gave a smoother picture of what was happening.

---

*Output touched bottom in the first quarter of 1981; and in the year to the first quarter of 1982, real GDP began its recovery, rising by 1.8 per cent. In the eight years 1981–9 it grew by an average of 3.2 per cent per annum. (The turning point in employment came a little later, in the first quarter of 1983, and in unemployment not until the third quarter of 1986.) The figures are average estimates of GDP at constant factor cost. Back series for quarterly data are taken from the Annual Supplement to Economic Trends.

Producer output price inflation peaked at 14 per cent in 1980 and was down to 9.5 per cent in 1981 and 7.7 per cent in 1982. Average earnings moved in line with this, falling from a peak annual increase of over 20 per cent in 1980 to 13 per cent in 1981 and 9½ per cent in 1982. The battle against inflation was being won.

CHAPTER 10

'THERE IS NO ALTERNATIVE'

Making the Case · High Unemployment For Ever?
Public Spending and Local Authorities · 'Funny Money'
The Civil Service Strike · Fresh Faces
The European Community Budget · The Dawn of the EMS
Appendix: Indexed Gilts

Making the Case

THE CASE FOR THE Government's economic policy was frequently summarized (not least, in derisory terms, by its opponents) by the acronym TINA, 'There is no alternative'. The sentence was actually Geoffrey's, but was soon attributed by the media to Margaret Thatcher, for whom it became almost a nickname. And indeed it encapsulated an important truth. I did try, however, to go beyond this and embark on a vigorous attempt to sell the 1981 Budget to a hostile Press and economic establishment.

The first and simplest point I had to make was that we were not perversely ignoring the effects of the recession. We were budgeting for a deficit of £3 billion above that implied by the MTFS: that £3 billion was our best estimate of the recession effect. But over half the threatened overrun was due to other factors, such as increased restructuring expenditure on British Steel and British Leyland. We could allow the recession to alter the time profile of the declining deficit we had set ourselves, but not to abandon the objective altogether, which we would have done if we had taken the easy way out and tried to attribute every aspect of the public expenditure overrun to some indirect effect of the recession.

My most substantial defence of the 1981 Budget was a lecture to a largely hostile audience at the Institute of Fiscal Studies (IFS) on 23 March. Part of what I had to say was inevitably defensive. We

100

had been pursuing a tight financial policy to reduce inflation. But the Budget did not make it any tighter. The tax increases were necessary to pay for the rising share of public spending in GDP which we had not yet succeeded in reversing. Paying higher taxes to finance higher spending could not be considered deflationary, however unpalatable it was to a Conservative Government.

But my principal point was that it was monetary policy which was the main Government influence on domestic demand, and we had no intention of allowing our monetary stance to be such as to lead output to spiral downwards. The main influence of the fiscal stance was on the pattern of domestic demand – in particular, the balance between public spending and private spending – rather than on its level. In a sentence which proved more prophetic than I might have wished, I asked, 'Is there any reason to believe that demand will fall if we replace lower public sector borrowing by higher private sector borrowing?'

The basic reason for being concerned about the Budget balance is the old adage: 'If you borrow too much you are in trouble' – whether you are a private individual, a company or Her Britannic Majesty's Government. At the very least, the higher the debt burden, the higher will be the future tax burden in servicing it. In particular, if debt increases faster than the national income, a debt trap is likely to occur in which the Government has to borrow ever more, simply to service the interest on past debts. In practice governments have nearly always inflated their way out of persistent and excessive deficits; in other words, they have defaulted by the back door.

High Unemployment For Ever?

The real academic venom was directed not so much against the Budget as against the notion of tight financial policies to reduce inflation. The House of Commons Treasury Committee was then and subsequently the home of model-based, technically advanced analysis, taking place in an intellectual time warp. The Committee's advisers accepted, superficially and reluctantly, that there might be no long-term trade-off between inflation and unemployment. But they sought to rescue the inflationist argument by attempting to quantify the short-term cost of moving from a higher to a lower rate of inflation in terms of the number of man years of unemployment involved. The Committee argued that to get inflation down by 1 per cent required, over a four-year period, a cumulative loss of output of 4 per cent and the equivalent of a year's additional unemployment for 650,000 people. As such mechanistic do-it-yourself formulae have remained in vogue, especially among the Eastern sea-board academics in the United States, it is perhaps worth repeating the refutation contained in my 1981 IFS speech, in which I employed the *reductio ad absurdum* method which can be particularly illuminating:

> Take first the so-called inflation/unemployment trade-off. If a lasting fall in the rate of inflation of about 1 per cent per annum can be achieved at a cost of 650,000 man-years' unemployment, presumably this calculation can equally well be reversed and thus provide us with a simple way of curing unemployment if only we are prepared to accept the higher inflation involved. Let us see what this would imply in practice. The Public Expenditure White Paper assumes an average unemployment rate of 2.5 million in 1981–82 and 2.7 million in 1982–83 and 1983–84. This level might imply a cumulative unemployment figure of about 10 million over four years. Suppose that we wished to have no more than a cumulative level of 4 million unemployed over the next four years; that is an average of 1 million. The solution, according to the Treasury Committee's ready-reckoner, is simple. All we need to reduce unemployment by 6 million over this period is 9 per cent higher inflation for ever . . . Who can possibly take this sort of nonsense seriously, particularly when we recall that the crucially important feature of the past quarter of a century is the way in which inflation and unemployment, under successive governments, have steadily and inseparably risen?
>
> In the 1960s the UK had an inflation rate of about 3½ per cent; during the lifetime of the 1974-79 Labour Governments this had risen to an average of 15 per cent per annum. At the same time unemployment rose from a level of under ½ million in the early 1960s to an average level of 1¼ million in the period of the last Government. Now we learn that apparently all that was preventing us from avoiding this deterioration in unemployment was a failure to let inflation rise still higher. Does it surprise you that we have got into our present difficulties of high inflation and high unemployment when we have a significant group of people who believe in such magic?
>
> It is claimed by the proponents of these ideas that the calculations are based on the Treasury model. It just goes to show how careful you have to be when handling a model

None of this is to deny that there is a painful transitional cost in reducing inflation, which can however be reduced by clarity and credibility in macroeconomic policy and by specific measures to improve the working of the labour market. The extent of the cost depends on specific circumstances, and is thus particularly difficult to predict. But the important point is that it is not a lasting cost.

The question asked in every recession by gloom-mongers and associated sceptics, not least businessmen, is 'Where will the growth come from?' (During the recession of the early 'eighties, this tended to take the allied form, 'Where will the jobs come from?', which became a constant refrain. However, in a world of unmet wants, increased productivity implies the capacity for increased output, rather than enforced idleness; so the two questions are much the same.) In my IFS lecture I dutifully gave the Treasury forecasters' answer, which was reduced savings, less destocking and some world economic upturn, which on this occasion turned out to be not too bad a prognosis. But I was provoked to the following outburst:

> Behind the prevailing scepticism lies the usually unspoken assumption that no economic recovery is ever possible other than by a conscious act of demand management by an expansionist government. This view, which is remarkably widely and deeply held, is not merely economic nonsense – implying as it does that the economy in general and the labour market in particular is incapable of adjusting to changing conditions, and that market forces are not merely blunted by the imperfections of the real world: but that they don't operate at all. It is also, and much more obviously, historical nonsense. If neo-Keynesian demand management were the necessary condition of economic growth, we would all still be living in caves and wearing woad, instead of listening to lectures at the centrally-heated Charing Cross Hotel. I am, needless to say, making no value judgement here.

Public Spending and Local Authorities

For all its watershed qualities, the 1981 Budget had in a sense simply made the best of a bad job. The 1979 Conservative manifesto had said 'The State takes too much of the nation's income; its share must be steadily reduced.' Yet General Government Expenditure, excluding privatization proceeds, had risen steadily from the 44 per cent of GDP which we inherited to a peak of 47½ per cent in 1982–83. It was because of this perverse development, not all directly attributable to the recession, coming on top of the excessive PSBR we inherited, that we had to increase the tax burden in flagrant conflict with our longer-term objective. Both the 1981 Budget Red Book and the 1981 Public Expenditure White Paper called for 'corrective action' in the next public spending round.

Our difficulties were further increased by a surge in local authority borrowing as well as nationalized industry borrowing. Although it accounted for about a quarter of total public spending, the constitutional principle of local autonomy meant that in practice the Government had no direct control over local government current expenditure. In 1981 Cabinet began to consider direct control of the rating powers of local authorities for the first time. The Environment Secretary, Michael Heseltine, secured Cabinet approval for a Bill which, *inter alia*, required councils to put excessive rate increases to their local electorate in a referendum. This was shot down by our own back-benchers, too many of whom had foolishly bowed the knee to their Conservative Councillors, who maintained that this would be an intolerable infringement of local democracy.

But other useful reforms contained in Michael's Local Government Finance Bill, introduced to the House in November 1981, survived. The Audit Commission for Local Government, which has done an excellent job in identifying waste in local government, was established. The ability of councils to levy a supplementary rate, in between the annual rate increases, was abolished. And, for the first time, the Government took the power to cap rates. While I supported the abortive referendum proposal as well as the abolition of supplementary rates and the introduction of the Audit Commission, I was initially apprehensive about rate capping, fearing that it would cause councils not to spend less but to borrow more, thus adding to the PSBR.

Fortunately, on the last point my fears were not realized; but the fact remains that the unsatisfactory constitutional position of councils, in which the bulk of their expenditure is financed one way and another by central Government, makes it all too easy for them to behave in an irresponsible way and avoid retribution at the polls by blaming everything on Treasury parsimony. I came increasingly to believe that the Treasury should either take complete control of local authority expenditure, or else require councils to fund all of their local services from local taxation. The battle for control of local government spending between the Treasury and the local authorities – which were supported increasingly as the years passed by successive Secretaries of State for the Environment – became one of the perennial themes of the Thatcher years. The Poll Tax was only the last, and most disastrous, attempt at a permanent solution.

'Funny Money'

The task of controlling public expenditure was also greatly complicated by the way in which spending was planned, and in particular by the way in which it accounted for inflation. This stemmed ultimately from the Plowden Report of 1961, which had led to the publication of an annual White Paper giving spending projections over the next five years. Less happily, Plowden introduced the planning of public expenditure in so-called 'volume' terms. Programmes for a series of years ahead were planned in the prices of the starting year. The jargon term was 'constant' or 'survey' prices, which eventually became known as 'funny money'. The theory was that this enabled spending Departments to plan resources – the number of teachers or doctors employed, or the number of miles of motorway built – without worrying about inflation. In fact 'funny money' meant that public expenditure was bound to get out of control. As Leo Pliatzky has pointed out:

> The object was to allocate real resources rather than money . . . The system was not designed to cope with a period of high inflation; when such a period arrived, the system facilitated it and was undermined by it. The method of adjusting to rising pay and prices offered no resistance to general inflationary pressures, and no incentive to economize in or switch from those items of expenditure which were particularly swollen by relative inflation.

Spending Ministers did not have to demand additional funds to cover the cost of inflation; it was accommodated automatically.

Programmes were adjusted not merely for the general rate of inflation, but by the particular price index of the services the Government was planning. This allowed the Ministry of Defence, for example, to argue that because the price of petrol was rising faster than retail prices, and the armed forces were particularly heavy users of petrol, it should be allowed an even bigger increase in spending. In the private sector the effect of an increase in the price of petrol is to use less of it. In the public sector, where spending was calculated in volume terms, consumption was not affected at all. The overall effect was inevitably a complete loss of control over public expenditure.

'Funny money' was such a dubious system that at the urging of Leo Pliatzky – then a Treasury official – even the previous Labour Government had introduced in 1976 a system of cash limits for a number of programmes for the year ahead. These could not be applied to demand-led programmes like pensions, social security payments or unemployment benefit, and were not even universally imposed elsewhere. We decided to build on cash limits when we took office, partly by bringing more programmes within their scope but also by abandoning volume planning altogether. The only question was whether we should calculate public expenditure in simple cash terms or in 'cost terms'. This last piece of jargon means taking account of general inflation only, but not the specific relative price changes, for particular items of public spending.

The Public Expenditure Survey Committee of the General Expenditure Policy Division of the Treasury explored the alternatives. I thought initially that there might be a case for the compromise of cost terms, but Geoffrey's and Leon's eventual decision to opt for cash planning was undoubtedly the right one. Virtually all the senior and middle ranking Treasury officials concerned with public expenditure were committed to the existing system and opposed to any change. They argued that if spending Departments were given cash budgets and told to spend them as they thought best, the budgets would always prove insufficient and there would be constant pressure for more money. But a group of less senior officials took a different view and recommended going over to cash planning in what became known within the Treasury as 'The Peasants' Revolt'.

The switch to cash planning was announced on Budget Day, 1981 and in the autumn of that year the public expenditure survey was carried out in cash terms for the first time. Although inflation in the base year had been 13 per cent, expenditure programmes were planned on the assumption that prices in the next three years would rise by 7 per cent, 6 per cent and 5 per cent. Happily, inflation did indeed fall rapidly, and public expenditure has been calculated in cash terms ever since. Cash planning proved successful, not because it meant that inflation could be ignored altogether – if it was significantly greater than forecast, spending Departments could seek an increase from the Reserve, which might or might not be granted – but because it required spending Ministers to justify demands for additional cash, rather than receiving the money automatically.

The Civil Service Strike

Not everything can be done by methodology. An important element in the increase in public expenditure in the early years was the surge in public sector pay which resulted from the recommendations of the Clegg Commission, which the Government had unwisely committed itself to implementing in full. The total public sector pay bill in 1980–81 rose by a quarter over the previous year, an increase twice as large as in the private sector. The resulting additional volume of taxation placed a burden on the private sector at a time when it was already hard pressed. Moreover, while the Treasury does have control over pay in the Civil Service, its influence over pay in the rest of the public sector, in particular in the nationalized industries and in local government, is almost non-existent, depending on the blunt instrument of overall cash controls and the Government's willingness to hold to them. My own preference was to demonstrate unequivocally our commitment to cash limits by resisting a public sector strike successfully. In August 1979 I remarked in a minute to Geoffrey that 'A successful stand taken at an early stage (the ground will need to be carefully chosen) is essential.' An opportunity did not arise until 1981.

In February of that year the Council of Civil Service Trade Unions, which represented 513,000 Civil Servants, rejected a final pay offer of 7 per cent (which could be accommodated within the official 6 per cent cash limits) and threatened to strike. On 9 March, there was a one day walkout at airports, social security offices and other Government centres. A campaign of selective strikes continued until the end of July, making it the longest industrial dispute since the General Strike of 1926. The bitterness was undoubtedly exacerbated by our commitment to reduce

Civil Service manpower by 100,000 within five years, and a general sense that the Thatcher Government was hostile to the public sector and all who worked in it. The strike's organizers concentrated their efforts on preventing Inland Revenue and VAT staff getting to work, in a deliberate attempt to wreck the public finances. Some £1 billion of tax went temporarily uncollected, costing millions in interest charges; and some VAT payments were lost for ever. The costs of the strike were reduced by the commendable response of British business which, at a very difficult time, made a tremendous effort to pay its tax bills to those Inland Revenue offices that remained open, and despite the strike the 1981–82 PSBR turned out better than forecast. The unions eventually settled in July for a pay increase of 7½ per cent and the promise of an inquiry into the Civil Service system of pay determination.

Christopher Soames, who as Lord President was the Minister responsible for the Civil Service, was very unhappy about the Government's stand and made known his view that the dispute could have been settled for 7½ per cent several weeks earlier. But even if this was so – and it was impossible to be sure – it ignored the beneficial demonstration effect of the Government's tough stance. My own view, stated in a speech at the time, was that:

> One obvious and major cause of unemployment has been the success
> – if that is the right word – of some union leaders in pushing wage
> costs above the level that companies can afford to pay . . . There
> are welcome signs that in private industry the vital lesson is being
> relearned. It is less clear that the message has got through to the
> public sector where the illusion still persists that the Government
> has some inexhaustible crock of gold.

The result of the strike was a victory for economic sanity. The Government was not seriously damaged and many of the strikers lost a great deal of money. But even today, in the closing years of the century, Britain's wage inflexibility remains the biggest avoidable cause of unemployment.

Fresh Faces

Despite the lesson of the 1981 Budget and the advent of cash planning the battle for public expenditure control was still far from won. Public spending, unlike most other key aspects of economic policy, is genuinely a joint Cabinet responsibility. There was little chance of real progress so long as the Cabinet, despite incremental changes, was a visible descendant of the Shadow Cabinet Margaret had inherited from Ted Heath.

The first of the promised Cabinet discussions of economic strategy duly took place on 17 June 1981, but it did not go well. Geoffrey presented a paper warning of 'a long and difficult haul' and stressed that it was vital not to ease up on public expenditure. 'Reflation – like import controls and incomes policy – is no answer to the real problems of the economy.' After the meeting at least six Cabinet sceptics made it known that they would resist any further curbs on government spending. Soon afterwards there was extensive rioting in several of Britain's inner cities, including the Toxteth area of Liverpool, Southall in London, and parts of Manchester. These followed similar disturbances in Brixton in April and provided ammunition to supporters of the 364 economists who asserted that the Government's economic policy threatened the 'social and political stability' of the nation.

The riots unnerved many in the Cabinet; and when Geoffrey presented his annual public expenditure proposals to Cabinet at two meetings on 21 and 23 July, he received an exceptionally hostile response to his call for further curbs. Quintin Hailsham likened Geoffrey to Herbert Hoover, the American President during the onset of the Great Depression. Peter Carrington, Ian Gilmour, Jim Prior, Francis Pym and Peter Walker made less apocalyptic, but no less disparaging noises. Geoffrey's critics even included two members of what was thought to be Margaret's ultra-loyalist breakfast group, John Biffen and John Nott.* Margaret and Geoffrey found themselves backed only by Keith Joseph, the Industry Secretary, and of course Geoffrey's number two at the Treasury, Leon Brittan, the Chief Secretary.

Margaret closed the discussion with the promise to resume it after the summer recess: but the meeting was a severe jolt for her. The result, as Jim Prior put it, was not 'a fresh examination – it was fresh faces'. Margaret Thatcher reshuffled the Cabinet before Parliament returned in the autumn, and I entered it as Secretary of State for Energy.

The European Community Budget

There was one particular public expenditure issue that was still unresolved when I left the Treasury in September 1981. This was the vexed question of Britain's contribution to the Community Budget. My own direct involvement in the issue was less than my official responsibility for the EC Budget would suggest. The size and nature of that Budget was largely determined by the Common Agricultural Policy (CAP) and to a lesser extent by initiatives agreed at Heads of Government level. The role of the Budget Ministers and of the EC Budget Commissioner was confined to the details of non-farm spending programmes and the implementation of guidelines largely agreed at a higher level.

---

*In the early years Margaret held a weekly economic breakfast meeting with a small number of like-minded Cabinet colleagues. The regular attenders were Geoffrey Howe, Keith Joseph, John Biffen and John Nott.

The Labour Government had favoured almost every conceivable increase in non-agricultural spending, as a potential gain for Britain. It did not take me long to stop officials briefing me along these lines. It would have made no sense to be striving to curb Government spending at home while boosting it at EC level. Moreover a very large increase in Community spending was required to achieve only a small net flow of funds, if any, to Britain. So I was extremely selective in the expenditure increases I supported.

The big issue was the strategic one, handled at Heads of Government level. The Treasury had made a study of the costs and benefits of EC membership. The need to pay more than world prices for food imports was a real cost to the British economy over and above the direct budgetary drain. But we decided to focus on the latter as it was itself a substantial sum and one that was quantifiable without any scope for argument. Had we sought to base our claim on the overall cost, we might have got bogged down in interminable controversies over what world prices would have been in the absence of the CAP. The issue was difficult enough without that.

The budgetary drain arose because Britain received only a tenth of Community agricultural expenditure, which accounted for nearly two thirds of its total Budget, while contributing a fifth of the Community's tax revenue. Our high level of agricultural imports and extensive trade with the rest of the world meant that our net contribution to the Community budget was far higher than our economic performance warranted. Britain, although at that time seventh in terms of GDP per head, was the largest net contributor to the Community Budget. Indeed, the UK and Germany were the only net contributors: all the others were net recipients.

The European Commission was reluctant to admit the cost of our net contribution even though it was readily calculable; but the Treasury estimated that, without adjustment, it would run at around £1 billion in 1980 which, as I remarked to the House of Commons, was 'manifestly and massively inequitable'. The Foreign Office, however, was unhelpful and defeatist. Peter Carrington, the Foreign Secretary, went so far as to tell the French that 'the net contribution problem was ultimately of our own making in the sense that we were not running our economy properly'. Fortunately, it was an issue on which Downing Street, rather than the Foreign Office, led.

Armed with Treasury briefing, Margaret launched her unforgettable campaign to 'get our money back'. At a memorable European Summit in Dublin at the end of November 1979, she rightly rejected an offer of only £350 million despite appeasing advice from the Foreign Office. Her efforts were made all the harder by the close relationship between the French President Giscard d'Estaing and the German Chancellor Helmut Schmidt; but the root of the problem was that, to the extent that the

UK contributed less, others would have to contribute more, and behind the pious protestations that we were being un-Communautaire it was this they found unpalatable.

It appeared at first as if Paris and Bonn thought we were complaining about the effect on the balance of payments, which was indeed adverse. But this was clearly not the case at a time of an almost embarrassingly strong pound. Once they grasped the budgetary nature of our complaint, the French haughtily accused us of the infamous crime of seeking a *juste retour* from the Community instead of being content with the profounder benefits of membership.

My own involvement in the issue arose mainly from the Treasury's role in briefing the Prime Minister rather than my specific job as, in Community terms, the UK's Budget Minister. I had minuted Geoffrey early on that 'sooner or later we have to be prepared to be bloody-minded (that is Gaullist) in the pursuit of our objective, and even before that to let it leak out both to our partners and to Parliament that we are prepared to be bloody-minded.'

It soon became clear the only serious threat we could make was to withhold our contributions to the Community Budget altogether. Under the joint guidance of the Treasury and the Law Officers, a Bill was prepared on a contingency basis to provide the legal backing for such a move and the modalities that would be employed. In the event, while we discreetly let it be known that the option of withholding was being considered, the Bill was never published, let alone introduced.

A considerable advance on the Dublin offer was secured at meetings in Luxembourg and Brussels in the spring of 1980, where rebates were negotiated for 1980 and 1981 worth £1,570 million in all. This success was due entirely to the obstinacy of Margaret Thatcher who was reluctant to accept even this improved offer, although she did in the end. She was right in thinking that this agreement, which went only up to the end of 1981, did not mark the end of the matter. A third rebate of £476 million for 1982 was later secured, accompanied by a Community commitment to find a permanent solution. This was finally concluded at the Community Summit in Fontainebleau in June 1984, where Britain won a £600 million rebate for that year plus an automatic formula for refunds on subsequent years. If Margaret's bloody-mindedness was the essential ingredient, the successful outcome owed a good deal to the skill of the lean and cerebral Michael Butler, Britain's Ambassador to the Community, whose understanding of the nuts and bolts of Community law and practice was as impressive as his unflagging zeal in carrying out his remit.

There was, however, a negative aspect to Margaret's triumph. Although the quality improved later on, the poor advice given by the Foreign Office over the Community Budget in 1979 and 1980 reinforced Margaret Thatcher's instinctive distrust of that Department; and the wetness of the diplomatic service became a perpetual theme in her thinking. Moreover the outcome of the Budget negotiations persuaded her that it always paid to be bloody-minded in dealings with the Community. This was to prove increasingly counterproductive in practice. Nor did it help when I sought to interest her in sterling's membership of the Exchange Rate Mechanism (ERM) of the European Monetary System (EMS).*

The Dawn of the EMS

By the summer of 1981, I had become persuaded of the case for making the discipline of the ERM, rather than targets for domestic monetary aggregates, the prime determinant of monetary policy and hence of the conduct of the battle against inflation. In my role as a columnist in the *Financial Weekly* in 1978–79, I had written in support of the idea of Britain's full EMS membership, but with a 6 per cent margin, in place of the normal 2¼ per cent. This was a concession which Italy had negotiated at the start in 1979 and which both Spain and Britain were to obtain when they eventually joined the EMS in 1989 and 1990 respectively. But when I joined the Government in 1979, inflation was rising so fast that I felt that the best bet for the time being was to concentrate on domestic monetary policy and leave sterling to market forces.

But two years later, with inflation on the way down, I had changed my mind. On 15 June 1981, I sent Geoffrey a long note, arguing that 'we should take advantage of our forthcoming presidency [in the second half of 1981] to join the EMS.' It was a conclusion I had reached with some misgivings. As I wrote:

> This is in many ways a second best course. Financial discipline is essential for the conquest of inflation; and there are two forms which financial discipline can take. It can be a self-imposed explicit monetary discipline, or a partly externally imposed exchange rate discipline . . . I have no doubt that ideally a straightforward monetary discipline is superior. But we are now getting into that phase, which will become increasingly evident as the election approaches, when the political pressures for relaxation of monetary discipline will start to mount. This raises the question of whether, in practice, we may not be able to enforce and maintain a greater degree of effective financial discipline if we were to embrace the exchange rate discipline, for all its imperfections. This is particularly apposite given that those

*The pedantic term 'ERM' came into vogue in the UK, for no good reason, towards the end of the 1980s. Prior to that, 'EMS' had been used to convey the exchange rate arrangement that the European Monetary System was all about, as indeed it still is so used outside the UK. In this book I have for the most part used the current UK terminology, but occasionally revert to the more sensible earlier (and internationally recognized) usage.

of our colleagues who are most likely to be pressing for relaxation of monetary discipline, are those who are keenest on the UK joining the EMS. In other words, we turn their sword against them. Essentially what this would mean is tying the pound to the German Mark . . . You will not be surprised to know that I have very mixed feelings about the course I have sketched out. At the end of the day the argument rests on political judgement.

The colleagues I had in mind were the Cabinet sceptics who even before the fateful July Cabinet meeting had made known their opposition to further public spending curbs and who were equally opposed to a firm monetary policy.

My advice was rejected on a number of grounds. It was argued that stability against the dollar was more important to British industry than stability against European currencies, an objection the force of which was somewhat weakened by the fact that stability against the dollar was not an offer; and that the prevailing sterling exchange rate against the Deutschmark was in any case too high a rate at which to join. More fundamentally, at that time Geoffrey, as well as Margaret, was still committed to the idea of an exchange rate determined by the free play of market forces. (While I became convinced of the merits of the ERM on hard-headed politico-economic grounds, Geoffrey's conversion derived initially from his Europeanism.)

Meanwhile, my own conviction of the case for the ERM was becoming steadily firmer. In the last memorandum I wrote to Geoffrey as Financial Secretary, on 14 September 1981, the day I joined the Cabinet as Energy Secretary, I pointed out that we were receiving 'increasing evidence of the weakness of £M3 as a reliable proxy for underlying monetary conditions, without any greater confidence being able to be attached to any of the other monetary aggregates. This clearly strengthens the case for moving over to an exchange rate discipline.' I left before I got a reply. But it was perhaps fitting that I should have joined the Cabinet secure in the same conviction that carried me out of it just over eight years later.

The issue did not come to a head until well after I returned to the Treasury as Chancellor in June 1983. There was only one Prime Ministerial meeting on the EMS during Geoffrey Howe's Chancellorship. This took place in the Cabinet Room of Number 10 on 22 January 1982, while I was at the Department of Energy, and I did not come to hear of it until some time afterwards.

Geoffrey at that time was not in favour of joining – indeed, he became fully convinced of the case for membership only after he became Foreign Secretary a year and a half later. At the 1982 meeting, he could see the attraction but was worried that the ERM might conflict with domestic monetary policy. He also sympathized with industry's view that the prevailing exchange rate (of around DM4.30) was too high a level at which to join. His most percipient objection (from the viewpoint of the committed European he always was) was that people might be turned off the whole European Community ideal if the ERM were, rightly or wrongly, held responsible for high British interest rates – which indeed happened after Britain eventually joined in 1990.

The principal supporter of the ERM at the time was the Governor of the Bank of England, Gordon Richardson. He correctly pointed out that the evolution of monetary policy under the Thatcher Government already indicated the need for a clearer role for the exchange rate, for which the ERM provided the right – and indeed the only practicable – framework. He was also afraid that the pound would depreciate outside the system. Unfortunately the post-Richardson Bank wavered in subsequent years, and at some key moments retreated into muttering that the timing was wrong.

Margaret summed up along lines that were to become increasingly familiar. She was not convinced of the advantages of the EMS and was worried about the loss of 'freedom to manoeuvre' . She conceded that the case would be stronger once British inflation and interest rates were closer to German levels (but when they were she found other objections). She concluded that the Government should maintain the existing position of being (supposedly) ready to join 'when the time is ripe'.

APPENDIX: INDEXED GILTS

MOST READERS WILL NEED no further demonstration of my belief that rampant inflation is an evil, moral as well as economic, and that inflation is a monetary phenomenon. But in the detailed formulation of strategy no weapon should be ruled out because of guilt by association. Indexation is a good example. In Chapter 2 I have recorded how, as an Opposition Whip, I played a key role in forcing a reluctant Labour Government to accept the Rooker-Wise-Lawson Amendment to the 1977 Finance Bill to index the personal tax thresholds. Soon after our election victory, I recommended to Geoffrey in a minute of 3 July 1979, the indexation of the entire personal tax system, both income and capital, 'as the only practical way of avoiding the tax system from becoming in an inflationary era steeply more progressive'. In his 1980 Budget Geoffrey duly indexed the thresholds both for the higher rates and for Capital Transfer Tax; and, in 1982, after I had left the Treasury, he took the much more complex (but thoroughly justified) step of indexing the Capital Gains Tax so far as future gains were concerned.

As Financial Secretary, however, my main energies in this field were devoted to the effort to launch indexed gilt-edged securities, on which I managed to initiate a discussion as early as December 1979. (Indeed, had it not been for this, as we shall see, it is unlikely that Geoffrey would have indexed the Capital Gains Tax.)

Margaret was instinctively opposed to indexation as in some way validating inflation. The Governor of the Bank of England, Gordon Richardson, was even more strongly opposed, regarding indexed gilts as redolent of a banana republic and not far short of the end of civilization as we knew it. To try to ease the atmosphere, Douglas Wass supervised the preparation of a well-argued Treasury Paper which demonstrated that it was senseless to be either always opposed to indexation or always in favour. The merits of the proposal depended entirely on what was being indexed. The indexation of wages, for instance, is a force for perpetuating inflation – Belgium was a prime example at the time. The indexation of personal tax does indeed mitigate some of the worst effects of inflation. But by removing the fiscal dividend the Government otherwise receives from a non-indexed tax system, it also removes some of the incentives for inflationary finance. The indexation of long-term Government debt was an even stronger deterrent. For, if both the principal and interest are indexed, the cost of servicing the debt increases as inflation rises. This is a stark contrast to conventional gilts, where the servicing burden declines when inflation accelerates.*

*The rest of this appendix will be of interest largely to financial readers.

But my immediate aim in pushing indexed gilts was more severely practical: to increase the range of options for financing the still substantial Budget deficit. The Bank of England traditionally offered gilts for sale at a fixed price. If the bonds were not fully subscribed, it then bought the surplus itself and dribbled it out to the market later, as and when conditions seemed favourable – this was known as the 'tap stock' method. Particularly frustrating was the Bank's insistence that funding could only take place – i.e. new gilt-edged issues made – when conditions were wholly propitious. One consequence of this was that there were periodic funding pauses, during which the market knew that the authorities must be becoming desperate to fund: which meant that the next issue had to be on conspicuously more generous terms. This became progressively truer as the financial year advanced. What I sought was a means of ensuring that the Government could fund steadily, almost irrespective of prevailing conditions.

My first attempt was to persuade the Bank to try the tender system, under which Treasury bonds were auctioned to the highest bidder so that the market determined its own price and yield. The idea was resisted point blank by John Page, the Bank of England Director in charge of the money and gilt-edged markets, who was wholly opposed to innovations of any kind: it was a great improvement when Eddie George subsequently took over in 1982.

It was after that that I had the idea of introducing index-linked gilts. The inspiration came from the indexed-linked National Savings ('granny') bonds which had been introduced by the Labour Government, available as the name suggests only to people above retirement age and then in limited quantities. Indexed gilts seemed to me to offer three important advantages:

- They would be saleable when conventional gilts were not.
- If, as we believed, the market's expectation of future inflation was too high, they would prove a particularly cheap way of funding.
- It would soon become clear that if they were introduced it would have to be by tender, thus establishing the tender principle, since there was no way of knowing what the 'right' price was.

My underlying purpose was to enlarge the range of options for the non-inflationary financing of the PSBR. 'A greengrocer selling apples and oranges would on the whole do better than one who insists on selling nothing but apples', as I put it in a speech at the time. A special attraction of indexed gilts was that they should be saleable at times of uncertainty without the need to push up long-term interest rates. An example occurred at the beginning of July 1981, when because of uncertainties about US interest rates and the overhang of a British Petroleum rights issue, we would have been unable to sell conventional stock even at the unacceptably high 15½ per cent long-term yield which then prevailed. Yet we were able to sell our second tranche of £1 billion of indexed gilts at a 2.8 per cent real interest rate.

It took time to reach this point. Gordon Richardson was uncompromising in his opposition. He no doubt felt that his prestige would plummet in the eyes of his central bank colleagues whom he met each month at Basle. He insisted that once we had issued an indexed gilt we would never again be able to sell a conventional one; yet another of the erroneous predictions the Bank made around this time. He found an unlikely ally in the shape of Ken Couzens, then the Treasury Second Permanent Secretary in charge of overseas finance, who objected on the different ground that if the UK alone were to issue indexed gilts, we would attract a massive influx of money from all over the world – notably from the Arabs – which would drive up the exchange rate still further, and at the same time alienate our partners in the Group of Five. I did not believe either of these solemn warnings, and in any case felt that we could live with the Couzens prediction even in the unlikely event of its being proved correct: it would not, after all, have been hard to make conventional gilts *less* attractive to overseas holders.

Armed with the Wass Paper on the general indexation issue, I was able to secure Geoffrey Howe's agreement to launch indexed gilts and suggest to him arguments he could use with Margaret. In this context it was clearly very helpful that Alan Walters, who had joined Number 10 at the beginning of 1981, was a strong supporter of indexed gilts. For all his faults, Walters had the great strength that he was prepared to argue with Margaret on issues when he was convinced she was mistaken. This was in strong contrast to Brian Griffiths, who headed her Policy Unit in her last years, who was inclined to tell her only what she wanted to hear. Nevertheless I did have to have one further meeting with the Prime Minister at Chequers, *à deux*, to secure her final acquiescence.

The final question to resolve was decided in September 1980, when we agreed to confine the initial issue of indexed gilts to UK pension funds and the pension businesses of the life assurance offices – so-called 'gross funds', which means that they do not pay tax. This did indeed deal with the Couzens fear of a torrent of overseas money, but the main reason for the restriction was different. It was to get round the tax problem which the Inland Revenue had, quite rightly, identified. The question was, should the capital gains on indexed gilts be liable to tax? On the one hand the Labour Government had, at Harold Lever's suggestion, taken conventional gilt-edged gains out of tax altogether when it had to fund excessive Budget deficits in financial markets conspicuously lacking in confidence. On the other hand, indexed gilts could be seen as being closer to equities, where gains were taxable, in their market characteristics and attractions. I was myself sensitive to the fact that, were we to legislate explicitly to make it clear that indexed gilt gains were tax free, the private sector would argue with some justice that this was thoroughly unfair and damaging to the equity market. Thus confining the purchase of indexed gilts to tax-exempt funds cut the Gordian knot on the tax issue. Moreover, pension funds seemed particularly suitable homes for index-linked gilts, given the growing trend towards at least partially inflation-proofed pensions.

Indexed gilts were announced in the 1981 Budget and the first issue was made on 21 March. The acronym internally used within the Treasury to describe the original issues was 'RIGS' (Restricted Indexed Gilts), although in one submission one Treasury wag suggested that they should be referred to as 'NIGELS' (New Indexed Gilt-edged Eligible Liabilities).

The initial issue of indexed gilts, much to the Bank's surprise, was highly successful and put them firmly on the map where they have stayed. The tax problem was fully solved by the indexation of the Capital Gains Tax by Geoffrey Howe in 1982, which meant that index-linked gilts no longer had to be restricted to gross funds for their gains to be tax free. When the restrictions were lifted the feared torrent of foreign purchases did not materialize.

Indeed the subsequent appetite for indexed gilts proved rather less than I had envisaged. Falling inflation boosted the attractions of conventional gilts, and a rising equity market made indexed gilts less attractive as the 1980s progressed. Nevertheless the proportion of total market holdings of gilts held in indexed form rose steadily from 1.3 per cent at the end of March 1981 to 9.1 per cent at the end of March 1986, and stood at 7.7 per cent at the end of March 1991. Indexed gilts have clearly proved a useful addition to the Government's funding armoury. The method of sale also provided a convenient precedent for the switch to the tender method of selling conventional gilts following the reforms instituted after the Stock Exchange's Big Bang in October 1986.

But the measure which probably impinged most on ordinary people was the removal of the restrictions on 'granny' bonds which I announced in 1981. First the minimum age for holdings was reduced to fifty-five and over and eventually they became open to everyone. The removal of restrictions on granny bonds was part of my general effort to increase the contribution of the hitherto moribund Department of National Savings, for which I was ministerially responsible, to funding the Budget deficit. Indeed, even a decade later, in 1990–1, index-linked certificates were the best selling National Savings product, netting the Treasury £1.2 billion out of a total of £1.4 billion raised. This was one Treasury initiative for which the Bank of England had nothing but praise, as a successful National Savings drive reduced the amount of funding it had to do. The irony is that their predecessor, granny bonds, were the true precursor of the indexed gilts it tried so hard in vain to stop.

PART TWO

Cabinet Minister

CHAPTER 11

ON BECOMING A SECRETARY OF STATE

Member of Cabinet · Life as a Minister
Cabinet Meetings · The Falklands Cabinets
The Thatcher Style · The Abuse of Information
Consent of the Victims

Member of Cabinet

THE MOST IMPORTANT EVENT, for me, of my time as Financial Secretary had been my marriage to Thérèse (with whom I had been living since the beginning of 1979) in October 1980, three months after my divorce from Vanessa whom I had married in 1955. Shortly afterwards Thérèse became pregnant and asked me if I would like to be present at the baby's birth. This unexpected suggestion took me by surprise, being of a generation for whom this was not customary, but I readily assented. I had not witnessed the birth of any of my five previous surviving children, and this was in all probability my last chance of an exciting new experience.

However, as the due date approached, it was clear that there was a real risk that when the baby arrived I would be away at Strasbourg addressing the European Parliament in my capacity as President of the Budget Council (the UK held the Community Presidency at that time). Thérèse's gynaecologist kindly solved this dilemma by offering to induce the birth a few days early. Accordingly on 10 September 1981, with me in rapt – and I hope helpful – attendance, Emily was born. Thérèse was characteristically brave throughout the process.

In the event, I never did get to make my carefully prepared speech to the European Parliament, scheduled for 15 September, and it had to be delivered by Peter Rees on my behalf. For four days after Emily was born, on 14 September, Margaret decided to purge the Cabinet of most of the 'wet' opponents of her economic policies, having already signalled her intentions by dismissing in January 1981 Norman St John Stevas, the Leader of the Commons, whose wit tended to get the better of his discretion, and effectively demoting the lugubrious Francis Pym from Defence Secretary to Leader of the Commons in his place. Out went the amiable Secretary of State for Education, Mark Carlisle, the sour number two at the Foreign and Commonwealth Office, Ian Gilmour (with the Foreign Secretary, Peter Carrington, in the Lords, Margaret had considered it necessary for the FCO to have a Cabinet Minister in the Commons as well), and the old-guard Leader of the House of Lords, Christopher Soames. Peter Thorneycroft, another distinguished representative of the old guard, was relieved of the Party Chairmanship: he had shortly before admitted to 'rising damp' and had written to Margaret to urge a change of economic course.

Margaret clearly considered Carlisle and Gilmour politically incapable of causing trouble on the back-benches, and the more heavyweight Soames and Thorneycroft constitutionally incapable of doing so as members of the House of Lords. Those wets whom she feared might cause trouble on the back-benches – notably Peter Walker at Agriculture, Michael Heseltine, only semi-wet anyway, at Environment, and the demoted Francis Pym she left in place; although Jim Prior was moved from Employment Secretary to the backwater of Northern Ireland Secretary. The affable but short-fused Heathite squire, Prior, made the mistake, when rumours of the impending move reached his ears, of letting the *Observer* know that he would sooner resign from the Government than be moved from his present post. When Margaret called his bluff and he accepted the Northern Ireland job, the episode effectively destroyed his standing as a significant political force.

The moral I drew from this was that resignation threats should not be lightly made, and if they are made, they should be made in private and must be in earnest. A threat withdrawn in the face of Prime Ministerial resolution fatally undermines the Minister concerned. Moreover, a serious resignation threat should be made with the probability in mind that it will have to be implemented and the Minister concerned out of office for a long time, if not for ever. If this personal fate is accepted, a resigning Minister can occasionally hope that his resignation will have some long-term effect. It is also probably salutary for Prime Ministers to be reminded from time to time that, while Cabinet colleagues may not be the equals that constitutional mythology makes out, they cannot be taken for granted either.

The four newcomers in 1981 were Janet Young as Leader of the Lords, Norman Tebbit as Employment Secretary, Cecil Parkinson as Party Chairman, in the Cabinet as Paymaster General, and myself as

Energy Secretary, this last post made vacant by the move of David Howell to Transport Secretary as part of a long sequence of changes arising from the departure of Mark Carlisle.

Janet, an old friend of Margaret's, likeable, brisk, with a distinguished career in local government behind her, was the only woman Margaret ever appointed to Cabinet. She never really made her mark and was dropped from Cabinet less than two years later. Norman Tebbit, Cecil Parkinson and myself, all committed Thatcherites, despite our very different characters, were to play larger and longer roles in the Thatcher Government.

Thus it was that in September 1981, two years and four months after taking office as Prime Minister, Margaret Thatcher at last secured a Cabinet with a Thatcherite majority. And after just over seven years in the House of Commons, I was a member of that Cabinet. It was a tremendous stroke of luck, and an equal privilege. Margaret herself very soon remarked – I think it was at the second Cabinet meeting after the reshuffle, but it may even have been the first – how much more agreeable the discussions were than they had been before the reshuffle.

Certainly, despite the Government's unpopularity, the spirit in Cabinet when I first joined it was excellent. Among most of us then was a clear sense of being bound together in a common endeavour, in which we believed, and of mutual trust. Those who had doubts concealed them. And Margaret herself, although she led from the front – that was always her style, and nothing wrong with that – had by that time developed neither the delusion of self-sufficiency nor the distrust of any colleague who was not a yes-man which were in time to make her so difficult and to contribute so much to her downfall.

Life as a Minister

Becoming a member of the Cabinet is in some ways like joining the first eleven (though the actual numbers were precisely twice that). But the most important difference from being a Minister outside the Cabinet is that of having one's own Department to run and the responsibility for taking the initiatives and solving the problems that fall within its sphere. Since I enjoy taking decisions, it was a great pleasure for me to have my own show to run, even though any major decision clearly required the endorsement of my Cabinet colleagues in general and of the Prime Minister in particular.

Thanks in particular to the brilliant *Yes, Minister* series of television programmes, most people are aware that British Ministers are treated with great servility to their face, and looked after hand and foot while on duty, but are also more overworked than their counterparts in most other countries. Moreover, all official support is suspended once a Minister is deemed to be engaged on private – or heaven forbid – party political work. Departments may stretch a point and allow a Minister's driver to pick him up after a private dinner in London, so that he can come home to his boxes more quickly; but this indulgence does not apply in his constituemcy. He will have a driver and a private secretary to accompany him if he opens a factory; but if his next engagement is a speech to his local party, he will have to make his own transport arrangements.

A Cabinet Minister's workload is in any case generally much heavier than that of lesser Ministers. This is a burden with which some new Cabinet members at first find it difficult to cope. The danger then is that they solve the problem by becoming the creature of their officials. This danger did not arise in my case, since my workload as Energy Secretary was no greater than it had been as Financial Secretary, who probably carries the heaviest workload of any Minister outside the Cabinet. It is also true that being Energy Secretary (or so it seemed to me in retrospect after I became Chancellor) is only a part-time job.

The demands made by the various Cabinet posts vary enormously. Apart from the Premiership itself, which is *sui generis* – carrying as it does not only awesome responsibility but a workload that varies enormously according to the way in which the incumbent chooses to exercise that responsibility – the heaviest load and toughest job is generally agreed to be that of Chancellor. That was certainly the view of Jim Callaghan, who held all three great offices of State – Chancellor, Home Secretary and Foreign Secretary – before becoming Prime Minister: I remember him telling me as much when we were chatting one sparkling November morning, waiting to take up our places on the politicians' side of the Cenotaph on Armistice Day early on in my time as Chancellor. The best job, short of Prime Minister, was in his view Foreign Secretary: 'Its a doddle' he told me, advising me to make that my ambition.

At the other end of the spectrum is the job of Employment Secretary which, despite the undoubted importance of trade union and other labour market legislation, involves the lightest of ministerial workloads – certainly for a Government determined to eschew corporatism. So long as it exists in its present form, it is best done by a consummate party politician since (unlike the occupant of other Departments) he has plenty of time to devote to party political speeches. That is what made Norman Tebbit's appointment to the job in the 1981 reshuffle particularly well chosen. When, later on, David Young, who was no politician at all, became Employment Secretary, he had to persuade Margaret to agree to the anomalous transfer of responsibility for small businesses to the Department of Employment to give himself enough to do.

Agriculture, too, would be a doddle were it not for the Common Agricultural Policy (and its domestic precursors) which we would all be better off without. Even Energy, to which I was appointed when I first entered the Cabinet, was, as I have mentioned, scarcely a full-time job. It was also, like the Treasury in this respect, but like very few other Departments, almost entirely a policy department, with very few executive functions of its own. This was particularly agreeable, since it is policy which should interest any normal Minister most. It was a small, compact Department, with little over a thousand officials, almost all of them located in its Millbank headquarters. Its subsequent reabsorption into the Department of Trade and Industry by John Major following the 1992 election was clearly sensible: indeed, it was something I had myself recommended to Margaret in 1987.

Cabinet Meetings

The least important aspect of Cabinet membership, certainly in Margaret Thatcher's time, were the Cabinet meetings themselves. The imprimatur of Cabinet was taken seriously, and there were occasional Cabinet meetings that really mattered, such as those that concluded the annual public expenditure round. But in general and for good reason, key decisions were taken in smaller groups – either the formal Cabinet Committees, of which the most important (such as the Overseas and Defence Committee and the two main economic policy Committees, Economic Strategy, which seldom met, and Economic Affairs, which met a great deal) were, like the Cabinet itself, chaired by the Prime Minister; or at still smaller informal meetings of Ministers which she would usually hold in her study upstairs. The Cabinet's customary role was to rubber stamp decisions that had already been taken, to keep all colleagues reasonably informed about what was going on, and to provide a forum for general political discussion if time permitted.

Thus, as Chancellor, I used to look forward to Cabinet meetings as the most restful and relaxing event of the week. This was all the more so since, by long tradition, Cabinet starts with a discussion of parliamentary affairs, initiated by the Leader of the House of Commons, followed by a discussion of Foreign Affairs, led by the Foreign Secretary. There then follows whatever specific items may be on the agenda for discussion. Towards the end of her long stint as Prime Minister, Margaret introduced a third regular item, Home Affairs, in which any colleague who had any important information to impart on the home front was expected to launch forth. But though the importance of the subject would have fully justified a weekly report by the Chancellor under the heading Economic Affairs, I was quite content to leave it to others to propose this break with tradition, which happily none of them did.

Perhaps they assumed that any Chancellor's report would be as uninformative as the Foreign Secretary's routine dissertation on foreign affairs, which could be delivered with elegance and wit, yet seldom revealed anything that was not already well known to the attentive newspaper reader. Indeed, during Geoffrey Howe's time, unkind colleagues would take to listening to the news bulletin just before Cabinet met, and embarrassing him by asking for his assessment of some reported new development overseas on which he had not had time to be briefed, not even as to whether the development had in fact occurred.

A normal Cabinet meeting has no chance of becoming a grave forum of statesmanlike debate. Twenty-two people attending a two-and-a-half-hour meeting can speak for just over six and a half minutes each on average. If there are three items of business – and there are usually far more – the ration of time just exceeds two minutes, if everyone is determined to have his say. Small wonder then that most Ministers keep silent on most issues or confine themselves to brief but pointed questions or observations.

Given the nature of Cabinet meetings, anyone who was inclined to talk too much would need to have something interesting to say if he was not to forfeit the sympathy of his colleagues and the patience of the Prime Minister. That exceptionally nice man, Patrick Jenkin, was one who fell into this trap. As Energy Secretary, and a new and junior member of Cabinet, I usually succeeded in restraining my natural inclination to air my views; subsequently, as Chancellor, I naturally took a fuller part in Cabinet discussions, but still less than I did at other meetings at which decisions were actually taken.

The Falklands Cabinets

The limitation of general discussion at Cabinet meetings became clear during the Falklands War in the spring and early summer of 1982, when Margaret introduced the practice of holding a second weekly Cabinet meeting in addition to the normal Thursday one. The conflict was, of course, the dominant event of 1982, and wholly preoccupied all our thinking while it lasted. Throughout the critical weeks of May and June, there was a full Cabinet meeting every Tuesday after the daily War Cabinet. The Chiefs of Staff were present and, although sensitive military matters were not discussed, it was possible always to gauge the balance of the conflict. It was at the special Tuesday Cabinet meetings that we discussed the various peace proposals put forward by the American Secretary of State, Al Haig, and the United Nations Secretary General, Javier Perez de Cuellar, during the weeks before the landings at San Carlos Bay.

I was convinced from a very early stage in the conflict that the various diplomatic manoeuvrings would amount to nothing and that it would be necessary to retake the islands by force, and said as much. This view may not have been universally shared. In any event, had the Galtieri junta accepted the British proposal of 20 May to place the islands under the indefinite jurisdiction of the United Nations, it is possible that the recall of the Task Force would have commanded a majority in Cabinet. Very foolishly it did not do so. As a result, there was no dissension within Cabinet throughout the war, even if one or two members may have nursed private doubts.

The Thatcher Style

Whether before Cabinet or the more effective smaller meetings, Margaret, who appeared to need only four hours' sleep a night, always did her homework on the subjects for discussion, almost as if she were about to sit an examination. In general this was a desirable characteristic, but it could lead to time-wasting attempts to show off her mastery of detail, at the expense of the main business in hand.

Some of the time saved through her economy of sleep was devoted to what was frequently her first appointment of the day: the visit of her hairdresser. She was convinced that her authority – in a world in which a woman's appearance is always a subject of comment, a man's only occasionally – would be diminished if she were not impeccably turned out at all times. She was probably right – and certainly this was one aspect of her with which the great mass of women voters could readily identify, however much it may have been derided in NW1.

Another and most attractive aspect of her femininity was the instant note (sometimes accompanied by flowers) sent to Thérèse when she was ill or had any problems. These notes were topped and tailed by Margaret in the early days, and written completely by hand when I became Chancellor and we were her next-door neighbours.

The practice of taking important decisions in smaller groups and not in Cabinet itself can clearly be taken too far, particularly if the groups are too small; but it makes obvious sense. Not only is twenty-two an unwieldy number for a good discussion. But Ministers whose interests lie elsewhere are unlikely to have informed themselves sufficiently to make a worthwhile contribution. Moreover, a Cabinet meeting is nowadays a highly visible and almost public affair. The Press and TV all know when Ministers arrive for it, and when they leave. Any unusually prolonged discussion thus leads inevitably to stories of splits, dissension and disarray, with attempts (occasionally assisted by the participants themselves) to identify who stood where. Thus meetings of Cabinet Committees or *ad hoc* groups, at times that are neither regular nor announced, with a membership that is not revealed – indeed their very existence used not to be officially admitted – are a more effective way to conduct business. (These special committees are normally called 'MISC' under Conservative Governments and 'GEN' under Labour ones.)

I have no doubt, however, that the best arrangement is for the Prime Minister of the day to develop an Inner Cabinet, which would be joined by appropriate additional participants to discuss specific issues. Key issues should initially be discussed by the Inner Cabinet alone. This is something that Margaret at one point, as I shall record later, came very near to doing, but never in fact did.

The Abuse of Information

Instead she sought to fragment any dissident voices. What had started off as a justified attempt to make effective decisions in small and informal groups degenerated into increasingly complex attempts to divide and rule. More and more, decisions were effectively taken in very small groups in which she had hand-picked the balance of membership to ensure the outcome she sought. Her conduct of meetings also became increasingly authoritarian. Some of her predecessors, such as Harold Macmillan, would allow other colleagues to have their say before summing up and stating a conclusion. Margaret on the other hand, when there was an issue on which she had already formed a firm view, would start with an unashamedly tendentious introduction of her own, before inviting the responsible and sometimes cowed Minister to have his say. Thus what began as a method for the most expedient conduct of business ended as a means of getting her own way irrespective of the merits or political costs.

This was not her only mode. In some ways far more irritating was her behaviour when her strongly held general views were not sufficient to reach a conclusion on difficult and complex detailed issues. She could then become unbelievably discursive, sounding off at random on various aspects of the matter, and generally going round in circles getting nowhere, reaching agreement only on the time and date of the next meeting. Broadcasting and education (where, however, she was not wholly to blame) were two cases in point. To busy Ministers seeking to get matters decided this was the most frustrating of all. Margaret, of course, was equally busy; but, presumably, being the star turn at these meetings was compensation enough. Eventually, after I became Chancellor, I took to offering to chair meetings of the key Ministers involved, in between her meetings, as the only way of making progress – I did this, with her full knowledge and consent, both over the Government's proposals for the development of broadcasting and over the year-long review of the health service.

Consent of the Victims

Why did the colleagues allow her to govern in the way she did? While spinelessness or careerism may be adequate explanation in the case of some, it will not do for all. And belief in her infallibility was even more narrowly shared. Of course all Prime Ministers are in a position of great power, so long as they can retain the office; and she was a particularly formidable Prime Minister who, over the years – she became, after all, the longest-serving Prime Minister this century – had acquired considerable experience.

But beyond this, her method of Cabinet Government was accepted because in many ways it was highly convenient to her colleagues. Most Cabinet Ministers, particularly after a longish period in government, tend to be preoccupied with fighting their own battles and pursuing the issues that matter within their own bailiwick, and lose interest in the wider picture. Most of the time it is comforting for them to feel that all they need to do is strike a deal with the Prime Minister, and not have to bother overmuch about persuading their other colleagues. (And if they are fighting the Prime Minister on an issue that means a great deal to them, all the more reason to concentrate on that.) It was noticeable that, towards the end, those colleagues who most bemoaned the lack of collective discussion of issues outside their own departmental field were busy making private bilateral deals with Margaret over issues within their own departmental responsibility.

Finally, if less important, was the fact that she was in practice at her best in bilaterals and other small gatherings. The larger the numbers, the greater her tendency to play to the gallery, either showing off her own knowledge on the subject or rounding, in a profoundly embarrassing way, on some hapless colleague whom she felt either bullyable by nature or objectively in a weak position at a particular time. Geoffrey Howe was a favourite victim.

Different Prime Ministers have different personal characteristics. But *mutatis mutandis*, I suspect that any Prime Minister so long in office is likely to develop much along the lines she did – which, to repeat, was far from inconvenient to individual Ministers most of the time – unless they have the wisdom to prevent it by the creation of a genuine Inner Cabinet.

CHAPTER 12

THE DEPARTMENT OF ENERGY

Policies and People · Economic Policy Revisited

Policies and People

BY 1981 NONE OF this pathology was apparent. Meanwhile, newly installed as Energy Secretary, my main problem, with which fortunately I had enough adrenalin to cope, was that for my first six months in Cabinet Emily did not allow me a single night's uninterrupted sleep.

Curiously enough, Secretary of State for Energy was a job I had in a sense invented. In the autumn of 1973 I was recalled from a sojourn at Oxford on the suggestion of my old friend Douglas Hurd, then Political Secretary to the Prime Minister, Ted Heath, to help give the Government what was described as a political cutting edge. It soon became clear to me that an early general election was advisable, and Michael Fraser, then the Party's Deputy Chairman, responded to my advocacy by inviting me to draft the manifesto for such an eventuality. Tony Newton, who was then a senior member of the Conservative Research Department, had already prepared a massive draft manifesto for a normal election in the usual way. This was given to me as background material.

It contained detailed prescriptions for virtually every area of public policy, but had not a word to say about energy, which had now become *the* political issue. It was an understandable omission. When Tony had completed the tome a year earlier, the coal miners were quietly and inefficiently producing coal, OPEC (Organization of Petroleum Exporting Countries) was unknown and oil was still selling at $2.50 a barrel. But a manifesto for an election in early 1974 when oil prices had rocketed following the Yom Kippur War and some miners were threatening to go on strike could scarcely skirt the issue altogether. Nor, I felt, would analysis alone be enough: there had to be some new Government policy proposal to deal with the drastically changed scene. The problem was that it did not have any, so I had to invent one; and for want of anything better I committed the Government in my draft to setting up a Department of Energy. Not surprisingly, this appealed to an exhausted Ted Heath, who always had a technocratic belief that problems could be solved by tinkering with the machinery of Government. Thus it was that the Department of Energy came into being in January 1974 with Peter Carrington as its first Secretary of State.

The Department of Energy could more aptly be described as the Department of Nationalized Industries. Within its purview lay three of the great industries nationalized by the Labour Governments of 1945 to 1951 – coal, gas and electricity – and the British National Oil Corporation (BNOC), created by Attlee's successors of the 1970s. All this meant that energy was also an important economic department, and so much more congenial to me than, say, the Department of Health and Social Security would have been. In fact, energy issues had become dangerously remote from economic policy. The nationalized industries then accounted for over a tenth of national output and over a sixth of total UK fixed investment. Characterized by weak management and strong unions, and untainted by market forces, they epitomized in an extreme form the problems of the British economy. Yet no government had found a satisfactory means of dealing with them.

Harold Wilson and Jim Callaghan had used the Department of Energy for the purpose of isolating its Secretary of State, the increasingly left wing Tony Benn. Callaghan distrusted Benn so deeply that he denied him access to virtually all sensitive Cabinet papers. This inevitably starved Benn's officials of influence as well and had completely destroyed the Department's morale.

Within less than two years of the Conservatives' return to office, morale, which had begun to improve with the departure of Benn and the restoration of normal relations with Number 10, was once again badly bruised. This time the cause was the débâcle of February 1981, when Margaret overruled David Howell, whom she had appointed Energy Secretary when the Government was first formed in 1979, and decided on a quick but abject surrender to the National Union of Mineworkers (NUM) over pit closures rather than face a confrontation which she felt the NUM were bound to win.

David had many political merits, being able to formulate ideas and sentiments with a speed and fluency extremely rare on the Conservative Front Bench. An old friend of mine since long before either of us entered the House of Commons (which he had done in 1970), he shared my own economic thinking and had been a close comrade-in-arms in Opposition. He was, however, in Harold Macmillan's words, a gown-man and not a sword-man. In the reshuffle of September 1981 he was moved from Energy to Transport, a post he held until the 1983 general election, when he was dropped altogether. According to David, the 1981 move was at his own request; but rightly or wrongly it was seen at the time as a demotion.

While my new officials professed to be glad to see me there, those who expected their Secretary of State to embark vigorously on the promotion of an energy policy were disappointed, as I did not believe in any such animal. I saw myself, quite simply, as having three main tasks: to bring to a successful conclusion the long struggle with the miners' union that had begun so disastrously in the last days of the Heath Government and, following the débâcle of January 1981, was now likely to be exacerbated by the growing power of the militant would-be revolutionary Arthur Scargill; to pursue Britain's interests in the international politics of oil; and privatization, which represented a continuation of work on which I had been deeply involved in the Treasury and was to continue as Chancellor.

David Howell had ended Labour's policy of subsidizing domestic gas and electricity prices, and courageously put in place the phased move to realistic pricing; but that alone was not enough. The endemic conflict between the nationalized industries and the Treasury, with the Energy Department as pig in the middle, was unresolved. It was not believed within either the Department, or the nationalized industries for which it was notionally responsible, that there was any sensible alternative to subsidy, compromise and intervention. Virtually all of the people and institutions associated with energy policy were still drenched in corporatism. All of the main nationalized industry chairmen were instinctively hostile to the Government's overall economic strategy. There clearly had to be changes both within the Department and in the coal, gas and electricity industries. These took most of my twenty months as Energy Secretary to complete.

One of the principal sceptics, in fact, was my own Minister of State, Hamish Gray, who had special responsibility for North Sea oil. Given the location of the vast bulk of the oil, it was thought desirable that the number two Minister at Energy should be a Scot, which Hamish, who represented the far northern constituency of Ross and Cromarty, most emphatically was. Despite our differing economic perspectives, he was a courteous and unfailingly loyal colleague. Anyone from the Scottish political culture, without a background in Smithian economics, was almost bound to be an interventionist. But he had no time for the cabals of the wets, for whom he had a healthy contempt. When I arrived he was still smarting from his defeat by the Treasury on a plan to build a £4 billion state-financed gas gathering pipeline in the North Sea. But he never allowed this to sour relations between us. Before long the unfortunate Hamish suffered a further blow, with the closure of an aluminium smelter at Invergordon in his own constituency, which almost certainly contributed to the loss of his seat to the SDP in the 1983 general election. Fortunately, through the good offices of Ian Gow, I was able to persuade Margaret to offer him a peerage, and he became Scottish Office Minister in the Lords during the Parliament of 1983–87.

By contrast, John Moore, the Parliamentary Under Secretary of State ('Pussy') with special responsibility for coal, was very much on the same economic wavelength as me – dry, free market, Thatcherite. He was both industrious and personable and I decided to give him special responsibility for nuclear power as well.

John got to know the coal industry better than any previous Conservative coal minister and almost certainly made more pit visits than any previous coal minister of either party. This was respected at all levels in the industry. He was an admirable lieutenant and when I became Chancellor I persuaded Margaret to let me take him to the Treasury with me as Economic Secretary. A few months later he moved up to Financial Secretary, when Cecil Parkinson was obliged to resign and the Cabinet vacancy was filled by the promotion of the then Financial Secretary, Nicholas Ridley. As such, he took over all Nick's delegated responsibilities, which included, to his great delight, privatization, in which he was a passionate believer – and, as an investment banker (in the US) before going into politics, he had a familiarity with the financial nuts and bolts involved.

The high profile he enjoyed over privatization secured his entry to the Cabinet as Transport Secretary. Indeed, for a short time he became Margaret's blue-eyed boy and was even canvassed in the press as a possible successor: she was always susceptible to good looks and in John's case she found loyalty, too. Unfortunately, this did not do him any good. After the 1987 election she over-promoted him to an unsuitable Department – that of Health and Social Security – believing, so she told me, that the overriding need at the DHSS was better presentation and that presentation was something at which John was exceptionally good. I demurred at both these propositions, but she was not to be deflected. Before very long she had unceremoniously dumped him – one of a number of examples of Margaret's carelessness in jettisoning her natural supporters.

The other member of my ministerial team was David Mellor. Whereas both Hamish and John had been in their posts since the Government was first formed in 1979, David was the first of his intake (that of 1979, which included John Major) to become a Minister – and, indeed, the youngest Minister in the Government.

THE DEPARTMENT OF ENERGY

A brash, self-confident, ambitious and not over-sensitive lawyer, David had at that time little understanding of the Government's economic strategy, but he was eager, hard-working and keen to impress. I gave him the least onerous responsibility: electricity (excluding nuclear), renewable energy and conservation. He still contrived to make some embarrassing (chiefly parliamentary) gaffes in his early days, stemming from aggression and an inability to recognize when he had gone too far. But he was a quick learner, and soon became an accomplished performer at the despatch box. His move to the Home Office in 1983 (to a job of equivalent status but in one of the great departments of state) was appropriate in that in his new job his legal background was of more use and his lack of any economic background less of a drawback. After a somewhat erratic progress through a number of middle-ranking ministerial posts he was eventually to enter the Cabinet when his friend John Major succeeded Margaret as Prime Minister.

But at the time John Moore felt understandably miffed that David Mellor's abilities were receiving such rapid recognition while his – he had now been in the same bottom-rung job for almost four years – were not, despite his impeccable Thatcherite credentials which David Mellor lacked. The explanation was that Margaret astonishingly left promotions at that level to the Whips' Office, where John Moore was not highly regarded.

David was succeeded at Energy by Anthony Eden's son, the Earl of Avon. He could hardly have been more different: tall, quiet, charming and exceptionally handsome, he was soon to die of AIDS – a distressing end. For my PPS I brought the suave Mark Lennox-Boyd with me from the Treasury. He stayed with me in all for four years, eventually becoming PPS to Margaret Thatcher and subsequently a junior Minister at the Foreign Office.

Since the Treasury has the first pick of graduate entrants, it is not surprising that outlying Departments, such as Energy, do not in general enjoy the same quality of Civil Servants, though there are some outstanding individuals in every Department. I found the overall difference particularly marked. I was therefore very fortunate that David Howell had seen to it that the key posts of Permanent Under Secretary* and Principal Private Secretary were exceptionally well filled, by Donald Maitland and Julian West. Donald was no kind of energy or industrial expert, but a first-rate administrator from the Foreign Office whom I had known for many years. Scottish, small, lively and politically aware (he had been Press Secretary at Number 10 during the Heath era) he was a man of total integrity with a giggling sense of humour. Julian,

---

*Commonly abbreviated to Permanent Secretary. Technically, however, in those Departments where the political head is (as in most cases) a Secretary of State, the official head is a Permanent Under Secretary of State.

tall, thin, bearded, pipe-smoking and soft spoken, had a maturity of judgement astonishing in one of his relatively tender years. He was a tower of strength to me. Together, they made a splendid team, with the convivial addition of my Chief Information Officer, the shrewd, experienced and robustly Tory Ian Gillis.

Below Donald there were three Deputy Secretaries – Philip Jones, David Jones (no relation) and Ivor Manley. Under Labour there had been no fewer than four, and it was David Howell who had cut it down to three. Under the so-called review of the open structure of the Civil Service, Cabinet Ministers were expected to trim the size of the senior echelons of their Departments as much as practicable, and it was clear to me that we could do perfectly well with only two Deputy Secretaries, a view from which Donald did not dissent.

The obvious one to lose was David Jones, whose submissions were incomparably the best written of any produced in the Department, but who had been a great favourite of Benn's and clearly found it difficult to adjust to the Thatcher Government. Since Civil Servants cannot be removed against their will, however, this was easier said than done. Donald, with great skill and making full use of his distinguished Foreign Office background, was able to secure for Jones a senior post with the International Energy Agency in Paris.

Sadly, however, Donald was due to retire in August 1982, and it was crucial that his successor was someone of his calibre on whom I could rely to manage the Department through the radical change of philosophy and direction on which I had embarked. I was able to secure an extension of his term to the end of the year while I prepared the ground. In the normal course of events, the job would have gone to the unchallenged internal candidate, Philip Jones, who had already been passed over once, when Donald had been brought in in 1980. But although undoubtedly able, he manifestly did not fit the bill. On the other hand, had he been passed over yet again in favour of an outsider he might have been a thorn in the side of the new Permanent Under Secretary.

Fortunately, the top (though not the most important) job in the nationalized electricity supply industry was about to fall vacant. In September 1982 I saw Jones and told him that I had firmly decided to go outside the Department for Donald's successor, but felt that he, Jones, would make an ideal Chairman of the Electricity Council. The idea suited him down to the ground; but persuading Margaret was rather more difficult. There was of course no reason why a Prime Minister, with so much on her plate, should be *au courant* with the complexities of the Electricity Council – itself the result of a misplaced attempt of an earlier committee of the 'great and the good' to rationalize its structure. But Margaret was not to distance herself from top appointments and I had the devil's own job to persuade her to agree to let Jones have the job.

Her main objection was that nationalized industry chairmen should be businessmen, not bureaucrats. I pointed out to her that no businessman of any calibre would want to be chairman of the Electricity Council, which was not a normal nationalized industry chairmanship, and that an able Civil Servant like Philip Jones, who knew the industry very well indeed, was the best bet. This was true so far as it went, though admittedly I had an ulterior motive. Reluctantly, she eventually acquiesced. Jones was delighted and quite impressed, since the official grapevine had predicted that she would block it. I was now free to go for the man I had decided I wanted as Donald's successor.

This was Ken Couzens, a Second Permanent Secretary at the Treasury, a small, clever, ebullient, highly articulate, untidy and somewhat disorganized dynamo of a man with a marvellous sense of humour. I knew him well, having worked closely with him when I was Financial Secretary. Ken did not have long to go before he, too, reached the Civil Service retirement age of sixty, and it was already clear that the successor to Douglas Wass as Permanent Secretary to the Treasury when Wass retired in 1983 was likely to be a younger man.

I invited Ken to dinner at the Garrick Club and wholly improperly asked him if he would be interested in succeeding Donald. He jumped at the chance of ending his career by running a Department of his own. He knew, of course, that this was not in my gift. Permanent Secretaries are appointed by the Prime Minister, after consulting the Cabinet Secretary and Head of the Civil Service who would in turn have sounded out the relevant Secretary of State. My unilateral short cut was clearly a breach of protocol. It displeased Geoffrey Howe, who felt I was poaching one of his key officials behind his back, and complained that I was weakening the Treasury. It displeased Margaret even more. But given that her veto would have been a bitter disappointment for Ken, which he scarcely deserved, she felt she had little choice but to acquiesce. The outcome, which would not have occurred had I played strictly by the rules, was clearly good for Ken, who thoroughly deserved to end his Civil Service career as head of his own Department, and was equally good for the Government, which secured the continuation of a harmonious partnership between Secretary of State and Permanent Secretary at the Department of Energy, where Ken fully lived up to my expectations.

Meanwhile, before getting the right policies and priorities in place, and securing the official support I required, there was one other matter which had to be dealt with. On becoming Energy Secretary I inherited a fine large room on the second floor (the traditional ministerial floor throughout Whitehall) of Thames House on Millbank, overlooking the river. But the furniture – which had been chosen by Tony Benn and left unchanged by David Howell – was an appalling example of the airport lounge school of decor. I recall with particular displeasure the armless tubular steel easy chairs, covered in an exceptionally hairy off-white fabric. I lost no time in replacing the lot – and for good measure put in pride of place on one of the walls the large eighteenth-century portrait of Henry Pelham which I had had in my room at the Treasury. I needed an environment in which I could work without being assaulted by ugliness on all sides. And there was no harm, either, in letting the Department know right from the start that they had not merely a new Secretary of State, but a new broom.

Economic Policy Revisited

During my time as Energy Secretary, I did not of course abandon my interest in general economic policy. My first public intervention occurred quite early on at the Conservative Party Conference of October 1981. This was the roughest I can remember, laying bare the deep divisions over economic policy that then existed within the Party. With unemployment at 2½ million (equivalent to 2¼ million on current definitions) and steadily rising, rioting in the streets, the newly formed Social Democrat Party (SDP) riding high and the Prime Minister weekly registering new lows in the opinion polls, the fainthearts in the party were calling for a U-turn. The leading dissenters, both inside and outside the Cabinet – Ted Heath, Ian Gilmour, Norman St John Stevas, Francis Pym, Peter Walker and Michael Heseltine – all made speeches in varying degrees of code in and around the Winter Gardens, warning that disaffected Conservatives would drift towards the SDP unless tight money policies were abandoned. Most of the critics were subtle enough to avoid the charge of disloyalty by accusing the Prime Minister and Chancellor of subordinating politics to economics rather than attacking the Government's policies head-on.

I decided to launch a counter-attack on the critics of the Government's economic policy at a fringe meeting of the Selsdon Group on the Thursday of the Conference. It was a speech I delivered from rough notes I had scribbled hours before in my hotel room; but it is still a vivid reminder of the battle we were fighting within our own party, and attracted considerable Press attention. In it I accused the dissidents of abandoning the economic programme on which we had been elected:

> Now today, halfway through our first term of office, one or two of those who had fought on the same platform and accepted Cabinet office in a Government committed to carrying it out, reveal that they reject it root and branch . . . I believe they are profoundly wrong, but at least I would ask them to drop their high moral tone, because there really is nothing that is moral or compassionate in prescribing policies which would engulf this country in a holocaust of inflation. What we are being offered is little more than cold feet dressed up as high principle.

The speech was also the first time that I alluded in public to the implications of British membership of the EMS. At that time membership was being peddled as a soft option – ironically in view of later developments – by critics who saw it as a way of escaping from the monetarist strait-jacket and lowering British interest rates. I was by then already convinced that the poor performance of £M3 as a monetary indicator, and the lack of an obvious replacement, made the EMS an attractive alternative financial framework. On this occasion I confined myself to pointing out to the Government's critics that, so far from being a soft option, its strength was that the external financial discipline of the EMS would be just as rigorous a financial discipline as the domestic monetary guidelines of the MTFS in its original form – as indeed they were to discover for themselves a decade and more later.

I mentioned in more historical terms the advantages of a pegged exchange rate when I spoke to the Association of Economic Representatives in London on 17 January 1982. 'Financial discipline', I reminded the gathering, 'was for a time maintained to some extent by a worldwide system of fixed exchange rates based on the dollar, whose value was assured by non-inflationary policies pursued by a strong and vigorous United States', but which had been brought to an end by the inflationary financing of the Vietnam War. With that constraint removed, Britain's GDP had more than quadrupled in nominal terms in the 1970s. But of that massive expansion only one twentieth represented higher real output. The rest was dissipated in higher prices.

Events in the Falklands briefly, but dramatically, diverted attention from the economic struggle. I had been in the Cabinet barely six months when the Falklands crisis erupted in April 1982. Although I was not a member of the War Cabinet, we all had a keen sense of responsibility for the lives that were at stake. We were also conscious that although the war enjoyed all-party support, a successful resolution of the conflict would transform the British people's view of the Government – and, more important, of themselves. I touched on this in a speech to Humberside businessmen ten days before the Argentine surrender of 14 June, when I said that the British people 'were sending out a signal that would strengthen our national security for years to come . . . All of us would have wished that the original act of aggression by the Argentine military regime had never occurred,' but recent events would lead to 'a new self-respect, self-confidence and sense of pride in ourselves. The years of retreat are over. And precisely the same is true in the economic and industrial sphere.'

The 'Falklands Factor' revived our electoral fortunes; but more importantly it gave a new momentum to the subsequent economic and industrial renaissance of Britain which, although later obscured by recession, has undoubtedly occurred.

The same mood to some extent permeated the Patrick Hutber Memorial Lecture I gave on 22 June 1982, under the title of *What's Right with Britain?* Patrick had been one of my oldest friends, whom I had recommended to Michael Hartwell, the then proprietor of the Telegraph group, for my old job as City Editor of the *Sunday Telegraph*, where he attained more fame than I had ever done, and attracted an audience well beyond the financial community. He did so in particular with his trenchant contributions to the long-running debate on the 'state of the nation'. Sadly he had been killed in a road accident in mid-career in 1980. My own father had died the day before the lecture after a long struggle with cancer. These events made me all the more determined to persevere with my own contribution.

I ranged widely, discussing the deep-seated and essentially non-economic roots of Britain's relative industrial decline over the past hundred years or so. As Patrick had written in his perceptive book, *The Decline and Fall of the Middle Class*, British business leaders and their natural allies in the opinion-forming classes for too long co-operated enthusiastically in their own downfall. It seems to me that middle-class guilt at enjoying the fruits of their parents' endeavours had replaced Victorian guilt about sex.

By the 1980s defeatism, although still endemic in many places, was clearly on the retreat. Reverting to my departmental concerns, I castigated those who contrived to make even the discovery of North Sea oil into a curse. In fact – as ordinary people sensed – it came on stream when it was of 'unprecedented value and strategic importance'. Looking ahead I dismissed the then current call of some industrialists for a national political consensus, saying that 'the consensus we most need is within the company, from the boardroom to the shopfloor'. The overriding need was to build on the new mood of realism, 'by seeking to promote employee participation and employee involvement' which I modestly tried to encourage as Chancellor. (See Chapter 35)

Finally, I turned to what were to be my major preoccupations at Energy, and which were then rising to the top of the national agenda. With the Scargill challenge very much in mind, I pointed out that it was no accident that the strike threats which threatened to bring to an end two years of unprecedented industrial peace were all in the state sector. Although improvements could and should be made in that sector, the only real answer was to create market disciplines and, whenever possible, competitive conditions through 'privatization', however ugly the word.

CHAPTER 13

COAL – 1
1. DIGGING FOR VICTORY

The Initial Retreat · Preparing for Conflict
The Battle for the Vale · Mobilizing Against Scargill
Increasing Endurance

The Initial Retreat

MARGARET THATCHER'S BRIEF TO me when she appointed me Energy Secretary in September 1981 was succinct. 'Nigel,' she said, 'we mustn't have a coal strike'. At the forefront of her mind was the half-truth, firmly believed in by the NUM, the media and most Conservative MPs, that it was the miners who had brought down the last Conservative Government in 1974; and the débâcle of the previous February had scarred her quite badly.

It was indeed a humiliating episode. David Howell had recognized from the start that the massive losses being incurred by the National Coal Board could be stemmed only by the closure of unprofitable pits. He had hoped to make this acceptable to the miners by offering 'social' grants and investment in new coalfields; and the 1980 Coal Industry Act, which guaranteed the Coal Board some £600 million a year in new investment for three years, was the centrepiece of this strategy.

But the strategy started to fall apart almost from the moment the Act was on the statute-book. As the recession bit, the demand for coal declined, but the output-obsessed Coal Board carried on producing as if nothing had happened. The result was a mountain of unsold coal, which was later to prove a blessing, but which at the time presented the Coal Board with a huge additional financing cost.

Throughout the Autumn of 1980 the Coal Board Chairman, Derek

Ezra, had warned David Howell and Donald Maitland that the market for coal had collapsed, and that unless still more public money was forthcoming, pit closures would be inescapable. David duly conveyed this to Margaret and other interested colleagues, and Ezra undertook to broach the matter with the NUM, promising David that he would in no circumstances mention a specific number of pits to be closed.

Yet no sooner had the meeting between the Coal Board and the mining unions ended on 10 February 1981, than a 'hit list' of plans to close between twenty and fifty pits was in the public domain. There were strong suspicions within the Department that someone in the upper echelons of the Coal Board had colluded with the NUM in revealing the number of pits to be closed. Arthur Scargill, then leader of the Yorkshire area NUM, had warned the meeting that closures 'could lead to one thing only – confrontation'. The wily Joe Gormley, then President of the NUM, had used the pressure from his left to threaten a national ballot on strike action.

Unofficial strikes soon started in the South Wales and Kent coalfields, the areas likely to be most affected, and all the signs were that a strike would be solid. John Moore was keen to make a fight of it. David was unsure. Margaret was not keen at all. She, rightly, felt that coal stocks at the power stations were insufficient to be sure of winning a prolonged strike, and promptly if less than heroically withdrew her support for the closure plans. Willie Whitelaw, Peter Carrington and especially Jim Prior, who fancied himself in touch with trade union thinking, were further worried that a coal dispute would spread to steel and the railways, the coal, steel and railway unions having announced the renewal of the old so-called 'Triple Alliance' to resist retrenchment in any one of the three nationalized industries with strikes in the others.

The climbdown was a severe embarrassment to Energy Ministers and officials. They had all privately assured the Coal Board, the NUM and the Press that the Government would resist a strike. The only redeeming feature of the decision to back down was the speed with which it was taken. The episode was over within a week of the 'hit list' leak, and before the media had really got their teeth into the story, but the surrender terms were even worse than they need have been. The Government undertook not only to relax the NCB's borrowing limits still further in order to keep the unprofitable pits open; but also to make the nationalized steel and electricity industries abandon their practice of buying a quantity of cheaper imported coal and rely exclusively on British coal instead. It was, to all intents and purposes, the formula that had been advocated by Arthur Scargill at the February meeting with the Coal Board, when he called for a 'complete ban on imports and for [further] subsidization of home coal production.' It was the first time the Thatcher Government had been defeated by militant trade union power.

COAL – 1: DIGGING FOR VICTORY

As Energy Secretary, I was determined that, if I had anything to do with it, it would never happen again.

This was an issue that had begun to preoccupy me well before Margaret appointed me to the job. I became convinced that the problems of the coal industry could not be resolved without the decisive defeat of the militant arm of the NUM, even if that meant facing up to a strike, for which we would need to be properly prepared. In April 1981, while still Financial Secretary, I minuted Geoffrey Howe:

> Our original aim was to build a successful, profitable coal industry independent of government subsidies; to de-monopolize it and ultimately open it to private enterprise . . . Then the events of February 1981 showed beyond any reasonable doubt we will make no progress towards our aim until we deal with the problem of monopoly union power.

This conclusion was not immediately drawn elsewhere. In the winter of 1980–81 the Prime Minister invited the Central Policy Review Staff (CPRS), popularly known as the think-tank, then newly headed by an Imperial Chemical Industries (ICI) director on secondment, Robin Ibbs, to analyse the nationalized industries. Its report was delivered at the end of July 1981. In the case of coal it advised a continuation of the failed policy of offering new investment in return for pit closures. At the Treasury I read the paper with a mounting sense of disbelief. It was already apparent that Joe Gormley would be succeeded as miners' leader by Arthur Scargill. 'The problem is essentially a political one, centring around industrial relations in general and outmanoeuvring Arthur Scargill in particular . . . [Yet] all that is really being claimed is that if large quantities of additional public money are poured into the industry this might persuade the NUM to agree more readily to pit closures in the long run,' I wrote to Geoffrey Howe after reading it. Within a few weeks I was charged with the responsibility for dealing with this problem.

Preparing for Conflict

On John Moore's advice, the first pit I visited was in Scargill's heartland rather than my own territory of Leicestershire. I chose Kellingley in North Yorkshire, where I went underground in July 1982, and I did not visit the Leicestershire coalfield until I went to Bagworth colliery in September. These occasions were rather like a State visit. Accompanied by Julian West and Ian Gillis, I was met at Doncaster station by the station master, sporting a bowler hat, who ushered us towards a motorcade of Stalinist dimensions, compered by the area manager, which conveyed us to a local hotel for a slap-up dinner with the pit managers. After dinner, and fortified by a large quantity of alcohol, they gave me their views of the industry's problems, notably Arthur Scargill, and how the Government had mishandled things. Next morning the motorized cavalcade sped us to Kellingley colliery, where I donned a miner's overalls and helmet and descended the shaft in the company of the pit deputies and overseers.

A miner's job is dirty, difficult and dangerous; but it has its attractive side, too. For one thing, detailed supervision is impossible underground, and the teams of miners working the seam enjoy a degree of independence unknown in any factory job. Miners are also – or were then – one of the last bastions of old-world courtesy. Whenever we came across a group of resting miners huddled in a corner of the long tunnel leading to the coal face we were wished a cordial and totally non-deferential 'good morning'. And a miner feels he is doing a real man's job – often reinforcing his macho image of himself by choosing to work semi-naked and in some cases even spurning the eye-protection that modern coal-cutting machinery, which sends splinters of coal flying in all directions, clearly requires.

I was then photographed emerging from the pit with a suitably blackened face. There followed a meeting with the local representative of the NUM, who said that investment in the pit was inadequate, that wages were too low and that management disregarded safety in pursuit of productivity. These lamentations were followed by an ample lunch, after which we boarded the train back to London, and I was promised a traditional miner's lamp (which turned out to be the slightly superior version carried by pit foremen as a badge of office) as a memento of my visit. It was quite a show, designed to persuade me that Kellingley was run by honest people doing a difficult job in trying circumstances, and that it was therefore a deserving home for public money.

It was on that visit to Kellingley that I first met Michael Eaton, who was then the Coal Board's North Yorkshire area manager. His blunt common sense and articulacy impressed me, and I was not surprised that he was subsequently plucked from North Yorkshire to play a key role on the presentational side during the coal strike of 1984–85. Unfortunately he and Ian MacGregor did not hit it off and the arrangement was not a success.

Meanwhile, on the coal front, I subordinated almost everything to the overriding need to prepare for and win a strike. It was not that I was seeking one. But it was clear that Arthur Scargill was, and I was determined that he should lose it when it came.

The débâcle of February 1981 left massive financial and managerial problems which could not be resolved without his defeat. When I became Energy Secretary, the Coal Board had the biggest External Financing Limit (EFL) – the amount of public money annually injected in loans and grants combined – of any nationalized industry. At £1,117 million, it was more than the EFLs for British Steel and British Telecom combined. Another £800 million was pledged to a huge programme of investment in new pits. Total subsidies to the industry, in the form of social, operating and deficit grants amounted to £550 million a year – or some £1½ million a day, or £5 for every tonne of deep-mined coal or £35 a week for every member of the Coal Board's workforce. The February setback had forestalled any immediate hope of stemming the financial haemorrhage. Instead of trading new investment for old pit closures, as planned by David Howell, the Government was now committed to subsidizing old pits as well as investing in new ones.

The Battle for the Vale

The first action I took, within weeks of my appointment as Energy Secretary, concerned a matter that had arisen, curiously enough, in my own adopted county of Leicestershire. Obscure though it may seem, the decision I secured here had a crucial impact on the strike when it did eventually begin in March 1984.

The Coal Board had discovered a rich seam of coal lying under the Vale of Belvoir, a lovely stretch of countryside in north-east Leicestershire. Geologically, it was a hitherto unknown southern extension of the massive Nottinghamshire coalfield. The Board wanted to sink three pits to exploit the deposits, two on the edge of the Vale but the third right in the middle of it. Unsurprisingly, the plan had provoked passionate opposition among environmentalists in Leicestershire and in the country at large. David Howell, then pursuing his policy of exchanging new pits for old, had endorsed the Coal Board proposals. But it was up to the Environment Secretary, Michael Heseltine, to give the Board the planning permission it needed. A special inquiry was held, under an eminent QC, which Michael hoped would find against the mining of the Vale. So, indeed, did Margaret. Not only did she have little time for the coal industry, but the Vale of Belvoir was close to her home town of Grantham and a member of her family had been postmaster of Asfordby, one of the three proposed sites for the pits. In fact, however, the inquiry came to quite the opposite conclusion.

Michael had to decide whether or not to accept this firm recommendation that the Coal Board should be given the green light to go ahead. Planning decisions, however momentous, and however great the political or economic consequences, are technically not matters for collective decision but have to be decided by the Environment Secretary alone, acting in a quasi-judicial capacity. Legally, he can listen to the views of his colleagues, but that is all. Having done so, Michael made up his mind to reject both the Coal Board's application and the Inquiry's conclusion lock, stock and barrel.

Even though I was myself a Leicestershire Member, this worried me greatly. There were two major mining areas in the country: Yorkshire and the Midlands. The Yorkshire miners could be counted on to support Scargill in a strike ballot whenever he chose to hold one. The only hope of defeating him, therefore, lay in detaching the traditionally moderate miners of the Midlands – all the more so since the lesser coalfields of Scotland, South Wales, Durham and Kent were all traditionally militant. The Midlands miners saw the opportunity to mine the Vale of Belvoir, which offered the prospect of new jobs to replace those that would be lost when old mines closed, as their most cherished objective.

The first meeting of any significance I attended as Energy Secretary, apart from the post-reshuffle Cabinet itself, was one called by Margaret to decide how and when Michael's decision should be announced. I told my closest officials that I would press for the matter to be reconsidered before there was any question of an announcement. They told me I was wasting my time: the battle had already been fought by David Howell and lost, and the Prime Minister was adamant against touching the Vale of Belvoir.

At the meeting Margaret got on her legal high horse and insisted that this was a matter for Michael alone, a doctrine that she had only barely respected so far as her own views were concerned (they said). By pointing out that this was a highly sensitive matter and that, as a new Energy Secretary, I wanted time to consider the matter more fully, I was able to secure a stay of execution so far as any announcement was concerned. When I got back to the Department to debrief them, my officials were pleasantly surprised. But the problem remained of how to change the smoke signals from Number 10.

I decided to write a long letter to my old and dear friend Ian Gow, who was later to be murdered by the IRA but was then the Prime Minister's Parliamentary Private Secretary, and the best PPS she ever had. I told him I would leave it to him to show it to Margaret as soon as he felt the mood was right. He was not opimistic, but promised to do so.

In my letter I pointed out, with the aid of a table giving a regional breakdown of the results of the last NUM strike ballot, that the Midlands miners were the most moderate of all the miners, and that it was vital to keep them on our side if we were to have any hope of preventing the NUM gaining a mandate for a strike. I explained how important Belvoir was to them, and how – especially since the inquiry had come out in favour – a refusal to allow the seam to be mined would be seen as a slap in the face for the Midlands miners from a government they would inevitably regard as hostile to them.

I added that I knew that Margaret had been told that, if the Vale of Belvoir were touched, a number of our Leicestershire seats would be at risk. As a Leicestershire Member myself, I could assure her that those who told her this were talking through their hats. The only serious hostility that existed on environmental grounds was to the proposed mine at Hose, in the heart of the Vale: the two other proposed mines were on its perimeter, at Asfordby and Saltby, and relatively uncontentious. The obvious solution was simply to veto Hose, and allow the other two.

Ian showed Margaret the letter in the first week of February 1982, and she responded in a note that Ian gave me a few days later, with a copy to pass on to Michael Heseltine. Ian expressed himself as 'agreeably surprised' by her reply. So, in the circumstances, was I. Margaret reminded me that this was a matter for Michael, and went on to imply that if he could be persuaded that there was an environmentally acceptable way of doing it – if, in other words, the two of us could agree on a compromise solution – then so be it. Accordingly, Michael and I met twice in mid-March and eventually agreed that I would ask the NCB to resubmit its proposals, this time seeking only one pit, Asfordby, on the edge of the Vale, from which it could, at slightly greater but by no means prohibitive cost, mine the entire rich Belvoir seam. This was something that Michael, for his part, would find environmentally acceptable, and we jointly informed Margaret of the agreement we had reached, which she duly accepted.

Although, incredibly, I then had some difficulty in persuading the Coal Board to play its part, it eventually did so; and in due course Michael announced that, while the original application was wholly unacceptable, the Board would be permitted to exploit the Belvoir seam from Asfordby. Understandably, this did not greatly please the Duke of Rutland, the then Conservative Chairman of the Leicestershire County Council, whom of course I had got to know very well, and who had led, with great passion, the campaign to save the Vale. But when the decision finally went against him, Thérèse and I were still generously welcomed for dinner at Charles Rutland's home, Belvoir Castle. I am not sure if he was ever persuaded that this was a necessary sacrifice in the battle against Arthur Scargill, but the crucial decision of the Nottinghamshire miners to carry on working during the coal strike of 1984–85 fully vindicated it so far as I was concerned. The coal they produced extended the Government's capacity to withstand Arthur Scargill's strike from months to years, if not indefinitely.

Mobilizing Against Scargill

When Arthur Scargill succeeded Joe Gormley as President of the NUM in April 1982 – with the support of 70 per cent of the miners who voted – a strike became inevitable. Scargill was a self-confessed class-war revolutionary, uninterested in rational discussion about the future of the industry. He first came to prominence during the 1974 coal strike as the leader of the so-called flying pickets who descended on the Saltley coke depot, where their behaviour led to a disastrous police withdrawal. After the 1974 strike, which was widely seen as having brought down the Heath Government, he told the *New Left Review* that the Transport and General Workers Union (TGWU) 'had a contractual arrangement with the working class and if they didn't honour that arrangement we'd make sure, physically, that they did. For we would have thrown their lorries and everything else into the dyke.' Thus violence was legitimate even against other trade unionists.

As NUM President-elect and subsequently as President he toured the country agitating ceaselessly for a strike; yet he never won a national ballot in favour of one (despite having engineered a change in the Union's constitution reducing the required majority from 55 per cent to anything over 50 per cent). This was not for want of trying. During my time as Energy Secretary the NUM polled its members no fewer than three times on strike action, over pay in January 1982, over pay and pit closures in October 1982, and over pit closures in March 1983. On the first occasion 45 per cent voted for a strike; on the second and third occasions the figure fell just below 40 per cent. It was these three failures that persuaded Scargill to call a strike, in the spring of 1984, without a national ballot; and it was his failure to hold a national ballot which in turn caused the Midlands miners to feel justified in carrying on working.

Although I had met Scargill on a number of occasions at television studios over the years, I did not meet him formally until immediately after he was elected President of the NUM, when I invited him to come and see me at the Department. He duly turned up, in April 1982, flushed with his overwhelming success in the presidential ballot. I had been warned that he always carried a tape recorder in his jacket pocket, so I was prepared to be more than usually guarded in what I said. I need not have worried, since he was determined to do almost all the talking himself. He spouted the most amazing nonsense, garnished liberally with spurious statistics 'proving' how even the least productive British pits were highly economic by comparison with their heavily subsidized competitors abroad. It was an extraordinary meeting, at which it became quite clear to me that Scargill's concept of the truth was heavily influenced by what he found it convenient to believe. After he had left I told my officials that there was no way we could do business with him.

At the end of March that year Joe Gormley, the outgoing NUM President, had also come to the Department to say farewell and let me know what he thought of his successor. Joe had deliberately stayed in his post longer than his colleagues had envisaged, so as to ensure that by the time he stepped down the formidable if somewhat unsubtle President of the Scottish NUM and former Chairman of the Communist Party of Great Britain, Mick McGahey, was too old (under union rules) to succeed him. Gormley had little more time for Arthur Scargill than he had for Mick McGahey. He described Scargill to me as an astute tactician but a poor strategist, committed to subverting the Government. Age and experience, he thought, might mature him. It proved a forlorn hope.

Gormley, who had outsmarted the Heath Government in 1973–74 and humiliated the Thatcher Government in February 1981, was able in the end to redeem himself. The strike ballot of January 1982, engineered by Scargill in the twilight months of the Gormley presidency, looked as if it would be a close-run thing. And, at that time, we were still not adequately prepared for a strike. Joe, with all the authority of President of the NUM, was prevailed upon to write an article in the *Daily Express* of 13 January, on the eve of the ballot, advising his members to vote against strike action. It may well have been this that denied Scargill his majority. Certainly, it cannot have done any harm. I later persuaded Margaret to offer Gormley a peerage, the first – and probably the last – time that a Conservative Government had ennobled a President of the NUM.

The NUM was not the only trade union with a part to play in any miners' strike, but Scargill's political posturing and unpopularity among his trade union colleagues made it difficult for him to build a coalition with other unions – notably those involved in the critically important power industry. I was careful to court John Lyons, the general secretary of the Electrical Power Engineers' Association (EPEA), whom I had got to know quite well in Opposition. (Indeed, he had given my son Dominic his first job, in the union's research department, in 1978.) He was a moderate with little time for Scargill, or the TUC, which had thwarted his plans to enlarge his union. Even so, representing as it did the skilled engineers and junior managers in the power stations, the power of his union was immense. His members were fully capable of closing down the power stations by themselves, as indeed they had demonstrated in Northern Ireland during the Ulster workers' strike of 1973. Equally, if they were prepared to co-operate with the army, they could keep the power stations going even if the other power unions decided to strike. Although a Labour man himself, Lyons told me that the majority of his members voted Conservative. But that did not mean that they could be taken for granted.

Fortunately, I was also on good terms with Frank Chapple, then the brave and tough Cockney leader of the industry's principal union, the Electrical, Electronic, Telecommunications and Plumbing Union (EETPU). Chapple, who detested Scargill, was at one with me in longing for a Coal Board management capable of standing up to him. It was Frank who probably gave me the best advice about the chairmanship of the Coal Board. 'Get someone who's not afraid of Scargill,' he said, after we had been discussing the matter over dinner *à deux* at my home one evening: 'Most businessmen will tell you they're not, but in their hearts they are.' The 'Chapple test' was one good reason why I went for Ian MacGregor.

Increasing Endurance

The overriding need in preparing for a coal strike was to increase substantially power station endurance – that is, the length of time the power stations could continue to meet the nation's needs in the event of a complete cessation of coal production in the UK. Preferably, too, adequate endurance should be secured without recourse to the three-day week that had featured so prominently and so unhappily in the coal strike of 1974.

Fortunately, the country's coal stocks were unusually high. The trouble was that they were in the wrong place. While the recession had severely reduced the demand for coal, the Coal Board, in true Stalinist style, had adhered rigidly to its production targets; and, although much of it was being mined at a cost far exceeding its value, pithead stocks were steadily accumulating. By December 1981 total coal stocks, largely at the pithead, amounted to 43 million tonnes, the highest level since the late 1960s, when the country's demand for coal was considerably greater.

The hard part was shifting the coal from the pitheads to the power stations. This could scarcely be left to be done during a strike, since the quantities involved were too large and the picketing problem introduced too much uncertainty. On the other hand, in advance of a strike, coal stocks could not be moved secretly, since the trains which ferried the coal to the power stations were as visible as the piles of coal themselves.

David Howell had begun the process of shifting the coal to the power stations, in a deliberately low-profile way, and had instituted the practice of the Central Electricity Generating Board (CEGB) reporting weekly to both the Department of Energy and Number 10 on the level of power station coal stocks and other relevant information. But it was all too clear when the February 1981 showdown occurred that they were insufficient to withstand a prolonged strike, and by the time I arrived in September the position was little better. I accordingly asked Donald Maitland to commission from the CEGB, as quickly as possible, a detailed and costed plan for increasing power station coal stocks, laying in extra supplies of the ancillary chemicals required in electricity generation, transporting coal by road rather than rail, and for conserving coal by increasing the amount of electricity generated by oil-fired power stations.

The most complicated part of this was probably the ancillary chemicals, where nothing at all had so far been done. Modern power stations cannot operate on coal alone. They need fuel oil to start the combustion process and carbon dioxide to cool their giant turbines. Other chemicals – oxygen, hydrogen and chlorine – are also required. Some of these could readily be stockpiled at the power stations in adequate quantities. Others could not, because of their short shelf-life, requiring them to be replenished during the course of a strike. Contingency plans would need to be made to fly these in by helicopter, a feasible operation given the relatively small quantities required, and potential helicopter landing sites were identified within the perimeter of every power station. I had not forgotten that the blockade of chemicals was one of the main causes of the power cuts of the 1970s.

The CEGB report was produced by the end of 1981, and going over it carefully with my key officials I put a proposal to a meeting with Margaret and other senior colleagues in February the following year recommending a dramatic acceleration in the build-up of power station coal stocks. For security reasons, I said nothing about the chemicals, feeling in any event that it was within my ministerial responsibility, without a need for collective discussion, to require the necessary contingency plans to be drawn up. This I duly did, and in due course was proudly shown by Walter Marshall, the newly appointed chairman of the CEGB, and Gil Blackman, the CEGB board member who had done most of the work, a meticulously detailed plan, complete with photographs of the helicopter landing sites that had been identified.

Meanwhile, the February meeting with the colleagues was by no means plain sailing. Jim Prior, in particular, speaking with the authority of a former Employment Secretary, considered my proposals dangerously provocative and likely to cause a strike. I conceded that a rapid build-up of coal stocks to the unprecedented levels I proposed (essentially the maximum the power stations could physically contain) would be a very high-profile policy. But I argued that, so far from provoking a strike, it would actually act as a deterrent, since the miners would know that, if they did vote for a strike, it would inevitably be a long one. Jim was also concerned that the railwaymen would refuse to carry the coal and go on strike themselves, supporting the miners under the terms of the Triple Alliance. In fact, there had been an unsuccessful train-drivers' strike in January 1982, and when they returned to work they were only too happy to recoup their lost earnings by working overtime transporting coal to the power stations.

But with Margaret's wholehearted backing, I secured the go-ahead, and pretty soon the so-called 'merry-go-round' – that part of the railway system dedicated to the transport of coal to power stations – was operating twenty-four hours a day, seven days a week. As a result power station coal stocks rose steadily, to 52.3 million tonnes in 1982 and 58 million tonnes in 1983, with a corresponding increase in power station endurance.

Indeed, Margaret was so keen that I found myself – much to the Treasury's relief – successfully resisting further suggestions of her own, such as the conversion of all coal-fired power stations to dual-firing (coal and oil), which would not only have been inordinately expensive but would have come to fruition beyond the timescale within which we were likely to be faced with a strike. She also set up an *ad hoc* committee of senior officials, initially under the Deputy Secretary to the Cabinet, Robert Wade-Gery, an outstandingly clever and likeable Wykehamist from the Foreign Office, subsequently our High Commissioner to India, to monitor the evolution of power station endurance and make recommendations, which I welcomed.

CHAPTER 14

COAL – 2
COMPLETING THE TASK

The Great Head-hunt · The Advent of MacGregor
A Famous Victory

The Great Head-hunt

THE TOP MANAGEMENT OF both the CEGB and the Coal Board were clearly crucial to the successful prosecution of a miners' strike. Fortuitously, the chairmanships of both organizations became available during my time as Energy Secretary. The CEGB Chairman I inherited, Glyn England, was civilized but unimpressive. He had been appointed by Tony Benn in 1977, when he was Chairman of the South West Area Electricity Board, after Benn had asked which of the Area Chairmen was a committed Labour supporter. The only one who qualified was England, who had been a Labour member of the Hertfordshire County Council. Ironically he subsequently went over to the SDP, having previously been very much on the Roy Jenkins wing of the Labour Party.

He had little stomach for a fight with the NUM and no enthusiasm for the Government's approach. In particular, he was anxious to avoid incurring the costs of stockpiling more coal than the power stations needed at a time when industry was already complaining to him about the high cost of electricity.

When his five-year contract came up for renewal in April 1982, I chose not to reappoint him. The decision was a great shock to him, and he wrote me a long letter threatening to make public his complaints about me. He alleged that I had seen him very little and had never taken him into my confidence, and that I had never expressed any dissatisfaction with his conduct or given him a chance to defend himself. For good measure, he appended a list of electricity issues – like flue gas desulphurization – which he alleged I had failed to address. In my reply I invited him to come and see me if he wished, but explained that I had no intention of rescinding my decision not to renew his contract. He evidently decided not to pursue the matter, and the great exposé never took place. While I was at fault in not giving him advance warning of my unwillingness to reappoint him, his list of neglected issues was remarkable, considering that he had never raised any of them with me during his chairmanship.

The only real problem of not reappointing England was that I had failed to find a suitable successor by the time he left, so I had to accept a hiatus at the top of the CEGB. In the interim, I asked Fred Bonner, England's deputy, to take over as acting chairman. I think he entertained the hope that I would one day appoint him chairman *faute de mieux*, but he was a CEGB man through and through, and I was looking not merely for the right man for the run-up to a likely coal strike and for the strike itself, but also for someone who would take a fresh look at this highly secretive organization so set in its ways. The new chairman had to come from outside.

The structure of the nationalized electricity industry in England and Wales was bizarre in the extreme. The business of generation was in the hands of the powerful CEGB, the chairman of which clearly had the most important industrial job in the whole set-up, while the business of distribution was in the hands of the twelve separate area electricity boards. Superimposed on all this was the Electricity Council, on which all the various chairmen sat, and whose sole managerial function was to conduct the industry's pay negotiations. Beyond that, it was responsible for 'co-ordinating' the industry and 'representing' it – notably in discussions with government on the industry's External Financing Limit and other matters.

This curious structure was a manifest nonsense, and *inter alia* institutionalized conflict between the chairmen of the Council and the CEGB. When Frank Tombs (later Sir Francis Tombs, Chairman of Rolls-Royce, but originally from the more rationally organized Scottish electricity industry) had accepted from Benn the job of Chairman of the Electricity Council, it was on the express understanding that legislation would be introduced to change the structure and merge the Council chairmanship with the chairmanship of the CEGB. When David Howell abandoned this, in the belief that it represented undesirable Bennite centralization, Tombs understandably decided to depart and had to be bought out of his contract at considerable public expense.

I had inherited the consequences, but soon decided that there was little point in going to all the trouble of restructuring the nationalized electricity industry, since the real answer was privatization and the consequent disappearance of the Council altogether. Meanwhile I had to find a new chairman both for the twilight years of the Council and for the effectively more important although technically subordinate CEGB. My choice for the Council I have described in Chapter 12. For the CEGB I eventually opted for Walter Marshall, who was then running the UK Atomic Energy Authority. He was a brilliant scientist and had a strong commercial instinct, although he was not really interested in the financial side at all, for which he had little feel.

I had chosen Marshall as CEGB chairman for a very specific reason. I needed someone to keep the power stations running in the event of a coal strike, and meanwhile to co-operate to the full with the Government in the preparations to withstand a strike. On both counts Marshall came up trumps. I knew, of course, that in addition to his scientific and technological ingenuity Marshall had the motivation, since at an earlier stage in his career he had been Chief Scientist at the Department of Energy and had been sacked by Benn, with whom he had fallen out over nuclear policy. So he had no affection for Benn's friend and ally, Scargill.

Opinionated, articulate, with a caustic wit, the large and shambling Marshall was, although very much his own man and no courtier, greatly admired by Margaret. This was partly because he was a passionate advocate, as was she, of nuclear power – which is why I had little difficulty in persuading her that he should be CEGB chairman despite the fact that he was not a businessman.

Marshall's commitment to nuclear power, incidentally, and his readiness and ability to take on the anti-nuclear lobby, although not the main reason why I had chosen him, was at that time an undoubted plus – not least because it relieved me of much of the burden of making the case in which I still believed.

He set to work with great zest and obviously enjoyed devising plans to smuggle essential chemicals into the power stations. Where I failed was in finding a top-class finance director for the CEGB which it badly needed. I made sure there was no shortage of financial expertise among the part-time members of the CEGB. David Howell had brought in Eric Sharp, then Chairman of Cable and Wireless, on this basis, and I persuaded Dick Giordano, then Chief Executive of British Oxygen (BOC) to join him. But that was no substitute.

The Advent of MacGregor

The managerial inadequacies of the CEGB, however, were as nothing compared with those of the Coal Board. It was the archetypal public corporation, where genuine business management was almost unknown. The pits around the country were run on a joint basis by mining engineers, who were unversed in management, and the local representatives of the NUM – the precise balance of power varying with the individuals concerned, although the greater cohesion of the NUM tended to give it the upper hand most of the time. As I had discovered on my visit to Kellingley, there was an *esprit de corps* between men and management in the coal industry, derived from the genuine need for teamwork and mutual support in the dangerous business of extracting coal. That was all very well, but neither management nor unions were much interested in either the costs of production or the demand for coal.

At the Coal Board's Hobart House headquarters in London, its chairman seldom lost an opportunity to warn the Government that any provocative action might bring the miners out on strike. The Board was also suffused with the paternalist, corporatist mentality of the post-war settlement. 'All I did deliberately was to seek the maximum area of agreement. That applied both within the management and with the union,' was how Derek Ezra, Coal Board chairman from 1972 to 1982, characterized his management style. He had in practice accepted the extraordinarily powerful role in the industry's affairs assumed by the NUM, the running of the industry to the NUM, which he relied on Gormley to control, and appeared to see himself chiefly as a super-salesman for the industry. Throughout Whitehall and Westminster, the Coal Board was known as 'the Derek and Joe show'. And just in case the management – prompted perhaps by the Government of the day – did make the occasional attempt to manage, Hobart House was riddled with NUM moles who would quickly report the offence to Gormley. It was scarcely surprising that productivity was lamentable and the losses astronomic. This was no basis either for turning the industry round, or for confronting Scargill.

Although the lugubrious Ezra was still only fifty-three when his second five-year term expired in 1982, I decided not to offer him a third term. Unlike Glyn England, he was not at all surprised. He had originally been appointed chairman by Heath in 1972, which his conduct during the 1973–74 strike soon demonstrated to have been a big mistake, and was less surprisingly reappointed by Benn five years later.

The really difficult question was Ezra's replacement, but fortunately there was an excellent stop-gap available while I looked around. This was the deputy chairman, Norman Siddall, a bluff Yorkshire mining engineer who had spent a lifetime in the industry and was widely respected at all levels. For years he had sat, appalled, alongside Ezra while the NUM effectively ran the show. He had never expected to be chairman: by the time I appointed him he was sixty-four years old and in very poor health, having recently undergone open heart surgery. But he welcomed the chance to start the much needed process of regaining the reins of management and sorting out the industry. Given the state of his health, the appointment could only be for one year; but during that year, and despite all Scargill's efforts, he succeeded in closing twenty heavily loss-making pits.

Discussion about Ezra's successor had begun long before his contract actually expired, but no compelling names had turned up. Indeed, the Coal Board chairmanship was among the topics considered by the Central Policy Review Staff in its report on the nationalized industries in the summer of 1981. It recommended an industrial rather than a political figure to succeed Ezra, an idea I then thought mistaken. In August 1981, while still Financial Secretary, I had minuted Geoffrey: 'Obviously a good industrialist would be better than a bad politician. But the fact remains that what we are discussing here is the most political job in the whole of British industry. Roy Mason, if he is willing, would be the ideal choice.'

Roy Mason was a tough Labour moderate, a mining MP and a former Minister of Power, Defence Secretary and Northern Ireland Secretary. He understood Scargill better than most in the talking classes and would not have been disposed to contract out the running of the industry to the NUM or give the unions a veto over national policy. Somewhat disconcertingly, however, Joe Gormley came up with the same name two months later when I asked him for his suggestions on a successor to Ezra. But then he, too, had little love for Scargill.

I regarded this appointment as so important that I even commissioned a leading firm of head-hunters to produce a list, without high hopes, just in case there was someone none of us had thought of who fitted the bill. Nothing of any value came from this, though there was no shortage of volunteers for this high profile job, among them the ebullient Walter Goldsmith, then running the Institute of Directors, who wrote to me to commend himself for the post, which he described as 'a logical career move'. The nearest also-ran, whom I did see, and who very much wanted the job (he had, most unusually in the private sector, begun his career in the coal industry) was Bob Haslam, a highly competent deputy chairman of ICI who had been passed over for the chairmanship in favour of the more flamboyant John Harvey-Jones. But despite his many qualities, I was not entirely confident that he passed the Chapple test – not being afraid of Scargill. Haslam in fact subsequently succeeded MacGregor as Coal Board chairman, an appointment I strongly supported as Chancellor, and did very well. But by then the strike was over, and Scargill a broken man.

The idea of Ian MacGregor had been put to me very much earlier by Keith Joseph. As Industry Secretary Keith had persuaded Margaret to appoint Ian as Chairman of British Steel, where he had done an excellent job. Keith had suggested to me that Ian should remain chairman of British Steel, and take on the Coal Board chairmanship as well – an idea I am pretty sure had come from Ian himself. Certainly Keith was confident that Ian would like to do this. Given the importance of the

Coal Board job, I was not impressed by the unusual suggestion of a part-time chairman, not to mention the unprecedented notion of one man being chairman of two major nationalized industries at the same time, however close the links between them – steel being a major coal consumer. So at the time I did not follow it up.

But the seed had been planted in my mind, and I began wondering whether Ian could be prised out of British Steel to do the Coal Board job on a full-time basis. Quite apart from the toughness and business skills that he had demonstrated he possessed at British Steel, he knew the coal industry well, having been chairman of the Amax Corporation in the US, which had substantial coal mining interests. There was no risk of his running scared of Scargill. In January 1982, before Ezra's term had expired, let alone Siddall's, I decided to see Ian and told him that I had no doubt that he was the right man for the job, but that equally I was sure that he could not do coal and steel simultaneously. This was something he found difficult to accept; but eventually, after a number of further meetings, he did.

I then had to persuade Margaret. This was far from easy. Patrick Jenkin, then Industry Secretary, understandably wanted to keep Ian at steel, and he was strongly backed by Geoffrey – the Chancellor is always consulted on nationalized industry chairmanships, and of course has to agree the salary. Margaret had a high regard for Ian, but she told me that he was doing such a good job at steel that he should not be moved, and that in any case his appointment to coal would be highly provocative: Ian was widely seen as an overpaid, over-aged, ruthless American whose main achievement at British Steel had been to slash the workforce. Eventually I secured her hesitant agreement, pointing out, first, that Ian had virtually completed the job he had been sent to do at British Steel, and that there was an excellent successor in his deputy, Bob Scholey, who could now pick up the baton; second, that the really big challenge now was coal, and we should put our best man in the biggest job; and, third, that while a coal strike sooner or later was highly likely, a strike simply as a result of the appointment of MacGregor was not on the cards.

Ian MacGregor eventually agreed to take the job in February 1983, after prolonged negotiations over his remuneration. We eventually settled for the Coal Board chairman's then salary (£58,325) plus a £1½ million fee payable to Lazard Frères, New York (in which Ian was a partner) in compensation for the loss of his services for another three years. The fee was a tidy sum, but its public presentation was eased considerably by its exact correlation with the amount the Coal Board was losing each day. Ian eventually took over as Chairman of the Coal Board in September 1983, three months after the election, by which time I had become Chancellor.

The news of his likely appointment leaked several months earlier, and the reaction showed that Margaret's fears were by no means peculiar to her. There were gales of protest in the Press. Large numbers of Tory back-benchers predictably panicked. Some, mesmerized by the end of the Heath Government in 1974, told me I had lost us the election. When I came to make my Statement to the House on 28 March 1983, the Whips were in a state of terror. They need not have been – as they had the grace to admit to me afterwards: it went very well.

The leak came, it seems, from 10 Downing Street. If it was a last ditch attempt by someone close to Margaret to prevent Ian from getting the job, it backfired. The leak took much of the sting out of my announcement to the House. Nor were Labour able to make too much of the fact that Ian MacGregor was seventy years old, as he was only a few months younger than Michael Foot, the then leader of the Labour Party who, as I reminded the House, was 'seeking even more onerous responsibilities' at the forthcoming election.

A Famous Victory

By the time the coal strike was called in March 1984, I was Chancellor of the Exchequer. Indeed the strike began effectively the day before my first Budget, when on Monday, 8 March, NUM leaders gave official sanction to strikes in Yorkshire and Scotland against pit closures and similar actions planned elsewhere. This was done without a strike ballot: the left-wing majority on the NUM executive insisted, however dubiously, that Rule 43 of the union allowed for a strike without a ballot. The plan was, of course, to get the militant areas out first, and then get them to intimidate the moderate areas into following suit. Even Martin Adeney and John Lloyd, in their standard book on the strike, concede that 'the preparation of the no-ballot option is one example of the premeditation with which the NUM leadership approached the strike'.

It also, of course, reflected their fear, after the failure of the three previous ballots, that if they did hold a strike ballot they would once again lose it. But what took me by surprise was not Scargill's decision to have a strike without a ballot – it had been clear for some time that he was determined to have one, come what may. The surprise was his astonishingly inept decision to start one in the spring, with the summer months, when coal consumption is at its lowest, immediately ahead. This inevitably greatly eased the power station endurance problem, which we had identified from the start as the key to winning any strike.

Margaret immediately set up a high-powered Cabinet Committee, Misc 101, under her chairmanship, to determine the Government's response to the strike as it evolved, while being careful not to usurp the role of the Coal Board against whom the strike had ostensibly been called. The committee met every week throughout the year-long strike – if necessary more than once – and at particularly critical moments there would be informal smaller meetings in her study upstairs. Misc 101 itself was a pretty large committee: in addition to Willie Whitelaw and myself, it included Peter Walker, my successor as Energy Secretary, Leon Brittan, then Home Secretary and responsible for the police, Michael Havers, the Attorney General, who provided legal advice, Michael Heseltine, then Defence Secretary, and a number of others. She also sought to set an example to us all by ostentatiously rushing around Downing Street turning off unnecessary lights.

The violent tactics used by the NUM pickets reopened the issue of 'Who governs Britain?' first raised in the 1974 election. Scargill himself had declared in his first presidential address to the NUM: 'Every trade unionist has to be determined to defy the law and to render it ineffective.' The physical intimidation of the many miners who wanted to work, and of the lorry drivers taking coal to the power stations, plumbed new depths.

Thanks to Scargill's folly in starting the strike in the spring, by the time the winter of 1984–85 came the striking miners had already foregone their wages for six months. With the Nottinghamshire pits running at full production, the winter came and went without making much of a dent in the massive coal stocks we had ensured that the power stations possessed. Thus it was hardly surprising that the striking miners had little stomach for enduring the long wait until the winter of 1985–86 – particularly since Scargill had falsely assured them that we would not be able to survive the previous winter. Both before and during the conflict, Scargill refused to accept that any mine was uneconomic and insisted that every pit must stay open as long as there was any coal at all to be extracted, irrespective of the fact that the costs of extraction far exceeded the market value of the coal. Having, as he thought, seen the miners bring down the Heath Administration in 1974, he was confident he could repeat the feat ten years later with the Thatcher Government.

He was, of course, totally mistaken. But it would have been a much more close-run thing if the Midlands miners had not carried on working, vindicating my earlier efforts to keep them sweet by persuading Michael Heseltine to consider a second application by the Coal Board to develop the Vale of Belvoir. Another factor in the successful resistance to the strike was the encouragement given by Leon Brittan to the police to uphold the law and not retreat as they had done during the 1974 strike – notably at the Saltley coke depot. Walter Marshall, too, deserves credit for the technological ingenuity he showed in increasing the amount of electricity generated from a given quantity of coal. The fact that the Cabinet remained united at all times in its determination to see the strike through to a successful conclusion was clearly of the first importance.

COAL – 2: COMPLETING THE TASK

The firmness of MacGregor throughout the strike vindicated my choice of him as Coal Board chairman, although he was pretty hopeless at public relations. In one bizarre episode he fled from journalists who discovered him in an hotel, departing down the back staircase and trying to conceal his face behind a newspaper. Fortunately, public relations was one thing that Peter Walker was good at. After a much predicted and long-delayed drift back to work, the strike finally came to an end exactly a year after it had begun, when an NUM delegate conference voted to return to work on 5 March 1985.

Although we were able to ensure that power supplies were wholly unaffected, the year-long strike inevitably inflicted considerable short-term economic damage. During the financial year 1984–85 it reduced output, worsened the balance of payments, exacerbated unemployment, increased public expenditure and borrowing, and undermined the pound. The effects were felt especially in the currency markets. The strike, which was very newsworthy, was widely reported abroad – unlike most events in the UK – and inevitably affected international confidence in sterling As usual, overseas observers knew nothing of the true state of affairs: they simply recalled the outcome of the previous UK miners' strike. They were also surprised – and therefore worried – by the duration of the strike. The miners' strike was thus partly responsible for sharp increases in interest rates in both the summer of 1984 and the early days of 1985 when – as Chapter 36 records – the pound fell sharply on the foreign exchanges.

This was not the only adverse effect. Although manufacturing output (which excludes coal) continued to grow vigorously during 1984, industrial production as a whole came to a virtual standstill and recorded GDP growth fell back sharply. Both the coal industry and its two main customers – the electricity industry, which consumed three quarters of the coal mined in Britain, and the steel industry which consumed another fifth – were then state owned, which meant that the impact of the strike on their costs and revenues fed directly into the public finances. The largest single cost was the additional expense of burning oil rather than coal at the power stations, but the Treasury had also to meet the cost of commissioning lorries to transport coal from the working pits to the power stations.

The miners' strike thus made 1984–85 the only year in my Chancellorship in which there was substantial overspending. The public expenditure planning total was exceeded by over £3½ billion in 1984–85, two thirds of the overspend being attributable to the strike. In the same financial year the strike added £2¾ billion to the Public Sector Borrowing Requirement.

These one-off costs did not in any way colour my attitude towards the strike. It was essential that the Government spent whatever was necessary to defeat Arthur Scargill. Inevitably, however, any robust Government language was deliberately misinterpreted. Margaret Thatcher's famous reference in a speech to the 1922 Committee in which she referred to the hard core of Scargillite activists as 'the enemy within' was a case in point. Labour politicians, from Michael Foot downwards, deliberately seized on it as a slur on the mineworkers as a whole. In fact, we were careful throughout to make it clear that we had nothing against the miners themselves. Those who continued to work were portrayed as heroes (and behind the scenes a considerable amount of private money was raised to help them resist the Scargillite intimidation to which they were subjected) and the strike was always referred to as a coal strike rather than a miners' strike.

I myself was involved in a parliamentary furore on 31 July 1984 when, winding up a major debate on Government policy initiated by the Opposition, I described resistance to the miners' strike as 'even in narrow financial terms . . . a worthwhile investment for the nation'. I explicitly stated that I had in mind the elimination of uneconomic pits, then running at around £1 billion a year, but Labour chose to regard my remarks as conclusive evidence that the Government had fomented the strike deliberately. This caused uproar in the Chamber. The atmosphere became so ugly that John Biffen, who was then Leader of the House, characteristically felt that I had gone too far, and perhaps ought to apologize. The following day the Opposition tabled a private notice question, to which I replied in measured but unrepentant terms, with the full and vocal support of our back benches. It was, of course, palpably absurd: if the defeat of the miners' strike was *not* a worthwhile investment, we would scarcely have spent so much public money to win it.

Adeney and Lloyd, writing from a left of centre perspective, are clear enough:

> Few episodes in the Thatcher Government's life went so well as its handling of the miners' strike. It won its main objective: it faced out the weightiest constitutional challenge it was likely to face on the UK mainland . . . and it wholly secured the right to make the coal industry – and thus any other industry, since that was the strongest bastion of non-market production – profitable and market oriented.

The miners' strike was the central political event of the second Thatcher Administration. Just as the victory in the Falklands War exorcized the humiliation of Suez, so the eventual defeat of the NUM etched in the public mind the end of the militant trade unionism which had wrecked the economy and twice played a major part in driving elected governments from office – James Callaghan's in the aftermath of the Winter of Discontent in 1979 no less than Edward Heath's in 1974.

COAL – 2: COMPLETING THE TASK

Both as a Leicestershire Member and as a former Energy Secretary it gave me no pleasure to see ordinary decent miners suffer (on whichever side of the barricades) and be humiliated. But the responsibility for this clearly lay with those who sought to subvert normal trade unionism to serve extraneous revolutionary aims. And although, with Scargill a pathetic and discredited figure, the coal industry since the strike has shrunk dramatically as it has come to terms with economic reality, sooner or later this was unavoidable.

As Adeney and Lloyd point out, the Government's victory owed a great deal not only to the careful preparations we had made but also to the lessons learned from the Heath episode. Although there was no doubt on whose side the Government was, it remained throughout an industrial dispute. Neither the Prime Minister, nor any other Minister, held any meetings with the NUM. The Government steered clear of the talks that did take place, the details of which were left to the Coal Board (though at critical moments Ian MacGregor was of course made aware of the Government's views). There was not even the shadow or hint of an incomes policy to inflame the situation, or lead other unions to rally to Scargill's support.

There was one disappointment for the Government at the time. During the course of the strike we had been languishing in the opinion polls, even though public opinion was overwhelmingly anti-Scargill. That was hardly surprising; but we did expect that victory would bring a political bonus in terms of our poll ratings. It did nothing of the sort. The British people were relieved the strike was over, and promptly turned their attention to other things. But at a more profound and lasting level, the political gain was immense. It was a gain not just for the Government, but for the country as a whole.

CHAPTER 15

ENERGY MYTHS

The Chimera of 'Energy Policy' · Fads and Forecasts
The Nuclear Delusion

The Chimera of 'Energy Policy'

DURING MY PERIOD AS Secretary of State there were many energy policy issues with a small 'e' to occupy my attention – uneconomic pits, energy prices, privatization, relations with OPEC and much else. I was, however, frequently criticized at the time and since for not introducing an Energy Policy with a capital 'E' and a capital 'P'.

Disappointing as this must have been to some people I did not – and still do not think – that it makes sense to have an 'Energy Policy', over and above the application of the Government's overall supply-side policy to the energy sector of the economy. This was not the view I found when I entered the Department, where the received wisdom was that projections should be made of energy demand at some date in the next century. There should then be projections of the supply of each of the forms of energy over the period and policies devised to ensure via the state sector that supply and demand equated. Indeed, there was considerable surprise and disappointment when I shot down a cherished departmental proposal to publish a White Paper setting out all this futuristic arithmetic. I gathered that the officials concerned were particularly chagrined because they had seen this as their 'monument'.

I was determined to break the *dirigiste* mentality that pervaded both the Department of Energy and the nationalized energy industries. In my first speech after taking office, I suggested to a CBI Conference that the real need was not dubious long-range projections but realistic pricing of fuel: 'We cannot have energy subsidies – which in essence is what our critics are calling for – without increasing government borrowing . . . Energy prices are even more important to the supply side of the economy . . . There would be little point to the great efforts which industry has made to become more efficient in terms of capital and labour if, at the same time, it were being given false price signals about the use of energy.'

This was tame stuff compared with alarmist projections of energy 'gaps' as fossil fuels became exhausted. The nineteenth-century economist Stanley Jevons managed to scare even as non-interventionist a statesman as William Gladstone with his prediction of a looming coal shortage. My own involvement with this sort of nonsense began as a novice *Financial Times* journalist writing features in the aftermath of the Suez Crisis of 1956. This gave rise to another wave of alarm about the so-called energy gap, and induced a world-wide programme for the construction of oil tankers, many of which had subsequently to be mothballed as the projected shortage turned into a glut.

I shall always remember a visit I made at the time to an energy expert of Austrian extraction, who took a different view from most of his fellows. 'Ze gap', he said in a rich Viennese accent, 'is in your mind.' I could not help remarking to a colleague that he was right, even though this somewhat emaciated the planned article.

Fads and Forecasts

After a number of years of *ad hoc* intervention, influenced by varying pressure groups and intellectual fads, the two successive oil price explosions of 1973–74 and 1979 gave renewed currency to the energy shortage scare, coupled with a belief in the need to combat OPEC. This approach reached its apotheosis at the Venice economic summit of June 1980, when the seven leading industrial nations pledged themselves to break the link between economic growth and oil consumption, through promoting conservation in the use of energy and the development of alternative sources of energy. The message of the Energy Policy enthusiasts in Britain went beyond this, and held that the Government should require the companies operating in the North Sea to slow down their rate of oil extraction. I was highly sceptical of all this, taking the view that the market was the best tool for allocating supplies between present and future needs – always provided governments were not so misguided, or so weak in the face of populist pressure, as to subsidize energy prices.

My most extensive exposition of the sceptical position was contained in an address I gave the 1982 annual conference of the International Association of Energy Economists (IAEE), held in the brick and fortress-like surroundings of Churchill College, Cambridge. I questioned the wisdom of guessing the unguessable – namely, what UK energy consumption will be in twenty, let alone fifty years' time – and then aiming to produce this amount judiciously divided up between the primary fuel sources.

I went on,

We will do far better to concentrate our efforts on improving the efficiency with which energy is supplied and used, an objective that will remain valid and important whatever the future may bring. This means, among other things, that public sector energy investment decisions should in general be based not on a simple-minded attempt to match projected UK demand and supply but rather, as in the private sector, on whether the investment is likely to offer a good return on capital.

Of course enterprises in some industries, such as electricity generation, have to take a view stretching decades ahead. But that is not an argument for 'co-ordinating' all plans around one central projection in which everyone is likely to be wrong together. In talking about forecasts and their successors, 'scenarios and projections', I remarked,

In the last twenty years – the period in which forecasting has become a major industry – we have seen some startlingly wrong predictions. For example, the Electricity Council in the 1960s and early 1970s produced forecasts for maximum demand seven years ahead which were never less than 20 per cent too high and in one year were about 50 per cent out. The Electricity Council were by no means unique in this and their error was in no small measure due to highly optimistic forecasts of economic growth provided by the Government of the day. By treating energy as a traded commodity we greatly reduce the need for, and importance of, projections of UK demand and production.

I conceded that projections could raise 'useful questions about the coherence of policy'. Moreover, until electricity privatization occurred, the Energy Department, as the custodian of the public interest, had to take an independent view as a check on that provided by the Electricity Council and the CEGB. Thus the Department continued under my stewardship to publish energy projections. But these were low key and in no sense at the heart of policy. Unfortunately neither I nor any of my predecessors or successors as Chancellor were to find a way of similarly downgrading Treasury forecasts.

Turning to North Sea oil, I remarked on the UK's genuinely free market regime, 'most unusual among the oil-producing countries of the world'. I confronted head on the question of whether Government should act to defer some of the expected surplus [of UK oil production over UK demand for oil] of the next ten years or so to help fill the gap that may start to emerge some time in the latter half of the 1990s. At first glance the answer may seem equally obvious; of course Government should ease the way. But behind the simple façade hide a host of complexities. Prospects for UK demand and supply, and for the world price of oil over the next ten or twenty years, are highly uncertain. We also have to consider whether action now would have any real economic justification. We have to consider whether it would damage either our more immediate prospects of general economic recovery or our longer-term objective of maximizing the economic exploitation of the North Sea. We have to ask ourselves whether we are really so unenterprising as not to be able to put to good use the wealth which derives from oil whenever it arises.

As it happens, a depletion policy of this kind would have meant selling less oil in the early 1980s in order to sell more in the 1990s and thereafter – when experience so far suggests that its real price in terms of other products has fallen by about half (see Chapter 17).

The Nuclear Delusion

Another important area where the received wisdom was eventually shown to be seriously flawed – although I was unaware of it during my time as Energy Secretary – was nuclear power. During the 1970s and the early 1980s, nuclear power was seen by much of the developed world as a means of liberation from the thrall of OPEC. In Britain, it was seen also as the means of emancipation from Arthur Scargill. The sharp rise in oil prices in 1979 had made oil-fired power stations uneconomic and thus substantially increased the CEGB's dependence on coal. By the winter of 1981–82, coal-fired power stations were generating as much as four fifths of the CEGB's electricity output, compared with two thirds five years earlier. None of the renewable sources of energy was anywhere near commercial application, and the price of gas, which tended to rise in line with oil under the regime then in force, was prohibitive. In any case the mystical doctrine that gas was a premium fuel too precious to burn in power stations could not be effectively challenged so long as the gas industry was nationalized and Denis Rooke remained its chairman. So nuclear power was the only practicable means of diversifying our sources of energy.

There was also a strong feeling, which I shared, that Britain, which in 1956 had been the first nation in the world to have a nuclear power station generating electricity for general use, had failed to capitalize on her early technological lead in nuclear power by a needless addiction to indigenous technology. It was quite different in France, where two fifths of the country's electricity was generated by nuclear power, relying on technology imported from America. At that time, only around a tenth of Britain's energy needs were being met from nuclear power stations. Strange as it may seem in the light of later revelations about the true cost of nuclear power, it was generally believed at the time that this proportion could be greatly increased, and electricity costs actually reduced, provided the Government reversed a mistaken decision taken by Tony Benn three or four years earlier.

After several years of indecision, Benn had decided in January 1978 to authorize the CEGB to build two British-designed Steam Generated Heavy Water Reactors (SGHWRs) rather than buy the popular American system, the Pressurized Water Reactor (PWR). The decision conformed to a pattern, nearly two decades old, of refusing to purchase American nuclear technology. It was the wrong decision, made for the wrong reasons. Even France, the most chauvinist nation on earth, had opted for the PWR whose technology was proven. The SGHWR soon showed all the signs of repeating the sad history of that earlier product of the British nuclear establishment, the Advanced Gas-cooled Reactor (AGR). Though technically exciting, AGRs had proved uneconomic to build and inefficient to operate. Five earlier versions had already fallen behind schedule, most notoriously Dungeness B, and they were all working at far below their planned capacity.

Unknown to me, it was an old saw at the Department of Energy that Dungeness B would be on stream 'within six months'. Unfortunately, the first time I was assured of this I took it seriously. When I told Margaret the news she scoffed and said she had seen all the reports since 1979 and that they had all forecast completion within six months. She confidently bet me £10 that it would be the same story all over again. Foolishly, I accepted. Of course she was right – despite a visit to the site by my Principal Private Secretary, Julian West, to impress upon the workforce the need for urgency – and, red-faced, I duly handed her a £10 note.

Rather than disrupt the nuclear programme again, David Howell and George Younger, the Secretary of State for Scotland, responsible for the electricity industry north of the border, authorized the continuation of work on two new AGRs at Heysham in England and Torness in Scotland. But at least the SGHWR was aborted and, prompted by Treasury distress at the mounting costs of the AGRs, David decided that all future nuclear power stations – and the CEGB was then demanding one a year for the next ten years – would be built using the proven PWR technology, suitably adapted to British requirements. He announced shortly before leaving the Department that the first PWR would be built at Sizewell in Suffolk. Inevitably, given the strength of the anti-nuclear lobby, largely on safety grounds, this would have to be preceded by an exceptionally thorough public inquiry, and in July 1981 David announced that it would be headed by the eminent QC, Frank Layfield. This was the legacy I inherited. In January 1982 I announced that the Layfield Inquiry would begin in January of the following year.

The PWR was seen as vital to demonstrate to the NUM that coal was not fundamental to the economy any longer, and that nuclear power stations could be built to time and to cost. The need for 'diversification' of energy sources, the argument I used to justify the PWR programme, was code for freedom from NUM blackmail. It is true that other countries had diversified into nuclear power to avoid dependence on the Middle East, including even the cautious Swiss. But that was earlier. By the 1980s, other sources of oil had been found and OPEC was no longer the bogey it once was – and was becoming progressively less so.

But before advising Margaret to recommit the Government to nuclear power, I gave Walter Marshall a lengthy and tough grilling on the subject about which he of course knew almost too much – even though I had always taken an interest in it myself, having at that time a major nuclear establishment in my own constituency. He succeeded in satisfying me – but I must admit that my questioning was mainly about safety. Perhaps I should have been more suspicious – the nuclear power industry had not had an unblemished record of achievement – but there was nothing I could do to challenge the CEGB's cost figures until the Sizewell inquiry was completed. The inquiry was still going strong when I left the Department in June 1983, and did not finally report until 1987. It was the longest public inquiry ever held in this country. And although at the end of the day it vindicated the Government, finding in favour of the PWR on safety and economic grounds alike, the victory was soon to prove a hollow one.

It turned out that for years the CEGB, wittingly or unwittingly, had been making a deceptive case in favour of the economics of nuclear power that had taken in even Frank Layfield and was not finally exposed until the Government was in the final stages of the privatization of the industry in 1989, and a detailed prospectus had to be drafted. And of course there was no greater enthusiast for nuclear power than Walter Marshall. The CEGB had always claimed that nuclear power was the cheapest source of 'base load' electricity. Although it is expensive to increase output from nuclear power stations to meet sudden surges in demand, the theory was that nuclear power stations could economically supply the country's unvarying minimum requirement for electricity, with oil or coal-fired stations meeting the upward fluctuations in demand. This claim had long been accepted by officials at the Department of Energy and by the CEGB's auditors alike, as it was to be by the exhaustive Layfield inquiry.

It is indeed true that nuclear operating costs are low. But it turned out that the CEGB had been underproviding for, and greatly understating the likely true cost of decommissioning a nuclear power station at the end of its life (and to a lesser extent the final cost of the reprocessing or safe disposal of the nuclear waste). They had been able to get away with this because no nuclear power station has so far been decommissioned; and it was only the intense scrutiny required for the privatization prospectus that brought it starkly to light years later.

This underestimation of the costs of nuclear power bedevilled the Government's plans to privatize the electricity generating industry. By 1990, decommissioning costs alone were put at £15 billion, against the £3.7 billion estimated by the CEGB in 1989 and the £2.5 billion subsidy the Government was prepared to make available. This made it highly unlikely that private investors would be willing to buy shares in a privatized company with any nuclear capacity.

The very last announcement that Cecil Parkinson, Peter Walker's successor as Energy Secretary, made to the House of Commons before he was moved to Transport in the July 1989 reshuffle, was that the Magnox stations, the first generation of nuclear power stations, were to be taken out of the sale. The background to this decision was that a few weeks earlier, as Chancellor, I had received a note from my officials warning me of the new decommissioning figures that were coming out of the Department of Energy. I concluded immediately that the Magnox stations were unsaleable, which made that part (and it was the greater part) of the former CEGB to which they had been transferred unprivatizable. The only solution I could see was to keep the Magnox stations in the State sector; and I minuted as such. Officials in both departments were astonished, presumably thinking that I would never oppose the privatization of anything.

I asked Cecil round to Number 11 and told him of my firm conclusion. He, too, was taken aback and said that, while he had realized from the start that there was a question mark over nuclear power, and had said as much at Margaret's original Chequers seminar on the privatization of the electricity industry, the Government was now firmly committed. Moreover, he added, Margaret, with her deep commitment to nuclear power, would never wear it. I pointed out that the situation had changed completely, and that it was now clear from the new figures that privatization would be impossible with the Magnox reactors included in the package. Not only did they give the enterprise a negative net worth, but the uncertainties alone would frighten off investors. We would have to see Margaret together. This was duly arranged; and although she found the conclusion distinctly unpalatable, she recognized that – to coin a phrase – there was no alternative.

When, after the July 1989 reshuffle, John Wakeham took over at Energy, he was far from pleased with his inheritance from Cecil. It was not surprising, however, that – alerted by the Magnox débâcle – he took a close look at the decommissioning arithmetic for the remainder of the nuclear power stations (the Magnox ones had been done first because, being the oldest, the date of decommissioning was fast approaching) and soon decided that they, too, would have to be removed from the sale. But by that time I had resigned from the Cabinet.

A passionate nuclear enthusiast to the end, Walter Marshall resigned from the CEGB almost immediately after the nuclear power stations were withdrawn from the privatization, and the Government's future nuclear power station building programme was put on ice. He had always opposed the privatization of the electricity industry, and in particular the splitting up of the CEGB, on which Cecil had rightly insisted, as inimical to the retention of a substantial nuclear programme. He continued to claim that, in the long term, nuclear power would be economic. He may be right; but not on present evidence.

The moral of the whole episode is twofold. First, that Ministers can always be led astray by scientific experts. Second, that the dangers of state ownership are greater than even the Thatcher Government had realized. Had it not been for privatization, who knows how much longer the country would have been paying the price of the phoney economics of nuclear power.

CHAPTER 16

THE PRICE IS WRONG

The Politics of Gas · Anatomy of a Row
The 1982 Party Conference · Electric Shock
Theories of Electricity Pricing

The Politics of Gas

THE POLICY PROBLEM WHICH caused me most political headaches was neither long-range projections nor the depletion issue nor even nuclear power, but the down to earth one of energy pricing, as part of general economic policy.

As I had put it in my Cambridge speech:

> If energy prices are below economic levels, then energy will be used wastefully and consumers will be encouraged to invest in inefficient energy-intensive processes. But what constitutes economic pricing of energy? Where there is a genuine market – as in oil – it is the price set by the market. Where there is no genuine market – as in electricity – prices will need to reflect costs of supply.

There is obviously no political mileage in raising prices to reflect costs. One unfortunate aspect of half a century of inflation is that most people think that all prices are always rising too quickly. The role of *relative* prices in allocating resources is scarcely understood, despite the millions of pounds that have been spent on economic education. The price mechanism is treated with particular uncomprehending hostility by the sort of people who become political activists in *any* political party. Margaret herself was not entirely immune, and David Howell had

had great difficulty in getting her to agree to very necessary increases in the price of domestic gas.

Whereas the Electricity Act, governing pricing policy in the nationalized electricity industry, contained a clause forbidding 'undue discrimination' between different consumers or classes of consumer, the Gas Act contained no such clause. This not only enabled Denis Rooke, the forceful Chairman of British Gas, to act in an arbitrary way. It had also allowed the Labour Government to lean on the industry to keep domestic prices artificially low at the expense of the industrial user. The purpose of this was to manipulate the Retail Price Index and buy a few votes.

The results were predictably absurd. By 1979, British Gas was supplying households at a loss. Gas was so cheap that demand for it had far outstripped the corporation's ability to supply. While taxpayers – a quarter of whose homes were not even connected to a mains gas supply – subsidized domestic supplies, British Gas limited the tapping of its massive North Sea reserves in deference to Rooke's own personal depletion policy. The situation was clearly intolerable and, backed by the Treasury, Howell had opted in 1979 to increase domestic gas prices by ten percentage points more than the rate of inflation in each of the three years to 1982. Since inflation over the relevant period averaged 14 per cent, this meant very large annual increases indeed. It was a brave decision, even though it had been endorsed to the letter by the Labour Government's Price Commission just before it was dissolved.

Inevitably this unpopular new policy came under severe attack, not only from the defeatists in the Government itself, but also from Rooke. British Gas enclosed a leaflet with every household gas bill, effectively blaming the Government for the rise in prices. Conservative MPs were inundated with complaints from constituents, and there were several tight votes in the House of Commons when members of our own side rebelled. When I arrived at the Department of Energy, several senior colleagues, notably Francis Pym, were sufficiently alarmed by the unpopularity to urge me to abandon the policy.

Industry, too, was deeply dissatisfied with British Gas, and thus with the Government, complaining that industrial gas was not only too expensive but unreliable. The latter charge had more substance than the former.

The problem stemmed from the Gas Corporation's statutory monopoly of the purchase of gas from the producers (principally the oil companies operating in the North Sea), which allowed it to dictate terms to all users of gas. Industry was obliged to buy gas on either a firm contract or an interruptible one, and both provided ample cause for complaint. Gas sold on a firm contract guaranteed a supply, but was priced by reference to the relatively expensive gas oil used in domestic central heating systems. Gas offered on an interruptible contract was cheaper, being priced by reference to the cheaper fuel oil used in power stations; but British Gas retained the right to interrupt the supply during any sixty- or ninety-day period they chose during the course of the year. They also insisted that interruptible users build a fuel oil plant in case the supply was interrupted, whether or not the customer was prepared to take the risk. British Gas reckoned, of course, that complaints against its policy would be even louder if the supply was interrupted and there were no alternative source of energy to hand. Businessmen were convinced that British Gas was overcharging industrial consumers to cover its loss-making domestic business, and deliberately holding back the development of new North Sea gasfields.

The Rooke doctrine was that gas was a so-called 'premium fuel', which meant that it had to be confined to 'premium' uses – which ruled out, in particular, its use as a power station fuel. British Gas would simply refuse to supply customers of whom it disapproved. Ironically today, since privatization, gas is increasingly burned in power stations; not surprisingly, since it is the most flexible and almost certainly the cheapest fuel available.

But although the increase in domestic gas prices was a highly unpopular policy, we succeeded in carrying it through in full, and no political disaster ensued. A large part of the art of politics in Government is judging correctly in advance the dividing line between the difficult and the disastrous, and determining which risks to take and which would be a bridge too far. Meanwhile, I sought to make a virtue of necessity by inserting in my political speeches the assertion that this was a Government that would always do what was right, regardless of short-term popularity. It usually went down pretty well. Subsequently, when I became Chancellor and was able to cut taxes, I rather enjoyed using this line against those who cited opinion polls purporting to show that people would far prefer increases in government spending.

Anatomy of a Row

The 1981 Cabinet reshuffle had taken place only four weeks before the annual Party Conference, which thus provided an ideal opportunity for the new team to present itself to the Party and indeed to the public at large. Unfortunately for me, however, no debate on energy had been included in the programme that year. I had a word with Cecil Parkinson, the new Party chairman, who undertook to use his good offices to ensure that energy would be the subject of one of the two balloted motions which are always added to the published programme. (Internal democracy within the Conservative Party has always, very sensibly, been of the guided variety.) I accordingly prepared a speech, ridiculing the case for subsidizing energy prices and blaming the price rises which were causing so much distress to the party workers on the state-owned monopolies. I promised to privatize the British National Oil Corporation (BNOC), the offshore oil business of British Gas and the gas showrooms. I concluded with a ringing peroration,

> We have talked about rolling back the frontiers of the State, about privatization, about curbing the State-owned monopolies, about liberating the forces of competition, about enlarging the freedom to choose – we have talked about all this long enough. The time has come to act, to translate words into deeds.

To my considerable annoyance, Cecil failed to deliver, and neither of the balloted motions was about energy. As a result, my first public utterance as Energy Secretary came when Parliament reassembled the following Monday, 19 October. I announced, first, the privatization of the entire oil-producing business of BNOC; second, the privatization of the British Gas Corporation's (BGC) offshore oil business and, third, the abolition of the Gas Corporation's statutory monopoly of the purchase of gas and thus of its resale to industry, which had prevented the full exploitation of our North Sea gas fields and denied British industry adequate supplies of gas.

Each Department answers questions roughly once a month while the House of Commons is in session. It so happened that in 1981 Energy questions fell on the very first day back after the long summer recess. By agreement with the Speaker, I answered an additional Question at the end of normal Question Time and made my announcement in reply to that, after which there was the usual flurry of supplementaries. It seemed to go down well with the back-benchers behind me, and was received with incredulous horror by all the opposition parties – including even the newly formed SDP in the person of David Owen. It meant that my career as a Cabinet Minister began with quite a bang, on my first appearance at the despatch box in that role, which in turn was on the very first day that the Commons had met since my appointment.

The steps I took to weaken Rooke's empire were of particular benefit to the industrial consumers of gas. Until the Oil and Gas (Enterprise) Act was passed in the summer of 1982, British Gas enjoyed by law the unfettered ownership and control of the onshore gas pipeline grid, and monopoly control over the purchase and sale of gas. This had naturally deterred private sector producers from exploring for or developing the ample gas reserves of the North Sea – although many oil companies produced gas as an inescapable by-product of oil extraction – because they knew they faced a take-it-or-leave-it price from British Gas. At a time when industrial companies were complaining that British Gas was either overcharging them or failing to supply them at all on the grounds that there was a shortage of gas, this was both damaging and absurd.

The Oil and Gas (Enterprise) Act made the first modest attempt to deal with this monopoly. The Act freed private companies to supply gas to large customers using over 2 million therms a year as they saw fit, and to customers using between 25,000 and 2 million therms a year with the consent of the Secretary of State, using the Gas Corporation's pipelines as a 'common carrier'. Competition was further reinforced in March 1986, when my successor, Peter Walker, permitted the export of gas. Meanwhile, access to the British Gas pipeline network under the 1982 Act exposed the excessive scale of the Corporation's transmission charges, which it promptly halved as a result.

None the less, competition has been disappointingly slow to develop. British Gas still controls nine tenths of the industrial gas market, and the industry is some distance from having a spot market where companies can buy gas for delivery as and when they choose. Maybe the removal of all remaining restrictions on the import of gas, announced in 1992, will expedite the transition to a truly competitive market. Meanwhile the regulatory authority set up when the industry was privatized in 1986 will continue to have an important part to play.

The 1982 Party Conference

The political row over the price of gas to the householder reached its climax in 1982. There was a Supply Day debate on gas prices initiated by the Labour Party on 2 March that year, during which several of our own Members spoke against the Government and a number abstained from supporting it in the division lobby. I had been warned to expect trouble when I met the executive of the 1922 Committee the week before the debate (I had told them to stop being so defensive, and start attacking British Gas rather than the Government). Margaret, who had never been happy with the policy, absented herself from the debate. The Opposition naturally revelled in the Government's embarrassment, and on our own side active support was hard to find. Although domestic gas was cheaper in real terms than it had been in 1970, and was at most half the price the French or German householder had to pay, the phased increases caused considerable disquiet in the party at large.

The rumpus reached a climax at the 1982 Party Conference in Brighton, where unlike the previous year an energy debate had been scheduled. Perhaps not surprisingly, all but three of the energy motions submitted for debate complained about the price of gas. Inevitably, it was one of the gas motions that was chosen for debate. My first Party Conference appearance as a Cabinet Minister would thus be in reply to the most hostile debate of the conference. I explained to the then chairman of the

National Union, responsible for these matters, that there was no way I could accept the motion, which was highly critical of the Government; equally, if I simply resisted it there would be the embarrassment of an inevitable defeat on the subsequent vote on the motion. The only way out was to allow an amendment to be moved – something entirely within the Chairman's discretion. Happily, he agreed.

I accordingly asked Peter Lilley, at that time not yet a Member of Parliament, but a prospective parliamentary candidate, to move an amendment praising the Government for its courage in correcting the chronic underpricing bequeathed by Labour. The debate began, but Peter was nowhere to be seen. After the motion had been proposed and notionally opposed, the Chairman called Peter to move his amendment. To my consternation, he failed to appear. It later emerged that the chambermaid at his hotel had thrown away his notes for the speech, and he had had to retrieve them from the dustbins at the back of the building. Eventually, late in the day, he turned up in the hall and made himself known, and the Chairman was good enough to allow him to move his amendment.

This bending of the rules angered the audience still further, and I began my reply to the debate in a distinctly unpleasant atmosphere. With 1982 having seen the last of the three 10 per cent real rises in the price of gas to the home, I was at least able to assure the party faithful that there would be no further large increase in 1983, which they knew was a possible election year. I also announced that I had asked the gas and electricity industries to look again at their standing charges, which many consumers judged excessive and unfair. I then rapidly changed the subject to the much happier theme of the forthcoming privatization of Britoil, which enabled me to end with a stirring peroration. Margaret for reasons of her own decided to sit this one out and watch the debate on TV in the safety of her hotel suite. As a result, the seat on my right was occupied by Cecil Parkinson, as Party Chairman, who redeemed himself for having let me down the previous year by leading the Conference in a standing ovation – the first time this had happened in an energy debate since the Government had taken office, and the last thing I had expected when I first got up to speak.

In January 1983, I secured agreement from both the gas and electricity industries to limit standing charges for domestic consumers to not more than half their total bill; and as I had envisaged, the gas price issue had disappeared altogether by the time of the 1983 election.

Electric Shock

Whereas it was chiefly the general public who were angered by the price of gas, industry was up in arms about the price of electricity.

The Confederation of British Industry (CBI) had persuaded itself that its members were paying more for electricity than their competitors abroad, and was lobbying Parliament and the Government for price cuts. ICI, which had plants in Germany as well as on Teesside, drew up comparisons of the price of electricity in Britain and Germany. These were distorted by the unusual strength of the pound against the Deutschmark in 1980, when the comparisons were made. But they were sufficient to persuade the National Economic Development Council (NEDC), which some industrialists used as a forum to pressurize the Government.

The Council commissioned a report on industrial energy costs from its own office (NEDO). The NEDO report, delivered to the Council in December 1980, concluded that the vast majority of Britain's industrial energy users were paying prices no higher than their European competitors, but that a small number of very large electricity users, such as the chemical, steel and paper industries, were indeed paying more.

One reason for this was that continental electricity suppliers pursued more commercial pricing policies in which they ruthlessly charged the captive domestic consumer more than the mobile industrial user. In addition some European countries deliberately used cheap electricity as a form of industrial subsidy – something I could never get the European Commission, to which I made vigorous representations, seriously to challenge despite its prevalence within the Community, notably in Italy and to a slightly less blatant but still appreciable extent in Germany.

A further specific CBI complaint was that UK firms were having to pay far too much for electricity in order to support uneconomic coal mines and thus overpriced coal. In fact there was little in this and eventually nothing, as the Coal Board moved to charging the full world market price for its coal, irrespective of its cost. The burden of keeping open uneconomic pits was indeed a substantial one; but it fell directly on the taxpayer via the massive subsidy to the Coal Board.

Nevertheless, the argument over the cost of electricity to British industry rumbled on. The NEDC task force monitoring the comparative costs of heavy industrial users had reported in November 1981 that many of the disparities between Britain and Europe had been drastically reduced. But the apparent price differential between Britain and Germany was not entirely eliminated by the fall in the sterling/Deutschmark exchange rate until 1983.

Throughout my time as Energy Secretary I had meetings with businessmen on the issue, who were well aware that the then Industry Secretary, Patrick Jenkin, was sympathetic to their pleas. On one occasion in October 1982 he unhelpfully decided to call a press conference to draw attention to the problem of excessive energy costs, prompted by the publication by the CBI of its regular international comparison of energy costs. Fortunately, the by then lower exchange rate made the figures look unusually favourable to British industry, and I decided to get in first by appearing on *The World at One*. This obliged Patrick to cancel his press conference and the incident predictably earned us a joint scolding at Number 10.

Electricity privatization was still some way off in 1982, but I was at least able to inject some competition into the market before I left the Department. At that time the private generation of electricity for sale to third parties was unlawful. Under the Electric Lighting Act of 1909, as amended, only the nationalized Area Electricity Boards were permitted to supply electricity. Private companies could generate electricity for their own use, and sell any surplus to the local Area Board, but they had no direct access to potential customers. The Area Boards, secure in their monopoly, usually offered a derisory price to private generators. These existed, although they were few and far between. Private electricity generation was responsible for just 6 per cent of total electricity supply in Britain, and some 15 per cent of all industrial requirements. The majority of it was derived from combined heat and power schemes, which made use of the waste heat generated as a by-product of industrial processes.

Unsurprisingly, there was no great clamour to enter the electricity generation business and there was unlikely to be one as long as the law denied private generators access to potential customers. Accordingly, in November 1982, I introduced an Energy Bill allowing private electricity generators for the first time to sell power directly to customers, using the national grid as a common carrier. To ensure there was no cheating, it also obliged the Area Boards to publish the tariffs they levied for use of the grid and the prices at which they would buy electricity from private suppliers. I just managed to get it on to the statute-book before the dissolution of Parliament in May 1983. Not surprisingly, it largely failed to attract private generators into the market. Since the industry was already characterized by substantial excess capacity, it was not hard for the state sector to frustrate the intentions of the Act. It was not until the national grid became a jointly owned subsidiary of the twelve area distribution companies (the former Area Boards) as part of the privatization of the industry in 1990, that the latter were given a serious incentive to encourage competition between generating companies.

Theories of Electricity Pricing

The last major exercise I put in train during my twenty-one months as Energy Secretary was a study of the best way to privatize the electricity industry. The prevailing view in the Department was highly sceptical, particularly since I had made it clear that I wished to see the giant CEGB split up. Over-influenced by the CEGB, they saw considerable difficulty in dispensing with the 'merit order' system. This was the arrangement according to which a unified CEGB graded all its power stations in a so-called merit order which allegedly reflected the cost of production, and then responded to fluctuations in the demand for electricity by feeding into the grid power from the next station down the order, or by taking out power from the lowest-order station then supplying the grid, as the case may be. They seemed to have no conception of how this might, with advantage, be replaced by a market system of bid and offer prices, something made all the easier by the fact that electricity is a homogeneous product and that modern technology had facilitated instant electronic pricing.

I felt I needed an expert second opinion, and commissioned the large accountancy firm of Coopers and Lybrand, which I knew had worked with electricity utilities throughout the world, to prepare a report for me on the prospects for the industry's privatization. The report was written, in the strictest secrecy, by two of the firm's partners, Lord (Roger) Chorley and Professor Chris Foster, with whom I had a number of meetings. On the whole it was positive, although it correctly identified the nuclear power stations as a major obstacle to privatization. It also made a series of recommendations designed to ensure that electricity prices corresponded more closely to market realities.

While the precise Coopers and Lybrand recommendations on pricing were open to question, I had myself become increasingly doubtful about the rigid adherence of the CEGB's economists to the doctrine of long-run marginal cost pricing. I was keenly aware that the problem of energy pricing is at its most acute in the case of electricity, which unlike gas is not an internationally traded commodity. But while it is as important to avoid the underpricing of electricity as it is of any other resource, the long-run marginal cost doctrine is much less helpful than some economists suppose.

According to textbook economics, price should be related to the extra (i.e. marginal) cost of the unit which it just pays to put on the market. At any one time this is the short-run marginal cost, which excludes all overheads and interest charges, which are for the time being fixed. Eventually price becomes equated to long-run marginal cost at which all additional costs – including the cost of replacing the plant at the end of its life, however far off that may be – are covered, not by deliberate pricing policy but by the exit and entry of new plants. Long-run marginal cost pricing is thus not a rule at all, but something which tends to happen under highly competitive conditions. The whole idea of a set of efficient pricing rules for the nationalized industries has been undermined by economists like the late Jack Wiseman, as well as by some of the more recent technical literature.

The Treasury had always insisted on long-run marginal cost pricing, as had the economists in the Energy Department. The result – characteristic of such Fabian rules – was that the demand side was overlooked altogether. The effect of the rule was that electricity was often overpriced, especially during periods of excess capacity, such as manifestly existed in the early 'eighties. This suited the Treasury, as high energy prices enabled it to reduce the External Financing Limits of the nationalized industries and thus save public expenditure. The Department of Energy, sandwiched between the industry on one side and the Treasury on the other, was disinclined to challenge the one and only matter on which the two historic enemies agreed. But the outcome was clearly harmful from a wider point of view.

I decided to have a private word with Terry Burns to ask him to persuade the public expenditure side of the Treasury to stop pressing for higher electricity prices for which there could be no real economic justification. I argued that the Treasury was perfectly entitled to impose taxes, but that a tax on electricity was not necessarily the best tax to levy. This seemed to have some effect and during my last year as Energy Secretary it was agreed that the price of electricity should be frozen, to correct the past overpricing. Unfortunately, my successor as Energy Secretary, Peter Walker, seemed to regard this as a precedent which should be continued indefinitely.

I cannot claim to have solved the mind-bending problem of pricing policy for monopoly public utilities. Some notion such as 'supply and demand' or 'the state of the market', however vague, is probably more useful than the deceptive precision of the long-run marginal cost rule. But as far as I know I was the first Minister to challenge the economic underpinnings – as distinct from the political feasibility – of the latter doctrine.

CHAPTER 17

FROM THE NORTH SEA TO THE GULF

The Oil Price Explosion · The Varley Assurances
What to do with Black Gold · Rent from the North Sea
Sheikhs of Araby · North Sea Retrospect

The Oil Price Explosion

OIL IS DIFFERENT. MORE than coal, much more than gas and infinitely more than electricity, it is *par excellence* an internationally traded commodity. The decisions of the UK Government can have only a trifling impact on its price, even though between 1975 and 1981 the UK moved dramatically from importing virtually all its crude oil to becoming a net exporter. Since the mid-1980s the oil surplus has been diminishing, but much more gradually than the fashionable predictions suggested; and the UK entered the 1990s with a modest trade surplus in oil.

Discussion of this 'black gold' is endless. Yet in practice there are only two aspects which call for a policy response. The first is the tax and licensing regime for North Sea exploration and extraction. The second is the direction in which the UK should exercise its very marginal influence over the world oil market.

The energy policies pursued by the Labour Government of 1974–79 and initially by the new Conservative Government were conditioned by the traumatic experience of the oil shock of 1973–74 following the Yom Kippur War, when the oil price rose fivefold. After a period of stability it then shot up again, this time a threefold increase, in 1979–80 in the aftermath of the deposition of the Shah of Iran, which was shortly to be followed by the outbreak of the Iran Iraq War.*

The expansion of the nuclear power and gas industries, the Labour Governments *Plan for Coal*, and the ten-year programme to raise output and investment in the coal industry, all dated from the first oil shock. The deposition of the Shah in 1979, the outbreak of the war between Iran and Iraq the following year and the loss of Iranian oil supplies were seen as a repeat of the events of 1973. In January 1981, David Howell warned the House of Commons that 'the worst danger facing Western economies at the moment is a further oil price explosion'. It was, and is, exceptionally difficult to disturb the widespread conviction that any rise in the price of oil is detrimental both to world trade and to the British economy.

The discovery of North Sea oil in 1969, which came on stream for the first time in 1976, greatly complicated the effects of a rise in the price of oil on the British economy. In 1981, the year I became Energy Secretary, Britain became a net exporter of oil for the first time. Even this did not shake the consensus that a high oil price was bad for the economy. This position had been adopted more or less unaltered from the previous Labour Government. But circumstances had changed radically since the first oil shock.

The world recession of 1974–75 and the subsequent slow-down in world growth reduced the growth of oil demand. As did the sharp increase in its price. The member states of the Organisation for Economic Co-operation and Development (OECD) reduced their consumption of oil as a proportion of GDP by 40 per cent. At the same time, encouraged by the higher oil price, the West began to develop alternative sources of supply such as the North Sea. All this made Middle East oil much less important to the world economy in the early 1980s than it had been in 1973, and the OPEC cartel began to fragment. Despite the temporary problems caused by Iranian developments, the outlook, at the start of the 1980s was, if anything, for a fall in the real price of oil. In February 1980 when our European Community partners were urging us to use our strength as an oil-producing nation to reduce the price of oil, I minuted Geoffrey Howe:

> What is the position today? Not only has the original (oil starvation) threat failed to reappear, but the cartel has also collapsed in disarray and effectively disappeared. Indeed, the major oil producer, Saudi Arabia, today seems chiefly concerned to do what it can to keep oil prices below what they would otherwise be if determined by supply and demand in a free market. The attitudes to OPEC (and oil) which were fashioned in the crisis of 1973–74 are thus now wholly

*Spot Arab light rose from $2.50 a barrel in January 1973 to $11.65 the following year. It then more or less stabilized, creeping up to $12.85 in October 1978, before exploding again to reach a peak of $41 a barrel in November–December 1979.

outdated. The oil price is probably now closer to being determined by market forces than it was when it was fixed by the international oil 'majors', and the oil market is no longer significantly different from any other commodity market. It follows that, as a producer of that commodity we shall, as soon as we become a net exporter by value (and I suspect we may be one already), have a clear interest in getting the best price we can. We cannot be accused, if we do so, of profiting from a cartel: there is no longer any effective cartel. We cannot even be accused of keeping the price artificially high (or seeking to do so) by restricting our production: we are producing as much as we possibly can.

The second oil price explosion was due to panic stockpiling and could have been dampened by sensible use of the West's strategic oil reserve. In the first quarter of 1979 there was a supply interruption of 2½ million barrels a day as Iranian exports were halted. This was significant – it amounted to 5 per cent of Western oil supplies – but essentially temporary, since much of it was quickly made good from other sources. Yet Western overreaction and stockpiling converted it into a trebling of the nominal price of oil.

In the absence of OPEC cohesion the price could not stay up. When the Iran–Iraq war broke out in October 1980 the Western economies did at last draw on their strategic reserves of oil and, after a temporary surge, oil prices fell back. The dollar price of oil gradually crumbled in the early 1980s before plunging in 1986 to a temporary low below $10. The real price – that is, its purchasing power in world trade – fell continually, if erratically, until the same year.

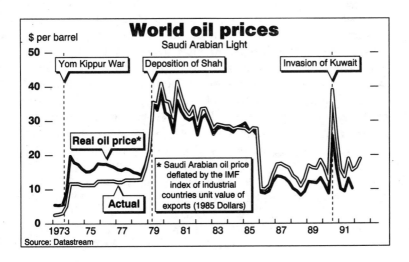

World oil prices
Saudi Arabian Light

$ per barrel

Yom Kippur War

Deposition of Shah

Invasion of Kuwait

Real oil price*

Actual

* Saudi Arabian oil price deflated by the IMF index of industrial countries unit value of exports (1985 Dollars)

Source: Datastream

183

There was another politically prompted doubling of the oil price in 1990 after Saddam Hussein's Iraq invaded Kuwait; but this time the price fell back to normal within a few months. I consistently argued that more could have been done to use the world's strategic stockpile to cut the tops off the huge politically induced speculative spikes both at the time of the deposition of the Shah and after the seizure of Kuwait in 1990. The primary responsibility for doing this lay very much in the hands of the US, which owns the greater part of this reserve, although the Paris-based International Energy Agency was too slow and insufficiently market-oriented in its reactions.

The Varley Assurances

There was a long-running debate in the UK over how fast our relatively modest reserves should be used up, and in particular on whether or not the Government should operate a 'depletion' policy, designed to prolong their life. The general arguments were discussed in Chapter 15. Hamish Gray, my Minister of State, with special responsibility for North Sea oil, was among those strongly in favour of such a policy; which could be implemented by imposing production cut-backs, restricting licences to explore and develop oil fields, or by tax incentives to defer their exploitation.

Norway, with whom we share the North Sea, did indeed have such a policy. In part this reflected a surrender to the blandishments of OPEC; but the circumstances were totally different, too. The Norwegian oil industry, which was almost entirely state-owned, completely dominated Norway's tiny economy. Indeed the main state-owned Norwegian oil company – Statoil – was widely considered to be more powerful than the Government. By contrast, the UK oil industry was predominantly in the private sector – a striking practical refutation, incidentally, of the standard argument of the Left that major industrial investments, where the return is only in the long term, have to be undertaken by the state since the private sector is allegedly interested only in the short term. Oil-producing countries in a similar position to our own, like the United States, did not have a depletion policy.

Uncertainty over whether the British Government would or would not introduce a depletion policy, however, was inevitably unsettling to companies operating in the North Sea and contemplating further investment there. The previous Labour Government had sensibly decided in December 1974 to deal with this problem by giving the so-called 'Varley assurances' (after the then Energy Secretary, Eric Varley). According to these, the Government undertook not to impose production cutbacks of more than 20 per cent on existing (i.e. pre-1975) fields, and then not before the earlier of 1982 or the recovery of the investment, provided that at least four years had elapsed.

By the beginning of the 1980s, these assurances were beginning to expire. David Howell was persuaded, on strategic and security of supply grounds, to announce in July 1980 that the Government would limit the sharpness of the production peak expected in the mid-1980s. While emphasizing that further exploration and development was the best way of achieving this, he had also hinted at delays in the development of fields discovered after 1975 (which were not subject to the Varley assurances) and even at cuts in production from fields on which the Varley assurances had expired.

The Treasury was, of course, fully involved in the discussion which led to David's announcement, not least because any depletion policy would in the short term lead to less tax revenue from the North Sea. There were also the wider economic effects to be considered. Oil was felt to have driven up the exchange rate, squeezing manufacturing industry out of its export markets. This was the point the debate had reached by the time I became Energy Secretary.

What to do with Black Gold

The depletion argument can be illustrated by a simple parable. A peasant finds gold in his garden. Should he be allowed to mine it at his own speed and be left to allocate the proceeds between extra spending and saving for the day when the gold has been depleted? Or should some authority force him to leave some of the gold in the ground to guard against profligacy? The argument for leaving him alone is not that he is perfectly far-sighted, but that no-one else is likely to take the decision better on his behalf.

When we talk about countries rather than individual peasants, the balance of payments arithmetic is used to sow confusion. As a matter of double-entry book-keeping, the balance of payments always balances. For any given current surplus or deficit, there must be a corresponding net outflow or inflow of capital. If the UK moves from being a large net importer of oil to being a net exporter, this means that there will be an offsetting adjustment elsewhere in the overall balance of payments. In the UK the swing factors tend to be the manufacturing trade balance, which duly moved into deficit in the 1980s, and the capital account, where a substantial capital outflow financed a corresponding increase in overseas investment. The capital gains from this investment did not show up in the published balance of payments accounts, but they were no less real for that.

As the oil gradually runs out, the manufacturing trade balance can be expected to show a corresponding improvement, a process which might (although it need not) be accompanied by a decline in the real exchange rate. That in turn can be accomplished without a depreciation of the pound if Britain can achieve a lower rate of inflation than its main competitors – a far from insuperable task, given the time-scale running into decades over which the process is likely to happen.

The depletion policy case was that, to avoid any erosion of manufacturing exports, the surge in oil production should be prevented. The advocates of planned depletion argued that, by deferring some of our oil income, we would assist in the eventual resurrection of manufacturing industry and – if the world oil price rose in real terms during the 1980s, as many then expected it would – also allow Britain to sell at least some of its oil at a better price later on.

I was highly sceptical from the beginning about this train of thought, which sought to convert North Sea oil from a blessing into a curse. 'This masochistic note can only reinforce the feeling among the British people,' I had remarked in my minute of February 1980, to Geoffrey Howe, 'that so far as the British economy is concerned, everything is for the worst in the worst of all possible worlds, and that nothing will ever go right for us.' Moreover, the economic arguments in favour of any sort of depletion policy were, as I argued in Chapter 15, badly flawed. It was impossible to predict the world supply of, and demand for, oil over the next decade or two, thus making any projections of its future real price absurd. Experience showed that almost all forecasts were falsified by events. But without some workable estimate of the future real price of oil, it was impossible to tell when the optimum time for selling our oil would be. (The Department was obliged to produce its own forecast of the future oil price as part of its evidence to the Sizewell inquiry: I insisted that it publish the minimum necessary.)

In addition to the arguments over depletion policy there was considerable support, particularly on the Left, for the proposition that the Government should ensure that North Sea revenues were invested. This was in large part based on the belief, disproved by the whole of Britain's post-war economic experience, that public investment was superior to private. Quite apart from the persistent tendency to attempt to shore up failing industries, Governments have a pretty poor record in trying to pick winners. Moreover, in both cases, political considerations inevitably loom large, with marginal seats counting for more than marginal costs.

The previous Labour Government had published in 1978 a much-trumpeted White Paper entitled *The Challenge of North Sea Oil*. This advocated the investment of North Sea revenues for the benefit of future generations. The idea was sensibly rejected by the Treasury even then – on the grounds that it could neither distinguish between different sources of revenue for public expenditure purposes nor make useful investment decisions for the whole economy. It seemed to me rather more sensible to use North Sea tax revenues to reduce Government borrowing, to cut taxes where this could be done on a sustainable basis, and generally to improve the climate for enterprise.

For all these reasons, I had little doubt that the Varley assurances should be extended; and in June 1982, the year when they were due to expire, I duly announced that the Government would not impose any production cut-backs before 1985 at the earliest, since when the power to improve cut-backs has effectively fallen into abeyance. My statement followed hard on the heels of the publication in May 1982 of a report into depletion policy by the House of Commons Select Committee on Energy. In 1981 and early 1982, members of the Committee interviewed officials from both the Department of Energy and the Treasury and representatives of the major oil companies active in the North Sea. Some economists also gave evidence, among them Tommy Balogh, who had been Minister of State for Energy in the previous Labour Government. Balogh had argued for years that the private sector was given too much latitude in the North Sea. He submitted a lengthy memorandum arguing for a new state oil corporation to throttle back output, on the grounds that the goal of saving oil for the benefit of future generations was 'politico-moral rather than economic in character'. It was not a view which much impressed the Select Committee, which dismissed the economic case for deferring North Sea production, highlighting the inaccuracy of all oil reserve and price forecasts, and concluding that:

> We do not believe that a convincing case has yet been made out for formal intervention by the Government to restrain production . . . We regard it as futile and probably self-defeating for the Government to substitute its own judgement for that of the oil companies in an attempt to overrule the technical and economic incentives with the aim of bringing about a desired production profile in the UK.

I had gone to considerable lengths to cultivate the Conservative members of the Energy Select Committee – which may have assisted it to reach the sensible conclusion on this sensitive subject that it did. The Treasury Select Committee was subsequently to prove stonier ground.

Rent from the North Sea

There was another North Sea issue which required rather more attention. That was taxation. It was common ground that a special tax regime for North Sea oil was justified because its low extraction costs, relative to the world price, gave rise to exceptionally large profits, known technically as 'economic rent', a term used by economists to describe a systematic excess of revenue over the minimum required to maintain the activity in being.

Identifying the concept however, is far easier than extracting the economic rent in practice, without overtaxing the 'normal' profit (including the risk premium) that provides the incentive to development. Since the possibility of enjoying the economic rent from North Sea oil derives from the allocation by the Government of the exploration licences in the first place, the theoretical answer is clear. It is to impose no special tax regime at all – simply the normal corporate tax regime – but to allocate the blocs by auction, leaving it to the auction price to capture the economic rent. Indeed I did, as Energy Secretary, hold some experimental auctions of North Sea oil blocs.

In the real world, however, the risk that a future Government might impose a special tax regime is bound to depress the level of bidding – thus making the imposition of a special tax regime the only satisfactory way of recovering economic rent. The practical question thus revolves around the characteristics of the North Sea tax regime. Ideally it should be price-sensitive (that so, it should not require to be changed every time the world oil price changes), and it should not make fields that are genuinely economic on a pre-tax basis uneconomic post-tax – nor, indeed, should it make fields that are uneconomic pre-tax economic post-tax. In addition, it seemed to me desirable that the UK oil tax system should be no harsher than the tax system in other major oil-producing areas of the world, as this is a highly mobile industry producing a largely uniform product.

Over the passage of time there had grown up a number of different levies which were designed between them to extract the economic rent from North Sea oil:

1. *Oil royalties* per tonne extracted, which raised over £1.6 billion in 1982–83;

2. *Petroleum Revenue Tax* (PRT). An addition to the normal Corporation Tax payable at 70 per cent on all North Sea profits ('revenues'), but only after the company had recouped the cost of its investment, which (including APRT: see below) raised almost £3.3 billion in 1982–83;

3. *Supplementary Petroleum Duty* (SPD). A special tax introduced in January 1981 on the value of all oil and gas extracted from the North Sea, which raised £2.4 billion in 1982–83;

4. *Advance Petroleum Revenue Tax* (APRT). The advance payment of PRT introduced as part of the emergency fiscal package of November 1980.

In addition, the North Sea oil industry paid a further £0.5 billion in 1982–83 in normal Corporation Tax (including Advance Corporation Tax).

I felt increasingly that the Inland Revenue were overdoing it. There was a danger of killing the goose that laid the golden eggs. By 1982 all the biggest and most accessible discoveries had already been made, and the exploration, appraisal and development of smaller, geologically more complex and proportionately more costly fields in deeper water hinged to a much greater degree on a more favourable taxation regime. The Energy Committee endorsed my own view that oil taxation policy was discouraging exploration and development in the North Sea. The same month that its report was published, I arranged for my Department, in conjunction with the Inland Revenue, to issue a consultative document on the taxation of North Sea oil and gas revenues.

It was common ground between the Department and the industry's principal trade association, the UK Offshore Operators' Association (UKOOA), that the tax regime was discouraging investment in new fields, which tended to be smaller than earlier discoveries. The problem lay in persuading the Treasury to forgo enough tax revenues to make a real difference. My officials, who like most of Whitehall had spent a fair part of their lives fighting the Treasury and more often than not losing, were not optimistic. Revenues from the North Sea oil and gas industries had soared from zero in 1975 to nearly £8 billion in 1982–3, at which point they accounted for nearly 8½ per cent of all tax revenues.

Knowing Geoffrey Howe's open-minded readiness to judge a well-argued case on its merits, I was more sanguine, and in the autumn of 1982 I initiated intensive discussions between my Department, the Treasury, the Inland Revenue and the industry, on future North Sea profitability and the fiscal regime. To enable a convincing case to be made, I persuaded the oil companies to reveal confidential information on the profitability of new North Sea oilfields, which they eventually submitted three days before Christmas. Armed with all this, my officials and I worked up a package of reforms which I put to Geoffrey in January 1983. They went considerably further than my officials thought the Treasury would be prepared to contemplate, but I was satisfied that they were fully justified.

Geoffrey was generally receptive, and after a number of further discussions, which also involved John Wakeham, then Minister of State at the Treasury, to whom Geoffrey had delegated special responsibility for North Sea tax matters, we were able finally to agree, just twelve days before the 1983 Budget, a far-reaching reform package broadly along the lines I had put to him. Geoffrey had already announced in his 1982 Budget the abolition of SPD. The measures announced on Budget day 1983 went considerably further. They included immediate PRT relief for the exploration and appraisal of new oil and gas reserves: the phasing out of APRT by the end of 1986; doubling PRT oil allowance; and waiving royalties on all new fields developed after April 1982. (The initials are explained on page 188.) The hardest job I had was persuading Geoffrey of the need for this backdating.

According to one of those procedural quirks that brighten the lives of Parliamentary clerks, oil royalties are not considered to be a tax, and so cannot be included in a Finance Bill. This meant that that part of the North Sea tax reform package would have to be enacted in a separate Oil Royalties Bill. That was the only blemish on what was otherwise a highly satisfactory outcome. I had secured far greater concessions from the Treasury than my officials had ever imagined possible. In particular, new fields would be liable only to Corporation Tax and to PRT once the companies involved had recouped the cost of their investment. The changes both simplified the oil tax regime and, by linking taxation exclusively to profits rather than to a mixture of profits and revenues, made the whole system far more sensitive to changes in the world oil price, ensuring that the Treasury would automatically receive more revenue when the price was high and less when it was low.

At the time, however, the Treasury soon began to regret that Geoffrey had agreed to such substantial concessions so readily. No sooner was the ink dry on the agreement we had concluded than the oil price not only began to weaken but threatened to fall precipitately. With only days to go before the 1983 Budget, the Treasury faced the awful prospect of a sharp decline in oil revenues causing a serious enlargement of the PSBR in the coming year. Geoffrey was sufficiently alarmed to instruct his officials to prepare two alternative Budgets, the second on the basis of a major slippage in the oil price. In the event, as we shall shortly see, this was averted, and he was able to introduce the Budget he had first thought of. But he was sufficiently chastened to warn in his Budget speech that 'if any further reduction in oil prices seemed likely to compromise the success of our economic strategy, I would be ready to take appropriate corrective action.'

The North Sea oil industry could scarcely conceal its delight at the tax changes, making Treasury officials even more suspicious, but the relaxation soon showed itself to have been fully justified. A great wave of fresh exploration and development followed the 1983 Budget. The number of exploration and appraisal wells drilled in the North Sea virtually doubled, averaging 160 a year in the seven years after 1983, compared with 83 a year in the previous seven years. The reforms also passed the durability test. A decade later the North Sea fiscal regime had hardly changed despite enormous fluctuations in the oil price.

Sheikhs of Araby

When I became Energy Secretary in 1981, OPEC members were still endeavouring to sell oil at a fixed price agreed between them; but the recommended price – the so-called 'Government Selling Price' or GSP, which varied according to the quality of the crude oil – bore increasingly little relation to the state of the market. The trading arm of the British

National Oil Corporation (BNOC), which continued to purchase 51 per cent of all the oil produced in the North Sea even after the exploration and production business of BNOC had been privatized, and then resold it to the trade, set a widely followed 'reference price' for North Sea oil. In accordance with the prevailing wisdom that the British economy benefited more from a low oil price than a high one, successive British Governments had encouraged BNOC to set lower prices than those of OPEC.

This policy greatly upset the Arabs, who feared that BNOC might lead oil prices down generally. This fear was not, however, immediately apparent to me. I first met Sheikh Ahmed Zaki Yamani, the long-serving Saudi Oil Minister and *de facto* leader of OPEC, when I was able to give a formal luncheon in his honour a fortnight after my appointment as Energy Secretary in 1981. I found the highly intelligent, soft-spoken, Western-educated Yamani a most congenial companion. While clearly conscious of the immense power he was widely supposed to wield, and of the fact that the world's press hung on his every public utterance, his courtesy and good manners prevented any sign of arrogance. He was, however, haunted by the fear of being kidnapped – a nightmare that had its origin some years previously when the notorious terrorist Carlos had hijacked an OPEC ministerial meeting in Vienna, and Zaki Yamani had spent several hours in fear for his life. At the time of our first meeting, the downward pressure on the oil price was still relatively modest, and Yamani was wholly relaxed about it.

By the spring of the following year, however, the pressure had intensified, and OPEC, in the shape of a series of visiting Arab oil ministers, began to lobby me heavily to support its efforts to sustain the price. They exerted public as well as private pressure. On 31 March 1982, Yamani addressed a packed committee room at the House of Commons, warning his audience that Britain was not doing enough to stabilize oil prices. Afterwards, he claimed to his hosts that BNOC's pricing policy was putting unfair downward pressure on the price of Nigerian oil. The assertion could not go uncontradicted. The same evening, I told the Press that:

> The British Government controls neither the price nor the volume of North Sea oil output. The price which BNOC negotiates has to reflect the realities of the market. It is not the policy of the British Government to lead prices down any more than it was our policy to lead prices up.

A year later, in March 1983, by which time the world oil market had weakened considerably, OPEC decided to step up its pressure on the

UK still further, convening a full ministerial meeting, for the first time ever, in London. It was hard to avoid the conclusion that the location had been chosen as a deliberate attempt to embarrass the Government. I could scarcely refuse to meet the assembled oil ministers, although I insisted on doing so in private, on an individual basis, and only if the Minister concerned specifically sought a meeting.

On this basis, during the last week of February and first week of March I saw Yamani's closest ally, the Kuwaiti oil minister Ali Khalifa, Humberto Calderon Berti from Venezuela, and Dr Oteiba from the United Arab Emirates. Each of them was accompanied by his country's ambassador in London, and I was flanked by Ken Couzens. Yamani himself finally called on me on the evening of 9 March. I saw him alone. As plainly as his dignity would allow, he in effect invited Britain to become a country member of OPEC. He explained that the weakness in the oil price would force OPEC to cut back on production to prop it up, and asked the UK to do the same.

This was obviously out of the question. I reminded him that in Britain it was the oil companies, and not the Government, which controlled the amount of oil produced in any given year. We were in any case in a very different position from the oil-dependent economies of OPEC. Oil accounted for less than 5 per cent of the UK's national output, and our primary economic interest was in the expansion of world trade. I pointed out, too, that unless BNOC's oil price came down in line with the market, and indeed did so without further delay, it would not be able to sell the oil it was contracted to buy. For all these reasons, we could not support any attempt to prop up the price artificially. Yamani must have known this before he came to see me, because I had already given the same message to the other OPEC Ministers who had visited me.

It was clear to me that the principal pressure to prop up the price came from the warring states of Iran and Iraq, who needed the oil revenues to finance the war, rather than from the Gulf states themselves. Saudi Arabia, Kuwait and the Emirates fully recognized that a modest fall in the oil price was inevitable. Even so, after the approach I had received, it would not have helped Anglo-Saudi relations to have sent Yamani away completely empty-handed.

I therefore undertook to persuade BNOC to lower its reference price for North Sea oil in the most discreet way possible. In addition, having first interrogated my officials responsible for forecasting the volume of North Sea oil output, I told Yamani that I expected North Sea output in 1983 to be no greater than the record level achieved in 1982. At the request of Yamani, Ali Khalifa and Oteiba, I subsequently included this projection in a press release. The OPEC meeting then agreed to a $5 cut in the oil reference price to $29 a barrel, and an overall level of output by OPEC members as a whole of 17.5 million barrels a day.

I was able to devise a method of fulfilling my promise to lower the North Sea oil price discreetly without too much difficulty. At that time the North Sea reference price was expressed in terms of the oil from the Forties field, the UK's largest. The Brent field, however, also produced a very large quantity of oil which, because of its higher quality, commanded a premium. It was a simple matter for BNOC to announce that in future, the North Sea reference price would apply to Brent crude. This of course produced an effective price reduction without any new price, in terms of dollars a barrel, being promulgated.

The danger, however, was that the Nigerians, whose oil was closest in quality to North Sea oil, and who regarded the UK with the deepest suspicion, would smell a rat and retaliate by lowering their price still further; and I had little confidence in my ability to talk them out of this myself. I therefore tracked Yamani down in New York, where he had gone after the London meeting, and told him over the telephone of BNOC's imminent announcement, which he greatly appreciated, and of my concern about the Nigerians, which he undertook to deal with himself. This he duly did, by persuading King Fahd of Saudi Arabia to make a direct appeal to President Shagari of Nigeria.

My ploy of providing an estimate of the volume of North Sea output in 1983 proved less successful, however. Although given on the basis of the best available official advice, like most short-term Government forecasts it proved to be wrong: Britain's oil output in 1983 was higher than in 1982. Yamani, who had a sophisticated understanding of these matters, knew full well that I had made a best guess and not a commitment – which, as he also knew, I was in no position to make, since under our system the oil companies decide how much oil to produce. But it may have suited him to hint to his less well-informed colleagues that he had extracted a commitment from me. In any case, OPEC leaders claimed that I had given them a guarantee that Britain would not increase its production in 1983. This gave rise to the subsequent Arab complaint that I had double-crossed OPEC.

But the erroneousness of the forecast did not come to light until later. In the short term, the new OPEC price held, the world price did not collapse, and when in April 1983 I visited Saudi Arabia, Kuwait, Qatar and the Emirates, I was given a warm welcome in all these Gulf states. Indeed, in Saudi Arabia Yamani gave a luncheon in his own home in my honour, to which he invited a number of his Cabinet colleagues and their wives – something our then Ambassador, James Craig, told me was a most unusual gesture of friendship. I was, however, slightly disappointed to discover, when I returned to London with the long-spouted Arab silver coffee-pots I had been given, that I had to hand them over to the Department, lest I be corrupted. I was able, however, to keep the amber worry-beads Yamani had given me.*

Meanwhile, the events of the spring of 1983 made it imperative for the Government to clarify its own thinking on the oil price, and during the week of the OPEC meeting in London Margaret convened a meeting of Ministers and officials from the Treasury and the Department of Energy at Number 10 to consider the matter. I argued that while, in general, the price of oil was bound to be determined by the market, in so far as the UK Government was able to exercise any influence it should, for economic and diplomatic reasons alike, seek to promote not lower oil prices but stability. I volunteered to submit a paper along these lines and Margaret invited the Treasury to put in a paper, too; both to be discussed at a further meeting. In the interim, the Energy Department was authorized to make a public statement, the key part of which read:

> Britain's position is perfectly clear. The Government does not control the price of North Sea oil: BNOC, quite simply, has to sell its oil at the best price it can get on the world market.
>
> Although appearances can be deceptive . . . this is also essentially true of the OPEC countries . . . Where the main difference comes is that . . . we in Britain operate a private enterprise system . . . under which it is the companies which decide how much oil to produce, on strictly commercial criteria . . . In the OPEC countries, it is the Government which controls the amount of oil produced in any given year . . . What we do most certainly share with the OPEC countries – and indeed with the rest of the world – is a desire not to see an exaggerated fall in the world oil price now which would inevitably be followed by a sharp and damaging rebound later on.

The two oil policy papers were duly considered at the second meeting a fortnight or so later. The Treasury, although still worried that its North Sea revenues would dry up, had submitted a rather unimaginative paper reiterating the orthodox view that on balance a low oil price was advantageous to Britain because it reduced inflation and promoted growth. Ken Couzens and I had written a rather more incisive paper which Margaret made clear she preferred. She added to the Treasury's chagrin by ruling that the Department of Energy should be the lead department on the issue.

*There are strict rules about ministerial gifts, designed to avoid the possibility of corruption. Any gift a Minister receives, even from a foreign government, has to be valued. If it is worth less than a fixed sum, which is adjusted from time to time to take note of inflation, and which in 1983 was something like £60, the Minister may keep it. If it is worth any more than that, he must hand it over to the Government; but he can buy it back from the Government at the valuation price less the monetary limit on acceptable gifts.

The Lawson/Couzens paper argued that the world economy was not assisted by sharp fluctuations in the oil price, and that an exaggerated fall in the world oil price now would only lead to a sharp rebound later on. This was subsequently borne out by events. A precipitate fall was averted for just three years. In the spring of 1986, the oil price plunged to below $10 a barrel, only to rebound a year later to $17 a barrel.

North Sea Retrospect

North Sea oil brought out our national genius for both gloom and exaggeration. First there was concern that its advent would crucify manufacturing industry on the cross of an overvalued exchange rate, then there was equal concern about the disaster that would ensue when the oil ran out. The initial impact was largely a matter of the speed with which the oil came on stream. The UK went from producing virtually no oil at all in 1975 to self-sufficiency in 1980 and a level of oil output in 1983 that was some 60 per cent higher than domestic consumption.

The alarmists never seemed to realize that the speed of the decline in North Sea output from its peak in the mid-1980s was always likely to be much slower than the build-up. In 1991 the UK was still a net exporter of oil and oil products. Moreover North Sea gas, which was equivalent to a quarter of North Sea oil production, at the time of the latter's peak, is likely to tail off even more slowly, and had actually risen slightly in the years to 1991.

Nor has the North Sea bonus been at all wasted. The abolition of exchange control facilitated a profitable investment of North Sea income overseas; and the yield from these investments (including the capital gain which, as I pointed out earlier, does not appear in the recorded balance of payments statistics) is easing the transition to lower oil production. This overseas investment was, of course, the mirror image of a series of current balance of payments surpluses totalling £23 billion over the years from 1978 to 1985 inclusive.

At its peak North Sea oil accounted for less than 8½ per cent of total tax revenues, a level from which it plunged back quite quickly, as a result of the fall in the oil price more than the moderate tailing off in production. But while it lasted North Sea oil gave a healthy kick start to the very rapid reduction in the Budget deficit in the course of the 1980s.

The crowding-out effect of North Sea oil, referred to in an earlier chapter, did hasten the decline in manufacturing as a share of GDP. But it did no more than reinforce a long-standing trend. Manufacturing industry's share of total output fell between 1970 and 1977 from 34 per cent to 30 per cent, a period when North Sea output was negligible and under Governments which attached a special importance to this sector. The share then fell further before stabilizing at around 23 per cent in the later 1980s.

FROM THE NORTH SEA TO THE GULF

As Chancellor, I devoted a speech in April 1984 to a Conference on International Energy issues at Cambridge to the explicit question of what would happen when North Sea oil ran out. I concluded that, just as the arrival of the black gold had crowded out some manufacturing exports, its decline would bring about some crowding back into the manufacturing sector. There has indeed been some movement in this direction. Thanks to the boom of the late 1980s, the manufacturing trade deficit did not reach its peak of £17 billion until 1989. The economic cycle has inevitably complicated the picture; but the fact that the manufacturing sector was less heavily hit by the recession of the early 1990s than the predominantly non-tradeable service sector suggests that the underlying trend has been in the direction I expected.

A more complex point was that, speaking in 1984, I accepted the view that re-entry to a world of falling North Sea output would require a decline in the *real* exchange rate, which I hoped would be achieved through lower British inflation rather than through sterling depreciation.

I was, however, determined not to try to predict in my Cambridge speech which of the industries with a larger tradeable content would expand relative to the others to replace declining oil exports. For it was not, and is not, the job of Government to guess the composition of production. But I could and did say that a gradual fall in oil revenues would still enable the Government to cut taxes as a proportion of GDP provided that public expenditure continued to fall as a proportion of GDP – a condition which remains valid.

The conditions I listed in 1984 for a successful transition from North Sea surpluses to a more moderate level of production from the UK Continental Shelf were:

1. A North Sea tax regime that encouraged development and thus made re-entry more gradual;
2. A firm control of public spending to offset the gradual rundown of North Sea revenues; and
3. Most important of all, supply-side policies to improve the working of markets faced with inevitable changes in the industrial structure, whether these changes were due to a decline in oil production or to other and larger forces.

These remain the key conditions.

CHAPTER 18

PRIVATIZATION – 1
THE JEWEL IN THE CROWN

The Coming of Privatization · Origins and Myths
Nationalization: the Experiment that Failed · Mules are not Zebras
Wider Ownership · A Low-key Start

The Coming of Privatization

> Privatization has been the most striking policy innovation since 1979
> . . . It also represents the Jewel in the Crown of the Government's
> legislation programme, around which all shades of Tories can unite.
> The idea has been taken up, and copied, with explicit acknow-
> ledgement of the British influence, not only by other industrialized
> countries, but also by the Third World countries.

So writes Peter Riddell, a leading political journalist who is no Thatcherite, but whose book on the period has far more to say on the substance of
policy than better-known works which have concentrated on the nature
of Margaret Thatcher's personality. If Riddell had gone to press slightly
later, he would have included the ex-Communist countries of Central
and Eastern Europe and indeed the Republics of the former Soviet
Union among the emulators.

By the 1992 general election, about two thirds of the formerly State-
owned industries in the UK had been transferred to the private sector.
Some forty-six major businesses, employing some 900,000 people, had
been privatized. Among the minority that remain in the State sector
are British Coal (formerly known as the National Coal Board) and
British Rail. The 1992 Conservative manifesto contained an unequivocal
pledge to privatize the former, but was somewhat cagey about the latter.

Yet despite the undoubted political difficulties, if we are ever to have an efficient railway service in this country, it will be achieved only by full-blooded privatization.

The expertise about privatization that Whitehall and the City have, sometimes painfully, acquired in the process has become a lucrative source of invisible earnings. Libraries could be filled with the books and reports written on the subject. What I can give in this book is an account of the origins of the idea, of the thinking behind it, and of how the initial difficulties were tackled. Not the least of those initial difficulties was the fact that, to all intents and purposes, it had never been done before. This is remarkably rare in Whitehall. Whenever a Minister has what he thinks is a new idea, the chances are that it is nothing of the sort. His officials dust down the relevant departmental dossier, and off they go. But with privatization there was no departmental dossier to dust down. Officials had to start from a blank sheet – an almost unheard-of experience. But they went to work with a will, and the good ones, who were very good indeed, soon found that while pioneering was hard work, it was actually much more enjoyable than re-treading a well trodden path.

First, however, a note on the semantics. Privatization means almost the same thing as denationalization. 'Almost' because industries such as the telephone service, which had always been in the State sector, and thus never been through a process of nationalization in the first place, were transferred to the private sector. Partly for this reason and partly because most of us felt denationalization did not sound positive enough, the process came to be officially described as 'privatization'. The word was, to the best of my recollection, David Howell's invention. It is an ugly word – and Margaret disliked it so much that for some time she refused to use it. But none of us could come up with anything better; and as this word, or quite literal translations of it, is now used from Siberia to Patagonia, we may as well stick to it.

A further terminological point is that privatization essentially means the transfer of control of a whole industry or firm from the State to the private sector. The sale of a minority stake which still leaves the organization concerned under State control is emphatically not privatization. Nor strictly speaking is the sale of State-owned shares in a business that has already been privatized, or where the organization is already effectively (and not just legally) run as a private enterprise concern. The sale of a tranche of BP by the Callaghan Government to reduce the size of its PSBR and to keep the IMF at bay – one of Harold Lever's many devices – was not privatization in any true sense and of course was not intended to be so. There was one Treasury term – 'special sales of assets' – which covered both privatization and these other kinds of sales, and this was indeed how the whole programme was officially known at the beginning. But by 1986 'privatization' had displaced it even in the Treasury Red Book, as the general term which it was convenient to use for any sale of State financial assets.

Another borderline case is contracting out and franchising, where State controlled organizations cease to carry out a particular activity and award a contract to a private firm instead. Obvious examples are municipal refuse collection or hospital laundries. A more spectacular case would occur if British Rail were to lease some or all of its track to private enterprise operators. But, to repeat: the essence of privatization is the transfer of the ownership and control of enterprises from the State sector to the private sector.

Origins and Myths

The limited and low-key reference to denationalization in the 1979 manifesto has led many commentators, even Peter Riddell, to suppose that privatization was not part of our original programme and emerged as an unexpected development into which we stumbled by happy accident. They could not be more mistaken. The exiguous references in the 1979 Conservative manifesto reflected partly the fact that little detailed work had been done on the subject in Opposition; partly that the enthusiasts for privatization were Keith Joseph, Geoffrey Howe, John Nott, David Howell and me, rather than Margaret herself; and, perhaps chiefly Margaret's understandable fear of frightening the floating voter. But privatization was a central plank of our policy right from the start. In Geoffrey Howe's first Budget Speech, less than six weeks after we had first taken office in May 1979, he referred (in a passage which I helped to draft) to a review

> of the scope for reducing the size of the public sector. It is already clear that the scope for the sale of assets is substantial. Such sales not only help in the short term to reduce the PSBR. They are an essential part of our long-term programme for promoting the widest possible participation by the people in the ownership of British industry. This objective – wider public ownership in the true meaning of the term – has implications not only for the scale of our programme but also for the methods of sale we shall adopt.

Geoffrey went on to announce that assets sales of some £1 billion would be made in 1979–80 of which the biggest single contribution would come from the sale of part of the Government's holding in BP, bringing it well below the 51 per cent at which it then stood. This was a simple operation, carried out in November, which raised £290 million. It needed no legislation: the shares were already quoted on the Stock Exchange, and the previous Labour Government had inadvertently paved the way

199

with its 1977 BP share sale. So the official Opposition could hardly complain with much conviction. Although the sale was not in fact a true privatization, since despite the majority Government stake, BP had always been run as a private sector company and had always been classified as being in the private sector, it clearly pointed the way.

In my 1980 lecture, *The New Conservatism*, I went a little further, saying:

> We have also embarked on a major programme of privatization of the state-owned industries, of which British Aerospace and British Airways will be among the first candidates . . . Throughout this exercise we are anxious to see the widest possible spread of private shareholding – so that the so-called public sector industries really do belong to the public – including in particular employee shareholding.

Meanwhile, immediately after the 1979 election, Margaret had set up a sub-committee of the main Economic Committee to explore candidates for privatization. Known as E (DL) in the Whitehall jargon, the 'DL' standing for 'disposal', it was chaired by Geoffrey Howe as Chancellor, and both John Biffen as Chief Secretary and I as Financial Secretary were members of it. It was unique for a Cabinet Committee to have no fewer than three Treasury Ministers in it, and it no doubt reflected Margaret's lack of confidence in most of the rest of her first Cabinet.

Not only was privatization opposed tooth and nail by Labour, but the Liberals (and the Liberal-Social Democrat 'Alliance' while it existed) sought to demonstrate their moderation by being opposed to privatization and nationalization with equal vehemence. This was a curiously conservative attitude (with a small 'c') to the boundary between the state and private sectors of industry for politicians who sometimes sought to portray themselves as radical to take. According to Roy Jenkins, on innumerable occasions, this stance was dictated by a distaste for the damage done by so-called 'pendulum politics', under which successive Labour and Conservative Governments reversed their predecessors' acts, and industries were deprived of all stability as they allegedly oscillated to and fro between the State and the private sectors.

His argument would have been more impressive had it borne any correspondence to historical reality. In fact, with the arguable exception of steel in 1951, when the incoming Churchill Government had declined to complete the nationalization embarked on in the twilight months of the Attlee Government, and the industry was thus spared that fate until the advent of the Wilson Government of the 'sixties, the motion had been not that of a pendulum, but of a one-way street – with the story prior to the Thatcher Government being one of ever-growing State ownership.

But devoid of principle and historical accuracy alike, the Liberal position accurately reflected the views of the British people. Opposed to nationalization, they were scared by privatization. In advance of every significant privatization, public opinion was invariably hostile to the idea, and there was no way it could be won round except by the Government going ahead and doing it. Then, when the scare stories which had been so luridly peddled by the Opposition about the consequences of a particular privatization in prospect were proved to be unfounded, the private sector status of the industry concerned became accepted as a fact of life.

This demonstrated, to my satisfaction at least, that while in an ideal world a Government would always persuade the people of the wisdom of a policy before implementing it, in practice that is often not possible, and becomes simply a recipe for inaction.

Nationalization: the Experiment that Failed

The climate in the 1990s is very different. Even economists who originally supported nationalization in the West are now advising ex-Communist countries on how to privatize as quickly as practicable. There are bound to be setbacks and disappointments in countries without any recent tradition of private enterprise and the culture that sustains it. The ultimate goal is more likely to survive intact if we remember why the experiment of State ownership failed and do not simply treat privatization as an unthinking article of faith.

My own most extensive early statement was made in a talk I gave in connection with the Oxford University Business Summer School, at Merton College, Oxford, on 23 September 1982. I had been provoked during the Britoil debates by the confusion between the State and the nation, which implied that no enterprise could be truly British unless it were owned by the State. (I also, incidentally, found it perverse to use the term 'public sector' to describe a part of the economy where, as often as not, the State posted a notice to potential competitors saying 'private: keep out'.)

I began by recalling the reasons put forward for nationalization by the Attlee Government of 1945–51 at the time. These were:

1. The improvement of industrial relations
2. The promotion of full employment
3. The gain in productivity from the removal of absentee ownership
4. The efficient regulation of monopolies (which were in themselves considered superior to 'wasteful competition')
5. The replacement of short term profit-maximization by wider national and social priorities

PRIVATIZATION – 1: THE JEWEL IN THE CROWN

There is no longer any need to labour the failure of nationalization to achieve these objectives. But the reasons I gave in 1982 may still be of interest.

The nationalized industries, so far from improving industrial relations, proved the source of the biggest threat to industrial peace – doubtless because of the combination of centralized union power and recourse to the bottomless public purse. On full employment I observed that 'while nationalization has enabled some industries to postpone job losses for a time, the resulting overmanning has usually proved unsustainable and the eventual job losses consequently greater.'

As for short termism versus national priorities, I pointed out that governments 'enjoy no unique hot line to the future'. But I went on to make the less obvious point that governments may well have more power in practice to influence the behaviour of the private sector by legislation (not least tax legislation) than they do that of supposedly State-controlled concerns. 'We have created industrial baronies not truly accountable to anyone – Parliament, Government, shareholders or the market place.'

But I concentrated more on the productivity and monopoly issues, speaking at a time when the rate of return on capital in the nationalized industries as a whole was negative. I was at the time particularly impressed by the findings of Richard Pryke, from whom I had commissioned an article when I was editor of the *Spectator* in 1966. He had just resigned from the Cabinet Office where he had worked under Tommy Balogh. He remained a champion of the nationalized industries in a book published as late as 1971. But he then began to develop doubts and, in the late 1970s, he brought out a fresh work which came to the conclusion that nationalized industries had performed less well than their private enterprise counterparts.

Nor was the failure due solely to the monopoly nature of some State industries. For Pryke also made a detailed study of three non-monopoly concerns – British Airways, British Rail sea ferries and the all-too-familiar appliance retailing outlets of British Gas and the Area Electricity Boards – which established that they had used capital and labour less effectively than their private counterparts, and were operating at a loss. The reasons Pryke gave for his findings remain fundamental. As I put it at Oxford, 'What public ownership does is to eliminate the threat of takeover and ultimately of bankruptcy, and the need, which all private undertakings have from time to time, to raise money from the market.'

The regulation of monopoly argument was, and is, perhaps the most insidious of all. For the belief that State ownership or regulation can be an effective substitute for competition leads governments to exaggerate the irreducible amount of natural monopoly and neglect ways of introducing competition. This brought me to what might be called the 'sub-text' of my speech, designed to answer the many faint-hearts in the Cabinet and Whitehall who believed that reforming public sector monopolies could be an alternative to privatizing them.

Most damaging of all was the inevitable *politicization* of nationalized industries. While governments find it hard to exercise strategic control over their industrial empire, the temptation to indulge in short-term interference in everything from prices and salaries to the placing of new plant in marginal constituencies is almost irresistible. The effect on nationalized industry management is equally bad: accommodating government or placating pressure groups becomes more important than commercial results.

Mules are not Zebras

At the time of my 1982 speech the nationalized industries accounted for over a tenth of total national output and more than a seventh of total fixed investment, and employed a workforce of some 1¾ million. For some private industries they were the only domestic customer; for some consumers the only suppliers. Yet no government, of either party, had found a satisfactory basis for running them. This was not for want of trying. 'The stream of White Papers, studies and reports has been unending,' I pointed out, 'Yet the problems have remained, more acute than ever.'

As my old friend Patrick Hutber used to say, you can no more make a State industry imitate private enterprise by telling it to follow textbook rules or to simulate competitive prices, than you can make a mule into a zebra by painting stripes on its back. There is no equivalent in the State sector to the discipline of the share price or the ever-present threat of bankruptcy. It is a commonplace of post-Communist economies that price reform is insufficient without introducing effective property rights to provide managers with an incentive to respond the right way. The same applies, albeit to a lesser degree, to the nationalized industries in Western mixed economies.

Of course, there are professional groups, such as doctors and academics, or members of the armed forces, who perform their tasks from a sense of vocation and not just for the financial rewards. This is excellent as far as it goes. But it is dangerous to press such non-profit motivation too far. A manager of a steel plant or an oil company needs much clearer day-to-day market signals to do his job effectively than does a surgeon or a musician. But, even in the non-profit-making sectors, as we have seen in education and health, it is important to have the right structure of incentives and rewards.

One of the key messages of my Oxford speech, directed in particular at my own colleagues, was that reform of the nationalized industries was no substitute for returning them to the private sector. One of the detailed reformist documents I had in mind was the Central Policy Review Staff (CPRS) report on the nationalized industries, commissioned by Margaret from its director Robin Ibbs and circulated in the summer of 1981. Its authors imagined that it was possible to transform the relationship between the Government and the nationalized industries. Its recommendations included defining strategic objectives for each nationalized industry; smaller boards dominated by outsiders; the establishment of 'Business Groups' within the sponsoring department headed by executives on secondment from the private sector; regular efficiency audits; and closer monitoring by government. This whole approach seemed to me to be fundamentally mistaken.

Only the Treasury exerted any external discipline over the nationalized industries, through its imposition of External Financing Limits (EFLs) in the annual spending round. The industries complained – with good cause – that the Treasury was obsessed with financial at the expense of commercial objectives. The sponsoring Departments for their part, always sensitive to the charge of surrendering to the Treasury, tended to side with their charges – something the 'Business Groups' proposal vainly was intended to cure.

The adoption of another of the CPRS recommendations demonstrated the limitations of trying to improve the efficiency of the nationalized industries without a change of ownership. At the beginning of 1982, the Treasury tried to formalize its relations with the nationalized industries by asking Departments to agree written policy objectives with them. These 'policy letters' would be signed by the Secretary of State and the chairmen of the industries for which he was responsible, and would be published by way of a written answer in Hansard.

Given the political sensitivity of nationalized industry spending and investment, however, this was easier said than done. In the case of coal, in particular, where pit closures could provoke a strike at any time, it was clearly dangerous to publish anything but the blandest list of overall objectives. The appointment of Norman Siddall to succeed Derek Ezra as Chairman of the Coal Board in the spring of 1982 provided an ideal opportunity to agree a policy letter with him, since its terms could be made a condition of the job. But the value of this exercise was somewhat limited by the need for the letter to take three forms: a list of general policy objectives, suitable for publication; an amplified version of the same, for private circulation; and a note of a frank meeting between Norman Siddall and myself, of which a single copy was kept locked in my office safe.

There were other unsatisfactory attempts to paint zebra stripes on the mule. The Westwell Report, a Conservative Party strategy document prepared in the winter of 1981, scarcely mentioned privatization at all despite the fact that it was drafted by John Hoskyns (head of the Number 10 Policy Unit), who continually stressed the need for Ministers to think strategically.

At an even earlier stage Leo Pliatzky, who had just retired from the public service as Permanent Secretary to the Department of Trade, was asked by the Government to formulate ideas on privatization. His report, produced in 1980 amid great secrecy, was not one of Pliatzky's happier efforts. He came up with two suggestions, each of them unsatisfactory. One was a single vast State holding company incorporating all the nationalized industries, shares in which could then be sold. The other was a new type of security, based on a French precedent, which was valued by capitalizing future revenue streams. This would have allowed the industries to raise fresh capital without the State relinquishing ownership, an idea which – for obvious reasons – attracted the Labour Party. As I minuted Geoffrey on 23 July 1980, both of Pliatzky's proposals would actually prevent true privatization; and I concluded that, 'The sole virtue of having conducted this study in such extraordinary secrecy seems to me to be the ability to drop the whole misbegotten idea without making any announcement whatsoever'. Which, in the event, is what happened.

In arguing the need to break up and genuinely privatize the large public utilities, I was originally in quite a small minority. Early efforts were directed at schemes to enable the nationalized public utilities to borrow directly from the public. The most notable example of this was the abortive 1982 plan for a British Telecom 'Buzby Bond'. The failure of these attempts to square the circle helped to swing Whitehall opinion behind privatization. I found it striking that the Treasury officials who worked in the Department's PE (Public Enterprise) division, whatever their political views and whatever the views on State-owned industries with which they had begun, nearly all ended up convinced that nationalization did not work and in practice was positively harmful.

Since the case for privatizing the so-called natural monopolies like gas, electricity and water is so rarely understood by the public and even by academics, I was subsequently driven to write a note to Nicholas Ridley in March 1989, in connection with water privatization, summarizing the case in terms which applied beyond water:

> 1. All experience shows that businesses are more efficient and successful in the private than in the public sector;
> 2. The water and sewerage industry is a business like any other;
> 3. A quarter of the industry is already in the private sector;
> 4. Of course it will need regulation – to protect the consumer as it is a natural monopoly and for environmental reasons (purity of water etc.) – but it is far better for the State's responsibility to be clearly

confined to that of regulator rather than to have the existing conflict of interest when it is both regulator and producer;

5. Even though water is a natural monopoly, the privatized water industry will still face (a) competition for capital in the private sector, and (b) a published daily share price – a comment on performance and a powerful spur to management.

6. Privatization not only widens share ownership (desirable in itself) but increases employee share ownership, which previous privatizations show leads to further improved performance.

Nick was, of course, totally committed to water privatization. But the arguments that he and his number two, Michael Howard, were then using to try to convince a hostile parliamentary and public opinion did not, in my judgement, get to the heart of the matter.

Wider Ownership

Although the primary aim of the privatization programme was to improve the performance of the former State-owned industries, there was a substantial spill-over benefit in the opportunities it provided for widening share ownership.

The references in Geoffrey Howe's first Budget Speech to 'the widest possible participation by the people in the ownership of British industry' was, of course, an extension of the Tory theme, central at least since Anthony Eden's day, of the creation of a property-owning democracy – which had hitherto been interpreted almost exclusively in terms of home-ownership.

I spelt out some of the reasons at the first Maurice Macmillan Memorial Lecture which I gave in June 1985:

> Those who, in the nineteenth century, argued the dangers of a mass democracy in which a majority of the voters would have no stake in the country at all, had reason to be fearful. But the remedy is not to restrict the franchise to those who own property: it is to extend the ownership of property to the largest possible majority of those who have the vote. The widespread ownership of private property is crucial to the survival of freedom and democracy. It gives the citizen a vital sense of identification with the society of which he is a part. It gives him a stake in the future – and indeed, equally important, in the present. It creates a society with an inbuilt resistance to revolutionary change.

Giving details of the decline of individual share ownership and the drift towards the institutions, I went on to remark:

Institutional investors are certainly powerful. But I give away few political secrets when I say that Governments are likely to be more concerned by the prospect of alienating a mass of individual shareholders
than they are by the lobbying of half a dozen investment managers.

The Thatcher Government introduced a number of measures to encourage share ownership. During the time of the Lib-Lab pact, the
Liberals had obliged Denis Healey to provide incentives for employee
shareholding in his 1978 Budget, and these were extended by Geoffrey
Howe in 1980 and further improved in subsequent Budgets. In 1982
Geoffrey indexed Capital Gains Tax to eliminate the taxation of future
inflationary gains. In my 1984 Budget I greatly improved the tax treatment of share options and halved the Stamp Duty on share purchase,
halving it again in 1986, prior to the eventual abolition promised by
John Major in his 1990 Budget. And in my 1986 Budget I introduced
Personal Equity Plans (PEPs).

But in practice the biggest boost was provided by privatization. Many
commentators made the wholly erroneous assumption that, since I was
a Treasury Minister, my interest in privatization could only be in the
proceeds, and my only policy the maximization of the proceeds. In fact
the Treasury was always on the side of introducing competition and a
tough regulatory regime where no competition was practicable, despite
that fact that either would reduce proceeds. There was no difference here
between officials and myself. What *is* true is that I believed in selling the
shares rather than in literally giving them away, a superficially attractive
policy that bristles with practical difficulties.

In fact no-one was keener than I to achieve the widest possible
distribution of shares in the privatized businesses both to small shareholders in general and to their employees in particular, who in most
cases were able to acquire shares on favourable terms. The most spectacular case of employee share ownership occurred in the relatively
modest privatization of National Freight in early 1982 where there was
a management-worker buy-out, suggested by the management and welcomed by Norman Fowler, then Transport Secretary. But even in the
larger flotations employee shares were invariably a major feature. In
the case of British Telecom (BT) no fewer than 96 per cent of the
eligible work-force took up shares: the average was 90 per cent. The
proportion of the adult population owning shares rose from 7 per cent
in 1979 to 25 per cent ten years later. This was not enough to reverse
the long-term decline in the proportion of shares held by private individuals rather than institutions – a worldwide trend – but it remains a
change of the first importance.

In addition to its many objective virtues, there was also a clear political
motive behind promoting the wider share ownership of the privatized

companies. For the more widely the shares were spread, the more people who had a personal stake in privatization, and were thus unlikely to support a Labour Party committed to renationalization. And if this forced Labour to abandon its commitment to renationalization, so much the better. For our objective was, so far as practically possible, to make the transfer of these businesses to the private sector irreversible.

A Low-key Start

Because of its responsibility for public finance, and because it had been specifically given the task by Margaret Thatcher, the Treasury was the lead department in charge of co-ordinating the whole privatization programme. When I was made Financial Secretary in 1979, I persuaded Geoffrey Howe to give me privatization as a specific delegated responsibility which has remained with the Financial Secretary ever since. Later, as Energy Secretary, I pushed through the privatization of Britoil, the former British National Oil Company (BNOC), at that time (1982) the largest privatization the world had ever known; and of course on becoming Chancellor in 1983, I was automatically in overall charge of the entire privatization programme. But it was while I was at Energy, with direct responsibility for more major nationalized industries than any other Minister, that I was able to give the greatest proportion of my time to the subject; and it is convenient to deal with it in this section of the book.

Initially it proved something of a struggle to get the privatization programme off the ground. David Howell was invited by the Treasury to submit plans for the sale of parts of the British Gas Corporation and the British National Oil Corporation (BNOC) nearly three weeks before the 1979 Budget. But obstacles developed. We eventually raised just under £1 billion from asset sales in 1979–80, although in a somewhat curious way, most of it coming from forward sales of BNOC oil. But there were also a number of small-scale sales, including the Government's minority holding in the Suez Finance Company (the successor to the old Suez Canal Company), various motorway service stations, and a mixed bag of assets owned by bodies such as the Water Authorities, the New Town Corporations and the National Enterprise Board.

In the following two financial years, 1980–81 and 1981–82, the scale of privatization was relatively modest, not least because the original plan to privatize British Airways, the legislation for which was on the statute-book by November 1980, had to be shelved because of the world recession. Even so, we managed to privatize some well-known firms which should never have been in the State sector. The principal public flotations during those two years were Cable & Wireless, British Aerospace, and Amersham International. In addition, Fairey Engineering, Ferranti, National Freight, International Aeradio and British Rail Hotels were sold.

These were concerns already operating in competitive markets. When I became Energy Secretary in September 1981, I found myself directly responsible for a larger industrial empire and was able to take action myself to get the privatization programme moving faster. My announcement in October 1981 of the privatization of the oil-producing assets of both BNOC and British Gas amounted to a substantial extension of the established programme of privatizing State-owned sections of the enterprises. But I became increasingly convinced of the merits of taking privatizations beyond the competitive sector into the realm of the giant monopoly public utilities. For me, this meant the privatization of British Gas and the entire electricity supply industry, the two main State-owned monopolies supervised by the Energy Department.

Among these early privatizations, the Energy Department had responsibility for Amersham International. This was an interesting little company, which was in the State sector simply because it had, under the name of the Radiochemical Centre, been a spin-off from the government nuclear research establishment, the Atomic Energy Authority. Its business was the manufacture of radioactive isotopes for use in medicine, a field in which the only other company of any significance in the world was by that time a wholly-owned subsidiary of the US chemical-based giant, DuPont. This sale, supervised by John Moore, was already at an advanced stage when I became Energy Secretary and the only important issue that remained to be decided was the pricing.

Nicholas Ridley, who had succeeded me as Financial Secretary to the Treasury, had wanted to offer the shares for sale not at a fixed price, as is customary in the UK, but by auction (technically known as the tender method). I had no objection in principle to the idea, having pioneered the issue of gilt-edged stock by tender when I was Financial Secretary myself, and Amersham, as the only company in its field, was unusually difficult to price. But I was anxious to use the issue to promote wider share ownership, and I had little doubt that this required a fixed-price offer, since small shareholders would have no idea what to bid in an auction and would be put off altogether. The advisers to the Amersham sale – Rothschilds advising the Government and Morgan Grenfell advising the company – were also divided on the matter. Nick and I agreed that the only way to resolve the matter was to invite Geoffrey Howe, as Chancellor, to adjudicate; and a meeting was arranged at Number 11 between the three of us. To Nick's amazement and disgust, Geoffrey – after having us put the respective cases – came down in favour of a fixed-price offer.

Since it is impossible to predict with any great precision either the demand for a new share issue or still less the state of the market when dealings in it begin (normally at least a fortnight after the offer price has been agreed with the underwriters of the issue) it is more a matter of luck than of judgement if the fixed price for any new issue turns out to be exactly right. Thus fixed-price issues invariably prove to be either underpriced or overpriced. In the latter case, when the bulk of the shares are left with the underwriters, the issue is always described in the financial Press as a 'flop', whereas the former case, when the issue is oversubscribed and goes to a premium, is described as a 'success'. There is thus a general tendency for issues to be deliberately slightly underpriced.

Unfortunately, in the case of Amersham, the merchant bank advisers who fixed the price – in those early days we did not equip ourselves, as we did later, with an independent adviser on pricing – overdid the underpricing by an embarrassingly wide margin. As a result, the £71 million issue was no less than twenty-four times oversubscribed, and shot to a premium of some 35 per cent when dealings began. This led to an enormous political storm, with Labour accusing the Government of ripping off the taxpayer and deliberately selling state assets on the cheap to its friends in the City. Nick Ridley understandably felt wholly vindicated, and I was acutely embarrassed. I felt obliged to announce an inquiry into what had gone wrong – not that there was any mystery about it.

In retrospect, the serious underpricing of Amersham, although in no sense deliberate, may have been no bad thing. The enormous publicity given to the profits enjoyed by subscribers to the issue conveyed the clear message to the general public that investing in privatization issues was a good thing. As for the general question of fixed price versus tender, it is significant that experience has led the Government to make fixed-price offers the norm for its privatization issues. But at the time I felt deeply humiliated, and resolved that the next privatization for which I was responsible, namely Britoil, would have to be a tender. Whatever happened, I could not afford a second Amersham.

CHAPTER 19

PRIVATIZATION – 2
THE BIRTH OF POPULAR CAPITALISM

*A Vector Quality · Showdown in the Showrooms
Compressing British Gas · No 'People's Stake'
BNOC into Britoil · The British Telecom Breakthrough*

A Vector Quality

ON 19 OCTOBER 1981, IN my first appearance as Energy Secretary, I announced to a surprised House of Commons the privatization of the entire oil-producing businesses of both BNOC and the British Gas Corporation, and subsequently other parts of British Gas, together with the removal of the Corporation's 'unique statutory rights over the purchase of gas and its sale to the industry in particular' and the conversion of its pipeline network into a common carrier. To maximize the dramatic effect, I had kept the announcement deliberately brief. I was able to expand on it, and indeed to make a good part of my aborted Party Conference Speech, in the Debate on the Address the following month.

My November speech contained two declarations which set the tone for the approach to privatization that I was to pursue throughout my time in Government. The first was the general slogan: 'The Conservative Party has never believed that the business of government is the government of business.' The second drew the inescapable conclusion: 'No industry should remain under State ownership unless there is a positive and overwhelming case for it so doing. Inertia is not enough. As a nation we simply cannot afford it.'

Meanwhile, my October announcement had pleased our own side and plunged the Labour Party into one of its customary frenzies. Replying for the Opposition, Merlyn Rees, then Shadow Energy Secretary, committed a future Labour Government to renationalize the oil assets at the sale price, presumably in part a vain attempt to frustrate the privatization, although it had of course to be prominently recorded in the prospectus. Even this did not go far enough for Tony Benn, the former Energy Secretary, then seeking to reshape the Labour Party in his own image, who threatened to renationalize the industry without any compensation at all. Apparently Benn's departure from the Party line provoked a resignation threat from Rees. The Conservative benches had been on the defensive for so long over unemployment and the economy that they were hugely cheered by Labour's obvious discomfiture.

The Bill to give my proposal legislative effect was published on 17 December 1981. At its heart was the biggest privatization hitherto attempted, anywhere in the world. I had originally sought two Bills in the 1981–82 session, one to deal with BNOC and the other with the British Gas Corporation, but Cabinet ruled that there was legislative time only for one, and I was obliged to put both sets of measures into a single Bill – which I was more than content to do.

I also had problems over the title of the Bill. David Howell had published in February 1981 what turned out to be his legacy to me, for which I was grateful: a Bill to deal with BNOC, though not as radically as I had in mind, entitled the Petroleum and Continental Shelf Bill. That scarcely set the pulse racing, but now I had to tack on to the title something about gas. I decided to start again and call it the Oil and Gas Enterprise Bill, making the most of the dual meaning of 'Enterprise'. I naïvely thought that would be that, but the chief Parliamentary draftsman declared it to be unacceptable. It had, he explained, a 'vector quality' - a euphemism, I took it, for being too political – and suggested instead the Petroleum, Gas and Offshore Licensing Amendment Bill.

There was certainly no 'vector quality' in that, but no meeting of minds, either. He insisted that he would have to draw the matter to the attention of the Lord Chancellor, Quintin Hailsham. When I subsequently took the Bill to the Legislation Committee of Cabinet, with its title still not agreed, I expected Quintin to raise the matter, but he failed to do so. Instead, as we left the room, he took my arm and said 'I hear you have been annoying Parliamentary Counsel'. I feared an explosion, but he went on, with a chuckle: 'I am wholly in favour of anything that annoys Parliamentary Counsel'. Finally, a further meeting with the Chief Parliamentary draftsman produced a masterly compromise. The Bill would indeed be called the Oil and Gas (Enterprise) Bill but the word 'Enterprise' would have to be in brackets. Thus bracketed, the Oil and Gas (Enterprise) Act reached the statute-book on 28 June 1982.

Showdown in the Showrooms

The privatization of Britoil was controversial enough, but initially, at least, the hottest political potato was the Government's earlier decision to privatize the British Gas Corporation's showrooms, opposition to which was exploited for all it was worth by the Corporation's Chairman, Denis Rooke.

The decision to sell the gas showrooms had followed the publication the previous year of a Monopolies Commission report on British Gas commissioned by the Labour Government. This found that the Corporation's monopoly of the supply of domestic gas appliances had reduced competition, raised prices and inhibited exports. Sally Oppenheim, the Minister at the Department of Trade with special responsibility for competition and consumer affairs, quite reasonably responded by securing colleagues' approval to a proposal to sell off the 900 gas showrooms over a five-year period starting in 1983. This was duly announced on 8 July 1981, shortly before I took over at Energy.

Few of us realized what a storm would be unleashed over what could scarcely be called one of the commanding heights of the economy. The Labour Party and the gas trade unions, encouraged by Denis Rooke who was incensed by the idea of losing any part of his empire, were up in arms. Even some of our own back-benchers were deeply unhappy. The Government's opponents were remarkably successful in portraying the privatization of this state-owned chain of shops, so damningly reported on by the independent Monopolies Commission, as an ideologically inspired attack on the British way of life. The heart of every community, it seemed, was neither the church nor the pub, but the local gas showroom.

This seemed to me a case for *reculer pour mieux sauter*. The much more far-reaching proposals of my October announcement enabled me to shelve the sale of the gas showrooms without egg on my face. I was also able to use the perfectly legitimate excuse that a showroom sale would have to wait on new safety legislation, for which there was at present no parliamentary time. But one way or another, I was determined to speed up rather than slow down the pace of privatization.

Compressing British Gas

For most of my period at the Department of Energy, Denis Rooke was my most formidable opponent. A large, craggy, overbearing, man, he has been described by normally reticent retired senior Civil Servants in language that I cannot reproduce in a book designed for family reading. He dominated British Gas and regarded the Energy Department as the principal obstacle to his plans for the gas industry, and indeed for the economy as a whole, treating Ministers and officials alike with a mixture of distrust, dislike and contempt. David Howell had unaccountably missed the only opportunity to replace him when his contract came up for renewal in 1980; so I was stuck with him.

Rooke had entered the gas industry in the 1950s when it was moribund, and he had seen it transformed from the Cinderella of the energy market into the most popular source of domestic power. He had personally played a large part in the important and successful switch from coal-based 'town' gas to natural gas from the North Sea. To break the Corporation up in any way was a negation of his life's work, and he opposed efforts to do so at every turn. He had been greatly impressed by the resourcefulness of the gas unions in opposing the showroom sale, and did nothing to discourage them from seeking to frustrate the Government's latest plans.

I tried to outflank him by appealing over his head to his Board of Directors, with whom power technically· resided; and in December 1981 I called a meeting of the entire Gas Corporation Board at the Department to see if any of them were amenable to reason; but they appeared to be quite overawed by Rooke. After that meeting I decided to make some changes on the Board. I appointed Martin Jacomb, then vice-chairman of the merchant bank Kleinwort Benson, Leslie Smith, then Chairman of British Oxygen (BOC), and Derek Birkin, now Chairman of RTZ, as non-executive directors. These three emminent businessmen could not be pushed around by anyone. They also kept me better informed than my officials were usually able to do.

Although there was no reason for British Gas to be in the oil business at all, it had acquired substantial minority stakes in a number of North Sea oil fields and a half share in Britain's biggest onshore oilfield, at Wytch Farm in Dorset, which it had discovered, but which was operated by the owner of the other half share, BP. David Howell, using his powers under the Heath Government's Gas Act of 1972, had required British Gas to dispose of its interest in Wytch Farm in June 1981. Rooke did everything he could to resist, but I persisted. It was obviously impossible to float Wytch Farm as a separate entity on the stock market, so the Department held an auction. Although a number of companies and consortia were interested, the outcome was most unsatisfactory.

The detailed information about Wytch Farm, which potential bidders required in order to decide whether and how much to bid, had to be supplied by British Gas; and extracting this proved very much more difficult than extracting the gas itself. As a result, when the auction closed, the prices offered were so low that I could not have justified the acceptance of any of the offers to the Public Accounts Committee.

Undeterred, I invited all the bidders to reconsider their offers, but not before I had acquired more adequate information from British Gas. On 30 March 1983, I called the entire Gas Corporation Board to the Department to complain about what had been going on, which I documented in detail. Several directors expressed considerable surprise and concern when they discovered what had been happening. Wytch Farm was not finally sold until well after I had left the Department.

Rooke was scarcely more co-operative during the preparation for the privatization of British Gas's offshore oil interests. These eventually became Enterprise Oil, which was floated on the Stock Exchange in June 1984, and named after the Act which had made its privatization possible. Thanks to Rooke's foot-dragging, I was just about to sign the instruction to him, under the terms of the Oil and Gas (Enterprise) Act, to dispose of the oil assets when the 1983 election was called. Constitutional propriety required that any further action be delayed until the outcome of the election was known.

Rooke clearly hoped that the election would bring a more compliant Secretary of State, but I was determined to have the last word if I possibly could. I therefore signed the letter to enforce the disposal before leaving the Department for the campaign trail, and gave it to Julian West, my private secretary, for safekeeping, with instructions to destroy it if we lost the election, but to send it on, on receipt of a telephone call from me, if we won. I duly telephoned him the day after the election, and the letter was sent. It turned out to be my last act as Energy Secretary: the following day I became Chancellor of the Exchequer.

My successor as Energy Secretary was Peter Walker, whose views on the privatization of British Gas were as different from mine as was his attitude on most other issues. Indeed, my former officials told me it was almost as if there had been a change of Government at Thames House.

After the election Margaret held a series of meetings at Number 10 to agree on the best way of privatizing British Gas. My strong preference was to break up the corporation both regionally and into separate gas and appliance businesses before privatizing it. It would have reduced the proceeds of the sale, but I judged competition a more important consid- eration than maximizing government revenue. Peter was totally opposed to anything of the kind. As he records in his autobiography, he maintained that 'The breaking up of the corporation was lunacy . . . I wanted a powerful British company which could compete around the world.'

This, of course, precisely echoed the views of Rooke, who was vehe- mently opposed to the dismantling of the corporation, and whom Walker describes as 'the best nationalized industry chairman I have met'. Rooke had originally been passionate in his opposition to gas privatization in any shape or form. It was only later, when it became clear that the Government was determined to privatize British Gas, that he fell back on his second line of defence: his insistence on the retention, intact, of the existing monopolistic and integrated gas industry.

Meeting followed meeting; but despite Margaret's support for the competitive route, we were getting nowhere. Meanwhile, time was running out. Eventually, after yet another wasted meeting I asked Peter to come next door with me to Number 11: I had a suggestion to make. I told him that I would agree to privatization *en bloc* provided he undertook to go ahead post haste with the privatization of British Gas without further ado. He promised to do so, feeling that he had won a great victory. When, at the next Number 10 meeting, Margaret learned of the deal, she no doubt felt I had gone soft, however relieved she was that the problem had been resolved. But I reckoned that this had become the only way privatization would occur during the lifetime of that Parliament.

As it was clear that Margaret was not prepared to move Peter, which would have been the only way around the impasse, I would have to rely on the regulatory authority, after privatization, to introduce competition. This was to be the Office of Gas Supply (Ofgas), with a regulatory regime based on that devised for British Telecom and described later in this chapter, except that the price control based on the formula $RPI - x + y$, where y represented the world oil price. (As for x, this was to rise from 2 per cent at the outset to 5 per cent in 1991.) But its remit would extend far beyond the relatively simple matter of price control. There is still much to play for.

No 'People's Stake'

But to return to my time as Energy Secretary. Far and away the most important privatization I secured during that time was that of BNOC. This had been set up by the Labour Government in 1976 to explore for, produce, refine and distribute oil from the North Sea. It accounted for some 7 per cent of total North Sea oil production. It also had the right, by a system of participation agreements, to buy up to 51 per cent of all UK North Sea oil, whoever produced it, and bring it onshore. This gave BNOC a predominant position in the purchase and trading of North Sea oil, even though nine tenths of it was produced by private sector companies, and in practice the BNOC offer price was, not surprisingly, kept close to the world market price. The Corporation was also equipped with an extensive list of privileges. It was exempt from Petroleum Revenue Tax, guaranteed access to interest-free funds, and enjoyed preferential rights in the licensing of new oil fields. It was also, along with British Gas, guaranteed the right of first refusal of any North Sea assets sold to third parties by private companies. This combination of preferential treatment and tax-subsidized competition had deterred some exploration and development by the private sector.

The 1979 manifesto promised to review all of BNOC's activities. The Corporation was made liable to PRT in Geoffrey's first Budget; and it was progressively stripped of most of its other privileges. It should really have been privatized well before I became Energy Secretary; but at the time such a radical step seemed fraught with political difficulties. It had an articulate Chairman and Board who were wholly opposed to privatization. But the main constraint was presentational.

The usual lack of enthusiasm for State ownership was reinforced in the public mind by the feeling that North Sea oil was a unique national asset which should remain strictly under national political control. Despite the fact that the private sector already accounted for the vast bulk of North Sea oil output, it was difficult to find a way of privatizing BNOC without succumbing to the charge that the Government was relinquishing ownership of a priceless national treasure to speculators, foreigners or multinationals. Indeed the main reason for David Howell's hesitancy was Margaret's acute sensitivity that privatization of BNOC's operating arm implied that Britain would somehow lose control of part of her oil. She rejected a number of BNOC privatization options on these grounds at an important meeting of the Economic Committee of the Cabinet in March 1980.

Prevented by Margaret from mounting a full frontal assault, David Howell had concentrated his efforts on preparing the ground by installing a pro-privatization chairman, Philip Shelbourne, with a City background – and, somewhat less constructively, on abortive plans for a so-called 'People's Stake' in North Sea oil. There have, of course, been various plans to hand over 'free' to all citizens a tradeable security entitling them to either all or part of government North Sea oil revenues, and – a completely separate proposal – to make a free gift of BNOC and other privatization shares to all citizens instead of selling them for cash. Because the word 'oil' occurred in both, the two proposals were frequently confused. The first idea was put forward by Samuel Brittan and Barry Riley of the *Financial Times* and the second by Samuel Brittan on his own. The first idea had nothing to do with BNOC, and the second would have applied to all privatization issues. Moreover the first idea, although the more ingenious of the two, failed to address the issue of the ownership of BNOC.

Whatever may be necessary in ex-Communist countries which need to privatize a large proportion of their industry rapidly in the face of a barely existing domestic capital market, the give-away idea had no real supporters in the Thatcher Government, least of all me, as I made clear to Samuel Brittan from the beginning. The reason was put very succinctly two centuries ago by Thomas Paine, the author of *Rights of Man* and hardly a right-wing figure: 'What we obtain too cheap, we esteem too lightly.' David Howell's idea, however, which he launched with a great fanfare in his speech at the 1980 Party Conference, was neither of these. What it amounted to was in effect a National Savings Certificate whose return would be linked to the value of Britain's North Sea oil output. Although a fair amount of work was done on it, I must confess that I could see little merit in it. As I argued at the time, there is no substitute, either industrially or politically, for full-blooded privatization.

BNOC into Britoil

The putative North Sea oil bond died a natural death. On becoming Energy Secretary I decided that the political damage Margaret feared could be minimized if BNOC were split in two, with the exploration and production business, where the value was, privatized, and the trading business, together with the participation agreements on which it was based, remaining for the time being at least in the State sector.

Assembling the best official team the Department could provide, led by an exceptionally able Under Secretary, Richard Wilson (he subsequently became Deputy Cabinet Secretary, and later Permanent Secretary of the Department of the Environment), I set to work to direct the separation of the oil assets from the trading arm of BNOC, the preparation of a suitably capitalized Britoil balance sheet and the writing of a prospectus. The name 'Britoil' was not in fact my choice. I would have preferred 'British North Sea Oil', but Philip Shelbourne was wedded to 'Britoil' since he wanted to convert it, post-privatization, to a global oil company rather than one confined to the North Sea. This he eventually did, to some extent, via a series of purchases which failed either to strengthen the company, or to impress the markets, and left it vulnerable to the takeover which a few years later occurred (see Chapter 62).

In preparing Britoil for privatization, ministers and officials alike were in uncharted territory. Even though we chose to sell only 51 per cent of the company in the first instance, it was still the biggest transfer of assets from the state to the private sector yet attempted. When we began work in the autumn of 1981, the Government's experience of privatization consisted of 51 per cent of British Aerospace and Cable and Wireless, neither of which sales exceeded £300 million in value, whereas 51 per cent of Britoil was worth around twice that amount. Moreover both British Aerospace and Cable and Wireless were straightforward Companies Act companies – as was Amersham International, whose bitter-sweet flotation preceded the Britoil offer for sale, whereas BNOC was a fully-fledged Morrisonian public corporation. The sheer size of the issue was also felt to be somewhat daunting. Both the Bank of England and Warburgs, the Department's financial advisers, were deeply worried that the equity market would be unable to absorb such a large amount of stock, especially in view of the campaign of vilification which preceded the sale.

Part of that vilification was caused by the fear that, once privatized, the company would fall into foreign hands; and it became politically imperative to find an answer to this. I recalled from my brief time as 'Lex', the stock market columnist of the *Financial Times*, in 1959–60, the curious voting structures I had occasionally come across (and invariably inveighed against), which enabled the owners of a very small slice of the equity to exercise quite disproportionate power. Inspired by this, I devised the so-called 'golden share', a special share which would be retained by the Government after privatization, and which would enable it to prevent control of the company from falling into unsuitable hands. (The term 'unsuitable' had to be used, rather than 'foreign', to avoid falling foul of Community law; but everyone knew what it was likely to mean.)

The 'golden share' has since become a standard feature in privatization issues, but in the early days both Philip Shelbourne and Rothschilds, whom he had brought in as advisers to BNOC, maintained that shackles of any sort on a free market in the shares of the privatized company would make the flotation more difficult. In this they were mistaken. However, we did not get the precise design of the Britoil golden share right, which was to prove awkward later on; but the details could be and were amended in subsequent privatizations: it was the concept that mattered.

The Labour Party inevitably made the Oil and Gas (Enterprise) Bill the focal point of their parliamentary opposition that session, obliging me to ask the business managers to introduce a guillotine motion, putting a limit to the time available for debate, in March 1982. The Press, too, as with most subsequent privatizations, was largely hostile, right up to the launch. So at the start, were many of our own back-benchers.

But the political difficulties were at least familiar ones: not so the technical problems that had to be overcome. Being a public corporation, it had first to be converted into a Companies Act company, and given an appropriate balance sheet. This was eventually achieved, not without a prolonged argument with Philip Shelbourne, who wished the new company to carry no debt at all on its books. I was less successful in my search for a high flyer from the oil industry to appoint as Chief Executive of Britoil – partly because of Labour's renationalization pledge. In the end I had to give up the search, as time was running out, and had to content myself with persuading BNOC's senior oilman to delay his impending retirement, and appointing three heavyweight non-executive directors whose clear remit was to find a new Chief Executive as soon as possible after privatization.

The biggest technical problem of all, however, was devising a wholly new method of sale. Following the Amersham affair, I had decided that Britoil would be not a fixed-price offer but a tender, which would be underwritten at the minimum tender price. Both Shelbourne and Rothschilds, the company's financial advisers, were opposed to this unfamiliar technique. But Warburgs, the Department's financial advisers, considered it a perfectly viable proposition, and with Margaret's full concurrence we set to work to devise a novel form of tender designed to avoid the danger, which had led me to oppose the tender for Amersham, of deterring the small investor.

What we came up with was a tender in which anyone who applied for shares, if they were uncertain as to what price to bid, could simply write in the box the words 'striking price' – which meant that they undertook to subscribe for the shares at whatever price emerged from the tender process. The application form itself was completely redesigned to make it simpler and clearer than in any previous share offer, whether by the Government or the private sector; and the fact that payment was by instalments, with the first instalment set at a fixed price, meant that despite the tender the investor knew exactly what cheque to send with his application. Finally, to encourage the genuine small shareholder, as against the 'stag' who applied in the hope of selling at a quick profit as soon as dealings in the shares commenced, I introduced (in addition to the employee share scheme customary in privatization issues) a 'small shareholder bonus', under which any small shareholder who retained his shares for three years would receive an additional allocation of shares, on a one-for-ten basis, free.

I finally agreed the minimum price for the tender with David Scholey, Warburg's Chairman, in early November 1982, after consulting Dundas Hamilton, a distinguished stockbroker whose firm had no connection with the issue, and whom I had formally appointed the Government's independent adviser on pricing. This was the first time this appointment, which was to be repeated in most of the subsequent large privatizations, had been made. It was, quite simply, designed to provide an extra line of defence against a possible investigation by the parliamentary watchdog, the Public Accounts Committee (PAC), the most powerful of all the select committees, which was by this time becoming restive at the apparent underpricing of privatization issues and consequent loss to the taxpayer.

On 10 November the underwriting of the issue was quickly and successfully completed. That night I said to my weary officials, 'Well done. Whatever happens now, Britoil has been privatized.' What did happen then, however, was something wholly unexpected. Over the critical weekend before the closing date for applications for the issue a fortnight later, Sheikh Yamani, the Saudi Oil Minister, then at the height of his power and prestige, gave an interview to an obscure Kuwaiti newspaper in which he expressed gloom about the future course of the price of oil. This was soon all over the wires. The oil price duly dipped, and sentiment about the Britoil flotation abruptly deteriorated. The issue was badly undersubscribed, with the underwriters being left with some

70 per cent of the shares, and dealings opened at a marked discount. In standard City parlance, the issue was 'a flop'.

But it was certainly no disaster. My old friend Godfrey Chandler, of Cazenoves, than whom there is no wiser observer of the City scene, wrote to me aptly describing the issue as 'a successful disappointment'. Britoil had been privatized. The momentum of the Government's overall privatization programme was in no way impeded. Although the tender method used for the sale had not been the cause of the undersubscription, it had certainly not helped, and fixed-price offers, or some variant of them, became accepted as the norm for future privatizations. There was one further silver lining to this particular cloud. The PAC, in its scrutiny of privatization, had been developing the theory that it was wholly unnecessary for the Government to have its share sales underwritten – influenced to some extent by Labour claims that this was simply a way in which the Tories lined the pockets of their friends in the City. After Britoil, little more was heard from the PAC of this canard.

Of the remaining 49 per cent of Britoil, one per cent had to be retained to distribute to those qualifying for the small shareholder bonus, and the other 48 per cent was disposed of in a successful offer for sale to the general public in August 1985. By that time all the political agitation had abated, and it was no longer necessary to pay lip-service to the idea that Britain's oil security depended on the state retaining the rump of BNOC as a trading arm. Peter Walker, with my support, initially merged it with the Government's long-standing strategic pipeline system to form the Oil and Pipeline Agency (OPA). In due course the oil trading operation, which was nothing but an intermittently embarrassing (and potentially costly) irrelevance, was quietly abandoned.

The British Telecom Breakthrough

With the transfer of Britoil to the private sector, the privatization programme was now gathering pace. But the cause of wider share ownership had yet to be greatly advanced. Britoil, even without Yamani's ill-timed (and some thought deliberate) intervention, was in any case not the right vehicle for the breakthrough. The general public are interested primarily in holding shares in companies they know and of which they are regular customers. The ideal vehicle was now at hand, in the shape of the telephone giant, British Telecom.

This had emerged through a number of stages. Originally, both the post office and the telephone system were, anomalously, a single government department staffed by Civil Servants and headed by a Minister known as the Postmaster General. The Wilson Labour Government of the 1960s, prompted by the then head of the Civil Service, William Armstrong, had separated them and converted them into two Morrisonian public corporations.

Shortly after we returned to office in 1979 Keith Joseph, as Industry Secretary, energetically set about breaking the British Telecom monopoly by fostering the birth of a partial competitor, Mercury Communications, owned principally by the newly privatized Cable and Wireless. Then, in 1982, his successor at Industry, Patrick Jenkin, announced that British Telecom was to be privatized. A Bill was duly introduced, but it had not completed its passage when the 1983 general election was called, and it was reintroduced in the subsequent parliament by the new Secretary of State for the (once again) merged Department of Trade and Industry, Norman Tebbit.

The length of time all this took was not wasted. When we first examined the nationalized British Telecom we discovered that, in true East European style, the corporation had not the faintest idea which of its activities were profitable and which were not, let alone any finer points of management accounting. All this clearly had to be changed. A new Chairman, George Jefferson, was brought in from the private sector and charged with the task of putting this right and otherwise preparing the corporation for privatization.

Our original preference had been to split up British Telecom so as to increase the competition in this fast-growing and capital-hungry industry which the birth of Mercury had begun. But Jefferson was insistent that his empire should remain intact. As it was, the trade unions representing its work-force – like all nationalized industries, it was totally unionized – were bitterly opposed to privatization and were making all manner of threatening noises. We felt that we could scarcely afford to have the management against us as well, if we were to achieve a successful privatization.

But the sale of even 51 per cent of British Telecom as a single entity meant a flotation far larger than any that had previously been contemplated. I vividly recall a small private dinner party held in the penthouse suite of the Dorchester Hotel by Kenneth Corfield, then Chairman of Standard Telephones and Cables (STC) in honour of the unusually named American, Rand Araskog, Chairman of the US telephone monopoly, ITT, which was about to be broken up under US anti-trust legislation.

Araskog naturally showed an interest in our plans for British Telecom, and views were sought from those present, who, myself apart, were all captains of industry and pillars of leading City merchant banks. With the exception of Martin Jacomb from Kleinworts, which had been retained by the Government to advise on the sale, each and every one of them roundly declared that the privatization was impossible: the capital market simply was not large enough to absorb it.

Needless to say, we went ahead, with Norman Tebbit in the lead, until he was severely injured by the IRA bomb which caused such devastation at the Grand Hotel, Brighton, during the Conservative Party Conference of October 1984. As Chancellor, I then took over for the last lap, and British Telecom was privatized by means of a fixed-price offer for sale in November 1984.

The final discussions involved, among other things, the regulatory regime that was to be put in place. This again was breaking new ground: British Telecom was the first more or less monopoly public utility to be privatized, and such animals clearly cannot be permitted to exploit that position. An independent state-owned agency, the Office of Telecommunications (Oftel) was set up to oversee the industry; and the key element in the regime was the rule that the company could increase its charges each year by no more than RPI-x; representing the rate of inflation for the previous year less a percentage designed to reflect the industry's scope for increasing efficiency. This formula, which had been devised by Professor Stephen Littlechild, was originally envisaged as a rough-and-ready short-term solution to the problem; but in practice it has endured and been used as the basis of the regulatory regimes for all the privatized public utilities.

It is undoubtedly greatly superior to the system used in the United States, the home of privately owned public utilities, where the regulatory regime is based on limiting the permitted return on capital, which inevitably leads to the inflation of costs of all kinds. By contrast, the price-based UK system means that the utilities can increase their profits only by reducing their costs. In the case of British Telecom, there was a major argument as to how big the x-factor should be, with the company (supported by Norman Tebbit) arguing for 2 per cent, while I wanted 4 per cent. Inevitably, we eventually compromised on 3 per cent. Since then, under the watchful guidance of the regulator, the x-factor has steadily risen, and has been set at 7½ per cent for 1993, implying a significant price reduction.

Another innovation of the Telecom privatization – and once again something hitherto unknown to the City – was the launch of a two-stage advertising campaign, particularly on television, designed to stimulate public interest in the share sale. Prior to the offer, this took the form of intensified corporate advertising; once the offer was launched, it advertised the offer itself – without, of course, going so far as to advise people to buy the shares.

The outcome of the offer for sale in November 1984 was a success that not only confounded our critics but exceeded even our own expectations. The price valued the total sale at almost £4 billion, to be paid in instalments over two financial years. It was comfortably oversubscribed. By tilting the allocation of shares in favour of the small investor we succeeded in almost doubling the number of Britons who owned shares overnight. Altogether some two million people, or 5 per cent of the adult population of the United Kingdom, bought shares in British Telecom, half of them applying for no more than 400 shares. As I put it at the time:

> The successful sale of British Telecom . . . reveals a vast and untapped yearning among ordinary people for a direct stake in the ownership of British enterprise. Investment in shares has begun to take its place, with ownership of a home and either a bank or building society deposit, as a way for ordinary people to participate in enterprise and wealth creation. We are seeing the birth of people's capitalism.

'People's capitalism' was my own coinage. Margaret Thatcher liked the idea, but not the precise formulation, which she thought sounded Communist, reminding her of expressions like 'people's republic'. She amended it to 'popular capitalism', and thus modified it became part of the stock-in-trade of Conservative speechmaking from that moment on

CHAPTER 20

PRIVATIZATION – 3
THE PROGRAMME REACHES
A CLIMAX

Trouble with the Lawyers · Privatization Gathers Pace
The Company Nobody Owned · Hot Water
The Exploding Share · The Nuclear Blight
An Assessment of Privatization
Appendix: Privatizations by Share Offer, 1981–91

Trouble with the Lawyers

THE TIMING OF THE British Telecom offer in November 1984, shortly after the Autumn Statement, was no accident. The Government's lawyers advised us that if the offer preceded the Autumn Statement, anyone who applied for the shares and subsequently experienced a loss might successfully sue the Government if the Autumn Statement contained anything that might be held adversely to affect the BT share price. As it was, with the Autumn Statement coming after the underwriting had been completed, the underwriters might sue the Government for release from their contractual obligations. This problem was to become increasingly vexing. The lawyers habitually took the view that if the Government was in possession of any piece of information which might in any way be relevant to the success or failure of a flotation, it should be disclosed in the prospectus. This was extremely awkward, to say the least, because the Government is almost always in the position of possessing information which it is not ready to reveal, either because final decisions have not yet been taken, or because there is a pre-arranged release date for a particular piece of statistical information, or for a number of other cogent reasons.

The Autumn Statement, in which the outcome of the public expenditure round was announced and the economic forecast for the year to come was made public, was a classic instance of this. The Budget was another. I usually adopted a fairly robust approach to the lawyers, far too many of whom are more interested in identifying potential problems than in devising solutions, but their advice could not be disregarded completely and it always influenced the timing of privatization issues. At one stage the lawyers even started taking an interest in the timing of gilt-edged issues. This was particularly absurd, since the Government has to deal in the gilt-edged market all the time, but it took Peter Middleton and myself a considerable amount of time and effort to talk them out of it.

Privatization Gathers Pace

The great success of the British Telecom privatization opened the way to the privatization of the next public utility, British Gas. As Energy Secretary, I had secured Margaret's agreement to include in the 1983 manifesto a somewhat cautious pledge to seek 'means of increasing competition in, and attracting private capital into, the gas and electricity industries'. I have recorded a little earlier on how my plans for making competition in the gas industry were frustrated, but the attraction of private capital on a massive scale was almost effortlessly achieved, assisted by the 'Don't tell Sid' (and subsequently 'Tell Sid') advertising campaign, which caught on to such an extent that small shareholders henceforth became known as 'Sids'.

Unlike the Telecom sale, a full 100 per cent of British Gas was successfully offered for sale in December 1986, raising £5.4 billion, payable in instalments, with the allocation of the oversubscribed offer tilted in favour of the small shareholder, thus increasing still further the proportion of British adults holding shares, if only in one or two privatization issues. This again took place while I was Chancellor, with overall responsibility for the privatization programme, day-to-day supervision of which I delegated to my Financial Secretary, John Moore. John went about his task with missionary zeal, something the City establishment was distinctly short of. 'But John,' the head of one broking house exclaimed to him, 'we don't want all those kind of people owning shares, do we?'

British Airways, which was eventually sold for £900 million in February 1987 was financially a very much smaller privatization than Gas. But it caused far more trouble than any other. It was originally intended to be the first privatization of all, and the enabling legislation was introduced as early as November 1979, and completed its passage through Parliament without any difficulty. It was then that the problems began. The airline industry is notoriously cyclical, and British Airways' profits were very badly hit by the world recession of the early 'eighties.

This would not have mattered so much in the United States, where airline shares are well known on the stock market and their cyclical nature fully understood. But in the UK no publicly quoted airline share existed, and the Government had no practical choice but to defer the issue until the recovery phase was firmly established. Meanwhile the rugged, astute, and politically aware industrialist John King – later Lord King, and rightly one of Margaret's favourite businessmen – was brought in as Chairman in 1981, and with the indispensable assistance of his excellent Chief Executive, Colin Marshall, set about doing the remarkable job of transferring British Airways from one of the world's least efficient major airlines to one of its most efficient. The massive overmanning, characteristic of almost all nationalized aviation, was drastically eliminated, and with the minimum of trouble from the trade unions; peripheral businesses were disposed of; unprofitable routes were discontinued; the airline's marketing strategy was greatly improved; and productivity was increased in every aspect of the business.

This dramatic transformation, incidentally, is an example of the difficulty of quantifying the great improvement in industrial efficiency that privatization invariably brings. It occurred while British Airways was still a nationalized industry, yet it would not have happened at all had it not been for the prospect of privatization. Had he not been able to take the airline into the private sector John King would never have accepted its chairmanship in the first place; and even if he had been prevailed upon to do so, he would never have embarked on the massive and difficult task of turning the company round as he did. Nor, equally, even if he had tried to do so, would the unions have been nearly as acquiescent had they felt that the bottomless purse of the State would always be there to shield them from the rigours of economic reality and the need to make a profit. This is a story that was repeated time after time, if not on so dramatic a scale, throughout the privatization saga.

Frustratingly, however, no sooner had the airline emerged from the rigours of the recession than it encountered a new and even more formidable obstacle to privatization. During the 'seventies the ebullient cockney, Freddie Laker, had built up the independent airline he had created, Laker Airways, into a serious competitor to the established scheduled airlines, not least on the transatlantic route. At the start of the recession Laker Airways went out of business altogether. The creditors of the failed airline, however, claimed that it was not the recession that had caused its collapse, but an illegal conspiracy by the established airlines to do Laker down.

Given the appallingly cartelized nature of the airline business (at that time throughout the world, and still, lamentably, within Europe), and the psychology and business methods that cartels invariably manifest, this was probably true. Moreover, unlike the US airlines involved, the nationalized British Airways, in the best bureaucratic tradition, had kept a note of every telephone conversation its senior officers held. Not surprisingly, the creditors filed a civil action in the US courts against all the airlines allegedly involved, including British Airways.

There was no way the company could now be floated with this open-ended financial liability hanging over its head, which clearly would have had to be fully disclosed in the prospectus. A prior out-of-court settlement was the only answer. English lawyers were a cross I learned to bear during my time as a Minister, but the complications they cause are as nothing compared with their American opposite numbers. Eventually, after a seemingly interminable delay, unbelievable complexity, and numerous meetings of the relevant Cabinet Committee over which Margaret presided, a satisfactory out-of-court settlement was reached, and the long-awaited green light could be given for the privatization of British Airways.

The flotation itself, the last of the 1983–87 Parliament, was embarrassingly successful, being no less than eleven times oversubscribed. As in many previous privatization issues, more than 90 per cent of the work-force subscribed for shares in the company. This had been an encouraging feature of most privatizations, and would continue to be. The trade union leaders would condemn the privatization with bell, book and candle, and enjoin their members not to touch it with a bargepole; and their members would take not the slightest notice of them.

The Company Nobody Owned

Meanwhile, as the British Airways problems were being laboriously sorted out, I introduced to Parliament in January 1985 legislation to permit the flotation of the Trustee Savings Bank (TSB). Since it was a bank, it was a direct responsibility of the Treasury; but it was not technically a privatization at all, since it was not owned by the State in the first place. The trouble was that it was not at all clear who *did* own it. It consisted of a constellation of somewhat curious organizations, whose origins lay in the Scottish thrift banks established during the Industrial Revolution for labourers too poor to afford the £10 minimum deposit then required by the joint-stock banks. The 1,600 odd branches of the bank are even now very heavily concentrated in Scotland, Northern Ireland and the north of England and their clientele continues to be drawn very largely from the lower income brackets.

It was then that the problems began. It so happened that I knew the Trustee Savings Banks (at that time they were a loose federation of more or less separate institutions) quite well, since as Financial Secretary to the Treasury, under Geoffrey Howe, I had liberalized their activities by allowing them to purchase assets other than gilt-edged securities, and brought in a new overall Chairman from the private sector, John Read, with a remit to put them on a more businesslike footing. That was just as well, for the story of the TSB sale is positively Gilbertian.

There was opposition from a vociferous minority from the outset, who felt that conversion of the TSB into a fully fledged competitor of the 'big four' commercial banks, complete with shareholders and a stock exchange quotation, was an affront to the social conscience and regional loyalties of the banks. This would not have mattered much – almost every privatization had been opposed by the public initially – had it not been for the vast scope for legal obstruction afforded by the uncertain ownership of the assets of the banks. They were neither companies (like other banks) nor mutual societies (like building societies) but trusts, whose trustees appointed professional managers. This appeared to mean that nobody owned them. The Government lawyers eventually decided that the banks effectively owned themselves, and that the proceeds of the sale should go not to the Government but to the new company itself.

This was contested by the objectors, who claimed that the Trustee Savings Banks were owned by their depositors, a view that, after pro- longed litigation in the Scottish courts, was surprisingly endorsed by a Scottish judge in November 1985. This was then overturned by the Court of Appeal in March 1986, but it was clear that the uncertainty was such that the case would have to go to the House of Lords, whose judgment endorsed that of the Appeal Court in July 1986. This meant the assets of the old Trustee Savings Banks could at last be trans- ferred to the new company, in readiness for a flotation in September. Then, in August 1986, a Law Lord, in a written judgment, delivered the bizarre ruling that the Trustee Savings Banks were owned not by the depositors, nor by themselves, but by the State. The idea that the Treasury was voluntarily forgoing many hundreds of millions of pounds had its comical side, but this last-minute spanner in the works was scarcely welcome. However, after further legal wrangling the way was cleared for a September flotation.

Had the Treasury in fact claimed the proceeds, on behalf of the State, all hell would of course have been let loose. But the conclusion that the company owned itself was not without difficulties of another kind. Suppose it was worth £1 billion, and was sold to the public for that amount. Since the company received the money, it would then be worth £2 billion. If, to take account of this, the company was sold for £2 billion, it would (after the sale) be worth £3 billion and so on, *ad infinitum*. In other words, the issue was bound to be underpriced.

Fortunately, neither the Press nor the Opposition tumbled to the conceptual and practical problem involved in this circularity. But it was scarcely surprising that, in City terms, the September sale was a great success. Over four million people applied for shares, and three and a half million received them, with preference given to those who had been depositors before the flotation was announced. As a hitherto entirely domestic operation, and thus without the Latin American and other overseas bad debts with which its competitors were saddled, the new TSB should have been in a strong position. But in fact the £1½ billion the flotation had raised for a relatively inexperienced board to spend as it saw fit marked the beginning of the TSB's problems. It had a very strong balance sheet already, and the sheer size of the dowry encouraged the company to engage in acquisitions, notably the purchase of the well-known merchant bank, Hill Samuel, which would have been a challenge to the strongest management team, and an imprudent expansion of lending. Not for nothing did the TSB advertise itself as 'The bank that says yes'. The worst thing after having no money is receiving a substantial windfall. No doubt it is now learning from its mistakes, and ruing what might have been.

Hot Water

The tide of ideas was now flowing strongly in favour of the market economy, and nothing illustrated this better than the Government's increasingly ambitious privatization programme. With telecommunications and gas now safely in the private sector, we turned our attention to the two remaining giant public utilities, water and electricity, starting with water, the purest natural monopoly of all. The water industry was also the first multiple privatization, with the ten regional water companies eventually being floated separately but simultaneously in November 1989.

The story began, however, as far back as the beginning of 1985. The nationalized regional water authorities were becoming increasingly restive about Treasury control of their ambitious investment plans and its insistence that they should earn a return that would finance those plans, which meant both cutting costs and raising prices. Roy Watts, the chairman of the largest authority, Thames Water, started to campaign publicly against the Government – unacceptable behaviour on the part of a nationalized industry chairman – and an ugly anti-Treasury mood began to emerge on the back benches. Fortunately, Watts had also made it clear that he favoured privatization, as a means of escape from Treasury control (a view not shared by most of the other Water Authority chairmen), and this seemed to me the ideal solution.

I discussed the matter with my old friend Ian Gow, then a Minister of State at the Department of the Environment under Patrick Jenkin, with special responsibility for the water industry, and a long-standing enthusiast for the privatization programme. I encouraged him to drop the following broad hint, the wording of which I had agreed with him, in a debate on the Water Authorities (Return on Assets) Order on 7 February 1985:

In our manifesto, we promised to transfer nine public sector businesses to independent ownership. The transfer of water authorities, which form a natural monopoly, presents special problems, not least because of their regulatory functions. Nevertheless, my Right Honourable Friends and I will be examining the possibility of a measure of privatization in the industry.

Within no time, privatization of the water industry had become firm Government policy, and announced as such. But it was out of one frying pan into another, for the proposal immediately aroused more hostility among our own back-benchers than any other privatization, before or since.

The initial privatization plans for water were published in the form of a White Paper in February 1986 by Kenneth Baker, who had succeeded Patrick Jenkin as Environment Secretary in Margaret's 1985 reshuffle, when Patrick was dropped from the Government altogether. They assumed that the various water authorities would simply be privatized as they stood. This reflected the strongly expressed views of the Water Authority chairmen, whose belief in the integrity of their empires was absolute. But it had little objective merit and served only to maximize back-bench opposition. Not that these empires were of long standing. They had been created by the Heath Government's 1973 Water Act, of which the author was the then Environment Secretary, Peter Walker.

The 1973 Act had introduced the concept of 'integrated river basin management', and set up ten statutory water authorities, each responsible for the full range of activities connected with a single river basin such as the Thames or the Severn-Trent. This meant, as Ian Gow had warned, that their functions included regulatory and environmental matters like water conservation, controlling beach and river pollution, land drainage, flood prevention and fishing rights as well as the core business of supplying water and sewerage services (which latter had previously been the responsibility of the local authorities).

Talking to back-benchers shortly before the House rose for the 1986 summer recess, it was clear to me that most of the objections to privatization on our own benches stemmed not from distress at the transfer of the core businesses of water and sewerage to the private sector, but from concern about the regulatory and environmental aspects, notably nature conservation and the defence of anglers' rights, about which they were receiving a large number of letters. England is a nation of anglers.

In the summer of 1986, Keith Joseph, to whom Margaret had been devoted ever since they had made common cause during the dark days of opposition in 1974, left the Government at his own request and was replaced as Education Secretary by Kenneth Baker. To the horror of the environmentalists in the Party, she made Nick Ridley Environment Secretary in succession to Ken Baker.

Nowadays it is probably the Environment Secretary who has the most important of the second division posts. Certainly, given the fact that he is responsible for the relationship between central and local government, his impact on public expenditure is considerable. Ken Baker's every instinct was to spend, spend, spend – a weakness mitigated only by the good humour with which he would normally retreat from the impossible positions he initially adopted. Nick Ridley, by contrast, was a firm believer in strict public expenditure control. He seemed to me, as he did to my then Chief Secretary, John MacGregor, with whom I discussed the matter after Margaret had consulted me, the best man for the job, and I duly told her so. I also thought, wrongly as it turned out (see Chapter 46), that Nick, as a former Treasury Minister much involved with taxation, would see the political dangers in the Poll Tax which had eluded Ken Baker.

What Nick did recognize pretty soon was that the Baker plan for water privatization was a non-starter. To the concern of my officials, who had pencilled the proceeds from water privatization into their financial planning, he warned me that he proposed to tell Cabinet that the flotation would have to be postponed until after the election. I could not but agree.

We then discussed the way forward, and had little difficulty in agreeing that, despite the devotion of the Water Authority chairmen to the doctrine of integrated river basin management, the obvious route was to privatize the water and sewerage business and hive off the regulatory and environmental responsibilities into a separate State-owned National Rivers Authority. Treasury officials were initially very unhappy at the idea of creating a new quango, and had nightmares about the numbers it would employ and the public expenditure it would incur. But these were practical problems of a kind that the Treasury, after all, had some experience of addressing. What was manifestly absurd – despite the fact that it had been the practice hitherto – was that the regulator and the regulated should be one and the same entity.

In due course, and in good time for the election, Nick announced the Government's revised proposals for water privatization; and despite opposition jeers at what they claimed was a U-turn, our back-benchers warmly approved the change and all seemed set fair for a flotation as soon as the Bill reached the statute-book in the new Parliament. Public opinion, however, remained overwhelmingly hostile, with opinion polls regularly recording a 75–80 per cent majority opposed to water privatization. Perhaps the British shared the Chinese belief – which has meant that even in that citadel of private enterprise, Hong Kong, the business of water supply remains in Government hands – that water, like air, is a divine element, and not a matter for commerce.

If so, it showed a remarkable lack of touch with reality. Most of the original waterworks were private, and operated under private Acts of Parliament, and they were only gradually taken over by the municipalities. Even after the 1973 Water Act, a quarter of Britain's water supply remained in the hands of twenty-nine private water companies, whose customers were perfectly content. In France, which ever since Colbert has countenanced far greater involvement by the State in the economy than Britain, the water industry was almost wholly in the private sector. Indeed, there was some embarrassment ahead of the flotation when a number of the smaller UK private water companies were gobbled up by the giant French water combines. Nick eventually decided to halt the traffic, making it clear he would refer any bid worth more than £30 million to the Monopolies and Mergers Commission.

The privatization programme had now been going long enough for us to face public hostility, even on this unusual scale, with equanimity. What we had not bargained for was the more serious problem of the European Commission, which almost on the eve of the flotation decided to take the Government to the European Court for non-compliance with an absurd Community Drinking Water Directive of 1980 – the Government had agreed to it in the very early days when we were somewhat less experienced in the ways of the Commission – which demanded quite unnecessary standards of purity. Needless to say, no other major Community member country had complied either; but they were not in the process of writing prospectuses which would have to spell out and quantify all contingent liabilities, whereas we were.

Eventually a settlement was reached; but it meant that the companies would have to commit themselves to a massive investment programme, financed partly by an expensive injection of public money prior to the flotation and partly by higher charges to water consumers after it. This solved the last remaining problem. Eventually, in December 1989, a few weeks after I had resigned from the Government, and almost five years after Ian Gow's original intimation, all ten new-style regional water companies were simultaneously and successfully sold to the public, raising more than £5 billion in an issue that, overall, was comfortably but not excessively oversubscribed. As with the other public utilities already privatized, a regulatory agency was simultaneously put in place – in this case the Office of Water Supplies, or Ofwat – to scrutinize the industry and prevent it exploiting its monopoly, with a similar regulatory regime based on the Littlechild price-control formula.

Willie Whitelaw, who stood next to me during the Cabinet Secretary's reading of the Queen's Speech at Margaret's traditional ministerial dinner at Number 10 on the eve of the opening of the new Parliament in June 1987, muttered that the Government would get into a great deal of trouble over the privatization of water. He clearly had grave doubts as to whether we were politically wise to go ahead with it at all. I replied that, in my opinion it was electricity, not water, that was going to be the difficult one. So it proved.

Most of the problems with water were presentational rather than fundamental. Once it was clear that the regulatory and environmental responsibilities would remain in the public sector, the success of the privatization never looked seriously at risk.

The Exploding Share

My forebodings about electricity were largely based on the fact that whereas water, although the more emotive of the two, was essentially a simple industry, electricity was very much more complex. But I do not claim to have foreseen all the hazards that did come to light. I had started the ball rolling, with the passage of the Energy Act making the national grid a common carrier and abolishing the statutory prohibition on private generation for sale, and the Coopers and Lybrand report on electricity privatization, during my last months as Energy Secretary in 1983. But my successor, Peter Walker, took the matter little further. There were one or two meetings on the subject under Margaret's chairmanship in early 1987 but it was clear that Peter was more anxious to maintain secrecy about what he was up to in this field than to make progress.

To mollify me and impress Margaret that he was serious, he arranged for a Treasury official to join his team; but it was not until Cecil Parkinson became Energy Secretary in June 1987 that preparations for the privatization of electricity began in earnest. The complications with electricity lay chiefly in the field of generation, not least nuclear generation, rather than in the sphere of distribution, which was the responsibility of the twelve area electricity boards. It was clearly sensible to privatize the latter first; and there were obvious similarities between the ten regional water utilities and the twelve area electricity utilities – similarities that extended to the technical financial problem, new to the privatization programme, and indeed to the City, of floating a number of different companies on the same day. For there was no time to float the companies seriatim, nor indeed any likelihood of the various chairmen agreeing on the batting order had we tried to do so.

It was the solution to this problem that caused the first unexpected headache. Schroders, the merchant bank advising the Government on the water sales, and Kleinwort Benson, which was advising on electricity, came up with two different ideas. Schroders favoured the straightforward approach of offering individual investors a choice of ten different regional water shares, each priced separately, with special incentives for the investor who subscribed to his own local company; and at the same time offering a package of all ten shares to institutional investors who wished to have a stake in the industry as a whole. Kleinwort, however, argued that it was impossible to price different companies simultaneously. They mentioned that unless the Government wished significantly to underprice all of them, which would be hard to justify, the outcome was almost bound to be that some would prove to be underpriced, and thus oversubscribed, and others overpriced, and thus undersubscribed. It was, of course, the latter that particularly concerned them.

Their solution, which they believed to be a stroke of genius, was something they termed 'the exploding share'. According to this, the original flotation would be of a single share in the twelve area electricity boards as a whole, with only one pricing decision having to be made. Then, after a suitable period of time had elapsed, it would 'explode' into twelve different shares in the twelve different distribution companies, each of which would find its own price in the market place.

It was clear to me that this divergence of view was unacceptable. The privatization of these two industries was difficult enough without bewildering the public by trying to explain, more or less simultaneously, two quite different methods of sale and thus of application for the shares. There must be a single method of sale, which could then be promoted. Nor had I very much doubt that this should be the simpler of the two, and that the Kleinwort wheeze – designed to solve a problem which was largely in their own minds – was too clever by half. The public would be utterly bewildered by the idea of the exploding share.

I therefore held a series of meetings at my room in the Treasury with Nick Ridley, in charge of the water privatization, flanked by his key officials and merchant bank advisers, and Cecil Parkinson, in charge of the electricity privatization, flanked by his key officials and merchant bank advisers; but it proved impossible to reach agreement. Not only had Kleinwort leaked their brainwave of the exploding share to the Press, with the result that to abandon it would involve a serious loss of face, but they had succeeded in selling their scheme to both Cecil and his officials, whose views became almost as deeply entrenched.

Eventually, after a number of inconclusive meetings, I had the idea of asking each side to come to the next meeting with a mock-up of the actual offer document which they proposed to issue to the public. This proved particularly telling. The Kleinwort document was of such mind-boggling complexity that even Cecil had difficulty with it. On that basis I secured agreement that we would go ahead first with water, on the simple basis advocated by Schroders, and should that prove to be successful it would be emulated for electricity. That, in effect, was the end of the exploding share.

The Nuclear Blight

But the real obstacle to the privatization of the electricity industry was elsewhere, in the field of generation, and in particular the economics of nuclear generation. The full horrors of this did not, however, become apparent until preparations for the sale were well advanced. There was no inkling of them when, on Saturday 14 September 1987, Margaret held a day-long meeting at Chequers for Cecil and his officials to present their plans. Newly restored to the Cabinet after four years in exile, Cecil was anxious both to please the Prime Minister and to secure her support. His plan to transfer ownership of the National Grid from the CEGB to a new company jointly owned by the twelve distribution companies was patently sensible. The National Grid was effectively the market place for electricity. As long as it remained in the control of the CEGB, which supplied 95 per cent of the electricity transmitted by it, there was little prospect of independent generating concerns breaking into the market. The privatization of the National Grid, and the concentration of purchasing power in the hands of independent distributors free to buy electricity from the cheapest source, was much more likely to encourage the emergence of private electricity generators.

The two contentious issues which emerged at the Chequers meeting in September 1987 both concerned the future of the CEGB. The key question was whether to privatize it whole or to break it up first; and, if so, into how many parts. The second (and related) question was whether or not to include in the sale the nuclear power stations operated by the CEGB in England and Wales and by the South of Scotland Electricity Board (SSEB) in Scotland. At that stage there seemed no compelling reason for excluding the nuclear power stations from privatization – after all, something like half the nuclear power stations in the world were in the private sector – but this conclusion had implications for the break-up of the CEGB. Cecil was convinced, and convinced Margaret, that, in order to be sure of securing the planning permissions necessary to implement a continuing programme of nuclear power station construction, the private sector company owning them must be of real substance, with proven expertise in this particular field.

This led him to conclude that all the CEGB's nuclear power stations would need to be kept within a single generating company which, to be saleable to potential investors, would have to own a large number of non-nuclear power stations as well. This in turn implied a company so large that there was room for only one other private sector generating company to be created out of the old CEGB. This was the origin of what were known in Cecil's original White Paper of 25 February 1988 as 'Big G' and 'Little G', subsequently privatized, in March 1991, as National Power and PowerGen. The twelve regional electricity distribution companies – or 'distcos' - had already been successfully privatized in December 1990, and with the privatization of Scottish Electricity in May 1991 the exercise was complete.

Or, at least, as complete as it could be. For right to the end, the nuclear problem cast a blight on the exercise. Initially, this took the form of Walter Marshall, the great nuclear power enthusiast and Chairman of the CEGB, threatening to resign if the CEGB were broken up. Walter was confident that Margaret would not allow Cecil to lose him: Cecil, to his credit, stood his ground and Walter duly went. Then the economics of nuclear power, on analysis, proved to be such that no private sector company would ever build a nuclear station without some artificial inducement, and a fossil fuel levy had to be introduced. Finally, as I have already described in Chapter 15, the nuclear power stations had to be removed from the privatization altogether, and the whole of the Government's nuclear power station building programme put on ice, as the financial and economic truths which State ownership had successfully concealed from successive Governments were at last exposed in the run-up to privatization.

An Assessment of Privatization

The success of the Conservative Government's pioneering privatization programme is accepted throughout the world. But it is only right to note some of the criticisms that have been levelled closer to home.

The first and least central criticism is that the fees paid to the Government's professional advisers and to the financial institutions as underwriters have been too high – and that where shares were firmly placed with the institutions in advance of the public offer the terms on which this was done were too generous. To the extent that this is valid, and it became progressively less true as we gained in experience, we developed new techniques – one of which, 'clawback', under which the more successful an issue was, the more the institutions had to surrender their allotments to the general public, I can claim to have devised myself. Privatization was an exercise in which Government found itself a financial innovator to an extent which is rare indeed.

A second criticism is that shares were offered to the public at prices that were less than could have been secured, in order to promote widespread share ownership. To this I would reply: 'Yes, and quite right too.' While the interests of the taxpayer had to be given adequate weight, the maximization of proceeds, despite what many commentators said, was never the main objective. To quote Pliatzky:

> The objective of raising money for the Exchequer by these disposals, which later became an important by-product of the privatization programme, played no part in the Conservatives' hostility to nationalization, and little or no part in the gathering impetus of its drive for privatization . . . The prime motives for privatization were not Exchequer gain but an ideological belief in free markets and a wider distribution of private ownership of property.

Wider share ownership was an important policy objective and we were prepared to pay a price for it – although this price declined as our techniques developed over time.

A third and related criticism is potentially more serious. This focuses not on Government revenues but on investor attitudes. Many well-disposed critics in the City and elsewhere have said that the process by which people apply for privatization issues, are allotted a fraction of what they bid for, and then immediately sell the proceeds at a profit, gives them a false idea of the nature and function of both capitalism and the stock market. While it would be unrealistic to expect all shareholders to abjure the chance of a quick profit, what is striking is how long-term many millions of shareholders have been. In some of the largest and most popular issues, such as gas and electricity, for example, more than half the new investors were still holding their stock at the time of writing.

Yet another criticism, which was very much in vogue at one time with the Treasury Select Committee and other less august commentators, is that the Government, in classifying privatization receipts as 'negative expenditure', was in effect cooking the books and – perhaps even more seriously – deceiving itself in this way to an extent that adversely affected the conduct of macroeconomic policy. Despite Harold Macmillan's jibe about making ends meet by selling the family silver, I believe there is nothing in this whatever. I made a point of publishing figures for both Government spending and the Public Sector Borrowing Requirement on two bases: one with the benefit of privatization proceeds, and the other without. No-one could possibly claim to have been misled; nor, needless to say, was there any self-delusion on the part of the Government. Any other presentation would have involved a major upheaval to no purpose.*

---

*It has been argued that the proceeds of council house sales, which are also classified as negative expenditure, should similarly be stripped out of the public expenditure figures. Certainly the 'right-to-buy' programme, under which some 1.7 million local authority houses and flats were sold to sitting tenants between April 1979 and March 1992, for a total of over £24 billion, was a form of privatization – indeed, it was the earliest form of privatization. It is equally true that the there was no concealment; figure for local authority receipts from council house sales was always separately identified and published annually. But the argument for a different treatment in the public accounts is even weaker in this case, not least because gross capital investment in public sector housing (which is of course classified as public expenditure) regularly exceeded the receipts from council house sales.

As it was, in fact, so far from flattering the public finances, the main consequence was probably to shed unwarranted doubt on what was by any standards a remarkable fiscal achievement. But that is for another chapter.

Probably the most serious criticism is that the Government concentrated too much on ownership and not enough on competition. This is the main charge made by John Kay in his studies with various co-authors. It reflects the standard mainstream economists' party line that it is only competition that matters and not ownership. This ignores both the theoretical importance of property rights and the practical experience of countries moving away from centrally controlled economies. Indeed, in a sense Kay comes to the same conclusion. His recipe for success is a combination of competition and privatization, so that there are both market disciplines and personal incentives for the managers of the concerns in question.

The difference between mainstream economists and the Government of which I was a member was about what to do as a second best in cases where a high degree of competition was not an immediate option, partly because of the natural monopoly characteristics of some public utilities, notably water, partly for supposed technological reasons, as in British Telecom, and partly as a result of political obstacles, as in the case of British Gas. I believed that it was important to privatize as much as possible as quickly as possible; and this would itself set up pressures for more competition and other structural changes.

It is, for instance, difficult to believe that Mercury would have been able to challenge BT, if the latter had remained a conventional public utility and had not been forced to allow competition initially as a direct consequence of legislation and subsequently by the independent regulator the Government put in place. Similarly, no conventional sponsoring department would have had the power to force BT to replace within a few months its vandalized public telephone boxes in the way that Bryan Carsberg, the head of Oftel, was able to do with the threat of further competition in the background.

The very issues which Kay is so keen to explore, such as contracting out and the form of relations between public utilities and Government, have come out into open debate in a way that simply did not occur when the industries were publicly owned monopolies and were assumed by definition to be acting in the public interest.

His main empirical finding is that all State-owned corporations improved their productivity remarkably in the 1980s, whether they were privatized or not. But that is scarcely surprising. It was the process of preparing State enterprizes for privatization, and the prospect of privatization, that initially enabled management to be strengthened and motivated, financial disciplines to be imposed and taken seriously, and costs to be cut as trade union attitudes changed. Without the privatization programme of the improvement identified by Kay would have happened. Neglect of the economic consequences of ownership is every bit as ideological as the neglect of competition, even if some British economists have difficulty in taking this on board.

But there remains another, more difficult, question about the State sector of the economy. The majority of public sector workers were never in the nationalized industries, but in the public services such as health, education and government itself, in particular local government. Although we were successful in reducing the number of Civil Servants and hiving off some government activities, there were never any plans for the wholesale transfer of the public services to the private sector – even though that could theoretically have been combined with continued public financing. How is this large and important sector of the economy, where the services provided (unlike those of the old State-owned industries) are largely free at the point of use, to be made more efficient and more responsive to public demand, and to provide better value for money? There is no easy answer, but I discuss the Government's approach to the reform of education and the National Health Service in Chapters 48 and 49.

APPENDIX:
PRIVATIZATIONS BY SHARE OFFER, 1981–91

Date	Company	% of equity initially sold	Proceeds £m
Feb 1981	British Aerospace	51.6	150
Oct 1981	Cable and Wireless	50	224
Feb 1982	Amersham International	100	71
Nov 1982	Britoil	51	549
Feb 1983	Associated British Ports	51.5	22
June 1984	Enterprise Oil	100	392
July 1984	Jaguar	99	294
Nov 1984	British Telecom	50.2	3,916
Dec 1986	British Gas	97	5,434
Feb 1987	British Airways	100	900
May 1987	Rolls-Royce	100	1,363
July 1987	British Airports Authority	100	1,281
Dec 1988	British Steel	100	2,500
Dec 1989	Regional Water Companies	100	5,110
Dec 1990	Electricity Distribution Companies	100	5,092
Mar 1991	National Power and PowerGen	60	2,230
May 1991	Scottish Power and Scottish Hydro Electric	100	2,880

PART THREE

The View From Number 11

CHAPTER 21

BECOMING CHANCELLOR

A Bland and Excellent Manifesto · The General Election of 1983
The Call Comes · An Unusual Politician
Press, Speeches and Papers · The 1983 Reshuffle
Life over the Shop · Running Number 11

A Bland and Excellent Manifesto

BY THE TIME OF the 1983 OPEC meeting in London, the Government was already on an election footing. After trailing in the opinion polls since the middle of 1980, the successful prosecution of the Falklands War had transformed the Conservative Party's re-election prospects. An upturn in the Government's fortunes had begun in the final months of 1981, as the recovery from the recession began to be apparent; and the Argentine surrender of 14 June 1982 secured it an unassailable lead. The 'Falklands Factor', the shambolic state of the Labour Party under the leadership of Michael Foot, the burgeoning economic recovery and the sharp fall in inflation all argued for an early general election. The reason why the so-called Falklands Factor was so powerful, and lasted so long, was that it was more than a military victory: it symbolized and reinforced the image of the Government, and of Margaret in particular, as tough, resolute and different from previous wishy-washy governments right across the board, not least in economic policy.

At the beginning of 1983, I was invited by Margaret to join the committee, chaired by Geoffrey Howe, whom she had charged with overseeing the drafting of the election manifesto. The committee members – Geoffrey, Norman Tebbit, David Howell and myself, plus Ferdinand Mount, then head of the Number 10 Policy Unit, and a writer of considerable style, to do the actual drafting – sifted the reports of various policy groups for items to include. A myth has grown up, which even Margaret came to believe, that the 1983 manifesto was too bland, that it lacked firm policy commitments and contributed to a lack of sense of direction during the 1983–87 Parliament. This fashionable view could not be more mistaken.

The 1983 manifesto was ideal for a Government whose policies and general approach were unusually clear and inevitably well known, as of course was its record. The bad manifesto was its much less well-written 1987 successor, replete with policy initiatives that had not been properly thought through. Had it not been for the strength of the economy, the 1987 manifesto would have been a disaster; as it was, it was merely an embarrassment.

The General Election of 1983

By the spring of 1983 there was a widespread feeling in the Cabinet, which Margaret on the whole shared, that if the local election results on 5 May were encouraging, we should go to the country without further ado. Headline inflation had fallen from over 20 per cent in the middle of 1980 to 12 per cent at the end of 1981 and 5 per cent in the early spring of 1983, and Geoffrey was worried that it would be rising again by the autumn. Margaret canvassed the opinions of her Cabinet colleagues in small groups. I was in a minority in arguing that Labour was in such a mess, with an unelectable leader, left-wing policies which the country would never stomach, and suffering badly from the Social Democrat defection, that we would win whenever the election was held, particularly with the economy recovering well and inflation low; and that an early election would merely trim a year from our term of office for no good reason.

But Margaret was superstitious. May 1979 was lucky for her and she wanted an early summer poll again; but waiting until May or June 1984, the last possible date, would leave the Government at the mercy of events. In retrospect I was probably wrong to counsel delay. The bird in the hand argument is so persuasive that it was right to go in June 1983. Margaret had already sensibly resisted the siren voices who had urged her to hold a 'khaki' election in the immediate wake of the Falklands victory in 1982. Her view was that a Government should always wait until the final year of the quinquennium, but once there should go as soon as it is confident it will win – a maxim that it is hard to fault.

All further policy initiatives were inevitably postponed until after the election, but Denis Rooke pursued me tirelessly to the end. My last meeting with him as Secretary of State for Energy was to discuss the Sleipner gas field, a large find on the Norwegian side of the North Sea. Rooke wanted to buy up its entire output, thus leaving British oil companies with no outlet for their North Sea gas finds, and no incentive to prospect for gas, as gas exports were then still prohibited. I was worried that he would strike a deal with the Norwegians while I was away on the campaign; so I warned him pretty starkly that he should do nothing until the election result was known. We parted as we had begun, on the very worst of terms. He found my successor, Peter Walker, whom he had known well since the early 1970s, a much more congenial Secretary of State, although not over Sleipner, where Peter rightly vetoed the purchase.

This was the first election I had fought as a Cabinet Minister, which meant that instead of spending my time in my own Blaby constituency I spent most of it visiting marginal constituencies throughout the country, but I did not play a prominent role in the campaign. The potentially difficult issue for us was unemployment. Using today's definitions, unemployment had risen from 1.1 million in the spring of 1979 to nearly 2.4 million at the end of 1981. Although output began to recover in that year, unemployment continued to rise, although at a slower rate, and reached nearly 2.8 million in the second quarter of 1983. Hitherto the conventional wisdom was that rising unemployment on this scale would mean certain disaster for the party in office.

This did not occur in 1983 for a mixture of reasons. The electoral potency of the trend of unemployment was always chiefly that it was a good indicator of the general sense of economic well-being. But unemployment caused by the end of decades of overmanning (unemployment on the job) at a time when the economy was manifestly improving and the living standards of those in work rising was a different matter altogether. Moreover the electorate at least half believed the official Conservative line (as in 1992) that the UK recession the country had suffered was essentially part of a world recession.

None the less, anxious to rebut the gloom-mongers who were predicting that unemployment would go on rising for ever, I was rash enough to venture in a speech at Moorsholm, Cleveland, that 'next year there is every prospect that unemployment would start to fall.' I added that I was talking as a former economic journalist and that this was in no sense an official prediction.

I was not wrong about the underlying forces. Employment indeed started to recover early in the second quarter of 1983. What I failed to foresee was that most of the increase in jobs over the next three years would consist of women newly drawn into the labour force, chiefly in the service industries, rather than re-employment of the men who had lost their jobs in the great shake-out in manufacturing. My qualified prediction was thus wrong as well as rash: recorded unemployment did start to fall again, but not until 1986.

The most important event in the campaign for me was probably a joint Press conference given at Conservative Central Office towards the end by Patrick Jenkin, the Industry Secretary, Leon Brittan, then Chief Secretary of the Treasury, and myself. It was quite clear that the Press and others present, not least Margaret, would be watching our relative performance with particular interest. For while none of us had played a prominent part in the campaign, we were generally regarded as the thr.e main contenders for the job of Chancellor if, as was widely expected, Geoffrey Howe moved over to the Foreign Office after the election. Fortunately, I acquitted myself reasonably well.

However, I was conscious that Patrick was comfortably the front runner. He himself expected the job both because of his seniority – he had been Chief Secretary in the Heath Government – and his long-established friendship with Geoffrey Howe. He had not realized how much he had irritated Geoffrey by his public lobbying for industrial support after he had succeeded the aggressively free-market Keith Joseph as Industry Secretary in 1981 – and in any event neither of these qualifications would weigh very heavily with Margaret, whose decision it would be.

The Conservative victory on 9 June 1983, by a landslide margin of 144 seats, was the largest majority any party had secured since 1945. In my own constituency of Blaby my majority rose to over 17,000, and my share of the vote increased for the third election in succession. The election had been held in the customary way on a Thursday: it was not until the following Saturday morning that I was telephoned at home in Stoney Stanton by Robin Butler, the Prime Minister's Principal Private Secretary, asking me to call on the Prime Minister at Number 10. Unable to locate my ministerial driver, I took a taxi from Euston to Downing Street, where Margaret unexpectedly offered me the Chancellorship.

The Call Comes

I was delighted to be offered the job, and phoned Thérèse as soon as I could to tell her the news. She was doing the ironing at the time and was so taken aback that she burned a hole in my shirt. At last, I had the opportunity to put my own economic ideas into practice. The whole of my previous professional life had been in effect a preparation for what – quite apart from its intrinsic importance – is in practice the number two job in the Government.

I had, however, greatly enjoyed Energy. Moreover, there was a great deal more to do – gas privatization and electricity privatization, to name but two of the tasks that lay ahead, not to mention the coming confrontation with Scargill – and I would not have wished to leave it for anything else on the domestic front. Indeed, in many ways my short stay at Energy gave me more pleasure than any other job I have had before or since.

It is true that I had occasionally complained that Energy was a 'Third Programme' department. By that I meant that the issues it dealt with were in general matters of interest to energy and industrial policy buffs rather than to the man or woman in the street. This has nothing whatever to do with weight in Cabinet. The ultimate Radio One department for example is Transport, which is often considered one of the lowliest jobs in Cabinet, but where a colourful personality like Ernest Marples, who held the job under Harold Macmillan, can make a large public impact. Of course the Secretary of State for Energy cannot carry the weight in Cabinet that goes with the top jobs of Chancellor and Foreign Secretary; but among the lesser jobs the weight a Cabinet Minister carries depends on the quality of the individual and his relationship with the Prime Minister. My 'Third Programme' comment, however, probably did reflect an occasional feeling of frustration at the inability to make more of a public impact in the job. I have always had an ambivalent attitude to the show business aspect of politics, being both attracted to it and repelled by it.

Now, however, I had been given the one job in Government which I had always coveted. But it was sad to leave the friends I had made among the officials at Energy and I threw a farewell party for them in the State Room at Number 11.* Ian Gillis, my splendid Chief Information Officer at Energy, came up to me. I knew exactly what he was thinking, and got in first. 'You are going to say that no Prime Minister but Margaret Thatcher would ever have given me this job, aren't you?' He was.

Ian was probably right. Unlike Geoffrey, who had always been seen as a safe pair of hands, I was a controversial choice, despite my generally acknowledged economic expertise, by no means a politically safe choice, somewhat irreverent, and scarcely an establishment figure. Although at fifty-one I was of a fairly standard age for Chancellors, I was unusually junior in political terms. I had been in the House of Commons for little over nine years and in the Cabinet for only twenty-one months. Margaret, more than any other Prime Minister, was unafraid of controversy, and generally devoid of the instincts and thought processes of the establishment.

Her admirable radicalism, however, stopped short with matters of personal deportment. As I left her study at Number 10 she gave me only one piece of advice. This was to get my hair cut, which I was then accustomed to wearing rather long. The story started to circulate long before anyone could possibly have known it to be true. I was at that

---

*Number 11 Downing Street, next door to Number 10, is the official residence of the Chancellor of the Exchequer.

time too grateful and overwhelmed to do anything other than make the earliest convenient appointment with my barber.

An Unusual Politician

As Chancellor, I was inevitably propelled into the political spotlight, and was widely regarded as a most unusual kind of politician – indeed as not much of a politician at all. This was certainly the view of most of the lobby correspondents (members of the journalistic cartel who have privileged access to both government and parliament) and of the parliamentary sketch writers. Edward Pearce, for instance, writing in *Humming Birds and Hyenas*, published in 1985, observed that: 'Publicly Nigel Lawson is a counterproductive man. Good looking, but stoutish and thick jowled, he looks like the Prince Regent on a diet . . . He has the sort of ineradicable arrogance of an intellectually consistent, honest and rational man . . . He is just as little of a politician as it is possible for a politician to be . . . Words worry and confuse him . . . Despite the Regency look, nothing about Heartless Nigel is for decoration.' Yet he added: 'In the spectrum of political sympathies, Lawson should be counted among humanitarians and liberals . . . as Mrs Thatcher should not. He is bone dry, but not remotely right wing.'

Pearce went on to say: 'If he fails, he will fail absolutely and the Government with him but should he succeed there are no political rewards . . . He is an unthinkable candidate for the Prime Ministership . . . He gives an impression of not envying the talents he lacks and of finding public debate a constitutional chore.'

Margaret to some extent shared this conventional view of me with two qualifications. She never regarded me as a political liability to the extent that she did Nicholas Ridley whom, for that reason, she never made Chancellor despite her great affection for him and a closer affinity of views. She may also have half-consciously thought that appointing someone who was technically proficient, but without any political base of his own, would enable her in effect to be her own Chancellor. If so, she was mistaken.

Margaret saw in me one who shared to some extent both her own strengths and her own weaknesses. According to Pearce, again, in his *The Senate of Lilliput* (1983): 'Lawson has never bothered to please . . . but the arrogance derives from a belief that markets, banks, the whole apparatus of capitalism are good things and not to be excused nervously or given PR treatment as deserving a small measure of tolerance.' Much the same, with the same degree of exaggeration, could have been said of her. But she did not of course suppose that I had anything like her own rapport with the British people.

The attribute that Margaret thought we both lacked she called 'presentation'. This was largely the ability to appear smooth on television, while putting across the Government's policies. A particularly effective exponent of this was Cecil Parkinson, Party Chairman during the 1983 general election, who shortly afterwards fell victim to the Sarah Keays affair. Margaret had originally promised Cecil the Foreign Office after the election. Because of the Keays complication, of which he had told her in confidence, she felt obliged to make him Trade and Industry Secretary instead. But within four months Press exploitation of the scandal forced her to drop him altogether. I had done my best to persuade her to keep him, which she did as long as possible. Despite Cecil's tendency to exchange gossip with the Press, it was a sad loss. Unfortunately, when he at last returned to the Cabinet, in my old post of Secretary of State for Energy in 1987, much of the old sparkle had gone.

But while I was no great shakes at 'presentation', certainly as Margaret used the term, neither was I the non-political technocrat of the lobby columnists' imagination. There are two qualities in particular, that the complete politician should possess. First he should appear stupider than he is (or be cleverer than he appears). The obvious example of this is Willie Whitelaw. Secondly he should appear to be less of a politician than he really is. The first of these assets confers the enormous advantage of being underestimated; the second that of being trusted, since the British distrust politicians almost as much as they do cleverness. At least I could claim the second of them.

As Chancellor I found this a mixed blessing. The big gain – especially when there is no independent Central Bank and the Chancellor is responsible for monetary policy – was that the financial markets were less likely to be suspicious of me than of an obviously political Chancellor, something from which Denis Healey had suffered. The partially offsetting disadvantage was that Cabinet colleagues were too ready to assume that I was always voicing an official Treasury view. For example, when I argued that the Poll Tax would be a political disaster, one of the reasons – although not the main one – why this cut so little ice was that colleagues were too ready to assume that my real objection was a Treasury fear that the Poll Tax would lead to increased public spending.

A further political quality, which is for example John Major's forte, is being good with people, and with back-bench colleagues and the Press in particular. This is the aspect at which I was worst. I suppose I am not sufficiently gregarious by nature. But although not gregarious, I am too ready to speak my mind, when engaged, without pausing to consider the likely consequences – or even on occasion without considering whether I may indeed be wrong. It may have been these defects which made Willie Whitelaw for so long determined to keep me out of high office, although happily his view subsequently changed.

BECOMING CHANCELLOR

Another obvious requirement for any senior politician is being good at the despatch box – from which Ministers and Opposition front-benchers speak. Here I was very uneven. Although no natural orator, I was effective in Opposition. My well-developed critical faculties and the ability to perform without the benefit of official advice stood me in good stead. Of course, the politics of Opposition are infinitely easier than the politics of Government, and there is far more time to prepare speeches in the enforced idleness of Opposition. But it remains an essentially unrewarding occupation. Someone like myself goes into politics to make the sort of contribution that can be made only in Government. Opposition is at best a preparation for office and very occasionally a relatively amusing way of passing the time, and at worst an exercise in futility and frustration. Although I gave the impression of enjoying Opposition, this was only because I try to enjoy whatever I happen to be doing. A prolonged period of Opposition would have been unendurable.

Although good at thinking on my feet, as a Minister I would tend to give distinctly lacklustre performances when I was not particularly interested and did not make a great effort. But on the really big or challenging occasions, I could usually be counted on to turn in a pretty effective performance. Apart from John Biffen, who always prided himself on being a parliamentarian first and a Minister second, I was the only Minister in the Thatcher Governments to be given *the Spectator*/Highland Park Parliamentarian of the Year award, which unexpected event occurred in 1987.* (I was also, incidentally, given the 'Speech of the Year Award' for my resignation speech in 1989.)

A parallel dimension is being good on television. Here again my record was patchy. When the adrenalin was not flowing I tended to be dull and to speak in bursts that were too fast to comprehend, interspersed with awkward pauses while I searched for the right word. But when the stakes were high enough and the adrenalin was flowing I could be effective, as for example my performances when I was belatedly fielded during the 1987 election campaign, my interview with Robin Day after the 1988 'missing tape' fiasco, or my post-resignation interview with Brian Walden in 1989.

Those who write about politics tend to be concerned with the visible side: that is, what a politician says in public and what is said about him. But to my mind the most important yet most overlooked dimensions of being a politician are the least visible. These range from being a loyal and reliable colleague to being a fertile source of workable political ideas and able to make correct political judgements – that is to say what both the short-term and long-term consequences are likely to be of a particular

*Lest unworthy suspicions are harboured, this was before my son Dominic was editor; but in any case the award is made by a panel of senior journalists from different papers.

course of action or turn of events; what the public will accept at a particular time and what it will not; or how best to present a particular policy, irrespective of who will be making the speeches.

Effective political judgement, moreover, involves thinking more or less simultaneously on two levels: assessing both the likely short-term electoral consequences and the longer-term political consequences – where political ideas become more important. These range from how to entrench – that is to say, render unlikely to be reversed – a particular policy, to how to affect the longer-term political climate. This sort of strategic and tactical thinking was probably my strongest suit, even if I was sometimes less successful in persuading others of my judgement. By contrast, Margaret's well-advertised gut instincts were not always a satisfactory substitute for a considered strategy, as both the disastrous Poll Tax and her counterproductive handling of the European issue amply demonstrated.

Nevertheless, one way and another, my political shortcomings were sufficient to ensure that I was most unlikely ever to be elected Party Leader and thus Prime Minister. Realizing this, I lacked the ambition and directed energy it takes to spend the necessary time in cultivating back-benchers with this object in mind – which was, of course, itself one of my main political shortcomings. Indeed I surprised a number of close observers – perhaps even disappointed a few friends and supporters – by publicly disclaiming all ambition for the top job when my standing was at its peak during the year following the general election of 1987.

I did not feel that I suffered greatly as Chancellor through not being a candidate for Number 10, although I know that others thought differently. On the one hand my actions did not excite the suspicions among my Cabinet colleagues aroused by those known to be motivated by personal ambition. On the other hand I had no faction on whose support I could rely in political conflicts, especially with Margaret. In other words, there was no future in being a Lawsonite.

There are many different kinds of politician, and most are probably needed. A paragon who combines the advantages of all and the drawbacks of none is unlikely to exist – and, if he did, he would almost certainly be impossible to live with.

Press, Speeches and Papers

Because I had once been a journalist, some people expected me to have a particular affinity with the Press. I enjoyed my time as a journalist and like to think that I can still turn my hand to an article at short notice. But I had embarked on a different career and, although a handful of journalists remained close friends, they did so purely as individuals.

Other journalists, I suspect, actively resented the fact that I had clearly crossed from their side of the fence to the politicians'.

Indeed, I discontinued immediately one practice that had been introduced when Denis Healey was Chancellor and was continued by Geoffrey Howe. This was to invite the leading political editors and correspondents to dinner at Number 11. Having accompanied Geoffrey on a number of these occasions, and noted how, despite his assiduous wooing and generous hospitality, the Press he received remained unremittingly hostile throughout his Chancellorship, I came to the firm conclusion that it was not worth the time and trouble. It may be, however, that when the going got rough I would have received a marginally better Press had I spent more time cultivating them.

There was another, more professional, shortcoming from which I suffered. Much of my most systematic thinking about policy took the form of carefully prepared speeches – usually not to the House of Commons, which is allergic to anything reminiscent of the lecture room – but to outside gatherings. To have gained maximum attention I should have made a point of completing the text of such speeches well before the event and then personally alerting editors to their importance. But I was temperamentally unable to do this, having a compulsion (so far as the written word is concerned) to leave things to the last moment and then make corrections even later than that. So I have only myself to blame if, for example, the academic literature on privatization scarcely mentions my contributions at all, except for highly political sentences extracted from short and unrepresentative newspaper reports.

Governors of the Bank of England have the advantage that their more important utterances are reprinted in the *Bank of England Quarterly Bulletin*, which is a standard reference source. The Treasury had no similar publication in my time. I am glad to say that since my departure it has started to publish a quality quarterly journal, *The Treasury Bulletin*, which is not yet on the scale of the Bank of England's, but could develop into a vehicle for the more considered utterances of Chancellors of the Exchequer and indeed other Treasury Ministers and officials.

I remained enough of a journalist to prefer to write my own key speeches. The length that comes most naturally to me is, not surprisingly, that of a rather long newspaper article. I find either the short Press release (the equivalent of a sound bite) or a complete book such as this more difficult. As Financial Secretary I was able to write most of my own speeches and to some extent to do the same as Energy Secretary. But as Chancellor the sheer volume of work, and the sheer number of speeches, made that impossible, except for the Budget speech, which I always wrote myself, my Party Conference Speech, and the bulk of my speeches at the Annual Meetings of the IMF and the Mansion House Banquet, as well as any major House of Commons occasions or outside lectures. Not that I was ever happy simply to read out the work of others. Where the speech was important enough to be written, rather than delivered from brief notes or completely off the cuff, my preferred method was to talk through the line I wanted to take, get it written up, and then extensively edit it. Sadly, Civil Servants or even special advisers with a genuine flair for speech-writing are few and far between.

Cabinet papers and similar documents which carry the Minister's initials are normally written by Civil Servants, with an occasional input from special advisers. Generally speaking, the Minister decides the line to be taken and the officials clothe it in the appropriate verbiage. I probably did more redrafting and restructuring than the average Minister. This was particularly the case with personal notes to Margaret. Nevertheless many of the key documents cited in this book are inevitably co-operative efforts in the sense I have indicated. Identifying the actual sources is often impracticable, not only because several officials usually play a part, but because they are not bound to agree with what they write. Indeed in hectic periods a good Civil Servant can allow himself the luxury of a personal opinion only after the draft has already been completed.

The 1983 Reshuffle

My own elevation was part of a much wider Cabinet reshuffle. The outgoing Foreign Secretary, Francis Pym, a gloomy Heathite, had never been an admirer of Margaret's (nor she of him) and he finally sealed his fate with a remark in the election campaign warning of the undesirability of a large Conservative majority. He was succeeded by Geoffrey Howe. Margaret saw Geoffrey as a patient and determined negotiator, with no strong views of his own; and Geoffrey himself, who still cherished Prime Ministerial ambitions, strongly supported by his formidable wife Elspeth, wanted to widen his experience. (I afterwards discovered, incidentally, that Geoffrey had unequivocally backed me for Number 11 rather than Patrick Jenkin.) A surprise elevation was that of Leon Brittan to be Home Secretary at the unusually early age of forty-four.

There was a pattern to the reshuffled Cabinet. Willie Whitelaw, who best represented the old Tory tradition, became Deputy Prime Minister and Leader of the Lords. Quintin Hailsham, then well into his seventies, but still a force, remained Lord Chancellor and a sparkling representative of continuity with the past. The three main Offices of State, however, were held by Geoffrey, Leon and myself, who were politicians of a different mould. We were all convinced supporters of Margaret's new brand of Conservatism. But in our different ways we had come to these beliefs through reason and experience, rather than through the sort of gut instinct that so powerfully animated her. We did not have Margaret's instinctive identification with the interests of the upper working and lower middle classes as she conceived them; nor were we part of her inner circle. Nor were we able to make up for her oratorical deficiencies. But we did have a capacity for clear thinking and hard work, a profound interest in policy, a toughness and an ability to deal with the higher Civil Service in their own language. She thus saw no threat at that time to her own position.

Press commentators tended to group Leon and myself very much together at the time, even though we were personally far from close. This may have been partly because we were both Jewish – as was Keith Joseph, a genuine confidant of Margaret's who remained at Education and David Young, who the following year was given a peerage and elevated to the Cabinet as Minister without Portfolio. As I subsequently told Kenneth Harris of the *Observer* : my parents were 'certainly Jewish, not orthodox, but it was something they took for granted, and something I took for granted. I've frequently been puzzled – not peeved or irritated, simply puzzled – by the way this is focused on.' There has been much speculation about the unusually large proportion of Ministers of Jewish origin in Margaret's Cabinets, but no generally accepted explanation. I cannot solve the riddle either; although it certainly demonstrated that there was not the faintest trace of anti-Semitism in her make-up: an unusual attribute.

Life over the Shop

My move to Number 11 meant a considerable upheaval both for Thérèse and the children. In particular it meant leaving our house in Walworth and moving into 11 Downing Street. We readily agreed with the Howes to defer this for a week, since they had in turn agreed to give the Pyms a week to clear their belongings out of the Foreign Secretary's official residence in Carlton Gardens. I duly turned up at the Treasury on the Monday morning after the election, to be greeted by John Kerr, the Principal Private Secretary I had inherited from Geoffrey, who said 'You'd better get over to Downing Street to get photographed'. He was quite right. When I got over to Downing Street, all the Press photographers and television cameramen were waiting for me. For the first of many occasions, I was photographed standing outside the front door. In the excitement of getting down to the job this obvious piece of PR had simply not occurred to me.

We then had to decide what to do with our own London home. That might seem a relatively easy decision to make. But Number 11 is an exceptionally large house to run and, so far as the private flat is concerned, no staff are provided. Emily was not yet two and Tom was only seven, so Thérèse had more to cope with than most Chancellor's wives. In the end we decided to sell our own house rather than go to all the trouble of finding suitable tenants – and my successor but one, Norman Lamont, was subsequently to discover how embarrassing an unsuitable tenant can be. This meant, of course, that we largely missed out on the property boom of the second half of the 'eighties. Nor was the avoidance of tenant problems the only reason for our decision to sell. British Ministers are extraordinarily underpaid by almost any yardstick, and I simply could not afford to keep both Stoney Stanton and a house in London while living in Number 11, which itself is a financial burden of sorts.

There is no absolute requirement for a Chancellor to live in Number 11; but it is both a long-standing convention and a practical convenience, at least so far as the job is concerned. And it is, of course, an attractive and comfortable home – though neither of us foresaw quite what a challenge living in Downing Street, with its conspicuous lack of privacy, would turn out to be from time to time.

Before we moved in, Elspeth Howe showed Thérèse round the private flat, which is separated from the official part of the building by its own front door, and which she found considerably larger than she had expected. In fact, it could have been larger still: when Margaret told me she proposed to make me Chancellor she immediately added that she needed the top floor of Number 11 to house Number 10 staff. At the time I was scarcely in a position to object, but I would not have done in any event. A large two-floor flat was quite big enough for us – indeed, it was slightly larger than the private flat in Number 10. Running it was no small enterprise; and it was a great coup when, after a few years, Thérèse succeeded in persuading the Treasury to contribute to the cost of employing a cleaner.

As it was, when we first went to live at Number 11 in 1983 the staff consisted simply of a single doorman. In addition to opening the front door to visitors, distinguished or otherwise, he had to man the small telephone switchboard, deal with the Treasury Messengers who were constantly delivering Government papers between Number 11 where I chiefly worked and the Treasury where my officials were, make and serve the tea, coffee and other drinks required at meetings or for my own consumption, and liaise with his opposite numbers, of whom there were several, next door at Number 10.

Even to me this seemed to be carrying Treasury parsimony too far, particularly since it meant that the place was completely unmanned during the doorman's lunch break. I sought and secured an assistant doorman, which proved a great stroke of luck, since he soon moved up to the number one slot, where he gave us five years of excellent service until he was forced to retire, having long passed the age limit. This was Arthur Woolley, a chain-smoking former butcher from Bermondsey, who had injured a foot quite badly in the Army during the war and become a Treasury messenger. The kindest and most loyal of men, with a secret passion for writing verse, his irreverent Cockney wit never deserted him.

Running Number 11

For more about life at Number 11 I can do no better than cite a talk which Thérèse gave on a private occasion in the constituency in 1984. She knew far more about the subject than I did.

> *Number 11 is a beautiful house, very Georgian-London. The exterior is of course familiar. But both Number 10 and Number 11 are much bigger than they look from the Downing Street façade – they grow not merely backwards but sideways. And because of the curious shape of the buildings, we have a marvellous range of views. From our kitchen you can watch all the comings and goings in Downing Street; if only there were time to stare! From the drawing room you see St James's Park and the new Mountbatten statue from the window on one side, and the garden of Number 10 and Horseguards Parade from the window on the other side. The laundry room looks out on to the Foreign Office. The position is also a great advantage. It is very central and has free parking. There is no worry about being clamped, which is such a perk for a Londoner. Nor is there any worry about being burgled. The place is guarded by those wonderful Downing Street policemen, day and night.*
>
> *Our bit of the Number 10 and 11 complex is on three floors. The ground floor is wholly official. There is the Chancellor's study, where Nigel works most of the time; a meeting room where at least half his official meetings take place; and a striking oak-panelled official dining room, which boasts a beautiful Soane ceiling. The entrance hall – like the front door that opens into it – is one that the family is obliged to share with official visitors: there is no back door.*
>
> *On either side of our hall are interconnecting doors to Number 10 on one side and Number 12 – the office of the Government Chief Whip – on the other. These can be useful in ways I leave to your imagination, of which the least important and most frequent is providing a throughway for all and sundry who wish to avoid the rain.*
>
> *On the first floor is the most spectacular room in the building – the state drawing room. At the moment some wonderful Turners on loan from the National Gallery are hanging there. This room is used for the large receptions we give, usually for 80 to 120 people. Some of these I have to do myself. Only if it is an official function is all the work done for me. Otherwise I do it – and pay for the food and drink. The same applies to the dinners we give: there is a set amount per head, given back to us, by the Treasury, for official guests; but not for any*

personal guests we invite to make these official gatherings more fun. The allowance is by no means extravagant and I always seem to end up subsidizing Her Majesty's Government.

Once past this magnificent stateroom, there is a door to our private flat. Everything beyond is now our home, up to us to organize and run, to clean and so on. Unlike the case with our Embassies abroad, no staff whatsoever are provided. People who believe the residence comes with butlers, maids and cooks are living in a fantasy. The flat is huge. Nigel prefers to do most of his entertaining upstairs. So that too is down to me.

And he does his homework on the red boxes up in the flat as well. But that is one of the best features of Number 11, of living above the shop. It means we see each other in spite of Nigel's absurdly busy schedule. His study is strategically placed near the kitchen, so he can easily call out to where he knows I shall be, for a cup of tea or something stronger. He can and often does pop up to see the children after school or to have lunch with me. I hadn't thought of this advantage before we moved in – not that there was much time to think about anything. But it has turned out to be a real perk.

In the same talk she went on to describe life inside the flat:

We had to move house in pretty much of a hurry of course. There was no time to recover after the campaign or to pack thoughtfully.

Elspeth Howe invited me to coffee at eight in the morning – which I thought at the time was strangely early. But now I know why she had to pick 8 o'clock. For, except between midnight and 8 a.m., there is never a quiet moment. There is constant activity, a constant stream of people coming in and out, and phones always ringing.

Some time after we moved in, I decided to have an early night – we had no function to attend and Nigel was working on his boxes in his study. It was about 11 o'clock and I had had a bath and thought I'd make a cup of tea. I went down to the kitchen in my dressing gown and to my amazement I found a man sitting at the kitchen table. Just sitting there. I hope I showed no surprise, in true British fashion, and carried on making the tea. But I was surprised and offered the man a cup. I was of course also a little embarrassed and enquired later on who it was in the kitchen. It was just someone from the Treasury, it turned out, waiting for an urgent paper from Nigel's box. He was also a very nice man I found as time went on. But it was a lesson learned pretty quickly about Number 11: never assume that you can behave as if no-one is there, at any point, in any part of the place!

So it's not like a normal home. And that, the lack of genuine privacy, is the real reason. It is a disadvantage, an extra strain.

BECOMING CHANCELLOR

So I am not going to pretend that living at Number 11 is all wine and roses. The most difficult thing about living above the shop is the impossibility of ever truly letting your hair down as you normally can in a real home, of wandering around with a face pack or hair in rollers at nine in the morning. It is a strain for me, anyway: I suspect Nigel is less worried about his face packs being spotted. You know how phlegmatic he is.

Family life is difficult to lead naturally in an official residence. You feel you are constantly on show. Similarly I do feel slightly sheepish, carting in carrier bag after carrier bag of the weekly groceries while the Press and television people and other onlookers stand and stare: I tell myself that this informal side is what is so endearing about British politics. I say that in public! I am not sure what I really think. Perhaps just that the contrasts are so odd.

Unfortunately, throughout the house we are obliged to have thick net curtains – they are a security measure to protect us from bomb blast. So I fear that the odd twitch of the kitchen net may reveal me as a nosy neighbour – or our young son, Tom, as a peeping Tom!

The Government has provided beautiful furniture, paintings and prints for the drawing room, dining room, study and hall in our flat. But a scrupulous dividing line is drawn. Rooms where visitors are likely to be are adorned with paintings from the Government collection, preferably by British painters. But none of the bedrooms or the upstairs landings is included, on the grounds that visitors are not expected to venture there.

The other outstanding features at Number 11 have all to do with time – the lack of it – and visitors. Our schedules look like nothing I have known before, and, in terms of hours and requirements, I consider this the hardest job I have ever had. It is also the least well paid. If anyone wants an example of voluntary work, here it is.

For a start the hours we keep are punishing. The average day is from 6 a.m. to 1 a.m., and I am not exaggerating – and Sundays aren't free either. The telephones never stop ringing. The pressures seem endless. Even my diary has to be planned months ahead – Nigel's is a year in advance. Yet – and this is perhaps the right note on which to end – we both thrive, and so I think do the children. I don't know why, and I can't explain. Our life at Number 11 is positively unhealthy by normal rules. But we are very lucky to have this challenge.

CHAPTER 22

ALL THE CHANCELLOR'S MEN

Finding the Right Ministers · Special Advisers
Prayer Meetings · The Changeover of the Mandarins
Surprise Choice for the Bank

Finding the Right Ministers

FINDING THE RIGHT MINISTERIAL team was as demanding as getting used to living above the shop, but in a different way. When Margaret saw me on the Saturday after the election to offer me the Chancellorship, she told me of her intention to make Peter Rees Chief Secretary. I had my reservations about his suitability for this particular job, but not having expected the Exchequer I had not come to Number 10 armed with an alternative candidate of my own. A convivial, dapper lawyer and son of a distinguished Welsh General, 'Tiger' Rees, Peter was a bon vivant whose gastronomic tastes were well indulged by his wife Anthea, at the time quite a chum of Thérèse's and a superb cook. He was however – perhaps because he yearned for the good life – not as well catered for in the Treasury as in his previous post, which involved a considerable amount of travel, which he loved. The no-frills hard grind of Chief Secretary was not quite his cup of tea. His very convincing portrayal of a dog while playing charades, at one of our pre-Budget meetings at Chevening, became a legend in Treasury circles.

Professionally Peter's forte was tax. As a former highly successful silk at the Revenue bar, he was an expert cross-examiner rather than a burner of the midnight oil. Margaret had chosen him because we had worked well together in both Government and Opposition, he had already had experience as a Treasury Minister and more recently had been a very successful Minister of Trade. Never having been a Treasury Minister herself, she tended to regard all Treasury jobs below Chancellor as virtually interchangeable, and did not realize the special combination of qualities required for the control of public spending. I made sure that his successors as Chief Secretary were colleagues I had personally earmarked for their suitability for the job.

Nick Ridley, my successor as Financial Secretary, was still in situ. Although we were at that time firm friends and comrades-in-arms of long standing, he had been in the House considerably longer than I had, and understandably did not relish serving under me. He was depressed, too, by the thought that, having been left in place during Margaret's big 1983 post-election reshuffle, his last chance of entering Cabinet had eluded him. Unexpectedly, both these problems soon passed. Within a few months the resignation of Cecil Parkinson had led indirectly to a Cabinet vacancy as Transport Secretary, which Nick filled.

I had persuaded Margaret to let me bring John Moore with me from Energy to become Economic Secretary to the Treasury. When Nick Ridley departed. John was the obvious choice for promotion to Financial Secretary; his successor as Economic Secretary was Ian Stewart who had once been Parliamentary Private Secretary to Geoffrey Howe and knew the Treasury well. Ian and I had known each other for a very long time, since we did our National Service in the Navy together in the 1950s. He did an excellent job piloting both the Building Societies' Act of 1986 and the Banking Act of 1987 through all their stages in the House of Commons.

Finally there was Barney Hayhoe, the Minister of State I had inherited from Geoffrey. Although our economic views were very different, this presented no problems while he was at the Treasury, which he had joined in October 1981 as Minister of State in charge of the Civil Service, as a result of the Treasury's absorption of the short-lived Civil Service Department. Margaret appointed him Minister of Health, under Norman Fowler, in 1985. In that much more exposed post his limitations became more apparent; and a year later Margaret gave him the sack, thus ending his ministerial career. This greatly embittered him; and thereafter, despite the fact that our relations at the Treasury had been excellent, his voice was always prominent in the attacks on my Chancellorship from our own side.

At least I had no problems over my choice of Parliamentary Private Secretary (PPS). Mark Lennox-Boyd, who had been with me continuously since the latter part of my time as Financial Secretary, and had been planning to move on, agreed to stay with me when I became Chancellor.

Special Advisers

I had also to make sure we had high calibre special advisers to inject some political awareness into the official machine and (if possible) to help with the absurd number of speeches a Chancellor is expected to make. Most Departments had only one special adviser, but the wide-ranging nature of the Treasury's responsibilities meant that we had three of them.

The principal one I inherited from Geoffrey was Adam Ridley. He had left the CPRS – the original think-tank started by Edward Heath – during Harold Wilson's final Premiership, to become the Conservative Party's principal economic adviser when we were in Opposition. I had thus worked with him both in Opposition and in Government (when I was Financial Secretary) for a considerable period. He stayed on with me for a couple of years, by which time he had probably been in the same job for too long. Certainly, he felt the need for a change, and left in 1985, eventually to become a Director of Hambros Bank. I was able to obtain as his successor an old and dear colleague, Peter Cropper, who had also worked with Geoffrey and me both in Opposition and Government, coming in as Adam Ridley's number two in 1979. He was then made Director of the Conservative Research Department, which was not a job that greatly suited him, and it was from there that I plucked him in 1985. I always had a great respect for his perceptive, if sometimes pessimistic, judgement.

The turnover of special advisers was inevitably on the high side, as the pay is not good and the job tends to attract bright youngsters who are contemplating a career in politics; so I cannot mention all the others who loyally served me during my six years and more as Chancellor. Three who were outstanding were Michael Portillo, later to become a Cabinet Minister himself, Howard Davies, who subsequently became Chairman of the Local Government Audit Commission and then Director-General of the CBI, and Andrew Tyrie.

Prayer Meetings

On the whole we had a very happy and relaxed team at the Treasury. I continued Geoffrey Howe's practice of holding a 'prayer meeting' on Monday, Wednesday and Friday mornings. In my time the congregation consisted of Ministers (including the Treasury Whip for the time being), special advisers, PPSs, and the head of the Economic Section of the Conservative Research Department. The object was to have a political discussion of current policy issues without the inhibiting presence of officials. To some extent it was the counterpart of the weekly meeting of the PCC – the so-called Policy Co-ordinating Committee – where senior Treasury officials met to discuss current policy issues without the inhibiting presence of Ministers. The most obvious difference was that a note of the matters discussed at each prayer meeting, although not of the views expressed or conclusions reached, was circulated to the Treasury mandarinate. That way, even if the conversation was private, they did at least learn what was on Ministers' minds. Not that it was impossible for the Chancellor to learn what was exercising PCC, should the need arise.

Prayer meetings were not the only ones that took place without officials present. I always made it clear that I would be happy to see any Minister or special adviser privately, should there be something on his mind that he did not wish to put down on paper or otherwise expose at that stage. And, starting with John MacGregor, who arrived in 1985, I held a regular weekly tête-à-tête with the Chief Secretary of the day. The one issue that I did not discuss even on these intimate occasions was that of my differences with Margaret over the exchange rate during the latter part of my Chancellorship – although I did talk it over with one or two, including Peter Brooke, subsequently an outstanding Northern Ireland Secretary, but for most of the time one of my Treasury Ministers and sometime Chairman of the Party, a man whose judgement I respected and whose discretion could be utterly relied on. I was, of course, well aware that Margaret herself was less discreet. But this was a matter that was highly market-sensitive as well as politically explosive; and I saw no advantage in taking any further risks on that front.

Like previous Chancellors, I held a weekly meeting with the Permanent Secretary, in my case Peter Middleton, which was essential to the proper running of the Department. My Principal Private Secretary would be present as a note-taker, except occasionally when we were discussing sensitive issues of personal moves within the official Treasury. I also instituted a weekly tête-à-tête with the Chief Economic Adviser, Terry Burns. I hoped in this way to free him of any inhibitions he might have felt in front of other officials or Ministers. Equally I was able to test out my own economic ideas before I was ready to have them circulate throughout the Treasury.

It was sometimes thought that I relied on Terry too much for the interchange of economic ideas. Certainly, I had a high regard for him. But I do not believe there is much in the charge. In the first place, there were others within the Treasury with whom I could and did exchange economic ideas – notably Peter Middleton and my long-serving Press Secretary, Robert Culpin. Among outsiders, and admittedly subject to the inevitable constraints imposed by the need for secrecy, I regularly exchanged ideas with that doyen of economic commentators, my old friend Samuel Brittan. Then, in 1986, I formed a group of outside economists of differing views to discuss the key issues with me on a confidential basis twice a year at Number 11. (There are those who would argue that that was when the conduct of economic policy began to go wrong. Even if that were so – and I discuss this in subsequent chapters – it would on the whole be unfair to argue *post hoc ergo propter hoc*.)

Nor is it right to overlook the written word. I remember talking to a visiting American Professor of Politics of some distinction, who observed that ministerial life was far too busy to allow senior politicians any time to think. 'What you guys need is a sabbatical,' he declared. 'We do have sabbaticals in our system,' I replied. 'We call it Opposition. And I've had enough of it.' But I did make a point of using part of the summer holidays each year as a time for thinking, including reading the economic literature on a subject that seemed to me particularly important at the time – provided that it was written in English and not in algebraic symbols.

Finally, of course, I was not devoid of the capacity to develop economic ideas of my own – even though the commentators tend to assume that that is the copyright of professional economists. A good example of that is the labelling of my 1988 IMF speech on the balance of payments as the 'Burns Doctrine'. Certainly I discussed it thoroughly with Terry, who was his usual constructive self. But it would be wholly wrong to saddle him with the responsibility for that 'doctrine', or any other 'doctrine' for that matter.

There are some who feel that, notwithstanding all that, a modern Chancellor needs to equip himself with a professional economist of acknowledged standing as his own full-time personal economic adviser, someone who can take on the Treasury's economic establishment on their own terms: in essence the role that Nicky Kaldor played under two successive Labour Governments, during the Chancellorships of Jim Callaghan, Roy Jenkins and Denis Healey. Healey's own verdict on the experiment, as contained in his autobiography, could scarcely be more damning, and I have to agree with him. A Chancellor who really needs a 'personal' economic adviser has got the wrong man as Chief Economic Adviser, and should be able to change him.

That is not to say that the state of affairs on the economic advisory front during my time as Chancellor was entirely satisfactory: it was not. But the gap I increasingly felt needed to be filled, though I never did fill it, was rather different from that described above. Partly because of the Treasury's obsession with short-term economic forecasting, partly because of the strong Keynesian tradition in the UK, the Chief Economic Adviser is invariably a macro-economist, and Terry was no exception. I increasingly felt the lack of a first-class micro-economist, with a good understanding of tax and financial issues, who was broadly sympathetic to what I was seeking to do. The obvious role for him, in the circumstances, would be the post of Deputy Chief Economic Adviser.

Towards the end of my time as Chancellor, Ian Byatt, the long-serving Deputy Chief Economic Adviser, who had been appointed to the post during Denis Healey's time as Chancellor, eventually left to run the Office of Water Supply, or Ofwat, the regulatory body for the newly privatized water industry. I tried hard to persuade Mervyn King, who fitted the micro-economic bill described above to a T, to take the post; but after much thought he declined. Two years later, after my resignation, the job of Economic Adviser to the Governor of the Bank of England (which carries with it an executive directorship of the Bank) fell vacant, and Robin Leigh-Pemberton very shrewdly snapped Mervyn up for that. A year later, in 1991, on Peter Middleton's resignation from the post of Permanent Secretary to the Treasury to take up a much more remunerative job in the City, Terry was unexpectedly promoted to take his place – the first time an economist had ever held it. Had Mervyn King accepted my offer of the job of Deputy Chief Economic Adviser in 1988, it is all Lombard Street to a China orange that he would now be Chief Economic Adviser to the Treasury.

The Changeover of the Mandarins

As I left Margaret's first-floor study in Number 10 on that Saturday in June 1983, the first person to congratulate me on my appointment as Chancellor was Robin Butler, whom I knew well as a former Treasury official, but who at that time was the Prime Minister's Principal Private Secretary (he was later to reach the top of the tree as Secretary to the Cabinet and Head of the Home Civil Service). He told me how pleased he thought the Treasury officials would be. I learned subsequently that the senior mandarins in Great George Street had discussed during the election campaign whom they would like to see as Chancellor and that I had emerged as their choice by quite a wide margin. I was not at all sure that this was entirely a good thing; but officials seemed to like a Minister who knew his own mind, enjoyed discussion and used the resources of the Department to the full. David Lipsey wrote in *The Sunday Times* of 19 June 1983: 'With Lawson they look forward to a kind of Denis Healey Mark II, with all the excitements of life in an intellectual rough house.'

It was also on the Saturday, shortly after my trip to Number 10, that I was telephoned by Peter Middleton, the recently appointed Permanent Secretary to the Treasury. I asked him to come and see me next day at Stoney Stanton. The Sunday turned out to be a beautiful summer's day and we spent most of it in the garden going over the whole range of Treasury issues. So when I arrived back in Great George Street on the Monday, to a warm welcome from officials, I had already been well briefed, and had had the opportunity to indicate my own priorities and concerns.

Peter Middleton was a man of outstanding ability, with whom I had worked closely on the formulation of the Medium Term Financial Strategy (MTFS) during my time as Financial Secretary. He was also an unorthodox choice, having ascended the Treasury hierarchy from Sheffield University and the Central Statistical Office. He had been a very skilful Press Secretary to both Tony Barber and Denis Healey before shrewdly specializing in monetary policy.

All Permanent Secretary appointments have to be approved by the Prime Minister of the day, but the importance of the Treasury is such that Margaret took a particularly keen interest in the Wass succession. Within the Treasury, the consensus was that none of the Second Permanent Secretaries were right for the job and that the choice lay between two up-and-coming Deputy Secretaries, David Hancock and Peter Middleton. Hancock would almost certainly have won in a Treasury vote. I have no idea what his politics were. But the majority of Treasury officials, as indeed of Whitehall generally, saw themselves for want of a better description as social democrats. David Hancock certainly fitted that picture, however he actually voted. Discreet, civilized, knowledgeable in the ways of the Treasury and very Oxbridge, he was very much the mandarin's mandarin. He had been immensely sceptical of George Brown's Department of Economic Affairs and the National Plan and was probably almost as sceptical of Tory radicalism. He was not the official who said in a public lecture that the good Civil Servant should 'avoid the last ounce of commitment', but it was not hard to imagine his making the remark.

He was clearly not Margaret's type. In her eyes, the choice lay between Middleton and the Second Permanent Secretary in charge of Public Expenditure, Anthony Rawlinson, for whom she had a soft spot. He was not only the best looking – in a tall, wiry, matinée idol way – something that always cut a great deal of ice with her. He was also the one undoubted Tory of the three.

Geoffrey, however, strongly favoured Middleton, as did Leon Brittan, then Chief Secretary – and as I made clear I did, too, when Margaret consulted me informally in the voting lobby at the House one evening. Rawlinson, who had been a reserve for the Everest team and was sadly killed in a mountaineering accident in 1985, lacked the imagination and the intellectual firepower required. Eventually, Margaret came to the same conclusion. Not yet fifty when he was appointed, Middleton, although lacking Rawlinson's good looks, had many of the other qualities she admired. He was not only an enthusiast for monetary policy. He strongly believed in supporting the government of the day – for instance in not thrusting an incomes policy down the throat of a Conservative Government which happened to be dead against the idea. Moreover his interpretation of the constitution was essentially Prime Ministerial, believing that all other Ministers and officials should toe the line. Margaret was also impressed by his support against the Foreign Office in the campaign to 'get our money back' from the European Community, and rightly regarded him as a doer and not just a talker.

A northern grammar school boy who had never been fully accepted as a member of the establishment, Middleton had none the less succeeded in rising to the top of the establishment-conscious mandarinate, even though he was disappointed in his ultimate ambition to become Cabinet Secretary and Head of the Home Civil Service. Although I always enjoyed his quickness, his intelligence, and his political sensitivity, and Thérèse got on particularly well with him, he and I were somewhat wary of each other. He worked very hard for me for over six years, and in many ways I could not have asked for anyone better; but I was never sure that his habit of cultivating the Press, which he had acquired during his years as the Chancellor's Press Secretary, was always helpful. A good Civil Servant, who has to serve with equal commitment Ministers of all types and of both political parties, has to become to some extent all things to all men; but in Peter's case this characteristic was particularly highly developed. Nevertheless, he was an outstanding Permanent Secretary to the Treasury.

There was, however, one curious parallel between Middleton and Wass, despite their many differences. Wass was originally a mathematician and had become a deeply committed Keynesian, particularly impressed by Nicholas Kaldor. During the Keynesian heyday Wass was seen as a welcome new broom uninhibited by earlier Treasury reverence for the sterling parity and the balanced Budget. But he had the misfortune to reach the top in 1975, just when the Keynesian orthodoxies were themselves being questioned, even by some Labour Ministers. Middleton, by contrast to Wass, had taken monetary economics seriously, but in a very technical sense. He was thus well acquainted with the monetary aggregates and the influences upon them, even attending Karl Brunner's highly specialist seminars at Konstanz. But by the time he became Permanent Secretary, the monetary aggregates were becoming an increasingly shaky guide to policy. This meant that it was financial discipline, rather than the technical means of securing it, that mattered.

Middleton and Burns worked very closely together, got on very well together, and formed a formidable partnership, rarely disclosing their differences in front of me. But the combination of the practical problems of technical monetarism and pressure of work made Middleton in some ways more like a traditional Treasury Permanent Secretary than might have been expected, taking the lead in discussions with lawyers, juggling with top-level appointments and keeping – as he saw it – the peace between Ministers. He was 'turned-on' most by the interface with the City, where he eventually ended up. He was at his best as a troubleshooter, taking a grip of a complex specific issue in a way few others could have done. An excellent example of this was the 1987 BP share sale, described in Chapters 61 and 62, when Peter played a key role under great pressure with impeccable skill and judgement.

The official whom a Minister sees most is not of course the Permanent Secretary but his Principal Private Secretary. I had inherited in that post a Foreign Office official who had for some years been on secondment to the Treasury, John Kerr, who had been chosen by Geoffrey Howe. I knew him well from my time as Financial Secretary. He was due to return to the Foreign Office in August 1983, but I managed to persuade him to stay on and see me through my first Budget. He had grown very close to Geoffrey and remained so throughout Geoffrey's time at the Foreign Office too. I came across him again towards the end of my Chancellorship, when he was handling the increasingly sensitive issue of our relations with the European Community, to which he became our ambassador in 1990. I also inherited John's excellent and immensely reliable number two, Margaret O'Mara, who worked long hours skilfully sifting through the mass of papers which flooded into my office every day, sending back what would not do and picking out what really mattered.

John Kerr himself was an amazingly lively and quick-witted character, whose love of plots and intrigue outdid any politician I have ever worked with. He worked extremely hard, but often could not be tracked down in the evenings, even though he had not officially packed up at the office. He was usually to be found at Number 10, picking up the latest gossip. These feats of over-assiduousness were faults on the right side, and John Kerr was one of the best Principal Private Secretaries I had during my time as Chancellor.

Outsiders seldom realize how important that role is in the life of the Chancellor. Indeed the key posts are very different from those the public supposes. They are, in probable order of importance, Principal Private Secretary, Chief Economic Adviser, Press Secretary and Permanent Secretary. The real point is not the precise order, which is arguable, but the fact that these are the four key people, which is unarguable. That is not to deny that there are other Treasury posts where the quality of the incumbent is very important. But on the whole they are posts where an indifferent number one can be compensated for by an outstanding number two. That is not the case with the key four – except to a limited extent with the Permanent Secretary, which is the only reason why I put him fourth.

Surprise Choice for the Bank

At least as important as the change at the top of the Treasury was that at the Bank of England. Although he was already sixty-seven years old and had served two terms as Governor, Gordon Richardson was disappointed not to be offered a third term. Although a sound, even stern, anti-inflationist by his own lights, he regarded the sometimes crusading radicalism of the Thatcher Government with ill-concealed distaste, which was more than fully reciprocated by Margaret. He is reported to have remarked: 'She is canine; I am feline.'

There was therefore little astonishment that she appointed a new Governor but some surprise at his identity. Six months before I went to Number 11 in December 1982 she announced that it would be an outsider – Robin Leigh-Pemberton, then Chairman of the National Westminster Bank. He took up his post in July 1983, a month after I had taken up mine. Although he was not initially widely respected within the Bank and at first had no great authority there, officials at both Great George Street and Threadneedle Street increasingly grew to like him. Unlike Richardson, he did not insist on controlling every aspect of the Bank's activities himself. This pleased senior Bank officials and made him a very much easier Governor with whom to work, both for me and for the Treasury as a whole.

Both Robin and I were keen to improve the rather prickly relationship that had developed between the Bank and the Treasury under Richardson. One of the first things we did was institute a regular monthly lunch to discuss areas of current or potential difficulty, and to compare notes on our views of monetary conditions. These lunches, held alternately at Robin's elegantly furnished gubernatorial flat in New Change and in the Soane dining room at Number 11, and attended only by my Principal Private Secretary as note-taker, allowed us to defuse a number of potential problems before they could cause trouble.

CHAPTER 23

A JOB WITH FEW FRIENDS

The Switchback · Range of Duties
The Finance Ministers' Trade Union · Mastering the Mint
Steering the Economy · A Spending Squeeze
The Shock of the Leaks

The Switchback

IN MY FIRST HOUSE of Commons speech as Chancellor, on 29 June 1983, I remarked that 'I am keenly conscious that few Chancellors of the Exchequer have left office with their reputations enhanced.' I could have added that these few had mostly stayed only a short time. The exception was my predecessor, Geoffrey Howe, who had four years in the post and to whom I paid tribute in that speech.

Part of the reason is that, more than other Ministers', the Chancellor's stock tends to follow a switchback course, and he is more likely to depart, for whatever reason, in a trough than at a peak. In my case I started with the usual honeymoon from my appointment in June 1983 to the summer recess of that year – a honeymoon, however, interrupted by a major embarrassment over some leaked spending cuts. Then came a poor, though not disastrous patch, from my rather indifferent 1983 Party Conference speech until my rapturously received first Budget in 1984.

But the glow lasted only a few months after which there was a very lean period, including my 1984 Conference speech (the least well received of the series) the nadir of which was probably the sterling crisis of early 1985, to my first enthusiastically received Conference speech, that of 1985. This triggered a steady climb back, leading to my really strong and supposedly 'unassailable' phase, which lasted from the 1986 Budget to the summer recess of 1988, when it was interrupted by an unexpectedly large deterioration in the trade figures. Finally there was a steady decline from the summer of 1988 until my resignation in October 1989, when the genuine problems of reducing inflationary pressure and the resulting unpopular rises in interest rates to a very high level were compounded by a prolonged conflict between Margaret and myself over the management of sterling.

Range of Duties

Before going into these events it is worth saying something about the job of the Chancellor of the Exchequer. It is an absorbing one, a difficult one, at times a frustrating one; but it is also a particularly demanding one. We are unusual in Britain in that the Chancellor has responsibility for taxation, for the control of public expenditure and for the whole of monetary policy, including interest rates and the management of sterling.

In other countries these jobs are normally divided up. In the United States for example, the Treasury Secretary is responsible for tax; the director of the Office of Management and the Budget (OMB) for public expenditure; and the Chairman of the Federal Reserve for the monetary side. Indeed, there could even be said to be four separate top jobs in the economic policy field if the Chairman of the Council of Economic Advisers is included. The latter post is of variable status but its holder, if he is close to the White House, can have considerable influence as part of a quartet who advise the President on economic policy. The only other important country in the advanced industrial world where the Finance Minister has a similar range of responsibilities to that of the British Chancellor is France.

Despite the very heavy demands it makes on the Chancellor, the concentration of responsibilities for the most part makes good sense. For public expenditure and taxation are after all two sides of the same coin. They are the income and expenditure sides of the State's budget. The coherence of policy is improved when they are in the same hands.

Monetary policy, however, is a different matter, and I eventually came to the conclusion that it would be best handled by an independent but accountable central bank, at arm's length from government, on the lines of the German Bundesbank or the US Fed, and towards which France and a number of other countries are now moving. This status will in any case arguably be necessary for those countries which wish to move to Stage Two of European Monetary Union as defined by the Maastricht Treaty of 1991, even if they do not wish (as I do not – see Chapter 71) to go all the way to stage three and the single European currency.

Nevertheless the monetary side of things was of special interest to me, probably more so than to many other Chancellors, I had specialized in it during my time as Financial Secretary, and it lay at the heart of the Government's economic policy.

Less well known, perhaps, is the fact that the Chancellor has his finger in pretty well every pie in government. This follows partly from his responsibility for Government spending and partly from tradition. As a result, he can exert a significant influence on policies which are announced by other Ministers and which the public does not associate with the Treasury at all.

If somebody had managed to penetrate security and called on me at a random hour of the working day, he would probably have found me, not considering interest rates or exchange rates or government borrowing – the issues so beloved of financial commentators – but playing a substantial role on a Cabinet Committee on any one of a vast range of subjects, from defence procurement to social security reform, from broadcasting to education reform, from the National Health Service to reform of the legal system. It is not for nothing that the Treasury is known in Whitehall as the Central Department.

The Chancellor, if he proceeds with care and caution, can affect the content and not merely the cost of other Ministers' policies and, in a limited number of carefully selected areas, generate the ideas which decisively influence the direction of government policy. Indeed, as I shall later describe, I played a significant part in both the health and education reforms of the late 'eighties. But at the end of the day the basis of the Chancellor's influence is in his control over finance.

This is exemplified by the long-standing rule that any Minister who has a proposal to put before Cabinet must first submit it to the Treasury. He can of course take it to Cabinet even if the Treasury disagrees; but in that case there has to be a paragraph in his Cabinet paper, written by the Treasury, which sets out the nature of the Treasury's disagreement and the reasons for it.

This influence is acquired at a price. For it inevitably ensures that both the Treasury as a Department and the Chancellor as an individual are regarded by most of the rest of the Government as the enemy. A Chancellor who is doing his job properly has few friends. That is one reason why it is of vital importance to the successful conduct of government that there is an extremely close and special relationship between the Chancellor of the day and the Prime Minister. They do not have to be cronies or soul mates, but they do have to be on the same wavelength. This was the case with Margaret Thatcher and myself for very many years. When that harmony came to an end I took the view that it was impossible to do the job effectively and therefore it was better not to do it at all.

There is another, less substantial but probably better known, way in which the British system differs considerably from others, even from the French. That is, the extraordinary ritual we have on Budget Day. Going round the world I was surprised to find that almost all the people I met had seen photographs of Thérèse and myself outside Number 11, with the old battered Gladstone budget box brandished in my hand. If truth be told, my opposite numbers in other governments were secretly envious of the British Budget.

In this country Press and academic commentators are predictably cynical. They describe it as a ridiculous survival, a foolish ritual and a meaningless tradition. That is not how I see it. Quite apart from the fact that it can be fun, it seems to me no bad thing that for one day in the year the attention of the entire nation should be focused on the national economy and on the issues involved.

The Finance Ministers' Trade Union

There is one consolation for unpopularity among one's colleagues at home. This is that other Finance Ministers around the world are in a very similar position. They too, if they are doing their job properly, have few friends among their own colleagues. As a result, there readily grows up a quite remarkable degree of cameraderie among the Finance Ministers of the various developed countries. For almost the only political friends they have are each other, and they are soon on Christian name terms.

I became particularly close to the long-serving German Finance Minister, Gerhard Stoltenberg, a tall, silver-haired man of total integrity, who subsequently became Defence Minister until he had to resign under something of a cloud. Gerhard and I used to ring each other up regularly to compare notes. On matters of mutual interest he would tell me on a strictly personal basis what was happening in the German Cabinet and I would let him know on the same basis, confident that it would go no further, the state of play in our own Cabinet.

More than mutual sympathy was involved. I recall one occasion when Gerhard telephoned me to discuss a projected European space venture he was seeking to resist within the German Cabinet. His opponent, as usual, was the seemingly perpetual German Foreign Minister, Hans-Dietrich Genscher, from the Free Democrat part of the ruling coalition, who held the job continuously from 1974 until his surprise resignation in 1992. Genscher, a man addicted to 'European' gestures and used to having his own way, had claimed in Cabinet that Germany had no choice but to support the proposal, irrespective of the cost, since the British had caved in to French pressure and if Germany were not to go along, too, it would find itself out on a limb, which would be intolerable. I was able to reassure Gerhard that Genscher was making it all up; that in fact we were resolute in our opposition to the project and would remain so. This enabled him to treat Genscher's intervention with the scepticism it deserved.

There were a number of occasions of this kind. In many ways I was sorry for Gerhard, who, despite the success of the German economy, had a tough time politically. This was an almost inevitable consequence of coalition politics, which follow from proportional representation. The Prime Minister of the day, in this case Helmut Kohl, always tended in any dispute to back the leader of his coalition partner, who posed no threat to him, against his own senior party colleagues, whom he saw as political rivals.

Since the Germans were our natural allies over so many issues within the European Community, it was unfortunate that my own relationship with Stoltenberg was not mirrored by Margaret's with Kohl. Whereas the Socialist President of France, François Mitterrand, was able to score a hit with her by treating her as a woman, Kohl's clumsiness served only to reinforce her pathological hostility to Germany and the Germans which in the end came to dominate her view of the European Community. Things might have been better, curiously enough, had the gloomy and highly intelligent Social Democrat leader, Helmut Schmidt, remained in office: Margaret had a considerable respect for him – as he had for her, to the extent that he was capable of holding a high opinion of any other politician.

Mastering the Mint

One of my more enjoyable responsibilities as Chancellor of the Exchequer was the Royal Mint. While the Bank of England is responsible for the issue of banknotes, it is the Royal Mint which designs and manufactures all British coins, medals and seals, including those used purely for commemorative purposes. The Chancellor is *ex officio* Master of the Mint, and as such responsible to the monarch for all new issues of coins. Although it was not the most important part of my job as Chancellor, for some inexplicable reason the coinage is a matter of intense and passionate interest to the public, far exceeding that in almost anything else I did.

The British are healthily conservative over the coinage, objecting to almost any conceivable change. I describe in a later chapter the outcry following my decision to withdraw the one-pound note in November 1984 in favour of the already circulating one-pound coin. Given this conservatism, I had little hesitation in rejecting the periodic advice I received from the Mint for rationalizing the UK coinage, and (apart from withdrawing the halfpenny and the one-pound note) confined myself to arranging for the absurdly heavy 10-pence piece to be reduced to the size of the old shilling, an event which at the time of writing has yet to occur, and preparing the ground for it by replacing the 5-pence piece (which formerly occupied the shilling slot) with a smaller coin the size of the old sixpenny bit. I was also technically responsible to the Queen for any new designs for existing coins, although this had long been largely delegated to the Royal Mint Advisory Committee, whose long-serving Chairman was the Duke of Edinburgh. This was to create the only occasion on which my dealings with the Royal Family over the coinage caused serious friction.

Ever since its inception, it had been the practice to change the design on the reverse of the pound coin every year. In 1987 the Advisory Committee sent me in the usual way, via Dr Gerhard, the Civil Servant who actually ran the Mint, with the title of Deputy Master, a series of photographs of the designs they had considered for the 1988 £1 coin, indicating which design they favoured. It seemed to me that the favoured design would be greatly improved by the omission of a wreath which surrounded the coat of arms, occupying all the spare space on the coin and making it look incredibly fussy. I therefore told Dr Gerhard that I would prefer to go ahead with the chosen design without the wreath. Unfortunately, he omitted to put this to the Advisory Committee.

I heard nothing further until, out of the blue, I received an icy letter from the Duke of Edinburgh saying that, if I did not value the advice of his Committee, I should wind it up. Deeply embarrassed, I swiftly despatched an apologetic reply, emphasizing my high regard for his Committee, and suggesting that misunderstandings could be avoided in future if he would agree to the attendance of a junior Treasury Minister, nominated by me, at all the Committee's meetings. This arrangement was duly put in place, and no further problems occured. As for the Mint, its response to the Duke's displeasure was to produce only a minimal number of 1988 pound coins, which as a result are a relative rarity – and to my eyes at least, quite a handsome rarity.

Where I did fear problems was when the time came to replace the young Queen's head that had adorned the coinage since she ascended the throne in 1953 with a more mature likeness. The Mint had commissioned the coin designer, Raphael Maklouf, who had done an excellent job; but when I went to the Palace to submit it to the Queen I was not quite sure how she would take it. Needless to say, she was at her most charming and approved the portrait without any reservations of any kind. I also took the opportunity of raising with the Queen the Mint's proposal to issue, over the years, a series of commemorative £2 coins. It was, I explained, always looking for ways to boost its profits by tapping the collectors' market, and had successfully produced a £2 coin in connection with the Commonwealth Games in Edinburgh in 1986. (Commemorative coins, incidentally, always used to be crowns; but by the time I had become Chancellor it was no longer economic to sell a commemorative coin for only 25 pence.) I added that in my view the suggestion was rather undignified – quite apart from the problem of finding sufficient memorable events to commemorate. The Queen wholeheartedly agreed, and that was the end of that proposal.

It was not, however, the end of the Mint's would-be money-making ventures. It had been left with a vast quantity of gold sovereigns, for which there was no longer any market overseas – the UK market having long since dried up, largely because gold coins were liable to VAT. The reason why they were unsaleable, The Mint assured me, was that they were the wrong size and weight. The South African Krugerrand had established that there was a vast market for one-ounce gold coins, and now that the Krugerrand was banned as part of the world's economic sanctions against South Africa, there was a great opportunity for the Mint to melt down its sovereigns and produce a new one-ounce gold coin for the overseas market.

I was sceptical. The profit came from selling an ounce of gold for significantly more than the market price of an ounce of gold, not the easiest of tricks to pull off. Moreover, as I pointed out, a number of other countries had been quicker on the uptake, and had already produced gold coins (such as the Canadian Maple Leaf) that had replaced the Krugerrand in the market place. The Mint was confident, however, that, such was its prestige, a large market was there to be conquered provided a sufficiently attractive design of Britannia – this was to be the name of the new gold coin – could be produced.

Still sceptical, I asked for the necessary market research to be carried out before I gave the go-ahead. I was told that this had already been done, and the result was encouraging. Accordingly, having secured the Queen's consent, I gave Dr Gerhard the green light, contingent on the design. In due course he came up with what was unquestionably a fine, if somewhat unconventional design. When I showed the first example of the coin as a matter of interest to Margaret, she remarked that Britannia looked like Rita Hayworth – a perceptive observation (although to my eyes she had more of the Ginger Rogers about her) and certainly no grounds for objection.

Sadly, the Britannia, attractive though it is, proved an embarrassing commercial flop. Dr Gerhard very kindly invited me to bring my then eleven-year-old son, Tom, to Llantrisant in South Wales, during the summer holidays of 1987, to strike the first Britannia. This was where Jim Callaghan, a loyal adopted son of Cardiff, part of which he had represented in the House of Commons since 1945, had moved the Mint from London during his time as Chancellor. It was only very much later that I discovered that the Mint had in fact done no serious market research at all.

It was in my capacity as Master of the Mint that I was expected to attend the annual Trial of the Pyx at the opulent Goldsmiths' Hall in the City of London and speak at the luncheon which followed it. The Trial of the Pyx is less of an ordeal than its name might suggest. Every year, according to a long-standing tradition, the Goldsmiths' Company conducts an impartial test of the coins produced by the Royal Mint. It takes a number of samples of each coin at random and checks that they are in every respect up to standard. The Trial of the Pyx – a word derived from the Greek for the small box in which the samples are kept at the Royal Mint – is the occasion on which the Company delivers its verdict.

It is a thoroughly surreal occasion. The Prime Warden of the Gold-smiths' Company and his fellow Wardens don their robes. The Queen's Remembrancer – originally the officer who collected debts owing to the sovereign – wears not only his best court garb but a wig and tricorn hat as well. The Master of the Mint cannot be outshone, and it was the only occasion in the calendar on which I attired myself in the Chancellor's magnificent black and gold robe of office, which my private office retrieved from the large metallic box in which it resided for the rest of the year. The elaborate costumes may to some extent account for the strange attraction the Trial of the Pyx continues to hold for senior Treasury officials, who never turn down an invitation to it.

The ceremony begins before the lunch, with the reading aloud by the Secretary to the Goldsmiths' Company of the results of the Trial of the Pyx. It always reminded me of Beachcomber's *Extracts From the Register of Huntingdonshire Cabmen*, which consists of nothing but a long succession of names. In this case it was a succession of the weights, sizes and metallic composition of each of the various coins tested, with the repetitive verdict that the outcome was 'more or less within the permitted variation' - a useful rubric which I always felt might with advantage accompany the publication of Government statistics. The Queen's Remembrancer marks the conclusion of this hypnotic procedure with a witty speech. The assembled company then proceeds into the Great Hall, where lunch is served on fine gold plates. After lunch both the Prime Warden and the Master of the Mint make speeches, usually fairly light-hearted disquisitions on some aspect of the coinage.

There was only one occasion on which the post-prandial speeches turned sour. One Teddy Hall, who was Prime Warden in 1986, used his speech that year to complain bitterly that the Royal Mint had reneged on a promise to allow its coin collection to be displayed at an exhibition the Goldsmiths' Company had organized. This was, by clear implication, an attack on me as Master of the Mint. He had not had the courtesy to inform me about it in advance. I knew nothing of the matter, since the Mint had not seen fit to tell me about it. The then Prime Warden's speech greatly embarrassed the other Wardens present, especially since – not having been warned that he planned to raise the matter – I was obviously unable to offer any explanation in my own speech, which followed, on a matter I knew absolutely nothing about.

There were other innocent pleasures in being Chancellor. One, which I happily shared with the enthusiastic and knowledgeable Peter Brooke, was choosing the Treasury Christmas card every year. Soon after I became Chancellor I discovered, flipping through the catalogue of the Manchester Art Gallery, an illustration of an allegorical painting by a minor Italian artist, entitled *The Blessings of Good Government*. It seemed an ideal choice for my first Christmas as Chancellor. Prompted by this, Douglas Wass drew my attention to the series of frescoes by Ambrogio Lorenzetti in the Sala della Pace in Siena on the *Effects of Good and Bad Government*, and I used each of the 'Good Government' frescoes in successive years until they ran out. I then considered cartoons but all the best ones had been used by my predecessors. So I embarked on a series of portraits of distinguished Chancellors of the last century, accompanied by a suitable panegyric on their achievements. The last Treasury Christmas card I was to send, in 1988, carried a particularly attractive sketch of Gladstone, the greatest Chancellor of all time. After my resignation the following year, the official Treasury were kind enough to present me with a full-sized framed reproduction of the National Portrait Gallery original.

Another rare pleasure, which Thérèse was able to share, was to stay overnight with the Queen at Windsor Castle in April 1985. These so-called 'dine and sleeps' are a much greater privilege – and much more fun – than an invitation to dinner. The Queen Mother and Princess Anne were among those present, as were Michael Heseltine and his wife, Anne. After dinner the Queen took us all on a long and fascinating guided tour of the Castle, which left only the then eighty-five-year-old Queen Mother as fresh as when we had started off on it. The Queen had taken great trouble to have on display something from the vast Windsor Castle collection which she thought might be of interest to each of her guests. For me, she had produced a letter from Benjamin Disraeli informing Queen Victoria what a tremendous success he had enjoyed with his latest Budget. The only royal occasion I dreaded was the annual reception at Buckingham Palace for the members of the Diplomatic Corps, where the guests are obliged to stand for an inordinate length of time while the Queen, followed by other members of the royal family, proceeds slowly down the long gallery, stopping to talk knowledgeably to each country's representative in London.

Steering the Economy

The economic situation I inherited from Geoffrey was one of resumed growth, following the quite severe recession of 1980–81 and inflation down to an underlying rate of some 5 per cent. But these generally satisfactory trends did not mean that everything was coming up roses when I first became Chancellor. Unemployment was high and still remorselessly rising; and although the pace of the rise had been gradually slowing down from the peak increase of some 800,000 in 1981, recorded unemployment did not start to fall, from a figure of well over 3 million, until three years after I had moved into Number 11.

Moreover the forecasts were extremely gloomy, not merely for future years but even for the course of events in 1983. The National Institute for Economic and Social Research (which has since improved) expected a complete standstill in output that year. The official statisticians were little better, understating what had recently happened, let alone what was likely. When the year 1983 was over, they reported that growth had been 2 per cent – a figure that has since been raised to 3.8 per cent in subsequent revisions – a sign of the statistical problems with which Chancellors have to struggle. At the same time the Treasury expected a rise in inflation towards the end of 1983 (this had been Geoffrey's main argument for holding the election in June rather than October), which happily did not occur.

During most of my time as Chancellor, I was assaulted by two groups of critics. The first and larger group wanted me to expand demand to absorb the unemployed: their recommended method was increased public spending. More sophisticated economists of this school argued that unemployment was above the supposed equilibrium rate consistent with stable inflation. The other, less vociferous, critics wanted an even tighter policy, designed to eliminate inflation altogether in short order – although they rarely spelled out what that would mean in terms of interest rates, pressure on profits and a still tighter labour market squeeze.

For my own part, I have always been extremely suspicious of analysis in terms of output gaps or equilibrium rates of unemployment. They are in practice extremely nebulous magnitudes; and estimates are contradictory and subject to huge variations, even when made by the same economist. I decided to try to keep the economy on a steady path, concentrating on a stable monetary framework as expressed by the MTFS, and not attempting to manage output and employment from the Treasury. The only concession I made to the clamour to 'do something' about unemployment was that I was content to make progress slowly towards the declared ultimate aim of 'zero inflation' - well defined by Alan Greenspan, the Fed chairman, as a state of affairs when the rate of inflation has ceased to be a factor in business calculations – rather than try for a quick kill. I saw my main macroeconomic task as that of keeping steady downward pressure on inflation in the face of international and domestic disturbances and pressures.

One practical warning against departing from the MTFS approach, certainly in the stimulatory direction the Press and the Opposition were urging on me, was that the growth in average earnings per head stopped declining in 1983 and remained astonishingly stable at around 7½ per cent a year up to and including 1987. Pay increases do not in themselves cause inflation, but they can be part of the transmission mechanism and are an important indicator of how much progress is being made.

For my first five years as Chancellor, up to the middle of 1988, I appeared to be broadly succeeding in achieving my objective. Total national output, as measured by real GDP, grew by an average of between 3 and 4 per cent a year – somewhat faster than was sustainable in the long run, but (at least until the end of the period) reasonable after the deepest post-war recession to date. At the same time inflation over the five years averaged not much more than 4 per cent a year (as measured by the Retail Prices Index excluding mortgage interest payments).

It was only then that it became clear how dubious an indicator unemployment had turned out to be of the gap between output and capacity, and of how that gap was changing. From the middle of the 1980s some other indicators, such as the CBI capacity survey, had been suggesting a very different picture, with capacity utilization high and increasing as the chart below shows.

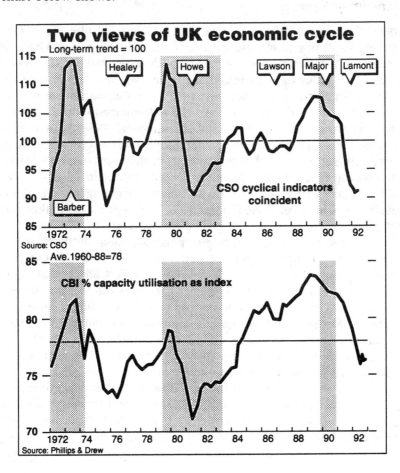

Two views of UK economic cycle

Long-term trend = 100

Healey   Howe   Lawson   Major   Lamont

Barber

CSO cyclical indicators coincident

Source: CSO

Ave. 1960-88=78

CBI % capacity utilisation as index

Source: Phillips & Drew

Sticking to a steady path did not, regrettably, mean putting the economy on auto-pilot and relaxing. On the contrary, a Chancellor's life is a never-ending struggle against destabilizing forces. Many of them are day-to-day pressures which come and go. But beyond these I decided to give priority to dealing with three major problems: how to improve the labour market by supply-side reforms, which – *pace* the expansionists – was the only lasting way of making inroads on unemployment; the problem of the monetary indicators which were not doing a good job in providing a stable financial framework; and keeping public expenditure to our chosen path. The first problem was long term and involved other Departments besides the Treasury. The second, or so it seemed to me when I took over as Chancellor in June 1983, could wait for a few months. But the public expenditure problem was staring me in the face, and was right at the heart of the Treasury's traditional responsibilities.

A Spending Squeeze

Indeed the urgent difficulty I faced on entering Number 11 was a very worrying surge in public expenditure. If uncorrected it would have meant increases in taxation or borrowing – or both. The pressure stemmed from the usual tendency to enter into new public spending commitments in the run-up to an election, coupled with an unwise decision made by Cabinet in the autumn of 1982 to encourage the nationalized industries and local authorities to increase their capital spending. The view was that, given the persistence of high and rising unemployment, the Government should listen more seriously to the demands from the construction industry for more capital investment. Margaret herself had been of this view, and had personally written to the local authority associations and nationalized industry chairmen on 2 November 1982 urging them to make 'full and proper use of the sums we have allocated to capital'.

In theory she was simply trying to persuade them to shift the balance from current to capital spending, and bring forward the use of sums already agreed. But I thought it an unwise invitation and said as much in Cabinet as Energy Secretary. Quite apart from the fact that investment of any sort is valuable only if it produces a worthwhile return, I was concerned at the signal Margaret's message was bound to convey that the period of public spending stringency was over.

To make matters worse, the spending forecasts on which Margaret's uncharacteristic and ill-advised exhortations were based turned out to be false, as she was duly furious to discover. In the autumn of 1982 the Treasury had predicted that the public sector would underspend significantly in the then current financial year, 1982–83. It need not have worried. As usual, there was a last-minute spending spree by Departments anxious to use up their allocations. Alas, the temporary weakening of Treasury control spilled over into the following financial year, 1983–84, and threatened to push the Budget deficit some £3 billion above target.

This upsurge in part reflected a change in the psychological climate. There was a feeling not only among back-benchers and the Press, but even among some officials in the Treasury and Bank of England, that, with inflation back well into single figures, the focus of policy should switch to the conquest of unemployment. Unaccustomed to the idea of any Government holding to a steady course for any length of time, it was felt to be inconceivable that the policies of the first term would be continued in the second. I was most emphatically not of that view, as I made clear to those journalists who interviewed me at the time. I did not believe that there was any trade-off to be obtained from a relaxation in the struggle against either inflation or excessive public spending and borrowing.

In my first speech to the House as Chancellor, on 29 June 1983, the final day of the debate of the first Queen's Speech of the new Parliament, I declared that I intended to 'maintain rigorous control of public sector borrowing . . . [which] in turn requires firm control of public expenditure, otherwise there will be no room for significant tax cuts throughout the lifetime of this parliament'. On public spending I said 'there is no scope for relaxation this year, next year or in any year . . . I stand ready to take action if our objectives are endangered.' But if I was to disabuse my colleagues (and indeed the commentators) of the idea that there had been a change in policy priorities, I had to make an early and dramatic move to wrench prospective public spending for 1983–84 back towards our original objective. Embarrassing though it was so soon after the general election, once I had revealed to Margaret the full horror of the Treasury's Summer Forecast* of the PSBR I had little difficulty in persuading her of the need for an emergency package of spending cuts. The Opposition were bound to claim that this justified their allegations during the campaign that we had a 'hidden agenda' of further public spending cuts; but I could readily demonstrate that all I was seeking to do was to get back as close as I could to the figures we had already published.

This would not be easy. With the financial year already in progress, I had to resort to the blunt instrument of a 2 per cent squeeze on general cash limits and a 1 per cent squeeze on the pay element. Most of this resulted in relatively modest cuts in specific programmes. But I needed to do more with defence, where the overrun threatened to be greatest. At a tense meeting between Margaret, Michael Heseltine, then Defence Secretary, and myself at Number 10, I managed to secure agreement on a £240 million cut in the defence budget.

*Treasury economists carried out three full-scale forecasts a year: the Winter Forecast, which was published on Budget Day, the Autumn Forecast, which was published in the Autumn Statement, and the Summer Forecast, which was not published at all.

The overall package came to £1 billion, half representing genuine savings and the other half a further sale of BP shares, to be held in September. Although the genuine savings were less than half of one per cent of total public expenditure they nevertheless had a profound psychological effect, reminding colleagues that the tight grip on public expenditure would not be relaxed simply because inflation had come down and unemployment was continuing to rise. They also set a new baseline for future years, which was particularly valuable in controlling the defence budget, since at that time the policy was to increase defence spending by 3 per cent a year in real terms, in accordance with the NATO guidelines.

As I explained in a Press interview: 'if we had done nothing this would have given the false impression that we no longer cared about what was happening to public spending and borrowing'. This was hardly an attitude which I had any wish to encourage, not least because public expenditure, partly as a result of inherited commitments, had risen by 3½ percentage points as a proportion of GDP during the first three years of a supposedly ferocious Thatcher Government.

The Shock of the Leaks

There was, however, an unfortunate personal fall-out. The £500 million package of genuine cuts was leaked to *The Times* of 7 July 1983, the very day that Cabinet was due to meet to agree the package. This created a sour atmosphere in Cabinet. To make matters worse, I had to tell my colleagues that because of the leak I had to announce the package that afternoon, since there would otherwise be a collapse of confidence in the financial markets. This led some colleagues to complain that I had arranged the leak to bounce them into agreeing to the cuts.

This was manifest nonsense, as there was no advantage for me in leaking spending curbs which I had already agreed with Margaret and the key spending colleagues. The leak brought only embarrassment; but this did not prevent the Lord Chancellor, Quintin Hailsham, from expostulating in Cabinet that 'this is no way to run the country'. It was a baptism of fire.

I also suffered a lesser embarrassment, which I put down to my inexperience. On 25 July, when I announced in a written answer the sale of a further slice of the Government's shareholding in BP, John Biffen, then Leader of the House, was barracked for some twenty minutes about the abuse of Parliament allegedly involved and he eventually took some pleasure in calling me to the chamber to deliver my written answer orally.

Thus in presentational terms at least my Chancellorship did not get off to a very good start. But there was worse to come. For unfortunately the public expenditure leak prefigured a much more serious leak of the contents of my first Budget early the following year, which I shall move ahead of the narrative and mention now.

The media coverage of the final days before the 1984 Budget was dominated by what was probably the worst breach of Budget security ever. An early draft of the tax section of the Budget Speech appeared to have fallen into the hands of the *Guardian*. Details of most of the tax measures I was then planning to announce were published in that newspaper on 1 March, less than a fortnight before Budget Day.

These included the ending of tax relief on life assurance premiums, the cut in corporation tax, the withdrawal of stock relief and 100 per cent first-year investment allowances and many other key details. There were some inaccuracies, including reference to a plan for taxing consumer credit, which reflected the date at which the stolen draft was written. But that was small consolation. I was deeply depressed, even devastated. I feared – wrongly, in the end – that the reception of my first Budget would be irretrievably soured. Indeed I find it difficult, writing several years later, to express the depth of the despair I felt on the night of 29 February 1984, when I was first told by my Press Secretary, Martin Hall, that the *Guardian* had got a jumbo Budget leak; and then was brought the first edition where I was able to see the full horror of it all.

The Budget leak was financially costly, too. The revelation of the withdrawal of tax reliefs from life assurance premiums on policies taken out after the Budget meant that, in the few days remaining before it, many thousands of people frantically took out new life policies. There are few salesmen like life insurance salesmen, and they made the most of the opportunity presented to them. It also caused immense complication and considerable ill will when unfortunate officials had to determine which new life policies had actually succeeded in beating the Budget and thus qualified for tax relief, and which had not.

The two leaks, on both public spending and the Budget, deeply scarred me in my first year as Chancellor and made me very anti-leak and security conscious. I am by nature fairly secretive; but I hope I am willing to listen to rational arguments for more open government, of which these leaks were certainly not examples. The first one could just have been some unauthorized and clumsy attempt by someone within the machine to prepare the Press for the public spending news; but as we did not get to the bottom of it, I do not know. The second leak was the pure theft of a Budget document and could only have been the result of deliberate malice or dishonesty. The combined result of the two was to reinforce my most secretive instincts, which may, I suppose, have increased the media's hostility towards me.

In the case of the Budget leak, I had no hesitation in authorizing a police investigation. This did not find a culprit, but it did propose a substantial tightening of Budget security procedures, which I accepted.

A JOB WITH FEW FRIENDS

Subsequently, under the amended Official Secrets Act, for which Douglas Hurd was responsible as Home Secretary, an act of liberalization which had my full blessing, leaks of economic information, including Budget leaks, no longer count as a criminal offence, but as serious breaches of discipline. The theft of documents, however, remains a crime under the ordinary law of the land and would still have justified a police inquiry.

CHAPTER 24

CONTROLLING PUBLIC EXPENDITURE

The Annual Round · The Star Chamber
There May Not be a Better Way · The Autumn Statement
Towards Greater Realism · Why No Capital Budget?

The Annual Round

THE EMERGENCY CASH LIMIT curbs which caused so much trouble in July 1983 were fortunately something I was not obliged to repeat. They should not be necessary if the normal machinery of spending control is working properly. This used to follow a regular annual cycle culminating in the Autumn Statement in November, when the Government's main spending decisions were announced.

The control of public expenditure is, to say the least, not the most gripping aspect of economic policy, let alone of Government as a whole. Yet without it the successful conduct of economic policy, and indeed of Government itself is impossible.

One of our first decisions when we took office in 1979 was to review, each year, the spending plans for the next three years. Previously, the Treasury had worked to a four-year time horizon; but the fourth year was so speculative that we decided to drop it. In any event, it is inevitably the year immediately ahead that is the main focus of attention. A more fundamental issue than the length of the planning period is the choice that has to be made between what might be termed the 'brick-by-brick' and the 'envelope' approaches. Under the 'brick-by-brick' approach, the process starts with negotiation over each individual spending programme, which is virtually guaranteed to ensure that the overall height of the resulting wall will be excessive. Under the 'envelope' approach, it is a guideline for the totality of public spending that is agreed by Cabinet first, and the individual programmes then have to be made consistent with the agreed overall guideline. This latter approach, which we adopted from the start, is clearly superior.

The round started in earnest with a meeting of the Cabinet in early July, at which the Chief Secretary presented a paper setting out in stern and measured tones the current public expenditure picture and trends, and recommending what the guidelines should be for the coming year in terms both of the 'planning total' and of total public spending, or 'general government expenditure' to use the jargon. (The difference between these two concepts is explained briefly later in this chapter.) This was accompanied by a paper from the Chancellor setting out the general economic context, drawing out the tax implications, and calling on colleagues to agree to the Chief Secretary's recommendations. With varying enthusiasm, they would do so. That was the time at which Cabinet would be made aware of the tax consequences of alternative spending decisions.

In the years immediately following the introduction of cash planning, the Chief Secretary's recommendation – which of course had emerged from exhaustive discussion within the Treasury with the Chancellor and senior officials, and then been agreed with the Prime Minister – used to be in terms of a precise cash total derived from the previous year's Public Expenditure White Paper. This eventually proved too rigid to be attained without either sacrificing realism – a dangerous path – or squaring the circle by some transparent device, such as increasing privatization proceeds. I eventually decided to switch to a double-barrelled guideline which permitted an adequate but not excessive degree of flexibility – something like 'as close as possible to the previously published planning total, and certainly a further decline in General Government Expenditure as a percentage of GDP'.

Cabinet agreement on the overall guideline was followed by bilateral discussions between the Chief Secretary and spending Ministers. Ministers taking part in the bilateral meetings were expected to agree the departmental totals in considerable detail, and the measures needed to secure any savings. The bilaterals started pretty soon after the July Cabinet; and after a break for the summer holidays, they resumed in September and continued right up to and usually during the Party Conference in October.

It was virtually unheard of for agreement with any spending Minister to be reached after one bilateral; there would invariably be a second and, if it was likely to prove productive, a third. It was a matter of virility for some spending Ministers, egged on by their officials, to put in bids well above anything remotely consistent with the overall envelope agreed by Cabinet. There were almost always Press reports in the summer and early autumn of excess bids, totalling anywhere between £5 billion and £15 billion. In so far as the reports represented more than the Press simply going through a regular annual routine – which they could do with impunity, since no official figure of the excess bids was normally revealed – the source would be talkative spending Ministers. I always found the latter both tiresome and bewildering. Their activities were unhelpful to the Government and, at the end of the day, made them look silly, since they never got what they were asking for; but some politicians evidently have a compulsion to leak, even when they have nothing to gain from it.

In any event, if an agreement could not be reached bilaterally, then the Chief Secretary would discuss with the Chancellor, who of course saw all the papers, how best to resolve it. There were basically three options, all of which were used on different occasions in my time. One was for the Chancellor to have a private meeting with the spending Minister, with no officials present, to agree a compromise acceptable to both, as I did, for example, with Nick Ridley when he was Environment Secretary in 1987. The second, which was likely to be used only when there were both large sums and major policy issues involved, was for the Prime Minister to hold a meeting with the Chancellor, Chief Secretary, and spending Minister involved, usually with no officials other than a Number 10 note-taker present – although on occasions the Secretary to the Star Chamber (see below) would also attend. The most dramatic of these occurred over the freezing of Child Benefit in 1988, when the then Social Services Secretary was on the brink of resignation (see Chapter 58).

The Star Chamber

The third option was to leave it to the Star Chamber, which – if required – would start work immediately after the Party Conference in October, to resolve the remaining disputed issues. 'Star Chamber' was the popular name for an *ad hoc* Cabinet Committee (officially known in my day as Misc 62) first set up in 1982 to adjudicate unresolved issues between the Treasury and spending Ministers.* Its first Chairman was Willie Whitelaw, who continued in the role until his resignation through illness in January 1988. The Secretary to the Star Chamber, who was the official keeper of the figures, and assisted the Chairman in devising compromises consistent with the guidelines agreed by Cabinet at the start

---

*The jocular nickname derives from a Tudor and early Stuart court, which met under a star-spangled ceiling in a chamber of the Palace of Westminster. Its authority derived from royal prerogative and it could dispense justice more quickly than other courts. But it lacked Common Law safeguards and became notorious for its intolerance and severity of punishment. See for instance S. T. Bindoff, *Tudor England*.

of the process, was normally one of the two deputy Cabinet Secretaries. Needless to say, he worked closely with the Treasury.

The Star Chamber had very little time, even sitting four days a week, to get everything buttoned up in time for the final public expenditure Cabinet, which was in those days usually held in the first half of November immediately prior to the Autumn Statement. It was thus important that it was not given too many outstanding programmes to resolve: five would be the absolute maximum. On the other hand, it would be foolish to set up the Star Chamber just to resolve one remaining programme – and difficult for the Star Chamber, too, which would be unable to do its main job of weighing up the relative merits of the cases put by different spending Ministers, and allocating the sum that remained within the original Cabinet remit between them. There would thus be heavy pressure on a sole spending Minister still in dispute to settle. That pressure would be exerted either by the Chancellor or by the Prime Minister with the Chancellor present.

The threat to activate the Star Chamber was always present and was intended to act as a deterrent to bloody-minded spending Ministers. Margaret and I would decide on its composition. The first question was, who is to be Chairman? In Willie's day the answer was obvious: he was an excellent Chairman. Quite apart from his great personal authority and political skills, he held to a small number of constitutional doctrines, one of which was that, while each individual issue had to be decided on its merits, overall the cause of good government required that the Treasury did not suffer many defeats. The fact, too, that by the time I had become Chancellor we were on good personal terms (strengthened by a similar rapport between Thérèse and Celia Whitelaw) did no harm either.

Following Willie's enforced departure, and given Margaret's profound hostility to Geoffrey Howe which ruled him out, the chairmanship went to less obvious colleagues – first to Cecil Parkinson and after John Major took over, to John Wakeham. This did not matter as much as it might have done, since during my time it never had to swing into action during the post-Willie phase, neither in 1988 nor 1989. Ironically, this was partly since some colleagues settled prior to the Star Chamber because they were not prepared to submit themselves to the arbitration of a tribunal to whose Chairman they were unwilling to defer.

The rest of the members had to be very carefully chosen. We would look for around four of them, in addition to the Chief Secretary and also the Chief Whip, who, as with the Cabinet itself, is not officially a member but who sits in and speaks if invited to do so by the Chairman. The four would ideally consist of three public spending hawks and one public spending dove, thus ensuring that while both wings of the Cabinet and the Party were represented, the balance was sound. Until he was dropped from the Government, John Biffen was usually the statutory 'dove'. There were other criteria. If, as in the overwhelming majority of cases, they were spending Ministers themselves, they should already have settled; for a Minister could hardly appear before a tribunal of which he was a member. Most of them should also have had previous experience of sitting on the Star Chamber. Membership of the tribunal was, in fact, quite sought after, partly because it was enjoyable in itself to sit in judgement on one's colleagues. Thus I could sometimes persuade a colleague to settle early with the incentive that, if he did, he would be asked to go on the Star Chamber. The most effective members in my day were, in their very different ways, Norman Tebbit and Kenneth Clarke.

There May Not be a Better Way

The much maligned Star Chamber system is in fact as near to a coherent system as any government has achieved. It evolved out of Margaret's understandable desire to have some method of resolving differences between the Chief Secretary and the spending Ministers short of Cabinet. At first we tried interposing a further round with Geoffrey, as Chancellor, in the chair. But this was invidious for him and – more important – hard for the colleagues to accept. So in 1982 Willie Whitelaw, as Deputy Prime Minister, was pressed into service to chair this stage, and this *ad hoc* arrangement was soon converted into an orderly and structured institution by the genius of the official machine. Pliatzky remarks that something like it 'seems to me an instrument which future governments, of whatever political complexion, should have available'.

Willie Whitelaw himself is far too modest about his own creature. For he worries in his memoirs that the Star Chamber 'is not in a position to judge priorities between departments'. Yet one of the main jobs of the Star Chamber was precisely to decide how a limited pot of money should be apportioned between various spending Ministers who appeared before it. (I would let Willie have a note telling him how much he had at his disposal if the July Cabinet remit was to be fulfilled.) It is true that, by the time things came to him, most of the original sum had already been allocated in the bilaterals. But in conducting these the Chief Secretary inevitably takes keenly into account the Government's known spending priorities. Indeed if he did not he would soon lose control of public expenditure. For example, if he were soft on low-priority programmes, neither he nor I would be able to offset this by being extra tough on the high-priority ones. For the Ministers responsible for the latter would take the matter to appeal, in one forum or another, and win.

The public-expenditure Cabinet meeting in the first half of November represented the final stage of the process. The Chairman for the Star Chamber would start the Cabinet discussion by listing the outcome of the programmes that had been settled bilaterally prior to the Star Chamber and the outcome of the agreements reached at Star Chamber. He would also draw to Cabinet's attention those settlements where politically contentious decisions had had to be taken. In years where there was no Star Chamber, it would be the Chief Secretary who would perform the analogous role.

Should, unusually, any issues remain to be resolved by Cabinet itself, he would inform the colleagues of the Chief Secretary's position, the spending Minister's position, and the Star Chamber's proposed adjudication. But I can recall only two occasions in my time when Ministers did go all the way to Cabinet: one was Patrick Jenkin and the other was Peter Walker. Patrick secured a little extra money for the housing programme in 1984. But the outcome fell far short of what he wanted and something very like it probably could have been secured in the Star Chamber. In the same year Peter Walker, the Energy Secretary, refused to accept the External Financing Limit for the electricity industry. But since he was abroad for the November public-expenditure Cabinet and was represented by his Minister of State, Alick Buchanan-Smith, this was little more than an empty gesture and the Star Chamber's suggested figure was agreed.

I always made a point of seeing Margaret alone before both the July and the November public-expenditure Cabinets, to discuss the sequence in which she called Ministers to speak – she would always make a point of inviting everybody to have their say. It was important to open and close the discussions with comments from Ministers who were dependable on public expenditure, leaving the less sound colleagues sandwiched in the middle – but not in a bunch, otherwise there was the risk of a momentum building up. George Younger, the Scottish Secretary and subsequently Defence Secretary, was always a reliable opening batsman, and Willie Whitelaw was ideal at the end. (After Willie's retirement, Geoffrey Howe was an excellent substitute in this role.) The one colleague who could be guaranteed to be unsound was Peter Walker: it was useful to have his contribution immediately followed by one from Norman Tebbit. Before Cabinet I would aim to see privately at Number 11 a number of Cabinet colleagues to whom I was close (such as Norman Tebbit, Geoffrey Howe, Douglas Hurd and Cecil Parkinson) to make sure that they were happy with the papers circulated before the meeting. I would also ask the Chief Secretary to see a few of his friends for the same purpose.

At the end of the November public expenditure Cabinet I would inform the colleagues whether the final outcome satisfied the original July remit – it almost always did – and reveal my plans for making the Autumn Statement announcement. I always kept a few cards up my sleeve, namely estimates of debt interest, plans for privatization proceeds, economic assumptions that had not already been revealed to departments, and of course the size of the Reserve. But clearly it was not in my interest to make any of these unrealistic. Nor would it look good to square an unsatisfactory circle by boosting the figure for privatization proceeds. I did so in the very early days, when I wished to enlarge the privatization programme in any event, but not subsequently, when in fact I made a point of publishing figures that took no credit for privatization receipts at all. It is true to say that the substance of the privatization programme was in no way affected by public expenditure or Budget cosmetics.

Finally, Cabinet would agree the brief statement summarizing what we had agreed (although of course without any figures) which would be given to the Press by Margaret's Press Secretary, the egregious Bernard Ingham. This would, of course, have been drafted by me and agreed by Margaret in advance of the meeting.

The Autumn Statement

The agreed public expenditure decisions were then outlined in the Autumn Statement, a document initiated by Geoffrey Howe in 1982, following a recommendation of the Treasury and Civil Service Select Committee Report on budgetary reform. It brought together a number of hitherto disparate announcements, including the rates of National Insurance contributions for the following year and the External Financing Limits for the nationalized industries. A third element, which the Press often focused on, in the absence, of any quickly assimilated message from the public spending decisions themselves, was the Treasury's latest economic forecast, which formed a foundation for speculation about the following year's Budget – an exercise which was assisted by the publication of an up-to-date ready reckoner showing the cost or yield of a wide range of tax changes.

A further element introduced by Geoffrey in the inaugural Autumn Statement of 1982, under pressure from the Treasury Select Committee, was the publication of a revised figure for the 'implied fiscal adjustment' for the year ahead. This derived from the format of the MTFS, where the projections for Government borrowing over the years ahead were buttressed by projections for the path of Government revenue and expenditure over the same years (see Chapter 7). The amount by which the excess of spending over receipts fall short of projected borrowing was shown in a separate line known as the implied fiscal adjustment, which was taken by commentators to indicate the scope for tax reductions – although it could equally well be used for reducing borrowing still further or even for increasing Government spending. It was an innovation I deeply disliked.

At Budget time the fiscal adjustment figure caused no problem: attention was inevitably focused on the Budget itself, and the projections for future years were taken as largely illustrative. But at the time of the

CONTROLLING PUBLIC EXPENDITURE

Autumn Statement, only four months before the next Budget, publication of an updated figure was inevitably taken as a preview of that Budget, despite all the uncertainties that in fact remained at that stage.

The presentational problem was particularly acute at the time of my first Autumn Statement, in November 1983, since the 'implied fiscal adjustment' for 1984–5 indicated a revenue shortfall of £500 million. 'On this basis the forecast implies the need for some net increase in taxes in next year's Budget,' I was forced to admit to the House on publication. This prompted a violent personal attack on me in the *Daily Express* the following morning under the headline 'Lawson in Blunderland', accusing me of smugness and lack of will in failing to cut public expenditure and make room for tax cuts: 'This Government was voted back to axe, not tax.' Attacks along similar lines followed from Walter Goldsmith, Director General of the Institute of Directors, and Terry Beckett, the Director General of the Confederation of British Industry. When I appeared on *Weekend World* the Sunday after the Statement, Brian Walden opened an entire programme devoted to public expenditure by saying that 'the whole strategy for economic recovery to which Mr Lawson is committed is being blown off course'.

These attacks reinforced my feeling that it was foolish in the extreme to advertise in advance the mere possibility of tax increases, especially when there was no statutory requirement to do so; and it would be just as foolish to advertise a tax reduction which I might not, in the event, be able to deliver. After one further year of this awkwardness, in 1984, I resolved to cease publishing any figure for the implied fiscal adjustment in the Autumn Statement. The Treasury mandarins were aghast when I informed them of my intention, because they felt that once MPs had become accustomed to receiving a particular piece of information no Chancellor would dare deny it to them. They were convinced that Parliament would force me into a humiliating climbdown. I assured them that I was fully capable of standing firm.

When I duly withdrew publication, in the Autumn Statement of 12 November 1985, it did indeed cause some astonishment. The Treasury and Civil Service Committee condemned me for withholding information from it; but as I explained to the Committee when I appeared before it on 26 November, the 'implied fiscal adjustment' was not in any true sense information at all, but merely a fallible guess at the future on which no operational decisions were based. I also pointed out that there was no reason why the Select Committee, with the aid of its own expert advisers and outside forecasts, should not make its own revised revenue forecast and derive its own estimate of the likely fiscal adjustment, should it so wish. Needless to say, it never did.

To make the change more palatable, I also decided in 1985 to add some genuine new information to the Autumn Statement, as well as subtracting some pseudo-information from it. Until 1985 the Autumn Statement contained figures for one year ahead only; even though Cabinet decisions, however shadowy, had been made for three years ahead. I decided that publishing the figures for the full three years in the Autumn Statement itself, instead of waiting until the Public Expenditure White Paper the following January, had advantages beyond the merely tactical. It would, for example, minimize the risk of Cabinet colleagues reopening public expenditure decisions between the November Cabinet and the publication of the White Paper.

In fact, no quid pro quo was really needed. Although it had upset the members of the Treasury Select Committee, most senior back-benchers on our side considered it a sensible move to get rid of it. Much to the astonishment of Treasury officials, its publication ceased without any serious disquiet. And with the proposed amalgamation of the Autumn Statement and the Spring Budget into a single event in December, it has clearly gone for good.

The practice I inherited was to defer making the Autumn Statement to the House of Commons until the full printed version was available some days after the final Cabinet decisions. For a time I went along with this, but eventually, in 1986, I switched to making my Statement to the House on the same day as Cabinet had met, accompanied by a duplicated summary of the document that was to go to the printers.

This was a tight schedule and I always prayed that there would be little need for last-minute changes. But the effort was worthwhile. It prevented selective and self-serving weekend leaks to the Press. Moreover the earlier the day of publication the more likely it was that it could be used in the Debate on the Queen's Speech, where the final day is traditionally devoted to economic matters, starting with a speech by the Chancellor. It was useful both to have some new material for an economic debate which was going to take place anyway, and to have an early parliamentary opportunity to develop the main themes of the Autumn Statement and to reply to any serious criticism that may have followed the original oral Statement. There was subsequently a full debate on the Autumn Statement as such after the Christmas recess when the Treasury Committee had reported.

Following the 1992 election, the Major Government announced a modification in the system of public expenditure control, which I discuss in Chapter 80. In practice it is unlikely that the new regime will prove very different from the old.

Towards Greater Realism

There are many different aggregates which are supposed to measure public expenditure; their definitions change over time. The confusion is reminiscent of that surrounding the money supply, although the two subjects are guarded by entirely different priesthoods who have almost nothing in common except their priestly nature. I described in Part I the shift from volume or 'funny' money to cash; and this was a big enough reform of definitions to be getting on with.*

There was one complication to which I have already alluded. General (meaning both central and local) Government expenditure, which is used to analyse trends for international comparisons, is a widely recognized aggregate corresponding to most people's idea of total public expenditure. But the annual spending round was conducted chiefly in terms of a narrower aggregate known as the Planning Total. The main item excluded from the Planning Total was debt interest. This essentially depends on the level of interest rates and the size of Government borrowing. Assumptions about both have to be made by the Treasury.

The planning total included a reserve to cover unexpected expenditure such as that caused by the Gulf War or the miners' strike. When I first became Chancellor, increases in demand-determined expenditure were not, however, charged to the Reserve. I decided to change that, and to charge against the Reserve all extra spending however incurred; in particular unavoidable increased costs of existing programmes as well as wholly new projects – for example, a higher take-up of existing social security benefits than had been officially estimated.

Getting the size of the Reserve right matters. An inadequate one is a foolish exercise in self-delusion, making it appear as if public expenditure is under tighter control than is in fact the case. But an excessive Reserve would be almost as bad, as it would encourage spending Ministers to put in extra bids during the course of the year. I always provided for a Reserve for the year immediately ahead a little above 2 per cent of the Planning Total, a practice which continued after my departure.

The Reserve is naturally bigger for Year Two than for Year One, and bigger still for Year Three than for Year Two, reflecting the simple fact that the further off the year is, the greater the degree of uncertainty. It is therefore right and proper that the Reserve for a given year is reduced as it moves closer. This inevitable process has, however, a number of consequences. In the first place it enabled my spending colleagues – and indeed the Government in general – to claim that they had won an increase in spending for the coming year, when all that had happened was that a portion of the Reserve for that year had been allocated among the various programmes. Secondly it meant that critics, including at times the Treasury Select Committee, would claim that public expenditure was out

---

*For a full guide to public expenditure concepts see the Treasury's Annual Autumn Statement Supplement, or Leo Pliatzky's readable books. As for the laws and traditional procedures, Sir Herbert Brittain's 1960 guide is still good value, or of course, Erskine May for full references.

of control, using as 'evidence' the increase in spending on programmes, when what had really happened was that sums already set aside were earmarked for specific purposes, as the year in question drew nearer. Although criticism founded on this confusion was occasionally tiresome, I can scarcely complain, since it was a confusion I exploited to the full when, usually for presentational reasons, it suited me to do so.

At the end of July 1987 I minuted Margaret, making the case for a further substantial narrowing of the definition of the Planning Total. This was in fact a joint initiative with Robin Butler, then the Treasury's Second Permanent Secretary in charge of public spending, and his last in that role. In January 1988, he succeeded Robert Armstrong as Cabinet Secretary and Head of the Home Civil Service – an unexpected but sensible choice on Margaret's part, although his departure was inevitably a considerable loss to the Treasury. Margaret was not immediately convinced, and Nick Ridley, by then Environment Secretary, had some objections of detail to what I proposed; but eventually agreement was reached and during the course of 1988 I was able to announce that the 'New Planning Total', as it was known, would come into force on 1 April 1990.

The essence of the New Planning Total was that it excluded all local authority self-financed expenditure, confining the local authority element in the Planning Total to the spending financed by central government grants of one kind and another, which are of course under central government control.

I had long been uneasy at the extent to which the annual Public Expenditure White Paper was a work of fiction. In the first place, the totality of local government current expenditure, although it could to some extent and with great difficulty be *influenced* by central Government, was in no sense *controlled* by central Government. And in the second place, within that total, the White Paper solemnly gave a detailed breakdown of the spending on everything from education to environmental services, figures for which were often the subject of fierce argument among spending Ministers and on which countless columns of Press comment were based, whereas in reality this reflected nothing more than Governmental aspirations: it was the local authorities themselves who, subject to meeting their statutory obligations, decided how the money they raised or received from central Government was in fact spent.

It seemed to me that the introduction of a new system of local government taxation, in the shape of the Poll Tax, notwithstanding the disaster I believed it to be, at least provided an occasion for a move towards a definition of the Planning Total that corresponded more closely to reality, while retaining an overall spending policy expressed in terms of the wider and much more important concept of General Government Expenditure.

CONTROLLING PUBLIC EXPENDITURE

Why No Capital Budget?

The definitions proved surprisingly controversial. Privatization proceeds, for example, count as negative spending and thus reduce both the Planning Total and General Government Expenditure, which is defined according to international convention. Although this was sometimes criticized, it was part of the whole corpus of government accounting conventions which the Thatcher Government certainly did not invent. Rather than go through the upheaval of a complete revamping of all definitions – which would still not have avoided controversy – I thought it right to show in all the main tables and charts public expenditure and the PSBR both with and without privatization receipts. But I did draw the line at deducting council house sales, which could not sensibly be done without making complex consequential changes to other items such as local authority property purchases and housing subsidies. In any case, their inclusion would not have affected the trend drop in the growth of public spending during my years as Chancellor.

Another recurrent criticism was that the Treasury mixed together current and capital items on both sides of its accounts and did not have a proper capital budget. In fact the Central Statistical Office, which is a Government Department (and since 1989 responsible directly to the Chancellor) does publish current and capital accounts for all levels of government in the National Income Blue Book; but it is true that such distinctions do not figure prominently in the presentation of public-expenditure decisions.

Behind this criticism is a lingering belief that capital spending is either superior to current spending, or at least safer to finance from borrowing. This really will not do. The current/capital distinction does not have the same meaning in the public as in the private sector. School buildings, for example – however desirable and productive in the larger sense – do not produce a cash return which will service debt interest. Nor are outlays on them inherently more productive of the non-cash return from education than, say, expenditure on better teachers, which counts as current. Those who seek to assimilate the system of public expenditure control to the conventions and methods used in the private sector always remind me of small children playing at shops. It has little relationship to the real thing. In so far as the disciplines of the private sector are superior, that is yet another powerful argument for privatization.

CHAPTER 25

THE TAMING OF LEVIATHAN

General Principles · A Science That is Not There
A Cabinet Riot · The Green Paper
The 1983 Spending Round · The 1984 Round and the Brighton Bomb
The Row Over Student Grants · Rage Over a Lost Pound Note
The 1985 Round – Leviathan Tamed · A Defence Concordat
1986 – The Pre-Election Round

General Principles

THE READER WILL BE as relieved as I am to move from the nuts and bolts of spending control to the policy issues raised. How much of our income should be spent privately as individuals or families or via voluntary organizations; and how much should be spent collectively through the State? The Government, of course, apart from relatively insignificant receipts from a few properties it owns, has no income of its own other than what it raises compulsorily by taxation or through the deferred form of taxation known as borrowing.

There is clearly no grand principle which will yield an answer in terms of a specific percentage of the national income as the appropriate level for public spending. There are some goods identified by economists as 'public goods', for which it is either technically difficult to charge or which are jointly provided to many beneficiaries. Standard examples are defence and the police. Others include lighthouses and parks (which benefit all those who look at them, even if they do not enter them). There' is also a generally accepted case for raising public funds to relieve poverty and provide for the needs of the sick and disabled which many economists misleadingly describe as 'redistribution'.

These objectives, however, can only be a general guide. They still leave the most important issues a matter of opinion. Whether a good is a public one or not is often a matter of degree. There is a 'public good' element in 'basic education, as the benefit from a literate body of citizens spills over to others. Higher and vocational education tends inevitably to involve the State because of the difficulties young people face in borrowing on their own security. There is also the problem that the benefits of training spill over from the employer who undertakes the training to his rival who poaches the workers. On the other hand there are private enterprise security organizations, and the police charge for keeping order at pop concerts. Where to draw the line is a political more than a technical issue. Moreover, even if there were universal agreement on the proper scope of State provision, this would still not determine how much should be spent on these agreed objectives.

There was one basic principle which guided my own efforts. Much writing on social choice and welfare economics implicitly assumes that all income belongs in the first instance to the State, and is then allocated by the State to individuals. Hence the Labour fury at the cuts in the higher tax rates in my 1988 Budget, which led to the temporary suspension of the House. The Tory belief should be the opposite one: that income or property belongs to the people who earn it or who have legitimately acquired it; and that a case has to be made for taxing it away. When the trumpets and drums are silent, and the last revisionist tract is off the Press, this is the abiding rift which still remains between Left and Right.

With that principle in mind, real world Tory politicians have to start off from where they find themselves: from existing structures, institutions, beliefs, political pressures and (sometimes unwelcome) manifesto commitments. Nevertheless, despite these handicaps, it is possible, with difficulty, to reduce public expenditure as a share of GDP. Where previous Conservative governments (with the rather special exception of a few years in the early 1950s, when defence spending was greatly reduced following the end of the Korean War) had merely succeeded in slowing down the seemingly inexorable onward march of the State, the Thatcher Government, by single-minded determination, succeeded in reversing it.

The following figures, all of which are after allowing for inflation, show that the Cabinet's public expenditure machinery was indeed able to discriminate between rival spending claims. (The full table is in Annexe 7.)

	% change in real terms 1979–80 to 1989–90
GDP	+23.3
General Government Expenditure	+12.9
of which	
Law and Order	+53.3
Employment and Training	+33.3
Health	+31.8
Social Security	+31.8
Transport	−5.8
Trade and Industry	−38.2
Housing	−67.0

The first three specific programmes listed above were clear Government priorities (although it must be said that the very high figure for law and order was swollen by the excessively generous formula for determining police pay we had inherited from the last days of the Callaghan Government). Social Security was not. But we had pledged ourselves to maintain most of the main benefit levels in real terms. Beyond this, social security expenditure was largely demand determined, reflecting the steady growth in the pensioner population, the alarming rise in the number of one-parent families, the greatly increased take-up of means-tested benefits (promoted by unofficial claimants' groups, who advised their 'clients' how best to exploit the system, rather like tax accountants at the other end of the income scale), and to a lesser extent the growth in unemployment.

At the other end of the scale, the run-down in transport, trade and industry and housing reflected the fact that they contained a large element of subsidy which it was Government policy to phase out. In addition, the standard accounting treatment ensured that the sale of council houses greatly reduced the figures for housing. The differences also reflect the general principle that State spending can more easily be cut back in those areas where there is a readily available private sector alternative. This explains, too, why Government expenditure on training, despite its rise over the decade as a whole, was allowed to fall towards the end of the period as company profitability recovered, and Government schemes were developed which involved substantial private sector funding.

A Science That is Not There

There was one recurring criticism of the PESC-Star Chamber system, which was made from time to time by (among others) the Treasury Select

Committee, which is based on a misunderstanding. It is argued that there ought to be an explicit and rational method for deciding priorities between rival claims on the public purse. Unfortunately there is no such science upon which we can draw. Even the economists' method of looking for the highest return at the margin does not work well here.

How, for example, do you decide objectively between building a new hospital, recruiting more policemen, increasing British Rail's investment programme or providing the local authorities with more money to spend on schools – which in any event you cannot ensure is all spent on schools, let alone determine what the schools do with the money? There should be nothing surprising here, since the same applies to how we decide our own personal spending priorities. All the time we are choosing between a more expensive holiday, a new music centre, restaurant meals or a new overcoat. But the process is scarcely an objective or scientific one.

Thus public spending is more like personal spending than it is like corporate expenditure. This is not very remarkable, given the high proportion that is either current expenditure on goods and services or transfer payments, rather than investment: the latter makes up only 10 per cent of general government expenditure. Moreover, even in the investment sector the greater proportion is in public services which provide no cash return.

There are of course techniques such as cost benefit analysis. These can to some extent be used to decide priorities *within* particular sectors of spending programmes: for example, where, if anywhere, a third London airport should be built; or priorities within the road programme; or the various investigations of where to put the rail link for the Channel Tunnel. As these examples show, not even studies such as these can avoid emotively charged assumptions and judgements. But they can at least help to organize information coherently. Attempts to use this technique to make comparisons *between* sectors – say military expenditure and the Health Service – are in practice a waste of time.

Just as revealed choice in the market place is a standard way of assessing consumer preferences, so the political market place is the only known method of making choices between different types of collective spending, or between the collective and private variety. Electoral choice has the disadvantage that the voter can choose only between two rival proclaimed policy bundles; he does not have the opportunity to make up his own bundles, as in a supermarket or other commercial market; which is an important reason why, other things being equal, private is preferable to collective provision. But within the public sector, the two-party system is a more subtle instrument for choice than the crude model suggests. Not only do parties offering unpopular bundles tend to stay out of office for long periods; but the political market works via changes of emphasis within the political parties as well as choices between them.

A Cabinet Riot

These reflections are not *a priori*. Towards the end of Geoffrey Howe's time as Chancellor, he made a serious attempt to produce a comprehensive review of how much public spending there should be and of what kind. The background was Geoffrey's very reasonable alarm about the implications of a Treasury study of public expenditure trends. The Cabinet accordingly authorized a survey of options by the Central Policy Review Staff – the so-called 'think tank'. The CPRS team was led by Alan Bailey, an official on secondment from the Treasury, who produced his report with an expedition rare in Whitehall – which may in part account for its political insensitivity.

Geoffrey's paper made grim reading. On a low economic growth projection, public expenditure seemed destined to remain at 47 per cent of GDP even in 1990; that is to say, still three percentage points higher than in Labour's last year. On a more optimistic growth projection, it might come down to just below 40 per cent by that year. Indeed this is exactly the ratio it did reach.

However Geoffrey and his advisers considered the optimistic projections unrealistic – if only because history showed that public spending tended to rise faster at a time of more rapid growth. Unfortunately, the implications of the pessimistic scenario did not bear contemplation. Taxation would have to rise to 45 per cent of GDP, even if the PSBR were not eliminated. The paper pointed out that this implied either a basic rate of income tax of 45 per cent or a single rate of VAT of 25 per cent, in place of both the zero rate and the then standard rate of 15 per cent.

It was in this context that Geoffrey brought in the CPRS paper, which canvassed various options, such as education vouchers in place of 'free' state schools; an increase in the pupil-teacher ratio; the replacement of part of the National Health Service (NHS) by compulsory private health insurance; and the cancellation of the Trident missile programme. This sounded like a Radical Right manifesto, but its inspiration was mainly Treasury-inspired arithmetic. Geoffrey certainly did not recommend all or any of these specific proposals, but urged the need for a new and fundamental study of public expenditure, with further exploration along the lines identified by the CPRS.

The result was the nearest thing to a Cabinet riot in the history of the Thatcher administration. Geoffrey's other and perfectly reasonable request – that no new spending commitments should be made, and that Ministers should avoid repeating old pledges that would otherwise expire – was not even properly discussed.

The episode played into the hands of the 'wets'. They not only managed to get the CPRS report shelved at the meeting; but made sure that its contents were leaked to the *Economist*, which obligingly described it as 'dismantling huge chunks of the welfare state'. Horrified articles duly appeared in the *Guardian* and the 'heavy' Sunday papers. Margaret, who in those pre-Poll Tax days knew how to beat a necessary retreat, was forced to state publicly that the Government had no intention of pursuing any of the options in the CPRS paper. It was this episode that formed the foundation of Labour allegations of a 'secret manifesto' in the 1983 election; and a full text of the CPRS report was released by the then Shadow Chancellor, Peter Shore, in the closing days of the campaign.

Although I strongly supported Geoffrey's emphasis on the need to curb the growth of public spending, and indeed achieved this during my own time as Chancellor, his September 1982 initiative was surprisingly maladroit for so experienced and cautious a politician. Had I still been at the Treasury I would certainly have counselled against it. As it was, his misjudgement (which Margaret, to say the least, had done nothing to restrain) was probably a product of his habitual over-estimate of his colleagues' and opponents' desire to be educated and of their readiness to respond to patient reasoning. Fortunately, little real harm was done. Indeed, the only casualty was the CPRS, which within a year Margaret, still smarting from the September 1982 episode, had disbanded for good.

The Green Paper

When I returned to the Treasury as Chancellor in June 1983, I discovered that it was all set to return to the charge. A Green Paper was in preparation, designed to demonstrate the nature of the long-term public expenditure problem and to encourage discussion of the consequences and possible remedies. It was based on a trawl of the spending Departments' own estimates of what they felt they would need to spend in the year ahead on the basis of current policies; and the idea was that these figures should be duly published to illustrate the scale of the problem.

This looked like yet another own goal, and I quickly put a stop to it. It seemed to me painfully obvious that public exposure of the various Departments' spending aspirations would give the figures a legitimacy that would make savings harder, not easier, to achieve. I decided instead to produce a Green Paper of a significantly different kind, and briefed one of my best officials, Michael Scholar, on what I wanted. He did an excellent job.

The Green Paper was published on Budget Day, March 1984 under the title *The Next Ten Years: Public Expenditure and Taxation into the 1990s*. It incorporated the published plans for public spending up to 1986–87, which projected a roughly unchanged spending total after allowing for inflation. This assumption was projected forward without departmental detail until 1988–89. Beyond that, it declared, there would be a margin for choice.

The Green Paper began, however, by quantifying some disturbing trends in the previous twenty years. In that period the UK's real national income had increased by about 50 per cent, but public expenditure had grown by 90 per cent. Taxes to pay for it already took up two fifths of GDP and were set to increase further if the trend were not halted and reversed. It was no consolation to Britain that other industrial countries experienced similar trends.

It then went on to discuss spending pressures in different sectors in terms that would repay rereading today. Its central message was that 'It is in the nature of the public services that demands are literally limitless, because they are not restrained by the price mechanism which forces those making demands to balance them against costs.' The Government would transfer provision to the market 'where possible and sensible' – no hostages to fortune here. Charges would be considered to limit demand. 'But over a wide range of services the only means of controlling costs is for the Government to limit the supply.' The so-called 'underfunding' of public services, in the sense of the Government having to say 'no' to demands for funds, is nothing more than an inescapable fact of life.

The Paper then spelled out the tax consequences of alternative spending trends, concluding that 'Government and parliament must reach their judgement about what public expenditure in total can be afforded, then contain programmes within that total'. In the past 'spending decisions, taken issue by issue, have steadily raised the burden of total spending without regard to what taxpayers will tolerate or the consequences for incentives and growth'. In advance of its publication there had been mounting demands from the House of Commons Select Committee on the Treasury and others for the Government to produce a Green Paper on the long-term public expenditure issue, as a basis for a great public and parliamentary debate. Characteristically, as soon as the Green Paper was published the Committee lost interest in the subject. The absence of political own goals must have come as a great disappointment.

The 1983 Spending Round

Largely as a result of the row which followed the leak of the 1982 CPRS report, the Government had effectively abandoned the attempt to secure tax cuts through real reductions in public spending, a policy formulation that had always been designed more to create a badly needed new climate than as a prosaic description of the likely outcome. I decided to switch to a new and more realistic objective which I put to the Treasury and Civil Service Select Committee just before Christmas 1983: holding the level of public spending steady in real terms while the economy grew. I subsequently refined it further to a slower rate of growth for public spending than the sustainable growth rate of the economy as a whole, with the result that public expenditure would steadily decline as a share of GDP.

Meanwhile, I referred to the concerns about public spending in my first Party Conference speech, in October 1983. Indeed, the main theme of the economic debate was that we faced a stark choice between a rigorous control of public spending and increases in taxation. As it was, the need to curb Government borrowing had caused the overall burden of tax to climb from 34¾ per cent of GDP in 1978–79, Labour's last year, to 38¾ per cent in 1982–83 (excluding oil revenues in each case). Although there were one or two calls from the floor for higher public expenditure to 'reflate' the economy, my emphasis on the need to restrain public expenditure before we could consider tax cuts echoed the mood of most of the speakers.

I listed some of the long-term pressures for higher public spending. 'They come from the ageing of the population, the development of costly technologies, the lobbying of vested interests, the innate desirability of many of the forms of public expenditure, the inherent desire of all bureaucracies to expand their empires, and the failure to recognize that what is provided free still has to be paid for.'

At an evening fringe meeting Ian Gilmour predictably attacked what he described as 'housewife economics', saying that the party had won the election in spite of its economic policies rather than because of them, describing potential cuts in social security spending as 'an affront to common sense' and calling for outright reflation and an incomes policy. John Biffen, the Leader of the House, appeared on *Weekend World* the Sunday before the Conference began, and unhelpfully asserted that the Tory Party had a very well-established tradition of the protective role of the State, and that 'very often means an expensive role'. As John Biffen had not previously been a 'wet', the media invented a new type of Cabinet split, between the consolidators and the radicals; but the fevered atmosphere of 1981 was not rekindled, and the prevailing mood at the Conference was clearly in favour of curbing public expenditure to finance tax reductions.

The 1984 Round and the Brighton Bomb

In the end, the plans approved by Cabinet for my first full financial year, 1984–85, were close to the declared objective of holding public expenditure steady in real terms: we agreed an increase of less than a half a per cent after expected inflation. In the event, the Planning Total was exceeded by some £3½ billion and rose by 3 per cent over the previous year after allowing for inflation, but the overshoot was overwhelmingly caused by the extra public spending incurred in resisting the miners' strike, above all to the extra borrowing by the coal and electricity industries. Needless to say, unlike the unfortunate events of the two previous years, this represented no loss of control of public expenditure, but was the result of a policy decision in wholly exceptional circumstances, and one that was fully justified.

At the time this emerged, however, I had been going through a bad patch, which caused the overshoot to be seen in a worse light than it warranted. The 1984 Party Conference will always be remembered as the occasion of the Brighton bomb, when the IRA attempted to murder the Prime Minister and the entire Cabinet, and came very close to succeeding. Five of those staying at the Grand Hotel, the Party's Conference headquarters, were killed, and two of my close colleagues, Norman Tebbit and John Wakeham, were badly injured. Although I was among the majority to emerge unscathed, it was a night of devastation which I shall never forget.

The previous day I had made the worst Party Conference speech of my career, and failed to secure a standing ovation. Since a Chancellor's authority depends to a considerable extent on his political standing, and since the media take their cue to a considerable extent from the Conference's response to a Minister's speech – it is almost the only occasion outside the House of Commons where the impact of a speech on those present actually matters – this was a very bad mistake. It was not that the speech was a poor one in itself; but it was far too cerebral for a Party Conference and I delivered it in far too perfunctory a manner. My first Budget, earlier that year, had gone down so well that I felt I did not really need to bother much with my Conference speech. It was not a mistake I was to make a second time.

The Row Over Student Grants

The Autumn Statement which followed shortly afterwards, in November 1984, was not a great success either, but for a very different reason. The main event was a huge row which blew up over student grants. Keith Joseph had become Education Secretary in 1981, as part of the reshuffle which brought me into the Cabinet as Energy Secretary, with a personal commitment both to university education and to the control of public spending. This led him to seek to finance extra spending on the universities by savings in the grants paid to parents for the cost of maintaining their children at universities. Under the system he had inherited, tuition fees were fully paid by the State, in other words the UK taxpayer, for all students, whether British or from overseas, irrespective of their parents' income. The cost of student maintenance, however, was theoretically the parents' responsibility; but so far as the UK students were concerned, means-tested grants were available to defray the cost, ranging from a minimum grant for comfortably-off parents to a grant that covered the full cost of student maintenance for the poorest parents.

The first change Keith made, in 1982, was to end the practice of asking the UK taxpayer to finance the tuition cost of overseas students: instead, these would have to be financed either by the overseas students themselves or by their own governments. This common-sense move aroused howls of protest both from the universities themselves and from the Labour Opposition. Since then, the number of overseas students at UK universities has continued to grow, and the change has long since ceased to be an issue: indeed, it is impossible to conceive of any future Government, of whatever political colour, choosing to reverse it.

But at the time, coming on top of our refusal to exempt the universities from the public spending stringency that we imposed on the rest of the public sector, it led to a seething hostility towards the Thatcher Government within the universities. The most striking manifestation of this was Oxford University's unprecedented decision to vote down the granting of an honorary degree to Margaret Thatcher, a courtesy which had been denied to no previous Oxford-educated Prime Minister. As an Oxford man myself, I was deeply embarrassed by this petty and boorish act. Since it was essentially all about money, I decided that the appropriate response was to consign to the waste-paper basket all the glossy appeals for funds I subsequently received from the university. Following my resignation as Chancellor, I was happy to accept the chairmanship of the Leicester University Development Committee, which exists to appeal for contributions from private benefactors. Not only is their need greater than that of a wealthy university like Oxford, but their manners are better, too.

So far as UK students were concerned, Keith's policy in his first three spending rounds as Education Secretary – in 1981, 1982 and 1983 -- was to agree to an increase in the minimum grant less than the rate of inflation. As he saw it, the rationale for this was clear. Not only was he diverting funds from student support – strictly speaking, the support of students' parents – to university support. He was also remedying an injustice, since the existing system was in effect taxing the parents of non-students, whose children's earnings in later life would be less, in order to subsidize the parents of students, whose children's earnings in later life would be greater. Moreover, by concentrating the real terms reduction on the minimum grant, he was reducing most the subsidy to the better off parents who received only the minimum grant. The poorest parents, by contrast, continued to receive the full grant.

But in 1984 Keith decided he needed to go further. The universities had convinced him that they urgently needed a substantial increase in their science research budgets. To finance this he agreed with Peter

Rees, the Chief Secretary, both that the minimum maintenance grant paid to all parents, regardless of means, should be abolished; and more controversially, that better-off parents should pay a means-tested con-tribution towards the tuition fees as well.

When the Autumn Statement was published, along with the usual Departmental Press releases filling out the details, on 12 November 1984, all hell broke loose. Keith was asked to appear before the back-bench Education Committee, where he robustly defended the changes, and was given a roasting. The back-benchers would have been up in arms anyway; but their fury was exacerbated by the fact that they had always suspected that Keith had no political judgement, a suspicion that was reinforced by an aside he dropped to the effect that the way ahead lay in students being partly financed via loans – as indeed was the norm in most of the rest of the civilized world.

The real problem was the people who would be hurt by the proposed changes. These were not the poor, who were fully protected, nor the rich, who could take the increased parental contributions in their stride, but the people in between. They were the people who comprised the bulk of the Party activists in the constituencies and, in particular, the local Party officers.

It soon became clear that we would not get the changes through the House of Commons, and that a tactical retreat was inevitable. Margaret held a meeting with Keith and myself at Number 10 on 5 December 1984 at which she asked us to sort something out between us. I asked Keith to come and see me at Number 11 the next morning. At that meeting I proposed to him that we should stand firm on the abolition of the minimum grant, but that we should drop the idea of seeking a parental contribution towards tuition fees. This would leave a shortfall of some £20 million, which I suggested we should split 50:50 – that is to say, I would give him an extra £10 million for his education budget from the Reserve, and he would reduce the proposed substantial increase in the science budget by £10 million. Keith agreed, and this did the trick. The revolt simmered down to containable proportions.

The next day, with characteristic courtesy, Keith dropped me a line in his own hand, thanking me 'for helpfulness at a crucial time – and for decisiveness'. But I had learned a lesson. Although both Margaret and I had of course known about the original settlement Keith had reached with Peter Rees, it had been buried away in the papers for the final public expenditure Cabinet in November, and had not been specifically drawn to the colleagues' attention. In all subsequent years I was careful to ensure that any politically controversial savings that had been agreed either in bilaterals or by Star Chamber were explicitly drawn to the attention of Cabinet.

Rage Over a Lost Pound Note

In the 1984 Autumn Statement I also announced, in addition to the main public expenditure plans, a twin decision to kill off the ½p coin – which by that time was costing considerably more than ½p to produce – and to phase out the £1 note. Geoffrey had introduced a £1 coin in April 1983 as a means of saving money, since inflation had reduced the life of the £1 note to nine or ten months before it became too grubby for further circulation. Thus although the coin cost more to produce, the fact that it was expected to last for forty years made it a much more economic proposition.

Unfortunately, however, while introducing the coin, Geoffrey had said nothing about the future of the pound note, to which a conservative British public remained wedded, as a result of which the Royal Mint was left holding a huge stock of unwanted £1 coins; and instead of the planned saving there was an additional cost.

The abolition of the ½p coin caused no trouble at all. Most people had been irritated to receive it in their change, and were glad to see the back of it. But the announcement that the £1 note was to go led to the most tremendous outcry, including a campaign by the *Sun* newspaper which issued large numbers of lapel badges featuring a picture of my face and the legend: 'Hands off our nickers'. Some commentators even believed that I had planned the whole thing as a diversion to obscure an unattractive economic prospect.

The truth was more prosaic. During the course of the public expenditure round, it embarrassingly emerged that the Treasury was likely to overspend its own very small departmental budget by some £3 million. This was largely because Margaret had decreed that the Treasury should pay for the cost of holding a Commonwealth Parliamentary Association jamboree in London. I had for some time been wondering how to persuade her of the radical proposition that the pound note should be phased out, an action that would save £3½ million in the first year alone; and saving the Treasury from the humiliation of an overspend, for which she had herself been in a sense responsible, seemed the ideal way to do it.

As I had expected, the initial outcry proved to be a storm in a teacup; the pound note disappeared (except in Scotland, where the Scottish pound note remains as symbol of the fact that Scotland is different) and elsewhere the pound coin was soon accepted. None the less, the episode was a reminder of the obsessive interest the public have in anything affecting the coinage.

The 1985 Round – Leviathan Tamed

There was, however, a much more serious shortcoming in the Autumn Statement. It rapidly became apparent that the overall public expenditure totals we had published for 1985–86 (and hence for the subsequent years) had been based on unrealistic assumptions and were thus far too low. I have never seen any virtue in living in cloud cuckoo land, not least because reality has an unfortunate habit of intruding at the most awkward moment. I eventually persuaded a very reluctant Margaret that the least bad course was to add a couple of billion pounds to the Reserve for each of the three survey years when it came to the Budget. It was profoundly embarrassing.

No sooner had that adjustment been made than a new threat to public expenditure control emerged from an unexpected quarter. Poor Keith Joseph, still smarting from the drubbing he had received over the student grants affair, decided that the heart of the problem was that Cabinet had never had a proper discussion of public expenditure priorities, and lobbied Margaret to hold one. He was supported by her then Principal Private Secretary, the normally sagacious Robin Butler, who should have known better, and she decided to go ahead as Keith had requested. I was distinctly cool. It seemed clear to me that, while in theory this was a wholly rational way of proceeding, in practice no spending Minister would agree that his own programme was a low priority, and each would seek to argue the reverse. Thus the only practical consequence could be a rash of new spending bids. All I succeeded in doing was persuading Margaret that the discussion should be held at Chequers, in the hope that colleagues would be less aggressive in a rural setting than they would be in Downing Street.

The priorities meeting duly took place at Chequers on Sunday, 23 June 1985, with Peter Rees giving a general presentation with charts, followed by a discussion round the table. Fortunately, although some colleagues, such as Peter Walker and John Biffen, argued the case for a more relaxed attitude to public expenditure altogether, it was less damaging than I feared. Needless to say, however, it served no constructive purpose and was never repeated.

Margaret did however make an important contribution to improved spending control in her Cabinet reshuffle of 2 September. This was to bring in my old friend John MacGregor as Chief Secretary in place of Peter Rees, whom she dropped from the Government altogether. In the same reshuffle Barney Hayhoe was moved from Minister of State at the Treasury where he was a relatively junior member of the four-strong team, to the much more exposed position of Minister of Health, to be replaced by another old friend, Ian Gow, subsequently murdered by the

IRA. The strategic gain was the acquisition of John MacGregor whose appointment I had long urged on Margaret. I had known John since we had worked together on Alec Douglas-Home's speeches before the 1964 election. Quiet and undemonstrative, he is easy to underrate. He combined a social liberalism with a Scottish determination (all too rare in today's Scottish establishment) to keep a firm rein on the public purse, assisted by shrewd political judgement.

The 1985 expenditure round was in the end uneventful – which means it went well. The July public expenditure Cabinet simply reaffirmed the cash figure for 1986–87 that had been published at the time of the Budget. I was helped by the drop in inflation in the second half of 1985, associated in part with a falling oil price, which reconciled the spending Departments to their cash allocations. A more fundamental gain was the expiry, at long last, of the UK's pledge to NATO to increase defence spending by 3 per cent a year in real terms.

Growth on this scale had been a long-standing NATO aspiration, accepted in principle by all its member Governments, but in practice honoured more in the breach than in the observance. A unilateral pledge that the UK would meet this target had featured prominently in the manifesto on which we had fought and won the 1979 general election. As time passed, this commitment became increasingly irksome to a Government desperately trying to curb the growth of overall public spending; particularly since it was quite clear that our European NATO allies, who as it was spent far less on defence both absolutely and as a share of GDP than we did, had no intention of following suit.

So by the time of the 1983 election, this pledge was quietly dropped from the manifesto. With a Labour Party led by the old CND campaigner Michael Foot and aggressively committed to the cause of unilateral nuclear disarmament, there was no need for us to repeat the NATO pledge to pose convincingly as the Party of strong defence. This meant that the first Autumn Statement of the new Parliament – my first, in November 1983 – could plan for the 3 per cent a year real growth, which we had scrupulously honoured since taking office in 1979, to come to an end in 1985–86. The new year that entered the plans for the first time, 1986–87, showed no real growth in defence spending at all.

This evolution had been eased, too, by the appointment of Michael Heseltine as Defence Secretary in January 1983, following the wayward John Nott's surprise decision to leave politics altogether. Contrary to his reputation, Michael (unlike, say, Peter Walker or Kenneth Baker) has never been an indiscriminate big spender, and he accepted without demur the dropping of the NATO pledge. He was also responsible, in 1984, for appointing Peter Levene as Chief of Defence Procurement – the first serious attempt by any Defence Secretary of either Party to get value for money.

A Defence Concordat

A further breakthrough was secured in the control of defence spending early in April 1986, following the resignation of Michael Heseltine over the Westland affair and his replacement by George Younger.

The defence budget is the largest programme of expenditure on 'goods and services' (as opposed to transfers like pensions) administered by a single Government Department. It is inherently difficult to control because, as with the health budget, thanks to the ever onward march of technological development, the cost of its hardware rises far faster than inflation generally. But on top of this there was a self-inflicted handicap. Hitherto Defence, unlike all other Departments, had operated a block budget – supposedly for reasons of national security. The Chief Secretary could negotiate with the Defence Secretary only over the total defence spending budget. There would be no discussion of individual items, which would not even be revealed.

Obviously there were exceptions. The Defence Secretary could not have complete *carte blanche.* Any major new procurement project would require Cabinet or Cabinet committee approval, which gave the Treasury an opportunity to probe its costs and those of alternatives. Any bid by the Defence Department for a slice of the Reserve in the course of a financial year would also need to be justified on its merits. Armed forces pay, too, was considered separately through the Pay Review Body. In addition, during the Falklands War, Falklands defence spending had to be put in a separate category, which continued for some time afterwards, given the need to fortify the islands. But despite the exceptions, the Defence allocation was essentially a block grant.

It was this system which at long last changed. Michael Heseltine had not been prepared to surrender the block budget which he had inherited, chiefly because he wanted to use the defence budget to implement a UK industrial policy, a notion that the Department of Trade and Industry (DTI) had largely and rightly abandoned. To the extent that overseas entanglements were inescapable, he wanted to see a European industrial policy. This, rather than defence considerations, was what really lay behind the Westland helicopter affair.

The sanctity of the defence block budget came to an end with the arrival of George Younger, which happily coincided with some outstanding promotions at the official level. Robin Butler moved from Number 10 to become Second Permanent Secretary at the Treasury in charge of public spending, very much at my instigation. The other key official was Clive Whitmore, another former Private Secretary to the Prime Minister, who had become Permanent Secretary at Defence.

All these moves paved the way for a hitherto unrecorded concordat between George Younger and John MacGregor, buttressed by a similar one between Whitmore and Butler. All of them deserve a share of the credit. The agreement laid down that Defence would henceforth open its books to the Treasury and allow the expenditure round to be conducted on an item by item basis. But the process would be very restricted. The only non-Defence individuals allowed to see them in the Treasury would be the Chancellor, the Chief Secretary, the Permanent Secretary, the Second Permanent Secretary responsible for public spending, and – operationally the key – one middle ranking Treasury official whose full-time job was vetting defence spending. That was quite enough.

The new defence arrangements could not of course be expected to make very much difference to the plans already agreed in the three-year programmes. But they almost certainly prevented the subsequent escalation which would otherwise have occurred.

One long overdue casualty of the defence economies was the UK-made Nimrod early warning aircraft, cancelled after massive cost overruns and delays and persistent operational shortcomings. Ironically, another item which did not in any sense leave the ground was the inordinately expensive Zircon spy satellite project.

This became something of a *cause célèbre* in January 1987 when details of it were procured by a left-wing investigative journalist called Duncan Campbell. He planned to broadcast them as part of a BBC Scotland television series, 'The Secret Society'. The Government managed to lean on the BBC to ban the programme. When Campbell published a *New Statesman* article instead, Margaret instructed Michael Havers, the Attorney General, to issue an injunction against him and every newspaper in the country. In a somewhat unfortunate blaze of publicity, the police raided the offices both of the BBC in Glasgow and of the *New Statesman* in London in an attempt to discover the source of his information. The irony lay in the fact that, well before all this blew up, I had succeeded in getting the Zircon project cancelled on grounds of cost.

In general, however, the security services, their establishments and their hardware, were one of the very few areas of public life virtually untouched by the rigours of the Thatcher era. Most Prime Ministers have a soft spot for the security services, for which they have a special responsibility. But Margaret, an avid reader of the works of Frederick Forsyth, was positively besotted by them.

1986 – The Pre-Election Round

The 1986 public-expenditure round was the only one that John MacGregor saw through from beginning to end. The pre-election round is always the toughest of the series and John deserves a tribute for what was in reality an outstanding result. Yet it did not look like that; for I was obliged to announce in the Autumn Statement of November 1986 a Planning Total (excluding privatization) for 1987–88 some £5 billion higher in cash terms than the figure previously published. This was intensely embarrassing to me, to John, and to our officials alike, and inevitably led to the accusation that I was engaging in a pre-election public spending bonanza.

In fact the previously published figure had once again been unrealistic; and the figure for which we settled represented only a minuscule real increase over the previous year. Indeed, the 1987–8 out-turn proved to be virtually identical to the previous year in real terms. This was a remarkable and almost unprecedented result in view of the electoral calendar.

Nevertheless, I felt it sensible to use the occasion of the 1986 Autumn Statement to change the presentation of the Government's public expenditure objective and provide a basis for making the whole process of spending control more realistic. I shifted the emphasis from the Planning Total to General Government Expenditure, and redefined the Government's public expenditure objective as ensuring that General Government Expenditure should continue to fall as a proportion of GDP – in the first instance, up to 1988–89.

The chief difference between General Government Expenditure and the Planning Total, as explained in the last chapter, is that GGE includes debt interest. But the main point, as the ever-reliable Pliatzky explains, is that the Planning Total corresponds to no recognized statistical aggregate in general use outside the Whitehall process, while GGE corresponds much more with a common-sense view of what Government expenditure is, as well as with international conventions, and indeed had been the concept used in the Green Paper.

I none the less had to insist on the reformulation almost over the dead bodies of the Treasury mandarins, who seemed to feel that simply aiming at a falling share of GDP was selling the pass. Critics from the political Right also attacked me for being content merely to cut the public spending ratio rather than the absolute level of spending. They were not living in the real world.

The problem of public expenditure, as the Green Paper had clearly shown, was that in the past it had consistently risen *faster* than the growth of the economy as a whole – as indeed was the case in most other countries. The new target, if attained, would mark a fundamental change of trend. Moreover, unlike the previous practice of defining the goal each year in terms of a specific cash figure for the Planning Total, it was a logical rule rather than an arbitrary number. The logic, of course, is that public expenditure falling as a share of GDP is the necessary and sufficient condition for tax cuts. It was helpful, too, that the original 1979 manifesto pledge had explicitly been to reduce the share of national income taken by the State.

Some too-clever-by-half commentators, such as *Financial Times* leader writers, attempted to ridicule the idea, asking whether the ratio was intended to fall indefinitely. Once again, they were missing the point; namely that, in the absence of any such guideline, the public spending share tends to rise inexorably. As it was, the goal of reducing public spending as a share of GDP over the three years to 1988–9 was, as the Soviet planners used to say, 'overfulfilled'.

Indeed, it is noteworthy that during the period 1978–9 to 1983–4, when the Thatcher Government was supposedly trying to cut public spending, the ratio of public spending to GDP rose embarrassingly. During the following five years, when we had on paper a less ambitious objective, the ratio fell dramatically to the lowest since the mid-1960s – even excluding privatization receipts. The fall in the public spending ratio from 1982–3, more or less continuously up to 1990–1, was something that had not been achieved under any government since the 1950s.

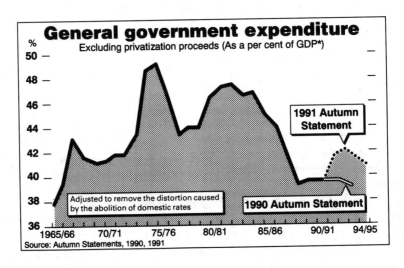

General government expenditure
% Excluding privatization proceeds (As a per cent of GDP*)

Source: Autumn Statements, 1990, 1991

By the eve of the 1987 election, while the commentators and Opposition were trotting out their clichés about a pre-election give-away, the truth was that my objective of ensuring that total public spending should rise less rapidly than the economy as a whole was being comfortably achieved. I was helped in this both by the improved prospect for debt interest as the PSBR plummeted and by the strong growth of the economy. But although the state of the economic cycle undeniably helped, it is clear from the zero real growth of public spending that this was no mere cyclical phenomenon. Public spending was genuinely under firm control – unprecedentedly so.

CHAPTER 26

THE MAKING OF THE BUDGET

The Preparations Begin · Chevening
The Budget Takes Shape · The Final Run-in
Prime Minister, Cabinet and Queen · Drafting the Budget Speech
The Ritual of the Day · The House of Commons
The Budget Broadcast and After

The Preparations Begin

WORK ON THE BUDGET used to start in earnest as soon as the Autumn Statement was out of the way in November. 'Budget starters', as they are called, are generated in one of four ways. First, there are the main tax rates and allowances which, by statute, have to be fixed annually anyway. Second, there are the technical proposals put forward by the Inland Revenue to close loopholes or to fulfil undertakings already given or to rectify acknowledged defects in the tax system. Third, there are the ideas put forward by the Chancellor and other Treasury Ministers, by Cabinet colleagues and by senior officials. Finally, the Treasury receives an enormous number of Budget submissions from various interest groups during the run-up to the Budget; and I initiated the practice of having a matrix constructed showing which outside groups were in favour of which particular changes. Where there was sufficient support for a proposition, I would always have it examined. By tradition, a small number of organizations were considered sufficiently important to warrant an oral hearing.

I would delegate the onerous task of sifting through the numerous Inland Revenue tax starters to the Financial Secretary, and those in the Customs and Excise field to either the Economic Secretary or the Minister of State, holding meetings on key issues myself. Only a small minority of starters will actually complete the course and appear in the Budget, and to avoid wasted effort, when time is inevitably so short, periodic culls are required. Towards the end of the year, Treasury officials were in a position to prepare two substantial papers for ministerial consideration.

One, prepared by the Chief Economic Adviser, was on the state of the economy and the MTFS. The other, written by the head of the tax policy division of the Treasury, covered tax policy and options. Both authors would discuss the contents of the paper with me before they were written, so as to ensure that we were all on the same wavelength, and these papers formed the basis of our subsequent deliberations. I insisted that they be ready in time to be read and fully digested by all Treasury Ministers and key officials – including the heads of the Inland Revenue and Customs and Excise – over the Christmas recess.

Chevening

I continued the practice which Geoffrey Howe had sensibly inaugurated in 1982 of starting the period of intensive Budget preparation in the New Year with a weekend meeting at Chevening, a fine country house in the Regency style, distinguished by a particularly splendid library, just outside London and into Kent. It had been left to a complicated hierarchy of public figures by the last Earl of Stanhope in the 1960s, but the tenancy was effectively in the gift of the Prime Minister of the day.

Until that time the Prime Minister had two country houses at his (later her) disposal, both of them in Buckinghamshire: Chequers, occupied by the Prime Minister himself, and Dorneywood, the customary country residence of the Foreign Secretary, who used it to entertain visiting foreign dignitaries. When Chevening was added to the portfolio, it soon displaced the less grand but delightful Dorneywood as the Foreign Secretary's country residence, and the Prime Minister was able to allocate Dorneywood to another senior Minister.

It was for the weekend Budget planning meeting at Chevening, more or less shut off from the outside world and the normal distractions of the working week, that the two main pre-Budget papers were prepared. The cast comprised the full Treasury ministerial team, the special advisers, the Permanent Secretary and the Second Permanent Secretaries (of whom the Chief Economic Adviser was one), the head of the tax-policy division of the Treasury, the Chairmen of the Inland Revenue and Customs and Excise, and my Principal Private Secretary as note-taker. Depending on the nature of the Budget measures I had in mind, a further Treasury or Inland Revenue official might be added to the list.

I was less convinced of the good sense of Geoffrey's decision to invite the wives of the participants to come along, too, since it was an intensive working weekend which meant that they were neglected most of the time. So far as I could make out, the main purpose was to satisfy the curiosity of the wives of the officials about the nature of the strange creatures their husbands were obliged to work for. At any rate, I concluded that, the precedent having been set, it would be churlish to depart from it.

We would usually assemble on a Saturday morning in the first half of January and leave after lunch the following day. This normally left the Saturday evening, after dinner, free for socializing, although in 1984 the complexity of the Budget, and the fact that it was my first, obliged me to fit in a further working session then, too.

The socializing took different forms in different years – the one constant being a snooker match between the Ministers, represented by the Chancellor and whichever member of his team was at all adept at the game, and the officials, represented by Peter Middleton and Terry Burns. This had a distinct air of Gentlemen v. Players about it. Middleton and Burns took the whole thing very seriously, and arrived with their own cues. The ministerial team would pick up whatever elderly and distinctly bent cues the Chevening billiard room could provide. It was naturally expected that the officials would win.

Much to their consternation, however, on the first occasion the match was held during my time John Moore and I succeeded in beating Middleton and Burns. The two mandarins took care that such a perverse result did not occur again, setting aside time for intensive practice at the Reform Club, that favourite watering-hole of the senior Civil Service, grand in scale and austere in character, with a name that appears to satisfy their modest appetite for change.

The Budget Takes Shape

The provisional Budget decisions taken at Chevening would be followed up by detailed official papers, principally from the two revenue Departments, on each of the measures under discussion, with the Financial Secretary chairing meetings to clear the ground on the more numerous Inland Revenue measures and the Minister to whom I had delegated day-to-day responsibility for the Customs and Excise, normally the Minister of State, chairing similar ground-clearing meetings on Excise measures. The key decisions would be taken at the weekly overview meetings, which could last up to three hours, in my room at the Treasury (this was the only time of year when I worked more at the Treasury than at Number 11). The core cast for the overview meetings would be the same as the Chevening cast, but other officials would be called in for individual items as appropriate, and at some stage I would add my Press Secretary as a full member: it was a matter of judging when the advantage of familiarizing him with the Budget in advance outweighed the bliss of ignorance when fending off Press speculation.

In addition to the papers covering the items on the overview agenda each week, there would also be a 'scorecard', compiled by the head of the Treasury's tax-policy division, showing, item by item, the overall cost or yield of the emerging Budget, for which a general ball-park figure would already have been provisionally agreed at Chevening. Costed notes on the main alternatives were also provided, not least because the estimated cost or yield of some individual items, if they were at all complex, could vary considerably from week to week as the Revenue refined its methodology. There was also a significant presentational issue to be decided. Different Budget measures can interact with each other, and this has to be taken into account to avoid double counting. But it does mean that the cost of individual measures will depend on the order in which they are assumed to be enacted. To take a simple example, an increase in personal allowances followed by a cut in the basic rate of income tax would show a larger cost for the former, and a smaller cost for the latter, than if the same two measures were assumed to take place in the reverse order, even though the overall cost would of course be the same in both cases.

Although, with no ambition to be Prime Minister, I spent rather less time than many of my colleagues on cultivating the back-benchers, I did think it desirable to canvass back-bench opinion in advance of each Budget. Our back-benchers were divided into five groups. Each Treasury Minister would then see about ten Members at a time over a drink. I would see the most senior ones. Elder statesmen such as Terry Higgins I would see individually. There were only one or two, like Ian Gilmour, who were so disaffected that I did not see them at all. I would also see organized groups of our back-benchers, like the Conservative Small Business Forum. All these invitations came from me. In addition, there were three regular pre-Budget meetings to which I was in turn invited. One, organized by the Chief Whip, was with Ministers' Parliamentary Private Secretaries (PPSs), a second was with the Executive of the 1922 Committee, and the third – to which I took my entire Treasury team – was with the Conservative Back-bench Finance Committee.

The purpose of the meetings with groups of back-benchers was to enable everyone in the Parliamentary Party to express their views before the Budget was finalized. On occasion, they could influence events: for example, the introduction of cash accounting for VAT for small businesses in my 1987 Budget (see Chapter 30) stemmed directly from views expressed at these meetings. I found them useful, too, in helping to keep back-benchers' minds focused on tax rather than public spending. On the whole, they were undoubtedly appreciated; and although the mood inevitably varied with the state of the economy, there was a wide welcome for an intensity of pre-Budget consultation greater than any previous Chancellor had apparently undertaken.

The demands of the Chancellorship were such that I seldom went to the

Chamber of the House of Commons unless it was absolutely necessary to attend a debate or answer questions, although I usually went to Prime Minister's Questions at least once a week to gauge the mood of the House, and to see how Margaret was performing. I obviously had to visit the House frequently but briefly in order to vote; but fortunately, despite the fact that I had no pair, the large majorities we enjoyed throughout my time as Chancellor meant that I could usually persuade the Whips to let me off late-night votes unless they were really important.

Occasionally I wandered into the Smoking Room or the Tea Room to get a feel for back-bench opinion, but not nearly as often as I should have done, and certainly not as often as most Cabinet Ministers do. Instead I invited groups of back-benchers to drinks at Number 11. This was much less intensive than the pre-Budget meetings; but by entertaining a different group every week, I hoped to talk informally to every back-bencher at least once during the course of the session. I also made a point of lunching at the House whenever I had no official lunch engagement, and dining there from time to time.

While I could shelve most other Treasury work during the Budget preparations, this did not of course apply to my role as a Cabinet Minister, and the procession of Cabinet committee meetings inevitably continued unabated.

The Final Run-in

Although the general shape of the Budget should be settled at least a month before the event, serious work on the Budget speech has to start long before all the individual tax decisions have been taken, and in some cases before the Chancellor has finally decided whether the Budget as a whole should involve a net increase or decrease in the tax take. This matters less than it might at first sight appear, since the early drafts of the speech, which are done by officials, consist largely of descriptions of individual measures where the need is to achieve the difficult ABC of accuracy, brevity and clarity.

The last day for Budget decisions can be surprisingly late. The precise date depends on their nature not their size. I made a very late change in the rate of tobacco duty in 1984, and in the basic rate of income tax in 1986. In both cases these were not more than ten days before Budget Day. The constraint in simple changes of this kind is essentially the printing schedules: the Customs and Excise notices to traders and the amendments to the Red Book (the Bible of the official Treasury and the economic commentators), including, if possible, the reworking of various aspects of the forecasts that may theoretically be necessary.

In the last week or two before the Budget, when pretty well all the decisions had been taken, the overview meetings would turn to the question of presentation. This involved *inter alia* deciding the Budget's theme and thus its epithet – in 1984 it was obviously 'a tax reform Budget', but in some other years an apposite epithet was harder to find – and allocating to each Treasury Minister a group of Budget measures to master and present. Although the Chancellor's Budget Statement is of crucial importance in setting the tone and determining the line to take on each measure and issue, the task of successfully 'selling' a Budget requires a sustained effort over several days.

Unlike my post-war predecessors, one important objective I set myself in my 1984 and subsequent Budgets was to confine the Budget to tax changes and rule out any new announcements, however politically attractive, on the public expenditure front. Public spending decisions having been taken in the previous autumn, and the plans announced in the Autumn Statement, it never seemed to me compatible with firm control of public expenditure to allow spending Ministers a second crack of the whip in the spring. I felt obliged to make a few rare exceptions to this rule, when unemployment was high and rising and special employment measures were called for; but on the whole I succeeded in getting the message accepted.

This is shown by the fact that, whereas in my early years as Chancellor, the pre-Budget argument was always over whether any scope there might be in the Budget should be used for increases in spending or reductions in taxation, by the end the debate was all about what form any tax reductions should take.

I have set out in Chapter 5 my reservations about the proposal to replace both the Autumn Statement and the March Budget with a unified Budget dealing with both spending and taxation in December. If, in addition, it serves to tilt the balance back towards the public spending lobbies, which it could well do, even though the intention is clearly the reverse, it could prove a big mistake. It is perfectly true that, in my day, a crucial part of the case for excluding spending decisions from the March Budget was the need to avoid allowing spending Ministers two bites at the cherry: one in November, with the Autumn Statement, and a second in March, with the Budget. The proposed amalgamation of these two events into one will certainly eliminate that danger altogether. But it will still require a strong Chancellor, who enjoys the full backing of the Prime Minister, to overcome the risks inherent in converting the most high-profile event of the parliamentary year, the annual Budget, from an event solely concerned with taxation to one shared equally by taxation and spending decisions.

Prime Minister, Cabinet and Queen

There is one particularly important respect in which – quasi-judicial rulings apart – the Budget is quite unlike any other government decision. It is not determined collectively. 'Taxation', goes the old Treasury saying, 'must not be put into commission': in other words, it is the exclusive preserve of the Chancellor. The only person the Chancellor is obliged to consult is the Prime Minister. The fact that Treasury approval is needed for most of the initiatives other Departments wish to pursue is a source of irritation to most Ministers, and if the Chancellor is doing his job he is likely to find himself a rather lonely figure in Cabinet.

Judging exactly when and how to involve Margaret in the Budget process needed considerable thought. I found it best to invite her and Denis to dinner at Number 11 with Thérèse and myself on a Sunday evening at the end of January or early February, after which I would let her know, informally and à deux, what I had in mind. She was a great believer in Budget secrecy, and I could rely totally on her discretion. I would then follow this up with at least two personal Budget minutes. One would be on the updating of the Medium Term Financial Strategy and the other on the tax changes I had in mind. Sometimes I would split this second one in two, with a paper on tax reform and a second paper on the other tax changes. This highly informal personal method of discussing the Budget strategy suited us both very well. In my early Budgets there was comparatively little dispute between us, although there were always some issues – in particular her opposition to any overt reduction in mortgage interest relief – on which she could not be budged.

The degree and direction of mutual influences vary with personalities and circumstances. In Margaret's case, while the idea of tax reform appealed to her, it was not something to which she gave much thought and she made no attempt to impose a tax strategy on me. What she did have firm views on were the politics of individual tax measures and, to a lesser extent, the overall size of public sector borrowing. On disputed issues, the bottom line was that I could not oblige her to accept something to which she was vehemently opposed; but equally she could not force me to introduce measures to which I was strongly opposed. Again, a good example of this stand-off was mortgage interest relief. I could not get her to agree to any reduction, but she for her part could not force me to raise the £30,000 ceiling for the relief, hard though she tried at first. The result was a stand-off, in which the ceiling remained stuck at that figure, leaving the passage of time to erode, quite significantly, its practical importance.

The Cabinet as a whole discussed the Budget only twice. The first occasion was a Cabinet meeting a month before the Budget, when the Chancellor provided a paper on the state of the economy, backed by a battery of statistical appendices on tax rates, National Insurance contributions and so on – including the tax burden at various income levels and as a proportion of GDP – over a number of years.* There would then be a round-table discussion in which all the colleagues would have their say about what they would like to see in the Budget, and I would for the most part stay silent, assiduously taking notes. Occasionally I would intervene, if it seemed that someone had clearly picked up the wrong end of the stick. But I would at no time give any indication of my own Budget thinking, nor would Margaret; and this was fully accepted and understood.

The second occasion when Cabinet discussed the Budget was at a special meeting on the morning of Budget Day itself, when the Chancellor reveals what he will be announcing to the House that afternoon. Theoretically, it is open to Cabinet to insist on some changes at this stage; but it is so late in the day that this could not be done without severe embarrassment, and in practice no-one would dream of suggesting it.

But while there is effectively no role for Cabinet in the Budget process, colleagues with interests in a particular area of taxation would rightly expect to be consulted on a bilateral basis about any tax changes in that field. Thus, for example, I would agree changes in Vehicle Excise Duty with the Transport Secretary and changes in oil taxation with the Energy Secretary. In addition, like other Chancellors, I would occasionally sound out a colleague to whom I felt particularly close and on whose discretion I could rely on matters outside his strict departmental sphere.

The final stage in the run-up to the Budget is the Audience with the Queen. The Chancellor is required to present himself at Buckingham Palace late in the afternoon before Budget Day, to inform the Queen of its contents. These are set out in writing, in a folder that he hands to her, but he is also expected to give an oral presentation, which I was always happy to do. Thanks to the dictates of Budget secrecy, no-one else is present, not even the monarch's Private Secretary. At my first such Audience, on 12 March 1984 I was feeling very depressed because of the Budget leak described in an earlier chapter, and she cheered me up considerably.

The conversation invariably ranged widely, going far beyond the Budget and the economy with which it would begin, and as the years passed the meetings seemed to lengthen, eventually stretching to the best part of an hour. The Palace has, of course, a special interest in the Chancellor, arising from his responsibility for the Civil List, the annual schedule of payments from the Exchequer to the monarch and the other members of the royal family to enable them to carry out their official duties in the style the British people at that time expected. Eventually,

---

*These useful appendices are based on published information and could be worked out by anyone with the know-how at the cost of some tedious labour. They are used in briefing journalists before the Budget and have become increasingly available in sanitized form to a select readership. In principle, there was much to be said for publishing these appendices, so that the interested public could have the information in systematic form without the filter of journalists. However, this might have upset Cabinet colleagues who understandably liked to be given special treatment.

the Queen decides that it is time for the Audience to end. She waits for the next convenient pause, discreetly presses a bell on the arm of her chair, and either the Private Secretary or a liveried flunkey, depending on the circumstances, enters to escort the Chancellor out.

Drafting the Budget Speech

Composing the Budget speech (strictly speaking, the Budget Statement) was a laborious exercise, but one which became easier once I had established a pattern in terms of structure and length in my first Budget. It always opened with a review of the economy before turning to the specific tax changes. Parliamentarians, political commentators and the general public are interested only in the tax measures, so unless the economic review came first there was a danger of losing the audience completely. As Margaret pointed out to me before my first Budget, it was also wise to impart an item of good news first, since the first hard measure to be announced in a Budget speech attracts a quite disproportionate amount of media attention. Terry Burns would supervise the early drafts of the economic section of the speech, and the Inland Revenue and the Fiscal Policy Division of the Treasury would draw up the tax sections.

I would then sit around the large table in my room at the Treasury with one or two key officials and a set of cards depicting all the different matters to be covered in the speech. My object was to establish a natural sequence, so as to avoid its sounding like a shopping list. This was easier said than done; for while it is accepted that not every Budget measure can be expected to feature in the speech, anything of any importance whatever must; and some of these may have precious little connection with anything else in the Budget. Finally, I would repair to Stoney Stanton with the official drafts, and rewrite the entire text myself, over the two weekends prior to the final pre-Budget weekend. I would write the tax passages on the first of these and leave the economic section until the second, to allow me to use the latest statistical information. The weekend immediately before the Budget was taken up by the ritual pre-Budget family photo calls, and by deciding what amendments to make in the light of Margaret's comments on the speech, in which she took a keen interest.

My standard Budget speech was some ten thousand words long and took me an hour and twenty minutes to deliver – a deliberate shortening of the previous norm for a Budget speech. The House of Commons prefers brevity and is impatient to hear the actual measures. It was not just the length of the speech, but the format, too, which I kept more or less constant throughout my time as Chancellor. I would begin with a list of the subjects I intended to cover, then cover them under a series of general sub-headings, leaving the best news to the last, and then conclude with a peroration, in which I tried to encapsulate the main themes of the Budget. It had to be a very short peroration – a minute at most – because anything more than a few sentences loses the attention of the House. As soon as MPs realize that the tax announcements are over they dash out of the Chamber to get their copies of the *Financial Statement and Budget Report* – the 'Red Book' – containing *inter alia* the MTFS and the full Budget, including those measures too detailed for the speech.

There was one lesson I learned early. Although my 1984 Budget speech was extremely well received, there was an audible and offputting muttering during the early sections dealing with monetary policy and the Medium Term Financial Strategy. I shrugged off Opposition interruptions by saying 'Opposition Members ought to sit quiet. They have a lot to learn.' But in fact not all the murmuring came from the opposition benches, and I concluded that the floor of the House was not the place to expound these matters. In future years I kept the monetary and macroeconomic sections brief, leaving the fuller message to the written text of the Red Book, on which I would expand at more suitable occasions, such as appearances before the Treasury Select Committee or lectures to gatherings outside the House.

The Ritual of the Day

Budget Day itself, as far as I was concerned, was best described as an enjoyable ordeal. It is a particularly full day, and sticking to a prearranged timetable is essential. This varied little, if at all, from one year to the next:

8.45–9 am	Walk in St James's Park
10.30 am	Pre-Budget Cabinet
1 pm	Light lunch at Number 11
3 pm	Press photo-call with Budget Box
3.15 pm	Departure for House of Commons
3.25 pm	Enter Chamber
3.30–4.50 pm	Budget speech
4.50–5.15 pm	Remain in Chamber for Leader of the Opposition's reply
5.30–6 pm	Conservative Back-bench Finance Committee
6–6.30 pm	Lobby briefing
6.30 pm	Return to Number 11; phone tabloid editors, record broadcast for BBC World Service
7 pm	Rehearse and record TV Budget broadcast in downstairs study, Number 11
8 pm	Post-Budget party in State Room at Number 11

The morning walk in the park, pursued by a phalanx of Press photographers and accompanied by a large police escort was an inherited ritual, but one which I was content to go along with, provided the rain held off. Although I am not particularly photogenic, Thérèse, the children and one or two dogs fully made up for this – indeed, Chancellors with young children are something of a rarity. Emily, who was only two-and-a-half at the time of my first Budget, was particularly self-possessed and photogenic and enjoyed the occasion enormously. Denis Healey, appearing on breakfast television during one of my early Budgets, pointed out correctly that 'the little girl' made the occasion. Tom, who is five years older, was understandably rather more self-conscious.

Once the walk was over, I returned to Number 11 to prepare for the special Cabinet at 10.30 a.m. at which I revealed to my colleagues for the first time the full contents of the Budget. Margaret usually cut the discussion short, reminding colleagues that I had a long day ahead of me. There was time for a light lunch at Number 11 with Thérèse and my Principal Private Secretary before I confronted the photographers again.

Several tiers of scaffolding had to be erected in Downing Street to accommodate the paparazzi who photographed my departure from Downing Street for the House of Commons at 3 p.m. The number of photographers and TV cameramen, some from overseas, was so large that I had to stand on the steps of Number 11, with Thérèse at my side, for quite a time, holding aloft the Budget speech in the battered little box said to have been made for Gladstone when he was Chancellor in 1860. The only Chancellor to have eschewed the Gladstone box was Jim Callaghan, who had a special blue box made for the purpose in 1965. Perhaps he thought it would project a more modern image.

When holding up the box for the massed photographers outside Number 11, my main concern was to avoid inadvertently obscuring Thérèse's face as I moved it around so that all the photographers could get the shot they wanted. This was a lesson I learned the hard way, from having made just this mistake the first time I did it. The transport of the Budget speech from Downing Street to the House of Commons is the only occasion when the Gladstone box is used at all. It reposes the rest of the time inside another, specially made, box in a safe at the Treasury. By now it has become too much a part of the Budget ritual, known throughout the world, to abandon.

The House of Commons

Once the photographers were satisfied, we entered the waiting car and were driven at high speed through cleared streets the short distance to the House of Commons. Thérèse would then be escorted to her seat in the Distinguished Strangers' Gallery while I had a brief chance to read through my speech for the last time, discover the state of the financial markets, and collect my thoughts in my room just behind the Speaker's chair, before entering the Chamber at about 3.25 p.m. just before the end of Prime Minister's Question Time, to an enormous roar from the Government benches, which persisted in a more subdued form even in my less popular periods. The drama of Budget Day is unparalleled in the parliamentary calendar. I can remember when many MPs used to dress up for the occasion – a practice now confined to one or two publicity seekers. But the Chamber is always packed to capacity, with Members having to sit on the floor in the aisles and others obliged to witness the occasion from the galleries upstairs. Budget Day is almost invariably on a Tuesday – evidently in bygone days Members from outlying parts of the British Isles could not rely on reaching London as early as Monday – and the debate continues until the following Monday.

The Budget speech itself – the longest and of necessity the most carefully scripted Ministerial speech of the Parliamentary year – is widely thought to be something of an ordeal for the Chancellor. I never found it so, although for my first Budget the alcoholic drink with which the Chancellor, exceptionally, is permitted to fortify himself on this occasion – at all other times the carafes by the Despatch Box are filled with nothing stronger than water – was certainly needed. To my surprise, the precise nature of the Chancellor's refreshment becomes a matter of absorbing interest to the media in the forty-eight hours before the Budget.

In 1984 I had my carafe filled with whisky and soda, a stimulant that had served me well throughout my time as Energy Secretary. After a year or so in the new job, however, I was forced to conclude, sadly, that whisky, however agreeable, was not altogether compatible with the Chancellor's much greater workload, and I gave up spirits for good, in favour of white wine, a regime that I find rather more compatible with keeping the brain working at high speed for long hours – and which has the added advantage of including champagne. So for my next three Budgets my carafe was filled with spritzer (white wine and fizzy water – my normal working drink), and for my last two Budgets I contented myself with water, which is what I would normally be drinking at half-past three in the afternoon, and I saw no real reason why Budget Day should be any different.

The main hazard in my time was the Ten-Minute Rule, under which, immediately before the main business of the day, a Private Member can make a speech of no more than ten minutes to introduce a Bill, which has no chance of securing legislative time, but is useful in drawing Members' attention to a particular issue. For an Opposition Member the opportunity to address a packed House was too good to miss. This would have been all good clean fun, were it not for the fact that I was working to a very tight timetable.

There was nothing for it but to beat the other side at their own game.

The Ten-Minute slot is allotted on a first-come-first-served basis. Led by the Treasury Ministers' PPSs, Conservative back-benchers took turns to keep a watch at the Public Bill Office right through the night before the day on which the Budget Day slot was allocated, so as to ensure that the winner was a Conservative Member who would then decide to drop his Bill at the last minute, thus ensuring that the Budget started on time. Fortunately for my successors, I was eventually able to persuade the House of Commons Procedure Committee that this whole absurd business should be ended by doing away with the Ten-Minute Rule Bill on Budget Day altogether.

My own Budgets were the last before television arrived at the House of Commons. The opportunity to deliver a televised Budget is a considerable advantage, since it enables the Chancellor to bypass the interpretation of journalists under pressure.

Immediately the Chancellor has sat down, it is the Leader of the Opposition's task to give a first, traditionally brief, response. This is not an easy speech to make, particularly for an Opposition Leader unversed in economic matters; and Neil Kinnock could be counted on to give a poor performance. The Opposition's considered response, by the Shadow Chancellor, opens the debate the following day; and this was considerably more effective once John Smith had replaced Roy Hattersley in that role in 1987.

As soon as Kinnock sat down I was free to leave the Chamber to return to my room to have a quick drink and a brief chat with my PPS and key Treasury officials, who had been sitting in the Officials' Box throughout the speech, before going upstairs to answer questions at a packed meeting of back-benchers under the aegis of the Conservative Finance Committee, chaired throughout my time by the admirably loyal William Clark.

After my meeting with the back-benchers, I had to hurry along to the Lobby Room of the House of Commons to answer questions from the Press. It was vital to be there as soon after six o'clock as possible and certainly by quarter past six at the latest, or the journalists would not turn up because if they did they would miss their deadlines. My innovation was to give these briefings on the record in the interest of accuracy. Later, I would telephone the editors of the *Daily Mail* and the *Daily Express*, to try and find out what line they were taking and influence it as best I could.

The Budget Broadcast and After

After the lobby briefing, I returned to Number 11, where I recorded a radio interview for the BBC World Service before getting made up for television and then recording the Budget broadcast for transmission later that evening. Although I always aimed to finish the script on the morning of Budget Day, it obviously could not be shown to the TV production team, supplied by the BBC, until after the speech, and usually needed some final polishing anyway. The charts, used to break up the monotony of what is known in the trade as a talking head, had to be slotted in very carefully to tie in with the precise wording of the script. I always hoped to complete the recording in a single take, but rarely did. Although I had no difficulty in reading from the autocue, there was nearly always one word over which I stumbled. But I never did more than two takes, since once the adrenalin has ceased to flow – and it was already near the end of an exceptionally full day – I would merely sound stale.

The text and visual aids for the Budget TV broadcast on the evening of Budget Day could be started rather later than the speech, although work on the two overlapped. The broadcast, which has a huge audience, was mostly about the state of the economy rather than actual tax measures in the Budget. The public is saturated with details of the Budget on the radio and television throughout the afternoon and early evening of Budget Day, so it was unnecessary for me to cover the same ground in my broadcast. It was also virtually impossible to do so in an entertaining way, since Budget secrecy precluded the preparation in advance of worthwhile visual aids about the tax measures. It was relatively easy, however, to develop charts depicting various aspects of economic progress on the basis of published information; and I would then summarize the main tax measures at the end of the broadcast.

As Geoffrey Howe had done before me, I always invited Tony Jay, the co-author of the outstandingly and deservedly successful television series, *Yes, Minister* and *Yes, Prime Minister,* and a great expert on writing for television, to help me with the text. We began work on the themes and charts well in advance of the Budget, but I did not finalize the narrative until Budget Day itself. On the whole, the Budget broadcasts worked very well.

Budget Day itself culminated in a buffet supper party in the State Room at Number 11, given by Thérèse (without official help and at our own expense) for my ministerial team and the key officials who had been involved in the Budget. As my birthday is on 11 March – just before the usual date of the Budget during my time – this party became a substitute for a usual birthday party. The television would be left on, for the benefit of those who wanted to see what sort of coverage the Budget was getting on the news programmes, or even to watch my Budget broadcast.

In the middle of the 1984 Budget party an ecstatic Margaret joined us from next door, shepherded by Ian Gow, her PPS, who had tipped me off in advance that this might happen. The following year, 1985, I was keenly aware that the Budget was bound to be an anticlimax (not least because expectations, which had been working in my favour in 1984, were inevitably now working against me) and I was feeling pretty low about it. So Thérèse and I decided to have only a small party in our own flat for those who had been involved on the day, and then go to bed relatively early.

At about eleven o'clock the doorbell to the Number 11 flat rang. I assumed it was a messenger from the Treasury with some urgent communication; so I got out of bed, shoved on a pair of trousers (I always sleep naked), and went downstairs to open it. There was Margaret, with a sheepish Ian Gow behind her. He had not tipped me off: it appears the decision had been taken on the spur of the moment. Margaret was very chic in a black, frilly dress, and had obviously come on from somewhere to look in, as she thought, on our post-Budget party. She was naturally somewhat taken aback to find me barefoot and naked from the waist up; nor was my composure sufficient to invite her in as if everything was perfectly normal. After a very brief and somewhat stilted chat in the doorway about the immediate reaction to the Budget, she returned to Number 10. In subsequent years we always had a full-scale party, and I took care to instruct my private office to inform Number 10 and let them know that the PM would be welcome. She always came.

The following day, Wednesday, after lunch at Number 11 with the Editor of *The Economist* and his senior colleagues, I would go to the Chamber for the opening speeches in the resumed Budget debate. This is the only occasion in the parliamentary calendar when the Minister who in effect has opened the debate is also required to wind it up. Wind-up speeches are quite different from opening speeches. Lasting from 9.30 to 10 p.m. and delivered to a distinctly post-prandial audience who may be in either a cheerful or a belligerent mood, but not in any case in a frame of mind for serious policy disquisitions, they are essentially occasions for rousing one's own troops. I had delivered a number of wind-ups earlier in my parliamentary career, but as Chancellor I had become rather out of practice at this particular art form, since apart from the Budget debate the only occasion on which the Chancellor is called upon to wind up is when there is a censure debate involving the Prime Minister.

Media interest did not end, of course, on Budget Day itself, and a large part of the remainder of the week was devoted to on- and off-the-record Press interviews and broadcasts. One of the most agreeable of these was the Thursday morning Jimmy Young show, which sometimes made me late for Cabinet, but which was not to be missed on that account. I am old enough to remember Jimmy as a crooner at the top of the hit parade with 'Slow Boat to China'. He was a professional through and through who always did his homework; and this, coupled with his native intelligence, made him a far more effective interviewer than many who affected to look down on him.

CHAPTER 27

AN AGENDA FOR TAX REFORM

A Chance to Surprise · A Memo to the Prime Minister
Only One Chancellor · Tax Objectives
The Tax Proportion · Lower Rates and Fewer Breaks
For and Against Neutrality · An Expenditure Tax?
A Discouraging Fiscal Outlook

A Chance to Surprise

THE FIRST BUDGET OF a new Government is the greatest opportunity a Chancellor has to introduce sweeping changes, and Geoffrey Howe had seized his opportunity in June 1979 with gusto. The next best thing is the first Budget after an election in which the Government has been renewed in office, when a Chancellor once again has the opportunity to introduce reforms which might be difficult later on, either because they are too controversial or because it takes too long for their beneficial effects to become apparent before the next election. The timing of the 1983 election meant I had to wait the best part of a year before I could introduce a Budget of my own, but I was determined to make the most of the chance it provided.

An innovative first Budget by a new Chancellor can lend economic policy a momentum and initiative that long outlasts the year of its introduction; and I think it is fair to say that my first Budget did have that effect. Every Budget has its critics, drawn both from the ranks of the official Opposition and from among the various interest groups affected, but a surprise first Budget, when nobody knows quite what to expect, can wrongfoot them completely.

In my case the element of surprise was no doubt assisted by the fact that I had not arrived at Number 11 with a detailed agenda for tax reform in my pocket. This was no accident. I have already explained how the odds were against my being made Chancellor. I was therefore careful not to invest too many hopes in its happening, or to tempt providence by making plans for what I would do in the event. But having written about tax policy quite extensively as a financial journalist, and been a member of every Finance Bill Standing Committee from my entry to the House in 1974 to my appointment as Energy Secretary in 1981, my mind was far from a blank sheet on the matter.

Some Chancellors used to regard the Budget as a means of fine-tuning the economy. Others saw it more as a statement from the chairman of the board on the state of the economy. But I conceived its role rather differently: as an essential part of a long-term programme to improve economic performance.

Of course the Budget is not the only part of such a programme (nor always the principal part). Indeed I pressed for supply-side reforms of various kinds in the appropriate Cabinet committees, and in the course of planning public expenditure, as other chapters demonstrate. Privatization, where as Chancellor I had the co-ordinating role, was something I was able to push particularly hard. But tax reform is the one major branch of supply-side reform which is unequivocally under the direct control of the Chancellor.

I started to plan my first Budget on the overnight flight from Washington on the evening of 28 September 1983 on my return from my first Fund-Bank meeting. Indeed I still have the piece of paper from the Spouses' Programme of the earlier Commonwealth meeting in Trinidad on which I jotted down eight tax reform ideas for the Budget and which I gave to John Kerr as an *aide-mémoire*.

Of the eight measures I jotted down on that flight from Washington six duly featured in the 1984 Budget – a reduction in capital allowances against Corporation Tax, abolition of the Investment Income Surcharge, a higher threshold for Development Land Tax, a widening of the base for Value Added Tax, a more generous tax treatment for stock options, and the abolition of life insurance premium relief. Of the other two, reform of the tax treatment of gilt-edged securities had to wait only until the Budget the following year, but the erosion of the enormous tax privileges of the pension funds, to the extent that it proved politically possible to move at all, had to wait rather longer. I put in hand work on all eight items, and in particular on the reform of Corporation Tax, as soon as I got back to the Treasury.

A Memo to the Prime Minister

The Budget preparations followed the course I outlined in the last chapter, including an exceptionally hard-working but otherwise successful

AN AGENDA FOR TAX REFORM

Chevening weekend in the first half of January. A few days later, on 19 January 1984, as a background to the specific measures I had in mind and of which I would shortly be informing her, I sent Margaret a fairly lengthy memorandum setting out the tax reform strategy I believed we should pursue during the course of the new Parliament. Some of the thinking in it I have since modified in the light of experience, as subsequent chapters explain; but not the main thrust. It began as follows:

TAX REFORM STRATEGY

In addition to tax reduction, I believe that we should aim to make substantial progress in the field of tax reform during the life of this Parliament. I have in mind a programme of reform covering both personal and company taxation.

Personal Taxation

2. The priorities here should be:-
   (i)   to increase the scope for income tax cuts by continuing the process embarked on by Geoffrey Howe in his first Budget of switching some of the burden from income tax to VAT;

   (ii) to improve incentives; and

   (iii) to remove or reduce distortions.

3. (i) above should not be pursued by increasing the 15 per cent rate of VAT still further, but by broadening the base of the tax, bringing into the VAT net some items at present zero-rated. Only half of all consumer spending is now subject to VAT. The need to have regard to the impact effect on the RPI in any one year points to the desirability of making gradual progress, starting this year. The political sensitivities are obvious, but I believe there is appreciable scope for action.

4. As to (ii) above, the priority here must be to increase personal tax thresholds. The married man's allowance has fallen as a percentage of average earnings from about 60 per cent in 1950 to just over 30 per cent today. The level of income at which people in this country start to pay income tax is well below that of our major competitors. A substantial increase in the thresholds would take many people out of the tax net altogether, ease the poverty and unemployment traps, and improve incentives. We also need to tackle the unsatisfactory 'kink' in the marginal rate of total deductions (income tax plus national

insurance) in the present system, which starts at 39 per cent, then drops to 30 per cent, and then rises again to 40 per cent; and to improve the tax treatment of share option schemes. When we have raised the income tax threshold to a reasonable level, we can again turn our attention to the rates of tax.

5. So far as (iii) above is concerned, the present system runs completely counter to our fundamental philosophy by encouraging the institutionalisation of savings and discouraging share ownership by the individual. The specially favourable reliefs for life assurance are the obvious example, but we shall also need to consider, when Norman Fowler's review is complete, the tax privileges of the pension funds. On the other side of the coin, I should like to get rid of the investment income surcharge.

Business taxation

6. At the present time we suffer from an excessively high level of Corporation Tax (52 per cent) made to some extent tolerable by an extensive and somewhat capricious system of reliefs.

7. Our long term objective should be to bring the corporation tax rate down to 30 per cent, which would remove the present distortion in the system against equity finance and in favour of loan finance. A gradual move in this direction could be financed for the most part by a correspondingly gradual reduction in the generous allowances and reliefs which at present bias investment between different types of assets and between capital and labour.

8. I believe that over the lifetime of this Parliament we should aim to abolish, in stages, the first year allowance for plant and machinery and for industrial buildings. This would leave the annual writing down allowances of 25 per cent and 4 per cent respectively to take account of depreciation. We should make corresponding changes in the less important allowances. We should also abolish stock relief, now that the high inflation which made it necessary is behind us.

9. We are pledged to abolish the National Insurance Surcharge during the lifetime of this Parliament. I am considering the right timing.

The remainder of the note mentioned a review of all the various capital taxes and the need to reduce stamp duty, 'as a tax on mobility and a disincentive to wider ownership, as well as a threat to the survival of a strong central securities market in London.' The note ended, predictably, by saying the tax reform would be easier against a background of tax reduction, to reduce the number of losers from any change to politically tolerable levels. These reductions in turn depended 'on the most stringent control of public spending'.

I never expected Margaret to be as enthusiastic as I was about my proposed Corporation Tax reforms. This idea of tax neutrality – the removal of special reliefs for this, that or the other, discussed later on in this chapter – held no appeal for her. Indeed, she was constantly proposing new tax breaks of one kind or another, usually arguing that this was preferable to higher public spending, which I was just as constantly rejecting. None the less, she acquiesced without demur in the proposed switch from capital allowances to a lower rate of Corporation Tax, at least partly because the package contained other items on which she was keener.

A reduction in income tax clearly had more appeal; and she was prepared to go along with the *principle* of widening the VAT base to help pay for it. But when it came to the point, the extension of VAT to building alterations (too close to home ownership for her to feel comfortable with it) and hot take-away foods was as far as she was prepared to go. She was delighted by the amount by which I was able to raise the tax thresholds and did not object to postponing basic rate cuts. She shared my enthusiasm for abolishing the Investment Income Surcharge and for reducing stamp duty. She was less keen on abolishing the tax relief on life assurance premiums, and in subsequent Budgets was against taking any further moves to reduce fiscal privilege.

Only One Chancellor

The nearest we came to a row in 1984 was over the involvement of Arthur Cockfield in the Budget preparations. Arthur had a long history of tax expertise. He had started his career in the Inland Revenue, where he claimed to have invented PAYE. He subsequently became Finance Director of Boots and then tax adviser to the Conservative Party, in both Opposition and Government, during the Heath era. I had happily worked with him in Opposition and we had served together as Treasury Ministers under Geoffrey Howe. In the run-up to the 1984 Budget he was in Ministerial limbo as Chancellor of the Duchy of Lancaster, where his only real job was to support the Prime Minister in Cabinet.

Ironically, in view of the acrimony which was to develop between them following his becoming as the UK's senior European Commissioner in 1985, Margaret was in 1984 a great admirer of Arthur's and wished me to involve him fully in the Budget discussions, starting with the Chevening weekend. This I was not prepared to do. Although Arthur has an outstanding knowledge of the tax system he is highly opinionated and inclined to be dismissive of others' ventures into fields he regards as his own. Some of his specific ideas, such as the abolition of the schedular system of income tax, would have required the diversion of scarce resources from other areas of far greater economic and political importance. But the main reason why I wanted to keep him at arm's length is that there can be only one Chancellor of the Exchequer; and I could not see his recognizing this fact. In a democracy, those people who are not prepared to put up with the humiliation of selection committees and the preoccupations of the House of Commons have to accept the price of this luxury.

In the end I was able to satisfy Margaret that I had taken sufficient account of his views by discussing my plans with him both before and after Chevening; and I sent him a copy of my Budget minutes to her. But to have involved him any further would have complicated matters in a thoroughly unhelpful way; and once Margaret realized that I was making good progress on my own, she did not press him on me any further.

The confidant of my own choosing was Norman Tebbit. As Trade and Industry Secretary, he would inevitably face a lot of flak for the changes I was proposing in company taxes, which were likely to be opposed by virtually the whole business establishment. He was also the colleague in whom I was keenest to confide my fiscal strategy. I had formed a close working relationship with Norman, who had entered the Cabinet on the same day as I did, since the days of Opposition. Although our characters are very different, our political and economic instincts were not. It became a particularly useful alliance once I had assumed the lonely occupation of Chancellor and he had succeeded Cecil Parkinson as Secretary of State for Trade and Industry, the key economic Department outside the Treasury.

Early in my Chancellorship Norman and I were able to devise an effective system (the so-called 'EuroPes') for deducting European Community subventions from departmental spending totals, denying Ministers the chance to treat them as a licence to spend more – an issue which the Commission was to take up again in 1991–92. I also supported Norman over the privatization of British Telecom, which he had been obliged to relaunch in the autumn of 1983 since the original Bill had lapsed because of the election. He was encountering considerable ill-founded scepticism both at Westminster and in the City that such a large offer could successfully be made. For my part, because I was planning the abolition of 100 per cent first-year allowances for business investment, I did not want him to be surprised by what promised to be a controversial Budget. He helpfully confirmed my own thinking by sending me a strictly personal *aide-mémoire* favouring combining the Corporation Tax reforms I had in mind with the abolition of the National Insurance Surcharge, to which we had pledged ourselves in the 1983 manifesto, so as 'to present the Budget as neutral towards industry [and] . . . avoid strong criticism that we have hit wealth creators'.*

Norman acknowledges our close relationship in his own memoirs where he writes: 'I was finding myself in too many difficult battles with the Treasury, so Nigel Lawson and I began to meet informally to try and head off some of our clashes. As the Prime Minister had said to me earlier, "You and I and Nigel must stick together": it was unhelpful if our Departments were constantly at war . . . Fortunately Nigel and I have a great deal in common. We are both pretty "leak proof", both liberal Thatcherites and we can both recognize when a disagreement is best settled. We soon found we could resolve many problems between us without involving other Ministers, and Nigel generously gave me plenty of opportunity to contribute to his thinking on budget policies at their earliest stages.'

Indeed the alliance with Norman was the most effective and closest I formed in the 1983–87 Parliament. As we shall see, he supported my November 1985 attempt to make sterling a full participant of the European Monetary System, before the issue had become entangled in political passions about 'Europe'. Even after his growing distance from Margaret contributed to his resignation in 1987 he continued to see me regularly at Number 11, although I had to be more careful about what I said. The fact that our relations sadly deteriorated after my resignation in 1989 and still more after Margaret's the following year is no reason to rewrite history.

Geoffrey Howe, of course, remained a close colleague and friend, and we continued to meet from time to time *à deux*. But his Foreign Office responsibilities left him little time for involvement in domestic matters. It was only after the 1987 election, when foreign and economic policy became intertwined on the European issue, that we were to see more of each other.

Tax Objectives

Right from the start, I devoted a great deal of time, thought and political capital to the question of tax reform. Moreover, despite the occasional carping of critics in the quality press and elsewhere – partly because my reforms did not coincide with their preferences – I think it is fair to

---

*The surcharge on employers' National Insurance contributions was introduced by Denis Healey at a rate of 2½ per cent in 1977 and increased to 3½ per cent in 1978, partly to raise revenue and partly to tighten fiscal policy following the failure of the TUC to support the latest phase of incomes policy. The Treasury saw it as an indirect tax which would be passed on in prices, but many in business saw it as a tax on business and jobs, which it plainly was. Geoffrey Howe had reduced it in stages to 1 per cent.

say that what I achieved, taking all six Budgets together, represented a coherent and substantial measure of reform.

Rather than presenting each of my Budgets as an isolated set of measures, it makes more sense to outline my approach to tax reform as it developed and place the individual Budgets in that framework.

My overriding purpose in reforming taxes was to improve the performance of the economy. In a nutshell the objectives were:-

1. To leave people more of their own money so that they could choose for themselves what to do with it.

2. So far as was practical, to reduce marginal tax rates, so that an extra pound of earnings or profits was really worth having.

3. To see that, as a general rule, people's choices were distorted as little as possible through the tax system.

4. But to be prepared, when sensible, to promote tax reliefs designed to make the economy work better.

5. To ensure, so far as possible, that the tax system both was simple and acceptable (not least to married women).

6. To adopt an economic rather than a social approach.

Certainly the Government has a responsibility for health, education, and assisting those who for whatever reason lack normal earning power. But these responsibilities are best discharged by those Government Departments, like the Department of Social Security, that are explicitly in charge of the various aspects of the welfare state, rather than by complicating the tax system.

The Tax Proportion

The Conservative Governments of 1979–92 cannot claim to have reduced the burden of tax as a proportion of GDP. Irrespective of whether North Sea revenues are included or not, the tax take was in fact a couple of percentage points higher in 1991–92 than it had been in 1978–79, the previous Labour Government's last year. (See Annexe 7.) This was understandably disappointing, but it arose as a result of the need to reduce the unsustainably large Budget deficit we had inherited from Labour, and its use as a debating point comes ill from the mouths of political opponents whose main complaint was that taxpayer-financed public spending was too low. Moreover, despite the inability to reduce the overall burden of taxation, a substantial measure of tax reform was carried out.

During my own time as Chancellor the proportion of GDP taken in taxes and social security contributions fell from 38¼ per cent in 1983–84 to 37¾ per cent in 1989–90, a decline of only a half per cent. Over the same period General Government Expenditure, excluding privatization receipts, fell from 46½ per cent to 40 per cent of GDP. As a result, the Public Sector Borrowing Requirement shifted from 3½ per cent of GDP to a repayment of ¾ per cent (again excluding privatization proceeds). These numbers are hardly consistent with a charge of fiscal laxity or of failing to allow for the effects of the boom in the conduct of fiscal policy.

The main way in which we were able to leave people more choice was by switching the tax burden from income to spending – itself a 'savings incentive' seldom acknowledged. The big move here was of course Geoffrey Howe's switch from income tax to VAT in his first Budget (Chapter 4), in which I had been involved as Financial Secretary. The switch went further with the modest extension of the range of goods liable to VAT that I was able to announce in 1984. The further increase of VAT from 15 to 17½ per cent by Norman Lamont in 1991 to reduce the severity of the Poll Tax, was theoretically a widening of choice; but it would have been far better not to have had to make it.

The Conservative Government was able in the end to reduce the basic rate of income tax to 25 per cent. Even if employees' National Insurance contributions, which were increased in Geoffrey Howe's time, are taken into account, there was an overall reduction in marginal tax rates for the generality of the population from 39½ per cent to 34 per cent, five percentage points of which occurred while I was Chancellor. Some would argue that employers' contributions are passed on to employees in one form or another. On this basis, and including the National Insurance Surcharge, the marginal tax rate was 53 per cent in 1978–79, 50½ per cent in 1983–84, and 44½ per cent in 1989–90. This merely underlines the fact that marginal rates are still too high.

The reconciliation between a rising or at best stable tax share and the periodic lowering of income tax rates is only partly due to the switch to indirect taxes. Just as important is the property of the tax system known by the ugly name of fiscal drag. This is the tendency of tax revenues to rise faster than the national income, which has two aspects. First, the tax system is not price-indexed in its entirety. The most obvious example is the mortgage interest relief ceiling. But non-indexation goes much wider than this, from the taxation of the inflationary element in fixed-interest income to the entire Corporation Tax system – particularly since I abolished stock relief. Second, even those parts of the system that are price-indexed are not earnings-indexed. The first aspect alone must be of the order of £2 billion a year.

This enables a Chancellor who can prevent public spending from rising faster than the economy as a whole to cut tax rates even when there is no real reduction in the tax burden. Equally, a Chancellor who wishes public spending to rise faster than the national income can, up to a point, do so without having to announce increases in tax rates – a process sometimes known euphemistically as 'using the fiscal dividend'.

A further reduction in the tax take amounting to some 2 per cent of GDP is estimated by the Treasury to have occurred between 1989 and

1992. Most of this fall was the automatic consequence of the recession, although the coming into force of independent taxation for married women has also had an effect. The key point, however, is that if my guideline that public spending should rise less rapidly than the economy as a whole is observed there will ultimately be scope for reducing not merely tax rates but the tax burden, too, over time.

The overall reduction in the total of the basic rate of income tax and employee's National Insurance contribution was part of a larger objective. For what really matters is whether, through a series of Budgets, a climate can be created in which people feel they are living in a country where tax rates are reasonably low and likely to come down further – a country where individuals and businesses are working less for the Government and more for themselves and their families, and for the causes they wish to support.

Lower Rates and Fewer Breaks

For any given level of public spending, the ideal way of achieving lower marginal rates is not through fiscal drag (or, as the Americans call it, bracket creep) or even by switching to indirect taxes. It is by eliminating privileges and exemptions of all kinds. A good tax system should be broadly based, with low tax rates and few tax breaks. The reason for this is not merely the avoidance of economic distortions, although that itself is important. There is also the practical point that tax breaks are inevitably abused as methods of tax avoidance, which means that the general level of taxation has to be still higher to bring in the required revenue. Moreover, the granting of one tax break inevitably increases the political pressures for others.

The higher rates we inherited when we took office in 1979 were frequently not paid. The well-heeled and well-advised took great pains to avoid liability through the perfectly legal use of tax shelters of one kind or another; and the tax avoidance (its practitioners liked to call it 'tax planning') industry flourished as never before. Needless to say, reducing or eliminating tax breaks is never popular with those who benefit from them. Reform plans here and abroad have foundered on this rock more than once. But the principle is clear: as somebody once said, 'If you want the Government off your back, you have to get your hand out of its pocket.'

So long as this approach is persevered with there is a virtuous circle to be had. Reducing or eliminating tax breaks provides increased revenue which can be used to bring down tax rates. Lower tax rates themselves reduce the value of tax breaks. So it is then a little easier to reduce the privileges that remain. This in turn releases more money to reduce tax rates. So just as high tax rates tend to bring with them high tax breaks, lower tax rates go hand in hand with lower tax breaks. Moreover, as high marginal tax rates are brought down, taxpayers will be less inclined to pay expensive accountants to devise complex schemes to reduce their liability or to seek remuneration in non-cash forms. These are among the reasons why a reduction in high marginal tax rates can lead in practice to a significantly smaller loss of revenue than the simple arithmetic would suggest.

This is the true virtuous circle. Some critics have confused it with another kind of virtuous circle promoted by some wishful thinking ultra-Keynesians – and ultra-supply-siders. This is the notion that tax cuts, without any spending cuts or substitute source of revenue will so stimulate the economy that the Budget balance will improve, enabling further tax cuts to be made, and so on. In fact, of course, long before anything like that could happen, the economy would be subject to massive inflationary pressures, and interest rates would have to be raised or tax policy reversed at the cost of severe recession. While excess demand can occur by inadvertence, this spurious kind of virtuous circle was emphatically not part of my thinking.

For and Against Neutrality

The trimming of allowances and reliefs was not only a matter of helping to find the revenue needed to pay for reductions in marginal rates. It was also intended to make the tax system more neutral. That is, to reduce the extent to which the tax system biases people's choices, by making it worth their while to spend or save in some ways rather than in others, purely for tax reasons.

The system we inherited in 1979 was not only badly biased, but biased in ways that could not fail to stultify the progress of the economy. It was biased against employment, biased against savings, biased against share ownership and biased against sensible business investment decisions.

There were three main biases against employment. First and most obviously there was the employer's National Insurance Surcharge, which Denis Healey imposed, and which Geoffrey Howe and I managed to get rid of entirely by 1984. Second, there was the bias against jobs inherent in the Corporation Tax system. In the form in which we inherited it, it provided tax subsidies for investment in capital equipment, even when more labour-intensive methods of production might be more economic. That was something I dealt with by the Corporation Tax Reforms of 1984. Third, National Insurance contributions acted as a deterrent to employers thinking of taking on lower paid and less skilled workers. This was something I remedied in my 1985 and 1989 Budgets, which both made it cheaper to employ people on low earnings and allowed such people to keep more of what they earned.

I attacked the bias against savings by a number of measures, among them the abolition of the Investment Income Surcharge, the replacement of Capital Transfer Tax by the far less penal Inheritance Tax, and the launch of Personal Equity Plans (PEPs); while my Corporation Tax reforms were the principal way of removing the bias against sensible business investment suggestions.

Not only do many politicians, mainly although not exclusively in the Labour Party, want to restore some of these biases. So too do some industrialists, who identify the national good not with the long-term profitability, but with the short-term cash flow of their own companies. Nevertheless, while most departures from tax neutrality are simply concessions to pressure groups, there are some that would be justified even on the most elevated principles.

Economists since Adam Smith have known that there are some so-called spill-over costs and benefits which are not captured in a conventional market system. Where the distortions are large and straightforward the use of taxes or subsidies to encourage or discourage certain activities, by operating through the price mechanism, is a more attractive remedy than outright prohibition. This is the theoretical case for the deliberately high excise duties on alcohol and tobacco. The pioneer of theoretical welfare economics, A.C. Pigou, proposed a tax on smoking chimneys before the First World War, although successive governments in practice preferred rules about permissible emissions. Nowadays there is a revival of interest in pollution taxes of various kinds.

The candidates for fiscal intervention which most attracted my attention, however, were in those grey areas where unimpeded market forces might in principle be sufficient but where the markets in question suffered from long years of ossification. To take the most significant examples, the labour market was notoriously rigid, while the market for private renting verged on the non-existent. Modest tax reliefs to complement our other policies to get these markets working better seemed to me well worth providing.

Well-directed tax reliefs can help to make the economy more flexible, adaptive and dynamic. That is why, for example, in my 1988 Budget I extended the Business Expansion Scheme (BES), a tax break introduced by Geoffrey Howe, to cover the provision of private rented accommodation. The lack of privately rented housing in the UK was – and still is – a serious blemish which greatly inhibits mobility of labour. Nicholas Ridley rightly sought to tackle it through housing legislation. I judged it worth helping by offering a new tax incentive for a limited period of five years. For similar reasons I introduced tax relief on Profit Related Pay in 1987: again a desirable carrot to get more flexibility into the labour market. Interestingly, the biggest response to it came from small businesses, confirming that these are in many ways the spearhead of the enterprise culture.

But while some tax reliefs can play a worthwhile role, the general presumption against them means that, as time passes, every relief must be reviewed with a critical eye. Is this one still needed for the purpose for which it was devised? Is that one now being used more as a tax planning device than for its original purpose? Is the other one showing diminishing economic returns in relation to the amount of revenue forgone?

The process can be illustrated by reference to the Business Expansion Scheme. When we first came into office, new business formation was in the doldrums; and it was still difficult, if not impossible, for small or medium sized companies to raise venture capital. So Geoffrey Howe introduced the Business Start-up Scheme, which developed into the Business Expansion Scheme. That provided tax incentives which have helped substantially to promote new businesses, to the undoubted benefit of the economy as a whole.

Meanwhile the spread of the enterprise culture, fostered by this and other policies, brought about a dramatic growth in the venture capital industry, from almost nowhere to over £1 billion of investment a year at the beginning of the 1990s. Thus much of the original purpose of the BES scheme was fulfilled. I therefore took steps in my 1988 Budget to limit the amount any one company could raise through the scheme each year, so as to concentrate BES money on the smallest companies where the need still existed. Moreover in extending the scheme to private renting I explicitly limited the relief to five years, running out in 1993.

In 1992, Norman Lamont decided to bring the whole scheme to a close by the end of 1993. This could be justified on two quite separate grounds. In the first place, the UK had by then a venture capital industry equal to that of any in the world outside the US, so over the longer term the scheme was no longer needed. And in the second place, the early announcement of the ending of the tax break might, with luck, lead to a rush of applications to take advantage of this before the guillotine came down – a useful ephemeral boost at a time of recession when bank finance was less readily available.

An Expenditure Tax?

There are two purist approaches towards the tax system: the Expenditure Tax and the Comprehensive Income Tax.

The Expenditure Tax proposal, described exhaustively in the Meade Report, tends to appeal to those who wrongly think of it as an extension of VAT and excise duties on a broader basis. Its name is in fact a misnomer. For in practice it would not be directly levied on personal spending at all but on income – after various complex subtractions and additions designed to exempt all savings and to tax drawings of capital. In its fully fledged form, all forms of savings would have to be registered, as would all capital disposals, including sales of pictures, homes, withdrawal of savings from the Post Office, even in principle the sale of second-hand furniture. In practice there would have to be many exemptions for small transactions and volumes of legislation to avoid cheating. The administration and information required would be similar to that needed for the Wealth Tax, which even the 1974–9 Labour Government decided to drop.

Another drawback is that, to the extent that it avoided taxing savings, the resulting tax rates would be higher – because levied on a lower base – than with income tax. There is also an *ad hoc* problem about an Expenditure Tax. In the present system corporate borrowing is tax deductible, whereas personal borrowing in general is not. This may be difficult to defend on first principles. But it does tilt the system in favour of companies. In other words a given level of interest rates bites harder on the personal than on the corporate sector, and any levelling of the playing field would therefore benefit the personal sector at the expense of the business sector. Both in the recent past and in any foreseeable circumstances, a tilt of this kind would look distinctly perverse.

In general, as Mervyn King has put it, 'It has not proved easy to design a satisfactory transition from our current hybrid system to a purer form of Expenditure Taxation.' For all these reasons, my enthusiasm for a wholesale switch to an Expenditure Tax was distinctly muted. I was also well aware that it was no accident that no country in the world operated an Expenditure Tax system.

It is true that Comprehensive Income Tax is also more complex than it looks. The idea is to remove special privileges and exemptions so that the lowest possible rates can be levied on the widest possible base. But while I welcomed the prospect of the elimination of the favours to special groups and eradication of the state-knows-best attitude, the practical political drawback of this route is that it involves the herculean task of fighting off one pressure group after another. In practice a tax reformer has to move in both directions: abolishing or reducing some privileges, and extending others, in order to level the playing field.

As a result, tax legislation has to be more complicated than is ideally desirable. Theoretical tax reformers who describe the outcome of this process as 'a mess' have not only never had to introduce a Budget themselves. They have not bothered to compare the tax system the Thatcher Government inherited with the one it left behind, and asked whether it was a net improvement or not. In the real world, tax will always be an irksome burden and a 'mess', but I believe I left it less of a mess than I found it.

AN AGENDA FOR TAX REFORM

A Discouraging Fiscal Outlook

Although there are obvious advantages for a Chancellor in introducing his first Budget in the first year of a new Parliament, after a stunning election victory, in other respects the timing of the 1984 Budget was distinctly unpromising. The immediate PSBR prospect seemed to rule out any early start on tax reduction. Indeed if I was going to make any impact in my first Budget, it would be by reforming taxation rather than reducing it – although without the lubricant of tax reduction, tax reform was not going to be easy.

Despite the emergency public spending cuts in July 1983, it was still clear that the Public Sector Borrowing Requirement for 1983–84 would considerably exceed the £8¼ billion target set by Geoffrey Howe in his 1983 Budget. The Autumn Statement forecast had put it at £10 billion, and the eventual outcome was not far short of that at £9¾ billion, or 3¼ per cent of GDP – equivalent to some £20 billion in 1992–93 terms.

Net tax cuts did not therefore, as I put it in my public utterances that autumn 'look a lively prospect for 1984'. Indeed the 'fiscal adjustment', which I then had an obligation to publish, indicated the need for a modest increase in tax receipts; and I have recorded how it attracted the fiercest opprobrium from the self-appointed keepers of Conservative conscience in the tabloids, despite my warning of the tentative nature of the forecast.

In the end the fiscal outlook improved sufficiently for me to get away with a neutral Budget, in the sense of no significant net increase or decrease in the tax take for the coming financial year. But taking expenditure and revenue together, my aim was to reduce the PSBR.

In the event, the public finances were knocked badly off course by the cost of the miners' strike, and the deficit in 1984–85 came to over £10 billion. The strike, was effectively called only the day before the Budget, far too late to alter the forecast. But even if I had ventured a guess, which I was prepared to reveal, of how long the strike would last, and Treasury economists had had the opportunity to estimate the consequences for the PSBR, it would not have affected my Budget judgement. For as I have already explained in Chapter 7, the essence of the fiscal strategy was that it was a medium term one, which *inter alia* implied refraining from raising or lowering taxes in response to short-term shocks, whether these shocks were due to the economic cycle or any other cause.

CHAPTER 28

1984 – MY FIRST BUDGET

The Tax Package · Strategy and Principles
Some Successful Theatre · Tax Abolition
The Reform of Business Taxation · The Results and a Postscript
Life Assurance and All That · VAT Vexations
An Unexpected Triumph

The Tax Package

THE FOLLOWING TABLE SUMMARIZES the main measures contained in my 1984 Budget. It will hardly by itself explain the success of the package, for which a little background is required.

1984 Budget Summarized

	Revenue effect £ billion 1984/85 full year	
	(All figures are on an indexed basis)	
Excise duties equalized on beer and wine	–	–
VAT to be paid earlier on imports	+1.2	–
National insurance surcharge abolished	−0.3	−0.9
Investment income surcharge abolished	–	−0.4
Corporation Tax reformed	−0.3	−0.3
Life assurance premium relief withdrawn on new policies	+0.1	+0.2
Stamp duty halved and reformed	−0.5	−0.5
Composite rate tax extended to bank deposits	–	–
VAT extended to hot take-away food and building alterations	+0.4	+0.7
Income tax personal allowances more than double indexed	−0.9	−1.5
Miscellaneous	+0.3	+1.0
TOTAL	–	−1.7

1984 – MY FIRST BUDGET

Strategy and Principles

In my Budget speech, I prefaced the tax measures with the declaration that 'this will be a radical, tax reforming Budget'. I went on to explain that the reforms were governed by two principles: 'First the need to make changes that will improve our economic performance over the longer term; second the desire to make life a little simpler for the taxpayer.' I rejected the notion of replacing the entire income-based tax system with an expenditure system. Even if such a root and branch change were desirable, 'it would, I believe, be wholly impractical and unrealistic'. My choice was the middle way: 'to introduce reforms, some of them far-reaching, within the framework of our existing income-based system'.

Even with this compromise approach I felt bound to utter the following warning:

> I am well aware that the tax reformer's path is a stony one. Any change in the system is bound, at least in the short term, to bring benefits to some and disadvantages to others. And the disapproval of the latter group tends to be rather more audible than the murmurings of satisfaction from the former.

This warning may have seemed otiose in March 1984 in view of the highly favourable reception the Budget received. But later events showed how necessary it was.

Some Successful Theatre

The speech was marked by some successful theatre. The European Court of Justice had recently upheld a Brussels Commission ruling that we were unfairly protecting beer, which was largely produced in the UK, by undertaxing it in relation to wine, which was largely imported. So there had been much speculation that I would have to impose a large increase in beer duties – guesses in the press had ranged from 4p to 7p on a pint. I did nothing to dampen this expectation and deliberately fostered it by saying in a suitably doleful tone: 'I now come to the most difficult decision I have had to take in the Excise Duty field . . . Accordingly I propose to increase the duty on beer by the minimum amount needed to comply with the judgment and maintain revenue . . . ' At this point I paused to take a sip from my beaker of whisky and soda, to allow Labour MPs ample time to guffaw in anticipation of my imminent discomfiture, as my own side braced itself for a shock increase.

I then continued '. . . 2p on a typical pint of beer including VAT' – which was only 1p more than normal indexation. The totally wrong-footed Labour benches went suddenly silent. To cheers from my own side, I went on to explain that the equalization would be completed by an 18p a bottle *reduction* in the duty on table wine, a rare event. The net effect on tax revenue of the two changes taken together was precisely zero. All this is a long way from the arguments that raged among the economic commentators about broad and narrow money; but it is what the House of Commons, like the public outside, understands and enjoys.

I was also able to extract a massive rabbit out of the hat for an unsuspecting audience. This arose in the following way. If I were to make the tax changes I wanted without any reduction in taxation overall, I needed extra revenue from somewhere. When I was Financial Secretary I had looked at the possibility of charging VAT on imports at the point of entry, as occurs with customs duties, instead of waiting (as was then the case) until their first sale within the UK. Geoffrey Howe had rejected the idea because British treatment was in line with the relevant EC draft directive. However, none of the other EC countries showed the slightest intention of agreeing the draft directive, and for some time he had been pressing them vainly to do the decent thing. He was also worried that business and industry might not welcome the switch to taxing imports at the point of entry because of its effect on their cash flow, for the sum involved was substantial. Several years later, and needing the money, I decided to take a different line towards our EC partners: if you can't beat them, join them.

Fortunately I was able to gauge what industry's view might be before the Budget since, wholly adventitiously, Ronald Halstead, the Chairman of the Knitting Industry Economic Development Committee, proposed this very change because that industry felt it unfair that we treated imports, for instance from the Far East, more favourably than other EC countries did. It was clear that industry's view was mixed, with as much support as opposition.

It subsequently became a cherished myth of the National Economic Development Council that they were responsible for this measure – something of which I did nothing to disabuse them, since it gave them harmless pleasure and helped with the reception. It is nevertheless a matter of record that this was a firm Budget starter long before Halstead raised it. Although the extra £1.2 billion of revenue it brought in was for one year only, since the change did not increase taxation but merely accelerated its collection, the improved fiscal prospect for subsequent years made this acceptable.

Tax Abolition

Yet another popular element in the Budget was that it included for the first time in living memory the complete abolition of a tax – indeed, I was able to do away with two taxes. Abolition, is, of course, the ultimate simplification, and I sought to abolish a tax in every Budget. Clearly the process would have to come to an end some time, but I was able to do it in six successive Budgets. The two taxes to disappear in 1984 were the National Insurance Surcharge and the 15 per cent Investment Income Surcharge. I was greatly helped in the case of the NIS by the fact that Geoffrey had already gone the greater part of the way by reducing it in stages from 3½ per cent to 1 per cent, and a pledge to abolish it had been in our 1983 election manifesto.

The abolition of the Investment Income Surcharge – although I had earlier mentioned its possibility to Margaret – was a last-minute decision which struck a chord on our own side. Yet it cost relatively little: £360 million in a full year and almost nothing in 1984–85. All the same, I was surprised that Labour accepted it so meekly. It is true that saving has a worthy image, but the return from saving had for generations been officially described by the derogatory term 'unearned income', and discriminated against accordingly. The main reason I gave for abolishing the Investment Income Surcharge was that it exacerbated the double taxation of savings (see next chapter); while the fact that half of those relieved by the measure were retired people, who otherwise would not have been paying taxes above the basic rate, may also have helped its favourable reaction.

The Reform of Business Taxation

The area where my reforms were most radical and based on clear fiscal principles was business taxation. These closely followed the lines I had set out in my reform memorandum to Margaret, which I reproduced in the previous chapter. Not only did I believe that the prevailing 52 per cent rate of Corporation Tax was too high, 'penalizing profit and success and blunting the cutting edge of enterprise'; it was also the 'product too many special reliefs, indiscriminately applied and of diminishing relevance to the conditions of today. Some of these reliefs reflect economic priorities or circumstances which have long vanished and now serve only to distort investment decisions and distort choices about finance.'

Although the details were inevitably complex, the basic thinking was quite simple. Because of a long prevailing belief that physical investment was good in itself, successive governments had tried to subsidize it in various ways. The subsidy applied more to manufacturing than to services; while investment in plant and equipment was more favourably treated than investment in buildings – not to mention investment in people.

The system I inherited was one of 'initial allowances'. In the case of industrial plant and machinery, 100 per cent of the cost could be written off immediately – that is, used to reduce taxable profits in the first year. The system was sometimes called 'free depreciation' and previous Ministers (of both Parties) had boasted that British incentives were the best in the world. It had proved wholly counterproductive. As I remarked at the time, 'We need investment decisions based on future market assessments, not future tax assessments.'

The new system of capital allowances which I announced – to come fully into effect in 1986–87 at the end of a three-year phased transition – was less artificial. Plant and machinery would in future qualify for annual tax allowances on a 25 per cent 'reducing balance' basis. This meant writing off 25 per cent of the cost in the first year, 25 per cent of the written-down value in the second year, and so on. For industrial buildings, which previously enjoyed a 75 per cent first-year allowance, the rate of write-off for tax purposes would be 4 per cent 'straight line' – i.e. 4 per cent of cost each year. The idea, in both cases, was to approximate to the rate of genuine commercial depreciation, erring on the side of generosity.

The quid pro quo was that the rate of Corporation Tax, levied on company profits, would be reduced in three successive stages to reach 35 per cent in 1986–87 – a lower rate than in almost any other competitor country including Japan. It was to remain there until Norman Lamont announced a further reduction, to 33 per cent, in his first Budget in 1991. At the same time I cut the small companies' Corporation Tax rate from 42 per cent to 30 per cent, equivalent to the basic rate of income tax, to which it has been linked ever since. The Inland Revenue had estimated that when these and the other changes to Corporation Tax had fully worked their way through, companies would on balance enjoy substantial reductions in their tax bills, for any given level of profits, since the reduction in the rate of Corporation Tax was a genuine remission, whereas the changes in capital allowances constituted not an increase in tax but merely bringing forward the date on which it became payable.

An incidental advantage of the switch was that it acted as a temporary investment incentive. This was useful in the early stages of an economic upturn, bringing forward investment to take advantage of the old system of capital allowances before they disappeared, the return on which would then be taxed at the new and lower rate.

But that was merely a beneficial side-effect. 'The more important and lasting effect', I argued, 'will be to encourage the search for investment projects with a genuinely worthwhile return, and to discourage uneconomic investment. It is doubtful whether it has ever been really sensible to subsidize capital investment irrespective of the true rate of return. But certainly, with over three million unemployed, it cannot make sense to subsidize capital so heavily at the expense of labour.'

351

Moreover, as I subsequently pointed out at the post-Budget meeting of the NEDC, the Corporation Tax reform removed the previous discrimination in favour of investment in hardware as against investment in either training or research.

One incidental but well-merited casualty of the Corporation Tax reform was the tax dodge involved in industrial leasing. The leasing business was estimated to be worth £3¼ billion by 1984 and to account for a quarter of all private business investment. What had been happening was that, because manufacturing firms often did not have the profits to be able to make use of the 100 per cent first-year allowance, new capital equipment would be bought by other companies who did have the profits – notably the banks – and then leased to the manufacturers. The banks claimed at the time that all the benefits they were getting from the 100 per cent allowances were being passed on to industry in better leasing terms; but their sour response to the Budget suggested that this might not always have been entirely the case. Some claimed that the entire leasing industry had been dealt a death blow. My reply was that if the leasing companies were really peforming a worthwhile service to industry, independent of the tax dodge, then I was confident that they would go from strength to strength – as indeed they did.

An important subsidiary aim of my Corporation Tax reform, which I stated explicitly at the time, but which is frequently forgotten, was to narrow the gap between the main Corporation Tax rate and the basic rate of income tax. When I became Chancellor the gap was between 52 per cent Corporation Tax and 30 per cent income tax – a difference of 22 per cent. It was reduced to 5 per cent by the 1984 reforms. My subsequent reduction in the basic rate of income tax caused it to creep up again to 10 per cent, and Norman Lamont's two-point cut in Corporation Tax announced in 1991 brought it back to 8 per cent. While any gap at all is in principle undesirable, this is at least substantially less than it was before I embarked on the reform.

The reason why the gap matters is that companies have a choice between financing themselves via equity capital and financing themselves via debt. So far as the tax system influences their choice, it is because debt interest is offsettable against Corporation Tax whereas equity dividends are not. The latter are paid by the company net of income tax at the basic rate. Thus the greater the amount by which the Corporation Tax rate exceeds income tax, the greater the encouragement to debt finance. I was always worried about the financing of the corporate sector, since an excessive reliance on debt finance was bound to lead to an underlying weakness which would be exposed at times of economic pressure.

Tax is of course only one of many factors influencing the way in which businesses choose to finance themselves. I believe that a case can be made that the most malign consequence of the Black Monday Stock

Exchange crash of October 1987 was that it killed the equity-raising market for at least a year and probably longer. This led to a massive switch to debt finance which in turn was one of the roots of the subsequent world recession, which was notably worse in the Anglo-Saxon world whose corporate sector is much more reliant on external finance. It may well be that the problem of corporate indebtedness would have been even worse without the 1984 reforms.

The aspect of the Corporation Tax package most strongly contested by some tax experts was the abolition of stock relief. This was a very rough-and-ready relief, introduced by Denis Healey in his autumn Budget in 1974, to deal with a corporate liquidity crisis. In essence, stock relief allowed profits from any appreciation in the value of stocks to be free of Corporation Tax altogether, even though some of the profits that escaped tax were not merely paper gains arising from general inflation, but real gains arising from the appreciation in the relative price of a particular commodity. Stock relief inevitably encouraged industry to hold inefficiently large stocks, which is not only undesirable in itself but also a source of instability in the economy as a whole, since the greater the volume of industrial stocks the greater the fluctuations in response to changes in final demand.

By 1984, with inflation under control, the original purpose of stock relief had largely disappeared. The Institute for Fiscal Studies criticized the ending of the relief on the grounds that at an inflation rate above 7 per cent companies would be worse off as a result of the overall Corporation Tax package. In the event, however, both producer price inflation and the underlying movement of the RPI averaged just over 5 per cent in the succeeding seven years (1984–91) – well below the IFS's 7 per cent – and seemed set to fall still further in the 1990s.

The Results and a Postscript

As I added in a mini-peroration to this section of the speech:

> These changes hold out an exciting opportunity for British industry as a whole: an opportunity further to improve its profitability, and to expand, building on the recovery that is already well under way. Higher profits after tax will encourage and reward enterprise, stimulate innovation in all its forms, and create more jobs.

This was a theme to which I returned in my winding-up speech on the Budget debate when I said:

> Under-investment has not been the problem. The problem has been the poor quality of so much of the investment, as measured by the

> return that it earns. I readily admit that my reforms will be bad for
> bad investment, but they will be good for good investment, because
> the lower rate of tax on the profits earned will stimulate investment
> in projects yielding a genuinely good return.

I concluded that 'The purpose of the reforms is to rehabilitate the role of profits in the British economy and in our national political debate'.

While it is always difficult to establish causality in political economy, the subsequent record is at least consistent with the hope I expressed then. Not only did business investment as a share of GDP rise to an unprecedented degree between 1984 and 1989, but even the subsequent trough in the depth of the recession of the early 1990s left business investment as a share of GDP still above the highest levels reached in the 1970s. More important, there was a parallel improvement in the profitability of investment, with the rate of return very nearly doubling between 1984 and 1989. Again, the subsequent decline during the recession of the early 1990s still left it well above the levels prevailing in the 1970s. The predictions of woe from the opponents of the change have been comprehensively confounded.

My decision to phase out first-year capital allowances did cause one hiccup just before the Budget. In 1981 Norman Tebbit, while Minister of State at the Department of Industry, had announced that Nissan, the Japanese car manufacturer, would establish an assembly plant in County Durham. Among the factors they had taken into consideration was the prospect of enjoying the 100 per cent first-year capital allowance, and the Chairman of Nissan had a letter from Margaret alluding to this carrot. But by the time they came to build the plant these allowances would have disappeared under my Budget plans. If nothing had been done, Nissan might well have gone ahead anyway, and certainly the new tax regime brought a considerable amount of new inward investment by overseas companies attracted by the low Corporation Tax rate. But there would have been loud and embarrassing allegations of bad faith which it would have been hard to gainsay.

Norman Tebbit and I had to find a formula to get round this. Simply making Nissan exempt from the change would not only have caused a public row but would have rendered the Finance Bill 'hybrid', the term used for any Bill that seeks to legislate about a specific named entity rather than a general class of entities. This would have been a parliamentary nightmare, and was unthinkable. For hybrid Bills – which are few and far between – are required to undergo a different and much more protracted legislative process before reaching the statute-book, making it impossible to enact a hybrid Finance Bill in time for the tax changes to come into effect at the start of the new financial year.

We therefore had to devise a general alteration to the Bill which would have the effect of exempting Nissan, while exempting as little else as practicable. This took the form of exempting investment projects in development areas, provided they had already been firmly announced, from the phased withdrawal of capital allowances. Fortunately in this context, the language in which Finance Bills are drafted is so arcane as to bear little resemblance to the English language, and no-one spotted what this particular clause was really about. Had they done so, there might well have been an outcry, and certainly the battery of claims for special treatment I received from industries that felt particularly hard hit by it would have intensified. Meanwhile our Ambassador in Tokyo was able to assure the Nissan Board that its 100 per cent capital allowance was safe, irrespective of the 1984 Finance Act. Nissan was suitably discreet.

Life Assurance and All That

The abolition of tax relief for life assurance premiums was highly controversial. In justifying its abolition for new policies, I mentioned that its main effect was 'unduly to favour institutional rather than direct investment'. But I was able to go beyond this generality and mention the multiplicity of well-advertised tax management schemes, all based on the exploitation of this relief, leading to 'no fewer than fifty pages of legislation concerned with its abuse'.

I halved the stamp duty on share transactions from 2 per cent to 1 per cent, and raised the threshold for stamp duty on house purchase by £5,000 to £30,000, which at that time excluded the majority of first-time buyers from the tax. At the same time I simplified the stamp duty on houses from a progressive scale, rising from ½ per cent to 2 per cent, to a flat 1 per cent, given the higher threshold. My aim was eventually to abolish stamp duty as an encouragement to labour mobility and wider share ownership. So far as share transactions were concerned, I halved it again in 1986, to coincide with the Stock Exchange's 'Big Bang'. By 1989 it was clear that sooner rather than later it would indeed have to go altogether, partly because an unusually enlightened Community Directive decreed it, and partly because the Stock Exchange would eventually get around to paperless (and thus unstampable) transactions. John Major accordingly promised to abolish the tax in his 1990 Budget, but at the time of writing it is still with us, as is the stamp duty on house purchase, despite a temporary remission designed to encourage the residential property market.

Another change I made in the taxation of savings was to create a level playing field for the banks and the building societies by bringing the banks within the system known as the Composite Rate of Tax –

a simple deduction of tax at source which had applied to the building societies since the late nineteenth century. This was one change that did not endure: my successor, John Major, decided in 1990 to achieve the level playing field by the opposite route of taxing interest paid on deposits with both institutions in the way that had previously applied only to the banks. This did away with the Composite Rate altogether, achieving greater equity at the cost of greater complexity.

VAT Vexations

VAT was in many ways a curious tax, falling as it did on little more than half of consumer spending. A flat-note tax on the whole of consumer spending would have been very much better, minimizing or even eliminating the distortion created by the present system, avoiding the administrative problem of policing difficult borderlines, and either allowing the tax to be levied at a lower rate, or bringing in more revenue from the existing rate, which would finance a reduction in income tax.

The problem was an amalgam of history and timidity. VAT was introduced by the Heath Conservative Government in 1972 as the replacement for Purchase Tax, which had been imposed at various different rates on a fairly narrow range of goods. The then Chancellor, Tony Barber, unified the rate at 10 per cent and extended the coverage, but did not feel able to extend it universally. In particular, the massive areas of food, fuel, housing and transport were zero-rated. But inevitably, once there are some exclusions (and these were not the only ones) this generates pressure for others. On the whole, that pressure has been successfully resisted, although during the passage of the original Bill a Conservative back-bench rebellion, supported by the Opposition, forced the Government to zero-rate children's clothes and shoes, too.

The 1979 manifesto on which we were first elected stated quite openly our intention to shift some of the burden of taxation from income tax to VAT – but added a pledge that food, fuel, housing and transport would remain zero-rated. When, in subsequent elections, we sought to keep our options open, the Labour Party would immediately accuse us of planning to put VAT on food, which Margaret would instantly deny, and this would be followed by pledges about the other 'basics', too.

So when, in 1984, I sought to broaden the base of the tax, the scope was disappointingly limited. I looked first at food – for despite the pledge, the definition of food was not as obvious as it might seem. Restaurant meals, for example, had been liable to VAT since the tax was first introduced; and Labour's obsession with the evil of VAT on food had not prevented Denis Healey, in his first Budget in 1974, from extending VAT to chocolates (including chocolate biscuits), sweets, ice-creams, crisps and the like. I concluded that the best bet for a further extension was take-away foods, a suggestion I owed to Thérèse, since these were clearly competing against restaurant meals, bar snacks and the rest, which were already liable to VAT. As a fast-growing sector I felt they would provide a buoyant source of revenue.

The question then arose as to the borderline between those foods, and groceries, which were to remain zero-rated. I recall a lengthy submission from the Customs and Excise, proposing a detailed schedule of the various items that would be liable to VAT, and seeking ministerial guidance on such earth-shattering issues as the treatment of filled rolls. The whole thing was in danger of degenerating into Nabarro-like farce, until I ruled that we should cut the Gordian knot by confining the tax to hot take-away foods and drink, which were unmistakably different from groceries.

Thus arose the notorious imposition of VAT on fish and chips, about which the popular press went to town. The *Daily Mail*'s headline was typical: 'Nigel's give and take-away Budget'. I doubt if the highly publicized criticism of this measure did me any harm.

The second VAT extension I decided to make was on building alterations and improvements. The logic behind this – once again a fast-growing market which should therefore produce a buoyant source of revenue – was that, since its inception, building repairs and maintenance had been liable to VAT. But improvements and alterations were zero-rated, producing what the Customs and Excise found the most difficult of all the VAT borderlines to police. It is well known that members of the building trade are not the most enthusiastic payers of tax of any kind, and it was common practice for repairs to be invoiced as improvements in order to escape VAT.

The disappearance of this problem by the extension of VAT to improvements and alterations aroused much less excitement in the popular press, but a storm of protest from every conceivable organization connected with the building trade. The heritage lobby, which had long cultivated support on the back benches for its case for assistance of one kind and another, was particularly vocal, too; and to head off an awkward rebellion I introduced an amendment retaining zero-rating for improvements and alterations to listed buildings.

I also planned, and had in the Budget until the very last moment, a third VAT extension – to newspapers and magazines (although not to books). But in what was scheduled as our final pre-Budget discussion Margaret advised against it. 'Look, Nigel,' she said, 'this is a wonderful Budget and you should get a wonderful reception. You don't want to spoil that by putting VAT on newspapers.' I told her I would reflect on what she had said. The next day I saw her again and told her I would take her advice, and raise the £200 million that VAT on newspapers would have brought in 1984 by an extra increase in the cigarette tax instead.

Had I decided to stand my ground on newspapers I could certainly have done so. That I did not is something I have regretted ever since. The opportunity never recurred: it is just the sort of thing that needs to be done, if it is done at all, by a new Chancellor in the first Budget of a new Parliament. I had a second go with Margaret in the first Budget of the subsequent Parliament in 1988; but by that time our relations had deteriorated and there was no way I could persuade her. With the benefit of hindsight, I have no doubt I could have got away with it in 1984. While the newspaper proprietors would have fumed, by no means all the newspaper editors would have allowed that to determine their reception of the Budget.

But at the time Margaret had used a shrewd argument. The Budget I had produced was a radical and highly controversial one. There was no guarantee that it would get the amazingly good reception it did. Not surprisingly I was obviously particularly keen that my first Budget should be thought a success. Moreover, it was emphatically my own Budget: in particular, the Corporation Tax Reform, which was its centre-piece, was entirely my own idea – although the Inland Revenue, once they learned what I wanted to do, gave me the most superb professional and technical support. Until her advice to drop VAT on newspapers, Margaret had gone along with everything I had proposed, even though much of it was very different from what she would have done in my place. Failing to extend VAT to newspapers in 1984 was, I believe, a mistake; but it is one for which I blame myself as much as I blame her.

The extra tax on cigarettes caused no political problem whatever. Such is the success of the anti-smoking lobby – whose intolerance even I, as a non-smoker, find intensely unattractive – that the tobacco duty is the one tax a Chancellor can increase and receive at least as much praise as execration for so doing. The only constraints are the risk of losing as much if not more revenue from people giving up smoking as is gained from those who continue to smoke – we are not quite there yet – and the immediate adverse effect on the RPI, which is particularly large.

So far as income tax was concerned, I left the basic rate unchanged and chose instead 'to use every penny I have to lift the level of tax thresholds'. The personal allowances were increased by more than twice the amount required by indexation, some 7 per cent in real terms. Around 400,000 people were taken out of tax altogether over and above the automatic effects of indexation. In presenting this I argued that 'it makes very little sense to be collecting income tax from people who are at the same time receiving means-tested benefits. Moreover low tax thresholds worsen the poverty and unemployment traps, so there is little if any financial incentive to find a better job or even any job at all.' This preference for raising pesonal allowances rather than reducing the basic rate was one I was later to abandon completely, as I explain in Chapter 30.

An Unexpected Triumph

Much to my surprise, despite the appalling leak described in Chapter 23, and the absence of any significant net tax reduction, the tax-reforming Budget of 1984 was extremely well received. This became clear as soon as I had sat down after delivering the Budget speech. The Conservative benches erupted in a tremendous cheering and waving of order papers, and even some Opposition Members congratulated me on it privately afterwards. Jim Callaghan told Mark Lennox-Boyd, my PPS, that he thought it was the best constructed Budget speech he had listened to – leaving aside (he was quick to add) his own efforts between 1964 and 1967.

The excellent reception continued when I went upstairs for the customary Budget day meeting of the Party's Back-bench Finance Committee, whose chairman, William Clark, opened by describing my first Budget as 'one of the most imaginative we have had'. The two hundred or so Tory Members crammed into Committee Room 14 banged their desks enthusiastically. The Budget undeniably lifted Party morale, which had been somewhat dented since the election by a series of embarrassments over issues ranging from the resignation of Cecil Parkinson to the ban on trade unions at GCHQ. Philip Howard, writing in *The Times*, told his readers that 'The Chancellor had some radical things to say and he delivered them with the oomph of an old pro. At the beginning he told the class what he was going to say. Then he said it. Then he told them what he had said and sat down, a lot sooner than some of his predecessors who have been as long-winded as the monsoon.' It was on the whole a difficult Budget to criticize. Terry Beckett, the Director General of the CBI – he of the bare knuckles – found it hard to attack the withdrawal of first year capital allowances in public, given the fulfilment of his long-standing wish to be rid of the National Insurance Surcharge, which I had presented as part of the overall business package, although he wrote to me to protest. The CBI as a whole has remained opposed to my 1984 Corporation Tax reforms and has continued ever since to favour subsidies for capital spending, which they could well obtain from some future misguided Chancellor. Nevertheless, at the time a number of individual business-men of distinction supported me; so, surprisingly, did the Engineering Employers Federation, which welcomed my Budget wholeheartedly.

One reason for the success of the Budget was the speech itself. According to Ian Aitken of the *Guardian*, 'Mr Nigel Lawson yesterday succeeded in restoring the tattered morale of the Conservative Party with his first Budget performance as Chancellor. In a pyrotechnic display of economic and financial skills, he raised the first genuine and unqualified cheer of approval for a Budget speech from the Tory back benches since the Government took office five years ago.' Peter Jenkins, also writing in the *Guardian*, described it as 'a triumphant tour de force', while Edward Pearce, of the *Daily Telegraph*, began his column: 'Once in a rare while a politician puts up a performance which not only transcends his broad reputation but which shifts him into a higher class altogether. Yesterday we learned that Mr Lawson is clever without inverted commas, for he gave a performance of sustained mastery which slew the Tories and left Labour drooping.'

It is probably true to say that nothing I have ever done has gone down quite so well as my first Budget in 1984. This was true not merely of the political and Press reception, but also in terms of the mass of letters and other private communications I received. The most poignant of these was from Bob Boothby, who sent me a copy of his memoirs, inscribed 'For Nigel Lawson, a rising star, with all good wishes from Robert Boothby, a fallen one.' It is a sad fact of political life that most of its rising stars end, one way or another, as fallen ones, even if rarely on the Boothby scale. But it is something to have been a star at all in that illustrious firmament.

The political commentators were surprised that I did not make any attempt to use my Budget triumph as a foundation on which to build up support on the back benches. The explanation lay in my lack of ambition to be Prime Minister. With hindsight, however, I was short-sighted in failing to take the opportunity to try to build a solid block of support that would not fade away with any adverse turn of economic events – not because it might have led to higher things, but because it would have been helpful to me in the storms that lay ahead, not least in the difficulties I was to have with Margaret.

The 1984 tax changes helped to launch a worldwide wave of new thinking on tax reform. Indeed if privatization was the Thatcher Government's prime claim to world leadership in economic policy making, tax reform must surely come second. The corporate side of the US tax reform package of the mid-1980s was consciously based on my 1984 Budget; other countries have followed much the same path. I cannot recall any previous UK Government exercising this kind of leadership in economic ideas and their practical implementation in one field, let alone two.

CHAPTER 29

1985 – PROTESTS AND PENSIONS

An Anticlimax · The Reform of NICs
Civilization in Danger · Home Dear Home
Nearly Taxing Consumer Credit · The Great Pensions Row
The Oblique Approach

An Anticlimax

IT WAS ALWAYS OBVIOUS that, whatever it contained, my 1985 Budget would be an anticlimax after the extraordinary success of my first Budget in 1984. On that occasion, the Budget's contents far outstripped political and public expectations. A year later expectations were working the other way, with politicians and commentators anticipating a similar display of fiscal ingenuity. There was widespread belief that, following the abolition of the life assurance premium relief, I would seek to finance a cut in income tax by getting rid of the tax privileges for some other forms of personal savings. The result was that every single lobby, and above all the pensions industry, had ample opportunity to agitate against a change and I was deprived of the benefit of surprise.

Nor was the budgetary outlook so comforting that I could float off tax reform on a sea of tax reduction. After the Budget deficit overrun caused by the miners' strike I did not want to take any chances, and concluded that the fiscal priority must be to bring about a decisive break from the plateau of 3–3¼ per cent of GDP on which the Budget deficit had been stuck for the previous four years, to 2 per cent, or just over £7 billion in cash, in 1985–86, in line with the Medium Term Financial Strategy. Some revenue boost was likely from the rebound after the coal strike, but I did not wish to rely on it too much in advance. On the basis of Treasury forecasts, I could reduce taxation by only £700 million in the coming financial year (on the usual indexed basis), which became some £1.3 billion in a full year.

The scope for tax cuts was reduced still further by the fact that I felt it necessary to announce additional expenditure on two measures designed to reduce unemployment, the Youth Training Scheme and the Community Programme, which together added £400 million in a full year. In addition I foreshadowed a non-Budgetary measure; a consultative document on Wages Councils 'which destroy jobs by making it illegal for employers to offer work at wages they can afford and the unemployed are prepared to accept'. But as so often happens with a consultative document approach, Wages Councils were in the event only limited in their scope, and not abolished; and so-called moderate socialists like John Smith became even more firmly committed to a worse evil: compulsory minimum wages across the board, which they denied would destroy jobs – just as they would refuse to accept that water flows downhill if they found it politically uncongenial to them.

The objective of my Budget was 'to continue the fight against inflation and help create conditions for more jobs'. To this end I had agreed with Norman Fowler, then Social Services Secretary, a major reform of the National Insurance Contributions system. But that inevitably meant that the 1985 Budget lacked the simple impact that only a cut in the basic rate of income tax can secure. There was, however, another reason why the 1985 Budget was an anticlimax. This was that the majority of the reforms I had hoped to introduce were controversial changes that I had to abandon, for the most part because Margaret was not prepared to swallow them. They included extending the coverage of VAT to newspapers and children's clothes, confining mortgage interest relief to the basic rate, introducing a tax on consumer credit, and taxing pension lump sums.

After delivering the Budget speech, I sat down to a distinctly muted reception from my own back benches. Supply-side measures to improve the working of the Labour market do not set the House of Commons or the media alight, however much they are demanded in principle. But the Party was rather more appreciative when I subsequently addressed it upstairs. The same applied to the more heavyweight press, if only because they wanted to use my Budget as a starting point for further discussions.

The Reform of NICs

The centrepiece of the 1985 Budget as I have indicated, was a reform of National Insurance contributions designed 'to cut the costs of employing the young and unskilled and to sharpen their own incentive to work at wages which employers can afford to pay'.

At that time National Insurance contributions for both employers and employees used to start at £35.50 a week at a flat rate of 9 per cent for employees and 10.45 per cent for employers. Unlike income tax, however, National Insurance contributions are levied not just on earnings beyond this level but, once the threshold is reached, on total earnings up to the so-called Upper Earnings Limit. In other words, while someone on £35 a week paid nothing, someone on £36 a week had to pay £3.24 (9 per cent of £36) in National Insurance Contributions: a considerable deterrent to earning the extra £1. Employers were similarly deterred from taking on low-paid labour, making it harder for the unskilled to find work.

I introduced instead a series of lower rate bands, starting at 5 per cent (for both employer and employee) before the full rates were reached. These reductions were paid for by abolishing the upper earnings limit for employers, while retaining it for employees. This did not affect the contributory principle, since it was the employee's contribution record that determined entitlement to benefit, and it avoided the enormous practical problems involved in abolishing the upper earnings limit for employees. I dimly sensed these in 1985, but the full force of them was brought home to me only when I contemplated taking this seemingly obvious and superficially attractive step in 1988.

In 1989 – to jump ahead – I went further. I removed the unsatisfactory feature of a single rate payable by employees on all their earnings. Instead I introduced a single rate of 2 per cent payable on earnings up to the lower earnings limit, then £43 per week, with the full 9 per cent payable only on earnings above the limit. This amounted in effect to an entry fee to the benefits of the National Insurance system of under £1 a week for employees. The effect of the 1989 changes is shown in Annexe 7: Reform of Employees' NICs. In essence it amounted to a much lower entry fee at the bottom and a lower burden of National Insurance contribution beyond that point for everyone, without the awkward 'steps' introduced by my earlier reform.

On tax proper I was able to take reform only modestly forward in 1985. I abolished one further tax, the Development Land Tax, at a modest cost of £50 million in a full year. This had been intended to cream off soaring land values at a time of high taxation, but its practical effect at 60 per cent was to discourage the bringing forward of land for development. Moreover, its disappearance swept away another 200 pages of complex legislation. The main measure of interest to the general taxpayer was the increase in the income tax thresholds by 5 per cent more than the rate of inflation. This cost a little under £1 billion in a full year, somewhat less than the cost of 1p off the basic rate. I was also able to improve the indexation of Capital Gains for tax purposes.

But for the most part, 1985 was a steady-as-she-goes Budget. I was able to gain modest additional revenues by raising excise duties, especially on vehicles, by rather more than the rate of inflation. My only notable extension of VAT was to impose it on newspaper and magazine advertising, which brought in some £50 million, with the prospect of higher sums in future. I also changed the status of transactions between credit card companies and retailers from zero rating to exemption. This actually brought in some revenue because of the absence of tax deductibility.

Civilization in Danger

The Budget was preceded by several unprecedented lobbying campaigns. Since my VAT extensions in the 1984 Budget, there was a feeling there would be further extensions and that the leading candidates would include books and newspapers. The publishing industry and various *literati* like Philip Larkin, Margaret Drabble and Antonia Fraser portrayed – under the slogan 'don't tax reading' – the extension of VAT to books as characteristic of Philistine Thatcherism. The House of Lords, where a number of university dons are to be found, staged an entire debate on the issue. In fact, the Great and Good could have saved their energies, because despite the fact that the vast majority of the 60,000-odd titles published in Britain every year are devoid of literary merit, I never had the slightest intention of extending VAT to books.

Even if I had been prepared to endure the hurricane of indignation, sales of books form such a small proportion of consumer expenditure that the relatively small and far from buoyant revenues raised would have made the game not worth the candle. Net home sales of books in 1990 were less than £500 million, suggesting net tax revenues of only £70 million. But as I told the House of Commons in the Budget speech: 'To have revealed this prematurely would not have stilled speculation; it would have merely concentrated it on those matters which were under consideration – a practice that no Chancellor, rightly, has sought to encourage.' While as a general rule this must be right, in retrospect it might have been better to have made an exception in this particular case.

The campaign against VAT on newspapers on the whole took the form of private pressure rather than public protest, although the President of the Newspaper Society publicly declared that a tax on newspapers represented the gravest threat to the freedom of the Press since stamp duty, which had been repealed in 1855. It was notable that two popular Conservative dailies, the *Mail* and the *Express*, attacked me fiercely over student grants and the taxation of pensions at the same time.

The two extensions I had in mind at the Chevening meeting in 1985 were newspapers and children's clothes. Unlike books, newspapers offered a very considerable source of revenue, but by 1985 the Government was trailing in the polls and Margaret was insistent that we could not afford to alienate the Press in this way. The zero-rating of children's clothes had become particularly anomalous, since it was based on size, with the result that small women escaped VAT and larger children (or, rather, their parents) paid it. But it was politically sensitive, and I decided that, while an extension to both newspapers and children' s clothes was just about acceptable, picking on children's clothes alone was not. To prevent a recurrence of the campaigning from the various VAT interest groups, which had caused consternation among the back-benchers, I announced that I had no further extensions to the VAT base to make during the lifetime of that Parliament.

Home Dear Home

Margaret's diary that year did not allow us to have our usual pre-Budget discussion over dinner and we had to move the meeting to Number 10 at 8 o'clock on the evening of Sunday, 3 February – a good time to catch her when she returned from the weekend at Chequers. I argued that the fiscal encouragement to invest in houses was far too strong, diverting funds from outlets like shares, and contributed to the housing booms and busts from which Britain had suffered in the past and was to suffer again. It was also, of course, an incentive to borrow.

Mortgage interest relief was costly in terms of revenue, too. I had worked out a self-financing package, in which the savings from the withdrawal of higher-rate mortgage interest relief would be used to reduce the higher rates of tax to a level sufficient to compensate most higher-rate mortgage payers. Margaret argued that this was out of the question, since it would contravene our manifesto pledge to retain mortgage interest relief. Indeed she countered by pressing me to raise the mortgage interest relief ceiling from £30,000 to at least £35,000. I replied that the Manifesto commitment would be fully honoured by retaining mortgage interest relief at the basic rate. Indeed this would concentrate the relief more on the first-time buyer, which was presumably where the Government's intent lay, since the first-time buyer was unlikely to be a higher-rate tax payer. I added that I had no intention of making matters worse by raising the £30,000 ceiling.

In the event, the restriction of mortgage interest relief to the basic rate was implemented by Norman Lamont in the first Budget after Margaret's deposition from the premiership. Structural changes have to be made when the opportunity arises. But if this one had been made when I proposed it in 1985, it might have helped to moderate the residential property boom and enabled the Government to curb the inflationary surge at the end of the decade at lower rates of interest. By the time

Norman made the change the property market was in serious decline and the short-term impact was to aggravate the recession.

Nearly Taxing Consumer Credit

One of the hitherto untold stories of the Thatcher era is how near we came to imposing a tax on consumer credit. I began to think about this, in fact, soon after becoming Chancellor in 1983. A number of different considerations seemed to point in the same direction. First, under European Community law financial transactions are exempt from VAT. So there was a clear 'level-playing-field' argument for imposing some other tax on this particular service to the consumer. Second, I needed revenue to finance income tax cuts, and a tax on something as buoyant as consumer credit could be a useful source. And third, since the traditional direct controls on consumer credit had become unworkable following the abolition of exchange control, a consumer credit tax was the only available supplement to high interest rates in curbing excessive growth in this type of lending.

I got my officials to work up the various options and, at a meeting I held on 15 February 1984, it was provisionally agreed to announce in the 1984 Budget the following month that there would be a duty of 1 per cent a year on all outstanding consumer credit, to come into force from July 1985, so as to give time for the banks and others to reprogramme their systems as well as providing a period for consultation. It was reckoned that if all forms of consumer credit were covered by the new tax – including, crucially, mortgages – it would raise up to £500 million a year. Although the concept was a simple one, however, the implementation bristled with practical difficulties; and I decided to drop it for 1984 with a view to doing more work on the outstanding problems and including it in my 1985 Budget.

The most intractable of the practical problems concerned the position of sole traders – unincorporated one-man businesses, where the individual concerned would borrow from the bank both for his own private purposes (consumer credit, and therefore taxable) and for business purposes (commercial credit, and therefore not taxable). The Customs and Excise, who would have been responsible for collecting this new form of indirect taxation, could see no satisfactory way of distinguishing between these two forms of borrowing in practice. This worried me a good deal less than it worried them. I decided that we could accept a rough-and-ready distinction, provided that in all borderline cases the sole trader was given the benefit of the doubt. This would certainly have led to a fair amount of evasion of the consumer credit tax by the proprietors of one-man businesses, but as a Minister in a

THE GREAT PENSIONS ROW

Government committed to promoting the enterprise culture, I felt it was something we could live with.

I was far less happy with the Bank's insistence that there would have to be a sixteen-month gap between the announcement of the tax and its coming into effect, largely to give time for the consultation with the banks which they saw as essential. While I understood their reasons, I did not relish the politics of the protracted public row which this would have guaranteed.

But the critical issue, as I saw it, was mortgages. Not only did lending on mortgage represent over 80 per cent of consumer credit, but if mortgages, in addition to their other tax advantages, were to be exempt from an otherwise general consumer credit tax, their share would be even greater. In other words, without the inclusion of mortgages the yield of a consumer credit tax would be so diminished that the game would not be worth the candle. With the details worked out, following a lengthy discussion at Chevening, and the practical problems solved at least to my satisfaction, I broached the new tax with Margaret in front of the 1985 Budget. She was hostile to the whole idea of introducing a new tax – a view which, in principle, I shared; but this seemed to me an exception. But on one issue she was adamant: there could be no question of a tax on mortgages. Given this veto, I lost interest in the idea, and dropped it from my 1985 Budget package.

My interest then revived with the start of the surge in consumer credit in the latter half of 1986, reinforced by the discovery I had made during a brief visit to Denmark that year, for an informal Ecofin, that the Danes had recently introduced a rough-and-ready consumer credit tax which seemed to be workable. At the Chevening meeting in January 1987 it was agreed to change the base of the earlier proposal and levy a 5 per cent tax on all consumer credit payments, with the exception of mortgage payments. Yet once again the Bank insisted that, with an announcement in the 1987 Budget, the tax could not be introduced until July 1988; and I decided to drop the whole idea without even bothering to put it to Margaret.

It admittedly would have looked odd to tax mortgage credit while at the same time continuing to give mortgage interest relief. But despite this presentational awkwardness, I believe that subsequent problems would have been less acute had I been able to introduce the comprehensive consumer credit tax I sought in the 1985 Budget, even if it had not come into effect until July 1986.

The Great Pensions Row

The campaigns against VAT extension were as nothing compared to the barrage that emanated from the beneficiaries of occupational pensions and the industry that catered for them. Following the abolition of tax relief for life insurance premiums in the 1985 Budget, it was not difficult to guess that the tax-free treatment of lump sum payments might come next. There followed the most astonishing lobbying campaign of my entire political career, devoted both to the preservation of the lump sum relief and to pension fund privileges in general.

Even the pensions industry accepted that the non-taxation of the lump sum was an anomaly. When an individual saves in the normal course of events, he has to save out of taxed income, and the income from his savings is then taxed again: there is, in a sense, double taxation. When he saves by contributing to an occupational pension scheme, he enjoys tax relief on his contributions to the fund and is taxed on the resulting pension: this might be termed single taxation. But when he saves by contributing to an occupational pension scheme and receives a lump sum at the end of the day, he enjoys tax relief on his contributions to the fund *and* pays no tax on the lump sum.

The industry was nevertheless determined to resist any change. The National Association of Pension Funds and the Society of Pension Consultants lobbied Parliament very effectively. The British Insurance Association, the Life Offices' Association and the Associated Scottish Life Offices, whose members marketed pensions, also mobilized. They commissioned a Gallup poll which, unsurprisingly, found 95 per cent of employees were 'extremely or very concerned' about the taxation of pensions.

The invention of the word processor has added enormously to the number and scale of the letters of protest mail to which Ministers and MPs can be subjected, and the deluge of letters organized by the pensions industry succeeded in arousing considerable anxiety on the back benches. William Clark, the chairman of the Conservative Back-bench Finance Committee, who had links with the life assurance industry, warned flatly that 'nothing should be done to harm occupational pensions'. In a number of private meetings with Conservative back benchers I was warned of a major revolt if I taxed lump sums. Of more immediate concern, there were rumours that senior managers, policemen and Civil Servants were contemplating early retirement to ensure they received their lump sums without deduction of tax; and there was even a modest boom in sales of personal pensions, encouraged by some fairly unscrupulous cash incentives offered by life companies.

I had learned by now not to expect any help against such lobbies from professed tax reformers – the Institute for Fiscal Studies for instance prepared a report, commissioned by the National Association of Pension Funds, which warned that a reduction in pension fund privileges would put an extra burden on the State Earnings Related Pension Scheme (SERPS). Even the TUC, whose members on balance might be thought to lose from what might be termed the middle-class welfare state, was up in arms. The CBI ran a slogan 'Hands Off Peoples' Pensions', while at the boardroom lunches I attended at this time all talk of the state of the economy, or of their own business, was suspended, as the directors turned the conversation to the all-important issue of their pensions.

After a hundred Conservative MPs signed a motion on similar lines, I decided to inform the House of Commons that any taxation of lump sums would not be retrospective – it had been clear from the start that, as with the abolition of life assurance premium relief the previous year, this could not be justified – but my stance did nothing to stem the tide of protest. The pressure against any change of any kind was reinforced at the traditional pre-Budget meeting of the Conservative Back-bench Finance Committee on 19 February 1985, when William Clark informed the Press that the lobbying had 'derailed' my plans. He was, of course, aware that the Executive of the 1922 Committee had privately but forcibly told me that the party could not cope with an attack on the taxation of pensions.

My intention had been to bring the lump sum into tax on a non-retrospective basis – that is to say, only that portion of any lump sum earned by contributions paid after Budget Day – or, if that was politically impossible, to find some other way of making the tax treatment of pension funds less generous to offset the lump sum anomaly. Margaret liked the tax-free lump sum, since it helped to spread a modest capital among more people. But I doubt if she would have stood in my way had it not been for the unrest on the back benches.

Not only was the lump sum issue political dynamite, but all the alternative measures I examined for tackling the pension funds' tax privileges either amounted to overkill or revealed technical problems to which I saw no solution. So, deprived of the lump sum option, I decided that discretion was the better part of valour; and that I would need to return to the subject at a later date in some wholly different way. This might well, I thought, have to take the form of a wider reform of the taxation of savings, on which it would be possible to demonstrate that there would be winners as well as losers – as the last thing I wished to do was increase the burden of income tax overall. But I was already in two minds about the wisdom of this when I finalized my Budget speech. Hence my somewhat tentative reference in it to the possibility of a Green Paper on the taxation of savings when I announced that I had no proposals to touch 'the anomalous but much-loved tax-free lump sum'.

However as time went by, having experienced the awesome power of the pension-fund lobby, I became increasingly convinced that a Green Paper would in practice serve only to assist the various vested interests to preserve the status quo – in other words, that reform would be more likely to be achieved by a well-directed side offensive with no prior warning. And that is what, in the event, I embarked on, starting the very next year.

The Oblique Approach

The side offensive began with the imposition in 1986 of a statutory limit on the size of pension-fund surpluses. This was much more difficult for the pension lobby to fight, and as a result, I was able to get it on the statute-book. The dramatic improvement in the financial climate of the previous three or four years meant that many occupational funds had accumulated assets far in excess of those needed to honour their liabilities to their pensioners – in other words, and even on the highly conservative basis used by pension fund actuaries, the funds were heavily in surplus. This was not simply due to inadvertence. For these excess funds enabled companies to accumulate income, free of any liability to Corporation Tax, in a gross fund – that is, once in the fund the money could be invested on an entirely tax-free basis, so far as both income and capital gains were concerned. Admittedly, the surplus could only be subsequently extracted from the fund with the consent of the Inland Revenue; but there was always the hope that, if the company could make out a case for it, that consent would be forthcoming.

The 1986 reform put an end to this: no new undue surpluses could be created, and existing surpluses would have to be run down over a period to a maximum of 5 per cent of total liabilities. The Revenue, characteristically, wanted to specify how the surpluses should be run down; but I concluded that it would be far neater to let the companies decide for themselves how they did it. A company could have a 'contribution holiday' – in which case, if, as was customary, it was the employer who took the 'holiday', the Corporation Tax yield would rise. Alternatively, the company could pay out more in pensions, in which case the income tax yield would rise. Or, finally, the company could pocket the surplus – in which case however, while Inland Revenue consent would no longer be required, there would be a new 40 per cent tax levied on the reclaimed surplus as a rough-and-ready payment for the 'free parking' the funds had hitherto enjoyed.

The course taken by most companies was the employer's contribution holiday, whose economic effects were a rise in company profits (and cash flow) and thus in Corporation Tax receipts, coupled with a fall in recorded personal saving, since employers' pension contributions are officially classified as personal saving.

In the pre-election Budget of 1987, I was able to level the playing-field in two further ways. First, the tax reliefs enjoyed by occupational pension funds were extended to the personal pensions whose promotion had been one of the main purposes of the Fowler reforms. They were taken up on a positively embarrassing scale, partly because Norman had persuaded me to provide, at least on a temporary basis, excessively favourable National Insurance contribution rates for those who contracted out of the

State Earnings Related Pension Scheme in order to invest in a personal pension scheme. Second, and under cover of the first, I introduced a number of measures to stop the abuse of the tax privileges accorded to pensions, including a limit of £150,000 on tax-free lump sums. To avoid retrospection, this involved only new members of pension funds. Even in the Thatcherite high noon, it was easier to slip in a tax reform that involved a limit for the better off than an outright abolition of a distortion or privilege. Moreover, it was the highest-paid employees, notably in the City, who were in the best position to influence their own remuneration package and abuse the tax-free status of pension lump sums.

One particularly thriving form of abuse I sought to curb was that, since pensions are related to final salary, those in a position to do so arrange to be paid a specially inflated salary in their last year of employment. Like all other abuses this one inevitably flourished particularly vigorously in the City; but it was also rife in, of all places, the NHS. Consultants there are paid on the basis of the proportion of the week they devote to their NHS work, boosted by a system of merit awards that are meant to be paid to those consultants who, in any particular year, perform particularly meritoriously. The assessment of merit was a matter for their peers. I could not help feeling that it was more than a coincidence that merit awards invariably seemed to go to consultants in their final year.

Encouraged by the acceptance of a lump sum cap in the 1987 Budget, I introduced in my last Budget, in 1989, a thoroughgoing limit on tax relief for occupational pensions. I decided to express the limit in terms of the pension that could be earned by someone on a salary of £60,000 a year. This implied a maximum pension of £40,000 a year (two-thirds of earnings) or a maximum lump-sum of £90,000 (one-and-a-half times earnings). The £60,000 was indexed to prices and not to earnings. To avoid retrospection the new rules applied only to new schemes or new members of existing schemes. Although the limit sounds and is high, over the years, as earnings rise faster than prices, its significance will steadily grow.

The imposition of the cap was allied to, and indeed permitted, a measure of deregulation that was welcome in itself. Under the old system all pension contributions were eligible for tax relief, but the Revenue could and did limit the size of pensions that could be paid, in terms of a proportion of final salary. The deregulation consisted of saying that henceforth any company could pay any pension it liked to an employee; but that there would be a cap on the amount of pension the contributions to which enjoy tax relief. Indeed it was as a deregulatory measure that I presented it to the House.

CHAPTER 30

1986 – PRINCIPLES AND A PENNY OFF

The Oil Factor Again · How to Use a Small Sum
The Politics of a Penny off · Basic Rate versus Thresholds
The Invention of PEPs · An Overall Assessment
The Charities Package

The Oil Factor Again

THE BACKGROUND TO MY 1986 Budget was mixed. Total national output (GDP) had risen the previous year by some 3¾ per cent, part of which represented the rebound from the coal strike. Despite this above average growth, unemployment was still rising. Inflation, happily, was coming down rapidly and averaged 3.4 per cent during 1986, the lowest for very nearly twenty years. It was to prove the lowest, too, of the Government's entire period of office.

But there was a snag in this very sharp drop. For, as with the similarly sharp drop in inflation in the rest of the world, it chiefly reflected the impact of the collapse in the oil price following Saudi Arabia's warning that it was no longer prepared to support the price in the world market by holding back its own production. Saudi Arabian light oil fell from around $27 a barrel in 1985 to $10 a barrel in the first quarter of 1986, thus more than reversing the explosion of 1979–80 (see chart in Chapter 17). Connoisseurs might have noted that my Budget speech was less sanguine on the supposed benefits to the UK of an oil price collapse than the Treasury's chapter on the economy in the Red Book.

Sterling had originally weakened somewhat, but had steadied after I increased base rates by one percentage point to 12½ per cent in January, which I was able to reverse the day after the Budget. The testing time for the pound was to come later in the year. My main direct concern over the oil price, which dominated all our economic thinking at that time, was its effect on tax revenue. In fact, despite the loss of oil revenues, the PSBR for 1985–86 turned out at only £5½ billion or 1½ per cent of GDP, thanks to firm control of public spending coupled with buoyant non-oil revenue.

In deciding on the appropriate borrowing requirement for 1986–87 there were two conflicting considerations. The medium-term strategy of smoothing out the impact of shocks and fluctuations suggested that a higher PSBR should be allowed, to let the oil price effect be absorbed gradually. On the other hand the projected rise in privatization proceeds argued for a lower figure. It seemed to me to be best to stick to the MTFS course, erring slightly on the side of caution. I accordingly aimed for a PSBR in 1986–87 of £7 billion, or 1¾ per cent of GDP.

My £7 billion target allowed me, on the forecast provided, to reduce taxation by £1 billion in 1986–87 on the usual indexed basis. In the end the outcome for that year was much better than I dared hope: a PSBR of £3½ billion, or £8 billion excluding receipts from privatization. This was so despite the oil price remaining depressed at around $10 a barrel for most of the financial year. Oil revenues in fact fell dramatically, from £11½ billion in 1985–86 to £4¾ billion in 1986–87, even faster than the forecasters expected.

How to Use a Small Sum

At the pre-Budget meeting at Chevening, electoral considerations began to loom. I toyed with the idea of giving myself more scope to cut income tax by exploiting the vagaries of the RPI and raising VAT to 16 per cent. Inflation would then appear to fall when the VAT rise dropped out of the index a year later, the probable election year, just as the effects of lower oil prices were falling off. In the end I felt that this would be too clever by half.

The clear consensus was to use any available scope we had to reduce income tax. The discussion was on whether to raise thresholds yet again or make a cut in the basic rate. The view at Chevening was that it was not worth cutting only a penny, taking it from the 30 per cent at which it had stood since Geoffrey's first Budget in 1979, to the somewhat bizarre figure of 29 per cent. It had to be two pence off, which would cost £2 billion in the coming financial year – or it would not be worth doing it at all. And it was hard to see, given the oil price fall, how we could possibly afford that sort of money.

But I continued to brood on it. In my usual pre-Budget note to Margaret on 13 February, I wrote:

> All in all, I believe we have reached a point where we have already done a great deal of what needed to be done on thresholds. Our next

> priority should be to reduce the basic rate. Once we have made sig-
> nificant reductions there, it will be time to look again at thresholds.

The pre-Budget Cabinet that month was steeped in gloom as a result of the sharp fall in oil revenues. At the final meeting of the overview group on the Budget a fortnight later, on 3 March, made up of Treasury Ministers, special advisers, senior Treasury officials and the Chairmen of the Inland Revenue and the Customs and Excise, the consensus was still to do nothing on the basic rate.

However, immediately after the overview meeting, each of the three special advisers, Peter Cropper, Rodney Lord and Howard Davies, wrote to me privately to argue in favour of taking a penny off the basic rate, primarily for political reasons. It was characteristically the shrewd Peter Cropper who put his finger on the fact that the very silliness of the 29 per cent figure – which he knew was what had concerned me at Chevening – was a strength and not a weakness. For as he wrote:

> A reduction to 29 per cent would be seen as an unqualified commit-
> ment to cutting the burden of taxation. It would be ludicrous to stop
> with a basic rate of 29 per cent for more than a year or two: people
> will see that.

The Politics of a Penny off

Although it was very late in the day, that convinced me; and I informed Margaret of my change of plan only eleven days before the Budget. She was delighted by the idea once I had reassured her that the overall Budget arithmetic was prudent.

Politically it proved a tremendous success. Here I was helped by the trap I had carefully laid for the Labour Party – and instant newshounds – in my Budget speech. Near the end I warned in pure Treasury-speak: 'Given the need for caution in the light of current circumstances, I do not have the scope this year for a reduction in the basic rate of income tax' – at this point I took a sip from the glass beside me, to give time for the predictable hoots of derision and *schadenfreude* from the Opposition benches, before continuing – 'beyond one penny in the pound'. The benches behind me erupted in triumphant cheers. I continued by saying that this represented 'the first cut in the basic rate of income tax since my predecessor took it down from 33 per cent to 30 per cent in 1979. So long as this Government remains in office, it will not be the last.'

The extraordinary impact of this modest reduction has to be seen against the political background. The year 1986 could not have opened worse. First Michael Heseltine resigned over Westland and then Leon Brittan. Margaret's position was shakier than at any time until the events which led to her downfall in 1990. Then came the one penny cut in the Budget in March, and the whole mood changed. Labour did not know what to do, so the Liberals decided to step into the limelight and divide the House against it. A predictable group of Labour rebels went into the Liberal lobby against the tax cuts, while the majority stuck to the Party line and limply abstained.

The 'penny off' allowed me to revive Geoffrey's 1979 aspiration of a basic 25 pence basic rate and make it sound more like a pledge. Margaret Thatcher, weakened by the Westland affair, was in no condition to oppose it, much as she disliked pledges of this kind. My main objective was to lock the Party into a publicly proclaimed tax objective, as a means of preventing the scope for future tax cuts from being eroded by public expenditure promises as the election approached.

But the last thing I wanted to do was to get the basic rate – as some back-benchers assumed – down to 25 per cent that Parliament. I wanted to keep it as a manifesto pledge. But it had to be a realistic one; and at the rate of a penny off every seven years it was not realistic yet. It was the further twopence off in the 1987 pre-election Budget that immediately made it realistic. The Opposition had been particularly sceptical. I recall appearing on television with Denis Healey, who had been Chancellor throughout the previous Labour Government, in a BBC *Question Time* programme during the course of the Conservative Party Conference at Bournemouth in October 1986. Speaking with all the authority of his own experience, Healey explained to the viewers that:

> the real problem for the Government is it is promising five times as much as it knows it can afford. Mr Lawson is promising, some time in the by and by, in the beautiful land beyond the sky, he will get it down to 25 pence in the pound.

There was a further political bonus from the 1986 penny. When I cut twopence off in 1987, Labour were determined not to be caught out by the Liberals again, and promptly decided to vote against the tax themselves. This was manna from heaven. No doubt they had taken at their face value (as indeed had the pundits) all the polls which showed a consistent and substantial majority in favour of public spending increases rather than tax cuts. Any politician with any understanding of the electorate, however, knows exactly what those particular polls mean.

There are large numbers of people in this country who have been conditioned to believe that it sounds better to say that they would like to see more money spent on worthy public services – however doubtful they may be about whether the worthy public services will improve as a result – than that they would like to receive a tax cut. But when it comes to casting a vote which might determine which of the two takes place, it is a different matter altogether. This was clearly demonstrated, to my complete lack of surprise, by the outcome of the 1987 general election. Yet, astonishingly, five years later, in the run-up to the 1992 general election, when the opinion polls once more predictably purported to show an overwhelming popular preference for increased spending on public services over tax cuts, both the pundits and the Labour Party were again taken in.

Basic Rate versus Thresholds

The desire of a Conservative Chancellor, given the scope to do so, to reduce the burden of taxation was not surprising. Despite having entered office pledged to reduce taxes, we had in fact, because of the need to reduce the budget deficit first, felt obliged to endure a net increase in the tax burden to date. Nor was it surprising that the focus was on income tax: again, that had been our declared objective from the start. But there was a lively argument on the relative desirability of cutting the basic rate and raising thresholds.

On this my thinking had evolved. I had started as a 'threshold' Chancellor, and raised the personal allowances substantially more than indexation required in both of my first two Budgets, those of 1984 and 1985. I then changed my mind, and became convinced that it was better to concentrate on reducing the basic rate, a view I hold to this day.

In a sense, of course, I had always recognized the unique importance of the basic rate. During the 1981 Budget I had as, Financial Secretary, fully supported the decision not to index allowances at all, but would have been aghast at any increase in the basic rate. When I first became Chancellor, however, I was seduced by the fact that one could fine-tune the amount by which the allowances were increased, so as to add up, with other measures, to precisely the overall reduction in revenue I had decided was prudent. The basic rate, on the other hand, lacked that flexibility since it had to be cut by a penny at a time, and each penny off cost a substantial sum in lost revenue. This made the rest of the Budget-making process far more difficult. Yet at the same time it seemed implausible that a single penny off would have any significant effect on incentives – unlike the threshold increase, which would have a considerable impact (via the poverty and unemployment traps) on an admittedly very small number of people.

Against that, however, it became clear to me that the threepence off the basic rate that Geoffrey had been able to achieve in his first Budget, financed by a substantial rise in VAT, was not something that I could repeat. So unless I was prepared to cut a penny at a time, I would probably never get the basic rate down at all: great distances can be travelled in short steps, but not with no steps at all. Moreover, the more the scope for reducing the burden of tax was used up by increasing the allowances, the less scope there would be ever to act on the basic rate. I also suspected that incentives were affected not merely by the rate of income tax, but also by the direction in which people expected it to move. In other words, a reduction to x per cent, coupled with a sense that tax was on the way down, would create a more invigorating climate than an increase to x per cent coupled with a sense that tax was on the way up – even though in each case the basic rate was the same x per cent.

I was struck, too, by the fact that, whereas probably an overwhelming majority of taxpayers knew what the basic rate of tax was, it was doubtful if one in a hundred knew what their threshold was.

Moreover we had already raised tax thresholds by over 22 per cent in real terms since 1979, and by 1986 they were close to the international average. By contrast, there had been no change in the basic rate since the Government's first Budget. The combined marginal rates of Income Tax and National Insurance Contributions for the bulk of the population had fallen by a meagre half of one point since Labour were in office, from 39½ per cent to 39 per cent, and our income tax rates were still, in general, higher than overseas.

The balance of the argument shifted still further following Norman Fowler's 1985 social security reform (see Chapter 47), which greatly reduced the effect of raising thresholds on the unemployment and poverty traps. For means-tested benefits were now to be paid on the basis of post-tax rather than the pre-tax earnings. Thus every pound by which I raised post-tax incomes by raising thresholds, would in future simultaneously reduce the entitlement to benefit. The high implicit marginal rate paid by the poorest households resulted in any event from the speed at which means-tested benefits (especially family credit, housing benefit and community charge benefit) were withdrawn as income rose, and tax changes were of comparatively trivial importance to this group.

Much the most important consideration, however, was that, if I wished to create a large constituency in favour of income tax reductions, as a counter to all the many vocal constituencies and pressure groups there always are for higher government spending on everything under the sun, the last thing I wanted to do was to reduce the size of that constituency by taking people out of income tax altogether by raising thresholds. I was struck by the number of people who complained to me after the tax cut of 1986 that I had done nothing for them. These were people who did not pay income tax at all, many of them thanks to the large real threshold increases in my first two Budgets. All these considerations, but perhaps most of all the last, made a compelling case for concentrating on cutting the basic rate.

The Invention of PEPs

As in the previous year, much of my speech was devoted to unemployment and the labour market. With some reluctance, I decided to include in the Budget some public expenditure measures on this front. But in contrast to the previous year, they could be financed out of the Reserve; and there was no overall increase in the Government's expenditure plans. My most innovative, if tentative, proposal – at this point there was not even a Green Paper – was for tax relief for Profit Related Pay. The proposal is outlined in another chapter, together with the rest of my labour market thinking. I gave a warning that despite rising productivity, pay was rising still faster, and that as a result labour costs were increasing faster than was compatible with high employment. These warnings, and the crucial linkage of pay to jobs, were sadly lost from sight in the boom of the late 1980s. But they were all too well vindicated by subsequent events.

The reforms I had made to the taxation of savings in my 1984 Budget, and those I had been stopped from making in my 1985 Budget, had been chiefly concerned with levelling down the playing field for institutional savings. By 1986 I felt the time had come to focus more on levelling it up for at least one form of direct personal savings: wider share ownership. This led to the invention of Personal Equity Plans (PEPs) and their launch in the 1986 Budget. Under the PEP scheme anyone could invest a specified annual amount in UK equities, in a properly supervised 'plan', and escape all liability to income tax and capital gains tax on the investment made, provided the sum remained in the plan for a full calendar year. Indeed, there would be no need to report it to the Inland Revenue at all. PEPs were deliberately designed to augment the progress already made in widening share ownership through employee share schemes and the privatization programme.

The scheme began in January 1987, with an investment limit of £200 a month or £2,400 a year. Once the year's qualifying period ended, investments could be realized without any penalty; but clearly the longer the investment remained in the PEP, the more the tax relief built up, and the greater the benefit. Anyone legally able to deal in securities could register as a PEP manager; but the investor himself could decide whether to use a plan in which he decided whether to make investment decisions himself, or one in which he delegated them to the PEP managers.

I was always very cautious about describing PEPs as savings incentives. Although I hoped they would encourage the growth of small savings, at a time when the personal savings ratio was falling away, I was well aware that they might simply divert money that would have been saved anyway, in National Savings for example. Any overall savings increase was a bonus over and above the main objective, an expansion in direct share ownership.

Although new to the UK, PEPs in a sense followed in the footsteps of the Loi Monory introduced in France in 1978 by the then Conservative French Finance Minister, René Monory. This allowed purchasers in French shares to deduct from their taxable incomes a limited amount of annual investment, so long as the money was locked up for at least four years.

The Loi Monory had long attracted interest among British Conservatives and there were numerous pamphlets and articles advancing a British version. But the PEP plan was significantly different. It originated when I asked John Moore, then Financial Secretary, to head a team of Treasury and Revenue officials with a remit to produce a range of options to encourage small investors to invest in equities. Of all the options he provided, the simple 'back-ended' relief idea seemed to me the best and most straightforward; and I asked him to develop it.

'Back-ended' relief simply meant that, while there was no tax relief on payments into PEP schemes, payments out – whether of dividends or of capital gains – were tax free. By contrast, the Loi Monory relief was front-ended. It was given on the initial investment, as with pension fund contributions, but all subsequent dividends and capital gains were liable to tax. The Monory method not only implied a high initial loss of yield to the Exchequer: it was also undesirably complicated. The long lock-up period was required to prevent investors simply 'churning' the same money in and out at the expense of the French Treasury. Indeed, the Socialist Government elected in 1981 extended the lock-up period to nine years. Even then small investors had to account to the tax authorities whenever they sold their stock. After several further modifications, the Loi Monory was scrapped altogether in 1989. The French Socialist Finance Minister, Pierre Bérégovoy, introduced instead a *Plan d'Epargne Populaire*, or PEP, remarkably similar to our own PEP.

Initially, PEPs looked like being a great success. In their first year of operation a quarter of a million people invested £500 million in PEPs. But the Stock Exchange crash of October 1987, only ten months after their inauguration, dealt them a savage blow, and it became necessary to give them the kiss of life. This took a number of forms: finding ways of reducing the burdens on the PEP managers so as to minimize the initially high management charges they levied; steadily increasing the permitted annual investment limit (by 1992 this stood at £6,000); and, most important of all, greatly enlarging the amount that could be invested in investment and unit trusts, where the big breakthrough came in my 1989 Budget.

This went against my original conception of PEPs as a means of encouraging direct popular investment in UK companies, with no institutional intermediary of any kind; but it was clear that the PEP scheme had to be promoted on a substantial scale, and it was only the Unit Trust companies that were prepared to do this.

As a result of all these improvements, PEPs, which at one point had seemed in danger of fizzling out altogether, went from strength to strength. By the end of 1990 over one million PEPs were in existence involving a total investment of some £3 billion, and the total was growing fast. Indeed the prospect of a Labour Government in the spring of 1992, and the risk of its bringing the PEP scheme to an end, led to a positive frenzy of PEP promotions and take-up.

An Overall Assessment

The overall package of reforms of the taxation of savings over the entirety of my term as Chancellor was considerable, and amounted to a significant levelling of the playing field for different forms of savings. No doubt more can be done; but not a great deal, I suspect, within the realm of the politically attainable. Indeed, a degree of determination may be needed to prevent some of my reforms from being undone.

A partial measure of what I succeeded in achieving is provided by the Chart in Annexe 8: Changing Effective Tax Rates, showing the striking narrowing of the range of the effective tax rates, as IFS economists calculate them, on different forms of savings. One reason why it is only partial is that the narrowing partly reflects the reduction in inflation, and the slight widening at the end its temporary resurgence. Nevertheless the chart is a good deal better than nothing, and gives some idea of the distance travelled.

The Charities Package

Finally, partly on merit and partly to give it an added political dimension, I included in the 1986 Budget a substantial package of reforms to help charities, at a cost of £70 million in a full year. This had one principle running through it, which I frequently enunciated, and which informed my other concessions in this field in other Budgets: namely, that the best way to make such concessions is to assist, not the charities themselves, but the act of charitable giving. To encourage corporate donations, I allowed companies to enjoy tax relief on one-off donations to charity up to a maximum of 3 per cent of their annual dividend to shareholders. To encourage personal giving, I invited employers to set up 'payroll giving' schemes, in which charitable donations of up to £100 a year deducted from pay packets would attract tax relief. In response to representations, there were also some minor VAT reliefs for charities.

The package as a whole was remarkably well received in the charity world. Yet the slow pace at which payroll giving took off was disappointing. To encourage it further, I convened a conference at Lancaster House on 18 July 1988, with a mixed array of bigwigs from the world of charity, employers, the Inland Revenue and assorted Ministers plus – to ensure publicity – one of my favourite comedians, Ronnie Corbett, whom I secured through the good offices of that tireless worker both for the Conservative Party and for charity, Basil Feldman. This was my one and only appearance on a public platform with Ronnie Corbett, and it seemed to do the trick. After the slow start in 1987, payroll-giving built up steadily by the end of 1988 to over 300,000 schemes, and has grown steadily, if unspectacularly, ever since.

CHAPTER 31

POWER TO THE TREASURY

*The Myth of the First Lord · Running a Small Department
They Don't Give You the Figures · The Advent of the 'Gooies'
Stumbles on 'Next Steps' · Civil Service Pay*

The Myth of the First Lord

MARGARET THATCHER, LIKE EVERY Prime Minister since Lord
Salisbury, held the title of First Lord of the Treasury, as well as that of
Prime Minister. The title of 'First Lord' meant that the Prime Minister
was head of the Board of the seven Commissioners of Her Majesty's
Treasury, which have since 1714 theoretically exercised the ancient office
of Lord High Treasurer. The Chancellor and the five junior Lords Commissioners (a title nowadays conferred on senior Government Whips)
were technically assistants. For well over a century, the Board of Commissioners has been a constitutional fiction: the last time it met on
serious business was in 1856. Margaret Thatcher did, however, re-
convene the Board once, in 1983, not to outvote the Chancellor, but
to mark the retirement of Douglas Wass as Permanent Secretary to
the Treasury. As this example suggests, she took the title half seriously, and Peter Middleton used to play up to her, addressing her as
'First Lord' when he thought it would please her. But as Leo Pliatzky
has observed, Ministerial responsibility for economic policy lies unequivocally with the Chancellor:

> In the more remote past, the position of First Lord, whether or not held
> by the Prime Minister, appears to have carried with it direct suzerainty
> over Treasury affairs, but that has long ceased to be the case. The
> Chancellor of the Exchequer is the minister in charge of the Treasury

just as much as the various Secretaries of State and other ministers with departmental portfolios are in charge of their Departments.

The Prime Minister's influence on economic policy comes from the same sources as his or her influence in other fields of policy. They are the 'hire and fire' power, the Prime Minister's position at the centre of the Whitehall machine, and the self-fulfilling belief of media and academe that the British system has become presidential. In addition, Margaret Thatcher paid intense, if spasmodic, attention to Treasury detail.

In some matters this could be a mixed blessing, but in others Margaret's interest in the activities of the Treasury was an unequivocal bonus. One of the most fruitful developments of the Thatcher years was the steady strengthening of the Treasury. Most Governments sought to reduce, rather than to enlarge its power. In the immediate post-war period, many of the national shortcomings of the inter-war years – both economic and military – were ascribed to the parsimony and orthodoxy of the Treasury and its satrap in the City, the Bank of England. Later, the Treasury was regarded as an obstacle to expansionist economic policies, and a succession of governments tried a variety of devices to reduce its power.

Harold Macmillan introduced the National Economic Development Council as a source of independent economic influence and advice; Harold Wilson set up a separate Department of Economic Affairs (DEA) to generate 'creative tension' with the Treasury, and transferred responsibility for the Civil Service to a new Civil Service Department. The Treasury survived all of these efforts to curtail its power. Harold Wilson's doleful explanation of the failure of the DEA, cited by Peter Hennessy, will do to explain them all:

> The one thing we need to nationalize in this country is the Treasury, but nobody has ever succeeded . . . 'Moles' was a phrase we very often used about the Treasury and it has been used many times since. The Treasury were very, very skilled chaps in more or less stopping you doing anything.

Even so, the Treasury did not fully recover its pre-eminence among Whitehall Departments until the accession of Margaret Thatcher. This was vital to the overall success of that Government. It re-established the truth that just as a company cannot be successful without a strong finance director, so the economy cannot be run successfully without a powerful Treasury.

Once its power was restored, the Treasury could capitalize on its dominance of all aspects of economic policy. Even the Bank of England was essentially the executive arm of the Treasury in the financial markets. Unlike its impact on some other Departments (such as the Foreign Office)

Margaret Thatcher's strengthening of the office of Prime Minister and of the role of the Downing Street staff within Whitehall was usually helpful to the Treasury during the 1980s. Leo Pliatzky has remarked:

> It does not seem to me that such limited build-up as has taken place in the Prime Minister's entourage adds up to a duplication or dilution of the Treasury's role, as the Central Policy Review Staff . . . were meant to bring about. Margaret Thatcher has wanted to have her own advisers, including the Policy Unit and the Efficiency Unit, which have sometimes been a nuisance to the Treasury. But the restoration to the Treasury of most of its old functions suggests that she has also wanted a strong Treasury capable of delivering the policies which she supports. Although in one sense No. 10 is at the very centre of government in Britain, in terms of allocation of functions, the Treasury and the Cabinet Office are now once again the only two fully fledged central departments in Whitehall.

Among the old functions which Margaret restored to the Treasury were primary responsibility for the Civil Service; while a new function *de facto* added (after Pliatzky's book had been published) was the transfer of ministerial responsibility for the Central Statistical Office to the Chancellor of the Exchequer. Pliatzky is right, too, in his judgement that the 'build-up . . . in the Prime Minister's entourage' never amounted to the creation of an Office of the Prime Minister as part of the machinery of government. What it did increasingly do, however, was to create a bunker, staffed by appointees of whose exclusive personal loyalty she felt confident, into which she could retreat – in the process distancing herself from her Ministers and gradually losing touch with the real world outside.

Running a Small Department

In addition to all his policy preoccupations and other duties, the Chancellor has overall responsibility for the administration of the Treasury. Fortunately, it is a small Department, consisting of just 1,400 staff at its headquarters in Great George Street, at the corner of Parliament Square and Whitehall, between the Foreign Office and the House of Commons; and the Chancellor probably enjoys a closer relationship with his senior officials than do most Ministers.

Given its informality, the smallness of its numbers, and the fact that it is almost entirely a policy Department, with virtually no executive function, it was absolutely essential to ensure that the right people were in the key positions at the Treasury; and staff appointments were a matter in which I always took the keenest interest.

Editor of the *Spectator*, 1968. *(Roger Jones/Campaign Haymarket Press Ltd)*

Prospective Conservative candidate for Blaby, 1972. *(Tom Blau/Camera Press)*

The Old Rectory, Stoney Stanton.

Leaving Number 10 after my first Cabinet meeting, with Quintin Hailsham, Septembe 1981. *(Express Newspapers)*

The Cabinet, December 1981. *(Back l-r)* Michael Jopling, Norman Tebbit, Janet Young, Norman Fowler, John Biffen, Humphrey Atkins, George Younger, Nicholas Edwards, Patrick Jenkin, David Howell, Leon Brittan, myself, Cecil Parkinson,

The original 1979 Treasury team. (*l-r*) Peter Rees, Minister of State (Commons); myself, Financial Secretary; Geoffrey Howe, Chancellor of the Exchequer; John Biffen, Chief Secretary; Arthur Cockfield, Minister of State (Lords). (The Financial Times)

Robert Armstrong (Cabinet Secretary). (*Front l-r*) Peter Walker, Jim Prior, Keith Joseph, Peter Carrington, Willie Whitelaw, Margaret Thatcher, Quintin Hailsham, Geoffrey Howe, Francis Pym, John Nott, Michael Heseltine.

Emerging from the coal face during a pit visit to Yorkshire as Energy Secretary, 1982. Ian Gillis is on the far left and Julian West is third from the right.

Arthur Scargill, with Mick McGahey, haranguing his supporters during the coal strike, 1984. *(David Muscroft/Rex Features)*

Numbers 10 and 11 Downing Street (Number 11 has the white stucco).
(Central Office of Information)

The State Drawing Room, Number 11. *(Royal Commission on the Historical Monuments of England)*

My first Conservative Party Conference as Chancellor, Blackpool, October 1983.

*(Ashley Ashwood/*The Financial Times*)*

Terry Burns.

(Universal Pictorial Press & Agency)

Peter Middleton.

(Universal Pictorial Press & Agency)

With my first Treasury team, June 1983. (*l-r*) Barney Hayhoe, Minister of State; Peter Rees, Chief Secretary; Nicholas Ridley, Financial Secretary; John Moore, Economic Secretary. *(Trevor Humphries/*The Financial Times*)*

With Michael Heseltine at the Conservative Party Conference, Blackpool, October 1983. *(Sally Soames/*The Sunday Times*)*

With Thérèse and Mark Lennox-Boyd on my first Budget Day, March 1984.
(The Financial Times) ·

The Budget ritual: being photographed at the Treasury with the Gladstone Box, March 1984. *(Rex Features)*

The Budget ritual: a quiet stroll in St James's Park with Thérèse, Tom (aged eight) and Emily (aged three), March 1985. *(Times Newspapers)*

A serious moment at the Conservative Party Conference, Brighton, October 1984. On my left, Leon Brittan; on my right, Norman Tebbit. (The Financial Times)

Margaret Thatcher's dinner for Ronald Reagan on the eve of the London Economic Summit, June 1984. (*Left of table, l-r*) Geoffrey Howe, President Reagan, myself, James Baker; *(right of table, l-r)* Margaret Thatcher, George Schultz, Don Regan. *(Press Association/ Topham)*

The IRA's handiwork at the Grand Hotel, Brighton, October 1984. *(Press Association/Topham)*

Willie Whitelaw. *(Rex Features)*

Margaret Thatcher leaving
Number 10 with her Parliamentary
Private Secretary, Ian Gow.
(Mike Pattison/Camera Press)

G5 Finance Ministers at the Plaza Hotel, New York, September 1985. (*l-r*) Gerhard
Stoltenberg, Pierre Bérégovoy, James Baker, myself, Noboru Takeshita.
(Associated Press)

Zaki Yamani . *(Popperfoto)*

Jacques Delors. *(Robert/SIPA Press/Rex Features)*

Paul Volcker and James Baker at the meeting of the Group of Ten, Washington, April 1986. *(Rex Features)*

The Daily Telegraph

WEDNESDAY, MARCH 18, 1987

LONDON AND MANCHESTER **25p**

No. 40,972

Cautious Budget cheers City and Tories

Lawson paves way for poll

Basic tax rate down 2p: lending rates set to fall

THE COST of borrowing is expected to start to fall sharply today as a result of Mr Lawson's Budget which cut the standard rate of income tax by 2p to 27p — and was hailed by the City for its caution and by politicians as preparing the way for a June or September election.

The Chancellor opened the way to reductions in interest rates — including home loan charges — by announcing a cut from £7 billion to £4 billion in the public sector borrowing target.

Predicting the seventh successive year of economic growth, Mr Lawson forecast that output would rise by three...

Borrowing target is cut to £4bn

25p still Tory tax target

BUDGET SPECIAL

MARRIED COUPLES — ALL INCOME EARNED			
ANNUAL FIGURES			
Income £	Charge for 1986-87 £	Proposed charge 1987-88 £	Reduction in tax £
5,000	390	325	65
6,000	680	595	85
7,000	970	865	105
8,000	1,260	1,135	125
9,000	1,550	1,405	145
10,000	1,840	1,675	165
12,000	2,420	2,215	205
14,000	3,000	2,755	245
16,000	3,5		285
18,000	4,1	3,795	325
20,000	4,		
25,000	6,		
30,000	9,		
40,000	1		
50,000	1		
60,000	1		
70,000	2		
100,000	3		

Calculations assu

EEK'S
E DAILY SALE

3,030

THE ‎ TIMES

WEDNESDAY MARCH 16 1988

30p

% higher tax rate laces five others

higher rate of income tax of 40 per cent replaces ting five higher rates up to 60 per cent. The basic ut from 27p to 25p and the Chancellor's target is a e of 20 per cent. Personal allowances go up by 7.4 — twice the amount needed to compensate for 's inflation. A single person's allowance rises by £2,605 and a married man's allowance by £300 to The threshold for the new higher rate of 40 per £19,300, up by £1,409. The rates apply to the tax ginning on April 6 and their impact on salaries will n the first pay day after June 14...............**Page 13**

ried taxation to go

sting taxation system for married couple's will be d from April 1990 and replaced with independent A husband and wife will be taxed separately on , savings, pensions and any other income and women will have complete privacy and indepen-he married man's allowance and the wife's ne allowance will disappear. All taxpayers will ....tion the single person's ....

BRITAIN

***

**NGES
ANCE**

which overall neither ellor Nigel Lawson. le helped the people out of the

Uproar at Chancellor's 'rich man's Budget'

Lawson's tax triumph

Basic rate cut to 25p in the pound
By David Brewerton and Robin Oakley

Mr Nigel Lawson, the Chancellor of the Ex-chequer, scored a per-sonal triumph yesterday with one of the most radi-cal tax-reforming Budgets this century.

At the same time he celebrated a victory over the Prime Minister, mak-ing clear that he will continue to run economic policy and that he will, if necessary, intervene in the foreign exchange mar-kets to prevent the pound rising too far.

Mr Lawson has slashed the top rate of tax from 60 to 40 per cent and taken 2p in the pound off basic rate. The tax cuts, adding up to £4 billion, will add an average of nearly £5 a week to pay packets. Nowhere in the tax system is there now a tax rate higher than 40 per cent.

The promise of a basic tax rate of 25p in the pound made in the election manifesto has been fulfilled in Mr Lawson's "tax reform Budget", which has swept away the numerous bands of tax which less than a decade ago went up to 83 per cent.

There will now be just two income tax bands, 25p and 40p. Allowances have been increased by double the amount required to keep them in line with inflation. Mr Lawson said the basic rate thresholds will be 25 per cent higher, in real terms, than they were in 1978-79 when the Conservative Government came to office.

Further cuts and overdue

education and at least £500 million more on law and order, than in the year just ending. There were no changes to those figures yesterday.

Mr Lawson is to reform the taxation of husband and wife to give married women "the same privacy and indepen-dence in their tax affairs as everyone else." And he is to bring to an end the ways in which the tax system can penalize marriage.

Mr Lawson told MPs he had been guided by four basic principles: "First, the need to

reduce tax rates where they are clearly too high; second, the need to reduce or abolish un-warranted tax breaks; third, the need to make life a little simpler for the taxpayer; and, fourth, the need to remove some manifest injustices from the system."

However, the changes are not all "giveaways". Mr Lawson has come down hard on company cars where he is doubling the car scales for 1988-89, instead of increasing them by 10 per cent as had already been announced.

He is also risking the wrath of some of his own supporters by removing the tax benefits of non-charitable deeds of covenant, which are used by parents and grandparents for student maintenance. Existing

Growth of 3% forecast in buoyant economy
By Rodney Lord, Economics Editor

Labour fury halts speech
By Robin Oakley
Political Editor

The Chancellor's sta sparked off a political which, for the first t living memory, led t suspension of the Co during a Budget speech

Left-wing Labour M ing it a rich man's promised the most fought Finance Bill th ever been, while famou ernment whips compla the failure of the Labo bench to control its MP their chanting of "sham continual uproar forc Harold Walker, the Speaker, to suspend the for MPs to cool down.

Angry ministers gest Mr Neil Kinnock duri disturbances to contr row behind him and furious that he and Mr Dobson, the shadow le the House, and Mr Foster, the Labour Whip, did nothing to r the angry Labour MP Mr Kinnock also later demn the disruption an his backbenchers: "Do mad, get even. Argum always superior to the fo action we have seen afternoon."

The Labour disruptio lowed a deliberately s protest by Scottish Natio MP Mr Alex Salmond w had him suspended from chamber.

Mr Brian Sedgemore, our MP for Hackney Shoreditch, and one o core of Campaign Group who headed the protests,

---

THE GUARDIAN

Printed in London, Manchester and Portsmouth

Wednesday March 19 1986   25p

AA 1986

Make the r your days out and away with your 198 Available now from and booksellers eve

Standard rate now 29p • Hint of pre-election cuts • 11p on cigaret

Pennyworth of jam from Lawso

Budget holding operation to rally troops
By Christopher Huhne, Economics Editor

Mr Nigel Lawson's third budget yesterday cut the standard rate of income tax by 1p to 29p in the pound with the promise of more cuts to come before the general election.

It was essentially a holding operation designed to rally the troops with some jam today without alarming the financial markets, although the Chancel lor said he intended to reduce income tax to 25p in the pound "in the long term."

The net tax giveaway was just under £1 billion, though the effect on the economy and hence on unemployment is broadly neutral once the fall in public spending as a share of national income is added in.

Mr Lawson's balancing act of net tax cuts despite plum-meting oil revenues was in

ownership schemes, and a tri-fling £100 million increase in special employment measures.

These were made easier by non-oil tax revenues £3 billion higher than expected as well as the predicted outturn for this year's government reve-nues and spending rather under the £7 billion originally predicted and the £6 billion forecast in the November statement.

The yield from indirect taxes like VAT was increased by 2p a gallon more in line with inflation, though the balance of taxes on spend-ing was shifted on to smokers, who will pay 11p more per packet (instead of 4.5 pence to inflation) while drinkers will see no rise.

Petrol duties were also in-creased by 2p a gallon more than required by 2p. Mr Lawson said that there should be a real fall in pump prices if companies passed on the reductions in the price of crude oil. He also used his extra revenue to hold the Ve-hicle Excise Duty at £100.

The City got off lightly, with a cut in the stamp duty on share transactions of 0.5 per cent point—justified on the grounds of competition with New York and Tokyo—financed by a new tax on vari-ous financial instruments.

Summing up his budget, Mr Lawson said that he had an-nounced "a further substan-tial range of measures to help the unemployed" and had proposed a radical scheme for

Crusade on course for a Cabinet clash
By James Naughtie, Chief Political Correspondent

The Chancellor yesterday turned his modest budget hand-out into a tax-cutting crusade for "popular capital-ism" which disappointed Conservatives hoping for a more direct attack on unemployment.

Mr Lawson's penny cut in the basic rate of income tax was seen as the centrepiece of a package, a foretaste of more to come. It was also a signal that the Cabinet ma-jority sceptical of his empha-sis on direct reductions has a fight on its hands against the Chancellor, the Prime Minister and Mr Norman Tebbit, the Tory Chairman.

After his speech Mr Lawson issued a warning to colleagues that his hopes for tax cuts next year would be put at risk

Basic tax rates cut by a penny
INCOME TAX cut on basic rates by a penny to 29p in pound and personal allowances up 5.7 per cent (£20 the married allowance and £130 for a single per worth about £2.60 a week to the average married c from mid-May. The first cut in the basic rate since t Higher thresholds all rise by £1,000. A discussion pa on the reform of personal tax has been published taining a number of options for change.

Petrol duty up 7.5p a gallon
MOTORING COSTS will rise less than expected, with only 7 on a gallon of petrol, less than 2p above the increase retail prices on the year and supposedly not enough prompt an increase in pump prices. Diesel fuel goes 6.5p. Vehicle Excise duty is unchanged. There will duty concessions to make lead-free fuel more attracti Company car fuel charges will be brought in line wi European levels and car scale charges increased 10 pe cent.

Cigarettes up 11p a packet of
SMOKING AND DRINKING will cost no more except fo cigarette smokers, who face an 11p a packet increase Cigars and pipe tobacco duties are unchanged, along wit beers, wines and spirits. Total income from the change in duty will be £795 million this year, in line wit inflation.

Community programme wage increase
JOB BOOSTING measures include small rises in the wage for community programme workers up £4 to £67 a week a "new worker scheme" for 18-20s which will pay £1 allowance scheme at a total cost of £795 million

part pulled off by a relatively rosy assumption that dollar oil narred" for 1986/87 computed ared" for 1986/87 computed with yesterday's in the

Speaking to journalists at Westminster, he said of his colleagues: "I can try to

transfer tax and virtually end the tax on gifts to indi-viduals at a cost of £35 million this year and £35 million in a full year.

Supplied by the John Frost Historical Newspaper Service

Part of June Mendoza's painting of the House of Commons in session, July 1986 (the first such painting this century). *(Camera Press)*

My favourite portrait of Gladstone; a copy hung in the hall of Number 11.
(National Portrait Gallery)

This was especially true of my Principal Private Secretaries. I have already referred to my first incumbent, John Kerr, whom I had inherited from Geoffrey Howe. After his return to the Foreign Office in 1984, he was replaced by David Peretz, a Treasury official whom Geoffrey had already designated as John Kerr's successor, and who was later to do a stint as the Treasury's man in Washington. David was gentle, quiet, kind and hardworking; but each Chancellor looks for the right Principal Private Secretary for him. After a few months I arranged for him to be moved to the monetary policy job he had always coveted and secured a Principal Private Secretary of my own choosing. This was Rachel Lomax, a professional economist and the first woman to serve a Chancellor as Principal Private Secretary, who did an excellent job.

Alex Allan, who took over from her in July 1986 was once again my own choice, although this time I had to secure him against the advice of the mandarins, who considered him too junior. A tall, good looking, well-built young man with a passion for sailing and computers, universally liked, and exuding good manners without a hint of the smarminess that so often goes with high-flying officials, Alex soon proved to be the ideal Principal Private Secretary. He possessed a quick and logical mind, was hard-working, loyal and straight as a die, and had a better understanding of the political and parliamentary dimensions than most officials – perhaps because his father had been an MP and junior Minister in the Macmillan Government. He was outstanding, and stayed with me for over three years, not leaving until less than three months before my resignation. Although he was then still under forty, he had done so well that I had little difficulty in persuading Peter Middleton that he should be promoted forthwith. After two Treasury posts as an Under Secretary, he was appointed Principal Private Secretary to the Prime Minister, John Major, after the 1992 general election.

The official I wanted to succeed him was Gus O'Donnell, but because he and his wife were planning to start a family he did not feel he would be able to put in the necessary long hours. There was no-one else of his calibre in the field; so I persuaded John Gieve, who by that time had become my Press Secretary, to be my Principal Private Secretary instead, leaving me free to appoint Gus O'Donnell as my Press Secretary, thus at least securing Gus as part of my personal team. I was glad that my successor as Chancellor, John Major, who inherited Gus as his Press Secretary, had the good sense to take him with him to be his Chief Press Secretary at Number 10.

But my personal involvement in Treasury appointments and promotion extended well beyond the Private Office. Peter Middleton would always discuss his thinking with me; and although they were matters strictly for him I was usually able to ensure that the best people were moved to what I considered to be the key jobs. This meant that policy advice and ministerial briefing was the best the Treasury could provide. A much harder task was securing adequate help with my speeches. A Chancellor of the Exchequer has to deliver an absurdly large number of speeches during the course of the year, and clearly does not have the time to compose them all himself. Unfortunately, few officials recognize the importance of the presentation and explanation of policy, and of those few, fewer still, however lucid their written submissions, know how to draft a speech.

My Principal Private Secretary was best placed to prepare a usable speech draft, because he knew me and my style well and understood my position on every policy issue; but he was also very busy. If the official covering a particular aspect of policy was invited to prepare a speech, it seldom worked. I eventually recruited a particularly talented young official from the Inland Revenue called Andrew Hudson, and he fulfilled the role of speech writer admirably until he secured the permanent transfer to the Treasury which he had long sought and was moved to a more orthodox job.

They Don't Give You the Figures

Unlike most other finance ministries in the world, which have ministerial responsibility for the regulation of the financial sector, in Britain the responsibility was divided, with the Treasury having responsibility for the banks and building societies and the Department of Trade and Industry being responsible for the securities and insurance industries. This division was always a mistake, but it became increasingly nonsensical as the distinctions between financial institutions became increasingly blurred. The nonsense was compounded by the fact that the Bank of England, which keeps an eye on the entire financial sector, has the Treasury as its sponsoring Department.

Although I was never an empire builder, I minuted Margaret in March 1987, arguing the case for using the opportunity of the new Government she would be forming after the general election to follow international practice and common sense and consolidate responsibility for the entire financial sector in the hands of the Treasury, as soon as the forthcoming general election was behind us. I suggested that, in return, the DTI could absorb my old Department, Energy, and possibly also the Central Computer and Telecommunications Agency and the Chessington Computer Centre, which were rather anomalous offshoots of the Treasury. Unfortunately Margaret, who was temperamentally averse to changes in the machinery of government, rejected my advice; and it was left to John Major to make this long overdue move after the 1992 general election.

As I have mentioned, one Department whose annexation I did secure, although not until 1989, was the Central Statistical Office (CSO). This was a perfectly natural acquisition which occurred regrettably late in the day. When Disraeli was unexpectedly offered the Chancellorship by Lord Derby in 1852, he demurred. Derby replied: 'You know as much as Mr Canning did. They give you the figures.' This remains an apt summary of the Chancellor's reliance on the facts and figures prepared by officials. The trouble is that they do not always give you the right figures.

The CSO, which was originally formed to monitor weapons production in the Second World War, had for that reason come under the control of the Cabinet Office, and therefore under the nominal command of the Prime Minister. Since the Prime Minister has no Department of his or her own, and a great deal else to attend to, this meant that, in practice, the CSO was effectively outwith ministerial control altogether. I have little doubt that this contributed to the deterioration in the reliability of the key statistics it provided. It was a monopoly producer of most economic statistics which felt itself under no obligation to meet the legitimate needs of its principal customer.

It did not, however, have responsibility for all of them. Some important series were gathered by statisticians working independently in other Government Departments. The Retail Price Index, for example, was prepared by the Department of Employment. This was a legacy of the days when its predecessor, the Ministry of Labour, was the only Government Department with a network of offices around the country – the labour exchanges – and its officials could be despatched to the local shops once a month to monitor the prices. In the last years of my Chancellorship, this accident of history severely restricted my ability to secure improvements in the Retail Price Index which would have led to a more accurate representation of inflation.

The traditional arrangements were not seriously questioned until the errors in the economic statistics, which had been a matter of growing concern for some time, reached a whole new order of magnitude in 1988. This led to the setting up of an interdepartmental committee under a Treasury official, Stephen Pickford, to scrutinize the quality of official economic data. Its report, which was published in April 1989, recommended the transformation of the CSO into a free-standing body and the transfer of ultimate responsibility for it from the Prime Minister to the Chancellor. This encountered vigorous opposition from within the machine, on the grounds that it would demoralize the statisticians and lead to accusations that the Government was fiddling the figures.

I pointed out to Margaret that the *status quo* had resulted in serious errors, on which key policy decisions had been based. I suggested that if the CSO were to absorb the statistical responsibilities and resources which had hitherto lain with the DTI and Department of Employment, and the enlarged Department be transferred to the Chancellor, he and his key officials (especially the Chief Economic Adviser) could insist that the CSO's finite resources were devoted to the statistical series they most needed to steer the economy. As for the CSO's integrity, the Inland Revenue was responsible to the Chancellor, but no-one had suggested that this compromised its integrity. To her credit, Margaret agreed, and the Pickford report's recommendation was duly implemented.

It is sometimes alleged that the deterioration in the quality of the official statistics was due very largely to the cut-backs in staff and statistical coverage that the Government imposed on the CSO in the early 1980s. In fact, most of the statistical series which were discontinued in 1980 and 1981 were appropriate to an age of detailed economic intervention, but not to one in which the Government recognized that its task was to influence the economic framework. There was little point in burdening businessmen with the responsibility to report statistics the Government no longer required.

In any case, apart from the failure to make the CSO responsible to its principal customer, the main reason for the deteriorating quality of the statistics was not staff shortages or discontinued series, but the deregulation of the economy in general and the liberalization of the financial markets in particular. Exchange controls, for example, greatly facilitated the collection of data about foreign exchange transactions. But once companies and individuals were free to pay, receive, invest or borrow sterling and foreign currencies without restraint, accurate statistics about foreign exchange transactions became almost impossible to obtain. The abolition of a host of other controls meant the economy began to develop in ways that were simply not picked up by statistical series designed to meet the needs of a different era. One obvious example was the growth of overseas trade in services, which the balance of payment figures consistently underestimated in the late 1980s.

These inadequacies were exacerbated by the fact that in Britain most statistics are collected on a voluntary basis, in order to avoid burdening businessmen with excessive form filling. Procedures were subsequently tightened; but it would be a mistake to make the collection of statistics an end in itself. Officials need to do more to frame their diagnosis and advice on the basis of accurate figures readily available – which are a thousandfold greater than anything Gladstone had at his disposal – without falling down on the job.

The Advent of the 'Gooies'

Discussion of the use of economic statistics inevitably leads to the question of economic advisers. In Chapter 22 I remarked that a Chancellor who needs a personal economic adviser has got the wrong Chief Economic Adviser to the Treasury, whom he should be able to change. But there is obviously a case for a Chancellor to test the economic advice he receives against the views of economists outside the Treasury. Samuel Brittan, in particular, had long advocated setting up a modified form of the US Council of Economic Advisers for this purpose.

While I did not favour the creation of a new institution, I did belatedly respond in an informal way by setting up in 1986 a group of outside economists of my own choosing whom I would invite to Number 11 for a prolonged discussion four or five times a year, rather along the lines that Gerhard Stoltenberg had told me he had organized in Germany. The 'gooies' (group of outside independent economists), as my officials soon christened them, originally were invited for about an hour and a half before dinner, over a drink, but I subsequently invited them for dinner, to give more time for discussion.

The membership of the group varied over time, but at one time or another included Alan Budd, then of the London Business School, who subsequently became Chief Economic Adviser to the Treasury in 1991, Walter Eltis, before his appointment as Economic Director and subsequently Director-General of Neddy, Geoffrey Maynard, a former Treasury Deputy Chief Economic Adviser, Harold Rose, the leading bank economist of his day, Patrick Minford, the strongly Thatcherite Liverpool economist, Samuel Brittan of the *Financial Times*, Gordon Pepper, the monetary economist I have referred to earlier, Mervyn King, who subsequently became Economic Adviser to the Bank of England, and John Muellbauer, the Oxford economist then specializing in the economics of the housing market. Terry Burns, of course, always sat in at our meetings, but deliberately adopted a low profile.

My office would inform all members in advance of each meeting of the two topics I wished to discuss; and anyone could put in a paper, but it was not mandatory. Originally, the sole note of the meeting was one made by Terry and sent only to me. Later on, I had my Principal Private Secretary sit in and make a note which was circulated to all participants. I deliberately sought a range of views, and did not confine the membership to political or personal sympathizers, but obviously I could not have economists likely to advise the Labour Party, as these were confidential gatherings. The idea was to represent a broad spectrum among those who were receptive to the new thinking of the 1980s. The split between the parochial monetarists and those who looked to the exchange rate (or the ERM) developed its needless bitterness only after the Group had been formed; otherwise I might have constructed it rather differently. As it was, I had to spend rather too much time in preventing Patrick Minford and Samuel Brittan from coming to blows.

There is, incidentally, an irony in the fact that it was only when, halfway through my time as Chancellor, I equipped myself with outside economic advice, that my conduct of macroeconomic policy got into difficulties. In general, the advice I received was so mixed as to be illuminating rather than operationally useful. While the 'gooies' were in no sense responsible for the policy I was pursuing, it is equally true that at no time was there a significant body of opinion within them, let alone a consensus, that policy was too loose. The one member of the group who came closest to this was Samuel Brittan. But the strongest criticism came from Minford, who was horrified by what he considered the brutal way I had wrenched up interest rates from 8 per cent in June 1988 to 12 per cent that August.

There is one other memory I have of those meetings, which points a moral. In the meeting we had in the wake of the October 1987 stock market crash, I vividly recall Pepper warning in stark tones that we were faced with the imminent danger of world recession or worse, brought about by an economy that had become far too 'loaned up' (that, or something very like it, was the unusual expression he used); as a result of which debt deflation stared us in the face. In one sense Pepper was very perceptive and ahead of the game; but because he got the timing so wrong, to have acted on his analysis would have been very much worse than anything I did do. The moral is that it is no use being right too soon. I made a modified form of the Pepper mistake myself, in the sense that I expected the long upturn of the 1980s to give way to a downturn well before it did, and was thus unprepared for the extent of the late 1980s boom.

Stumbles on 'Next Steps'

Margaret had entered office in 1979 fired with a desire to root out waste and extravagance in Whitehall and in Government generally. To this end she invited Derek Rayner, of Marks & Spencer, to set up an Efficiency Unit in the Cabinet Office. By the autumn of 1986, the Civil Service payroll, which had been steadily expanding under previous administrations of both Parties, had been cut by almost 20 per cent; and through this and other economies cumulative savings of some £1 billion had been secured. Derek Rayner also launched, in 1982, the Financial Management Initiative (FMI), which introduced into the public service for the first time in any systematic way such useful disciplines as the clarification of specific objectives, the assignment of individual responsibilities, the delegation of authority and a detailed awareness of costs. Rayner left to return to Marks and Spencer in 1983, and was succeeded as Head of the Efficiency Unit by Robin Ibbs of ICI.

Ibbs conducted himself in a wholly different fashion from Rayner. He believed that the route to efficiency in the public sector was to mimic the private sector as closely as possible. Conscious that in the private sector it is necessary to spend money in order to make money, he was always sympathetic to the predictable complaints of the spending Departments that they could make themselves much more efficient, provide a much better service to the public, and give much better value for money if only the Treasury were less stingy and ceased to deny them the resources they needed to do the job properly.

I tried hard to get him to see the light. As early as July 1984 I wrote to him:

> We need to do all we can to ensure that increased efficiency shows up in lower expenditure. We cannot afford changes in financial management which become a means of institutionalizing present levels of expenditure, and then try to console ourselves that public sector output has risen.

I explained to him that I myself considered Treasury control of spending to be very much a second-best form of financial discipline: the discipline of the market place was altogether superior. That was why there was no-one more zealous for privatization than I was. But so long as public services existed, insulated from the discipline of the market place, with no 'bottom line' and, indeed, in most cases providing services free at the point of use so there was not even a price mechanism at work, Treasury control was essential. The alternative was no financial discipline at all.

This truth was later to be paralleled in an unexpected context. Following the collapse of the Soviet Union, it soon became clear that, where market disciplines were not quickly put in place following the abandonment of the Communist command system of control, the result was chaos.

With this background, I was inevitably suspicious when, towards the end of 1987, I and other Cabinet colleagues were informed by Number 10, out of the blue, of a new Ibbs initiative, which apparently had Margaret's enthusiastic support. It seems that in May of that year, the Efficiency Unit had submitted to her a report entitled *Improving Management in Government – The Next Steps*, the main burden of which was a recommendation that the executive functions of Government should be hived off into separate executive agencies, to be run like businesses by chief executives, some of them appointed from outside the Civil Service.

It was clear that Ibbs had not addressed either of the two principal problems involved in a change of this kind, however sensible the concept may have been. The first was the question of parliamentary accountability. Members of Parliament would not take kindly to the idea of a Minister being able to shrug off a constituent's complaint as being nothing to do with him, since the wrong suffered by the constituent had been inflicted by an autonomous executive agency, whose head was, according to the original Ibbs blueprint, effectively accountable to no-one.

But even when this was solved there remained the second problem, that of maintaining effective control of the agencies' expenditure, in which Ibbs showed no interest. Having persuaded Margaret that this had to be addressed, a long battle ensued, resulting in a lengthy written concordat negotiated by Peter Middleton on behalf of the Treasury and Robin Butler on behalf of Number 10.

This achieved two things. First, an understanding that agency status would always be seen as a second best to privatization, which would have to be explored first. Second, that the chief executive of the agency, and his 'board' would be set stiff financial targets which would have to be agreed with the Treasury in the first place and monitored by the Treasury thereafter. This agreement made the proposal acceptable, and the public interest was further secured by the appointment of a senior Treasury official, Peter Kemp, as the manager of the 'Next Steps' project, with the rank of Second Permanent Secretary.

Kemp was an unusual official, an accountant by training who had joined the Treasury from the private sector. He was to do a remarkable job. By 1991 he had created fifty-one free-standing executive agencies covering 200,000 Civil Servants, or one third of the entire Civil Service. Only the Foreign Office escaped his attentions altogether. An enthusiast for the project, Kemp set himself the aim of converting half the Civil Service into agencies by June 1993, and three quarters of it by the mid 1990s. I myself, early on, volunteered three of my outlying Departments, the Stationery Office (HMSO), the Royal Mint and the Central Office of Information, as executive agencies.

I did not, however, support Kemp's desire to convert the Inland Revenue and the Customs and Excise into agencies. These politically sensitive Departments, with a small but important policy role, had long enjoyed a high degree of autonomy from political control so far as their executive functions were concerned, and converting them into agencies would have created no discernible advantage. Moreover, the only way in which it could have been achieved would have been to transfer their policy role to the Treasury, leaving them as purely tax collecting agencies. This was something to which the Chairmen of the two Revenue Departments were implacably opposed, arguing with some plausibility that policy advice was improved if it was informed by practical experience on the ground.

Agency status has undoubtedly reversed some of the negative effects on Civil Service morale of the economies of the early 1980s, by giving the staff a sense of ownership. But most of the chief executives are still drawn from the Civil Service and the agencies inevitably lack the ultimate sanction of financial failure. The main practical advantage I see is that by creating accounts, boards of directors and saleable assets, future privatization may prove less difficult.

Civil Service Pay

Peter Kemp had previously been the Treasury Deputy Secretary in charge of Civil Service pay; and it was largely through his efforts that I was able to effect a major change in Civil Service attitudes and practice. By the time I became Chancellor, Civil Service pay negotiations were in a chaotic state. The Civil Service strike in the first half of 1981 had ended with an inquiry into the matter headed by a judge, John Megaw. His report, delivered in July 1982, was full of brave talk about a greater role for market forces in the determination of Civil Service pay, but its recommendations were in practice a compromise. Megaw replaced the old idea of pay awards based exclusively on comparability by what was called 'constrained informed bargaining', in which pay rises were to lie between the upper and lower quartiles of the rises awarded in the private sector.

Although the Government committed itself to the 'principles of Megaw', we also had other objectives which, at that time, the unions were not prepared to accept. The result was five years of free collective bargaining in which the Government, on the whole, managed to hold pay settlements below the levels prevailing elsewhere. There were a few strikes and other disputes, but they were all unsuccessful, and it was the trade unions which eventually proposed to the Government a more organized system of pay negotiations. In mid-1987 the Institution of Professional Civil Servants (IPCS) approached the Treasury and agreed a special deal which incorporated for the first time both performance criteria and regional differentiation as well as comparability studies à la Megaw. The other Civil Service trade unions, which continued to bargain freely, had to settle for rises of just 4¼ per cent that year.

In subsequent years they opted to follow the example of the IPCS, and by the time I resigned as Chancellor every Civil Service union was negotiating pay agreements which at least made a gesture towards market considerations. The weakening of the idea that all Civil Servants should be treated in the same way, and the introduction of market forces into

Civil Service pay negotiations, was a triumph of sorts. The success was secured largely by Peter Kemp, who was an exceptionally patient and skilful negotiator, and who knew he could count on me to see the key Civil Service trade union leaders on the few occasions when it was helpful for me to do so.

Paradoxically, the Government's biggest blunder over Civil Service pay had nothing to do with the unions whatever. This was the decision in July 1985 to honour in full the recommendation of the Top Salaries Review Body (TSRB) that senior Civil Servants, officers in the armed forces and judges should receive pay increases of between 12.2 and 17.6 per cent. Moreover, these large increases, of more than double the rate of inflation were averages: the salary of the Cabinet Secretary, Robert Armstrong, rose by 46 per cent.

Sizeable increases were certainly necessary to staunch the flow of talent from the Civil Service to the City and to attract sufficient bright graduates to replenish the losses, but the real problem lay not at the top but lower down, among the Assistant Secretaries and Principals. That was where the 'brain drain' had become serious, and where morale was dangerously low. Not surprisingly, these huge increases for the mandarins caused a tremendous political furore at a time when the private sector was still under pressure and the Government was seeking overall restraint in public sector pay. After six years as Prime Minister, Margaret had appointed many of the top Civil Servants. She valued them very highly, and failed to foresee that others might not see them in quite the same light. She misjudged the unpopularity of the increases among Conservative back-benchers in particular, many of whom came under pressure from their constituency associations.

The salaries of the mandarins, military top brass and judiciary covered by the TSRB awards are an administrative matter, and do not require the endorsement of the House of Commons. However, in 1983 the Government had accepted a TSRB recommendation that the Lord Chancellor should always be paid more than the Lord Chief Justice. An increase in the Lord Chancellor's salary as a Minister – which the 1985 TSRB award to the Lord Chief Justice obviously implied – did require an Order which had to be approved by Parliament. It was this which enabled the TSRB recommendations to be debated in the House of Commons on 23 July 1985, when the Government's majority slipped to a mere 17 votes, the smallest since it first took office in 1979. Indeed, had a number of Labour Members not failed to vote – perhaps because the Government's business managers had arranged for the vote not to take place until a quarter to two in the morning – the Government would have been defeated.

I had opposed the granting of the TSRB increases in full, but was overruled. In October of that year I sent a minute to Margaret and other interested colleagues proposing a more radical solution: the abolition of the TSRB altogether. It seemed to me that segregating 'top people' in this way was almost bound to create political difficulty, to no great advantage. I suggested, instead, that senior Civil Servants' pay should be part of the overall Civil Service pay arrangements; that the senior officers in the armed forces should come under the Armed Forces Pay Review Body which covered the rest of the armed forces, and that a specialist body could be set up to make recommendations for the pay of the judiciary.

As for the other two groups notionally covered by the TSRB, the pay of MPs was already effectively out of their hands, since Parliament had agreed a linkage with the pay of middle ranking Civil Servants, and Ministers' pay was in any event always in practice decided on an *ad hoc* basis by Cabinet (which invariably led to very small increases for the non-Parliamentary portion of Ministers' pay). Although I secured the support of John Biffen, who as Leader of the House of Commons had had the unenviable task of defending the 1985 TSRB recommendations to the House in the debate on the Lord Chancellor's salary, other colleagues showed little interest in the matter and Margaret was able to reject this radical suggestion and insist on retaining the *status quo*, as she did so often.

CHAPTER 32

FRAUD AND THE CITY

Divided Against Fraud · Reforming the Stock Exchange
Big Bang and After · The Johnson Matthey Débâcle
Strengthening Bank Supervision · A New Banking Act
The Role of the Bank of England · Reflections on BCCI
How to Put Fraudsters Behind Bars

Divided Against Fraud

IT MIGHT SEEM SURPRISING at first sight that a Government, and a Chancellor, so committed to deregulation, including financial deregulation, should have spent so much time over, and been so concerned with, financial regulation. Indeed, some have even seen it as a tacit admission that financial deregulation went too far. But this is to be confused by words. Financial deregulation in no way implies the absence of financial regulation for prudential purposes and for the prevention, so far as possible, of fraud. Economic freedom, as much as political freedom, is possible only within the framework of the rule of law.

I mentioned in the previous chapter the unsatisfactory division of responsibility for the oversight of the financial services industry between the Treasury and the Department of Trade and Industry which existed throughout my time as Chancellor, and Margaret's refusal to authorize the obvious remedy – an error subseqently rectified by her successor, John Major.

My March 1987 proposal to give overall departmental responsibility to the Treasury was based on the lessons of experience. For a number of reasons, I had been plunged into this particular corner of the Chancellor's bailiwick right from the moment I entered Number 11. One of the first worries Peter Middleton expressed to me after welcoming me as the new

Chancellor in 1983 concerned the inadequacy of Whitehall's machinery for dealing with commercial fraud. He was absolutely right. He suggested that I might set up and chair an inter-ministerial group on the subject, which I readily agreed to do, with Margaret's acquiescence. As 'Lex' of *The Financial Times* in 1960, I had seen the exposure of financial skullduggery – in so far as the lawyers permitted me to engage in it – as a major part of my job, and had continued this intermittent crusade as City Editor of the *Sunday Telegraph* in 1961–63. I was thus fortunate in having some background knowledge of the subject, if of a somewhat mature vintage.

But the inter-ministerial group which I chaired in my room at the Treasury in 1983 and 1984 was a depressing if instructive experience. It soon became clear that a *sine qua non* of an effective Government response to financial fraud was the fullest co-operation between the various departments with responsibility in this area. That was not to say that the component parts themselves were adequate: they were not. But there was no need to make matters worse by a refusal to subordinate departmental *amour propre* to the common cause.

Yet that proved to be the case. The Department of Trade and Industry, with its wide-ranging regulatory responsibilities and the statutory power to initiate the most searching investigations into suspect companies, felt that it should head the combined Government effort. The Attorney General, to whom the Director of Public Prosecutions (DPP) and his Department reported, had no doubt that a consolidation of the Government's capability under any other auspices than his own would be grossly improper. And the Home Office, with responsibility for the police in general and the fraud squad in particular, and a strong sense of its high place in the Whitehall pecking order, was adamant that not an inch of its departmental turf should be surrendered.

Eventually, as a new Chancellor, the best I could secure was the setting up of the Fraud Investigation Group (FIG) as a new permanent body, backed by additional resources, to deal with serious cases of commercial and financial fraud. It would be located in the DPP's Department and would comprise accountants seconded from the DTI as well as lawyers. The Home Office promised that it would enjoy the fullest co-operation from the police. I minuted Margaret on 29 June to inform her of this modest proposal, which she endorsed. It was announced on 3 July 1984 and came into effect on 1 January 1985.

The FIG was eventually superseded as a result of one of the recommendations in the report of the committee set up by the Government in 1983, shortly after I had instituted my own inter-ministerial group, under the chairmanship of the distinguished Law Lord, Eustace Roskill, to examine the conduct of serious fraud trials. Regrettably, Cabinet rejected what I regarded as the most important of Roskill's recommendations: the setting up of a special Fraud Trials Tribunal which would replace the normal trial by jury in particularly complex and serious fraud cases. Quintin Hailsham, the Lord Chancellor, and I appeared to be its only supporters, with the Government's law officers and the other lawyers in Cabinet – apart from Quintin – particularly hostile. Subsequent events have served only to reinforce my belief in the necessity for this reform .

Most of the other Roskill recommendations, however, were accepted by Cabinet, including the setting up of a new specialist Serious Fraud Office. This was eventually enacted in the 1987 Criminal Justice Act, and once it had been set up replaced the more modest FIG.

Reforming the Stock Exchange

My other early Chancellorial involvement in the broad area of financial regulation concerned the Stock Exchange. Shortly before we first took office in 1979 the Office of Fair Trading (OFT) had begun an investigation of the restrictive practices of what was then still known as the London Stock Exchange. As the investigations rumbled on, the Stock Exchange became increasingly alarmed. The end of the road could only be an inordinately expensive case before the Restrictive Practices Court, which it was bound to lose, and to have reform imposed upon it. In 1980, while I was Financial Secretary, Nicholas Goodison, the tall, urbane, civilized, effective and deceptively languid chairman of the Stock Exchange, called on the then Trade Secretary, John Nott, asking him to call off the OFT, for which he had ministerial responsibility, promising that the Stock Exchange would reform itself. John Nott refused to play. Goodison also saw Geoffrey, who was much more sympathetic, but pointed out that John Nott was the lead Minister in this field. This served only to reinforce Goodison's ardent support for the transfer of ministerial responsibility for the oversight of the securities industry to the Treasury.

When John Biffen replaced John Nott as Trade Secretary in January 1981 he unsurprisingly saw no reason to change what had become the departmental line. But when Arthur Cockfield in turn replaced John Biffen in April 1982 he saw the sense in striking a deal, and began discussing with Geoffrey the form this might take. That was the state of play I discovered when I became Chancellor in June 1983, as did Cecil Parkinson who was appointed to the enlarged post of Trade and Industry Secretary at the same time. Moreover the matter had become urgent, with the first hearing of the OFT's action against the Stock Exchange scheduled to take place the following January.

Cecil came to see me about it immediately after the election, and told me he favoured a deal in which the Stock Exchange would be exempted by law from the ambit of the Restrictive Practices Act in return for an undertaking that it would reform itself. I told him I agreed, provided the reform was genuine and adequate. The Bank, of course, had been urging a deal along these lines right from the moment we took office in 1979. There was little to be said for long drawn out litigation, which in addition to its inordinate expense – the point which weighed heaviest with the Stock Exchange's own members – would in practice delay reforms which were urgently needed.

The specific restrictive practices included 'single capacity', which meant the enforced separation of the securities business between brokers, who were agents acting for their clients for a fixed commission, and jobbers, who made the markets and theoretically provided liquidity by holding lines of stocks and shares on their books; fixed minimum commissions; the insistence that brokers and jobbers should be independent and not part of any larger financial group; and the exclusion of foreigners from stock exchange membership.

The old system had many virtues, but in addition to being intellectually indefensible it had one fatal practical defect: it was woefully undercapitalized. In the heyday of the old, clubby, system, in which the Exchange's proud motto 'my word is my bond' proclaimed a truth which made it an attractive place in which to do business, adequate capital had been provided by the personal fortunes of the jobbers. But in the new era of the emergence of a highly competitive and rapidly evolving global securities market, the capital required had multiplied many times, the private fortunes of the jobbers had dwindled, and social changes had eroded the club ethos. As a result, while the City of London remained one of the world leaders – if not *the* world leader – across a whole range of financial markets, such as the foreign exchange market, in the securities market it was in danger of becoming a backwater.

Cecil asked me to help him to persuade Margaret of the need for the deal. He himself was not at his best, and in the strictest confidence he explained to me why. He was, at that time, totally preoccupied with the personal complications of the Sarah Keays affair, which was about to erupt into the public prints and eventually to force his resignation after only four months in his new job. When he told me of his problems I urged him not to resign; and when it had become public and the pressure began to intensify I urged Margaret not to yield to it. That was her instinct, too; but eventually she felt she had no option.

With Cecil in this state, I had to play a larger part than would normally have been necessary in getting the right decisions taken. This was notably the case at the key meeting held shortly after the election in Margaret's room at the House of Commons. Margaret was fearful of the politics of intervening at the eleventh hour to rescue the Stock Exchange from the embrace of the Restrictive Practices Court, leaving its would-be prosecutor, the Director-General of Fair Trading, angrily deprived of the quarry he had been patiently hunting for so long; and her misgivings were powerfully reinforced by Willie. There was no doubt that the politics were uncomfortable: the Labour Party would inevitably accuse us, as indeed they did, of rushing to protect our wealthy friends in the City who, it would be alleged, had financed our election campaign, while leaving manufacturing industry to face the full rigours of the law and the marketplace.

At that meeting I supported Cecil strongly, and for the reason I have indicated had to make most of the running myself. I argued that Cecil's proposal was right on the merits of the case, and that the politics could be ignored at the start of a new Parliament, with the next election several years hence. Well before that, it would have become clear that the reforms on which we were insisting were genuine. Eventually, Margaret acquiesced.

Big Bang and After

Cecil gave Goodison the green light on 1 July 1983, after which a period of intensive negotiation began, culminating in Cecil's statement to the House four weeks later. There were three key issues. First, whether Goodison would agree to the reforms we believed were essential. After some discussion, but without too much difficulty, he did. Second, whether he could persuade his members to agree to them. This was less straightforward, and Goodison showed considerable skill, patience and firmness over a prolonged period in achieving this. The third key issue was whether the changes should be phased in over a period or whether everything should happen at once, on a single day. This became known as the choice between the gradualist and the big bang approaches. Goodison felt that it was only by introducing all the changes in full overnight that he could be confident of securing his members' agreement. The Government concurred, and the chosen date was 27 October 1986 – subsequently to become known as 'Big Bang', a name which was also attached to the package of reforms itself and the far-reaching changes these reforms set in train.

The coming of Big Bang underlined the need, which had been identified during the early years of the Thatcher Government, for a new and improved regulatory framework for all aspects of the savings and investment industry. This eventually came into being in the shape of the 1986 Financial Services Act (FSA), and the various agencies set up under that Act. The FSA was based on the idea of what was somewhat misleadingly termed 'self-regulation'. It was in fact – necessarily – a fully statutory system; but the rules were made by the various so-called self-regulatory organizations (SROs) set up under the Act, manned by practitioners rather than bureaucrats, under the aegis of a Securities and Investment Board (SIB) on which practitioners were also represented. The system had been greatly influenced by the Gower Report on investor protection, which had been published in January 1984, and which *inter alia* sapiently observed that the level of supervision should not 'seek to achieve the impossible task of protecting fools from their own folly' – an observation of wide application which was sadly forgotten towards the end of the 1980s – but should rather 'be no greater than is necessary to protect reasonable people from being made fools of'.

The concept, in fact, was admirable; but what eventually emerged was something far more cumbersome and bureaucratic than I or, I believe, any of us in Government had ever envisaged. The fault lay largely in the rules promulgated by the SIB, under its first chairman, Kenneth Berrill, a somewhat peripatetic member of the Whitehall establishment. Norman Tebbit, who had succeeded Cecil Parkinson as Trade and Industry Secretary, had left the task of finding the first chairman of the SIB to the Governor, Robin Leigh-Pemberton; and Robin's first choice had been my old friend Martin Jacomb, founder-chairman of the investment bank BZW. Martin would have done the job very well; but he was too busy to take it on, agreeing only to serve as a member of the SIB, from which he resigned in frustration some two years later. One of the practical problems with practitioner-based regulation is that most of the ablest practitioners are too busy making money to be able to devote adequate time to the task of regulation. Perhaps that is why, despite the massive SIB rule book, the SROs did not always prove as vigilant against fraudsters as might have been hoped.

The dominant figure on the Berrill SIB, however, was neither Berrill himself nor Jacomb, but the Deputy Chairman, Mark Weinberg, a South African lawyer who had come to London and made a fortune by building up an innovative and highly successful life assurance business. When he was asked to take on the role of poacher-turned-gamekeeper the lawyer in him came very much to the fore, and played a large part in framing the excessively legalistic rule book that emerged.

But the bankers and brokers who complained so bitterly were themselves partly to blame, by failing to make good use of the lengthy consultation period before the rules were promulgated. This was particularly the case over the so-called polarization issue. A number of institutions, notably banks, were in the habit of selling a range of savings products, such as life assurance policies and pension plans, and the SIB was concerned that a bank, for example, would advise a customer faced with this range to purchase its own in-house product even when that was not the best suited to his needs or best value for money. To solve this problem the SIB evolved the extraordinary doctrine of 'polarization', which obliged banks and other financial institutions to choose between selling exclusively their own products or exclusively the products of other firms.

As a result, most chose, reluctantly but inevitably, to sell exclusively their own products, thus greatly limiting consumer choice. The banks complained bitterly when the rules were promulgated, but by then it was too late. A far better protection for the consumer would have been transparency – that is, full disclosure of the intermediary's commission hidden away in the price of each savings product, and of its effect on the true value of the investment; which would *inter alia* have diminished the risk of salesmen recommending those products which carried the highest commissions. No doubt the life assurance industry had made powerful representations to the SIB against transparency; since the massive hidden commissions buried away in the price of most life policies might, if known, have led to considerable sales resistance.

As a result, it was not until 1988 that mounting pressure led the SIB to introduce commission disclosure rules of a sort; and even then they were inadequate, as the information that came to light following the collapse of the Levitt Group at the end of 1990 made painfully clear, and the DTI belatedly instructed the SIB to redraft them. The degree of transparency still falls short of what is called for, while polarization remains in the rule book. But while the regulatory system ushered in by the FSA still suffers from a number of its early defects, there has been considerable improvement and simplification since the Government and the Bank replaced Berrill as SIB chairman in 1988 with the Bank's David Walker.

The Johnson Matthey Débâcle

The aspect of financial regulation which concerned me most was the supervision of the banks. Anyone who has read their Bagehot will be aware of the economic importance of banking and its effective supervision. The latter is not an easy task. If the supervisory authority were to be prepared to allow banks to fail as readily as governments should allow other unsuccessful or unlucky businesses to fail, this could lead to a major collapse of confidence throughout the banking system with devastating consequences for the economy as a whole. If, on the other hand, it were to ensure that no bank ever failed, this would inevitably encourage irresponsible and imprudent banking. Thus the supervisory authority has to be very careful both in deciding when to intervene and when not to intervene, and to keep banks on their toes by creating uncertainty as to whether it would intervene in any particular case.

It is essentially the acceptance that the Bank of England will, in appropriate circumstances, save banks (and thus their depositors) from the full consequences of insolvency, that creates the 'moral hazard' which makes it necessary for the banks in return to submit to a degree of official supervision unknown to other businesses. For the main – although not the only – task of bank supervision is to prevent banks from getting into a situation that is likely to lead to failure in the first place.

The event which was to focus my mind on it occurred at six o'clock in the morning of Monday, 1 October 1984. It was then that the telephone rang in the Number 11 flat and I found Peter Middleton on the line with the news that the Governor and Deputy Governor wished to see me before the markets opened about a banking matter. I agreed to see them at Number 11 at half-past seven. I asked Peter Middleton to come along too, and to bring Frank Cassell, the relevant Treasury Under Secretary, with him.

Robin and Kit McMahon duly arrived, and told me that Johnson Matthey Bankers (JMB), a bank of no great consequence, was on the brink of collapse. The problem was that its parent company was the prominent City bullion dealer, Johnson Matthey; and the difficulties of JMB were on such a scale that the Bank feared that, if nothing were done, they could bring down the parent company too. The Bank believed that this could create a crisis of confidence in the London bullion market as a whole, the most important gold market in the world, accounting for half of all world business in the metal. It did not want to see the centre of the world gold market decamp from London to, say, Zurich. It was also worried about the contagion spreading to other members of the small and select bullion market. It was particularly concerned about Samuel Montagu, since this was a subsidiary of the Midland Bank, already by then in a fragile state, and in no position to take a further knock.

The Bank had therefore decided, on the merits of the case, that JMB had to be rescued. The decisive factor, in the Bank's eyes, was the damage that might be done to the London bullion market were JMB allowed to fail: something that was not, strictly speaking, within the ambit of bank supervision – which is concerned with the protection of depositors and the probity and stability of the banking system – at all. Be that as it may, the Bank had tried to be midwife to a private sector rescue, but had failed. In particular, its discussions with the Bank of Nova Scotia, on which it had pinned great hopes, had finally broken down late the previous evening. There was now no alternative but for the Bank to take over JMB itself. Moreover, an announcement would have to be made when the markets opened that morning, at 8 o'clock.

This was something the Bank of England, as the supervisory authority for the banking system, was fully entitled to do if it felt it to be necessary: it did not require my authority or approval. The snag was the amount of money that might be required. The Bank was in the process of extracting financial contributions of one kind or another from JMB's parent company, Johnson Matthey; from Johnson Matthey's principal shareholder, the giant mining group Charter Consolidated; and from the clearing banks, the other members of the London gold market, and some merchant banks. Some of this was already in the bag, some was yet to be secured. But it was clear that a very large part of JMB's loan book was bad, and it was possible that the Bank – which proposed to acquire JMB for the token payment of a one pound coin – could be faced at the end of the day with a loss of up to £100 million. This was a very large sum in relation to the Bank's own free reserves, which it maintained for such purposes, and it might therefore require a guarantee from the Treasury to make good any shortfall from public funds.

If the news itself was unpalatable, the very late stage at which I was informed of it made it even worse. The crisis had evidently erupted the previous week, while I was in Washington for the annual Bank and Fund meetings, along with both Robin and Kit McMahon. Yet no-one had seen fit to mention it to me. Since then, the Bank had been working night and day to try and discover the facts, evaluate the situation, and effect a rescue; still without a single word to me. As a result, I was being given only a few minutes to decide whether or not to give an open-ended guarantee of taxpayers' money in support of a rescue about whose wisdom – as I made clear to Robin and Kit at the time, and subsequently in a minute to Margaret – I was far from convinced. I had to make up my mind with no time to secure the information on which to base a considered decision. In the circumstances, I had no option but to rely on the Bank's judgement. I protected my position so far as I could by emphasizing that I could give no undertaking that the Treasury would be prepared to give a guarantee, should it be asked to do so; but if the Bank was prepared to go ahead on that basis, so be it.

Needless to say, it was and did, as soon as the meeting was over. I could have prevented it only by making it clear that in no circumstances would the Treasury make public funds available. Leaving the issue open, as I did, enabled the Bank to go ahead confident that, once the rescue was a *fait accompli*, there was no way in which the Government could fail to provide the Bank with funds if it were to need them. The only stroke of luck was that the House of Commons was still in recess and not due to reassemble for a further three weeks. This meant that I had time to mount an urgent investigation without being required to make a statement to the House before I had the evidence on which to form a view.

Strengthening Bank Supervision

It turned out that JMB had been founded in 1965, and had grown particularly rapidly in the early 1980s by lending very large sums to a small number of little-known Asian businessmen. The more I discovered about it the less surprising its collapse became – but by the same token the more inexplicable the Bank's failure, as the supervisory authority, to step in at a much earlier stage. But my interest was not in raking over the JMB issue as such: it lay in strengthening the system of banking supervision in the UK so that a débâcle of this kind was far less likely to occur in future. Moreover, while the implementation of bank supervision was strictly an autonomous matter for the Bank of England, in which I had an interest to the extent that it raised issues of economic or political importance, the legislative framework within which the Bank carried out its duties was inescapably my responsibility.

On 17 December 1984 I made a statement to Parliament announcing the setting up of a Committee to look into the UK system of bank supervision and make recommendations. Astonishingly, although the House had by that time been sitting for the best part of two months, the official Labour Opposition had never once raised the matter. The only remotely serious probing had come from the Opposition back benches, in the person of the austere left-wing xenophobe and conspiracy theorist, Denis Skinner, the maverick Member for the mining constituency of Bolsover – an accomplished parliamentarian with the best and quickest repartee in the House, and a better sense of where the Government was vulnerable than the whole of his Party's front bench put together.

It was clear, even without an enquiry, that the supervisory side of the Bank of England had badly fallen down on the job over Johnson Matthey, and its reputation had suffered as a result. Not wishing the Bank to be humiliated any further, I decided on an internal rather than a public enquiry, and asked the Governor, Robin Leigh-Pemberton, to chair the committee. But I was careful to put on it a strong Treasury team headed by Peter Middleton, together with a distinguished commercial banker, Deryk Vander Weyer, a former Deputy Chairman of Barclays Bank and arguably the outstanding commercial banker of his generation.

It cannot be said that my concern for the Bank's problems was entirely reciprocated. In the questioning that followed my statement, the chairman of the powerful Public Accounts Committee, Bob Sheldon, asked me what the Bank's liability was in respect of JMB. I replied, truthfully as I thought, that apart from the £1 spent on the purchase of JMB, there was only the Bank's half share of a £150 million indemnity, but that it was too soon to say how much of that indemnity would be required. It was only subsequently that it came to light that on 22 November the Bank had placed a £100 million deposit with JMB, which it had subsequently converted into permanent capital. It emerged that this had been authorized by Kit McMahon while Robin was away in the Soviet Union, and no-one had seen fit to inform me of it. I felt badly let down, as I made clear when I learned about it. While it is true that at the end of the day the money was recovered, misleading the

House, however inadvertently, is a serious business.

I published the report of the Committee on banking supervision on 20 June 1985, and made a statement to the House the same day. Also on the same day, the Bank published its annual report, which contained a special Annexe on the JMB débâcle, together with a press notice announcing that, through JMB, it would be suing the accountancy firm of Arthur Young, who had been JMB's auditors prior to its collapse, for substantial damages.

Certainly neither the Bank nor the auditors emerged well from the report. The supervisory side of the Bank had effectively disregarded all manner of danger signals – including the failure of JMB's representatives to turn up at meetings called by the Bank to discuss its accounts – and the auditors had performed little better. The company appeared to have lost no less than £248 million; yet its records were in such a state of disarray that it was extremely hard to discover the circumstances in which the bad loans had been made. Inevitably, the Leigh-Pemberton Committee's report recommended a substantial strengthening, in terms of quantity, quality and expertise, of the supervision division of the Bank of England; and this Robin agreed to put into effect without delay.

There was, however, in my view a structural problem, which the report perhaps understandably did not address, but which had and still has important implications. By tradition, the Bank of England had two principal tasks: the implementation of monetary policy, including funding and exchange rate policy, and the supervision of the banking system. In the monetary policy field it was the Chancellor who was responsible for taking the decisions, with the Bank providing him with advice before the event and conducting the necessary financial market operations after it; whereas in the area of bank supervision, responsibility lay fairly and squarely with the Bank of England. Yet despite the Bank's subordinate role in monetary policy and its leading role in bank supervision, the high fliers were all attracted to the former, much sexier side, while the humdrum but important bank supervision side was always in danger of becoming something of a backwater. This problem would take on a new dimension with an independent Bank, as I discuss later in this chapter.

A New Banking Act

While indicating the non-legislative changes it felt to be necessary, the report also recommended a significant strengthening of the statutory framework within which the Bank carried out its task. I therefore took the opportunity of my statement of 20 June 1985 to announce my intention of publishing a White Paper on Banking Supervision later that year with a view to the early introduction of a new Banking Bill. The White Paper was duly published in December 1985 and the Bill, which was to become the 1987 Banking Act, the following December. The Bill embodied all the legislative recommendations of the Leigh-Pemberton committee, but went a great deal further.

Until 1979, banking supervision in the UK had been conducted on an entirely informal and non-statutory basis, with the Bank relying on what was officially termed 'moral suasion', and more commonly 'the Governor's eyebrows', to secure its objectives. In the clubby City of the past this could be a formidable weapon. But the change in the composition of the City made it increasingly inadequate, as the secondary banking crisis of the early 1970s had demonstrated – and in any case a European Community directive required all member states to have bank supervisory legislation in place. Hence the Banking Act of 1979, the last piece of legislation the outgoing Labour Government had been able to put on the statute-book.

But the 1979 Act, which the 1987 Act was to supplant, was defective in a number of ways. The powers it gave the Bank were seriously inadequate, and I strengthened them very considerably in the 1987 Act. The new Act also made it, for the first time, a criminal offence to provide false or misleading information to the supervisory authority, which had occurred in the case of JMB. The 1979 Act had divided all deposit-taking institutions into two categories: banks and licensed deposit-takers. The powers it gave the Bank of England in respect of the supervision of banks were appreciably less than those given in respect of the supervision of licensed deposit-takers. This reflected an assumption that serious problems would arise only among those below the salt. It was significant that JMB was a recognized bank.

The Leigh-Pemberton committee recommended the abolition of this distinction, which the 1987 legislation duly enacted. Any sensible supervisor will know that he has responsibility for a whole spectrum of institutions. But the main effect of the artificial separation of them into two distinct categories, sheep and goats, was to disadvantage British licensed deposit-takers vis-à-vis their foreign competitors. This arose because UK licensed deposit-takers were not permitted to call themselves banks, whereas licensed deposit-takers that were the UK offshoots of overseas banks – such as, most notoriously, the Bank of Credit and Commerce International (BCCI) – were allowed by the Bank to call themselves banks.

But to my mind a much more important recommendation of the Leigh-Pemberton committee – even if it did not go far enough – was the recommendation that the iron curtain of confidentiality that separated bank supervisors from bank auditors should be replaced by 'a regular dialogue'. This was an attempt to address a two-way problem. The accountancy profession considered itself prevented by a duty of confidentiality to its client from passing any information to the bank supervisors; while the supervisors were effectively prevented by the terms of the 1979 Banking Act itself from passing information to the auditors.

Clearly, the interests of effective supervision made this double barrier a nonsense. My original plan was to lay a statutory duty on bank auditors to disclose relevant information to the bank supervisors. This was regarded with horror not merely by the accountancy profession but also by the Bank, who felt that all that was necessary was to enable bank auditors to disclose information to the bank supervisors if they felt it right to do so, by protecting them from any action for damages in such cases. Eventually, I reached a compromise with the Bank, agreeing, somewhat reluctantly, to accept the Bank's weaker formulation, but with the addition of a power for the Treasury to make regulations in effect requiring the auditors to disclose information to the regulators should this appear to be necessary.

The Role of the Bank of England

The other key feature of the 1987 Act, which went well beyond the recommendations of the Leigh-Pemberton report, was the setting up of a Board of Banking Supervision, chaired by the Governor, but with a two-thirds majority of independent (i.e. non-Bank) members, in effect to oversee the Bank's execution of its supervisory duties and to give the Bank advice on difficult cases. The Bank remained technically free to reject the advice of the independent members; but should it do so it would be required to inform the Chancellor of the Exchequer. Moreover, the independent members would have the right to inform the Chancellor of the reasons for their advice – which seemed to me to ensure that the Bank was most unlikely to overrule the Board of Banking Supervision in practice.

The Bank found the whole idea of a Board of Banking Supervision along these lines particularly unattractive. In the end, however, Robin went along with it quietly when I pointed out that he should see it as a satisfactory way of meeting the arguments of those who wished to take the task of bank supervision away from the Bank of England altogether. He knew – because I had told him privately of her views – that I was referring to Margaret. I had, of course, kept her fully informed about the Johnson Matthey affair and its aftermath throughout, and discussed the issues with her. She was so incensed by the extent of the Bank's failure over JMB that she argued strongly that the task of bank supervision should be removed from the Bank of England altogether, and entrusted to a new agency set up for the purpose.

Objectively, Margaret was absolutely right. This sort of separation was the practice in a number of countries overseas, notably Germany, where bank supervision fell not under the Bundesbank in Frankfurt but under the quite separate Bundesaufsichtsamt für das Kreditwesen in Berlin. It would have been the best way of overcoming the problem I identified earlier in this chapter of bank supervision becoming something of a backwater. It would also have removed the inherent conflict of interest between the task of monetary policy and that of bank supervision, with the former requiring a stern unbending and single-minded stringency and the latter favouring a judicious laxity to prevent bank failures.

I none the less resisted Margaret's proposal, despite its innate good sense, for one practical reason. Under the UK arrangements, with monetary policy clearly in the hands of the Chancellor, it was the unfettered responsibility for banking supervision that, as I saw it, largely gave the Bank its authority in the eyes of the City and thus more widely. If that were removed, I feared that the standing and authority of the Bank, not least in the eyes of its peers around the world, would suffer greatly; and I did not believe this to be in the national interest.*

If, however, we were to move, as I strongly favour (see Chapter 69) to an independent Bank of England, in the sense of responsibility for monetary policy, then it would indeed be right from every point of view to remove from it all responsibility for banking supervision, which would be entrusted to a separate agency created for that sole purpose. In my 1988 minute to Margaret recommending the creation of an independent Bank of England I proposed that 'The Bank would, at least for the time being, retain responsibility for supervising the banking system.' This was because I felt that to introduce a further unheaval at the same time as the others contained in my proposal – which included the transfer to the Treasury of responsibility for funding the Government's borrowing requirement – might be too much. This was probably a mistake.

Reflections on BCCI

The next major banking scandal, the BCCI affair, which once again highlighted the whole issue of the adequacy of banking supervision, did not come to light until well after I had left office. But it obviously raised the question of whether the legislative framework I had put in place, the 1987 Banking Act, was in any way defective. The Bingham Inquiry set up by the Major Government to look into the supervision of BCCI

---

*This was the only difference between Margaret and myself over the 1987 Banking Act. The claim in Stephen Fay's book, *Portrait of an Old Lady*, that the Board of Banking Supervision and certain other aspects of the 1987 Act were included at Margaret's insistence and against my wishes, is mistaken.

will clearly shed considerable light on this, but its report had not been published by the time this book went to press. I should be surprised, however, if the 1987 Act, with the enormous powers it gave the Bank, is found to be inadequate: if there were any failings, they are more likely to be found to lie elsewhere.

There were, however, two areas of potential weakness which worried me during my own time in office, and which the 1987 Act itself was unable to address. The first concerned the relationship between the Bank of England and the law. I have already mentioned how up to 1979 the Bank had operated without any statutory framework at all, an arrangement of sadly but inevitably diminishing efficacy. I got the impression, even a decade later, that it had never fully come to terms with the task of taking tough supervisory decisions within a statutory framework. Whether it did not take sufficient high-level legal advice, or whether it took the wrong sort of legal advice, or whether it failed to grasp the interaction between the law and practical common-sense reality, I do not know. But on a number of occasions during my time, in a number of different fields, I found the Bank fearful of taking a particular course of action because of a misplaced fear of being successfully taken to court if it did.

A more serious shortcoming, however, lay in the worrying fragmentation and compartmentalization of the various law enforcement agencies involved in the financial area in one way or another, to which I referred right at the start of this chapter, in the context of fraud. BCCI was, of course, a case of fraud on a massive scale. But in my experience it is very rare indeed for there to be a major supervisory problem in which fraud is not involved. Even if the origins of the problem lie elsewhere, as they usually do, fraud is characteristically resorted to subsequently to conceal the scale of the difficulties that have arisen.

That is why, in my personal foreword to the 1985 White Paper on Banking Supervision, I observed that 'an important deterrent to financial fraud is effective supervision'. The Bank tended to see very much less of a connection between the two: regulatory supervision, for which it was responsible, was one thing; the extirpation of fraud, for which the police in the shape of the sadly inadequate fraud squad were responsible, was another. This compartmentalization could lead the Bank to be surprisingly innocent: on the very day the White Paper was published, I answered a question in the House on JMB by saying, on the firm advice of the Bank, that 'no *prima facie* evidence of fraud has so far been uncovered' – something I subsequently bitterly regretted. It may have been strictly true at the time: that depends on what is held to constitute 'evidence'. But of course fraud was involved in the JMB affair.

The real mischief, however, in the mistaken compartmentalization of supervision and the detection of fraud is the dangerous lack of effective liaison, and in particular the failure to exchange relevant information, between the supervisors and the fraud squad. Moreover, as I have already indicated, this failure to co-operate effectively and to exchange relevant information is by no means confined to the Bank of England and the police. As emerged in the BCCI case, a number of other law enforcement agencies, in the widest sense, were involved, including the Customs and Excise, the Inland Revenue, and even the security services; but for most of the time they might almost have been living on different planets. I do not deny the difficulties involved and safeguards required in the exchange of information between different law enforcement agencies. But the traditional compartmentalization culture is a fraudster's benefit.

Remedying this is at least as important as improvements in international co-operation between the various bank supervisory authorities around the world, which was widely, and rightly, felt to be one of the lessons of the BCCI scandal. Indeed there is nowadays probably more co-operation between central banks in the UK and overseas, between the police in the UK and overseas, and between the tax authorities in the UK and overseas, than there is between the Bank of England, the fraud squad and the revenue Departments within the UK.

How to Put Fraudsters Behind Bars

One final area where a different approach is, I believe, badly needed, is that of prosecution – although here, paradoxically, co-operation of a malign kind is part of the problem. The expensive, time-consuming and complex task of the investigation of fraud and financial skullduggery, sometimes of a highly sophisticated nature, loses much of its point if there is not a successful prosecution at the end of the day. Successful prosecutions, leading to criminal convictions and prison sentences, are the most effective deterrent to financial fraud. Equally, the absence of a criminal prosecution tends to promote suggestions, however ill-founded, of a government cover-up, and to lead to a degree of cynicism among the public at large.

For all these reasons I always felt that putting fraudsters behind bars should be an important objective of policy. In some areas the failure to achieve this was less serious than others. The unique dependence of banking on confidence and trust, coupled with the immense battery of powers given to the Bank of England by the 1987 Act, meant that successful banking supervision and effective deterrence – and indeed to some extent the punishment of wrongdoers – could sometimes be achieved without the need for a criminal conviction.

Outside the banking field, the exposure of skullduggery in a DTI Inspector's Report, written by a distinguished lawyer or accountant, and protected by privilege from the libel laws, could serve a useful purpose. That is, of course, once it was published: I found myself constantly battling against pleas from the Attorney General and Director of Public Prosecutions of the day that DTI Inspectors' Reports should be held back since their publication might prejudice a successful prosecution. This was a dubious proposition at the best of times, made even more absurd by the infrequency of the occasions on which, at the end of the day, the DPP ever felt he had sufficient evidence to mount a successful prosecution. Not that publication of a damaging Inspector's Report was a fool-proof stratagem. The measured and carefully documented report on Robert Maxwell in 1971, which all but branded him a crook, did not prevent him from re-emerging in the 1980s to practise his fraud and skullduggery on an even larger scale, assisted by the unbelievable credulousness of the banks. To repeat the dictum of the good Professor Gower in a different but germane context, no system can perform 'the impossible task of protecting fools from their own folly.' Unfortunately others got badly hurt too.

Returning to the question of prosecution, it was inevitable that a time of boom and optimism such as the second half of the 1980s should see an upsurge in financial fraud: hence my desire to see some high profile fraudsters behind bars. Yet on more than one occasion this was prevented by foolishly allowing the best to be the enemy of the good. Under the English legal system, the two Revenue Departments are, very sensibly, independent prosecuting authorities: unlike other Departments, they do not need to go through the DPP to mount a case. Moreover, for obvious reasons, fraudsters tend to be averse to paying tax.

On more than one occasion during my time, the Inland Revenue was about to prosecute a leading fraudster for tax evasion – which, if successful, would have led to a prison sentence – only to be held back by the DPP who insisted that this would obstruct the process of securing the evidence required for a conviction for the fraud itself. At the end of the day, the DPP discovered that he did not, after all, have sufficient evidence to mount a prosecution – by which time, however, the Inland Revenue trail had gone cold. It should not be forgotten that the US authorities managed to jail the notorious gangster Al Capone only by prosecuting him for not paying his income tax. There is a clear lesson for us here, in the extirpation of financial fraud in an increasingly complex world.

CHAPTER 33

MY MONETARY PRINCIPLES

'The British Experiment' · No Jobs – Inflation Trade-off
A Nominal Framework · Exchange Rate Mechanism
Principles and Practices · Reaction to Shocks
The Counter-revolution in Retrospect

'The British Experiment'

MONETARY POLICY RESEMBLES THE detection of financial fraud only in its complexity. This very complexity makes it all the more important to state the main principles without sinking in a sea of technicalities. My essential beliefs about money, jobs and inflation were outlined in Part 1 and there is no need to go through all the theory again. In brief, inflation is a monetary phenomenon. This does not mean to say that the quantity of money is easy to measure or that there is any simple relation between money and prices. The basic point is that if everybody had twice as much money to spend, the main result would be to drive prices upwards. Any beneficial effect on output and employment would be transitory, as David Hume explained more than two centuries ago.

Unfortunately there is a long and tortuous route from these home truths to devising a framework of monetary control for a modern economy. So, far from inheriting a smoothly working system of monetary control, the system I inherited was – through no fault of Geoffrey's – full of puzzles and confusions. In the chapter on the Medium Term Financial Strategy, I explained that, although the monetary targets were missed, the spirit of the strategy was observed, as a result of which inflation fell far more than our supporters – let alone our critics – would have believed possible; and that the framework was useful in resisting calls for 'reflation'. But there remained a problem both of how best to state our policy and how best to carry it out technically.

As soon as I became Chancellor, therefore, I asked the Treasury to carry out a full-scale review of internal and external monetary policy, including the exchange rate and membership of the ERM. I also thought it important to try to pick out the wood from the trees: that is, to state the underlying beliefs which united practitioners of the new approach and to avoid getting lost in technical disputes.

Accordingly I was delighted to accept an invitation from the City University Business School to give the fifth Mais Lecture in June 1984, in which I tried to lay down the basic principles behind the new approach to economic policy.

The title I chose was 'The British Experiment', which I described as providing increasing freedom for markets to work within a framework of firm monetary and fiscal discipline. The opposite approach of ever-more *ad hoc* interference with markets coupled with financial indiscipline had often been embarked upon simply 'because British governments believed that political and electoral pressure gave them no option'. The British experiment was at the same time a political one: 'to demonstrate that union power could be curbed and inflation eradicated within a democracy'.

The basic doctrine I sought to set out in the Mais lecture was straightforward. It divided economic policy into two branches: macroeconomic policy – interest rates, exchange rates and Budget deficits; the matters which get Chancellors into the headlines – and microeconomic (or supply-side) policy – the whole range of detailed measures designed to influence specific aspects of economic behaviour. It then challenged what had hitherto been the conventional wisdom head-on, by reassigning the roles of these two arms of economic policy:

> The conventional post-War wisdom was that unemployment was a consequence of inadequate economic growth, and economic growth was to be secured by *macro*economic policy – the fiscal stimulus of an enlarged Budget deficit, with monetary policy (to the extent that it could be said to exist at all) on the whole passively following fiscal policy. Inflation, by contrast, was increasingly seen as a matter to be dealt with by *micro*economic policy – the panoply of controls and subsidies associated with the era of incomes policy.
>
> The conclusion on which the present Government's economic policy is based is that there is indeed a proper distinction between the objectives of macroeconomic and microeconomic policy, and a need to be concerned with both of them. But the proper role of each is precisely the opposite of that assigned to it by the conventional post-War wisdom. It is the conquest of inflation, and not the pursuit

of growth and employment, which is or should be the objective of macroeconomic policy. And it is the creation of conditions conducive to growth and employment, and not the suppression of price rises, which is or should be the objective of microeconomic policy.

. . . The most important point to emphasize is that this Government is pursuing simultaneously both a macro and a micro policy, that the one complements the other, that the macro policy is unequivocally directed at the continuing reduction in inflation, with the ultimate objective of stable prices, and that the micro policy is equally wholeheartedly designed to make the economy work better and thus generate more jobs.

In reality, the distinction may not always be quite as clear-cut as this. In certain circumstances, which history suggests do not occur very often, macroeconomic policy could also play a role in supporting economic activity. This was a point I made, not in the Mais Lecture, but in some of my Budget speeches and one or two other speeches I made at the time. It was in reply to those who worried that, if pay settlements were to decline at a time of falling inflation, spending power would also decline and that a downward spiral of depression might be created. The prospect of a serious depression being threatened in this way is much more remote than it appears; but the answer I gave applied irrespective of the cause – namely, that a properly functioning monetary policy is a safeguard against cumulative depression as well as against inflation. With this caveat the assignment of macro policy to the defeat of inflation and micro policy to the promotion of conditions favourable to growth is both accurate and the heart of the matter.

No Jobs – Inflation Trade-off

The Mais Lecture was also a product of its time. Its aim was to tackle the then common view that macroeconomic policy either had changed or should have changed to give more emphasis to growth and employment over reducing inflation. It was an example of the cultural and intellectual lag of so many British economists and economic journalists that these doctrines were regarded as startling and disturbing. In many other countries the criticism would have been that they were too obvious.

As I put it in the lecture, 'double-digit inflation never persisted long enough to become embedded in expectations or a part of our economic bloodstream.' Yet 'stable prices are a blessed condition, but one that we in this country have not experienced other than very fleetingly for fifty years.' To achieve it required 'fighting and changing the culture and the psychology of two generations'. Here a policy of gradualism was required – 'bearing down on inflation' in the Treasury jargon, and taking advantage of every opportunity to lock it in at lower rates. The failure to take advantage in this way of the opportunity presented by the oil price collapse was the real error of the mid-1980s, for which those who opposed joining the ERM at the right time must take their share of the blame.

At the time of the Mais Lecture, the mainstream view was that the Government had intentionally or by inadvertence produced high unemployment, which in turn had reduced wage demands, which in turn had reduced inflation. What in fact had happened was a tight monetary policy had brought down inflation, largely, although not exclusively, via the exchange rate. But this reduction in inflation had only gradually permeated through to wage settlements. Thus profits were under squeeze; and it was 'the slowness of wages to adjust that was such an important factor in the rise of unemployment'.

A Nominal Framework

What I was seeking to do as Chancellor was to keep total spending in the economy rising rapidly enough to allow reasonable real growth in an environment of price stability. But, in contrast to earlier post-war concepts of full employment policy, we did not attempt to sustain output and activity in the face of rising prices. Such attempts nearly always came to grief, as the wiser Keynesians realized: which is why they began to call themselves 'reconstructed' Keynesians. The key is to abandon the attempt to set 'real' variables – objectives for real economic growth, full employment or whatever – and instead to define objectives in money terms.

There are many different ways of doing this. The way that has been used throughout most of human history has been to maintain a metallic standard, usually gold or silver. This is obviously not very sophisticated. But in a rough-and-ready way it worked astonishingly well. For instance there was virtually no trend either way in the British price level for about two and a half centuries after the accession of Charles II in 1660. In recent times, there have been four candidates. In no particular order, they are:

1. A nominal GDP objective;
2. A money supply target;
3. A price level objective;
4. An exchange rate objective.

Nominal GDP, as its name suggests, is fundamental to the idea of a nominal framework. It simply means the total amount of national income in money terms, without adjusting by a price index. It is also roughly equal to the toal amount of national spending on goods and services, and to the total value of output produced. (If the balance of payments is moving into deficit, nominal GDP will understate total spending, as some spending spills over into imports or into goods diverted from exports. So there are other related concepts, which have sometimes appeared in the Red Book, such as domestic demand or domestic expenditure. But these are refinements of the general principle.)

The weakness of nominal GDP and its variants is that they are too far removed both from the instruments that the policy-maker has at his disposal and from the information available to him. Estimates of GDP, whether real or nominal, are not normally available until two or three months after the quarter to which they refer – and then there are three separate measures, which should be the same but seldom, if ever, are. They are also among the numbers most subject to revision. Both for statistical reasons, and because of the inherent variability of the economy, the path of nominal GDP will inevitably wobble in the short term. To try to iron out these variations, by some misguided fine-tuning exercise, is contrary to the whole idea of a nominal framework. Even if it were possible, it would not be desirable. For some variation in the movement of output and income is almost certainly a necessary safety valve. None of the earlier students of business cycles ever thought that quarter-to-quarter stability was either possible or desirable.

Moreover it is not obvious how to translate an objective for nominal GDP into the kind of decisions that policy makers actually take, such as whether to move interest rates up and down and by how much. Any attempt to use nominal GDP too directly is far too dependent on fallible forecasting models. Its real use, which can be very important, is as a guide to the medium term.

It is less often realized that many of the same difficulties apply to money supply targets. In virtually all modern economies, the Central Bank operates through its control of short-term interest rates. But the relationship between interest rates and the money supply is as uncertain as is the relationship of the quantity of money, however controlled and defined, to either the price level or to nominal GDP.

I do not want to go to the other extreme. A money supply target, in a country where financial institutions and practices have been fairly stable, can be a very useful aid to policy, as for instance in Germany. But it can never be an automatic pilot. Judgement is always required; in selecting the monetary rule, in deciding how to enforce it, and in assessing when short-term departures in either direction are acceptable.

A direct price-level objective has the great advantage of simplicity. Indeed if it had been followed in most of the post-war period we would almost certainly have benefited. Just as the Romans used to say, 'if you want peace, prepare for war', there is something to be said for the maxim 'if you want high employment, concentrate on price stability'.

Again such a rule is not nearly as automatic as it looks. There are many different price indices – producer prices, consumer prices and commodity prices, all of which can be constructed in various different ways. In the case of the UK RPI, a rise of 1 per cent in short-term interest rates adds more than ⅓ per cent to the RPI. It would be quite absurd for the authorities to respond to the mechanistic effect of their own tightening by tightening further. There are also obviously one-off events – such as the Gulf War – which have a temporary shock effect on the price level, to which it might be perverse to react.

A price-level rule works best when there is some authority removed from day-to-day political pressure, such as an independent central bank, which is free to choose its own method, but which is held strictly to account for the results achieved in terms of price stability. The purest model of this at the time of writing is the contract between the New Zealand Central Bank and the New Zealand Treasury. A more conventional version consists of the rule that applies to the Bundesbank, which gives price stability as the overriding aim – and, *subject to that*, the duty to support other aspects of government economic policy.

A simple price-level objective may be more dubious when there are powerful recessionary tendencies. In the modern world, with its wage and price rigidities, it is possible that an unnecessarily severe recession could occur without prices actually falling. The monetary authorities might find a nominal GDP guideline more helpful in telling them when they can support activity by reducing interest rates without running an inflationary risk.

Exchange Rate Mechanism

The final option on the list, an exchange rate objective, is the clearest from the operational point of view. The exchange rate is a price available day by day and minute by minute in the markets. The range of policy choice is limited to short-term intervention in the foreign exchange markets and interest rate changes. Moreover, being readily understood, an exchange-rate rule also has enormous expositional advantages over nominal GDP or money supply objectives. The study of the money supply or even of nominal GDP is inevitably very much a minority activity. Everyone remotely concerned with business can on the other hand understand the idea that if costs increase too quickly, British goods will be priced out of foreign markets, imports will displace British goods at home and bankruptcies and unemployment will result. It does not take the Nobel Prize in economics to see that if sterling is tied to, say, the Deutschmark, the long-run movement of prices of internationally traded goods and services cannot be too different in the two countries.

But nothing is without problems. An exchange rate target requires an anchor country with reasonably stable prices to which the domestic currency can be tied. For a long time the US dollar admirably fulfilled this function; and as I explained briefly in *The New Conservatism* (see Annexe 1 at the end of this book), under the Bretton Woods system governments had the illusion that they were pursuing domestic full-employment policies, whereas in fact they were following some form of international monetarism. Germany has been a very useful anchor country within Europe. It is impossible to say whether this will continue or whether the unification problems will prove too much.

Another problem is that of non-traded goods, whose price is not directly governed by an exchange rate link. This is much more important in relation to very large economies such as the US and Japan, where the external sector is relatively speaking much smaller and for whom periods of neglect of the exchange rate are at least a partial option, which is not the case for middle-sized European countries. If a country like Britain or France could achieve long-run stability in the prices of all the many goods and services which are, or potentially can be, subject to international competition, this will be as good an approximation to price stability as is necessary or likely in the real world. Nor is it possible for wages and prices in the non-traded goods sector to take off in the long run in a completely different direction.

A more fundamental objection is that, as a matter of logic, not every country can follow an exchange rate objective. The anchor country has to have some domestic objective, whether a price-level or money supply or a nominal GDP rule, or some mixture of these. Some technical monetarists, such as Alan Walters, produce this point triumphantly as if it demolished the case for an exchange rate link. But of course it does nothing of the sort. It is obvious that an exchange-rate objective is monetarism at one remove; and that is indeed its attraction. The question is – or should be – a severely practical one: which form of monetarism is the least difficult to operate successfully? If a country such as Germany, because of its track record, the independence of its Central Bank and many other factors, has anti-inflationary credibility, pegging other European currencies to the Deutschmark clearly makes sense.

The point of membership of the ERM, which is the obvious choice for an exchange-rate-based policy in today's world, is not that the Bundesbank is able to run UK monetary policy better than the UK. It is, first, that, for a mixture of historical, cultural and institutional reasons, Germany is able to maintain a reasonable degree of price stability with less difficulty than other European countries; second, that recognizing this, the financial markets attach greater credibility to a monetary policy based on adherence to the Deutschmark link than they do to one which lacks it – and without financial market credibility it is hard to make a success of any monetary policy; and third, that within the ERM, companies know that if they fail to control their costs they are unlikely to be saved from bankruptcy by devaluation, and both companies and individuals will lower their inflationary expectations and act accordingly. Moreover, so long as the ERM exists, for one Community country to refuse to join it is likely to be interpreted, however wrongly, as that country wishing to retain the right to devalue – from which the markets (and UK companies) will draw their own conclusions.

It is of course possible to combine a number of different intermediate goals. Treasury officials during my time liked to give some weight to all of them, for instance to look at both domestic monetary indicators and the movement of the exchange rate. While a case can be made for this, the most obvious objection to such a combination is the lack of clear guidance that it gives to businessmen and the public generally.

Needless to say, none of these options is some sort of automatic pilot: all need to be operated with judgement. But one thing is clear. When all is said and done they are alternative means to common objectives. We can all make mistakes. But to go on heresy hunts against those whose intermediate monetary objectives are different from one's own would be laughable, if it were not for the damaging effect of such scholastic controversies on the British politico-economic debate and on the supposedly common-sense Tory Party in particular. Indeed one day somebody will write the history of the Conservative Party in terms of its disruption by economic controversy, from the Corn Laws in the last century to Empire Free Trade in the early part of this century and fixed versus floating exchange rates in our own time.

Principles and Practices

One of the greatest challenges I had when I became Chancellor was in putting over the logical structure of the Government's approach. Debate in the UK seems to swing between market and academic technicalities – which ultimately and quite rightly lead even the most diligent lay-man to switch off – and vague partisan slogans. Serious argument on policy principles is much more difficult to launch, as I realized when I overheard people coming out of the Mais Lecture complaining that I had not announced any specific measures. The logical point I found most difficult to ram home was the distinction between 'first-order' and 'second-order' decisions. By this I mean the difference between the principles of economic policy – first order – and the precise means by which these principles are implemented – second order. (The analogy is with first and second orders of magnitude in the physical sciences.)

The point I sought to make was that the choice between the various methods of specifying the nominal framework was second order. The big choice was whether to aim at output and jobs directly, as in the post-war interpretation of Keynesianism, or whether to focus on nominal variables, such as money flows and prices. All of us who opted for the second alternative were monetarists of sorts, and the civil wars which have broken out between the varying schools are absurd.

The choice between the various methods of achieving nominal objectives must vary between time and place. It is perfectly sensible to target the money supply in some countries and at some times, and to target exchange rates at others. At the international level, say that of the Group of Seven, nominal GDP might come more into its own – especially when there is a serious risk of deflation or contraction, perhaps through the weakness of the banking system.

Reaction to Shocks

This brings me to one omission in the Mais Lecture, which I intended to tackle on a subsequent occasion, but never in the end got round to doing. That is the reaction to shocks.

In general, as I argued, the task of monetary policy is to ensure reasonable price stability; and the task of supply-side policy is to promote growth and employment. There can nevertheless be periods of shock, such as the collapse of the American banking system in 1931, when the assignment might differ. A more vigorous monetary policy then might have prevented or reduced the fall in prices that took place and thus have mitigated the severity of the Great Depression. But it would be pedantic to treat an anti-depression financial policy simply in terms of the price level. It should, rather, be aimed at maintaining the national income, *but still in nominal terms*.

I very much doubt if we are ever likely to return to an inter-war state of affairs in which we can forget about inflation altogether. But since the international debt problem of the early 1980s and the more general problems of banking and corporate indebtedness, which emerged a decade later, the possibility of a systemic collapse has been lurking in the background. Were it to become a more imminent threat, a large part of the preventative and curative policy would need to be in the field of banking supervision, lender of last-resort operations and the like. The complete divorce of banking and corporate expertise from macroeconomics, inside both the Treasury and the Bank, and among outside commentators too, is a cross that the policy-maker has to bear.

The Counter-revolution in Retrospect

Looking back from the vantage point of the 1990s, it is possible to simplify further the difference between the post-war approach to macroeconomic policy and the counter-revolution of the 1980s.

The new approach of the 1980s was concerned with nominal variables; that is, amounts stated in cash. It did not pretend to guarantee particular rates of growth or employment. It laid down a financial policy tight enough to prevent any outside events, such as oil price explosions or an outbreak of union militancy, from acting as an inflationary trigger. On the other hand, had the circumstances arisen, the counter-revolutionary approach was meant to be as vigilant as Keynes could have desired in fighting off any cumulative contraction of national or global income. A satisfactory counter-revolution does not just go back to the *status quo ante*, but incorporates what is of value in the intervening revolution.

Stated in this way, a nominal framework covers both the normal case when macroeconomic policy is concerned with containing inflation and the more exceptional episodes when it is concerned to stop deflation or depression. Where my thinking did develop was in a growing belief that many of these tasks could be more readily accomplished by co-operative action among the main industrial countries rather than by each country confining itself to putting its own house in order, as in the early Reagan–Thatcher version. Such co-operation does not in my view require a European, still less a world, federal state. But it would *inter alia* be facilitated if the central banks of the main participating countries were independent of day-to-day control by governments.

CHAPTER 34

'WHERE WILL THE JOBS COME FROM?'

Unemployment – Cause and Cure · Job Losses of the 1980s
Pay and Jobs · The Truth Continues to Shock
An American Example · Unions or Employers?
Government's Role · Restart In, Workfare Out
Jobs in Boom and Recession

Unemployment – Cause and Cure

IT FOLLOWS FROM THE thesis set out in the Mais Lecture that the promotion of jobs and employment is not the Treasury's principal responsibility. But it does not follow from that that either the Thatcher Government as a whole or I as Chancellor was indifferent to the problem of unemployment. Indeed, as I have already indicated, we were firmly committed to the view that the key to improved economic performance was allowing markets of all kinds to work better. It is a commonplace that one of the most serious weaknesses of the British economy – one that it shares with most other European countries, but that is small consolation – is the way in which the labour market operates.

The diagnosis and treatment of unemployment shares one feature in common with monetary policy. It attracts every variety of crank and purveyor of misbegotten schemes. The contrast is that the cranks have even greater popular appeal when talking about jobs; and many supposedly down-to-earth political and business leaders share the approach of these cranks.

Most popular discussion of unemployment is governed by the idea that there is a limited amount of work to be done and that the wonders of modern technology threaten to produce a chronic and increasing shortage of work. Samuel Brittan has revived the term 'lump of labour fallacy' for this belief. But a more accurate label would be the

423

'lump-of-output fallacy'. For it assumes there is a limited amount of goods and services to be produced and that, if anything happens to enable these goods to be produced by fewer people, the result will be unemployment – unless there is compulsory work sharing, forced reduction in hours, early retirement and so on.

British industry was substantially overmanned during the 1970s, especially in manufacturing; and the strains of structural change were greatly increased by the emergence into the open of this disguised unemployment. The resulting dislocation engendered the deepest pessimism about the ability of the market economy to restore high employment.

This pessimistic mood exhibited the tendency, common to both booms and recessions, of extrapolating existing trends indefinitely into the future. This was as true of the recession of the early 1980s, which was not only both deeper than previous post-war economic downturns, but more uneven in its impact, as it was to be of the more prolonged recession of the early 1990s. There were calls from all sides to cut the supply of labour by reviving military conscription and other equally drastic measures. Some particularly sensational soothsayers talked of the need to educate people for a life of perpetual leisure. Their line of reasoning was both fallacious and debilitating.

The question I was most frequently asked at this time was 'where will the new jobs come from?' This succeeded in combining the lump-of-output fallacy with the collectivist fallacy of supposing that some central planner can or should be able to predict the future pattern of output and employment, which in fact depends on the unforeseeable development of technology and taste interacting in thousands of different markets.

Nevertheless it was a question that was put to me everywhere, not least by industrialists; the assumption being that, unless I could tell them precisely where the new jobs would come from, they would not believe there would be any respite from ever-increasing unemployment. It was clear by the time I became Chancellor that growth had resumed and that recovery from the recession was in train. But the immediate impact of technological progress, the failure of pay to adjust, greater efficiency, and the determination of businessmen not to return to the overmanning of the past seemed to be remorselessly rising unemployment. This was held to demonstrate that we had entered a new era in which unemployment would not only be a permanent feature but would rise inexorably.

Job Losses of the 1980s

The first half of the 1980s provided particularly fertile soil for nonsense of this kind. By the spring of 1984 the economy was in its third consecutive year of growth, but recorded unemployment was rising for the fifth year in succession. Although the number of people in work had been rising since March 1983, the official unemployment figures, on which attention had always been focused, did not even start to fall until the second half of 1986. This translated into very considerable political pressure which increased as 1984 wore on.

UK job trends

Source: Datastream

Among the many prominent adherents of the lump-of-output fallacy was Francis Pym, the disaffected former Foreign Secretary whom Margaret had dropped from the Government after the 1983 election. In 1984 he brought out a book, which became something of a bestseller, part of which was devoted to promulgating this fallacy. It advocated reductions in the working day and in the working week, longer holidays, earlier retirement and artificially long training periods to raise the age of entry into industry. Pym cited 'some industrialists' who expected unemployment to reach nine million by the end of the century.

Francis Pym was quite the gloomiest politician I have ever met. He would dilate in the watches of the night on how democracy was doomed and the world was racing to perdition. But his despair over the outlook for jobs was shared by others of an altogether jollier disposition. Hector Laing, for example, the long-serving paternalist chief of the successful food manufacturing group, United Biscuits, and a strong supporter of the Conservative Party, persistently lobbied Margaret and myself to adopt an 'imaginative scheme' he had devised to stimulate employment. At the same time the Labour Party was advocating solving the problem by a massive expansion of public sector, particularly local authority, employment.

Schemes for reducing the size of the working population and increasing the numbers of those dependent on them seemed to me to be particularly

425

perverse. To advocate early retirement at a time when the Fowler review of social security was rightly beginning to focus on radical solutions to the problem of the huge demands that existing policies would place on the taxpaying workforce, in a world in which the population was steadily ageing, was manifest lunacy. In the long run it clearly made a great deal more sense to raise the retirement age, rather than to reduce it.

Although I successfully resisted most of the work-sharing nostrums, the climate of the times, coupled with official Treasury resistance to anything that added to public spending, did cause the postponement of one common-sense reform: the abolition of the pensioners' earnings rule, which I was to announce in my last Budget in 1989.

The background to all this agitation was the shake out in manufacturing described in Chapter 6, which led to the loss of two million manufacturing jobs which obviously could not be absorbed overnight in the expanding service sector. There tends to be a special resonance about the word 'manufacturing', and the quality of debate over this was not helped by the prevailing confusion between manufacturing output and manufacturing employment. Given the appalling degree of overmanning with which we had started, weakness in manufacturing employment was in fact likely to be a necessary precondition of strength in manufacturing output, which clearly depended on improved competitiveness.

It is true that I did not even pay lip service to the contemporary House of Lords report on manufacturing, which advocated deliberate Government preference for that sector; and I was attacked as being anti-manufacturing because I declined to label any sector of the economy as uniquely meritorious. Yet without any special State stimulus UK manufacturing productivity during my Chancellorship rose more than in any other comparable period within living memory, and UK manufacturing output rose more than in any comparable period for a very long time. By contrast, during the lifetime of the previous Labour Government manufacturing output had actually fallen. There has seldom been a greater gulf between rhetoric and reality.

Pay and Jobs

The labour market is more complicated then most other markets. But it is still true that, as in other markets, the higher the price the smaller the volume sold. Other things being equal, higher pay means fewer jobs. I have to confess to taking a moderate relish in bringing home to people unpalatable truths, as I did in my speeches on jobs in the mid-1980s. A moment's reflection is all that is needed to grasp the simple truth that for employers, the total real wage bill (including social security contributions and the cost of meeting employment protection legislation) is a cost which, if they cannot recover it in their selling prices, they will strive to reduce by economies in manpower.

As a Government, however, we were handicapped in explaining these elementary relationships by decades of propaganda about a supposed wage-price spiral in which the evils of excessive pay were seen almost entirely in terms of inflation rather than unemployment. The true causal chain in the 1970s – the most inflationary decade the UK has ever suffered – was different. High wage awards led to unemployment, which Governments felt obliged to combat by 'reflating' - that is, increasing spending in the economy. It was this that led to inflation, which made British goods uncompetitive in world markets. This was then offset by a falling exchange rate. The falling pound gave inflation a further boost, which encouraged still higher wage awards. Hence the supposed vicious circle. But the heart of the matter was Government financial accommodation of excessive pay awards – whether this was seen in terms of internal accommodation through lax monetary policy or external accommodation through allowing sterling to depreciate.

In fact, the relationship between pay and jobs was blindingly obvious. But to many, especially in the world of opinion formers, it appeared outrageous, provocative or even just a personal hobby horse of my own. Above all, it was seen as politically motivated: an attempt by the Government to escape the blame for unemployment and to pin it on the trade unions instead, just as previous Governments had sought to blame the unions for inflation. (In fact it was employers, not unions, that I consistently claimed were primarily responsible for determining pay.)

To demonstrate that it was none of these things, I decided to publish in January 1985 a Treasury Paper entitled: *The Relationship between Employment and Wages: Empirical Evidence for the UK*. It had a yellow cover and the unusual byline 'Review by Treasury Officials'. This was, of course, a correct description, in that the Treasury had done no first-hand research of its own into the subject, and could only bring together the research that had been conducted by others. But the purpose of publishing a paper explicitly by Treasury officials was to demonstrate that there was nothing political or opportunist about it: it was an analytical, if unpalatable, statement of the economic facts of life. The fact that it appeared at all demonstrated how great a change there had been in the intellectual climate. In the 1970s, the then deputy head of the Economic Section of the Treasury, Geoffrey Maynard, had found his life made impossible for merely suggesting that excessive real pay had something to do with high unemployment.

The central numerical estimate of the Yellow Paper – hedged with countless conditions and qualifications – was that a change of 1 per cent in real wages would be associated with a change the other way in employment of some ½ to 1 per cent, equivalent to 110,000 to 220,000 jobs. One still finds this numerical relationship as the best available guess in many much later studies.

The big question, of course, is why real wages rose too rapidly. Cannot employers prevent this from occurring? One theory, associated with Professor Richard Layard, is that unemployment has to be high enough to moderate wage earners' otherwise unrealistic expectations: it is thus the *attempt* to obtain excessive real wages that is responsible for high unemployment. Economists on the 'radical right' such as Patrick Minford put most emphasis on the level of social security benefits as the key. For this produced a 'floor' which discouraged workers, displaced by union monopoly, from pricing themselves into work in the non-unionized sector. It also provided the floor above which collective bargaining took place. I was fiercely attacked early in my Chancellorship for merely alluding to this relationship. While this was part of the story, another factor was that employers expected inflation to be higher than it turned out to be, thus expecting wage rises to be eroded more than they were. I have no doubt that more deep-seated cultural factors were also at work.

The Truth Continues to Shock

A brief passage about joblessness in my IMF speech of 25 September 1984, which focused primarily on the international debt problem and the difficulties caused by the American Budget deficit, was greeted by the British Press with astonishment, which, although undeserved, was useful in drawing public attention to the pay-and-jobs relationship. What I actually said was:

> While maintaining this [stabilization] policy intact we need to place more emphasis on supply-side policy in the true sense of that much-abused term: that is, in dealing with the structural problems that are the cause of the continuing high level of unemployment which so many countries face today . . . To some extent, of course, the rise in unemployment is the temporary consequence of the long overdue success of British industry in making itself more competitive by cutting costs and improving productivity . . . [But] the heart of the problem – and here the contrast with the US is particularly striking – has been the steady growth in real wages . . . We must not be seduced by the wonders of high-tech into overlooking the fact that many of the jobs of the future will be in labour-intensive service industries – not so much low-tech as no-tech.

It was that last sentence that caused all the fuss. Like many other visitors to the US, I had observed the number of Americans who were prepared to take on simple jobs, such as carrying goods purchased in supermarkets to the customer's car, at prevailing market rates of pay. Modern technology is most unlikely to reduce the demand for such jobs; it is more likely to increase it. It is no accident that even in the UK, whereas at the start of the 1970s more than one worker in three was employed in manufacturing industry, by the 1980s the figure had fallen to nearer one in five, with a commensurate rise in employment in services of all kinds. During that time, moreover, manufacturing *ouput* had increased by some 20 per cent. My remark about 'no-tech' jobs was subsequently viciously attacked by the self-appointed tribunes of the people in the media. It was in fact a simple statement of the truth; and even now I am not sure whether my critics considered it to be false or simply immoral.

A month or so after returning from Washington I appeared on the television programme *Weekend World* and caused renewed surprise in the Press by telling Brian Walden, a Labour MP who had given up the Commons, where he had been one of its few outstanding speakers, to become an equally distinguished (and considerably better remunerated) interviewer, that I considered unemployment to be a human problem rather than an economic one. The *Guardian* announced that I had launched a 'We Do Care Campaign'. Bernard Ingham sent me a congratulatory note – the only time I can recall his doing so.

What I meant was perfectly straightforward. The economy was doing well by most of the normal indicators: output, productivity, inflation and so on. Yet unemployment was high and still rising. The Government's critics maintained that this was because so much capacity had been destroyed in the 1980–81 recession. Yet businessmen themselves conceded that much of the scrapped plant and equipment was obsolete or unsuitable anyway, and the recession had merely accelerated its departure. All the same, the undoubted economic improvement was obviously little comfort to those who had lost their jobs in manufacturing and could not see their way to another job elsewhere.

The Labour Party believed it could make considerable political capital out of the high level of unemployment, using the days on which the Opposition chooses the subject of parliamentary debate to mount a series of debates on unemployment, taking the various regions in turn. But I could not help noticing that the Opposition benches were even more deserted than usual during these debates. They clearly did not have their hearts in it, recognizing perhaps that there was no groundswell of anger in the country as a whole, which seemed pretty content. Paradoxically, the Government's main worry was that Conservative Members in marginal seats were becoming increasingly restless about the relentless rise in the number out of work, and that this anxiety had communicated itself to Margaret herself.

'WHERE WILL THE JOBS COME FROM?'

An American Example

It is often forgotten how frequently the ballooning US Budget deficit was held up by domestic critics as an example for the British Government to follow. The hope was that this would stimulate growth and employment in the UK. These sentiments were uttered at the very same time that the harmful effects of the US deficit became a subject of condemnation at one international meeting after another. The American Budget deficit was applauded in the US by the more extreme Reaganites and in the UK by their less comprehending camp followers, such as *The Sunday Times*, as a magnificent example of supply-side economics. It was also warmly espoused by the Labour Party as a good old-fashioned Keynesian demand stimulus. An astonishing number of people got drawn into praising the US deficit, including at one time even the Duke of Edinburgh.

There was some superficial evidence to support this view. American real GDP shot up by about 6 per cent in 1984, and although the Fed then reimposed the brakes, there were none of the 're-entry' problems that Britain and other countries customarily experienced in returning from an unsustainable to a sustainable rate of growth. Nor was there any notable re-acceleration of inflation in the US, which until 1989 rarely strayed outside the corridor of 3 to 4½ per cent a year. Long-term bond yields, where the effects of deficit finance were supposed to show themselves first, rose in 1984 and then subsequently fell in the remainder of the 1980s to around 8 or 9 per cent – less than in the UK – even though the President and Congress never succeeded in seriously tackling the deficit.

The sharp rise in the dollar undoubtedly helped to contain inflation during the most rapid phase of American growth, however embarrassing it was for other countries and for US exporters. But the policy mix of currency appreciation, large budget deficits and tight monetary policy, which some purveyors of instant wisdom urged on us, was not sustainable for more than a short period. Competitive appreciation is almost as self-defeating as competitive depreciation.

The US experience did, however, strengthen my view that monetary rather than fiscal policy was the key counter-inflationary weapon. The main harm inflicted by the high US Budget deficits, which were not financed by 'printing money', was long term. The burden of Federal Government debt service spending steadily rose, which was among the factors which made it difficult for the Americans to take the same lead after the collapse of Communism in Europe that they previously took in the Marshall Plan period that followed the collapse of Nazism.

In any case, as soon as Ronald Reagan had been re-elected as President in November 1984, the US Administration abruptly stopped defending the Budget deficit and accepted that it was its number one economic problem. This abrupt change of tune was signalled by Don Regan, and preceded his imminent replacement as Treasury Secretary by James Baker. President Reagan had always believed in a balanced Budget, and blamed the deficit on the spending proclivities of the Congress. He defended his refusal to close the gap by increasing taxes, as we had done in 1981, by arguing that under the US system, with its separation of powers, any extra revenue raised would only have been spent by Congress. While there may have been some truth in this, it was undoubtedly a highly convenient belief.

From the point of view of employment, the US Budget deficit was a red herring. A superior US employment record went back to well before its Budget deficit began to climb. In the ten years up to 1983, as I pointed out in the Mais lecture:

> . . . the total number of people in work in Western Europe has fallen. In the US over the same period the number of people in work has risen by over fifteen million. This sharp contrast has not been the product of macro policy. It has been almost entirely due to the more efficient, competitive, innovative and adaptive labour and goods markets in the United States. Over the past ten years, the workers of Western Europe have seen their real earnings rise by around an eighth; over the same period their American counterparts have been prepared to accept a small reduction in real earnings. Relatively free markets, the spirit of enterprise, and workers who prefer to price themselves into jobs rather than out of them, are a powerful engine of employment. There is indeed an important lesson to be learned from the American experience, but it has nothing to do with the deficit.

Unions or Employers?

When the Thatcher Government came to office in 1979, the most obvious influence in pricing workers out of jobs was union power. For all their protestations about unemployment, unions were primarily concerned with those workers who already had jobs and (in their judgement) were likely to retain them.

The issue is too often presented in Treasury documents and elsewhere in terms of broad national averages. But the demand for labour depends as much upon relative as on average real wages. Pay did not adjust sufficiently to occupational, sectoral and regional differences in the supply and demand for workers. The long-standing preference among trade unions for centralized pay bargaining and nationwide rates of pay is one reason why heavy unemployment in some areas during the 1980s coincided with labour shortages, particularly of skilled labour, in others. Moreover these shortages, by depressing overall output, further aggravated joblessness everywhere.

A reduction in union power was an important aim of Conservative policy even though it was couched in the language of checking abuses, democratizing procedures and so on. Union power was duly reduced by a series of Acts covering strike procedures, picketing, the closed shop and much else. Just as important was facing up to a number of strikes, above all the 1984–85 coal strike, and providing police support for employers who stood up to intimidation, such as Rupert Murdoch at Wapping. The development of the less unionized service sector and the mushrooming of small firms all further served to weaken trade union influence. Its main redoubt is now the State sector.

As the 1980s wore on I became more and more convinced that employers rather than unions were responsible for pay settlements incompatible with high employment. British employers had a marked preference for cutting unit labour costs by cutting payrolls rather than by cutting pay rates. Like the trade unions, their concern was with their employees rather than with those who had left their employment, and they felt inhibited by guilt in taking a tough line on pay at a time when profits were rising rapidly and top managers were paying themselves substantial increases.

Labour market rigidity is a weakness in many European economies and not just the UK. The curious feature on this side of the Atlantic is that an employer who wishes to cut his labour costs evidently finds it easier to persuade his workforce to accept large-scale redundancies rather than to forego a pay rise – let alone to take a pay cut. This is in sharp contrast to the US, where the labour market is more flexible, both in terms of pay and of labour mobility. American employers are also much less inhibited than their UK counterparts either by rising profits or by their own pay levels when it comes to taking a firm line on wages.

Government's Role

In a market economy and a free society it is plainly a matter for business and industry itself to determine rates of pay, which in turn in the long run determine the level of employment; and the responsibility of government is essentially to provide the right overall economic climate. But there were some specific areas in which government action was needed, and to a considerable (although incomplete) extent that action was taken.

One such area was that of the long-established statutory Wages Councils, which set minimum pay rates in certain low-pay industries. These were not, as I would have liked, abolished; but their powers were greatly limited and (outside agriculture) those under twenty-one were removed from their scope altogether. It is not surprising if unqualified and untrained youngsters find difficulty in getting started in the world of work, if the first rung of the ladder of employment is removed by law.

On other fronts, Geoffrey Howe early on made unemployment benefit taxable – a brave step politically, but essential if the 'why work?' problem was to be solved – while the National Insurance reforms in my Budgets of 1985 and 1989 made it more worthwhile both for people with a low earnings capacity to take a job and for employers to employ them. Again, Norman Fowler's social security reforms shifted the basis of means-tested benefits from pre-tax to post-tax incomes. This meant that, although the combined marginal rate of tax, National Insurance and benefit withdrawal could be very high (a necessary evil if benefits are to be concentrated on those whose need is greatest), at least it could not reach (and indeed exceed) 100 per cent as it could before. Another way in which the Social Security Act of 1985 helped was that early leavers from occupational pension schemes were entitled to take their pension rights with them to a new employer. This eliminated a major discouragement to job mobility.

Restart In, Workfare Out

One of the most important innovations of the 1980s which has survived into the 1990s was at that time called the 'Counselling Initiative and Jobstart Allowance'. This was the brainchild of David Young, the new Employment Secretary, and was launched nationally after the success of local pilot projects. Every single person on the register who had been unemployed for more than a year was invited to an interview at the local Job Centre and offered either a job or a place on a training scheme. It paid those prepared to take a job paying less than £80 a week a temporary £20 a week 'Jobstart Allowance' to top up the wage. David Young generously records in his own memoirs that 'the Treasury' – meaning the Chancellor and Chief Secretary – 'gave me all I asked for, except that interviewing and counselling had to be called "Restart" and the allowance "Jobstart".'

Of all the schemes introduced by the Government, 'Restart' had the most marked effect on the unemployment figures. Over two million interviews were carried out each year. Of those who took the short course offered, 60 per cent were in – or about to start – a job within six weeks. Others found jobs unaided when faced with what they saw as the threat of a Restart interview; and there were those who decided they were not looking for work after all and left the register. The scheme not only helped those who were genuinely looking for work, but weeded out those

433

who were not – either because they had decided to take early retirement, or because they were already hard at work in the black economy.

Both Margaret and I were also interested in developing a fully fledged 'workfare' scheme in which the unemployed would be required to work rather than to do nothing, by the simple device of making the payment of benefit conditional on participation in a 'workfare' scheme. This was an American idea, which was subsequently taken up by Michael Heseltine as part of his long-running campaign for the Party Leadership. Under the federal constitution of the United States, this is a matter which comes within the authority of the individual State – something the centralists of Brussels would doubtless regard with horror if it were proposed for Europe. As a result, it operates in some States and not others, and better in some than in others. But there is ample evidence that it can work very well, not only in economic terms but in human terms, too. A number of meetings were held, under Margaret's chairmanship; but unfortunately an alliance on the issue between Norman Fowler, as Social Security Secretary, and David Young, as Employment Secretary, produced so many alleged practical difficulties that the idea was dropped. It is surely time to pick it up again.

Jobs in Boom and Recession

I was always convinced that, once economic growth had attained sufficient momentum, smaller businesses had started to grow rapidly, and confidence recovered, larger established companies would start to recruit again. This took longer than I had expected because of the slowness with which wages responded to market pressures. But after years in which many feared that nothing would reverse the upward trend, unemployment suddenly started to fall dramatically. It fell from over three million (on current definitions) in mid-1986 to 2.8 million at the end of that year, 2.3 million at the end of 1988, 1.8 million in 1989 and 1.6 million (or 5.6 per cent) at its low point in early 1990.

Unfortunately the boom proved unsustainably vigorous, which inevitably exacerbated the subsequent recession. Unemployment rose by a million to 2¾ million, or 9¾ per cent, by the middle of 1992; and it would clearly be no surprise to see the 3 million level regained before it starts falling again. Clearly some, although I do not believe all, of the earlier fall in unemployment was cyclical. But none of this in any way undermines the important pay-and-jobs link. No sensible exponent of that link denies that unemployment can fall in a boom or rise in a slump. The point is that the rigidities of the British pay culture (a) increase the cyclical fluctuations in unemployment and (b) raise the underlying level of unemployment over the cycle as a whole.*

. There was, moreover, one important silver lining to the sharp rise in unemployment in the recession of the early 1990s. Productivity, after a brief pause, resumed its rapid increase, especially in manufacturing. Precisely because there was much less overmanning to reduce this time round, the gain was even more impressive than that achieved in the recession of the early 1980s. This strongly suggests that the reforms of the 1980s have indeed improved the economy's long-term growth potential.

*Some economists would say that during my period as Chancellor, unemployment started off above the so-called NAIRU and ended up below it. The NAIRU stands for the 'Non-Accelerating Inflation Rate of Unemployment'. But since we do not have much idea of what the NAIRU is, I do not find it a helpful concept. To give an example: there was in the 1970s a great deal of suppressed unemployment due to overmanning. When this came out into the open was there really a sudden increase in the NAIRU which would normally be interpreted as increased malfunctioning of the British labour market? Richard Layard attempts to cope with such dilemmas in his *magnum opus* by envisaging a whole family of NAIRUs – a short- to medium-term one, which reflects such shocks, and a long-term one reflecting underlying economic behaviour. But even that can change. All of which confirms my instinctive suspicion of the whole concept.

CHAPTER 35

TRADE UNIONS AND THE LABOUR MARKET

Taking on the Unions · The Role of the Treasury
Focus on Training · Profit Related Pay
Pay and Productivity · The So-called Regional Problem
Ending the Dock Labour Scheme · Nil Desperandum

Taking on the Unions

WHEN WE FIRST TOOK office in 1979, at the heart of the problem of Britain's malfunctioning labour market – and of a number of other ills besides – clearly lay the much-discussed trade union question. Among the Thatcher Government's most important pieces of legislation were the Employment Acts of 1980 and 1982 and the Trade Union Act of 1984, which eroded the closed shop, introduced compulsory ballots before strikes and outlawed flying pickets and most secondary industrial action.

This was not the first time, of course, that an attempt had been made to reform trade union law. Throughout the 1960s there had been a growing sense that the unions had become over-mighty subjects, an affront to the rule of law and an obstacle to economic success. The first attempt to remedy this unacceptable state of affairs had been made by the Labour Government led by Harold Wilson in 1969, with the publication of the White Paper *In Place of Strife*, which was intended as a precursor to immediate legislation. Wilson himself had no doubt of its importance: 'The Bill we are discussing tonight is an essential Bill', he told the Parliamentary Labour Party; 'It is an essential component of ensuring the economic success on which the recovery of the nation, led by the Labour Government, depends. That is why I have to tell you that the passage of this Bill is essential to its continuance in office. There can be no going back on that.'

But there was: a TUC-inspired Cabinet revolt prevented the Bill from ever seeing the light of day; and the following year Labour was out of office. The incoming Conservative Government led by Ted Heath lost no time in picking up the baton, and duly enacted the Industrial Relations Act of 1971. Although defective in a number of important respects, given time it could no doubt have been amended into reasonable shape. But within three years Labour was back in office, to embark on the opposite course of conferring yet further privileges on the unions. The Government was repaid for its pains by the notorious winter of discontent of 1978–9, an outbreak of union mayhem in protest against Labour's pay policy, acceptance of which was meant to be the *quid pro quo* for the new privileges.

This in turn ushered in the Thatcher Conservative Government a few months later, and with it the third, and at last successful, attempt to reform trade union law. Despite overwhelming popular support, Margaret – as so often – moved cautiously, rejecting the idea of a single all-embracing Act in favour of moving one step at a time, with a series of Acts over a period of years, each dealing with different aspects of the problem. The outcome was as important as it was successful. A Government which its critics had confidently predicted would plunge the nation into a maelstrom of civil strife, saw the number of days lost through strikes plunge dramatically. The balance of power within industry was changed decisively, with management at last being able to manage. The individual union member was emancipated from the thrall of the union to which he had hitherto been compelled to belong.

But there are two key points that tend to be overlooked when this story is told. The first is that the transformation of the industrial relations scene in Britain depended just as much on the economic policy the Government pursued as it did on the reform of trade union law. In particular, the eschewing of pay policy, which conferred undue importance on trade union leaders while creating unnecessary grievances among their members, and the abandonment of the unfulfillable commitment to full employment, which had enabled the unions to hold previous governments to ransom, were both essential components of the new order – and of the 'new realism' which the union leaders felt obliged to embrace. The privatization programme, too, which no previous Government had attempted, was important in this context: trade union leaders are least inclined to feel constrained by the economic facts of life when State ownership both politicizes the context and appears to provide a bottomless purse.

The second key point is that the Thatcher Government's attempt to reform Britain's labour market was by no means confined to the reform of trade union law. It is with the battery of other measures we took, and the issues we addressed, that this chapter is concerned.

TRADE UNIONS AND THE LABOUR MARKET

The Role of the Treasury

The Government as a whole clearly has a role both in removing obstacles to the functioning of markets, not least the labour market, and in taking positive steps to improve them. But the Treasury is only one of several Departments involved in these areas and is not in any formal sense the lead Department.

I have been careful to say 'Treasury' rather than 'Chancellor'. For the Chancellor, as the senior economic Minister, who sits on all key Cabinet committees and chairs some of them, has to be concerned with all aspects of economic performance, and especially anything as important and as sensitive as jobs.

The public seems to sense the allocation of responsibilities better than many commentators. For the Chancellor's reputation is most obviously affected adversely by such events as sterling crises, rising interest rates, shock inflation figures or soaring budget deficits, or favourably by tax reductions or lower inflation. But if the unemployment news is bad, the Chancellor suffers politically more as a leading member of the Cabinet than in his departmental role. This is just as well. For it is clearly desirable to have as the senior economic Minister in the Cabinet someone who does not have an interest in taking risks with inflation for the dubious purpose of buying a very few, very temporary, jobs.

Indeed, the whole idea of 'buying jobs' was something I continually sought to demolish; pointing out that if this were really possible there would be no unemployment anywhere, since the one thing that any government can do is to spend money.

Focus on Training

There were a great many specific policies introduced in the Thatcher years to improve the working of the labour market. By the time I became Chancellor in June 1983, some £2 billion a year was already being spent on special employment and training measures for 850,000 people. New Government measures included the Youth Training Scheme; the Community Programme to give work to the long-term unemployed; and the Enterprise Allowance Scheme, which paid people unemployment benefit while they set up in business on their own. These programmes were further expanded after the energetic and innovative David Young, the former Chairman of the Manpower Services Commission, joined the Cabinet in the September 1984 reshuffle with a special brief from Margaret to tackle unemployment. A year later he replaced Tom King as Secretary of State at the Department of Employment.

Among the contributions I myself was able to make to improving the labour market as Chancellor, perhaps the most important was the

438

creation of a climate in which profitability improved dramatically. This meant that employers could at last afford to invest in training; while at the same time I introduced a tax system in which such investment, for the first time for decades, was not discriminated against *vis-à-vis* investment in hardware.

It is a pernicious myth, to be found particularly but by no means exclusively on the political Left, that the effort a country devotes to training its youngsters is measured by the amount of Government spending on training. I always argued strongly that, to the greatest extent possible, the employer, rather than the taxpayer, should pay for training. This is far more likely to lead to the sort of training the market requires. As industry became more profitable, larger companies found it was far more sensible to invest in training, even if they lost some of their trained staff to other and often smaller companies, than to bid up the wages of an ever-decreasing pool of skilled labour. Company-based training is the norm in Germany, for example, which is often cited as a model in this field. It is much easier and cheaper to train people today than it used to be. Modern equipment is so advanced and user-friendly that school-leavers who are literate and numerate can be trained to do almost anything in six months. The real problem was the appalling standard of education in far too many state schools, where pupils sometimes left scarcely able to read, write or do simple sums.

In so far as new Government labour market schemes required public money, of course, this meant that the Treasury had to agree the expenditure. This allowed me and my officials to ensure that the schemes concerned were designed in an economically sound, market-based way.

Profit Related Pay

In my 1986 Budget I announced an initiative designed to reform the labour market from a totally different perspective: the reduction of pay rigidity. 'If the only element of flexibility' I observed 'is the numbers of people employed, then redundancies are more likely to occur.' I had got the idea from a book I had read, during the *longueurs* of the Bonn Economic Summit, by a Harvard professor, Martin Weitzman, who argued in favour of what was in effect a two-part package for paying workers. One element would be a normal wage negotiated, or set by employers, as at present. The other part would vary with profits. This second part of the pay packet would thus act as an automatic shock absorber, reducing the total pay bill during a downturn in demand, thus avoiding the need for redundancies, or at least minimizing the number required.

I decided to call the idea Profit Related Pay (PRP), because the term 'profit-sharing' was already used, somewhat misleadingly, for employee share ownership schemes (which I had also encouraged in various Budgets). Such schemes may have worked in the same direction as PRP, and certainly both should tend to strengthen the identification of the employee with the profitability of the company for which he or she works, and erode the 'them and us' divide which is the bugbear of British business. But PRP was intended to do more than this.

If PRP was to be of value as a shock absorber and job promoter, it would have to amount to a significant part of the employee's total remuneration, and could not just be an add-on as in so many existing schemes. This was not something that could happen very quickly. I could hope only to make a start which might be developed further in later years.

The reason why the announcement was in the Budget was, of course, that there had to be tax relief attached to the scheme if it was to get off the ground. My original intention was to introduce the PRP tax relief in the 1986 Budget, too; but the Chevening discussion highlighted a number of difficulties. One was that the relief could be dissipated in higher pay for existing workers. For the trade unions might try to dissuade employers from taking on additional workers in order to prevent the dilution of the profit-related element.

It was obvious that Profit Related Pay was more likely to take off if there were a period of consultation. So I contented myself with launching the idea in the 1986 Budget Speech. Margaret did her best to talk me out of the scheme, which she regarded as a gimmick. But I insisted that we should see what came out of the consultations.

Uncharacteristically, I began my post-Budget exercise in persuasion by taking the idea to the National Economic Development Council on 12 May 1986. The overall response was predictably cautious, but sufficiently encouraging for me to publish a Green Paper on 15 July. I made some alterations to make it easier for firms to phase PRP in gradually. The minimum qualifying PRP element was 5 per cent of normal pay, with an option to build up gradually to 20 per cent over a period of years. Schemes could apply to separate factories or even work units. Moreover new workers would have to be employed for a qualifying period to become eligible to join the scheme. This was an idea of my own, and not part of the Weitzman scheme at all. It seemed to me an effective way of neutralizing any objection by the unions to an employer who wished to take on more employees.

One criticism I was not prepared to accept was the frequent argument that, if they were given a share in the profits of a company, employees would press for greater involvement in decision making. The Green Paper remarked: 'Increasing employee identification should bring about improved communication between management and the workforce . . . That will be a benefit of PRP, not a drawback.' The majority of responses to the Green Paper were welcoming if unenthusiastic; and the scheme was eventually enacted in the 1987 Finance Act. I decided that half of an employee's profit-related pay would be tax free up to a ceiling of 20 per cent of total pay or £3,000, whichever was less. The cost would not be large even if the scheme were a runaway success; and in his 1991 Budget Norman Lamont doubled the amount of relief.

Not surprisingly the take-up was small at first. But the numbers of firms with PRP schemes grew steadily, with a remarkable spurt in the last quarter of 1991. By the end of 1991 there were 3,000 such schemes in operation covering almost 600,000 workers, or 2 per cent of the working population.

One question I had to decide when designing the scheme was whether the tax break should go to the employee, the employer, or be split between the two. I took the view that the advantages to the employer were clear, and that the problem was trade union hostility. I therefore concentrated the relief on the employee. This may well have been a psychological error, and it might have been better to have saved some of the carrot for the employer.

Not that the scheme has been a failure. Indeed, the official figures of take-up understate the force of the idea. Whenever tax relief is involved, rules have to be laid down to prevent the scheme being used simply for tax avoidance. It is true that the PRP rulebook was on the large side, but this was because I wished to provide employers with a number of options, rather than seeking to force them into a single straitjacket. Even so, a number of employers preferred to introduce their own tailor-made profit-related pay schemes, at the expense of foregoing the tax relief. Moreover, the launch of the PRP scheme took the idea of profit-related pay – which of course was not new, even if the context was – from the outer margins of consideration to close to the centre of business debate, as a result of which there can be no doubt that the idea of variable pay, related to corporate performance, is steadily gaining acceptance.

Not surprisingly, statistical investigation of profit-linked pay has so far produced varying results. But it is worth citing a 1991 study by the London School of Economics Business Performance Group which concluded that even modest levels of PRP led to a significant reduction in the volatility of employment in firms that introduced it. The director of the project, Greg Clark, added that there was a clear connection between this and training, since the more stable the workforce the more worthwhile it was for an employer to invest in training it.

Pay and Productivity

Productivity, however, was another matter altogether. The frequent ministerial exhortations under all governments to link pay to productivity were more misleading than helpful. If wage increases were literally related to increases in output per person, then all sorts of bizarre consequences would ensue. Wages in high-technology sectors would shoot ahead and people like teachers and doctors, whose productivity is more difficult to measure, would lag badly for reasons which have nothing to do with effort. Bus drivers whose productivity diminishes as a result of increasing congestion on the roads would have their pay cut. A technological improvement which greatly reduces the number of workers who are needed to do a particular job would result in the workers concerned being paid more, even though the demand for them is less. One way and another, all labour markets would be well and truly gummed up. The true principle is the simpler, but less moralistic, one that pay should be related to the state of the labour market; that is, supply and demand in particular sectors and areas.

What gives the pay-productivity link some credence is that, on the one hand, it is broadly true for the economy as a whole, and on the other, there are occasions where it makes sense for an employer to bribe a labour force to accept some uncomfortable change that would improve productivity. But the bribe has to be modest and the extra effort appreciable for such deals to be worth promoting.

The pay-productivity exhortation is so familiar and uncontentious that it is very difficult to do without it, especially at the despatch box at the House of Commons, where blunter market-related arguments go down extremely badly, even on the Conservative side. I made a point of seeking to avoid it myself, although I may not invariably have succeeded.

The So-called Regional Problem

We were constantly criticized for not tackling Britain's regional problem with sufficient vigour, and often for not tackling it at all. This was no oversight. The regional and industrial policies of previous governments had perversely subsidized investment in machinery at the expense of men, usually in uneconomic locations. This was not a path we had any desire to tread; and Norman Tebbit, as Secretary of State for Industry from 1983 to 1985, with my full and active support, embarked on a long-overdue rationalization and scaling down of regional assistance. The 1984 Corporation Tax reforms reinforced this new approach.

But the main reason for the regional imbalance in terms of unemployment rates was the dependence of the North on manufacturing in general, where overmanning had been greatest in 1979, and in particular on declining industries such as steel and shipbuilding. Until the overmanning had been eliminated and the industrial structure changed – instead of fossilized as under previous so-called industrial policies – there was no avoiding the imbalance.

As these problems were gradually tackled the imbalance dwindled, to the amazement of the advocates of highly interventionist regional policies. Indeed, by almost abolishing regional policy and letting market forces work better, we did more to solve the regional problem than any previous post-war Government.

The other dimension of regional imbalance was, of course, inadequate mobility of labour. In my own area of responsibility I sought to improve mobility by greatly reducing the distortions caused by mortgage interest relief (a) by freezing the amount of mortgage on which interest was allowable against tax at £30,000 over a period during which house prices rose substantially, (b) by reducing income tax rates, which reduced the value of the relief and (c) by abolishing both multiple mortgage relief and home improvement loan relief. These changes should also reduce the future volatility of the housing market, which made the conduct of economic policy in the 1980s so difficult. But a genuine improvement in labour mobility required not merely a curbing of mortgage interest relief, but also positive measures to rehabilitate the private rental market.

This was the main purpose of the Bill which Nick Ridley, as Environment Secretary, introduced after the 1987 Election. Its most important provision was the removal of new tenancies from the ambit of rent control. In time, especially if the election of a Labour Government committed to the reimposition of rent control appears remote, it should do the trick. In the meantime, a kick start was required. Nick asked me to give rental accommodation the same degree of tax relief as owner-occupiers enjoyed. This I was not prepared to do. But, after a thorough study of the options by a group of my officials and his, I included in my 1988 Budget an amendment to the Business Expansion Scheme to include within its scope, for five years only, the provision of accommodation for private rental. Meanwhile, although it is true that people remain disinclined to move far to find a job, as the 1980s progressed companies started to move, through market forces and without Government bribes, to where labour was readily available.

All in all, the labour-market reforms carried out by the Thatcher Government amounted to a substantial package. Over the years the improvement should be considerable.

Ending the Dock Labour Scheme

One highly specific issue that had to be addressed, and which in the end was addressed, was the notorious Dock Labour Scheme. At the same time it must be said that the long drawn out saga of the demise of the Scheme provides a good illustration of the need there was for constant pressure from like-minded colleagues if Margaret was to live up to her radical principles, particularly (although not only) where the trade unions were involved.

TRADE UNIONS AND THE LABOUR MARKET

The National Dock Labour Scheme was arguably the biggest institutionalized scandal in British industry, for which previous governments of both Parties were culpable. The essence of it was that all Britain's major ports were manned exclusively by registered dockworkers, all of whom were guaranteed a job for life, and who had to be paid whether or not there was work for them to do. In the event of a port closing down, the dockers involved would be allocated to other ports, which had to take them whether they were needed or not. This whole bizarre arrangement was enforced by statute, and could therefore be changed only by repealing the relevant legislation.

The result was inevitable. Britain's ports were grotesquely overmanned, high cost and generally inefficient. The only saving grace was that more and more business was moving to ports outside the scheme, such as Felixstowe. But the damage being done to the economy was still considerable, and as sanity returned to industrial relations elsewhere, the lunacy of the Dock Labour Scheme became a notorious anomaly.

Within Government, responsibility for the scheme lay technically with the Department of Employment, but the Transport Department clearly had a considerable interest in it, too. The first attempt to abolish it came in the summer of 1985. Nick Ridley, then Transport Secretary, rightly judged that, with the miners' strike over and Scargill humiliated, the time was ripe to put an end to the indefensible Dock Labour Scheme. Moreover, the port employers, who had previously been rather wet, were now firmly in favour of abolition and wanted the Government to act.

Accordingly, he and Tom King, then Employment Secretary, put in a joint paper to Margaret, setting out the facts and calling for a decision. On 29 July 1985, Margaret called a small meeting of Nick, Tom and myself to discuss the issue in her room at the House. Nick argued the case for abolition, and Tom supported him. So, without reservation, did I. Margaret, however, displayed cold feet to a quite remarkable degree. She suggested, first, that it would be more sensible to do nothing and simply let the Scheme wither on the vine. Nick demonstrated that this was not an option: if we did nothing, the Scheme would survive indefinitely. She then expressed acute anxiety about the effect of a dock strike on the balance of payments and sterling. I replied that if anyone should be worried about that, it would be me, and I was not. Not only had the growth of the non-scheme ports and of air freight made a strike in the scheme ports far less serious than it had been at the time of the previous dock strike in 1972, but the strength of sterling was no longer dependent on the monthly balance of payments figures. The only threat to sterling would be if we were to back down in the face of a strike.

But Margaret was adamant. Arguing, somewhat inconsequentially, that we needed to 'reconstruct' the coal industry first, she concluded that in her view there was no serious prospect of abolishing the Dock

Labour Scheme this side of the election – then still some two years off. A disappointed Nick Ridley accepted her verdict, and that was that.

The 1987 General Election brought with it a new Employment Secretary in Norman Fowler and a new Transport Secretary in Paul Channon. Paul, who had been Leon Brittan's number two at the Department of Trade and Industry – he was an ideal number two – had found himself propelled unexpectedly into the Cabinet as Trade and Industry Secretary the previous year as a result of Leon's unhappy resignation in the wake of the Westland affair. Margaret had intended to drop him altogether after the Election, but relented at the last moment for compassionate reasons – he had recently suffered the tragic death of his student daughter – and demoted him to Transport instead. She was finally to drop him in the ill-fated reshuffle of July 1989. Norman, by contrast, was an experienced Cabinet Minister who had been the Thatcher Government's first Transport Secretary.

I saw Norman in the House after the Election and urged him to scrap the Dock Labour Scheme. He was clearly receptive to the idea. Shortly afterwards, Margaret called a small meeting at Number 10 to have a preliminary discussion of the matter. Apart from Norman, Paul and myself the only others present were Willie Whitelaw and John Wakeham. It was clear that both Norman and Paul were keen to press ahead with abolition, as of course was I. Margaret no longer contested the case for going ahead, but remained terrified at the prospect of a dock strike, and made various unconvincing excuses for delaying any action. She did, however, agree to a further meeting, with the same deliberately restricted cast, to discuss how it might best be done.

At the subsequent meeting Paul argued for a major all-purpose dock reform Bill, of which abolition of the Dock Labour Scheme would be only a part, to be introduced early in the 1988–9 session. Norman, with my strong support, made the case for a short, sharp Bill confined to scrapping the scheme. Paul's proposal smacked of the usual official desire to use any Bill as a vehicle for everything the Department had been wanting to do, but made little political sense: it was obviously right to give the unions the shortest possible time to mobilize their opposition. That, at least, was agreed; but Margaret continued to argue that the time was not ripe.

As 1987 was succeeded by 1988, meeting followed meeting, at which nothing was agreed except contingency plans. A Bill was drafted on a contingency basis, as was a White Paper, and contingency plans were drawn up to minimize the effects of the prolonged strike that Margaret was certain would occur, including mobilization of the police and the army. All this was completed by the autumn of 1988. Eventually, Margaret agreed to go ahead early in the New Year, so that any strike (she reckoned) would be over by the summer recess. But she insisted that the registered dockers should be paid compensation for the loss of the scheme, and asked Norman and me to agree a figure. He proposed a pretty large sum, expecting me to reduce it, which I duly did, and we went back to Margaret with an agreed figure. This she considered far too small, and insisted on £35,000 a head – more even than Norman had originally asked for. By that time I was so anxious to give her no further excuse for procrastination that I grudgingly agreed.

The New Year came, and still Margaret was afraid to act. By this time the small group had been enlarged by the inclusion of Douglas Hurd, then Home Secretary, and responsible for the police, and Malcolm Rifkind, then Scottish Secretary, because of the Scottish Scheme ports. More to the point, the discussions had now been continuing for a year and a half: it was a miracle that there had not been a single leak, not so much as a whisper – a very rare occurrence indeed. When, out of the blue, Margaret did at last agree to go ahead at the beginning of April 1989, and Norman promptly announced it to the House, it burst on an astonished world as a complete surprise.

In the event, there was no prolonged dock strike – merely some half-hearted unofficial industrial action that petered out within a month of the Act becoming law at the beginning of July. I suspect that the dockers were surprised that it took the Thatcher Government no less than ten years before it did away with their statutory racket. The objective, of course, was not to deprive the dockers but to secure an efficient ports industry. And thanks to the 1989 Act, we are now well on the way to achieving it.

Nil Desperandum

In writing of the British labour market it is difficult to strike the right balance between on the one hand its continuing rigidities and on the other hand the improvements that have undoubtedly occurred. The Thatcher period witnessed a big transformation for the better in industrial relations, which had seemed so intractable in the 1970s. There was also a large decline in union power and union membership – and, just as important, the emergence of the 'new realism' on both sides of industry. Despite disappointing unemployment figures, there was an increase of no less than 1½ million in the number of people in work between the cyclical peak of 1979 and that of 1990. In almost every respect, the British labour market of the 1990s was a very different one from that which had attracted the pity of the world during the winter of discontent.

CHAPTER 36

THE MYTH OF A MONETARIST GOLDEN AGE

Far From Plain Sailing · What is Money?
Monetary Policy Reviewed · Transactions Balances
Black Box Monetarism? · White Tie Monetarism
Appendix: Overfunding and the Bill Mountain

Far From Plain Sailing

I HAVE SET OUT THE purposes and limitations of monetary policy as I saw them when I became Chancellor in Chapter 33. The difficult task was to find a practical form in which to embody these principles.

There is a myth that all was plain sailing in the conduct of monetary policy until I began shadowing the Deutschmark in 1987 – or at least until my announcement at the Mansion House of the suspension of the £M3 target in the autumn of 1985. The truth is very different. It was never plain sailing, neither in Geoffrey's time nor mine.

According to this myth, monetary growth was kept within its target range until the policy was wantonly abandoned in either 1985 or 1987 to launch an irresponsible boom. Indeed, this appears to be what many students are nowadays taught at university; and something like it has been adopted for political purposes by many commentators who are far from being monetarists, but are glad of any stick with which to beat the Government of that period. It is not hard to demonstrate that this convenient picture represents a tendentious rewriting of history and distortion of the facts. If there is to be any real understanding of this difficult but important aspect of policy, it is necessary to take the trouble to get at the truth.

The Thatcher Government took over the targeting of £M3 from its

Labour predecessor and maintained a target range for this aggregate during its first seven or eight years in office. But, contrary to the myth of a monetarist golden age, the target was hit only twice – in Geoffrey's last year and in my first (1982–83 and 1983–84). In every other year it was overshot, usually by a wide margin. It was overshot despite a large increase in the target range by Geoffrey in 1982 and an even larger increase by myself in 1986, in one last attempt to make something out of the aggregate. The problems with it were already apparent as far back as 1980 when I was Financial Secretary, and have been explained in Part One of this book.

To recapitulate briefly. The poor performance of the original target aggregate £M3 (which consisted essentially of cash and bank deposits) and the consequent need to supplement it with other indicators, were not surprising in the light of the changes taking place in the financial markets as a result of deregulation. The abolition of exchange control had exposed the London financial market to international competition, while the Latin American debt crisis persuaded the banks that they would be better off at home, competing with the building societies for mortgage business for the first time. At the same time, the building societies, gradually breaking free from their interest-rate cartel, were beginning to compete aggressively with the banks for deposits. Both were offering increasingly generous terms in competing for the same business; yet £M3 did not even include building society deposits. As inflation tumbled and real interest rates turned positive, money was left with the banks not for spending purposes but to earn a worthwhile return. As a result of all these developments, the money statistics were constantly changing their meaning.

At this stage the general reader may care to be reminded of the warning of Miss Prism to her charge in *The Importance of Being Ernest*: 'The chapter on the Fall of the Rupee you may omit. It is somewhat too sensational.' The remainder of this chapter can indeed be omitted without losing the main thread of this book. But those interested in the truth about what did and did not go wrong with the conduct of economic policy during my time as Chancellor should grit their teeth and read on. It may help them to refer back to Part One of this book, where I outlined the Medium Term Financial Strategy, the idea of monetarism as I saw it, and 'the black art of monetary control'.

What is Money?

Doubts had arisen both about the relationship of £M3 to inflation, and about its appropriateness as a definition of money. In the first place, underlying inflation had plummeted from 16½ per cent in the last quarter of 1979 to 6¾ per cent in the last quarter of 1982, despite a massive overshoot in monetary growth, as measured by £M3. In the second place, it was increasingly argued that the £M3 definition was too wide. As real interest rates rose, bank as well as building society deposits took on many of the characteristics of financial investments and were much more a home for savings than a means of spending. This school therefore advocated a move to so-called narrow money – that is, cash plus only those balances likely to be used in settling transactions. Some of the monetarists closest to Margaret Thatcher, such as Alan Walters and Patrick Minford, belonged to the latter group. And there was no-one more contemptuous of 'your M3' than Karl Brunner, the Swiss-American economist of whom Margaret was such an admirer.

In the light of all this, Geoffrey Howe decided to change the monetary target in his 1982 Budget (while I was at Energy), introducing two new target aggregates alongside £M3. One of them was known by the off-putting name of PSL2 (the initials stood for private sector liquidity). Essentially this included building society as well as bank deposits. It was later rechristened M4 and became the main definition of broad money used in this book and in most other studies. The other new target aggregate, M1, was composed of cash and current account balances, which at that time did not pay any interest, but excluded deposit accounts. To his great delight, Geoffrey at last hit his targets – for all three aggregates – in 1982–83. But this was only after he had set a revised target range which, in the case of £M3, was nearly twice that laid down in the original MTFS.

Moreover, this success had been achieved in part by a device known as overfunding. I discuss this technique and its implications, which are still a matter of lively debate, later on. But basically it meant the Government selling more gilt-edged securities than it needed to do to finance its own Budget deficit, in order to attract money that would otherwise have been left with the banks. It was a peculiarly British practice, being unknown in other countries, such as the US and Germany, where the central bank has nothing to do with selling long-term securities for the Government. It was essentially cosmetic; being undertaken simply because the money raised by the sale of additional gilt-edged securities was a subtraction from £M3.

In the light of all these problems, the Government had begun to place increasing reliance on other financial evidence, including in particular the exchange rate. Although it was not yet pursuing an exchange rate target, it had experienced the effective discipline exerted by a high exchange rate during the squeeze of 1980–81. That, indeed, is why, during my time as Financial Secretary, we had been rightly prepared to let £M3 overshoot its range. The first official avowal of the importance attached to the exchange rate in the conduct of monetary policy occurred in the turgid prose of the 1982 Red Book, which stated that:

> The exchange rate is a route through which changes in the money supply affect inflation. It can also be an important influence on financial conditions. External or domestic developments that change the relationship between the domestic money supply and exchange rate may therefore disturb the link between money and prices, at least for a time . . . They are a reason why the Government considers it appropriate to look at the exchange rate in monitoring domestic monetary conditions and in taking decisions about policy.

Following my appointment as Chancellor in June 1983, I received a personal note from David Willetts, an astute young Treasury official, who had been my private secretary when I was Financial Secretary and was later to become a Conservative MP, but who at that time was working on monetary policy, which he clearly felt had become distinctly muddled.

> Probably the main change since your time has been the way policy has degenerated into 'looking at all possible indicators of monetary conditions'. On occasions there is more than a hint of muddling through. Maybe this is inevitable given the failure of the target measure of money always to give a reliable indication of the degree of financial laxity or tightness – especially given the importance of the exchange rate. But it does leave the City unclear about what our intermediate targets really are: they suspect that it is now too easy for us to find a *post hoc* justification for anything we want to do.

Monetary Policy Reviewed

Accordingly, when I first became Chancellor in June 1983, I asked Peter Middleton to organize a number of official papers on macroeconomic strategy, including a review of monetary policy, and in particular a review of whether or not we should join the ERM. I also received at the time a letter from Kit McMahon, the Deputy Governor of the Bank of England, asking about my intentions on monetary policy, although making no reference to the ERM. This was a reasonable request, although it made no practical difference as I had already set the wheels of a review in motion.

What was sad, however, was that the Bank had no contribution to make to the answer. On reflection this is not so surprising. The new and then inexperienced Governor, Robin Leigh Pemberton, had only just taken over; and during the hiatus McMahon was effectively in the driving seat at the Bank: hence of course his authorship of the letter. McMahon's reflexes were essentially neo-Keynesian; and he had little time for monetarism in any shape or form and the role of monetary policy was for him a subordinate one. While McMahon was at the Bank, Eddie

George, the Bank's real monetary expert and later Deputy Governor, was given no role in policy at all, being seen mainly as the Bank's market expert and operator.

The ERM aspect was covered by a paper from Geoffrey Littler, the Second Permanent Secretary in charge of Overseas Finance, who was one of the very few senior Treasury officials at that time in favour of ERM membership. After recalling Margaret's earlier rejection of the idea in 1982 (see Chapter 10) the paper went on to state that the climate for sterling's participation in the ERM was more favourable than it had been in recent years. It referred to the benefit that France had derived from ERM membership, and went on to argue that the case for sterling's participation would be strengthened if a number of conditions were satisfied.

First, the oil market should continue to be relatively settled; second, UK and German policies and economies should continue to converge; third, a clearer way should be seen through the negotiations currently going on over the Community Budget; and fourth, and most important, that the dollar should fall against the Deutschmark. The reasoning was that the dollar was at that time unrealistically high and that it was bound to – and indeed should – fall against the Deutschmark. But when it did, sterling would inevitably fall part of the way with it, making it difficult if not impossible to maintain its ERM parity.

The paper suggested that these conditions might well be fulfilled some time in 1984. In fact it took somewhat longer for the foreign exchange market condition to be fulfilled. The dollar continued its vertiginous rise and did not turn down until 1985. The paper concluded that, in the meantime, private discussions with the Germans about practical UK–German co-operation might be desirable to prepare for membership. I did in fact initiate such discussions, but that was some while later.

At the meeting I held in the summer of 1983 to discuss the ERM paper, the other Treasury mandarins were far less enthusiastic, not least because by that time considerable intellectual capital had been tied up in the existing domestically based policy. Nevertheless, they were well aware – and this had been amply covered in the papers on domestic monetary policy – that there were considerable uncertainties over causal relationships in domestic monetary policy. There were particular difficulties in interpreting the behaviour of monetary aggregates which appeared to be subject to structural velocity changes that could not readily be identified or explained.

The official Treasury line by then was to differentiate between the monetary stance – the total effect of policy on nominal GDP and inflation – and the policy mix. The idea of the latter was that the same overall effect could be achieved by varying combinations of interest rates, exchange rates, and fiscal policy. Thus a low exchange rate would not matter so much if interest rates were high, or vice versa; and weakness on either front could to some extent be offset by a tighter fiscal policy. I confess that I was never entirely happy with this 'policy mix' model, and felt increasing misgivings at the toleration of a falling pound to which it from time to time pointed. Moreover, quite apart from my personal misgivings, it was an almost impossibly difficult concept to put across in a convincing way.

The outcome of the review, which had of course been conducted in close collaboration with the Bank, was somewhat inconclusive. There was general disillusion with £M3, but no interest in Monetary Base Control (MBC has been explained in Chapter 8). Here the Bank's hostility, coupled with the considered rejection in 1981, were decisive. Dissatisfied by the unsatisfactory nature of the outcome but still not entirely clear in my mind as to the best way ahead, I arranged a couple of private meetings in the summer of 1983 with Gordon Pepper, whom I had known for over a decade, and who was at that time the leading monetary analyst in the City.

Pepper was scornful of broad money and favoured going over to Monetary Base Control (MBC). He knew, however, that the Bank, which would have to operate MBC, was very hostile to it; and agreed that in those circumstances to impose it on the Bank would be asking for trouble. He saw some value in using M0, whose composition is essentially the same as that of the monetary base, as an *indicator*; but in general felt that nothing short of full-blooded MBC would do, a view that he has consistently reiterated since.

Pepper was particularly derisory of £M3. Its link with fiscal policy, which so much appealed to Treasury and Bank officials, was seen by him as a neo-Keynesian contamination of monetary policy. Pepper also claimed that the Bank favoured £M3 because its close links with the PSBR meant that any excessive growth in the aggregate could be attributed as much to failures of Treasury as of Bank control. I pointed out that the official preference for £M3 was based not only on the link with fiscal policy, but also on the fact that during the Heath inflation it was the movement of £M3, rather than that of M1, which had provided the warning. Pepper replied that M0 had provided the earliest warning of all.

Transactions Balances

Inside the official Treasury, Terry Burns was as almost sceptical as Gordon Pepper about the continued value of targeting £M3. But most officials were nervous about downgrading £M3, which was the only aggregate accepted by the financial markets. Indeed, both the City and the financial Press were incapable, at that time, of conceiving that 'money' could mean anything else – a form of myopia that is not wholly eradicated, even today. In the light of this, I was not yet willing to abandon broad money targets altogether, but insisted on having a separate target for narrow money – that is the kind of money that is actually used for settling transactions. Here I was at one with Alan Walters (who had by then left the Government service).

The choice of a narrow aggregate boiled down to a choice between three different totals known as M0, M1 and M2. The first, M0, consisted of notes and coins in the hands of the public, plus till money in the banks, plus an extremely small quantity of deposits kept by the banks at the Bank of England for operational reasons. It was to all intents and purposes cash. M1 included money in current accounts (called sight deposits in the US) as well as cash; while M2, which was nearly fifteen times as large as M0, included almost all bank and building society deposits. It was claimed to be a measure of transactions balances which were held for spending rather than saving. The basis of this claim was that it excluded so-called wholesale deposits – that is, deposits in excess of £100,000, and smaller ones that could not be quickly withdrawn.

The Bank, where Eddie George was by then in charge of monetary policy, argued strongly in favour of M2. I was sceptical. Not only was the definition somewhat arbitrary, but this was a newly constructed aggregate for which we had no significant track record. It was just as well I was, since its behaviour proved to be impossibly wayward.

Terry Burns and I both favoured a non-interest bearing narrow aggregate, since this came closest to a true measure of transactions balances. The choice was between non-interest bearing M1 (or NIB M1 as it was known to monetary policy afficionados) – that is, M1 excluding all interest-bearing current accounts – and M0. Terry on balance preferred NIB M1 because it showed a clearer and more robust relationship with interest rates. Nevertheless, I decided in favour of M0. I was concerned that NIB M1 might be too interest rate sensitive, since the borderline between non-interest bearing and interest-bearing current accounts was exceptionally fluid. Terry subsequently became an eloquent advocate of M0. It was undoubtedly a primitive measure of money, but its track record showed an impressively stable relationship with Nominal GDP. I announced tentatively in my first Mansion House Speech, on 28 October 1983 that 'M0 could have a more important part to play in monitoring monetary conditions'.

Black Box Monetarism?

As the account I have just given shows, nearly all the reputable monetarist gurus – with the exception of the City analyst Tim Congdon – so far from urging broad money targets on me criticized me for giving too much influence to broad money in general and £M3 in particular. The enthusiasm of the hard-core monetarists for M0 was to some extent based on wishful thinking, since many of them hoped it would be a staging post to Monetary Base Control, even though I had made it clear that that was not what I had in mind. The problem, however, was that M0 went down very badly with City opinion and financial journalists; and the Bank of England initially treated the measure with open contempt. Non-monetarist and anti-monetarist economists (who are in a majority) found an M0 target even more absurd than monetary targets in general.

This was because it consisted overwhelmingly of notes and coins. Students had long been taught that cash was only the 'small change of the monetary system'. People find it hard to believe that the amount of spending had anything to do with people's supply of ready cash. If people needed more notes and coins they could always get them by drawing on their bank, building society, or Post Office savings accounts. There were complaints, too, that using M0 was what was termed a 'black box' form of monetarism. In other words, however good its track record as an indicator, there was no way in which M0 growth could be said to be the *cause* of inflation. An excessively large increase in M0 was no doubt a sign of inflationary pressure, but could not be the cause of it.

This objection missed the point. Had there been a monetary aggregate with a clear and predictable causal connection with inflation, I should certainly have used it. The whole problem was that no such aggregate existed. In its absence an accurate and up-to-date indicator of what was happening to Nominal GDP would be invaluable. If such an indicator causes warning bells to ring in time and leads the monetary authorities to take action, such as an increase in interest rates, when danger threatens, then it serves its purpose. I was well aware that, in an ideal world, it might have been better to have had a reliable measure of all genuine transactions balances, including not only cash but all those bank and building society deposits held as a reservoir for spending rather than as a home for savings. M2 had been specifically constructed for this purpose. Unfortunately, changes in the banking system made it impossible to find a reliable measure of transactions balances. I opted for M0 simply because statistical studies made by the Bank as well as the Treasury showed it to be a very good 'proxy'. All case studies going back over many decades suggested that M0 was much more closely related to Nominal GDP – and thus ultimately to the price level – than any of the larger aggregates. Despite inventions like credit cards, the trend relationship of cash balances to the national income has changed surprisingly little over the years.

It was striking that for several years the Bundesbank had been pursuing a successful anti-inflation policy in Germany, using as its monetary target a weighted index known as Central Bank Money, just over half of which consisted of M0. In 1988 the Bundesbank switched from this index to the broad aggregate, M3, only to experience much the same kind of problem that we had suffered with £M3 – to the considerable discomfort of other ERM members.

It was clearly a disadvantage of M0 that it was not much of an advance indicator. Some of its strongest supporters claimed that it gave a very short lead. But I always regarded it as essentially an up-to-date contemporaneous indicator – which was a great deal better than the tardy and uncertain figures for Nominal GDP itself, even though by the time M0 was clearly signalling danger, the economy would already be experiencing inflationary pressures. A rather more serious shortcoming was the failure of M0 to give a true picture at one or two crucial points, notably in early 1988.

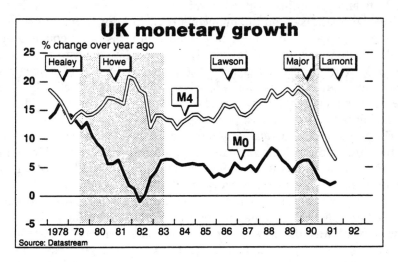

White Tie Monetarism

I announced the preliminary outcome of the monetary policy review in my first address to the Lord Mayor's Banquet at the Mansion House on 20 October 1983. This was one of the regular slots in the Chancellor's diary, and one of the few official occasions on which I was invited to bring Thérèse. Much to her astonishment, she was whisked away as soon as we arrived at the Mansion House, the convention then being that the wives of the speakers, who are all invited to the banquet, had dinner by themselves in a room upstairs. They emerged after dinner on to the gallery, from where they were expected to gaze admiringly at their husbands making speeches below.

It was not until the subsequent first-ever election of a woman Lord Mayor of London, Mary Donaldson, that this archaic practice ceased. Thereafter Thérèse always sat at my side at the Lord Mayor's table. But it was the other diners at this great white-tie occasion who suffered the real hardship, since they had to endure a quite excessive number of rather heavy speeches. The Chancellor had the great advantage of speaking early after a review of his year in office by the outgoing Lord Mayor, but was followed by the Governor of the Bank of England, the Chairman of the Stock Exchange and (in my day) the Chairman of Lloyd's of London. My own speech in 1983 was rather too long, and I was careful in future years to make it shorter.

The formal title of the occasion is 'The Lord Mayor's Banquet for the Bankers and Merchants of the City of London', and it is assumed that this is therefore a fitting audience to listen to the Chancellor and the Governor dilating on monetary policy. In fact most of them are interested in more profitable if less cerebral pursuits, and leave such matters to advisers, analysts and subordinates down the line.

But the markets – and the financial press, too, for that matter – expect an annual explanation of monetary policy, and this was a convenient and well-reported (and indeed televised) occasion on which to provide one. I simply had to accept the fact that I could not expect a particularly responsive audience; as the few who, well fed and well wined, kept themselves alert among the brandy fumes and cigar smoke, did so only by laying bets on the length of my speech.

The immediate practical consequence of the review was that in place of the three monetary targets Geoffrey had bequeathed me, I substituted two in my first Budget in 1984. One was for the old standby £M3. Despite all its faults – of which the most serious was its omission of building society deposits – this measure had been in every previous statement of the MTFS, and was familiar to, and beloved by, the financial markets. The second was the newcomer M0 – or the 'wide monetary base' – which I have already explained. In both these aggregates I included a declining path stretching to 1988–89. But because of the predictable long-run trend for the public to economize on holdings of cash I set lower growth ranges for M0 than for £M3.

As I explained to a restless House of Commons in the course my 1984 Budget Speech:

> One important development has been the decision to give a more explicit role to the narrow measures of money. Sterling M3 and the other broad aggregates give a good indication of the growth of liquidity. But a large proportion of this money is in reality a form of savings, invested for the interest it can earn. In defining policy it is therefore helpful also to make specific reference to measures of money which relate more narrowly to balances held for current spending . . . The two target aggregates will have equal importance in the conduct of the policy. And the authorities will continue to take into account other measures of money . . . as well as wider evidence of financial conditions, including the exchange rate.

In my first Mansion House Speech, in October 1983, I had stated that: 'None of the Ms is a perfect guide to the underlying concept they seek to reflect.' It was obvious that the exercise of judgement and discretion was an inescapable consequence of the evolution of the monetary system. Yet it was hard to persuade the financial markets of this necessity: the City was inclined to believe that any departure from the original rules was politically expedient and therefore economically unsound. I tried to reassure the markets in the Mansion House Speech by shifting the emphasis of policy from the monetary targets to the explicit commitment to 'a continuing decline in the growth of money GDP . . . The rules are clear, but must necessarily be interpreted with discretion.'

In time it became clear that the real problem with M0 was that it lacked street credibility. That meant that none of the feedback mechanisms were in operation. The achievement of the M0 target – or even its undershooting – had no great effect on inflationary expectations. Here it was at the opposite end of the spectrum to the exchange rate target, where the mechanisms at work are much more obvious and, so long as the official commitment is credible, the feedback is very powerful indeed.

APPENDIX: OVERFUNDING
AND THE BILL MOUNTAIN

OVERFUNDING WAS ESSENTIALLY A way of massaging the money numbers to make it look as if monetary policy was tighter than it was. But as some influential commentators see ending it as a grave error, responsible for our subsequent inflationary difficulties, a brief account is necessary.

The Bank of England and the Treasury stumbled on this technique during the early 1980s when they were anxious to meet the Government's £M3 target, but did not want to raise base rates any higher than they were. Overfunding averaged £3.4 billion a year over the four years 1981–82 to 1984–85. On average £M3 grew by nearly 4 per cent a year less than if there had been no overfunding.

Overfunding means that the Government sells more of its own debt (principally gilt-edged securities, or 'gilts' for short, but also including National Savings bonds and certificates) than it requires to finance its Budget deficit. The essentials are simple. Imagine that Mr X – or more likely company treasurer X – buys more Government securities and runs down his bank balance. The quantity of bank deposits declines and with it most broad measures of the money supply.

What did the Bank of England do with the proceeds? It bought bills from the market. If these were Treasury bills, Government debt was extinguished. If they were commercial bills, the Bank of England took over the debt. In either case commercial bank lending fell – the counterpart on the assets side to the fall in private deposits. In effect, a part of bank lending was being nationalized: a curious activity for a Conservative Government to promote.

Looking at it from the point of view of the banks, deposits are normally raised to whatever level is necessary to finance a desired level of bank lending to the public and private sector. When bank lending falls off, so do bank deposits. The ability of the banking system, taken together, to decide its own level of deposits, within prudential limits, is one of the paradoxes of banking explained in most banking textbooks.

But does the overfunding operation tighten monetary policy to any significant extent? In the first place, the type of bank deposit that is most readily shifted into gilts is much more likely to be held as a savings deposit than for transaction purposes. In the second place, and more fundamentally, by buying bills from the market, the Bank of England was reinjecting in a different form the liquidity it had extracted by the original funding.

The complications to which overfunding led were, however, immense. The Bank of England accumulated a vast and ever-growing bill mountain, which made the day-to-day conduct of monetary policy increasingly diffi-cult. Moreover, as the policy continued, the Bank began to be worried about running out of bills to buy, and started to investigate increasingly desperate measures, such as making special deposits with the clearing banks. This would have been a bizarre way of 'tightening' monetary policy. The Bank had only a few years earlier been asking the clearers to make special deposits with itself to immobilize some of their resources.

All that was in practice achieved was a tilt in the yield curve, so that short-term interest rates, influenced by the Bank's purchase of bills, were slightly lower, and long rates, influenced by its extra sales of gilt-edged, slightly higher. This was clearly an own goal; since, other things being equal, it made it more attractive for companies to finance themselves by borrowing from the banks rather than issuing longer-term corporate debt or raising equity.

In addition, the reduction in short-term rates created what was known as the 'bill leak'. That is, corporate treasurers found it profitable to sell commercial banks' bills to the banks and deposit the proceeds in the wholesale ('interbank') market to obtain a higher return. Apart from its inherent undesirability, 'round tripping' (as it was called) created additional bank deposits and undermined the cosmetic purpose of the whole overfunding operation. At the time the Bank of England under-played the importance of round tripping; but it now freely admits that it was a significant problem.

By the time of my Mansion House Speech of 17 October 1985, the position had become ridiculous. The bill mountain had grown to fresh heights; yet £M3 had in the latest twelve months grown by 14 per cent compared with a 5 to 9 per cent target rate. The conclusion I reached was that overfunding should be abandoned and net sales of gilts confined, as in the old days, to financing the Budget deficit.

The new funding rule, which I had devised with the help of my officials, was that gilt-edged and National Savings sales to non-banks should total the amount needed to fund the PSBR plus the amount needed to offset (or 'sterilize') net Government sales of sterling in the foreign exchange (or minus the amount needed to offset the net purchase of sterling in the foreign exchange market, as the case may be). This rule was continued even when the Budget went into surplus: that is to say, debt was repaid. This was both logical and classic; but like everything else in this field, it inevitably attracted criticism. The idea that the repayment of part of the national debt was either improper or inflationary would have amazed Gladstone, and he would have been right.

The new procedure meant, however, that the £M3 target became even more transparently meaningless, since the only means of hitting it would be via short-term interest rates, whose effect on bank lending and bank deposits was uncertain and delayed. This did not cause me sleepless nights, however, since the relationship between £M3 and Nominal GDP was itself demonstrably uncertain and unpredictable, M0 was a more reliable indicator of Nominal GDP; and I had by that time become convinced that the best guide to the conduct of monetary policy, which meant in practice the appropriate movement in short-term interest rates, was in British circumstances, at any rate, the exchange rate. Indeed as the following chapter will make clear, this is how we were in fact operating, and it is clearly desirable that the rhetoric should match the reality as often as possible.

There were no real problems about the idea of bringing systematic overfunding to an end with either the Treasury or the Bank of England. But Margaret, who liked anti-inflationary symbols as much as she disliked tightening monetary policy in practice, needed some persuasion to agree to the suspension of the £M3 target.

It is open to anyone to say that monetary policy should have been tighter, so long as they realize that real interest rates in 1985 averaged some 7 per cent; very much higher than they had been in the early 1980s. But the case should be argued directly with acknowledgement of the consequences that tightening would have had for short-term interest rates, and not stated in terms either of dubious monetary targets that were seldom if ever hit or of a cosmetic technique that created far more trouble than it was worth.

CHAPTER 37

THE STERLING CRISIS OF 1984–85

The Trauma of July 1984 · Ours Not to Reason Why
The July Hike Undone · The Ingham Run on the Pound
Damage Limitation, January 1985

The Trauma of July 1984

WHILE M0 LACKED CREDIBILITY and thus the ability to influence the markets, the exchange rate manifestly had it. That in itself was reason enough to pay increasing attention to the exchange rate.

In my first year at Number 11 sterling had gradually fallen back somewhat from its pre-election peak, but it still remained above the low point of early 1983 (see chart in Chapter 8). Moreover, from early in 1984 the pound had levelled off against all major currencies apart from the dollar. So it was reasonable to speak in terms of a rising dollar rather than a falling pound. With underlying inflation moving gradually downwards from 5 per cent towards 4 per cent, I was content to leave base rates fluctuating around 9 per cent, where they had been since June 1983.

The first real trauma did not occur until July 1984. Three sources of upward pressure on base rates developed very suddenly. The combination of rapid growth in the US and anxiety about the continuing large Federal deficit led to a sharp rise in US short-term interest rates between May and July; and the dollar started on one of its upward spurts. The financial markets began to worry about the miners' strike and the threat of a national dock strike (which in the end proved short lived, starting in August and ending in September). Lastly, the money supply figures for June were erratically high and, in the prevailing nervous atmosphere, increased financial market anxieties. When the Bank of England made a 'technical adjustment in the profile of its bill dealing rates' on 25 June, it

461

took the unusual step of making a statement saying that it saw no need on monetary policy grounds for a general increase in interest rates. Within a few days that statement had backfired.

On 5 July sterling fell sharply against all currencies, not just the US dollar, and I increased base rates up to 10 per cent. On 9 July, the dock strike was called and on 10 July the shock-horror money supply figures appeared. During those few days three-month market interest rates shot up to almost 12 per cent, as the money markets had anticipated that the Government would respond to events by raising interest rates to defend sterling. The markets' move steadied the pound, but left the 'authorities' (as the Treasury and the Bank are collectively known) with a level of market interest rates quite incompatible with 10 per cent base rates. There had of course been many previous occasions when sterling weakness had forced the Government to raise interest rates. But this occasion, when the market had acted first, was a disconcerting new experience, subtly different from past periods of pressure.

There was a feeling of impotence in the air at a meeting I held at the Treasury on Wednesday, 11 July. The Bank recommended accepting the rise in interest rates. Otherwise the credibility of monetary policy would be put into question and sterling would fall sharply. They pointed out that in the circumstances they were powerless to influence the market by the usual mechanisms. They therefore favoured a two-point rise in base rates to 12 per cent, which would have the bonus effect of allowing large sales of gilts to be made, thereby reducing £M3 growth.

Ian Stewart, the Economic Secretary, to whom I had delegated the monetary policy responsibilities I used to have when Financial Secretary under Geoffrey, because of his understanding of the City and the financial markets, strongly endorsed the Bank's position. I tried to put the Bank's anxieties into relatively simple words later on in my Mansion House Speech of 18 October, when I said that the rise in interest rates in the money market could not have been resisted 'without temporarily injecting cash into the system on such a scale which, had we done it, might have created dangerous doubts about the Government's central anti-inflationary strategy.'

The Treasury mandarins, however, were unhappy with the Bank of England's advice, on three grounds. First they did not like being dictated to by the foreign exchange market in this way. In particular, they feared that if we let the markets do this to us once, it would set a most undesirable precedent, and we would have lost control of interest rates altogether. Second, they did not believe there was any objective reason why interest rates should go any higher – indeed they would have liked on 'economic' grounds to see them lower. And third, they did not want to see the option of a lower pound, which on balance they regarded as the lesser evil, ruled out in this way.

I had of course warned Margaret of the likely need for a further rise in interest rates, and told her that I was holding a meeting with the Bank that morning to discuss the situation. Halfway through the meeting my office heard from Number 10 that Alan Walters was over on one of his occasional visits to London (he was by then living in Washington) and the Prime Minister would like him to join us. I replied that he was welcome to do so. When he arrived I asked him for his opinion and he suggested splitting the difference. He saw no monetary reason for an increase in interest rates, but because of the pressures from the US, he thought it might be right to go up by one percentage point. That seemed to me almost guaranteed to get the worst of both worlds, and would certainly fail to get funding restarted. I believed we had no option but to raise interest rates enough to regain control of the situation, as the Bank had recommended.

The Treasury mandarins reluctantly concurred. I fully understood their reluctance. I did not relish being dictated to by the money market any more than they did, and subsequently commissioned a paper on how we might regain control. But I had no doubt at the time that I had to bite the bullet. I then went to see Margaret, to give her the unwelcome news. She accepted it with ill grace, expressing the desire that we should get interest rates down again as soon as possible.

Ours Not to Reason Why

There was still the problem of how to present the two-point rise, which I raised at the end of the meeting at the Treasury. The financial Press did not seem to realize what was novel about the situation and treated it as an old-fashioned sterling crisis. Yet in previous such crises the authorities had, or felt they had, a choice of three responses to pressure on the pound: intervention (i.e. the Bank of England buying sterling), letting the exchange rate take the strain, and raising interest rates. Given that choice, I would have liked to try intervention; Treasury officials would have preferred sterling to take some of the strain, at least initially. But as things were, we did not – as I saw it – have the luxury of a debate: the financial markets had already imposed their own rise in interest rates.

At that time it would have been difficult to justify, on the domestic grounds we customarily used, a rise which took real interest rates to their highest levels since the War. On the other hand, had we given pressure on sterling as the reason (which, as I have indicated, was in any case true only indirectly), it would have been an open invitation to the financial markets to repeat the episode. As the main event in the foreign exchange markets – then and for many months to come – was the seemingly irresistible rise of the dollar, which put downward pressure on all other currencies, it was unlikely to be long before another such occasion arose.

After considerable discussion, we reached a rather complicated conclusion. The Bank would conduct its daily operations in the money market so as to leave the clearing banks technically with the option of whether to increase their base rates to 11½ or 12 per cent, knowing full well that they would in fact choose 12 per cent. The Treasury's and the Bank's press officers would then give informal guidance to the effect that the banks had been obliged to move by the structure of market rates and hoped that base rate would not stay up for long.

A message along these lines was duly disseminated, but it did not go down very well in the markets, especially in the Bank's version. The conclusion I drew from this episode was that it was best on all future occasions to say as little as possible, and to get the Bank to do likewise. Not only would this reduce the likelihood of the Bank and Treasury saying different things, but it is invariably better to let interest rate changes speak for themselves and to give no hostages to fortune.

Throughout my time as Chancellor I made a considerable effort to ensure that both Treasury and Bank sang the same song. This was for the most practical of reasons. The Press were always trying to discover differences, not to say rows, between the Treasury – and in particular me – and the Bank, and anything that enabled them to do so risked undermining the effectiveness of the day-to-day conduct of monetary policy. So far as I was concerned I had two sets of advisers on monetary policy: the official Treasury and the Bank. Usually, of course, they were agreed; but when they were not, I was if anything more likely to come down on the side of the Bank when it came to interest rate changes.

Inevitably, I discussed the background to the July interest rate hike in my Mansion House Speech of 18 October 1984. This was to be my last significant utterance as an unreconstructed parochial monetarist. I reiterated the standard Treasury line:

> It is the monetary aggregates that are of central relevance to judging monetary conditions and determining interest rates. That has always been our policy and it remains so. We take the exchange rate into account when its behaviour suggests that the domestic monetary indicators are giving a false reading, which they are not. Provided monetary conditions are kept under firm control, excessive movements, whether in the money or exchange markets in response to outside influences, will tend to correct themselves relatively quickly.

This line was a fiction even when I uttered it, as the exchange rate played a much larger part in policy than I was prepared to admit in public. But there was a genuine difficulty about any alternative presentation. The Commons Treasury Committee and others were continually asking Ministers and senior officials who came before it what our exchange rate policy was; and outside the ERM it was a very difficult question to answer. The idea of giving weight to the exchange rate as a factor in monetary policy decisions, but not having an exchange rate target, was extremely hard to put across. In late 1984, opinion veered between attributing to the Government a secret sterling target and believing that we were completely indifferent as to where the pound went.

This difficulty was compounded by the fact (which again ERM membership would largely have avoided) that the exchange rate, in those days, was still seen almost exclusively in terms of the sterling/dollar rate, and the dollar was soaring ludicrously into the stratosphere at the time. This 'misplaced preoccupation with the sterling-dollar rate', as I described it in my 1984 Mansion House speech, was a hangover from Bretton Woods when all parities were stated in terms of the dollar. It became out of date when the dollar finally floated in 1973. But the habit remained for a ludicrously long period – no doubt reflecting among other things the City's continuing preoccupation with the English-speaking world and reluctance to become seriously involved in what was going on in Europe.

It was about this time that Peter Middleton, at his suggestion and with my blessing, began a campaign to persuade the broadcasting media, and particularly BBC TV and ITN, to refer to the exchange rate index (ERI) for sterling in their bulletins. The custom then prevalent of referring exclusively to the pound/dollar rate meant that every time the dollar soared, we got a 'pound plunges' story on the TV news. Knowing how sensitive the BBC in particular was to any hint of political pressure, I felt it better for my Permanent Secretary rather than me to do this. Peter's campaign was ultimately successful, although it took a considerable time to get there.

The July Hike Undone

Meanwhile, the weeks following the July interest rate hike had seen a welcome calm return to the foreign exchange markets, and I was able to undo 1½ points of the two-point rise, in stages, by the middle of August. Despite this reduction, throughout the autumn of 1984 the advice I continued to receive from both Treasury officials and the Bank of England was that monetary conditions remained tight, and that there was a convincing case for lower interest rates. Although I queried the advice at the time, I mistakenly accepted it, and authorized a further one percentage point reduction to 9½ per cent, in two stages, in November. My misgivings were based partly on a general sense that we were being imprudent, but more particularly because sterling was continuing to slide – something to which I felt the Treasury mandarins gave too little weight.

Pressure for an increase in interest rates did not start to build up again until the publication on 11 December of another large and erratic increase in £M3 in November, this time attributable for the most part to a surge in personal borrowing to finance the massive oversubscription of the British Telecom flotation. This unsettled the market, and in the last few weeks of the year, ominously, the pound, which had hitherto suffered from the superdollar no more than any other currency, started to slide against other currencies, too.

In the middle of December, I decided to take a long weekend off and spend it with Thérèse and the children at an hotel on the Kent coast. Although it might seem rather odd to go to the seaside in December, the sea breezes on the beach were wonderfully invigorating and the children were able to swim in the indoor pool at the hotel. It was from the hotel that I telephoned Peter Middleton to tell him that I thought events in the foreign exchange markets were looking increasingly dangerous and that it might be necessary to raise interest rates. He replied that there was no need to worry and that I should concentrate on enjoying my brief holiday. I was soon to regret having allowed him to talk me out of an interest rate rise in this way. For the result was a larger increase than anything I had in mind a few weeks later. Although sterling stabilized before the markets closed for the Christmas holidays, it began to weaken again when trading resumed in January.

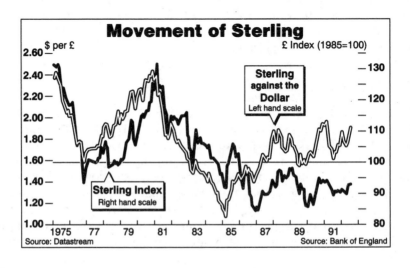

Movement of Sterling

2.60 $ per £   £ Index (1985=100)

Sterling against the Dollar
Left hand scale

Sterling Index
Right hand scale

Source: Datastream   Source: Bank of England

The Ingham Run on the Pound

One of the most self-defeating aspects of the Thatcher regime was Margaret's excessive and increasing reliance on Bernard Ingham, her long-serving Press Secretary and personal confidant. A blunt, sometimes thuglike, xenophobic Yorkshireman, and inordinately proud of it, Ingham became a tremendous admirer and promoter of the Prime Minister and her activities; but he never escaped from his Labour background sufficiently to understand the market economy – still less to persuade others of its merit. He was only really at home with the tabloids – above all the *Sun* – and once rebuked a newly appointed Press Secretary of mine for wasting time lunching with a senior *Financial Times* writer, instead of cultivating those who really mattered.

At quite an early stage, Margaret decided that she had no time to read the newspapers during the week. Instead, Ingham would get into Number 10 very early each morning, go through the papers himself, and prepare her a crisply written press summary. This had a selection and a slant that was very much his own. It would usually start with the *Sun*, the paper he himself was closest to and which he had taught Margaret represented the true views of the man on the street. It was also the paper whose contents he could most readily influence. This led to a remarkable circularity. Margaret would sound off about something, Ingham would then translate the line into *Sun*-ese and feed it to that newspaper, which would normally use it. This would then take pride of place in the news summary he provided for Margaret, who marvelled at the unique rapport she evidently enjoyed with the British people.

In his own way, Ingham was an outstandingly competent and thoroughly professional operator; but his successes were obtained at a high price. Margaret Thatcher was promoted, but her political and economic beliefs were not – with the exception of a truculent chauvinism, which was originally a caricature of her views but eventually became almost indistinguishable from her own as she started to live up to her caricature. Moreover, his concept of promoting her included denigrating her Cabinet colleagues. This not only irked the colleagues, but was plainly unhelpful to the Government as a whole.

He was unhelpful in other ways, too. In private, Margaret was in the habit of letting off steam in a thoroughly indiscreet and intemperate way, going far beyond the rather attractive outspokenness that marked her utterances in public. Ingham frequently failed to discern the distinction, and relayed to a wide audience sentiments that should never have been given a public airing. His view of the relative importance of her political colleagues and himself was well illustrated by the story he himself told on television in the wake of her resignation in 1990. Margaret, in her last days at Number 10, was evidently bitterly lamenting how the Party had turned against her. 'Don't worry about *them*, Prime Minister', he claimed to have told her, seeking to comfort her, *'We're* right behind you.' That his perspective could be so distorted as to say this in the final stages of a leadership election in which it was the colleagues ('them') who had the voting power, and the courtiers, on whose behalf he spoke, who had none, is in its way even more revealing.

There is no doubt that he served her with dog-like devotion for eleven long years. But he reinforced all her worst characteristics and, unwittingly, did her a profound disservice. Willie Whitelaw, seeing this clearly, several times sought to persuade her that the time had come to find a new Press Secretary, but she would never hear of it. Although it was the last thing Ingham wanted, he undoubtedly contributed to her downfall.

This digression may seem a long way removed from the currency turmoils of the winter of 1984-85. But alas it is not: the continuing upward surge of the dollar in the first few months of 1985 would have made life difficult for sterling in any event, but matters were made far worse by a self-inflicted wound suffered by the Government, thanks to Ingham.

There had been no intervention to support sterling in December and very early January. It seemed to me folly to squander our then very limited reserves against a strong adverse tide of sentiment. Unfortunately the pound was given a downward shove by a story in *The Sunday Times* (a paper to which the business world tends to pay exaggerated attention) on Sunday, 6 January 1985:

> According to the highest sources in Whitehall yesterday, Mrs Thatcher, supported by the Chancellor of the Exchequer, Nigel Lawson, is determined to maintain a 'hands off' policy even if the pound falls to parity (£1 = $1). Mrs Thatcher, according to the sources, believes the pound will eventually find its own level. The Government's decision last summer to raise rates to protect the pound is now officially regarded as a mistake, and not to be repeated.

The story came from Ingham, who was aware of Margaret's theoretical distaste for 'bucking the [foreign exchange] market' and her hatred of high interest rates, but had concocted out of them a false account not only of my views, but even of hers.

Although Margaret was in principle a free floater, she was in practice schizoid about the issue. She deeply disliked a falling pound, particularly against the dollar. Her fixation with the United States made her share to the full the conventional exaggerated attention accorded to the sterling/dollar rate. Anyone who thought she would be indifferent to a 'one dollar pound' did not know the lady. She was most definitely not Milton Friedman in drag.

Predictably, *The Sunday Times* story knocked sterling not only against the dollar, but against the Deutschmark and other currencies as well. A good set of money supply figures was set aside early the following week as the market concluded that the Government was unwilling to defend the pound. I protested strongly to Margaret and received an assurance from her that all future questions about sterling would not be answered by Ingham but would be referred to the Treasury. But I did not feel that words alone would be enough, and on Friday, 11 January, with the pound worryingly weak, I insisted on a 1 per cent rise in base rates from 9½ to 10½ per cent, in large part as a clear demonstration that *The Sunday Times* story was wrong. This action should have demonstrated to anyone at all *au fait* with monetary policy that the Government was indeed concerned with sterling. I went off to Chevening for the normal pre-Budget weekend on Saturday, 12 January, imagining that I had seen the end of the Ingham affair.

The newspapers arrived late at Chevening that Sunday; and my officials had failed to check on the early editions available in London on Saturday night. I was therefore taken completely by surprise when I was telephoned by an excitable Margaret Thatcher at Chevening early on the Sunday morning. She had heard on the BBC radio news a summary of the main stories in the early editions of the Sunday newspapers, several of which led with a report that the Government was prepared to let the pound fall as far as the currency markets cared to push it. *The Sunday Times* carried the story under the banner headline 'Thatcher Ready to Let £1 Equal $1'. Variations on the same theme appeared in other papers. Only the *Observer* took a different line, saying that the Government had 'switched to determined defence of the exchange rate'. The paper's economic editor, William Keegan, was no friend of the Government's economic policy, but he had good contacts at the Bank and successfully withstood pressures from his own paper to toe the Number 10 line and not go out on a limb.

Margaret was horrified that I had not, as she saw it, done anything about the stories. I told Margaret that I was even more horrified that they had appeared in the first place. I also undertook to get my Press Secretary to speak to the BBC forthwith to let them have an authoritative denial of the story, which he did, and this was duly broadcast. What I did not know was that, in answer to questions following the previous Friday's lobby briefing for the Sunday papers, Ingham had totally undermined the interest rate rise in terms which were outrageous if he understood what he was doing, and totally improper and a breach of his earlier undertaking if he did not. He has himself admitted subsequently that he 'vehemently stated that the Government was not going to waste its reserves on supporting the pound'.

The following day I summoned Ingham to my study at Number 11 and gave him a roasting. He seemed subdued, and apologized. But Margaret, when I tackled her about it, flatly refused to believe that he was responsible for the Sunday paper stories. Robert Harris remarks in his biography of Ingham, 'Had the error been made by anyone else, especially a Minister, she would surely have turned the flame thrower of her wrath fully upon him. But Ingham was different. She went out of her way to ensure that everyone knew he was still in favour.' Indeed, at a party that very Monday evening she showed him around, saying 'He's the greatest'.

Damage Limitation, January 1985

The Ingham story was the end of all hopes of a reflective weekend on the Budget. I left Chevening to return to Downing Street straight after lunch on Sunday to try and further limit the damage Ingham had done. Treasury press officers telephoned the daily newspapers to ensure that the Monday Press rebutted the Sunday stories, and indicated the Government's willingness to accept a further rise in base rates to defend sterling. Robin Leigh-Pemberton was away for the weekend; I arranged a meeting at six o'clock that Sunday evening with Eddie George, then the executive director of the Bank in charge of monetary policy.

It was obvious to both of us that, when the markets opened on Monday, the pound would come under very severe pressure, and that interest rates would have to be increased. I went next door to see Margaret at Number 10 at half past eight that same evening, and warned her that unless interest rates were raised quite sharply the pound would go into free fall. The thought of the pound dropping below one dollar had put the fear of God into her. The sterling/dollar rate touched a new low of $1.10 in the Far East before the London markets opened; and the Bank literally unveiled a 1½ per cent rise in its Minimum Lending Rate (MLR) to 12 per cent. (Until the abolition of MLR on 20 August 1981, the Bank had advertised changes in the rate by drawing the small pair of green velvet curtains which covered the notice board on which it was pinned. Ever since then – until January 1985 – they had remained drawn.)

Of course the temporary restoration of MLR was little more than a dramatic symbol. The authorities, as I explained in Part One, had never really abandoned their responsibility for determining short-term interest rates. Giving the markets a greater role was always a charade and one from which I steadily departed. The main effect of the charade on the markets was to make the authorities look weak and indecisive.

Nor did I rely on higher interest rates alone. After staying out of the foreign exchange markets in December the Bank of England, along with other central banks, intervened to support sterling, to the tune of a published $500 billion of intervention in January and February combined. But neither the 12 January interest rate rise nor the intervention proved sufficient to halt the run on the pound. One worry was a weakening of the oil price, which seemed much lower than it was, given that the price was denominated in rising dollars.

On 28 January, with sterling still suffering from both Ingham and a weak oil price, and with uncertainty on the latter front compounded by an OPEC meeting starting that day, I authorized another 2 per cent increase in base rates to 14 per cent – the highest level for three years and a level they were not to attain again until May 1989. Nevertheless it was much less of a trauma than the 14 January increase – or even than the increase the previous July – largely because it was widely seen as the necessary completion of the 14 January rise. (See base rate chart in Chapter 67.)

I made no attempt to postpone the 28 January hike even though I had to appear before the Treasury Committee that very afternoon – something I normally enjoyed but on this occasion it made me feel uncomfortably like Daniel in the lion's den. In fact I came out of it reasonably well, mainly by explaining factually and carefully the nature of the turmoil in the currency markets.

But in less specialist circles the Government was seen to be very much on the ropes, and it was no surprise that Labour tabled one of their rare censure motions for debate on 31 January. Margaret opened and I wound up for the Government. Fortunately for us the Kinnock/Hattersley team took charge for Labour. (Roy Hattersley was then Shadow Chancellor, a post he was eventually obliged to relinquish to the more effective John Smith.) Kinnock's proposal for bringing back exchange control and 'taking power' to set interest rates at a low level carried little conviction.

Both Kinnock and Hattersley made the mistake of not seriously probing the monetary side (where Labour tends to be badly informed) and instead broadening their attack into a general indictment of the Government's performance and notably of the level of unemployment. But given the increasing signs that Scargill was about to lose the miners' strike, our back benches were solidly behind us, and it was not hard to see off the Opposition attack. According to the political correspondent of the *Daily Telegraph*, it was 'another dismal performance by Labour on a major Commons occasion'. We were very lucky.

CHAPTER 38

JUDGE AND JURY

The US Financial Cavalry · Getting the Words Right . . . and Wrong
Chancellor and Mandarins · Savaged at a Seminar
'Judge and Jury'

The US Financial Cavalry

BY A HAPPY COINCIDENCE there was due to be a meeting of the Group
of Five Finance Ministers at the United States Treasury in Washington
on 17 January 1985. The G5 had begun in 1973 as the Group of Four,
with a membership consisting of the US, UK, Germany and France; but
it was not long before Japan was invited to join. During the first two
years of my time as Chancellor, 1983–84, its meetings were informal
and genuinely private, and received mercifully little press attention.
Despite the enlargement of the Summit to seven, and its gradual change
of character, the G5 happily went on as before, avoiding the limelight,
and constituting without doubt the key forum for international economic
co-operation. The January 1985 meeting had been instigated by Gerhard
Stoltenberg, the German Finance Minister, since he and indeed the rest
of us were keen to have a first-hand account of the likely direction of
American economic policy in Ronald Reagan's second term: he had
been re-elected the previous November. But the turmoil on the foreign
exchange markets meant that I also had some more immediate matters
to discuss with my counterparts.

Shortly before leaving for Washington on the afternoon of 16 January,
I saw Margaret and told her I thought the G5 meeting would be an
excellent opportunity to garner some international support for sterling.
The principal obstacle I faced was the US Treasury Secretary, Donald
Regan, who still adhered to the *laissez-faire* exchange rate policy of
Reagan's first term. The best means of influencing him was to draw

on Margaret's exceptionally close relationship with President Reagan, to whom Don Regan could be expected to defer. I drafted a letter for Margaret's signature on the worrying effects the excessively strong and seemingly ever-rising dollar was having on the pound, which, after making a few amendments, she sent to the President.

My first working engagement in Washington was a breakfast meeting on 17 January of the European members of the G5, at the Four Seasons Hotel, where Stoltenberg always stayed when in Washington. France was represented by the then French Finance Minister, Pierre Bérégovoy, and we were each accompanied by our central bank governors and senior officials, known as the 'G5 deputies'. Stoltenberg had brought Karl Otto Pöhl, the then President of the Bundesbank, and Hans Tietmeyer, who was then a State Secretary at the Finance Ministry in Bonn. The governors and deputies, with the exception of Pöhl, took little part in the discussion. I urged the others to join me in pressing the Americans to agree to joint action to curb the rise in the dollar and achieve some stability.

The French took little persuading, as they were always keen on exchange-rate management. Their support, however, was much less important than that of the Germans. Pöhl said he was in total agreement with me on the unwarranted rise of the dollar, but earlier experiences had convinced him that the Americans would never acquiesce in a policy of suppressing their currency, and that it was a waste of time asking them to do so. He recalled with particular bitterness an occasion when the Bundesbank had intervened heavily in support of the Deutschmark against the dollar, only to find the Americans intervening in the opposite direction, which he considered distinctly unfriendly.

Pöhl was of course unaware that Margaret had written to Reagan, and I did not enlighten him. The President had also by that time replied warmly, though without committing himself:

> Regarding your message on the pound. We understand your concern, and recognize that on occasion disorderly markets may develop. We take seriously our joint commitment made at the Williamsburg Summit which, as you recall, was to pursue closer consultation on policies affecting exchange rates and on market conditions. In that connection, we also discussed co-ordinated intervention where it was agreed such intervention would be helpful. Secretary Regan will be prepared this Thursday to discuss the current and prospective exchange market situation and related issues with Chancellor Lawson and the other G5 Finance Ministers. I have asked Secretary Regan to give me a full report on the meeting on Friday morning. I look forward to seeing you in February.

It was certainly encouraging enough for me to feel it worth my while to persuade the other Europeans that we should at least broach the subject of action to rein back the dollar with Don Regan. I left the Four Seasons Hotel for the US Treasury, where the main G5 meeting was being held at 10 o'clock that morning, and saw Don Regan privately beforehand. Unlike Pöhl, he was of course well aware of Margaret's letter to Reagan. He was tiresomely condescending, reminding me of the numerous occasions in the past when the Americans had come to the aid of the British. But what mattered was that he agreed for the first time to consider what might be done to curb the rise in the dollar.

At the G5 meeting itself, which lasted for the rest of the day, I left it to the ever-loquacious Pöhl to introduce the subject of our concern at the strength of the dollar. To the great surprise of the Germans, the French and the Japanese, Don Regan agreed that action was necessary to stabilize the currency markets. To make the views of the meeting known to the markets, we instructed our deputies to draft the first ever G5 communiqué. Previously, communiqués had been confined to the annual Economic Summit and the G5 had been kept deliberately private, informal and communiquéless. It is arguable that it might, after all, have been better kept that way; it is equally arguable that the modern investigative Press – and talkative Ministers – would never have enabled secrecy to persist. Once secrecy goes, a communiqué is bound to come, if only to prevent rival and conflicting accounts, and a consequent impression of disarray.

In any event, the 17 January 1985 communiqué was at least refreshingly short, which enabled Don Regan to read it out in its entirety to the mainly US journalists gathered in the marble corridor of the US Treasury Building, outside the room in which we had been meeting.

The key sentences read that the participants 'expressed their commitment to work towards greater exchange market stability'. After the usual sentiments about convergence and non-inflationary growth, and 'in light of recent developments in foreign exchange markets', the Ministers reaffirmed their commitment made at the Williamsburg Summit to undertake co-ordinated intervention in the markets as necessary.

The significance, of course (apart from that of having a communiqué in the first place) lay in the commitment to co-ordinated intervention, not merely in the event of 'disorderly markets' but 'as necessary' – i.e. whenever the G5 considered it necessary, with the clear presumption that this might happen at any moment. In fact there was very little intervention by the US in the wake of the January 1985 G5; but both the Germans and the Japanese were active, and this, coupled with the communiqué, appeared to achieve the G5's objective.

Thus, contrary to widespread belief, international co-operation in exchange rate management did not begin with the Plaza agreement of September 1985, but had originated at the meeting of the Finance Ministers of the G5 on 17 January that year. I was able to tell the Treasury Select Committee when I appeared before them ten days later that the agreement went beyond Williamsburg in the readiness of the signatories to intervene to curb the rise in the dollar.

I had left Washington on the Friday morning after the meeting in a more relaxed frame of mind than when I had arrived, thanks also to some important changes within the Reagan Administration. Don Regan and James Baker, the White House Chief of Staff, had hatched a plan to swap jobs, which the President agreed to while I was in Washington. There was a dinner on the Thursday evening, hosted by Federal Reserve Chairman Paul Volcker, to mark Regan's departure from the Treasury. It was at drinks beforehand that I met Jim Baker properly for the first time. It was obvious even from our brief conversation that he would be a much more amenable colleague than Regan. Less doctrinaire than his predecessor, he was greatly concerned at the impact of the high dollar on American business and industry.

Co-operation to bring down the dollar afforded Baker a means of defusing protectionist sentiment and portraying the Europeans, and especially the Japanese, as allies. Although it was not perceived at the time as a radical change of policy, Baker himself later pinpointed the January G5 meeting in Washington as the moment at which American resistance to a lower dollar began to weaken.

Neither Jim Baker nor I believed that prolonged intervention could protect a currency for ever from economic fundamentals. Nor did I for a moment imagine that intervention could be more than a supplement to the interest-rate weapon whose primacy I emphasized to the Treasury Select Committee when I was back in London. But the possiblilty of concerted intervention by the central banks of the United States, Germany, Japan, France and Britain did lend intervention (or even the threat of intervention) a credibility in the financial markets it had previously lacked.

The importance of concerted intervention is not simply its short-term effect in the currency markets. More important, it is, or should be, the outward and visible symbol of a more fundamental policy commitment, to fulfil which domestic monetary weapons, notably interest rates, have to be used as and when necessary. If the fundamental policy commitment secures credibility then intervention can take a significant part of the strain from interest rates. If, on the other hand, the credibility is lacking, then the role of intervention is inevitably a more modest one.

Getting the Words Right . . . and Wrong

The dollar eventually reached its peak at the end of February 1985, some six weeks after the watershed meeting of the G5; and it was on

26 February that we came nearest to the dreaded 'parity', with the pound briefly at a record low of just under $1.04. After that sterling began to recover against all the main currencies. So when the dollar began another upsurge in late April, sterling was safely above $1.20; and with the shift of the US to a lower dollar policy under Jim Baker and his successor, the 'one-dollar pound' had become a distant and unreal nightmare.

But I was taking no chances; and the Budget of 19 March 1985, was suitably cautious. In a sense the main thrust of the Budget was devoted to improving sentiment in the currency markets. In my Budget Speech I devised a form of words for bridging the gap between the old and new ways of presenting our strategy:

> There are those who argue that if we stick to sound internal policies, the exchange rate can be left to take care of itself. In the long run that may well be true, but significant movements in the exchange rate, whatever their cause, can have a short-term impact on the general price level and on inflationary expectations. This process can acquire a momentum of its own, making sound internal policies harder to implement. So benign neglect is not an option.

The last sentence is worth dwelling on. Even in the US, with its much smaller dependence on external trade, there are usually limits to how far the authorities will allow the dollar to move in either direction, as was shown by the Volcker squeeze of 1979, and the Baker initiative of 1985. But even the option of temporarily disregarding currency weakness, which the US adopted in an attempt to counter the recession of the early 1990s, is not open to any European government. For the United States is unique in the combination of its large size, its relatively small exposure to external trade, and the special position of the dollar in the foreign exchange firmament. Many British Prime Ministers – not just Margaret Thatcher, but Macmillan, Heath and Callaghan, too – have toyed with the idea, but none of them has been prepared to see it through. Attempts to do so – as in the events chronicled in the previous chapter – have usually led to higher interest rates, as well as higher inflation, than might have been necessary had the sterling exchange rate been accepted as a constraint from the outset.

The 1985 Budget Speech also put some emphasis on Nominal GDP, which had previously been mainly a matter for the Red Book. As my subsequent evidence to the Treasury Committee showed, I had no doubt that in practice the economy had to be steered by more immediate indicators, such as the money supply and the exchange rate. But I did now emphasize that our setting of policy instruments to bring down the rate of inflation would ensure a reasonable level of demand in money terms: 'The Medium Term Financial Strategy is as firm a guarantee against inadequate money demand as it is against excessive money demand.' There was, however, one short paragraph in this section of the Budget Speech which I subsequently came to regret. This was when I said:

> There is nothing sacrosanct about the precise mix of monetary and fiscal policies required to meet the objectives of the Medium Term Financial Strategy. But this is not the year to make adjustments in either direction. The wisest course is to stick to our pre-announced path.

The origin of this passage was the controversy then raging over the appropriate size of the PSBR for 1985–86. I had decided to stick to the £7 billion (2 per cent of GDP) envisaged in the previous year's MTFS – a significant reduction from the coal-strike-affected 1984–85 out-turn of over £10 billion (3 per cent of GDP). This was the product of considerable reflection on the issue; but in the Budget Speech, in the interests of brevity, I merely asserted it. The purpose of the previous sentence (the first in the passage quoted above) was to indicate that my bald assertion should not be interpreted as dogmatism.

Unfortunately, it succeeded both in incensing a number of stern unbending monetarists, who believed I was saying that inflation could be cured by fiscal rather than monetary means – somewhat bizarre in the light of my subsequent reputation as a 'one-club golfer' - and giving ammunition to those who mistakenly argued, at a later date, for a return to fiscal activism as a means of restoring macroeconomic room for manoeuvre within the constraints of the ERM. Needless to say, I never repeated the sentiment, but the damage (such as it was) was done. A Chancellor cannot be too careful in his choice of words, even those of no operational significance.

Chancellor and Mandarins

There may, however, have been more to it than that. Subconsciously, I may have been to some extent reflecting the received wisdom of the official Treasury, which did indeed hold, at least up to a point, that in the battle against inflation there was a choice between fiscal and monetary tightening. I did not. This difference was one reason why the Treasury top brass did not wholeheartedly approve of the tax cuts I made, even when Government borrowing and spending were lower than projected and better than on track; whereas when it came to monetary policy the boot was on the other foot. I had been suspicious of their eagerness to lower interest rates in the autumn of 1984 and I was generally keener than they were to raise rates in the face of inflationary threats from sterling.

There was another reason, too, I had always regarded interest rates as a vitally important *instrument* of policy. But during my absence at Energy, the Treasury had come to elevate low interest rates into an *objective* of policy. The mandarins were not helped to break out of this mould by the fact that low interest rates had an unfailing appeal for Margaret. Despite her reputation as a diehard opponent of inflation, and her dislike of it was undoubtedly genuine, she was almost always in practice anxious to reduce interest rates, and thus the mortgage rate. All this powerfully reinforced the traditional Treasury desire to get Government borrowing on a downward path, which it imagined would enable interest rates to move down in parallel. For somewhat different reasons, cutting back Government borrowing was an objective of mine, too: indeed, I was to succeed in eliminating it altogether. Where we differed on the fiscal front was that the official Treasury's disapproval of public spending – which is an essential part of its job – carried over to a distrust of private spending, too, and an austere quasi-moral disapproval of any significant reduction in tax rates, even to prevent the tax burden getting larger. Saving was always worthier than spending and investment superior to consumption.

These temperamental differences were not a serious problem. I simply learned to allow for them at Budget time. But I also began in time to realize that the traditional Treasury view greatly exaggerated the extent to which reducing or eliminating the Budget deficit could bring down domestic interest rates. They still had subconsciously in mind a world of exchange control and domestic financial regulation in which the balance of the Budget was a decisive factor in a national capital market, instead of one modest factor in an international capital market where interest rates were largely determined.

I have no wish to exaggerate these differences. In general, throughout my long stint as Chancellor, my senior officials and I worked together in remarkable harmony. When we got things right, we got them right together; and when we made mistakes, we made those mistakes together. Indeed, it was because this harmony was so pronounced that I took some time to appreciate the differences that did exist.

Savaged at a Seminar

Given the mistakes of 1984 and their consequences, and having arrived at high interest rates by the end of January 1985, I was determined to be ultra-cautious in lowering them. I brought base rates down in gradual steps after the Budget and eventually reached 11½ per cent by the end of July – still 2 percentage points higher than at the beginning of the year – after which there were no further changes in 1985. The tough monetary stance, coupled with the anti-climax of my

1985 Budget, did not make me popular; but that was just too bad. Newspaper articles started to appear on my alleged inability to command the confidence of the City. Articles of this nature always appear, whoever is Chancellor, whenever real interest rates are persistently high. The CBI, too, were restive, as they always when high real interest rates were accompanied by a strong pound: sterling had recovered to within a whisker of DM 4.

It was around this time that another member of the Prime Minister's kitchen cabinet, one David Wolfson, who from 1979 to 1985 gloried in the title of 'Chief of Staff' of the Political Office at Number 10, advised Margaret to sack both Norman Tebbit and myself in the next reshuffle, since we were manifestly electoral liabilities. As we were at that time Margaret's two most effective supporters in Cabinet, it was not surprising that this advice went unheeded. Nevertheless, Wolfson showed prescience in one sense: Margaret's growing tendency, as her Premiership developed, to dismiss or alienate her 'Thatcherite' colleagues, while retaining and promoting those who were opposed to everything she believed in.

There were, I think, two main explanations for this self-defeating behaviour. First, I use the term 'Thatcherite' to indicate like-minded colleagues, rather than those who considered her infallible. And while, in the beginning, she was desperate to find like-minded colleagues, as time went by she saw them as political rivals to be cut down. She felt she had changed the Party so much that a non-Thatcherite succession was inconceivable. Second, she came increasingly to believe in her self-sufficiency, that she *was* the Government and had no need of allies. There can be little doubt that these traits led to the isolation and behaviour pattern that contributed to her eventual downfall.

Meanwhile, my main domestic financial task was to clean up the presentational mess we had got into over monetary targets, which gave quite the wrong impression of how tight or loose policy was. As 1985 proceeded, the long-standing target aggregate, £M3, was once again soaring, despite historically very high real interest rates; and even the Bank of England was becoming disenchanted by it.

I have described in an earlier chapter how I suspended the target for £M3 and abandoned overfunding. What I have not described are the 'seminars' at which the decisions were taken. When I told Margaret that I felt the time had come to end overfunding, she decided that she should hold one of these occasions at Number 10 to discuss the matter – partly because she enjoyed them and had not held one for some time, partly because she had become alarmed by the inflation 'blip' in mid-1985 which I had foreshadowed in the Budget Speech. She clearly did not believe it was just a blip.

The seminar duly took place on 25 June 1985, with a second leg on

16 July. She began the first of these with an extravagant attack on me (she always behaved worst when she had an audience of this kind to play to) for undoing all the good work of the Government's first five years in bringing down inflation. The year on year headline RPI had indeed reached a peak of almost 7 per cent in the second quarter of 1985 as a result of the automatic effect of mortgage rate increases on the year on year comparison. The absurdity of a so-called inflation index which inevitably rose whenever the Government took action against inflation was subsequently to haunt me and my successors.

But such statistical disturbances are broadly predictable and I had warned about them in the Budget Speech. Indeed the underlying rate of inflation, as measured by the RPI, excluding mortgage interest payments, was 5¼ per cent over the same period – admittedly higher than the 4½ per cent of 1984, but exactly the same as the figure for 1983, the year that Margaret had considered such a triumph. She complained that my failure meant that the objective she had unilaterally announced, to the *Evening Standard*, while on an overseas tour, of 3 per cent inflation by 1988, was no longer attainable. In fact a headline rate of below 3 per cent (3¼ per cent on an underlying basis) was attained in each of the two middle quarters of the following year, 1986, which we might have partially 'locked in' if she had given me a free hand.

As it was, I pointed out to her in the first 1985 seminar the absurdity of looking at the headline RPI rather than the underlying rate (i.e. excluding mortgage interest payments), which showed a very different picture. I also pointed to her failure to recognize the significant monetary tightening that had occurred in early 1985. In any event, after she had finished letting off steam I secured exactly what I wanted: agreement to announce at the Mansion House the end of overfunding, the launch of the 'full fund' rule and the suspension of the £M3 target. At the second seminar, which was attended by Alan Walters, Margaret once again raised the issue of Monetary Base Control, which the Bank of England again found technically difficult. The issue was satisfactorily put to bed with the promise of 'further studies' of the US and German systems.

'Judge and Jury'

My Mansion House Speech of 17 October 1985 is probably best remembered for a single frequently quoted sentence – invariably out of context. The actual passage went as follows:

> The acid test of monetary policy is its record in reducing inflation.
> Those who wish to join the debate about the intricacies of different

measures of money and the implications they may have for the future are welcome to do so. But at the end of the day the position is clear and unambiguous. The inflation rate is judge and jury.

The much-quoted last sentence clearly refers exclusively to monetary policy. I was seeking to rise above the internecine war between the different schools of monetarists, and certainly not talking about the Government's record as a whole.

The heart of my Mansion House Speech that year, however, was my announcement of the new formulation of the Government's monetary policy in my Mansion House Speech of 17 October 1985. Since it caused such a sensation at the time, and has become so much part of the mythology subsequently, I hope the reader will forgive me for quoting the words I actually used:

> The aim of monetary policy is to ensure sustained and steady downward pressure on inflation. This can be secured only by delivering an appropriate growth of money GDP over the medium term . . . But to achieve this, it remains operationally necessary to conduct monetary policy through the use of intermediate targets – taking account of relevant information such as the behaviour of the exchange rate – rather than by attempting to target money GDP directly.
>
> In the 1980s . . . liquidity has grown faster than money GDP. Over the past five financial years, for example, while £M3 has grown by 82 per cent and PSL 2 by 84 per cent, money GDP has grown by only 54 per cent – and prices by 43 per cent . . . We can maintain, and are maintaining, progress towards our inflation objective while £M3 is growing at a rate well above the top of the range set in this year's Budget Statement.
>
> . . . I shall as usual be considering what target to set for £M3 for 1986–87 at the time of the next Budget. In the meantime, we shall continue to monitor £M3, and indeed other measures of broad money, as part of the task of forming an overall judgement about monetary conditions. That judgement has to take into account the level of interest rates, where a cautious approach continues to be indicated. It must also be influenced by the behaviour of M0, which, as a relatively undistorted narrow aggregate, is more closely related to spending patterns . . . The other good and early guide to changing financial conditions is the exchange rate.

The suspension of the £M3 target was described by superficial commentators as the 'death of monetarism'. Tim Congdon and Patrick Minford joined in attacking what they saw as the substitution of discretion for rules in a publication by the Centre for Policy Studies. This would have carried more weight had not the rules they preferred pointed to dramatically opposite policy conclusions. Minford agreed with his mentor, Walters, both that 'M3 was a dog that barked too often to be taken seriously' and that monetary policy was not too loose. For Congdon it was the downgrading of broad money which was the act of rank treason – as if the mere publication of unattained, and to all practical purposes unattainable, numerical targets had some profound significance. From then on the alliance of sectarian monetarists (later known as the 'Liverpool Six') has essentially been one of convenience, united only by a detestation of any emphasis on the exchange rate.

CHAPTER 39

—————

ENTER THE ERM

Anglo-Saxon Attitudes · Ripe and Unripe Time
Tackling the Treasury · Tackling the Prime Minister
The Meeting of 13 February 1985 · Strengthening the Reserves
The ERM and the Election

Anglo-Saxon Attitudes

THE ATTENTIVE READER WHO has followed the account of the sterling crises of 1984–85 will have noted that British monetary policy was in practice constrained by the sterling exchange rate. In other words, our decisions had many of the characteristics of an explicit exchange rate policy but without the advantages that might be derived from public commitment and organized international support.

Moreover, partly because of the surge in the dollar and partly because of the lag in political and financial attitudes, there was a danger of getting hooked on the wrong exchange rate, that with the dollar. Indeed, Margaret had been fleetingly attracted in the earliest days to a proposal by the financial journalist, successful businessman and *bon vivant*, Patrick Sergeant that we should pursue a two-dollar pound policy. The sterling/dollar rate (known as the 'cable') remains important for financial transactions. But the rate against European currencies has long been much more important for trade – which means both for UK inflation and for international competitiveness.

This line of thought inevitably pointed to exploring once again the arguments for British membership of the Exchange Rate Mechanism (ERM) of the European Monetary System (EMS). The decision not to join it had probably been the most important decision taken by the last Labour Government during their final months of office. As

483

a result, it had started without the UK, after two and a half months' delay, on 12 March 1979, two months before the Thatcher Government took office. A Green Paper published by the Treasury the previous November had sought to give a balanced statement of the case for and against membership. But in common with most British economists, the official Treasury was in fact hostile to joining.

Technically speaking, the UK *was* a member, and a founder member at that, of the EMS, since the Labour Government had bizarrely signed the Treaty while abjuring the exchange rate stability that it was all about. What this meant was that the UK had agreed to a modest pooling of reserves, would take part in EMS realignment meetings, and would maintain sterling as a component of the European Currency Unit (Ecu) – which was then just a currency basket and played little role in stabilizing exchange rates.

The heart of the system was of course the ERM. This had many complex paraphernalia; but in essence was a parity grid, giving a lower and upper margin of fluctuation of each member currency against every other. Although parities were formally stated against the Ecu, which the founding fathers vainly hoped would be the core of the system, governments and traders alike soon saw that the key range for every currency was between its upper and lower limit against the Deutschmark. It was *de facto* – although not *de jure* – a Deutschmark zone.

Labour's main fear in 1979 had been that membership would inflict an excessively high exchange rate for sterling, to the detriment of the economy as a whole. Whereupon, as is so often the case, the pundits were proved wrong as the pound soared outside the ERM – and the business and academic argument advanced in favour of membership became the need to put a cap on the pound. But there was also a political element, equally ironic in the light of subsequent events. In Andrew Britton's words, 'The attitude of the Labour Party to Europe was still (at best) ambivalent', and there was no enthusiasm 'for a commitment which might restrict the action of British Governments'.

Ripe and Unripe Time

As I have recorded earlier, I became convinced of the desirability of British membership of the ERM as Financial Secretary before I left the Treasury in September 1981. Although I returned as Chancellor in June 1983, the first serious meeting I convened in the Treasury on joining the ERM was on 11 January 1985. Why did I wait those nineteen months?

The answer is that I felt I had to wait for the right opportunity. During the whole of that period the dollar had been rocketing upwards; and it was this problem – on which the ERM had no bearing – which was the overwhelming focus of concern so far as the exchange rate and its impact on monetary policy was concerned. Nor was it going to be easy. Joining the ERM was a far bigger issue for a widely held currency like sterling than it was for any other European currency. The official Treasury had always been opposed, although it was subsequently to change. The predominant Bank of England view was also hostile, with the conspicuous exception of the new Governor, Robin Leigh-Pemberton, who had still to make his mark on the Bank. The opposition from officials would not have mattered had Margaret Thatcher been sympathetic. Indeed it might scarcely have continued to exist. But in view of her position the official attitude added to the difficulties. I had to wait until the time was ripe, to coin a phrase.*

In other words, Margaret was the key. The manifest absurdity of the rise in the dollar in 1984 had started to shake her faith in the foreign exchange markets; and the traumatic nature of the pressure on the pound in early 1985 frightened her as similar events had frightened every previous Prime Minister. That was essentially what created the 1985 opportunity, as I saw it. This was reinforced by the shift in the American position in President Reagan's second term away from free floating: Margaret's eyes were always focused across the Atlantic.

Throughout my period as Chancellor the holidays were the only time I had to sit back and reflect on policy. It was during the Christmas and New Year break of 1984–85 that I came to the conclusion that the time had arrived for a serious attempt to join the ERM. This was partly because I had become increasingly concerned both with the weakness of sterling (charts in Chapters 37 and 52) and with the continuing problems I was having with the conduct and presentation of a domestically based monetary policy.

Tackling the Treasury

The first internal Treasury meeting I held on the ERM membership was on the fateful Friday, 11 January, the day before the Chevening weekend, the day when I raised base rates by one percentage point to protect the pound, and also the day that, unknown to me, Bernard Ingham was briefing the Press that the Government was happy to leave sterling to its fate. The case for buttressing the pound and firmly dispelling the increasing uncertainty over monetary policy was clear to me.

*There is a minor ambiguity here. The official position was that Britain would join the ERM 'when the time is ripe'. Some years later it changed to 'when the time is right'. There was never a formal decision to adjust the wording. The change may have started off as a typing mistake or a mishearing. But elision probably occurred because the doctrine of unripe time was something of a Whitehall chestnut. In any event, the two formulations are so similar in meaning and sound that few noticed the difference; and when they did it was not worth the bother of debating their relative merits.

Nevertheless most of those I invited to the meeting, including both Ian Stewart, the Economic Secretary, and Peter Middleton and Terry Burns, were at that time still opposed to membership. The principal reservation that Treasury Ministers and officials voiced in public – for instance at the Commons Treasury Select Committee – centred on sterling's continuing, although diminishing, role as a petrocurrency and the possible destabilizing effects on the ERM itself of the entry of sterling, which was much more widely traded than other member currencies. There was also the question of how well the ERM would in fact hold together once the pressure from a strongly rising dollar was lifted. (When the dollar rises, funds move out of all European currencies into the dollar; but when the dollar falls, funds tend to move out of the dollar preponderantly into Deutschmarks, thus putting a strain on ERM parities.)

These were, however, essentially questions of timing and tactics. The true objections of officials were different. In the first place, they felt that the Government – and they personally – had invested a great deal of intellectual capital in the existing monetary policy framework and were loth to abandon it; second, they were also loth to lose control (as they saw it) over the level of interest rates; third, they were keenly aware of Margaret's strong views and fourth, the 'snake' episode had left some scars. (The 'snake' was an earlier ill-fated attempt to narrow the extent of exchange rate fluctuations among EC currencies. It had been agreed to by the Heath Government on 1 May 1972; but a massive run on the pound forced the UK to abandon it, in the most humiliating way, the very next month.)

After I had raised the matter, Peter Middleton moved fairly quickly from the anti-ERM camp and on to the fence: like many good Civil Servants, that was his instinctive position on most issues. Terry was slower to shift, because he was keen to try and operate a policy based on M0. At the Bank of England Eddie George also shifted, partly in deference to the Governor. While the subsequent thinking of Treasury officials moved steadily in what I regarded as the right direction, Eddie's thinking pursued a more volatile and erratic path – like the markets he loved to monitor with his portable pocket screen.

At any rate, the conclusion of the meeting of 11 January was that officials would examine the mechanics of ERM membership and also of contingency plans to increase the foreign exchange reserves. In the course of 1985 I gradually brought my officials around to my way of thinking on the ERM. Since in the end Civil Servants have to support their Minister, they had no real choice; but as far as I could see their conversion was genuine, if in some cases unenthusiastic.

I also raised the issue with Geoffrey, in his capacity as Foreign Secretary. He was anxious to join the ERM, not only to strengthen his political hand in Europe, but because he now shared my assessment of the economic attractions. Needless to say, confiding in him did not constitute a plot against Margaret. We were old friends and colleagues and discussed a variety of policy matters over the years. Rightly or wrongly, there was only one occasion when, under extreme provocation, four years later, we acted in concert to put pressure on Margaret.

It was clear that more intervention in the foreign exchange markets was going to be the order of the day. Such intervention would be required to sustain the pound within the ERM; it would be required as part of any G5 or G7 concerted intervention in the currency markets; and it would help with any informal and unannounced targeting of sterling. Ultimately the main instrument would have to be domestic monetary policy – that is, interest rates. But intervention could supplement the use of interest rates and minimize or even avoid their use in the face of purely temporary shocks and disturbances.

Intervention on a worthwhile scale requires the holding of substantial reserves of foreign currency. Largely as a result of a deliberate policy of repaying the foreign debts run up by the last Labour Government, which we had embarked on in 1979 when we were seeking to underline the new Conservative Government's wholly different approach to economic policy, the UK's gross official published reserves had fallen from $27 billion in 1980 to just under $16 billion at the end of 1984, of which less than $8 billion consisted of readily usable convertible currencies. British reserves were not only very much smaller than those of Germany, but only a little more than a third of those of either France or Italy. A submission made to me by Treasury officials on 21 December 1984, emphasized the inadequacy of the UK's reserves and recommended (probably on the advice from the Bank of England) a dollar bond issue to replenish them. This proved a timely initiative.

Tackling the Prime Minister

The question of the reserves came up again at a meeting in Number 10 on 28 January 1985, held (at my request) to secure Margaret's approval of the final two-point increase in base rate to 14 per cent. After we had concluded the main business, Margaret reported that she had recently asked the Dutch Prime Minister, Ruud Lubbers, for whom she had a high regard, why, although the Netherlands was also a major energy producer (of gas rather than oil), it did not experience similar currency turbulence to Britain. His reply had been that ERM membership protected it, as changes in the parity were not expected by the foreign exchange market. Margaret concluded by herself asking me to look into the question of whether in present circumstances it was right for the UK to join the ERM.

Needless to say, I was happy to do so, and took the opportunity to raise the matter again at one of my regular weekly bilateral meetings with her on 3 February. I told her that there was growing interest both among our back-benchers and within the business community in the possibility of joining the ERM. The Government had always said that it would join when conditions were right, and I believed this was a question which should be considered before the Budget. I remarked that financial discipline, which was the key to bringing down inflation, could be provided by either monetary targets or a fixed exchange rate. We should choose between the two on practical grounds.

New arguments, I reminded her, were now being put forward in favour of the ERM. The financial markets were having difficulty in understanding the Government's position so far as the exchange rate was concerned, and the ERM would provide clearer rules of the game. Moreover, as there was now substantial support for ERM membership within the Conservative Party in the House of Commons, it would be helpful in future arguments about spending and borrowing if our back-benchers in effect faced a discipline of their own choice. I added that membership would have the additional advantage of moving attention away from the misleading sterling/dollar exchange rate. It would also help domestically, as £M3 was becoming increasingly suspect as a monetary indicator.

For once I took the opportunity myself of urging a Prime Ministerial seminar on the issue. I suggested that in addition to a Treasury team headed by me and a Bank team headed by Robin Leigh-Pemberton, both Geoffrey Howe, as Foreign Secretary, and Alan Walters should be invited. She agreed, and asked her private secretary, Andrew Turnbull, to set it up.

I held a further internal Treasury meeting on the subject on 8 February. With sterling still very weak, I was worried about declaring an intention to join the ERM at the time of the Budget, by then only some five weeks away. It seemed to me that it would be better to reach agreement in principle as soon as possible, with a view to making the announcement and joining the ERM in the summer, when I expected sterling to be stronger.

The Meeting of 13 February 1985

The ERM seminar duly took place at Number 10 on 13 February 1985, attended by the cast I had suggested, with the exception of Alan Walters, who was in America, and with the addition of John Redwood, then head of the Number 10 Policy Unit, and subsequently a middle-ranking Minister. I opened the meeting by making clear that I was not seeking agreement to enter the ERM then and there, with the pound still under pressure, and that we needed to re-establish a reasonable degree of confidence in the currency first if the move was to be credible. But the balance of argument had shifted markedly in favour of joining, which would make the maintenance of financial discipline easier, and the time was now very close when it would be right to do so.

Geoffrey said that he recognized that a decision had to be taken on economic rather than political grounds, but doubted if there were any insuperable problems. He accepted that current circumstances were not right, but thought that the UK should be looking for the first opportunity to join. Robin Leigh-Pemberton said that the Bank was looking more sympathetically at the arguments in favour. He agreed that current circumstances were not right, but the Bank leaned towards joining at some stage, although he added that Bank opinion was not unanimous.

In her summing up, Margaret chose to dwell on the consensus that now was not the right time to join, and ignored the majority feeling that the right time was not far off. Nevertheless, I felt that some progress had been made. This was not least because one of the pre-conditions for joining, identified at the meeting, had been an increase in the UK's foreign exchange reserves. Margaret was alarmed to discover how small our reserves were, compared with those of other major European countries, and she asked me to investigate ways of increasing them. Once they had been increased, she concluded, the question of joining the ERM could be looked at again.

Needless to say, I was more than happy to get on with the job of rebuilding the reserves, but for the time being this would have to wait. The following month I had a Budget to present, and there was a great deal of work to be done on it. After the Budget was out of the way, I got down to the reserves issue without further delay.

Strengthening the Reserves

The best way of increasing the reserves, when this is possible, is to intervene directly in the markets, selling pounds for foreign currencies. This improves the net reserve position as well as the gross. But with the pound as weak as it then was intervention to buy dollars or other currencies was scarcely an option. Indeed, the intervention going on in early 1985 was the other way round – selling foreign currencies in order to buy sterling to support it.

In the circumstances, therefore, there was no practical alternative to borrowing dollars on the international capital markets, and I discussed this with officials who in turn had been consulting the Bank of England. The Treasury had considerable experience of borrowing abroad, particularly during the previous Labour Government when – quite apart from the notorious crisis borrowing from the IMF and elsewhere – it had been official policy to have a steady, low profile, foreign borrowing programme by inducing the nationalized industries to meet their borrowing needs in this way. But the chances of strengthening the reserves on the scale I had in mind by this route were nil. Some of the potential candidates had already been privatized, others were earmarked for privatization, and most of the rest had improved their finances to the point where their new borrowing needs had been greatly reduced. In short, there was nothing for it but for the Government to borrow abroad in its own name – for the first time since Labour had done so in 1978.

The Bank advised doing it by the issue of floating-rate notes (commonly known as FRNs: securities whose rate of interest is not fixed but fluctuates in line with the general level of short-term rates). Even this way, they reckoned, we could count on raising only $1 billion, or up to $1½ billion if market conditions were ideal. While I was content to accept their advice about the method, I was extremely sceptical of their modest estimate of the likely scale of demand. I saw Margaret about it at the end of April, and confirmed in a minute of 8 May that I proposed to issue, in the Government's own name, a dollar-denominated FRN to boost the reserves, to the tune of at least $1½ billion and probably $2 billion. She agreed to my proposal, in writing, on 16 May.

The Bank's original plan had been to raise the money straight away, in the middle of May. Annoyingly, however, just before we could launch the FRN, the European Community stepped in with a badly handled $1.8 billion issue, which was a conspicuous flop. This so soured the market that the Bank advised me either to scale our own issue down or postpone it until the Community's had been absorbed. I had no hesitation in opting for postponement.

There was, after all, much to be said for raising the money when Parliament was in recess. Although the circumstances of the issue could scarcely have been more different from the distress borrowings of the Labour Government in the 1970s, foreign borrowing by the UK Government had acquired an unfortunate political image. Moreover, it was not so long since we had been claiming political credit for repaying overseas debt. Had the House of Commons been sitting, there could have been some awkward questions to answer.

The only risk in a delay of this kind was that our intentions might leak in the interim. Fortunately, absolute secrecy was successfully maintained. On 16 September, while MPs were still enjoying their summer recess, and four months after receiving Margaret's formal green light, I announced a $2 billion FRN. Despite the terms being the finest ever attempted by any borrower in this market, demand for it was such that I immediately authorized an increase in the amount to $2½ billion. Apart from a single isolated barbed intervention from Dennis Skinner, who seldom missed a trick, when the House reassembled in the autumn, there was no political flak of any kind.

The notes were due to mature in 1992; but well before then I had been able to strengthen the reserves so much through intervention, notably in 1987, that I felt able to repay the issue in full three years ahead of time, in 1989. Meanwhile, pleased with the success of the operation, I decided to repeat it the following summer, but on a larger scale. Once again the Bank was pessimistic, suggesting that a second issue would undermine the market price for the first, and advising me to desist; although if I insisted on going ahead, they would recommend a fixed-price issue this time, for a maximum of $1½ billion. Once again I had to tell them I was highly sceptical, and suggested they consult, in strict secrecy, the lead managers of the 1985 FRN, Credit Suisse First Boston and Warburgs.

They duly did so, and came back with the rather different story that they now felt we could raise up to $3 billion by a further FRN. I told them that would do as a minimum, and saw Margaret to get her agreement, which she gave me and confirmed in writing on 1 September. Two days later, on 3 September 1986, a $3 billion issue, maturing in 1996, was announced; and once again it was oversubscribed, bringing in $4 billion before I instructed the Bank to close the offer.

But to return to 1985, and the ERM. At the beginning of August, while I was still biding my time, waiting for the FRN issue which would not only strengthen the reserves but demonstrate to Margaret that we had a simple and politically acceptable means of achieving this at any time, Geoffrey mentioned to me that the Economic Section of the Foreign Office had just completed a paper on sterling and the ERM. I asked him to let me see it, which he did.

It was a workmanlike effort, although it added nothing new. Its slightly rum conclusion was that conditions then were not as favourable for joining as they had been some nine to twelve months earlier, but that we should be alert to the possibility of joining at some time over the next few months. Its real weakness, however, as I saw it, was that it seemed to envisage automatic realignments in order to cope with the different inflation rates in different member states – which rather destroyed the point of joining in the first place.

I then went on a brief family holiday, and on my return towards the end of August saw Margaret privately and pressed once again the case for ERM membership, indicating that in my opinion, as soon as the FRN issue had dealt with the problem of inadequate reserves in the sense I have just indicated, the time would be right for sterling to join. Margaret was sceptical, but indicated that her mind was not completely closed on the issue, and argued that it was for those who favoured joining to make their case. She suggested that we should have a further seminar towards the end of September, which I welcomed.

ENTER THE ERM

The ERM and the Election

I told my officials that, in preparing the Treasury's paper for the seminar – which should be done in close collaboration with the Bank – they should address two central questions: first, precisely why we believed that the time was right to join, and, second, how the decision to join could be most positively presented in public. I also told them that Margaret was particularly exercised about a problem that Alan Walters had put to her when she last discussed it with him. (Although Walters had no official post, and was an academic living in Washington, she remained in frequent contact with him: indeed, our Washington Embassy used to grumble about being instructed by Number 10 to send him confidential Government papers.)

The problem that Walters had posed at that time, and which so worried Margaret, was that if sterling were in the ERM it could seriously damage our chances of electoral success. The scenario he painted was one of a General Election campaign in which an opinion poll showing Labour ahead, or even a sharply narrowing Conservative lead, would lead to a run on the pound, which would force us to put up interest rates then and there to defend the parity, thus making a Labour win certain.

As an argument against joining, I did not find this convincing. In the first place, a purely political and intrinsically transitory problem of this kind was just the sort of situation in which massive intervention would be warranted; and I had little doubt that the Germans, who had no wish to see a Labour Government in Britain, would be helpful. In the second place, a pre-election run on the pound was at least as likely to occur with sterling outside the ERM, and it was highly unlikely that the Government (as Walters clearly envisaged) would be content simply to sit back and let it happen, unabated.

Finally, if the worse came to the worst, and interest rates had to be increased in the circumstances envisaged, I did not feel that it would be too difficult to make the political point (a) that this demonstrated the world's conviction that a Labour Government would be an economic disaster and (b) that if this was what even the prospect of Labour in power could mean, then it was not hard to imagine how much worse the reality would be. Certainly, there was no evidence that the Labour Party ever imagined that it would be in their electoral interest to engineer a pre-election sterling crisis: quite the reverse.

Despite this, however, I thought it prudent to arm myself with a fallback position when dealing with this point at Margaret's seminar, and asked the ever ingenious Geoff Littler to let me have one. He replied with a submission suggesting what he was later to term the *congé* : when senior officials suggest something they consider faintly disreputable, they evidently feel that the French language adds tone and a cloak of respectability. The proposal was that the Government might *in extremis* formally declare that the pound would be allowed to float until polling day, and couple this announcement with 'a strong statement' that, on re-election, it would immediately restore sterling to the ERM at the previous parity.

This seemed to me a reasonable contingency plan if one were needed: our partners would not welcome the *congé*, but in practice they would be powerless to stop us; nor was it conceivable that, in the circumstances, they would refuse us readmission. It should be recalled that, at that time, not only did the Labour Party have no commitment to ERM membership, let alone to any particular parity, but its subsequent love affair with the European Community had not even begun. None the less, during the 1992 election campaign, by which time its position on Europe and the ERM had changed completely, there were still tremors in the foreign exchange market when it looked as if Labour might win; but the situation was successfully contained with only modest amounts of intervention.

While my officials were busy preparing the papers for the seminar, I had to fly to New York for a special meeting of the G5 at the Plaza Hotel, where on 21 September we signed the so-called Plaza Agreement to take concerted action to reduce the international value of the dollar, as described in Chapter 43. I was very happy with this timing. There was reason to hope that the Plaza Agreement, which marked in the most formal way a major change in US exchange rate policy, away from free floating and the doctrine that you cannot (or should not) 'buck the market', might, at least subconsciously, soften Margaret's resistance to sterling's ERM membership. On my return from Washington I saw her to debrief her fully, in the usual way, on the events at the Plaza Hotel, and found that this had indeed modified her scepticism about the ERM: she remarked to me that the agreement created a favourable prelude to ERM membership, should we decide to join. She proposed 30 September as the date for the forthcoming seminar.

CHAPTER 40

THE AUTUMN ASSAULT OF 1985

The Meeting of 30 September · The Meeting of 13 November
Secret Mission to Germany · Retrospect
If the UK Had Joined in November 1985 . . .
Appendix: The 'Walters Critique' and All That

The Meeting of 30 September

THERE WERE ABOUT A dozen of us present round the Cabinet table at Number 10 for the seminar which started at 4 o'clock in the afternoon of 30 September. From the Treasury I brought Ian Stewart, the Economic Secretary, Peter Middleton, Terry Burns and Frank Cassell. The Governor, Robin Leigh-Pemberton, brought with him Kit McMahon, then still Deputy Governor, Eddie George, the executive Director in charge of monetary policy at the Bank, and Anthony Loehnis, the executive director in charge of the overseas side of the Bank. Geoffrey Howe was also present.

Margaret was flanked by Brian Griffiths, a former professor of economics at City University who had replaced John Redwood as head of the Number 10 Policy Unit, and by one of her private secretaries, David Norgrove, as a note-taker. Walters was in the United States and unable to attend. This was on balance a pity, since he was the only economist who influenced her and I would have welcomed the opportunity to meet his arguments head-on. Griffiths, by contrast, simply presented her with a pale echo of Walters' views in private and said little on occasions such as this.

I opened by speaking to the paper which I had circulated in advance. I pointed out that, since our previous discussion in February, the recovery of the pound on the foreign exchange markets and the replenishment of the reserves had disposed of the two main arguments against joining then. The overwhelming case for joining now was the desirability of reinforcing our anti-inflationary strategy. While this continued so far to be successful, the monetary indicators were proving increasingly difficult to interpret.

In the light of this, we were already having to place increasing weight on the exchange rate in the conduct of monetary policy, and joining the ERM would thus be seen as a natural development. It would undoubtedly strengthen our strategy in the eyes of the markets, it would make it clear to industry that they could not look to exchange rate depreciation to solve their difficulties, and it would create a helpful context for the Government's public-expenditure decisions. While monetary conditions were at that time adequately tight, we were still facing problems of presentation and market psychology.

Robin strongly supported me, claiming that the need to make subjective judgements about the interpretation of the monetary indicators, coupled with our resistance to the increasing pressure from the market to disclose an exchange rate 'target', were undermining the credibility of policy. Geoffrey pointed out the significance of the fact that both the Treasury and the Bank, who had for so long been sceptical of the merits of ERM entry, were now both unequivocally in favour of it. He added that it was clear that the exchange rate was already dominating economic decision-making, and he believed that joining the ERM would strengthen the MTFS by which he continued to set great store.

Margaret then responded. It was clear that she had been speaking to Walters since I had seen her on my return from Washington. She argued that an exchange rate discipline would increase interest rate volatility and would mean a much tighter monetary squeeze than any internal discipline. It would reduce the Government's room for manoeuvre (by which she meant its ability to reduce interest rates and let the pound depreciate) and might require unattractively high interest rates in order to keep up with the Germans, leading to higher unemployment. Moreover, sterling was different from other Community currencies, not least because we were a net oil exporter and they were substantial oil importers. Finally, she made the point that, given the absence of exchange controls, there could be massive speculation against the pound in the run up to a General Election, requiring a politically embarrassing rise in interest rates.

I replied that it was clear from the events earlier that year that the exchange rate was already having a powerful influence on interest rates, and ERM membership, by stabilizing the exchange rate, could actually reduce the volatility of interest rates. As for the oil factor, the extent to which the markets regarded sterling as a petrocurrency had greatly diminished. The problem of pressure on the pound in a run up to an election, I pointed out, could occur whether we were inside or outside the ERM, and might actually be easier to handle within it; were we to join in 1985, we would have fully established the credibility of ERM membership and the parity we had chosen by the time the election came. In the last resort, I added, we could take the *congé* route I have already described.

Perhaps the most depressing aspect of Margaret's response was the renewed evidence that, despite her reputation for sound money, in practice she was too ready to allow sterling to depreciate rather than raise interest rates. Geoffrey's remark that ERM membership would actually strengthen the MTFS had been very much to the point. As I said to her, the significance of the MTFS was that it represented a public commitment to the pursuit of an anti-inflationary policy. Linking the pound to the Deutschmark via the ERM would represent exactly the same sort of public commitment to an anti-inflationary policy, and one that would by that time carry greater conviction.

Margaret concluded that she had not been convinced that the balance of argument had in fact shifted in favour of joining the ERM. There would need to be a further discussion, to which other colleagues should be invited. She would circulate a list of questions which needed to be answered which could form an agenda for that meeting. She no doubt felt that, with the Treasury and the Bank both now solidly ranged against her on the issue, supported by the Foreign Office, she was becoming dangerously isolated, and that she needed to bring in other colleagues (whom she would, of course, choose) to redress the balance. I for my part welcomed the wider ministerial discussion she had proposed, since, given her own scepticism, at the end of the day it might be through a collective decision of this kind that ERM membership could be obtained.

After the meeting, which had lasted a little over two hours, I asked Peter Middleton to have a word with me next door at Number 11. I told him that, in addition to providing the answers to the Number 10 questions, it was essential that we circulated a very persuasive paper of our own to all those who were going to attend the meeting, and that we should involve the Bank fully in the preparation of that paper. A joint Treasury and Bank team was put together, under the chairmanship of Frank Cassell, to draft both this paper and the answers to the questions, which I asked to be done in a coherent and logical way of our own choosing, rather than in whatever sequence they happened to emerge from next door. Over the next few weeks I held a succession of meetings on the papers, which went through a number of drafts before I was satisfied.

When the Number 10 questionnaire arrived, it proved to contain no fewer than twenty-three questions, and read rather like a rag-bag of every objection to ERM membership that anybody could come up with. In so far as there was an underlying theme, it was that sterling would be subject to greater pressure inside the ERM than if it remained a non-member, and that the economy was not strong enough to sustain a fixed parity against the Deutschmark. There were also practical questions, such as the Deutschmark parity at which sterling should join. Curiously, about the only objection that was not included in the list of questions was that dubbed (by Alan Walters) the 'Walters' critique'. Because of the importance he and some others attached to it, I deal with it later in this chapter; but it was never raised by Margaret herself.

The Meeting of 13 November

The ministerial meeting was fixed for 9 o'clock in the morning of Wednesday, 13 November, the day after the Autumn Statement – and less than a month after the Mansion House banquet at which both Robin and I had been unable to conceal the fragility of the presentation of the Government's existing monetary policy. The colleagues Margaret had invited to the meeting were Willie Whitelaw, Geoffrey Howe, Norman Tebbit, who had recently been moved from Secretary of State for Trade and Industry to Party Chairman, Leon Brittan, Norman's successor at Trade and Industry, John Biffen, the Leader of the House of Commons and John Wakeham, then Chief Whip.

Of these six, three – Willie, as Deputy Prime Minister, Geoffrey, and Leon as head of the second economic Department of Government – were there because she could scarcely exclude them. The other three had been chosen largely because she felt sure they would support her, either on political grounds or, in John Biffen's case, on economic grounds. Apart from Geoffrey and myself, none of them had given any previous indication of support for ERM membership. Biffen was a committed free-floater of long standing, and I regarded him as a lost cause. All the others I saw individually, before the meeting, to go over my paper with them, and answer any doubts they may have had about any of the arguments it advanced. The full text of my paper is published in Annexe 2.

The main paper was accompanied by a second paper giving the full answers to Margaret's written questions, but put in a logical sequence; a third paper which gave a brief history of the EMS, and how the ERM worked in practice, and a number of charts, of which probably the two most important were one which showed how, for many years now, base rate changes, and in particular base rate rises, had tended to coincide with movements in the exchange rate; and another which demonstrated that the close relationship between changes in the external value of the pound and changes in the oil price had largely broken down.

The meeting was not a formal Cabinet committee meeting, but an *ad hoc* gathering to which others besides Cabinet colleagues had been invited. I myself was accompanied by Peter Middleton and Terry Burns while Robin Leigh-Pemberton was also, of course, present, accompanied by Eddie George. Margaret was once again flanked by Brian Griffiths and a private secretary. None of us, however, was in any doubt of its importance.

As someone wholly outside the Government machine, Alan Walters clearly could not be present at a meeting of this kind. But Margaret had a short letter from him among the papers in front of her. He was evidently concerned that we were now on the brink of joining the ERM, since his chief point was that the oil price was clearly weakening and would weaken still further, and that we should therefore defer entry until the following Easter, by which time the oil price fall would have been completed and we would then be able to join, should we wish to do so, at a lower and more realistic parity. He was, of course, quite right about the oil price; but equally he knew full well that, if a November 1985 meeting towards which I had taken so much trouble and time in working were to decide against entry, it was most unlikely that I would be able to get the horse to jump the fence at a second attempt the following Easter.

I opened the meeting by summarizing the main points of my paper. The paper was not of course intended as an exhaustive analysis of the pros and cons of ERM membership, but was much more specifically designed to meet the particular concerns that Margaret had raised with me in our earlier conversations on the subject. It recalled that the Government's clearly stated policy was to join the ERM when the time was right, and argued that that time had now come. It pointed out – and I elaborated this in my opening remarks – that the position was not one of deciding whether, on balance, we would be better off with a fixed or a floating pound in the abstract. The plain fact was that the ERM existed, and thus the question asked by the markets was why we refused to join it; and I pointed out that this led them to the inevitable conclusion that it was because we sooner or later wished to see sterling depreciate, which in general made the conduct of economic policy harder than it would otherwise be, and in particular required interest rates to be kept higher in the longer run than would otherwise have been necessary.

My paper also went into the potential pre-election problem, and floated the *congé* option. It concluded with these words:

> My judgement that the advantages of joining now outweigh the risks is shared not only by the Governor of the Bank of England, but also by senior officials in both the Treasury and the Bank. They all believe that it makes operational sense to join, and that they can now deliver our policy objectives more effectively in the EMS than if we remain outside it.

From then on the discussion did not go as Margaret had expected. Geoffrey, of course, spoke in favour, along the lines that he had done at the 30 September seminar. But then Leon Brittan said that while he had been opposed to ERM membership in the past, because of the problems of sterling's petrocurrency status, since the importance of this factor had diminished and given the declining credibility of the monetary aggregates, he now believed we should join. Norman Tebbit, who was to turn against the ERM later when it was seen as part of the essentially political argument about European monetary union and the single currency, also declared himself in favour if I thought it would be helpful economically; and added that, as Party Chairman, he felt that it would be easy to carry the Party and that a decision to join now might silence some of the back-bench critics of our economic policy.

A nettled Margaret promptly asserted that what it would do would be to split the Party in Parliament right down the middle; to which John Wakeham replied that as Chief Whip, he had no worries on that score: there would be very few rebels and he was in fact surprised that so far there had been relatively little back-bench pressure to join, but he expected this to increase. John Biffen unsurprisingly declared himself very doubtful of the merits of ERM membership. Robin Leigh-Pemberton then had his say arguing that the difficulties of sterling outside the ERM were greater than they would be inside the ERM.

Margaret then weighed in. She recited what had become a familiar litany of objections. The United Kingdom had low foreign-exchange reserves and a more open capital market than anyone else. The Government would be left with no discretion on interest rates; and the UK could not pull out of the ERM, even on a very temporary basis, in advance of an election, without looking as if it had lost all faith in its own policies. A 'rigid grid' would deprive the Government of all freedom of manoeuvre.

Willie, as was his custom, had held himself back to the end. Unless he disagreed with it, it was his habit to formulate what he thought was the clear consensus of any meeting (equally, if there was no consensus, he would make that plain), as an aid to Margaret in her summing up. On this occasion, having listened attentively to the discussion he declared, 'If the Chancellor, the Governor and the Foreign Secretary are all agreed that we should join the EMS then that should be decisive. It has certainly decided me.' I suspect he was as surprised as the rest of us when Margaret instantly replied, 'On the contrary: I disagree. If you join the EMS, you will have to do so without me.' There was an awkward silence, and the meeting broke up.

There is just one other point to be made about that fateful meeting. Whatever differences there might have been in the extent of their own personal enthusiasm for ERM membership, both then and at the earlier meetings, all my officials fully, loyally and competently backed my position. Despite Margaret's attempts to drive a wedge between them and me, she completely failed to do so.

At the end of the meeting Margaret swept out, with Griffiths trotting behind her. I asked Willie, Geoffrey and Norman to accompany me next door to Number 11 to discuss what had happened. I was extremely depressed, and told them that, in the circumstances, I saw little point in carrying on and probably ought to resign. Willie, too, had clearly found it a depressing as well as an embarrassing occasion, but urged me not to resign, as did both Geoffrey and Norman. Norman said he was convinced that she would eventually come round, and Willie agreed.

In a sense, they were right; but no-one could have foreseen the sequence of events which took her there. Given the emphasis that she had laid on the political arguments – despite a warning from Willie, among others, that the political pressure was likely to stem from not joining rather than joining – it was clear that it would be difficult, to say the least, to reopen the issue before the next General Election, which was at least eighteen months away. An historic opportunity had been lost, when the time really had been right.

Secret Mission to Germany

Having, after much reflection, decided to accept the advice of Willie, Geoffrey and Norman not to throw in the towel, I gave the green light to a secret mission I had planned in advance in the hope of a favourable outcome of the meeting. Accordingly on, 7 December, Peter Middleton, Geoff Littler and (from the Bank) Anthony Loehnis went on a highly confidential visit to Bonn to discuss contingency planning in the event of Britain deciding to join the ERM. The two key figures on the German side were Leonhard Gleske, the Bundesbank board member in charge of external affairs, and Hans Tietmeyer, then a top Finance Ministry official who was both Stoltenberg's Deputy in the G5 context and Chancellor Kohl's 'sherpa' for the annual economic summit. Although something of a rough diamond for an official, Tietmeyer is a highly competent and agreeable man, who in 1991 was appointed Vice President and President-elect of the Bundesbank.

The Germans made it clear that they would welcome sterling's membership of the ERM, which in their view would help to maintain the soundness of the system despite the weakness of its southern members (they were particularly concerned about Italy). They also found British thinking about the further development of the EMS very close to their own and 'sensibly pragmatic'. Two days later Loehnis had a separate talk with Gleske about possible swap arrangements with the Bundesbank – that is to say a substantial line of short-term credit – to support British entry, and reported back that 'the reaction was unexpectedly favourable'.

In his report to me on his secret talks, Geoff Littler said that in his opinion, after the coming French elections, there was likely to be an ERM realignment, particularly if the Right under Chirac won. (This proved accurate in every respect.) One possibility would be for the UK to wait until the system had settled down following the realignment, and then join. While, in a purely rational world, there would have been much to be said for this, I could not see Margaret changing her mind so soon after the drama of 13 November.

For their part, the Germans were more interested to hear our views on the parity at which sterling should enter the system than to suggest a figure of their own, but they made it clear that they regarded somewhere in the region of DM3.50 to DM3.75 as reasonable. They believed that if the UK were to join from strength on a credible basis there would be an inflow of funds into London and upward pressure on the sterling exchange rate – something which we did indeed experience when I subsequently shadowed the Deutschmark, albeit at the appreciably lower rate of DM3.

I was able to confirm the German view for myself when I discussed the matter privately with Gerhard Stoltenberg in the margins of the next Ecofin meeting early the following year, 1986. He greatly welcomed my desire to see sterling in the ERM, which he believed would strengthen the system as well as benefiting the UK. He saw no problem whatever with the kind of practical co-operation the Treasury and Bank officials had discussed on their visit.

Retrospect

Looking back with hindsight on all this, the saddest event of my time as Chancellor and the greatest missed opportunity, two obvious questions need to be answered. The first is whether, if I had played my cards better, I could have secured the outcome I sought. The second is in what way subsequent events would have been different had I been successful in securing agreement for sterling to join the ERM in November 1985, five years before we did eventually join. As to the first of these, I believe that the only serious mistake I made was to underestimate the influence that Alan Walters exerted over Margaret.

I subsequently discovered that copies of his first book on the Thatcher period, *Britain's Economic Renaissance*, published in 1986, were circulating in draft in London in the latter part of 1985, and in advance of the 13 November meeting. He had of course sent a copy to Margaret, although not to me. A curiosity of the book is that it contains a seemingly abruptly inserted section on the evils of the ERM, with no explanation of why it is there. Treasury officials, although thoroughly supportive on the issue itself, could usefully have alerted me to this.

·   A paper setting out a point-by-point rebuttal of Walters' case might, in the circumstances, conceivably have shaken Margaret's faith in his judgement on this issue.

But apart from that, and I accept with hindsight that it was an error, I believe that my handling of the issue was about the best I could have done. I had waited until the time was right, and chosen a moment when Margaret's misplaced faith in free floating had been shaken by events. I had replenished the reserves, and demonstrated how painlessly this could be achieved. Although the Plaza agreement was, of course, primarily Jim Baker's doing, I had been urging something of the sort on him ever since he was first appointed Treasury Secretary in February 1985, and this had provided the right international context. And I had secured a meeting of senior Ministers on the issue, on which the line-up was what should have been a decisive 6 to 2 in favour of joining (5 to 1 excluding Margaret and myself).

Perhaps, constitutionally, the most extraordinary aspect of all was that the Government's official and collectively agreed position on the ERM of the EMS was that it was in favour of, and indeed committed to, joining, as soon as the time was ripe – a position that Margaret herself had publicly stated and repeatedly restated. Yet here was a Prime Minister allowing herself to be guided on the issue by someone who made no bones about the fact that, in his opinion, the ERM was the work of the devil and that we should never, in any circumstances, join it. Had Margaret come to that conclusion, too, she could at any time have sought Cabinet's endorsement of this fundamental change of policy.

Had she done so, I would of course have opposed it; and had Cabinet been persuaded by her I would have been faced with the choice between giving up my repeated attempts to secure ERM entry and resigning. It is hard to say with honesty which of the two it would have been – probably the latter – but it would have had to be one or the other, and in either event there would subsequently have been a greater degree of harmony in the conduct of policy than in fact, towards the end, proved the case. But she never once sought Cabinet's endorsement of a fundamental change of policy of this kind. Until after my resignation at the end of October 1989 she simply acted as if Government policy were different from what she herself repeatedly avowed it to be.

If the UK Had Joined in November 1985 . . .

At the time of the November ministerial meeting, the ERM was not in practice a completely rigid system. During its first eight years, from its inception in March 1979 to March 1987, there was an average of one major realignment against the Deutschmark a year (defining a major realignment as one involving either the French franc or the Italian lira, and usually both: there were also three involving only the Danish kroner, the Belgian franc or the Irish punt over the same period).* Subsequently, the system hardened: up to the middle of 1992 there was only one, involving the lira – and that was a special case, being a consequence of Italy's decision to move from the wide band to the narrow band in January 1990. Given the downward pressure on the pound in the wake of the oil price collapse in the first quarter of 1986, sterling would almost certainly have moved down with the franc in the realignment of April of that year. Had we entered the ERM, as I had recommended in November 1985, at a parity of DM3.70, this would imply a move to some DM3.50 in April 1986.

This puts into perspective Walters' claim in his curious book *Sterling in Danger* that an attempt to hold the pound at DM3.75 would have involved interest rates of 17–20 per cent when sterling came under pressure as a result of the oil price collapse – quite apart from the fact that the particular way in which he reaches his estimated interest rate is wholly spurious. But I readily accept that some increase in interest rates would almost certainly have been required to maintain a parity of DM3.50 in 1986 – and a good thing, too. It would have been a small price to pay to prevent the collapse from DM3.45 in March 1986 to DM2.85 in December 1986 that actually occurred. Those who wish to criticize me for not taking sufficient action soon enough to curb the credit boom, cannot complain about the higher interest rates a more restrictive stance would have entailed.

I am not, of course, suggesting that Margaret's veto on ERM entry in November 1985 absolves me from responsibility for any mistakes I may subsequently have made. But it undoubtedly made the conduct of economic policy more difficult, and thus errors more likely. In particular, it was very difficult, outside the ERM, to handle the

---

*French and Italian realignments from the inception of the EMS in March 1979 to the end of April 1992:

	Franc	Lira
	% decline against the DM	
24 September 1979	-2	-2
23 March 1981	-	-6
5 October 1981	-8.5	-8.5
14 June 1982	-10	-7
22 March 1983	-8	-8
22 July 1985	-	-8
7 April 1986	-6	-3
12 January 1987	-3	-3
8 January 1990	-	-3.6

effects of the 1986 oil price collapse and prevent sterling from falling too far. Moreover the advantage of rules over discretion in the conduct of economic policy is not merely that this can save policy makers from their own mistakes. It also – and this is equally important, although usually overlooked in discussion of the subject – affects decision-makers in the private sector, persuading them to conduct their affairs in a more prudent way.

It is hardly an extravagant exercise in hypothetical reasoning to claim that ERM entry in November 1985 (or indeed soon after it) would have put a dampener both on pay and price increases in the internationally exposed sector of the UK economy – most importantly on the prices of products sold at home and subject to competition from imports – and, through higher interest rates, on the credit explosion and the housing boom, thus moderating the excessive spending by businesses and consumers alike which those developments fuelled.

Not the least of the advantages is that Margaret would not have been able to prevent me from raising interest rates in 1986, as in practice to some extent occurred. Margaret was right in arguing that what I was advocating would constrain the freedom of Governments to do whatever they like. But a constraint of this kind is highly desirable, and should be welcomed by all true 'Thatcherites', even though it was evidently anathema to Margaret herself.

Although I was not aware of it at the time, there would have been two further advantages in ERM entry in November 1985, rather than five years later as eventually occurred. The first is that it would have been unequivocally an act of economic policy, clearly distanced from the wider political argument over the future of Europe which later threatened to split the Conservative Party. The second is that, in those days, German reunification was nothing more than a distant and eccentric dream. In other words, we would have enjoyed a clear run of five or six years during which the Deutschmark would have served us, as it served the other member nations, as a very satisfactory low-inflation anchor, without the strain of the relatively high interest rates that unification was eventually to impose on the system as a whole.

APPENDIX: THE 'WALTERS CRITIQUE' AND ALL THAT

THE REASON WHY simon-pure monetarists detest managed, pegged or fixed exchange rates is not hard to understand. If interest rates are used to maintain a given exchange rate – or even if the exchange rate is merely 'taken into account' in setting interest rates – they plainly cannot be dedicated exclusively to controlling the domestic money supply.

But suppose that, for whatever reason, different measures of money supply move in different directions, and there is serious uncertainty about the relationship between any of these measures either to inflation or to the national income in money terms. Then the simon-pure monetarist will insist on trying even harder to find a relationship of this kind that does exist, and the various sects will argue among themselves over what that might be. The exchange rate monetarist, however, will adopt the common-sense approach of deriving all the help he can get from linking his country's currency to that of another country with a proven track record of reasonable price stability.

That, in a nutshell, is what the debate was about. What, then, was the new element that Walters was supposed to have brought to it? In *Britain's Economic Renaissance* – overall a much better book than his later *Sterling in Danger* – his central critique is that two countries linked by a fixed exchange rate, say France and Germany, would be forced to have the same interest rates as if they had a common currency, even though their inflation rates were very different. Thus France, the (traditionally) high-inflation country would be forced to have interest rates that were too low, and Germany interest rates that were too high.

Incredibly, this assertion was greeted as a major contribution to economic policy thinking by a number of economists who should have known better. Being a practical man myself, I could not help noticing that, so far from being the same, short-term interest rates in France exceeded those in Germany by 5½ per cent in 1985, by 3 per cent in 1986, and by 4 per cent in 1987 – a gap even greater than that between the two countries' inflation rates in each of those same three years. Seeing the reality staring us in the face, and given that Margaret never included the 'Walters critique' (his own name for this particular application of what has long been known to economists as the interest parity theorem) among her litany of objections to ERM membership, I found it hard to take it seriously.

It might have been a serious matter, of course, if Germany had watered down its anti-inflationary policy to make things easier for France. But this was not the case, since the Bundesbank was able to use its statutory obligations and publicly respected independence to insist on putting price stability first, leaving it to other member countries to pursue sufficiently tight policies to maintain the Deutschmark link.

How, then, were interest rates held apart? By the time he came to write *Sterling in Danger* in 1990, Walters was forced to admit that in the real world they were not the same, and he explained it in terms of uncertainty about the timing and size of the next realignment. This caused the financial markets to insist on an interest rate premium for holding the traditionally weaker currency. In other words, the 'Walters critique' had been based on a simple confusion between what the economists like to call *ex post* and *ex ante*. After the event, if two currencies have had a fixed parity for a period of time, it would indeed look foolish to have held the currency with the lower interest rate: the only stable state of affairs is one in which the two countries' interest rates are the same. The only snag is that decisions about which currency to hold cannot be taken after the event: they have to be taken before it. And before the event there is no cast-iron guarantee that the parity will in fact be held for any given length of time.

Of course, if inflation rates converge towards the German rate, and realignments become very rare (as subsequently occurred), interest rates will tend to converge, too; and this phenomenon became particularly marked when the adverse short-term consequences of reunification caused doubts about German price stability in the early 1990s. But this in no way justifies the flawed nature of the 'Walters critique', which was expressly concerned with the alleged perversity of the ERM at a time when inflation rates greatly differed.

Moreover this was by no means the only fallacy in the 'Walters critique', or even the most important one, particularly in the context of the ERM as it actually existed in 1985. For ERM parities, even without a realignment, are not fixed in the sense on which the 'Walters critique' depends. They are allowed to fluctuate within a range of 2¼ per cent on either side of their central parity, giving a total band width of up to 4½ per cent. Indeed, some member countries – Italy from 1979 to 1990, Spain since 1989 and the UK since 1990 – have been allowed, on an officially temporary basis, margins in principle as great as 6 per cent either side of the central parity.*

But even the narrow band provides a degree of fluctuation that can keep interest rates apart. Nor is that all it does: it can allow realignments of modest proportions to occur without any destabilizing change in the market rate and without offering speculators a one-way bet. The simple

---

*In practice, when there is more than one wide-band member, and one of them is at or near its limit, the rules of the EMS grid prevent the others from enjoying the full width of the 6 per cent margin. But this is a technicality which need not detain us.

rule, which I was to set out in my IMF speech in 1987 in the context of what I described as 'managed floating' between the world's major currencies (but the principle is exactly the same), is that the change in the central rate at any realignment should normally be less than the size of the band.

There is, however, a much more interesting question about the ERM than the 'Walters critique', and it is this. How is it that Germany could secure low inflation by pursuing a domestic monetary policy, whereas others felt they had to use Germany and the Deutschmark as their anchor? Exchange rate systems either have a particular commodity as the anchor to which every country chains its currency, as with the classical, and in its day highly successful, gold standard; or else one of the currencies in the system has to act as the anchor to which the others are chained, as with the dollar under Bretton Woods or the Deutschmark in the context of the EMS. In the latter case the anchor currency clearly cannot secure price stability by chaining its currency to one of the others: the anchor currency (which strictly speaking need not be the same one for all time) has to be able to pursue a successful domestic monetary policy. But if one country can do this, why not all of them? Why just Germany?

This is a mystery only to economists, or at least the large number of them whose universe is bounded by what can, at least in principle, be measured. For the answer lies in a web of cultural, historical and institutional factors which are no less real for being unquantifiable. In Germany, the horror which memories of the Weimar hyper-inflation of the 1920s had left behind, a horror which was refreshed by the appalling post-war inflation of the 1940s, led to a virtuous circle. There was overwhelming public support for counter-inflationary measures, which enabled them to be successfully implemented. This success in turn led to the expectation that such measures would be successful, as a result of which inflationary expectations were low and easily dampened, and it did not take a savage recession or sky-high interest rates to stop incipient inflationary surges in their tracks.

The whole beneficent process was further assisted by the existence of an independent central bank, the Bundesbank, bound by law (as America's independent Federal Reserve system is not) to put price stability first, and which enjoyed far too much public esteem and popular support for the politicians to dare to threaten it. In addition, the degree of financial innovation in Germany was much less than in the English-speaking world (which is why Germany leads in manufacturing but not in financial services), making the choice of monetary targets easier. Even so, the targets were in practice quite often missed – and in 1988 the Bundesbank made an important change in the monetary aggregate targeted, which has not proved a great help to it. But so great was the confidence commanded by the Bundesbank, that the overshooting of targets and changes in definition were taken in their stride by the financial markets, leaving inflationary expectations unimpaired.

This cultural, historical and institutional mix created a public good which it would have been folly for other European countries, with different cultures, histories and institutional arrangements – in many cases at least as admirable from other points of view – not to choose to borrow.

CHAPTER 41

MONEY TALKS EVERYWHERE

Summits and Circuses · Trinidad No Holiday
The Washington Scene · Countries Can Go Broke
Buying Time

Summits and Circuses

My conviction that sterling's membership of the ERM was desirable for the successful conduct of economic policy generally and the battle against inflation in particular can be dated back to the minute I sent Geoffrey Howe when I was Financial Secretary in 1981. But it developed in the context of the wider interest in the international financial scene which was a major part of my job as Chancellor. This tended to revolve around a regular annual round of meetings.

The most high-powered, but rarely the most important, of these was the summit of the Group of Seven major industrial powers – the United States, Japan, Germany, the UK, France, Italy and Canada. The economic summit meetings had begun in 1975 when two of Europe's leading Finance Ministers, Valéry Giscard d'Estaing and Helmut Schmidt became President of France and Federal German Chancellor more or less simultaneously. They decided to try and replicate the recently established Group of Five Finance Ministers, of which they had been a part, at Head of Government level. Gerald Ford, then filling in as President of the United States, Jim Callaghan for the United Kingdom, and Takeo Miki, Prime Minister of Japan, for the time being all agreed, and the summit was born. Giscard, who was the host at the first Economic Summit, then decided to invite Italy as well, which made it more or less inevitable that the following year, 1976, when the US was the host country, they should invite Canada to join.

The next year, 1977, it was the UK's turn to play host. Roy Jenkins, the then President of the EC Commission, prevailed upon a misguided Jim Callaghan to extend an invitation to the European Community, whose representatives would be the Commission President and the President of the Council of Ministers for the time being. As it was, Europe, with four countries (all of them Community members) out of the seven, was over-represented; to have the Community as such there as well made the over-representation ridiculous, and particularly irked the Americans. Nor did it help the European members there in their own right, since the Brussels delegation, and especially the Commission President, tended to see their principal objective as the assertion of the Community's 'competence' in whatever area happened to be under discussion. The implication was that the four Community countries directly represented should leave him to speak for them – something that none of them were ready to accept.

The early meetings were successful in their most important initial object, which was to prevent an international trade war. They had also been responsible for one bad mistake: persuading a reluctant Germany, at the Bonn Summit of 1978, to stimulate its domestic economy in return for US pledges to deregulate its oil market. Like many domestic experiments in fine-tuning this international one proved ill-timed and took effect at a time of rekindled world inflation, during the second oil price explosion.

By 1983 the summits had become, in Bagehot's terminology, part of the dignified rather than the efficient machinery of Government. Once they were established international events they ceased to be informal gatherings and became media circuses. Meetings of senior officials, (known as 'sherpas' because they prepared the way to the summit) started many months beforehand to draft the communiqués. Once both Giscard d'Estaing and Helmut Schmidt had departed, economic issues were largely left to Finance Ministers – who, along with Foreign Ministers had been added to the cast list – to discuss separately. This was so that the heads of Government could escape from economic issues, in which most of them had little interest, to discuss world politics. The summits were still officially 'Economic Summits', but the reality increasingly belied the description. So I cannot say that I was devastated to become Chancellor just too late to attend the 1983 Williamsburg Summit, which had been held during the General Election campaign, in late May.

The two main economic topics at that meeting were the soaring dollar and the emergence of America's so-called twin deficits – the Federal Budget deficit and the current account balance of payments deficit. Finding himself in a minority of one, President Reagan none the less refused to contemplate a tax increase, to reduce the US Budget deficit, despite Margaret's homily on the virtues of Geoffrey's 1981 Budget. But he did endorse a communiqué which referred in an extremely guarded way to the desirability of stabilizing exchange rates.

Trinidad No Holiday

For a Chancellor of the Exchequer the key international meetings are not the annual Economic Summits in the summer, but meetings of the G7 (formerly G5) Finance Ministers, which can occur at any time; the spring meeting of the Interim Committee of the IMF in Washington; and of course the annual meeting of the IMF and World Bank each autumn.

This last is far and away the most arduous occasion, involving, with the other meetings held on its margins, a solid week of speech-making and economic diplomacy. It is held in Washington, where the two institutions have their headquarters, in two years out of three, and in different non-US cities, where the facilities are seldom adequate, in the third. Fortunately, the first of these meetings I attended was in Washington in September 1983. With world growth still sluggish and the debt problem of the middle-income developing countries still threatening, the meetings promised to be lively.

But before I could reach Washington I had a somewhat unpromising diversion. For I first had to go to Port of Spain, Trinidad, where the Commonwealth Finance Ministers were gathering for their annual meeting, an event which always preceded the Bank and Fund gatherings. Anything more different from a few days relaxation on a Caribbean beach would be difficult to imagine. I have never been the greatest admirer of the Commonwealth as an institution. In political terms it is a largely meaningless relic of Empire – like the smile on the face of the Cheshire cat which remains when the cat has disappeared.

The Trinidad meeting was conducted in the unpleasant and acrimonious spirit that had become customary at Commonwealth gatherings. Many Commonwealth countries were aggrieved that the sovereign debt crisis, which had erupted a year earlier, was invariably thought of in terms of Latin America. There was a grain of truth in their complaint. Because the Latin American governments had the largest debts, they posed the biggest threat to the world's banking system; and because it was American banks that were the most exposed and the countries themselves lay within what the United States had historically considered its own sphere of interest, Latin American debtors did receive a disproportionate amount of aid and attention.

Yet many of the smaller Commonwealth countries had debts which were, in relation to the size and strength of their economies, equally burdensome. Those which had no bank debts at all were generally in that normally fortunate condition because they were so poor that no

Western bank would lend to them. Both these groups felt neglected and forgotten, and used the Commonwealth Finance Ministers' meetings to berate the West in general, and Britain in particular, for parsimony and lack of assistance. In 1983 it was the Nigerians who, not for the first time, led the assault.

The vehicle of their anger was a report drawn up by Professor Gerald Helleiner of the University of Toronto, entitled *Towards a New Bretton Woods*. Commissioned at the 1982 Commonwealth Finance Ministers' meeting at Lancaster House, it called for more funds for the IMF and the World Bank; greater representation of Third World views in their management, easier terms for IMF loans; and of course an international conference to discuss the reforms. Shridath ('Sonny') Ramphal, the then Commonwealth Secretary General, opened the meeting with a call to accept the principles of the Helleiner Report. I made clear, with some support from my Canadian opposite number and the representative of Australia, that I could not do so.

The unlikely hero of the oppressed at that time was the then Prime Minister of New Zealand, Robert Muldoon, who doubled as Finance Minister. By that time Bob Muldoon was pursing interventionist policies to such disastrous effect that his Labour opponents in New Zealand became wholly converted to the market economy. It was of course true that prosperous New Zealand, like many poor Commonwealth countries, was greatly affected by the fluctuations in commodity prices; but the fact was that Muldoon loved playing to the gallery. In reality, the Helleiner scheme amounted to no more than a demand for increased subventions from the West, and especially from Britain. It did not at that time occur to any Commonwealth Finance Ministers that their economic problems might be at least partly due to the policies they themselves were pursuing.

The whole experience was both pointless and disagreeable, and I then and there decided that I had better things to do than submit myself to annual meetings of Commonwealth Finance Ministers – happy as I always was to see them individually whenever they visited London, which they did frequently. There were six further such meetings during my time as Chancellor, of which I attended two – which was at least two more than my Australian opposite number, the acerbic Paul Keating, who was subsequently to become his country's Prime Minister.

Happily, however, by the end of my time as Chancellor the mood of the meetings of Commonwealth Finance Ministers had changed completely. Even before the collapse of Communism in eastern Europe, many developing countries came to realize that their problems originated not in Western parsimony but in the interventionist policies they had themselves consistently pursued since independence. This change of emphasis greatly improved the atmosphere at the Commonwealth meetings; where, instead of berating the UK, the various Finance Ministers vied with each other to demonstrate their free-market credentials. Moreover, because most countries were at last making genuine attempts to remedy their mistakes, I was able to persuade the international financial community at a series of meetings culminating in the Toronto summit in June 1988 to offer the sub-Saharan African countries substantial relief from their mounting debts.

The Washington Scene

Commonwealth Finance Ministers tended to meet in the West Indies in September, not so much because of the attractions of the Caribbean, but because the islands are conveniently located for most Ministers en route to the annual meetings of the IMF and World Bank in Washington later that month. I arrived in Washington, via Miami, on Friday, 23 September 1983, where I was joined by Thérèse, whose presence on my trips overseas was to prove sadly infrequent. This was partly because she hated flying, partly because she did not want to abandon the children, and partly because even if she did pay these two prices, the reward was to take part in a 'wives' programme – which did not greatly enthuse her – while I worked. It thus had to be in a part of the world she found unusually congenial – such as Cap d'Antibes during the French presidency of the Community – for her to agree to venture overseas.

Thérèse and I stayed in great comfort at the official residence of the British ambassador, at that time Oliver Wright, whom I had known ever since we worked together for Alec Home in 1964. Designed by Lutyens, and lavishly furnished and decorated, the Washington residence is, quite simply, the best hotel in the world for those fortunate enough to be able to stay in it, as I was to do, usually twice a year, for several years. The service is impeccable, the food and wine second to none. Both Oliver and his successor, Anthony Acland, who had been at Christ Church, Oxford, with me, were understanding hosts. They recognized that I had come to Washington to work, and left me to get on with it, ensuring that their excellent domestic staff looked after all my needs.

Robin Leigh-Pemberton, the Governor of the Bank of England, accompanied by his kind and energetic wife, Rose, also stayed at the Residence on these occasions, which greatly eased liaison between us. Robin's Washington visits, however, were considerably less demanding, except on the social front. In every respect the job of a Central Bank Governor is more agreeable than that of a Finance Minister.

Apart from my Principal Private Secretary, who was also put up at the Residence, my official team was housed elsewhere, and we would gather in the sitting room of my suite to prepare for the key meetings and draft the numerous speeches. This culminated in the speech to the annual meeting itself, over which I always took a great deal of trouble, seeing it as an opportunity to develop economic thinking on one of the major international issues of the day. Since the days were occupied by wall-to-wall meetings, the speech writing would normally start after a small working dinner, and could often go on late into the night.

My team for this would normally consist of Terry Burns; the top official responsible for international matters at the Treasury (for most of my time the chain-smoking Geoff Littler, later with the National Westminster Bank) and his number two; our Economic Minister from the Washington Embassy, a Treasury man on secondment who also doubled up as the UK executive director of both the IMF and World Bank, and my Principal Private Secretary and Press Secretary.

The annual meetings were remarkable affairs. Since they were the one occasion on which the Finance Ministers and Central Bank Governors of the world would gather together in one place, bankers and other financial intermediaries from all over the world would be there in vast numbers in the hope of doing business, throwing extravagant parties as a bait. The fact that a large part of the business done was a disaster for the banks' shareholders scarcely deterred them. And of course nothing deterred the world's financial Press, also there in force.

But for me and my fellow Finance Ministers from the major nations, at any rate, all this was essentially a sideshow. What mattered were the meetings, both formal and informal, in the days preceding the start of the annual meetings themselves, which is where the real governmental business is transacted.

Far and away the most important of these meetings in 1983 was that of the Group of Five Finance Ministers and Central Bank Governors, usually known as the Group of Five or G5.

While it was the Finance Ministers who took the lead at its meetings, which were chaired by the Finance Minister on whose territory the meeting in question was held, the participation of Central Bank Governors was particularly important in the case of Germany and the United States, given the statutory independence of the Bundesbank and the Federal Reserve. The fact that, by contrast, Central Bank Governors do not attend the annual Economic Summit is yet a further shortcoming of the Summit as a forum for economic co-operation. In fact, each country fielded a team of three – the third being a senior Treasury or Finance Ministry official, known as the Minister's 'Deputy'. The G5 Deputies would meet separately, whenever this was needed, to prepare for the G5 meetings – a process which also enabled them to brief their Ministers more or less accurately on the positions of the others.

There were thus a total of only fifteen present at a G5 meeting (plus the occasional interpreter: the discussion took place in English, which was frequently a genuine problem for the Japanese contingent and a policy problem for the French) and since the Deputies seldom spoke, an uninhibited exchange of views between the Ministers and Governors could and did take place. I recall Geoffrey Howe telling me shortly after he had become Foreign Secretary that the Group of Five was the most useful international gathering of which he had ever been a member, and that he greatly missed it. That was my experience, too.

My first attendance at a G5 meeting was on the evening of Saturday, 23 September 1983. We met for a working dinner in a private room at an old and well-established Washington club without the Press even knowing the meeting was taking place, let alone where it was held. It was hosted and chaired by the then US Treasury Secretary, Donald Regan, flanked by Paul Volcker, then Chairman of the Federal Reserve, and the free-market zealot Beryl (he pronounced it 'Burl', which was just as well) Sprinkel, Don Regan's Deputy. One important purpose of these meetings was to agree a common view on the issues likely to arise at the various IMF and World Bank meetings which followed, since it was obviously desirable that the major industrial nations at least should pursue a common approach when discussing the problems of the world economy.

The meetings always began by a session on what was known in the jargon as 'surveillance'. This meant a presentation on the state of the world economy by the Fund's Managing Director, at that time Jacques de Larosière, followed by a round-table discussion, during which each Finance Minister would comment on the Fund's assessment and speak briefly and frankly about the situation in his own country. The Managing Director would then withdraw and leave us to our private deliberations.

The G5 meeting was followed the next day by a brief Ministerial meeting of the so-called Group of Ten. With a membership consisting of the G5 countries plus Italy, Canada, Belgium, Holland and Sweden, with Switzerland (later to become a full member) sitting in as an observer, the G10 had already been to all intents and purposes marginalized by the emergence of the G5, and this was further emphasized when the G5 was eventually enlarged to become the G7. The meeting of the twenty-plus Interim Committee of the IMF – the Fund's key policy-making committee – also took place on the Sunday, and then it was the turn of the Development Committee on the Monday. The formal annual meeting of the Fund and Bank then opened on the Tuesday.

The two official Committees – the Interim and Development Committees – were by no means of equal importance. The Interim Committee, genuinely did determine IMF policy, and the Fund's Managing Director enjoyed a free hand only to the extent that he retained the Interim Committee's support and trust. The Development Committee, by contrast, chaired by a Finance Minister from one of the developing countries, was a curious hybrid offspring of the Bank and Fund jointly, and was primarily a forum where Ministers from both the developed and developing world could meet to discuss matters of particular interest to the latter.

Countries Can Go Broke

The big issue at the 1983 meetings was the international debt problem. Like the world recession of the early 1990s, it owed much to herd-like bank folly. It started with massive and careless bank lending to Third World governments prompted by the erroneous belief, voiced most prominently by Walter Wriston, the large and publicity-seeking Chairman of Citibank, that 'countries can't go broke'. Among the many fallacies in that remark was overlooking the fact that developing countries raised taxes in their own currencies but borrowed in dollars.

The remuneration of loan officers in US banks according to the quantity rather than the quality of the business they did, aggravated matters by ensuring that loans were advanced with the minimum of risk assessment. In so far as the banks thought about this at all, they were either comforted by the Wriston doctrine, or else assumed that the sovereign borrowers would be indefinitely floated off by rising commodity prices (including the oil price) and low or negative real interest rates. The lectures by Western political leaders in the 1970s on the valuable and essential public service the banks were performing in recycling the oil surpluses did not help matters either. The two oil price explosions of 1973–74 and 1979, which had created a temporary export surplus among the oil producers and a large increase in the import bill of the non-oil developing countries, and the banks were given to believe that it was their profitable duty to use funds from the former to lend to the latter. But the flow of bank lending soon acquired a momentum of its own and went well beyond the passing on of the original OPEC surpluses.

Sooner or later nemesis was inevitable: the only question was when. In the event, it was triggered by the sharp rise in US and world interest rates consequent upon Paul Volcker's anti-inflation drive after the second world oil price shock. Because the squeeze succeeded in reducing inflation rates faster than expected, short-term real rates shot up from around zero or even negative levels in the 1970s to 4 or 5 per cent by the early 1980s. An associated development was the global W-shaped recession with a dip in 1980 and a much sharper one in 1982. Real commodity prices tumbled to their lowest level since the middle 1960s and oil prices started to crack a little later.

The crisis was precipitated by Mexico's consequent announcement in 1982 that it was unable to service its international loans; and this was soon followed by similar statements by the governments of the Argentine,

Brazil, Venezuela, Nigeria and a number of other large sovereign borrowers. The American banks abruptly stopped their sovereign lending; and this sharp 'improvement' in the US capital account sent the dollar, which had already risen in real terms by 30 per cent between the election of Ronald Reagan and the autumn of 1982, soaring further, which in turn made the (dollar-denominated) debt problem even worse. All this was further exacerbated by the huge US fiscal deficit and the need to finance it, which turned the biggest economy in the world into a massive international borrower, as well as by the unstable nature of the foreign exchange market in the leading world currencies.

The Mexican announcement on Friday, 13 August 1982 that it was no longer able to service (that is, pay the interest on) some $80 billion of foreign debt, came as a shock of seismic proportions. Had Mexico defaulted, 70 per cent of the equity capital of the two largest US banks would have vanished overnight. The OECD estimated that at the end of 1982 the total bank debts of the non-OPEC developing countries came to $640 billion – more than the entire UK national income at the time – and this ignored altogether bond issues and loans from governments and international organizations. Mexico, Brazil, the Argentine and South Korea accounted for nearly half this sum. The entire world banking system was under threat and with it the world economy. It was the sovereign debt crisis as much as the domestic recession that caused the US Fed to ease monetary policy at the end of 1982 and throughout 1983, to abandon its brief experiment with Monetary Base Control, and to pay more explicit attention to interest rates in the determination of monetary policy.

But it was clear that a co-ordinated international response was required, and the only existing body capable of rising to the challenge was the IMF, even though this was no part of its official remit. A number of emergency aid packages were hurriedly put in place, but the 1983 meetings were the first real test of the Fund's ability to develop a coherent and effective response. In its Managing Director, Jacques de Larosière, the IMF was fortunate in possessing an exceptionally able and influential leader, well versed in international banking.

Larosière, a short, silver-haired, urbane, highly intelligent, cultivated and meticulously correct French public servant (he was, inevitably, an *énarque** and an *Inspecteur des Finances*), possessed an impeccable

---

*After the war, President de Gaulle was determined that France should be governed by an élite, all of whose members would know eath other personally and be informed by a commom commitment to the idea of public service (at the highest levels, of course). He had been impressed by the nature and contribution of the Oxbridge élite to the government of Britain. To achieve this he set up the *Ecole Nationale d'Administration*, or ENA, whose graduates accordingly became known as *énarques*. Entry to the ENA was by competitive examination, and much sought after. The rigorous education it provided was designed to be more attuned to the demands of the modern world than were the traditional disciplines of Oxbridge. Those

(continued over)

command of English and was deeply proud of his aristocratic descent ('Larosière' was an abbreviation, which he accepted in deference to the democratic instincts of the United States, of his full name of Jacques de Larosière de Champfeu). He did an outstanding job of redirecting the Fund's energies to spearheading the international response to the sovereign debt crisis that had burst upon the world with the Mexican bombshell of 1982.

Larosière's effectiveness was considerably increased by the excellent working relationship he developed with the six-feet-eight-inches-tall, cigar-smoking, sceptical, impressively competent Paul Volcker. His disappointment was that his wife, France, loathed America and the Americans, and was always hankering to return to Paris. She eventually had her way in 1986, when the Right won the French parliamentary elections and offered her husband the Governorship of the Banque de France, which he accepted more for her sake than his own.

Larosière's first priority had been to increase the funds available to the IMF to deal with the crisis. In February 1983 the IMF Interim Committee, chaired by Geoffrey Howe, had sanctioned a 50 per cent increase in the IMF quotas which determine both the scale of contributions to the Fund by its member governments and the amount debtors can borrow. But Congress, unattracted by what it saw as bailing out the banks, was refusing to ratify the US quota increase, and at the same time was holding up approval of a $6 billion loan to the IMF to cover its share of unexpected commitments in 1984. It took President Reagan to break the deadlock, by throwing his personal prestige behind the quota increase. I was able to help by introducing a compromise formula for adjusting the borrowing rules, which had been worked out at the Commonwealth Finance Minister's meeting the previous week. Under it, debtors were allowed to borrow smaller proportions of the enlarged quotas, with variations to take account of the seriousness of their problems.

who secure the top places in the ENA leaving examination are allotted to one of the three so-called *Grands Corps*, of which the *Inspecteurs des Finances* is the largest. Members of the *Grands Corps*, whatever career they choose to pursue, always remain members, and enjoy the security of jobs for life, in the sense that they are guaranteed a senior post in the bureaucracy whenever they wish. More important, they provide France with a tightly knit ruling class, who signify their consciousness of their membership of it by addressing each other, automatically, in the second person singular rather than the customary second person plural (*tu* rather than *vous*). In short, in the post-war decades, when Britain was engaged in stamping out élitism and the idea of a ruling class, France was engaged in creating it. There are no prizes for guessing which country had the better of the exchange.

Buying Time

The essence of the IMF's debt strategy was the so-called case-by-case approach. This meant dealing with each country's problems separately, on its merits.

This was widely considered at the time to be a heartless and cynical approach. Between 1982 and 1985 there was a great outpouring of literature and speeches claiming that the debts were a global problem in need of a global solution. From time to time the Latin American countries would form debtors' cartels in an effort to secure more favourable terms, but the major countries which effectively controlled the IMF quite rightly refused to deal with them. Instead, they insisted that each country be treated on its own merits. In return for sensible economic reforms, the IMF would promote rescheduling packages, in which the borrowers were given more time to pay and thus avoid default. Its own 'new money' was nearly always the smaller part of the total package, and acted chiefly as an essential lubricant. More important was the fact that its seal of approval became a *sine qua non* of persuading the banks to reschedule.

The Western world was wise to choose the IMF rather than set up some new organization, because it imbued the response from the outset with its particular approach and ethos, which derived from the fact that the IMF was the principal vehicle for international co-operation between the Finance Ministries of the world, and its executive board was composed of their representatives. There is always a risk in any international crisis that the Foreign Ministries will regard its resolution as their task. Had this occurred in the case of the debt crisis of the early 1980s, it would have rendered impossible the relatively hard-headed approach the West eventually and quite rightly adopted.

A hard-headed approach was just as necessary from the point of view of the debtor countries as it was from that of their Western creditors. For while the debt problem as such was largely a product of the folly of the banks, the core of these countries' difficulties lay in poorly performing economies. It is, of course, perfectly sensible for developing countries to import capital, since they are unlikely, at least for some time, to be able to generate what they need for economic development themselves; but the supply of capital is useless unless the policies are in place to allow it to be put to productive and profitable use. In general, that was not the case. Moreover (and this was another point I was to make at countless international meetings on the issue over the years), until the debtor countries put sound economic policies in place, their own citizens would continue to send their own capital abroad – so-called 'flight capital' – as fast as the rest of the world was persuaded to put it in.

Moreover the developing countries had compounded their problems by the form in which they chose to import capital. Instead of encouraging private sector equity investment from overseas, and to some extent raising debt finance through bond issues where the risk is widely spread and investors usually make a realistic assessment of the risks of default, they chose the highly dangerous course of relying on floating rate bank finance. As I put it in my speech to the Annual Meetings on September 18 1983: 'Many [developing countries] ought to look again at their attitudes towards private investment and to reflect on the advantages they could draw from encouraging long-term flows in that form, rather than the short-term borrowing of which they have had such uncomfortable recent experience.'

As I have indicated, the international debt problem was of particular concern to the United States, for foreign policy and domestic reasons alike. It was this that led to the so-called 'Baker Plan', named after its author, the then US Treasury Secretary. It was unveiled at the annual meetings of the Bank and Fund in Seoul in October 1985, which provided for additional loans by the World Bank and other international agencies to a specified group of major debtors, linked to the pursuit by those countries of what were described as growth-oriented adjustment policies, designed to attract the financial support of the commercial banks. The 'plan' succeeded in buying more time which was probably the most that could realistically have been expected of it.

Indeed, the principal – although largely undeclared – objective of the Western world's debt strategy, ably co-ordinated by the IMF, was to buy time. When it first broke, the debt crisis posed a real systemic threat. Defaults in Mexico and Brazil alone (the two largest debtor nations) might have precipitated the collapse of the entire Western banking structure and imperilled the prosperity of the world. Time was needed not only to enable the debtor countries to put sensible economic policies in place, but also for the Western banks to rebuild their shattered balance sheets to the point where they could afford to write off their bad sovereign debts. For it was perfectly clear that the vast bulk of these debts would never come good and be repaid – even though there was an understandable conspiracy of silence over admitting this unpalatable fact.

In these terms the debt strategy was largely successful. The policies being pursued by the debtor nations, although far from impeccable, are more sensible today than they were during the 1970s. As a result, some of the debtor countries now have healthier economies than ever before. And the very real threat to the world banking system in the first half of the 1980s was averted. Indeed, this is one of the very few examples where buying time in order to delay the inevitable was the right strategy. Generally speaking, in both politics and economics, any delay in tackling an identified problem only stores up more acute problems later on.

Alas, happy endings are all too rare, and this was no exception. Having escaped from the jaws of disaster overseas, it did not take the banks – notably in the US, Japan and not least the UK – long to discover new forms of bad lending closer to home. But that is for another chapter.

CHAPTER 42

REAGAN AND HIS PEOPLE

Hong Kong Excursion · Debating the US Deficit
A New Realism in the Third World · The London Summit
No Global Debt Solution

Hong Kong Excursion

MY DEPARTURE FROM WASHINGTON after my speech to the 1983 plenary session of the IMF and World Bank, in which I spoke about both the international debt problem and the state of the UK economy was delayed by a meeting at the Residence with Margaret, who had just arrived in Washington, to discuss the financial crisis that had erupted in Hong Kong. Talks with China on the future sovereignty of Hong Kong had started in July 1983. They were not going well, and in the week before the IMF meeting the *People's Daily* carried a vitriolic attack on the British negotiating position. The bottom fell out of the Hong Kong stock market and property market, and the Hong Kong dollar plunged on the foreign exchange markets, despite a sharp increase in interest rates, precipitating panic in the Colony.

I telephoned a beleaguered Philip Haddon-Cave, the Chief Secretary of the Government of Hong Kong, from Washington and told him that we were willing to assist in stabilizing the situation in any way that we could. I had known Haddon-Cave well since meeting him on a visit to Hong Kong while in Opposition, when he was the Colony's Financial Secretary (equivalent to Finance Minister), a job he had held for many years with great distinction. Indeed, at one time I had hoped that Geoffrey would persuade Margaret to make him Governor of the Bank of England.

The Hong Kong Government had already let it be known three days earlier – on the Sunday after the disastrous plunge in the market – that it was developing a scheme to ensure the exchange rate would 'more accurately reflect the fundamental strength of the economy'. This had halted the slide, and (having already discussed the matter both with my officials in Washington and over the telephone with Peter Middleton in London) I told Margaret that it looked as if the best way of consolidating the position would be to link the Hong Kong dollar explicitly to the United States dollar. Fortunately, despite her theoretical belief in the impossibility of bucking the market, she needed little persuading of this – largely because Alan Walters, who had returned to academic life in the United States after the 1983 election, had a former star pupil in Hong Kong who had put forward a scheme along these lines which Walters had already commended to her.

Although it had had a floating currency, to which Haddon-Cave was devoted, for some years, Hong Kong had amassed huge (though undisclosed) foreign exchange reserves. This was because it had no public debt, having always run a budget surplus. Without a borrowing requirement of its own, the only way the administration could conduct open market operations was through the foreign exchange market. As a result, its foreign exchange reserves actually exceeded its note issue. The simple concept of backing every Hong Kong dollar with a US dollar had instant credibility in the marketplace. Haddon-Cave was initially resistant to the idea, but he reluctantly agreed. I offered to send a team of two key officials, one from the Treasury and one from the Bank of England, to help his people put it into practice. He was happy to accept the offer, and a team consisting of David Peretz from the Treasury and Charles Goodhart from the Bank duly travelled to Hong Kong to carry out their task, without the Press ever getting wind of it – a necessary precaution in as imaginative a rumour-factory as Hong Kong.

The pegging of the currency at HK$7.80 to the dollar was announced to the markets on 16 October 1983 and proved an extremely successful solution. Confidence in all the financial markets was restored very quickly and, despite all the political vicissitudes that have subsequently occurred, the relationship between the Hong Kong dollar and the United States dollar proved to have considerable staying power.

Debating the US Deficit

The main international financial question of 1983 persisted into 1984 and beyond: the interrelated problems of the high US fiscal deficit, high world real interest rates, the high dollar and the Third World debt problem. A syndrome emerged – dubbed 'the trend is my friend' by the markets –

in which foreign buyers of US Treasury bonds, enjoying gains from the appreciation of the dollar as well as a handsome income from relatively high interest rates, purchased US Treasury bonds, thus pushing up the dollar still further. The simple-minded view was that the resulting high dollar 'caused' the US current account payments deficit. But what really caused the deficit was a deficiency of US savings relative to domestic investment, to which the Federal Budget deficit clearly contributed. The gap was met by an inflow of foreign capital, of which the current account deficit was the necessary mirror image, since overall the balance of payments of any country – taking capital and current transactions together – has to balance. The level of the dollar thus had to be high enough to be consistent with the current account deficit.

This was the background to my next visit to Washington, in April 1984, to attend the spring meetings of the Interim and Development Committees. In the discussions, most of us argued that the debt problem was being prolonged by the effects of the Federal Budget deficit in keeping American interest rates at relatively high levels and driving up the value of the dollar. This not only increased the cost of servicing dollar borrowing but, by impeding economic recovery in the developed world and encouraging protectionist sentiment, reduced the income debtor countries earned in the commodity markets.

Unfortunately, it was virtually impossible to persuade Donald Regan, the United States Treasury Secretary, that the deficit was of any importance at all to other countries – not that he would have worried unduly even if he had been so persuaded. A silver-haired and sharp-suited former Merrill Lynch bond salesman, who had married the boss's daughter and enjoyed a successful career on Wall Street, Don Regan was a rough diamond with nothing in common with the Ivy League establishment. He cultivated a tough guy image and revelled in it, almost as if he had modelled himself on the poker-playing villain of the standard Western. As a result, he was viewed with the utmost distaste by most of Washington, not least by our own Embassy.

This was an overreaction. Although Regan could go too far – I recall one occasion, at an Interim Committee communiqué-drafting dinner, when he threatened to walk out if he did not get his way, and was made to look distinctly foolish when his bluff was called – and was not the ideal Treasury Secretary, he was basically straight and one knew where one stood with him. Certainly, I found no difficulty in getting on with him, repaying bluntness with equal bluntness, with no acrimony on either side. Unlike US foreign policy, which has traditionally taken wider concerns into account, US economic policy is invariably dictated by the domestic political considerations of the moment. The only difference between Don Regan and other incumbents was that he made no attempt to conceal this.

Beyond that, he had no economic or political views of his own, whatever. He therefore relied for his economic thinking on his G5 deputy, Beryl Sprinkel, a short, balding, pipe-smoking academic economist of extreme free market and monetarist views. Sprinkel tended too readily to believe that the market was infallible; but he was on the whole right more often than he was wrong, and was wholly devoid of either political ambition or personal malice. His view that the US Budget deficit was a matter of no importance which would sort itself out in the fullness of time brought him into conflict with Paul Volcker, who had no compunction in putting him down at G5 meetings, which added to the entertainment value for the other participants.

If Don Regan's economic views were borrowed from Sprinkel, his only political desire was to please the President. It was this that persuaded him to swap jobs with Jim Baker, who had been White House Chief of Staff throughout President Reagan's first term, in the early days of Regan's second term. Baker wanted to switch to a job with a policy content where he could, to the extent that the Presidential system makes it possible, be his own man; Regan wanted the power that came from proximity to the President. They agreed the swap between themselves, and then jointly presented the proposal to Reagan, who accepted it. It proved a better deal for Baker than for Regan, whose complete lack of diplomatic finesse, though little more than an embarrassment as Treasury Secretary, made him totally unfitted to be White House Chief of Staff. As a result, he soon acquired powerful enemies, none more powerful than the President's wife, Nancy, who eventually secured his dismissal. Don Regan characteristically repaid her with a particularly vituperative, although not conspicuously inaccurate, book of memoirs.

It was in deference to Reagan's view that, after the President's triumphant re-election in November 1984, Don Regan abandoned Sprinkel's advice and completely changed his tune on the US Budget deficit, making a number of speeches in which he described it as America's number one problem, prior to his departure as Treasury Secretary in February 1985.

It was, and to some extent is, fashionable to mock Ronald Reagan. I suspect that the verdict of history will be that he was America's most effective post-war President. When he entered the White House US power was in decline, its people demoralized and its currency distrusted. When he left it, America had become the world's only remaining superpower, and its people had rediscovered their pride – even though like the British peoples rediscovery of their pride during the Thatcher era, this was subsequently to be severely tested by the recession of the early 1990s.

Reagan was the most unusual political leader I have met. He had no time for detail, and little for policy in the everyday sense of the term. His mind worked exclusively on two contrasting levels. He had a small number of principles, which he clung to unswervingly, and which informed all his decisions. (Difficulties arose only when two principles came into conflict.) That was the higher level. The lower level was that of anecdote, of which he was a master, which he used as a substitute for argument, to communicate and to persuade.

His main principles were anti-communism, strong defence (although he was no warmonger), free trade, the work ethic, low taxes and a balanced budget. His foreign policy stance, including the much derided 'Star Wars' project, undoubtedly hastened the collapse of communism and of the Soviet empire (although he was saved from a colossal blunder at the Reykjavik summit of 1986 only because Gorbachev overplayed his hand when a major triumph was in the Russian's grasp). He opposed the protectionist proposals that regularly emanated from Congress more bravely and more effectively than any other President. (An old man when he became President, Reagan vividly remembered the protectionist Smoot-Hawley legislation of the 1930s, and the damage this had done.) The US tax reform package of the mid-1980s – the only serious attempt there has ever been to reform America's loophole-ridden tax system, which incidentally was launched during Don Regan's last days at the Treasury and merely inherited by Jim Baker – found its way to the statute book only because Reagan, at the height of his power and influence, was prepared actively and tirelessly to put his full weight and authority behind it.

Every President has a problem with Congress under a constitution in which the separation of powers is so genuine that coherent and effective government is rarely possible. Reagan solved this problem more successfully than almost all other Presidents, and in a unique way. Essentially, he ignored Congress, appealing over its head direct to the American people, with whom he had such a remarkable rapport that for most of the time most Congressmen were afraid of the popular consequences of thwarting him. His most conspicuous failure was over the US Budget deficit, where his principled belief in a balanced budget (which he would have liked to see written into the Constitution) came into conflict with his principled beliefs in a strong defence and low taxes, and lost. He always maintained that even if he had raised taxes, Congress would simply have spent the money, and the Budget deficit would have been no lower. Under the extraordinary US system of government this may well have been true: it was certainly politically convenient for him.

Meanwhile, by borrowing abroad, the US Treasury hoped to reduce both the upward pressure on domestic interest rates and the invidious political choices involved in cutting the deficit. As befitted a former bond salesman, Regan facilitated this process by devising new Treasury bonds aimed at foreign buyers, and axed the 30 per cent withholding tax levied on overseas investors. His methods with important foreign investors could involve sticks as well as carrots. At the IMF meeting in April

1984 he withheld American approval of a $9 billion replenishment of the International Development Association (IDA), an affiliate of the World Bank, dedicated to lending at concessionary rates to poorer countries, to put pressure on the Japanese to liberalize their capital markets, which to some extent they duly did the following month.

A New Realism in the Third World

More progress was made on debt in 1984 than on the imponderables of US macroeconomic policy. At the spring meeting of the Interim Committee in April I warned once more against: 'the dangers of excessive reliance on short-term banking finance. What is needed is long-term capital, which will not burden borrowers with servicing costs dependent on fluctuations in US interest rates and with repayment schedules threatening recurrent crisis.' Fortunately, since 1984 most debtor and developing countries have recognized the value of foreign investment. A substantial market in debt-for-equity swaps developed in the late 1980s, in which banks exchanged non-performing debt for equity stakes in new and old enterprises. It was a pity that the switch was delayed for so long by political posturing.

As its title suggests, the Interim Committee was originally set up as a temporary device. But as the French have it, '*Ce n'est que la provisoire qui dure*', and its twice-yearly gatherings in April and September have become a permanent and important feature of the international economic scene. Those responsible for determining the Fund's constitution were obviously aware of Lawson's Law – that the effectiveness of an international institution decreases in proportion to the number of its members – since the number of IMF executive directors and the size of the Interim Commitee, in each case just over twenty (roughly the same as the UK Cabinet), makes it a manageable international forum, unlike most.

This is made possible by the fact that only the major nations of the IMF – the G5 countries plus Saudi Arabia and China (and, after my time, Russia) – enjoy untrammelled full membership. All other countries are grouped into a series of constituencies, of between four and twenty-four members according to the size of the economies concerned, with each constituency allowed only a single spokesman at each meeting. As a result, there are some very mixed groupings, such as the constituency headed by the Netherlands, whose other members were in my time Yugoslavia, Romania, Israel and Cyprus, for whom arriving at a common view was not always easy. By tradition, the Interim Committee Chairman is always either a European or a Canadian.

The other main forum, the Development Committee, is considerably less important. A joint committee of both the IMF and the World Bank, it is always chaired by a senior figure from the developing world. In 1984 it was chaired by a tough but charming elderly moustachioed Anglophile from Pakistan called Ghulam Ishaq Khan, who always opened the committee's meetings with a prayer invoking the blessing of Allah upon our deliberations. He subsequently had the Presidency of his country rather unexpectedly thrust upon him.

The London Summit

The international debt problem and the US Budget deficit were back on the agenda for my first Economic Summit, in London in June 1984. We made no progress on the latter; but on debt the communiqué called on bankers to engage in what were known as multi-year rescheduling agreements (MYRAs) and on developing countries to attract more private equity investment.

There was also some pressure at the London Summit for an international initiative on environmental matters, which were then emerging as a fashionable concern. Geoffrey Howe was keen to launch a British initiative, if only to neutralize any unattractive proposals advanced by others. I was opposed to it, and secured Margaret's support. Any British initiative, which might well have been accepted, was likely to be both costly and politically unhelpful, in that it would increase the pressure on Britain to conform with expensive European Community directives on pollution. In the end, a working group was invited to select suitable areas for further research – a typical Summit compromise.

My most agreeable recollection of the London Summit is of a very small dinner party Margaret hosted at Number 10 for President Reagan on 5 June 1984, two days before the Summit officially began. The President was accompanied by George Shultz, his Secretary of State, Don Regan, and Jim Baker, then his Chief of Staff at the White House. The home team consisted of Margaret, Geoffrey and myself. It was the first time I had met either Reagan or Baker. Reagan was on sparkling form, reeling off the homespun anecdotes that defined his political philosophy. It was clear that Margaret was somewhat in awe of Reagan, despite his disarming manner. She had no great respect for his intellect, and his hands-off approach to government could not have been more different from hers, but she both respected and envied his power. Margaret was mesmerized by power, and she recognized in the American President a man whose writ far exceeded her own. It may have been this awe of power that subsequently led her to become so besotted with Gorbachev.

But in the case of Reagan, there was another factor, too. Margaret was an instinctive Atlanticist, judging the relationship with the United States to be far more important to Britain than the European Community.

This was an attitude common to all post-war British Prime Ministers – with the exception of Ted Heath, who was obsessively pro-European and almost equally anti-American. And since one of Margaret's earliest rules of thumb was to do the opposite of whatever Ted Heath had done in any particular set of circumstances, his position on this further reinforced her own instincts.

The London Summit of June 1984 was also notable, so far as I was concerned, for a much more parochial reason. It was the first major occasion on which I used my new Press Secretary, Robert Culpin. Robert's was a controversial appointment. A large man, with the most luxuriant beard in a generally clean-shaven Treasury, he claimed that until I offered him the job he had never had the slightest desire to read the newspapers. Like the Foreign Secretary, whose Press Secretary is always a rising young diplomat rather than a professional 'press officer', the Chancellor needs an official who has both a good grasp of economic policy and a personal rapport with his Minister. Robert had both, he eventually became an outstanding Press Secretary.

No Global Debt Solution

The serious business of 1984 continued after the summer break with my visit to the annual meeting of the IMF and World Bank in Washington in September. Accompanied on this occasion by Thérèse, I dropped in first on the Commonwealth Finance Ministers' meeting in Toronto. Apart from the ritual denunciations of British parsimony, the meeting was dominated by the debt question. Harold Lever, the former Labour Chancellor of the Duchy of Lancaster, had prepared an apocalyptic report for the meeting which warned of the imminent collapse of the Western banking system. Parts of the report, like its advice that debtor countries should do more to attract private equity capital, were eminently sensible, as one would expect from Harold. But his call for the increased subsidization of debtor countries by the West was not something I could accept. I praised the IMF debt strategy of treating each country on its merits and buying time for mismanaged economies to recover.

Sonny Ramphal, the Commonwealth Secretary General, was much more warmly received when he too forecast the collapse of the world financial system unless the Lever report was endorsed in full and financial aid to poorer countries vastly increased. Commonwealth opinion had not yet swung in favour of the market economy and private capital investment, and most of the speeches in Toronto were hostile. The likeable and sincere Mike Wilson, who had been appointed Finance Minister in the new Conservative Government led by Brian Mulroney that had swept to power in the recent Canadian general election, found himself chairing an international gathering of deeply unsympathetic Finance Ministers within a few days of taking office and had a pretty tough time of it. The Commonwealth meeting wound up with a call on the United States to cut its Budget deficit and lower both interest rates and the dollar. With that at least, I was able to agree.

I was glad to get to Washington where Don Regan once again chaired a private meeting of the Group of Five, this time over dinner at Blair House, a charming old residence which the US Government reserves for overnight stays by visiting Heads of State or Government. It is, however, made available during the day to lesser beings like the Finance Ministers of the Group of Five.

The Federal Budget deficit, rising interest rates and the overvalued dollar were high on the agenda. Unless the dollar weakened, it looked as if European interest rates would have to rise further. Karl Otto Pöhl, the President of the Bundesbank, despite his later proclaimed hostility to intervention, pressed hard for direct action in the currency markets to restrain the dollar, bolstering his argument by instructing his colleagues at home in Frankfurt to sell dollars in the market the same day. I was sympathetic, and urged co-ordinated intervention by all central banks (including the Federal Reserve) to depress the dollar, but Regan stuck rigidly to his non-interventionist line. In my speech to the plenary session on 25 September, I gave full vent to European exasperation about American fiscal policy and concluded with a quotation from Thomas Jefferson, the third President of the United States, who judged economy the 'first and most important of republican virtues, and public debt as the greatest danger to be feared'. Although Regan promised some accommodating measures, it seemed clear that so long as he remained Treasury Secretary progress on the deficit was unlikely.

The bulk of my speech dealt with the debt issue, where I felt it was necessary to rebut the 'global solutions' being peddled by the developing countries, which invariably – if not always explicitly – involved new and inflationary methods of financing, or the assumption by the taxpayers of creditor countries of the obligations of the debtor countries or the risks of the banks, if not both. It was bad enough that an insidious process, at that time unavowed, was taking place whereby, as the chastened banks stopped all new lending to the problem countries, the burden of risk was gradually shifting to the taxpayers of the creditor nations as a result of the continued activities of the national export credit agencies and to a lesser extent of the World Bank and of the IMF itself.

The London Summit in June had endorsed my belief that the long-term solution to the debt problem lay in a switch to market economics in the developing countries, in the increasing use of bond finance rather than bank debt, and in the growth of private equity investment, both by multinational companies and by the citizens of the debtor nations themselves. As Britain's contribution to this process I announced the resumption of official export credit insurance cover to those countries which had rescheduled debt, where it would assist the economic recovery of those countries.

But on this occasion it was the domestic section of my speech which attracted most attention. I always thought of this section of my IMF speeches as 'home thoughts from abroad'. I was well aware that the Press, in order no doubt to justify their travel expenses, would give fuller coverage to home thoughts from abroad than they would to the same home thoughts uttered at home. Which on this occasion, as I have already recounted in Chapter 34, they most certainly did.

CHAPTER 43

———

FROM THE PLAZA . . .

The Dollar Peaks · Baker's Beginning
The Road to Plaza · From Secrecy to Ballyhoo
Exchange Market Follow-through · Common Cause, Different Aims
Another Oil Shock · The G5 in London

The Dollar Peaks

MY ABORTIVE ATTEMPT TO put sterling into the ERM in November 1985 took place in parallel with wider moves to introduce some order into the pattern of world exchange rates.

I referred in Chapter 38 to the landmark agreement announced in Washington on 17 January 1985 to undertake co-ordinated intervention when necessary to achieve greater exchange monetary stability. The first practical results were seen in February 1985. During that month the dollar advanced again to new record highs against all the major currencies, in line with rising American interest rates and in the wake of an unfortunate remark by President Reagan on 21 February that he opposed attempts 'artificially' to depress the currency. This clearly breached the spirit of the January agreement, a point made to the Americans particularly forcefully by Karl Otto Pöhl. On 26 February, the dollar reached its peak against the Deutschmark at over DM 3.47 (the same day that the UK came nearest to the 'one dollar pound').

The European central banks, led by the Bundesbank, supported by the Bank of Japan, sold dollars aggressively in the markets the following day, and for several days thereafter. The intervention amounted to at least $10 billion, including a modest contribution from the UK. Coupled with a more sober assessment of US economic growth, which clearly could not continue at the unsustainable 1984 rate of between 6 and 7 per cent and a change in financial market sentiment, this caused the dollar to fall sharply for the first time in over four years. In the seven weeks to mid-April 1985 it dropped 20 per cent against the pound, 15 per cent against the other European currencies and over 6 per cent against the yen. At the time, it was widely felt that this could well be merely a short-term correction, and not the long-awaited change of trend.

Baker's Beginning

But before the G5 Finance Ministers could consolidate their work on currency co-operation, their governments were very nearly diverted into a huge time-wasting spectacular. President Mitterand formally proposed an international monetary conference, which I viewed with considerable alarm. It was entirely politically inspired, designed to enable France to launch a great international initiative and appear a major player on the world stage. It would have led to a series of high profile international meetings, which would have achieved nothing except increased turbulence in the foreign exchange markets.

It was true that the French did have a long-standing proposal for so-called target zones for currency parities, of a more ambitious nature than that which I was later to espouse; but this seemed to me at the time highly unlikely to secure international agreement. The Germans wholly opposed to it, and I was sure that, when it came to it, the Americans would be, too.

It was thus something of a blow when President Reagan appeared to be calling for an international monetary conference in his second-term inaugural speech in February 1985 – no doubt the State Department thought it was clever to hijack the Mitterand initiative. The new US Treasury Secretary, James Baker, followed it up at the OECD Ministerial meeting in Paris soon afterwards, where I made my reservations clear; but there was no time (there never was at these events) for a serious discussion. My first opportunity for a proper talk with him came with the IMF spring meetings in Washington on 17–19 April. I found him encouragingly receptive to the case I made for dropping the idea of an international conference on the world monetary system, and concentrating instead on bringing about a lower dollar. In a sense, this was the start of the process that led to Plaza.

Shortly before flying to Washington I attended an agreeable informal Ecofin Council under the Italian presidency of the Community. It was held in the middle of April at the Villa Igieia Hotel in Palermo, Sicily – a city with strong English connections, many of which were still visible, dating back to the heyday of the Marsala trade in the last century. Nevertheless, it seemed to me a somewhat unsafe location for a high - profile meeting of European political leaders; but the soft-spoken, heavily bearded Giovanni Goria, who was then Italy's Finance Minister, assured me that as a matter of policy the Mafia never murdered politicians. I told the Press who had come to cover the Palermo meeting that there was 'no disposition to regard the rather confusing US intervention [at the OECD meeting] in Paris as an important event'. The Germans in particular shared my doubts about the usefulness of such a conference, which was likely to raise false hopes of a new Bretton Woods.

The customary G5 meeting on the eve of the IMF spring meeting in Washington in April 1985 was the first under Jim Baker's chairmanship, and the change in atmosphere from the Regan era was almost palpable. Only David Mulford, the Assistant Secretary of the Treasury for International Affairs, had survived the change of regime. The free-floating ideologue Beryl Sprinkel had become chairman of the Council of Economic Advisers, which effectively took him out of the international policy-making sphere. Baker kept him under-informed about developments, and his influence waned accordingly. Baker's Deputy Treasury Secretary was Dick Darman, who had moved with him from the White House. Baker and Darman were very sensitive to the sky-high dollar, mainly because they had a clearer grasp of its impact on American industry and farming and the consequent danger of irresistible political pressure for protection and an all-out trade war.

The undervalued yen and the burgeoning Japanese trade surplus – the mirror-image of the problems of the United States – were an easy target for the protectionist lobby in the United States. In the spring of 1985 both Houses of Congress passed resolutions attacking Japan for unfair trading practices. I agreed that some Japanese policies – the managed undervaluation of the yen, the laws designed to protect small shopkeepers which ensured that the Japanese retail trade had a low propensity to import, the exclusion of foreign banks and securities firms from the Tokyo capital markets and the subsidization of domestic savings – were 'unneighbourly'.

I subsequently came to believe that I may have been wrong in urging the Japanese to end their subsidies to small savers – even though it had been recommended in their own Maekawa Report. In the context of the global economy, in which the medium-term problem, once the world recovers from the recession of the early 1990s, is likely to be inadequate world savings, the high Japanese propensity to save, unusual among the major economies, is on balance a good thing. But in 1985 my concern was that, since Japan's surplus savings were flowing overseas, the consequent capital outflow had to be matched by a current account surplus, as the overall balance of payments must by definition balance. Thus less saving by the Japanese would mean a smaller export surplus, which I felt might head off the alarming protectionist pressures in the US. I was also, of course, instinctively against subsidies.

The Road to Plaza

It was Jim Baker who initiated the negotiations which led to the Plaza agreement of 22 September 1985 on international agreement to reduce the excessive value of the dollar. Having first sounded out the Japanese, he telephoned me at my home in Stoney Stanton in the middle of August and suggested a meeting of the G5 Finance Ministers to agree on a co-ordinated strategy. He was extremely worried by the protectionist legislation Congress was threatening to pass on its return from the summer holidays, and believed that its passage into law would be facilitated by any further strengthening of the dollar. The best he could hope to do, he said, was prevent the legislation securing the two-thirds majority support needed to override a Presidential veto. He asked how I felt about this, and mentioned that he would be speaking to Gerhard Stoltenberg next. He also swore me to secrecy, saying that he had not yet broached the matter with the Fed Chairman, Paul Volcker – even though he enjoyed a far better rapport with the Fed Chairman than the awkward arm's length relationship which had existed between Volcker and Don Regan.

I warmly welcomed the idea, and we discussed the broad outlines there and then. We agreed that there should be no prior announcement of the meeting, believing that an unexpected event would have a greater impact on the market. During late August and early September the G5 Deputies – in my case, Geoffrey Littler, and in his, David Mulford – met amid conditions of great secrecy to draw up what became known as the 'non-paper'.

Initially Baker tried to put pressure on Germany and Japan – and to a lesser extent Britain – to take action to 'stimulate growth', and thus impress Congress. This we all resisted; but both Stoltenberg and I thought it should be possible to re-state our existing policies in a positive form in a communiqué. Coupled with the threat of concerted intervention, we reckoned it might suffice to depress the dollar. The resulting communiqué eventually reflected this. The crucial details were largely resolved at a meeting of the Deputies in London on 15 September, although they did not appear in the final communiqué. An extraordinary meeting of the Finance Ministers of the G5 was then scheduled for 22 September, at the Plaza Hotel in New York. Both the draft communiqué and the 'non-paper' were approved individually by each of the Finance Ministers before the meeting. The European members of the G5 were able to consider both papers jointly in Luxembourg on 20 and 21 September when we met for an informal Ecofin council, before flying to New York for the meeting with the Japanese and Americans on the Sunday, a meeting whose existence was successfully kept secret until it was announced only the day before.

FROM THE PLAZA . . .

The 'non-paper' prepared by the Deputies before the meeting aimed at a '10–12 per cent downward adjustment of the dollar . . . over the near term'. It envisaged a six-week blitz on the dollar, with the central banks jointly selling up to $18 billion of foreign currency reserves, mainly for Deutschmarks and yen. It was not lost on the British Press that the agreement came less than a week after the UK Government had raised $2½ billion for the reserves on the Euromarkets.

The initial US plan had suggested that the United States, Germany and Japan should each assume a quarter of the intervention burden, and France and Britain an eighth piece. This was amended at the meeting itself, following an agreement between the three European members, in favour of the United States and Japan being responsible for 30 per cent each, Germany (claiming in effect to speak also for other EMS members not in the G5) 25 per cent, France (which wanted a relatively large share on prestige grounds) 10 per cent and the UK (I was conscious of the still relatively low level of our reserves) 5 per cent. The overall European contribution thus amounted to 40 per cent rather than 50 per cent of the total, a scaling-down amply justified by the fact that the misalignment causing most concern was between the dollar and the yen – indeed, it was explicitly agreed at the meeting that the yen needed to rise more than the Deutschmark against the dollar.

After a five-hour meeting in the White and Gold Room of the Plaza Hotel, the communique was issued. They key passage read:

> The Ministers and Governors agreed . . . that in view of the present and prospective changes in fundamentals, some further orderly appreciation of the main non-dollar currencies against the dollar is desirable. They stand ready to co-operate more closely to encourage this when to do so would be helpful.

It was Paul Volcker who insisted on the word 'orderly' to guard against a free fall of the dollar. He was supported by Pöhl and myself. The full communiqué was, at Jim Baker's urging, inordinately prolix and ranged far beyond the foreign exchange markets, with each member of the G5 giving specific policy commitments; all of which, however, reflected existing known policy intentions.

The United States undertook to reduce the Federal Budget deficit, although President Reagan remained adamantly opposed to any commitment to raise taxes; the Japanese to open their markets to foreign imports, increase public spending and allow the yen to appreciate; and the Germans to continue their programme of tax reduction and reform. For the UK, I cobbled together a series of pledges to operate an anti-inflationary monetary policy, to pursue a prudent fiscal policy, to reduce public spending as a share of GDP, to undertake further privatization, to reduce the burden of taxation, to improve the working of the labour market and to liberalize the financial markets. All of the signatories pledged themselves to co-ordinate macroeconomic policy and to resist protectionism. This last point was regarded as very important by all of us, although it was inevitably overshadowed by the unprecedentedly specific words about exchange rates.

The word 'intervention' was not explicitly mentioned. But it had been in the January communiqué which was quite enough to leave no doubt as to the meaning of the last sentence in the extract quoted above. Few of us, of course, imagined that exchange rate stability could be achieved by intervention alone. Interest rate policy, in particular, would need to be consistent with our objective. But that was far too politically sensitive a matter to feature in any communiqué, even in code.

From Secrecy to Ballyhoo

By the standards of the G5, which normally met in secret and had never issued a communiqué at all until the January meeting in Washington, the publicity that came after the Plaza agreement was astonishing. Although I recognized the immense pressure the Reagan Administration was under from the protectionist lobby in the Congress, I had not realized the extent to which Jim Baker had envisaged the Plaza agreement as a great domestic political event in the United States. At the conclusion of the meeting all the US media were summoned to a hastily convened televised Press conference in the slightly shabby gilded grandeur of the ageing Plaza Hotel. In order to impress Congress that there was an alternative to protection as a way of solving the world's and especially America's problems, the hitherto secret society of the G5 went public in a big way.

There is no doubt that Jim Baker hoped to derive some personal and political advantage from the Plaza agreement, as well as to silence the protectionist lobby. He was a very close friend of George Bush, who was then Vice President and the front-runner to succeed President Reagan. Baker would almost certainly have shared the Presidential ticket with Bush in 1988, were it not for the fact that both were Texans, and he explained to me the convention that the Vice President should come from a different State than the President. Nevertheless, Baker's association with an important agreement to avert a potential domestic and international economic catastrophe clearly contributed to his becoming Secretary of State under Bush in 1989.

There was another and more important benefit from the Plaza agreement. The extremely well co-ordinated publicity did not end at the Plaza Hotel. I gave a large Press conference as soon as I got back to London, and most of my opposite numbers did the same on their own return.

What was evident to the world's Press, and to the financial markets, was that for the first time in many years the Finance Ministers of the major nations had genuinely got their act together, had reached an agreement of substance, and were all speaking about it in much the same terms. This gave a new credibility to the idea of international financial co-operation in general and to the G5 (and its successor) in particular. This in turn gave a boost to financial and economic conferences throughout the world – that unquantifiable but essential ingredient of economic success.

This needs to be set against the less happy consequences of the ballyhoo at the Plaza. Meetings of the G5 were never the same again. Press knowledge of a meeting increased the pressure on us to issue a communiqué, if only to prevent journalists speaking to Finance Ministers individually and – if they found that Ministers were not all singing from the same hymn book – circulating stories of discord among them. Secret meetings became impossible, and the expectations that built up ahead of meetings whose existence was publicly known were almost impossible to fulfil. If the communiqué was too bland, the Press judged the meeting a failure and the financial markets became nervous; but if it went beyond the familiar platitudes the Press would announce that the policy had changed, and the markets would take fright. The loss of privacy exacted its price. Today the only way Finance Ministers can have a genuinely secret meeting is by telephone – an innovation I suggested in 1987 and which was implemented in December of that year – but it is less satisfactory.

It was also the blaze of publicity at the conclusion of the Plaza meeting that effectively turned the G5 into the G7 that exists today. Bettino Craxi, the Italian Prime Minister at the time, found it intolerable that it should be exposed to the whole world that there was a top table to which Italy was not invited, and within a year he had found a defence issue over which he could threaten Reagan, who knew little about the G5 anyway, into promising to secure Italy's membership. This duly occurred, and inevitably Italy's inclusion meant Canada's too, thus replicating the Economic Summit membership, although thankfully no-one was so unwise as to suggest following in Jim Callaghan's footsteps and inviting the European Community to be represented. It was, however, agreed, as part of the deal among the G5 to submit to America's arm-twisting over the creation of the Finance Ministers' G7, that the G5 should continue to have a shadowy existence alongside it. This was the cause of a great diplomatic row on the occasion of the Louvre agreement in February 1987; but with the passage of time the separate G5 became progressively more spectral.

Arguments about the Group of Seven and the Group of Five – let alone the economic summits, the Group of Ten (with its eleven members), the IMF Interim Committee and other gatherings – must remind the reader of a hastily guided tour of the splendid Gothic- Renaissance Doges' palace in Venice, where council chambers for a bewildering variety of combinations are to be found. But there were serious matters at stake. In particular, there was to my mind a real danger in the demise of the G5 and its *de facto* replacement by the somewhat unwieldy G7, with its seven Finance Ministers and seven Central Bank Governors, as well as seven Deputies. The real focus of co-operation could easily become an informal G3 consisting of the US, Japan and Germany, from which the UK would be excluded. The only reason why this did not happen after the Plaza was that the US was at least half-persuaded that it was better for it to deal bilaterally with both Japan and Germany, rather than risk being 'outvoted' in a G3. But that view could change, as it showed signs of doing under Nick Brady who took over as US Treasury Secretary towards the end of 1988. In any event the resort to bilateralism, with its counterpart on the trade front, carries dangers of its own.

Exchange Market Follow-through

The noise made by the Plaza agreement led some observers to conclude that it merely put a gloss on what was happening anyway. In retrospect, that might appear to be so. The dollar had peaked in February and was already declining, partly under the pressure of central bank intervention. But at the time, it was by no means clear that that decline would continue. Indeed a modest rise in the dollar shortly before the Plaza meeting is just discernible in the chart overleaf. The experienced Karl Otto Pöhl was so convinced that the markets would be sceptical of our resolve that he warned us that they would test the agreement as soon as they opened on Monday morning. I suspected at the time that he was right, and it was agreed that the central banks should intervene jointly and decisively as soon as the markets challenged the agreement.

In fact the markets accepted the Plaza agreement at its face value, and by the end of the year the dollar had fallen by a further 15 per cent and more against both the yen and the Deutschmark. It went on falling throughout 1986, with sterling appreciating against the dollar and depreciating against the Deutschmark – arguably a better mix, even though the net depreciation went too far.

The Japanese were much less pleased. Despite the collective desire of the G5 to see the yen rise more than any of the European currencies against the dollar, the scale of the yen appreciation was rather greater than the Japanese had bargained for. It put their Finance Minister, Noboru Takeshita, under considerable political pressure from industrial interests at home and earned him an unkind pun on his name, which in English means 'the riser'. He thought it would finish his political career – he told me that they were saying at home 'as the yen rises, the riser

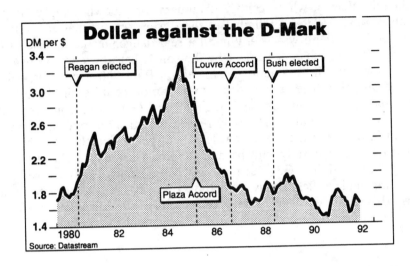

Dollar against the D-Mark. Source: Datastream

falls' – but in fact, after a period of difficulty, Japanese manufacturing industry adapted impressively to a strong currency, and Takeshita later served briefly as Prime Minister, before his enforced resignation in the wake of the Recruit Cosmos scandal.

Although he spoke very little English, which made it hard to get close to him, he was an obviously likeable man, albeit a politician in the traditional Japanese mould, concerned with politics and power rather than policy. His successor, as Finance Minister, Kiichi Miyazawa, who took over from 1986 to 1988, was unusual in having policy ideas of his own and being prepared to articulate them. At the time of writing Takeshita remains the most formidable presence in the ruling Liberal Democratic Party in Japan, and still takes a personal interest in international economic co-operation. He was largely responsible for securing the premiership for Miyazawa in 1992.

Common Cause, Different Aims

It is important to recognize, in the context of the Plaza and subsequent accords, that although I was able to make common cause with Baker most of the time, there was in fact a fundamental difference in our thinking. His objective, which he first mentioned to me in his August telephone call to me at Stoney Stanton, and which became a constant theme thereafter, was to get other countries, especially Germany and Japan, to give their economies a Keynesian demand boost in order to solve the US current account deficit and make a contribution to world growth. Baker was always terrified that high interest rates would push the United States into recession. There were clear echoes of the disastrous 'locomotive' approach of the 1978 summit in this line of thinking, despite the switch from Jimmy Carter to Ronald Reagan in the White House.

Unlike me, Baker believed in a 'real' rather than 'nominal' framework for economic policy, and his approach was essentially Keynesian. In other words, he believed that a monetary and fiscal stimulus would boost real activity rather than be frittered away in higher inflation. The fundamental change in the approach to macroeconomic policy described in my Mais Lecture, and implicit in the Medium Term Financial Strategy, never really took hold in the US Administration. The Americans continued throughout my time and afterwards to talk the old neo-Keynesian language and seemed incapable of accepting either the nominal framework or the reason for its adoption. The Administration left it to the Fed to deal with any inflationary dangers, which it did in a pragmatic way.

The earlier Regan–Sprinkel regime was in many ways much nearer to the UK Government's approach and to my own thinking; but a combination of its resolutely hands-off attitude to the dollar and its determination that US views should prevail at all costs – whereas Baker was always looking to do a deal – made it more difficult to do business with than was the case with the Baker–Darman regime.

In any event, the ideological differences that divided us mattered little so long as the dollar was clearly overvalued by almost any yardstick. Moreover the preoccupation with the US current account deficit was useful to the extent that it made the US Administration pay attention to the supposedly 'twin' Budget deficit. It would have been harmful only if it had succeeded in persuading the world's leading nations to give their economies an inflationary boost in order to help the US.

But the main reason why the process in fact developed on the whole more in the direction that I sought rather than the direction Baker sought, despite the immense power of the US, was that the Germans were simply not prepared to play ball and repeat the locomotive errors that followed the 1978 summit. When the secret Middleton–Littler mission went to Germany in December 1985, they were told that the inflation target for the next five years was an average of 2½ per cent. In fact it averaged less than 1½ per cent, and was slightly negative in 1986, the year oil prices plunged. Despite its refusal to follow the Americans' advice and stimulate demand, Germany still achieved a respectable growth rate of some 3 per cent a year between 1985 and 1990.

The Japanese were not too keen to stimulate their economy either, for much the same reasons. But they were always more inclined to defer to the Americans, partly because they relied on US military protection for their defence and partly because they feared US protectionism. So they placated the Americans by giving periodic boosts to their economy via grandiose plans for public works. They had the engaging habit of announcing the same programme several times, in order to make the

Americans feel they were doing more than they were. But there was a genuine expansion of public works in Japan, not unconnected with the fact that the Japanese construction industry is the principal financial backer of the ruling Liberal Democrat Party, and the Japanese political system is money-based to a remarkable extent. Fortunately the Japanese economy was robust enough, at least until the early 1990s, to take these boosts in its stride. Moreover, given the chronic surplus that developed in the Japanese Budget and the country's inadequate public infrastructure, the relatively moderate boosts (after allowing for the repetition factor) were probably objectively justified.

Another Oil Shock

The first half of 1986 was dominated by yet another oil shock, but this time it was a price collapse rather than an explosion. After the fall from its previous peaks which occurred during my talks with OPEC Ministers as Energy Secretary (see Chapter 17) the spot oil price had remained remarkably stable at $27 to $28 a barrel until almost the end of 1985. But all the time demand was being undermined by the search for energy-saving and for oil substitutes triggered by the previous two price increases. And as happens in this sort of market, when the price fell, it dropped like a stone, the trigger being the failure of OPEC to agree on production quotas. Saudi Arabian light crude was selling in the first half of 1986 at an average spot price of $10 a barrel – below the level prevailing before the Iranian crisis of 1979. It recovered slightly afterwards. But apart from a brief flare-up when Iraq seized Kuwait in 1990, it remained in real terms well below the 'pre-Iranian' levels.

Just as the impact of the two oil price explosions had given an upward shove to inflationary expectations and a downward one to growth and employment, the plunging oil price was widely expected to have the opposite and much more desirable effect of ushering in a period of non-inflationary growth. The falling oil price did indeed have a beneficial immediate impact on the rate of inflation throughout the G7, which fell from just under 4 per cent in 1985 to just over 2 per cent in 1986. But just as we in the UK sadly failed to 'lock in' the oil-induced fall in inflation, the same failure was evident to some degree in the G7 as a whole, where inflation rates began to creep upwards, starting in 1987 and continuing up to 1990.

As for growth, the likely impact of lower oil prices had been greatly exaggerated by the economic forecasters. For the OPEC countries had by now learned how to spend their oil revenues (governments soon learn how to spend: it is how to refrain from spending that creates headaches); and the main impact of the lower oil price was simply a transfer of spending power and thus of demand from some countries to others. So far from boosting demand there may even have been a modest pause: for what they are worth, the official statistics show a temporary dip of half a percentage point in a very steady 3 to 3½ per cent growth rate in the industrial world as a whole over this period.

But just as the Weimar inflation had given Germany a low toleration of inflation, so the slump of the 1930s had given the United States a low toleration even for the smallest degree of hesitation, pause or uncertainty – let alone recession. These underlying fears are magnified a thousandfold by the many very short-term analysts who live off the American financial markets. The perennial American tendency to lecture other countries about their over-restrictive policies and to call for a stimulus thus re-doubled at the time of the largely mythical growth pause.

The G5 in London

The resulting US pressure for co-ordinated international interest rate cuts was supported by France at a G5 meeting I chaired at Number 11 on 18 January 1986 – the first to be held in London for a very long time. Pierre Bérégovoy, then in his first incarnation as President Mitterand's Finance Minister, was, with good reason, worried about the forthcoming French Parliamentary elections in March, which the Socialists lost – leading to the brief period of 'cohabitation' between a Socialist President and a Conservative Cabinet. But the rest of us were unmoved.

The advantage of holding the meeting at Number 11 was that even if the ballyhoo of the Plaza had made it impossible to hold meetings in secret any more, the barrier at the entrance to Downing Street would at least keep the Press at a reasonable distance. During the lunch I gave in the Soane dining room at the end of our discussions, however, the atmosphere took a marked turn for the worse when Jim Baker revealed that President Reagan had assured the Italian Prime Minister, Bettino Craxi, that Italy would be invited to all future meetings of the G5. It turned out that Reagan had made the offer, without consulting any of the other member governments, in response to a fierce Italian complaint backed by a threat to close American military bases in Italy. Both Gerhard Stoltenberg and I felt badly let down, and made this clear to an embarrassed and apologetic Jim Baker. But there was little we could do in the face of this *fait accompli*, apart from insisting that the old G5 should continue alongside the new arrangement.

The London meeting ended with no more than an expression of hope that interest rates might come down in the next twelve months – which to some extent they did, in response to the improved inflationary out-look – and was of historic significance only in being the last old-style free-standing meeting of the G5. It will, however, live in my memory as the occasion on which Paul Volcker went off with my navy blue Aquascutum overcoat, leaving his own behind: an amazing exchange to anyone who has seen a picture of the two of us together.

Not long afterwards the French Socialists duly lost the March election. But although I was pleased in political terms, and developed a warm personal regard for his Gaullist successor, Edouard Balladur, this did not prevent the customary exchange between Pierre Bérégovoy and myself going beyond the normal courtesies. In reply to my letter saying how much I had enjoyed working with him, he replied:

> *Nous avons démontré, l'un et l'autre, qu'il était possible aux responsables des finances de nos deux pays de coopérer efficacement, bien que leurs conceptions politiques fussent différentes.**

Bérégovoy, who became Finance Minister again in 1988, wrote me a warm letter after my resignation the following year; and I was delighted to see him appointed Prime Minister of France in 1992, as I made clear (to the best of my French-speaking ability) in an interview I gave French television at the time. A short, bespectacled man of working class and trade union background and simple tastes, he had not the slightest trace of a chip on his shoulder; and his cheerful demeanour gave no sign of the admirable toughness he displayed as a Minister. He was also one of the few active survivors of the generation whose formative years were during the war, which left him with a warmth towards Britain which is not universally shared among the French political classes today.

It was at an informal Ecofin at Ootmarsum in Holland in April 1986 that I first met his successor, Edouard Balladur, a true product of the French establishment, as dignified in appearance as Bérégovoy was not, and in political terms a kindred spirit. His first task was to negotiate the devaluation of the franc against the Deutschmark at the EMS realignment meeting held in the midst of the Ootmarsum Ecofin, and he carried it off well. I felt it would be helpful to get closer to him, so I invited him to private talks in London a couple of months later. The meeting ended with lunch in the Soane dining room at Number 11, for which the Government Hospitality Services produced a claret of such splendour that Balladur talked longingly about it whenever he saw me for months afterwards.

Our political fellow-feeling was cemented by his passionate espousal of privatization. He changed his own official Ministerial title from the traditional 'Minister for Finance and the Economy' to 'Minister for Finance, the Economy and Privatization', and was determined to have

---

*We have together shown that it is possible for the financial leaders of our two countries to co-operate effectively even though their different political outlooks are different.

an even larger privatization programme than ours. There was certainly great scope for surpassing the British, since the French public sector was among the largest in Europe; but the re-election of the Socialists less than two years later, in 1988, sadly put an end to his privatization programme. It was disappointing that the Chirac government lasted such a short time and that Balladur never enjoyed the fruits of his eminently sensible policies.

But despite such happy exchanges with individual opposite numbers, none of the meetings of early 1986 advanced exchange rate co-operation, or indeed any form of international financial co-operation, much further. At least I was able, when in Washington for the 1986 IMF spring meeting, to sign on behalf of the UK the Multilateral Investment Guarantee Agreement (MIGA), for which I had been pressing for some time, making the UK a founder member. MIGA established common codes, conventions and guarantees on the treatment of private investment in the developing world, which I hoped would encourage a much-needed flow of private capital to those countries. It imparted some substance to the generalized call at the 1984 London Summit for greater private sector investment in the developing world.

CHAPTER 44

. . . TO THE LOUVRE

Tokyo Interlude · Managing Director of the IMF?
The Road to the Louvre · Fives, Sixes and Sevens

Tokyo Interlude

THE TOKYO ECONOMIC SUMMIT at the beginning of May 1986 was organized with characteristic Japanese thoroughness. The streets between the gigantic New Otani Hotel, where the UK contingent headed by Margaret, Geoffrey and myself were staying, and the Aksaka Palace, where the meetings were held, were cleared of all forms of traffic and lined without interruption on both sides of the road with soldiers with their backs to us as we sped to and fro – an unusual sensation in Tokyo of all cities.

While the Americans were, as ever, chiefly preoccupied by misplaced worries that global economic growth was slowing down, the Japanese had become acutely concerned about the extent of the dollar's decline. By mid-year it had fallen by well over 30 per cent against the Mark from its 1985 peak. Against the yen it had fallen by over 40 per cent. Japan, much more than Germany, wanted the US to halt the slide in the dollar, which Jim Baker refused to do unless the Japanese and Germans 'increased growth' – by which he meant fiscal stimulation and interest rate cuts. This dance was more like a scherzo than a stately minuet; and it was to be repeated many times with small variations for the next six years.

Jim Baker, subsequently attached considerable importance to the Tokyo Summit, partly because it was in that summit's communiqué that the compromise resolution of the G5/G7 row was finally and formally agreed and set out in writing with the authority of 'the Heads of State and Government present'; but even more because it was there that he secured agreement to the 'indicator' initiative by which he set such store. The communiqué declared that the new Group of Seven (G7) Finance Ministers would meet at least once a year between the annual Economic Summits, and would use a new range of economic indicators to assess the economic performance of the G7 and to guide policy. There were originally ten of them, but I managed to get them whittled down to seven: growth, inflation, unemployment, budget deficits, trade balances, 'monetary conditions' and exchange rates.

The description 'indicator' was chosen carefully, after much haggling, to distinguish them from objectives. My officials played an active part in the indicator exercise, which would probably have gone completely off the rails had they not done so. But even in the improved form in which they eventually emerged, they were essentially a device to put pressure on the Japanese and Europeans to take 'expansionary measures' and in this way to take the heat off the falling dollar. There was never any agreement – or even proper discussion – of what to do if the various indicators pointed in different directions, or even any analysis of the relationship of the different indicators to each other. I found it impossible to take the exercise very seriously – and it certainly played no part, for all Jim Baker's combination of nagging and enthusiasm, in the subsequent course of world economic policy.

During my visit to Tokyo, I had some bilateral fish to fry, outside the context of the Summit, in the shape of seeking to persuade the Japanese to open their markets to British goods and services. Indeed I saw Noboru Takeshita, the Japanese Finance Minister, mainly for this purpose, as soon as I arrived on Sunday, 4 May. Japanese securities houses had for many years been able to trade freely in London, but no British securities firms had been given licences to deal in securities or manage funds in Tokyo. These efforts to secure trading licences were reasonably successful, with the number of British securities firms operating in Japan jumping from just two at the end of 1983 to fifteen by the end of 1987. Partly as a result of the Summit, the first British firm was admitted to membership of the Tokyo stock exchange in 1986. This was an issue I had first raised with Takeshita in private during the London Summit in 1984. The Japanese could scarcely be accused of acting quickly, and it was in an effort to speed the process up that I insisted on the insertion into the Financial Services Act of 1986 a clause allowing the UK authorities to refuse to authorize, or remove authorization from, any institution whose national authorities did not provide reciprocal access to British houses.

The Japanese unwillingness to liberalize trading practices was not confined to financial services. At the Sunday morning meeting I also spent some time trying to persuade Takeshita to lift the heavy duty

Japan imposed on imported Scotch whisky, which was finally halved three years later, in April 1989. Margaret, who had a strong mercantilist streak, was always fretting about the imbalance of trade between Britain and Japan. But although I did not share her concern with bilateral balances, she undoubtedly had a case on the many visible and invisible barriers to consumer goods and agricultural imports into Japan, some, although by no means all, of which were gradually removed after much diplomatic pressure. Indeed, she played a considerable part in battling on behalf of Scotch Whisky – her own favourite tipple.

The most memorable feature of the Tokyo Summit, so far as I was concerned, was the dinner that Takeshita gave for his G7 counterparts in the private room of a well-known Tokyo restaurant on the Monday evening. It was an up-market establishment of the traditional Japanese variety, with highly trained and unfailingly solicitous *geisha* girls, whose concession to the official nature of the occasion was to confine entertainment to card tricks, dancing, and karaoke: the only time I have ever experienced this apparently popular contribution of Japanese electronic skills to Western civilization.

The girls' card tricks were amazing, leaving Jim Baker, who fancied himself as something of a connoisseur of this genre, totally baffled. The evening came to a spectacular and unscheduled conclusion with Takeshita and Michio Watanabe, then the Minister for Industry and International Trade (MITI), putting on make-up and mounting the dais to perform a dramatic cameo from the classical Japanese repertoire. I was surprised when, the following day, Takeshita begged me not to tell his wife, Naoko. It seemed to me he had done nothing of which he could possibly be ashamed.

Before leaving Tokyo on the evening of 6 May, the Ministers from all the summit countries were invited to an audience with the Emperor Hirohito at his palace in the centre of the city. He was very old and frail, and could manage only a very few words in English, but it was remarkable to be greeted by a man who had become Emperor in 1926, well before I was born, when Baldwin was Prime Minister and Winston Churchill was Chancellor of the Exchequer. He was also the only man I am ever likely to meet who officially resigned from being God.

There was a court banquet at the Imperial Palace afterwards, where we dined to the accompaniment of a group of musicians playing seventeenth-century Japanese music on authentic instruments; and producing the most monotonous cacophony it has ever been my misfortune to endure. Not even the good food and Hans-Dietrich Genscher's endless fund of political jokes could make it tolerable, and I was relieved that Margaret, Geoffrey and I had to leave the dinner early and rush to Haneda airport to board the ancient RAF VC10, which contained a bed for Margaret, for the flight back to London. On the return journey, the aircraft refuelled at Anchorage, which lingered in my mind as a place of such remote desolation that I successfully resisted Jim Baker's attempt to hold a G7 Finance Ministers' meeting there at the end of the following year.

Managing Director of the IMF?

Britain assumed the Presidency of the European Community for six months from 1 July 1986, which meant that it fell to me to host the September informal Ecofin Council. There are a number of differences between the normal monthly Ecofin Council meetings and the so-called informal meetings, of which there is one in each Community Presidency, making two a year. Whereas the regular meetings can be fitted into a normal working day, the informal ones stretch over an entire weekend. This gives time not only for relaxation and entertainment, to which wives are invited, but for more work to be done as well. The two other main differences are that Central Bank Governors attend the informal Ecofins, but not the regular meetings of the Council; and whereas the regular meetings are always held in Brussels or Luxembourg, each informal Ecofin is held in the country of the Presidency for the time being.

In my case I decided to hold the informal Ecofin of 19–21 September 1986, at Gleneagles in Scotland – the first time the Council of Ministers of the European Community had ever met in Scotland. It proved to be a popular venue, particularly among the central bankers, who have more time than Finance Ministers do to spend on the golf course.

We met at a time when the dollar was diving, largely because Jim Baker was deliberately talking it down, threatening that he would not stop doing so until the Germans gave their economy a boost by cutting interest rates. Talking a currency down is, of course, very much easier than talking it up; and Stoltenberg was not amused. There was no case in terms of German domestic policy for them to cut their interest rates, nor was there any substance to Jim Baker's belief that the world economy was flagging and in need of a boost. I was very much on Stoltenberg's side over this – as was Edouard Balladur, the French Finance Minister – and felt that Jim's behaviour was verging on the irresponsible.

I called a private breakfast meeting on the Sunday morning of my European G5 colleagues, Stoltenberg and Balladur, and our Central Bank Governors, to discuss the problem of the dollar and what our response should be. Balladur and I agreed to support Stoltenberg against Baker in return for a promise from Karl Otto Pöhl that the Bundesbank would step up its intervention in the foreign exchange market with a view to supporting the existing pattern of parities.

This agreement subsequently became known as 'the spirit of Gleneagles', and it was agreed that I should communicate our joint views by telephone to Baker. I duly did so, adding to Baker that in my opinion megaphone diplomacy of the type he was conducting was something that Finance Ministers would do better to eschew. Jim did not particularly welcome the advice, but he could see that for once his diplomatic skills had deserted him: the Germans were not going to move, and all he had achieved was a united European front against him on the issue. I then gave a rather windswept *al fresco* press conference in the bracing Highland air.

It was during the Gleneagles meeting, too, that I first learned that Jacques de Larosière had decided to step down prematurely, halfway through his second five-year term as Managing Director of the IMF. Our excellent Treasury man in Washington, Tim Lankester, who combined the functions of Economic Minister at the British Embassy and UK executive Director of both the Fund and the Bank, rang me at Gleneagles in a state of great excitement and urged me to put my name forward. Just as the President of the World Bank is always an American, the Managing Director of the IMF is, by tradition, a European, and there had never been a British Managing Director.*

To Tim's palpable disappointment I indicated that I had considerable reservations. The job is undoubtedly an important one, and in different circumstances I might well have been tempted. Perhaps I should have let my hat be thrown in the ring. But at the time I did not see how I could possibly leave the Government just in front of the General Election, and in any event there were a number of tax reforms I was keen to introduce before I gave up the Chancellorship. No sooner had I put the telephone down than I received a letter by hand from Balladur, seeking my support for Michel Camdessus, who had only recently moved from being Director of the Treasury to Governor of the Banque de France. What the French had in mind was a straight swap between Camdessus and de Larosière, whom they planned to install as a more politically compatible Governor of the Banque de France.

When I got back to London, I discovered that President Mitterand had written along the same lines to Margaret, and indeed to all the other European Community Heads of Government, which gave the French a flying start. They did not, however, have it all their own way: Onno

---

* The Japanese, incidentally, have never held either post, and there have been increasing suggestions in recent years that it is about time Japan, as the world's second economic power, held the IMF post. The problem is not so much a lack of suitable talent: Japan does possess some able English-speaking individuals of the right age with international financial experience. It is rather that the tightly knit and ultra-consensual character of Japanese public life, coupled with its inward-looking leaders' reluctance to take a world view of anything, may contribute to domestic economic success but make it inappropriate for a Japanese to head any major international organization. When this self-created disqualification disappears, as one day it surely will, it might be more sensible for Japan to provide the Bank President rather than the Fund Managing Director. There are always high calibre Europeans willing and able to do the Fund job, whereas the United States invariably has the greatest difficulty in finding an adequate candidate for the Bank post.

Ruding, the young but long-serving Dutch Finance Minister, was desperately keen to get the job, and had secured the backing of Germany. The tradition on these occasions is that the European Community countries agree on a candidate, who is then accepted by the rest of the Fund's membership. As President of Ecofin for the time being, it fell to me to try and secure agreement on a single Community candidate – something on which the Americans were particularly keen, as they wished to avoid the embarrassment of having to make a choice, which, with their large voting power in the Fund, could well be decisive.

I discussed the matter with Margaret. Although I had nothing against Camdessus, we both felt that the French proposal, while a convenient way of solving their own domestic problems, was too greedy. The French already held the other main international economic post available to a European, with Jean-Claude Paye as Secretary General of the OECD, not to mention Jacques Delors as President of the European Commission. They had the outgoing Managing Director of the IMF, and now they wanted to have his successor, too. On the other hand, Margaret was opposed to the idea of a Dutchman, since the Dutch at that time were being singularly unhelpful within the Community over sanctions against South Africa, to which she was strongly opposed.

The answer was to try and find a Brit; but whom? Margaret asked me to sound out Tony Barber, who had been Chancellor during the Heath Government, but he was not interested. In any event, the best bet, all things considered, seemed in my opinion to be Jeremy Morse, the Chairman of Lloyds Bank, who had been well known in the international financial field at an earlier stage of his career; and when I sounded him out he told me he was indeed interested in the job. I sought to persuade my Community colleagues of the desirability of agreeing on a single candidate, since the alternative was an election which would be determined by non-European votes; and suggested to them that, if there was no agreement as between Camdessus and Ruding, the best solution would be for both to withdraw in favour of Morse as a compromise candidate.

While this suggestion secured a measure of support, it was abundantly clear that the French were determined to secure the post for their man. Even when, at the final Ecofin discussion I chaired on the matter, I held a vote which Ruding narrowly won by 7 to 5, the UK voting with the majority, the French still refused to bow out. They were confident that, in an election between Camdessus and Ruding among the entire Fund membership, their man would win. And in the event, that is exactly what happened. The developing and debtor countries, in particular, believed that Camdessus would be a softer touch than the austere Dutch Conservative.

In fact, a strong case could be made for Camdessus on merit, and he has demonstrated himself to be a worthy Managing Director. Wiry, bespectacled, likeable, suffused with nervous energy, self-conscious at not being an *énarque* while proud of having (unusually) got to the top without it, lacking his predecessor's easy command of English, Michel Camdessus has proved hardworking, practical and businesslike. But I was left with the firm conviction that British Government's need to take a great deal more trouble than they have done in the past to think ahead and ensure that there is always a strong British candidate for any major international post that falls vacant. That is what the French do, and over the years it has served them well.

The Road to the Louvre

My first meeting with Jim Baker after Gleneagles was over breakfast at the US Treasury on the morning of Saturday, 27 September 1986. I had flown to Washington for that year's Fund/Bank annual meeting. Baker was prepared to abandon his policy of talking down the dollar, and told me that the United States was in principle prepared to enter into an international agreement to stabilize exchange rates. He was prepared to discuss two versions: preferably a 'hard' one, which would include an interest rate understanding, but failing that a 'soft' one, in which the understanding would be confined to intervention. It was abundantly clear, however, that the interest rate understanding he sought concerned exclusively European, and in particular German, interest rates, rather than US rates. Indeed, either way he wanted an undertaking from the Germans at the G5 meeting that afternoon that they would cut their discount rate by half a point. I met Gerhard Stoltenberg later the same morning. He was content to see a half point cut in the German discount rate, but said that Pöhl would not budge. Any hopes of a deal between the Americans and the Germans eventually foundered, thanks to Pöhl's opposition. This was only partly because he believed that an interest rate cut was not objectively warranted. What concerned him more was the failure of the Americans to recognize the importance of the independence of the Bundesbank, which he felt obliged to assert.

The deadlock was not broken until the Louvre Accord, some five months later. In essence, the well-prepared G5/G7 meeting in Paris over the weekend of 21 and 22 February 1987, and chaired by Edouard Balladur in that corner of the Louvre in which, as Finance Minister, he still had his office, was the sequel to the 'spirit of Gleneagles'. The French, the Germans and ourselves had agreed there that something needed to be done to arrest the plummeting dollar, and we had also agreed that Jim Baker should cease his megaphone diplomacy – and on behalf of the three of us, I had told him so. It followed that we needed to have a private meeting with Jim, where we could count on Japanese support.

Since the Plaza meeting less than eighteen months earlier, the dollar had fallen almost 50 per cent against the Deutschmark and more than that against the yen. The situation had become absurd. It was not simply a matter of German and Japanese concerns about American competitiveness. That was the least of my worries. The real problem, as I saw it, was different, and more fundamental. Not surprisingly, given the 'J curve' phenomenon (a devaluation initially causes a deterioration in a country's trade balance, before there is any improvement, since prices adjust before volumes do, rather like the shape of the letter 'J'), the US current account was still in substantial deficit.

This was causing many Americans who should have known better to argue that the dollar should continue to decline until the current account deficit was eliminated. At the same time, the foreign exchange markets were happily selling dollars on the way down in the same spirit as they had been buying them on the way up. In other words, we were headed for a dollar overshoot in the downward direction which could well prove as massive as the earlier upward overshoot had been. If nothing was done, there was no reason why this violent switchback – wholly unrelated to economic fundamentals – should not become the norm, causing severe dislocation to the world economy.

In these circumstances, it did not require a genius to discern the need for the G5 to reach an agreement to stabilize the dollar, at least for a time. Nor was this disputed by Jim Baker (still less by Paul Volcker). But Jim was determined to get something in return for his agreement: an undertaking by the Germans and the Japanese to boost their economic growth. They duly obliged – the Japanese modestly, the Germans entirely cosmetically; but it was enough to save Baker's face, which was important. There remained only the precise details of the concerted intervention scheme to be worked out and the wording of the communique to be agreed; both of which, after prolonged discussion, achieved.

Once the meeting was over, a press conference was arranged at one of the grander rooms in the Louvre, all chandeliers, gilt and mirrors, at which it was agreed that all the Ministers present should make a short statement. Baker, Stoltenberg and I were the only ones who had also taken part in the Plaza agreement; and when it came to my turn I was anxious to promote the thought that this was not an ephemeral response to an immediate crisis but part of a continuing process of international financial cooperation. Accordingly, I described the Louvre agreement (somewhat to Balladur's dismay, I suspect), as

> Plaza 2 . . . I see this meeting as the lineal descendant of the Plaza meeting . . . Then we all agreed that the dollar should fall; now we all agree we need stability.

There was another reason why I wished to link the two. The markets knew that the dollar had indeed fallen following the Plaza, and I wanted them to expect a similar success following the Louvre. For sterling, an agreement to peg the three main world trading currencies offered the prospect of a welcome respite from the pressure the pound had been under for most of the previous year. For that reason, as well as for the contribution it could make to currency stability in the world as a whole, I was a strong supporter of the Louvre Accord.

The communiqué issued by the G6 on 22 February 1987 contained a great deal of routine prose pledging the signatories to eradicate current account imbalances, fight protection and co-ordinate economic policies. The Germans agreed to a package of tax cuts (mostly the bringing forward of measures which were already part of Stoltenberg's policy) and the Japanese to reform taxes, raise public spending and cut their discount rate by half a point. For their part, the Americans undertook to stabilize the dollar and once again promised to cut the Federal Budget deficit. The key paragraph in the communiqué was the tenth and last:

> The Ministers and Governors agreed that the substantial exchange rate changes since the Plaza Agreement will increasingly contribute to reducing external imbalances and have now brought their currencies within ranges broadly consistent with underlying economic fundamentals, given the policy commitments summarized in this statement. Further substantial exchange rate shifts among their currencies could damage growth and adjustment prospects in their countries. In current circumstances, therefore, they agreed to co-operate closely to foster stability of exchange rates around current levels.

The original draft had 'present' as the penultimate word, to which Miyazawa, who spoke excellent English, objected, claiming that when translated into Japanese it was much too precise. I was able to resolve the impasse by suggesting 'current' instead, which Miyazawa was happy to accept.

The unpublished central rates agreed for the dollar were 1.825 Deutschmarks and 153.5 yen. There was no explicit range for sterling, but it was understood that sterling would conform to the spirit of the agreement. Needless to say, it suited me to let the market think there was a floor under the pound, which had been having a rough time. Indeed, in effect I put one there at my Press briefing immediately following the Louvre Accord, when I declared, with deliberate asymmetry that I did not wish to see sterling fall any further or rise significantly, from its then level.

There was an inner range of 2½ per cent either side of these central rates within which intervention would be discretionary and an outer range of 5 per cent on either side beyond which it would be obligatory.

A modest war chest of $4 billion was established for intervention, with the US, Japan, and Europe contributing a third each. Much scholastic argument was devoted to what to call these ranges: the agreed jargon was 'reference ranges'. These ranges would have 'soft edges'. This was partly a reference to the inner and outer ranges. But it also meant – although this was much less explicit – that if the outer ranges came under pressure there would be consultations on whether to continue defending them or to move the centre point.

The Louvre Accord worked reasonably well for a time, after an upward adjustment of the yen central rate to Y146 to the dollar at the G5 held in Washington in April 1987 on the eve of the IMF spring meeting. The weakness of the Accord, which eventually undermined it, was its failure to bolster the pledge to intervene in the foreign exchange markets with an undertaking to adjust domestic monetary policies to validate the agreed ranges.

There was in fact much discussion and general agreement on the need to be prepared to validate the ranges by interest rate changes, although nothing about interest rates appeared in the official declaration partly because of American political sensitivities (shared to a lesser extent by others), partly because of the Bundesbank's insistence that nothing could be allowed to derogate from its independence, and partly because the agreement in principle on interest rate differentials did not in practice solve the problem of how any change in differentials should be shared between the country whose interest rate needed to rise, in relative terms, and the country whose interest rate needed to fall in relative terms.

In itself, the absence of any explicit reference to interest rate changes was in line with historical precedent, and thus scarcely surprising. Bretton Woods was a highly formal exchange rate system, and it contained no express provision for accompanying domestic monetary policies. But Bretton Woods contained a key currency or numeraire, the dollar, which in effect told everyone what they had to do – that is, to adjust their policy to maintain the dollar parity. The Louvre lacked this. As a result, when the dollar weakened against the Deutschmark (or the Deutschmark strengthened against the dollar), the Germans were convinced that the US should raise interest rates, something the Americans refused to do; while the Americans for their part were equally convinced that the Germans should reduce *their* interest rates, something to which the Germans were equally adamantly opposed.

The resolution of this dilemma might have been helped had I been able to persuade Baker to agree a global nominal framework, since this might have indicated whether a net loosening or a net tightening of global monetary conditions was appropriate. As it was, while my relationship with Baker worked well in personal terms and on the basis of immediate deals and strategies, there was a very practical disagreement on whether the main dangers facing the world in 1987 were recession or incipient inflation, which could not be papered over so easily.

Later that year, in September, Jim Baker made no effort to conceal his irritation at a German decision to raise interest rates shortly after the Federal Reserve had done the same, thereby nullifying its effect. When the dollar slipped outside its Louvre trading range against the Deutschmark the following month he refused to support an increase in interest rates, arguing that it would tip the American economy into recession. This fear was manifestly unfounded – the American economy at that time was growing strongly – and may have mainly reflected his exasperation with Pöhl. Unfortunately, his very public dispute with the Germans erupted at a time when Wall Street had enjoyed a particularly large and substantial rise and was ripe for a correction. By undermining market confidence in G7 co-operation, he undoubtedly helped to precipitate the stock market crash of Black Monday, 19 October 1987, a few days later.

Fives, Sixes and Sevens

I have been deliberately vague about the signatories of the Louvre Accord since the exact participation caused as much argument as the detailed contents, and attracted rather more attention.

The most important aspects of the deal were agreed at a meeting of the G5 in the Salon de Famille of the Palais du Louvre on the Saturday afternoon, and the Italians and the Canadians were invited to join the G5 Ministers and Central Bank Governors for dinner that evening in the adjacent dining rooms of the French Finance Ministry. The splendid Palais du Louvre used to house the entire French Finance Ministry, but the administrators of the museum had succeeded in colonizing most of the space for more cultural purposes.

During Jacques Chirac's term as mayor of Paris, the city had begun the development of a new financial quarter at Bercy, northwest of the Arc de Triomphe, which Chirac intended should one day rival the City of London. A futuristic building of unrelieved ugliness was built there to house the Finance Ministry, whose presence was intended to attract other financial institutions to the district. Although the new building was equipped with all the latest information technology, it was inconvenient for the top Ministers and officials to be so far from the city centre. Edouard Balladur, the Finance Minister during Chirac's premiership, flatly refused to move to Bercy and he and the top brass of the French Finance Ministry continued to work amid the gilded and ornate splendour of the Louvre. Those days, sadly, are gone for good: after Balladur the entire French Finance Ministry decamped to Bercy.

The decision to hold a meeting of the G5 before the G7 dinner on the

Saturday evening upset the Italians, despite the attempted compromise at Tokyo. When Craxi heard of the G5 deal he threatened to cancel the Venice Economic Summit scheduled for June 1987, on the grounds that Italy could not possibly host a meeting of industrialized nations without being a full member of the club. As I said in my note to Margaret:

> Having succeeded in getting the G7 formally off the ground at the Tokyo summit, Craxi is now set on getting the G5 abolished. All G5 members are opposed to that, and we and the French have particular reason to fear it. But Jim Baker is fearful that President Reagan will succumb, given the threats Craxi is prepared to make. You will recall this was precisely how the Italians secured American backing for the Finance Ministers' G7 in the first place.

Meanwhile, Craxi instructed his amiable Finance Minister, Goria, who had arrived in Paris for the G7 dinner, to return to Rome forthwith. Balladur interrupted the G5 meeting to plead with Goria to stay; but to no avail. The less touchy Canadians did stay. This was thus the one and only meeting of the G6. The Louvre Accord was devised by the Five, announced by the Six and subsequently endorsed formally by the Seven. Giovanni Goria's absence in fact affected nothing substantial. Carlo Ciampi, the much-respected Governor of the Bank of Italy, who had for so long sought to keep his country to the path of rectitude as one weak and unstable coalition government succeeded another, gave assurances that Italy would abide by the agreement; and Italian officials subsequently referred quite happily to the Louvre Accord as an agreement between the members of the Group of Seven, which from then on took the lead – the Five gradually fading away.

The incident had an amusing coda. When we got back to London Nigel Althaus, then the Government Broker and sometime Master of the Skinners Company in the City of London sent me a tie dotted with the numerals 6 and 7. It turned out that Skinners and the Merchant Taylors had in the distant past disputed which ranked sixth and which seventh in the hierachy livery companies. The Lord Mayor of the day had resolved it by ruling that they should each in alternate years rank sixth and seventh, which gave rise to the expression 'at sixes and sevens'. On the centenary of this ruling the two City livery companies had commissioned a commemorative tie, which still serves as an equally apposite memento of the G6 meeting at the Louvre.

PART FOUR

Policies and People

CHAPTER 45

THE STORY OF THE POLL TAX – 1

Prologue · Basic Issues
Early Reform Efforts . . . · . . . and Early Problems
Alternatives to Rates · Scottish Revaluation
Lord Rothschild Lights a Fuse

Prologue

IN RETROSPECT, IT IS clear that all the elements which were to bring down
Margaret Thatcher five years later had emerged in embryo in 1985: the
row over ERM; and the dawn of EMU; the Poll Tax; the Prime Ministerial
ambitions of Michael Heseltine; and the quasi-presidential aspirations of
Margaret herself. But on the most comprehensible of these issues – that
of the Poll Tax – many of the charges against Margaret Thatcher are
unfair. It was a colossal error of judgement on her part to seek to turn a
form of taxation which had been notorious throughout the ages into the
flagship of her Government. Yet it is quite untrue to say that her Cabinet
colleagues were 'bounced' into accepting it.

Despite her profound personal commitment, she observed the proprieties of Cabinet government throughout. For month after month in 1985
she chaired innumerable meetings of the Sub-Committee of the Economic
Committee of Cabinet known as E(LF), the 'LF' standing for Local
Finance. In view of the wide range of local government responsibilities,
the membership of that Committee comprised two thirds of the entire
Cabinet, including such politically aware colleagues as Willie Whitelaw,
Douglas Hurd, Norman Fowler and Norman Tebbit; and because of its
obviously political nature the Chief Whip, John Wakeham, also attended.

So far from the tax being a product of haste and inadequate preparation,
it was preceded by the most detailed Departmental studies, by no less

than two-and-a-half years of intensive ministerial discussion, and by a Green Paper which ushered in a period of public consultation. Nor is it true that Ministers were uninformed about how the tax would work in practice. We were all provided with a very full 'Specification Report' by the Department of the Environment. Having failed to persuade the Prime Minister in private of the folly of what she had in mind, I had no alternative but to table a dissenting Cabinet paper, which I did in May 1985, drawing on that report and explaining precisely what the consequences would be.

Unfortunately, I received no support from any of my colleagues on the 1985 Cabinet Sub-Committee – with the exception of my two Chief Secretaries, Peter Rees until the 1985 reshuffle and, more vigorously, John MacGregor thereafter; but inevitably they were not seen as an independent voice. The main blame for this lies not with Margaret Thatcher, who certainly made clear her impatience with dissent (on one occasion, when I was unavoidably absent and left it to John MacGregor to carry the torch, he had his head well and truly bitten off for his pains), but with a general characteristic of Cabinet government in practice.

Ministers too often see themselves first and foremost as departmental chiefs with their own departmental battles to fight. When an issue arises, as it did with the Poll Tax, where the Prime Minister of the day and the responsible Minister (in this case Kenneth Baker) are wholly and indeed enthusiastically at one, their colleagues – who have causes of their own over which they are either seeking Prime Ministerial support or resisting Prime Ministerial pressure – are disinclined to raise objections. That the Poll Tax was a disaster is beyond dispute; but it is important to learn the right lessons and not the wrong ones from this sorry story.

Basic Issues

The battle between central and local government for control of local authority expenditure was one of the perennial themes of the Thatcher years. Its persistence reflected the failure of the Government to re-solve satisfactorily the two fundamental problems which bedevilled dealings between central and local government. One was the unsatisfactory constitutional position of the local authorities. Throughout my time as Chancellor local authority spending accounted for a quarter of total public expenditure, of which roughly half was funded by the Treasury. Overspending by local authorities could thus have a pronounced effect on the public finances. Yet central government had in practice very little control over local government spending. I remarked to the Treasury and Civil Service Select Committee on 28 January 1985:

We suffer from an unfortunate constitutional set-up in this country as a result of our consistent pursuit in every way of the middle way. There are countries like West Germany and the United States which have a genuine federal constitution and where local authorities, whether they be states, as in the case of the United States, or *Länder*, as in the case of Germany, are genuinely held to account. They are independent authorities and the electorate understands the responsibilities that these authorities have for managing their own affairs. That does not work too badly. You also have the opposite. The French, very logically, have a unitary constitution and carry it to the extreme where nearly every decision is dictated from the centre – Paris – and the head of the *Département*, the *préfet*, is appointed from the centre. That works out not too badly. We have a curious mixture because our constitution is mid-way between the two: we have a unitary constitution but nevertheless the local authorities have considerable autonomy.

It was unusual for me to go out so far on a limb in public. But the Press entirely missed the significance of these remarks – presumably because it was off the beaten track of Chancellorial pronouncements.

The second and closely related problem was the inadequacy of the rates as a tax base for fulfilling the many responsibilities either imposed upon or voluntarily assumed by local authorities. The rates were invented in 1601, but extended rapidly during the nineteenth century. At that time most local authority services – refuse collection, roads, gas, water and electricity – were supplied to properties. A property rate, based on the rental value of the house, was a sensible way of paying for such services. Moreover, in those days the franchise was restricted to property owners; so those who did not own property were unable to vote to receive services at the ratepayers' expense.

By the 1970s most of the original local authority services had long since been nationalized and councils were obliged to provide a variety of other services, of which education and personal social services were only the most obvious and the most expensive. Successive Governments responded by substantially augmenting the rates with grants from the Exchequer. The principal mechanism for this, the Rate Support Grant (RSG), was calculated according to an incomprehensible formula designed to take account of local needs and resources, and there was a variety of other, more specific, grants from central government.

Early Reform Efforts . . .

A succession of devices was introduced during the 1980s to enhance central government's influence over the amount of local spending. These included taking a tough line on the overall size of central government grants, a complicated system of allocating grants which penalized overspending, abolition of the power to levy supplementary rates, compulsory tendering to provide certain services, scrapping the Greater London Council and the six metropolitan authorities, the establishment of the Audit Commission for Local Government and, via the Rates Act of 1984, taking powers to cap excessive rate increases. According to one count, the Government passed roughly fifty separate acts affecting local government in its first decade, almost all of them designed to restrain council spending. Every measure was easily caricatured as an affront to local democracy.

Throughout this saga there were always two distinct perspectives within the Government. The Department of the Environment, which dispensed central government grants to local authorities, maintained throughout the tenureship of several different Secretaries of State that, unless the local authorities were treated generously by central government, they would raise the rates and alienate local businessmen and voters from the Government. The Treasury view, on the contrary, was that a generous central government grant would only encourage the local authorities to spend even more.

In fact, both sides were right. Faced with a smaller grant than it would have liked to receive, the typical council would respond partly by trimming back its spending plans, as the Treasury always maintained, and partly by increasing the rates. Given our muddled constitution and muddled system of local government finance, part of the blame for any large rate increase would be laid at the council's door and part at the Government's, as the Environment Department claimed. The strength of the Treasury's case was that, given the overriding need to curb the growth of public spending, its truth was a more important truth than the Environment Department's was. Moreover the Government had a reserve power to cap the rates.

The annual battle within Government over the size of the rate support grant invariably exposed Margaret's ambivalence. Her low regard for local government, particularly that large part of it under Labour control, made her unsympathetic to the Environment Department's case for generosity; while her fixation with the evil nature of the rates made her reluctant to endorse the Treasury's case for parsimony. In the event, the Government did take a tough line over central government grants to local government, but probably not tough enough.

Although the relationship between central and local government had started to turn sour during the latter part of the previous Labour Government, when the then Environment Secretary, Anthony Crosland, uttered his celebrated warning that 'the party is over', it was during the Thatcher Government that it degenerated into something close to open warfare. The reason for this was the collapse of the traditional understanding that, irrespective of the colour of the Party in power at local level, a local authority would conduct its affairs in more or less conformity with the economic policy of the Government of the day. This understanding broke down for two main reasons. The first was the arrival in office, for the first time within living memory, of a Government committed to imposing severe curbs on public spending, and this at a time when local councillors – Conservative almost as much as Labour – had come to believe that their sole *raison d'être* was to improve the services for which they were responsible by spending ever more public money. The second was the emergence of a new breed of Labour councillor, of which the Militant Tendency group which for some years controlled Liverpool were only the most extreme example, dedicated to pursuing a policy diametrically opposed to that of the Government.

As a result, the tendency of local government to exceed the spending forecasts the Government made and on which its grant disbursements were based, became endemic. It was this that led to the gradual decline in the share of local government spending financed by central government grants from 57 per cent in 1979–80 to 48 per cent in 1989–90. Had the overspending been validated by the Government maintaining the share unchanged, public expenditure control would clearly have disappeared out of the window altogether. This was particularly acute because of the differences between the behaviour of different councils. At one end of the scale there were still some councils that sought to abide by the traditional understanding. At the other end there were those whose ambition was to establish a high-spending Socialist republic. In these circumstances, to validate overall overspending would have meant rewarding the worst overspenders, which would have been as counterproductive politically as it was unthinkable in economic terms.

Indeed, as it was, the annual battle between the Treasury and the Environment Department was accompanied by a separate but parallel battle between the Government and its back-benchers. The Government, conscious of the acute problems of the inner cities, distributed a large amount of grant to those areas (even if it was considerably less than they sought). Tory back-benchers tended to consider this as the sacrifice of their own constituents' interests in favour of the irresponsible extravagance of doctrinaire socialist authorities. Parochial though the back-benchers often were, they had a case; which increasingly led the Government to seek more effective and imaginative ways of dealing with the inner city problem, involving a larger role for the private sector and the sidelining of uncooperative local authorities. This is clearly a field in which there is still much to do.

. . . and Early Problems

In general, the public and Party alike were not unduly affronted by the Government's unceasing battle against local authority overspending (although I found it a wearisome business being in the thick of it). The argument that local government spending was being discriminated against, since central government spending was rising faster, was palpably meretricious. The fastest rising public expenditure programmes – law and order, employment and training, health and social security – happened to be entirely or largely central rather than local government responsibilities; but their position at the top of the pecking order represented either conscious Government priorities or the inescapable consequences of demographic trends. Equally, the spending programme that was cut back most – council housing – would have been cut back just as much, if not more, had it been a central rather than a local government responsibility. And the slow growth of what was far and away the local authorities' most expensive area of responsibility, spending on the schools, was a consequence of the demographic accident of falling school rolls.

The one policy decision in this whole area of whose merits, throughout my time as Chancellor, I found enormous difficulty in convincing anyone, and which was maintained thanks to the persuasive power of the Whips' office rather than my own, concerned the proceeds of council house sales.

The policy of obliging councils to sell council houses to those sitting tenants who wished to buy them, and on attractive terms, was one of the Government's greatest successes. Not only did it lead to a massive increase in home ownership, with the value of council houses sold in this way rising from £¾ billion in 1979 to over £5½ billion in 1989, but it also greatly improved labour mobility, since home-owners can sell up and buy a house elsewhere with far less difficulty than a council tenant can find a suitable council house in an area where he has never lived before. (Mobility is, of course, even greater in the private rented sector; but as explained in Chapter 35, that scarcely existed.) Moreover, one had only to pay the briefest visit to a council estate to see how much better maintained and cared for were the houses that the tenants had bought.

The problem emerged because the 1980 Local Government, Planning and Land Act, which created the tenant's right to buy, had been badly drafted so far as the use of the sale proceeds was concerned. As a result, what was intended as a modest and arguably unnecessary financial incentive to the local authorities to implement the Act without undue delay, turned out to be an almost untrammelled ability on their part to spend the entire proceeds. This did not matter too much when the amounts were relatively small, but by 1984–5 local authorities had accumulated sales receipts amounting to some £6 billion – with no obligation whatever to use the money to repay some of their indebtedness. This worried me. Not only did it give the local authorities the means, at any time, to drive a coach and horses through the Government's public spending and borrowing policies; but it also gave them an opportunity to increase their spending in a particular year to a level which could not subsequently be maintained without substantially increased Exchequer assistance. The PSBR problem derived from the not unreasonable public accounting convention that borrowing consists of the amount by which spending in any year exceeds that year's income – which old sales receipts manifestly were not. The spending problem was more obvious.

In 1984 I brought the matter to the relevant Cabinet Committee, but the discussion was inconclusive. Accordingly, in November of that year, Margaret asked me to chair a group of interested Ministers charged with finding an agreed solution. After a number of meetings, and with great difficulty, I was able to discharge this remit, securing agreement on a system under which the expenditure of the accumulated sales proceeds by the local authorities would have to be spread over a considerable number of years. But in the eyes of most people it always remained a case of a bloody-minded Treasury needlessly preventing local authorities from spending their own money.

Another serious problem arose in June 1985, when Patrick Jenkin, the then Environment Secretary, regrettably abandoned local authority spending targets, as a sop to the House of Commons to secure the passage of that year's Rate Support Grant settlement. This was a scheme we had introduced under which each local authority was given a current spending target, and overspending was penalized by an increasingly steep withdrawal of grant. There was no doubting that the targets were deeply unpopular with local councillors. But since the main complaint of Tory back-benchers was about the extent to which the better-off Conservative areas were obliged to subsidize high-spending big-city Labour councils, the ending of targets made little sense. And of course it badly undermined Treasury control of overall local spending.

Alternatives to Rates

It may be a surprise to some readers that rates and their successors taxes were not under the control of the Chancellor of the Exchequer. Unfortunately, although all forms of local taxation are undoubtedly taxes, they have always been seen as an aspect of local government, and thus fall within the responsibility of the Secretary of State for the 'Environment' (a trendy version of the more accurate earlier title 'Housing and Local Government'). The Chancellor has his say, as he

THE STORY OF THE POLL TAX – 1

does in all matters affecting public finance, but his unique personal responsibility for national taxes does not extend to the local level.

As Chapter 2 records, the centrepiece of the housing section of the Conservative Manifesto for the second 1974 General Election had been a pledge to replace rates by 'taxes related to people's ability to pay', although no-one in the Party had the slightest idea what the replacement would be. When the Conservatives lost the October 1974 election the whole package automatically lapsed. Moreover, the election-winning 1979 Manifesto clearly stated: 'Cutting income tax must take priority for the time being over abolition of the domestic rating system.' But Margaret Thatcher did not forget the promise she had made to the voters in 1974. She was determined to return to the issue at some stage.

The rating system attracted a variety of criticisms. Because domestic rates were levied on the basis of houses, irrespective of the number of occupants, a widow living alone on a pension complained that she paid the same amount as four adults in paid employment living in exactly the same kind of house next door. People who improved their home, and thereby increased its notional rental value, had to pay higher rates – something that Margaret considered particularly reprehensible. Local businesses, which paid more in rates than did householders, had no vote at all in local elections and were therefore suffering from taxation without representation. To cap it all, the egalitarian grant system was so complicated as to be completely incomprehensible.

By 1981 the difficulties the Government was experiencing in controlling local authority expenditure, and increasing complaints that excessive rate increases were driving firms out of business, had reawakened Margaret's interest in the iniquities of rates. Michael Heseltine, then the Environment Secretary, published on 16 December 1981 a Green Paper entitled *Alternatives to Domestic Rates*, which explored a wide range of options. It remains a valuable summary of the three main alternatives to some sort of rating system – a local sales tax, a local income tax and a poll tax – and of the reasons why none of them would work.

A sales tax, it pointed out, would merely encourage people to shop in neighbouring areas where the sales tax was lower. A local income tax was the solution favoured by most local government professionals; and the Layfield Committee of Enquiry into Local Government Finance, set up by the Labour Government, had recommended supplementing the rates with a local income tax collected via the national PAYE system. But the Green Paper was lukewarm both about this idea and about local income taxes in general, warning of additional staffing needs at the Inland Revenue, of delays in introducing it and of a variable yield. Moreover, as part of the PAYE system, it would merge imperceptibly into the national income tax, defeating the goal of making councillors more accountable to their electorates. It was in any event of little attraction to a Government pledged to reduce the overall burden of income tax.

The 1981 Green Paper was also unenthusiastic about a flat rate Poll Tax, calculating it would cost every adult in Britain the politically unacceptable sum of about £120 a head, or more if there were significant exemptions. It concluded: 'The Government believes that a flat-rate annual capitation charge of this order of magnitude would almost certainly not be a practical proposition.' In fact, the poll tax averaged roughly £400 when it was introduced in 1990, or more than twice the level the Green Paper judged impractical, even after allowing for inflation since 1981.

Scottish Revaluation

The consultations on the Green Paper, which were formally concluded in March 1982, led to the conclusion that there was no satisfactory alternative to the rates. This was greeted with relief by almost everybody in the Cabinet, and the issue went to sleep for the remainder of the Parliament. But although asleep, it was not, alas, dead. Patrick Jenkin, who succeeded Michael Heseltine after the 1983 Election, and whose desire to seek after truth invariably exceeded his political judgement, felt he ought to launch yet another review of local government finance which, with Margaret's enthusiastic support, he duly announced at the 1984 Party Conference. Even so, this might not have come to anything had it not been for the problems raised by the 1985 Scottish rating revaluation.

Under English law, which also covers Wales, rating revaluations are meant to occur periodically, but it is left to the Government of the day to decide exactly when. They are obviously highly unpopular, and there had not been one in England and Wales since 1973. The delay was not entirely cynical. The private rental sector had been virtually eliminated, and there was scarcely any evidence on which to base a revaluation. It was for this reason, among others, that the Layfield Committee had recommended in 1976 that the next revaluation be carried out on the basis of sale prices rather than on notional rental values. Although evidence of sale prices was plentiful, a revaluation on that basis would, as the Heseltine Green Paper demurely put it, lead to 'some redistribution of the rate burden between households.' It therefore recommended banding to reduce the extent of the changes which were bound to take place. This, ironically, was the essence of the system which Michael Heseltine, once more Environment Secretary a decade later, was to announce in April 1991 as the replacement for Poll Tax.

In Scotland, however, revaluation was unavoidable, since Scottish law explicitly required it every five years. All revaluations are unpopular, since there are bound to be losers, but the Scottish rating revaluation of 1985 was particularly explosive, since commercial properties gained at the expense of the domestic ratepayer. Household rates rose by an average of 20 per cent, and in many cases, of course, the increase was substantially greater than this. The politics were uncharacteristically badly handled by George Younger, who was then Secretary of State for Scotland. The new valuations were announced without any transitional arrangements to ease the shock, and many Scottish voters, particularly in the more prosperous areas represented by the twenty-one remaining Conservative MPs north of the border, found themselves facing massive rate increases overnight.

A huge political row broke out in Scotland and George Younger had an exceptionally rough reception at the Scottish Conservative Party Conference in May 1985. I was obliged to shore up his position and eventually agreed to make the best part of £100 million available in transitional relief to ease the burden of the revaluations, of which more than half was spent on domestic ratepayers. This put the rates issue right at the forefront of the political agenda. George Younger argued passionately in Cabinet that quinquennial revaluations were political suicide for the Conservative Party in Scotland and that the Government had to abolish the rates before the next one was due in 1990. Margaret added that a revaluation could not be put off indefinitely in England and Wales, either, and that would be far worse. She was adamant that the rates had to go.

Lord Rothschild Lights a Fuse

Patrick Jenkin, asked by Margaret to devise an alternative to the rates, was at a loss to know what to do. He asked his two junior Ministers on the local government side of the Environment Department, Kenneth Baker and William Waldegrave, to re-examine the territory covered by the 1981 Green Paper to see if they could come up with anything. Waldegrave in turn asked his hero the late Lord (Victor) Rothschild – the former head of Ted Heath's Central Policy Review Staff, in which William had served in the early 1970s – to let him have a paper on the principles of local taxation.

This was a fatal invitation. Rothschild prided himself on having no political judgement: he was above that sort of thing. Unfortunately, William Waldegrave seemed to consider it an advantage that Rothschild would examine the issue with a mind uncluttered by political preconceptions. The central proposition of the paper Rothschild eventually produced was that a poll tax was the best solution. William added his gloss to it and submitted the paper to Patrick Jenkin, who passed it without much further reflection to the Prime Minister, who in turn convened a meeting to discuss it at Chequers on Sunday, 31 March 1985, to which I was of course invited. I never liked giving up a Sunday in this way;

and having been assured that this was simply a preliminary discussion at which no decisions would be taken, I foolishly decided not to go and to send Peter Rees, then my Chief Secretary, in my place. Before leaving for the weekend, I briefed him to register my firm opposition to a poll tax, and gave him the arguments to use.

In fact, the Chequers meeting moved the discussion on much further than I had been led to expect. It apparently began with a description by Kenneth Baker of the existing state of affairs in local government. He argued that many councillors and voters were extremely unhappy with the rating system and its lack of accountability, which he defined as the absence of any strong connection between local expenditure and local taxation. Any solution, he said, must act on that central issue. One option was to bring local expenditure and taxation into line by shifting the cost of education to central government. Perversely, he rejected the idea as failing to improve local accountability: in fact (see Chapter 48) the reverse was the case.

William Waldegrave then presented the preferred alternative of the Environment Ministers. This was the creation of a national business rate to replace non-domestic rates, coupled with the abolition of domestic rates and their replacement by a local residents' charge falling equally on all adults in each local authority area. He maintained that only this idea achieved true local accountability, by making local voters responsible for local spending and bringing home to them the real cost of local authority services. There would be rebates for those on low incomes, but not so generous as to insulate them completely from spendthrift councils. In this way a 'graduated residents' charge' would gradually replace the rates. He also recommended a move over the long term towards single-tier local authorities.

The discussion which followed these two presentations was a lengthy one, during which the immense political disadvantages of a poll tax became apparent but were ignored. The meeting evidently agreed that the case against the rates was a strong one, both politically and financially. (In fact, in England and Wales it was a sleeping dog that could perfectly well have been allowed to lie.) But it was also recognized that the proposed residents' charge would be much more difficult and costly to collect, and that the effects of an increase in the tax would be felt much more keenly and immediately by the voters than increases in rates. That, of course, was meant to be part of the attraction of the scheme. Margaret, summing up, congratulated Waldegrave and his officials on their proposal and invited them to develop the idea, by drawing up illustrative examples of the effect of a poll tax on particular authorities and individuals.

She rejected outright the idea of single-tier authorities, perhaps because it would only delay the rapid timetable she was already formulating in her mind. The aim was to publish a White Paper in the autumn of 1985, and to introduce legislation in the 1986–87 Parliamentary session. A second ministerial discussion was scheduled for the second half of May.

Once I found out from Peter Rees what had happened at the Chequers meeting I was horrified. There were some aspects of the Waldegrave proposals – like the national business rate – which I could support, but it was clear to me that the idea of replacing domestic rates with a poll tax would be a political disaster. I asked William Waldegrave to come round and see me privately at Number 11 and told him as much. He noted my dissent but defended his ideas vigorously, apparently confident that there was considerable Prime Ministerial momentum behind them. This prompted me to explain the political dangers as I saw them to Margaret directly at one of our regular bilaterals. She played down the advanced state of the discussion, assuring me that I would be a member of the Cabinet committee responsible for the reform of local government finance and that I could lay all my objections before it. This led to the memorandum of dissent which I circulated ahead of the committee's initial meeting on 20 May 1985. It was the most strongly worded attack I launched on any policy proposal throughout my time in Government.

CHAPTER 46

THE STORY OF THE POLL TAX – 2

'Unworkable and Politically Catastrophic' · *The Steamroller Rolls*
'Everyone Pays' · *The Death of Dual Running*
The Disaster Unfolds · *Operation and Outcome*

'Unworkable and Politically Catastrophic'

IN DRAFTING MY MEMORANDUM of 16 May 1985, I was able to draw much of my ammunition from the exemplifications of the Poll Tax in practice which had been drawn up by officials at the Department of the Environment (who were privately astonished that the tax had been taken seriously) and circulated to the Committee in the Specification Report:

> I agree that our system of local government finance cannot be left as it is, and that radical change is needed . . . I believe it is well worth pursuing further the proposals which Kenneth Baker and William Waldegrave have made to enhance local accountability by making radical changes both in the system of Exchequer grants to local authorities and in the way revenue is raised from non-domestic properties . . . I am also attracted by the subsidiary proposals for annual elections, for the greater use of fees and charges, and for overhauling local authorities' budgetary framework . . . Fixed needs grants and *per capita* grants also have clear attractions . . .
>   It is only when we come to the question of what local tax we should have that I have to depart altogether from the proposals in the Specification Report. The report recognizes that a flat-rate poll tax would be politically unsustainable; even with a rebate scheme the package would have 'an unacceptable impact' on certain types of household.

The biggest gainers would be better off households in high rateable value properties; the losers would be poorer households, particularly larger ones. Tables 3 (a) to 3 (e) give a horrifying picture of the impact. A pensioner couple in Inner London could find themselves paying 22 per cent of their net income in poll tax, whereas a better off couple in the suburbs would pay only 1 per cent. We should be forced to give so many exemptions and concessions (inevitably to the benefit of high spending authorities in Inner London) that the flat-rate poll tax would rapidly become a surrogate income tax. That is what a 'graduated residents' charge' is. The Introductory Report, for very good reasons, rejects local income taxes . . .

Whatever system we adopt, we should learn from this year's experiences in Scotland: we should always ensure that revaluations – and other changes – are phased in over a reasonable period. The problems of an old-style revaluation upheaval would, of course, be magnified many times during the period of transition from rates to poll tax. This is not simply a hideous political problem: local authorities would seize the opportunity to bump up their spending and revenue and blame it all on the imposition by the Government of an alien system of taxation . . . The proposal for a poll tax would be completely unworkable and politically catastrophic. A radical reform of the rating system seems a more attractive option.

My paper was unequivocal in its condemnation of a poll tax, not least because even if it were transformed into a surrogate income tax it would have exactly the same disincentive effects as an increase in national income tax. The radical reform of the rating system I proposed in its place had the following features:

● There would be a shift to capital values as the basis of reformed rates.

● The change could be simplified and the redistributive effects reduced by 'banding': that is to say, houses within a particular price range would be taxed on the basis of the bottom of the range.

● Shocks caused by revaluation would be much reduced by 'rolling revaluations' in which the new valuation would be phased in very gradually over a period of, say, ten years, or when the property changed hands, whichever was sooner.

● The most deeply felt injustice of the rating system would be met by a fixed percentage reduction for pensioners living alone.

● The problem of accountability would be met by central government taking over complete responsibility for the financing of, and key aspects of the management of, education – desirable in itself on educational grounds.

● The educational expenditure taken over would be financed either by the Government retaining the proceeds of business rates as a national tax or by eliminating the bulk of the Rate Support Grant, which local authorities, relieved of the cost of education, would no longer need.

These proposals would have greatly improved local accountability by substantially reducing councils' reliance on central government funding and producing a much closer link between local spending and local revenue. Moreover, as I pointed out, taxes on property are cheap to collect and difficult to avoid. They have a clear local base and have a rough-and-ready relationship to ability to pay.

My proposals would also have had the bonus of acting as a dampener on the great housing boom that was to make the conduct of economic policy so difficult in subsequent years. But even without any such boom, a tax on property values is abundantly justified as it reduces the fiscal privilege attaching to home ownership over alternative investments (see Chapter 30). Indeed a Treasury economist's paper might well have started with this point. The interaction of extended fiscal privilege (due to the prospective demise of the rates, superimposed on mortgage interest relief) with the effects of credit liberalization was undoubtedly a potent and aggravating force in the boom of the late 1980s. Kenneth Baker's own 1986 Green Paper acknowledged that abolishing domestic rates would raise house prices by about 5 per cent. Most outside economists put the figure at around 20 per cent.

The Steamroller Rolls

To my intense disappointment and some surprise, since the case seemed to me so clear, my objections received no support at all at the meeting of 20 May. Margaret invited Patrick Jenkin to develop the Waldegrave proposals further, but I was asked merely to circulate further details of my modified property tax proposal. The Poll Tax was then given fresh momentum by the removal of Patrick Jenkin as Environment Secretary in the first week of September 1985 and his replacement by Kenneth Baker, who as Minister of State in charge of local government was part-author of the original proposal. This was Kenneth's first Cabinet post.

Partly because he had managed Ted Heath's leadership campaign in 1975, Margaret had not had much time for Kenneth. When the Government was first formed in 1979 he languished on the back benches until he wrote his own job specification by persuading her in January 1981 that the Department of Industry needed a Minister for Information Technology. In that post he presided over such wonders as 'IT Year' in 1982. These essentially presentational skills commended him to her in the autumn of 1985, when the Government was trailing badly in the opinion polls. Kenneth sought to secure his new status as a Cabinet Minister by outdoing Margaret in his enthusiasm for the proposed new tax. His performances for Cabinet and the Press, using slides and charts and blackboards, clearly demonstrated his talent for presentation. It was only the policy that was wrong.

At a two-and-a-half hour meeting of the Cabinet sub-committee on 23 September 1985, I again voiced my grave misgivings about the poll tax, and was loyally and effectively supported by my new Chief Secretary, John MacGregor. Kenneth, to my relief, said he now proposed to supplement a flat-rate poll tax with a property tax along the lines I had suggested. But the meeting was inconclusive, and a second meeting of the committee had to be convened before Cabinet on 3 October, to clarify what Kenneth could tell the Party Conference the following week. I lobbied some of my senior colleagues on the committee; but they tended to view the matter very much from a departmental perspective rather than a political one. The Poll Tax seemed unstoppable and was the centrepiece of the new Green Paper *Paying for Local Government*, unveiled by Kenneth Baker on 28 January 1986.

At this stage, the proposal was to freeze domestic rate bills in 1990 and introduce a 'residents' tax' on everyone over eighteen to make up the amount of local authority income lost to inflation every year. The new tax would rise gradually as frozen rate bills produced falling real income for councils, until by the turn of the century domestic rates would have disappeared altogether. This became known as 'dual running'. It was hoped that, by phasing the rates out and the Poll Tax in, the voters would gradually become accustomed to the Poll Tax as the primary source of local authority revenue.

While this made sense on its own terms, I saw an additional advantage in dual running. If the Poll Tax were to prove as counterproductive and as big a political liability as I had warned my colleagues it would, it would be a relatively simple matter to 'stop the clock' as soon as this started to become apparent, leaving us with a hybrid system consisting largely of the rates, but with a small poll tax superimposed on them. This might not be very elegant, but it would be in every way preferable to a state of affairs in which rates no longer existed and the Poll Tax was the sole form of local government taxation.

The Green Paper estimated that the average Poll Tax bill might rise from £50 a head in 1990 to £250 a head in the year 2000. A rebate system would vary the level of the charge from 20 per cent for the least well-off to 100 per cent for the wealthiest individuals. The non-domestic rate was to be abolished altogether and replaced by a uniform business rate levied on all commercial and industrial property, which would have been revalued by 1990. Indexed to inflation, it was designed to rescue business from the swingeing rate increases levied by local authorities on a sector which, as such, had no vote.

The Green Paper was well received on the Conservative benches, where there was no love for the rates, and they accepted Kenneth's sales patter without wishing to probe too deeply – as indeed, to their discredit, did the Press. It was greeted, rather more ominously, with universal hostility among the local authorities, Conservative as well as Labour, who would have to operate the new system. The consultation period was due to expire on 31 October 1986. By then Kenneth had moved on to the Department of Education, where Margaret hoped his presentational skills would help to solve the teachers' pay dispute. Nick Ridley, who as Transport Secretary had served on the Cabinet Sub-Committee on the Poll Tax, replaced Kenneth as Secretary of State for the Environment in the same reshuffle, which was prompted by the resignation of Keith Joseph, on 21 May 1986.

At the time, I greatly welcomed the change, partly on public spending grounds – since for Kenneth no level of spending was too high, whereas Nick was thoroughly sound on that issue at least – but partly, too, because it seemed to offer the last chance to draw back from the Poll Tax. And, indeed, initially Nick did not feel at all comfortable with the Poll Tax. However, he soon recognized Margaret's enthusiasm for it, and became a convert himself. Sadly, Margaret had lost all her usual political judgement about the issue. By 1986 it had become a matter of principle to her to abolish the rates, about which she had developed a phobia rivalling her sentiments towards the ERM. By that time, too, it had acquired its official name of the 'Community Charge', and at informal lunches, on completely different topics, she would become very agitated if the 'Poll Tax' was mentioned, drumming her fingers on the table as if it were a piano, and saying that it must *not* be called a poll tax but a 'Community Charge'.

'Everyone Pays'

Supporters of the Poll Tax – and even some opponents – were mesmerized by its supposed great merit that, unlike the case with the rates, 'everyone pays'. This was one of the arguments stressed most strongly by Kenneth Baker, when he first presented the tax to his Cabinet colleagues, and it was eagerly taken up by Margaret. In this, as so often, I found myself marvelling at her inconsistency. While eloquent on the 'everyone pays' argument for the Poll Tax, she welcomed increases in personal tax allowances which took people out of the income tax net altogether. And of all the imposts on the statute-book, the one she detested most was the television licence fee, the closest approximation to a poll tax in the entire system, with precisely the same regressive characteristics.

But in any case the distinction between the rates and the Poll Tax, on these grounds, was largely spurious. While it was true that only one rate bill was sent to each household, the vast majority of the alleged non-payers of rates were the wives of householders, few of whom can have been unaware that the family had to pay rates. The only other sizeable class of adult non-ratepayers consisted of those at the bottom of the income scale, whose rate rebates (later subsumed into housing benefit) were large enough to exhaust their liability to rates altogether. But this problem had already been dealt with, before the advent of the Poll Tax. In time for what was to prove the last year of the rating system, the law had been changed to ensure that rate rebates could not exceed 80 per cent of the rate bill.

The principle of the 20 per cent rule (which was offset by a commensurate increase in the general level of benefit, not linked to the rates, for those on very low incomes) was one that I endorsed. It was clearly undesirable that there should be a section of the local electorate, which in some areas could be quite sizeable, who would always support higher local expenditure in the knowledge that they would not have to pay a penny towards it. The important point in this context, however, is that the 20 per cent principle had nothing to do with the Poll Tax, and indeed had already been introduced before the poll tax came into being.

Just as the Poll Tax was logically distinct from the 20 per cent rule, so it was quite separate from the other changes to local government finance introduced by the Thatcher Government – though, once again, many people laboured under the delusion that they formed an inextricable package. These other changes had two main aspects. First, there was the move to a fixed central government grant to each local authority based on an 'objective' (and greatly simplified) determination of needs. Second, there was the move to a centrally determined Uniform Business Rate, the proceeds of which were to be distributed to local authorities according to their population. The level of the new business rate was constrained in that it could not be increased each year by more than the rate of inflation.*

The first change was meant to bring home to local voters the true cost of excess spending, and the second one to prevent businesses,

---

*The impact of the introduction of the Uniform Business Rate was subsequently to become hopelessly confused in businessmen's minds with that of the revaluation of business properties that came into effect in 1990.

which had no vote, suffering from the excesses of spendthrift councils. The two changes together meant that the amount of tax paid by local residents was highly geared to spending above Whitehall-determined needs. But they could have been introduced without any move to a poll tax; and would have worked much better without being accompanied by that hated impost, which even made many of those who gained financially from it feel uneasy.

The Death of Dual Running

Nick Ridley initially recognized some of the problems inherent in the Poll Tax, which I had spelled out in my 1985 memorandum, and came to see me at Number 11 for a heart-to-heart talk about them. He was particularly concerned about the politics of the duke paying the same as the dustman, and we discussed how the tax might be changed to make it less regressive. Following our meeting, he wrote to me saying that he would be working up an alternative to the Community Charge along the lines we had discussed, but would bring it forward only if the issue went badly at the Party Conference in October.

Despite these doubts, Nick was opposed from the start to the Green Paper's proposal that there should be dual running – on the grounds, as he later put it, that it 'never seemed to me right to have two taxes in operation at once, and the accountability advantages of the Community Charge would be completely obscured'. This was apolitical to the last degree. Even though it was costly in administrative terms, 'dual running' was the one safeguard against disaster that Kenneth's Green Paper had incorporated.

Initially I won the argument. The merits and demerits of 'dual running' were debated exhaustively in the Committee over two Parliamentary sessions, and I succeeded in July 1987 in securing agreement to a five-year transitional period. This was duly announced. Nick Ridley and his new number two, Michael Howard, who had become Minister of State at the Department of Environment thereupon began an energetic lobbying campaign to persuade Parliamentary colleagues that 'dual running' was an abomination and that a clean switch from the rates to the poll tax was preferable. At the Party Conference in October 1987 they contrived a succession of speakers from the floor – led by the then recently unseated MP for Aberdeen, South, Gerry Malone – who called for the immediate abolition of the rates, with no transitional period. Margaret, who was on the platform with Nick, was duly impressed. According to his account, she whispered in his ear: 'We shall have to look at this again, Nick.'

When the Committee reassembled in London after the Conference, Nick formally announced that, in the light of the views expressed at the Party Conference, he wished to reopen the decision to retain dual running. This seemed to me the height of folly, and I wrote to Margaret on 10 November 1987:

> We should stick to the policy which we agreed and announced in July. It is a complex area, but we should do ourselves no good in 1990 if we change our minds now on the basis of what is, I have to say, generally, if understandably, ill-informed pressure.

The Committee duly met to discuss the issue, and once again the case on both sides was argued long and hard. This time, however, at the end of the day the majority on the Committee, including Margaret, was against me. Nick was delighted, and felt he had won a famous victory. In fact, it sounded the death knell of the Community Charge. It repeated precisely the blunder of the Scottish rates revaluation of 1985, despite the fact that it was in order to avoid such horrors that the reform of local government finance was being carried out at all.

Meanwhile, as a last desperate attempt to salvage something from the wreckage, I had urged that the Poll Tax be introduced in Scotland a year earlier than in England and Wales. This was welcomed by the new Secretary of State for Scotland, Malcolm Rifkind. There had to be separate Scottish legislation in any case, and he was keen to forge ahead. The Scottish Bill received Royal Assent before the 1987 election. As I saw it the Scottish tail had been wagging the English dog for far too long; and there was an outside chance that, if implementation of the Poll Tax in Scotland demonstrated its horrors, there might still be time for the Government to have second thoughts about its introduction in England and Wales. In the event, however, despite all manner of trouble when the poll tax was introduced in Scotland in April 1989, Margaret was by that time far too committed to the tax, which had figured prominently as a 1987 Manifesto commitment, to contemplate drawing back.

The Disaster Unfolds

The events that followed had a grim inevitability about them. As late as 1988 the Department of the Environment envisaged a poll tax averaging £200 a head rather than the £400 or so which eventually emerged in 1990. Nick Ridley attributes the doubling of the charge to local authorities using the occasion to increase their spending and staffing and blaming the consequences on the Government – precisely what I had predicted would happen. It was, indeed, a rich irony that a measure designed to curb local government spending led directly to the biggest increase in local government spending of the entire Thatcher period. In May 1991 the Government admitted that 10 per cent of budgeted revenues from the poll tax, or some £2 billion, went uncollected in its first year of operation. This, too, could scarcely have been a surprise to anyone who had glanced at my original 1985 memorandum.

Meanwhile, before the 1988 Budget, Nick had the gall to try and persuade me to abandon my tax-cutting plans, in order to offset the regressive effects of the poll tax; going so far as to draft a mock statement in pseudo-Treasury language. He must have known there was no chance I would fall for this. The reduction in the higher rates of income tax had enormously important incentive and supply-side effects, whereas the windfall gain to the better off from the switch to the Poll Tax brought no economic benefit whatever, and merely added further distortions to the housing market.

After this, one expedient followed another, most of which had the effect of reducing the distinctive characteristics of the Poll Tax and moving it towards a clumsy, arbitrary and ill-drafted caricature of an income tax, as I had warned would be the case. Chris Patten, who succeeded Nick Ridley at Environment in July 1989, characteristically sought far larger injections of public money than Nick had ever done. With considerable misgivings, I agreed in 1989 an unprecedented increase of £2.6 billion in the total central government grant to local authorities for the following financial year – an increase far in excess of the rate of inflation. Yet what the Press described as 'sources close to Patten' suggested I was deliberately trying to kill the Poll Tax by providing inadequate financial lubrication.

Not content with the £2.6 billion, Patten then pressed, in the autumn of 1989, for a further £2 billion, which he must have known was unacceptable. But what astonished me most about Patten's behaviour was that, while he was well aware that the Poll Tax was a political disaster, he made no effort whatsoever to abort it, even though he was in a strong position to do so.

The overall impact of the new system of local government finance involved, *inter alia*, a switch in the tax burden from richer to poorer councils. The switch was so great that a 'safety net' had been set up to phase in the change over four years. The safety net in turn led to an outcry from Tory back-benchers representing the more affluent areas, who objected to their constituents having to pay an extra amount of Poll Tax – even for a transitional period only – in order to cushion the blow for those living in the less affluent areas. They pointed out that many of those adversely affected in this way were not themselves particularly well off.

But although this was the focus of the discontent on the back-benches, the really sensitive political problem concerned not different local authority areas and the safety net, but the effect of the Poll Tax on those – generally of modest means, and often pensioners – living in low-rated property, wherever they happened to be. It was clear that we had to address both these shortcomings. It was equally clear, and here Margaret was in full agreement with me, that there could be no question of spending anything remotely approaching the £2 billion that Patten had demanded to deal with it. Time was pressing, and Margaret was busy preparing for the Party Conference, so she asked Geoffrey – exceptionally – to exercise his role as Deputy Prime Minister and chair a meeting with Patten and myself to work out a detailed solution.

The meeting began in a somewhat ill-tempered way; but thanks to Geoffrey's soothing chairmanship we eventually reached a reasonable agreement within the overall figure I had set myself. I dealt with the grievance of the richer councils easily enough – by offering to end the safety net after the first year, and for the rest of the transitional period undertaking to pay for the cushioning of losers out of the Rate Support Grant. Since the Rate Support Grant for subsequent years had not yet been fixed, this was a costless concession. Meeting the problem of hard hit individual local taxpayers was not, however, costless, and consisted largely of reaching agreement on the precise categories of individuals in greatest need of extra assistance through the benefit system, and on the amount of extra benefit they should have.

I was in no doubt that the tax was so fundamentally flawed that no amount of tinkering could make it acceptable; and it was tiresome to have to spend so much time on this complex and futile patching up exercise on the very morning that the Bundesbank had just raised German interest rates, immediately ahead of the 1989 Party Conference. But I could not be confident that Norman Lamont, then a relatively new Chief Secretary, and not yet familiar with the issue, would be able to maintain a sufficiently tough line with Patten, who was behaving in a thoroughly unreasonable way. As it was, I was able to secure agreement on a package of help for the hardest hit costing, in all, an estimated £345 million; and this was put to Cabinet, and endorsed, the next day. The amount involved was by no means a derisory sum, but just about modest enough for Margaret to be able to stipulate, without testing the bounds of realism too much, that it should come wholly from the Reserve, leaving the overall spending plans for 1990–1 unaltered.

Operation and Outcome

At the time these discussions were taking place, the Poll Tax had been in force in Scotland for some six months, and stories of disaffection and non-payment were widespread. But since the Scots had made a practice over the years of complaining bitterly about every initiative the Government had ever taken, this occasioned little surprise, let alone alarm. In any event, we were regularly assured by the then Scottish Secretary,

Malcolm Rifkind, who had inherited his enthusiasm for the tax from his predecessor George Younger, that in reality it was all working out pretty well. No doubt he was keenly conscious of the key role the Scottish Conservatives had played in bringing the Poll Tax about in the first place.

Six months later, in April 1990, the tax was duly introduced into England and Wales. By then, of course, I was no longer a member of the Government. All I could do was watch from the sidelines, with mounting horror, as all that I had warned about five years earlier came to pass. Whatever theoretical arguments may be advanced in its support, no new tax can be introduced and sustained that is not broadly acceptable to the majority of the British people. The Poll Tax failed this basic test in the most fundamental way imaginable. There was, of course, an organized hard Left 'can't pay – won't pay' campaign against the tax, with all the usual demonstrations and one particularly violent riot in Trafalgar Square, the television pictures of which, beamed round the globe, convinced half the world that the UK was on the brink of bloody revolution. But opposition of that kind was something the Government could have taken in its stride.

What was insupportable was the anguish caused to millions of ordinary people, with no political axe to grind, up and down the land. In all my years as a Member of Parliament, I had never encountered anything like it. Constituents of modest means would come to me, asking me why they should suddenly be faced with this huge increase in their local tax bills; and there was no convincing answer I could possibly give them. We had asked people, on numerous past occasions, to accept tough decisions because they were part of the only route to economic salvation. I had found no great difficulty in explaining the case, and the British people by and large accepted it. But the Poll Tax was another matter altogether.

There may be some surprise that I did not resign over the Poll Tax. This would, in fact, have been extraordinary conduct, which was given retrospective credibility only by my subsequent resignation in October 1989 over the conduct of economic policy. Senior ministerial resignations are few and far between – I was the first Chancellor to resign for more than thirty years – and there are good reasons for this. If Cabinet Ministers resign whenever they disagree with a policy being pursued, Cabinet Government would be impossible. You certainly fight for your own corner, but you can never expect to win every battle. In this case what was at issue was a proposal that did not lie within my own range of ministerial responsibilities, and which was not a matter of high principle but simply a grotesque political blunder. When I did resign, it was because a situation had arisen which made it impossible for me to carry out my job successfully. Whatever other troubles the Poll Tax may have caused, it did not do this.

Some back-benchers had seen the Poll Tax disaster coming, and had staged a revolt, on an amendment designed to relate Poll Tax liability to the individual's income, thus converting it into a form of income tax, when the Local Government Finance Bill which introduced the tax was in the later stages of its passage through the House of Commons; but they were too few in number to win the day. The amendment had been moved by Michael Mates, a close associate of Michael Heseltine.

It was, incidentally, curious that neither the Press nor the Opposition noticed the omission of my name from the list of 'backers' of the Bill. When a Bill is first published, it carries on the back the name not only of the Minister who is presenting it to the House of Commons, but also of those Ministers who are listed as its supporters, commonly known as its backers. The Minister presenting the Bill asks those of his colleagues whom he considers appropriate to back the Bill in question, and they normally agree. It is virtually unheard of for the Chancellor not to be a backer of a major financial Bill presented by a colleague. The backers of Nick Ridley's Local Government Finance Bill were Margaret herself, Peter Walker, Kenneth Baker, Kenneth Clarke, Malcolm Rifkind, Paul Channon, John Major, Michael Howard and Christopher Chope (a junior Environment Minister). I was of course asked to be one, but declined. Nor could I once bring myself to make a speech in support of the Poll Tax; although collective Cabinet responsibility obviously prevented me from speaking in public against it.

Once the tax had been in operation for a short time, however, the number of back-benchers who had become thoroughly alarmed far exceeded those who had supported the Mates amendment. They did not need the opinion polls to tell them that the Poll Tax had become the issue of greatest concern to the voters, and the issue most likely to determine how they voted at the next general election. They noted, too, that they were stuck with the hated tax so long as Margaret remained leader. Within seven months of its introduction in England and Wales, she was leader no longer. In the subsequent contest for the succession, the appeal of Michael Heseltine's pledge to review the tax – and his position on it was well known – forced his two opponents, John Major and Douglas Hurd, to promise that they, too, would review it.

The Poll Tax was without doubt Margaret Thatcher's greatest political blunder throughout her eleven years as Prime Minister. I pointed out to her very early on the many dangers it posed; but without any support from Cabinet colleagues I was unable to persuade her that they were real. Indeed, at the time of its initiation in 1986, she had openly boasted to her favourite journalists about how she had 'seen me off'. Ironically, in the end it played a large part in seeing *her* off as Prime Minister.

Nor was that all it did during its relatively brief and dismal existence. It was also one of the roots of the gradual loosening of public spending control that characterized the period from my resignation up to the 1992 election, and in particular after the departure of Margaret. For the concessions I had been obliged to make in 1989 marked only the beginning of the subsidization of the Poll Tax. Michael Heseltine, who succeeded Chris Patten as Environment Secretary after John Major became Prime Minister in November 1990, felt obliged to supply a further £3 billion of central government support in January 1991, to fund the so-called 'Community Charge Reduction Scheme'. This was financed in the 1991 Budget by a 2½ per cent increase in VAT, which was used to reduce every Community Charge bill in the country by £140.

Finally, at long last, at the end of April 1991, the Major Government published its plans for replacing the Poll Tax with a new Council Tax, based largely on banded property values – not dissimilar to the scheme I had put forward, as the desirable alternative to the Poll Tax, some six years earlier.

CHAPTER 47

REFORMING SOCIAL SECURITY

A Finger in Every Pie · The Fowler Review
The Struggle over SERPS · The Age of Retirement
Some Sensible Changes · Priorities and Politics
Benefits and Taxes

A Finger in Every Pie

As I MENTIONED SEVERAL chapters back, the Treasury is not simply a Finance Ministry. It is also, both in name and in reality, the central Department, with a finger in pretty well every pie that the Government bakes. While this stems principally from the fact that there is a financial dimension to everything, it is entrenched in the UK by the conventions and procedures of Government. How much time a Chancellor spends on matters outside the field of economic policy proper depends partly on the extent of his own interest in these matters and partly on the degree to which the Government of the day is engaged in reform. For the issues involved in reform are clearly very much more important than those involved in the effective operation of the *status quo*. On both these counts, my involvement was, I suspect, well above average.

It would be foolish to imagine that my colleagues welcomed this interference. But they would have been wrong if they imagined that my sole concern was to ensure that whatever they were proposing did not cost too much. That was obviously one of my concerns: if the Treasury fails to keep a beady eye on cost, then no-one will, and all is lost. But in addition, I was keenly aware that many of these other matters, from social security to education, could have a profound bearing on economic performance, at least in the long run. And even where that was less obviously true, such as health care or the legal system, there was always the political dimension, which should in theory engage the interest of every member of Cabinet, irrespective of his or her departmental responsibility.

The Fowler Review

The social security system is of profound concern to the many millions of people who to a greater or lesser extent rely on it, and represents far and away the biggest item of Government spending, costing more than the *total* yield of income tax. From every point of view, Norman Fowler was right, as Social Services Secretary, to decide in 1984 that this was far too important an area of Government to escape the searchlight of reform.

Norman set about his task in an admirably thorough way. He had been Social Services Secretary for over two years before he did anything at all, which gave him ample time to make up his mind about the weaknesses of the existing system. Then, in the early months of 1984, he set up no fewer than four separate reviews of different parts of the system, all of them manned by interested outsiders as well as Ministers and officials, with Norman himself chairing the most important of them, that on pensions. The reviews produced their recommendations by the end of the year; and the buck was then passed to a specially convened Cabinet Committee, MISC 111, chaired by Margaret and of which I was of course a member, which went over the ground intensively and arrived at the Government's conclusions during most of the first half of 1985. This was followed by a Green Paper in June of that year, a White Paper the following December, and legislation in 1986 – to come into effect in April 1988.

The Struggle over SERPS

It was over pensions, and more particularly SERPS – the State Earnings-Related Pension Scheme – that Norman and I had our only serious disagreement. SERPS was the product of the last Labour Government, and had been put on the Statute Book by Barbara Castle, whose Social Security Pensions Bill had been given an unopposed second reading by the Conservative Opposition in March 1975. We were clearly wrong to have done this; but at the time Margaret had been leader for only a month, and was clearly influenced by the view of the saintly Keith Joseph that pensions ought not to be a political football and by the fact that the Labour Government had squared the private occupational pensions industry.

What SERPS did was to promise a generous second State pension, over and above the basic old age pension, based on the individual's earnings (up to a limit). Like the basic State pension, SERPS is an unfunded, pay-as-you-go, scheme: that is, the taxpayers of each generation do not put money aside for their own pension when they come to retire, but are taxed to provide for the pension of those of an earlier generation who are currently retired.

Although, by the mid-1980s, it was still in the process of being phased in, and nothing like the full cost of the scheme was yet being felt, it was clear to anyone who took the trouble to analyse the scheme that it was a doomsday machine. The combination of the irresponsible generosity of its provisions and the ageing of the population – according to the Government Actuary, the pensioner population would rise by some 40 per cent over the fifty years from 1985 – implied a massive rise in public expenditure. Moreover, since the Government Actuary also foresaw no increase in the population of working age, this meant that the burden of tax and National Insurance contributions on the working population in the next century (SERPS was expected to reach its peak cost by the year 2030) would be intolerable. All this assumed, of course, no change in the age of retirement – an important qualification which I come back to later.

Norman's pensions review team had accordingly recommended that the benefits payable under SERPS should be cut back sufficiently to make the scheme affordable. But Norman, quite rightly, wished to go further, and abolish SERPS altogether. While the provision of an adequate basic pension was a legitimate responsibility of the State, any further pension provision over and above that should be entirely a private matter. That is to say, each individual should be free to purchase from the private sector whatever level of additional pension provision he or she wished to possess. To make this possible, Norman was anxious to develop personal portable pensions, wholly independent of whatever company scheme an employer chose to operate.

Up until then the idea of personal portable pensions had never got anywhere, for two good reasons. First, with SERPS so generous, most people could rightly see no reason to look any further. And second, those who *were* anxious for something more would seek employment where a good company scheme was in place, since the tax concessions made this a much better buy. Thus what Norman envisaged was the abolition of SERPS coupled with the extension of the favourable tax treatment of occupational pension schemes to personal portable pensions. I had made it clear to him that, in principle, I was happy to give personal pensions comparable tax relief. All this was fully in accord with my own political philosophy and principles.

Although the abolition of SERPS would produce a substantial public expenditure saving in the next century, the immediate effect on the PSBR was bound to be adverse. This was an inevitable consequence of the switch from a pay-as-you-go scheme to properly funded private provision, the contributions to which enjoy tax relief at the time they are made. This was something I was prepared to accept; but all sorts of alarm bells started to ring when I discovered in April 1985, as the time was fast approaching when MISC 111 was scheduled to take a decision on these matters, that one of the options being considered was that of *compulsory* private provision.

During the first three months of 1985 I had been fully occupied with dealing with the sterling crisis of early January and preparing for the Budget of 19 March. Officials from the social security division of the Treasury had been fully involved in the Fowler reviews, and I had taken it for granted that they would alert me to any major problems, and enter a Treasury reservation until I had had time to come to a view on them.

On this occasion they had failed to do this. When I inquired about the PSBR costs and economic implications of the various options under discussion, I discovered to my horror that they had done no work on this at all. I immediately asked Peter Middleton to undertake a crash costings exercise, with Terry working on an economic analysis – a high-falutin' term for the burdens on business which the various options implied. With the MISC 111 proposals about to be finalized, and to be put to Cabinet in two parts, on 25 April and 2 May – SERPS being due for discussion on the latter date – there was no time to lose. Peter and his team worked through the weekend of 20 and 21 April, and the figures they produced for me on Monday, 22 April were sufficiently alarming for me to fire off a minute to MISC 111, stating that I could not accept the imposition of compulsory private pension provision at the level envisaged.

I had never seen Norman so cross. He insisted on cancelling the Cabinet discussion planned for that Thursday, 25 April – even though it was entirely concerned with other items of the social security review over which there was no disagreement between us – and came round to see me at Number 11 on the morning of 24 April. He was furious at what he saw as a last-minute attempt to sabotage his plans, and claimed that I had no right to act in that way. I had considerable sympathy with him. It was pretty intolerable to have a fundamental objection raised at the eleventh hour. But he was wrong to imply that I was reopening matters that had already been fully discussed and agreed. Through no fault of his, the key issues had never even been put to MISC 111. However late in the day, it was clearly important that they *were* put to the Committee before the final decision was taken.

In general, I have nothing but praise for the high standard of service I received as Chancellor from my officials. Of course I was served up erroneus advice on occasions – the most obvious example, perhaps, being the serious forecasting errors of the late 1980s – but these were honest errors of judgement which are bound to occur from time to time. Examples of sheer incompetence were very few and far between. In all my time as Chancellor, this was the worst.

Ironically, Norman's position had originally been the same as mine. It was the abolition of SERPS, coupled with the availability of private provision through personal pension schemes which he sought. It had been Margaret – backed by the majority of the Committee – who had argued that there would be no political support for the abolition of SERPS unless an adequate replacement private sector scheme were made compulsory. I disagreed, pointing out that we were the Party of individual freedom; that different people had different views about how much pension provision they required; and that to make the taking out of a particular level of private provision compulsory was wholly contrary to our political philosophy. Margaret replied that compulsory private provision had long been the practice in Switzerland. 'But Prime Minister,' I countered, 'it is well known that in Switzerland everything that is not forbidden is compulsory' – a pardonable exaggeration in the circumstances. At least I never had Switzerland thrown at me again. But she remained firm that SERPS could be abolished only if a compulsory private sector scheme were put in its place; and Norman, anxious to see the back of SERPS, was content to go along with this.

It was true that, in the ten years of its existence, SERPS had become something of a sacred cow – partly because it had been introduced, however mistakenly, with all-party support. However, it was far from being the holiest animal in the herd; and the main reason why no-one expected it to be slaughtered was that no-one expected a Government to be concerned about problems that would not present themselves for another twenty-five years at the very earliest. Moreover, to my mind she had got the politics all wrong: the burdens imposed by a compulsory private sector scheme would make far more political difficulty than the simple abolition of SERPS. But at that time I did not have the figures – and so neither did anyone else.

There was, however, one thing I was able to agree with Norman when he came to see me on 24 April. There is nothing I find more tiresome than arguments about facts and figures. Arguments about policies, principles, priorities – all these are the very stuff of politics. But such arguments should always be conducted, so far as is possible, against a background of agreed facts and figures. I accordingly suggested to Norman that his officials and mine should, without further delay, get together and produce an agreed set of statistics showing the impact of the alternative options. He was content to go along with this, and the exercise was duly done. It confirmed my worst fears. The following Monday, 29 April, I sent a hard-hitting minute to those whose views I had to move if the Government was to come round to my way of thinking: Margaret, Willie, John Wakeham (as Chief Whip) and, of course, Norman himself.

I opened by explaining that the figures in my minute had been agreed by Norman and myself and by our respective officials, and had never before been put to MISC 111. What they showed was that the compulsory private pension scheme envisaged would increase the PSBR in 1988–89 by £1 billion. This was overwhelmingly a result of the tax relief on the additional pension contributions; but there was also some public expenditure cost arising from the burden on public sector employers, since the compulsory private scheme required a compulsory contribution from the employer as well as the employee. It should be recalled that, at that time, the MTFS was indicating only a very gradual reduction in the PSBR between 1985–86 and 1988–89: with an extra £1 billion in 1988–89 there would have been no reduction at all as a share of GDP, and an actual increase in cash terms.

Nor was that the end of the story. Although the overall burden on employers would not change significantly, there would be both winners and losers. This was even truer of employees, who overall would have their take-home pay reduced by some £300 million, a relatively modest amount which masked the fact that there would be some very substantial winners and losers who cancelled each other out. Most striking of all, the self-employed, who were not in SERPS at all but who, it had been agreed by MISC 111, should be compelled to take out private pension provision on the same basis as everyone else, would be mulcted of £600 million – an average of something like £200 a head.

I readily conceded in my minute that, in the absence of compulsion, there would still be consequences for the public finances of the abolition of SERPS, since many people would voluntarily take out private pension provision which, given the generous tax relief, would involve a PSBR cost as well as a loss of take-home pay, and I gave the agreed estimates for this alternative, too. It showed, however, a much lower PSBR cost, at least in the short term, since the level of pension take-up would initially be less. More important politically, a voluntary reduction in disposable income, as people chose to contribute to private pension schemes, would clearly not cause the resentment that would undoubtedly be engendered by one that was forced on people, whether they felt they could afford it or not.

I concluded the analysis with the warning that, if we were to proceed as was then envisaged, 'it would be more than a banana skin: it would be evidence of an electoral death-wish.' Not wishing to be wholly negative, I added that, if it was considered unthinkable to abolish SERPS unless compulsory private pension provision were put in its place, it would be better not to abolish SERPS at all, but instead to modify it to make it affordable, as Norman Fowler's own review had recommended. A wholly defensible modification could cut the additional cost of SERPS to the taxpayer from an estimated £22 billion in 2030, the peak year, to an estimated £8 billion.

Although Norman was angry at my last-minute intervention, as he not unnaturally saw it, it was a case of better late than never. My colleagues were clearly shaken by my minute, and at a meeting held to discuss it it was agreed that the self-employed should be excluded from the compulsory scheme. The self-employed aside, however, Margaret was still determined there should be a compulsory private scheme for all, as was Norman, as the only means of seeing the end of SERPS. It was this amended proposal that was duly put forward as the Government's preferred way forward in the Green Paper Norman published in June.

The reaction to the proposal in the Green Paper soon become clear enough. Both the CBI and the Engineering Employers Federation were strongly opposed to the costs that the proposed compulsory private scheme would impose on business, a fact that caused me no surprise. When MISC 111 met again, after the Party Conference, on 15 October, there was little disposition to argue with my contention that the misbegotten notion of a compulsory private scheme should be dropped, and we should simply make SERPS a good deal less generous – something which in itself would encourage the growth of voluntary private provision. Norman writes in his memoirs that

> Even at this stage I would have proceeded had I been sure of my political support. Margaret Thatcher remained totally stalwart in her support throughout, but not everybody took the same view. In particular . . . Nigel Lawson had made no secret of the fact that he saw the proposals as financially prohibitive.

In fact, as the blunt conclusion of my 29 April minute made clear, I saw them as at least as politically prohibitive as they were financially prohibitive.

Be that as it may, it was the compromise that I had put forward of no compulsory private scheme but a drastic scaling down of SERPS – involving in particular a reduction in the level of the pension from 25 per cent of the best twenty years' earnings to 20 per cent of a person's lifetime earnings, with half the pension and not the whole pension passing to the widow or widower – that duly featured in the White Paper published in December 1985 and found its way on to the Statute Book the following year. I shared Norman's regret that SERPS had not been done away with altogether. But I could not share his apparent regret at the loss of the compulsory private scheme – something that in any event he himself had not originally put forward. The compromise now in place has removed an intolerable burden from the shoulders of future generations.

The Age of Retirement

Curiously, however, the more obvious way of reducing the cost to future generations of workers, not only of SERPS but of the basic State pension, too, was never even considered. I refer to raising the age of retirement. Norman was never prepared to propose it, and Margaret, whenever I raised it with her informally, was strongly against it. She seemed to identify with the women involved, who would inevitably be particularly affected by this, since any change in the age of retirement would be bound at the same time to remove the anomaly of women reaching pensionable age a full five years earlier than men – currently sixty rather than sixty-five. But it was evidently a wholly disinterested identification, as her own dismay at having to retire from arguably the most demanding job in the country at the age of sixty-five in 1990 was to testify.

Norman's successor, John Moore, did however take up the charge. He minuted Margaret in June 1989 arguing the case for a common retirement age for men and women of sixty-five, to be phased in from the year 2010 so as to ensure that no woman then (in 1989) over 40 would be affected. I promptly sent Margaret a minute strongly supporting John, adding only that in my opinion the common pension age should be sixty-seven rather than sixty-five. Margaret refused to have anything to do with the issue. But given the steady deterioration in the ratio of pensioners to working population that is bound to occur over the next forty years unless something like this is done, coupled with the indefensibility of the difference between the male and female age of retirement, I have no doubt that this change must come, and the sooner the better. Whether it is accompanied by the introduction of a so-called decade of retirement, according to which a pension can start to be drawn at any time within five years either side of the central retirement date, the size of the pension rising the later it starts to be drawn, is – however sensible – very much a secondary consideration. It is the central State retirement age that is crucial.

Some Sensible Changes

As for the rest of the social security review, this produced no comparable drama. I failed in my bid to secure significant immediate savings out of the reform of this massive programme, but the changes Norman made, with my full support, undoubtedly checked the escalation that would otherwise have occurred. This was particularly true of the replacement of the system of 'single payments' by a cash-limited Social Fund empowered to make interest-free loans to the poor in appropriate circumstances. The single payment procedure, under which those on social security benefit could apply to their local office for a special payment to enable them to buy an expensive item such as a washing machine, had become the most notoriously abuse in the whole system. Claimants' advisory groups, often politically motivated, had emerged all over the country advising social security beneficiaries how to exploit the single payment scheme. As a result, the cost had got completely out of control – and those not on social security, and who knew what was going on, had become increasingly resentful.

Another important and highly desirable change was Norman's long-overdue decision to base entitlement to means-tested benefits on post-tax rather than pre-tax income. This made it impossible for anyone to be actually worse off by earning more – which had not been the case hitherto. Again, the introduction of personal portable pension schemes, to which I extended tax relief in my 1987 Budget, represented an important advance in privatization and wider ownership, which I enthusiastically supported. Indeed, I may have been too enthusiastic: to get these schemes off to a good start, I agreed to Norman's request to me to allow those who took them out a 2 per cent reduction in their National Insurance Contributions. The response was far greater than either the DHSS or the Treasury expected, which made the concession quite unnecessarily costly.

Norman made a number of other changes, all of a sensible nature. The most notable was the introduction of a belated measure of justice to members of company pension schemes who left the company, whether of their own volition or not, well before they reached retirement age. Hitherto the rules of company schemes ensured that these 'early leavers' subsidized those who stayed. This enabled companies to reward their remaining employees at no cost to themselves. But it was an undesirable disincentive to job mobility and a manifest injustice.

Priorities and Politics

There was one important area, however, where I believed Norman to be mistaken. As he puts it in his memoirs:

> My view was that we should examine whether the money was reaching those that most needed it and whether the priorities of the system laid down in 1945 were still the same. In the 1940s the elderly, often totally without pensions, were the first concern. More and more, I became convinced that the priority for the 1990s should be families with children.

The case for this switch had long been an article of departmental faith, where officials had been exposed to years of effective lobbying by that most professional of all social security pressure groups, the Child Poverty Action Group. It also appeared justified, as Norman demonstrated to us, by a simplistic one-dimensional analysis of the incidence of poverty. He duly achieved it by making means-tested benefits less generous to the elderly and more generous to 'families with children' , to use the jargon. But it was a major political blunder; and I was surprised that someone as politically shrewd as Norman undoubtedly was should have swallowed the fashionable case for the switch so uncritically.

I recalled Dick Crossman, when he was the first ever Secretary of State for the Social Services in the 1960s, telling me how he had discovered to his surprise that an increase in Family Allowances – the then name of the social security benefit for poor families with children – was invariably unpopular with the electorate at large. Whereas the DHSS sees things in terms of the children, the electorate sees them in terms of the parents (or parent) to whom, after all, the benefit (whatever its name) is actually paid, with no guarantee that it will be spent on the welfare of the children. Moreover, the parents who receive the bulk of means-tested benefits for families with children tend to be either those with large numbers of children or unmarried mothers, who of all the categories of social security beneficiaries tend to evoke least sympathy among the public at large – the feeling being, rightly or wrongly, that to a large extent they are the deliberate authors of their own misfortune.

By contrast, the category of social security beneficiary which evokes the greatest degree of sympathy among the general public are the poorer pensioners. No-one can accuse them of having brought their misfortune upon themselves, they suffer other disabilities besides low incomes, and they lack the ability that the able-bodied possess to increase their income by their own efforts. There is a general moral sense, too, that those in the last phase of their lives, who may have contributed a great deal to society over many decades, should not have to suffer poverty on top of the infirmity and loneliness that is their unavoidable condition. Perhaps there is a sense of guilt, too, among the increasing numbers of the able-bodied who choose not to have their elderly parents living with them.

Whatever the reason, Norman's switch of support, at the very sensitive margin, from the elderly to 'families with children' ran clean counter to the moral sense of the nation. It was bound to be unpopular – which it was, massively, when the reforms came to be implemented by Norman's unfortunate successor, John Moore, in April 1988; while the emasculation of SERPS caused no trouble at all. It was also bound to lead to irresistible pressure both to moderate the withdrawal of benefit from the losers and to do more for the elderly poor – which, again, it did. But that was not my main worry. Any upsurge of popular feeling about pensioner hardship was bound to lead to renewed pressure for a general increase in the basic state pension, over and above indexation; and this – given the vast and growing size of the elderly population – would be inordinately costly.

I have to confess that, while I was aware at the time that Norman

595

was making a mistake, I kept quiet about it. Priorities within the social security budget were pre-eminently a matter for him; and had I raised the matter he would undoubtedly have responded that he was obliged to take money from the elderly to finance improved support for poor families with children, which he was determined to do, only because I was not prepared to allow him to increase his budget overall: indeed, I was urging him to reduce it. Since my immediate bone of contention with Norman was SERPS, I had no wish to open a second front; but I subsequently regretted not having spoken up. Whether it would have made any difference if I had is more doubtful.

Benefits and Taxes

There was one fundamental issue, where, to his chagrin, I felt obliged to baulk Norman right from the start. He announced that he wished to look not only into the social security system, but into the tax system as well, in so far as it affected the clients of the DHSS. I refused, holding fast to the hallowed Treasury doctrine that taxation is a matter for the Chancellor and must not be put into commission. Towards the end of April 1985 he came back to me again, and suggested that we announced the setting up of a joint Treasury–DHSS study group on the links between the tax and social security systems. Again I refused. There was thus no discussion of either a tax-credit scheme of the kind that had been advocated by the Heath Government, and which enjoyed considerable sympathy among Conservative back-benchers, or of any of the so-called 'basic income' schemes that had more recently been advocated.

My objection to Norman's superficially sensible proposal was not, simply an obscurantist defence of my own turf, although the Treasury is entirely right to believe that for any Chancellor to agree to put tax into commission would be disastrous. I had enough trouble as it was with Margaret, who was always urging me to introduce special tax concessions for anything she wished to promote or protect. My objection was based on a careful assessment of the issues involved. I subsequently published that assessment in my March 1986 Green Paper, *The Reform of Personal Taxation*, chapter 6 of which is devoted entirely to an analysis of the pros and cons of bringing together the tax and benefit systems. This lucidly demonstrated the overwhelming practical case for keeping the two systems apart – a case which, significantly, no-one even attempted to rebut.

The key point is that the tax and social security systems are *not* simply mirror images of each other, with social security payments a form of negative taxation. Whereas liability for tax is measured over a period of twelve months, which makes life simpler for the taxpayer and Inland Revenue alike, income-related benefits have to be assessed on a weekly basis to ensure that poor families can always meet their basic needs. Again, tax liability is based on individual income; whereas means-tested benefits are based on the finances of the household, which is essential if benefit is to flow where the need is greatest. Moreover, income-related benefits look at circumstances, such as the capital resources of the claimants, which the income tax system does not and should not do. It may be that the social security authorities pry too far; but the features of a system for taxing income to pay for p. blic spending can hardly be the same as those of a system of payments to relieve poverty.

In any event, even if these practical difficulties could be overcome, which they manifestly cannot be, it is hard to see what great gain would arise. The problem that worries many people is the disincentive effect that there is at the bottom of the income scale, as people discover that, by earning more, they are very little better off. By basing eligibility for means-tested benefits on post-tax rather than pre-tax income, Norman removed the possibility of people being actually worse off by earning more; but even after this reform, the amount by which they were better off could be very small indeed. The illusion, however, is to suppose that this could be prevented by some kind of amalgamation of the income tax and social security system. Indeed, the problem has nothing whatever to do with income tax as can be readily seen by imagining a world in which income tax did not exist at all.

Suppose the Government of the day has a fixed sum of money to apply to the relief of poverty (raised, for example, from VAT). The choice before it is whether to spread the money evenly among the population at large, which would be manifestly absurd and would not relieve poverty, or whether to concentrate it on the poor. The latter course is the only one that relieves poverty; but equally it means that as the poor become less poor – essentially as they earn more – their eligibility for benefit is reduced. It is this withdrawal of benefit, and not the tax system, which creates the inevitable consequence that the poor are little better off from earning more. The only practical way of mitigating this debilitating disincentive effect is to embrace the US concept of workfare, in which the payment of benefit is contingent on doing work for the local community, as I have already discussed in Chapter 34.

The 'basic income' concept, too, becomes less attractive the more it is studied. The essence of this is that every adult should be paid a basic income from the State, sufficient to live on, which is then progressively clawed back through the income tax system as the individual's other income rises. The idea is to overcome the problem of the poor not availing themselves of their entitlement to means-tested benefits. But a heavy price would have to be paid for this advantage. A large part of the population would be saddled with the disincentive effect of a significantly higher marginal rate of tax than they suffer at present. And the critically important distinction between what individuals earn by their own efforts and what they receive from the State would be blurred.

Indeed, at bottom, it was the inability to grasp the importance of the fundamental philosophical difference between tax and social security which worried me most. It may have been the Thatcher Government's passionate desire to curb public spending that led Norman to support Margaret's unsuccessful attempts to persuade me to reintroduce the old child tax allowance. For here was a way of helping a large number of his Department's clients without incurring any extra public spending at all, even though it would have meant complicating the tax system in order to give maximum relief to the better-off parents who needed it least. Even that excuse does not apply to the simple failure to recognize the fundamental difference between the tax and social security systems.

The tax system enables the State to take money in the simplest, least economically damaging and fairest way it can devise in order to finance necessary Government spending, with no 'social' dimension of any kind. This is a wholly different activity from that of the social security system, which is the State *giving* (other people's) money to alleviate poverty. The distinction may seem obvious. But any Minister who seeks to use the tax system, rather than public expenditure, to achieve social objectives, is failing to observe it. So, too, is any Opposition spokesman who describes tax cuts as 'hand-outs' (whether to the rich or any other undeserving group); for taking less can never be the same as giving, whether it is a benign Government that is doing the taking or the meanest protection racketeer. So, too, is any Chancellor who boasts how much money he has 'given away' in tax reduction: it is not his to give. I trust that, whatever other mistakes I may have made, I was never guilty of this elementary political and philosophical howler.

CHAPTER 48

_____

REFORMING EDUCATION

A Secular Saint · The Hard Path to Student Loans
Constitutional Confusion · The Teachers' Pay Trauma
After Burnham · Taking the Initiative
My Diagnosis and Prescription · Onward to Opt-out

A Secular Saint

THE SECRETARY OF STATE for Education during my first three years as Chancellor was Keith Joseph. Keith was the founder-member of the group of Tory radicals which, under Margaret's leadership, were the Government's driving force during the first two Thatcher parliaments. The only other full members of that group were Geoffrey Howe, Norman Tebbit and myself. There were other Tory radicals – such as Cecil Parkinson, Nicholas Ridley and John Moore – but for various reasons they did not carry the same weight and were not part of the driving force.

Although Keith could turn in a first-rate despatch box performance when he was really in the mood, he was too unworldly to be a really effective politician in the practical sense. Tormented by self-doubt, devoid of guile, and with a passion to educate, he laboured under the delusion that everyone else, friend or foe, was as intellectually honest and fundamentally decent, as lacking in malice and personal ambition, as he was. He had embraced monetarism with a fervour founded on a need (as he felt it) to atone for the sins of his inflationary past; but there was nothing arid about him. This was partly because his belief in the beneficence of capitalism and the need to recreate an enterprise culture was even stronger than his monetarism.

During the five years that Keith and I sat in Cabinet together, he was a loyal and trusted colleague. I was always aware, of course, that his only profound personal loyalty was to Margaret, whom he had first to a considerable extent made, and subsequently came to admire and adore. But he remained a loyal colleague because he believed in loyalty and because we were politically like-minded. But despite the fact that he believed passionately in education, he was not a particularly distinguished Education Secretary. The Department of Education and Science was a most unfortunate Department to have. While a few able officials no doubt lurked there, in general the calibre of its key personnel was poor. And its ethos was wholly opposed to that of the Government: collectivist and steeped in the once trendy nostrums of progressive education that have so much to answer for. Keith was aware of this up to a point, but he was far too nice a man to realize fully what he was up against, or to do anything about it.

The Hard Path to Student Loans

The one radical reform for which Keith did secure Cabinet agreement was the abolition of university tenure,* although the necessary legislation was not enacted until 1988, under his successor, Kenneth Baker; but he attempted another: the introduction of a system of student loans. On economic grounds and in terms of equity alike, the case for switching from student grants to student loans was overwhelming. Graduates have higher lifetime earnings than non-graduates, and a subsidy to them from the general taxpayer is perverse. What students need is essentially bridging finance to see them through the period when they are earning little or nothing. Moreover, as there is bound to be greater taxpayer resistance to outright grants than to loans, a system of student support which contains at least an element of loan is more likely to provide students with an income they consider adequate. It was no doubt for all these reasons that pretty well every other country in the civilized world had long included a substantial loan element in its system of student support. The UK was almost alone in relying entirely on outright grants.

As soon as I became Chancellor, Keith had a quiet word with me to find out where I stood on student loans, which he told me he favoured. He knew, as I did, that the official Treasury view was hostile to the idea. I told him that I did not share that view, and that he could count on my full support. In addition to the conventional arguments, I also suspected that a loan element would make it more likely that those who chose to go to university were properly motivated, and that those who were merely

*The system under which a university post was a job for life, irrespective of the quality of the incumbent's performance.

putting off their entry into the real world might have second thoughts.

Student loans represented one of those areas where there was a conflict between the Treasury's mission to control public spending in the short-to-medium term and economic common sense. Since the main purpose of introducing a loan element into student support was to enable a higher level of cash to be paid at a lower overall cost, it was clear that public spending would rise in the early years. The savings would come many years later, as the loans were repaid. Not only is the official Treasury line on public spending issues always heavily influenced by the three-year time-horizon of the annual public expenditure survey exercise, but over the years the Department had become understandably cynical of promises that short- or (as in this case) medium-term spending would produce long-term savings. But when I told my officials that I expected the Education Secretary to come forward with a proposal for student loans and that I wanted them to help his officials to work up a sensible scheme, they of course accepted it.

In fact, Keith made no formal approach until early 1985. With the help of my officials, we then worked out a scheme to introduce a limited loan element into student support. The loan would be interest free, but the repayment would be indexed to take account of inflation. I then convened a small group of interested Ministers, of whom the key members were Keith and George Younger, then Scottish Secretary and responsible for education in Scotland, to discuss the proposal and agree the details. The group held a number of meetings at my room at the Treasury and agreement was duly reached. The way was then clear for Keith to put the proposal to Cabinet. He had a terrible time. I had assumed that, given Keith's close relationship with Margaret, he would have secured in advance at least benevolent neutrality from her. I could not have been more wrong: she was implacably opposed to it, seeing any flirtation with student loans as political dynamite. When they saw which way the wind was blowing, those colleagues who had assented in the earlier discussions promptly ratted, and I was left as Keith's sole supporter.

The issue had in fact been discussed, informally and in general terms, once before, as a possible runner for the 1983 election manifesto. Cecil Parkinson, who was at that time Party Chairman, revealed himself to be passionately opposed to the idea on the grounds that, had there been a loan scheme, people like him from modest backgrounds would never have got to university. I told him I thought he was mistaken: that was not the experience abroad, where loan schemes were the rule. In Germany, for example, where the average student loan was some £2,000 a year, the proportion of students from the lower income groups was about three times as high as it was in the Britain of the 1980s. None the less Cecil's view, and the fervour with which he held it, had made an impression on Margaret.

Poor Keith was so shattered he never made a second attempt. But the seed had been planted; and as the years went by the opposition to what became known as 'top-up' loans gradually diminished. After a considerable amount of work both by Keith's successor, Kenneth Baker (who had been put up to it by his enthusiastic junior Minister, Robert Jackson) and by Kenneth's successor, John MacGregor, a top-up student loan scheme at long last came into operation in 1990–91, after I had resigned. Maintenance grants were frozen at their levels of the previous year; but together with the top-up loans they provided students who applied with a 25 per cent increase in the cash available to them. This restored the total cash support to the equivalent in real terms of what it had been in 1979, from which it had subsequently been reduced by almost 20 per cent.

Constitutional Confusion

The real education problem had nothing to do with the universities: it was in the schools, where Keith had the constitution ranged against him. For – unlike the case with universities – responsibility for education in the schools lay, constitutionally, not with central government but with local government. Indeed, it was far and away local government's biggest responsibility, in terms both of its national importance and the money spent on it – substantially more than every other item of local government spending taken together.

The situation was a profoundly unsatisfactory one. I had for years been concerned at the generally low level of state education in England, compared with most of the rest of Europe, despite the massive sums of taxpayers' money lavished on it, year in, year out. This concern was reinforced when I became Member for Blaby, where I found the biggest single local issue to be parents' dissatisfaction with the standards of education and conduct in the schools most of their children were obliged to attend.

The idea that one could reply to these understandably dissatisfied and in some cases deeply anxious parents, 'Frightfully sorry and all that, I agree it's a dreadful business, but there's nothing we can do: we're only the Government. Don't you know that the schools come under the County Councils?' seemed to me absurd. Yet that was the constitutional position to which the Government – and for that matter the Opposition, too – clung. It was absurd partly because, rightly or wrongly, the concerned public found it unacceptable. But it was also absurd for a more important reason: I did not see how any Government could honourably wash its hands of all responsibility for something so vital to the country's future. It would have been a different matter, of course, if the local authorities had been doing a splendid job and Britain's schools were leading the world. Sadly, the truth was the precise opposite of this.

I tried hard to persuade Keith that the standard of education in the state sector, about which he cared so much, would never be improved so long as the schools remained the responsibility of local government; but he would not hear of it. He had had responsibility for the National Health Service as Secretary of State for the Social Services (the old DHSS job) in the Heath Government, and did not relish the idea of a National Education Service in its image. Yet the plain fact was that the National Health Service, for all its faults – and it was clearly in need of reform, too – was doing a far better job in the field of health care, by any objective measure or comparison with its counterparts overseas, than Britain's schools were in the economically and culturally vital field of education. This was despite the fact that the problems of health care, as every country had found, were far more intractable than those of education.

Moreover, this was where the logic of our own constitution clearly pointed. In Germany, with an explicitly federal constitution, it was natural that education should be the responsibility of the provincial (Länder) governments. On the other hand in France, with its explicitly unitary constitution, education was the responsibility of central government, which required and secured educational standards which put ours to shame. True, we had no written constitution at all; but we had a constitution none the less and, with the complex exception of Scotland, it was manifestly a unitary one, and well understood by the public as such. Indeed, one of the reasons – although not the only one – for the poor performance of local government in Britain was that good local administrations were not rewarded at the polls nor poor local administrations punished: when the local elections came round the public for the most part treated them as an opportunity to pass judgement on the central government, and voted accordingly.

The Teachers' Pay Trauma

Keith, alas, was adamant – and this despite the fact that the latter part of his time as Education Secretary was dominated by the teachers' pay dispute, which dragged on for over a year, from the start of 1985 until March 1986, only to resume at the end of 1986 and continue, sporadically, until the eve of the 1987 election. It began with selective strikes, in which schools in the constituencies of Cabinet Ministers were targeted, but soon spread nationwide. Teaching did not of course come to a complete halt; but during that time it was seriously disrupted, and parents were fearful that their children would fail to meet examination standards and thus blight their future career prospects. The strike had followed my refusal, with the full support of the Cabinet, to provide the funds to enable the local authorities to finance the massive pay rise the teachers' unions were demanding.

It was a dispute that caused Keith considerable anguish. Not only was education seriously disrupted; but the teachers, by their irresponsible and unprofessional action, gravely damaged their standing in the eyes of the public. It also demonstrated, so far as I was concerned, yet another unsatisfactory aspect of local authority control of the schools.

Ever since the First World War, teachers' pay had been determined by what was known as the Burnham Committee. This comprised representatives of the local authorities, as the teachers' employers, and of the teachers' unions, with one or two officials from the Education Department, as representatives of the Secretary of State, sitting in merely as observers. The fundamentally unsatisfactory nature of this arrangement was for many years largely obscured by the existence of the so-called concordat. This was an understanding on the part of both sides that they would reach a settlement which did not depart significantly from the amount the government representatives had indicated was the maximum that could be afforded. It was understood that the Education Secretary would in return do what he could to persuade the Chancellor to interpret this as generously as possible.

But even if the concordat worked so far as the overall average increase was concerned, the Burnham arrangement was always a disaster in terms of the structure of any award. For the union side was dominated by what was far and away the largest of the teachers' unions, the National Union of Teachers (NUT), whose policy was in turn dominated by the more junior and less skilled teachers, among whom the bulk of the membership lay. Thus the awards that were made invariably had an egalitarian bias, failing adequately to reward either responsibility, in the shape of head teachers and deputy heads and the like, or the special skills of which there was a severe shortage, such as the teaching of mathematics.

Things went from bad to worse, however, during Keith's time, when the unions repudiated the concordat. The Government still retained a fall-back sanction in theory: an excessive Burnham award could be overridden by a resolution passed by both Houses of Parliament. There was at least one occasion when Keith contemplated using this device. But Margaret was never prepared to put it to the test, having no doubt been advised by the Whips that it was too risky.

At the same time as the unions were repudiating the concordat, the composition and attitude of the employers' side was changing, too. It is normally the case that the Party which enjoys a majority at Westminster is in a minority at the local level, and the longer a Government has been in office the likelier this is to occur. So it was not surprising that the employers' side of Burnham was Labour-dominated. What changed was that the Labour majority started to field its education 'experts', who were usually members of the NUT. Thus, as Kenneth Baker was graphically to inform the Cabinet Committee wrestling with all this, soon after taking over from Keith as Education Secretary in May 1986, Burnham had largely become a matter of the NUT negotiating with the NUT – a manifestly intolerable state of affairs.

After Burnham

It was clear that Burnham would have to go; and Kenneth lost little time in introducing legislation to abolish it, which took effect in March 1987. But it was less clear what should take its place. What Kenneth wanted was an independent pay review body, something to which I was strongly opposed, and with Margaret's support was able to prevent.

The main problem with pay review bodies was that public sector pay accounted for a very large part of total public spending. There was clearly a limit to the number of public sector employees whose pay could be left to outside bodies to decide without the Government effectively losing control of public expenditure. Nor was this the only problem. We had inherited pay review bodies covering the armed forces, the doctors and the dentists, and those on so-called top salaries – by that time confined to the judiciary, the military top brass, and the Whitehall mandarinate. Although the Government could in theory refuse to implement what it considered excessive awards in full, it was always an awkward business – doubly so in the case of the Top Salaries Review Board, whose periodic fits of extreme munificence created a situation in which the awkwardness of rejecting an award was exceeded only by the acute political embarrassment of endorsing it.

But at least the existing pay review bodies could be justified on the grounds that the groups they covered had forsworn the use of the strike weapon. Thus not only could review bodies be seen as a guarantee that the Government would not exploit this self-denial, but the number of other groups who could conceivably qualify for a review body would, on this criterion, be very limited. Indeed, the only new pay review body created during my time in government was that for nurses and other health service professionals. When Norman Fowler announced it in 1984, he explicitly stated – as Cabinet had agreed – that the Government felt it right to do this only because the groups concerned had abjured the strike weapon. (While this was not strictly true of all nurses, it was true of the overwhelming majority – those who were members of the Royal College of Nursing.)

So Kenneth Baker's advocacy of a pay review body for teachers not only threatened to take a massive pay bill outside effective public spending control, but manifestly broke the rule that review bodies were a special protection for non-striking groups of workers. Indeed, it could almost have been seen as something the teachers had won from the Government by the unrestrained use and threat of strike action.

Instead of a pay review body, we set up what was known as the Interim Advisory Committee on Teachers' Pay. It was interim, since it was a stop-gap until we had decided what permanent arrangement we wanted to replace Burnham. It was advisory, since technically its job was not to determine teachers' pay but to advise the Secretary of State, whose decision it was. But – and more importantly – unlike the review bodies, which had *carte blanche* as to what they awarded, the Interim Advisory Committee was told by the Government, at the start, how large an overall increase it had at its disposal, and its remit was to advise how that should be apportioned among the various categories of teacher. The whole point was to reverse the Burnhamite egalitarianism that had wreaked such havoc, and to ensure that those teachers carrying special responsibilities, or of special merit, or in subjects where there was a serious shortage of qualified teachers, were adequately rewarded.

This arrangement began in 1987, as soon as Burnham was abolished, and worked pretty well for the remainder of my time in Government. It lasted longer than was originally intended, as interim arrangements are always inclined to do, because of our inability to agree to a permanent successor – Kenneth continuing to argue for a full-blooded pay review body, and I resisting it. For my part, I would have much preferred to see something like the pay arrangements I had, with the invaluable assistance of Peter Kemp, already put in place for the Civil Service (see Chapter 31). In the end, the Major Government did, in 1991, concede a full-blooded pay review body for teachers, which I fear it may live to regret.

Taking the Initiative

My main concern, however, was not teachers' pay; it was education standards. I was therefore particularly sad to see Keith go in May 1986 and be replaced by Kenneth Baker. Kenneth is a most civilized man with an agreeably sunny disposition, but not even his greatest friends would describe him as either a profound political thinker or a man with a mastery of detail. His instinctive answer to any problem is to throw glossy PR and large quantities of money at it, and his favoured brand of politics is the instant response to the cry of the moment. It would have been hard to imagine anyone less like Keith. More to the point, it was hard to imagine that we would get from Kenneth the fundamental thinking about education reform that I was sure was needed.

By early 1986 I had become even more convinced of the importance of this issue after reading Corelli Barnett's newly published book, *The Audit of War*, which impressively documented the British educational failure stretching back into the last century, and linked it persuasively with the reasons for our disappointing economic performance over that period, with particularly ominous implications for the future. Of course, in narrow political terms, genuine educational reform is a particularly unattractive prospect for any government. Like all reform, it upsets from the start all those with a vested interest in the *status quo*; whereas the nature of education is such that the return from even the most successful reform will not become apparent within the lifetime of even the longest-lived administration.

Nevertheless, we prided ourselves in being a Government which, unlike others, did believe in taking a long-term view and was prepared to act accordingly, regardless of short-term popularity – as we had recently shown, for example, over the state earnings-related pension scheme. I also sensed from my own constituency experience that the time had come when the general public, and in particular parents of children of school age, would instinctively feel that we were doing the right thing in seeking to tackle this issue. In an age, regrettably, of interest group politics, diffuse public benevolence of this kind may not count for a great deal; but at least it is better than diffuse public hostility.

Moreover, the more I thought about it the more I saw the possibility of killing two birds with one stone: not only could we make possible the improvement in standards of education the country so badly needed, but we could also solve the linked problem that had plagued us for so long. That was of the relationship between central and local government, and the lack of local government accountability, which it was quite clear to me could never be achieved by the dreadful Poll Tax.

Accordingly, soon after Keith's departure and Kenneth's appointment, I saw Margaret and told her I would like to let her have, on a strictly personal basis, a paper on educational reform. Education was, of course, a subject in which she was particularly interested and on which she considered herself to be an authority, having served as Education Secretary in the Heath Government. Indeed, this had been her only Cabinet post before she became Prime Minister. She fully recognized the need for radical change, and welcomed the idea of a paper on it.

Back at the Treasury, I called a meeting with John MacGregor, my Chief Secretary, who, like me, happened to have a long-standing interest in education and had thought a great deal about it, the special advisers, and a small group of Treasury officials including Peter Middleton and John Anson, a dry (in the non-political sense), shy, Wykehamist Under Secretary, with a good logical mind and an ability to write clear prose. I told them of the paper I had undertaken to put to Margaret, and warned that they were not to breathe a word to anyone at the Department of

Education: not only would they be unhelpful, but I had little doubt that Kenneth would be more inclined to embrace an initiative which he believed had emerged from Margaret than he would one that had emanated from me. I then outlined my thinking and we had a prolonged discussion.

My Diagnosis and Prescription

So far as the local government problem was concerned, accountability was a mockery because the voters had no idea who – central or local government – was responsible for what, a confusion that was further compounded over the greater part of the country by there being two tiers of local government, again with overlapping responsibilities. Nor was the public's confusion at all surprising, since there was a parallel muddle over the financing of local government, which was a mixture of grants from central government and the money the local authorities themselves raised by local taxation – at that time, still the rates. Among other things, this made it quite impossible for the voter to judge whether any problems with local services were, as local councils claimed, the fault of central government for providing an inadequate grant or, as the Government claimed, the fault of waste and incompetence on the part of the councils. The overriding need was to inject some clarity into the situation; and this was where the changes, which to my mind were in any case needed if education was to be radically reformed, came in.

It so happened that, at that time, the amount of money given by central government to local authorities by way of the Rate Support Grant was almost exactly equivalent to the amount of money spent by the local authorities on schooling – some £9 billion in 1986–87 money. It seemed to me that the obvious first step was for central government to take over the entire responsibility for the schools, and simultaneously to abolish the Rate Support Grant. (To the extent that it was felt desirable to retain a measure of equalization – the system that channelled rate revenue from the richer to the poorer areas – this could be achieved via non-domestic rates.) This would leave local authorities with a range of other matters for which they were entirely responsible, a responsibility that would be recognized by the fact that, apart from a limited number of specific grants from the centre, they would have to finance them entirely out of their own tax revenues. Moreover, with education removed, there would no longer be a case for two tiers of local government, which would remove the subsidiary cause of confusion. The public would at last be clear where responsibility, both for the services and their finance, truly lay; and only in this way would genuine democratic and financial accountability be secured.

Next, the wresting of the schools from the so-called local education authorities would provide the essential basis for educational reform. The State would be able to lay down, and enforce, both a core curriculum and the standards of attainment required, without which there was no hope of securing the badly needed improvement in the standard of education in Britain's schools which was the object of the whole exercise. The practice in France was highly relevant here, and we could learn from it: it was striking that the latest figures then available showed spending per pupil to be the same in France as in the UK, yet the average standard of education was considerably higher.

Then, with nationally determined standards, the actual running of the schools could and should be devolved to the schools themselves – which would still be subject, of course, to an improved national schools inspectorate – a devolution which it was clear would never occur on any significant scale so long as responsibility for the schools lay with local government. Within that context, each school would be given its own budget to use as it thought best; each school would have the right to hire and fire teachers; and with each school's income based largely on the number of pupils it attracted, a system of open enrolment could be introduced, enabling state schools to accept pupils in much the same way as the private sector does.

After a number of further meetings to discuss the problems that a change of this kind would throw up and how they might be solved, John Anson wrote an excellent paper along these lines – starting, of course, with the need to improve education in the schools and how to achieve it. The paper also showed how the various objections and difficulties that might be raised could be dealt with. I sent the paper to Margaret in July 1986, with a covering note offering to discuss it with her. We had a couple of lengthy meetings, to the second of which I brought John Anson, so that he could answer any of the technical points she might raise.

Onward to Opt-out

Initially, Margaret was attracted to the proposal; but on further reflection she decided that it was too radical and that she was not prepared to take on the local authorities, who would greatly resent the loss of their responsibility for the schools. She did, however, decide to set up a Cabinet Sub-Committee on the reform of education in the schools, under her chairmanship, and on which I served.

The Cabinet Sub-Committee on Education Reform proceeded in a way unlike any other on which I have served. The process would start by Margaret putting forward various ideas – in addition to the Anson paper she had the Number 10 Policy Group heavily involved in the subject, and its then head, Brian Griffiths, was engaged in little else at this time – and there would then be a general discussion, to which I would contribute my four pennyworth. At the end of it, Margaret would sum up and give Kenneth his marching orders. He would then return to the next meeting with a worked out proposal which bore little resemblance to what everyone else recalled as having been agreed at the previous meeting, and owed rather more to his officials at the DES.

After receiving a metaphorical handbagging for his pains, he would then come back with something that corresponded more closely to her ideas, but as often as not without any attempt by his Department to work them out properly, a gap that I tried to fill as best as I could by having John Anson do the work, which I would then present to the next meeting. This procedure was repeated on most of the aspects of the reform. Kenneth remained in unruffled good humour throughout this process, and the outcome was the raft of proposals that appeared in the 1987 Conservative manifesto, before – as became embarrassingly clear right at the start of the campaign – some sensitive issues had been settled. These were summarily dealt with immediately the election was over, and the proposals were duly enacted early in the new Parliament through the agency of what Kenneth liked to call 'the Gerbil' (the great Education Reform Bill).

The substitute Margaret came up with for my proposal to remove all the schools from local authority control was the 'opt-out' system, under which individual schools could escape from local authority control provided a majority of parents voted so to do. It remains unclear whether this will ever, in practice, happen on a sufficient scale to secure the improvement in national education required – although it is true that the mere possibility of dissatisfied parents voting to opt out could theoretically cause local education authorities to provide the better education all parents desire for their children. Nor, of course, can the opt-out solve the local government accountability problem.

Not surprisingly, however, things were still in a somewhat unsatisfactory and untidy condition when Kenneth left the DES to become Party Chairman in 1989, and it was left to his successor, John MacGregor – a particularly appropriate choice in the circumstances – to start to make it work. In the reshuffle that followed Margaret's replacement as Prime Minister by John Major, the baton of education reform was energetically picked up by John's successor, the robust and effective Kenneth Clarke, who in turn was reshuffled to the Home Office immediately after the 1992 election. He was succeeded by John Patten, who in July 1992 published a white paper containing some radical proposals designed to speed up the process of reform. All this chopping and changing caused some problems in the schools – although it had already become apparent that even the relatively modest degree of devolution known as LMS (Local

Management of Schools) was producing worthwhile improvements that would never have occurred otherwise. Above all, what really mattered was that, for the first time within living memory, a Government had committed itself to the long overdue and all-important task of raising the standard of education in Britain's schools.

CHAPTER 49

REFORMING THE DOCTORS
AND LAWYERS

Health Care: an Intractable Problem · The Health Service Review
A Private Diversion · How the Reforms Emerged
Taking on the Lawyers · The Green Paper Proposals
A Remarkable Lord Chancellor

Health Care: an Intractable Problem

As THEY WERE TO do in the 1992 General Election campaign, the Labour Party sought to make the National Health Service a major issue in the 1987 Election campaign. It was an issue – one of the very few – which found us on the defensive. Margaret could quote back at them, *ad nauseam*, the statistics which demonstrated how much extra taxpayers' money we had poured into the Health Service, even after allowing for inflation; how much better we had done on this score than the previous Labour Government; and how many more doctors and nurses there were than when we had first taken office in 1979. But it cut very little ice.

After we had returned with a handsome majority, the Opposition continued the onslaught in the House of Commons. At Prime Minister's Questions every Tuesday and Thursday afternoon, Margaret had thrown at her case after case of ward closures, interminably postponed operations, and allegedly avoidable infant deaths, all of them attributed to Government parsimony. Labour may have been using this stick to beat us because they had no other; but they were clearly on to something. A number of our own back-benchers were becoming increasingly uneasy; and I knew from my own experience as a constituency Member that we had a real and growing problem on our hands.

My economic policy group that had sat before the election had, at my suggestion, interpreted its remit widely; and, among the recommend-ations it had made were a number of proposals for the reform of the Health Service. Understandably, Margaret would not touch them with a bargepole. The provision of health care is an issue where the intractability of the problems is matched only by the acute political sensitivity of the issue. The intractability stems chiefly from the fact that the demand for health care, particularly if it is to embrace caring as well as curing, is infinite. In this it is quite different from, say, education, for which most people's demand is, rightly or wrongly, strictly limited. There is no limit to the demand for health care; and as medical science progresses, and new treatments are discovered, the demand grows still more and the cost of meeting it rises even faster.

There are in practice only two ways in which health care can be financed. One is by the taxpayer, and the other through the individual taking out an insurance policy. The latter method, which is the basis of the US system, inevitably results in a massive further escalation in the cost of health care – even in the UK it is not unheard of for bills to be higher when it is known to the provider that an insurance company will foot them. This in turn means insurance premiums that are so high that the taxpayer has to come to the rescue of those who cannot afford them. And many US employers, who have provided free health care, often extending beyond retirement, as part of the remuneration package, now find themselves sitting on a contingent liability which, when it crystallizes, could bankrupt the company.

The UK system of taxpayer finance avoids these problems. But it cannot escape the fact that, when finite resources, however substan-tial, are faced with infinite demand, there will always be frustrated demand; and the consequence of this in terms of human suffering will all too often be held to be the direct responsibility, if not the deliber-ate policy, of the Government.

As if this were not sensitive enough, the political problem in the UK was compounded by two other factors. The first was the sheer size of the Health Service. It was the third biggest employer and bureaucracy in the world, after the Indian railway system and the former Red Army, with well over a million employees. The second factor was even more delicate. The National Health Service is the closest thing the English have to a religion, with those who practice in it regarding themselves as a priesthood. This made it quite extraordinarily difficult to reform. For a bunch of laymen, who called themselves the Government, to presume to tell the priesthood that they must change their ways in any respect whatever was clearly intolerable. And faced with a dispute between their priests and Ministers, the public would have no hesitation in taking the part of the priesthood.

All the same, it was clear to me that we could not allow things to carry on as they were. The National Health Service, although remarkably successful by international standards in terms of straightforward cost control, was in many respects highly inefficient and fundamentally flawed. When Margaret and Denis came to have dinner at Number 11 with Thérèse and myself on a Sunday evening towards the end of January 1988 as the prelude to our annual post-prandial private talk during which I outlined to her my plans for the forthcoming Budget, I decided to use the occasion to return to the charge on Health Service reform. After a full discussion of the Budget, about which she was enthusiastic, I turned to the subject of the National Health Service.

I told her that in my judgement we had reached the point where the pressures to spend considerably more money on the Health Service were almost impossible to resist. But I was very reluctant to give the money to the Health Service as it was at that time: we had to ensure that, if we were going to give significant extra taxpayers' money to the NHS, we would get real value in terms of improved patient care. This meant that we had to have some kind of review to decide what changes to make to achieve that objective. Margaret appeared to agree. Had we said anything about it in the manifesto, it would have been disastrous. The start of a new Parliament was the only practical time to consider the matter. We decided that, because of the sensitivity, the enquiry would need to be small and entirely internal. The professionals, once they knew it was going on, would not be backward in giving us the benefit of their advice – and, more fruitfully, we could always get the opinions of politically well-disposed practitioners informally.

When, the next day, I told John Moore, who had been one of my junior Ministers at both Energy and the Treasury, and was now the Secretary of State at the DHSS and responsible for the Health Service, of this conversation, he was delighted. He had suggested embarking on the reform of the Health Service to Margaret shortly after his appointment the previous June, and she had firmly warned him off it.

The Health Service Review

On 28 January 1988, Margaret duly set up a small ministerial group under her chairmanship, whose terms of reference were to undertake a fundamental review of health care in general and the hospital service in particular. It was unusually intimate in size, consisting of only five members: apart from Margaret herself there were John Moore and his number two, Tony Newton, plus myself and my number two, John Major. There were two other regular attenders: Roy Griffiths, the Sainsburys executive who had conducted the 1983 inquiry into the management of the Health

Service and was then advising the Department on the implementation of the management changes that had been agreed, and John O'Sullivan, a political journalist at that time seconded to the No. 10 Policy Unit. When Margaret decided to split the DHSS into two in July 1988, and consigned John Moore to the Social Security side, John was replaced by Kenneth Clarke and Tony Newton by Kenneth's number two, David Mellor.

My own idea had been that the review should be confined entirely to the hospital service. It was here that all the obvious problems were, from waiting times for operations to babies dying. Moreover the general practitioners came face to face with the public all the time, and the political cost of alienating them could be very high. I felt that it would be politically prudent to leave the reform of general practice until later, after the reform of the hospital service had been completed. Margaret, however, having initially been too nervous to do anything at all, once she had accepted the idea, characteristically decided to go the whole hog, and reform everything at once. She was probably right. Somewhat eccentrically, she announced the formation of the group during the course of an interview on the television programme *Panorama*. We sat for the best part of a year, meeting every week – and more often than that, towards the end – before Kenneth Clarke published the outcome in his January 1989 White Paper, *Working for Patients*.

The Labour Party subsequently alleged that what we were proposing amounted to the privatization of the Health Service; and even those who do not subscribe to this foolish charge often suspect that that was what we wished to do. As both an arch-promoter of privatization and one of the only three members of the review group from its inception to its conclusion, I can state quite categorically that there is not a word of truth in it. Some, I realize, will say 'So much the worse' - to which I would have to reply that the provision of medical care is *sui generis*, and should not be assimilated to other activities where full-blooded privatization is entirely appropriate. In this particular area the ground on which to stand firm is support for the parallel availability of private medical treatment, against those who inveigh against a so-called 'two-tier' system and imply that the provision of private health care should be a criminal offence. This would not only be an intolerable restriction of individual freedom but almost certainly contrary to both the UN Declaration of Human Rights and its European counterpart, and thus itself illegal.

Of course, the maintenance of a largely tax-financed Health Service in no way rules out the use of specific charges for particular items and facilities. Indeed, it is highly desirable that people should be reminded that nothing is free: it is simply a matter of how it is paid for. During the course of the review discussions I argued for a considerable extension of charging, pointing out how absurd it was that the proportion of total NHS spending financed by charges was lower in the 1980s than it had been in the 1950s, despite the huge increase in real incomes in the meantime. But Margaret was not prepared to touch it, fearing the political unpopularity.

One of the sticks with which the Opposition had sought to beat us was the low level of spending per head of population on health care in the UK. At a very early stage I put to the group a paper showing that, despite this, by all the conventional objective tests of the medical health of the nation, such as life expectancy or the rate of infant mortality, we compared perfectly respectably with other North European and North American countries. I concluded that this suggested that the Health Service was in fact serving us pretty well: what we had to concentrate on was making it even better.

Not that we were complacent. We looked first, albeit rather briefly, at other countries to see whether we could learn from them; but it was soon clear that every country we looked at was having problems with its provision of medical care. All of them – France, the United States, Germany – had different systems; but each of them had acute problems which none of them had solved. They were all in at least as much difficulty as we were, and it did not take long to conclude that there was surprisingly little that we could learn from any of the other systems. To try to change from the Health Service to any of the sorts of systems in use overseas would simply be out of the frying pan into the fire.

A Private Diversion

I sought to set out what I saw as our objective in a note I sent the group in July 1988, in the course of which I wrote:

> In the work we are doing in the Review, it is vital that we do not lose sight of some of the basic features of the economics of health care. Simply stated, the demand for health care exceeds the supply; and that is inevitable in the public sector with a free service financed out of general taxation, which means that demand is virtually unlimited – hence the persistence of waiting lists. Our objective has to be to see that, despite the absence of the price mechanism, the NHS provides health care as efficiently and effectively as possible – in other words, we get the best possible value for money.

That is why, incidentally, talk of 'underfunding' is, quite literally, meaningless. The occasion for my note was, however, rather more specific. In the early months, while we were not making a great deal of progress on the reforms proper, despite the inordinate amount of paperwork the DHSS was producing, I came under heavy pressure from Margaret, strongly supported by John Moore, with Roy Griffiths voicing his approval, to introduce tax relief for private health care. More precisely, what they wanted me to do was to make all subscriptions to BUPA and similar private health insurance schemes tax-deductible, and to cease to tax as a benefit in kind the provision of private health care to employees under a company scheme – a rapidly growing perk. I thus concluded my note by saying:

> If we simply boost demand, for example by tax concessions to the private sector, without improving supply, the result would not be so much a growth in private health care, but higher prices. The key is the supply side, as we have recognized in most other areas of policy. Moreover, of course, increasing demand in the private sector pushes up prices and therefore pay. That would inevitably spread across all staff costs in the NHS, and we would end up getting less value for money.

I was also, of course, concerned that a tax concession in this field would lead to pressure for similar tax concessions in other fields, such as private education.

In the end the pressure was such that, mistakenly, I offered Margaret a compromise. There would be no change in the tax treatment of the benefit of company health insurance schemes. Nor would there be a general tax relief for contributions to private health insurance schemes; but what I was prepared to offer, I told her, was tax relief for contributions to private health insurance schemes by or on behalf of the over-sixties. Not only was this much smaller beer, but it was clearly less repercussive, and could just about be justified on the grounds that those who had been members of company schemes during their working life would be assisted to maintain the benefit to which they had become accustomed in retirement. Even so, had I known that, within weeks, John Moore would have been replaced by the robust Kenneth Clarke, I would not have made even this concession.

Margaret eagerly snapped up my compromise – for which there had for some time been a back-bench campaign, led by Philip Goodhart – pausing only to wonder whether there was a catch in it. I duly introduced it, trying to conceal my embarrassment, in my 1989 Budget.

How the Reforms Emerged

So far as the review proper was concerned, a number of key issues quickly surfaced. There was the confusion between the *provision* of health care and the *financing* or *purchase* of health care. Hitherto the local Health Authorities had been indiscriminately responsible for both within their area. Yet there was no reason why they should be. Drawing the distinction between these two quite separate functions was the key step towards creating a genuine internal market within the Health Service, along the lines proposed by my pre-election economic policy group report. It meant that the money followed the patient. Hitherto each hospital had been allocated a fixed budget by its local Health Authority. Thus if it was efficient, and had the capacity to perform more operations than it did, it could not afford to take the additional patients since to do so would involve it in increased cost and attracted no additional revenue. This elementary but crucial reform paved the way to a significant reduction in waiting times for operations – not that this consideration stopped the British Medical Association (BMA) from running, as part of its vitriolic and ultimately counterproductive campaign against the reforms, large posters featuring a lonely granny in a hospital bed hundreds of miles from family and home.

This was reinforced by two further key reforms. Hospitals were allowed to withdraw from the control of the local Health Authority and become self-governing trusts within the Health Service, funded from general taxation but free to settle their own pay and staff conditions and to sell their services to any Health Authority, to other hospitals and even to the private sector. And doctors' practices with large patient lists were allowed to take control of their own budgets, enabling them to buy health care for their patients, including non-emergency operations, from wherever they could obtain the best service at the best price. The aim was to encourage these fund-holding GPs to improve their services, attract more patients, and thereby secure a bigger budget. The reform would also reward the more efficient hospitals.

There was much criticism when the White Paper was published that the Government was being characteristically doctrinaire and arrogant in imposing its reforms without even having a series of pilot projects first. I found this very puzzling. No hospital was obliged to become an NHS Trust Hospital: those that did volunteered to do so. Similarly, no doctors were obliged to become fund-holders: those that did volunteered to do so. This seemed to me the best possible form of pilot project, with the guinea pigs volunteering for their role rather than having it unwillingly thrust upon them.

The mistake, although it was a minor one, which I now believe we did make in this area was to use the phrase 'trust hospitals'. Margaret always had a weakness for the word 'trust', which certainly went down well in financial circles. But in the NHS context it encouraged absurd talk of such hospitals opting out of the Health Service. In fact, in many ways we were harking back to the time, not so long ago, when the great London teaching hospitals were constitutionally independent Health Authorities of their own, and not part of any larger Health Authority. Even 'direct grant hospitals', on the analogy of the old direct grant grammar schools, would have been less open to malicious misconstruction than 'trust hospitals'.

Among the other aspects of the Health Service reforms in which I played a key role was bringing the Health Service within the ambit of the Local Government Audit Commission. Clearly, if improved value for money, in order to improve the service to patients, was the heart of the matter, then a high-calibre watchdog, as the Audit Commission had proved itself to be in the local government field, was, I felt, highly desirable. This was bitterly – but, I am glad to say, vainly – opposed by the DHSS, which took the view that it was perfectly capable of monitoring Health Service performance itself.

Indeed, throughout the course of the review the relative weakness of the official DHSS and of its successor, the Department of Health, meant that a remarkable amount of the work, both in terms of the analysis and the working-up of solutions, as well as the knocking down of nonsenses, fell to the Treasury. I was fortunate to be able to entrust this work to a very small, but hand-picked, team headed by a lively senior official, Hayden Phillips, on secondment from the Home Office.

By the time of the Autumn Statement of November 1988 I was sufficiently confident of the value of the reforms we were preparing to justify announcing an increase in Health Service spending for the year ahead of some 4½ per cent in real terms – the largest increase the Health Service had ever had. But the implementation of the reforms was inevitably a gradual process, and at the time of writing it is still too soon to pass a final verdict on their success. Teething troubles are inevitable, but the balance of judgement so far is that they have made a substantial improvement.

The old argument that nothing whatever needed to be done except inject more taxpayers' money is no longer heard, other than from the less enlightened sections of the Opposition benches of the House of Commons. The opposition from the BMA, once so strident and vituperative, is now little more than a whimper. Perhaps most striking has been the experience of the GP fundholders, who are convinced that they are performing a far better service for their patients than they ever could before. Despite the official opposition of the BMA to fundholding, large numbers of doctors voted Conservative at the 1992 election simply because they were terrified by Labour's pledge to reverse all the Health Service reforms we had introduced. I very much doubt if, at the next election, the Labour Party will again be foolish enough to pledge itself to undo all the Thatcher Government's health reforms. If I am right, that itself is success of a sort.

Taking on the Lawyers

There are few pressure groups as redoubtable as the BMA; but they were easy meat compared with the lawyers. The Government's proposals to increase competition in the provision of legal services emerged from a sub-committee of the Cabinet's economic committee known as E(CP), the 'CP' standing for competition policy, of which I was chairman. Although most of its work was concerned with restrictive practices in business and industry, its remit was in no way confined to that. I had always felt that restrictive practices in the legal profession were a particularly ripe subject for critical scrutiny, not least because no previous government had ever dared touch the subject. There was widespread public dissatisfaction over the high costs of legal services; while another contentious issue was the barristers' monopoly of the right of audience in the higher courts, which meant the exclusion of solicitors however eminent. There was also the question of conveyancing, which had been the subject of a long-running battle within the Government.

However, I saw little point in opening up the issue while Quintin Hailsham was Lord Chancellor. Not that there was any animus between us personally. Nor was he oblivious of the need for reform. Indeed, in many ways his ideas on the reform of legal practices were more radical than those of the eminent left-wing lawyers who graced the Upper House, whose radicalism extended to everything except their own profession, about which they were dyed-in-the-wool reactionaries. But as someone who had first become Lord Chancellor as far back as 1970, Quintin had clear ideas of which reforms he would support and which he would not; and he would certainly not take kindly to the matter being discussed in as lowly and lay a forum as E(CP). So it was not until he had been replaced by Michael Havers, after the 1987 election, that I formally put the matter on the E(CP) agenda and asked for a paper on the subject.

Michael duly submitted his paper, which read as if it had been written entirely by his officials. It was a thoroughly complacent document which concluded that there was no case for change of any kind. However, by the time it came before the committee for consideration Michael had been obliged to retire on health grounds – making him both the longest serving Attorney-General and the shortest serving Lord Chancellor.

Michael was succeeded as Lord Chancellor by James Mackay, the first Scottish lawyer ever to hold the post, who had been an outstanding Lord Advocate (the Scots equivalent of Lord Chancellor) during the first Thatcher administration, when I had got to know him well. He duly turned up at E(CP), flanked by the Attorney-General, Patrick Mayhew, to discuss the Havers paper. I instinctively felt that this was a mistake. Before he had a chance to speak, I used my chairman's prerogative to say that I felt it was quite unfair of the committee to expect him to give his considered views on this important matter so soon after his appointment, and to require him to speak to a paper he had not himself written. I said that the committee would be happy to defer the issue until its next meeting, which would enable him to withdraw the Havers paper and submit one of his own instead. My colleagues concurred, and James agreed to do just that.

As I had hoped, his paper, when it arrived, was totally different from its predecessor. He had clearly written it himself, after considerable thought. By conventional legal standards remarkably radical, it was nevertheless cautious and measured; and its original approach to the issue of solicitors' right of audience in the higher courts was remarkably ingenious. James was someone who, when faced with a major problem, did not start by considering the opposing views and choosing a position on the spectrum between them. He looked at the matter afresh, and thought through his position from first principles.

The Mackay paper, which covered pretty well all the outstanding issues, was discussed by E(CP) at a number of meetings, during the course of which James warned us that his proposals would be bitterly opposed by the judges. I duly submitted them, only minimally amended, to Margaret with E(CP)'s blessing, for presentation to Cabinet. The subsequent Cabinet discussion was prolonged but, with Margaret's unqualified support, the proposals emerged unscathed. The Cabinet also agreed James Mackay's desire to publish them in the form of a Green Paper. He had originally intended the next stage after the Green Paper to be legislation; but in the event he decided that it would be wiser to interpose the conventional White Paper stage.*

The Green Paper Proposals

In fact the proposals were split into three Green Papers, all of them published in January 1989: the main one on the structure of the legal profession, another on the totally separate but vexed question of conveyancing, and the third on contingency fees, where James was able to draw on his experience of the wholly different practices which applied under Scots law.

The Green Paper proposals were broadly supported by the Press and lay opinion generally, and received partial support from the Law Society (representing the solicitors); but were violently attacked by the rest of

---

*A White Paper sets out the Government's considered opinion on a subject, and the reasons for that opinion. It is invariably the prelude to legislative (or, as in the case, say, of the annual Defence White Paper, non-legislative) action along the lines indicated. A Green Paper by contrast is a discussion document, which normally sets out the Government's provisional conclusions on an issue, and which may or may not be a prelude to action. If legislation is intended, there will normally be a White Paper stage first, which might demonstrate that the Government's position has been modified in the light of the response to the Green Paper. However, progression from Green Paper to legislation, without the intervening White Paper stage, although rare, is perfectly possible – one example of this being my introduction of independent taxation for married women.

the legal profession in the shape of the Bar Council (representing the barristers) and particularly the judges, whose intemperate and injudicious assault did their cause no good at all – Lord Lane, the then Lord Chief Justice, going so far as to call the principal Green Paper 'one of the most sinister documents ever to emanate from government'. Unlike the doctors, the lawyers suffered from the political disadvantage of being deeply unpopular with the general public. On the other hand lawyers are highly articulate and – more to the point – well-represented in both Houses of Parliament. It was clear that we had a battle on our hands.

Conveyancing (the legal processes involved in the transfer of ownership of houses) had been largely deregulated already, under the Administration of Justice Act of 1985. Until then it had been the sole preserve of independent solicitors; but the Act had created the new profession of licensed conveyancer as an alternative. Since most licensed conveyancers were former solicitor's clerks, who had in practice done the work for which the solicitor submitted the bill, the net result had been to provide the public with precisely the same service at considerably lower cost. Quintin, however, had insisted, to the point of threatening resignation, that we draw the line at allowing qualified solicitors employed by building societies, banks and other institutions to enter this market, arguing that there would be intolerable conflicts of interest. James's Green Paper proposed removing the bar on employed solicitors, with safeguards to deal with the conflict of interest problem. The Law Society, which had been outraged by the original act of deregulation – conveyancing had been its members' most lucrative business – was predictably appalled.

But it was the main Green Paper, *The Work and Organisation of the Legal Profession*, which proved the most contentious. This proposed granting rights of audience in the higher courts to anyone with relevant professional qualifications and experience; the relaxation of the rules of admission to the Bar; the abolition of the requirement for barristers to be accompanied by solicitors; and freedom for barristers to enter partnerships or form companies, even with members of other disciplines. An Advisory Committee on Legal Education and Conduct was to be established in the Lord Chancellor's Department, to enable him to decide who was qualified to appear in court or to provide legal services.

The Bar Council and the judges bitterly opposed extending the right of audience, and portrayed the other proposals as an affront to the cherished principle of professional self-regulation. There were murmurings of an unconstitutional interference by the executive in the work of the judiciary. The Law Society gave a strangely muted welcome to the proposed extension of the right of audience.

The third Green Paper, on contingency fees, described both the American system, under which a lawyer takes a percentage of the damages awarded if he is successful in a case, and nothing if he is not; and the Scottish system, under which a lawyer is allowed to agree that he will be paid his so-called taxed costs if he is successful, but nothing if he is not. Both versions were rejected by all the interest groups during the consultations on the Green Paper as both improper, since they gave lawyers a financial interest in the outcome of a case, and potentially ruinous, since lawyers would have worked for nothing in the event of failure. While there were undoubtedly arguments against going the whole American ambulance-chasing hog, I found the opposition to the Scottish system quite extraordinary.

A Remarkable Lord Chancellor

James Mackay displayed admirable steadiness under fire, his roots in Scottish jurisprudence allowing him to view the fulminations of the English legal establishment with a certain detachment. But it was clear that the reforms would have to be modified if they were to reach the statute-book. This modification was apparent in the White Paper of July 1989 and in the subsequent legislation which became the Courts and Legal Services Act of 1990; but the main thrust of the reforms was preserved.

It will be possible only in the light of experience to judge just how successful the reforms, as modified, have been. On conveyancing, I have no great concern. The Act allowed employed solicitors to engage in conveyancing, but strengthened the safeguards against conflicts of interest. But the really important deregulation had in any case been done in the 1985 Act. Contingency fees, hitherto illegal, were permitted on the basis of a 'moderate percentage uplift' on the normal lawyer's bill in the event of success. It remains to be seen whether lawyers are prepared to accept clients on this basis; but judging from the success of the long-standing practice of lawyers taking on 'speculative cases', as they are known, in Scotland, they should be.

The big question is whether the right of audience has or has not been genuinely opened up. It is encouraging that by the summer of 1992 the Advisory Committee set up under the Act had already given a clear indication that rights of audience for qualified solicitors would not be long delayed. The compromise enshrined in the Act maintains the key Mackay principle of anyone qualified being able to appear; but the senior judges were effectively given the last word in determining who was adequately qualified. It is to be hoped that, whatever their prejudices, they will not, when it comes to it, feel able to act in an unreasonable manner – not least because it would be singularly embarrassing for them to be taken to court themselves for so doing.

REFORMING THE DOCTORS AND LAWYERS

One thing is clear. All credit for any liberalization that has been achieved belongs to James Mackay. But I was proud to be a member of the first government that had even been radical enough to wish to take on the legal establishment in the interest of the people, and brave enough to do so. And I was pleased to have been able to play a part in it.

CHAPTER 50

DEREGULATION AND THE CREDIT BOOM

The Effects of Deregulation · Building Societies Unleashed
The English Language Disease? · Banking Fever
Too Much Optimism · Not So Permanent Income
Lament for Loughborough
Appendix: The Building Societies Act, 1986

The Effects of Deregulation

IN THE TWO PREVIOUS chapters I gave an account of my involvement in measures to improve the supply side of the economy in areas such as health and education where there is inevitably a large role for Government. In the great bulk of the economy, however, the need was not to secure higher standards of performance and better value for money from activities largely carried out by the State, but to get the Government off people's backs.

When the Thatcher Government first took office in 1979 it inherited an economy beset by all manner of government controls and regulations. We judged these controls and regulations to be among the causes of Britain's economic weakness, and we wished to be rid of them. The same applied to monopolistic restrictions imposed by the private sector.

The programme of deregulation thus needed to be, and was, a comprehensive one, and one embarked on without delay. In the financial area the Bank of England was a strong supporter of deregulation on the practical grounds that the controls were ineffective, produced their own distortions, and diverted business from reputable financial institutions to fly-by-night operations.

Any radical reform, even if it achieves its objectives, as I believe deregulation did, was also likely to bring about unforeseen side-effects.

DEREGULATION AND THE CREDIT BOOM

This proved particularly true in the case of financial deregulation. Moreover, given that deregulation in general and financial deregulation in particular became part of a continuing worldwide trend, the subject is one of more than parochial relevance.

Although financial deregulation is a somewhat imprecise term, it is possible to identify at least ten specific events, of varying degrees of importance, that qualify as acts of financial deregulation, most of which occurred during the early part of the Government's term of office. In chronological order, these were:

1. The unannounced ending, virtually as soon as the new Government took office in May 1979, of the restrictive guidelines on building society lending.
2. The abolition of exchange controls in October 1979.
3. The abolition of the so-called 'corset', the Supplementary Special Deposits Scheme designed to curb bank lending, in June 1980.
4. The abolition of the Reserve Assets Ratio requirement, under which banks had to hold at least 12.5 per cent of their deposits in a specified range of liquid assets, in August 1981.
5. The abolition of hire-purchase restrictions in July 1982.
6. The collapse of the building societies' cartel in October 1983.
7. Some aspects of the Building Societies Act, 1986.
8. The ending of the restrictive practices of the stock exchange in the so-called 'Big Bang'of October 1986.
9. The withdrawal of mortgage lending 'guidance' in December 1986.
10. The effective abolition of the Control of Borrowing Order in March 1989.

Two of these events stand out as being of particular importance. The first, and most important of all, was the abolition of exchange controls. At the time a radical and highly controversial act, it became the norm throughout the major industrial nations of the world – partly because of a genuine belief in freedom and deregulation, partly because the information technology revolution made controls on capital movements increasingly difficult to police. As a result we were returning to a degree of economic freedom last seen in the early years of this century, before the First World War – but with international capital flows on a very much larger scale.

The consequences of this for the conduct of economic policy were considerable. In the first place, it transformed the foreign exchange markets. Whereas for well over half a century the movement of currency across the exchanges had been largely associated with trade flows, and the external value of currencies largely determined by the state of the balance of payments on current account, this ceased to be the case in the 1980s. But in the second place, and of greater relevance to the events considered in this chapter, the ending of exchange control rendered ineffective any form of direct national controls on credit. For in a world in which capital can flow freely across the exchanges, the effect of such controls would merely be to drive lending offshore.

Building Societies Unleashed

This bears directly on the second of the two main acts of financial deregulation in this country: the collapse of the building societies' cartel. Unlike exchange control abolition, this was not brought about by the Government – indeed, although I was philosophically in favour of it, I always feared the short-term consequences. That was why, as Financial Secretary, I resisted official advice to take Government action to break the cartel; believing also that in any event market pressures would sooner or later cause it to disintegrate. That was what duly occurred, shortly after I became Chancellor.

Until 1981 the building societies, and to a lesser extent the local authorities, had almost a monopoly over housing finance. Building societies took in funds on retail terms – that means they were easily withdrawable in small quantities – and lent them to home buyers at rates of interest fixed by the Building Societies Association. The cartel broke up as a result of a burgeoning of the competitive instinct among the bigger building societies themselves, followed by the massive invasion of the mortgage lending business by the banks, who were growing increasingly disenchanted with the joys of lending to Latin American and other governments overseas.

Competition for mortgage business was further increased in the second half of the 1980s by the entry of specialist mortgage lenders, many of them American, who raised finance in the wholesale capital markets – in other words, they borrowed large sums of money from the financial markets to lend in smaller packages to householders.

The collapse of the building societies' cartel, under which mortgage rates were kept well below market clearing rates, and advances were rationed by a queuing system, thus occurred in a new world in which direct credit controls were out of the question; and the only checks on excess were the price of credit, which the Government remained able to control, and prudence, which it could not. Moreover the previous existence of the cartel had created a pressure of pent-up mortgage demand of unknowable size until it unleashed itself following the cartel's collapse. But the adjustment from regulation to deregulation took some years fully to work through.

The consequent explosion of lending, and of spending financed by lending, for both consumption and investment, by both consumers and business, was thus on a wholly unprecedented and unforeseen scale – despite UK interest rates which both in nominal and real terms were consistently well above those of the other major economies. This is now a generally accepted explanation of the switchback course the UK economy followed in the late 1980s and early 1990s.

Compared with the two principal acts of financial deregulation just identified, the other eight had little real impact, since the restrictions they abolished were either ineffectual (particularly, in the case of the corset, following exchange rate control abolition), or purely technical, or (as in the case of Big Bang) not directly connected with bank and building society lending at all.

Arguably, the one exception to this is Big Bang, which had one important and unpredictable, or at least unpredicted, side-effect. Against the background of the huge worldwide rise in equity prices and turnover – until it came to an abrupt halt on Black Monday in October 1987 – Big Bang clearly contributed to the massive rise in investment spending by the financial services industry in the UK. This in turn was probably one of the major contributors to the unforeseen scale of the surge in domestic demand in the late 1980s.

The English Language Disease?

In looking at this period, it is important not to be too parochial. Of the seven major industrial nations that comprise the G7, three – the United Kingdom, the United States and Canada – underwent a recession at the beginning of the 1990s of a remarkably similar nature. It is hard to believe that the economic consequences of the English language provides the common thread. What seems a far more likely explanation is that these were the three economies that travelled furthest along the road to financial deregulation. A similar phenomenon occurred in Japan.

There always has been, and always will be, an economic cycle. But with credit in all its forms facilitated by financial deregulation, these three economies experienced a particularly virulent form of credit cycle. In other words, individuals and companies alike came to borrow excessively. And while this was bound to be a self-correcting process – which the authorities could by their monetary policy to some extent expedite – it was not surprising that the correction involved a period of recession as individuals and companies alike reined back their spending in order to correct their over-extended balance sheets.

Clearly, with hindsight, I greatly underestimated the demand effect that financial deregulation, a supply-side reform, was to have. But borrowers and lenders alike also made their mistakes. Hence the hardships of many of the former and the unprecedented bad debts reported by the latter.

If the switchback was somewhat sharper in Britain than across the Atlantic, that is perhaps not too surprising, since the extent of deregulation was significantly greater here – chiefly because we started from a greater degree of regulation in the first place. There was subsequently an interesting parallel, among a number of the smaller economies in Scandinavia. In the words of a 1991 *Financial Times* article on the region:

> The banking crisis has its origins in the financial deregulation that swept the region in the 1980s . . . The banks, breathing the heady air of liberation, vastly expanded their lending – and their risks. But risks appeared minimal during the 1980s . . . as property prices rose sharply. Since then, however, the recession that began in Norway and has spread to Finland and Sweden has exposed the weaknesses of the banking system.

Happily, the UK banking system, although battered, was incomparably stronger than its Scandinavian counterpart. But the echoes were striking.

Banking Fever

What were the respective responsibilities of the building societies and banks for the 1986–8 credit boom? Building societies remained the largest source of mortgage finance for housing. A substantial proportion of that finance leaked into consumer spending – a process known as 'equity withdrawal'. The societies still accounted for nearly a third of all lending by the banks and building societies to the private sector in the peak year of 1988; and they certainly went beyond the bounds of prudence in their lending policies in the second half of the 1980s.

They lent an ever higher proportion of house valuations – in some cases over 100 per cent. They also lent an unusually large multiple of people's earnings. Instead of the traditional maximum loan of two and a half times earnings, they went up to three and a half and even four times earnings. Moreover the loan was usually based on the applicant's own estimate of his or her income. This was often exaggerated and seldom checked – quite apart from the numerous cases of straightforward mortgage fraud by deliberate lying.

Even so, the building societies were not as imprudent as the banks. Most of the societies insured against default – which is why the insurance companies subsequently found themselves in such trouble. Nor were the building societies able, under the Building Societies Act, to follow the banks into Maxwell-type lending. Mortgage lending is, other things being equal, the least risky form of lending – which is why the Bank of England refused my request to it to intervene on prudential grounds.

DEREGULATION AND THE CREDIT BOOM

The combination of artificially stimulated demand for housing and some of the tightest planning controls on land use in Europe puts a long-run upward pressure on house prices. But the upsurge is unsteady and characteristically takes the form of a series of heady booms punctuated by downturns when people have difficulty in selling their homes at all. Between the start of the housing boom in 1985 and its peak in 1989, average house prices in the UK more than doubled: in real terms they rose by 70 per cent. Moreover, with the increase in home ownership, this had an even greater effect on the economy than previous housing booms.

The banks, for their part, only dimly recognized the extent of their vulnerability to the credit cycle, and in particular to the fact that, as interest rates rose, home-buyers would inevitably cut back on their purchases in the high street in order to keep up with their mortgage payments. Thus by fuelling the housing boom with easy lending against the apparently reassuring security of bricks and mortar (which they continued to do even after interest rates had begun to rise sharply in response to emerging inflation), they were not only taking bigger risks than they imagined on their housing business. Far more seriously, they were inadvertently undermining the quality of their lending to the smaller and more vulnerable end of the corporate sector.

We are left with some key questions: was the Government responsible for the banks taking leave of their senses? Were the banks, by contrast, largely responsible for the excesses of the credit binge? The point here is not that the banks should put the public interest above profit. The point is that by acting in the imprudent way they did, they inflicted terrible damage on their own profit-and-loss accounts and balance sheets. The 'authorities' cannot fine-tune bank lending. That is one of the reasons why the economic cycle cannot be avoided. Had I been able to foresee how excessive the lending would become, my only useful weapon, whether some call it 'one-club golfing' or not, would have been to have raised interest rates sooner and even more sharply than I did.

There are at least three conclusions to be drawn from our first experience of a world in which freedom of capital movements and an uncartelized lending industry are facts of life. The first is that a financially deregulated economy, while more efficient and dynamic, is also probably less stable, by virtue of an amplified credit cycle. The second is that, recognizing this, borrowers need to exercise prudent self-discipline and lenders to develop a far more sophisticated risk analysis than they have hitherto found necessary. It is clearly not good enough for a bank to look at a potential corporate borrower – his accounts, his track record, his business plan, his management and so on – in isolation. The industry risk also needs to be assessed, including its links with other industries and *their* risks. Above all, its vulnerability to changes in economic conditions has to be fully taken into account.

The third conclusion, and the most reassuring, is that what Britain went through in the later 1980s was to a considerable extent a once-for-all occurrence: the change from a financially regulated to a financially deregulated economy. Others may still have this pleasure in store.

Too Much Optimism

The most important acts of deregulation and increased financial market competition – the ending of exchange control and the building societies' cartel – took place respectively in 1979, when I was Financial Secretary (although heavily involved: see Chapter 4), and in 1983, not long after I arrived at Number 11. Yet inflation did not start to take off until the second half of 1988, after I had been Chancellor for five years, and did not reach its peak until the autumn of 1990, a year after I had departed. This is an example of 'long and variable lags' in the financial system, extending far beyond anything Milton Friedman had in mind when he promulgated the phrase.

An increase in the ratio of debt to income was only to be expected as householders and businesses adjusted to the end of credit rationing; and the timing of both the adjustment and its effects were inherently unpredictable. Borrowing as a proportion of disposable income rose to new peaks in 1986 for the corporate sector and in 1987 for the personal sector. Companies borrowed on a larger scale to finance takeovers and overseas investment; but also to purchase capital equipment made in the UK, which while itself desirable, added to the pressures on productive capacity. In the personal sector, much of the increased investment was in land and housing already in existence, pushing up the price of land and housing, which made households feel wealthier and thus able to borrow more. This played a large part in the fall in the personal savings ratio (saving, less borrowing, as a proportion of income) from an average of 11½ per cent between 1979 and 1984 to 8 per cent in 1986 and a low of 5 per cent in 1988.

But was there not something more? One of the most balanced and comprehensive treatments of the forces behind the credit boom which I have so far seen is by Dick Sargent (a former economic adviser to the Midland Bank and an academic economist in his own right). His main stricture on my policies and statements is that I encouraged excessive optimism – a point to which I return when I discuss the 1988 Budget. As Sargent writes:

> The scale of the credit increase is larger than seems plausible to attribute to credit liberalization alone. There was also an increase in the extent to which the private sector was willing to incur debt at given levels of income and interest rates. This increase was a direct

result of a climate of over-optimistic expectations which developed in the 1980s about the economy's performance. This hypothesis is consistent with the fact that the boom in the second half of the 1980s was characterized, to a much greater extent than most previous booms, by inflation of asset prices as distinct from producer prices, wages or retail prices.

Not So Permanent Income

One of Friedman's early pioneering works was his *Theory of the Consumption Function* in which he related consumer spending to two variables: a person's 'transient' income in a particular period and the 'permanent' income he thought he was likely to obtain in a normal year of his or her working life. In the mid to late 1980s, there was a substantial upward revision of this permanent element, particularly if we include capital gains, notably from home ownership. In part this was wholly justified, given the undoubted supply-side improvements that had occurred. But it clearly went too far.

In the six years from 1982 to 1988, the only one in which output growth fell below 3½ per cent was 1984, when it was artificially depressed by the miners' strike. This was a considerably stronger performance than either I had expected or the Treasury had forecast at the time. The Central Statistical Office commented in a 1991 post-mortem in *Economic Trends* that growth was exceptionally steady for many years in the mid-80s, with much smaller cyclical variation than in the past. This phenomenon, coupled with the exceptional duration of the upswing, led too many borrowers and lenders to believe that it would go on for ever, and that the economic cycle, with its alternation of upswing and downswing, was a thing of the past. This was the fatal error.

With hindsight, however, I must accept my share of responsibility for the excessive optimism that characterized the climate of the time. Given the all-pervasive defeatism that was the grimmest aspect of our 1979 inheritance (see Chapter 3), I regarded the creation of a climate of confidence as a major objective of policy, and the tone of my speeches tended to reflect this. And of course my speeches on the economy set the tone for those of my colleagues, from Margaret downwards. But, while these things are difficult to calibrate, I probably overdid it. There is a link here, too, with my tax-cutting Budgets. Those who, in retrospect, argue that those Budgets (notably the 1988 Budget) caused the overheating, are on any quantitative analysis clearly wrong, as Chapter 65 demonstrates. But in psychological terms they did contribute to the climate of optimism – which does not invalidate the Budgets, but reinforces the case for more measured speech-making.

A similar but more abstract analysis has been provided by Mervyn King, an economist who is more sympathetic to the supply-side revolution. He demonstrates, with a command of algebra which makes me nostalgic for my former self, that even a moderate change in underlying growth, if it is suddenly perceived, can lead to a very sharp temporary rise in both investment and consumption, which would subside after a short period once the adjustment had been made. As he writes:

> Any successful attempt to raise the rate of growth of a small open economy will, in a world of integrated liberal financial markets, lead to a rise in investment, and a step-jump in consumption which will have all the appearance of an unsustainable Government demand stimulus, including a swing into deficit in the balance of payments.

A question worth considering is whether we could have ridden out a temporary rise in investment, consumption and imports, which was the once-for-all effect of a shift to a higher growth path, without applying the monetary brakes in the way that I did. Theoretically, we might have been able to do so if, *per impossibile*, the economy had been 100 per cent open to international trade instead of 50 or 60 per cent open. In that case a temporary increase in consumption and investment could readily have been supplied from abroad, without any rise in prices at home. But since some goods and services, such as new construction, can come only from home suppliers, overheating inevitably appeared.

Nevertheless, analysis underlines the usefulness of a current account deficit as a safety-valve.

Lament for Loughborough

There are three further questions about the credit boom. When exactly did it begin? Why were its effects not diagnosed earlier? And what was – or could have been – done about it?

The table overleaf shows that from 1979–80 to 1987–88 bank and building society lending consistently rose rapidly, at rates fluctuating between 17 and 21 per cent a year. There was then a surge to over 24 per cent in 1988–9 and a sharp plunge in 1990–1. This makes it very difficult to give a date to the boom. The actual numbers were however moving more quickly than these percentages would suggest. A 20 per cent growth of bank and building society lending in 1979 represented around £14 billion, equivalent to 7 per cent of total national income. By 1988–9, the 24 per cent growth of credit represented no less than £82 billion, equivalent to 18 per cent of GDP.

The growth of bank and building society lending is approximately equivalent to the growth of broad money, best measured by M4. This

DEREGULATION AND THE CREDIT BOOM

follows from the balance-sheet identity for the banking system, linking
the increase in bank assets to the increase in bank liabilities. The numbers
are different because the banks also have non-deposit liabilities (mainly
their capital) and because building societies also borrow overseas to some
extent.

CREDIT AND BROAD MONEY
annual % growth

	Bank and Building Society lending	M4
1979–80	20.3	14.0
1980–81	17.7	17.5
1981–82	20.3	13.9
1982–83	18.9	14.3
1983–84	17.1	11.5
1984–85	18.3	13.8
1985–86	16.6	14.5
1986–87	19.2	13.9
1987–88	21.0	16.8
1988–89	24.3	17.6
1989–90	20.5	17.9
1990–91	11.1	10.0

Note: The figures refer to growth over the twelve months
of each financial year. Source: HM Treasury

There was no lack of rationalizations designed to explain why the
growth of credit was harmless, both in itself and in the effect it had
on broad money. The most high level and detailed of these was incorporated in the lecture delivered by the Governor of the Bank of England,
Robin Leigh-Pemberton, at Loughborough on 22 October 1986, and
given star billing in the following issue of the *Bank of England Quarterly
Bulletin*, accompanied by no less than twelve explanatory charts. The
Governor's assessment was that:

> A good part of the increase in personal sector liquidity since 1980,
> which is held with building societies rather than banks, can be at-
> tributed to a redistribution of personal sector assets as a response to
> changes in the behaviour of financial intermediaries. To this extent
> it does not carry the same threatening message about future infla-
> tion as the same increase in liquidity would in the absence of the
> changes in financial behaviour.

He concluded by questioning whether, in view of the changes in the
financial system, 'it might not be better to dispense with a target for

broad money'. I duly did so in the 1987 MTFS: my own thinking had, albeit by a slightly different route, reached a similar conclusion.

The Loughborough lecture, whose principal author was Eddie George, was an intelligent analysis of the consequences of financial change, which can still be read with profit. The 'velocity of circulation' of M4 had indeed embarked on a falling trend since the early 1980s (see chart *Velocity of Circulation* in the Annexe 7). But in the event the fall turned out to be neither steep enough nor steady enough to prevent the dangerous blip in inflation at the end of the decade, which was so painful to reverse.

APPENDIX:
THE BUILDING SOCIETIES ACT, 1986

THE BUILDING SOCIETIES, WHICH had lost a substantial slice of their core business to the banks in the early 1980s, complained that the were unable to counter-attack effectively while they were barred from raising money on the capital markets or from offering services such as cheque books. They successfully lobbied the Treasury to liberalize the regulatory regime. They had a legitimate desire for a level playing field with the banks, at least where their business overlapped.

The building societies had been pressing for fresh legislation for considerable time. They pointed out that the statute under which the operated dated back to the nineteenth century and was wholly out of date. It also happened to be at odds with European Community legislation in this field, something which sooner or later would have to be rectified. Indeed, Treasury officials urged me to persuade Geoffrey to legislate on all this when I was Financial Secretary, with delegated responsibility for the building societies, but I declined to do so, telling them that it would have to wait.

When I returned to the Treasury as Chancellor in 1983, it was clear to me that it would be wrong to procrastinate any longer. But I had to wait until the 1985–6 session before I could persuade my Cabinet colleagues to give me a slot for it in the busy legislative timetable. had entrusted responsibility for the Bill to Ian Stewart, the Economic Secretary, who had issued a Green Paper in July 1984, which eventually became the immensely complex Building Societies Act of 1986. This enabled societies to issue cheque books and cheque guarantee cards make personal loans and carry on a number of other quasi-banking activities.

The societies had sought even greater powers to compete with the banks, but I was unwilling to go the whole hog. Under the new Act they still had to raise the bulk of their funds from retail deposits, and put most of their assets into straightforward home mortgages. A new supervisory authority, the Building Societies Commission, replaced the Registrar of Friendly Societies.

There was some criticism that the Government was being unreasonably restrictive; but those societies which found the restriction unduly irksome were given the option of converting themselves into joint stock banks, provided that borrowers and investors approved by a large and complex majority. As banks, of course, they would come under the supervisory authority of the Bank of England and, more important, be subject to the capital adequacy requirements applicable to banks. Up to the time of writing, only the Abbey National has chosen to exercise this option and convert itself into a bank. It is proving an effective and low-cost competitor in the field of retail banking.

CHAPTER 51

FROM GROWTH PAUSE
TO OVERHEATING

Rewriting History · A False Dusk
Fallible Forecasts

Rewriting History

THE BANK OF ENGLAND'S regular commentary on the contemporary scene was in similar terms to those of the Loughborough lecture. Its June 1986 *Bulletin* stated that 'there is little indication that liquidity is unwillingly held at current real interest rates or that monetary conditions are loose'. By December it had moved no further than the neutral 'Monetary conditions continue to be difficult to assess . . . on account of far-reaching structural changes in the financial system'. A closer analysis of the housing component of bank and building society lending might have given a clue that something was afoot. Net advances for house purchase rose from £19 billion in 1985–86 to £27 billion in 1986–87, a jump of almost 50 per cent. Too many economists, including most of my 'Gooies', were satisfied that house prices were essentially relative prices and not a symptom of general inflation.

This was unfortunate, since it turned out that, during this period, rising house prices were an important part of the transmission mechanism from credit creation to inflation – namely the effect of a sharp rise in house prices in increasing perceived personal wealth, and the increase in personal wealth in leading to an upsurge in consumer spending. I myself, however, was reassured at the time not merely by the arguments of my advisors both at the Treasury and the Bank, but also by the observation that a similarly sharp rise in domestic property prices was occurring in Japan, and there was no sign there of it spilling over into general inflation. It was not until the summer of 1987 that the Bank began to worry that monetary conditions may not be tight enough; a concern that I then shared and met by raising interest rates by one percentage point on 7 August, which at the time was regarded as a bizarre move by most monetarists and the financial Press.

The Bank's concern started to re-emerge in the autumn, but it was once again met, this time by the Wall Street crash of 19 October 1987, which the Bank believed, like almost all other commentators at the time, implied 'a tightening of monetary conditions', to quote its own *Bulletin*. The only occasion in all my years as Chancellor when the Bank can be interpreted as having wanted a tighter policy than I was pursuing, was in the difficult period subsequent to that event when Eddie George argued that sterling should be allowed to rise in the autumn of 1987. Everything else that has emerged from some Bank quarters since my resignation amounts to an attempt to rewrite history with the benefit of hindsight; an understandable activity, but scarcely a commendable one. It is, I suppose, theoretically possible that the Bank from time to time believed that monetary policy should be tighter, but refrained from telling me – even at the markets meetings I regularly held with the Governor and his senior officials. But this would have amounted to a dereliction of duty so grave as to be unthinkable.

A False Dusk

A failure to foresee the consequences of financial deregulation in a climate of unusual optimism, the consequences which were greatly exacerbated by the follies of the lending institutions and in particular the banks, was not the only reason for my slowness and that of my advisers to recognize the full significance of the credit boom. There was also an apparent marked slowdown in the growth of the real economy at a crucial period in the first half of 1986. Indeed, when the official statistics were first published the public perception was that the upswing that had begun in 1981 was drawing to a close – it had already lasted if anything longer than the average of previous upswings – and that a period of recession lay ahead.

I have already mentioned in an earlier chapter how the oil price collapse of early 1986, so far from providing the expected stimulus to the industrial countries, seemed initially to be accompanied by a setback to output. This was especially the case in Britain. The false dusk emerged with the publication in the third week of May, 1986, of the GDP figure for the first quarter, as measured on an output basis. This is the first measure of GDP to be calculated: it is subsequently also calculated on two other bases, income and expenditure; and the three calculations should produce the same result, but never do. However, the Central Statistical Office always maintains that it is the output measurement that provides the best guide to the short-term trend.

The GDP figure for the first quarter of 1986, on this basis, suggested that the annual growth rate was ¾ per cent down on a year ago. Indeed, when the figures were adjusted for the fact that output in the first quarter of 1985 had been artificially depressed by the coal strike, the slowdown was much steeper: from 3½ per cent in the first quarter of 1985 to a mere ¾ per cent in the first quarter of 1986. It was this that set the alarm bells ringing. It was only some years later, when the figures had been revised several times, that it emerged that the bulk of the reported decline in the rate of growth was simply a statistical error. According to the latest estimates for the period, the drop, adjusted for the distorting effect of the miners' strike, was only from an annual rate of growth of some 3 per cent in the first quarter of 1985 to a little over 2 per cent in the first quarter of 1986.

Shortly after the original figures for the first quarter of 1986 were published, purporting to show that, after adjusting for the coal strike, growth had virtually come to a standstill, I felt it necessary to use the occasion of a lunchtime meeting of the Association of Economic Representatives in London on 28 May to give a robust, confidence-boosting speech. The mood of the time, which is seldom remembered today, can be gauged from the following extract:

> Some are even asking whether the British economic recovery – whose end has been regularly predicted every year since the recovery began in 1981 – may at long last really be petering out. I am confident that it is not. Some pause in growth was to be expected, if only because fluctuations are a fact of life. But I see no reason to change the analysis of the effect of lower oil prices I set out in my Budget Speech. What *is* happening – here as elsewhere – is that we are getting the inflation benefits of the oil price fall before the output benefits . . .
>
> I can see a number of forces which, before many months have passed, will sustain a vigorous resumption of growth in this country as well as in the major oil consuming nations – growth in the private sector, not an artificial and short-lived stimulus provided by the public sector. Critics have been caught out in the recent past by underestimating the current strength of the British economy, and they look like being caught out again.

The speech was received by industry and the Press with ill-concealed scepticism. No doubt the fact that I was suffering at the time from one of my infrequent bouts of laryngitis, and could summon up only an apology of a voice, did not assist me to carry conviction. But even those who were not aware of this, and only read the speech – which I had distributed as a handout in its entirety – felt that it was one of the most contentious I had made.

Given the figures as they appeared in 1986, there was particular alarm that the upturn seemed to be coming to an end before unemployment had even stopped rising. At the time I made my speech to the Economic Representatives, unemployment had been increasing for seven years without a break; and although the rate of increase had previously been slowing down, in the spring of 1986 it started to accelerate again. On 8 May the Government had lost the ultra-safe Yorkshire seat of Ryedale in a by-election caused by the death of the sitting Member. Even committed supporters of the Government's economic strategy were insisting that reducing unemployment should now have priority.

I developed two arguments to deal with the political difficulties these events were causing. First, I insisted that what we were experiencing was merely a pause and not a recession. I told the House of Commons on 3 June, in reply to an uncharacteristic brief Opposition motion condemning 'this Government's economic policies which have led to the highest ever level of unemployment', that what was happening was a mirror image of the two great oil price shocks of 1973 and 1979. There was then a delay of several months before output was hit decisively. This time there was a delay before output rose, as 'oil producers tend perforce to be prompter in cutting back their spending than oil consumers are in increasing theirs'. I was drawing here on Treasury economic analysis which, if correct, would have been more useful if it had been available before the event, or even before the event was nearly over.* Second, and more effective in speechmaking terms, I developed a 'weathering the storm' theme. A typical example was my speech to the Party the Party's Wales Area Conference on 20 June:

> There could be no greater testimony to the success of our policies than the strength the British economy has shown over the past couple of years. Who would have imagined that we could have survived – and survived successfully – a twelve-month-long coal strike with so little damage to our country's economy? And who would have imagined that we could then brush aside, as we have done, a complete collapse in the price of oil, on which, it was alleged, our economy depended?

I was similarly upbeat in my July 1986 'end-of-term' letter to all Conservative MPs, a practice which I had initiated the previous July

*There was no kind of pause or slowdown predicted in the Red Book forecasts, either in the text or the table.

and which I maintained throughout the rest of my time as Chancellor. The passage survived in almost identical form in my Party Conference speech that October. This turned out to be a particularly successful speech in a particularly successful Conference, which proved to be a turning point in the Government's fortunes, as a subsequent chapter records. Meanwhile, my end-of-term letter was well received.

It was in July, too, that unemployment at long last peaked, at well over three million (11.2 per cent), although this was not yet apparent in early September, when I made one of my visits to Scotland to test the temperature there. It was a perfect late summer's day, and the Highlands had never looked lovelier. But as I flew to Inverness the rows of mothballed oil rigs clearly visible in the Moray Firth seemed to give the pause a palpable form.

It was on this trip, incidentally, that, thanks to an administrative blunder, I only narrowly avoided bumping into Margaret in the small Highland town of Forres, where I was due to attend a teatime meeting in the house of one of the local Party worthies and she was scheduled to hand over the keys to the purchasers of the one thousandth council house sold in Scotland. Such was the obsession with security in general and Prime Ministerial security in particular that neither of us had been told in advance that the other was to be there. The good people of Forres, accustomed to reading in the Scottish Press of the London Government's shameful neglect of Scotland, must have wondered what they had done to warrant visits from both the Prime Minister and the Chancellor of the Exchequer on the same day.

The first clear-cut evidence that the pause was over did not emerge until the GDP figure for the third quarter of 1986 was published on 19 November. At the same time it was now clear that unemployment had started to turn down after its July peak, and it was to fall without interruption for the next three and a half years. There was much debate in the early stages about how far the fall was a reflection of economic growth and how far it was due to the Government's labour market measures, such as David Young's 'Restart' programme. As Chancellor, so far from having an interest in massaging the figures, I needed to know the underlying trend as accurately as possible. I launched a Treasury inquiry which concluded that the greater part of the fall had nothing to do with the Government's mixed bag of special employment measures, some of which performed an invaluable task in improving the working of Britain's arthritic labour market, but others of which did little more than remove people from the unemployment register.

In fact, while commentators were still arguing about whether we faced recession, slowdown or merely pause, the upturn was if anything becoming uncomfortably vigorous. But I had not waited for the November GDP figure to act against the danger of inflationary excess. Certainly, inflation was gratifyingly low in 1986; but I was aware that the figures were flattered by the oil price collapse, as I made clear in speeches at the time. I had already been alerted to the risks by the renewed weakness of sterling, which was in part a symptom and in part a cause of growing inflationary pressures. Indeed, I would have done more had I been allowed to do so, as the next chapter explains.

My conviction, even when the misleading first quarter GDP figures were published in May, that the recovery would resume of its own accord, was indeed largely based on the low inflation we were enjoying in 1986. This worked through two different channels. First, other things being equal, low inflation makes people confident enough to save less and spend more. Second, with the rate of growth of earnings still stubbornly stuck at the 7½ per cent to which it had fallen in 1984, real incomes were growing unusually fast. This last phenomenon was not, of course, something I welcomed. It would clearly have been better if pay per head had risen less, in which case the same increase in overall national earnings could have been spread among more people, bringing forward the fall in unemployment and reducing the inflationary pressure at any given level of unemployment.

Fallible Forecasts

I cannot, however, claim to have foreseen the full extent of the boom that began to develop. Moreover, I was not helped by the Treasury's economic forecasts, which despite being regularly castigated by Labour as ludicrously optimistic, in fact seriously and consistently underestimated the strength of the upturn. In each of the three years 1986, 1987 and 1988, growth was forecast at 3 per cent – only some half a percentage point at most above the best guess of the underlying growth of productive capacity. In the event, growth in those three years averaged over 4 per cent a year; which was too much to be borne without inflationary consequences. As I showed in the last chapter, the outside forecasts underpredicted the boom by an even greater margin than the Treasury did.

Still greater errors were made in forecasting the strength of domestic demand. This inevitably led both to a strong growth in imports and the diversion of exportable goods to the home market. Hence the extreme inaccuracy of the current account balance of payments forecasts in each of the three years, which transformed what I called 'a readily financeable current account deficit' into the £15 billion and £19 billion current account deficits we experienced in 1988 and 1989. I was right in one respect, however: even these unexpectedly high deficits proved, in the new world in which we now lived, to be 'readily financeable'.

FROM GROWTH PAUSE TO OVERHEATING

It was in 1986 that the forecasters, both within and outside the Treasury, started to get domestic demand seriously wrong. With hindsight, however, it is clear that there were two important clues that something was amiss. The first was the weakness of sterling, which at the time was seen by the Treasury as for the most part an inevitable and acceptable consequence of the oil price collapse. The second was the behaviour of house prices. These began their stratospheric climb in 1986, when they rose by over ten percentage points more than inflation. Yet few foresaw in 1986 that this was but the prelude to a rise of 12 per cent more than inflation in 1987 and no less than 22 per cent more than inflation in 1988. Certainly, neither I nor my advisers, either at the Treasury or at the Bank, did.

Contrary to much that has been written since, the rapid increase in domestic demand in the second half of the 1980s was not just a consumer boom. Indeed, whereas the average annual increase in consumption in the three years 1986, 1987 and 1988 is now reckoned to have been around 5 per cent a year, investment rose by more than 8 per cent a year.

Exports of goods continued to grow strongly in 1986 and 1987, at over 5 per cent a year. But by 1988 the pull of the home market had become so great that exports did not grow at all. Import growth, on the other hand, shot up from 7 per cent in 1986 and 8 per cent in 1987 to almost 13 per cent in 1988. The strain of excess demand at home was taken mainly on the balance of payments in the boom years themselves, and relatively little was reflected in higher prices. The underlying rate of inflation averaged only 4½ per cent in 1988: the inflationary peak came in 1990, after the boom in spending had at last come to an end and had given way to recession.

FORECAST AND OUTCOME
percentage increase on previous year

	Real GDP (at factor cost)		Domestic Demand (at market prices)	
	Budget Forecast	Outcome	Budget Forecast	Outcome
1983–85*	2.5	3.2	n.a.	3.6
1986	3.0	3.6	3.5	4.6
1987	3.0	4.6	3.5	5.3
1988	3.0	4.2	4.0	7.8

*Three-year average, to eliminate coal strike effect.   Source: *Treasury Review* 1990

On the basis of the information that was available to me at the time, it would have been thought highly eccentric to have pursued a tighter policy than I did. Inflation, however measured, was down to 3½ per cent in 1986 – reflecting of course the impact of lower oil prices. (Indeed, the headline rate went below 2½ per cent in July 1986.) Producer price inflation was also at the lowest level for decades. House prices did, as I have already remarked, start to take off; but this followed several years in which there had been virtually no increase in real terms at all. Moreover, at this stage the housing boom seemed confined to central London, and around the turn of 1986–87 the Bank advised me that it was probably petering out.

The domestic monetary indicators also showed a high degree of tightness. Real interest rates were around 7 per cent in 1985 and 1986 – probably the highest level experienced since the 1920s and some 2½ percentage points higher than the G7 average. The growth of M0, at 4.2 per cent (year on year), was well within its target range. Even the growth of the broader aggregate, M4, dipped slightly compared to the previous year.

Interestingly enough, the Treasury's inflation forecasts were almost spot on, predicting a rise in the headline RPI in 1986 and 1987 very near the actual outcome of 3.4 per cent and 4.1 per cent respectively. The serious deterioration in the Treasury's inflation forecasts did not take place until 1988 and 1989, showing the importance of time-lags. It also shows the value of the current account balance of payments deficit as a safety valve, so long as underlying policies are sound and errors unhesitatingly corrected. A failure to grasp the long time-lags between excessive demand growth and its inflationary consequences is one reason why most of my critics have focused on minor errors in the winter of 1987–88 rather than the more serious errors of 1986. Another reason why critics play down the errors of 1986 is their ideological reluctance to recognize the value of the exchange rate as a warning signal.

At the time, the relationship of any measure of the growth of money to either the national income or to the price level seemed highly unreliable. M4 rose by a cumulative total of 50 per cent in both the first and second halves of the decade 1975–85. In the first half it was accompanied by a rise in nominal GDP twice as great as this, whereas in the second half it was accompanied by a rise in nominal GDP only half as great. So whatever people may say today, and whatever technical adjustments are made to the series, it did not appear to be a reliable indicator. Indeed, for the first half of the 1980s, the Bank of England's 'Loughborough' analysis seemed to fit the facts perfectly. Extra money balances were willingly held, and the increased bank credit did not stimulate excess spending on goods and services.

The fact is that throughout our period in office we suffered from the operation of Goodhart's law,* the financial equivalent of the better-known Murphy's law, which states that any monetary aggregate ceases to be reliable the moment it becomes a target for policy purposes.

There were some other warning signals, of varying significance. It was worrying that pay increases got stuck at 7½ per cent a year, despite falling inflation and seven years of steadily rising unemployment, right up to the summer of 1986. And I have already referred to the evidence of house prices, for what that was worth in 1986. But the warning signal which influenced me most was the fall in sterling, which I instinctively did not like and which I tried to halt at various times in 1986, with little support from most of those who subsequently blamed me for the upsurge in inflation. That is a story for the next chapter.

*So called because it was first enunciated by Professor Charles Goodhart of the London School of Economics when he was adviser on monetary policy to the Bank of England from 1969 to 1985.

CHAPTER 52

AN UNWANTED DEVALUATION

The Hidden Sterling Crisis of 1986 · Base Rate Cuts, Spring 1986
The ERM Again · The Sterling Crisis Surfaces

The Hidden Sterling Crisis of 1986

THE EARLIEST AND CLEAREST warning that policy might be too lax came from the behaviour of sterling, which during the course of 1986 – that is, from December 1985 to December 1986 – plunged by some 12½ per cent as measured by the official exchange rate index. This was the largest fall of any year during the lifetime of the Conservative Government, and towards the end of it, in November, the pound reached what at the time of writing remains its lowest level ever recorded on this basis. Yet curiously it gave rise to little of the hysteria that had accompanied previous sterling crises, and featured scarcely at all in the political debate at the time.

There were two main reasons for this: oil and the dollar. It had been the dramatic collapse in the oil price in the first half of 1986 that had triggered the sterling plunge in the first place. Between December 1985 and June 1986, the oil price dropped like a stone from about $28 a barrel to only $10 a barrel. During the second half of the year it then staged something of a recovery, reaching over $14 a barrel in December 1986. But what should have set the alarm bells ringing was that, of the overall fall of 12½ per cent in the sterling index during the year, less than half occurred in the first half of 1986 when the oil price was plummeting. The greater part occurred in the second half of 1986 when the oil price was recovering.

The fact that, by and large, it did not, can be explained partly by the belief, then widely held, that the fall in the second half was essentially a delayed reaction to the oil price collapse. But it also owed much to the false comfort derived from the behaviour of the dollar. Since the Plaza meeting of September 1985, the dollar had been declining sharply from the stratospheric heights it had earlier reached, as indeed the G5 participants had hoped and intended; and this continued throughout 1986. As a result, the 12½ per cent fall in the sterling index over the year was composed, *inter alia*, of a small *rise* (of some 2½ per cent) in sterling against the dollar, and a fall of almost 20 per cent against the Deutschmark. In those days the focus of attention still tended anachronistically to be the sterling/dollar rate, which had caused Margaret such panic when it looked as if the pound might actually fall to below parity against the then mighty dollar in the wake of the Ingham crisis of January 1985.

Even so, it was disturbing that, once again dividing the year into its two halves, sterling's rise against the dollar was entirely confined to the first six months: in the second half of the year it even fell slightly against the dollar, too.

When the sterling plunge began, the political and public debate, in so far as it was not distracted by the Westland affair (see Chapter 54), focused not on the pound at all but on the damage that the collapse of the oil price would do to the UK economy as a whole. The Labour Party had convinced itself that anything good that had happened to the economy, notably the recovery from the recession, which the Opposition had gradually and grudgingly admitted had to some extent occurred, had happened solely as a result of the windfall of North Sea oil. The media, too, were convinced that the prospect for tax cuts depended entirely on the tax revenues from North Sea oil, which had now gone down the drain. In general, it is difficult today to recall how widespread was the absurd view that the British economy depended entirely on oil, as if we were some Gulf state, and that with the collapse in the value of our North Sea oil the UK ship – as a *Daily Telegraph* cartoon of the time graphically portrayed it – was heading straight for the rocks.

While I was aware, of course, that all this was nonsense, that did not help with the problem of perceptions – particularly the perception of overseas holders of sterling, who even more than domestic holders tended to believe it. I was deeply worried that, as a result, the slide in sterling would turn into a rout. Nor was confidence assisted by the Government's evident disarray over the Westland affair. On the morning of Wednesday, 8 January, I asked Robin Leigh-Pemberton to come over to the Treasury, with his key officials, to discuss the situation at one of the frequent markets meetings I used to hold. We rapidly reached the conclusion that interest rates should be raised by a full percentage point, from 11½ per cent to 12½ per cent, forthwith.

I was under no illusion about Margaret's likely reaction. It would be the first rise in interest rates for almost a year, the first since I had hoisted them to 14 per cent in the aftermath of the crisis of January 1985. Given the certain prospect of a sticky meeting, I decided to take Robin and

Eddie George with me to Number 10 to acquaint her with the decision I had reached. I pointed out to her that the markets were clearly expecting us to raise interest rates, and that if we did nothing at all the prospect for sterling could be very ugly indeed. She took it every bit as badly as I feared. She argued that the markets were being their usual hysterical selves, and that if we succumbed to their pressure they would simply try it on again the following week. Eventually, after prolonged resistance, she conceded with a conspicuously bad grace, insisting that any further pressure for higher interest rates should be firmly resisted.

For a time the 1 per cent increase seemed to have done the trick, but the position of the pound was still a precarious one. The oil price continued to crumble; the very day after the interest rate hike Michael Heseltine resigned from Cabinet over Westland, plunging the Government into a political crisis; and the mood could not have been worse. It was not long before sterling was under severe pressure again, and on 23 January I took the unusual step of getting the Treasury press office to distribute to all and sundry a one-page 'Factsheet on oil and the UK economy'. This pointed out that, at its peak in 1985, North Sea oil and gas represented only 8½ per cent of our total tax revenues, only 8 per cent of our total exports, only 5½ per cent of GDP, only 5 per cent of UK capital investment, and less than ½ per cent of UK employment. Having attempted to put the UK's alleged total dependence on North Sea oil into perspective, it concluded that 'The overall effects [of the oil price collapse] on both output and inflation in the UK are expected to be broadly neutral – if anything, slightly beneficial'.

The intention, of course, was to steady the markets. My great fear was that the counter-inflationary benefits of lower oil prices would all be lost in an excessive depreciation of sterling, which Margaret's refusal to allow me to take the pound into the ERM the previous November made it particularly difficult to avoid.

The following morning, Friday, 24 January, against a grim background, I held a further markets meeting with my top Bank and Treasury advisers. Once again, I concluded that interest rates should be raised a full percentage point, this time to 13½ per cent. On this occasion I took just Robin with me to Number 10 to see Margaret. I told her that the pound was under severe pressure, and I was afraid that if we did not act that day the bottom might fall out of the market. She was even worse than on the previous occasion, insisting that it was quite unnecessary, that it would be a positive disaster, and much else in the same vein. Eventually, after a particularly unpleasant harangue, she concluded, 'Go ahead if you insist, but on your own head be it'. After we had left her room, the small study on the first floor, Robin said to me 'I don't know how you put up with this sort of thing'. I explained that she had a great deal on her mind. By then she was fighting for her own political survival over

Westland (Leon Brittan was to resign later that day). But that did not excuse her intolerable behaviour.

Robin returned to the Bank to implement the interest rate increase so bruisingly agreed, only to discover that the pressure on sterling, on which I had largely based my case, had suddenly eased, and even to some extent reversed. He telephoned me to acquaint me of this unexpected and, in the circumstances somewhat embarrassing, turn of events. With considerable reluctance, I felt honour bound to rescind my earlier decision. I then went to see Margaret, to tell her that we would not be going ahead with the interest rate rise after all: she was suitably pleased. I have regretted doing so ever since.

The difficult analytical question we now faced throughout 1986 was how far the exchange rate should be allowed to fall in response to the sharp fall in oil prices, without weakening monetary policies.

I myself had accepted the need for some real depreciation of sterling in the speech I had made at Cambridge in 1984 when speculating about 'What happens when the North Sea oil runs out?' But I had hoped that a fall in the real exchange rate would be secured via a UK inflation slightly below the international average over a period of years, rather than by a depreciation in the nominal exchange rate, which, quite apart from its inflationary dangers, might well, on the basis of recent experience, not even bring about a real depreciation at the end of the day.

The view of officials, both Treasury and Bank of England, was that an oil price fall would lead to higher interest rates, a lower exchange rate, a higher PSBR and relatively little effect on output or inflation. The official Treasury had produced a set of ready reckoners based on their expectations of what might happen following an oil price fall. They had been reworked each year for some time as there were constant rumours of a sharply lower oil price.

Based on this work, they had developed the concept of the oil-adjusted exchange rate. This was designed to show changes to the exchange rate that would leave the inflation rate unchanged following an oil price fall. It was at no time challenged by the Bank.

The oil adjusted exchange rate was often mentioned as a point of reference in the Monthly Monetary Reports I received. In the early months of 1986 it suggested that the exchange rate had in fact fallen rather less than would have been needed to compensate for the fall in the oil price in terms of its implications for future inflation. It was not until August that it was suggesting that the exchange rate had dropped to a level where it was putting upward pressure on inflation.

I was never convinced by this sophisticated anaylsis, which seemed to me too clever by half. While I accepted that a halving of the oil price made some exchange rate depreciation inevitable and necessary, I soon came to feel that sterling was falling too far and too fast.

Base Rate Cuts, Spring 1986

The economic strategy paper Terry Burns presented to the pre-Budget Chevening meeting, in January 1986, argued against any further tightening of monetary or fiscal policy and maintained that further downward pressure on inflation could be combined with a respectable increase in output if policy was left unchanged. The official Treasury view throughout 1986 was that allowing the pound to fall in line with oil prices would not only restore the competitiveness of exports but also allow interest rates to be lower – which would in turn give a further boost to investment, growth and employment. They maintained that the adverse impact of a lower pound on domestic inflation would be offset by lower oil prices, which indeed it was in the short term.

When the Budget of 18 March was well received in the markets and sterling strengthened slightly I took the opportunity the following day to reverse the January increase. Over the following two months, with the rise in unemployment, already over 3 million, apparently accelerating again, with the oil price appearing to have bottomed out and sterling reassuringly steady, I concluded that the pound was now safe and gradually reduced interest rates further, half a point at a time, to 10 per cent in May.

I now regret this far more than anything focused on by my critics. For my confidence that sterling had weathered the storm was distinctly premature. Not only had I acquiesced in the relatively modest depreciation that had already occurred, but the second half of 1986 was to see a much more serious sterling slide. As a result, I lost the opportunity to lock in the marked fall in inflation that the oil price collapse had temporarily secured, and allowed policy to become looser just when the credit boom was starting to take off. Needless to say, I disliked intensely sterling's depreciation in the second half of 1986; but there was a limit to what I could do, outside the ERM, particularly given Margaret's profound hostility to raising interest rates or maintaining any kind of sterling target. The net result was that the exchange rate exerted no downward pressure on inflation in 1986; and interest rates, although high in real terms – they averaged over 7 per cent in real terms in the second half of 1986 – were, with the benefit of hindsight, clearly not high enough to stifle at birth the excessive growth of credit which was to lead to the resurgence of inflation in 1988–90.

The ERM Again

The collapse of the oil price should have had one beneficial effect: it removed what remained of the petrocurrency argument against joining the ERM, as Leon Brittan, by then a back-bencher, pointed out in his contribution to the Budget debate. Support for membership was growing. A survey of CBI members showed some 85 per cent declaring themselves in favour, and support also came from the Institute of Directors, the quality Press and numerous other bodies. But with the possible exception of the Institute of Directors, these were not names to conjure with so far as Margaret was concerned.

She could in any case have responded by pointing out the apparent lack of support for ERM membership from any eminent academic economists. It was certainly striking how Alan Walters' periodic blasts in the newspapers, though invariably flawed, seldom if ever elicited an academic counterblast. One reason for that was that those who favoured free floating tended to be fired with purist zeal, whereas those who favoured ERM membership on economic grounds did so (as I did) for pragmatic reasons, as probably the least bad alternative in a wicked and imperfect world. The only pro-ERM zealots were those who wanted it on political ('European') grounds.

Be that as it may, in my Lombard Association speech in April 1986, I myself dropped a broad hint. After expressing my misgivings about the various definitions of the money supply I went on to say:

> In the right circumstances membership of a formal fixed exchange rate system can itself provide a very effective framework for monetary policy. Indeed, the gold standard was the earliest and most durable form of financial discipline. Modern fixed exchange rate systems are more flexible. But the exchange rate can still provide a very clear and tough discipline, obliging the authorities to take timely action when domestic policies are out of line with other low-inflation countries. Of course the exchange rate will not signal the right policy action every time, any more than the monetary aggregates. But, over the medium term, maintaining a fixed exchange rate against countries who share our resolve to reduce inflation is a pretty robust way of keeping domestic monetary policy on the rails.
>
> But I see no role for an exchange rate target outside a formal exchange rate system, shared by other countries, and supported by a co-ordinated approach to economic management and intervention. And that, for the UK, means outside the exchange rate mechanism of the EMS.

So far as the phrasing of this last paragraph is concerned, it has to be remembered that, at the time I gave my Lombard Association speech, the Louvre Accord had not even been envisaged, let alone signed. In any event, not wishing to mislead the market into thinking that I was signalling sterling's imminent membership of the mechanism, I added that 'the Government does not believe the time is yet right for us to join the ERM'. The use of the expression 'the Government' rather than the word 'I' was, of course, deliberate. It so happened, however, that on the very same day Geoffrey Howe made a speech to the Conservative Group for Europe saying that 'a decision cannot be postponed indefinitely'; adding that it should be left to the Chancellor. Meanwhile Margaret took the opportunity of congratulating herself in the House for refusing to join the ERM at the relatively high sterling/DM rate that had prevailed before the oil price collapse. But for me the ERM realignment earlier that month was a good illustration of how the system, when working normally, engendered market expectations that any realignment would be small.

Geoffrey was keen to follow up our speeches with more private pressure on Margaret. I told him that I thought it best to wait a little before returning to the charge. Not that I would have objected in the slightest had I thought that his proposed approach would have been productive, but unfortunately it was far more likely to prove counterproductive. Geoffrey had been one of the principal architects and most articulate expositors of Thatcherism, but his relationship with Margaret had never been a particularly close one, and even by 1986 the signs of tension were beginning to become apparent.

This was largely a matter of personal chemistry: he for his part never sufficiently treated her as a woman, while she found his quiet, dogged manner intensely irritating. Increasingly, over the years, she felt compelled – to the acute embarrassment of everyone else present – to treat him as something halfway between a punchbag and a doormat. At least while he was Chancellor they were at one on most issues of policy. Even this bond steadily weakened after he became Foreign Secretary, and was taken over, as she saw it, by the Foreign Office, a Department she deeply distrusted as being congenitally 'wet' and always on the foreigners' side rather than ours, even though she admired individual Foreign Office officials, sometimes excessively. Towards the end matters went from bad to worse, as Geoffrey became steadily more pro-European Community while she moved violently in the opposite direction.

The Sterling Crisis Surfaces

As I have mentioned, the foreign exchange markets reacted well to the Budget in March and the pound remained firm for the next three months. It then began to slide again, this time at a more alarming rate, with the pressure becoming intense by September. In the three months from June to September, 1986, it fell a further 10 per cent on the index, and considerably more than this against the Deutschmark, for the first time ever threatening to fall below DM3.

AN UNWANTED DEVALUATION

I was rather more concerned than my advisers by sterling's depreciation. No doubt some depreciation compared with the previous autumn's
DM3.7 was inevitable given the fall in oil prices. But the oil price was
by then well off the bottom and the further depreciation late in 1986
simply risked an upsurge in inflation. I had become convinced that
the time had come to act, initially through intervention, but standing ready to raise interest rates if intervention alone was not enough.
My intention was to defend a *floor* of DM3 – an interesting figure in
the light of subsequent events.

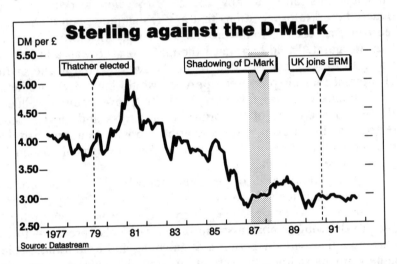

The week before I had to fly off to Washington for the annual Bank and
Fund meetings, I asked Peter Middleton at our regular weekly bilateral
on 19 September what he thought the implications for interest rates
were of 'tracking' the Deutschmark at around that level. He replied that
the prospects for interest rates had deteriorated, but that no-one had
suggested an increase. Nevertheless, when I saw Robin the following
day I remarked that we were hanging on by our fingertips.

The pound came under further pressure with the publication on 23 September of a then record monthly current account deficit of £886 million for
August. I instructed the Bank to use the reserves unstintingly to defend
the pound, and to sell Deutschmarks in particular, given the agreement
at Gleneagles that it was desirable to halt the fall in the dollar.

The markets not unreasonably concluded that the Government was
trying to avoid a politically damaging increase in interest rates before the
(very likely pre-election) Conservative Conference in the second week
of October, which indeed I was. Gerhard Stoltenberg, however, was
persuaded by an angry Karl Otto Pöhl, the President of the Bundesbank,
to telephone me the following day to complain that by selling dollars at all

654

the Bank of England was contravening 'the spirit of Gleneagles'. By this he meant that it was acting in opposition to the Bundesbank's purchases of dollars to prop up the US currency. I pointed out that I had explicitly instructed the Bank to sell more Deutschmarks than dollars, which was (in my interpretation) fully in accord with the 'spirit of Gleneagles'. This was something of which Pöhl had evidently omitted to inform him. As I flew to Washington on 25 September, sterling had closed in London at just under DM2.94, ominously below the Bank's objective.

Occasional sterling crises are an inescapable part of any Chancellor's life, and he soon learns, if not to enjoy them, at least not to lose any sleep over them. But I particularly disliked those that blew up while I was abroad, and they seemed to have a perverse tendency to occur during the week of the annual Bank and Fund meeting. The problem was essentially one of divided command, with me in Washington with Robin and Terry, while Margaret was in London holding meetings with Peter Middleton and Eddie George. The danger of wires getting crossed was accentuated by the five-hour time difference between Washington and London, and only narrowly averted by my daily telephone conversations with Peter, and occasionally Margaret. Nor did it help that the massed ranks of the UK financial media were in Washington, waiting to descend as a pack on Robin or me whenever we appeared, and, when we did not, looking for anyone who could be persuaded to utter an unhelpful word.

In September 1986 the mood of the media was particularly hysterical; but even discounting media hysteria it was clear that interest rates would have to rise. The question was how much, and when. Nevertheless, market sentiment had not been helped by Robin's remark to a journalist who had taken him unawares in the spacious atrium of the Fund building. Asked whether we would be raising interest rates, Robin replied that we had no intention of doing so 'today'. On 28 September I held a meeting with Robin and his and my senior officials in Washington in the office of Tim Lankester, the admirable Treasury official who was then the UK's executive director of the Fund and Bank and economic Minister in Washington. I had not yet made up my mind whether or not more than one percentage point was required, and in any case I wanted to defer the move at least until I was back in London and fully in control of events, and if possible until after the forthcoming Party Conference. What we needed to do now, I concluded, was to buy a small amount of time.

Accordingly, the same day I took Robin with me to see Stoltenberg and Pöhl to ask for their help in supporting sterling on the foreign exchange markets. Stoltenberg was sympathetic, but Pöhl said there was nothing he could do. It was Bundesbank policy to hold nothing but dollars in their foreign exchange reserves, which meant that they could not buy sterling on their own account, but only as an agent acting on behalf of the Bank of England.

655

AN UNWANTED DEVALUATION

While the sight of the Bundesbank supporting sterling, even though it was not really the Bundesbank doing it at all, might, I reckoned, help sentiment in the foreign exchange market in the short term, it still implied a substantial loss of UK reserves which, despite the strengthening I had secured over the previous year and a bit, we could ill afford. I therefore floated the idea of entering into a standby swap arrangement, of the kind that the Bundesbank had long had with France, under which the Germans would in effect stand by to lend us Deutschmarks for a specified period of months. Pöhl undertook to consider the matter.

At the crack of dawn (Washington Time) the next morning, 29 September, I telephoned Margaret to put her in the picture. She was furious that the Germans were not being more helpful, and went into her gut anti-German mode, which was never far from below the surface. If the Germans would not play ball, she declared, she would pull the British Army out of the Rhine. More practically, she endorsed my proposal to secure a substantial swap arrangement.

I then drove with Alex Allan at high speed to see Stoltenberg and Pöhl in Stoltenberg's room at the Four Seasons Hotel, where the German delegation to the meetings always stayed. It turned out to be Stoltenberg's birthday. After a quick drink to celebrate this important event, I reverted to the question of the swap, explaining to them that this was a very serious matter indeed and that I had discussed it with the Prime Minister, who fully shared the importance I attached to securing an adequate agreement without further delay. Stoltenberg replied that he fully accepted this; and Pöhl said that the Bundesbank would be happy to enter into an immediate swap agreement with the Bank of England along exactly the same lines as had long existed with the US Federal Reserve and the Bank of Japan. I told him I would inform the Governor forthwith, and meanwhile I would like the Bundesbank to support sterling in the foreign exchange markets as an agent of Her Majesty's Government.

Leaving the Four Seasons Hotel, I went straight to the UK office in the IMF Building to see Robin and inform him of the swap arrangement I had in principle agreed. This was then formally negotiated between Anthony Loehnis on behalf of the Bank and Leonhard Gleske on behalf of the Bundesbank, and so far as I am aware remains in force to this day. The form of the swap was, as is customary, a standby agreement, which we duly made use of, not so much because we needed to but because I was anxious to establish the precedent. Needless to say, the money was repaid well before the due date.

Meanwhile, it was understood in the markets the following day that the Bank of England and the Bundesbank were acting in concert, and the pressure on sterling immediately subsided. As one City analyst put it: 'It is always more impressive if the Germans are buying sterling because the markets know that they have more ammunition in their locker'. The concerted intervention also revived speculation that Britain was about to join the ERM and that the Government was already pursuing a covert exchange target for the pound. This was premature. Although the Bank of England was now aiming to stop sterling falling too much below DM3, this was purely a matter of short-term tactics. It was not until the framework of the Louvre Agreement was in place, five months later, that I started to see it differently. At my Washington press conference - a regular annual event – I made a light-hearted allusion to Robin's earlier gaffe when I replied to the inevitable question by saying that the UK had 'no intention of joining the ERM . . . today'.

Before leaving Washington I decided to take some time off to go on a shopping expedition, using the amazingly long black stretched limo which the Ambassador always kindly hired for my use when in Washington. Taking Alex, Terry and Robert Culpin with me, I bought presents for Thérèse and the children. On our return to the Fund building Robert discovered that the Press, noting my disappearance, had concluded that I had been so overcome by the crisis I had hidden away in some bunker.

As soon as I had returned to London, I called a meeting on 2 October with Robin and the usual cast of senior Treasury and Bank officials. Terry was struck by the change of mood, remarking that only a few weeks earlier the Treasury had been thinking that industrial confidence was fragile and monetary policy too tight. By now, however, I reckoned that the increase in interest rates that was clearly necessary could wait until after the Party Conference the following week. Before going off to Bournemouth for the Conference on 6 October, I held one further meeting with Robin and the others. Pressure on sterling had re-emerged, and the position was undoubtedly uncomfortable with the pound now below DM2.90. The only real subject for discussion was whether, after the Conference, interest rates should rise by one percentage point or two. I suggested that we should decide that in the light of conditions at the time.

One small stroke of good fortune was that the end-September figure for our foreign exchange reserves, published in early October, showed – despite the sizeable intervention – a healthy increase, thanks to the receipts from the $4 billion floating rate note issue I had organized at the beginning of the month (see Chapter 39). Indeed, in the event, the September 1986 reserve loss never really showed up in the published figures at all, since it was more than absorbed by the massive reserve gains we were able to secure the following year while shadowing the Deutschmark in the wake of the Louvre Accord.

CHAPTER 53

POLITICS AND INTEREST RATES, 1986

Conference Success at Last · Another Seminar
Tories for ERM · The Row Goes Public
Looking for a 'Trigger'

Conference Success at Last

I WAS DETERMINED TO make an impact at what promised to be the
last Party Conference before the election. Norman Tebbit, now Party
Chairman, had chosen as the 1986 Conference theme 'The Next Moves
Forward', and every Minister who spoke was asked to include a section setting out his objectives for the immediate future. This suited me
well enough. Alistair Ross-Goobey, whom I had got to know when he
contested the neighbouring (Labour) constituency of Leicester West
in the 1979 General Election, and whom I recruited to the Treasury
as a special adviser in April 1986 when Howard Davies returned to
McKinseys, successfully negotiated the pre-lunch slot for me on the
Thursday morning of the Conference.

In 1984 and 1985 I had been given the slot immediately after lunch
on the Thursday, when the audience were less alert and there was the
risk of the BBC's live coverage of my reply falling a victim to children's
television. Unfortunately Alistair, who could never resist a joke, told the
Financial Times that the purpose of the change was to ensure a standing
ovation, since everyone would get up to go for lunch immediately after
the speech. This was duly published.

An enthusiastic standing ovation was indeed highly desirable. This
meant that I needed to equip myself with a good peroration. I wrote one
myself, but also asked Tony Jay, who combined a genuine philosophical
commitment with a writer's flair, to do one for me, intending to use

whichever was better (almost certainly his). In the event I liked them both so much that I used both, so the conclusion of the speech was like a two-tiered wedding cake. The standing ovation at the end was both refreshingly enthusiastic and embarrassingly prolonged. Indeed, it had gone well from start to finish: from my topical jokes at the start, through the assertion of the importance of the tide of ideas, which clearly struck a chord, and the pledges of a 25 pence basic rate of income tax, more privatization, and zero inflation (final score: two out of three), to the two-tier peroration. I included some stern words about public spending and borrowing, and dealt with the tricky issues of interest rates and the pound by ignoring them altogether.

The speech was much better delivered, too, than my previous Conference efforts. I decided to have a second crack at using the 'magic screens': the almost invisible autocues – indeed, they are completely invisible to the television viewer – which President Reagan had introduced to the UK and which enable the speaker to read a speech while apparently looking his audience straight in the eyes and using no notes at all. My first go with them had not gone well; but this time I took the precaution of rehearsing it first, under the skilled guidance of Harvey Thomas, and it made all the difference.

More important than my speech, however, the entire 1986 Conference was an outstanding success, and marked a turning-point in the Government's fortunes so marked that you could sense it at the time. We had started the year in the shadow of the Westland affair, which had not only cost two prominent Cabinet resignations but left Margaret herself so badly wounded that at one point it looked mortal. The economy appeared to be faltering badly after seven successive years of inexorably rising unemployment, and we were losing safe seats in by-elections. Even as late as September, the month before the Conference, when Westland had already receded into a distant memory, we were still five points behind Labour in the polls. Immediately after the Conference, we leapt into a lead which continued right up to the 1987 general election.

Meanwhile, as soon as I got back to London from Bournemouth on the Friday I called a markets meeting with Robin and the customary cast and decided without much difficulty to raise interest rates by one percentage point, deferring the implementation until the following Tuesday to prevent it from being indecently close to the end of the Conference. The markets had recovered sufficiently from the fevered mood of the Washington meetings to enable that to 'stick', and Margaret was sufficiently relieved that I had not gone for a two-point rise to agree to it with relatively little resistance. For myself, I disliked going up by more than one point at a time partly because it looked like panic and partly because I wanted to educate the markets that this was the norm. Recorded inflation was just 3 per cent and real interest rates were already at their highest level ever. I had no wish to confirm the incipient market view that interest rates always rose by 2 per cent when the pound was under pressure.

The Mansion House speech on 16 October was a far more difficult hurdle to negotiate than the Party Conference. The rise in base rates had obviously been triggered by the fall in the exchange rate, and I saw no point in denying it – although I gave a somewhat unconvincing mention to M0 as well. But I was determined that, if I could possibly avoid it, there should be no further fall. Against the strong advice of the mandarins, who felt I was being rash to the point of insanity, I said:

> Given the precipitate collapse of the oil price, it was inevitable and indeed necessary that the exchange rate should fall . . . But there are clearly limits to the necessary and desirable extent of that fall.

This message was reinforced by Robin, who spoke after me, and described the fall in the exchange rate as 'fully sufficient to effect the necessary current account adjustment'. Sterling was still not out of the woods, however, especially after the OPEC meeting broke up on 22 October without reinstating firm oil production quotas. The dismissal of my old opposite number Sheikh Zaki Yamani on 29 October, who was regarded the best hope for their restoration, added to the uncertainty. Fortunately, the so-called Baker-Miyazawa accord of 31 October, in which Jim Baker agreed to stabilize the dollar in return for a pledge from the Japanese Finance Minister Kiichi Miyazawa to cut Japan's discount rate and undertake a fiscal boost, took some of the pressure off the pound. Following the Gleneagles agreement among the European members of the G5, this paved the way for the multilateral currency stabilization agreement reached at the Louvre in Paris the following February.

Another Seminar

On Sunday 19 October, Margaret decided to hold one of her occasional economic 'seminars' at Chequers. Those present included, in addition to John MacGregor, the Chief Secretary, and myself, Peter Middleton, Terry Burns and Brian Griffiths. She began by expressing deep concern at the underlying economic position. She said that the combination of shrinking savings, high consumer spending, booming retail sales, growing current account deficit and the falling pound, smacked of another 'Barber boom'.* Stop there and Margaret looks impressively prescient. But in fact she was far more wrong than right; and it was hardly surprising that I chose not to alter course as a result of the seminar. She had

---

*A reference to Anthony Barber (later Lord Barber), Chancellor of the Exchequer from 1970 to 1974, who was widely blamed for the lax policies which led to record inflation in the mid-1970s, but which were in fact largely instigated by the then Prime Minister, Edward Heath.

called the gathering in the wake of the very necessary sterling-induced one per cent base rate hike of 14 October, which she had not liked. Her three main complaints were:

1. That the current account was swinging from surplus into deficit for the first time since she had become Prime Minister.* Like the Labour Party, Margaret never managed to emancipate herself from the early post-war belief in the current account balance as a key indicator of economic success. A pure monetarist would have paid little attention to the current account, leaving it to a market-determined floating exchange rate to balance all movements, current and capital, across the exchanges. Even an 'exchange rate monetarist', as I became, would know that, in a world without exchange controls, a current account deficit in itself revealed little beyond the fact that the country was a net importer of capital.

2. That the pound had been falling. Yet she herself had insisted, only a few months earlier, on rejecting what was then clearly the best means of preventing this slide – membership of the ERM – and had opposed interest rate increases designed to stop the pound falling.

3. That fiscal policy was too lax, and more specifically that the £7 billion PSBR set at the time of the last Budget was too large. Here she was simply ill-informed: the 1986–87 PSBR was in fact running well below the Budget estimate and turned out to be £3½ billion, equivalent to only 1 per cent of GDP, the lowest level for a very long time.

Indeed, the conclusion she drew, that fiscal policy ought to be tighter and monetary policy looser, was wholly perverse and if anything the reverse of the truth. It represented her perennial harking back, whenever she was uneasy, to the 1981 formula, which was appropriate to a special situation when the Budget deficit was in excess of 5 per cent of GDP and sterling had soared to an unsustainably high rate. Now the whole situation had gone into reverse. The Budget deficit was well under control, but sterling was weak.

As the autumn of 1986 went on and my political and personal standing started to rise, I remained worried about the low level of sterling. I did not see how it could be stabilized at a reasonably satisfactory level on the basis of any politically feasible interest rate changes in the run-up to an election – or even on the basis of a level of interest rates justified by the state of the domestic economy as we saw it at the time. I was convinced that we needed to bolster the effect of interest rate policy by a public commitment to a stable exchange rate system,

*This was, however, entirely a consequence of the collapse of the oil price and should not have been a cause for concern at that time even for those who took the recorded current account figures at face value. The current account went back into surplus during the last quarter of 1986 and the first quarter of 1987.

such as the ERM, not the least of whose virtues was an obligation to engage in short-term intervention on the part of the central bank of the strong currency as well as that of the weak currency. It was true that this obligation meant less than met the eye, since it came into effect only when a currency was right up against the limit of its parity range, which in practice seldom occurred. But the knowledge that this rule existed was itself a stabilizing force, which was intended to be further fortified by the Basle/Nyborg changes agreed the following year (and described in Chapter 59).

Fortunately (as I mistakenly thought at the time), the day after the Chequers seminar, Karl Otto Pöhl, the Bundesbank President, was due to visit London to deliver a lecture. While in London he had arranged to see not only Robin and myself, but also Margaret. Short, bespectacled, well-built and usually sun-tanned (his holidays in South Africa saw to that), Pöhl, with whom I always got on well although he was never the friend that Stoltenberg became, was one of the most powerful and most colourful characters on the international financial scene. He and his deputy (and successor) Schlesinger formed a well-balanced combination; with Schlesinger, the archetypal central banker, quietly providing the technical grasp and Pöhl, the flamboyant former sports journalist, the international awareness.

Pöhl was affable, highly articulate (in English as well as German), intelligent, quick-witted, vain, and somewhat too talkative to the Press. He was also extraordinarily volatile – at one moment a confirmed sceptic about intervention in the foreign exchange markets, for example, and a prominent advocate of it the next. (There may have been some consistency in this instance, however: he tended to favour intervention when the dollar was strong *vis-à-vis* the Deutschmark and to be philosophically opposed to it when the dollar was weak.) He has two outstanding achievements to his credit. The first was to persuade the world outside Germany that it was his outstanding qualities that made the Bundesbank the force it was. Only inside Germany was it understood that in fact the reverse was the case: it was the Bundesbank which gave Pöhl the stature he so enjoyed. The second was to know when to quit: just before reunification (the dangers of which he had warned against in advance) was to throw the German monetary scene into turmoil.

But if the Bundesbank is to disappear as an independent force, and with it the Deutschmark whose value it was committed to preserving, as the current proposals for European monetary union envisage, then it will be Pöhl who is largely responsible for its death. It was the way in which Pöhl openly revelled in his role, via the EMS, of the ruler of Europe's monetary affairs and arbiter of its destiny, and encouraged the world's Press to see him in this light, that the French in general and de Larosière in particular found so intolerable that they were prepared to sacrifice their own national independence in order to see the Bundesbank abolished. A more sensitive and discreet Bundesbank President could have avoided this. It was striking that even the easy-going Robin Leigh-Pemberton, despite not then being tied to the ERM's apron strings, was frequently irked by Pöhl's behaviour.

Even so, as a key member of the Delors Committee which produced the EMU proposals, Pöhl could have prevented them from emerging in anything like the radical form they did – as indeed he had promised Robin he would. But when it came to it, Pöhl never bothered to read all the many papers the Committee had before it, confident he could, if necessary, play it by ear; as a result of which the hardworking and well-briefed Delors, ably supported by Larosière, was able to run rings round him.

For some time Pöhl had been arguing in public in favour of British membership of the ERM, and I knew that Margaret held him in high – perhaps exaggerated – regard. I hoped he might persuade her of the desirability of the move where I had so far failed to do so, and I said as much to him when I saw him at Number 11. I was later told that she began the meeting (which was with Pöhl alone) by making it clear that she did not wish to discuss the EMS, and that as a result they never did.

The newspapers the next day mentioned Pöhl's visit. They also carried a story, clearly emanating from Number 10, to the effect that the UK had no intention of joining the ERM before the next General Election. When I sought to raise the matter with Margaret at my bilateral with her later that day, she brusquely declined to discuss it with me. I was feeling increasingly frustrated. I was also becoming somewhat isolated, since my senior officials had come to take the view that the Prime Minister had vetoed entry, and that was that – at least for the forseeable future.

Tories for ERM

But I was far from isolated within the Party as a whole. Margaret had asked most Cabinet Ministers to chair a policy group on each of the various aspects of policy that would feature in the forthcoming Election Manifesto. As with most of these exercises, the purpose was primarily public relations: to give the impression that others besides the Cabinet, and in particular senior back-benchers, were fully involved in the Manifesto-drafting process; although she also hoped that one or two useful ideas might be generated. To sit on the group on economic policy, which I chaired, I sought individuals of ability who represented a good cross-section of opinion within the Party.*

*The full membership was myself (chairman), Peter Cropper, Nigel Forman, Peter Hordern, David Howell, Peter Lane (the chairman of the National Union), Peter Lilley, Professor Stephen Littlechild, John MacGregor, John Major, Cecil Parkinson and John Redwood, with Judith Chaplin as Secretary.

We met six times between September and December, and submitted our final report on 19 December. The group was overwhelmingly in favour of ERM entry, recording a division only between those who believed that membership 'would provide a more credible economic policy in the pre-election period' and those who wanted to join after the election, but still believed that a commitment to join should be in the Manifesto. In fact, the only dissenter was John Redwood, and even he was prepared to go along with a unanimous recommendation in favour of 'Membership of the ERM (if not already implemented)'.

The arguments adduced for early membership were: (a) the need for another financial target now that £M3 had been discredited, (b) the fact that a reasonably sustainable pattern of international exchange rates now existed, (c) the greatly reduced risk to sterling from a slump either in the dollar or in oil prices since both had already fallen so far, and (d) the fact that uncertainty about exchange rate policy on the one hand made exporters reluctant to invest and sell, since they feared the exchange rate would rise, and on the other hand prevented the exchange rate from acting as an anti-inflationary discipline, 'since wage negotiators assume that the pound will sink further to offset pay awards'. Needless to say, Margaret refused to accept either variant of the group's recommendation; but the weight of opinion, coming on top of my own strong views, led her to suggest to me that I should return to the matter after the election.

The Row Goes Public

What could not be postponed until after the election were immediate decisions on interest rate policy and how to respond to the continuing downward pressure on sterling. By now Margaret was becoming sufficiently careless to allow the disagreement between us to emerge into the open. In an interview she gave to the *Financial Times*, which was published on 19 November, she conceded that, after the election, 'I will expect to have to reconsider membership'; but the hostility she showed towards the ERM was so extreme that it was difficult to imagine her doing so objectively. She also came out in the open about her threat to 'do another 1981' – that is, to raise taxes. She seemed curiously unable to believe the massive improvement in the public finances I had told her about at the Chequers seminar the previous month.

Much more serious was her refusal even to hint that there might be any limit to the downward movement of sterling against the Mark. Asked about my statement at the Mansion House to the effect that the pound had fallen far enough she said:

> I do not think there are a great many consequences of that statement. We may believe it has gone far enough, but it is what the market

believes [that matters] and you know what the market is: 95 per cent of the movement is speculation and the other 5 per cent is trade.

It is indeed precisely the febrile and anchorless nature of a freely floating exchange rate which make it both possible and desirable for national monetary authorities to give a lead. Even more dangerously, after seven and a half years in Number 10 she was clearly coming to see loyalty as a one way street: something her Ministers owed to her but not she to them – a mistake which the old Margaret Thatcher would never have made. Despite this public rebuff I held my ground and told the Treasury Committee the following day that the 'step change' in the exchange rate due to the sharp collapse of the oil price had now come to an end:

> So we are back to the policy of having an exchange rate which is exercising a financial discipline and that means I do not want to wish to see it fall further . . . I think there is clearly a case for being a part of an explicit regional fixed exchange rate system.

Looking for a 'Trigger'

But sterling could not simply be talked into stability, and the pound was under constant pressure during both November and December. My worries about sterling were reinforced by the growth of M0. This had been rising on a seasonally adjusted basis for some months, almost certainly reflecting the strength of consumer spending.

On Thursday, 20 November, the day on which I appeared before the Treasury Select Committee, I warned the Bank that I would probably want to raise interest rates by one percentage point to 12 per cent the following Monday (24 November). It was disappointingly resistant to the idea. Whereas I was now convinced by the evidence both of sterling and of M0 that monetary policy was in danger of becoming too lax and should be tightened forthwith, the Bank was above all concerned to avoid surprising the markets, which were not expecting an interest rate hike, given my firm declaration at the time of the October increase that one per cent was enough.

I accordingly convened a full-scale markets meeting for Wednesday, at which I argued that if it was necessary in the Bank's view to have a 'trigger' before raising interest rates, we should use either the publication of the next M0 figures or the next bout of pressure on the pound, whichever was the sooner. On a seasonally adjusted basis, M0 was growing at a rate slightly above the top of the range I had set in the Budget. The Bank which was always hostile to using M0 as a trigger for an interest rate change, agreed in principle that we were likely to need to raise rates, but maintained that we should wait until the pound began to fall sharply from its already low level.

I felt I had little option but to accept this advice. It was hard enough to persuade Margaret of the need to raise interest rates when I had the Bank with me. If she were to get wind (as she almost certainly would) of the fact that the Bank were against the idea, it would be impossible. If there is one thing I learned about the timing of pressure on the pound, it is its innate perversity. It comes when you want it least; but now that I did want it, it failed to materialize. However, anxious to avoid the risk of enabling Margaret to exploit a rift between the Bank and myself, I eventually persuaded Robin that we should take the unusual step of sending her a joint note making the case for an interest rate rise.

At my weekly bilateral with her on 9 December, I told her that I was concerned that monetary conditions were too loose and believed that interest rates ought to go up by a further one percentage point. I promised her a note on the matter that evening, on the basis of which we could have a proper discussion the next day. The key passages of the joint Chancellor–Governor note I sent across to her that evening read as follows:

> We have been considering our stance on interest rates in the light of the latest monetary indicators, with an eye also on the pressures which have beset us in the past two Januaries . . . There is considerable advantage in moving well before our hand is forced by the market. Last January the fact that we were prepared to raise interest rates promptly by 1 per cent enabled us to avoid the sort of drastic action we had to take in July 1984 and January 1985 . . . The consequent improvement in market sentiment will also enable us to replenish the reserves . . . The next set of money numbers to be published on 18 December could provide a suitable opportunity; but in any event we need to be prepared to move quickly should financial confidence start to deteriorate.

This was drafted a good deal more tentatively than I would have liked, but I wrongly assumed that it would not be long before sterling came under pressure again. Moreover, as I saw it, the need was to tighten policy, and it was absurd to allow the technicality of the trigger to get in the way of it.

The meeting to discuss this took place the following evening, 10 December. Brian Griffiths was present. Margaret was every bit as resistant as I had expected. After I had put my case, along the lines of the note, which I pointed out represented the considered opinion of both Robin and myself that monetary conditions had become too lax, she reeled off all her objections. Nothing had changed since we had decided to raise interest rates by 1 per cent rather than 2 per cent in October. Raising interest rates now would hit people with mortgage. So far from bringing down inflation it would increase it (this was a reference to the RPI effect), and it would also increase public expenditure. She suspected, too, that the seasonal adjustment of M0 was defective (a point she had no doubt got from Brian Griffiths) and would like the Treasury to prepare a note on this – a palpable delaying tactic.

Most bizarre of all, she argued (as she had done at the Chequers seminar in October) that in so far as we were experiencing any problems at the present time, they all stemmed from the PSBR having been set too high in the 1986 Budget, and the right answer was therefore not a rise in interest rates, but a 'very prudent' Budget in 1987: she suggested that I should aim for a PSBR 'as low as £5 billion', even if that left no room for tax cuts.

It was difficult to decide which was the more perverse: her refusal to accept that inflation had to be fought by the use of monetary policy, or her persistent misunderstanding of the fiscal position. The 1986 Budget may have set a PSBR of £7 billion, but the out-turn for 1986–87 was only £3½ billion. Thus in urging me to aim, in the 1987 Budget, for a PSBR 'as low as £5 billion' she was unknowingly knocking at an open door: I was to aim for a PSBR for 1987–88 considerably less than £5 billion, even after cutting taxes by some £2½ billion (as described in Chapter 55), and to achieve a surplus.

I duly countered all her various points, and reiterated the importance I attached to taking no avoidable risks with inflation. After a long discussion, she concluded that everything should be done to avoid a rise in interest rates in advance of a Budget which, she reiterated, would need to be prudent enough to obviate any conceivable need to raise interest rates (indeed, it might make possible a reduction in interest rates). However, she conceded with the utmost reluctance that it might nevertheless be right to raise interest rates – but if, and only if, there was 'a clear trigger' for an increase.

We left it at that. However unconvincing most of the arguments she had used, her final conclusion was so similar in substance (if very different in tone from) to the Bank's position, that to have pushed it any further would merely have destroyed the common front I had taken so much trouble to construct. And I was of course unaware that the clear (exchange rate) trigger was not to materialize until the run-up to the Louvre Accord of February 1987, by which time I was thinking in terms of a different way of keeping sterling strong.

These two occasions in 1986 – one towards the start of the year, the other towards the end of it – were the only occasions during my time as Chancellor on which Margaret actually prevented an interest rate increase I sought. Conceding an interest rate rise with ill grace was, most of the time, par for the course. There were, needless to say, no occasions when she made any attempt to stand in the way of a proposal of mine to reduce interest rates; and there was one important time when, as we shall see, she foisted on me an interest rate cut I had not wanted.

No doubt every Chancellor has experienced the same difficulties as I did in persuading the Prime Minister of the day that interest rates should be increased. Some may have encountered even greater difficulty. Essentially, Margaret was no different from the others so far as this was concerned. The picture she liked to present of herself as a uniquely doughty fighter against inflation was, in this sense, largely mythical. Where she was unusual was in her courage and resolve, most of the time, to see a tough policy through, once it had been embarked upon, irrespective of short-term unpopularity. This was highly commendable. But it was not the same thing.

CHAPTER 54

A SURFEIT OF RESIGNATIONS

The Curse of Ulster · The Resignation of Ian Gow
A Future Party Chairman · Prelude to Westland
The Westland Affair · The Resignation of Michael Heseltine
The Resignation of Leon Brittan · The Bunker Beckons
A New Policy for the Pound

The Curse of Ulster

THE YEAR LEADING UP to the successful 1986 Party Conference had been politically disastrous. It began with little more than a hiccup: the resignation from the Government of Ian Gow over the Anglo–Irish Agreement of 15 November 1985.

The Agreement, which essentially gave the Irish Republic, for the first time, a locus in the affairs of Northern Ireland, in return for undertakings which Margaret had been persuaded would be helpful to the British Government in the discharge of our responsibility for governing the province, had been negotiated in total secrecy, largely by the Cabinet Secretary, Robert Armstrong. Not without cause, Margaret clearly regarded the Cabinet as far too leaky to be taken into her confidence. Geoffrey, as Foreign Secretary, was of course fully in the picture, as were Tom King, who had been appointed Northern Ireland Secretary in the reshuffle two months earlier, and his predecessor, Douglas Hurd. But with the possible exception of Michael Heseltine, then still Defence Secretary, the rest of us, so far as I am aware, knew nothing of it until it was presented to us for our approval, almost as a *fait accompli*.

I had considerable doubts about its wisdom myself, and indicated as much in Cabinet, but did not go so far as to oppose it – nor did anyone else. Over the years there had been a succession of well-intentioned political initiatives launched to deal with the Irish problem, and each of them had ended in tears, if not in bloodshed. It had made me highly sceptical of the wisdom of any Northern Ireland initiative. I had no doubt that the Anglo–Irish Agreement would be a political liability, in the sense that the resulting alienation of the Unionist majority would far outweigh any accretion of support from the Republican minority, and I could not imagine that any objective observer would believe otherwise. The question, however, was whether the domestic political cost would be outweighed by the military benefits that might be expected to come from greater co-operation from Dublin in the struggle against IRA terrorism and greater co-operation from Washington in preventing the supply of Irish American money and weapons to the IRA. As I say, I was sceptical; and the subsequent black comedy of attempts to persuade the Irish courts to extradite suspected terrorists did not make me any less sceptical. But I was not sufficiently confident of where the balance of advantage lay to oppose the Agreement.

For Ian, who was one of my closest political friends and who had only just become one of my Treasury team, having replaced Barney Hayhoe as Minister of State in the September reshuffle, it was all very much clearer. Ian was a solicitor by trade, and looked like one, too. But looks can be deceptive; and he was one of the greatest romantics in the House of Commons. With an orotund wit, a complete absence of malice, and a practical generosity which reflected a rare generosity of spirit, Ian was a man for whom loyalty – personal loyalty and loyalty to whatever 'regiment' he was serving in at the time, or had ever served in, or to which he had attached himself – was everything. National Service with the Hussars had made a profound impression on him.

He had been an outstanding PPS to Margaret throughout the 1979–83 parliament; dedicated to his job, devoted to her, yet without a trace of sycophancy: the best PPS she ever had. His next job, as Minister for Housing under the then Environment Secretary, Patrick Jenkin, was less happy; his instinctive loyalty to the Department and its causes getting the better of his judgement. His move to the Treasury would, I was confident, enable him to demonstrate just how able a Minister he was capable of being.

The Resignation of Ian Gow

Alas, he was not to give himself that opportunity. One of the causes to which he had pledged his loyal support was that of Ulster Unionism. The intensity of this sprang chiefly from his friendship with Airey Neave, who would have been Margaret's first Northern Ireland Secretary had he not been murdered by the IRA, and was reinforced by his long-standing friendship with Enoch Powell, whose economic views he had largely adopted. For Ian, the Anglo–Irish Agreement was a bombshell and a betrayal, and he could not be part of a Government that had negotiated it and would demand his support for it in the House of Commons. That Margaret, of all people, could have headed a Government that had done this made his sense of betrayal all the more intense.

I spent hours with him trying to persuade him not to resign, telling him that while I, too, thought it probably a mistake, it did not in fact alter the constitutional position of Northern Ireland one iota. But his mind was made up. With great difficulty, I did manage to persuade him to see Margaret before sending her the resignation letter he had written and which he had shown me, in the hope that she might succeed where I had failed; but their meeting was brief and changed nothing.

After his resignation, he wrote to me in characteristically generous terms:

> I am writing to thank you for the real privilege of having served as a junior member of your Treasury team . . . and to assure you of my continuing support for the whole of the Government's economic strategy, under your direction. Jane and I remember your character-istic support in having come to sit beside me during the only two speeches which I made in the House as a Treasury Minister; and we remember, too, that happy dinner party which you and Thérèse gave on the second of last month to welcome your new team, when I sat next to your brave Thérèse.
>
> Now it is all over. I have severed ministerial links with the Prime Minister whom I love and with her Chancellor and her Foreign Secretary who are two of my closest friends in politics. But though the ministerial link is severed, there remains an unbreakable personal and political affection for the three of you in the heart and mind of your ex-colleague.
>
> With all my heart, I hope that the Cabinet will be proved right and that I will be proved wrong. I shall follow your continuing success with a combination of pride and happiness.
>
> We are both feeling shattered by what has happened, but not nearly as shattered as the Conservatives and Unionists in Ulster.
>
> Please give our love to Thérèse.

Although he behaved impeccably on the back-benches – indeed it was impossible to conceive of his behaving otherwise – he was in fact thor-oughly miserable at no longer being at the centre of things. And as the years passed, his grief at being on the sidelines was joined by increasing concern at Margaret's behaviour. I saw him regularly, either dining with him alone at the Cavalry Club, or – when Jane, his immensely talented pianist wife, was in London – with Thérèse at their London flat, south of the river. While his devotion to Margaret never faltered, he was never an acolyte and never part of that tedious faction that considered her infallible. Indeed, he became increasingly critical in private, although never in public; and I recall a dinner with just the four of us in the spring of 1990 at which he expressed himself as appalled by her treatment of Geoffrey in the 1989 reshuffle. It was not that he questioned her right to have a change at the Foreign Office. It was the way in which she had done it that he found unforgiveable. By the summer of that year brave Ian, too, had been murdered by the IRA.

A Future Party Chairman

Meanwhile, the one consolation for me in Ian's resignation in November 1985 was that I managed to persuade Margaret to replace him at the Treasury with Peter Brooke. I had not known Peter for as long as I had known Ian, but I liked him and admired his qualities, and we were to become steadily closer during the three and a half years he served as a member of my Treasury team. A descendant of the white rajahs of Sarawak, Peter was in the best sense a politician of the old school, both in his style and his values. His political judgement, rather like Willie Whitelaw's, who in some ways he resembled, was both acute and instinctive. In Peter's case it no doubt stemmed from having been brought up in an exceptionally political household, his father having been (a rather unlucky) Home Secretary and his mother a key figure in the Central Office hierarchy for a considerable number of years.

When, shortly after the 1987 general election, Margaret had to find a new Party Chairman, David Young proposed himself for the role – his equivocal stint at Central Office during the election campaign had evidently given him a taste for the job – and Margaret was disposed to agree, despite the strong opposition of the outgoing Party Chairman, Norman Tebbit. It then transpired that David expected to do the job while remaining Trade and Industry Secretary – arguing that as a Minister in the Lords, with no constituency to look after, he could do the two jobs simultaneously without any difficulty. At first Margaret was disposed to agree, since she could see no satisfactory alternative, but she was somewhat shaken when she discovered how unhappy Willie was with the whole idea.

I raised it with her at one of my bilaterals, saying that it was to my mind out of the question that the Party Chairman, one of whose jobs is to bully industrialists into contributing to Party funds, should also be Trade and Industry Secretary: a conflict of interests, I suggested, which would not be lost on the Opposition. David would have to choose which of the two jobs he wanted more. She replied that, in that case, he would (as I knew) choose Trade and Industry, and she would be left without a Party Chairman. I suggested she made Peter Brooke Party Chairman, for which I thought he would make an excellent choice.

That was what she did, although whether my suggestion had anything to do with it I would not know. After a couple of years as an excellent Party Chairman, during which time, I am glad to say, he remained a Treasury Minister (I removed from his remit those responsibilities where there might have been a conflict of interest), she brought him into the Cabinet as Northern Ireland Secretary. Apart from one silly but unimportant gaffe, he was outstanding in that thankless post, and was without doubt one of the ablest of Margaret's Cabinet Ministers whom John Major inherited. I found John's decision to drop Peter after the 1992 general election inexplicable.

Prelude to Westland

The resignation of a Minister of State, as Ian Gow was, is not normally a matter of great political significance: Ian's resignation in November was of unusual interest at the time because none of her Ministers was closer to Margaret than he was. But it was soon eclipsed by the much greater disaster of the Westland affair. An essentially trivial matter, it exploded into a major political crisis at the turn of the year, which Margaret survived only by the skin of her teeth. Looking back, there were two events early in 1985 that had an important bearing on it.

Margaret had inherited Michael Heseltine from the Heath shadow cabinet, and had initially been very wary, not to say distrustful, of him. But as her first Environment Secretary she had become rather impressed by him, in particular by the businesslike way in which he ran his Department, which she felt was an object lesson to those of us who appeared to be interested only in policy. Indeed, during this time it was Willie who took against him far more than Margaret did, as Michael brought modern gimmicks like massive computer print-outs to the Cabinet table and generally tried to blind us with science. She, by contrast, was sufficiently impressed to appoint him Secretary of State for Defence in January 1983, replacing John Nott who had announced his intention of leaving parliament at the next general election.

This was only partly because she saw in Michael a flamboyant campaigner against the folly of Labour's then policy, under the quixotic leadership of Michael Foot, of unilateral nuclear disarmament – a task he performed admirably. It was also because she felt that the Ministry of Defence could do with the businesslike approach that only Michael could bring to it. Michael, however, saw it differently. As someone whose sole ambition other than the premiership was to be Trade and

Industry Secretary – an ambition eventually realized under John Major's premiership in 1992 – and organize what he saw as a Japanese-style industrial policy, the defence procurement budget offered him the chance to achieve this from another Department.

As Margaret began to realize what was afoot, relations between them deteriorated rapidly, with her old distrust of him once again in full bloom, while he became increasingly frustrated by what he saw as her excessive interference in his departmental business. The first portent of the Westland crisis occurred very early in 1985, when the question came before the Economic Affairs Committee of the Cabinet, which Margaret almost always chaired herself (I did so only when she was unable to), of whether an order for a Type 22 frigate should be given to Cammell Laird of Merseyside or Swan Hunter of Tyneside. Michael urged the former, but Margaret, backed by a clear majority of the Committee, of whom I was one, preferred the latter. Margaret hurriedly closed the meeting, and then asked Willie and me to come with her upstairs.

There she told us that Michael had indicated to her that, if the decision did not go his way, he would resign. She would rather avoid that; and since the issue was such a minor one she hoped Willie and I would agree to letting him have his way at a subsequent meeting. Despite the emotional commitment to Merseyside that Michael had developed at Environment in the wake of the Toxteth riots of 1981, I was astonished that he could seriously contemplate resigning over so trivial a matter. I had not previously realized the extent of his frustration with Margaret. The further meeting was duly held, and Margaret blithely opened by announcing that we had had a preliminary discussion at the previous meeting; now we had to reach a decision. Willie nobly did his bit, and Cammell Laird duly got the Type 22. She did not show it, but she was seething. Michael had humiliated her: from then on, she was as determined to do him down as he was determined to run his own Department in his own way.

The second portent came a little later in 1985, when the same Cabinet Committee had to decide on a replacement for the RAF's ageing Phantoms. The official Treasury advice, which was entirely predictable but none the less in my judgement almost certainly correct, was that, in the high-tech microchip-controlled missile age, there was no point in making a massive investment in a new generation of highly sophisticated manned fighter aircraft at all – something the Gulf War was to vindicate in a spectacular way. If that was too radical a course, then the cheapest and most reliable course was to buy the next generation of American fighter aircraft off the peg. As I had expected, I could get no support for either of these propositions: the Committee was persuaded that we had to have a fighter and we had to keep the technological skills alive in the UK.

Margaret then characteristically proposed that we went into partnership with the Americans, only to be told by Michael that he had sounded them out and they were not interested: not altogether surprisingly, since they had already embarked on their own project. The choice then came down to either the UK going it alone, favoured by Margaret, or a European joint venture, favoured by Michael. At this point I supported Michael: going it alone would have been absurd. That led to the decision to go for what was to be known as the European Fighter Aircraft (EFA).

In the event, the French were outmanoeuvred. They refused to participate in the agreement unless a cheaper and less sophisticated aircraft was specified than that envisaged by the UK. They were confident that the powerful Franco–German special relationship that dominated the European Community would ensure that Germany would never dare participate unless France did, thus frustrating the entire venture unless something closer to the French specifications was agreed. They may well have been right about the specifications, but – partly thanks to Michael's negotiating skill – they were wrong about the Germans. To their immense chagrin, the agreement was signed in August 1985 by the UK, Germany, Italy and Spain, with the French left out in the cold. Seven years later, with a massive budget deficit problem thanks to the costs of unification, the Germans did decide that, in the age of the missile, they did not need an expensive new fighter aircraft at all, and threatened to pull out of EFA. But at the time Michael was seen as having pulled off a coup – and had acquired a taste for European joint ventures.

The Westland Affair

Meanwhile, in the early summer of 1985, I received a message one weekend that Margaret was calling an urgent meeting about Westland on the Sunday evening and she would like me to come. All I knew about Westland at that time was that it was Britain's only helicopter manufacturer, based in Yeovil, and very badly managed. My source was my good friend John Peyton, who had been the Conservative Member for Yeovil for many years until he was ennobled in 1983, whereupon the Liberal candidate, Paddy Ashdown, captured the seat, and John was invited on to the Westland board. By 1985 he had already resigned, since although the company was in some difficulty, the management never seriously sought his opinion or advice.

As it happens, crisp, wise advice is something John is particularly good at. When I first entered the House of Commons in 1974, it was John who was kind enough to be my mentor, and I could not have had a better one. Minister of Transport (not then a Cabinet post) in the Heath Government, Margaret had inherited him from Ted Heath and given him the agriculture portfolio in her shadow cabinet – something he was singularly unsuited for, since farmers in those days were used to flattery and soft soap, which are not part of John's stock in trade. A combination of farmers' complaints and the fact that John had been on reasonably good terms with Ted Heath led her to drop him altogether, to his great disappointment, as soon as she took office in 1979. It was a bad misjudgement by her, too; since apart from his considerable qualities John's views were unequivocally dry, a scarce commodity in those early days.

In any event, I was sent the Treasury brief, and went off to Number 10 on the Sunday evening, where Margaret was in the white state drawing room. It was a small and informal meeting, the only others present being Michael Heseltine and Norman Tebbit, at that time still Trade and Industry Secretary. Michael said he felt we should know that Westland had informed his Department that unless they were given Government assistance they would have to go out of business. Michael said he was not prepared to divert any of his existing budget to Westland, since its survival was of no strategic importance to the UK. Norman was not prepared to divert any funds from his much smaller budget and I made it clear that I was not prepared to make any new money available. Michael said that he now knew what answer his people must give the company, and that was that. Norman and I were left wondering why, if Westland was of no strategic importance, it was necessary to have had a sudden Sunday evening meeting at all.

Westland, *in extremis*, then acquired a new Chairman, John Cuckney, a very able businessman and financier whom I had known off and on for a fair number of years, who set about finding a private sector solution; and by the autumn had emerged with a wealthy suitor in the shape of the American helicopter firm, Sikorsky. This perfectly satisfactory solution galvanized Michael, who sought the permission of the Economic Affairs Committee of the Cabinet, on Monday, 9 December, to see if the various European National Armaments Directors, as government defence procurement chiefs are known in NATO-speak, could cobble together a European alternative. It was clear that he had already been actively exploring this informally, and was fairly confident they could.

I was wholly opposed to Government intervention of this kind. Rescue operations were bad enough when the alternative was closure; when there was not even, as in this case, a threat of closure any longer – indeed the intervention had only been suggested when the closure threat was removed – it was absurd. The moral hazard involved was enormous: a European consortium which had emerged not spontaneously but at the prompting of the National Armaments Directors would inevitably expect government orders to keep it in business; and governments could scarcely 'rescue' a company one day and let it go to the wall the next.

Margaret, too, was opposed to the idea, and sought to condition the Committee by, most unusually, holding the meeting in two parts. In the first part John Cuckney and his managing director were present. They explained why they believed the Sikorsky deal was best for the company, and answered questions. They then withdrew, and we had the Committee meeting proper. Although Cuckney was a very polished performer, Margaret's ploy was predictably counterproductive. Cabinet Ministers dislike being told by outsiders what conclusion they should reach. Although there was still a clear majority in favour of the perfectly coherent line that the Government should stay out of it altogether, Margaret was visibly shaken by the degree of support, which included Norman Tebbit, for Michael's plea to be given a chance. While the balance of argument was clearly against Michael, sentiment was with him. Unwisely, I think, she changed the summing up she had intended to give and instead gave him the green light, coupled however with what she may have imagined was an impossible deadline: four o'clock on the afternoon of Friday the thirteenth – in other words, only four days away.

The Resignation of Michael Heseltine

Michael has subsequently claimed that it was agreed that the Committee should meet again then. As I recall it, the understanding was simply that we might need to, not that we would. In any event, Michael did succeed in getting a somewhat vague European alternative together just before the deadline, but the next Ministerial discussion was not until Cabinet the following week, on 19 December, the last Cabinet meeting of the old year. Margaret now realized she had got herself into difficulties; and the discussion in Cabinet hinged on the question of whether it was a matter for the shareholders to decide which offer they preferred, or (as Michael insisted) for Ministers, given the nature of Westland's business. Cabinet decided it should be the shareholders, and Michael's blood was up.

Throughout this saga, Leon Brittan, although still smarting from his loss of the job of Home Secretary in the September 1985 reshuffle, when he was made Trade and Industry Secretary instead, loyally supported Margaret. But I had the sense that his normally clear judgement had been affected. His brother Samuel, *The Financial Times* assistant editor, told me he was going to stay with Leon for Christmas and had bought him a toy helicopter as a Christmas present. 'I wouldn't, if I were you', I told him, 'this is no laughing matter'. After Christmas he could not wait to tell me that I had been quite wrong, and that Leon had thought it an excellent joke.

But if Leon was losing his judgement, Michael had by now thrown caution to the winds. Over the Christmas recess, while the rest of us were taking a break (or at worst quietly reading the papers for Chevening),

677

A SURFEIT OF RESIGNATIONS

Michael was busy campaigning for the European consortium, in open defiance of the Cabinet decision that Ministers should stay out of it and leave it to Westland's shareholders to decide; while Number 10 was equally busy campaigning against Michael. The extraordinary climax came with the leaking, on 6 January, of a Number 10-inspired warning letter to Michael from the then Attorney General, Patrick Mayhew. The letter turned out to be ill-founded, having been based on incorrect information; but the real scandal was the leaking of confidential advice from a Law Officer, which by strict convention is never made public. Mayhew was furious, and threatened to resign unless there was an inquiry into the source of the leak.

None of this was mentioned, however, when Westland came up as the first substantive item on the agenda at the first Cabinet meeting of the new year, on 9 January. By then Margaret realized she was in a desperate position, and that desperate measures were called for. Having gone out of her way to prevent his resignation over the absurd issue of the Type 22 frigate only a year previously, she now set out to humiliate Michael, in the full knowledge that this would almost certainly lead to his resignation over an issue on which he could cobble together a colourable case. Indeed, she had already decided whom she would appoint Defence Secretary in his place. The issue before Cabinet, Margaret said, was quite simply the restoration of the doctrine of collective Cabinet responsibility (not something of which she was at all times the most devoted adherent herself). To that end Michael would have to be gagged, by the requirement that he could say nothing on the issue without first clearing it with Robert Armstrong, the Cabinet Secretary.

Michael objected that this was wholly impracticable, and that in any case collective Cabinet responsibility could scarcely apply since she had not permitted a proper collective discussion of the issue. He spoke quietly, and not at all aggressively, and sought to find some compromise arrangement. But Margaret was adamant. She could see that Michael was now isolated in Cabinet. The general view of the colleagues was that Michael had become obsessed with the issue, and had lost all sense of proportion; while as for gagging, it was a great pity that everyone had not been gagged a good deal earlier. She pressed home her advantage; whereupon Michael slammed his Cabinet folder shut, saying 'If this is the way this Government is going to be conducted, I no longer wish to be part of it', picked the folder up and strode out of the room. It was the most dramatic moment in any Cabinet I have attended. In the stunned silence that followed Margaret announced that there would be a short break for coffee (to enable her to brief Bernard Ingham) after which Cabinet resumed with the rest of its agenda. When we were once again in our places, Margaret announced that the new Defence Secretary was George Younger.

The Resignation of Leon Brittan

The Opposition wanted Margaret's blood. The back-benchers, too, felt that they had been badly let down by the Cabinet, as indeed they had been, and wanted blood. Some of them wanted Margaret's, but most of them wanted Leon's; as it emerged that it was he who had authorized the leak of the Mayhew letter, having been given the clear impression that that was what Margaret wanted him to do. There was an unpleasant whiff of anti-semitism, and Leon resigned on 24 January.

Once again, I was amazed by his uncharacteristic lack of judgement. No doubt he was frustrated by the fact that, in the unorthodox and improper political game that had been played during the Christmas and New Year break, Michael had outsmarted him. But for any Minister to leak a confidential Law Officer's letter was amazing enough; for a lawyer of Leon's distinction to agree to do so, whether Margaret wanted him to or not, was mind-boggling. Yet once again his lack of judgement was equalled only by his amazing loyalty to Margaret. Had he made public all he knew, she could not possibly have survived; but he chose not to do so. As it was, he meekly accepted the role of scapegoat. It was a ghastly time for him. Despite having to a considerable extent brought it on himelf, I felt deeply sorry for him.

Margaret was at the lowest ebb I had ever seen her. Leon had resigned on the Friday. Thérèse and I had invited her round to Number 11 the following Sunday evening, so that, after Thérèse had withdrawn, I could outline to her my plans for the 1986 Budget. It was pretty hopeless: she was totally exhausted and unable to focus or concentrate on anything. Never the best of listeners, that evening she simply did not appear to be able to hear what was being said to her, and when she spoke it was like the automatic responses of a zombie. When Emily, then four years old, entered the room, Margaret said in a tired voice, 'What a pretty dress.' Emily replied 'Yes, it comes from Marks Expensive'. Thérèse explained that Emily was under the impression that that was the name of Marks and Spencers. Margaret, completely missing the point, replied a trifle tetchily, 'Yes, I know little girls' dresses are expensive.'

The Bunker Beckons

In some ways Margaret's period of acute weakness, while her own job was on the line, was helpful to me. Not that it lasted very long: she was nothing if not resilient. But it was during that patch that the oil price collapsed. The Saudi royal family started leaning heavily on my successor as Energy Secretary, Peter Walker, to persuade us in effect to become an honorary member of OPEC, by agreeing to restrict production so as to support the oil price. Peter was initially undecided how to respond.

A SURFEIT OF RESIGNATIONS

Had Margaret, with her soft spot for the Saudi royal family, been in a condition to intervene, we might well have acceded to their request, which was certainly what the Foreign Office would have liked. As it was, it was left to Peter and me to determine our response. As in 1983, I was clear that there could be no question of our joining forces with OPEC. Peter agreed and duly made this known to the Saudis.

A few months later, King Fahd dismissed his very long-serving Oil Minister, Zaki Yamani, for having (as he saw it) badly mismanaged things. I felt I had now played a part in seeing off both the energy tsars who had sought to dominate the scene when I was Energy Secretary: Scargill and Yamani. While I was delighted with the political castration of Scargill, I was sorry to see Yamani, whom I liked, go. Both had made the mistake of imagining that they could dictate terms to the British Government.

The longer-term effects of the Westland affair, however, were wholly adverse. The lesson Margaret took from it was that her colleagues were troublesome and her courtiers were loyal. From then on she began to distance herself even from those Cabinet colleagues who had been closest to her – certainly those who had minds of their own – and to retreat to the Number 10 bunker, where the leading figures were Charles Powell and Bernard Ingham.

I have already written of Ingham, against whom she would not hear a word said. On the occasions when I complained about his activities, she roundly denied that he could possibly have been guilty of what I was alleging, even though it was well known to the Press that that was exactly what he had been doing. Other Ministers met precisely the same response. Charles Powell, the Foreign Office man who had become her foreign affairs private secretary, and for most of the time the dominant force in her private office, was as polished as Ingham was blunt. Highly intelligent, he wrote the best and wittiest notes of meetings of anyone in Whitehall. His closeness to her was reinforced by the unlikely friendship Margaret developed with Powell's vivacious and somewhat less polished Italian wife, Carla. He never saw it as his role to question her prejudices, merely to refine the language in which they were expressed. And like Ingham, he stayed at Number 10 far too long – despite all Whitehall's efforts to persuade her to make a change and the Foreign Office's repeated attempts to lure him away with the promise of ever more attractive Ambassadorial posts.

With things drifting in this undesirable direction, I was both surprised and immensely heartened when, on the flight back from the May 1986 Tokyo Summit, Margaret took me aside and said she was considering forming an inner Cabinet: what did I think? It was, of course, what I had for some time felt to be the crucial missing ingredient in the Thatcher Government, and I told her I thought it an excellent idea. Soon afterwards she asked Geoffrey to join us, and we discussed the membership. It seemed to boil down to herself, Willie, Geoffrey, Norman Tebbit, John Wakeham and myself. But no sooner had she arrived back in London, than the plan changed. Perhaps she changed her mind unaided, perhaps she was persuaded against it by the courtiers, whose role would have diminished. There was no point in asking her, as she would inevitably have replied that it was her unaided decision.

The group was set up all right, but instead of being an inner Cabinet it was constituted as a group to oversee the contents of the manifesto for the forthcoming general election, known in the Press as the 'A team'. In particular, this meant going over the reports of the various policy groups, each headed by a Cabinet Minister, which Margaret had set up. I have already referred to this in an earlier chapter, in the context of the economic policy group which I myself chaired. My group produced a sensible and radical report, ranging far beyond the economy in the narrow sense, which reads quite well even today. But it was all pretty much of a waste of time, since it was essentially nothing more than a PR exercise, with the real contents of the manifesto being hammered out in the appropriate Cabinet committees. The only greater waste of time were the regular weekly meetings of the 'A team', whose job it was to discuss these reports. Indeed, Margaret did nothing to disguise her view that the only valuable part of these meetings was the first item, which consisted of Ingham reciting the main events of the coming week, and our discussing the best way to handle them politically. So much for the inner Cabinet.

Apart from the discussions in the various Cabinet committees of our new policies for education reform, housing reform and so on – for Margaret had mistakenly persuaded herself that we needed a really meaty manifesto for the 1987 general election, unlike the wrongly criticized bland offering of 1983 which had served us so well – the most important preparation for the election was occurring on the currency front.

A New Policy for the Pound

As I have already recorded, 1986 had been a terrible year for the pound. Essentially, what had happened was that, as the dollar fell from the stratospheric height it had reached in 1985, sterling fell with it, dropping very nearly 20 per cent against the Deutschmark. But sterling had not been grossly overvalued in 1985 as the dollar had been. And Margaret's veto of the interest rate rise I had sought in December 1986 made the prospect for the foreign exchange markets in the run-up to the 1987 general election even more worrying.

The slide continued into January 1987. But by then relief was at hand. For we had agreed to hold meetings of the G5 and G7 at the

A SURFEIT OF RESIGNATIONS

Louvre in Paris in February, with a view to ending the dollar's long decline and ushering in a period of stability. And just as the pound had been falling with the dollar, so there was a reasonable prospect that stabilizing the dollar would also stabilize the pound – just what was needed in the approach to a general election, when markets always tend to be nervous. Before going off to the Louvre, I discussed all this with Margaret, who was in full agreement with my objective. On my return I sent her a minute, explaining what had been agreed. After setting out the 'readiness to engage in concerted intervention' to defend the key parities specified in the Accord – the dollar/Deutschmark rate and the dollar/yen rate – I added:

> No limits of this kind were suggested for the pound or the Canadian dollar, but I indicated that I would expect sterling to fit into the general climate of stability, and should we need to intervene we would endeavour to avoid doing so in a way which was contrary to the spirit of the overall agreement . . . We can be well content with an outcome which does not involve us in onerous commitments, and which if successful could helpfully provide a more stable external background for us in the coming weeks.

I also attached to my minute – since, contrary to much subsequent insinuation, I was scrupulous in keeping Margaret fully informed about the Louvre – a transcript of my brief press conference, at which I said:

> The agreement applies to all currencies, though the principal focus, as with Plaza, is the dollar, and the key rates are the dollar/Deutschmark and dollar/Yen. So far as the UK is concerned, I have said many times that I do not want to see sterling fall further. By the same token I have no desire in current circumstances to see a substantial rise.

The assymmetry of the last two sentences was of course deliberate, as was appreciated at the time. And the Louvre duly did the trick, causing a sudden resurgence of confidence in sterling. I sat back while the pound rose from DM2.79 on the eve of the Accord of 22 February to DM2.94 on 10 March – an increase of more than 5 per cent in just over a fortnight – before trimming interest rates by half a point to 10½ per cent. The Budget a week later was well received in the financial markets, and I shaved interest rates by a further half point to 10 per cent, with the pound at DM2.95. It was clear, both to me and to the financial markets, that the Louvre framework had for the first time made a policy of exchange rate stability credible. So far as the pound was concerned, the markets started to infer that my intention was to keep it below DM3. At the markets meeting I held on 18 March, at which the reduction to 10 per cent was agreed, I told the senior Treasury and Bank officials present that this market view was useful, and that we should validate it, by being ready to intervene as and when necessary, making sure that the intervention was sterilized in order to neutralize any monetary consequences. This should be a simple matter, given the very low PSBR; while the intervention would be useful in enabling us to rebuild our reserves, which had been severely depleted in the previous year. Thus it was that the policy of shadowing the Deutschmark, at DM3 to the pound, was born.

A Chancellor's life, however, is never predictable. At the post-Budget meeting of NEDC on 1 April (an appropriate date for a Neddy meeting) I was asked what level of sterling exchange rate I would like to see, and I replied that I was perfectly content with the pattern of exchange rates we then had. Seeing some blank looks on the TUC side of the table, I added, unwisely seeking to be helpful, that the current levels were around $1.60 and DM2.90. At his subsequent routine press conference the Director-General, John Cassels, unhelpfully translated this into an announcement by me of an exchange rate target of $1.60 and DM2.90. I felt obliged to deny this, and explain what I had said at the NEDC meeting, at the press conference I happened to be holding the following day in the State Room of Number 11 prior to going to Washington for the Spring Meetings – although I rather enjoyed the implication that I had my own target for the exchange rate between the dollar and the Deutschmark.

What was much less predictable, however, was the strength of the upward pressure on the pound, as the confidence created by the Louvre was augmented by the markets' conviction that we were going to win the general election – an astonishing turn-round compared with only a year before. This meant intervention on a much larger scale than anything previously experienced, leading to a strengthening of the reserves that my predecessors would have given their eye teeth for, as well as two further half point cuts in interest rates on 28 April and 11 May, this last on the very day the general election was announced, taking rates down to 9 per cent. It was a helpful prelude to the election itself, but I saw it as essentially an interim measure. My hope was to replace the policy with full membership of the EMS, as soon as practicable once the election was out of the way.

CHAPTER 55

1987 – A PRE-ELECTION BUDGET

My Own High Noon · Two Pence Off . . .
. . . But Still Cautious · A Twentieth-Century Record
The 1 per cent Borrowing Rule · Pre-Election Reforms
'Yes, Of Course I Do' · Tailpiece: Stirling Devalued

My Own High Noon

MY 'UNASSAILABLE' PERIOD BEGAN in the late autumn or early winter of 1986. The reception of the Autumn Statement on 6 November had been badly received by the financial markets. As described in Chapter 25, John MacGregor's success in limiting public spending in a pre-election year was largely disguised by the shift to a more realistic projection and presentation. The disappearance of the misbegotten autumnal 'estimated fiscal adjustment' did not prevent gloomy reports from appearing of the likely fiscal outlook for the present and coming financial year.

But then quite suddenly the atmosphere changed. To be fair, the lead was taken by the City analysts – not always my favourite scribes – who suddenly concluded from the monthly Exchequer returns that the PSBR outlook was much better, rather than much worse, than the Treasury had thought. Recorded unemployment had at long last peaked in July (at some 3.1 million) and the subsequent fall provided helpful mood music. Those of the chattering classes in more contact with business and industry were beginning to accept that some things had changed for the better. It was the time when the left wing intelligentsia, in organs such as the briefly influential *Marxism Today*, began to talk seriously of 'Thatcherism' and how to learn some of its lessons.

Too much talk of 'economic management' has obscured the fact that the reputation of a modern Chancellor is to a substantial extent dependent on much the same factors (with many more noughts added) as those on which a Chancellor's reputation in Gladstone's time depended. If public spending is under control, revenue is coming in well and there is a margin to divide between tax reductions and judiciously targeted public spending measures, he will be riding high. If not, not. The big difference from Victorian times is that a good fiscal prospect is now a necessary, but not a sufficient, condition of perceived success. Other factors are needed, such as the absence of uncomfortable increases in interest rates, or too much recession gloom and doom. But spending and revenue are still the key. Nor will this ever be changed by sophisticated (and speculative) cyclical correction of the figures.

Two Pence Off . . .

I did my best to dampen expectations of a pre-election Budget bonanza. At the time of the Autumn Statement in November 1986, for example, I told the House that 'Clearly the same pound cannot be used twice. A pound which is used in higher public expenditure is not available for a reduction in taxation.' This was in the context of my pledge to stick to the 1987–88 Budget deficit indicated in the previous year's Red Book.

Since the commentators at that time were convinced that the PSBR was spiralling out of control, dampening expectations was not too difficult. But it was clear to me that the commentators had got it wrong. On 23 November, 1986, I scribbled on the back of my diary card eight items I hoped to include in the 1987 Budget. They were to cut the basic rate of income tax, simplify the higher rates, introduce tax relief for profit-related pay, allow cash accounting for VAT, raise the Inheritance Tax threshold, reform corporate and individual Capital Gains Tax (CGT) and levy either a credit card tax or a consumer credit tax. The date of the card shows that, unlike the case with the 1986 Budget, the 1987 decision to cut the basic rate was there from the start. Four of the other measures listed on the card were wholly or partially effected in the 1987 Budget. Two of those left undone or half done – simplifying the higher rates and reforming CGT for individuals, as well as businesses – were merely postponed until the immediate post-election Budget. The consumer credit tax was the only failed candidate, for reasons I have already explained.

Not surprisingly, the Chevening meeting of 10 and 11 January 1987, was one of the easiest and pleasantest of any during my time as Chancellor. The house was snow-bound, which added to the happy atmosphere – marred only by Norman Lamont's wife, Rosemary, slipping on the ice and breaking her wrist. We provisionally agreed to raise the income tax allowances and thresholds strictly in line with inflation and to cut the basic rate by 2p to 27p, which is exactly what happened.

1987 – A PRE-ELECTION BUDGET

The Treasury mandarins never sought to prevent me from cutting income tax, since they accepted that it was the Government's clearly stated policy; and, with Government borrowing coming down faster than taxes were, they could scarcely argue that I was being imprudent. None the less, there was no disguising the fact that they disliked it, and hoped that I would do it as little as was consistent with Government policy. The ethos of the official Treasury – and for all its quirks, I retain both respect and affection for the Department – is unremittingly austere. They disapprove of tax cuts almost as much as they dislike increases in public spending. They cannot imagine what the public have done to deserve tax cuts, which will inevitably be put to frivolous use. Interest rates were a different matter altogether.

Curiously enough, though for rather different reasons, Margaret's views on all this were closer to those of the official Treasury than mine were. She was positively soft on interest rates. Indeed, what with that and her opposition to the ERM, it always seemed to me that, so far as the battle against inflation was concerned, she willed the end without being prepared to will the means. Her softness on interest rates was primarily dictated by her overriding concern to promote home ownership and to look after those who were buying their homes with a mortgage. But she also saw her Government's finest hour, her equivalent of the Battle of Britain, to which in her mind she was always harking back, as having been the 1981 Budget, in which taxes were increased and, as a trade-off, interest rates (although admittedly not for long) reduced. This was the turning point, as she saw it, in the battle against inflation, and the event which finally confounded her critics.

As a result, throughout most of my time as Chancellor, I found myself favouring both lower taxes and higher interest rates than either the Treasury mandarins on the one hand or the Prime Minister on the other.

But to return to 1987. After Chevening, Margaret pressed me to raise the £30,000 mortgage interest relief ceiling – she had successfully induced Geoffrey to raise it from £25,000 in the pre-election Budget of 1983, and had wanted to go considerably higher – but when I made it clear that I was prepared to do so only as part of a package in which the relief was restricted to the basic rate, she quickly desisted.

It was as well that the 1987 Chevening was so straightforward, as I had to leave punctually, with Alex Allan, on the Sunday morning to take part in a hurriedly called EMS realignment meeting in Brussels. My own driver, Cindy Ash, was stuck in the snow somewhere, as was Robin Leigh-Pemberton; and I had to borrow Peter Brooke's car and driver for a hair-raising drive to the airport in thick snow along deserted roads, the police and motoring organizations having warned people not to venture out. But by then the outline of the Budget had been firmly decided.

. . . but Still Cautious

When I presented my Budget on 17 March 1987, it looked as if the PSBR for 1986–87 would be a little over £4 billion, some £3 billion less than originally forecast. According to the Treasury's projections, it was possible to reduce taxation by getting on for £3 billion and still bring the Budget deficit below the £4 billion the MTFS had indicated for 1987–88. The result was much better still: a deficit of little more than £3½ million in 1986–87 and – what I christened a Public Sector Debt *Repayment*, or PSDR – that is, a Budget surplus of almost £3½ billion in 1987–88.

There was nothing in the 1987 Red Book economic forecast to indicate inflation or overheating. It was thought by the forecasters at the time that GDP had risen by 2½ per cent in 1986 and would rise by 3 per cent in 1987, if anything falling back slightly in early 1988. These rates straddled the then estimated growth of productive capacity and were expected to be accompanied by a small current account deficit. Unfortunately, this was the period when both the statistics for the recent past and the projections of the future started to go seriously off the rails. The 1986 growth rate was subsequently revised upwards to 3.9 per cent, and growth in 1987 came to no less than 4.8 per cent – a very substantial difference in each case. Not surprisingly, a large part of the excess demand spilled over into imports, leading inevitably to a greatly enlarged current account deficit.

Despite the reassuring forecasts, I decided to err on the side of caution. First, there was my decision to aim for a very low deficit. Second, and more controversially, anxious about the inevitable rebound in recorded inflation as the effects of lower oil prices passed out of the year-on-year comparison, I decided to refrain from revalorizing the excise duties. Thus, for once, there was none of the usual x pence on a pint of beer or packet of cigarettes in the Budget speech. Instead, after telling the House about some very minor changes, I simply said: 'I have no further changes to propose this year in the rates of excise duty', and passed on. It was some time before anyone realized what had happened.

My failure to revalorize the excise duties shocked senior Treasury officials, who regarded it as 'tinkering', if not worse. They also argued that I would find it impossible to present, certainly so far as cigarettes and alcohol were concerned – a view shared by some of my ministerial colleagues. I saw no great difficulty. The man in the street was unlikely to protest about the failure to increase the price of cigarettes and drink. And by doing nothing at all (rather than, say, merely increasing the duties by less than inflation) there would be no need for any clauses in the Finance Bill, and thus no occasion for a parliamentary debate. The fundamental belief of the official Treasury is that the Chancellor should never knowingly give away revenue which might be difficult to recover. They have a point. But I was worried about the likely consequences of the depreciation of sterling in 1986. Not that I thought, of course, that leaving beer and tobacco duties unchanged was a barrier against the forces of inflation. But I was anxious to do what I could to prevent a rekindling of inflationary expectations, and to buy time while more fundamental measures – which I saw increasingly in terms of ERM membership – were put in place.

A Twentieth-Century Record

It was in 1987, too, that I decided to attempt, and just managed to achieve, the record for the shortest Budget speech this century. It lasted precisely fifty-nine minutes, speaking at my normal measured Budget pace. This was still some way short of the all-time record of forty-five minutes set by Disraeli in 1887, but that was beyond my ambition. In fact, the speech might well have been even shorter but for a minor mishap. As usual I arrived at my room at the House of Commons a short while before I had to enter the Chamber. I used the time to get an update of the position in the financial markets and to have a final quiet read through my speech, making one or two stylistic improvements as I did. On that occasion the improvements were to a particularly turgid technical tax passage, which nevertheless was of sufficient importance to oblige me to include it in the speech. Unfortunately, when it came to putting the edited pages back, I put them in the wrong order – the pages of my Budget speech were never strung together, since this makes reading them easier. When I reached the passage in question, I saw immediately that the text skipped a page, so I improvised from memory while looking for the missing page. My fear was that I might inadvertently have misrepresented the complicated point in question.

Fortunately, my memory of the missing page was pretty good, so my improvisation was very close to the actual text which I found pretty soon – although it seemed longer – and no harm was done. However, Peter Lilley, then my PPS, recognized that something had gone wrong, but mistakenly thought that the page was missing altogether. He became visibly agitated, rushing towards the officials' box to procure me a duplicate. It was this, unfortunately, that alerted the Opposition and gave the Labour wag, Willie Hamilton, a chance to make a spurious point of order which wasted a precious minute or two. The fault was, of course, mine for not having made a final check of the page number-ing before getting up to speak.

Although it was a nasty moment, I was able to keep cool and unflustered partly because I was accustomed to this sort of pressure. Indeed I used to drive my officials to despair by writing my speeches for parliamentary occasions at the very last moment. On one occasion, when I was Energy Secretary, I had to go to the House to open a debate when half my speech was still being typed out. I got up at the despatch box and started my speech with the notes for the first half only. As I had hoped, just before I had got to the end of them, the notes for the second half arrived, neatly typed (on cards, in large type, as I preferred), via the officials' box and my PPS. I was thus able to complete the speech, which was quite an important one, without any hiatus or problem.

The way in which I shortened my 1987 Budget speech to achieve the record was by abstaining from any substantial economic homily – since the tax measures could scarcely be omitted. This did not best please the highbrow commentators, who had to wait for the economic section of the Red Book – available only after the Chancellor has sat down, and a messenger journey away from those who do not come to the House – before finding the material to get their teeth into, when working against a tight deadline. No-one can say that I tried too hard to ingratiate myself with those on whom I depended to disseminate my message.

Nevertheless the brevity of the speech added to the impression of competence, and there was a good reception among the back-benchers, the markets, and even the Press. 'Lawson opts for Prudence in Last Budget Before Election' was the headline in *The Financial Times*, not always my greatest fan. (Not bad for a package which took two pence off the basic rate.)

'What a Lot You Got' was the typically crude verdict of the *Sun*, after due reflection on lower income tax, no increase in alcohol and tobacco duties and the prospect of a cut in the mortgage rate. I was later to discover the unpleasantness of having that sort of vulgarity directed against myself. But at that time I was ignorant of the traumas that lay ahead. For although the 1987 Budget was certainly not my most important one, it was my happiest. The March 1984 triumph achieved against the odds was inevitably a more tense affair, and what should have been my genuine triumph in 1988 was marred by the row with Margaret over sterling.

Our back-benchers thought the 1987 Budget a good election Budget, without being blatantly so. As within the preceding Autumn Statement, the politics were mainly a matter of presentation. Despite the two pence off the basic rate, there was no pre-election giveaway. The overall tax burden (taxes plus National Insurance contributions as a percentage of GDP) was unchanged in 1987–88, and, thanks to firm control of public spending, the Budget deficit (even discounting privatization proceeds) was all but eliminated.

1987 – A PRE-ELECTION BUDGET

The 1 per cent Borrowing Rule

There was one new piece of macroeconomic doctrine I introduced in the 1987 Budget on which the pundits could bite. Since its launch in 1980, the Medium Term Financial Strategy had, as one of its key features, a steady decline in the PSBR as a proportion of GDP. No thought had been given, however, as to how the process should go. In March 1987, the Treasury forecasters envisaged a PSBR for 1987-88 amounting to 1 per cent of GDP, as in the previous financial year. In the Budget speech I described this as 'an appropriate destination' for the MTFS path.

The 1 per cent formula derived from the fact that, when the MTFS was launched in 1980, the net public sector debt was approaching 50 per cent of GDP. Even on the most conservative basis, the British economy's sustainable rate of growth must be in excess of 2 per cent. Thus an annual deficit of 1 per cent of GDP would ensure that there was no increase in the public debt ratio even in a world of zero inflation. (See Chapter 7.) As it proved only a staging post to the doctrine of the balanced budget ('over the cycle as a whole') which I put forward in 1988, it is not worth dwelling further on the many complications involved in the 1 per cent rule. My attitude in 1987 was that I would have welcomed a balanced budget, not least on presentational grounds, but did not believe it worth torturing myself or the economy to achieve it, as stability could in theory be secured with a modest deficit.

Pre-Election Reforms

The Government's desire to encourage the growth of personal pensions had been one of the most important outcomes of Norman Fowler's 1985 review of social security, and I decided to bring the starting date for this forward to January 1988. The 1987 Finance Bill thus included legislation to put personal pensions on the same attractive tax footing as occupational schemes and retirement annuities. I also agreed with Norman to allow members of occupational pension schemes to make additional voluntary contributions (AVCs) with full tax relief, up to the pension limit set by the Inland Revenue, to a separate personal pension plan of their own choice, instead of being restricted to their employer's scheme. Employers were not best pleased, since it meant they had to reveal to their employees precisely what they stood to receive from their existing occupational pension. Yet it was clearly essential to ensure there was no tax advantage in choosing an occupational scheme, or few would ever take out a personal pension. Portable pensions, which people could take from job to job, were important both to increase labour mobility and to widen the ownership of capital.

690

The taxation of capital gains was more difficult. I had long felt it was highly undesirable that Capital Gains Tax should have given rise to a substantial tax avoidance industry dedicated solely to converting income into capital gain, which were taxed very much more lightly. I had noted with approval the fact that the American tax reform package introduced by President Reagan had, in the jargon, 'assimilated' (that is, equated) income tax and capital gains taxes. Accordingly, I decided in the 1987 Budget to tax corporate capital gains at the relevant corporation tax rate, which at that time meant 35 per cent for larger companies and 27 per cent for smaller companies (the definition of which was in terms of profits), instead of at the long-standing Capital Gains Tax rate of 30 per cent. It was an astonishing stroke of luck that no-one guessed that I envisaged this merely as the first stage in a two stage process, with the principle being extended to individuals in a subsequent Budget. It thus came as a complete surprise in the 1988 Budget when I brought Capital Gains Tax for individuals into line with the basic and higher rates of income tax.

I also introduced a worthwhile measure of assistance to small businesses, for whom cash flow is so important. It was something I would have done years before, had it been brought to my attention earlier. As it was, it was something that emerged from my pre-Budget drinks with back-benchers. Under the rules of VAT, the date on which businesses had to pay VAT to the Customs and Excise was determined by the date of the invoice they issued. Plagued by late payment of their bills, often on the part of very much larger companies, this meant that they often had to pay VAT to the Customs and Excise before they had received the money from their business customers. To avoid this, I introduced cash accounting for VAT for small businesses – meaning that they would not have to pay the VAT until they had actually received the cash. However this required a derogation from the relevant European Community Directive, to which the French tax authorities churlishly objected when in June 1987 they discovered what I had done. Fortunately I was able, through the good offices of my friend Edouard Balladur, the then French Finance Minister, to get their objections overruled.

Another change was to exempt from Inheritance Tax not only charitable gifts, but gifts for what are officially described as 'political and public' purposes. As far back as 1976, the Conservative Opposition had persuaded the Labour Government, behind the scenes, to reinstate the traditional parity of treatment for charitable and political giving, which they had done away with when they replaced Estate Duty by the much more savage Capital Transfer Tax. But when Geoffrey Howe exempted charitable gifts entirely from Capital Transfer Tax, he separated the two again. I decided to bring them together in the 1987 Budget in response to a representation from Keith Joseph, who had been going round his wealthy friends and acquaintances urging them to remember the Conservative Party in their wills. Happily the change went almost unnoticed.

'Yes; Of Course I Do'

Naturally, I was beginning to think of my future after the election. I did not believe in going 'on and on'; but the likelihood of a 1987 election meant that some of my most cherished tax changes had to be postponed. So quite apart from any hopes I may have harboured on the EMS front, I still wanted to present at least one more radical Budget.

I therefore took the opportunity of my usual informal pre-Budget informal discussion, this time unusually held in the Long Gallery at Chequers, on 1 February, to ask Margaret if she wanted me to continue as Chancellor after the election. Her reply was unequivocal: 'Yes; of course I do.'

Tailpiece: Stirling Devalued

In preparing my tax reforming Budgets I had not been greatly assisted by the existence of a massive Treasury-financed academic study of the effects of tax on personal incentives by Professor C. V. (Chuck) Brown of Stirling. I knew nothing of its existence until I saw a report in the *Guardian* in December 1986 alleging that the Brown study had demonstrated that reductions in marginal tax rates had no beneficial effect on incentives. I was furious that anything so politically sensitive had been concealed from me. I immediately demanded to see it and to be given an explanation. It emerged that it had been commissioned many years previously, apparently at the suggestion of Douglas Wass, by Ian Byatt, the Treasury's Deputy Chief Economic Adviser, and authorized by Geoffrey Howe when his mind was on other things. Since then it had been trundling on, year after year, at a total cost of some £½ million – an expenditure which had got completely out of control and which represented an inordinate share of the Treasury's modest economic research budget. The return for all this expenditure was a particularly unimpressive piece of work, which even then had not been finally completed.

It did indeed claim to show that tax reductions had no positive effect on incentives (except among part-time workers). The basis on which it concluded this was that the vast majority of full-time workers had no opportunity to earn more by working longer hours. Since the bulk of the fieldwork had been done during the recession of 1981, when little overtime was indeed available, this 'finding' was hardly surprising, and seemed to me to prove nothing. In any event the case for low taxation is first and foremost a moral one. It is the case for enlarging individual freedom of choice and keeping to a necessary minimum the area where decisions are taken for people by the State. It is within that context that it makes obvious economic sense to have a system which does least damage to incentives and is least likely to drive the enterprising and the talented overseas.

I read my officials the Riot Act over this unnecessary episode. I insisted, first, that there should be no more funding of this particular project beyond any sums to which the Treasury was contractually committed; second, that if the findings were to be published, they would have to be published not by the Treasury but by Professor Brown on his own responsibility (to avoid any charge of suppression I told Parliament I would place a copy in the House of Commons library); third, that there must in future be much closer Ministerial control of the Treasury's Economic Research budget, a responsibility I delegated to the then Economic Secretary, Peter Lilley, who was particularly well-qualified for the task; and fourth, that nothing commissioned by the Treasury must ever again be released to the Press before the Chancellor has been informed of it. I also made it clear that I was in any case highly sceptical of the Treasury funding *any* studies. There is a vast amount of worthwhile economic research undertaken by academic institutes around the world as it is. Treasury economists would be better employed on bringing to the Chancellor's attention, in summary form, the best of that, rather than playing the patron at the taxpayer's expense.

CHAPTER 56

AN ELECTION WON ON
THE ECONOMY

*The Date Chooses Itself · The Campaigns Compared
Costing Labour's Pledges · Divided Counsels
Of Lice and Fleas · The Effort to Keep Me Out
My Freelance Election Campaign · The Tide Rolls on*

The Date Chooses Itself

BY 1987 IT WAS clear that an election was imminent. Not only would we soon be in the final year of the Parliament, but having won in May 1979 and June 1983, Margaret was convinced that May and June were her lucky months. There was thus a strong presumption that the election would come in June 1987, and the Budget had provided the ideal launching pad. All that remained was to take the political temperature by analysing the results of the local elections held throughout England and Wales on 7 May. Margaret asked me to come to Chequers on the morning of Sunday, 10 May, by which time all the analysis would have been done and we could choose the election date.

I duly arrived at Chequers that sunny Sunday morning. In addition to me, she had invited Willie, Geoffrey, Norman Tebbit (then Party Chairman) and David Young, who had been allotted a somewhat ill-defined role in Central Office once the starting pistol had been fired. What it really amounted to was that Margaret was becoming uneasy about Norman's growing popularity, and suspected that he was using Central Office to build up for himself a rival power base. David's job, essentially, was to keep an eye on him: an unhappy augury. Norman presented his analysis, which showed that we ought to win a June General Election quite comfortably. We then fell to discussing dates, and had very soon settled on 11 June. It was the easiest choice of election date in which I have ever been involved. It was announced the following day.

The only complication, so far as I was concerned, was that there would not be time to get the Finance Bill through in its entirety before Parliament was dissolved. But this merely involved truncating it, and reintroducing the more complex and less important measures in a new Finance Bill at the start of the new Parliament. There was never any risk of not being able to enact the income tax cut before the dissolution. This brought with it a double benefit. First, under the PAYE system, the new and lower rate of tax would start to show up in people's pay packets by the middle of May, roughly four weeks before polling day. Second, there was obvious propaganda to be made from the fact that both Labour and the Alliance (as the Liberals and Social Democrats called themselves) had voted *against* the two-pence cut in the basic rate.

The Campaigns Compared

The Labour campaign undeniably began well, with the smoothly professional filmed 'profile' of Neil Kinnock, by Hugh Hudson of 'Chariots of Fire' fame, showing him in various photogenic settings, notably walking hand-in-hand with his wife, Glenys, on the cliff tops with the birds circling above them. It was also the only election broadcast I can recall which did not close with the Party's name. Instead of 'Labour' the film ended with the screen filled with the one word 'KINNOCK'. Sentimental and corny though it was, it made the Conservative TV broadcasts look old-fashioned and amateurish by comparison, and was said to have raised Kinnock's personal opinion poll rating by no less than 19 percentage points overnight – although if it did it was too ephemeral to affect voting intentions.

The Labour campaign did not really start to unravel until 25 May, when Kinnock told David Frost in a television interview that if the Russians invaded a non-nuclear Britain they would be resisted by guerilla bands who had taken to the hills. The Conservative poster depicting a soldier with his hands up in the surrender position above the simple slogan 'Labour's Policy on Arms' was the most memorable image of a less than vintage campaign for political posters. The Alliance campaign, initially regarded as a great threat, never really took off, largely because neither David Owen nor David Steel could trust each other, let alone agree on a single leader.

It was just as well that we entered the election comfortably ahead, as demonstrated by the local election results, since the Conservative Party campaign was in every way the most incompetent in which I have ever participated – and my participation dates back to 1964. The manifesto, crammed with pledges which caused considerable difficulty in the early days of the campaign, was launched at Central Office on 19 May. Margaret highlighted the three 'flagships', as she called them, of the poll tax, education reform and housing. This clearly contravened Lawson's law of election campaigning, which I first enunciated in an article in *The Financial Times* in April 1965, reflecting on the 1964 General Election. In it I wrote:

> Do you try and win votes over on the 'important' issues (which means fighting the battle on basically unfavourable ground) or do you forget about winning votes over and concentrate on trying to convince them that the 'unimportant' issues (on which they are already on your side) are really important? For a variety of reasons the Tory strategists eventually plumped for the second course. I believe they were right to do so.

The words 'important' and 'unimportant' referred to the opinion polls of the time, which asked voters to list issues in order of importance. Since people tend to interpret this as a question about the issues that are worrying them most at the time, it is not surprising that the 'important' issues are usually those on which the standing of the Government of the day is weakest. But the main point of Lawson's Law is that the key strategy in fighting a General Election is to determine the territory on which the main battle is fought. The most favourable territory for the Tories in 1987, as in most years, was defence, central government taxation, and the economy in general.

As for the three 'flagships' themselves, the only saving grace of the Poll Tax was that, as it had not yet been introduced, the full extent of its horrors was not widely appreciated. Nevertheless, we were extremely lucky that Labour unaccountably ignored this juicy target altogether. As for the education and housing reforms, these had been cobbled together so hastily to get them ready in time for the manifesto that a number of details had still not been finally worked out; and even where they had been they were not wholly familiar to those fighting the campaign, not least to Margaret herself. On 22 May, after the formal press conference was over, she made remarks which were taken to imply the introduction of fees in state schools. Norman Tebbit felt obliged to issue a specific denial that evening. She also spoke about the reintroduction of selective entry, implying a revival of the grammar schools, which Kenneth Baker felt obliged to deny categorically. These embarrassing contradictions reflected not only the failure of Ministers to agree answers to difficult but obvious questions about the new policies, but also how ill-thought out various aspects of the policies still were at that stage.

Costing Labour's Pledges

A major contribution made by my Treasury team to the campaign was the careful costing of the policies proposed by the Labour Party. Labour was still lumbered with all of its historical commitments to reverse pretty well every spending cut and multiply every benefit. As far back as the summer of 1986 I had asked John MacGregor, the Chief Secretary, to supervise an exercise in which Treasury officials would cost specific policy proposals put to them by the Special Advisers, who had taken these proposals from commitments made by Labour front-bench spokesmen, resolutions passed at Labour Party Conferences and the proposals made in various *ad hoc* policy papers produced by the Labour Party. The sums were then added up, and it was calculated what they would mean in terms of the extra taxation needed to finance them.

There was some criticism at the time that it was improper to use officials for party political purposes, but the Cabinet Secretary ruled that it was entirely proper for Ministers to ask officials to cost alternative policy proposals, as indeed the previous Labour Government had done. The 'costings' rose as new Labour commitments were made. After Labour's social security spokesman Michael Meacher, added a raft of new and uprated benefits at the 1986 Labour Party Conference, they reached a grand total of £34 billion, which implied a basic rate of income tax of no less than 56p in the pound or VAT at almost 50 per cent, or some combination of the two. In reality it was of course more likely that had Labour been elected, the pledges would have been dishonoured; but that was not the most impressive of defences. Right from the start, the Shadow Chancellor, Roy Hattersley, had considerable difficulty in sustaining his claim that only those earning more than £25,000 a year, or the top 5 per cent of the population, would pay more tax under a Labour Government.

To my astonishment, I discovered that those responsible for organizing the campaign had made no plans to use this meticulous work. Fortunately I had my own personal campaign team, in the shape of the three Treasury special advisers. I based Peter Cropper in Central Office to keep an eye on what was happening there and to keep me informed; Andrew Tyrie remained at the Treasury to be my link man there; while Alistair Ross-Goobey travelled with me wherever I went. Using Peter as an intermediary, I managed to organize an unscheduled Central Office press conference on the morning of Saturday, 23 May, at which, with whatever visual aids Peter could get them to rustle up at short notice, I introduced the John MacGregor costings of Labour's spending plans. Saturday morning is not a very good time (that was why no press conference had been scheduled for then); but at least it helped to get the issue into orbit.

Divided Counsels

It was, in fact, extremely difficult to discover just who was running the campaign. As Party Chairman, it should have been Norman Tebbit; but as I have indicated, even though Norman had been one of her closest colleagues, both personally and politically, Margaret had come to distrust him and fear him as a future rival for her job. She was particularly worried that he would take the credit for an election victory. Hence her decision to put David Young in Central Office, too; reporting directly to her. The effect was predictable. Central Office, throughout the campaign, was divided into two warring factions, who spent far more energy trying to get the better of each other than they did in fighting the enemy.

As if the idea of divided leadership were not bizarre enough, the choice of David Young as Norman's *alter ego* was unbelievably perverse. David had many excellent qualities. He was a genuine believer in the enterprise culture, had useful business experience, and had a particularly fertile mind, which was always coming up with ingenious ideas and schemes, all of which, given his business background, were practical, and many of them had merit. But David was a businessman who had gone straight into the House of Lords and the Cabinet via a back-room advisory role and the chairmanship of a quango, without ever having stood for political office or even been a local Party worker. As a result, he knew less about election campaigning and had his finger further from the public pulse than any other Cabinet colleague.

He was, however, a great believer in the power of advertising. As Employment Secretary he had spent copious amounts of public money on promoting the advertising campaign 'Action for Jobs'. He seemed to believe that it was the choice of advertising agency which would determine the outcome of the election. Margaret, who was always in-clined to think that if a policy was unpopular it could only be because of poor presentation, had a weakness for this line of thinking. Norman had retained the Party's usual advertising agents, Saatchi & Saatchi, for the 1987 election. Margaret, however, had turned against them when Norman presented the results of opinion research they had done which suggested that the public found her 'bossy' and 'fussy'. He had presented it, too, at the very time when her own relations with him were at their lowest ebb, and it certainly did nothing to improve them.

David decided that the solution was to bring in a new advertising agency (Tim Bell, with a walk-on part for Young and Rubicam), initially behind Norman's back. This introduced yet further tension at Central

Office, which came to a head on the so-called 'wobbly Thursday', a week before polling day, when a rogue and clearly faulty adverse opinion poll caused David Young to panic completely, a panic which he succeeded in communicating to Margaret Thatcher. It was in fact abundantly clear, to anyone who had any sense of what was actually happening on the ground, that there had been no change in electoral intentions at all. However, according to David's own account, he got Norman 'by the shoulders and said "Norman listen to me, we're about to lose this f--- election! You're going to go, I'm going to go, the whole thing is going to go. The entire election depends on her doing fine performances for the next five days – she has to be happy, we have got to do this." ' By 'this' he meant the campaign that the second agency had come up with.

Of Lice and Fleas

So far as the battle of the advertising agencies, which dominated David's account of the 1987 election, is concerned, I am inescapably reminded of Dr Johnson's remark: 'Sir; there is no settling the point of precedency between a louse and a flea'. Politics and the media always tend to exaggerate the importance of election campaigns. In most elections – and 1987 was one of them – the overwhelming majority of people have already made up their minds how they are going to vote before the campaign starts; and then wait more or less patiently for polling day to arrive. But in so far as the campaign does matter – and obviously the closer the election the more important it can be – the least important aspect of the campaign is that of paid advertising. The relative contributions to the ultimate victory of the two agencies concerned were, in Johnsonian terms, those of a louse and a flea.

I was unusually well placed to judge the mood of the people during the 1987 campaign since I was asked to spend most of my time making speeches and visiting businesses in an inordinately large number of marginal constituencies up and down the country. Between these engagements I was able to fulfil my commitments to deliver both the main address to the CBI annual dinner at the start of the campaign and the first Arnold Goodman charity lecture in the middle of the campaign.

I cannot recall a campaign in which both public and business opinion was better disposed to the Government of the day than it was in 1987. I was particularly struck by the enthusiastic welcome I received from those youngsters, particularly in the Midlands and the North of England, who had started their own businesses. Irrespective of their backgrounds, they all instinctively identified with the Conservative Party. Much of that enthusiasm and support will inevitably have been destroyed by the recession of the early 1990s; but it would be a tragedy if none of it has survived.

AN ELECTION WON ON THE ECONOMY

I always asked the Party workers wherever I went what their canvass returns were showing. They had been greatly impressed and therefore worried by the Hugh Hudson film on Kinnock, and were relieved to find on the doorsteps that it had not led to any loss of Conservative support. If anything, while no doubt reinforcing existing Labour support, it seemed it had also fortified existing Conservative support. As for wobbly Thursday, they were totally mystified. There had been no wobble in *their* constituency.

The Effort to Keep Me Out

The time I was able to spend touring marginal constituencies was in large part a consequence of the decision made at the start of the campaign to keep me out of sight, so far as the wider public was concerned, in case I frightened the voters or stole the limelight – the first being the ostensible reason given. It was, from the outset, a particularly foolish decision. This judgement says nothing about me personally. It is simply that the economy is always a major issue in any election, and it is invariably in the Tories' interests that it should be a major issue. Given all the exposure he receives during the course of the year, year in year out, the public comes to know the Chancellor as the man who talks about and takes decisions about the economy. Thus to try and hide the Chancellor – any Chancellor – during an election campaign is a folly that can only harm the Government.

Nevertheless, that was the decision originally taken in 1987. In particular, those in charge of the campaign sought to keep me off television, despite the constant requests by the media to have me appear. Margaret had originally asked John Wakeham, who had been Chief Whip since 1983, to be in charge of deciding which Ministers did which broadcasts. In 1987, for the first time, the long-standing radio phone-in programme, *Election Call*, compèred by Robin Day, was televised, and the novelty attracted a great deal of attention.

Somewhat rashly, John decided to do the first of these himself. As Chief Whip, the arch behind-the-scenes operator, John had had little opportunity to gain television experience. As a result, his broadcast was a disaster: his eyes wandered all over the place and he looked unbelievably shifty. Margaret was furious, and John's influence on the television side of the campaign was never the same again. The man who moved swiftly to fill the vacuum was, inevitably, the ambitious David Young, who judged that as Employment Secretary he should be the Party's principal economic spokesman on television. When *Weekend World* told Central Office that they wanted me to represent the Government in an hour-long analysis of unemployment they planned to run, I was not informed of the request; and Central Office replied that David would do the programme instead of me – which he did. When journalists asked Central Office what they had against me, one of the *apparatchiks* was reported as having replied 'He's hardly in the Kenneth Baker class'.

Margaret, by this time, was not greatly interested in who did what, feeling that all that really mattered was her own conduct and performance. The media's predilection for presidentializing general election campaigns, and focusing to such an inordinate extent on the Party Leaders, reinforced her own growing view of the political process. In the event, I made only two major television appearances throughout the campaign. The first was on *Election Call*, towards the beginning of the campaign, and the second was the third and last *Question Time* programme, also with Robin Day in the chair, in the final week of the campaign. My *Election Call* was thought to have gone well. According to Alan Watkins in the *Observer* the following Sunday:

> Though Mr. Lawson made perhaps the most telling and certainly the most pleasant ministerial contribution so far on Robin Day's 'Election Call', this was, in a sense, by inadvertence. The Party managers considered it prudent to slip in the Chancellor, who is thought by them to be overweight (which he may be) and unsympathetic (which he is not) early in the campaign, when no-one was looking.

And Allan Massie, writing about the same programme in *The Times*, judged that:

> He [Lawson] looks less now like a young man who has been doing himself undeservedly well, and he has acquired a quite becoming authority. There is also a certain diffidence, a polite hesitation that serves to mitigate the impression he gives of thinking rather better of Nigel Lawson than anyone else. He turned what might have been a dodgy occasion into a personal and Party success because he conveyed the impression that he was master of his brief and really believed in his policy . . . His Party should come to see Mr Lawson as an electoral asset, not a liability.

The *Question Time* programme was conveniently held in Leicester, not far from my Blaby constituency, where I was pitted against Roy Hattersley, Labour's Deputy Leader, and Roy Jenkins for the Alliance. This went equally well, although by that time the commentators were less surprised. I was lucky to be able to secure the last word – always the most important word to have in any television debate, and I used it to link the themes of a strong defence and a strong economy.

David Young's perspective, however, according to his memoirs, was rather different:

> I was appalled at what I saw – there seemed to be an enormous amount of Nigel Lawson . . . The Prime Minister . . . said 'Nigel's got to get his hair cut – will you tell him?' 'No, Prime Minister,' I said, 'you've got to tell him.'

In the event it was Thérèse who did, unprompted.

My Freelance Election Campaign

My principal frustration about the campaign, however, was not my lack of television exposure, absurd though that was in an election in which the economy was (as it frequently is) the most important factor. It was rather the persistent failure of the official campaign to highlight the implications of Labour's tax and spending plans, where I was convinced they were highly vulnerable. After making no headway with several telephone calls to Norman Tebbit, and after Peter Cropper had reported to me that he had been unable to get Central Office interested at his level, either, I decided to forget about the official Party election campaign and run a separate one of my own in parallel. This meant using to the full my three special advisers, who were all first class; with Andrew Tyrie in particular playing a key role.

Up to the point at which I intervened, at the beginning of June, Labour spokesmen had been instructed to stick to the line that no-one who earned less than £25,000, or some £500 a week, would be worse off. This worked well enough to start with. I then fired my first salvo, with a couple of press releases from a tour I had been making of marginal constituencies in Yorkshire on 1 June. This was essentially to prepare the ground for the Central Office press conference which Norman Tebbit had at last decided I should give on the economy, and Labour's threat to it the following day, 2 June, only nine days before polling day. I focused hard on the tax issue. The Press at long last began to sense that there might be a good story in all this.

Two days later, on 4 June, Labour's position started to crumble, when friendly journalists who had been well-briefed by Andrew Tyrie forced Neil Kinnock to admit that Labour's plans to abolish the ceiling on employees' National Insurance contributions meant people earning between £15,000 and £17,000 a year would have to pay a 'few extra pence a week'. He further conceded that the abolition of the married man's tax allowance and its replacement by higher child benefit (another Labour policy which I had been vainly trying to get Norman Tebbit to exploit) would hurt married couples without children earning as little as £10,000 a year. Labour had also admitted – they could scarcely deny it, having voted against it in the House of Commons – that they would, if elected, reverse the two-pence reduction in the basic rate of income tax in my 1987 Budget.

It was the exposure of Labour's plan to abolish the married man's tax allowance which really destroyed their credibility. The abolition of the upper earnings limit for employees' National Insurance Contributions was at least something to which they were openly committed. But when it came to their earlier proposal to abolish the married man's tax allowance in order to finance an increase in child benefit, they had decided to put in their manifesto only the increase in child benefit. Very carelessly, however, they had stated that the increase in child benefit would be not £7 a week, or £8 a week, but the extraordinarily precise figure of £7.36 a week – which happened to be the value of the married man's tax allowance in 1986–87 prices. Apparently Roy Hattersley and John Smith had removed the abolition of the married man's tax allowance from the Labour manifesto at the last minute, but had forgotten to amend the child benefit pledge, which was in a different chapter. It was this tell-tale figure which gave the game away, and obliged them to admit – under cross-examination – that they were proposing what amounted to a substantial tax increase for millions of married couples without children under eighteen. This came as a revelation to the Press.

The meticulously reliable Peter Cropper then made a series of calculations illustrating the total increases in taxation and National Insurance contributions that would be payable by married couples in the event of a Labour victory, and compared the outcome with the Government's plans. The extra taxes ranged from £6.80 a week for a husband earning £70 a week to £29.75 for one earning £400 a week. On 5 June, the *Daily Mail*, carefully briefed by Andrew Tyrie, and supplied with a suitable quote from me, led with 'Labour's Lies over Taxation'. A similar Tyrie/Lawson operation caused the *Daily Express* to run a story headed 'Exposed: Labour's Tax Fiasco' the following day, 6 June. At last those responsible for organizing the Conservative campaign realized that we had Labour on the run; and that same morning I gave yet another unscheduled Saturday press conference at Central Office, on the tax cost of voting Labour, and made public the full figures. As events had turned out, I was able to mount an attack on two fronts: Labour's would-be tax increases themselves, and their deceit in attempting to hide the fact. The broadcasters then took up the story for the first time.

Labour's response to this barrage was gratifyingly muddled. On the day of the press conference, Neil Kinnock reiterated his admission that 'some people' earning less than £25,000 a year would be worse off under a Labour Government, but Bryan Gould and Roy Hattersley stuck to the original line. It was easy for me to accuse Roy Hattersley of, as I delicately put it, 'lying through his teeth' – a charge he was unable to rebut when we appeared on the *Today* programme together. The Labour campaign was in shreds. One account described those three days as the turning point in Labour's fortunes.

> In the course of that Saturday before polling, Labour lost its initiative. It was not merely a matter of fading away: by the evening Labour's campaign had broken into several pieces, cracked apart by a Tory attack on Labour's precarious tax policy . . . The newspapers were telling Labour's target voters that they would be clobbered for tax if they succeeded in earning what seemed a relatively modest income. That would have been damaging enough. But it was immediately compounded by muddle among Labour's senior politicians over what the Party policy actually meant.

Peter Mandelson, the highly professional Labour Party official who masterminded the 1987 campaign, has himself admitted that his plans were disrupted only twice during the campaign. The first was Neil Kinnock's defence gaffe; the second was the exposure of the incoherence of the Party's tax and spending plans in the final week. The subsequent 1992 campaign, which included John Smith's maladroit 'Shadow Budget', showed that Labour had still not fully learned the lesson.

The exposure of what I called Labour's 'deliberate deceit' had finally placed the economy and taxation at the centre of the campaign. Norman Tebbit later acknowledged that:

> It was not easy to get the economic issue going . . . Nigel Lawson, by sheer persistence and the strength of his personality, finally focused attention on the economy just as our heavy advertising campaign did the same. Labour were in a mess, as Hattersley's figures clearly did not add up and in the last few days – unlike 1983, when we lost several points – our support remained rock solid.

The Tide Rolls on

Even before the polling stations closed on the evening of Thursday, 11 June, it was clear that the Government had won an overwhelming victory, despite the BBC making themselves look foolish by giving great publicity to a final poll they had done which purported to show the two Parties neck and neck. The eventual Conservative majority over all the other Parties was 101, with my own share of the traditional three-cornered poll at Blaby going over 60 per cent for the first time ever.

It was a remarkable achievement for the Government to have won a third term by such a handsome margin, and marked the intellectual ascendancy of the market economy even more surely than the Labour landslide of 1945 had marked that of socialism. 'Never underestimate the tide of ideas,' I had told the Scottish Party Conference at the start of the campaign:

No British Government has ever been defeated unless and until the tide of ideas has turned against it. And so far from turning, the tide of ideas that swept us into office in 1979 is flowing even more strongly today. And that, after all, is what will sweep us back into office on the 11th of June.

It was a theme to which I was to return, at greater length, in a major speech at the Carlton Club in January 1988, published by the Centre for Policy Studies the following month as a pamphlet entitled *The New Britain: the tide of ideas from Attlee to Thatcher.*

By April 1992 the tide had still not turned.

CHAPTER 57

———

POLITICS AFTER THE POLLS

Not for Two Terms · Election Aftermath
Cabinet-making · How Neddy Escaped the Axe

Not for Two Terms

IT WAS NEVER MY desire to stay for two full Parliaments as Chancellor. Nor, for a variety of reasons, has any Chancellor ever done so. A Minister is not a senior Civil Servant. He is there to achieve specific political objectives, and while he is there he also provides personal impetus and political leadership to the work of the Department more generally. Once he has achieved his objectives to the extent he is able to do, he should depart and move on to fresh challenges. Moreover, of all the ministerial posts, the job of Chancellor, certainly approached in the way I approached it, is exceptionally demanding, and takes a heavy toll of personal and family life.

Parallel considerations apply to the Premiership. The Americans, after their experience with Roosevelt's last years, wisely limited their President's tenure to two terms. Either Prime Ministerial exhaustion or the other diseases which come with staying too long at Number 10 can be concealed from the incumbent by the intoxicating effects of power and publicity, making a strong case for some conventional limit on his or her period of office. At any rate, I pointed out publicly on a number of occasions that it was not normal for a Chancellor to stay for two full terms. This – together with my public disavowal of prime ministerial ambitions – may have been politically unwise. But my instinctive

706

secretiveness has always been seasoned by a tendency to blurt out the truth when it is not conventional to do so.

I had no fixed date in mind for leaving Number 11. There were two things I wanted to achieve in my second Parliament as Chancellor – income tax reform and full EMS membership. Given that, I saw myself laying down the burden amicably, at the time of a reshuffle. This meant that the earliest date would be the summer of 1988, after the tax reforming 1988 Budget was on the statute book – and the very latest the summer of 1990. If I stayed on any further I would inevitably be stuck for the rest of the Parliament. Leaving it until the summer of 1990 would have made me the longest serving Chancellor this century. But although this had some attraction, it was not a major consideration, and an earlier date – such as the summer of 1989 – was more the sort of thing I had in mind when I was reappointed in 1987.

In retrospect I should have gone immediately after the 1988 Budget, as Thérèse urged me at the time; but I was sufficiently conventional to leave it until the summer of that year, that being the customary season for reshuffles, by which time the current account deficit had soared, overheating had become apparent, and I felt I could not honourably leave my post until I had dealt with it.

Where would I like to have moved if things had gone according to plan? The only other senior offices of State, apart from the Exchequer, are those of Foreign Secretary and – more arguably – Home Secretary. The latter never held any appeal for me. Foreign Secretary, although nothing like as important a job as Chancellor in today's world, had compensating attractions which did appeal to me. But even if there had been a vacancy, I would probably have been too unconventional an appointment for even Margaret to make. It was perhaps just as well that the job of Chancellor kept me too occupied to spend time brooding on all this.

Election Aftermath

Meanwhile, it was back to business as usual. I knew that my first task after the election would be to equip myself with a new Chief Secretary. For it was always clear that John MacGregor, who was the best Chief Secretary I had, would be given a Department of his own after the election. Fortunately, however, I was in a particularly strong position to influence the choice of the new Chief Secretary, since the informal meeting Margaret held on 12 June, the day after the 1987 election, to discuss the membership of the new Cabinet, initially consisted solely of her, Willie Whitelaw and myself. After some hours we were joined by Norman Tebbit, and a little later by John Wakeham.

The fact that Margaret had asked me to be part of her Cabinet-making troika was to some extent simply a reflection of the fact that I was a senior Cabinet Minister whom she had already decided, as indeed she had told me before the election, to keep where I was. So I had no personal interest in this particular game of musical chairs. But Geoffrey Howe, whom Margaret had also decided to leave where he was, was an even more senior Cabinet Minister than I was, and she had no intention of inviting him to join us – a clear indication of her increasingly strained relations with him.

In other words, my presence also underlined the fact that, at that time, despite our differences over the ERM and the Poll Tax, and our tiffs over interest rates, Margaret and I remained politically very close, as we had been since the Government was first formed in 1979. But almost from that moment on, to my intense regret, our relationship started to deteriorate.

The trouble began when she discovered that I was widely seen in the Party as the man who had won the 1987 election. For the first time, she started to see me in a completely new light, as a potential rival. I have already explained why, rightly or wrongly, this was never the case; but it was her perception, and not the reality, which counted. Our relations then took a further turn for the worse in the wake of my IMF speech that September, of which she disapproved and her acolytes disapproved even more. But even then Willie was still at hand, a voice of sanity to calm her down whenever the need arose. It was only after his sudden departure at the end of the year that the rift became irreparable. Indeed, after his going the Thatcher Government, which for more than eight years had been such a great and glorious adventure, was never the same again.

Willie had collapsed during a Christmas carol service at St Margaret's, Westminster, on 14 December 1987. Doctors diagnosed a minor stroke. Wisely, he took their insistent advice to retire at once. But it was a dreadful loss to the Government, as I was well aware at the time. I wrote to tell him so, and received a characteristically over-generous reply:

> In my heart I know that I am right to take the strong medical advice. Had I been sixty, I might have thought differently. But one has to go sometime and in my case 70 is about right. I shall miss it all very much, but I am determined to look forward to a new life and not back at an old one. Of course I shall always be at your service. I shall never interfere but will equally come if wanted. You know how much I admire what you have done for this country as Chancellor of the Exchequer. Again and again you have been proved right. You deserve all the support in the world, which you will continue to get from me.

Only someone who served at the heart of the Thatcher Government can fully appreciate the key role Willie played. He was irreplaceable. It was not simply that he was a wise elder statesman of immense experience and acute political instinct, unfailingly loyal and devoid of personal ambition, to whom Margaret could always turn. He also resolved many of the tensions that arise between Cabinet colleagues in any government before they even reached Margaret. And when she was involved, it was he alone who could sometimes, although inevitably not always, prevail upon her to avoid needless confrontations or eschew follies. Certainly, from my own point of view, he could scarcely have gone at a worse time.

Nor was Margaret's reaction to his departure encouraging. His generous offer, 'I shall always be at your service. I shall never interfere but will equally come if wanted', was one that I took him up on when my problems with Margaret became acute during the last year or so of my Chancellorship. Although he did once come to Number 11 at a particularly low point, I would normally see him at his room in the House of Lords. He was always sensible, sympathetic and supportive; but I cannot say that I left our meetings feeling much better.

Although his usual robust and loyal self in public, I found him steeped in gloom in private. 'I don't know who she listens to now' he would say. For while he had made exactly the same offer to her as he had to me, to his surprise and disappointment she seldom if ever sought him out and consulted him. And he was certainly not going to 'interfere', as he had put it, by giving unsolicited advice. It was she who had uttered the immortal words, as accurate as they were unfelicitous: 'Every Prime Minister needs a Willie'. Yet when she needed him most she ignored him completely, and instead retreated even further into her Downing Street bunker.

Willie's departure at the end of 1987 raised the question as to which Minister would be fortunate enough to take his place as the resident of Dorneywood, where he and Celia had lived since the Government first took office in 1979. There are, in all, three country houses at the disposal of the Prime Minister of the day: Chequers in Buckinghamshire, Chevening in Kent, and Dorneywood in Buckinghamshire. Chequers is by tradition occupied by the Prime Minister, and the elegant Chevening, once the home of the Stanhope family, by the Foreign Secretary, who has a heavy burden of entertaining and impressing visiting firemen from overseas. Willie, as Deputy Prime Minister, was inevitably given Dorneywood; but on his departure the succession was less obvious.

Easily the smallest of the three ministerial country houses, and the only one built this century, Dorneywood none the less possesses a remarkable charm. Its setting, too, is so idyllic that it is hard to believe that it is in fact only a few miles from downtown Slough, where I had cut my political teeth. Thérèse and I had first visited it at a dinner party given by the Whitelaws in June 1985, and adored it from that moment. I therefore let it be known through the Permanent Secretary net (that is to say, I had told Peter Middleton with a view to his conveying the message to Robin Butler) that I would be delighted if Margaret were to offer me Dorneywood, but decided to say nothing to her myself and simply wait and see what she chose to do with it. With Willie gone, I was now number three in the Cabinet pecking order, after Margaret and Geoffrey; but that was not in itself decisive. It was in the Prime Minister's unconstrained gift, and she could have taken the view, however eccentric, that since the Chancellor had Number 11, Dorneywood should go to a senior colleague who had no official residence of any kind.

On Sunday, 24 January 1988, Thérèse and I had invited Margaret and Denis to dinner at Number 11 to let her have my by now customary post-prandial summary of my plans for the forthcoming Budget. She chose the occasion, not least because she wanted Thérèse to hear the good news direct from her, to tell us that we could indeed have Dorneywood. We were suitably grateful. The great advantage of Dorneywood, where we spent eighteen happy months, apart from the house and grounds (including the swimming pool, which the children made good use of during the summer) was that, unlike Number 11, it was staffed – modestly but admirably. For the first time, entertaining became painless. Far nearer to London than Stoney Stanton was, and with amenities that the Old Rectory inevitably lacked, it was ideal for recharging the batteries at the end of a busy week.

The Sunday evening at Number 11 on which we were told the welcome news was an agreeable occasion altogether. After dinner, I told Margaret of my plans for my tax reforming and tax cutting 1988 Budget. She was so delighted by the main lines of what I had in mind that she did not cavil at those reforms which, in other circumstances, she would have sought to persuade me to drop.

Cabinet-making

But to return to the Cabinet-making meeting of 12 June 1987. It was just as well that I was present. Margaret first decided, as had been widely expected, to drop John Biffen, an astute Parliamentarian who was never cut out for ministerial office. She further decided to replace him as Leader of the House of Commons with John Wakeham, who had proved a wily and effective Chief Whip throughout the previous Parliament – except for a period when he was out of action, having been seriously injured in the IRA's murderous bomb explosion at Brighton in October 1984, in which his wife, Roberta, had been killed. John Wakeham's replacement as Chief Whip was to be John Major, at that time Minister of State for Social Security.

It was at that point I objected. As soon as Margaret indicated to me at the beginning of February, 1987, that she wanted me to continue as Chancellor after the election, I started to think about whom I should ask her for as Chief Secretary. I still have the diary card, for 4 February 1987, on which I scribbled my conclusion: John Wakeham, who had entered the House of Commons with me in 1974 and had been a Treasury Minister under Geoffrey when I was at Energy, or – failing him – John Major, who had seemed to me the pick of the 1979 intake.

Shortly before the election I asked John Wakeham to pop round from Number 12 to Number 11, and told him that I would very much like him to be my next Chief Secretary, a job whose importance he, as a former Treasury Minister, could fully appreciate. He thanked me, but indicated that the job did not greatly appeal to him. He obviously hoped for something better. I could understand that. The Chief Secretary to the Treasury, although holding a key post, is very much the Chancellor's subordinate, and as a successful Chief Whip John Wakeham could reasonably expect to secure for himself a job in which he would be his own man.

This left me with John Major, whom I had first come across during his time in the Whips' Office, when he was responsible for assisting the passage of the 1985 Finance Bill through the House of Commons, and I had formed a high opinion of him. Subsequently, as Minister of State for Social Security, he had demonstrated an impressive grasp of the complexities of the Social Security rules and an ability to put the Government's case across in a firm, clear and agreeable way. This relatively unusual combination of mastery of detail and likeable manner would, I felt, make him an excellent Chief Secretary.

Now Margaret wanted him to be Chief Whip. I told her I would much rather see him as Chief Secretary. 'It's very hard to find a good Chief Secretary,' I argued, pointing out that of the four she had appointed so far, only two – Leon Brittan and John MacGregor had been able to master the job: 'It's much less difficult to find a good Chief Whip.' She immediately countered by asking who, in that case, I thought could do the job of Chief Whip, if not John Major. 'David Waddington,' I replied, much to her surprise. Waddington had been Minister of State at the Home Office for a number of years, where – as I pointed out to her – he had handled the difficult and sensitive immigration issue with a notably deft touch.

After some discussion, Willie, who had earlier endorsed Margaret's original plan, agreed, with the added authority of a former Government Chief Whip himself, that Waddington would be perfectly all right in that job, and declared that if I felt that John Major was the only strong candidate for the job of Chief Secretary, I ought to have him. Margaret consented, and that was that. I was greatly relieved. Thus it was that John Major entered the Cabinet, as Chief Secretary, in June 1987. It is ironic that, had he instead become Chief Whip, as Margaret had intended, he could never have been a candidate to succeed her when she stepped down in 1990.*

As for John's predecessor, John MacGregor, Margaret had decided to make him Minister of Agriculture. He knew the Ministry well, having earlier been Minister of State there; but it was a great waste of a particularly able and consistently underestimated Minister. I tried to persuade Margaret to give him the Department of Health and Social Security (DHSS), which Norman Fowler wanted to give up after a particularly long stint there; but because he had said to her shortly before the election that he believed that we would sooner or later have to make some move on the pensions front, she quite wrongly regarded him as unsound on public spending, and did not wish to entrust him with the biggest spending programme of all. What John had in mind – indeed, we had discussed it together and come to the same conclusion – was the need for additional help for the poorest pensioners, about which he was right and which we subsequently gave.

We then went on to the rest of the Cabinet. Margaret told us, to my surprise and sorrow, that Norman Tebbit had decided to resign from the Government to look after his wife Margaret, who had been paralysed from the neck down in the Brighton bomb explosion. The reason he had given was genuine enough, and so were Margaret's regrets. But I very much doubt if he would have left had he not been thoroughly disillusioned by her treatment of him during his time as Party Chairman, and in particular during the election campaign itself.

The only compensation for her in losing Norman was that she could at least bring Cecil Parkinson in from the cold, where he had languished since the Sarah Keays affair became public in 1983. I suggested to Margaret (who had already rejected my first idea of giving the job to John MacGregor) that she might make him Social Services Secretary. This she immediately vetoed on the grounds that he would be ridiculed every time the question of one-parent families came up in the House of Commons. So Cecil was given my old job of Energy Secretary.

Margaret insisted on giving the DHSS, instead, to John Moore, who had been in the Cabinet, as Transport Secretary, for only a year, on the grounds that this was a job where what she always called 'presentation' was crucially important, and John looked good on television – an odd basis on which to make such a key appointment. We then went on to discuss the other posts, and at the end it was a pretty strong Cabinet that emerged, with the loss of Norman Tebbit the only serious weakening. I suspect that Leon Brittan may have been disappointed not to have been recalled: when he had been hounded into resigning in January 1986, Margaret had expressed a clear desire to have him back in the Cabinet as soon as possible. But when it came to it, in the wake of the 1987 election,

*Pace Mr Michael Dobbs, and his entertaining political fantasy, *House of Cards*.

she did not feel that it would be possible to bring Leon back without bringing Michael Heseltine, who had much more support in the Party, back as well; and there was no way in which she was going to do that.

With John Major taking John MacGregor's place as Chief Secretary, my Treasury team for the new Parliament was almost complete. Norman Lamont, whom I had persuaded Margaret to bring in as Financial Secretary in May 1986 stayed on, as did Peter Brooke as Paymaster General. She decided to move Ian Stewart sideways, however, to the Ministry of Defence, leaving a vacancy as Economic Secretary, the most junior post in the team. I had long been trying to persuade her to give a job to my PPS, Peter Lilley. This was not because he was (although entirely my own choice) far from an ideal PPS, for which a more gregarious and clubbable nature than Peter's is really required, but because I was convinced that with his high intelligence and commitment to free-market principles he would make a good Minister. Hitherto, the Whips' Office, which has a considerable say in junior appointments, and which had taken against him for reasons I never fully understood, had always blocked him.

This time, however, Margaret said 'You've always been telling me I should make Peter Lilley a Minister. Well, you can have him at the Treasury.' I was pleased that, shortly after my resignation, Margaret put him in the Cabinet. Meanwhile, I was happy to have him to complete my Treasury team, both for his sake and mine, even though it meant I had to look for a new PPS. To general astonishment, I plumped for Nigel Forman, who had entered the House eleven years earlier, since when he had languished on the back-benches, as some long-forgotten incident in the past had caused him to be *persona non grata* with Margaret. Thoughtful and conscientious, he was a member of an inordinate number of back-bench dining clubs, and his friends were chiefly on the wetter end of the Party spectrum, where I had least rapport. This was quite useful, although I would not have chosen him had his views on economic issues not steadily moved closer to mine over his decade and more as a back-bencher. I was glad that he was eventually given ministerial office by John Major in the reshuffle that followed the 1992 election. Nigel, who was to be the last of my three PPSs during my time as Chancellor, served me loyally and well.

How Neddy Escaped the Axe

The first few months after a general election – particularly a very successful general election, as that of 1987 was – provide a window of opportunity for radical measures which it is folly not to make the most of. I had long felt that no useful purpose was being served by the National Economic Development Council (NEDC or Neddy), of which I was ex-officio Chairman, and that it should therefore be abolished. It was a symbol of a half-hearted corporatist past which had no place in a Britain which had decisively turned its back on the corporate State.

Founded by the Macmillan Government in 1961, the Council was intended to provide a forum in which representatives of the Government, the TUC and the CBI could discuss and agree measures to improve economic performance. It was serviced by a secretariat, the National Economic Development Office (NEDO) which had originally been conceived as a very watered-down version of the French *Commissariat du Plan*. Particular issues were pursued in a series of so-called 'little Neddies' for specific industries.

By 1987 the Council had been reduced to little more than a political platform from which the trade unions tried to embarrass the CBI into making common cause with them against the Government. Although the reports published by the Office (NEDO) were usually of a quality that caused them to be widely used by journalists and academics, the deliberations of the Council itself were a complete waste of valuable ministerial time. This was far from being simply my own opinion, as Chairman of the Council. My private office regularly had the greatest difficulty in preventing my Cabinet colleagues on the Council from sending a junior Minister in their place, and every so often I had to keep a straight face when signing a round-robin letter to my colleagues castigating them for their poor attendance.

There is to some extent a parallel here, in the international field, with the Paris-based Organization for Economic Co-operation and Development, the successor organization to the post-war Marshall Plan. This, too, has outlived its usefulness as an institution. Its economists, who do some excellent work, particularly in the microeconomic sphere and in putting different countries' statistics on a comparable footing, could and should be preserved by putting them under the wing of the IMF. It is the ministerial talking shop at the top which is now such a waste of time and money, and which even causes member countries to maintain a full-time Ambassador to the OECD, ensconced in an expensive Paris residence.

Much earlier on I had hoped that the NEDC might abolish itself. In March 1984 the TUC contingent walked out in protest against the Government's ban on trade union membership among employees at the security service's Cheltenham radio monitoring establishment known as GCHQ. Since this spelled the end of tripartism (as the British version of corporatism was officially known), which was the NEDC's sole *raison d'être*, this seemed a good opportunity to wind up the Council altogether. Unfortunately, the CBI wanted to carry on with it. So for some nine months the Council continued to meet without the TUC. The discussions were far less acrimonious, but since Ministers and leading industrialists regularly met anyway, they were also otiose.

Needless to say, before long the TUC began to regret their precipitate decision to walk out, and Len Murray, the Oxford-educated and like-able, if (understandably) somewhat cynical, TUC General Secretary, accompanied by the unbelievably self-important Chairman of the TUC's Economic Committee and leader of the General and Municipal Workers' Union, David Basnett, came to see me at the Treasury to negotiate, as they saw it, the terms of the TUC's return.

Basnett had a shopping list of TUC demands which he claimed were the TUC's conditions for returning to Neddy. Most of them were wholly unrelated to Neddy itself, and concerned some outstanding public sector pay issues. I waited until he had finished, and then politely pointed out that, while I would of course be happy to see the TUC back, whether they came back or not was entirely a matter for them, in which I would not dream of interfering. The question of negotiating the terms of their re-entry, therefore, did not arise. There was nothing to discuss. Murray quickly took the point – I suspect this was how he had expected me to respond. Basnett, however, clearly found it difficult to grasp, and started again. I suggested that the two of them should think over what I had said, and, when they had done so, I would be happy to see them again to hear their response. I felt it would be better to leave it to Len Murray to explain to Basnett, when they were alone, the facts of life.

When, in due course, Murray and Basnett came to see me again they announced that the TUC would be returning at the next meeting. In the interim they had gone to the CBI, and unfortunately hammered out between them a joint TUC/CBI document setting out the various improvements in the working of NEDC they would like to see. It was a pretty anodyne list, and the only undertaking I gave, to both the CBI and the TUC, was that I would take their points into account. The TUC considered this piece of paper a sufficient face-saver, and came back.

Since then, and particularly after Len Murray had been succeeded as TUC General Secretary by the markedly less sophisticated Norman Willis, the TUC had taken to giving impromptu and tendentious press conferences after each Council meeting. Hitherto, there had been an understanding on all three sides – Government, TUC and CBI – that the press briefing would be done only by the supposedly impartial Director-General of NEDO, who was also a member of the Council. After failing to persuade the TUC to stick to this practice, I felt obliged to respond by having the Treasury issue a short press release of my own, after each meeting, embodying some point that I particularly wished to get across. In order to make the link with the Council meeting genuine, I would weave the text of the press release into my summing up of the discussion of an appropriate item on the agenda. When the TUC tumbled to what I was doing, they complained that I was abusing my position as Chairman. Of one thing I was completely confident, however: they would not again make the mistake of walking out. Nor did they.

But it was all very tiresome. On the industrialists' side, I made a practice of telling each incoming CBI President that my door was always open whenever there was any aspect of Government policy that was troubling them and which they wished to discuss with me, frankly and in private. They invariably took me up on this. And in addition I dined regularly with groups of leading businessmen. On the unions' side, the institutional channel of communication with the Government was of course the Department of Employment and its Secretary of State; but all other Cabinet colleagues saw trade union leaders in fields for which they were responsible whenever either side wished it – as, indeed, I had done when at Energy. All the NEDC added was tripartism, whose preservation was irrelevant to the success or failure of the Government's economic policy. Geoffrey, who had a profound belief in the process of education by patient, reasoned argument, always saw the Council as having a value as an adult education establishment. I was sceptical of this, believing that, for the individuals in question, it was events, rather than argument, that would educate; and that the preservation of the anachronistic NEDC was more likely to stand in the way of the unions' coming to terms with what Len Murray had called 'the new realism' than to facilitate it.

Given the scale of the Government's success in the 1987 general election, the NEDC could clearly be abolished without any serious political difficulty, provided we struck while the iron was hot. Immediately the election was over, I raised the issue privately with my two Cabinet colleagues most closely concerned: Norman Fowler, the newly appointed Employment Secretary, and David Young, the newly appointed Trade and Industry Secretary. Both of them agreed that the NEDC should go. David, who knew the Council very much better than Norman, having served on it for several years, first as Chairman of the Manpower Services Commission and subsequently as Employment Secretary, was particularly supportive of my suggestion. To get a purely political reaction, I also had an informal word with Norman Tebbit, who, although he had just stood down from the Cabinet, was still Party Chairman for the time being, and possessed the added advantage of having previously been both Employment Secretary and Trade and Industry Secretary. He, too, was strongly in favour of the Council's abolition.

I had, of course, informed the relevant Treasury officials of what I had in mind, most importantly Peter Middleton. As he saw it, this was essentially a political matter; and the official Treasury's greater interest was in the future of the Office (NEDO) and the thirty-eight Sector Working Parties (or 'little Neddies') for various industries which it serviced. It saw the opportunity for a worthwhile public expenditure saving in sharply reducing the public funding for the Sector Working Parties, with consequential savings from reducing the size of the Office which serviced them. This was, it seemed to me, a fair point. Although

716

I would not have myself invented Sector Working Parties (SWPs) in the first place, they existed; and some of them were doing sufficiently good work to make a case for continued public funding. At least as many, however, were not. If, in any case where the Government withdrew public funding, industry genuinely believed the Government was making a bad mistake, there was nothing to stop them putting their money where their mouth was and funding it themselves. (It was significant that, when it came to it, they never did.)

About a week after the election, I broached the matter with Margaret. To my disappointment I found her wholly opposed. She was terrified of what the unions might do. It was true that she had never been a member of the NEDC herself, and so was unaware of quite what a waste of valuable time it was – not least for officials, who had to prepare and in principle co-ordinate the ministerial briefing for its meetings, and much else besides. Even so, her response, however true to form, was depressing. I arranged a further meeting at Number 10, this time accompanied by both Norman Fowler and David Young, who gave me particularly robust support. In the end, the best I was able to negotiate with Margaret was a compromise, in which the number of Council meetings was reduced from one a month to one a quarter. I told her that in that event the chairmanship could rotate among the key ministerial members, and that I myself would attend and chair only one meeting a year, that which followed the Budget. It was also agreed that there would be a drastic cull of the little Neddies, at least so far as public funding was concerned.

I had taken the precaution, meanwhile, of sharing my thinking with David Nickson, the then CBI President. David was not only a highly successful Executive Chairman of Scottish and Newcastle, the brewing and hotel group, but a businessman who combined to an unusual extent a clear understanding of the climate needed for business success with a keen sense of public duty. This made him one of the best Presidents the CBI has ever had. He undertook to deliver the CBI's backing for the compromise proposal that had emerged.

The first meeting of the NEDC after the June 1987 election was on 1 July. I opened by reading a prepared statement setting out the new arrangements for the Council and the cull of the SWPs, the precise details of which would be subject to a period of consultation. When the CBI then came in and supported my changes, the TUC, for whom the whole thing had come as a bolt from the blue – there had been no leaks, for once, of any kind – realized that with two out of the three constituent parts of Neddy in agreement, and one of these the Government, they were faced with a *fait accompli*. They huffed and puffed, and issued a suitably outraged statement, but that was the beginning and end of it. The Director General of NEDO, John Cassels, was equally shocked, although in his case he kept his feelings to himself.

Fortunately, Cassels was rapidly approaching retirement; and I was able to side-step the usual problem involved in the appointment of a successor – the fact that each of the three parties to Neddy has a veto, something the TUC always made the most of – by arranging an internal appointment. A short while earlier, I had been able to secure the appointment of the distinguished Oxford economist Walter Eltis, a founder member of my 'Gooies', as part-time Economic Director of Neddy. A man of great gentleness and integrity, who had already been accepted by the TUC as Economic Director, Walter was not someone to whose promotion to Director-General the TUC could object.

I subsequently made further improvements to the composition of the reprieved if somewhat diminished NEDC. I broke the TUC monopoly of the union side by inviting on to the Council Eric Hammond, the leader of the main electrical trade union, the EEPTU, which had been expelled from the TUC over the Wapping affair.* To demonstrate even handedness, I simultaneously broke the CBI's monopoly of the employers' side by inviting on to the Council Jim Ackers of the Association of British Chambers of Commerce.

But, although the new arrangements represented a signal improvement, the failure to abolish the NEDC altogether in June 1987 was a sadly missed opportunity. As a result this obsolete organization limped on, pointlessly, until Norman Lamont, Chancellor in the Major Government, announced its abolition in June 1992 – citing precisely the same reason as I had used when vainly seeking to persuade Margaret to show the same radicalism and courage exactly five years earlier. Needless to say, there were no untoward consequences whatever.

Margaret's extraordinary timidity over the abolition of the NEDC was part of a wider syndrome. Despite her tough talk and her iron lady reputation, she was fearful of the trade unions throughout her time as Prime Minister. Her enthusiasm for nuclear energy derived largely from the belief that it reduced the country's dependence on coal and thus on the National Union of Mineworkers (NUM). She never really understood the implications of the Government's victory over Scargill in 1984–85, and continued to worry about being unprepared for a strike for years afterwards. Similarly, as an earlier chapter records, she had to be dragged kicking and screaming into belatedly authorizing the abolition of the infamous National Dock Labour Scheme in 1989.

---

*The EEPTU co-operated with Rupert Murdoch in the secret overnight removal of his newspaper operations, which included both *The Times* and *The Sunday Times* as well as some of the worst examples of the gutter press, from the Grays Inn Road, where militant trade unionism held sway, to Wapping, where EEPTU members got the jobs and the militants were excluded. This led, for a considerable period, to the worst excesses of trade union violence and intimidation the country had seen outside the coal strike.

CHAPTER 58

PUBLIC SPENDING REVISITED

The New Chief Secretary · Television Interlude
The Child Benefit Drama · Still Fresher Faces
Public Spending in Retrospect

The New Chief Secretary

FOR A TIME AFTER the 1987 election I was concerned that I might have
made the wrong choice of Chief Secretary after all – a view I suspect
was shared by John Major himself. He found the job far more difficult
than anything he had ever done before, and had to work very hard to try
and master it. He would come and see me at Number 11, ashen faced,
to unburden himself of his worries and to seek my advice. Before too
long, however, he was thoroughly on top of the job. But throughout his
two years in the job, which were to constitute the greater part of his total
Cabinet experience before becoming Prime Minister, he made a point of
sticking to his last. Apart from the Budget-making process, and of course
the political matters we discussed at ministerial prayer meetings, he chose
not to contribute to the discussion of any Treasury matter which did not
have a public expenditure dimension.

He was assisted in his public spending task by the fact that he had
the good fortune to become Chief Secretary at the start of the new
Parliament. This helps in several ways. For one thing, there is not the
pressure from colleagues to increase spending for electoral reasons that
always emerges in the second half of a Parliament. For another, the
large scale reshuffle that follows a general election means that a great
many spending Departments have new Ministers in charge who do not
know the subject at all well, and moreover do not feel bound by the
aspirations of their predecessors.

719

Spending control was further helped in 1987 by three other factors. First, strong economic growth meant that less money was needed for those social security benefits which are related to unemployment – which was falling fast – and for the nationalized industries, whose profits were looking very much healthier. In addition the proceeds of council house sales, which count as negative public spending, had risen significantly. Secondly, there was a helpful trend of debt interest as the public finances moved into substantial surplus.

Thirdly, Margaret had appointed to the DHSS, the biggest spending Department of all, John Moore, who was determined to be more Thatcherite than his predecessor, Norman Fowler. Indeed it soon became clear that the problem with John Moore was not the normal one of overbidding, but the fact he had not asked for enough. This was to cause a number of problems; but the great gain was that John Moore's helpful attitude enabled John Major to secure a freeze in the rate of the indiscriminate and untaxed Child Benefit, in return for a substantial rise in the means-tested Family Credit for poorer families. This switch, which saved a large sum of money, had been a long standing ambition of the official Treasury. Moreover, we were able to maintain this policy, not without some difficulty, throughout the rest of my time as Chancellor.

Thus it was that it proved possible in 1987 for the first time in many years to secure a public spending outcome in line with the summer remit, without even requiring recourse to the Star Chamber. This was helped by the fact that, when John Major had succeeded in whittling down the non-settlers to a hard core of three, I decided to see each of them privately myself. At these tête-à-têtes I indicated that everyone else had either settled or was on the brink of settling except my interlocutor, suggesting that I could not believe that he would want to incur the odium of having the whole apparatus of the Star Chamber activated simply to deal with him. That seemed to do the trick.

Television Interlude

As I indicated a few chapters ago, a Chancellor's job spans a far wider range than is commonly realized. Another example of this was the debate on the future of broadcasting, and in particular television, which occupied a surprising amount of my time in 1987. Television in Britain had hitherto been dominated by a duopoly in which the BBC enjoyed a monopoly of tax finance and the regional ITV contractors had a monopoly of television advertising in their own regions. It was also highly regulated, as befits a duopoly in such a sensitive area. The sensitivity arose because what was technically a publishing duopoly acted not like book publishers, whose material is provided by a multiplicity of independent authors, but more like newspaper publishers, whose whole *raison d'être* is to originate themselves the material they publish. The one exception to this was Channel Four, which the Government had set up a few years previously in a way deliberately designed to provide an opportunity for independent programme makers; and after a poor start it had proved a success.

The main forces for change were technological – especially satellite and to a lesser extent cable television – rather than any Government initiative. Cable television was deregulated under the Cable and Broadcasting Act of 1984, although its growth was initially slow. Another major event was the report of the committee, chaired by the market economist Professor Alan Peacock, which had been set up in 1985 by the then Home Secretary, Leon Brittan, ostensibly to review the future of the licence fee after several futile battles between the Government and Corporation over its size. As Leon had intended, the Peacock Committee interpreted their brief very widely, and their report emerged as something of a libertarian manifesto. Its key conclusion was that:

> British broadcasting should move towards a sophisticated market system based on consumer sovereignty. That is, a system which recognizes that viewers and listeners are the best ultimate judges of their own interest, which they can best satisfy if they have the option of purchasing the broadcasting services they require from as many alternative sources of supply as possible.

The main long-term impact of Peacock was to give a push to technological developments already in train. In terms of immediate policy, its two most important recommendations concerned the licence fee and access to the viewing public for independent programme makers.

The Committee favoured continuing for the time being the licence fee and, to end the regular haggle with the Government over its level, automatically linking increases in the licence fee to the Retail Price Index. But more important ultimately were the recommended provisions for greater access by independent producers to both the BBC and the former ITV (now ITC) contractors. So long as most households were confined to the two main alternative terrestrial networks, quotas for independent producers, guaranteeing them a minimum share of airtime, were a way of widening both competition and consumer choice.

A medium-term recommendation by Peaccok was that the BBC should move to subscription television – a form of pay-as-you-view. However, a follow-up technical report by Charles Jonscher, then of Booz Allen & Hamilton, the US-owned consulting firm, who had been commissioned by the Department of Trade and Industry, raised serious doubts about the desirability of subscription for the BBC, but recommended it strongly for the fifth terrestrial channel – which

721

Peacock had wrongly been told was a technical impossibility.

Faced with the need to devise a coherent Government response to both the Peacock Report and the enormous technical possibilities that were opening up, which clearly required a wholly new statutory framework, Margaret set up a Cabinet Committee on broadcasting on which I served, and which she chaired. It was not the most cost-effective way of spending time. Broadcasting was a subject on which Margaret held a great many firm views and prejudices, which she would air at some length, irrespective of whether this had any bearing on the Committee's pressing need to reach decisions on a number of complex and critical issues. Indeed, her Chairmanship became so discursive, and hence indecisive, that, with her full knowledge and consent, I took to chairing smaller meetings between the meetings of the main committee, without which it was hard to see how any decisions would ever have been taken. At these smaller meetings I would be assisted by the Treasury official who specialized in this area, but the key participants were the two Ministers with the main departmental interest in broadcasting: Douglas Hurd, then Home Secretary, and David Young, then Trade and Industry Secretary – each of them assisted by one senior official.

In general, Margaret was excited by the prospect of breaking the duopoly and encouraging diversity, which *inter alia* caused her to welcome with open arms the Peacock recommendation to set quotas for independent producers, which duly came into being. It was, after all, a cause the Government had already made its own. We were all conscious, too, that in addition to its own merits, the universality of the English language meant that a strong UK independent television production industry would have a world market. But at the same time Margaret was deeply concerned at actual and potential political bias on television, especially in news programmes, and with the prospect of moral degradation. I had a great deal more sympathy with her concern than I had with the sort of remedies she sought. It is a fact of life that bright young people on the left tend to seek and get jobs in broadcasting and journalism, just as those on the right tend to choose the City. The only way to diminish the resulting bias is through increased choice and competition.

As for moral degradation, she suffered from the delusion that tends to affect all politicians, even professedly free-market ones, that they can regulate anything if they really wish to. In this case she found it hard to grasp that, once a viewer has a satellite dish, there is no preventing him from receiving material from transmitters that lie wholly outside UK jurisdiction. One can do little more than trust that the benefits of freedom exceed the price that has to be paid. I have little doubt they do. The problem in the UK is not the evil influence of television, but the failure of many parents, teachers and clerics to be an influence for good.

In part to assist the Committee in its deliberations, but rather more to demonstrate the Government's willingness to listen and learn, Margaret decided to hold one of her 'seminars' on broadcasting, to which leading figures from all parts of the industry were invited. It was held in Number 12, whose 'open plan' ground floor provides the largest single room in the Downing Street complex, and followed by a lunch at Number 10. Meetings which generate more heat than light are not uncommon: this one, held on 21 September 1987, generated neither heat nor (despite one or two eloquent contributions) light; merely the deafening sound of axes being ground.

Despite the welcome outbreak of broadcasting freedom and diversity that the new technology promised us, there would still be franchises to award; and the basis on which this should be done occupied many hours of the Committee's time. There was general dissatisfaction with the old system of entirely subjective and discretionary decisions, qualified only by inertia, and a strong disposition to follow Peacock's (majority) advice and include an auction element in the process. The tricky question was precisely where and how the balance should be struck.

By the time the Broadcasting Bill, which became the 1990 Broadcasting Act, was finalized, I was no longer in the Government. I could therefore be a dispassionate observer of the first test of the new system, the 1991 semi-auction of ITV franchises, which proved to have an unusually high farce content. This reflected partly defects in the Bill as originally published and, to a limited extent, deficiencies in the way it was implemented by the new Independent Television Commission. But most of all it reflected amendments to the Bill insisted on by Parliament during its passage to the statute book, which Home Office Ministers (responsible for the Bill's passage) showed little disposition to resist. On this issue, as on many others, the new thinking and the radicalism came from the Government; and it was Parliament – on both sides of the House – that argued in effect that the man in Whitehall knew best. They simply wished him not to be located in Whitehall.

However, the curious letter Margaret wrote, after she had ceased to be Prime Minister, to Bruce Gyngel, Chairman of TV-AM and hammer of the television trade unions, saying that she was heartbroken that the company had lost its franchise and apologizing for her error in promoting legislation that made this possible, suggests that the free-market convictions of her senior colleagues on the Committee were greater than her own.

The Child Benefit Drama

Although membership of Margaret's Cabinet Committee on broadcasting took a surprising amount of my time, much more central to my job as Chancellor were my last three public expenditure rounds. I have already outlined my general approach to Government expenditure and my earlier efforts to bring public spending under control in Chapter 25.

The 1987 public spending round, John Major's first, had proved a highly successful one. The plans in the Autumn Statement showed general Government expenditure (excluding privatization) falling from the equivalent of 42½ per cent of GDP in 1987–88 to 42 per cent in 1988–89. The reality turned out to be a very much greater decline, from 42 per cent to 39½ per cent of GDP. This represented an overall fall of 7 percentage points from the Thatcher Government's peak of 1982–83, and the lowest ratio achieved since 1966–67. I fear that it will also be the lowest ratio for several years to come. While the scale of the reduction in 1988–89 was obviously in part a consequence of the unsustainably rapid rise in GDP, that was by no means the whole story. Government spending, in real terms, actually fell, for the second year in succession. Other countries, whose economies were also forging ahead in 1988, achieved nothing comparable on the public spending front.

However, two successive years in which public spending, in real terms, actually declined, as the economy grew rapidly, made it impossible to avoid some let-up in the 1988 public spending round. I announced in the 1988 Autumn Statement an increase in real public spending of 1¼ per cent, which I expected would lead to a further modest decline in the public spending ratio. In the event things did not turn out quite so well: there was a real increase in spending of 3 per cent and a modest rise in the public spending/GDP ratio from 39½ to 40 per cent. There was mounting pressure throughout 1988, by no means confined to the Opposition benches, for still further increases in spending on the National Health Service, in particular.

Nevertheless, all in all, the 1988 spending round was satisfactorily uneventful until very near the end, when there were two hiccups. The lesser of the two concerned Nick Ridley, then still Environment Secretary, who refused to settle his housing budget with John Major, then Chief Secretary. Nick wanted more public money over a wide front, and contended that the Treasury should permit him to use some of the excess receipts from council house sales, which had been exceptionally buoyant in 1988, for this purpose. John, rightly, insisted that the proceeds of council house sales had no bearing on the merits of spending more money on the housing programme.

In the normal course of events an impasse of this kind would have been resolved by Star Chamber. But in this case both of them were anxious to avoid this. John was proud that he had succeeded in achieving a good result in the 1987 spending round without recourse to Star Chamber. He was determined to maintain his record if he possibly could. With Nick the problem was a different one. Willie's departure had, among other things, left a vacancy as Chairman of Star Chamber. I had suggested to Margaret that Geoffrey, as her most senior Cabinet colleague now that Willie had gone, and a former Chancellor, would make the best replacement. I had already seen Geoffrey, then still Foreign Secretary, to make sure that he had no foreign trips during the brief but intensive Star Chamber period. Margaret, however, was by that time already in no mood to confer any mark of preferment on Geoffrey, even when it was in the Government's interest to do so. It had been bad enough that she had felt obliged to reappoint him as Foreign Secretary; she was certainly not going to let him think that he was a second Willie, a *de facto* deputy Prime Minister. She therefore gave the Star Chamber job, to the astonishment of many, to Cecil Parkinson – which incidentally led to unfounded speculation in the Press that she was planning to make him Chancellor.

This had an unexpected consequence. A number of colleagues, who had regarded a Star Chamber presided over by Willie as part of the natural order of things, could not adjust to the idea of having Cecil sitting in judgement over them. All of these had settled bilaterally, except Nick. There was only one solution. I saw Nick privately at Number 11, with no officials present. We went over his programme together, and I offered him a number of modest concessions – which I had discussed with John in advance. We soon reached what was from the Treasury's point of view a very satisfactory agreement on all the outstanding issues between us.

The other, and much more serious, hiccup was over child benefit. In 1987, for the first time, this had been frozen in cash terms instead of being uprated in line with inflation. The argument was that help should be concentrated on the poorest families – which meant that what mattered was not the indiscriminate child benefit, but the means-tested Family Credit. This had long been the Treasury's position, but it was not until 1987 that the DHSS had, in John Moore, a Secretary of State sufficiently in favour of selectivity to accept it. John defended the decision very effectively at the despatch box, and there was no serious back-bench revolt.

Needless to say, having established the principle, John Major, with my strong backing, was anxious to consolidate it with a further child benefit freeze, accompanied by a further large increase in Family Credit, in 1988. When the 1987 freeze had been announced, the Press had characteristically described it as a defeat for John Moore at the hands of the Treasury. This was something John could have taken in his stride, had it not been for Margaret's decision in July 1988 to split the DHSS in two, adding insult to injury by giving him the Social Security job, the political inferior of the two jobs created from the one he had previously held. Feeling his political position on the slide, and knowing full well how a further child benefit freeze would be interpreted by the media, he became determined to resist it, and unwisely let this be known to the Press.

He was rapidly painting himself into a corner, and as he did so he felt driven to raise the stakes still higher. As the impasse between John Major and himself over the issue continued, he saw David Waddington, the Chief Whip, and told David that unless child benefit were increased he himself would resign from the Government. David immediately informed Margaret, who, on the afternoon of 18 October, 1988, hastily arranged a meeting in her first-floor study at Number 10 with John Moore, John Major and myself. It was a tense and difficult occasion. John Moore was quiet, but highly emotional. The arguments on both sides of the child benefit case were gone into in considerable detail. His case became no better as the argument developed, but at the end he said that he had not changed his mind about resignation. He simply could not carry on with his job unless child benefit were increased.

Margaret wisely asked him to sleep on it, and he left the room, as did John Major. I stayed behind for a bit, and told Margaret that, in my judgement, his Department had been of no help to him over this. It was repeating the mistake that had been the source of so much trouble over the Fowler reforms, but in an even more foolish way. It had become obsessed – a tribute, perhaps, to that tireless pressure group, the Child Poverty Action Group – with the problem of child poverty. Yet although child benefit had a strong following among supporters of the middle-class welfare state, not least among Tory back-benchers, the greatest sense of grievance, so far as the level of welfare benefits was concerned, was felt by the poorer pensioners whose average age was well above that of pensioners generally; and it was their plight that evoked the greatest public sympathy, too.

If I had not been aware of this before it had certainly been borne in on me while campaigning in the 1987 election. If John wanted to make a stand, it should have been over these people. Margaret agreed, and said she hoped that John would not be so foolish as to resign. I warmly endorsed that. John was an old friend, who for five years had worked for me, first at Energy and subsequently at the Treasury, with energy, enthusiasm, commitment and total loyalty. The last thing I wanted was to see him resign, particularly over such a wrong-headed issue. I told her I would do what I could to talk him out of it.

I managed to get a message to him that evening that I would like to see him, completely privately, at Number 11 at 8 o'clock the next morning. When he called round his mood had changed. He was less emotional, clearly did not wish to resign, and was looking for a way out. After explaining to him how much I personally wanted him to stay in the Government, and what an impossible position he would be in if he were to resign over a policy which he himself had defended so robustly only a year earlier, I offered him something for the poorer, older, pensioners as a way out. He rejected it, insisting that it was child poverty that the argument was all about. I then offered him what the official Treasury had had in mind all along: a freeze in child benefit, but extra money for Family Credit. This he accepted; and after he had left I sent a message to Margaret to let her know that the crisis was over. On 27 October 1988, John announced the child benefit freeze and Family Credit increase to the House of Commons, defending it with all the verve he could muster. At the next reshuffle, some nine months later, she sacked him.

It was a sad, unnecessary, heartless and foolish act; for apart from that one aberration over child benefit, John had been loyal to a fault throughout his ministerial career, one of the few unwavering free-market Ministers in the Cabinet. It was true that he had not been a great success as Secretary of State at the DHSS; but the mistake was Margaret's in appointing him in the first place. On top of all that, he had to grapple – as his more politically nimble predecessor, Norman Fowler, had not – with the question of reforming the National Health Service. Small wonder he was slightly out of his depth.

Still Fresher Faces

For what was to prove my final public expenditure round in 1989, I had once again a new Chief Secretary, my fourth, in Norman Lamont. For in the first of his astonishing leaps, Margaret had made John Major Foreign Secretary in place of Geoffrey Howe, in the same fateful reshuffle of July 1989 that had seen the dismissal of John Moore.

Margaret suggested to me three possible successors, all of them un-doubtedly able: Peter Brooke, Michael Howard and Michael Portillo. I knew that she would quite rightly put Peter Brooke, who had done an excellent job as Party Chairman, and for whom I had a high personal regard, into Cabinet anyway. But I told her that Chief Secretary was not the right job for him: he was too much of a gent. She gave him Northern Ireland instead. Michael Howard, very much a QC, might have been successful in the job, but he had a reputation for putting his colleagues' backs up. In the event, he was to enter the Cabinet as Employment Secretary in the reshuffle caused by my resignation some three months later. Michael Portillo, who had worked for me as a special adviser before entering the House, was the outstanding member of his generation in the House, who would clearly and rightly go far. But at thirty-six, with only two years' ministerial experience behind him, I was not entirely confident that he would carry the clout a Chief Secretary requires. Three years later he did enter the Cabinet as Chief Secretary after John Major's 1992 election victory – an excellent appointment, and the right time both for the Government and for Michael himself.

But my reasons for rejecting the strong candidates Margaret had offered me would not have been decisive, had it not been for the fact that I felt it would be very unfair to Norman Lamont. Norman had been a Minister since the Government was first formed in 1979, and after a disappointing start had been serving me loyally and well as Financial Secretary, a post he had held for the past three years. I did pass him over in favour of John Major in 1987. But to have passed him over yet again in 1989 was something he would have taken very hard, and understandably so. It had come to the point where he felt that this was his last chance of making it into the Cabinet. I felt that he deserved to be given that chance.

Margaret did her best to talk me out of it; but in the end, and with considerable reluctance, she conceded that her Chancellor should be allowed the Chief Secretary he wanted. Thus it was that, little more than a year later, Norman was in a position to run John Major's leadership campaign following Margaret's enforced departure, and to succeed John as Chancellor of the Exchequer. If politics does nothing else, it develops an appreciation of irony.

To complete my last Treasury team, the promotion of Peter Lilley from Economic Secretary to Financial Secretary was an obvious move. As his replacement I chose Richard Ryder, then languishing in the most junior job at the Ministry of Agriculture. He was a politically shrewd young man who, for personal reasons, needed a fresh start. He made the most of it, and became John Major's Chief Whip when John succeeded Margaret as Prime Minister. He, too, had not been on the short list Margaret had offered me. Finally, in place of Peter Brooke as Paymaster General she asked me to take Malcolm Caithness. The Lords had been asking for a third Cabinet post – they were now down to the minimum possible of two: Lord Chancellor and Leader of the House of Lords – and she had denied them. Having the Paymaster General in the Lords was, she felt, the best she could do. In the circumstances I could hardly object.

I do not recall the precise details of the 1989 public spending round so well, since it was a particularly traumatic time for me, coinciding as it did with the events leading up to my resignation. Indeed, although little of substance remained to be done, I did not quite see it through to the end. In the circumstances, it was just as well that my Chief Secretary, Norman Lamont, was someone who had been working for me for a considerable time. Although the pressures were beginning to build up as they always do in the second half of a Parliament, the outcome was not at all bad. Two factors made large contributions to this satisfactory result. First, 1990–91 saw the fourth successive Budget surplus – or public sector debt repayment – which helped greatly so far as the burden of debt interest was concerned. And second, it was the third year in succession in which child benefit was frozen; in return, as John Major had negotiated in the two previous years, for a substantial rise in Family Credit for the poorest families. This caused much less furore than on either of the two previous occasions. To all intents and purposes, the Government had won the argument.

Sadly, it was John Major himself, who, as one of his earliest acts as Prime Minister, was to overrule his Chancellor at a time when the new policy had at last been widely accepted, and caused it to be announced in March 1991 not only that Child Benefit would be increased, but that it would henceforth be increased every year in line with inflation. This was a big mistake. Child Benefit, the overwhelming bulk of which goes to people who do not really need it, was estimated to cost some £5¾ billion in 1992–93 money. Compared with that, the cost of a substantial advertising campaign to overcome the problem of inadequate take-up of Family Credit, which concentrates help on poor families, is chickenfeed. Moreover, not only is the untaxed child benefit a straight addition to the income of better-off parents, but in the normal course of events any increase in it is of no help to the poorest families who suffer a pound for pound deduction from their means-tested benefits. The difficult task was to break the habit of the annual Child Benefit uprating. Once that had been accomplished, and the ground had been consolidated, giving it up again – unnecessarily and irrevocably – has made the task of curbing the growth of public spending, which has once again become one of the main challenges facing the Government, very much harder.

Public Spending in Retrospect

The accompanying table shows the record of public spending since the mid-1960s. Under both the Wilson Labour Government of the 1960s and the subsequent Heath Conservative Government it was growing much faster than any conceivable rise in the national income. It slowed down under the Wilson–Callaghan Government of the 1970s, at the behest of the IMF, but only enough to make a very small dent in the public spending ratio, since economic growth had also declined.

Under the first three Conservative Parliaments following the 1979 election, public spending rose only slightly more slowly than under the previous Labour Government, but economic growth was a great deal faster and the spending ratio fell by two percentage points – an unusual achievement. A worrying acceleration of public spending is officially expected in the period up to 1996, which cannot all be put down to recession. This is a clear danger signal, particularly since there is a tendency for the out-turn to be worse than the plans.

I trust that it will not be considered unforgivably immodest to look in particular at my own period as Chancellor. Of course it was somewhat easier for me than for Geoffrey Howe, who initially had to cope with a recession. Even so, the table, which excludes all benefit from privatization proceeds, shows that the unprecedented fall of up to 8 percentage points in the public spending ratio during my stewardship of the Exchequer, cannot be written off as simply a boom phenomenon. The very low growth in public spending in real terms clearly demonstrates that this was a time of genuine public spending restraint.

The growth of Public Spending (General Government Expenditure excluding privatization proceeds)

	Average annual percentage growth (real terms)	Overall change as % of GDP
Labour (1964–70)	4.7	+4.2
Conservative (1970–74)	4.9	+2.4
Labour (1974–79)	1.8	−0.6
Conservative (1979–92)*	1.7	−2.1
Conservative plans (1992–96)	2.7	−0.7

*of which:

Howe (1979–83)	2.3	+3.5
Lawson (1983–89)	0.6 (0.9)	−8.0 (−7.6)
Howe/Lawson (1979–89)	1.3 (1.4)	−4.5 (−4.1)
Major/Lamont (1989–92)	2.0 (1.4)	+2.4 (+2.0)

NB: The figures in both the table and the footnote refer to the financial year ending in the year in question. The figures in brackets show the effect of taking 1989 to refer to the financial year 1989–90 rather than 1988–89.

CHAPTER 59

'MANAGED FLOATING'

*A Promise Broken · From Europe to the World
To Washington via Nyborg · My 1987 IMF Speech
Reactions to the Speech · The Poorest of the Poor
The Toronto Terms*

A Promise Broken

TOWARDS THE END OF Chapter 54, I pointed out how the Louvre Accord of February 1987 created a framework which for the first time made a policy of exchange rate stability credible. My decision to take advantage of this to embark on a period of what later became known as 'shadowing the Deutschmark', arose from my desire to put a floor under sterling, which had fallen more or less continuously from its somewhat artificial peak of over DM5 to the pound in January 1981 to a low of DM2.75 in January 1987. But a floor would not be credible without a ceiling. If the markets saw a 'hands off' policy on the way up, they would take it for granted that there would be a 'hands off' policy on the way down, too – at least until a very low point indeed had been reached. Hence the DM3 ceiling. Moreover I had no wish to inflict on British industry the unnecessary trauma of an appreciation of sterling which would in the event prove unsustainable. The sterling overshoot of 1980 had provided a much-needed shock. But since then the Government had fully established its credentials and the economic climate – and expectations – had changed completely. There seemed to me to be no cause for a repeat dose of the same medicine seven years later.

Shadowing the Deutschmark (and nudging up interest rates when I had an opportunity to do so) provided both a welcome period of exchange rate calm in the run-up to the election, and a practical demonstration of sterling's ability to keep station with the Mark. But I saw it essentially as a short-term expedient which would keep the show on the road until after the election. Despite earlier setbacks, I had not lost hope of securing my long-term objective of full EMS membership.

Within that framework, I wanted to err on the side of caution. Towards the end of July 1987, the Bank, supported by the Treasury, began to urge a base rate rise. I had no hesitation in agreeing; and a slight weakening of sterling provided me with an opportunity to raise rates by 1 per cent to 10 per cent on 9 August, thus reversing the two pre-election reductions. The markets were taken completely by surprise. But I had little doubt at the time that the next move in interest rates would also be upward – as it almost certainly would have been had it not been for the stock market crash two months later.

Margaret had explicitly indicated to me that she felt the right time to consider the EMS was after the election, at the start of a new Parliament, so that ERM membership was fully bedded in by the time of the subsequent election campaign. I reminded her of this at my bilateral with her on 27 July, some seven weeks after the election. I went on to point out that the reserves were now very much stronger, and that ERM membership would provide a stability that would help business confidence and reassure the financial markets. Moreover the Treasury was engaged in negotiations to improve the technical working of the ERM (these were to lead to the Basle–Nyborg agreements) and their fruition would be a good opportunity to announce British membership.

Margaret responded as if our earlier discussions had never happened. She attacked the ERM with every debating point that occurred to her (or to whomever had written her brief). I said I was not prepared to let the matter drop: it was too important for that. I told her I would want to discuss it further in the autumn, after the summer break. She dissented insisting the autumn was too soon: she would not be prepared to hold a further discussion on ERM membership with me until the New Year. Finally, she was adamant that, whatever happened, she would not be prepared to hold meetings of the kind she had held in the autumn of 1985 – when she had found herself heavily outnumbered in a meeting of senior Ministers and had to threaten to resign herself.

I was dismayed. It was clear that she had simply been stringing me along in everything she had said before the election, which obviously had not been uttered in good faith. Perhaps I should have resigned then and there. Rightly or wrongly, I did not do so, since I could not see what good it would do. There was no way in which I could force her to join the ERM at that time against her will. It was true that my political position was stronger than it had ever been before: I had been widely credited, much to her annoyance, with being the true author of the 1987 election victory. But by the same token Margaret, as the leader who had just won a third election victory in succession – an unprecedented achievement – was at the peak of her authority.

From Europe to the World

In any event, I felt I could never trust her completely again. She complained afterwards that I played my cards close to my chest. There is something in this – even if it was a case of the pot calling the kettle black. For by then it was the only alternative to either resignation or confrontation. For the time being, I decided to shift the focus of my exchange rate efforts to the wider international field. Since the Plaza and Louvre Agreements I had been reflecting on how to take further the informal G5/G7 accords on exchange rates. Partly because G5/G7 currency management had been enshrined in international agreements to which we were a signatory, and partly because the process had been initiated by the US Administration, Margaret was not inclined to make a full frontal assault on it, or prevent my co-operating in its working, on which I had duly briefed her at every stage.

The Election campaign had been quite exhausting, and my then Constituency Chairman, Paul Hyde-Thomson, generously offered us his charming villa in the Costa Smeralda in Sardinia for our August family holiday. Instant recognition is something that any public figure has to become inured to (although Thérèse always loathed it) but it does mean that one can relax on holiday only if there is complete privacy. From this point of view, and indeed from every other, the Villa Tartuga was ideal. Before going away, however, I decided that, since the forthcoming Fund/Bank Annual Meeting would be the first since the Louvre Accord, the obvious theme for my main speech would be exchange rate policy. Accordingly, I asked Terry Burns to let me have as somewhat unusual holiday reading copies of the best academic articles he could find on the subject, from all points of view, ranging from that of the fixed-rate scheme-mongers to that of the untrammelled free floaters. Once in Sardinia I settled down beside the swimming pool with my reading list, and – having sorted out my thoughts – wrote down on a single sheet of foolscap the main points of my subsequent IMF speech on 'managed floating'.

To Washington via Nyborg

Immediately prior to the IMF, however, there was the usual informal Ecofin meeting, this time at Nyborg on the Danish island of Funen. The main business was the technical improvements in the EMS which I had mentioned to Margaret. The French had been arguing for what they liked to describe as more symmetry in the system. Under the EMS rules, when (for example) the franc was at the bottom of its permitted ranges against the Deutschmark, there was an obligation on both France and Germany to intervene to maintain the parity. What the architects of the scheme had strangely not foreseen, however, was that Central Banks would not normally want to wait until their currency was right up against the buffers before intervening; and thus so-called intra-marginal intervention had become the norm.

But this was something which, in the example I have quoted, the Banque de France found it had to do on its own, since, unlike the case with intervention at the margin, the Bundesbank was under no obligation to do anything at all, and did nothing in practice either. The Bundesbank's argument was, essentially, that it was the responsibility of the weak to keep up with the strong; but this was reinforced by its long-standing policy of holding no European currencies, only dollars, in its reserves – not to mention its fear that intervention might be inflationary. This was the 'asymmetry' to which the French objected. They were clearly on to an important point; and I supported them in particular over the Bundesbank's unhelpful – and for that matter distinctly un-communautaire – reserves policy.

In the event, the French did not achieve the legal obligation they sought, but they did secure an understanding that there would in future be co-operation between central banks over intra-marginal intervention. There were also other, more technical, changes agreed; but this was the most important. In fact, most of this had already been agreed by the European Community's Committee of Central Bank Governors, of which Karl Otto Pöhl was Chairman, at Basle the previous weekend. Pöhl was characteristically anxious both that the Finance Ministers' role should be little more than that of ratifying changes the Central Bank governors had already agreed, and that the Press should be made fully aware of this. Nevertheless the proprieties were observed and the improvements became known as the 'Basle–Nyborg Changes'.

The Nyborg Ecofin also endorsed, to no great effect, a mutual surveillance system though the Community's Monetary Committee, involving the UK as well as ERM participants, which aimed to use a version of the G7 indicator system. What was much more important was that it also marked the start of the long negotiations which eventually led to the Community's Capital Movements Directive requiring the removal of all exchange controls by July 1990 – thus knocking down another stock objection of Margaret's to the ERM.

As usual, the G7 (as it by then firmly was) met in Washington on the eve of the annual Bank and Fund meetings, and on Saturday, 26 September issued a worthy communiqué reaffirming the adjusted Louvre currency ranges, but remaining silent on the accompanying interest rate moves necessary to underwrite them. The dollar continued to be under pressure, and the row about whether the Americans should increase their interest rates or the Japanese and Germans reduce theirs continued to rumble on, and could not be papered over by the indicator exercise. While I saw little case for a rise in *average* world interest rates, I had no sympathy for the US refusal to contemplate any increase in their interest rates.

In my address to the IMF Interim Committee, I focused for the first time on the so-called problem of the trade imbalances. This had long been (in my view mistakenly) a major preoccupation of international gatherings in the context of the US trade deficit and the German and Japanese surpluses, but I had largely ignored it, preferring to focus on genuine problems. With the UK now moving into current account deficit, I was conscious that this was likely to re-emerge as an issue in the UK, and I decided to break my silence, saying:

> It is easy to overstate the problem. There is no iron law that dictates that the current accounts of the major industrial countries should always be in balance. We have an integrated world economy and we encourage the free flow of capital and goods. Investment opportunities and savings propensities inevitably differ from country to country and it is natural for this to produce substantial, and often sustained, capital account flows. These flows are bound to have their counterparts in current account surpluses and deficits. But . . . there are clearly limits to the accumulated external liabilities or assets that can be sustained without creating major anxieties for capital markets.

I was to develop this thesis much more fully in my main address to the annual Bank/Fund meeting in both 1988 and 1989.

My 1987 IMF Speech

The major event of my Fund/Bank visit of September 1987 was my formal address to the Joint Annual Meeting on Wednesday, 30 September. Fortunately I had a little time to do further work on it. The traditional reception given by the British Ambassador on the Monday evening in honour of the Chancellor of the Exchequer and the Governor of the Bank of England was not very taxing. The American bankers present tended to be figures from the past – more likely the product of an out-of-date Embassy guest list than anything else. The informal lunch given the following day by Tim Lankester, the Embassy's Economic Minister, was much more useful, but left the rest of the day free. This was needed. Although a draft speech had been prepared for me, with a considerable input from Terry Burns, on the basis of my Sardinian notes and subsequent briefings, it was not quite what I wanted and I decided to rewrite it completely.

'MANAGED FLOATING'

The main section of the speech discussed the evolution of exchange rate policy since the breakdown of the Bretton Woods system in the late 1960s and early 1970s, with particular reference to our experience in the 1980s. I went on to sketch how, based on that experience, I thought the world's exchange rate régime should develop in the years ahead.

So far as the past was concerned, I pointed out how the period of free floating had in practice led to wild gyrations in exchange rates, especially for the dollar, which still dominated the world's money markets and accounted for 97 per cent of all transactions on the London foreign exchange market. The problem with 'global 24-hour foreign exchange markets' was the absence of players who 'take a longer view and so provide a stabilizing influence'. As a result, exchange rate movements 'have often acquired a momentum of their own, which has not been reversed until they have reached extreme levels of over- or under-valuation'. These gyrations were harmful to the growth of world trade, caused businesses to divert scarce management time and skills to coping with currency fluctuations rather than improving company performance, inhibited risk-taking, and required shifts in resources from the home to the export market and back again, at a pace that was wholly unrealistic.

It was in response to this unsatisfactory state of affairs that the major nations, first at the Plaza and then more fundamentally at the Louvre, had moved to a regime of what I called 'managed floating'. (I thought at the time that I had invented the term myself, but subsequently discovered that, unknown to me, it had been used before, albeit in a rather different context.) This had proved possible in the 1980s, whereas it would not have been in the 1970s, essentially for two reasons: first, the fact that we had moved from a world of high inflation to one of low inflation; and, second, because a new consensus had emerged over the conduct of economic policy – broadly speaking, greater reliance on market mechanisms within the framework of a firm monetary and fiscal policy.

On the basis of my account of the recent past, I then turned to the future, and I quote that section of the speech in full since it was to prove somewhat controversial:

> I believe that we can and should use the experience we have gained to build a more permanent regime of managed floating. I do not see the past two years as a temporary phase. Our objectives should be clear: to maintain the maximum stability of key exchange rates, and to manage any changes that may be necessary in an orderly way.
>
> Let me make it clear that I am not suggesting that we can or should return to Bretton Woods. That system was undermined by its rigidity; the margins were too narrow; it required a predictable and mechanical response from the authorities that made them an easy target; necessary realignments were postponed too long, and consequently, when they

came, they were inevitably large.

For the future, it is important, therefore, that we continue to keep an adequate degree of flexibility in terms of the width of the bands within which currencies are able to fluctuate. And, if and when the time comes to adjust one of the rates, that adjustment should be made by moving the midpoint within the confines of the existing range. This means that the markets are not given a one way bet, and the authorities retain tactical flexibility.

As I have already emphasized, what made the Plaza and Louvre agreements possible was that the countries participating were, and remain, in effect, members of an anti-inflationary club, with a clear commitment to taking whatever steps are necessary to curb their own inflation. It is vital that that commitment continues, individually and collectively. A resurgence of inflation in any individual country would make it difficult for that country to remain within the club.

At the same time, we must also ensure that there is no persistent inflationary (or for that matter deflationary) bias for the group as a whole. This can be helped by:

● the development of indicators for the group as a whole; these will be mainly financial but special attention should also be given to the trend of world commodity prices;

● a nominal framework for policy, in terms either of a path for GDP growth for the group as a whole, or one for the average inflation rate; and

● a medium-term perspective when setting out the path and in gauging actual performance. We should not become involved in an exercise in short-term fine tuning.

In recent meetings we have put a lot of effort into developing performance indicators for individual countries. I have to say that I have considerable doubts whether we can usefully take that exercise much further. I believe it would be far more useful to devote our efforts to monitoring the performance of the group as a whole, so that we can ensure that we maintain the correct non-inflationary policy stance.

Reactions to the Speech

Much of the subsequent press comment said that I had come out in favour of target zones, a perennial French proposal for the conduct of exchange rate policy and something with which the US Treasury team, notably Jim Baker's number two, Dick Darman, had been flirting. Indeed Baker, whose own speech immediately followed mine, spoke (without any collusion) in remarkably similar terms – although in his case Press comment largely latched on to his proposal to add the gold price to other commodity prices as the anchor for the system.

'MANAGED FLOATING'

In a sense it was true that I had come out in favour of target zones, although with important qualifications and accompaniments. But what I myself thought was important about the speech was its analysis of what had actually happened and why, of where we found ourselves as a result, and what its essential logic was. Beyond that, what was 'new' in the speech – apart from the fact that it was the first time it had been uttered by a British Chancellor – was the thesis that it was not a matter of proposing a new international monetary order: that we were already three quarters of the way there.

In this I was much too optimistic. Within a matter of weeks the Wall Street crash of Black Monday, 19 October, had thrown everything into confusion. There were even those who contrived to claim that it was the Louvre Accord that had caused the crash – claiming bizarrely, that there was somehow a fixed quantum of instability in financial markets, and that stable exchange rates channelled all the instability to the stock market. By the time the world had recovered from the crash, Jim Baker had resigned as Treasury Secretary to organize his old friend George Bush's 1988 Presidential campaign, taking Dick Darman with him; and when he returned to office after the election it was as Bush's Secretary of State. At the same time, Darman was appointed to head the Bureau of the Budget, which is concerned solely with public spending.

Given the uniquely important position of the dollar, a necessary (although not a sufficient) condition of international financial co-operation, particularly on the exchange rate front, is American leadership. Baker's successor at the US Treasury, Nick Brady, had neither the desire nor the capacity to exercise international leadership in this or indeed any other field, and the situation degenerated into one of *ad hoc*cery and drift. There was neither the ideological belief in free floating that characterized the Regan period, nor the commitment to a structured form of managed floating that characterized Baker's term of office.

Meanwhile my speech was well received by the more thoughtful observers on both sides of the Atlantic, with one important exception. Although she never said a word to me herself, I learned indirectly that Margaret had been complaining that my speech had not been 'cleared' with her in advance – the implication being that she would have stopped it if it had been.

I also learned, again indirectly, through friends in the City and in the Press, that Brian Griffiths, whose capacity for causing trouble was considerable, had been letting it be known that my speech did not represent Government policy. It appears that he did not consider that the Louvre Accord, to which the UK was a signatory, and which had been formally endorsed by the seven Heads of State and Government at the Venice Summit, represented Government policy, either.

Needless to say, and contrary to what some of her apologists have subsequently sought to maintain, Margaret knew all about the Louvre agreement and about my understanding of how sterling fitted into it, since I had made a point of keeping her well informed at every stage. She also knew all about the intervention in the foreign exchange market to implement the policy, receiving a market report every evening showing *inter alia* the full extent of that day's intervention.

Indeed, until September 1987 she welcomed not merely sterling's stability and strength (for while remaining steady against the Deutschmark, the pound was rising against the dollar), but the intervention itself. Whenever she saw Robin Leigh-Pemberton during this period she would greet him with the question 'how much have you taken in today, Mr Governor?' (that is to say, how much foreign exchange had been added to the reserves that day through sales of sterling on the foreign exchange market), and the larger the answer the happier she would be.

But around September 1987 (perhaps during a visit to the United Nations in New York, when she may have seen Walters) she turned against the intervention involved in shadowing the Mark, seeing it as the UK almost single-handedly financing the US deficit, but above all as somehow inflationary. It was against this background that she reacted so badly to my IMF speech – although, as I have already mentioned, saying nothing about it to my face. Then, before I had fully appreciated the extent of her *volte face* , the focus of attention switched abruptly with the irruption of the Wall Street crash of Black Monday, 19 October.

The Poorest of the Poor

Fortunately there was more to life and even to international economics than arguing about exchange rate policy. Before the 1986 Fund and Bank Annual Meetings in the Autumn of 1986 I asked my officials to let me have an up-to-date analysis of the international debt situation, with a view to launching a UK initiative. The picture they came up with was a remorselessly realistic one, and very gloomy reading it made. It was clear that the position of most of the debtors was not improving but deteriorating, and that the assumption that they would ever be in a position to repay their debts in full was pure moonshine. Any UK initiative, the official paper concluded, would have to start from a recognition of this reality.

It was impossible to dissent from either the analysis or the conclusion. Nevertheless, I shied away from making any move so far as Latin American and similar sovereign debt was concerned. This was owed largely to the commercial banks, and I felt it was for them to come to terms with reality in their own way, just as they have to do with bad loans to industrial customers. Government intervention could easily do more harm than good. But it was a different matter so far as the poorest countries, largely in sub-Saharan Africa, were concerned. By Latin American standards, the sums involved were small. But in terms of what their enfeebled economies could actually withstand, the Africans were in a far worse position than their Latin American counterparts. Their GNP per head was typically less than $350, and their overseas debt per head averaged $250.

These countries faced a heavy burden of debt service at a time when their ramshackle economies were going from bad to worse, with many of their people close to starvation. Those that were simply unable to service their debts found that the capitalization of unpaid interest meant that their indebtedness was steadily increasing. Straightforward debt rescheduling (there had been eighty-eight rescheduling agreements in the previous decade) was clearly leading nowhere. These countries were so poor that even the banks had refused to lend to them, with the result that, in contrast to Latin America, the money was owed to Western governments (not least to their export credit agencies) and, to a lesser extent, to international financial institutions. This meant that the problem was clearly one where direct official action was appropriate.

I abandoned my idea of an initiative at the imminent Annual Meetings, and asked my officials to work up a scheme to help those whom I termed the poorest of the poor, which I could launch in the spring of 1987, after the Budget was out of the way. The plan they came up with had three parts. These were, first, to convert official aid loans into grants; second, to allow longer repayment periods (of up to twenty years) for other types of official loan; and third (the only really new element, and one that was absolutely critical) to reduce the rate of interest on the outstanding debt to well below market rates. These concessions were to be confined to those debtors which were pursuing sensible economic policies.

Some commentators found my interest in helping the countries of sub-Saharan Africa out of character. I was not known, for good reason, as a bleeding heart. But that was not out of any lack of sympathy for black African suffering, as anyone who recalled the campaign I had waged as Editor of the *Spectator* on behalf of the Ibos of 'Biafra' during the appalling Nigerian civil war of the 1960s would have recognized. It was rather because government, for me, was not about fine-sounding words but about achieving practical results. It was clear, on a straightforward practical basis, that there was no prospect of the governments who had lent the money to these desperately poor countries ever getting it back.

It was, I reckoned, more sensible to recognize this fact, and use it to manoeuvre the governments of those countries into pursuing sensible economic policies for the benefit of their own people, than to pretend for cosmetic budgeting reasons that the loans were good. But it was also clear that I would have to secure the agreement of all the creditor nations, which would not be easy, since unilateral action by the UK, although it might be emulated by some other countries, would benefit not the debtors, but the remaining creditors.

I decided to broach my plan first, privately and in the most general terms, at the informal Ecofin at Knokke, on the Belgian coast, on 5 April 1987. This was not a matter of canvassing support: it was essentially a courtesy to my Community colleagues, since my intention was to launch the plan officially at the spring meeting of the IMF Interim Committee in Washington, a few days later, when I would have the wider world audience I needed. On the eve of the Interim Committee meeting, again as a courtesy, I mentioned that I would be launching an initiative to help the poorest of the poor to my G5/G7 colleagues.

It was clear that the main practical effect of these two advance warnings would be to alert the French, who always looked on sub-Saharan Africa as their own sphere of interest (even though there were at least as many anglophone as francophone black African countries that were likely to qualify) and would not wish to be upstaged by the UK. I therefore took the precaution of informing the Press, immediately after the G5/G7 meeting, of the broad outline of the initiative I would be putting forward at the interim committee meeting the next day, at which I managed to ensure that I was called to speak before my French opposite number, the estimable Pierre Bérégovoy. I am afraid the French did not relish being beaten at their own game in this way.

Not surprisingly, my initiative was extremely well received by the black African Ministers present. But it quickly ran into formidable American and West German opposition over the question of offering sub-Saharan debtors sub-market interest rates. They believed that it would encourage the so-called 'middle income debtors', mainly in Latin America, to press for a similar concession, deter commercial lenders and give the Africans no incentive to pursue more realistic economic policies. This kind of thinking was either confused or self-serving.

There were, as always, awkward borderline cases (the Caribbean countries were a case in point); but the difference between the poorest of the poor in sub-Saharan Africa and the Latin Americans was, as I have already described, clear and indisputable. Moreover ring-fencing already existed, in various contexts, not least the internationally-accepted World Bank criteria for eligibility for assistance from IDA (the International Development Agency), the World Bank affiliate charged with lending to very poor countries at concessional rates.

From the April 1987 Interim Committee meeting onwards, it became a matter of drumming up support from the rest of the world outside the United States, Germany and Japan (the last of which could be counted on to drop its objections if and when the United States did so), and wearing the United States and Germany down by a mixture of persistence and their unease at their increasing isolation.

The cause was helped by the fact that the IMF, sensing the way the wind was blowing, developed a different but complementary initiative of their own to help the poorest of the poor. This was formally communicated to the Economic Summit held in Venice in June 1987, in the midst of the UK election campaign. As a result, and at the strong urging of the UK, it was accepted in principle, for the first time at one of those gatherings, that the problems of the poorest countries, chiefly in sub-Saharan Africa, were different in kind from, and warranted different treatment from, the general international debt problem.

Clearly, however, I needed to make further progress at the Annual Fund and Bank meetings in September. But I decided first to make a rare appearance at the preceding Commonwealth Finance Ministers' meeting, which in 1987 was held in that most English of all the Caribbean islands, Barbados. My speech there was warmly received, and I won the endorsement of the Commonwealth for my plan, although not without some carping from some of the countries that realized they would not qualify for assistance under it, and hesitation right up until the last moment from the Canadians. Getting Canada on board was one of the main purposes of the exercise, since the United States tended to count on them to support the US position on international financial issues. The other main purpose was to keep up the momentum, and to secure a backing I could quote and use when I got to Washington.

The overall atmosphere at Barbados could scarcely have been more different from that which had greeted me at my first Commonwealth Finance Ministers' meeting in Port of Spain four years earlier. The ritual denunciations of Britain, coupled shamelessly with pleas for additional aid, had given way to boasting about the free-market policies which they were now pursuing. It was a most encouraging change.

The Toronto Terms

Patience and persistence are the two main requirements of any successful international initiative. I had first launched my plan in April 1987. It did indeed gain further momentum of a kind at the IMF in September. Even so, it was far from being in the bag. The crucial breakthrough did not occur until the summer of 1988, on the eve of the Economic Summit which that year was to be held in Toronto. Up to that point Margaret had tolerated my initiative, without showing any great enthusiasm for it, although it had been agreed that it should be one of the UK's objectives to secure the plan's endorsement at the Summit. Then President Mitterrand, out of the blue, announced with a great fanfare a French initiative which he proposed to put to the Summit. This was similar to the UK initiative (of which he made no mention), save that instead of an interest rate reduction on all debt there would be a complete write-off of one third of the debt, with full market interest rates continuing to be payable on the rest.

This seemed like a clear attempt to steal the UK's thunder, and it transformed Margaret's attitude. She was determined that Toronto should be the scene of a successful UK initiative rather than a successful French one. Meanwhile Jean-Claude Trichet, who as *Directeur du Trésor* was Bérégovoy's deputy and, even more important in this context, chairman of the Paris Club, the forum at which the policies of the various national export credit agencies are coordinated, not least in respect to bad payers, sought to defuse the situation by working out a synthesis of the British and French plans.

At Toronto my first task was to have a private talk with Jim Baker, who at last said he was prepared to do something, simply to get me off his back; but for budgetary and Congressional reasons this could not be either the interest rate reductions I had proposed or the partial debt write-off the French were pressing. The best he could offer was ultra-long rescheduling – up to twenty-five years – with a very long period of grace before any interest would be payable at all. After considerable discussion, it was clear that it was not possible to push him any further.

Thus it was that, in June 1988, the Heads of State and Government agreed to what was to become known as the Toronto terms. This was a package in which every creditor country would offer the poorest of the poor, in addition to the conversion of aid loans into outright grants (or the equivalent), one of three items from a menu which consisted of an interest rate reduction as proposed by the UK, a partial write-off of principal as proposed by France, and an ultra-long rescheduling, with a very long period of grace, which the Americans had made clear was the best they could do. The Paris Club was charged with working out the details, and the intention was that the resulting scheme would be agreed by the entire world financial community at the forthcoming Bank and Fund annual meeting in September.

Trichet, who exemplified, both professionally and personally, the French Civil Service at its impressive best, duly worked out a matrix in which the details of the various options made each of them, in theory at least, of equal value to the recipient. By the time we arrived at the Annual Bank and Fund meeting, all the details had been fully worked out, and the only country of any significance not to have agreed was Germany. Since, however, the annual meeting that year was in Berlin (it takes place in Washington two years out of every three, but rather absurdly becomes peripatetic in the third), Stoltenberg had little choice, as host, but to give in gracefully. At long last, eighteen months after I had first launched my initiative, full international agreement was finally secured.

It did not, of course, transform the appalling position of the debt-laden countries of sub-Saharan Africa, but it was the best that could be agreed at that time. It was, moreover, a breakthrough, which could be built upon subsequently. Among the Africans, no-one was in any doubt that, despite the 'Toronto terms' appellation, it was a UK initiative that had started it all off. The episode earned the UK quite remarkable goodwill from those benighted countries, at a cost which, however it appeared in the official accounts, was in reality almost nugatory.

CHAPTER 60

THE WALL STREET CRASH

Blackpool Parade · Black Monday
Policy After the Crash · Base Rates After the Crash
The US–German Row · International Co-operation Survives
An Important Non-Meeting

Blackpool Parade

THE CONSERVATIVE PARTY CONFERENCE in Blackpool in the second week of October 1987 was more or less a victory parade, and my own speech was tailored to the triumphal mood of the Party. In it I coined the phrase 'a nation of inheritors'. There seemed no point in pretending that all personal property was the result of lifetime personal savings. An element is inherited: and a good thing, too, in giving people a cushion to fall back upon, a capital base with which to start their careers or take a few risks, and a stake in the capitalist system. But I was keen that inherited wealth should be diffused and not confined to a few. The notion of a nation of inheritors was not merely, as I saw it, the logical sequence to the property-owning democracy. It was also an essential means of *entrenching* the political, economic and cultural changes we had sought to bring about – an objective that increasingly preoccupied me.

Black Monday

Less than a fortnight after I had spoken, the triumphal mood of the Party Conference was abruptly shattered by what came to be known as Black Monday.

The Wall Street crash of Monday, 19 October, cannot be described as a bolt from the blue. The New York stock market had been falling

745

quite steeply in the two weeks before the crash, as had London. The crash was essentially a reaction to an earlier excessive stock market boom. At its peak in September the New York equity market was no less than 44 per cent above its level at the start of the year, and the Tokyo market 42 per cent up. The London market had peaked in July, some 46 per cent above the level at which the year had begun.

In England, nature provided a suitably Gothic overture to the cataclysm which followed. During the night of Thursday 15 October, southern and south-eastern England were devastated by a freak hurricane. (Among the many victims was the Governor of the Bank of England, Robin Leigh-Pemberton, whose Kent estate was stripped of many of its finest trees.) Blocked roads and railways prevented more than a handful of people getting to work in the City on the Friday morning, and the stock exchange and the money markets were both officially closed. This postponed any further downward pressure on the London market until Monday morning.

On Black Monday itself the Dow-Jones fell by 23 per cent – an unprecedented fall in a single day – taking the index to 34 per cent below its early October level. The fall in London was of similar dimensions but less concentrated into a single day. Continental bourses fell by equivalent amounts, but Tokyo fell much less. There were then modest rallies and further falls to strain the nerves. The equity markets eventually bottomed out in early December. After the large correction markets resumed their more normal fluctuations. By the second half of 1989 London was back at pre-crash levels. Other markets regained their pre-crash levels somewhat sooner. So there should have been no lasting damage to the cause of wider share ownership. And if investors had a spectacular lesson in the fact that security prices can move in both directions, no harm was done.

Such phlegm may be all right after the event. Indeed by 1988 I was publicly calling the crash an economic 'non-event'. But at the time it seemed to many the end of financial civilization as we had known it.

Because the Wall Street crash of 1929 had been the prelude to the Great Depression, every subsequent major stock market setback tended to be followed, like a conditioned reflex, by predictions of 'another 1929'. But there had never been a setback as sharp as that of 1987. For a few days, sheer panic reigned. The institutions, who had been buying equities hand over fist as the market rose to its peak, were now too frightened to enter the market at all. The august former Editor of *The Times*, William Rees-Mogg, warned his readers to expect what he called a 'drunken M' along the lines of the early 1930s, when the crash was followed by a modest recovery and several much larger downward movements, culminating in a huge slump in the real economy. *The Economist* ventured that 'the crash of 1987 could lead to the slump of 1988 . . . The immediate task is a Keynesian one: to support demand at a time when the stock market crash threatens to shrink it.'

Even after I had modestly reduced interest rates, the Labour Party called for still more cuts. At the end of December 1987, after rates had come down by one and a half percentage points, Bryan Gould, Labour's trade and industry spokesman, still accused me of 'fiddling', of 'staggering complacency' and of 'wringing my hands . . . while continuing to saddle industry with excessively high interest rates.' John Smith was no more restrained.

The mood in the boardrooms was, to say the least, alarmingly fragile. I remember a morale-boosting dinner Margaret hosted at Number 10 for David Nickson, the President of the CBI, Denys Henderson, the Chairman of ICI, and a number of other business leaders. Their deep gloom and despondency bore no relation to the roaring economic boom of 1987 which the statistics subsequently conveyed. When I asked Nickson and John Banham, the CBI's Director-General, round for drinks at Number 11 nearly a month after the crash, maintaining business confidence was still their primary concern.

Policy After the Crash

While I myself did not share the general crash hysteria, for the first and only time during my period as Chancellor I judged the risk of serious recession as greater than the risk of inflation. On the Tuesday after Black Monday I spent most of the day giving television and radio interviews trying to spread reassurance. I told the Stock Exchange Conference for Industry exactly one week after Black Monday:

> One well-known characteristic of financial markets is their tendency to overshoot . . . It was neither unexpected nor in any way unprecedented that sooner or later there would be a sizeable correction . . . It is abundantly clear that market corrections of this kind do not require there to have been any change in economic fundamentals. Still less do they imply that the world's economies are fundamentally unsound.

Inevitably, I devoted the major part of my Mansion House speech that year to the stock market crash. I said the fact that share prices were actually at much the same level as a year ago was 'something that needs very much to be borne in mind when assessing the likely scale of the economic effects of the stock market falls.' I added that the effect in the 'UK may not be very large and should reduce any risk of overheating there may have been.' William Keegan, an unremitting political and economic critic, gracefully conceded: 'Lawson's comments so soon after the crash read well in retrospect and he made his contribution to diffusing the panic.'

It seemed nevertheless likely that there would be some real effects from the crash, if only because of the collapse of financial and business confidence. There was also some concern that the US, where the stock market impinges most on personal wealth and the public mood, might by its sheer size lead the world into recession. In the regular economic forecast which accompanied the Autumn Statement on 3 November 1987 the growth prospects for 1988 had to be revised in a rough-and-ready way. They showed growth falling by almost a half, from 4 per cent in 1987 to just 2½ per cent in 1988. In the event, the crash had very little impact on the real economy at all, which expanded all too vigorously.

There was one thing I was determined not to do: that was to abandon my budgetary guidelines. If the crash had been followed by a recession the Budget would have moved automatically into temporary deficit. This I would have been prepared to accept, since it was consistent with underlying balance over the cycle as a whole. But I did not see anything on the horizon which would justify discretionary anti-slump spending increases, despite all the advice showered on me to institute emergency public works programmes from the Opposition front bench and even from some of my own senior back-benchers.

Base Rates After the Crash

The crash had a significant effect on the conduct of domestic monetary policy. Until then I had regarded it as almost certain that the one percentage point increase in base rates to 10 per cent in August would soon be followed by another. During September and the early part of October evidence of overheating had gradually been growing. Once the immediate trauma of the crash had passed, it seemed as if it had been a blessing in disguise – a douche of cold water just when it was needed. In the words of the November Bank of England *Bulletin*, 'the sharp fall in equity prices . . . implies a tightening of monetary conditions, by raising the cost of equity capital to firms and, through the effect of wealth reduction, by depressing consumption demand by households. It is far from easy . . . to judge just how powerful these last effects will be . . . but they are unlikely to be negligible.'

There was another way in which developments at the time of the crash eased some policy problems. It was never my practice to look only at the sterling—Deutschmark rate. I always kept a weather eye on the sterling index too. Because of the weakness of the dollar, sterling strengthened against the currency basket, even when it was up against the DM3 ceiling. There was a particularly strong rise in the sterling index in November; and in the whole year of shadowing the Mark – up to March 1988 – it rose by 5 percentage points, thus tightening the policy stance.

Indeed, whereas before the crash I had been discussing with senior officials at the Treasury and the Bank whether, and if so when, interest rates should rise further, discussion after the crash turned to the question of interest rate reductions. I called a meeting of the usual cast – with the exception of Robin Leigh-Pemberton, who was abroad – to assess the situation the day after Black Monday, 20 October. There was a general concern that normal forecasting methods might not take sufficient account of the effects of the stock market crash on personal and corporate wealth. This was stressed especially by Terry Burns. He was supported by the Bank, which warned that if the US was dragged into recession the British economy would follow. At the end of the week there were further meetings, and I decided to make a half per cent cut in base rates 'for psychological reasons only', in order to bolster business confidence. It was also agreed to have a short funding pause to ease any liquidity problems, which lasted only a few days.

Alan Greenspan, who had succeeded Paul Volcker as Chairman of the Fed, declared on 20 October:

> The Federal Reserve, consistent with its responsibilities as the nation's central bank, affirmed today its readiness to serve as a source of liquidity to support the economic and financial system.

These words were widely thought to have stabilized market sentiment. But I saw no need for them to be repeated in the UK.

I cut interest rates by a further half per cent on 4 November, after a further plunge of 80 points in the London equity market that morning had touched a raw nerve, coming only a fortnight after Black Monday. At the same time sterling was rising against all currencies. Thus both external and internal considerations argued for a cut, which was concerted with similar action in most other financial centres. As I told the City bankers – who were for once probably listening carefully – at the Mansion House that evening:

> I fully understand – and sympathize with – the hesitations of those who are fearful of the risks of inflation. I have made it clear in the management of the UK monetary policy that I am as conscious as anyone of such risks. But if interest rates were the right levels three weeks ago, then it is unlikely that those levels are still right after all that has happened since . . . What is needed in the world today, above all, is the avoidance of any major blow to industrial confidence. It was not the 1929 crash that caused the depression of the 1930s, but the policy response to it: the failure to provide

adequate liquidity to the system, leading to a rash of bank failures, which in turn led to further monetary tightening; and of course the lurch into beggar-my-neighbour trade policies . . .

The third and final half per cent cut in base rates in response to the crash was made as part of a co-ordinated move by European countries to stem the falling dollar, and to encourage the US to commit itself to a hands-on policy. The Germans cut interest rates on 3 December, accompanied by the Benelux countries, France, Switzerland and Austria. On 4 December, British base rates came down from 9 per cent to 8½ per cent, implying a real interest rate of a shade under 5 per cent, comfortably above the G7 average. The co-ordination, which required a large number of telephone calls, was also intended to boost confidence by demonstrating that international financial co-operation remained alive and well.

Throughout this difficult and somewhat fraught phase, there was no rift whatever between the Treasury and the Bank. A few days after the 1987 election I had received a note from George Blunden, the Deputy Governor in which he wrote that 'I don't think there has been a time since the war when Treasury Ministers, the Treasury staff and the Bank have worked so well together.'

Even with several years' hindsight, I cannot regret the action which we took, along with our partners, to avert the risks from the Wall Street crash. One does not regret a fire insurance policy because there has been no fire. Nor, indeed, can we be absolutely sure (and here the analogy breaks down) that there would not have been a fire had we all simply sat on our hands and done nothing. It might well have been one of those relatively rare occasions on which there was no 'right' course to take: it was rather a matter of choosing the lesser of two evils. If so, however, this emphasizes that the real mischief occurred in 1986, when the sharp fall in the exchange rate, exacerbated by my inability to secure the interest rate increases I sought, created an excessive degree of laxity. On 5 November, the day after the second of the three half-point reductions in interest rates I made in the wake of Black Monday, the Labour Party moved a motion in the House of Commons urging the Government, *inter alia*, 'to significantly cut interest rates [and] to target increases in public expenditure in order to prevent an economic downturn'.

Opening the debate, John Smith declared:

Following the crash in the financial markets, and with the threat of an international crisis looming, the House should concentrate its mind on the lessons to be learned from the turbulent events of recent weeks with one overriding objective – the urgent steps that need to be taken to ward off the threat of economic downturn.

Winding up for Labour, Bryan Gould argued that

> Interest rates are the crucial determinant of the policy stance . . .
> If interest rates are kept high, the City will applaud, but the real
> economy will be damaged. Unfortunately for that economy, it is
> already clear that the Chancellor has again opted for the money men
> and the financial establishment. Yesterday's feeble half per cent cut
> did no more than complete the reversal of the mistake of August.

The Liberal Democrats also urged me to bring interest rates down
further, as did a number of Conservative back-benchers, echoing the
almost universal message of the Press and other commentators. If, in
the event, I overreacted to the 1987 crash, it is clear that matters would
have been incomparably worse had I heeded the advice that was being
showered upon me from all sides.

The US–German Row

The Wall Street crash had a diplomatic prelude and postlude. I have
alluded more than once to the simmering row between the Americans and
the Germans as to whether the former should tighten monetary policy or
the latter loosen theirs to maintain the Louvre ranges.

Intervention had been taken almost as far as it could go in 1987. The
American authorities possess a great deal of gold, but are remarkably short of foreign currency. The Germans, and the Bundesbank
in particular, were concerned that under their system, endless intervention to sustain the dollar was inflationary. The subsequent German
inflation figures did not bear this out in Germany itself; but evidence
does suggest that the average G7 policy stance was too inflationary,
not because of intervention but because average short-term interest
rates were not high enough. In any case the 1987 position – when
the greater part of the US current account deficit was financed by
overseas monetary authorities acquiring dollars – was highly abnormal,
and could not and did not recur.

In the US both growth and inflation were rising to unsustainable
rates and the Federal Reserve had perfectly good domestic grounds
for raising its discount rate at the end of September. Baker had pressed
Greenspan to use his contacts with the Bundesbank to dissuade them
from negating the American increase by raising their own interest rates.
But the Bundesbank went ahead and raised its discount rate a few days
later, thus necessitating a second rise in American rates towards the
end of September. In the second week of October – the week before
the crash – Baker publicly expressed his exasperation, saying that the
German monetary tightening 'violated the spirit of our consultations' and

that the Louvre accord did not require further increases in US interest rates to stop the dollar depreciating.

However understandable Jim Baker's annoyance may have been, this was a doubly unwise statement to have made. Indeed, the standard study by Destler and Henning described it as 'the greatest mistake Baker made as Treasury Secretary'. In the first place, the financial markets' confidence in international financial co-operation was bound to be seriously damaged by a public row between two of the main participants. And in the second place, Baker appeared once again to be threatening to let the dollar go into free fall. To his credit, the US Treasury Secretary repented of his remark very rapidly, and flew to Germany from Sweden where he happened to be at the time, to meet Stoltenberg and Pöhl in the immediate wake of the crash. In a joint communiqué released that day both sides reaffirmed their commitment to a 'flexible application' of the Louvre Accord with a view to 'exchange rate stability at around current levels'. The agreement was understood to provide for an easing of German monetary policy.

Ever since then a controversy has rumbled between those who maintain, somewhat implausibly, that the Louvre Accord was the cause of the Wall Street crash and the rival view that it was the failure to observe the Accord that was the culprit. A third school, following the Brady Commission, places emphasis on various technical innovations in the New York stock exchange such as automatic computerized programme selling, which magnified any incipient downturn.

As I saw it, some market correction was overdue and probably desirable, and the US–German row may have provided the trigger for something that would have occurred sooner or later anyhow. As for computerized programme selling, this did not so much magnify the downturn but rather sped it up, telescoping what might have taken a week into a single day. While it was the unprecedented rapidity of the decline that caused the panic at the time, there is nothing intrinsically wrong with a rapid correction; and now that we have safely survived the first of these it must be more likely that the next time it occurs the refrain will be not the alarmist 'remember 1929' unless the conditions genuinely warrant it, as they did not in 1987.

International Co-operation Survives

There is a myth that monetary and exchange rate co-operation collapsed in the wake of the crash. In fact it continued, and did not evaporate until 1988 brought new problems and a new US Treasury Secretary.

I was in constant touch with my opposite numbers in the other G7 countries from the day of the crash onwards. Indeed, during the fortnight following Black Monday, I was on the telephone to my fellow-G7 Finance Ministers at what seemed to be all hours of the day and night. I recall one conversation with Jim Baker in full evening dress, immediately after the Mansion House banquet at eleven o'clock that evening. My first conversation with Jim, however, was when he rang me to plead on behalf of the Wall Street investment houses exposed to the BP issue, which I come to in the next chapter. I suggested in turn that confidence would be better restored by a co-ordinated round of interest rate reductions. The problem was the Germans, who had refused to follow the Anglo–American example in the week of the crash. Until then I had supported German resistance to American pressure for more expansionary policies. But I now thought that a new situation called for a new attitude; and in my speech to the Stock Exchange industry conference on 26 October I remarked:

> What is not required in current world circumstances is either a lurch into protection or undue monetary tightening. It was this which quite unnecessarily turned the 1929 Wall Street crash into the Depression of the 1930s. I believe the lesson has now been widely learnt. But it would certainly be helpful if the German authorities were to show more obvious awareness of this.

Jim Baker's main priority, however, was to secure agreement with the Democrat-controlled Congress on a package of policies to reduce the American Budget deficit, which was then a main concern in the financial markets. He secured this on 20 November, the deadline set by the Gramm-Rudman-Hollings legislation for supposedly automatic deficit cuts. The US Budget deficit had in fact already started to fall in 1987 and on nearly all measures shrank substantially in 1988 and 1989, only to balloon again with the subsequent Savings and Loan Rescue Operation and the onset of recession.

Meanwhile, the Americans, nursing what was at that time an unwarranted fear of recession, were happy to let the dollar slide for a while after the crash, and Louvre ranges were set aside. By early December UK businessmen were starting to complain to me about the effect on their competitiveness of the falling dollar exchange rate. Other European Finance Ministers and central bankers were similarly concerned about the falling dollar and were looking for firm evidence that the Americans were prepared to stabilize it. In view of the US Administration's continued preoccupation with recession, the only feasible move was a co-ordinated cut in European interest rates. It was something the Americans had frequently called for, but this was the first time in my Chancellorship that it had seemed appropriate. Robin Leigh-Pemberton told me that Karl Otto Pöhl was prepared to cut the

Bundesbank's discount rate by half a point on the understanding that other countries would follow suit.

A co-ordinated cut in European interest rates was intended to entice the Americans into committing themselves to a stable dollar. There was much talk of whether there should be a meeting of the G7. Indeed, in the UK the Opposition had been calling for one ever since Black Monday. I took the view that it would be better to have no meeting at all than one at which the Americans refused to accept such a commitment. I told the American Chamber of Commerce in London on 24 November that a get-together would be useless 'unless all those involved were prepared to contribute wholeheartedly to the stabilization of the dollar'. On 3 December, I wrote to Jim Baker setting out the conditions I felt essential to a successful G7 agreement. After some flattering remarks about the 20 November US budgetary agreement, I got to the point:

> We must address the two basic and linked problems of exchange rates and the financing of the US fiscal and current account deficits . . . Official intervention has in effect financed the major part of the US external deficit this year. Though intervention has an important part to play, it obviously cannot be the sole or major source of external funds. Spontaneous private flows have to meet this need. I believe it is unrealistic to hope to restore sufficient private capital flows to the US as long as the market harbours expectations of dollar depreciation which could be self-fulfilling. Unless we can co-operate to prevent this, I see a real risk of further dollar depreciation spiralling out of control . . . I cannot see how the US could then avoid serious inflationary consequences, and sooner or later the market would inevitably drive up US interest rates.

I suggested that the G7 should endorse prevailing exchange rates and demonstrate its ability and willingness to support them with all measures including interest rate changes. I also suggested the US should consider foreign currency denominated borrowing both to bolster its own reserves and to minimize the risk of having to push up American interest rates when it did not wish to do so. The point about foreign currency denominated borrowing was that the return to the purchaser depended on the movement of interest rates in the package of currencies in which the bonds were denominated. This severed or at least weakened the link between US domestic rates and the rate at which the US could borrow overseas.

Unfortunately, President Carter had made a similar move in the face of a weakening dollar, and the device, which had become known as 'Carter Bonds', had been strongly attacked by Reagan and his colleagues in Reagan's first Presidential campaign. Although Baker was sympathetic to the idea, he explained that, given what the Republicans had then said, it was politically impossible for the Reagan administration to issue bonds denominated in foreign currencies.

An Important Non-Meeting

Baker eventually agreed to commit himself to dollar stabilization. But the question then arose of where we should meet. Baker felt he had to remain on American soil while the budgetary legislation was grinding through Congress; and Japan's Kiichi Miyazawa claimed that parliamentary obligations made it difficult for him to manage the long trip to Europe. Baker eventually suggested Anchorage in Alaska, a god-forsaken place whose sole claim as a venue (apart from the fact that it was US soil) was that it was more or less equally inconvenient for all of us.

This did not appeal to me at all, nor were my European counterparts very much keener. It occurred to me that in the circumstances, we did not really need to meet at all. What we needed was a communiqué that would steady the markets. It so happened that an Ecofin meeting was due to be held in Brussels on 7 December. I got in touch with Stoltenberg, Bérégovoy (who had returned as French Finance Minister) and Amato, and fixed a meeting between the four of us and our deputies at the office of the British Ambassador to the European Community an hour before the Ecofin was due to begin.

I put it to them that we had got into the habit in the G7 of meeting and issuing communiqués, and pointed out that in the good old days the G5 used to meet without issuing a communiqué. Why should we not avail ourselves of the remaining option, a communiqué without a meeting? The telephone had, after all, been invented some time ago; it would avoid an inconvenient trip to Anchorage; it would serve the purpose of having the US signed up; and it would be a useful shot in our locker for the future, since the markets could never be sure when we were going to do it again.

The others were attracted by the idea, and Stoltenberg, as the senior European Finance Minister, undertook to sell the idea to Baker, which he did. The Japanese then had no option but to concur. An agreed text was hammered out by telephone. It took a number of lengthy calls; but the reason for the delay in issuing it was Jim Baker's understandable desire to postpone it until Congress had finally ratified the US Budget reduction programme.

The communiqué, which was published on the evening of 22 December, US time, or 23 December, European and Japanese time, reaffirmed the 'basic objectives and economic policy directives agreed in the Louvre Accord'. The key paragraph was Number 8, which read – with deliberate assymmetry – as follows:

> The Ministers and Governors agree that either excessive fluctuation of exchange rates, a further decline of the dollar, or a rise of the dollar to an extent that becomes destabilizing to the adjustment process, could be counter-productive by damaging growth prospects in the world economy. They re-emphasized their common interest in more stable exchange rates among their currencies . . . In addition they agreed to co-operate closely on the exchange markets.

Predictably, the communiqué was disparaged by the Press when it was released. The Press hate being taken by surprise, and on this occasion they were. Not only was no-one expecting a communiqué without a meeting, but no-one was expecting anything at all on the day before Christmas Eve. The markets were equally taken by surprise, and on the first day of trading in the New Year, 1988, the central banks of the G7 were able to spring a highly successful and large-scale 'bear trap'. Expecting a continuing dollar decline, the markets had gone short of dollars over the Christmas and New Year period – that is to say, their obligations to supply dollars exceeded their holdings of dollars. The central banks then went into the market to purchase dollars on a large scale, forcing it up, which meant that the market had to square its position at a heavy cost. Worldwide intervention during the first few weeks of January exceeded $3 billion. The dollar may not have responded to a communiqué alone, but it certainly responded to the combination of a communique followed by well-timed intervention, and revived strongly in 1988–89.

It is notable that throughout all the turbulence of the five years that followed the Louvre Accord of February 1987, the dollar stayed largely within the DM1.50 to DM2 range and during that period the wild currency gyrations of the mid-1980s were not repeated. No doubt convinced floaters could argue that the markets were at last beginning to operate floating rates as the textbooks had expected. Believers in currency co-operation could retort that the diplomacy and intervention of the years 1987–8 had their effect; and the markets were aware of a strong possibility of official action if they went to absurd extremes in either direction. There may be something in the first of these views; but, given the nature of the foreign exchange markets in the real world, there is, I believe, a great deal more in the second. However, in the absence of any further initiative, by the second half of 1992 the stabilizing effect of actions taken several years ago had inevitably waned, to the general detriment. The torch will have to be taken up again.

CHAPTER 61

THE BP AFFAIR – 1
THE EVENTS OF 14–28 OCTOBER 1987

The World's Largest Share Sale · To Pull or Not To Pull
Force Majeure *and Clause 8 · The Underwriters' Complaint*
The Pressure Mounts

The World's Largest Share Sale

THE WALL STREET CRASH of Monday, 19 October 1987, with its repercussions on the rest of the world's stock markets, was a major and seemingly doom-laden international event in its own right. But for the British Government, and for me in particular, it had a special dimension to which I had to pay equal attention.

The postponement of the water flotation in July 1986 had created a gap in the privatization timetable, and I had announced in March 1987 that it would be replaced with the sale of the Government's remaining 31.5 per cent shareholding in BP. It was also my intention to use the BP sale to widen share ownership beyond the privatized utilities like British Telecom and British Gas. Indeed, in May 1985, when James Hanson, the Chairman of Hanson Trust, had paid a secret visit to me at Number 11 and offered to buy the entire stake outright, I had told him I was not interested because I wished to offer the shares to the general public, although there was no way in which it would have been proper to do a deal of that kind anyway. BP was not only a household name, but a massive company. Moreover, it wanted to raise £1½ billion of equity for its own purposes. This was accordingly packaged with the Government's stake, making the total sale worth £7¼ billion, dwarfing even the £5 billion privatization of British Gas a year earlier. In fact, it was the largest share sale the world had ever seen.

By a malign coincidence, the world's largest ever share sale collided with the world's most dramatic stock market crash. The preparations for the BP sale, which had actually begun as early as January, culminated in a meeting at the Treasury at 11 o'clock on Wednesday, 14 October, to settle the price at which the shares would be underwritten. The underwriting of share sales is an insurance policy. In return for a fee, the underwriters undertake to buy any shares which are not taken up in the offer for sale. In fact, the normal practice in London is for the underwriters to take very little risk themselves, off-loading their obligation on to their largely institutional clients, who are known as the sub-underwriters, who receive a 1 per cent fee for their pains. Michael Richardson, the head of corporate finance at the merchant bankers N.M. Rothschild & Sons, the advisers to the Government, joined my officials and me at the meeting.

I had known Michael Richardson for at least twenty-five years, having met him first when he was a stockbroker with Panmure Gordon. While at first sight too suave and smooth to be true, his unfailing charm, courtesy and good manners disarmed all who came into contact with him. And that was an unusually wide circle, for as well as fellow financiers and businessmen he cultivated prominent politicians (not least Margaret Thatcher) and was a leading freemason. Like Siegmund Warburg, although from a very different background (Harrow and the Brigade of Guards), Richardson was an investment banker who owed his considerable success to manipulating people rather than money.

At my meeting on 14 October, Richardson said that, given the uneasy tone of the market, he could not guarantee success, but that he would try and secure an agreement with the underwriters at £3.50 a share. I did not much like the smell of the equity market, either. Heavy falls in the American stock market were beginning to affect the London and Tokyo markets as well. After a short discussion, Richardson duly went off to negotiate with the underwriters. When he returned at a quarter to three, I was not surprised by his discovery that they would pay not more than £3.30 a share. This would be payable in three instalments, spread over well over a year; with only £1.20 payable on application. In most privatizations a reappraisal of that magnitude would have precipitated lengthy bargaining between the Government, which has a duty to the taxpayers to secure the highest possible sale price for its assets, and its advisers, who want the easiest possible task and tend to pitch the underwriting price as low as possible. In fact, I astonished both Michael Richardson and my officials by crying 'Done!' as soon as the price, for which Richardson apologized, was put to me. It was the shortest pricing meeting in which I ever participated. In the light of subsequent events, it was also one of the best bargains I ever struck on behalf of the taxpayer.

Richardson then returned to Rothschilds to conduct the underwriting auction, which we had agreed would replace the conventional standard underwriting fee of 0.5 per cent. The average commission bid was an unprecedentedly low 0.018 per cent, or a fee of £180 for each £1 million of BP shares underwritten. The following morning the Financial Secretary, Norman Lamont, who was responsible under me for privatization, Michael Richardson and Peter Walters, the Chairman of BP, announced the price to the world, and it was quickly sub-underwritten by hundreds of investment institutions, despite falling stock markets in London and New York. BP closed at £3.47 in London on Thursday, 15 October, but the underwriters and sub-underwriters clearly thought the issue was still cheaply priced.

As if to underline that belief, the underwriting banks insisted on taking 5 per cent of their underwriting commitments on to their own books. Rothschilds and S.G. Warburg, which was advising BP, took 10 per cent each. This not only earned them additional fees for sub-underwriting, but offered them the prospect of selling the shares at a higher price as the market rose. Several underwriters complained to Rothschilds that they had been allocated insufficient stock, and one institution complained bitterly when it was left out altogether.

The freak hurricane of Thursday, 15 October, prevented most people from getting to work in the City on the Friday morning. Richardson, who had made it to the office, has since claimed that he became increasingly pessimistic as the day wore on, but if so he did not communicate this to me. The London market re-opened on Monday, 19 October – Black Monday. From one point of view, the underwriting of the BP issue had been completed only just in time. From another, the issue was absolutely beached. On the Tuesday the London market plunged another 250 points and dragged the BP share price down to £2.85, well below the offer price of £3.30. It implied a very much larger percentage discount to the partly paid price of £1.20. The question naturally arose as to whether the issue should go ahead at all under these circumstances.

To Pull or Not To Pull

At half past nine on the morning of Tuesday, 20 October, I had a brief meeting with Norman Lamont and senior Treasury officials at Number 11 to review the state of the market and decide whether or not to call off the BP issue. I took one decision immediately: to cancel all further advertising. It was unthinkable to continue to encourage individual investors to buy BP shares in the offer when they were available at far cheaper prices in the marketplace. 'Pulling' the issue, to use the market jargon, on the other hand, was an unattractive option. It would have been inconvenient, blowing an enormous hole in the privatization receipts expected in both 1987–88 and 1988–89. It would also have meant giving up the certainty of very large proceeds in the immediate future for an uncertain sum months, or possibly years, later. As steward of the public finances, and trustee on behalf of the taxpayer, that was not a chance I wished to take. Most worrying of all, it might have seriously damaged the credibility of the rest of the Government's privatization programme. Pulling the issue would also have been expensive. The £50 million the Treasury had sunk into the advertising and sales campaign would have had to be written off.

Given the enormous profits that underwriters and sub-underwriters had made in past privatizations, there were also political hazards in bailing them out on only the second occasion – the first having been Britoil – that the market had gone against them. Nor was there much point in the Treasury taking out an insurance policy if, when the event against which it had insured took place, it chose not to claim. Last, but by no means least, pulling the issue would, in my judgement, have badly damaged the reputation of the City of London. The countervailing argument was that, with all the major financial centres in such a fragile state, going ahead with the issue could cause further damage to the markets and to the reputation of BP itself.

I decided that the balance of argument was heavily on the side of going ahead with the issue. The Deputy Governor of the Bank of England, George Blunden – Robin Leigh-Pemberton was then on a tour of eastern Europe, and did not want to add to the panic by cutting short his visit – reinforced this view when he joined me at ten o'clock, immediately after my meeting with Norman Lamont. He said that although some banks and investment institutions in the City of London were facing heavy losses, none was seriously imperilled by its underwriting commitment. The London-based primary underwriters had spread most of the risk across 400 sub-underwriters, and themselves faced collective losses of 'only' some £70 million. It was a large sum, but not a disastrous one. Warburgs and Rothschilds, which had the largest underwriting commitments, faced losses of about £10 million apiece. The sub-underwriters, who between them had shouldered the bulk of the risk, took a robust view. Indeed, the investment committee of the Association of British Insurers put out a statement saying:

> ABI members are quite prepared for the issue to go ahead, and they will, of course, meet the obligations they have undertaken. There is no question of the ABI membership seeking to put pressure on the Government to have the BP issue postponed.

Nicholas Goodison, the Chairman of the London stock exchange, also expressed the view that the BP sale was not an issue the City could disown. The American underwriters were less accommodating, partly because ethical considerations of the kind exemplified by the ABI statement were wholly alien to the leading Wall Street investment bankers, and partly because they were much more exposed. Sub-underwriting has no place in the United States system, and the four American underwriters – Goldman Sachs, Salomon Brothers, Shearson Lehman and Morgan Stanley – had chosen to take 480 million BP shares on to their books. They faced collective losses of £330 million.

Other foreign underwriters faced similar problems. In Japan, five underwriters led by Daiwa Securities were carrying potential losses of £110 million. The issue would cost the European underwriting group, led by Swiss Bank Corporation, £75 million. In Canada, the situation was worst of all. A small group of thinly capitalized underwriters headed by the investment bank Wood Gundy faced losses of £75 million, which was sufficient to drive some of them out of business. It was not hard to foresee strong overseas pressure to pull the issue. In fact, a Goldman Sachs partner flew over from New York to plead with Treasury officials for exactly that. Similarly alarmist representations came from Salomon Brothers. Needless to say, none of them pointed out that the collapse of the equity market had led to a flight into government bonds which had accordingly risen in price, enabling a number of them to make huge profits.

Force Majeure *and Clause 8*

Over the next nine days I was subjected to intense pressure, and not only from the overseas underwriters, to pull the issue. On the afternoon of Friday, 23 October, Michael Richardson telephoned the Treasury to say that he had convened a meeting that day with the seventeen British underwriting banks to discuss Clause 8 of the Underwriting Agreement they had all signed on 14 October. The Underwriting Agreement was an extremely long legal document which I myself had never read, and I was wholly unaware of the existence of Clause 8. It was, in fact, a *force majeure* clause, which stipulated the conditions and procedures under which the underwriters could ask to be released from their obligation to purchase the BP shares. Richardson said that the underwriters were unanimously agreed that *force majeure* had occurred but were evenly divided as to whether or not they should invoke Clause 8. The clause itself read as follows:

> If, between the execution of this agreement and the time this agreement becomes unconditional, there shall in the reasonable opinion of the Treasury, or a majority in number of the underwriters, have been any adverse change in national or international financial, political, industrial or economic conditions, or currency exchange rates or exchange controls which, in the reasonable opinion of the Treasury,

or a majority in number of the underwriters, is of such magnitude and severity as to be material in the context of the offers, or the fixed price offer, and which in the case of an opinion formed by a majority in number of the underwriters should not, in the reasonable opinion of the majority in number of the underwriters, be regarded as a proper underwriting risk, the Treasury and Rothschilds, after consulting with BP, shall consult as to what action shall be taken in relation thereto, and if the Treasury and Rothschilds on behalf of the underwriters shall not agree whether or not the offer should proceed, the Treasury and Rothschilds shall jointly consult the Bank of England, and shall before reaching a decision take full account of the Bank of England's assessment.

This lengthy sentence was a standard *force majeure* clause copied from previous privatization underwriting agreements, to which neither the Treasury nor the banks had hitherto paid much attention. However, the agreement stipulated that only if a majority of the underwriting banks wished to do so would the *force majeure* procedure be set in motion. Initially, no such majority existed. While they agreed unanimously that the crash constituted an 'adverse change' of the sort described, they were divided eight to eight (with one abstention, Kleinwort Benson) on whether or not it constituted a 'proper underwriting risk'. A second meeting was therefore scheduled for Monday, 26 October, to reach a majority view. However, even if a majority of the underwriters decided that the *force majeure* clause *had* been triggered, that was far from decisive. Clause 8 merely entitled them to ask the Treasury to call off the issue. If the Treasury disagreed, the dispute was then referred to the Bank of England to make a recommendation, which the Treasury, after due consideration, was free to reject.

None the less, there were two unsatisfactory features of the Clause 8 procedure. I was alerted to the first by George Blunden, when he came to the Treasury on the morning of 20 October. He warned me that, because the Bank of England was cast in the role of umpire, the normal relationship between the Treasury and the Bank of England would have to be suspended while the procedure was followed. The arbitration of the Bank in a private sector issue was reasonable enough, but anything that stood in the way of the normal close relationship between the Treasury and the Bank, particularly at a time of some financial turmoil, was clearly undesirable.

The second unsatisfactory feature was that Rothschilds, although still nominally advisers to the Government, were now acting on behalf of the underwriters. Indeed, it was soon pretty clear that Rothschilds had in effect changed sides. The document they had asked Freshfields, the solicitors, to prepare for the Friday meeting of the underwriting group was apparently heavily slanted in favour of postponing the issue. These developments caused some reconsideration in subsequent privatization issues both of the terms of the *force majeure* clause and of the practice of appointing the advisers to the Government as the lead underwriters to the issue.

Abandoned by both the Bank and my merchant banking advisers, I was left to my own devices. I took soundings over the weekend, telephoning a number of City friends whose views I respected. They were all quite clear that the issue was not only a proper underwriting risk but that it would reflect very badly on the reputation of the City if it failed to shoulder the burden. I was sure they were right. Not only was the crash a normal underwriting risk, but it did not constitute an 'adverse change' of the sort described in Clause 8 either. International political, industrial and economic conditions were barely altered, and exchange rates and exchange controls remained as before. The only adverse change the underwriters could plausibly point to was in international *financial* conditions, and it was not at all clear to me that a fall in stock market prices alone constituted any such thing. There had been no significant problems in the bond, money, foreign exchange or commodity markets.

I felt on strong ground over my interpretation of Clause 8. The real worry was the wider impact on the market, in its then highly nervous state, of going ahead with the issue. At a meeting at Number 11 with senior Treasury officials, accompanied by Juliet Wheldon from the Treasury Solicitor's Department, and Giles Henderson of Slaughter & May, the solicitors to the Government for the purposes of the BP offer, I indicated that I was prepared to consider some sort of safety net under the BP share price to shield the market from the possibility of a complete collapse in the price. This worried the lawyers, who argued that it was tantamount to admitting that the Treasury was wrong to go ahead; but I was concerned that the BP share price could drop like a stone if the underwriters were forced to unload stock into a market devoid of buyers.

In the circumstances, I thought it was entirely reasonable to seek to put a floor under the shares provided it did not recompense the underwriters for the losses they had already incurred. I accordingly asked Treasury officials to draw up a specification for such a safety net and to let me have a note on a strictly personal basis, copied only to Norman Lamont and Peter Middleton. I suggested to them that the operation could be conducted by the Issue Department of the Bank of England, following the rather apposite Burmah Oil precedent.* I also asked Treasury officials

---

*In 1975, when the Burmah Oil Company got into difficulties, the then Labour Government somewhat controversially rescued it by purchasing its main asset, a large holding of BP shares, at a knock-down price, and placed them with the Issue Department of the Bank of England.

to convey my thinking to the Bank of England, using informal channels which would not compromise the strict neutrality to which the Bank was committed by the terms of Clause 8.

The Underwriters' Complaint

In the afternoon on Monday, 26 October, Michael Richardson sent a letter by hand to the Treasury informing us of the result of the second meeting of the underwriting group. Although he had come under intense pressure from the foreign underwriters, the terms of the Underwriting Agreement made it clear that the decision over whether to involve the *force majeure* clause and ask the Treasury to pull the issue lay exclusively with the UK underwriters. It turned out that, by a narrow majority, they had concluded that the *force majeure* clause had indeed been triggered. There is some suggestion that they were influenced by fanciful ideas that they could be sued for damages by angry foreign underwriters if the issue went ahead, although this was almost certainly not the case. Richardson's letter contained a great deal of tendentious supporting evidence, but its essence was clear enough: the underwriters were seeking a consultation with the Treasury under the terms of Clause 8, with a view to terminating the BP issue. On the following day Richardson elaborated on their reasoning in a second letter:

> There were two meetings with the UK underwriting group, held respectively on Friday, 23 October, and Monday, 26 October. The opinion of a majority of the UK underwriters, that the circumstances should not be regarded as a proper underwriting risk in the context of the offers or of the fixed price offer, was formed after a number of points had been made. They included the following:
>
> 1. There had been a very severe upheaval in world equity markets in terms both of the scale of the falls and of their volatility.
> 2. It is both multi-national and international in character – multi-national in that it affects all major markets, and international in that each major market influences the others.
> 3. It may be thought to be structural – it is not limited to concerns about a particular stock market sector or the economy of a particular country.
> 4. It has been described as unprecedented – parallels have had to be sought with situations such as the 1929 Crash, but in the equity markets it has been even more extreme.
> 5. Quite apart from the reflection of underlying factors, it has had a significant weakening effect, not least, in the context of the offers, on investor confidence.

6. In time its effect will no doubt attenuate, but the effect must be considered within the context of the time periods of the offers and fixed price offer, and in those contexts, including the arrangements with respect to sales by underwriters, it is fundamental.

7. Its effects on the after-market in BP shares, having regard to the scale of the offers and their international spread, will be serious.

. . . We hope that this letter identifies the reasons underlying the opinion with greater precision. We look forward to proceeding with the consultation as a matter of urgency.

None of these matters seemed to me to be outside the scope of a normal underwriting risk, but the invocation of Clause 8 nevertheless presented a considerable additional awkwardness. I had to be extremely careful in my private and public pronouncements on the issue, in case an unguarded comment or snap judgement breached the obligation on the Treasury under the Underwriting Agreement to confer, consult and consider seriously both the approach from the underwriting banks and the assessment of the Bank of England before reaching any decision. Otherwise, there was a risk that any decision I took would be successfully challenged in the courts.

The Pressure Mounts

Meanwhile, pressure to pull the issue was intensifying in other quarters. Mike Wilson, the Canadian Finance Minister, telephoned me to say that there was a real danger that Wood Gundy would collapse and that, in the interests of international financial stability, I should withdraw the sale. Unwisely, he had already declared on Canadian television his view that the issue should be pulled. The Deputy Finance Minister of Canada, Stanley Hart, telephoned Peter Middleton with the same message. It was tough talk, although not as tough as that which followed from Jim Baker and the Americans. Baker telephoned me on 27 October to urge me, in the strongest possible terms, to call off the issue. David Mulford, the Assistant Secretary to the US Treasury, reiterated that view to senior Treasury officials. Mulford also warned that Alan Greenspan, the Chairman of the Federal Reserve, would be contacting the Governor of the Bank of England with the same purpose in mind. Greenspan's letter was not shown to the Treasury, although the Bank later quoted from it to support their view that the BP issue should be pulled.

The Americans all claimed that the BP issue would precipitate another fall on Wall Street, and that it was the duty of responsible Finance Ministers to avert that possibility. There was no direct pressure from the Japanese Government, though Daiwa Securities, the leading Japanese underwriter, wrote to Rothschilds advising pulling the issue and the bank forwarded the letter to the Treasury. I took a firm line with all these pleas for mercy, pointing out that they were inviting me to abandon the right to claim on an insurance policy. It would also be extremely difficult to justify to the House of Commons a lavish gift from the UK taxpayer to financial institutions in New York, Toronto and Tokyo.

The Americans then stepped up the pressure. When it became clear that I was not going to yield, a senior member of the White House staff telephoned Charles Powell at Number 10, and asked him to intercede on their behalf with Margaret. I was not pleased at this attempt to go behind my back. I told Margaret, who had called me over to Number 10 to inform me of this development, that I felt very strongly indeed that we should not yield to American bullying. I suspect she felt I was becoming over-excited, but I knew how much she disliked upsetting the Americans. To her credit, she stood firm, and sent back a message saying that she fully supported the line I had taken with Jim Baker. I cannot recall a time when I was under heavier pressure.

The domestic outlook was little better. BP had lost its nerve. The company had told Treasury officials immediately after the crash that it thought the issue should be pulled – it had no immediate need for the £1½ million that would go to BP, and was worried about the damage the offer would do to its standing in the markets. On 28 October I myself received a long letter from Peter Walters, the Chairman of BP, pleading directly for the issue to be withdrawn.

The political temperature was rising, too. On 26 October the Labour leader, Neil Kinnock, absurdly accused me of 'cowardice' for failing to make a statement to the House of Commons about the crash in general and the BP share sale in particular. Since the House had still been in recess on Black Monday, as it was on the following day, too, I obviously had to give my prompt response and words of reassurance on television. There was no way in which I could sensibly have waited until the House returned on the Wednesday. Moreover at Business Questions the following day, 22 October, when Kinnock had his first opportunity to ask for Government Statements on issues the Opposition regarded as important, he had asked for Statements on help for victims of the recent hurricane and on space research, plus debates on a number of issues ranging from the Scottish economy to security at the House of Commons. He had not uttered a word about either the crash or BP.

Labour's recently appointed principal Treasury spokesman, John Smith, who had replaced the somewhat discredited Roy Hattersley, then claimed that I had added 'insult to injury' by preferring to address the Stock Exchange Conference for Industry that evening rather than attend the House. This was an equally foolish allegation: I was fulfilling a long-standing commitment (to an event which, ironically, had originally been devised to celebrate the first anniversary of Big Bang) and had I pulled out at the last minute it would obviously have deepened the panic which was then gripping the Square Mile. Margaret came under pressure from Neil Kinnock at Question Time on 27 October but, as she pointed out to him, there was a legal obstacle in the way of a Statement on BP. I was precluded from saying anything substantive about BP until I had fulfilled the contractual obligation under Clause 8 to consider in full the representations of the underwriters and the assessment of the Bank of England.

The Labour Party had persuaded itself that the crash had left the Government vulnerable over privatization and wider share ownership. This would no doubt have been true had the BP issue been pulled, and partly accounted for my determination that it should go ahead. John Smith eventually decided to table a Private Notice Question on the financial situation and the BP share offer on 27 October. After referring briefly to the previous day's half-point cut in interest rates and to the underlying strength of the British economy, I turned to BP, saying:

> There is provision under Clause 8 of the BP fixed price underwriting agreement for the underwriters to seek consultation with the Treasury if a majority of them form the opinion that there has been an adverse change of circumstances, as specified by the agreement, in the light of which they believe that they are no longer assuming a proper underwriting risk. I have been informed by N.M. Rothschild & Sons, on behalf of the United Kingdom underwriters, that a majority of them now take that view. They therefore sent a written representation to the Treasury yesterday afternoon seeking consultation with a view to terminating the offer for sale. I have to say that I was surprised by this.

The irony in the last sentence, which was appreciated in some, although not all, parts of the House, was designed to indicate the drift of my own thinking without transgressing the procedure laid down by Clause 8. I concluded by saying:

> The House will understand that, now that the underwriters have invoked this consultation process, I cannot say more until the process is concluded; but I will gladly listen to the views of right honourable and honourable Members.

In his reply, Smith worked himself up into a considerable lather. His calls for an emergency summit meeting and dire predictions of the final crisis of capitalism were easily brushed off. He was able to make more headway on BP, where I was effectively gagged by the Clause 8 procedure; but I was glad to note that most of our own back-benchers, including those with City connections, were against conceding to the pressure from the underwriters.

I had seen no point in meeting Richardson myself, and asked Peter Middleton to put the Treasury case in the consultations with the underwriters that formed the first stage of the Clause 8 procedure. It was clear from the outset that there would be no agreement, and that the matter would have to be referred to the Bank of England. This duly took place; but unhelpfully the Bank took an inordinate time to make its assessment. It did not even begin its hearings until Wednesday, 28 October, despite the fact that the procedure had been initiated two days earlier and the arguments on both sides had been very well aired already. Once again I sent along Peter Middleton to put the Treasury's case, as he had done at the meeting with the underwriters. The Bank indicated that it expected to deliver its recommendation to the Treasury by midday on 29 October.

With Noboru Takeshita (*right*) at the Tokyo Economic Summit, May 1986. (*Associated Press*)

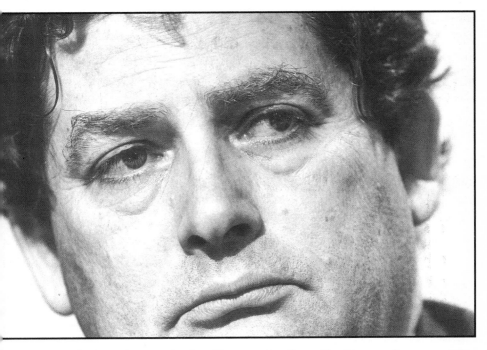

Listening attentively at the pre-election Conservative Party Conference, Bournemouth, October 1986. (*Ashley Ashwood*/The Financial Times)

G6 Finance Ministers at the Louvre, Paris, February 1987. (*l-r*) Michael Wilson, myself, Gerhard Stoltenberg, Edouard Balladur, James Baker, Kiichi Miyazawa. *(Popperfoto/Reuter/Mike Theiler)*

Karl Otto Pöhl, Jacques de Larosière and Edouard Balladur at the IMF/World Bank spring meeting, Washington, April 1987. *(Robert Trippett/SIPA Press/Rex Features)*

With Thérèse and Emily at the fish-and-chip shop, Stoney Stanton, during the 1987 general election campaign. (Independent)

Emily contributing to pre-election publicity in the garden of Number 10, May 1987.

Making my 'managed floating' speech at the IMF/World Bank annual meeting, Washington, October 1987. (*Terry Kirk*/The Financial Times)

With Robin Leigh-Pemberton at the IMF/World Bank annual meeting in Washington, October 1987. (*Terry Kirk*/The Financial Times)

Margaret Thatcher and myself at the reception given by George Jefferson (*left*),
Chairman of British Telecom, to mark the company's privatization.

Alan Greenspan. (*Popperfoto/Reuter*)

Norman Lamont and BP Chairman Sir Peter
Walters at the unveiling of the price of the BP
share offer, October 1987. (*Trevor Humphries/*The
Financial Times)

In full flow: 1986... (*Roger Taylor*/The Financial Times)

...1987... (*Ashley Ashwood*/The Financial Times)

and 1988. (*Alan Harper*/The Financial Times)

Proceeding to the House of Lords to hear the Queen's Speech at the State Opening of Parliament, November 1987. (*l-r*) Myself, Geoffrey Howe, Roy Hattersley, Margaret Thatcher, Denis Healey, Neil Kinnock. *(Rex Features)*

Dorneywood. *(P. J. Baldwin)*

(*Opposite*) My 1988 Treasury team: (*l-r*) Myself; John Major, Chief Secretary; Norman Lamont, Financial Secretary; Peter Brooke, Paymaster-General; Peter Lilley, Economic Secretary. *(Ashley Ashwood/*The Financial Times)

Acknowledging the applause for my speech at the Conservative Party Conference, Brighton, October 1988. (The Financial Times)

The Cabinet, May 1989. (*Back l-r*) David Waddington, John Major, John Belstead, John Moore, Malcolm Rifkind, Kenneth Clarke, Kenneth Baker, John MacGregor, Paul Channon, John Wakeham, Cecil Parkinson, Tony Newton,

With Thérèse, seeing off President and Mrs Bush at Northolt, June 1989. James Baker is on my left. *(Tim Ockenden/Press Association)*

Robin Butler (Cabinet Secretary). (*Front l-r*) Nicholas Ridley, Norman Fowler, Peter Walker, James Mackay, Geoffrey Howe, Margaret Thatcher, Myself, Douglas Hurd, George Younger, Tom King, David Young.

With the other G7 Finance Ministers at the Economic Summit, Paris, July 1989. (*l-r*) Helmut Haussmann, Theo Waigel, Nicholas Brady, Michael Wilson, Pierre Bérégovoy, myself, Giuliano Amato, Tatsuo Murayama, Henning Christopherson. (*Ashley Ashwood*/The Financial Times)

With US Treasury Secretary Nick Brady at the IMF/World Bank annual meeting in Washington, September 1989. (*Popperfoto/Reuter*)

'The Right Team' applauding Margaret Thatcher's speech at the Conservative Party Conference, October 1989. (*l-r*) Kenneth Clarke, myself, Nicholas Ridley, Geoffrey Howe, Norman Fowler, Margaret Thatcher, Tom King, John Major, Kenneth Baker, Cecil Parkinson, John Belstead and Douglas Hurd. *(Press Association/Topham)*

With Thérèse in the garden of the Old Rectory, Stoney Stanton, making a statement of support for John Major the day after my resignation, October 1989. Behind me are (*l-r*) Tony Potts, Special Branch, and my agent, Graham Smith.

(*Alan Harper/*The Financial Times)

The Daily Telegraph

TABLISHED 1855   NO. 41,786 •   FRIDAY, OCTOBER 27, 1989   LONDON

Walters 'steps aside' in row over economic policy

Crisis for Thatcher after Lawson quits as Chancellor

Major is moved to No 11: Hurd for Foreign Office

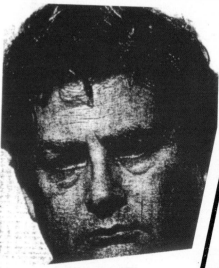

By George Jones, Political Editor

MR NIGEL LAWSON stunned the political world and plunged Mrs Thatcher into her biggest crisis in 10 years as Prime Minister by resigning as Chancellor of the Exchequer last night in protest at the continued presence of Sir Alan Walters as her personal economic adviser.

Mr Lawson's simmering discontent over the way his economic policies had been "second guessed" in No 10 Downing Street by Sir Alan finally boiled over into the most sensational Ministerial resignation since Mr Michael Heseltine walked out of the Cabinet over Westland in January 1986.

In a night of dramatic developments at West-minster, Sir Alan — who is in America — ~l~ as Mrs Thatcher's econ~ ing of M~'

Fvit '

Major yesterday: from Ign Office to Treasury

I resign without rther ado'

~wson's letter to ''

FINANCIAL TIMES

Friday October 27 1989

● HURD IN AT FOREIGN OFFICE ● WADDINGTON IS NEW HOME S

Lawson replaced by Major

THATCHER She stay

BABY

By Philip Stephens, Political Editor

MR Nigel Lawson threw Mrs Margaret Thatcher's Govern-ment into turmoil yesterday by resigning as Chancellor of the ~chequer over his differences

also

the Chief Whip, was appointed Home Secretary.

Amid tense scenes at West-minster, senior Conservative MPs counselled against panic. But they and Government min-isters were acknowledging that Mrs Thatcher now faced per-~ political

article by Sir Alan.
Sir Alan had referred to the European Monetary System, into which Mrs Thatcher is for-mally committed to taking sterling, as "half-baked" and in the Commons yesterday the Prime Minister refused to be drawn into publicly disowning

198~.
nomic ~ Thatcher.

MARCH 1988 rift between Thatcher ove down the pou

APRIL — We that Britain the exchange of the EMS.

JUNE — W eral articles ing of "trag full EMS m

JULY 15 Walters Washing adviser t

~ILY 18

Daily Mail

FRIDAY, OCTOBER 27, 1989   22p

Agony of a boxer SEE BACK PAGE

THATCHER DAY OF DISASTER

Lawson quits, Walters goes too and Major is promoted Chancellor

THE Prime Minister was forced into an aston-ishing crisis reshuffle of her Cabinet last night after the quarrel between her Chancellor Nigel Lawson and her economic adviser Professor

IRA kill airman

No 951

Lawson says his position untenable; Walters goes t

Govern as Cha

By Anthony Bevins
Political ~

Daily Mirror

DAILY Mirror

YOUR NEWSPAPER OF THE YEAR

INCORPORATING THE DAILY RECORD

National Sale 3,900,158

22p

RESIGNED!

CHANCELLOR: Nigel Lawson

...ATCHE...
CRISIS

...nent totters as
...wson and

By ALASTAIR CAMPBELL
Political Editor

MRS THATCHER faced the gravest crisis of her Premiership...

Daily Express

FRIDAY OCTOBER 27 1989

WEATHER: RAIN

INSIDE TODAY
£1 Million
WAITING TO BE WON

Millionaires Club

PLUS
GIRLS W...
DARE TO...

Major is new Chancellor in shake-up

I RESIGN

Tory crisis as Lawson quits then Thatcher guru goes too

CHANCELLOR Nigel Lawson and his arch-rival Sir Alan Walters both sensationally quit last night — plunging Mrs Thatcher into the greatest crisis of her decade in power.

Mr Lawson resigned over the Prime Minister's refusal to sack or silence her...

By ROBERT GIBSON Political Editor

...arily appointed to replace Mr Lawson. And in what rapidly became a full-scale Government reshuffle, Home Secretary Douglas Hurd was moved to the Foreign Office and Chief Whip David Waddington took Mr Hurd's place.

In Downing Street, Lawson's departure was received with a sigh of relief. His sensitivity and argumentative nature...

THE ☙ TIMES

FRIDAY OCTOBER 27 1989

...Major goes to Treasury, Hurd and Waddington move...

...awson quits over Walters

...huffle as adviser ...eaves office too

...and Richard Ford

...NDEPENDENT

FRIDAY 27 OCTOBER 1989

∗ ∗ ∗ Published in London   30p

...ster moves ...Treasury

Hurd is Foreign Secretary; Waddington to Home Office

A deep crisis of confidence in...

...t in turmoil
...or resign...

WE HAVE a crisis of confidence in the Prime Minister. By refusing to dispense with her personal economic...

'**I should be censured for not having shot down the communist missile targeted on Britain** --- "

8 September 1984. (*Cummings*/Daily Express)*

22 July, 1988. (*Garland*/Independent)**

"WE ARE RIGHT ON COURSE ..."

'**Would you believe it! Nigel Lawson says that not everything has gone right!'** 12 March 1981. (*Osbert Lancaster*/Daily Express)

'THE DEATH OF GORDO

17 October 1986. (*Garland*/Independent)**

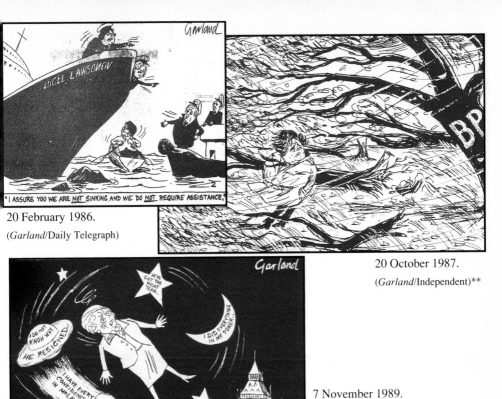

20 February 1986.

(*Garland*/Daily Telegraph)

20 October 1987.

(*Garland*/Independent)**

7 November 1989.

(*Garland*/Independent)**

21 July 1988. (*Garland*/Independent)*

CLAP HANDS, HERE COMES FERGIE! · THE HIDDEN TREASURES OF WATERHOUSE
INNER CITIES INITIATIVE SHOCK · THE YELLOW PERIL · WIN A MAXWELL BIOGRAPHY

PUNCH

18TH MARCH 1988 £1

CUT!
NIGEL
THE SIMPLIFIER
IS UNLEASHED

Pre-budget edition of *Punch* magazine,1988. *(Illustration by Simon Dewey/Reproduced by permission of Punch)*

CHAPTER 62

THE BP AFFAIR – 2
DÉNOUEMENT AND AFTERMATH

The Bank's Assessment · The Buy-Back Offer
My Statement to the House · Enter the Kuwaitis
The Judgement of the MMC · Britoil and its Golden Share

The Bank's Assessment

When I entered the House to answer Treasury Questions at half-past three on the afternoon of Thursday, 29 October, the Bank's assessment had still not arrived; and all I could do was say that I hoped to make my decision about whether the issue should go ahead later that day, and would inform the House of it. The need for a decision that day stemmed from the fact that, if the offer went ahead, dealings in the new shares were due to start the following day, 30 October. The Bank's five-page recommendation, largely the work of Eddie George, finally arrived by fax a little after six o'clock. This left very little time in which to complete the legally required procedures and honour my promise to come to a decision and inform the House of Commons that day, especially since the latest acceptable time for making a Statement was ten o'clock.

To my horror, I found that the Bank had concluded that the safest course was to postpone the issue; but that, if I insisted on going ahead with it, the Issue Department of the Bank of England should guarantee to buy back the BP stock in the market at a price of 90p a share until the second instalment was due in August 1988. In other words, and for no comprehensible reason, the Bank was recommending a substantial premium over the market price – then a shade over 70 pence – which would have saved the underwriters about £750 million and left the Bank, on behalf of the taxpayer, with most of the shares. Among other things, this would have defeated the whole purpose of the sale.

The recommendation was obviously unacceptable. It even failed to address itself to the terms of Clause 8. It was based not on the view that the crash constituted an adverse change in international financial conditions which transcended 'a proper underwriting risk' but on the Bank's assessment of the effect of proceeding with the BP issue on wider market and economic conditions. Indeed, the Bank had quoted to this effect from the letter it had received from Alan Greenspan. The Treasury was as well equipped as the Bank to make judgements of that sort.

Nevertheless, the Bank's assessment had to be fully considered under the terms of Clause 8. At half past six I called a meeting of all the Treasury Ministers and special advisers I could locate – all but Peter Brooke turned out to be available – and all my most senior officials, together with my legal team of Juliet Wheldon, Giles Henderson and John Chadwick QC, the Treasury counsel. We had a brief discussion, during which both Peter Middleton and the lawyers confirmed my own view that the recommendation contained no new arguments against proceeding with the issue, and that those that it did contain had been fully considered already.

In particular, there was nothing in it to cause me to question my provisional conclusion that, since the main concern of both the underwriters and the company itself was that the BP share price would go into free fall, all that was needed to prevent this was to put a floor under the then implied market price of 70p (part paid). This had been fully covered in the note I had commissioned from Treasury officials, which went on to explore the possibility of alleviating the difficulties faced by the 270,000 small investors who had applied for shares in the offer at what had become an excessively high price. Sadly, it emerged that there was nothing I could do, since it would have been illegal to treat individual shareholders differently from the underwriters without the latter's agreement, which would clearly not have been forthcoming at a time when the Government was in serious conflict with them.

The next step, given that I had decided to reject the Bank's recommendation, was to inform Margaret and secure her endorsement for the course I proposed to take. There was just time to do this before the Bank team, headed by the Governor, was due to arrive at the Treasury to hear my verdict. To avoid the press and TV who keep constant watch in Downing Street, I took Norman Lamont, Peter Middleton and the three lawyers up Whitehall, into the Cabinet Office, and thence by the twisting corridors to Number 10, passing through the locked door which divides the two buildings and to which, as Chancellor, I held one of the very few keys.

Margaret met us in the Cabinet Room. I summarized the state of play, stating that, while I accepted the need to place a floor under the BP share price, I had deep misgivings about the Bank's recommendation.

It took no account of the principle that the underwriters should meet their obligations, and clearly went much further than was necessary to deal with the problem of sending the BP share price, and possibly the rest of the stock market with it, into a tailspin. I then pointed out that to offer a premium over the prevailing market price would constitute an improper use of public money which would be impossible to justify either to Peter Middleton, as the Treasury's relevant Accounting Officer*, or to the Public Accounts Committee of the House of Commons. Peter confirmed this so far as he was concerned. John Chadwick then assured Margaret that the care the Treasury had exercised in following the procedures laid down in Clause 8 would make it extremely difficult for the underwriting banks to mount a successful case against it under either the Underwriting Agreement itself or by way of judicial review. This was of considerable comfort, since American banks were notoriously litigious.

As she carefully listened to the case being put to her Margaret became increasingly outraged that the Bank had given so little weight in its deliberations to the sanctity of contract and the reputation of the City of London. Her only problem with the course of action I proposed, she said, was her concern about the impact on the American markets of a decision to go ahead. I pointed out that the American banks, having the largest exposures, would benefit most from any buy-back scheme.

The Buy-Back Offer

Once we had returned to the Treasury, by the same indirect route, the consultative gavotte continued. Under the terms of Clause 8, the Treasury was obliged to give Rothschilds an opportunity to make further points, which it then had to consider. This requirement was solemnly followed to the letter. Peter Middleton rang Michael Richardson at ten minutes to eight that evening, and told him that the Bank of England recommendation had been rejected, that the issue was going ahead and that a support mechanism would be put in place at the prevailing market price.

Richardson, claiming the support of a majority of the underwriting banks, said unsurprisingly that he would rather see the issue called off than proceed without the generous buy-back proposal that had been

---

*Each Whitehall Department has at least one Accounting Officer, who is responsible for the propriety of any expenditure his Department, or the relevant part of his Department, incurs. The Accounting Officer is normally the Permanent Secretary; but whereas *qua* Permanent Secretary he takes his instructions from the Ministerial Head of Department, *qua* Accounting Officer he does not, and is responsible to Parliament. This responsibility in turn is in practice enforced by the Public Accounts Committe of the House of Commons, whose role goes beyond the exposure of any impropriety in the expenditure of public money, and encompasses also the exposure of waste and inefficiency in public spending.

devised by the Bank of England – the Bank had sent a copy of its assessment to him at the same time as it had sent it to me. He declared that his 'heart was uplifted' by the Bank's proposal (as well it may have been), which he considered 'very imaginative', and that he would have to reserve judgement on the Treasury alternative until the details were available. Peter Middleton duly reported this to me; I confirmed my decision that the issue should go ahead; and the lawyers were then able to confirm that the Treasury had finally met all its obligations under Clause 8. Shortly after eight o'clock, Robin Leigh-Pemberton, flanked by an intense Eddie George and other Bank officials, arrived at the Treasury to be told of my decision.

Once they had learned that their own proposal had been rejected, the discussion turned to the implementation of my decision. It was agreed that from the end of the following week, the Issue Department of the Bank of England would stand ready to buy the partly-paid shares at 70p each for at least one month but for no more than two. I had decided that the buy-back offer should close on 11 December at the earliest, and 6 January at the latest, rather than linger on until August the following year as recommended by the Bank. Any shares acquired by the Bank as a result of the safety net would not be re-sold within the subsequent six months, unless the price rose above £1.20. Peter Middleton telephoned Richardson again at ten past nine to inform him that his advice, after due consideration, had been rejected.

Richardson, having reluctantly accepted that I had decided to go ahead, and that the decision was mine to take, then inquired what was the nature of the support operation we had in mind. When told that it was similar to the Bank's, but at a lower price, he argued unconvincingly that there was no risk to the Government in a 90p support price, since the market would push the shares above the support price to around £1. Thus no buying back, in practice, would be required. He was thanked for his view, which I saw no reason to accept. That left only one more telephone call to make which, although not required by the agreement, common courtesy demanded. This was to inform BP of the Government's decision. The BP Chairman, Peter Walters – who, of course, knew that this was the day of decision – turned out to be absent and unreachable, and Peter Middleton conveyed the message to BP's Finance Director, David Simon, instead.

While all this activity was going on in my room at the Treasury, across the road the House of Commons was becoming increasingly restive. They had been promised a Statement by me that day, and as the hours went by and I failed to appear, the mood showed signs of becoming very ugly. Just after half past six, the business of the House was interrupted by very nearly half an hour of points of order, led by Kinnock and John Smith, about my failure to deliver the promised Statement. The Whips were sending messages of increasing urgency, at increasing frequency, asking me to come across to the House and make the Statement, and I was sending messages back that I would come as soon as I could, that I hoped to be able to make it at ten o'clock, but that there was no way in which I could make any Statement until I had fully complied with the legal procedures.

The truth was, the Bank had let me down. They had promised they would get their assessment to me by around midday. In fact, it did not arrive until after six that evening. There was no good reason for the delay: they had had ample time to prepare it. No doubt they regarded the parliamentary dimension as of little account; but they knew it was of considerable importance to the Government.

As a result of the delay it was a real struggle to complete the procedures that the law required, have an unscheduled meeting with Margaret to explain to her why I had decided to overrule the Bank's advice, explain the same to the Bank and secure their agreement to the use of the Issue Department of the Bank to implement my alternative buy-back scheme, agree with them the nuts and bolts of how the scheme would be operated, secure the consent of the Takeover Panel to the buy-back offer, and draft a statement which had to be both legally watertight and politically persuasive – all in time for me to make the Statement at ten o'clock, the latest practicable deadline.

My Statement to the House

As it was, I only just made it. I was drafting the Statement, with the help of my officials, at the long meeting table in my room at the Treasury, while Peter Middleton was still making the final telephone calls in another part of that large room. There was no time to prepare answers to likely supplementary questions: I would have to improvise. I arrived just before ten o'clock to a packed, noisy and expectant House, and sat down next to Margaret, who was already in her place – as were a large number of my Cabinet colleagues. The business then before the House – the Scottish Development Agency Bill (Money Resolution) – was rapidly wound up, and by five minutes past ten on the evening of Thursday, October 29, I was on my feet, making the Statement. To cheers from the benches behind me, I told the House that I had decided the offer should go ahead. I then went on to describe the buy-back arrangement I proposed to put in place, the impact of which was heightened by the fact that no hint of this had leaked out in advance, nor had the financial commentators even envisaged it as a possibility. I concluded:

> I would like the House to be quite clear about the objectives of my decision: first, and most important, to allow taxpayers to secure the full proceeds of the BP sale to which they are entitled; secondly, to

ensure that there are orderly after-markets in BP shares; thirdly, to make quite sure that the sale does not add to present difficulties in world markets. It is not my objective in any way to bail out the underwriters, whether in this country or elsewhere. By proceeding as I have indicated, the City will uphold its reputation as the world's leading international financial centre.

My Statement appeared to wrong-foot John Smith completely. He had evidently prepared his response on the assumption that I would cave in to the underwriters. Perhaps the press coverage over the previous week, which had been heavily influenced by the tireless Michael Richardson, had persuaded him this was inevitable. He nevertheless felt obliged to attack the decision, arguing that the sale should have been withdrawn in the interests of BP. This might have carried more conviction had he not earlier described the pleas from the underwriters to pull the issue as 'hard to justify'. He was easily mocked. 'The Labour Party today', I declared, 'is simply the friend of Goldman Sachs.' Until I spoke, the Opposition thought they had me on the ropes, and many on our own side feared that they were right. When, in the event, they found that I had completely turned the tables on them, they were lost; and our own immensely relieved and impressed back-benchers cheered to the echo almost every reply I gave. Although the Speaker allowed the cross-examination of me to run for a full hour, at the end of a long and tense day, it was one of the most satisfying Parliamentary occasions in which I ever participated.

The following morning the partly paid BP shares opened at 88p and, despite heavy trading that day, never dipped below 85p. The premium to the floor price of 70p was not, of course, maintained, but, in the end, the buy-back programme cost only £27 million and left the Bank, on behalf of the taxpayer, owning just 1.8 per cent of the share capital of BP. As soon as it became clear that there would be no substantial overhang of BP stock in the hands of the Government, institutions started buying again and the problem evaporated altogether. To his credit, Mike Wilson, the Canadian Finance Minister, generously wrote to congratulate me for having devised such a satisfactory means of going ahead with the issue against such strong advice from him and others.

The Bank of England behaved less graciously. In the circumstances, a period of silence on their part would have been appropriate. Although they had made life difficult for me by producing a perverse assessment and doing so inexcusably late, I had never uttered a word of criticism of them. I was therefore distinctly unamused to discover from the Saturday press that the Bank were claiming that it was they who had first conceived of what was by then regarded as a brilliantly successful buy-back plan. A Bank official had apparently told James Long of the BBC that

Threadneedle Street had forced the buy-back option on to a reluctant Chancellor and that, although it would have preferred a higher price, it was grateful that I had eventually seen reason.

This was pretty galling, considering that it was I who had first conceived the idea and ensured that the Bank were made aware of it, that their first preference had been for me to call the issue off altogether, and that their fallback recommendation had been that I should bail out the underwriters at a substantial premium over the market price. As soon as I read the story, I telephoned Robin Leigh-Pemberton at his home in Kent to complain. He was genuinely horrified, and I am sure was entirely innocent. The Bank of England had, of course, been smarting ever since I had suggested at the time of the Johnson Matthey scandal three years earlier that it had fallen down on the job. Someone at the Bank presumably had the notion that taking credit for the coup of the BP buy-back scheme would be a good way of restoring its slightly tarnished reputation.

For what was the first and last time I decided to enlist the services of Bernard Ingham. I rang Margaret at Chequers, who, of course, clearly recalled the meeting we had had round the Cabinet table the previous Thursday, and was appalled to discover the Bank's shameless attempt to deprive the Government of the credit for its coup. She got Ingham to telephone me, I briefed him, and he ensured that a suitably robust correction to the Bank's version appeared in the Sunday press. The episode soured relations between the Bank and Treasury, albeit only temporarily, and was an unedifying end to an otherwise remarkable example of snatching victory from the jaws of defeat, in which I had been invaluably assisted by Peter Middleton, who had taken a firm grip of the official side of the issue from an early stage.

Enter the Kuwaitis

There was, however, a much more worrying sequel to the BP share flop. In his letter to me of 28 October Peter Walters, the BP Chairman, had warned that if the issue went ahead 'there will be the possibility that an unwelcome buyer could obtain a major stake in BP for a very low initial cost. Twenty per cent of the company may be procured from desperate sellers for around £1 billion.' It very soon began to look as if his worst fears were being realized. Within days the market was alive with rumours that a large buyer was taking advantage of the substantial number of BP shares being unloaded on to the market, by the US underwriters in particular, to accumulate a major stake in the company. Sure enough, on 18 November, the Kuwait Investment Office (KIO) declared that it held 10 per cent of BP, and was still buying. Questioned about this in the House, Margaret replied that it was a straightforward commercial matter, and no cause for concern. There was little else she could have said.

The Gulf Sheikhdom of Kuwait (over which the 1990–91 Gulf War against Saddam Hussein's Iraq would be fought) had long generated an oil income far in excess of what this pocket handkerchief of a country could absorb. To provide a home for the surplus funds it had long ago set up the Kuwait Investment Office, a highly secretive and shrewdly managed investment fund based in London. Given the generally unintelligent and herd-like behaviour of western investment institutions – the UK pension funds, who fit this description to a T, had invested the highest ever proportion of their funds in equities in the quarter immediately prior to Black Monday, when the market was at its all-time peak – the KIO had not had too much trouble in spotting investment opportunities and seizing them. This was clearly the case with BP. The western investment institutions, who had fallen over themselves to underwrite the BP issue for a derisory fee at 120 pence a share (part paid) on the eve of the Wall Street crash, would not touch it with a bargepole as it languished, in large quantities, just above the buy-back price of 70 pence a share (part paid) on the morrow of the crash.

That the cash-rich KIO could recognize a bargain, always attractive to the Arab mind, and a major buying opportunity when it saw one, was hardly surprising. Unfortunately, however, the reality was rather more complicated. While the KIO itself was run on purely commercial lines and guided by intelligent investment criteria, it was owned by the Kuwait Investment Agency, which existed to further the political and strategic interests of the Kuwaiti Government. Thus a KIO operation on behalf of the KIA had a very different significance from one conducted off its own bat.

Not surprisingly, as the KIO steadily built up its BP stake to the point where it represented the largest single investment in its entire portfolio, BP became increasingly concerned. On 17 December Peter Walters wrote to me to express his anxiety. He was worried that the KIO was engaged in building up a shareholding sufficiently large for the KIA to demand representation on the BP Board, as it had already done, for example, with Daimler-Benz in Germany. While BP would resist any such demand – not least because the Kuwaiti Government was a direct competitor of BP, having built up its own worldwide oil business, the Kuwait Petroleum Company, with its own 'Q8' brand name – it would be distinctly uncomfortable to have a serious competitor as far and away BP's largest shareholder, now that the UK Government's holding was reduced to below 2 per cent. He was also worried that BP's business prospects in the US, where it had been actively expanding, would be jeopardized if it were seen to be partly owned and controlled by one of the leading members of the OPEC cartel.

While I sympathized with Walters' anxieties, my sympathy was qualified by the extent to which he had made matters more difficult for himself. Under the terms of the agreement concluded when the State first acquired a majority stake in BP (then the Anglo–Persian Oil Company) shortly before the First World War, the Government had had the right, under the company's articles of association, to appoint two directors to the BP Board with special veto powers. In the preparations for the 1987 sale of the Government's remaining holding in the company, it was obvious that the company's articles would need to be changed to remove the Government's right to appoint directors to the BP Board. I wrote to Peter Walters asking him if he would like the Government, in exchange for giving up this right, to take a special or 'golden' share in BP, analogous to the golden shares involved in a large number of privatization issues, which would enable the Government to prevent an unwelcome takeover of the company. Walters replied that he would *not* want the Government to have a golden share.

By the time I received Walters' letter of 17 December he was out of the office; but I managed to track him down and suggested to him, over the telephone, that he might have a word himself with the KIO Chairman, pointing out that any further increase in its holding would be damaging to BP and thus to the value of the KIO's own substantial investment in the company. He thanked me for the suggestion, but did nothing. The Government's official attitude remained that this was a normal commercial transaction, and that there was nothing to worry about. But I took the precaution of having a quiet word with Geoffrey Howe, asking him if he would find out what the Kuwaitis were up to.

It so happened that David Mellor, then one of his Ministers of State at the Foreign Office, was about to visit Kuwait, and Geoffrey promised to get him to probe the Kuwaitis when he was there. Mellor discussed the matter with them on 23 December, and on his return reported to Geoffrey that he had been given an assurance by the Kuwaitis that they would at no time seek to exercise any control over BP, nor any management role in the company.

That was fine as far as it went; but the KIO went on adding to its holding of BP shares, and by the end of the year had acquired 18 per cent of the company. Meanwhile, Walters was fully occupied with the BP bid for Britoil (described later in this chapter), and had still done nothing. I remained concerned, however, that the assurances the Kuwaitis had given to David Mellor did not prevent them from selling their stake to a foreign predator interested in bidding for BP. Accordingly, on 6 January 1988 I wrote to Geoffrey, with copies to Margaret and Cecil Parkinson, then Energy Secretary, explaining my concern and asking him to speak to the Kuwaitis himself with a view to getting a threefold undertaking from them: first, that the KIO would not increase its stake in BP beyond 20 per cent; second, that they would not dispose of their stake to a third party without first ensuring that the potential purchaser was acceptable to the Government; and, third, reiterating the assurances reportedly given to David Mellor.

Geoffrey, however, was unwilling to press the matter, so I decided to pursue it myself. It had become clear that, however shrewd an investment the KIO had made, this was no normal KIO commercial operation. It was an opportunistic political move by the very able KIA Chairman and long-serving Kuwaiti Oil Minister, Sheikh Ali Khalifa, a member of the ruling al-Sabah family and someone I had known for many years, since he had been his country's Oil Minister when I was Energy Secretary. I had always got on well with him, and asked him to come and see me at Number 11 when he was next in London. He duly turned up at Downing Street on 28 January, bringing with him Fouad Jaffar, the KIO Chief Executive. I was accompanied by Peter Middleton.

Ali Khalifa was his usual urbane and courteous self, but resolutely declined to give the undertakings I sought. Stripped of all the verbiage, his position was that the Kuwaitis would always respect British law, but nothing they were doing was illegal. He was also able to add, annoyingly, that he had received no complaints from BP about the KIO's share purchases. He was unmoved by my response that legal, or not, it was clearly unwise to risk seriously damaging Anglo–Kuwaiti relations, which were so important to Kuwait. He was equally unmoved when I said that if the law was all he would heed, he should not forget that we could refer the matter to the Monopolies & Mergers Commission (MMC) whose recommendations, if accepted by the Trade & Industry Secretary, at that time David Young, had the force of law.

I was, of course, aware that an MMC referral would be something of a gamble: it was seldom possible to predict which way that inscrutable body would jump. I therefore had two further meetings with Ali Khalifa in February 1988, this time accompanied by the Energy Secretary, Cecil Parkinson, in an attempt to conclude a voluntary agreement; but to no avail.

The Judgement of the MMC

By early March, by which time the KIO holding in BP was well above the 20 per cent limit to which I had sought to get Ali Khalifa to agree – indeed it was not far short of 22 per cent – I told Margaret that I thought there was nothing for it but to refer the matter to the MMC. With some reluctance, she agreed. As soon as they had got wind of this, the Kuwaitis responded by halting KIO purchases of BP stock. Claiming that the shares were now overvalued, they announced that they would not take their shareholding above 22.5 per cent. If they hoped this would halt the process of law, they were mistaken. On 3 May, David Young, referred the KIO shareholding in BP to the MMC. He explained that 'the implication of BP coming under the influence or control of a Government with substantial oil interests, and which is a member of OPEC, raises issues of public interest which warrant investigation by the MMC. The decision to make a reference to the Commission does not in any way prejudge the question whether or not the Kuwaiti shareholding is against the public interest.' The Kuwaitis undertook not to buy any further shares in BP, pending the outcome of the investigation.

The MMC referral clearly unsettled the Kuwaitis. On 8 August, the KIO executed a formal deed specifying that it intended to reduce its stake in BP to 20 per cent, not to seek board representation, and voluntarily to limit its voting rights to no more than 14.9 per cent of BP's share capital. It hoped that this would reassure the MMC that the BP shareholding was merely a portfolio investment without implications for the future of the company. It even offered to ensure its shareholding rose no further, by undertaking to opt always for cash rather than scrip dividends, and not to take up its shares in any rights issue. But the Kuwaitis had left it too late. What would have been an acceptable offer in February, before the referral to the MMC, was acceptable no longer. David Young rightly declined to sign the deed, on the grounds that he could not pre-empt the findings of the MMC.

To my relief and some surprise, the MMC reported in September 1988 that the KIO should be required to reduce its shareholding in BP to below 10 per cent within twelve months. It was a much tougher ruling than I had expected. The report concluded:

> While it is not possible to predict the future of the oil markets or of the Middle East, we believe that there is a high degree of probability that sooner or later situations will arise in which Kuwait's national and international interests will come sharply into conflict with BP's and HMG's interests. Such conflicts of interest would be even more likely to occur if a future government in Kuwait was less well disposed to the West and the United Kingdom. We consider that if and when these conflicts occur Kuwait will seek, and be able, to use its shareholding to influence BP in the ways we have set out . . . and that this may be expected to be detrimental to, and will operate against, the United Kingdom public interest.

The following month David Young formally accepted the MMC finding, modifying it only by giving the KIO three years, instead of only a year, to get their holding below 10 per cent. BP, however, was still worried that the KIO would dump its shares on the market in a fit of pique, enabling them to be picked up by a predator; and concluded that the only safe course was for the company to buy back the shares itself. Discussions to this end began, and by the end of 1988 agreement was reached between the company and Ali Khalifa. The sale was completed the following month, January 1989, when BP purchased 790 million of its own shares for almost £2 billion. The KIO had made a useful profit on the deal, but Ali Khalifa had gambled and lost. He had clearly wanted Kuwait to have a quasi-strategic stake in BP, and could have settled for 20 per cent. By refusing to do so, the Kuwaitis had damaged their relationship with the British Government and ended up with under 10 per cent; and Ali Khalifa's personal standing within the ruling al-Sabah family was considerably diminished.

Britoil and its Golden Share

While all this was going on, BP was deliberately getting involved in a complication of a different kind. On 8 December 1987 the company staged a £225 million 'dawn raid' on Britoil, formerly the operating arm of the British National Oil Corporation, which I had privatized when I was Energy Secretary in 1982 (see Chapter 19), and secured 15 per cent of the shares. It then made a tender offer for another 14.9 per cent, which took its stake to just below the threshold where a full takeover bid became mandatory. BP clearly wanted to acquire Britoil, but recognized that before going any further it needed to secure Government consent. At the time Britoil was privatized, I had created a special (or 'golden') share in the company designed to give the Government, which held the share, an effective right of veto over any takeover.

By enabling the Government to appoint its own nominees to the board of Britoil as soon as any potential bidder's share stake passed 50 per cent, and to win any votes taken at subsequent general meetings of shareholders, the Britoil golden share allowed the Government to deny BP any representation the board and thus any role in the management of the company. There was no legal impediment preventing BP from acquiring 100 per cent of Britoil if it chose to do so, but not even 100 per cent ownership would give it control without Government consent.

As it happened, the Britoil golden share was held anomalously by the Treasury. I had concluded a satisfactory agreement with Cabinet colleagues before the 1987 election under which all residual Government shareholdings in privatized companies were transferred to the Treasury, which was responsible for their eventual sale, with the exception of golden shares, which were, of course, not for sale, and which until can-celled would remain with the appropriate policy Department. The Britoil golden share, however, had been transferred from the Department of

Energy to the Treasury in 1985, before the 1987 agreement had been concluded, and the Treasury had not got around to transferring it back again. So it fell to me to decide whether to use it to frustrate the BP bid.

The BP share raid placed the Government in a somewhat embarrassing position. The Britoil golden share was less well designed than later versions. It had failed to deter a potential bidder from acquiring a potentially commanding stake in the company, and gave the Government the power to frustrate the bidder only via the unsatisfactory device of divorcing ownership from control. Not that there was any clear reason why the Government should exercise that power. The purpose of the golden share had been twofold: to prevent an overseas takeover of what was considered an important British asset, which clearly did not apply in this case, where the potential bidder was itself British; and to give the new company a chance to prove itself in the private sector. Britoil had had that chance, but unlike its sister privatized oil company, Enterprise Oil, had not made good use of it. It was more than likely that BP would manage the company better. But there were two complicating factors. First, the Britoil Chairman, Philip Shelbourne, backed by a majority of his board, was opposed to a takeover by BP. He preferred a rescue deal with Atlantic Richfield (Arco) of the United States, in which the American oil company would acquire 49.9 per cent of Britoil through share purchases and an exchange of assets for shares.

Second, and much more sensitive, there was the Scottish dimension. The Britoil headquarters were in Glasgow, most of its oil prospecting was in Scottish waters, and it was generally regarded as Scotland's most important company. Scots MPs, and particularly Scottish Labour MPs – of which there were a great many, some of them very able, unlike my early days in the House of Commons – inveighed against the idea of control of Britoil leaving Scotland. Malcolm Rifkind, the Scottish Secretary, told me that he felt that this was a sufficiently sensitive issue to consider using the 'golden share'. The golden share had been a useful device in making the original privatization more acceptable to Parliament and public; but now it had become an embarrassment, obliging the Government to make choices that would have been far better left to the company's shareholders.

As long as there were two rival suitors for Britoil, one of them a foreign company, it was difficult to disavow the special share. On 18 December, 1987, ten days after the BP raid, I authorized a Treasury statement saying that 'in the present circumstances' the Government intended to use its special share to prevent any bidder from gaining control of the Britoil board. On 11 January John Smith, himself a Scottish MP, asked me by a private notice question how I intended to use the Britoil golden share. I replied that 'the powers of the special share will be used for so long as it is in the national interest to do so.' This was a clear signal that there were circumstances in which I would be prepared to waive the use of the golden share, and it was not lost on either BP or Arco. On 22 January 1988, Arco agreed to sell to BP, at a profit, the 24 per cent stake in Britoil it had acquired. BP then made an offer for the rest of the shares. This gave BP a launch pad of almost 54 per cent of the shares in Britoil and the near-certainty of acquiring the rest. The question then became one of how the Government could extricate itself from an awkward situation at the smallest political cost. On 1 February I minuted Margaret suggesting what seemed to me the best solution.

In essence, I recommended that the Government should use the golden share as a negotiating card. In return for allowing BP control of the Britoil board, the Government should seek firm and public undertakings that Britoil would remain committed to Scotland and to the North Sea. The golden share would remain in place until BP had demonstrated satisfactorily that it intended to fulfil its undertakings, at which point it would lapse. This was consistent with my pledge to the House of Commons that day, in response to a further Private Notice Question from John Smith, to use the golden share in the national interest but also to 'take fully into account what is best for Scotland and for the development of the North Sea'. Margaret concurred; and, after discussing with Malcolm Rifkind and Cecil Parkinson the details of the sort of undertaking we required, I asked Peter Middleton to set about negotiating the terms of the deal with BP.

I announced the agreed terms to the House of Commons on 23 February, 1988, by which time BP already owned 80 per cent of Britoil. Under them, BP undertook to increase North Sea exploration (Britoil's forte), to manage the combined North Sea oil operations of BP and Britoil from Glasgow, to transfer its research and development operations north of the border, to move between 50 and 75 senior executives to Scotland, to endow research fellowships at Scottish universities and to retain Aberdeen as its main operating centre for North Sea activities. It was enough to give Malcolm Rifkind the ammunition he needed to use against his Scottish critics. On 25 February 1988 the Britoil board, with evident reluctance, recommended the offer from BP; Britoil duly became a wholly owned subsidiary of BP, BP lived up to the undertakings it had given; and the golden share was cancelled. But well before that I had transferred it from the Treasury back to the Energy Department from which it should never have strayed.

CHAPTER 63

SHADOWING THE DEUTSCHMARK

Exchange Rate Policy After the Crash
The Financial Times *Interview*
The Switch to Marks · A Near Realignment

Exchange Rate Policy After the Crash

The relief provided on the sterling front by the Wall Street crash was short-lived. Indeed, the problem of the inflow into London re-emerged as early as 30 October. The very fact that interest rate cuts were internationally co-ordinated meant that the comparative attractions of holding money in London and other centres had not changed very much.

It cannot be emphasized too strongly that, although I was obviously interested in demonstrating that sterling was fully ready for ERM membership by giving it a dry run, the main purpose of the policy of shadowing the Deutschmark was to arrest the fall in sterling which, both in terms of the index and against the Mark, had been going on, intermittently but inexorably, since the peak in 1980–81, and about which I had already become worried both in 1984 and 1986. My original post-Louvre policy was to secure sterling stability at a level higher than the pre-Louvre rate of some DM2.8, but with no specific parity in mind. The markets, however, assumed that we must have had a desired parity and tried to guess what it was. Their guess was DM3. As I have already recorded, this occurred well before the 1987 election. As a result, the market started to do much of the stabilizing for us, selling sterling when it approached DM3 and buying sterling whenever it dipped below it. So we decided to ride on the back of that.

As for the scale of the intervention required by the policy, I was anxious at least to recoup the sizeable loss of reserves that had been incurred in the defence of sterling in the closing months of 1986. The official monthly reserve figures, so conscientiously quoted and commented upon by the financial press and by analysts, are in fact a far from accurate indicator either of the amount of intervention over the month or of the true level of reserves at the end of it. This is so even if the figures are adjusted for special borrowing to replenish the reserves, annual revaluations, the proceeds of privatization offers (the large ones always had an overseas component) and many other complications.

Far more important is the fact that the published figures relate solely to the spot book and not to the forward book, the size of which is never revealed. (The forward book consists of foreign exchange already acquired or sold, but for delivery at a later date.) During 1987, when money was flooding into London, I understated the size of the inflow by tucking some of it away into the forward book – that is to say, by getting the Bank to resell part of the foreign exchange inflow before the end of the month with a matching repurchase for delivery some months later. This was partly to avoid the danger that a large inflow might make the market so optimistic about the pound that still more foreign money flowed in. But it was also in part so that when sentiment turned, as I had little doubt one day it would, I would be able to offset much of the cost of intervention to support the pound by taking delivery of some of the hidden reserves in the forward book, thus minimizing the reduction in the published reserves.

The idea of making use of the forward book to conceal the true position was not an innovation of mine. I believe that, during the acute run on sterling in 1976 under Labour, the true reserves were completely exhausted and actually became negative; and that this was concealed from view by selling dollars the UK did not possess in the forward market and buying them back spot, relying on IMF funds to save the Government from the day of reckoning when the time came to deliver the dollars that had been sold in this way. Be that as it may, whatever was concealed from the press or the financial commentators, it goes without saying that the Treasury's own market report, which was sent to Margaret every evening without fail, always gave the full and true figure of UK intervention.

Her own view of all this underwent an astonishing transformation. During the first half of the period of shadowing the Mark, up to my September 1987 IMF speech, she positively loved the steady accumulation of reserves. Alan Walters, however, who deeply disapproved of my IMF speech, got on to her about it and thoroughly put the wind up her; as a result of which she completely changed her tune.

It is worth underlining that the rows I had with her at the end of 1987 and in the early part of 1988 were entirely about intervention. She had convinced herself that this was inflationary, even though it was fully sterilized – a point more fully discussed in the next chapter. She at no time suggested that interest rates should be higher, which she should have done if she had really wanted a stronger counter-inflationary stance. Indeed, she made it clear that, if we stopped intervening and let the pound rise, one of the attractions for her was that this might enable interest rates to come down. I vividly recall, too, how cross she was as late as May 1988 when the main article in the Bank of England *Bulletin* that month suggested that a better policy mix, if achievable, would be to have a lower exchange rate and higher interest rates.

There was, of course, an international dimension. Although there was no specific Louvre range for sterling, the purchase of dollars clearly fitted in with the agreed G7 policy of preventing any further fall in the dollar. But my chief concern was the defence of sterling. The foreign exchange market may appear at times to be a one-way street, but nothing could be more unwise than to assume it will stay that way. By resisting *upward* pressure on the pound I sought to create credibility for a commitment to resist renewed *downward* pressure. Although I was no longer a believer in the old orthodoxy that exchange rates always moved in line with the current account of the balance of payments, I still expected that the UK's swing into current deficit, which had taken place in the second quarter of 1987, would sufficiently unsettle the financial markets that they would be reminded that the underlying UK inflation rate remained stubbornly above that of our main competitors, and start to sell sterling. The fact that UK short-term interest rates were more than 5 per cent above German rates in late 1987 (they were also more than 2 per cent above German rates in real terms) seemed to me a reasonable assessment of the relative risks of holding the two currencies.

Neither in our regular weekly bilateral meetings nor on any other occasion did Margaret make any complaint to me about the exchange rate policy I was pursuing until December. But it is clear in retrospect that she was getting more and more worked up about it. She was increasingly seeking advice from other sources and biding her time to act.

The Financial Times *Interview*

A portent of the wrath to come was another interview Margaret gave to *The Financial Times* published on 23 November 1987, when she categorically and repeatedly denied that there was any exchange rate target for the pound. She rejected completely the notion of the pound being tied, even unofficially, to a rate of just under or around DM3. 'There is no specific range' she said. 'We are always free.'

The objection she gave to both shadowing the Deutschmark and to joining the ERM gives the lie to the notion that she saw the inflationary dangers ahead and wanted a tighter policy. On the contrary, she argued that the 'DM at the moment is slightly deflationary. That means that the whole of Europe is geared to a slightly deflationary policy. Now, we have not been so geared and we have had a degree of freedom in relation to both the dollar and the D-Mark and I just think that I am grateful for that.'

Her interlocutors reminded her that a year previously she had told the paper that Britain could not become a full member of the EMS because the domestic economy was still too weak. In her reply she shifted, as she had done in our conversation in July, to opposing ERM entry outright, even though it was Government policy to join. She also expressed scepticism about the possibility of a more managed international system.

Opinions such as those she expressed on the record to *The Financial Times* could have been elicited from her at any time had the Opposition been more alert. Although she was ultra-scrupulous about Budget secrecy, on currency questions Margaret indulged in a stream-of-consciousness response, apparently oblivious to the sensitivity of the foreign exchange markets to her words. At the time I was thankful that no-one else did press her. My attitude, when publicly questioned about the apparent contradictions between us, was to point out that 'actions speak louder than words', a formula I first used before the 1987 election and was still using when I was questioned by the Treasury Select Committee on 30 March 1988.

The Switch to Marks

The first rumblings of trouble on the operational front came in the early days of December 1987. The co-ordinated European base rate cut of ½ per cent had been agreed on 2 December and implemented on 4 December. Between these two events, on 3 December, there had been further upward pressure on the pound, and the Bank had intervened heavily to hold the rate, acquiring a further $1 billion. When I held a meeting on Friday, 4 December, to review the situation in the immediate aftermath of the ½ per cent cut, the pressure had abated somewhat, but the position was still uncomfortable. The pressure might flare up again at any time, and I was clear that we would not be justified in cutting interest rates any further – indeed, I would not have considered the 4 December cut had it not been a concerted European move designed, as I indicated in a previous chapter, both to demonstrate to the markets that international co-operation was still alive and well and to meet the American terms for their active participation in stabilizing the dollar.

The main purpose of intervention, from the UK's point of view, had been to maintain the DM3 parity. Yet the intervention hitherto had consisted entirely of purchases of dollars. This was partly because the

Bank preferred it, since the dollar market is far and away the largest and easiest to deal in, and partly because we had committed ourselves under the Louvre agreement to participating in the stabilization of the dollar. But by that time I reckoned we had already (admittedly for our own purposes) contributed more than our fair share to supporting the dollar and fulfilling our Louvre obligations. It would be far more logical and effective, in the event of any resurgence of pressure, for us to buy Deutschmarks, which was clearly possible, whatever the Bank felt about the size of the market.

Indeed, in a sense the smaller the market the better, since it might mean that a given amount of intervention would have greater immediate effect. I therefore told Robin that, from then on, should there be further upward pressure on sterling, we should buy Deutschmarks and not dollars. The ownership of, and responsibility for, foreign exchange reserves as between the Government and the central bank varies from country to country. In the UK the reserves belong to the Treasury, and policy for the reserves is a Treasury responsibility. The Bank acts in the foreign exchange markets explicitly as the Treasury's agent.

What I was not aware of, however, when I told Robin of the change of policy, was that one of the clauses of the March 1979 agreement setting up the EMS, which had been concluded shortly before we took office, stated that no member country would purchase the currency of another member country without first securing the permission of that country's central bank. And, although sterling was not in the ERM, we were of course technically a member of the EMS – a perfect example of the British art of compromise securing the worst of all worlds. My officials, who did know of this, had not sought to trouble me with it since there was a clear understanding that the necessary permission would normally be granted, and there would need to be a compelling reason for its not being, which they did not see in this case.

But when Robin returned to the Bank and telephoned Karl Otto Pöhl to inform him that we would be purchasing Deutschmarks, he received a flea in his ear and was told in no uncertain terms that we could not do so. In Germany, unlike in the UK, the foreign exchange reserves are owned by the Bundesbank and policy for the reserves is the responsibility of the Bundesbank. The Finance Ministry's only statutory right is to receive a substantial share of any profits the Bundesbank makes from its reserves. The Bundesbank was strongly averse to the Deutschmark becoming a reserve currency, believing that this caused problems far greater than any offsetting reward, and in particular that the more Deutschmarks were held overseas, the harder it would be for it to exercise monetary control. But it was generally accepted that this was not a sufficient ground for withholding consent. Instead, Pöhl's ostensible objection was that the purchase of Deutschmarks was contrary to the Louvre Accord.

Robin reported Pöhl's refusal to me, which seemed to me wholly un-reasonable, and I undertook to take the matter up with Stoltenberg, whom I would be seeing the following Monday, 7 December, at the Ecofin meet-ing in Brussels. There is a strict protocol in the conduct of international financial relations, requiring that, outside joint meetings such as the G7, Finance Ministers speak only to Finance Ministers, and central bank Governors only to central bank Governors. When I saw Stoltenberg I was armed with the figures showing the amount of dollars we had purchased since the Louvre Accord, an amount far greater than the Bundesbank's purchases of dollars, for which I also had figures. Given that, I suggested that it would require far larger purchases of Deutschmarks than anything I had in mind for the UK to be vulnerable to the charge of breaching the Louvre Accord. Moreover, we were not selling dollars, but pounds. Stoltenberg replied that he would have a word with Pöhl, but it was all very difficult. I concluded that we should go ahead regardless.

The following day, 8 December, I had my regular weekly bilateral with Margaret. I found her in an extremely agitated and aggressive mood. She told me that she was deeply concerned about the continuing large-scale intervention required to hold sterling below DM3, which already amounted to some $27 billion since the beginning of the financial year. (This information was one of the items contained in the evening report which the Treasury sent her every day.) She argued that the resulting extra liquidity would lead to renewed inflation. I pointed out that there was no increase in liquidity at all, since the intervention was always sterilized (that is, the equivalent amount of liquidity was removed from the system by the sale of gilt-edged securities).

I had, in fact, sought to explain the position, in my Mansion House speech the previous month, when I said:

> To prevent there being excessive liquidity in the economy, our policy is to ensure that, over time, any net intervention is sterilized – in other words fully funded, and that will be done, as and when appropriate although not necessarily entirely within the financial year in which the intervention takes place . . . Nor should there be any doubt about commitment to maintain a stable exchange rate, with the rate against the Deutschmark being of particular importance. It gives industry most of what it wants, and provides a firm anchor against inflation. And we now have very substantial reserves with which to maintain a stability in the future.

I reiterated the point, at my bilateral, that not only was there no problem of increased liquidity, but we were gaining the advantage of a significant strengthening of our foreign exchange reserves, something she had earlier agreed was needed. She then changed tack, arguing that we were losing money by acquiring dollars which depreciated in value. This gave me the cue to suggest that, if this was her fear, the answer was to intervene to maintain the DM3 ceiling by purchasing Deutschmarks instead, which in any case seemed to me the sensible thing to do. The problem, however, was Pöhl's invocation of the March 1979 EMS agreement, to which the Bank of England was a signatory (it was technically an agreement between the central banks of the member States). This made Robin very reluctant to buy Deutschmarks.

Margaret was attracted by this. She said that although she was still worried about the scale of the intervention, she agreed that it would be worth attempting in the first instance to hold sterling below the DM3 ceiling by intervening in Deutschmarks, not least because she very much hoped that considerably less intervention would be required. She told me to instruct the Governor that, as from the next day's opening, the purchase of dollars should cease, and all intervention should be done in Deutschmarks – irrespective of the 1979 agreement.

The whole nature and context of this discussion, incidentally, gives the lie to the extraordinary suggestion, put about by her acolytes after the event, that Margaret was somehow unaware of my policy of shadowing the Deutschmark. It was always an implausible insult to her formidable intelligence to suggest that she could possibly have been unaware of it, even if I had wished to keep her in the dark, which, of course, I did not. In fact, we discussed it openly on a number of occasions, of which the 8 December bilateral is merely one instance. What is true is that there was no meeting at which the DM3 ceiling was formally agreed. That was because, as I have already explained, it evolved gradually over a period of weeks from the Louvre Accord, of which she was also fully aware.*

Following the decision to confine intervention to Deutschmarks, I telephoned Robin and confirmed that this was to be the policy from now on. I added that Margaret, too, was clear that this was what we should do, despite the 1979 agreement, of which I had made her fully aware. This was clearly most unwelcome to Robin, who said that he could carry out this policy only if he were given clear instructions in writing to do so. This would enable him to explain to Pöhl that the Bank had no choice in the matter. I agreed to do this, and first thing the following morning, Wednesday, 9 December, sent him a letter by hand, the key section of which read as follows:

From now on all intervention. . .should be in Deutschmarks and not in dollars. Where it is necessary to intervene in markets where the direct

---

*In an interview with Simon Jenkins in *The Times* of 29 June 1991, Margaret publicly admitted that she had known about my policy of shadowing the Deutschmark, claiming however that her decision to allow it was her 'great mistake'. Despite this, the myth that she did not know about it continued to be peddled by some of her acolytes.

sterling/Deutschmark market is thin, and hence for technical reasons intervention has to be in some other currency, the proceeds should be switched into Deutschmarks as soon as possible . . . We have bought enormous amounts of dollars since the Louvre Accord, far more than the Bundesbank: our market intervention in dollars has totalled some $25 billion, compared with intervention by the Bundesbank of under $3 billion. In these circumstances it is wholly unreasonable for the Bundesbank to object to what we shall be doing.

Later that day, Robin telephoned me to say that he had received the letter, but was still very unhappy. He had now heard from Jacques de Larosière, who had clearly been approached by Pöhl. De Larosière urged Robin very strongly not to buy Deutschmarks, since this would put strains on the ERM which could be very dangerous for the franc. Robin felt he could not carry out the new policy without first having the opportunity to put his case to Margaret himself. This was fair enough, and I arranged for Robin and myself to see Margaret about it the following morning, 10 December. I felt that de Larosière was on to a much better point than Pöhl, although it was, of course, the Bundesbank's permission that was formally required, not that of the Banque de France. It obviously was possible that sizeable purchases of Deutschmarks could put upward pressure on that currency, making it harder for the French to maintain the Deutschmark/franc parity. I concluded that we should accommodate de Larosière's point by amending the policy to one of purchasing Deutschmarks and francs in equal quantities. This would avoid any conceivable strain being put on the Deutschmark/franc parity; and although it formally meant that the Bank of England would need to secure the permission of the Banque de France to purchase the francs, they could scarcely object, since it was being done for their benefit.

Robin and I accordingly went to see Margaret the following morning, after Cabinet. Robin made his case. I then chipped in with my suggestion for meeting the French objection, and Margaret agreed that the policy should be amended in this way. There was a brief further discussion, at which it was agreed that other currencies might also be purchased: Margaret's chief concern at this point was that we should purchase no further dollars. Robin then pointed out that he still had a letter from me instructing the Bank to purchase exclusively Deutschmarks. I undertook to let him have a new letter which would supersede the earlier one, which I sent him later that same day. The key passage read as follows:

I am writing to confirm what we agreed at our meeting with the Prime Minister this morning . . . It was agreed this morning that intervention in French francs should broadly match intervention in Deutschmarks, and that intervention in Swiss francs and yen would

also be permitted. But details of intervention should be settled between the Treasury and the Bank.

The letter then went on to cover various other details, including the
fact that the Bank could make purchases of Ecus (the artificial currency
created from a basket of all the Community currencies) as and when
feasible. The main argument for buying Ecus, which it was not easy to
do in large quantities at that time, was that it was to some extent a means
of buying Deutschmarks through the back door, since the Deutschmark
was far and away the largest component of the Ecu basket. But it was
not covered by the 1979 agreement – even though Pöhl at one point had
the gall to argue that implicitly it was and that no European Community
central bank could buy Ecus without the Bundesbank's permission.

Meanwhile the upward pressure on sterling was continuing. By the
following day, Friday, 11 December, it stood at DM2.997 – only a whisker
below the DM3 ceiling. I arranged to have a meeting with my three key
Treasury advisers on the Monday morning. Sterling was still under
heavy pressure, despite renewed intervention, this time under the new
policy guidelines. As a result, on Thursday, 17 December, Stoltenberg
telephoned me to protest about our purchases of Deutschmarks. It was
clear that the originator of the protest was Pöhl who had been told by
Robin that there was nothing he, Robin, could do: he was acting under
instructions from me; and protocol prevented Pöhl from speaking to me
himself: he had to go through Stoltenberg.

However, Stoltenberg added his own four penn'orth by arguing that
what we were doing would make it much more difficult to get a satisfactory section on intervention in the G7 'communiqué without a meeting'
which, as I explained in the previous chapter, we were at that very
moment engaged in drafting. I told Stoltenberg that I understood the
problem, but that what we were engaged in was essentially a temporary expedient to overcome an immediate problem with which we
were faced. I did not envisage it being a permanent feature of our
policy. This seemed to satisfy him: Stoltenberg and I knew each other
well, trusted each other, and had been working together closely for
the past four and a half years.

A little over a year later I discovered from Mariano Rubio, then
Governor of the Spanish central bank, that Spain had been in exactly
the same position. Following the entry of the peseta into the ERM, the
Spanish currency had been under enormous upward pressure which had
been met by intervention. Rubio had soon tired of purchasing dollars and
switched to Deutschmarks instead, only to be told by Pöhl, in the strongest possible terms, that under the rules of the EMS this was not possible
without the Bundesbank's permission, which was not forthcoming.

Rubio was, in a sense, in a stronger moral position than that into which I had put the unfortunate Robin. Unlike the UK, Spain was not a signatory to the 1979 agreement, not having been a member of the Community at that time. Nor, of course, not being a member of the G7, was it a signatory to the Louvre Accord. On the other hand, by joining the EMS, Spain was as much bound by the rules of the system as any other member. But it was clear to Rubio, as it was clear to me, that this particular rule had been inserted at the behest of the Bundesbank, and was wholly unnecessary for the effective functioning of the ERM, and indeed did not serve the interests of the EMS in any wider sense. In any event, Rubio in effect told Pöhl to get lost, in language more appropriate to the intercourse between central bank Governors, and carried on purchasing Deutschmarks.

A Near Realignment

What I had in mind when I assured Stoltenberg on 17 December 1987 that what we were engaged in was only a short-term expedient was that it was clear to me that intervention on this scale could not continue very much longer – not least because it was becoming subject to the law of diminishing returns. Before long, either the sterling tide would turn, or else, if the upward pressure continued, we would have to 'realign'. Indeed, we had come very close to a realignment only three days previously.

I had opened the meeting with my three key Treasury advisers on 14 December by asking 'Have we run out of road?' For the decision I had to take was whether the time had come to abandon the DM3 ceiling and allow the pound to rise – and, if so, how the policy change was to be presented to the markets. A number of views were expressed. One was that we should not abandon the DM3 ceiling. Another that any uncapping should be accompanied by a cut in interest rates, in the sense that a modest cut would not be taking great risks with inflation, as it would merely offset the contractionary effect of sterling appreciation. Yet another was to cut interest rates sharply, to break the bullish mood by leaving markets in no doubt that the next interest rate move would be upward. The consensus was that if it really was impossible to hold the line, it would be better to uncap the pound and cut interest rates afterwards, with a view to restoring the DM3 ceiling as soon as possible.

Listening to the discussion, I came to a clear conclusion. We should not rush into anything. But if the *status quo* became unsustainable, we would allow the pound to rise through the DM3 ceiling and then seek to stabilize it at a new, slightly higher level. We would, in short, have an informal realignment. Quite apart from the drawbacks to all the other courses, this seemed to me to be the least difficult to present as essentially a continuation of the existing policy, while avoiding taking any risks with inflation. It was agreed that this was what we would do.

However, as it happened, my caution about doing anything straight away proved justified. The upward pressure on sterling abated that very week and the pound, in fact, fell slightly against the Deutschmark. At the time, it seemed like a last-minute reprieve. In the light of subsequent events, it might have been better to have had the realignment.

CHAPTER 64

FROM SHADOWING TO SHOWDOWN

Sterling Uncapped · 'No Way One Can Buck the Market'
Griffiths Tries to Draft · Shadowing the Deutschmark: a Post-Mortem
Appendix: Intervention and Inflation

Sterling Uncapped

BY THE BEGINNING OF MARCH 1988 sterling had returned to virtually DM3, a level last seen in mid-December. In forty-eight hours on Wednesday and Thursday, 2 and 3 March, some $1.8 billion of intervention had been required in the effort to hold the pound. Sudden movements in the reserves are always inclined to cause a panic, even when, as in this case, the movement was in an upward direction; and the advice of Bank and Treasury officials on the morning of Friday, 4 March, was that I should uncap the pound forthwith.

I told my officials I would think about it over the weekend and let them have an answer first thing on Monday morning. It was not that I failed to recognize the inevitable. It was simply that we were by then only eleven days from the Budget, and I very much wanted to hold the line until then. I felt that an orderly realignment would be easier to achieve in an orderly setting, on a day on which I clearly held the initiative. Moreover, I was planning to leave London at 2.30 that afternoon for Stoney Stanton to work on the Budget speech. It was an important Budget, and I wanted to focus my mind on that. I then received a message that Margaret would like to see me at two o'clock.

I found her in a highly agitated state. She said she was deeply worried by the scale of the intervention in the foreign exchange markets needed to suppress the pound over the previous two days. She argued that it was adding to the inflationary pressure in the economy, and that the defence of the DM3 ceiling was attracting speculators to sterling, so adding to the upward pressure on the pound. I explained to her once again that there was no question of the intervention being inflationary, since all the excess liquidity was being 'sterilized' by sales of gilt-edged securities. I added, 'The time will come when you will be very grateful we have acquired all these reserves.'

I explained to her my intention to try to hold the position until Budget Day and then, if the pressures had not abated, make an informal upward realignment. But she had the bit between her teeth and would not hear of it. I told her I would discuss the situation with my officials, and come back to her. I returned to the Treasury to discuss with Treasury and Bank officials the best means of uncapping the pound. My intention was still to lift the informal range rather than to leave sterling to its own devices. Robin was away, but the rest of the normal cast was present. It was agreed to uncap the pound from Monday morning, and to try and brake its rise through intervention and, if necessary, interest rate cuts, once it breached DM3.08. As for presentation, I decided that the least bad course was to insist that policy was unchanged, and that stability had never meant immobility.

I then returned to Number 10 at half past four. I told Margaret that, as she wished, the pound would be uncapped from Monday morning, but that intervention would continue in London and New York that evening because it would be unwise to let the pound breach the ceiling just before the weekend. I also explained that further intervention might be necessary to prevent the pound rising too sharply the following week. This greatly upset her. She insisted that sterling should be left to find its own level without any intervention at all. I told her that it would be absurd to abstain from intervention altogether.

After a heated discussion, she agreed to allow some limited intervention to smooth market movements and mentioned the sum of $50 million. This was a ridiculously small amount in the circumstances, and I told her that I could not possibly accept this constraint. She replied that my private office should contact Number 10 every half hour during the course of Monday and that she reserved the right to convene another meeting at short notice to review developments if she did not like the way policy was unfolding. It was an unpleasant meeting, and I particularly resented her manner on the eve of a Budget that was to achieve so many of the objectives we shared. Equally, there was no way in which I could contemplate resigning then: I was determined to introduce the 1988 Budget for which I had laboured so long and so hard. And Margaret knew this.

What was striking was that Margaret's entire concern in all this was with the level of intervention – and the fact (although she did not say this in terms) that I was using it to circumvent, in an informal way, her ERM veto. Not once did she suggest that interest rates needed to be higher, monetary policy tighter.

The uncapping of the pound in March 1988, coupled with her adamant refusal to contemplate British membership of the exchange rate mechanism of the EMS, removed a major plank of my counter-inflationary policy. A substantial current account deficit was already looming, and I could see sentiment in the markets turning against sterling before long. The massive reserves the Government had acquired during the previous year were bound to be useful, but the fact that the authorities had been driven off their declared policy of stabilization would not be forgotten in the markets. So it proved.

The credibility earned in resisting upward pressure, so important when it came to resisting downward pressure, was largely dissipated. By denting the already wavering confidence among businessmen that the Government was committed to exchange rate stability, the uncapping of the pound, as David Nickson, the CBI President, was to point out, represented a major threat to British industry since it lowered the resistance of his members to high pay awards.

I was also irritated by the style in which Margaret had conducted the meeting. I was particularly outraged by her claim that I had misled her about the conduct of exchange rate policy, and reminded her very firmly during the meeting that she had been fully briefed by me both before and after the Louvre Accord – when the policy of shadowing the Deutschmark was initiated – and that she had received every evening a report of daily intervention in the markets in pursuit of it.

I detected in her allegation that I had misled her about the policy – which she knew to be untrue – the influence of Alan Walters. He knew nothing of the Louvre agreement, except what he had read of it in the newspapers, and I suspect that she was articulating his ignorance of what was going on rather than her own. I knew also that he contacted her fairly regularly, usually by letter, and that the British Embassy in Washington passed him information on Margaret's instructions. His advice was never copied to me, although I would sometimes find out through informal official sources. Coming so soon after her disparagement of my IMF speech five months earlier, it was increasingly clear that Margaret preferred the advice of an academic economist observing the British economy from 3,000 miles away to that of her Chancellor of the Exchequer.

'No Way One Can Buck the Market'

Some journalists subsequently reported to me that she had been particularly incensed by my evidence to the Treasury Committee on 9 December when I had said: 'Obviously interest rates are something I watch carefully all the time and when I think they ought to go up they go up and when I think they should come down they come down.' It may not have been the most felicitous formulation, but, as the context made clear, I was simply emphasizing the point that interest rates could not somehow be left to the market, or determined by a formula: they were an inescapable responsibility of the authorities, and in the last resort the buck stopped with the Chancellor. Perhaps she felt it stopped with her. Margaret had a habit of talking in the first person singular about every aspect of policy, as if no other Cabinet Minister existed. But when I once slipped into a similar usage in an area which, in the absence of an independent central bank, was unquestionably my own, it was evidently too much for her.

Not surprisingly, on Monday, 7 March, the pound rose to DM3.05. The Treasury Press Office was still talking along the lines that 'stability does not mean immobility' and I still wanted the policy to be seen as some sort of realignment. But Margaret was evidently determined to sabotage even this hope by saying at Question Time the next day that she ruled out action to hold down the pound through either intervention or interest rate cuts:

> The only way to deal with that is either to have excessive intervention
> . . . or to deal with the matter by interest rates, which would not be
> in the interests of inflation at the present time.

In the circumstances, this could only be construed as an encouragement to the market to run the pound up still further.

This was the last thing either industry or the economy wanted; and during Treasury Questions in the House of Commons two days later I countered with the opinion that any further appreciation of the pound against the Deutschmark was 'unlikely to be sustainable'. Treasury Questions are always followed by Prime Minister's Questions, and Margaret lost no time in making a bad situation worse. Under pressure from the Labour leader, Neil Kinnock, to explain the apparent difference of opinion between us, she said:

> My Right Honourable Friend the Chancellor and I are absolutely
> agreed that the paramount objective is to get inflation down. The
> Chancellor never said that aiming for greater exchange rate stability
> meant total immobility. Adjustments are needed, as we learnt when
> we had a Bretton Woods system, as those in the EMS have learnt
> that they must have a devaluation from time to time. There is no way
> in which one can buck the market.

Up to that last sentence she was sticking reasonably closely to her prepared position, and it would have caused no comment had she stopped there. But it was that simplistic last sentence, which she added on the hoof, that was all that was remembered, and which did the damage. There may indeed be circumstances in which one cannot buck the market. But in the context Margaret's remark was inevitably taken to mean that any policy for sterling was being thrown out of the window.

As it happened, in the short term we got away lightly, in that the pound closed that week at DM3.0775, still short of the level at which I had thought further intervention would be justified a week earlier. But the unprecedented and highly damaging public spat between Prime Minister and Chancellor threatened to overshadow the Budget itself.

Griffiths Tries to Draft

There was one further argument between us before the Budget, although this time, thankfully, it was at least in private. It was over the passage on monetary policy and the exchange rate in the Budget speech. I sent the final draft of the speech to Margaret, for her to read and let me have her comments, on the morning of the Friday before the Budget (which by tradition is always on a Tuesday). That afternoon Brian Griffiths, the head of the Number 10 policy unit, came to see me at Number 11 with a fresh draft he had done of that section of the text. It was wholly unacceptable, describing monetary policy without any reference to the exchange rate at all; a formulation we had abandoned as far back as 1981, and one which bore no relation to the way in which policy was in practice conducted. I rejected it out of hand. But it was equally clear that Margaret would not swallow my original draft, and there was no time to thrash out the underlying issues ahead of the Budget. With Terry's help, I drafted a compromise version, and sent it to Number 10 with a message saying that I had gone as far as I could to accommodate the Prime Minister's views, taking the Griffiths version into account. I then went off to Dorneywood, saying that I looked forward to receiving her comments on the rest of the speech over the weekend.

The essence of the exchange rate section of my compromise version, which she did not challenge, and which I duly delivered, read as follows:

> The objective of greater exchange rate stability [has been] given an explicit role in the process of international co-operation . . . for well over two years now. I can assure the House that we shall continue to play our full part . . . Exchange rates play a central role in domestic monetary decisions as well as in international policy co-operation. I believe that most businessmen have welcomed the greater exchange

rate stability over the past year. It is important that they also accept the financial discipline inherent in this policy.

Margaret wasted no time, and sent the speech back to me, with a number of minor comments, some of which I accepted, on the Saturday. She attached a fulsome note in her own hand: 'Marvellous – extremely clear . . . Congratulations – I am sure it will be a great success.' I was irked that she thought I could be mollified so easily. It was never praise that I sought from her: just trust, honesty, and the loyalty she expected of others.

Meanwhile, I recall telling the Queen, the one person to whom I could unburden myself in complete confidence, during my usual pre-Budget audience with her the following Monday, that I thought the 1988 Budget would be my last, because the Prime Minister was making the conduct of policy impossible.

Shadowing the Deutschmark: a Post-Mortem

Whatever may have been said subsequently, by the autumn of 1987 senior Treasury officials were fully supportive of the policy of shadowing the Mark, particularly following the stock market crash. They believed that the real policy dilemma would come when sterling started to weaken again, and that economic policy needed both an intellectually coherent framework and to be something that could be presented to the outside world. By that time it was clear to them that the £M3 doctrine with which we had started was no longer viable; and we now had something which was both viable and actually working. They feared that if we were to lose that, we would be without any anchor at all, floundering about in no-man's land.

The only objection any official raised to shadowing the Mark came, as I have already recorded in Chapter 51, from Eddie George in the autumn of 1987. This was partly because he did not like fighting the market, but also because Margaret Thatcher had been getting at him. To be fair, he did worry about domestic inflationary pressures more than most other officials at the Treasury or the Bank. Nevertheless, his main concern was with the level of intervention. At a meeting just before the internationally concerted half-point cut in interest rates of 4 December 1987, he said that, although he was still concerned about domestically generated inflation, he preferred another small cut in base rates to yet more intervention.

Over a year after the March 1988 uncapping I asked the Treasury to let me have an honest post-mortem on the policy of shadowing the Deutschmark. Most of what they came up with represented common ground. Because of lags, we had, they said, to look back to the conduct of policy from mid-1986 onwards. In retrospect we had failed to spot both the extent of the decline in the savings ratio and the strength of the investment boom. They believed that the assessment of events in 1986–88 had been complicated by the oil price collapse of 1985–86 and the stock market crash in 1987. Further distractions were the mythical 1986 growth pause and the IMF's unfounded economic pessimism in the spring of 1987. They believed that, as a result, the shadowing of the Deutschmark had probably taken place at too low a parity.

Their main conclusion, however, was that the shadowing of the Deutschmark had no bearing whatever on our underestimation of the strength of the boom. Both the size of the decline in the personal savings ratio and the strength of private sector investment were unprecedented. (They might have made more of how they were both affected by financial deregulation.) They did not believe that the intervention had been inflationary. The problem, with hindsight, was simply that the overall stance of policy – taking both exchange rates and interest rates into account – was not tight enough. Had we made the right diagnosis from 1986 onwards, it was possible that on average interest rates might have been around 2 per cent higher and the exchange rate some 10 per cent higher – say DM3.30: a remarkably similar level to that at which I suggested earlier we would have eventually settled for, had my 1985 bid for ERM entry succeeded.

APPENDIX: INTERVENTION AND INFLATION

THE CHARGE THAT PURCHASES of foreign exchange to stop sterling rising above DM3 caused the resurgence of inflation in the late 1980s, although I believe manifestly mistaken, was not without precedent. Only a few months earlier, there were those who sought to blame the Wall Street crash of October 1987 on the substantial intervention undertaken to stabilize the dollar following the Louvre Accord. The argument here was that intervention by the Bundesbank had rekindled inflationary forces in Germany, thus provoking the sudden German discount rate increase of October 1987. This in turn evoked an aggressive US response, which triggered the crash.

The relationship between intervention and inflation ought, one might have thought, to be a straightforward matter about which there is no dispute. Regrettably, as in most areas of monetary economics, there is no real consensus. The nearest thing to an agreed text in the 1980s was the report of an intergovernmental team of officials chaired by the young French Treasury official Philippe Jurgensen, after the Versailles summit of 1982. The report was a compromise draft with no clear conclusions. The body of the text concentrated on the difference between 'sterilized' and 'unsterilized' intervention. If a central bank is to buy foreign exchange to prevent its currency from rising, then it needs domestic currency to finance its purchases. If that currency is created for the purpose and allowed to have its normal effect on the monetary system, the intervention is said to be unsterilized. If the central banks or governments in question sell securities to offset the monetary effect, then the intervention is said to be sterilized. The interpretation that was put on the Jurgensen Report was that unsterilized intervention was inflationary (or deflationary if it went in the opposite direction) while sterilized intervention was ineffective.

The simplest and most effective reaction has come from Paul Volcker:

> I can testify to an important fact: central bankers don't consciously think that way in conducting their operations. Almost every central bank has its own objectives for monetary policy, and these are not framed in terms of the amount of its foreign exchange intervention. If that intervention either enlarges or contracts the monetary base, the natural instinct is to offset it by monetary action. In other words they automatically sterilize intervention to the extent they can. That is the way the Federal Reserve behaves and so does practically every central bank in countries with a well enough developed money market to permit offsetting large operations.

In the UK the effect of intervention on the monetary base (M0) is automatically offset within the day, through the Bank of England's normal day-to-day money market operations, which are designed to hold bankers' balances with the Bank broadly constant.

The effect on broad money is more complex. Ever since I promulgated the 'full fund' rule in 1985, the authorities had financed through the sale of gilt-edged securities, outside the banking system, all the Government's borrowing requirements, including not only the Budget deficit but the currency required to purchase foreign exchange as well. So any increase in reserves was offset by a corresponding increase in sales of long term Government debt. Strictly speaking there can be complex secondary effects depending on precisely who is buying sterling in the first place and who buys the gilts, which can go in either direction. A reasonable assumption is a rough neutrality.

Thus in the UK, as in most other countries, intervention, by and large, is sterilized. But I have never accepted the so-called Jurgensen doctrine that this means it must be ineffective. Of course, if a currency is persistently in high demand, like the dollar in the mid-1980s or sterling in 1987–88, ultimately the monetary authorities – if they cannot change market expectations – must either let the exchange rate rise or reduce interest rates to offset the attractiveness of their currency.

But in my experience sterilized intervention can affect the market trend before the 'ultimate' is reached. The foreign exchange market likes to ride a trend, which can create bandwagon effects taking the currency far above or below that justified by any plausible view of fundamentals. Thus if, by relatively modest intervention, the authorities can create an expectation in the market of a movement in a particular direction – or even the absence of a previously expected movement – this can attract private sector funds, several times the size of the original intervention, in a benign direction.

In addition, concerted intervention is very much more effective than unilateral intervention, especially when the currency is under pressure. Intervention to support a falling currency is constrained by the level of national reserves, which the foreign exchange market roughly knows. Concerted intervention, however, also involves those countries that are selling their own currency and adding to their reserves, for whom there is no theoretical limit to the amount of intervention. The obligation of central banks of both the weak and the strong currency to intervene when the exchange rate comes up against the limits of the parity grid is theoretically a strong point of the ERM: the problem in practice has been the Bundesbank's reluctance to act in the spirit of the EMS rules, as strengthened by the Basle–Nyborg agreement (see Chapter 59). The Bundesbank's 'excuse', that intervention to restrain the Deutschmark might be inflationary, is not endorsed by economists at either the US Federal Reserve or the Bank of England.

There is some evidence to suggest that unilateral intervention is most effective when it is unexpected – which it can be even in the ERM if it takes place before a currency reaches its limit. On the technical issue, it is worth remarking that intervention and its sterilization do not of course (except in the case of the monetary base in the UK) occur simultaneously: characteristically the intervention takes place when a currency is under pressure and its sterilization after the pressure has subsided.

The main role of successful intervention is probably in changing the expectations of the private sector about where the authorities would like to see the exchange rate in the future. The immense trouble the foreign exchange markets take to try to discover the authorities' intentions does not suggest that they think that intervention is immaterial. Intervention can in some cases have a powerful effect, even if sterilized, provided that the authorities' intentions are credible in the sense that markets believe that interest rates will be used if necessary to support the desired exchange rates. In other words intervention is a useful short- to medium-term technique but, as I often put it, should not become 'a way of life'.

But however limited one may believe the efficacy of sterilized intervention to be, and whatever the circumstances necessary to make it a sensible weapon to use, there is no reason *pace* the Bundesbank, to believe it to be inflationary.

CHAPTER 65

BACKGROUND TO THE 1988 BUDGET

*The Overheating Debate · The Prospects at Chevening
Forecasting: The Moral · A Tight Budget
A Balanced Budget*

The Overheating Debate

IN THE SUMMER OF 1987, roughly a year after unemployment – that most lagging of indicators – had peaked, a debate began in the economic and financial press about whether the economy was overheating. There were two aspects to it. How much of a supply-side improvement had taken place in the British economy? And was demand increasing excessively?

On the first of these issues I stuck my neck out when I told the Edinburgh Chamber of Commerce on 23 June:

> As this upswing goes on, more and more people, at home and abroad are realizing that what we are seeing is much more than a recovery from recession, or than the operation of the normal cyclical pattern . . . Instead of wondering whether the recovery will last, people are asking what has caused this transformation.

In the immediate aftermath of the election optimism was rampant. City economists were revising their growth projections upwards, and both the OECD and the IMF were forecasting higher growth in the United Kingdom than in any other industrial country. Business surveys by the CBI and the DTI predicted continuing increases in output and investment.

Did I, in fact, mistake an unusually long cyclical upswing for a permanent supply-side improvement? When the two are occurring simultaneously it is never easy to apportion the contribution each has made, and

I probably exaggerated the extent of the latter. But I remain convinced that the massive supply-side changes that occurred have produced a fundamental long-term improvement in the performance of the British economy. It was, however, never my intention somehow to use 'growth' as a substitute for the proper control of monetary demand. I have already recorded how the extent of the upturn was vastly underestimated not only in the forecasts, but also in the statistics of the recent past which were afterwards revised heavily upwards.

There were some warning signs from business surveys, particularly the CBI survey of capacity utilization, and from house prices. The monetary data were, however, reasonably reassuring. £M3 was rising particularly rapidly, but that was now so distorted and had performed so misleadingly in the recent past that its predictive success in this one instance must be considered something of a freak. The growth rate of the best indicator of broad money, M4, was in double digits, but no greater than for many years past. The narrow measure of money, M0, which we did target – as an indicator and not as a cause of inflation – was well within its target range.

At a meeting of the 'Gooies' (see Chapter 31) on 24 July 1987 Samuel Brittan was almost the only one who raised the question of overheating. Patrick Minford and Alan Budd were among the more dismissive of this suggestion. An example of the false reassurance offered at the time was an article in the London Business School *Financial Outlook* of September 1987, purporting to demonstrate econometrically that 'any causal relationship between house prices and retail prices is spurious'.

The Bank of England's view was almost equally reassuring at that time. The author of a lengthy article in the Bank's May 1987 quarterly *Bulletin* was not worried about any inflationary threat, pointing out that rising personal indebtedness was more than offset by increased holdings of financial assets like bank and building society deposits, life policies, pensions and stocks and shares. 'To some extent,' as the Governor put it in the Mais Lecture which he delivered the same month, 'the personal sector's monetary behaviour . . . may reflect simply a redistribution of its portfolio of assets and liabilities without serious implications for future inflation.'

The Prospects at Chevening

The economic prospects were still far from clear when we met for the Budget planning meeting at Chevening in January 1988. The growth of credit and the consequent fall in the personal savings ratio were pointers, but they were not conclusive. The personal savings ratio was already well below its historic norm: it clearly could not go on falling for ever. At some point people would decide that they did not wish to get any further into debt. The difficult, if not impossible, question was to forecast when that would be. One Treasury economist's paper, circulated before the Budget, was entitled 'Are we about to experience a cyclical downturn in demand?' Life was relatively simple for the Treasury forecasters in the days when personal spending rose more or less in line with personal incomes. But the credit revolution, which allowed people, to an unprecedented and unknown extent, to bring their spending forward, ahead of their incomes, left the forecasters fumbling in the dark. There were of course other indicators of buoyancy, too – most notably the state of the housing market. Although that was in part simply another aspect of the same credit phenomenon, that was not all it was.

I mentioned in a previous chapter Gordon Pepper's warnings at a meeting of the 'Gooies' towards the end of 1987 of the imminence of a severe recession – indeed he excused himself for leaving early to give a talk on that very subject. The danger to the financial system which so alarmed him was not mythical. He simply got his timing wrong and was ahead of the game.

There is some similarity here with my own error in believing the Treasury forecasts which indicated a slowing down in the economy in 1987 and again in 1988. Clearly, although the forecasters did their best, they let me down badly. But I believed them not because I had any faith in Treasury forecasts as such, but because they reinforced my own instinct. That instinct was based on the fact that, while the banks and many others seem to have believed that the economic cycle had been abolished and that the upswing would go on for ever, I believed nothing of the sort. I was convinced that it would be followed by a downswing, and felt that the upturn had gone on for so long already that the downswing must be imminent. Moreover, I fully expected the payments deterioration and the early signs of a rise in inflation to put downward pressure on sterling which would need to be checked by higher interest rates. In all this I was not so much wrong as premature; for the downward pressures I feared were to emerge in 1989 in a big way.

Nor was this false reassurance confined to the Treasury. Robin Leigh-Pemberton, speaking on 29 January 1988, was doubtful whether credit expansion had been too fast. He told the annual luncheon of the News-paper Conference that day that the rise in borrowing:

> . . . has much to do with more intensive competition between financial intermediaries, particularly in the mortgage field, which has made it easier, for example, for home-owners to borrow against the accumu-lated equity in their houses. Not all of this increased borrowing has fed through immediately into higher consumer spending. Much of it has gone into a parallel increase in the personal sector's holdings of

financial assets, including deposits with banks and building societies
. . . We need to be wary of over-simple and over-hasty conclusions
. . . There could be a danger of overreaction if we simply took the
credit figures at their face value.

Indeed, as late as May 1988, the lead article in the Bank of England *Bulletin* had sub-headings saying 'Rapid growth of the economy continued to
the end of 1987 . . . But signs are gathering of a more sustainable pace.'

Forecasting: the Moral

There is, I suspect, a moral in all this – probably several – which may be
of interest and possibly even of some help to my successors. The first is
that the nature of a modern economy is such that, while there will always
be turning points, it is impossible to predict when those turning points will
occur. Thus when speaking in a timeless sense about the economy, one
should *always* forecast a turning point, while when speaking about the
year immediately ahead, one should *never* forecast a turning point – since
in any given year the odds are that it will not occur. The second is that the
absurd 1975 Industry Act requirement that the Treasury must maintain
a forecasting model and use it to make and publish forecasts should be
repealed, as I unsuccessfully sought to persuade Geoffrey Howe to do
when we first took office in 1979 (see Chapter 5).

The third is that, unless and until this is done, Treasury forecasts should
in practice be replaced by what is explicitly a conventional assumption
that the immediate future will be a repetition of the immediate past (as
has long been done, incidentally, in the case of the exchange rate implicit
in the forecast).* The fourth, following on from this, is that the effort
and skills of the economists and statisticians should be concentrated on
establishing what in fact *has* been happening in the recent past. Unlike
the future, the past is at least in principle knowable; yet the greatest
source of error in assessing the economic situation has in practice been
a misperception of the recent past. Fifth and finally, economic policy
decisions should be based as little as is humanly possible on short-term
forecasts, or even on conventional assumptions about the future: that is
one of the principal reasons for steering by the exchange rate instead.

I was aware of most of this at the time, but there were other reasons,
besides the mistaken advice I was receiving, that led me for a time to
be more relaxed about monetary conditions than I should have been. In

---

*By a repetition of the immediate past, I have in mind the same inflation rate as in the
previous year and the same (positive or negative) real growth rate. To repeat, this would
be a conventional *assumption*, and in no sense a true *forecast*; even though in practice it
might well be no further from the actual outcome than most self-styled forecasts.

the first place, when we met at Chevening, the growth of the targeted monetary aggregate, M0, was still comfortably around the middle of its target range of 2–6 per cent. This proved to be another illustration of Goodhart's Law – exacerbated, in this instance, by the fact, which did not emerge until some time later, that the Bank of England had got its seasonal adjustments wrong. Second, the exchange rate was strong, which is seldom a sign of lax monetary conditions.

Third – and this is frequently forgotten – the underlying rate of inflation (as measured by the RPI excluding mortgage interest payments) was below 4 per cent. Not only that, but it had been below 4 per cent consistently for the previous year and a half, with scarcely any sign of acceleration. To be precise, it had risen from a low point of 3.3 per cent in the second quarter of 1986 to 3.9 per cent in the fourth quarter of 1987 – and was to fall back to 3.7 per cent in the first quarter of 1988, when I presented my Budget.

This, then, was the mixed background to the January 1988 Chevening discussions. Before the Budget I had become concerned that monetary conditions were not tight enough for comfort, and on 2 February I took advantage of a modest weakening of sterling to raise interest rates by half a point. At that time the strengthening of the dollar and disputes in the motor industry kept sterling slightly subdued. But by mid-February overseas funds were once again being attracted by the relatively high level of UK interest rates, compared with German rates; by market perception of the UK's political stability and economic strength and, in the words of the Bank of England *Bulletin*, by 'the growing perception of the strength of the UK fiscal position'.

A Tight Budget

That strength was in no way dissipated by the 1988 Budget itself. Indeed, it is not sufficiently realized that it was a tight Budget in overall terms, and the occasion on which I re-established the target of a balanced Budget to be achieved in a normal year. How could a Budget that reduced taxation by £4 billion in the coming financial year and by £6¼ billion in a full year be regarded as prudent and tight? That this could be seen as an outrageous suggestion is a reflection of the nonsensical post-war habit of judging the fiscal stance, and thus the appropriateness of the Budget, entirely on the tax side, omitting all consideration of expenditure. Even on the tax side the outraged commentators ignored the effects of 'fiscal drag' in increasing the tax burden so that rates have to be cut simply to stand still.

Few critics of this supposedly irresponsible Budget have noticed that general Government expenditure, even *excluding* privatization proceeds, did not rise at all in real terms in 1987–88 and actually fell in 1988–89. As a percentage of GDP it fell between 1987–88 and 1988–89 by 2½ percentage points, having fallen as much in the previous financial year, too. (See Chapter 58).

The result of these favourable trends was that, instead of the small Budget deficit the Treasury had predicted for 1987–88, there was a Public Sector Debt *Repayment*, or Budget surplus, of £3.4 billion. For 1988–89 the Treasury projected another Budget surplus of £3.2 billion. In the end the surplus came to £14.7 billion, or £7.6 billion even without privatization proceeds. The more thoughtful commentators, well outside the Conservative ranks, realized that the 1988 Budget was very far from a reckless giveaway. Hamish Macrae, writing in the *Guardian* the following day, said: 'The final thing to get clear about this Budget is that it is not a tax-cutting Budget . . . In its big numbers it is quite a cautious Budget.'

As we now know, the Budget arithmetic was based on notoriously bad economic forecasts. By then the Treasury and CSO realized that they had greatly underestimated the expansionary forces at work in 1987 – when by the time of the final revision, GDP was seen to have risen by 4½ per cent. The forecasts, however, as is their wont, showed a return to a more sustainable growth rate – 3 per cent in 1988 and 2½ per cent in the year to the first half of 1989. In fact, growth stayed well above trend, at 4½ per cent, in 1988; and the *level* of demand remained above trend in 1989. As a result, a further 2 per cent of demand was deflected into the balance of payments – that is, into extra imports or goods diverted from exports to the home market – making well over 6 per cent overall growth in domestic demand in 1988.

Suppose I had had both a perfect forecast and a completely free hand from Margaret to manage the economy – two extreme counterfactuals – would my Budget judgement have been very different? I hate to disappoint the unreconstructed Keynesian reader, looking for a *mea culpa*. But (and it is *fiscal* policy that we are discussing here) the answer has to be 'no'. Innate caution led me to budget for a substantial surplus for 1988–89 rather than anything approaching balance. I find it difficult to imagine that even the most unreconstructed Keynesian Chancellor would have budgeted for a still higher surplus for 1988–89 than the unprecedented £14.7 billion or 3 per cent of GDP actually achieved – especially at a time when sterling was experiencing upward rather than downward pressure.

According to estimates published by the OECD – which puts every country's Budget on the same standardized basis – UK fiscal policy was strongly tightened in the calendar year 1988 even on a cyclically adjusted basis. According to other reputable estimates made by Goldman Sachs, the fiscal tightening was even greater, namely a reduction of the PSBR on a *cyclically adjusted basis* in each of the four financial years from 1985 to 1989 – amounting in total to over 4 per cent of GDP. As for the

Public Sector Financial Deficit, which excludes privatization proceeds, there was an even larger cumulative tightening on this basis.

I did not rely overmuch on such calculations, but generally aimed to keep public borrowing as low as practicable, and eventually zero, over the medium term, and not be deflected by shocks and windfalls in particular years (see Chapter 4).

With foreknowledge and a completely free hand, the main difference in my policy decisions would have been on the interest rate and exchange rate side. The difference on the budgetary side would essentially have been one of tone rather than substance – that is, a different speech rather than a different Budget. I would probably have dwelt much more on the sentence 'It will not be possible in this Budget to reduce taxation as a share of GDP'.* I would have dwelt on the inevitability and the nature of the economic cycle. And I might have engaged in a homily on savings, much as such exhortations go against the grain. The idea would have been to talk down exaggerated expectations of real income growth. In other words it would have been a less buoyant and very much more boring 'economic' speech.

INDICATORS OF FISCAL STANCE

Change in General Government financial balance as a percentage of GDP

	Actual	Cyclically Adjusted
1980	−0.1	+1.3
1981	+0.7	+2.2
1982	+0.2	+0.8
1983	−0.9	−1.2
1984	−0.6	−0.6
1985	+1.1	+0.7
1986	+0.5	−0.3
1987	+1.0	0.0
1988	+2.4	+1.7
1989	+0.1	0.0
1990	−2.0	−1.4
1991	−1.4	+0.2

+ = tightening   − = loosening   Source: OECD

---

*In the event, there was a slight and unintended ¾ per cent reduction in the tax taken as a proportion of GDP in 1988–89, due probably to the lag of tax receipts in the boom. But that hardly counts as a relaxation of fiscal policy, given the sharp swing to surplus in the overall balance. Throughout my whole period as Chancellor the tax burden, as defined in terms of the revenue from non-oil taxes as a proportion of non–oil GDP, never moved outside a range of more than half a percentage point either side of 38 per cent. I would, of course, have liked to see a steady decline, but this would have to be earned by continuing to keep public spending growing more slowly than the economy as a whole.

When all is said and done, I must stress what I made clear at the time. The Budget was in no way an attempt to give the economy a boost. Nor, in any strict economic sense, did it. Taxation and public spending have to be seen together, and the expenditure side in those days was under the most rigorous and effective control. As the OECD table above shows, in orthodox fiscal policy terms the 1988 Budget, even cyclically adjusted, was the tightest since 1981. To put things further into perspective, the scale of the growth in consumer credit in the ensuing year was ten times as great as the reduction in taxation. The purpose of the 1988 Budget was simply and solely to improve the supply-side performance of the economy through tax reduction and reform, which is what Budgets ought to be about. The long-term benefits of that will become apparent in the recovery from the recession of the early 1990s. But in the short term, it may have unintentionally contributed to a climate of excessive optimism and dangerously unrealistic expectations.

A Balanced Budget

I took advantage of the strong fiscal position in 1988 to reinstate the doctrine of a balanced Budget. As I said in the Budget speech:

> At one time it was regarded as a hallmark of good Government to maintain a balanced Budget; to ensure that in time of peace, Government spending was fully financed by revenues from taxation with no need for Government borrowing. Over the years this simple and beneficent rule was increasingly disregarded, culminating in the catastrophe of 1975–76, when the last Labour Government had a Budget deficit, or PSBR, equivalent in today's terms to some £40 billion*. This profligacy not only brought economic disaster and the national humiliation of a bail-out by the IMF; it also added massively to the burden of debt interest, not merely now but for a generation to come.

Before my time as Chancellor, a balanced Budget had been achieved on only one isolated occasion since the early 1950s. But now that it was achieved, it represented

> . . . a valuable discipline for the medium term. It represents security for the present and an investment for the future. Having achieved it, I intend to stick to it. In other words, henceforth a zero PSBR will be the norm. This provides a clear and simple rule, with a good historical pedigree.

*Equivalent to some £55 billion – £60 billion in 1992–93 terms.

BACKGROUND TO THE 1988 BUDGET

My prime difference from the Gladstonians was in being consciously medium term. I warned that 'In the very nature of things, there are bound to be fluctuations on either side from year to year'. It was no part of my doctrine to raise taxes in a recession, if the underlying balance was sound (as it was not in 1981), or in the face of a temporary deterioration due to, say, a war or a strike. Equally I had no intention of dissipating purely cyclical surpluses achieved in periods of boom.

The discredited neo-Keynesian idea of cutting the Budget deficit by raising tax rates to curb a boom, and increasing the deficit by lowering them to counter a recession, did not, in practice, stabilize the economy but merely destabilized tax rates. By the same token, I had no wish to inflict the supply-side damage caused by volatile tax rates in order to balance the Budget in fair weather and foul alike. But this in no way detracted from the importance of the doctrine of the balanced Budget as the norm – that is to say, over the cycle as a whole, or when the economy was growing at its normal trend rate.

While senior Treasury officials, over-impressed perhaps by the degree of arbitrariness inherent in the definition of the PSBR, would never have rehabilitated this doctrine if left to their own devices, they were happy to go along with my decision to espouse it. For they saw in it a useful weapon in the unending battle to control public spending – particularly as the alleged connection between public borrowing and the level of short-term interest rates became increasingly implausible. Moreover the fiscal side of the MTFS clearly had to have *some* terminus – an ever-increasing Budget surplus was manifestly absurd – just as the monetary side, in its heyday, had as its terminus the rate of monetary growth consistent with stable prices.

Of course, the new doctrine was a departure from my previous objective of a PSBR of 1 per cent of GDP, which I had described at the time as 'the modern equivalent of a balanced Budget'. But why bother with the complications of a 'modern equivalent' which could not in any case stand up to rigorous examination as a scientific doctrine, if balance was within reach? Leaving aside the problems of the transition, it is a delusion to suppose that economic activity will be any lower if the medium-term objective is a balanced Budget than if it is a 1 per cent deficit as I had previously suggested – or an ill-defined 3 per cent ceiling, as in the Maastricht Agreement of 1991.

Nor does the choice between such medium-term goals have any direct bearing on the control of inflation. Where it does make a difference is, first, in providing a readily comprehensible rule of thumb which is less likely to be fudged than any other more complicated rule which would mean nothing to the average voter; second, in reducing the burden of debt service and therefore the tax level in years to come; and third, if one day it could be the basis of a global agreement, in reducing the demands made by governments on the savings of the private sector.

One detail needs to be clarified. My objective of zero borrowing was for the PSBR as conventionally defined. But proceeds from privatization – and for that matter council house sales – were bound to dry up once all saleable assets had eventually been realized. So in the long term – say by the end of the century – the balanced Budget would have to be achieved without asset sales.

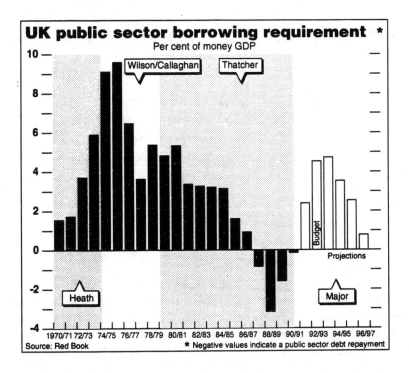

UK public sector borrowing requirement *

Per cent of money GDP

Wilson/Callaghan   Thatcher

Budget

Projections

Heath   Major

1970/71 72/73 74/75 76/77 78/79 80/81 82/83 84/85 86/87 88/89 90/91 92/93 94/95 96/97

Source: Red Book   * Negative values indicate a public sector debt repayment

---

CHAPTER 66

1988 – A PROVOCATIVE BUDGET

Reforming Personal Taxation · Cutting Tax Rates
Uproar in the House · Aligning Capital Gains
Restricting Mortgage Interest Relief · Ending Tax Breaks
A Triumph Marred · The Kink and the Elephant Trap

Reforming Personal Taxation

DURING MY TIME AS Chancellor, I developed two overriding ambitions, to which I devoted considerable time and thought. These were international monetary reform and tax reform. Having been largely frustrated in the first, I came to give priority to the second.

I had always intended the 1988 Budget, like that of 1984, to be a major tax-reforming Budget, this time focusing on personal rather than company taxation. Indeed, my desire to be reappointed Chancellor after the 1987 election was principally in order to introduce just such a Budget; just as my failure to have a real showdown with Margaret in early March 1988, over the issue of shadowing the Deutschmark and her subsequent disloyal remarks in the House, which in other circumstances might well have led to my resignation then, was caused by my determination to introduce the tax reforms.

I was clear, too, that a key element in the tax reforms should be a reduction in the higher rates of income tax. Controversial changes to the tax system are best implemented in the first Budget of a new Parliament, to allow time for the inevitable opposition to die down and for the benefits to become apparent – as in 1984 with Corporation Tax. I told the House in my Budget speech on 15 March, 1988, that I was guided by four basic principles: 'First, the need to reduce tax rates where they are clearly too high; second, the need to reduce or abolish unwarranted tax breaks; third, the need to make life a little simpler for the taxpayer; and, fourth, the need to remove some manifest injustices from the system.' The objectives had hardly changed since 1984.

Cutting Tax Rates

The centrepiece of the 1988 Budget was the establishment of a single higher rate income tax of 40 per cent, in place of the previous sliding scale going up to 60 per cent, coupled with the fulfilment of our manifesto pledge to reduce the basic rate of tax to 25 per cent.

The reduction and reform of personal tax rates had become more necessary than ever before in the light of the changes that were occurring elsewhere in the world. Most conspicuously, the United States had cut personal taxes and eliminated a series of tax breaks in 1986. But major reforms were also taking place in countries as diverse as Australia, New Zealand, Canada, Ireland, Japan, Sweden, France, the Netherlands, Germany and Denmark. There was increasing recognition throughout the industrialised world of the importance of tax reform and low marginal rates in raising economic performance through improved incentives and encouraging enterprise – and in maintaining revenue by containing avoidance and keeping talented individuals within the jurisdiction. In a world in which the international barriers to capital and labour mobility were steadily diminishing it would have been folly to ignore what was happening abroad. But my ambition was not merely to keep up with the Joneses: I wished to see the UK reap the advantages of being, if possible, ahead of the Joneses.

The income tax reductions of 1988 were not confined to the basic and higher rates. With some misgivings, but in order to improve the 'social' balance of the Budget, and thus its presentation, I increased the personal allowances by twice as much as the inflation rate, bringing the tax thresholds to a level 25 per cent higher in real terms than where Labour had left them in 1979; and, in the case of the still-existing married man's allowance, to its highest real level for nearly half a century.

Having at last achieved the 25 per cent basic rate which Geoffrey had first advocated in 1979, which I had revived as an objective in 1986, and which had become a Manifesto pledge in 1987, I persuaded a reluctant Margaret that I should announce in the Budget speech a new objective of reducing the basic rate to 20 per cent 'as soon as we prudently and sensibly can'.

Some people, even among those sympathetic to my general objective, regarded the new target as appallingly crude, and could think of many more reformist and radical changes to make if there were scope for reducing tax revenue. They overlooked the politics and the psychology. The basic rate is the flagship of the tax system. A public commitment to reduce it sends the right signals about the commitment of a Conservative Government to continue to reduce both taxation and the share – not the level – of public spending in GDP. Without this kind of commitment it is extremely difficult for a Chancellor and a Chief Secretary to hold the line against spending pressures.

Moreover, I was keenly conscious of the fact that the tax burden even by the middle of a third Conservative term was still virtually unchanged from when I first became Chancellor in 1983 (and still above what we had inherited from Labour in 1979, when the tax burden was artificially kept down – not that it felt like that at the time – by an unsustainably high level of public borrowing). The rate reductions I had been able to make had been almost entirely absorbed by so-called fiscal drag. If we were to show that we were in earnest about reducing taxation and to move the centre of debate away from how much to increase public spending, we had to keep the basic rate of income tax at the centre of the political debate.

Uproar in the House

By long-standing tradition, the Budget Statement is listened to without interruption (although sedentary mutterings are by no means unknown). But that tradition was flouted, in the most lamentable way, in 1988.

The first interruption occurred well before I reached the higher rates, when I had just announced the cut in the basic rate. The Scottish Nationalist member Alex Salmond began shouting: 'The Budget is an obscenity. The Chancellor cannot do this.' He would not stop when the Deputy Speaker (who always occupies the chair for the Budget speech) 'named' him. The motion was then put that Mr Salmond be suspended 'from the service of the House' for five days. This was then voted on, with the Labour front bench voting with the Government in support of the Deputy Speaker's decision. A handful of the Labour left joined the Scottish and Welsh Nationalists in the No lobby. But the voting figures – 354 to 19 – for the suspension show that most Labour Members abstained. I could not help wondering what kind of democracy the Nationalists would establish in Scotland if ever they had the opportunity.

All this however, was no more than a curtain-raiser compared to what occurred when I came to the higher rates. Here are the supposedly provocative, not to say obscene, words:

> It is now nine years since my predecessor, in his first Budget in 1979, reduced the top rate of income tax from the absurd 83 per cent that prevailed under Labour to 60 per cent, where it has remained ever since. At that time this was broadly in line with the European average

for the top rate of tax. It is now one of the highest. And not only do the majority of European countries now have a top rate of tax below 60 per cent, but in the English-speaking countries outside Europe – not only the United States and Canada but in Labour Australia and New Zealand too – the top rate is now below 50 per cent, and sometimes well below. The reason for the worldwide trends towards lower rates of tax is clear. Excessive rates of income tax destroy enterprise, encourage avoidance, and drive talent to more hospitable shores overseas. As a result, so far from raising additional revenue, over time they actually raise less.

By contrast, reduction in the top rates of income tax can over time result in a higher, not a lower, yield to the Exchequer. Despite the substantial reduction in the top rate of tax in 1979, and the subsequent abolition of the Investment Income Surcharge in 1984, the top 5 per cent of taxpayers today contribute as much again in real terms as they did in 1978–79, Labour's last year; while the remaining 95 per cent of taxpayers pay about the same in real terms as they did in 1978–79.

After nine years at 60 per cent I believe that the time has come to make a further reduction in the top rate of income tax. At present there are no fewer than five higher rates of income tax: 40 per cent, 45 per cent, 50 per cent, 55 per cent and 60 per cent. I propose to abolish all the higher rates of tax above 40 per cent . . .

This major reform will leave us with one of the simplest systems of income tax in the world, consisting of a basic rate of 25 per cent and a single higher rate of 40 per cent, and indeed a system of personal taxation in which there is no rate anywhere in excess of 40 per cent.

Although I had to resort to it in my Budget speech for reasons of brevity, comparing top rates of tax is a manifestly inadequate way of comparing different tax systems. Just as important is where the rates tend to bite. Japan had a top rate of 93 per cent in 1979 which was reduced in the 1980s to 65 per cent. But this top rate came in at such a high level of income that it was much less penal on the top executive earners and professionals than the apparently lower British rates. It is possible that, had I kept a top rate of 60 per cent, but reserved it for incomes in excess of £1 million a year, the reaction would have been less extreme. But this would have made it very difficult indeed to align the income tax and capital gains tax rates – an important reform in its own right.

The ellipses before the last paragraph of the quotation from the Budget speech cover some of the most amazing scenes ever to have taken place on Budget Day. Dave Nellist, the Labour MP who was subsequently expelled from his party because of his close involvement with Militant Tendency (a group of far Left anti-Parliamentary extremists within the Labour Party), not to be outdone by the Scottish Nationalists, started shouting and interrupting. Other Labour Members, to their great discredit, joined in. In the words of *Hansard*, 'grave disorder having arisen in the House, Mr Deputy Speaker suspended the sitting for ten minutes.' If all income belongs to the State, then my reliefs were indeed outrageous handouts to the rich. But if it does not, then the Labour explosion was nothing but a particularly loutish display of the politics of envy.

The tax reductions in the 1988 Budget were a vital part of the Government's sweeping reform of the supply side of the economy, to which privatization, trade union reform and employee share ownership were also central. The actuality and expectation of cuts in tax rates were part of an important cultural change, which fuelled business confidence and economic growth in the 1980s, and benefited the population as a whole. Few doctrines are more insidious than the view that poverty is relative. None of this means that we can ignore the hardships of the homeless or the increase in the number of beggars on our streets. But the prosperity of the many, which is to be welcomed, is not the cause of the poverty of the few.

Aligning Capital Gains

Reducing top rates of tax to 40 per cent enabled me to introduce a further radical tax reform. This was the alignment of capital gains and income tax rates. Instead of the special 30 per cent tax on capital gains which had existed since the tax was first introduced in 1965, I legislated to tax capital gains, after deduction of the exempt amount and the exclusion of purely inflationary or paper gains via the indexation provision, as if they were income – that is, at either 25 per cent or 40 per cent as the case may be. Not surprisingly, this change was, and remains, very unpopular with many Conservative back-benchers, who saw it as an increase in the Capital Gains Rate from 30 per cent to 40 per cent – although they were in no position to complain too loudly in a year in which the higher rates had been significantly reduced.

But the case for the reform was overwhelming. Before 1988 anyone paying tax at the higher rate paid less – often much less – on capital gains than on income. A whole tax avoidance industry had therefore grown up whose sole purpose was to dress up income as capital gains. I had been reinforced in my desire to bring this unproductive activity to an end by the US Tax Réform Act of 1986, which had similarly provided for capital gains to be taxed as income. (A so far unsuccessful campaign to reverse this has been raging ever since.) There is little genuine economic difference between income and most capital gains, and no obvious reason why one should be taxed more heavily than the other. With the reduction in the basic rate below 30 per cent, we had reached the bizarre position in which some people were being taxed more heavily on capital gains than on income, while others were being taxed more heavily on income than on capital gains. Moreover, contrary to popular supposition, the new UK capital gains tax regime was less onerous, even at low levels of inflation, than its American equivalent, in which there was neither indexation nor a separate capital gains tax threshold.

At the same time, I converted the capital gains tax system from a partially indexed to a fully indexed regime. The indexation provisions introduced by Geoffrey Howe in 1982, which I had extended in 1985, applied only to future, i.e. post-1982 gains. Gains made between the introduction of the tax in 1965 and 1982, many of them purely paper gains reflecting the high inflation of the 1970s, remained untouched by the indexation relief. I removed this injustice in the only way practicable: by exempting pre-1982 gains from tax altogether. This would bring the added economic advantage of unlocking those assets, particularly land, where the unindexed capital gains tax liability had been so great that the owners would never dispose of them during their lifetime – knowing, of course, that on death the liability would disappear altogether.

Yet a further 1988 reform was to the Inheritance Tax I had introduced in 1986 to replace Labour's Capital Transfer Tax. In place of the ascending scale of rates inherited from the Capital Transfer Tax (and before that the Estate Duty) I introduced a single flat rate of 40 per cent, after raising substantially the (indexed) threshold for the tax. This reduced the number of estates liable to tax by a quarter, allowing many more people to inherit the family home free of tax. It was only the impending and misguided abolition of local authority rates, to be replaced by the disastrous Poll Tax, that made me unwilling to go even further in this direction. As it was, the change not only helped to realize the ideal I had set out at the 1987 Party Conference, of making Britain a nation of inheritors; coupled with the income tax changes, it also meant that no personal tax anywhere in the system would be levied at a rate higher than 40 per cent. In other words, every taxpayer in Britain would remain the majority shareholder in his or her own income and capital.

Restricting Mortgage Interest Relief

There were many other clear-cut reforms, some discussed in earlier pages. In particular, I restricted mortgage interest relief to £30,000 per property, instead of (as previously) £30,000 per borrower, thus ending the practice by which a group of 'sharers' could secure very substantial relief on the purchasing of a large property – and also the unfairness and perversity of enabling an unmarried couple to draw a £60,000 double ration of relief, whereas the married couple were confined to a single ration. The complete removal of interest relief on home improvement loans stopped the most notorious abuse of mortgage interest relief to finance consumer spending.

Unfortunately, the effect of the first of these two restrictions – the ending of multiple mortgage interest relief – was perverse in the short term, and added further fuel to an already booming house market. The Inland Revenue, whose advice was normally of a very high quality, insisted that the restriction should not come into force until 1 August: more than four months after the Budget announcement. They maintained that the lending institutions, whose responsibility it was to collect the mortgage interest due to them net of tax (under the so-called MIRAS – Mortgage Interest Relief At Source – system) could not reprogramme their computers any sooner than this.

After the meeting at which this was provisionally agreed, Terry Burns mentioned to me that he was worried that it would lead to a wave of additional borrowing to take advantage of the relief while it lasted. I told him that I shared his concern – so much so that I would hold a further meeting with the Revenue and press them on this specific point. This I did; but they remained adamant, arguing that any earlier date would lead to a shambles, and the Government would be left with a large amount of egg on its face. As I am no computer expert myself, I felt obliged to accept this advice.

The result fulfilled my worst fears. Foolishly, considerable numbers of people pushed house prices up still higher in their rush to secure the extra income tax relief, despite the fact that this could not possibly recompense them for the excessive price they were having to pay for the house in the first place – and thus the excessive sum they were having to borrow. What this, in practice, did was to add froth to an already heady housing boom, which made the subsequent inevitable downturn all the more painful. It was inevitable both in the sense that excess always ends in tears – every binge is followed by a hangover – and because multiple mortgage interest relief, did, of course, come to an end of 1 August.

I have no regrets over the end of multiple mortgage interest relief. It was clearly the right thing to do: what was wrong was the long delay between announcement and implementation. It was scant consolation that the Revenue subsequently concluded that perhaps their firm advice had been wrong, and that the institutions possibly could have reprogrammed their computers more quickly had they been requested to do so.

It would have been better, of course, if multiple mortgage interest relief had been ended much earlier, as I had wished. It had first emerged as a proposal in my March 1986 Green Paper, *The Reform of Personal Taxation*, in the context of independent taxation (since the logic of this was either that husband and wife would each have to be given their own £30,000 ration of relief, as already occurred with unmarried couples, or the whole basis of the ration would have to be changed from the individual to the property, which was indisputably preferable). But it was clearly a free-standing proposal, desirable on its own merits, which could be introduced well in advance of the rest of the package.

Although I had sought to do this in both the 1986 and 1987 Budgets, on each occasion I ran up against the brick wall of Margaret's passionate devotion to the maximum amount of mortgage interest relief the Exchequer could afford. Indeed, it was only because the 1988 Budget was such an exciting one overall that Margaret reluctantly agreed to my going ahead with the announcement of independent taxation,* and it was only the logic of independent taxation that persuaded her that this restriction on mortgage interest relief was unavoidable.

Ending Tax Breaks

There were other measures, too, which the overall scale of the tax cuts made possible, and which otherwise Margaret would have resisted. I felt strongly that the sharp reduction in tax rates on cash incomes should be accompanied by an increase in the tax on benefits in kind, or 'perks'. I had a great deal of work done on a general fringe benefit tax; but both the political and practical problems proved far more daunting than I had hoped, and the likely yield at the end of the day was limited. So I decided to cut the Gordian knot, and concentrate on company cars, which had a value far in excess of all other perks put together, and which were still, despite the increases I had introduced in each of my four previous Budgets, manifestly undertaxed. I decided to double, with immediate effect, the tax on the benefit conferred by the possession of a company car, as measured by the so-called scale charges. This brought in a healthy £300 million.

I also ended all tax relief on covenants, apart from charitable covenants, which (once the inevitably complex transitional arrangements had been worked through) greatly simplified the system as well as ending an indefensible tax avoidance device. I similarly simplified the tax treatment of maintenance payments. Both these changes, but especially the latter, raised complicated legal questions. I decided to take James Mackay, the Lord Chancellor, into my confidence. He was characteristically helpful and constructive.

One of the most blatant tax shelters I closed concerned forestry. The previous system, (as I explained in the Budget speech) enabled 'top rate taxpayers in particular to shelter other income from tax, by

---

*This major reform is dealt with fully in Chapter 70.

setting it against expenditure on forestry, while the proceeds for any eventual sale are effectively tax free'. Forestry, of course, genuinely is different, given the long time that elapses between the initial planting and the production of saleable timber. Moreover, the Government, for a mixture of political, agricultural and environmental reasons, had foolishly made a public commitment to a specific level of tree planting. Nevertheless the existing system gave top rate taxpayers such a ludicrously generous tax break that the overall yield from the taxation of forestry was negative – the Inland Revenue was giving more in tax relief than it raised in tax revenue.

I decided that the most elegant solution was to remove forestry from taxation altogether – a measure that could scarcely be portrayed as unduly harsh – and, given the Government's pledge, to use the money thus saved on improved planting grants, which at least could be given with environmental considerations uppermost. Thus not only was a long-standing tax break eliminated, and the system greatly simplified, but rural Scotland (in particular) was saved from having its environment further ruined by the eyesore of plantations of Sitka spruce, that unattractive but previously tax-efficient conifer. Indeed, my action on forestry, coupled with a further twist in the taxation of petrol in favour of unleaded petrol (I had originally introduced this uncharacteristic departure from neutrality in my 1987 Budget), was the main reason why Jonathan Porritt, at that time Director of the high-profile environmental pressure group, Friends of the Earth, was moved to declare that my 1988 Budget had done more for the environment than any action by any other Minister – a most unexpected bouquet.

The Inland Revenue had wanted me to go for perks in a much more detailed way. Shortly before the 1987 pre-election Budget they came to me with a long list of allegedly taxable benefits, ranging from corporate Christmas presents (diaries, calendars and the like) to the provision of car parking spaces for employees on the company's premises. They warned me that unless I legislated explicitly to exclude these from tax, they would have to pursue each and every one of the beneficiaries for tax. I told them to go away and come back to me after the election, which they did. The 1988 Budget accordingly took some benefits (such as car parking) out of tax altogether, and simplified the tax on others above a *de minimis* level. It was a very tedious business. The Revenue was always a rich source of odd and usually counter-productive revenue proposals which would have required large numbers of extra staff to monitor for little revenue and at the cost of considerable annoyance to the taxpayer.

I even found yet another tax to abolish. This was Capital Duty, of which most people had never even heard. It had to be paid at a rate of 1 per cent when companies raised new capital or sold shares to the public. It was an understandable irritant and a further deterrent to equity finance as distinct from debt finance. At a cost of £100 million a year it was well worth abolishing.

A Triumph Marred

The 1988 Budget completed what I then thought was more or less the maximum politically feasible transformation of the British tax system, certainly so long as Margaret was Prime Minister. The Cabinet, when it first heard of it the morning of Budget Day, was enthusiastic. I ended my Budget speech with the following perotation:

> I have announced a radical reform of the taxation of marriage, which for the first time ever will give married women a fair deal from the tax system. I have eliminated the long-standing injustice of taxing inflationary gains, and abolished a fifth tax. I have radically reformed the structure of personal taxation, so that there is no rate anywhere in the system in excess of 40 per cent.
>
> After an Autumn Statement which substantially increased public spending in priority areas, I have once again cut the basic rate of income tax, fulfilling our manifesto pledge of a basic rate of 25 pence in the pound and setting a new target of 20 pence in the pound,
>
> And I have balanced the Budget.

I sat down to tremendous cheers and waving of Order Papers. Conservative back-benchers were genuinely ecstatic, and they were determined to outdo the earlier hostile disturbances I had endured. I received an equally warm reception at the back-bench Finance Committee.

But it is a general rule that when something really angers the Labour Party there will be timid Conservative members who think the Government has gone too far. And this rule was reinforced by my anxiety about how the Budget changes would square with the implementation of the Fowler social security reforms due to come into force in the following month, which although expenditure-neutral, introduced a marked tightening-up of entitlement to some benefits.

Inevitably, the press reception tended to divide along standard Left-Right lines, which had not on the whole been a feature of my earlier Budgets. The *Guardian*'s political commentator, Hugo Young, wrote that it marked 'the final disappearance of the last vestiges of the post-war consensus . . . Fairness and social justice, as registered through the tax system, have ceased even to be the pretended aspiration of the Conservative Party'. My favourite headline from the popular press was 'Nigel The Tax Terminator' in *Today,* which borrowed from the cover of *Punch* the week before the Budget a portrait depicting me as the sword-wielding Conan the Barbarian, poised to cut taxes. A few months later the editor of *Punch* kindly invited me to lunch, where I was presented with the framed original.

Given that a Budget as controversial as this was hardly likely to be welcomed by those of a contrary political philosophy, my 1988 Budget must be accounted a signal success, in terms both of the reception it secured and, more importantly, of the amount of radical reform it embodied. But for me personally the triumph was marred by the continuing row with Margaret over the exchange rate.

The Kink and the Elephant Trap

The far-reaching reforms in the 1988 Budget went considerably further than anything Margaret had in mind: her own ambitions were essentially confined to implementing our manifesto pledge on the basic rate and reducing the top rate of income tax to 50 per cent. With one important exception they were, however, broadly along the lines I had explicitly laid down well before the 1987 general election and on which the Treasury and Inland Revenue had been working ever since. Seldom can any Budget have had such lengthy and thorough preparation.

That exception was the abolition of the Employee's Upper Earnings Limit (UEL) for National Insurance Contributions. In my 1985 Budget I had abolished the UEL for employers; and in my original plans for the 1988 Budget I envisaged as the key to the reform package the abolition of the employees' UEL, too. This had considerable support among those outside government interested in tax reform, largely because of the anomalous pattern of the combined marginal rate of income tax and national insurance - that is, the percentage of an extra pound earned taken by both imposts – under the current system.

The position before the 1988 Budget, for example, was that an employee on average earnings paid a combined marginal rate of 36 per cent, composed of income tax at 27 per cent (the then basic rate) and a further 9 per cent in employee's National Insurance Contribution. Once his or her earnings reached the UEL, then just under £300 a week, the marginal rate dropped to 27 per cent. It continued at 27 per cent until his or her taxable income reached around £400 a week, when the taxpayer entered the first higher rate band of income tax, and the marginal rate rose again to 40 per cent. The chart immediately below shows the analogous picture both for 1978–79, Labour's last year, and for 1989–90, my final year as Chancellor. The curious dip between the UEL and the upper limit of the basic rate band became known as the 'kink'.

THE TAX TRAPS

Effective marginal tax rates* (married man, two children)
Including effects of benefit withdrawal

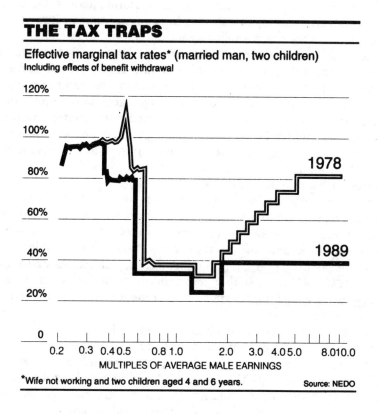

Wife not working and two children aged 4 and 6 years.   Source: NEDO

Unlike the obsessively tidy-minded would-be tax reformers, the existence of the kink did not greatly affront me. It was certainly anomalous, but it was difficult to believe that it was doing any economic harm, since disincentive effects are created by the level of the marginal rate rather than by changes in that level. As for the progressive or regressive nature of a tax system, that is measured not by the marginal rate but by the average rate of tax and National Insurance Contributions – that is, the proportion of the individual's total income paid in income tax and NICs. And despite the kink in the marginal rate, the average rate steadily rose in line with income. Moreover, the seemingly obvious way of eliminating the kink, making the UEL the same as the upper limit of the basic rate band, was not available.

This is because the two imposts have quite different bases. The base on which income tax is levied is total income, including investment income and pensions, after deduction of all allowances and reliefs. The basis on which NICs are levied is earned income only, but without deduction of any allowances or reliefs. (There are other differences, too, but these

825

are the main ones.) Thus, since different individuals have different mixes of earned income, investment income, pensions, allowances and reliefs, there is no universally applicable point at which the UEL coincides with the basic rate limit. Indeed, that is one of the main reasons for the existence of the kink in the first place: if there were not enough clear water between the UEL and the basic rate limit for the average taxpayer, those with above-average investment income or pension, and/or with below average allowances and reliefs, would find themselves paying, for a time, a marginal rate of 49 per cent (40 per cent higher rate income tax plus 9 per cent NICs). And the adverse incentive effects of an anomalously high marginal rate are obviously worse than the effects of an anomalously low one.

So the only practical way of eliminating the kink is to abolish the UEL altogether; and at first sight this seemed to me to be well worth doing for reasons going far beyond mere tidy-mindedness. For one thing, it would enable me to reduce the higher rates of income tax by a correspondingly greater amount. Thus, for example, the single higher rate of 40 per cent that I eventually went for could have been replaced by a single higher rate of income tax of 31 per cent, plus 9 per cent employee's NICs.

A further gain I saw from abolishing the UEL, and offsetting it by a compensating reduction in the higher rate of income tax, was that, since tax reliefs do not apply to NICs, there would be a reduction in the distortions caused by those reliefs. In other words, both aspects of the direction in which I was seeking to move – that is, towards a system of lower rates and lesser reliefs – would see real progress.

I accordingly asked my officials, in both the Treasury and the Revenue, to work up a scheme. There was, of course, no question of my being able to move to a simple flat-rate proportionate income tax system in the immediate future. By 1988 we were already, regrettably, in the shadow of the impending introduction of the hideously unpopular and regressive Poll Tax. This made it politically imperative to retain a higher rate of income tax.

The more work that was done on the abolition of the UEL, however, the more the disadvantages seemed to outweigh the advantages. One stemmed from the fact that the National Insurance system is a contributory system. It is fashionable to mock this; but I suspect that the mockery is itself based on a confusion between the insurance principle, which clearly does not apply to the misleadingly named system, and the contributory principle, which manifestly does. That is to say, the benefits paid depend on the beneficiary's contribution record.

In particular, this applies to the State Earnings-Related Pension (SERP); with the result that the abolition of the UEL would mean higher SERPs for those on higher earnings, without any limit – an extension of state provision for the better off that would have been palpably absurd, quite apart from the increased public expenditure involved, and wholly contrary to the Government's pension policy so recently reinforced by the Fowler reforms.

To avoid this, my officials recommended the retention of a 'shadow' UEL in place of the old UEL, with contributions above it not conferring any additional benefit entitlement. This somewhat bizarre arrangement, moreover, would have solved one problem only to create another. For 'contributions' above the shadow UEL would become a straightforward tax, risking undermining the contributory principle and leading to increased pressure to assimilate employees' NICs into income tax altogether.

This would have been undesirable on a number of grounds. It would have had the unfortunate appearance of an increase in income tax. It would have weakened in the public mind the truth that social security benefits have to be paid for. Moreover, assimilating employees' NICs into income tax would mean that all reliefs and allowances would have to be extended to NICs, further distorting the system; while at the same time NICs would have to be levied, like income tax, on (*inter alia*) pensions. So far as the state pension was concerned, there could be rough-and-ready compensation, at the cost (once again) of increased public spending, via a higher state pension; but nothing could be done to help the hard-hit occupational pensioner.

All these difficulties paled into insignificance, however, compared with the plight of the people in the kink, and in particular those in the upper half of the kink (that is, with incomes close to the top of the basic rate band). Over 1¼ million taxpayers, the Revenue calculated, would face a sharp increase in their marginal rate, and several hundreds of thousands of these would suffer an unconscionably large increase in their total tax bills. And whereas I had always envisaged compensating those on the higher rates of income tax with a reduction in those rates, there was no possibility of being able to afford to reduce the basic rate sufficiently to compensate the heavy losers at the top of the basic rate band. Nor could it possibly be justifiable (particularly in the context of a tax-cutting Budget) to inflict such heavy losses, and on people who were not particularly well off: the UEL was at less than one and a half times average earnings. My officials looked at every conceivable way round the problem, but none of them really worked.

In short, abolition of the UEL, so logical and desirable at first sight, turned out on examination to be an elephant trap. Despite all the man hours of high-quality work that had been done on it, I had decided even before we met at Chevening in January 1988 to walk round it, and leave the UEL undisturbed – although I allowed a brief discussion at Chevening before formally closing the books on it. This led to an uncovenanted political bonus. Before the Parliament was out, the Labour Party had walked straight back into the elephant trap themselves – a fact that was widely believed to have been one of the reasons for their defeat at the 1992 General Election.

CHAPTER 67

THE BATTLES OF DOWNING STREET

After the Hat Trick · Hammering out the Concordat
'You'll Pay for This' · The Four-to-One Rule
Ghosts from the Past

After the Hat Trick

TO THE POLITICAL ACTIVIST on either side, the aftermath of the 1988 Budget must have seemed extraordinary. The Government had achieved the hat trick – higher spending on public services, lower tax rates and a Budget surplus. Moreover, contrary to what unhistorical commentators assumed, such a hat trick was not normal in the boom phase of the economic cycle. The missing element in the past had been a Budget surplus, which had last been achieved by Roy Jenkins in 1969–70 with the aid of a good deal of pressure from the IMF following devaluation. Normal UK experience since the mid-1950s was for public expenditure to rise faster than GDP, with control being effected only by periodic sterling crises such as those accompanying the 1967 devaluation or the 1976 borrowing from the IMF. The unusual element in the 1980s was the maintenance of very firm public expenditure control in the absence of any crisis imperative. This, rather than the boom alone, was what made the hat trick possible.

Yet although the Budget itself was met with widespread acclaim, the passage in the Budget speech dealing with the exchange rate was obviously a compromise, which left a number of options open. The multiplying tribe of City analysts – and even bankers and holders of sterling – were demanding a resolution. In the circumstances, nothing short of ERM membership would have been accepted as a resolution, and that looked further away than ever.

Sterling soared after the Budget and looked like breaking above DM 3.09. Contrary to City gossip that Margaret had forbidden all intervention, there was a sizeable amount of intervention on Budget Day. Nevertheless the City view was substantially correct. In accordance with my undertaking to Margaret on 4 March, there was to be no further large-scale intervention (not that 'large scale' was ever defined) and any further actions to restrain the pound had to be through interest rates. She had got what she wanted – an end to intervention on any significant scale, and a bias towards unduly low interest rates. But as a glance at the interest rate chart on page 839 shows, her victory was to prove Pyrrhic.

At the markets meeting I called immediately following the Budget there was universal agreement that the Government could not be seen to be indifferent to the exchange rate. As I had accepted Margaret's veto on any further shadowing of the Deutschmark, there was no point in pretending that there was another hard ceiling at, say, DM 3.10. But we did have to demonstrate that sterling was not a one-way bet. The pressure was so strong early the following day, Thursday 17 March, that I authorized a half point cut to 8½ per cent. It did not help relations in Downing Street that the media reported the decision as a defeat for the Prime Minister – which was far from the case, as she never objected to lower interest rates.

Hammering out the Concordat

Until the row in March 1988 my personal relations with Margaret had remained generally harmonious; but once she had disowned me in public things could never be the same. All the pundits said that open warfare between the Prime Minister and Chancellor could not be allowed to continue – which meant that they assumed that it would. But an agreed policy clearly had to be hammered out. To this end, Margaret called a meeting in Number 10 for 25 March, ten days after the Budget.

Meanwhile the stakes were getting higher. David Young, the Trade and Industry Secretary, made some remarks about the ERM in which he came down rather ineptly on Margaret's side, while the day before the meeting at Number 10 Geoffrey Howe gave me unsolicited support in a speech he made in Zurich, in which he said 'exchange rates have necessarily come to play a more significant role in both domestic monetary decisions and international policy operations'. The same day I received from Peter Brooke, by then Chairman of the Party, and still a Treasury Minister, a letter offering help, encouragement and the assurance of support, but also expressing his concern at the impact of the dispute on the Government. 'I am very conscious', he wrote, 'of how trying it must be at the moment;

and that your friends feel for you is, I admit, as much because of your centrality to this Administration and its success as it is because of their profound liking, respect and admiration for you personally.'

It was an extraordinary situation: a private policy meeting between the Prime Minister, the Chancellor, the Governor, and various advisers was treated in the media as if it were a truce meeting between warring generals with trumpets blazing off-stage. As the basis for the discussion, I asked Terry Burns to produce a paper analysing the role of the exchange rate and setting out the options for the future conduct of policy. He made a good job of it. It was, of course, written in full consultation with me, and thus expressed my views as well as his own. But within that context it bent over backwards to try and accommodate Margaret's.

The paper began by explaining how an appreciating exchange rate tightened monetary conditions – for example, by putting pressure on the profit margins of companies that made internationally traded products, whether for the home market or for export. It argued that it also had significant 'secondary effects' in restraining wage negotiations in this sector and reducing inflationary expectations more generally. A depreciating exchange rate had the opposite effects. The paper contained a chart showing clearly the strong connection, over a long period, between exchange rate and interest rate moves. It also cited the increasing role of the exchange rate as an anti-inflationary anchor for many other countries – such as Switzerland, of which Margaret was a great admirer, where the Swiss franc was at that time closely linked to the Deutschmark. It also rebutted the notion that the Louvre Accord had caused the Wall Street crash, citing Paul Volcker in support.

The paper then went on to discuss the problem of speculative capital movements that had caused periodic exchange rate misalignments. The actions of the authorities in such circumstances were important, since they formed part of market expectations. The paper accepted that on rare occasions a conflict could arise between the needs of internal monetary stability and those of exchange rate stability: indeed, one such occasion provided the background to the meeting. In such cases domestic stability should come first. But the paper argued that the resulting exchange rate change should be presented as a realignment and not as abandoning the long-term policy of currency stability.

The paper then listed the three broad options for the future conduct of policy. These were:

1. To take sterling into account in formulating monetary policy, as we had during most of the 1980s.
2. To announce an explicit commitment to exchange rate stability, but within an unpublished band.
3. To join the ERM.

It deliberately did not include the theoretical but, in my judgement, wholly unrealistic option of untrammelled free floating. The last of the three options listed was the easiest to explain and, once credibility had been established, would be a powerful bulwark against inflation. If this at any time produced insufficiently tight domestic monetary conditions, the solution would be an upward realignment rather than abandoning the whole policy.

It is worth noting that this presentation of the ERM was very much geared to the conditions and mood at the time. Thus it did not consider the possibility of a situation in which ERM membership produced excessively tight domestic monetary conditions. Nor did it canvass the so-called 'hard' ERM, in which realignments are eschewed in all but the most extreme and unlikely circumstances, relying on the fact that, if sterling were to be tied more or less irrevocably to the currency of a low-inflation country such as Germany, any period in which domestic monetary conditions in the UK were looser than they ought to be must of necessity be short-lived. But there was no point in exploring the ERM case in depth since there was no chance at that time of persuading Margaret to accept it. The immediate purpose of including the third option was to try and persuade her to reinstate the second option, an informal target range supported by both interest rates and intervention.

After considerable discussion, Margaret and I accepted what the press began to call a concordat. She conceded the desirability of a measure of exchange rate stability, subject to the overriding importance of sound policies to control inflation. She also conceded a role for intervention, but insisted that it be a much smaller one than before, and said that we should avoid commitments to specific levels of sterling. Her main point was that, however desirable exchange rate stability might be, it should never be an *objective* of policy, or presented as such. This, however, begged the question, which concerned the role of the exchange rate in securing and maintaining the agreed objective of near-zero inflation.

Although clearly better than conflict, a concordat between the Prime Minister and her Chancellor was a pretty rum notion. Rather more seriously, it had been reached by a process of compromise and fudge, which meant that even if it was just about workable as a basis for policy decisions, it was incapable of explicit articulation in the way the markets sought.

When sterling rose above DM 3.12 on 8 April the Bank and I agreed that, in the circumstances, there should be a further half-point cut in base rates to 8 per cent. Needless to say Margaret was happy to go along with this. But although I had not yet appreciated the full extent of the boom, it was a cut that ideally I would not have made. I would have preferred a higher interest rate to damp down domestic demand offset by a lower exchange rate to reinforce business expectations of exchange rate stability. But my ability to achieve this combination was fatally undermined by the foreign exchange market's conviction that Margaret favoured leaving sterling to its own devices.

When I went to Washington for the spring meeting of the IMF Interim Committee in early April the international outlook was little better. There had been intervention to support the dollar, but with the Presidential elections looming the Americans were unwilling to support it with higher interest rates. I made a further plea for exchange rate stability, but without going into the sort of detail that I had the previous September. I flew home to find the concordat already starting to fall apart.

'You'll Pay for This'

On the financial front, sterling was continuing to rise, as the markets now believed there would be no appreciable intervention to restrain it. Politically, too, the situation was getting out of hand. The rift between Number 10 and Number 11 was getting headline and feature treatment by journalists who would normally have walked the other way if anyone had so much as mentioned interest differentials or the policy mix. When I was pressed on the matter on the BBC television programme *This Week Next Week* on Sunday, 24 April, I repeated that I did not want to see the exchange rate appreciate further: 'It would be an unsustainable appreciation. That does nobody any good and is damaging for business and industry.'

I also observed somewhat pointedly that it was 'unfortunate' and 'not sensible' that the question of the exchange rate 'was discussed as much as it was in public, because these are very sensitive matters.' I added, however, that this problem was now 'behind us' and that both the Prime Minister and I were interested in securing 'the maximum possible exchange rate stability within the context of a sound anti-inflation policy.'

I had weighed my words carefully; but perhaps it was inevitable that when, the following evening, in the division lobby of the House of Commons, Margaret beckoned me over for a brief and perfectly amicable discussion of the row that had erupted over the social security reforms which had been implemented a fortnight earlier, some troublemaker told the press that she had been seen angrily wagging her finger at me. The myth duly appeared in most of the newspapers.

But the real mischief did not occur until Prime Minister's Questions in the House of Commons on Thursday, 12 May when at last Neil Kinnock seized the opportunity that had been staring him in the face for so long. The Labour leader asked Margaret whether she was content to see the pound going on rising against the Deutschmark. She gave an evasive reply, complimenting me on the way in which I had been running the economy. Kinnock then quoted at her my observation that I did not want to see the pound rise further, and believed that any such rise would be unsustainable. 'Does the right hon. lady agree with the point the Chancellor made?' he asked. Once again Margaret was evasive, replying that 'The Chancellor runs the economy extremely well.' Kinnock then rose a third time, asking with uncharacteristic brevity 'That is all very interesting. Can the right hon. lady give us a straight answer? Does the Prime Minister agree with her Chancellor of the Exchequer?' Yet again, Margaret conspicuously refused to say 'Yes', and gave a complete non-answer about the Government having achieved low inflation, excellent growth, high living standards and a high standard of social services.

It was an astonishing and immensely damaging performance. All she had to do was to reply 'The Chancellor and I are in full agreement about everything', which the conventions of Cabinet Government and collective responsibility required, and she would have defused the situation without in any way compromising herself. No doubt few, if any, would have believed her; but Kinnock could not have called her a liar, which, apart from anything else, is an unparliamentary and therefore impermissible expression. But she simply could not bring herself to defuse the situation in the conventional way – and, as a result, made it infinitely worse.

She nevertheless realized that the exchange had, to say the least, not gone well. At the end of Prime Minister's Questions we left the Chamber together, and went straight to my room – the Chancellor's room in the House of Commons is almost immediately behind the Speaker's chair, and the nearest Ministerial room to the Chamber. She was accompanied by the bevy of officials and advisers who helped her over Question Time. 'Was that all right?' she anxiously asked me. She was trying to pretend to herself that her praise of my handling of the economy had somehow saved the day. 'I only hope so,' I replied, grimly; 'but I doubt if we have heard the last of it.' Needless to say, it was manifestly not all right, with the press buzzing about her pointed refusal to say that she and I were in agreement over the exchange rate; and it was hardly surprising that the following day the pound rose to DM 3.18, its highest level since the end of 1985.

That day I had to travel to Travemunde, on the Baltic coast of Schleswig-Holstein, Stoltenberg's political base – the Germans had the European Community presidency at the time – for an informal Ecofin Council. No sooner had I got there when I began to receive reports that Geoffrey Howe had just made a speech to the Scottish Conservative Party conference at Perth, in which he had departed from his prepared and press-released text to say that the Government could not go on for ever repeating the formula that sterling would join the ERM when the time was right. Needless to say, I had known nothing about this in advance; but coming on top of Thursday's damaging episode in the Commons, Geoffrey's apparent challenge to Margaret on the Friday led to an orgy of speculation in the weekend press. One story was that she would move me to the Foreign Office and Geoffrey to some other job, thus silencing two turbulent Ministers at a stroke.

I returned from Schleswig-Holstein on the Sunday, and called Alex in. It was clear to me that Kinnock, having scored a bull's-eye beyond his wildest dreams, was bound to return to the subject at the next opportunity, which meant Prime Minister's Questions on Tuesday, 17 May. With Alex's help I drafted an answer for her to give to Kinnock's inevitable question. It was carefully designed to indicate that she did agree with me, but in a way that was within the terms of the 25 March concordat. Alex then telephoned his opposite number at Chequers to tell him that I would like to see the Prime Minister privately at Number 10 as soon as she returned that evening.

I went next door to see her after dinner. We met in her upstairs study, alone. I explained that developments both in the financial markets and on the political front had made it clear that her answers to Kinnock on the Thursday had not had the desired effect, and that the Government was now in serious trouble. The only way to save the situation was for her to make it quite clear on Tuesday, when Kinnock would inevitably return to the charge, that she did agree with me. I then handed her the draft answer to read, pointing out that it was fully in line with the concordat.

Amazingly, while she recognized that there was nothing for it but for her to remedy on the coming Tuesday the damage she had done the previous Thursday, she still could not bring herself to indicate that she agreed with her Chancellor. It was conspicuous how, during her last three years in office, she was always eager to claim that her Ministers agreed with her, but found it extraordinarily difficult to say that she agreed with her Ministers.

Rejecting my succinct draft on the grounds that it would not sound right from her, she took up her pen and a piece of paper and embarked on a fresh draft of her own. The atmosphere was calm and businesslike. Her draft was considerably longer than mine, and went into the details of policy much more. We then went over it carefully together, with my making a number of suggestions for changes, some of which she accepted. After a prolonged drafting session – we went over it several times, altering it each time – she called in a private secretary to get it typed. While we were waiting for the typed version, I said that her draft would undoubtedly help – she had made an unexpectedly positive reference to intervention, a subject which my draft had not mentioned at all – but I still felt that the simple affirmation that she and I were in agreement would be far safer.

To my astonishment she suggested that the best way to strengthen the effect of her proposed reply to Kinnock on Tuesday was not to alter the draft we had agreed but to accompany it by a half point cut in interest rates, from 8 per cent to 7½ per cent. The May Bank of England *Bulletin* had just infuriated Margaret by declaring that:

> The combination of a stronger currency and lower interest rates does not represent an ideal response to current concerns and a different balance would be desirable if it could be achieved.

It may be that Margaret was determined to snub the Bank's implicit call for higher interest rates. But whatever her reasons, to my eternal regret, I accepted this poisoned chalice. While nothing had been farther from my mind than a further interest rate reduction, I could see when Margaret suggested it that it would clearly demonstrate that we took sterling into account in our interest rate policy; and I was confident that I could reverse it fast enough to prevent it from bringing about a reduction in mortgage rates. And this indeed is what came to pass: I allowed the 7½ per cent base rate to persist for only a fortnight before reversing it, and mortgage rates never went down at all.

When I returned to Number 11 I gave Alex a copy of the revised draft answer and asked him to keep closely in touch with Number 10 the next day in case Margaret, having slept on it, had second thoughts. I also asked him to fix a markets meeting for the following day, with the usual cast, explaining to him that Margaret and I had decided that interest rates should go down another half point to 7½ per cent, and that I felt that this could do no harm provided it was a purely temporary move to deal with the current difficulty. The markets meeting was duly convened on the Monday morning, and the temporary half point cut agreed. The following day, 17 May, the reduction was implemented around midday and then, in the afternoon, came Prime Minister's Questions, with me sitting beside Margaret on the front bench. Kinnock asked the inevitable question, but in terms which filled me with foreboding as soon as he uttered them:

> May I warmly welcome today's cut in interest rates and the Chancellor's victory over the Prime Minister? Does this cut mean that

the Prime Minister has changed her position and now wholeheartedly agrees with the Chancellor that further rises in the pound would be unsustainable and would damage British business and industry?

After a short impromptu response on the interest rate cut, Margaret got down to reading the response she had drafted during my meeting with her on the Sunday evening:

> I am sure that he [Kinnock] would like a detailed reply. My right hon. Friend and I entirely agree [*interruption*] that we must maintain a firm monetary policy and a downward pull on inflation. I agree completely with my right hon. Friend's Budget speech, every bit of it, which is more than the right hon. Gentleman the Leader of the Opposition does.
>
> The right hon. Gentleman asked about exchange rate policy. It is a part of overall economic policy. As I indicated a moment ago, he will note that we have taken interest rates down three times in the last two months. That was clearly intended to affect the exchange rate. We use the available levers, both interest rates and intervention, as seems right in the circumstances, and [*interruption*] it would be a great mistake to think at any time that sterling was a one-way bet.

Our back-benchers were delighted by what seemed an unequivocal endorsement of my policy and the end of the rift between Margaret and myself. William Clark, the long-serving Chairman of the back-bench Finance Committee, who had been among those most concerned by the rift, asked her 'Does not today's reduction [in interest rates] prove beyond peradventure that there is complete and utter unanimity in the management of our economy under the capable management of the Chancellor?' Margaret replied with the single word 'Yes'.

If only she had been able to bring herself to utter that single monosyllable five days earlier, there would have been no need whatever for the prepared answer on 17 May – and the question of an interest rate cut would not have arisen. I do not believe for a moment that Margaret had deliberately proffered me a poisoned chalice: it was just that, whereas the thought of saying that she agreed with me was repugnant to her, she was always keen on an excuse to cut interest rates. But there was no doubt that – even though, ironically, it was at Margaret's instigation and not mine – the fact that I had reduced interest rates (albeit for only a fortnight) to 7½ per cent, the lowest level ever reached during the entire Thatcher era, and that I did so at the height of a boom, was subsequently to do considerable damage to my reputation.

But that was not the only damage the half point cut inflicted. Kinnock's response that it was a victory for me over Margaret – particularly ironic given the true origin of the interest rate cut – was inevitably, personalities being so much more interesting than economics, the theme of all the newspaper headlines the following morning. It was something that Margaret had never before experienced, and I knew she would hate it. So did Thérèse. 'You'll pay for this,' she said to me. We all did.

The Four-to-One Rule

The official Treasury, understandably anxious to find some firm policy bedrock among all these shifting sands and political turbulence, fell back on a rule of thumb which had apparently emerged from the Treasury's computerized economic model. This was that a 4 per cent rise in the exchange rate was roughly equivalent in terms of its restrictive effect on demand and inflation to a 1 per cent rise in base rates. The equation was based on the sterling index, but it was so rough and ready that it could almost equally well be applied to the DM rate. This had risen by just over 6 per cent since the March uncapping, conveniently equivalent to the 1½ point cut in base rate which we had made in total since the Budget.

I myself never went overboard for the 4-to-1 rule. Interest rate and exchange rate changes worked their way through the economy by such different channels and through such different sectors that to treat them as equivalent with this degree of quantification was too great a violation of reality even for macroeconomic policy.

But the real problem was not the precise nature of the interest rate/exchange rate trade-off. It was that the overall combination was not tight enough. My critics have subsequently alleged either that I lost interest in the battle against inflation, which is demonstrably untrue, or that I took my eye off the ball. There may be some truth in this latter charge for the brief period of April and May 1988, when I became so absorbed in my battle with Margaret over exchange rate policy that I was unable to devote the attention to the state of the economy that I should have done. But it was soon remedied.

Critics who have focused on the 17 May half point cut in base rate to 7½ per cent have got it wholly out of proportion. Because I had never sought it in the first place I was determined to reverse it as soon as practicable. As a result, as I have said, it lasted a mere two weeks, during which, as the chart shows, it had no influence whatever on mortgage rates. Nor, of course, did I stop there. As the bullish sentiment towards sterling began to falter, as I had expected it would, I raised interest rates by a rapid series of half point steps to 11 per cent by 5 August. The purpose of doing it by half point steps was to demonstrate that this was a tightening of monetary policy for its own sake, and not a macho move designed to impress the foreign exchange market in order to protect the pound. The pound did not, in fact, recover its mid-May level against the Deutschmark until late July.

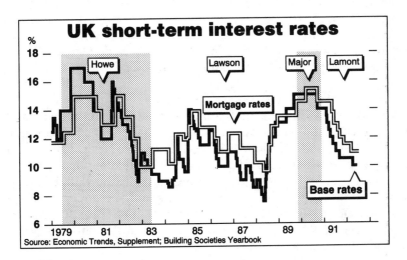

By 22 June I had reversed all the post-Budget base rate cuts, and by 4 July, when base rates were back at 10 per cent I had reversed all the post-crash reductions. By 8 August, I had raised base rates to 11 per cent, their highest level since 1986. The chart shows, moreover, that mortgage rates never fully followed base rates down, reaching a low point of 9¾ per cent in May, which lasted for less than three months before they were on their way up again. In 1988 as a whole UK *real* short-term interest rates averaged well over 5 per cent, compared with 3½ per cent in the US and 3 per cent in Germany – not high enough, but hardly the degree of laxity with which some have charged me.

The monetary tightening in the late spring and summer of 1988 was a relatively harmonious process, with Margaret, for once, in agreement with the interest rate increases I proposed. By this time, moreover, I had become worried about the massive expansion of mortgage lending on prudential grounds. It did not seem to me conceivable that lending growth at this rate, and in the indiscriminate way anecdotal evidence made it clear was occurring, could possibly be prudent. I was confident that I could prevail upon the Building Societies Commission, headed by the former Treasury official Michael Bridgeman, with whom I had worked closely when I was Financial Secretary, to lean on the building societies; but this would work only if the Bank of England could be prevailed upon simultaneously to lean on their competitors in the mortgage market – the clearing banks, whose supervisory authority was the Bank.

Astonishingly, the clearing banks had totally failed to recognize that the relentless interest rate increases in the summer and autumn of 1988 presaged difficult times ahead. Just as management exacerbated the cost of defeating inflation by obstinately continuing to negotiate excessive pay awards, so the banks worsened the pain of disinflation for themselves and their clients by imprudent expansion of their loan books. My particular concern with mortgage lending derived from the key role the housing boon was playing in the overheating process. This was not least because of its effect on public psychology – in effect, the excess of optimism, to which I referred in Chapter 50.

Accordingly, in May 1988 I convened a meeting in my room at the Treasury with Robin and his key Bank of England officials, including the head of banking supervision, Brian Quinn, to encourage them to lean on the clearing banks on prudential grounds. I pointed out that, if they did, I was confident that the Building Societies Commission would do the same with the building societies. They declined to make any serious attempt to do so. I tried, on more than one subsequent occasion to persuade the Bank to ask the clearers to be more prudent in their mortgage lending, but with similar lack of success.

The reason the Bank gave, at my May meeting, for its refusal to act was essentially threefold. First, the Bank's duty as supervisor was the protection of depositors, and in its judgement there was no risk to bank depositors. Second, there was no threat to the banking system as a whole, in the sense of a core bank getting into serious difficulties, even though some loans were bound to turn sour. In particular, there was no danger in the UK of a collapse on the lines of the Savings & Loan débâcle in the United States. (The spectacular UK failures of the early 1990s were in the commercial property sphere.) Third, mortgage lending was probably the safest form of lending in which the banks engaged, secured as it was on domestic bricks and mortar: it would not make sense to caution the banks about this form of lending, when much of their lending to business and industry was less well secured or even unsecured.

While there was undoubtedly substance in all these arguments, I believe that at the more fundamental level at which central bank thinking ought to be pitched the Bank was both unimaginative and misguided. In the first place, the grossly imprudent bank lending which took place in 1988 and 1989 may not have led to the collapse of any core bank, let alone the collapse of the banking system as a whole. But it gravely weakened it – something which ought to have been of concern to the Bank of England. And in the second place, while it is true that mortgage lending is in normal times the safest form of lending, there are three important qualifications to be made.

The first is that when it leads to the sort of house price bubble that occurred at the end of the 1980s, which at some point was bound to burst, this type of lending is less secure than it seems. Second, the credit-based house price bubble of the late 1980s, by creating an exaggerated impression of personal wealth and prosperity, led to a great deal of other borrowing and lending of a less secure nature. And third, it was inevitable that at some point the burden of rising mortgage payments would mean that other forms of spending would be cut back, thus making much other lending even less secure. A central bank needs to be aware of these connections, and of their implications.

The Bank's strongest argument for inaction was probably the one that it left unsaid: that the commercial banks, driven by a desire to maintain and if possible increase their share of the mortgage market, come what may, would have taken no notice of a call for greater prudence and caution from the Governor of the Bank of England. But although it was true that the Bank's authority had diminished over the years, I very much doubt if it had vanished completely. And if the worst came to the worst, it would have been better to have tried and failed than not to have really tried at all.

Ghosts from the Past

The summer of 1988 was a time for the return of two ghosts from the past. The first of these was our old friend the current account balance of payments deficit. This took a marked turn for the worse in 1988. I was giving a press conference in support of the Conservative candidate at the Kensington by-election that had been caused by the death of the sitting Member, the redoubtable if lonely back-bencher, Brandon Rhys-Williams. I had said my usual piece about the fundamental strength of the British economy, when one of the journalists present asked me how I could possibly claim that the economy was strong when the May current account figures, which had just been published, had shown an unexpectedly large deficit, and all the City pundits were preaching doom and gloom. I lightheartedly replied that I would not advise him 'to take too much notice of the teenage scribblers in the City who jump up and down in an effort to get press attention'.

There are, of course, a very small number of economists of distinction and perception who work for various City firms. But, allowing the element of polemical exaggeration in the adjective 'teenage', so far as the generality is concerned my remark was as accurate as it was unwise. Not only was it deliberately misconstrued as an attempt to dispute the accuracy of the analysts' revised forecasts of the current account for the year as a whole; but I was seen as belittling the entire self-important tribe of City analysts. For the rest of my time as Chancellor, they were determined to get even and were unremitting in their hostility towards me – something I could have done without.

However, the more threatening ghost from the (more recent) past was Alan Walters. In July 1988 I got wind of the news that Margaret was negotiating with him for his return as her personal economic adviser, the post he had held between 1981 and 1983 before leaving to take up a couple of academic posts in the United States. This caused me considerable concern. Between 1981 and 1983 he was a relatively little-known figure who worked quietly behind the scenes. But once he had escaped from the conventions of the civil service he had traded heavily on his self-proclaimed importance as Margaret's economic *éminence grise* and became a minor celebrity, giving his forceful views to the press at the drop of a hat. All this had rather gone to his head. The fact that, by 1988, he was writing articles in the UK press attacking me and my policies, made matters considerably worse; but it could not make sense, as I saw it, for a Prime Minister to have as a special adviser anyone as opinionated as Alan Walters, when their opinions have been widely publicized and become so well known, and when they continue to feel free to utter them irrespective of Government policy.

I went to see Margaret privately to express my concern. We met in the white state drawing room of Number 10. I told Margaret that I did not for one moment dispute her right to have her own personal economic adviser if she felt she wanted one. But I foresaw serious trouble ahead if she gave the job to Walters. His hostility to various aspects of Government policy was well known; and he had become far too high-profile to be able to reassume the conventions of civil service discretion. She replied that he had done an excellent job when he had worked for her before; and she had never wanted him to leave. Now he had accepted her request to him to return, and she could not go back on that. I repeated why, in my judgement, to reappoint him would cause considerable trouble for the Government, which we could well do without; and for the Government's sake, I begged her to think again. But she had clearly made up her mind.

For good measure, however, I went to the Whips' Office and told a more or less comple·e gathering of the Government Whips of my concern and foreboding: they were entirely sympathetic; but, so far as I am aware, David Waddington, the Chief Whip, took no action of any kind. The mandarins for their part, appeared to be under the illusion that Walters would do less damage 'inside' Whitehall than outside, as his views would be properly circulated and rationally discussed, instead of creeping through the back door into Margaret's personal brief. They did not realize how much he had changed since his departure from full-time Government service in 1983. In his second incarnation, he attended only a small number of meetings and when he did he kept very quiet, giving the impression he was keeping his real opinions for his *tête à tête* talks with Margaret, and was there merely to gather ammunition.

In the short term the political fall-out from Walters' activities was entirely favourable to me. This was the third time that Margaret had appeared to disown me within a few months – first by torpedoing my exchange rate policy in early March, then by conspicuously failing to back me over the 'unsustainable' rise in sterling in mid-May, and finally by refusing to disown Walters' remarks and by taking an unconscionable time before getting her Number 10 staff to tell him to desist from further public pronouncements.

Parliamentary colleagues who had no interest in monetary or exchange rate policy – and even some who did not particularly like me personally – were enraged that a non-resident economist should be treated, in John Smith's words, as an 'unelected Chancellor' and allowed to rock the boat in the way he was doing. On the evening of 19 July I was given a resounding vote of confidence at a packed meeting of the Party's back-bench Finance Committee, at which the back-benchers banged their desk to show their approval of me and disapproval of the way Margaret was treating some of her Cabinet colleagues. Ian Stewart, my former Economic Secretary, who since the 1987 election had been Minister for the Armed Forces, wrote to me on 20 July:

> I have been appalled (and astonished) at the circumstances to which you have been subjected these last few days. I had hoped and thought that things had got back to a reasonable working relationship with next door after the previous bout of public angst. Anyway, you have my profound sympathy and I know you have the same from most of our colleagues.

One back-bencher told *The Times* after the Finance Committee meeting that I was 'unsackable'. William Clark, the chairman of the Committee, wrote to me a few days later to say that 'there was no question as to your standing in the Party'. Margaret herself did not respond to this unaccustomed display of back-bench concern until Prime Minister's Questions on Thursday, 21 July, when she fell back on the usual generalities that I was pursuing 'excellent economic policies'. Later, at the final meeting of the 1922 Committee of all Conservative back-benchers before the 1988 summer recess, she declared that I had 'handled the Crash marvellously' and that the Budget was 'quite the best Budget we have seen. Brilliant in concept, brilliant in drafting and brilliant in delivery.' 'Unassailable' could not be far away.

CHAPTER 68

MY LAST STRUGGLE WITH INFLATION, 1988–89

Locked into Number 11 · Figures Sent to Try Us
On to 14 per cent · The Ludicrous RPI
Why Not Overkill? · Mythical Golf Clubs
My Balance of Payments Heresy · A Self-Correcting Mechanism?

Locked into Number 11

MARGARET HAD NO INTENTION of making it easy for me to resign in the summer of 1988, when my standing within the Party was still high. It was not that, however, which kept me at Number 11, but the increasing signs of overheating in the economy. I had a word with Peter Brooke, whose disinterested and shrewd political judgement I valued, one evening when we were both stuck at the House just before the July reshuffle. I told him that I was fed up with Margaret's behaviour, and was thinking of telling her that she should use the occasion of the reshuffle to find a new Chancellor. We went round and round the subject, in my room at the House, and the next day he sent me a note summing up his view:

> Your friends (and our benches) would reject outright a charge of 'cut and run', but Smith (who has touches of Asquith about him) would lend it a gravitas not available in Sparkbrook*. I am conscious this is more a Treasury and Party view, but it does have a personal component too: I recognize it would not be decisive against any new class of cruiser (HMS Intolerable, HMS Impossible etc.) but it should weigh.

I took the point; but was still wondering whether I had taken the right

---

*The constituency of Roy Hattersley, John Smith's predecessor.

844

decision when, on 22 August, I was given advance warning of the trade figures for July which were due to be published three days later. The current payments deficit for the month was put at a staggering £2.2 billion; as large as that for the previous two months, which had been bad enough, taken together. It was clear to me that demand in the economy was pressing against the limits of capacity to a much greater degree than I had previously realized, and that decisive action was required. It was not the current account deficit itself which concerned me: quite apart from its changed significance in the new global economy, our foreign exchange reserves stood at all-time record levels. It was the message it conveyed.

I had already surprised the financial markets with my half point increase in base rates to 11 per cent on 8 August. On learning of the July trade figures I immediately drove from Stoney Stanton to Downing Street to see Margaret and told her that I believed we should raise interest rates by a further full point to 12 per cent on 25 August, the day the figures were due to be published. She was even more shocked by the figures than I was, since she attached importance to them in themselves rather than, as I did, as a symptom of something else. I informed my officials, asked them to arrange a markets meeting with the Bank on 25 August to decide the nuts and bolts, and returned to Stoney Stanton to resume my summer break. Fortunately, confidence in sterling was still robust.

In retrospect the August trade figures and the consequent rise in base rates marked the turning point in my Chancellorship. It was then that it finally became clear just how strong the boom was, and the difficulties I would have in curbing it if inflation was not to get out of hand. It was then that my colleagues realized that I was no longer the miracle worker that some had imagined me to be. It was then that I recognized that there could be no thought of resignation: I owed it to the Government and myself to see the thing through.

Figures Sent to Try Us

It was obvious long before August 1988 that most of the official economic statistics were seriously unreliable – indeed some were little more than a work of fiction. In May 1988 the Government had set up the Pickford Inquiry into the quality of economic statistics, which ultimately led in 1989 to the decision to place a reformed Central Statistical Office (CSO) under the ultimate supervision of the Chancellor, as recounted in Chapter 31. A relatively minor indication of the sort of problems from which we suffered comes from comparing the monthly trade figures as they originally appeared in 1988 with the latest available revisions:

Monthly Current Account Payments Deficit, 1988
£ billion

	Original Figures	Latest Revisions (as of 1992)
January	0.9	0.8
February	0.7	1.2
March	0.3	1.2
April	0.5	0.8
May	1.2	1.1
June	1.0	1.2
July	2.2	1.4
August	1.3	0.9
September	0.6	1.0
October	2.4	2.2
November	1.6	2.0
December	1.3	1.7

Both sets of figures may well overstate the true deficit, as there remains an unexplained so-called balancing item of almost £6 billion for 1988; and how much of that represents unrecorded current account receipts and how much unrecorded capital receipts is shrouded in mystery. But the revised figures would have been more helpful had they been available at the time – not least because the extent of the deterioration would have been clearer much sooner, leading to a much earlier tightening of policy. There is one particular aspect of this that deserves a special mention. One of the reasons why I did not believe the sharp rise in the sterling exchange rate in the aftermath of the uncapping of March 1988 would prove sustainable was that I expected the markets to become nervous about the current deficit and what it portended. Had the deficit for the first quarter been the £3.2 billion, on a rising trend, now recorded, rather than the £1.9 billion, on a declining trend, originally published, sterling might well have been weaker – in which case the circumstances which led to the 1½ per cent cut in interest rates over the ten weeks following the uncapping might not have occurred.

Whatever improvements flow from the full implementation of the Pickford Report, the likelihood is that accurate trade figures in future will become even more difficult to obtain as the European single market becomes a reality. This is bound to strengthen still further the case for a rule-based approach to policy, with greatly reduced dependence on instant statistical diagnosis. The practical problem, however, which is unlikely to go away, is that the financial markets are always liable to react sharply to the latest piece of statistical information, however dubious its quality.

On to 14 per cent

Needless to say, I was far from alone in hoping that 12 per cent base rates would do the trick. Indeed, with real interest rates at 6½ per cent, the prevailing view both in business and industry and among my parliamentary colleagues was that they were already too high. Some economists took a similar view. I recall the domestic monetarist, Patrick Minford, at the autumn 1988 'Gooies' meeting, inveighing against the 'savagery' of a four-point rise in interest rates in under three months. But by the late autumn there was uncomfortable evidence that domestic demand was continuing to increase too rapidly.

The recorded current account deficit had initially subsided somewhat after the then all-time record of July. Indeed, by September it had apparently fallen back to some £600 million. But then came the next bombshell: towards the end of November I was informed that the current account deficit for October had come out at £2.4 billion, larger even than that of July. Moreover, other indicators – such as retail sales, underlying inflation, mortgage commitments, manufacturers' margins, house prices and earnings – were by then telling a similar story. There had also been an acceleration in the growth of M0 to 7¾ per cent, well above the 1 to 5 per cent target range. It was clear that interest rates would need to be raised again. At the markets meeting I held my advisers were divided, but I settled for a further one point increase to 13 per cent.

As in August, I timed the interest rate increase to coincide with the publication date of the trade figures – which also happened to be the day I was due to travel to Birmingham to present the Midlands Businessman of the Year Award, under the auspices of the Variety Club of Great Britain. In the circumstances, my audience was remarkably civil and good-natured. But it was a reminder of the unwisdom of agreeing to undertake commitments of that kind on a day on which significant economic statistics were scheduled for publication.

The interest rate rise also took place in the middle of the six-day debate on the Queen's Speech which, at the start of each session of Parliament, sets out the Government's programme for the coming parliamentary year. By tradition, the opening speaker for the Government on the final day of what is technically known as the Debate on the Address is the Chancellor. Not surprisingly, I had a pretty sticky time when I spoke on 29 November. The only memorable contribution that day came from Ted Heath, not normally a great phrase-maker, when he said:

MY LAST STRUGGLE WITH INFLATION, 1988–89

> In golfing terms, the Chancellor could be described as a one-club man, and that club is interest rates. But if one wishes to take on Sandy Lyle and the rest of the world one needs a complete bag of clubs. The Chancellor flatly refuses to have that. He has turned down any other measures to influence the economy.

The accusation that I was a 'one-club golfer' stuck. It was an excellent example of how a good phrase can transfigure a bad point. As the contents of this book amply demonstrate, I was engaged in implementing a whole range of measures, not least tax reform, to 'influence the economy'. But interest rates are the essential means of curbing inflation, just as a golfer confines himself to the use of his putter for putting.

As it happened, after six months during which I had felt obliged to raise interest rates by almost as many percentage points, there then followed six months during which they remained unchanged at 13 per cent. But in the second half of May 1989, there were clear signs that sentiment towards the pound, which I had expected to turn sour considerably earlier, had at last begun to do so. There was nothing dramatic about sterling's weakness, but there was no mistaking the change in the market climate; and it was a change across the board, not simply against the Deutschmark, since the early months of 1989 had witnessed a modest recovery in the dollar. At the same time, evidence that the steady monetary tightening that I had embarked on as far back as the beginning of June 1988 was cooling the economy down adequately was disappointingly thin on the ground. In particular, bank and building society lending in May 1989 was still growing at an annual rate of over 23 per cent – precisely the same explosive rate of growth as when I began the tightening about a year earlier.

I was due to fly to Spain for an unusually important informal Ecofin Council meeting on Friday, 19 May (see chapter 73). That morning, I called a markets meeting with a view to increasing base rates by a further percentage point to 14 per cent – the highest level since the sterling crisis of January 1985. In addition to the usual cast I invited Alan Walters, who had just arrived back as Margaret's personal economic adviser. Curiously, the Bank, which the previous November had toyed with the idea of moving straight from 12 per cent to 14 per cent, was now in two minds as to whether we should move to 14 per cent at all. Walters, who arrived late for the meeting, said that in his opinion 13 per cent was quite high enough. My senior Treasury advisers, like me, felt uneasy at the prospect of leaving things as they were.

I decided to defer a final decision until my return, when on Tuesday, 23 May, there was a further run on the pound. So far as I was concerned, that clinched it. The following morning Margaret reluctantly went along with my proposal to move base rates up a further point, from 13 per cent to 14 per cent. Politically, the timing could scarcely have been more awkward: I was due to address the annual Conservative Women's Conference that afternoon; and for the first and only time that normally well-mannered congregation gave me a rough ride.

The Ludicrous RPI

Throughout this period I was not helped by the composition of the generally accepted measure of inflation in the UK, the Retail Price Index or RPI. This had been very foolishly amended during the early period of the previous Labour Government, in 1975, to include as a proxy for the cost of owner-occupied housing the level of mortgage interest payments. Hitherto the housing component of the index had been confined to rents – both private sector rents and council house rents – and local authority rates. At the time the Treasury, driven, as ever, far too much by the public expenditure side, had unwisely supported the change in the belief that it would weaken the opposition to reducing local authority rent subsidies – since a lessening of the weight of rents in the RPI would clearly reduce the effect of rent rises on recorded inflation.

But the inclusion of mortgage payments was both ludicrous and perverse. Not only are mortgage interest payments not a retail price in any normal sense of that term, but their inclusion meant that the principal means of fighting inflation – raising interest rates – showed up as an increase in the rate of inflation. For both these reasons, few other countries would dream of including mortgage interest payments in their consumer price index. Indeed, of the twelve countries of the European Community, the only other one to do so was Ireland, which takes its cue from the UK in most things. For this reason, sensible international comparisons of inflation are impossible given a UK index which includes them.

The effect of this UK own goal was considerable. In 1989 as a whole, for example, while the 'underlying' rate of inflation, as measured by the RPI excluding mortgage interest payments, was 5.9 per cent – which was bad enough – the headline rate of inflation, as measured by the RPI, warts and all, was 7.8 per cent. The perversity was further compounded in 1990, when the Poll Tax – which is manifestly not a price of any kind – was included in the RPI in place of local authority domestic rates, which had been classified as an indirect tax on housing. For a time the distortion of the RPI was self-reinforcing. For in the short term the rate of pay settlements was strongly influenced by the headline RPI, particularly when employers were able to pass on their increased costs in higher prices. This did not really start to change until unemployment started to rise, and that in turn did not occur until May 1990. Thus the net effect of the exaggeration of inflation by the RPI was to bring about a longer and deeper recession than would otherwise have occurred in reversing the inflationary momentum.

In a sane world the obvious answer would have been to undo the mistaken 1975 change in the composition of the RPI. But in the real world this was a good deal easier said than done. The constituent parts of the RPI were determined not by the Government acting alone but on the advice of the RPI Advisory Committee, a body at that time appointed by the Secretary of State for Employment. By convention, while it included representatives of the Government, the majority of its members were outsiders, in particular nominees of various interest groups, such as the TUC and the CBI.

The Committee was ostensibly set up to ensure the Government did not tamper with the RPI. In practice it reflected the interplay of the various pressure groups which served on it. The trade unions were interested in including anything which made the RPI go up, because of the link between wage bargaining and the RPI; and in general the outsiders seemed to regard it as their duty to take the opposite view to that of the Government, whatever the merits of the case. The 1975 change had been possible only because it enjoyed the wholehearted support of the TUC.

Baulked of the possibility of reforming the RPI, I decided as early as 1986, at a time when there was no difference between the two measures, that it might at least be helpful to publish on a regular monthly basis, alongside the headline RPI, the RPI excluding mortgage interest payments as a better measure of underlying inflation. Even so, such is the interest in preserving the *status quo*, that I had to have a long drawn out battle with successive Employment Secretaries, first David Young and then more particularly Norman Fowler, merely to get the Department to publish such an index.

Once this had at long last occurred in the latter part of 1988. I was at least able to quote the underlying rate of inflation in all my speeches. But the benefit of this was severely weakened by Margaret's insistence on referring to the headline rate in all *her* speeches, and never once mentioning the underlying rate. Stirred up by her acolytes, she was in a permanent state of resentment with me for having – as she saw it – allowed inflation to rise, and she was determined to rub my nose in it. Ingham had consistently briefed the press on the basis that everything that went right was Margaret's own personal achievement, while everything that went wrong was the fault of her Ministers; and Margaret herself increasingly came to see things in these terms.

Meanwhile, I was able to make what I hoped would be a useful preparatory step towards reforming the RPI. As a result of the Pickford Inquiry into the quality of official economic statistics, responsibility for all economic statistics, including the RPI, eventually in 1989 passed to the new enlarged CSO, which in turn reported to the Chancellor. At least the obscurantist Employment Department was removed from the picture.

But there was another and far trickier minefield to traverse. When index-linked gilts were first introduced in 1981, the Treasury and the Bank of England had agreed that the prospectus for each issue should contain an undertaking to the effect that, if the RPI were materially changed in any way which was disadvantageous to holders of the bonds, the holders had the right to demand immediate repayment in full at par. The exclusion of mortgage interest payments from the RPI, however justified, would clearly be a material change, and in the light of the experience of the 1980s, when the inclusion of mortgage interest payments exaggerated the recorded rate of inflation in seven years out of ten, it might be difficult to persuade the Courts that their exclusion was not disadvantageous to holders of indexed gilts. Even so, the extent of the consequent problem for the Government depended on the extent to which indexed gilts stood below par, which would determine how great would be the rush by bondholders to exercise their right to sell the bonds back to the Government at a profit.

During my time there was no way through this minefield. The composition of the RPI Advisory Committee was loaded against the Government, and most index-linked gilts stood well below par. As a result, the terms of the indexed gilts prospectus, exacerbated by the membership of the Advisory Committee, effectively meant that the RPI could be changed only in a way which made recorded inflation look worse. But that does not mean that a way through it cannot be found. The switch of Ministerial responsibility for the RPI from the Employment Secretary to the Chancellor, which I secured shortly before my resignation, has provided an opportunity – not yet seized – for the radical reconstitution of the RPI Advisory Committee, which ought to exclude the interest groups and confine the outside members to respected professional statisticians and economists. There will surely be a time when the bulk of indexed gilts are standing above par. When the opportunity to remove mortgage interest payments from the RPI at a relatively low cost arrives, it would be a foolish Chancellor who did not seize it with both hands.

Why Not Overkill?

Looking back, it may be argued that I should have deliberately gone in for shock treatment, and raised interest rates much more sharply in the early stages. This might have led to a more pronounced recession; but it might well have started to bite much sooner and lasted less long. Hindsight is a wonderful thing. At the time, even what I did do was considered pretty severe. Moreover, the real problem, for which I had not bargained, was the extraordinary slowness of borrowers and, even more, of lenders to react to the tightening. My interest rates moves represented a sharp change of policy fully backed by tough talk. Had I foreseen the inability of the credit markets to grasp the inevitable consequences of this – and I vividly recall spelling out some of them in radio interviews at the time – I would indeed have gone in for a greater degree of shock treatment.

The figures tell the story. Bank and building society lending had been growing at a steady rate of between 16¼ per cent and 18¼ per cent from the first three months of my Chancellorship in 1983 up to and including the third quarter of 1986.* It then rose to an annual rate of growth of 19½ per cent and stayed in the 19½ – 20½ per cent range until 1988, when it surged further ahead. The peak annual growth of 24¾ per cent was in the first quarter of 1988. Lending then continued at a remarkably high rate, despite the very high level of interest rates, right through to the middle of 1990: it did not fall below an annual growth rate of 19¼ per cent until the third quarter of that year. From then on, of course, it fell rapidly, as the economy slid into recession.

The extraordinary and unforeseen continuation of the rapid expansion of bank and building society lending, right through to the middle of 1990, two years after the sharp monetary tightening began, is a major reason why the boom went as far as it did; why the banks and so many of their customers subsequently got into difficulties; why the subsequent recession was as bad as it was and lasted as long as it did; and why the recovery was delayed as it was. In other words, my own misjudgements were enormously compounded by the mistakes of the private sector in general and of the banks in particular.

Mythical Golf Clubs

The advocates of shock treatment were few and far between, and would almost certainly have melted away had it been put into effect. More serious politically were those who urged me to find other weapons, apart from interest rates, to use against inflation. A refrain that has frequently punctuated this narrative has been the desire of those who should have known better for a painless technical gimmick to secure low inflation, a call that came from left and right alike. I gave this wishful thinking no quarter, telling the House on 7 June 1989 that there was no alternative to setting interest rates and holding them at the level needed, and for the time needed, to do their work.

It was not difficult to rebut the simple-minded advocates of direct controls, who tended to be chiefly concerned about credit cards and hire purchase. I needed only to point out that some 85 per cent of total

*The quarterly figures are the growth over the same quarter of the previous year.

household debt consisted of mortgages. Credit card and hire purchase lending taken together amounted to only a little over 5 per cent of total household debt. So it was absurd to imply that introducing controls on hire purchase or credit cards would do anything significant to reduce the growth of consumer credit, or to allow interest rates to be one whit lower. In any event any such controls would have been simplicity itself to get around in a deregulated financial market without exchange control. As for direct controls on bank lending; these had proved increasingly ineffective even before exchange control was abolished. By the late 1980s they would simply have provided a field day for foreign lending institutions.

The novel feature of the 1989 debate was the alliance between left-wing financial columnists and right-wing City critics who both supposed that there must be sophisticated methods of controlling the money supply which would slow down monetary and credit growth without having to ration credit by interest rates. The devices usually suggested had been aired for a very long time, and I have already dealt with them in Chapter 8, covering events in 1980 when I was Financial Secretary to the Treasury and Monetary Base Control was attracting Margaret's attention for that very reason. Although I did not share the Bank's abhorrence of MBC, I had no doubt, either at the beginning or the end of the 1980s, that it was essentially just another way of generating the level of short-term interest rates needed to curb inflation. It was in no sense an alternative to high interest rates – as the Americans discovered during Paul Volcker's experiment with MBC in 1979–81, when short-term interest rates at times exceeded 20 per cent.

Another frequent variation on the same theme, which was taken up both by the Labour Opposition and within the Cabinet by Peter Walker, then Welsh Secretary, was a variable assets ratio for the banks. I explained to him that his proposal reflected a common misunderstanding about the way in which monetary policy operated in Germany, and in some other countries as well. In normal circumstances, the German banking system was short of reserve assets and the Bundesbank operated regularly in the course of each month to provide the required reserves, normally by means of repurchase agreements against the banks' holdings of public debt. The key to the system was the price at which the Bundesbank provided reserves. This set the level of short-term interest rates in the economy, and it was changes in the level of interest rates which represented the mechanism for monetary control. What the Bundesbank system did not do (and still does not do at the time of writing) was to operate a direct quantitative control on credit. There was no question of the Bundesbank refusing to supply the quantity of reserves that banks needed.

Thus in essence the German system was little different from that operated in the UK by the Bank of England. As in Germany, the banks normally needed assistance from the central bank to build adequate reserve holdings. It was the price at which the authorities provided the cash that they needed, by way of money market operations, that set the level of interest rates. The only substantive difference between Britain and Germany was that in Germany there were mandatory, and much larger, reserve requirements – idle balances so far as the banks were concerned. The high German reserve requirement did not make German interest rates any lower: it merely encouraged the Frankfurt banks to escape the impost by channelling business through offshore centres such as Luxembourg, to the annoyance of the Bundesbank. This explanation had, in fact, been given numerous times in the Bank of England *Bulletin*. But the myth was so much more attractive than the bleak reality that it seemed indestructible.

Yet another technocratic attempt at a painless short cut was overfunding. I have already chronicled the Government's unhappy experience with this in the early 1980s. The only effect of overfunding – insofar as it has any effect at all – is to make long-term interest rates slightly higher relative to short-term rates; which is scarcely a solution to anything. I told the *Weekend World* Sunday lunchtime television audience that unless we were to bring back mortgage queuing, which would soon be circumvented and would be grossly unfair on first-time buyers in the meantime, people had to adjust to the new climate of freedom and borrowers had to learn self-discipline. Until they did, interest rates, at whatever level was necessary, would have to hold the balance.

My Balance of Payments Heresy

I have mentioned earlier that I always sought to make my speech to the annual Fund and Bank meeting more interesting by developing some original thinking on a topical economic issue. At the 1988 meeting, which was held in West Berlin, I chose as my heretical theme the thesis that the balance of payments on current account did not have the central importance as an indicator of success or failure that popular comment supposed. This thesis did not, in fact, come as a bolt from the blue. I had touched on it at the spring meeting of the Interim Committee in 1987 and had discussed it on several subsequent occasions, most fully in my IEA lecture in July 1988 on the 'State of the Market'.

As the title of that lecture suggests, it was a serious if broad-brush account of my thinking on a number of prominent issues, including the superiority of the market economy, privatization, deregulation, tax reform, monetary policy and the exchange rate, as well as the current account of the balance of payments. Needless to say, the popular press concentrated exclusively on the passage dealing with the exchange rate, where their interest was in perpetuating the story of the rift between Margaret and myself. On the exchange rate I had the temerity to state the following:

> With separate national currencies in an international financial market-place, it is inevitable that the exchange rate plays an important part in determining monetary conditions. So governments have to come to terms with the behaviour of the foreign exchange market. Left entirely to its own devices, we have seen in recent years how destabilising and disruptive that behaviour can sometimes be.

The journalists could not wait to tell Margaret's press secretary, Bernard Ingham, that I was once again attacking the Prime Minister; and he did nothing to discourage them from the most troublemaking interpretation possible. This duly enabled him to describe my speech in his press summary for Margaret the next morning in these terms:

> While you defend the Chancellor and praise his Budget and handling of the stock market crash, he makes a speech to IEA which is interpreted as yet another 'declaration of independence'.

This interpretation was then backed up by selective extracts from various newspapers, starting with one from Ingham's favourite organ, the *Sun*:

> I'll do it my way – Lawson puts job on line in row with Maggie. But he receives a pat on the back from you. His speech is an amazing challenge to your authority and a massive gamble over his future.

Since Margaret never read the daily newspapers herself, and relied entirely on the daily press summary Ingham prepared for her, the effect of this sort of poison, week in, week out, month in, month out, on Margaret's attitude towards me is not hard to gauge.

But to return to my balance of payments heresy: my proposition was not that the current balance of payments could be ignored. No piece of economic information should be thrown away. My point was that the current balance of payments deficit was *not* like a company running at a loss – 'Britain in the red', as the headlines were inclined to put it. As I explained to the IEA:

> A better analogy is with a profitable company raising funds externally – either by borrowing or by raising new equity. A company with greater investment opportunities than it could finance from retained profits would look for additional funds from outside. A country in a similar position will draw on the savings of the world, which is particularly easy in today's global markets.

I accepted that part of the UK current deficit was a symptom of an excessively rapid boom at home, but went on to say:

> But that is only part of the story. For there is no iron law that the private sector's finances must be in balance, in any given year or indeed any given period of years. Sometimes savings will exceed investment; sometimes investment will exceed savings. If domestic savings exceed domestic investment, there will be a capital outflow and a current surplus; if domestic investment exceeds domestic savings, there will be a capital inflow and a current deficit.
>
> Looked at like this, it would in fact be very surprising if the current accounts of the major countries were always in balance. Net capital flows are inevitable and indeed desirable, given differing propensities to save and differing investment opportunities. And a country whose investment opportunities are sufficiently attractive to generate a net capital inflow will by definition have a current account deficit.

The dethronement of the current account balance as a sensible objective of policy can also be seen as a consequence of financial deregulation. In a world of rigid foreign exchange controls, a current account deficit could be financed only by a country running down its foreign currency reserves, which was clearly something that could continue only for a very short time. It was this state of affairs which justified the IMF emphasis on the balance of payments in the post-war world, and its continued preoccupation with the balance of payments of its clients in the Third World and the former Soviet bloc, whose enterprises do not have a sufficient credit rating to borrow on the private international capital market.

In today's world, by contrast, an advanced industrial country that can maintain a reasonable degree of confidence in its currency can finance a current account deficit for a considerable number of years – as for example the United States did – by importing capital from overseas. This in turn can be seen in terms of the relationship between savings and investment. For a mixture of cultural, historical, institutional and economic reasons, countries differ in their savings ratios. Similarly, profitable investment opportunities vary from country to country. While these things, of course, change over time, at any given period those countries whose capacity to generate savings exceeds their indigenous investment opportunities will experience a capital outflow, which will finance the current account deficits of those countries whose capacity to generate savings falls short of their indigenous investment opportunities.

I concluded this section of my IEA address by saying that, given a firm financial framework, a period of private-sector-induced current account deficit should give no cause for concern. But the proviso about a firm financial framework is crucial. It has a number of facets. As I explained:

● It depends on the public finances staying in balance. The current account deficits of the 1970s reflected excessive Government borrowing and spending, which it was certainly the Government's job to correct.

● It means remaining vigilant for signs of inflationary pressure, whatever the source, and standing ready to tighten monetary conditions by raising interest rates whenever such pressures emerge.

● And it implies not accommodating increases in costs by a depreciation of the exchange rate.

These provisos are frequently forgotten both by critics of my balance of payments thesis and by those who accept it too readily.

A Self-Correcting Mechanism?

The IMF staff – not surprisingly in view of the history of the organization – were initially sceptical of what I was saying. However, a remarkably similar analysis crept into the IMF's *Economic Outlook* in the following year. In a sense all I was doing was harking back to the assumptions of an earlier age. No Chancellor of the Exchequer in the days of the classical gold standard before the First World War – the only previous occasion when complete freedom of capital movements existed – lost any sleep over the balance of payments. Indeed, since the only figures available then were for visible trade, and these were even less accurate than those we have today, he had little idea of what the size of the UK current surplus or deficit was. It is, incidentally, interesting that six out of the eight economies for which reasonable data for that era are available ran current account deficits averaging more than 2½ per cent of GDP – that is, in terms of the UK and the money of 1992, more than £15 billion – in the years prior to 1914.

Treasury officials, notably Terry Burns, continued to defend the downgrading of the current account at hearings of the Commons Treasury Committee after my resignation in October 1989. But in the absence of a Ministerial lead, efforts to develop the Lawsonian heresy further – at least for public consumption – inevitably lapsed. Be that as it may, a number of practical questions clearly arise from my thesis. For example, how does one distinguish between a current deficit that is a symptom of domestic overheating and one that reflects merely the normal international flow of borrowing and lending? Domestic overheating apart, when – if ever – is a current deficit excessive? When is a currency depreciation the right answer?

So far as the first question is concerned, there is no foolproof way of deciding if a deficit is a sign of overheating. But a clue is provided by *changes*. A deficit that has been running for several years without much change and been readily financed is unlikely to be a symptom of inflationary pressure. But a sudden increase, such as that experienced in the UK when it went from zero in the early part of 1987 to some 4 per cent of GDP in 1989, is indeed likely to be a sign of such pressure. The second question, whether a purely private sector deficit can ever be too great, is more difficult. The answer I suggested in my September 1988, IMF speech was in two parts. I mentioned first:

> . . . the arithmetic of debt accumulation and debt service costs. Persistent large imbalances do become a problem as flows compound and therefore by definition become unsustainable. But even for deficits of the size we have seen recently in the major countries, this problem emerges quite slowly. As the OECD has suggested, the effective constraint is not so much the size of the current account imbalance as the country's overall creditworthiness, in which net overseas assets play an important part.

But this was clearly an extreme and unlikely constraint; and in general I was sceptical of the case of Government action even when the deficit was due to low net private sector savings. Here I came to the most controversial part of my speech, the 'self-correcting' doctrine:

> The main source of fluctuations in net savings is changes in the amount of borrowing by the private sector. There is a limit to the amount of debt which the private sector will be willing – or can afford – to undertake. Once that limit has been reached, the savings ratio will rise again. Moreover higher debt means higher interest payments in the future, which will reduce disposable income and consumption . . .
> It is only in the unlikely event that the self-correcting mechanisms threaten to stretch over so long a period that the creditworthiness constraint to which I have alluded comes into play that it would be appropriate for the Government to run a large budget surplus in order to offset the lack of private sector savings.

The heart of the matter was that the obsession with the current balance of payments was a hangover from the period when the Government was expected to manage the whole economy. A corollary of the switch to market ways of thinking in the 1980s should have been that the Government was responsible for its own finances and the private sector for *its* finances. If the Government's finances are in order, then excessive borrowing, whether at home or overseas, is a private sector matter, which will be automatically corrected. For the non-bank private sector does not have access to a lender of last resort and cannot get out of its debts by depreciating the currency. As for the self-correcting thesis, the UK experience of the early 1990s showed clearly that it does indeed operate. The savings ratio, after falling very sharply, did indeed rise again as borrowing was cut back severely. But it can be a painful process. And meanwhile the Government's finances went into sizeable deficit.

Needless to say, my IMF speech was not intended as a purely theoretical dissertation. I had a number of practical objectives, of which probably the most important was to question the automatic assumption that a country which was running a deficit of, say, 2 per cent of GDP was an automatic candidate for devaluation, and one running an equivalent surplus was an automatic candidate for revaluation. In the first place there might not be a problem at all. But even if there were, it is the savings/investment balance which should be tackled in the first place.

It is when a normal stabilization programme would require a country urgently to deflate costs and prices that depreciation should be considered. It is probably most appropriate for a country such as Poland, re-entering the world market economy after a period of rigid controls during which its cost levels had been allowed to lose touch with the rest of the world. In a normal Western economy, persistent unemployment is much more likely to be a symptom of labour market failure than an overvalued currency; and frequent devaluations will serve only to entrench a high inflation mentality without improving job prospects at all.

CHAPTER 69

TOWARDS AN INDEPENDENT BANK OF ENGLAND

Latin America: the Brady Plan · Not in Our Back Yard
An Accident-Prone Month · The Tape that Never Was
An Independent Bank of England · Margaret Thatcher's Response

Latin America: the Brady Plan

WHILE I HAD DECIDED not to resign after the 1988 Budget when, in retrospect, and as Thérèse advised me at the time, I probably should have done, my US opposite number, Jim Baker, exhibited a better sense of timing. Jim stepped down from the job of US Treasury Secretary at the end of August 1988, in order to manage his friend George Bush's presidential campaign, in the confident and correct expectation that Bush, if elected, would appoint him Secretary of State.

We had worked closely together throughout his term at the US Treasury, and I was sorry to see him go. In his farewell letter to his G7 colleagues Jim wrote that 'our common effort to develop and implement an effective economic policy co-ordination process to address global economic problems represents an enduring monument to economic co-operation among our countries'. Regrettably, 'enduring' was scarcely the *mot juste*. Effective international co-operation in the economic field, as in most other fields, is impossible without the full-hearted participation of the United States; and with Jim Baker's departure the process more or less ground to a halt.

Jim was succeeded as Treasury Secretary by another old friend of George Bush, Nick Brady, the courteous, old-money chairman of the blue-blooded Wall Street investment bank, Dillon Read. But whereas in their different ways both Jim Baker and his predecessor, Don Regan, had been political heavyweights, Nick Brady was not. Nor did he have any interest in international financial co-operation in any real sense. I first met him at the Fund and Bank annual meetings in Berlin in September 1988. At that time he had been in office for less than a month, so his unfamiliarity with the matters under discussion was hardly surprising. But when, in early January 1989 I took a day trip to Washington – such are the wonders of Concorde – to have a full-length discussion with him, à deux, it was clear that the economic centre of gravity in the United States had moved to Paul Volcker's successor as Chairman of the Federal Reserve Bank, Alan Greenspan. The new Chairman's lugubrious appearance and slow speech belied the man himself, who was clever, quick and excellent company.

It was at Berlin, incidentally, that I was formally nominated 'Finance Minister of the Year' by the remarkably successful *Euromoney* magazine, the first Chancellor of the Exchequer to have received the award. It seemed that I had been a contender for some years, and that the tax-reforming Budget of 1988 had clinched it – just in time, some would add. The modestly proportioned inscribed silver salver was within the financial limit of gifts Ministers are permitted to accept. It was also about this time that I became the longest-serving Treasury Minister this century.

Looking back on Berlin in the autumn of 1988, it is strange to recall that the main focus of political attention was the violent demonstrations by crowds of Red and Green militants, not all from Germany, protesting against capitalist exploitation – as represented by the IMF and assembled bankers and finance ministers – of the developing world. This led to the tightest security I can ever recall at a Bank and Fund meeting, and may well have caused the Germans to regret their coup in securing Berlin as the venue for the meeting in the first place. But of the momentous events that were to lead to the dismantling of the notorious Berlin Wall and the acknowledged triumph of capitalism little more than a year later, there was at that time not the faintest inkling.

Nick Brady's sole interest in the international scene was the Latin American debt problem. This arose partly from his Wall Street background and his concern for the US banks which had the greatest exposure to Latin American sovereign debt, but even more – as he made abundantly clear – from George Bush's concern, as President, that without some alleviation of their debt burden the United States' southern neighbours would acquire governments hostile to the US. There had been a number of riots in Latin American capitals which had made the White House distinctly nervous. Brady set out, with some success, to make this the focus of G7 attention.

He began by launching in early January 1989, in broad-brush terms, what inevitably became known as the Brady plan, with a view to securing the endorsement first of the G7 when it met in Washington on 2 February, on the eve of a meeting of the IMF Interim Committee, and then of the Interim Committee itself. The plan had been largely worked out by David Mulford, the long-serving US Treasury official who had been elevated to be Brady's number two on the international side – Jim Baker's number two, Dick Darman, having left when Jim did, subsequently to emerge as Bush's Director of the Office of Manpower and the Budget. The moustache-sporting Mulford, with his somewhat self-conscious good looks, was remarkably unpopular among his European opposite numbers. This was largely by virtue of his attempt to railroad often ill-considered proposals through meetings of the G7 deputies not by force of intellect or charm of personality, but by the assumption that the representative of the superpower called the tune.

The Brady plan, which Mulford had largely devised, contained two main proposals. One was for the World Bank and the IMF to divert a quarter of their lending to Latin American governments to enable those governments to buy back their own debt at a discount. The other was for the two international financial institutions to underwrite, by means of funds or guarantees, the payment of interest by the Latin American governments to the creditor banks; in return for which the banks would agree to accept a lower rate of interest.

Not in Our Back Yard

I did not like it at all. It had, most unwisely, been launched with a great fanfare and little detail, in a way that had inevitably aroused expectations among the debtor countries of a far greater degree of debt relief than was remotely realistic.

I had long been aware, as I recorded in Chapter 41, that the great bulk of these debts would never be repaid in full. But that was a different matter, as I saw it, from the taxpayer relieving the banks of part of the risk of existing sovereign debt, which not only partially baled out the banks but was bound to lead to further demands by the debtor countries for the world's taxpayers to get them out of their difficulties.

I was particularly unenthusiastic about all this because the pre-Brady debt strategy had by that time succeeded in its objective of enabling the world's commercial banks to strengthen themselves sufficiently to remove the threat to the banking system as a whole that had originally existed. What this was about was essentially solving a political problem in the United States' back yard; and that, as I saw it, was a matter for them. If they wished to increase their aid programme to Latin America that was their concern. But to expect the taxpayers of the western world as a whole to shoulder the burden of financing this aspect of US foreign policy was something I found profoundly unattractive. Indeed, it was to be only a matter of months before events in Eastern Europe were to provide the European members of the G7 with a far more persuasive case for economic assistance considerably closer to home.

But when it came to the G7 discussion on 2 February, the only serious opposition to the Brady plan came from Gerhard Stoltenberg, the German Finance Minister, and myself. The Americans had already struck a deal with the Japanese before the G7 meeting, in which Japan had agreed to support the Brady plan in return for US support for Japan's ambition to supplant the UK in the number two spot in the IMF hierarchy. The French, persuaded by Brady that his plans were in harmony with the proposals that President Mitterrand had earlier put forward, also supported the Americans, while the Canadians would never cross swords with the US unless a clear and distinct Canadian national interest was involved. Giuliano Amato, the likeable, intelligent, and somewhat birdlike Italian Socialist Treasury Minister who was shortly to lose his job, only to reappear as Prime Minister in 1992, made it clear to me in private that his views were close to those of Stoltenberg and myself; but he was unwilling to stick his head above the parapet.

At the end of a very long and at times heated G7 discussion, a compromise was struck. There was no agreement on any extra money for the World Bank and the IMF to lend to Latin America; but it was agreed that a proportion, yet to be decided, of their *existing* resources could be set aside to finance the repurchase of debt at a discount, provided proper economic reforms were being implemented. There was agreement neither on the amount of debt to which the arrangements would apply, nor on the interest support proposal.

It was essentially this compromise proposal that was then agreed by the Interim Committee. In my speech to that committee, I argued that we should continue to stick to the two key principles by which we had effectively been guided hitherto. The first was that responsibility for solving their economic problems lay with the debtor countries themselves; only they could put in place the essential economic reforms, without which international aid would be merely throwing good money after bad. The second was that it was up to the debtors to negotiate directly with their creditors – that is, for the Latin American governments to negotiate directly with the banks – just as occurred in the case of normal industrial and commercial bad and doubtful debts.

An Accident-Prone Month

A short while earlier, in November 1988, I suffered the most accident-prone month of my Chancellorship. The famous Great Ormond Street Hospital for Sick Children had for fifty years been living off the royalties from James Barrie's *Peter Pan*, which Barrie had left to the hospital in his will. As the fifty years drew to a close, and the copyright expired, a fresh source of income was required; and an ambitious campaign known as the 'Wishing Well' appeal was launched, with a mass of fund-raising events.

One of these was a so-called 'flower power ball' at the Camden Palais in north London, with a 1960s theme. A friend of Thérèse's who was organizing the event was anxious that we should be there and bring with us our good friends Adam Faith and his wife Jackie; since Terry (to give him his real name) had originally sprung to fame as a 1960s pop star and might be persuaded to perform. The event, on 21 November 1988, coincided with Margaret's annual eve-of-session dinner at Number 10. But it was no trouble, after the dinner, to get out of my black tie and into an open-necked red striped shirt and red velvet smoking jacket – my minimal concession to the 1960s theme – and arrive with Thérèse, Terry and Jackie in good time at the Camden Palais. Nor was I particularly surprised to find, on the way out in the small hours, at least one press photographer waiting to take a picture of any celebrities (the film actress Joan Collins was also at our table) who emerged.

Unfortunately, I had to get up at six the next morning, as usual, to go through my boxes. So I had had little sleep when, next morning, we all trooped to the bar of the House of Lords, in the customary way, with senior Cabinet Ministers and their Labour opposite numbers to the fore, to listen to the Queen reading the speech we (the Cabinet) had written for her, setting out the Government's programme for the coming session. As I stood there, my eyes momentarily closed. It was only for a split second; but with the whole thing recorded live on television it was a simple matter for that particular frame to be frozen and the photograph published in all the papers alongside that taken outside the Camden Palais, with a 'morning after the night before' story. It was all good-natured; and although undoubtedly embarrassing, my sole real concern was that it might have appeared disrespectful to the monarch. But knowing the Queen's lively sense of humour, I was not too worried.

The much more serious gaffe had occurred a little earlier that month. It had always been my general policy to avoid mass briefings on 'lobby terms', a phrase that means that full use may be made of what is said provided that both direct quotation and direct attribution are avoided. Obviously I had private conversations with individual journalists, but press conferences in which journalists are expected to restate one's words in lobbyspeak ('senior Ministers are concerned that . . . ') seemed a recipe for misunderstanding and trouble. If I had something to say, it was better to put it in my own words and take the responsibility.

However, there had been four annual exceptions to this: the meeting with the journalists who composed the parliamentary lobby proper after both the Budget and the Autumn Statement, and the meetings with the political correspondents of the Sunday papers, who called themselves the Sunday lobby, on the Friday after the Budget and the Autumn Statement. When Robert Culpin became press secretary we agreed on two important but unrelated innovations. The first was that the two briefings of the parliamentary lobby paper would be entirely and explicitly *on* the record: the status of my two Sunday lobby briefings would be clearly established at the time. The second innovation was that all my on the record conferences at the Treasury and at Number 11 would be openly – indeed ostentatiously – taped. This was partly so that the Treasury knew exactly what I had said, but partly for my own protection against misquotation or misrepresentation.

Despite these sensible precautions, the briefing I gave the Sunday lobby after the 1988 Autumn Statement, on Friday, 4 November, proved a total disaster. Margaret was on her travels, and most of the senior political correspondents were with her, so it was for the most part a rather less experienced second eleven who attended my briefing at Number 11. Robert Culpin had just ceased his long and successful stint as my press secretary, and this was the first lobby briefing at which his new and at that time inexperienced successor, John Gieve, had officiated. There was confusion over whether the briefing was on the record or on conventional lobby terms: he had said nothing at the meeting itself, but when he was asked afterwards he said it was on the record, believing this to be my wish. When he reported this to me, I told him that, on the contrary, I had been speaking on lobby terms. He agreed to telephone those who had been present to explain the position. This was embarrassing for him and sounded very suspicious to them; but I was not too concerned because (as I thought) I always had the tape transcript to fall back on.

The reader will recall that the main purpose of the Autumn Statement was to set out the Government's public expenditure plans, and that the main drama in 1988 had been over the continued freezing of child benefit. It was no great surprise, therefore, when the journalists' questioning concentrated on social security issues, particularly since there had been a Tory back-bench revolt over charges for eye tests that very week. What was a great surprise, and shock, was the banner headlines in the press the following Sunday, alleging that I was planning to do away with universal benefits for pensioners, in particular, in favour of means testing; and to cease uprating a number of benefits in line with inflation. These highly coloured scare stories were backed by leading articles, of which the worst was probably that in the *Mail on Sunday*, which pontificated 'The Government's determination to "means test" every single benefit available from the State to the ordinary citizen will be met with predictable cries of outrage.' Even the *Sunday Mirror*, no friend of the Government's, had conceded that 'the state pension is safe'.

What, in fact, I had said, according to one of the journalists' shorthand notebooks that subsequently came to light, was that 'We have to see in the evolution of the social security system whether we can do better, so that we can help the minority of pensioners who genuinely do have difficulty in making ends meet.' My purpose in all this was to head off the pressure for a *general* increase in pensions, over and above inflation; and I made my remarks in the knowledge that John Major (as Chief Secretary) and I were already engaged in discussion with the Social Security Secretary, John Moore, about a targeted scheme to provide additional help to the oldest and neediest pensioners.

The Tape that Never Was

When this damaging travesty appeared in the Sunday papers, I got hold of John Gieve as soon as I could and told him to publish the full transcript of the meeting as the best means of killing the story. It was only then that he revealed, to my horror, that – due to his own inexperience – he had failed to set the tape-recorder properly, as a result of which nothing had been recorded at all: there was no transcript. Furious though I was at this, the real villains were clearly the members of the Sunday lobby; and when I agreed to appear on the radio programme, *Today*, on the Monday morning, I laid into them for their fevered imagination and deplorably low standards, which led them to publish stories that bore no relation to what I had said.

The Opposition clearly thought they were on to a winner. The same day, Monday, 7 November, Neil Kinnock tabled a Private Notice Question to me asking me to make a statement on my intention to introduce further means-tested benefits for pensioners. This was the first occasion in more than 30 years that a Leader of the Opposition had asked a Private Notice Question of anyone other than the Prime Minister: the normal convention is for a Minister to be asked a Private Notice Question by his opposite number. I replied simply that:

> I have no such intentions except in one respect. I have been discussing with my right hon. Friend the Secretary of State for Social Security a scheme to give special help to poorer pensioners. This would be over and above the existing level of benefits. We shall announce the outcome of this consideration in due course.

This did not prevent the mild-mannered and normally sensible Labour back-bench social security expert, Frank Field, from saying 'We in the Labour Party have rarely got our teeth near an election winner. We have one today and we do not intend to take them out.'

However, one of the journalists who had been present at my briefing,

Jack Warden of the *Sunday Post*, had taken full shorthand notes of the meeting, and had decided there was nothing worth publishing on the Sunday. He made his notes public in the *Daily Telegraph* and *Evening Standard* early the following week. They entirely corroborated my own version of the incident. I was reminded of the true story of a distinguished political correspondent I knew who, many years previously, when he had first become a member of the lobby, was telephoned by his editor one night to demand why he had not got a story which, as the first editions showed, the other papers were all running. My friend explained that he had not filed the story because he happened to know that it was not true. 'That doesn't matter,' his editor replied, 'if the others have all got it, we must have it too.'

That does not mean that Governments cannot make good use of the lobby system: they can and do. The prime example is the Number 10 press secretary – in Margaret's time, Bernard Ingham; but other Prime Ministers' press secretaries before him had done much the same, albeit in a very different style. This works, however, because the Number 10 press secretary is such a regular source of information that no journalist is likely to risk biting the hand that feeds it. By contrast, a Minister whose contacts with the lobby are few and far between has no such leverage.

But by the time the full account – with which I had no quarrel – of what I had actually said came out, the press had changed the subject. The new issue that transfixed them was the mystery of the missing tape. The following Sunday the *Sunday Times* ran the banner headline 'Lawsongate' – a reference to Nixon and Watergate – strongly implying that I had been guilty of suppressing the tape because of its incriminating nature, and by implication lying about it. A number of other papers took a similar line, despite the fact that, as the full account had shown, I had no motive whatever to suppress it: indeed, its absence was a severe handicap to me. As a result of my November 1988 experience I never gave another briefing on lobby terms, nor did I ever again speak to the Sunday lobby.

An Independent Bank of England

But for me the most important event of November 1988 was my submission of a five-page memorandum to Margaret on 25 November* setting out a carefully worked-out proposal for an independent Bank of England – a proposal I first revealed publicly in my resignation speech to the House of Commons eleven months later. I had first thought seriously of the idea during the summer recess of 1988. When I returned from holiday in September of that year I amazed and horrified my officials by asking them

*See Annexe 3 for full text.

to devise a concrete proposal for an independent but accountable Bank of England. When they realized that I really meant it, a small but high-level group was formed, which worked with the utmost dedication and in the greatest secrecy throughout the autumn, with periodic meetings with me. The Bank of England was not told: it was important that the Government should make up its own mind itself.

The purpose of my proposal was to entrench the use of monetary policy to fight inflation and secure price stability. This would be a far more useful constitutional reform than any advocated by Charter 88 and other constitution-mongers. Part of the background to it was the repeated rejection by Margaret of ERM membership. An independent Bank was to some extent an alternative way of entrenching the commitment to stable prices and, as I put it in my paper, 'making it a permanent feature of UK economic policy, while at the same time assisting us in the completion of our present task'.

An independent Bank would not, of course, have had the merit of ERM membership of replacing discretion by rules. But it would at least, in the words of my paper, 'be seen to be locking a permanent anti-inflationary force into the system, as a counterweight to the strong inflationary pressures which are always lurking'. In particular, it would do something to 'depoliticize interest rate changes'. I also sought to persuade Margaret that an incidental advantage of creating an independent national central bank, with a proper statutory framework, would be to demonstrate that we did not envisage the absorption of the Bank of England into a European central bank.

The advantages I envisaged sprang not from the illusion that the Bank of England possesses any superior wisdom, but from the logic of the institutional change itself. I was certainly not proposing to hand over responsibility for monetary policy to the Bank of England for it to interpret in any way it liked. I had in mind a Bank working under a completely new statutory framework, with an explicit statutory obligation to preserve the value of the currency. Three important consequences would flow from this. First, monetary policy decisions would be taken not by a Government, which has a number of objectives, but by a central bank statutorily charged with the achievement of one sole objective. Second, unlike Ministers, who are subject to political and electoral pressures, central bankers would be largely immune to such pressures. An incidental consequence of this is that international financial co-operation is likely to be very much easier between independent central banks, all charged with the same task, than it is between governments with different domestic electorates to appease.

But third, and in many ways most important, even if there were to be a Government genuinely committed to put the conquest of inflation above all other objectives, and genuinely determined to ignore all political and electoral pressures to stray from the path of virtue, it would never enjoy the same degree of market credibility that an independent central bank has. And this extra market credibility is what would make the successful conduct of monetary policy less difficult. It is no accident that it was the independent Bundesbank, and not the German Government, that possessed the market credibility to be the anchor authority for the ERM.

At first sight, without a written constitution, it might seem that the independence of the Bank of England would be pretty flimsy. But I argued that there would in practice be powerful market sanctions against the repeal of the legislation by a future Government: the mere announcement of the intention to do so would be so damaging to confidence that a future Government would be extremely reluctant to attempt it. The longer and better the independent Bank's track record, the more powerful this sanction would be.

Despite its deep dislike of the loss of power involved, the official Treasury, on investigating the matter, had to concede that the change was technically feasible. The Bank would be responsible for setting short-term interest rates and monetary targets, while the Government would remain responsible for the exchange rate régime. The Bank would then carry out monetary policy within that framework. Of course, all sorts of examples can be constructed in which there is a tension between the two assignments. Yet there is a similar division of responsibility in both Germany and the US, which works better than the UK arrangement under which, so far as monetary policy is concerned, the Bank of England takes its marching orders from the Chancellor of the Exchequer. Anyone looking for perfection will not find it in this world.

I concluded my minute by saying that the proposed change 'would provide a beneficial jolt to inflationary expectations and would help lock into the body politic of this country a permanent anti-inflationary force'. My plan was to publish a White Paper on Budget Day of 1989 and have the necessary legislation introduced in November of that year.

Going into slightly greater detail, I proposed that the Bank of England should be obliged, like the Bundesbank, to co-operate with Government economic policy 'but only so far as that is consistent with its primary function of safeguarding the currency'. One big change was that the Treasury would be responsible for Government borrowing, and for repaying debt when the Government was in surplus. But it would be required to sell exclusively medium-term and long-term debt, so as not to add to money or liquidity. The Bank would be able to use a portion of the Government's foreign exchange reserves for intervention within limits which could not be exceeded without Government permission.

Although independent, the Bank would be accountable: in particular, it would be answerable to Parliament in the sense that the Governor would regularly appear before a suitable select committee constituted explicitly for that purpose. A further safeguard, both for independence and for accountability, might be to make the appointment of the members of the Court (or Council) of the Bank, other than the Governor himself, subject to the Select Committee's approval. To secure independence, members would be appointed for eight years at a time.

Margaret Thatcher's Response

When, a few days later, I discussed my paper with Margaret, I was disappointed but not surprised to find her wholly unreceptive. She did not ostensibly reject it out of hand, but argued that it was something that could be considered only when inflation was low and coming down. At the time of our discussion the latest headline rate of increase in the RPI was a shade under 6 per cent, and edging higher; and although the more reliable underlying rate was lower, at 5¼ per cent, it too was edging higher. In those circumstances, she contended, an announcement that the Government proposed to hand over the responsibility for monetary policy, and thus for the fight against inflation, to an independent Bank of England would look as if the Government were admitting that, after all, it was unable to bring inflation down itself, which would be highly damaging politically.

There was undoubtedly something in this, although at the time I did not myself consider it a decisive argument. No-one at that time expected inflation to go on rising as much as it did or for as long as it did. The Treasury forecast in the Autumn of 1988 was that headline inflation would peak at under 7 per cent in the summer of 1989; and by November 1989, when I had suggested the Bill be introduced, the forecast suggested that headline inflation would be back to around 5 per cent and edging lower. I saw no problem in introducing a Bank of England (Independence) Bill in those circumstances. In the event, of course, headline inflation in the autumn of 1989, when I revealed my proposal in my resignation speech, was some 7½ per cent, and the underlying rate a shade over 5 per cent. Moreover, even then few expected that – partly thanks to the effect of the Poll Tax, and partly to the temporary effect of the Gulf War on oil prices – it was not to peak for a further year, at a shade under 11 per cent on the headline basis and a true underlying rate of 7½ per cent.

Nevertheless, a long historical look suggests that the 1990 bulge in the rate of inflation was indeed a blip rather than a change of trend. Yet it did not seem so at the time, and might not have remained so without the firm and unpopular, if belated, action I took on interest rates in 1988–89. Indeed in October 1988, when I discussed the proposal with Margaret, base rates were already at 12 per cent, implying almost 7 per cent in real terms, on the basis of the underlying RPI – and, of

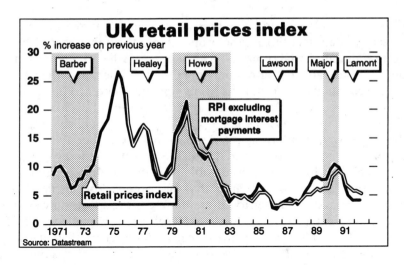

UK retail prices index

% increase on previous year

Barber Healey Howe Lawson Major Lamont

RPI excluding mortgage interest payments

Retail prices index

1971 73 75 77 79 81 83 85 87 89 91

Source: Datastream

course, the rate for borrowers is always appreciably above base rate. I certainly did not feel that I was running away from the measures needed to bring inflation down, and proposing to pass the baton to an independent Bank of England as a gesture of defeat. On the contrary, I was anxious above all to entrench our counterinflationary commitment and policies against the vagaries of future governments, possibly of a different political complexion

Even so, I would have been content for my proposal to have been put on the back-burner until not merely the Treasury forecast of inflation, but inflation itself, was coming down, had I believed that that was Margaret's sole concern. However, I strongly suspected she was using the unripe time argument over an independent Bank of England just as she had used it over the ERM. And as the discussion developed I became increasingly convinced that her opposition to the idea went far beyond the question of timing.

She seemed quite incapable of accepting the possibility that there might be another government some day, and that it was in the national interest to entrench counter-inflationary policy against that eventuality. So far as she was concerned, she really was going to go on and on and on, as she had told a television interviewer she would. While she was there, she was not going to give up the levers of power which the control of interest rates, as she saw it, represented.

It was, in a sense, the ERM argument all over again. Unlike the ERM, however, there was at least no problem of losing face, even though by that time this undoubtedly told against any proposal, at least in the monetary policy and exchange rate area, that emanated from me. I concluded that

871

my best bet was indeed to come back to it later, but in the meantime to choose a good moment to get the proposal into the public arena, in order to secure a groundswell of back-bench support – which I felt was, on this issue, a considerably better bet than my Cabinet colleagues. In the event, the preoccupations and problems of my final year in office prevented me from getting round to this; and it was indeed to make up for my failure to do so when in office that I launched the proposal publicly in the most high-profile way, in my resignation speech of 31 October 1989.*

It appeared to have the desired effect. Support for the proposal from senior back-benchers was considerable, and the serious press began to take up the issue. The Labour Party was predictably hostile; but the Liberal Democrats, in order to differentiate their product, duly espoused it. So, more significantly, did Michael Heseltine, who made it one of his policy planks in his campaign to succeed Margaret in 1990. However, despite the fact that Margaret had departed, and Michael was once again a senior Cabinet Minister, the Government formed by John Major after the election victory of 1992 showed no sign of movement on this issue. I sense that its time will come – as indeed it should.

It is, incidentally, sometimes forgotten that the Conservative Party, under Margaret Thatcher, stated in its 1977 policy document *The Right Approach to the Economy* that 'we favour a more independent role for the Bank of England'. Although that was only some 18 months before we took office for the first time, nothing became of it. In fact, it is not difficult to see why. A close reading of the text shows clearly that what was envisaged was a Bank of England with an independent voice but with no independence of action – the sort of ill-considered if well-intentioned compromise that oppositions, who are themselves condemned to voice without action, tend to espouse. A moment's reflection reveals that this would achieve the worst of all worlds. Whereas a genuinely independent Bank of England, responsible for setting interest rates in the context of a statutory obligation to promote price stability, could greatly enhance credibility, a central bank empowered only to criticize publicly the economic policy of the Government of the day would, in fact, diminish credibility. All the same, the 1977 policy document could be a foundation on which to build.

In Heathite terms, it may be argued that what I proposed would turn the Chancellor of the day from a one-club golfer to a golfer who has to remain in the clubhouse because he has no clubs at all. But this serves only to demonstrate the folly of the original analogy. With responsibility for monetary policy transferred to an independent Bank of England, a future Chancellor would still have everything that a Finance Minister in a country with an independent central bank has to do.

*See Annexe 4 for full text.

872

That is no sinecure, including as it does the control of public expenditure; tax reform; the whole of the rest of the supply side, from labour market measures to privatization; and a whole raft of international financial issues, both within the European Community context and in the wider world – to name but a few of the non-monetary matters that occupy a large part of this book.

For good or ill, however, there was a limit to how much I could brood over these issues at that time. Within a very few weeks of presenting my proposal for an independent Bank of England I was fully occupied with the 1988 Autumn Statement, after which I had to get down to preparing what was to prove my last Budget.

CHAPTER 70

1989 – MY LAST BUDGET

Down to Earth at Dorneywood · Colleagues Against Alcohol
The Search for Savings Incentives
The Lingering Death of Stamp Duty
The End of Earnings Rule · Official Secrecy
Envoi: A Fair Deal for Married Women

Down to Earth at Dorneywood

SINCE I NOW HAD the use of Dorneywood, it would have been absurd to have decamped to Chevening for the traditional January Budget planning weekend. Because of its modest size, however, there was no possibility of providing overnight accommodation at Dorneywood. This meant no wives, and concentrating on getting through the business in a single day – Saturday, 7 January. The Dorneywood staff rose to the occasion magnificently, and everyone was well looked after. We made an early start, and succeeded in finishing by dinner time; leaving those who wished to do so to stay on after dinner for snooker and bagatelle.

The Dorneywood bagatelle book, in which anyone who makes a score of a thousand or more is invited to record the event for posterity, goes back quite a long way, with Churchill's one of the earlier signatures. A little application enabled me to add mine to the long and distinctly mixed list. It was while the others were snookering and bagatelling after dinner that Peter Middleton saw me privately and told me of his intention to get married again. I was delighted, as was Thérèse; and we lost no time in inviting Peter and Connie to dinner at Number 11. The warm and outgoing Connie was to be a great comfort to him following the tragic death of his only son in a climbing accident some three years later.

874

The background to the 1989 Budget was clear: the overriding need to ensure that the inflation blip remained only a blip. This meant that interest rates, which at the turn of the year stood at 13 per cent, would have to be kept high enough for long enough to put inflation on a firm downward track, whatever the short term cost.

The usual pre-Budget economic paper warned that the struggle could be harder and longer than the official forecasts envisaged. Consumers might choose to borrow even more to sustain their standard of living through what they might imagine would be a temporary monetary squeeze. The net wealth of the personal sector was still sufficient to allow banks and other lenders to churn out yet more credit. That would postpone the adjustment in behaviour, and necessitate higher interest rates for longer, increasing the eventual agony by raising the overall level of indebtedness. That is more or less what happened. All forms of personal borrowing continued to increase sharply in 1989 and even in the first half of 1990.

The official forecasts for once slightly over-stated the growth of output; but they continued to understate its *level* and therefore the pressure it was putting on resources. However their biggest flop by far was the inflation forecast. The rise in the headline RPI, which had reached 6½ per cent in the last quarter of 1988 was expected to decline steadily to 4½ per cent by the second quarter of 1990. In the event it rose unsteadily to 9¾ per cent in that quarter before peaking at not far short of 11 per cent in September and October of 1990. The error was due to the failure to forecast the momentum of the rise in underlying inflation, which required further interest rate increases not expected by the forecasters, thus magnifying the rise in the headline RPI, thanks to the absurd inclusion of mortgage interest payments in the index. On top of that, the Whitehall machine failed to foresee either the full impact of the poll tax on the index, or (with considerably more excuse) the short-lived rise in oil prices following Saddam Hussein's seizure of Kuwait in August 1990.

So far as the Budget itself was concerned, I consciously aimed at a surplus – of no less than £13¾ billion, similar to the latest estimate of the outcome for the previous year. This still allowed me to reduce taxation by almost £2 billion in the coming financial year. Half of that – rising to four-fifths in a full year – went on the National Insurance reduction for the lower paid described in a previous chapter.

Nevertheless, I did not want the 1989 Budget to be called a 'Budget for the Poor'. To do so would be inviting the 1988 Budget to be indelibly labelled a 'Budget for the Rich', with 1989 as a penance for it. More fundamentally, such a label would have entrenched just the sort of confusion between the tax system and the social security system from which I was trying to get away: that is to say, the misconception that tax cuts are handouts, like benefits, but differ from them because they are usually given – with immoral perversity – to the rich. In fact the tax system, as I saw it, was about how much was taken from people and how it was taken, with a view to what was best for the economy. It was the purpose of the social security system to help the poor. Indeed, I never liked the idea of budgets 'for' any particular section of the population. They were intended to benefit the economy and thus the country as a whole.

As it happened, the 1988–89 Budget surplus turned out, at £14¾ billion, to be even higher than expected, while that for 1989–90 eventually came out somewhat lower at just under £8 billion. Such variations are to be expected given the vagaries of the economic cycle, interest rate changes and so on. But I was still well on target for the medium-term aim of a balanced Budget.

Because of my deliberate policy of allowing surpluses to accumulate in years of above trend growth, the Government repaid in the three years to the end of March 1990, as I told the House of Commons, 'roughly a sixth of the public debt that had accumulated over more than two centuries'. But I was anxious to scotch the idea of repaying the whole National Debt as an objective of policy, which had attracted Margaret and which Cecil Parkinson had misguidedly promoted in public speeches. I specifically rejected the idea as 'deferring for a long time the benefits of a reduction in the burden of taxation'.

In 1989–90 the economy actually slowed down somewhat faster than the official forecasts envisaged; but the starting point was a higher level of activity and of pressure on resources than was realized; and both the current account balance of payments deficit and the inflation rate continued to rise and did not start to turn down until the following financial year. As in 1987 I omitted to revalorize of the excise duties, at a cost of just over £1 billion. At a time of large Budget surplus this temporary way of shaving the top off what was then forecast to be a brief blip in the RPI seemed worth trying. But the recrudescence of inflation proved to be a rather more substantial blip than that of 1985.

Colleagues Against Alcohol

My failure to revalorize the excise duties was despite the fact that I had received – as in the previous year – a solemn deputation from a group of colleagues Margaret had asked to look at all aspects of the problems of alcohol, particularly among the young. It was headed in 1989 by the then Home Secretary, Douglas Hurd, and came to Number 11 to plead the case for an increase in the excise duties on alcohol on grounds of social policy. Though deeply unpopular with the general public, increases in the duties payable on alcohol always meet with almost as much approval among the *bien pensants* of Parliament and the serious press as do increases in the tobacco tax.

This perennial puritanism was lent additional weight in 1989 by the fact that Margaret had become greatly concerned about football hooliganism the previous summer, and had set up a committee to explore methods of combating it. It led, *inter alia*, to the launch in January 1989 of the ill-fated Football Spectators Bill, which aimed to establish a national football club membership scheme. The committee also concluded that alcohol consumption by football hooligans might be reduced if its price were increased through higher excise duties. This was unlikely. If experience was anything to go by, hooligans would simply consume less of the more highly taxed drinks and more of the less highly taxed ones. For that reason, raising the excise duty on alcohol – unlike petrol, the demand for which is almost completely unaffected by an increase in the duty – rarely raises the tax yield. However, it does have a disproportionate effect on the Retail Price Index, as the Hurd delegation was well aware.

The Search for Savings Incentives

Savings incentives were at the time much in vogue. I learned on the grapevine that Margaret had held an informal seminar at Chequers on the subject the previous autumn without inviting me – an instance of her growing desire to keep me at a distance. If any good practical ideas had emerged I would presumably have been made aware of them, so it was clear they had not.

Despite that, as previous chapters have made clear, I was interested in the idea of fiscal incentives to increase savings in the long run. The problem was that most such incentives simply substituted the transfer of existing savings from one medium to another at the expense of the Exchequer. What I did not believe was that fiscal incentives of this kind could help in reducing inflationary pressure in the short term. I was in no doubt that the best short-term deterrent to borrowing was a sufficiently high interest rate. As I was to say in my Budget speech, 'inflation is a disease of money; and monetary policy is the cure. The role of fiscal policy is to bring the public accounts into balance and to keep them there and thus underpin the process of re-establishing sound money.'

Base rates were already 13 per cent and I reaffirmed that interest rates 'will stay as high as is needed for as long as is needed'. I also said, in a passage which bears on the depth of the recession of the early 1990s:

> The question of just how 'soft' or 'hard' the so-called landing will be is not in the hands of Government alone. The Government's task is to reduce inflation by acting through monetary policy, to bring down the growth of national income in money terms. The task of

> business and industry is to control their pay and other costs. The
> more successfully they do so, the less costly in terms of output and
> employment the necessary adjustment will be.

I did, in fact, take the opportunity to increase the attraction of PEPs, as outlined in Chapter 30. In addition I raised the annual limit on employee share schemes and on SAYE share option schemes as well as trying to encourage employee share ownership plans (ESOPs). Deterrents to unit trust investment were removed.

There were also some tightening-up measures. The life assurance tax regime, which dated back to the First World War, was hideously complicated. The Inland Revenue very much wanted to clarify and simplify the tax rules, and in June 1988 I authorized it to issue a consultative document on the taxation of life assurance. The changes I made in response to that document were highly technical, but resulted in some increase in the tax burden on life offices. The net effect of the changes was expected by the Revenue eventually to increase the tax yield from the life assurance industry by £250 million. It was a further modest step towards the erosion of the excessive tax privileges of the institutional investment industry.

Much more important was the cap on occupational pensions, whose long-term effects I have already discussed (see Chapter 29) and which led to a vitriolic pamphlet from the National Association of Pension Funds, entitled *Truth, Honour and Democracy*. The most awkward resistance, however, came from within the official machine. The cap on tax relief applied to public sector pensions as well as private. The Treasury mandarins made a determined – but unsuccessful – attempt to persuade me to exclude them. I am sure they have subsequently secured adequate compensation for this setback.

The Lingering Death of Stamp Duty

The major omission from the 1989 Budget was the abolition of Stamp Duty on share transactions. I had decided at the Dorneywood meeting to announce its demise in the Budget. The precise timing of its disappearance would be linked to the switch planned by the London stock exchange, and then expected to occur at a relatively early date, from the traditional system of settlement via share transfer (which were the documents that were actually stamped) to its proposed high-tech paperless settlement system, Taurus. (The process was known by the engaging name of 'dematerialization'.) The fate of the tax was sealed anyway, under European Community legislation, which forbade transaction taxes of this kind, and its abolition was much sought after in the City, where turnover had still to recover from the slump which followed the 1987 crash. I had halved it in my first Budget from 2 per cent to 1 per cent, and halved it again in 1986, but it had remained unchanged since then. I thought it preferable to abolish it as an autonomous act rather than wait until it was forced upon us by Brussels.

As work went on after Dorneywood, however, it became clear that the total cost of the emerging package was becoming too great. That was Margaret's main concern, too, when I discussed the Budget with her. The choice boiled down to either a less substantial reform of National Insurance Contributions or deferring the abolition of Stamp Duty on share transactions. Despite the fact that Stamp Duty abolition would have been something I could present as an encouragement to savings, at a late stage I decided to defer it.

The Inland Revenue was deeply disappointed by my last-minute reprieve for the tax: they were concerned about the practical problems of taxing dematerialized transactions. In fact they need not have worried: the stock exchange made such a mess of Taurus that delay followed delay in its introduction. At that time, however, this unhappy saga was far from clear, and I placated the Revenue by promising them to abolish the tax in the following year's Budget. My successor, John Major, did indeed announce his intention to abolish it in his first and only Budget in March 1990, although the much-delayed introduction of Taurus meant that Stamp Duty on share transactions was still with us in 1992.

The End of the Earnings Rule

The last-minute removal from the 1989 Budget package of the abolition of a Stamp Duty on share transactions meant that I had to forfeit my record of abolishing at least one tax in every Budget I presented. In 1989 I had to make do instead with the abolitions of the pensioners' earnings rule. Under this long-standing rule, pensioners who continued to work during the five years after they had reached the age of retirement had their pensions docked. It was an understandable source of grievance, which was why we had promised to do away with it in our original 1979 manifesto. However, nothing had hitherto been done about it, partly because it was felt that, with unemployment high, it was folly to encourage the elderly to get jobs which younger workers badly needed. But quite apart from other considerations, demographic trends clearly showed that the 1990s and beyond would see a steady deterioration in the ratio of the working population to the non-working population, as youngsters stayed longer in education and, more importantly, people lived longer. To deter from work fit men and women in their sixties who actually wanted to work made no sense at all.

Official Secrecy

The 1989 Budget did include one minor curiosity. It is often forgotten, particularly in the light of the much-publicized GCHQ and *Spycatcher* affairs, that it was in fact the Thatcher Government that liberalized the Official Secrets Act of 1911, a far more important event than either of the other two. At the time of the Budget the Bill which became the Official Secrets Act of 1989 was passing through Parliament. The new legislation repealed the notorious catch-all Section 2 of the 1911 Act and replaced it with six clearly defined categories, broadly speaking confined to matters involving national security in the strict sense and relations with other countries.

When consulted, I had readily agreed that economic and financial information should not fall within the ambit of a reformed Official Secrets Act. But it was clear to me that, for totally different reasons, taxpayer confidentiality remained as vital as ever. I therefore included in the 1989 Finance Bill provisions making it a specific criminal offence for officials or former officials of the Revenue Departments to reveal information about the tax affairs of private taxpayers. The need for this was fully accepted both by my ministerial colleagues and by Parliament, where the relevant clauses were agreed without a division.

That, I thought, was the beginning and end of my involvement with the Official Secrets Act, of whose reform I had long been a strong supporter. Alas, I was wrong. Out of the blue, all Cabinet Ministers were informed that the traditional classification of Government papers – as 'Restricted', 'Confidential', 'Secret' and so on – duly marked on every page, would henceforth have to be confined to the narrow range of matters convened by the 1989 Act. If there were matters outside this range which a Cabinet Minister wished not to be disclosed, the papers could simply be marked 'private'.

This was not something that had even been raised at any of the consultations that preceded the publication of the Bill, and it seemed to me madness. A number of matters discussed in Treasury papers are highly market-sensitive – the most obvious examples being matters concerning the exchange rate and many of the pre-Budget papers. I had no desire to make it a criminal offence to reveal their contents, but equally I had no wish to let it be thought that their confidentiality was no longer so important, which the abandonment of the traditional system of classification would inevitably mean. The proposal was clearly seen as the logical consequence of the liberalization of the Official Secrets Act. It seemed to me the triumph of Whitehall tidy-mindedness over common sense; which, if agreed, would create a wholly unnecessary problem. I argued that far and away the simplest and safest solution was simply to continue with the old system of classification, which served a clear and useful purpose. I ran into considerable ministerial and mandarin opposition, but eventually Margaret agreed.

Envoi: A Fair Deal for Married Women

Although it has nothing whatever to do with the 1989 Budget, ostensibly the subject of this chapter, it is fitting to conclude my accounts of the tax changes for which I was responsible during my six years as Chancellor with the reform which, I believe, is least likely to be reversed by any of my successors. I refer to the independent taxation of married women.

Income tax law, as it stood when I first entered Number 11, made no bones about married women being second-class citizens. In a form of words unchanged for the best part of two centuries, it roundly declared that 'A woman's income chargeable to pay income tax should be her husband's income and not hers.' However simple this made life for the Inland Revenue, in the 1980s it was, I felt, an unacceptable anachronism, completely denying married women either independence or privacy in their tax matters. It is true that the system had been, to some extent, mitigated in 1914 by the introduction of the option of separate assessment, which allowed a wife to file her own separate tax return and receive her own separate assessment for tax. But the basis for that assessment remained unchanged: her income was still taxed as if it were her husband's.

The old system was indefensible in pecuniary terms, too. Under it a husband enjoyed a married man's allowance amounting to rather more than 1½ times the single person's allowance. A wife who was earning enjoyed the wife's earned income allowance, which was the same as the single allowance, while a non-earning wife had no allowance at all. Thus a couple with two earners would have a combined allowance equivalent to roughly 2½ times the single allowance, compared with roughly 1½ times the single allowance for the couple where only the husband was an earner.

This seemed to me manifestly unjust. A couple where the wife ceased paid work to have, and look after, a baby suffered a double blow at that point: not only did the wife's income disappear, but the tax system turned against them, too. Moreover, because there was a wife's earned income allowance but no allowance at all for savings income, the system was particularly harsh on a wife who had managed to accumulate some savings of her own. This, coupled with the fact that the wife had to reveal the full details of her savings to her husband, since the income from them was taxed as if it were his, was an increasing source of resentment. Finally, in most cases the old system meant that there was a financial penalty on marriage, as distinct from living together unmarried.

There had already been one Green Paper on the subject of the taxation of husband and wife, produced by Geoffrey in 1980, but the response had been inconclusive. It certainly showed that the status quo had very few friends, but as so often, there was no agreement whatever over the various options for change that were clearly set out. Despite Geoffrey's strong desire to right this wrong, the unhelpful response to his Green Paper, coupled with Margaret's pronounced hostility to doing anything at all (partly, I suspect, because she believed it was all inspired by Geoffrey's wife, Elspeth), ensured that no further action was taken.

It therefore fell to me, when I became Chancellor in 1983, to pick up Geoffrey's baton. It seemed to me that the next stage should be a White Paper, setting out the Government's preferred option. After careful study, I came to the firm conclusion that this should be a system of independent taxation, with the allowances freely transferable between husband and wife. This would remedy all the grievances created by the old system.

When I discussed this with Margaret, however, she made it clear that she did not like the idea at all, and felt that there was nothing really wrong with the status quo. She was emphatic that a White Paper was out of the question. Although my officials had warned me of her views, I had expected a woman, and a married woman at that, to be more receptive to the strong sense of grievance felt by so many married women about the old system. But it was clear that, despite her oft-pronounced and no doubt deeply felt belief in the importance of the family, in practice she strongly identified with the two-earner couples, who (in financial terms) were the beneficiaries of the old system. I suggested that there was a long-term electoral bonus to be secured from being the party that emancipated married women so far as the tax system was concerned. She countered by claiming that all we would do was alienate working wives, on whose votes we depended.

En passant, I have to say that I have never liked this distinction between 'working' and 'non-working' wives. There are, of course, idle married women, but they are very few. Most of the wives who are described as 'non-working' are so described because they work at home (frequently very hard) and not outside it, have no employer and receive no wage. Moreover, among a very large number of pensioner couples, it is often the so-called non-working wife (and pensioner wives were bound to be particularly numerous among the beneficiaries of any move to independent taxation) who works the harder of the two.

Be that as it may, I clearly had my work cut out if I was to get anywhere on this issue; but I was disinclined to give up. Following the success of my 1984 Budget, in which I radically reformed company taxation, Margaret accepted my proposal that I should have a go next at reforming personal taxation, and that this should be preceded by a Green Paper.

Although the Green Paper procedure is not one to which I was often attracted, least of all in the field of tax, my 1984 Budget had propelled tax reform into the centre of the political debate, certainly within the Conservative Party. As a result, there were a number of reforms being floated (or re-floated), such as a tax credit scheme, involving a degree of integration of the tax and benefit systems, along the lines that had been proposed, but never enacted, by the Heath Government, and the amalgamation of the National Insurance Contribution and income tax systems, which had been exhaustively studied within the Treasury (under the unattractive acronym NICIT) during Geoffrey's last year as Chancellor.

Both these proposals were superficially attractive, and could not be dismissed lightly; on the other hand, I had pronounced reservations about both. A Green Paper seemed to me the best means of getting the disadvantages as well as the advantages of these schemes into the public arena – which should then give me a freer hand to introduce those reforms I wished to bring about. Moreover, I pointed out to Margaret that, if we were going to have a Green Paper on the reform of personal taxation, we could not avoid a chapter on the taxation of husband and wife, which we had left hanging since Geoffrey's 1980 Green Paper. On the clear understanding that this was a Green and not a White Paper – that is to say, a basis for discussion without any commitment on the part of the Government – she consented to this, and agreed to my announcing the Green Paper in my 1985 Budget speech.

This I duly did, and took the opportunity to make the case for a system of independent taxation with transferable allowances. I explained it in these terms:

> Everyone, man or woman, married or single, would have the same standard allowance. But if either a wife or a husband were not able to make full use of their allowance, the unused portion could be transferred, if they so wished, to their partner.
>
> This reform would produce a more logical and straightforward system. Far more people would be taken out of the poverty and unemployment traps, and indeed out of tax altogether, for a given sum of overall tax relief, than is possible under the present system. It would end the present discrimination against the family where the wife feels it right to stay at home, which increasingly nowadays means discrimination against the family with young children.

Under the scheme I had in mind, the revenue for providing the wife with her own personal allowance under the new system would in essence have come from phasing out the 'bonus' enjoyed by the two-earner household. I proposed to move gradually to the new system, on the 'no cash losers' principle. This is always possible so long as there is inflation: while I would far rather have seen inflation eradicated, if one is suffering all the evils it brings, it is folly not to put it to good use when one can.

At the time of the Budget I had planned to publish the Green Paper in the autumn of 1985. I entrusted the work of drafting it to Frank Cassell, a senior Treasury official (and Kent cricket fanatic) who had originally been a financial journalist and was a master of good, clear English: he did an excellent job. But any thoughts that I was home and dry were soon disabused when Margaret insisted that that particular chapter would have be cleared by an *ad hoc* Cabinet Committee which she would chair. It required a large number of meetings, at which I was ably supported by John Moore, then Financial Secretary, and was quite a struggle.

Margaret showed herself to be out of sympathy with the project altogether. A number of spending colleagues, in particular Norman Fowler, then in charge of the DHSS, saw it as a plot by me to outflank Cabinet by pre-empting for tax cuts resources that otherwise might have been available to increase public spending. This was not, fortunately, an argument that had much resonance for Margaret; but she insisted that what I was proposing was the wrong kind of tax cut: the right way to help families with children was by reinstating the old child tax allowance – a proposal of singularly little merit which I knew to be a hobby-horse of hers (she was always proposing it).

I was rather more surprised to find it enthusiastically supported by Norman. Fortunately I was able to head it off, with the help of David Young, whom I had seen privately and demonstrated to him the benefits of my proposed scheme in terms of the so-called unemployment trap. In addition, although not of course on the Committee, the formidable Emma Nicholson, whom Margaret had made Women's Chairman at Central Office, was a strong supporter, and I persuaded her to lobby Margaret with her customary vigour.

In the end, Margaret reluctantly agreed to authorize the publication of the Green Paper on Budget Day in 1986 – insisting yet again that she was doing so only because it was a Green Paper and therefore did not commit the Government to acting on it – despite the strong preference it expressed for independent taxation with transferable allowances.

I had hoped that the response to the Green Paper would be so strongly favourable that I could use this as the clinching argument for action at long last. Unfortunately, it was nothing of the sort. Very few ordinary people responded at all – although those who did were generally in favour. Response came for the most part from the various women's lobbies and pressure groups, many of which had their own pet scheme they wished to promote. Moreover some women, whose support I had hoped for, argued that transferable allowances would destroy all the gains to privacy that they and I both sought, since husbands and wives would still have to reveal their incomes to each other to decide which of them should have the allowance. This surprised me, since the wife for whom privacy was important could always purchase it cheaply enough by letting her husband keep the transferable allowance.

What I plainly lacked was the mandate for action for which I had hoped. There was a real risk that, as a result, we would be left with the status quo – the one thing that almost everyone agreed they did not want. Still determined to find some way out of the maze, I drafted a holding statement for Norman Lamont, who had taken over from John Moore as Financial Secretary in the 1986 reshuffle, to make in the course of the 1987 Budget debate. The key passage went as follows:

> The Government do not yet feel that there is sufficient support to take a decision now to go ahead with so far-reaching a reform . . . We will be considering the matter further and will be exploring whether there is any satisfactory halfway house to the approach in the Green Paper.

At the time, I had not the faintest idea what any 'halfway house' might be; but there the matter rested until after the 1987 General Election. Reconfirmed as Chancellor, I resumed discussions with the Inland Revenue. By now the earliest I could act was in the Budget of 1988, and the Revenue warned me that the implementation of a system of transferable allowances was so complex that, with the computerization of income tax still being bedded in, there was no way my preferred scheme could start before 1993. That was the other side of the *next* General Election, and I was determined to have a scheme up and running during the lifetime of the Parliament that had just begun.

So a halfway house it had to be, and one without fully transferable allowances. When I got down to it, it did not take too long to work out the specification of the new system. There would be genuine independent taxation, with everyone, man or woman, married or single, having the same standard allowance, being legally responsible for their own tax return, and being taxed at the rate appropriate to them as individuals. The allowances would not be transferable.

On top of that, however, all married couples would have an additional married couple's allowance (equivalent, initially, to the difference between the single allowance and the married man's allowance, but which ideally should be allowed to wither on the vine). This would, for administrative simplicity, initially go to the husband; but in the event of his not having the income to make use of it, he would be able to transfer it to his wife. On this basis, the Revenue assured me, they could have a scheme legislated for in 1988 up and running in 1990.

I decided to go ahead. Although inferior to independent taxation with fully transferable allowances, it was so superior to the old system, and went so far towards remedying all the existing grievances, that it would have been folly not to go ahead. But there was still the matter of persuading Margaret. I decided that, for once, I could make good use of the Party Conference. I was due to reply to the debate on the economy and taxation on 8 October 1987, and the chairman for that session was to be Joan Seccombe, then Vice Chairperson of the National Union (the organization representing the voluntary Party workers), and an ally on this issue. I invited Joan to Number 11 before the Conference, and she agreed to call in the debate a number of women speakers who were likely to be in favour of independent taxation. She did, and they were; enabling me to begin my reply to the debate with some ostensibly impromptu opening remarks:

> I was struck by the number of speakers today who raised the question of the tax treatment of married women. Let me say to them, and to you, Madam Chairman, that I agree that the traditional tax treatment of married women is no longer acceptable, and that change will have to come.

Margaret, who was on the Conference platform alongside me, heard for herself the tremendous cheer that pledge evoked. When we returned to London, I told her that I had revised my plans for independent taxation in the light of the views she had expressed, and remarked on the strength of feeling expressed at the Party Conference. I gave her a persuasive outline of the 'improvements' I had made, and said that I wished to announce the reform in the coming Budget and legislate in the 1988 Finance Bill, with a view to embarking on the new system in 1990. She asked to see a paper on it, but agreed in principle.

Thus it was that, at long last, independent taxation came into being, and for the first time married women were given a fair deal by the tax system. The announcement in my 1988 Budget received a warm welcome on all sides, and the Revenue kept to their side of the bargain with implementation in 1990. In both his 1991 and 1992 Budgets, Norman Lamont sensibly refrained from indexing the Married Couple's Allowance, and attracted no criticism for so doing. Moreover, he was able to announce in 1992 that the one discriminatory feature I had been obliged to leave in the system, the payment of the Married Couple's Allowance in the first instance to the husband, which at that time was all that the Revenue could administratively cope with, would as from 1993 be removed. The couple would opt to which one of them it should go, with it split down the middle if they were unable to agree.

Throughout the rest of my time in the Commons, I could still get a cheer among an audience of women whenever I wished by referring to independent taxation. Yet it came to pass only after the best part of five years' struggle by me, built on the foundations of four years' battle by Geoffrey. The moral is clear. The achievement of worthwhile radical reform requires the continuity in office of a single Party for a considerable period of time, and preferably a similar continuity among its senior Ministers, too.

CHAPTER 71

EUROPE AND THE DAWN OF EMU

1985 and the Single European Act · The Role of Jacques Delors
My Opposition to Monetary Union · The Road to 1992
The Tax Approximation Row · Margaret Thatcher Unites Europe

1985 and the Single European Act

IN WRITING THIS ACCOUNT of my time as a Minister, and in particular my unusually long time as Chancellor, I have tried to inject a degree of coherence by dealing with different issues in different chapters in a broadly logical sequence. But in one sense this gives a false picture of the job, since the overriding reality is that, to a considerable extent, everything is happening at the same time. Perhaps the abrupt leap from the independent taxation of married women to the issues of Europe in general and Economic and Monetary Union in particular serves at least to give a flavour of the true nature of Chancellorial life.

I observed in an earlier chapter how, in retrospect, 1985 was in many respects a watershed year: it was then that all the elements that were to bring about the downfall of Margaret Thatcher five years later originally emerged. This was certainly the case with Europe. I refer here, however, not to the ERM, although it was indeed in November 1985 that I made my first and most substantial unsuccessful attempt to persuade Margaret that the time had come for sterling to join the mechanism. That, although of the first importance, was never something I saw primarily in European terms. Certainly, I was conscious that our self-imposed exclusion from the ERM greatly diminished our authority and influence within the Community. But that was never why I wanted to see sterling within the ERM. My case, as readers will be aware, was wholly in terms of the balance of economic argument: the assistance that ERM membership could provide in the conduct of economic policy in general and the fight against inflation in particular.

The important event on the European front in 1985 was the meeting of the European Council in Luxembourg at the beginning of December, where Margaret agreed to the first ever substantial amendment to the Treaty of Rome, known as the Single European Act.* It was a fateful step.

The Single European Act covered a wide range of issues, but three stood out as being of particular importance. The first was an explicit target for the completion of the European common market, rechristened, to make it sound as if it were a new initiative, the Single Market, by the end of 192. The legal obligation to bring into being a genuine common or single market within the Community was, of course, enshrined in the original 1958 Rome Treaty; but once internal tariff barriers had been removed and the common external tariff established, progress had more or less ground to a halt. The second was a substantial extension of majority voting on matters where previously unanimity had been required by the Treaty, in order to make it less difficult to meet the end-1992 deadline. Indeed, in the economic field majority voting was extended to cover almost everything, the most conspicuous exception being taxation.

Margaret had originally been opposed to any extension of majority voting, since the requirement for unanimity gave her a precious blocking power, which she was more than happy to use, over any new Commission proposal in any of the areas where the unanimity rule applied. When she grudgingly allowed herself to be persuaded that a major move to majority voting was essential if the single market was ever to be achieved, she consoled herself by assuring the House of Commons, in her Statement announcing the outcome of the Luxembourg European Council, that 'The Luxembourg compromise, whereby a member state can invoke a very important national interest to prevent a decision being taken, is unaffected.'

Whether this unwritten article of the Community's constitution, a legacy of de Gaulle, could in practice amount to anything was never put to the test, thanks to the bizarre policy the Foreign Office had developed over the compromise. It had been invoked by the UK just once during the Thatcher years, by Peter Walker when he was Minister of Agriculture. What Walker had done, however, was to make it quite plain that he had no serious reservation about the matter concerning which he had threatened to invoke the Luxembourg compromise, but that he would carry out his threat unless he received satisfaction on another front. This was, of course, a wholly illegitimate use of the

---

*The actual signing of the Single European Act was not until February 1986; but that was purely a formality. The UK was represented by the junior Foreign Office Minister, Lynda Chalker.

compromise, and the others quite properly ignored it altogether, leaving Walker with egg on his face.

The Foreign Office was horrified and, believing that the Walker episode had severely, if not mortally, wounded the Luxembourg compromise, developed a policy designed to ensure its survival. This consisted of two principles. The first was that if any other member country sought to invoke the compromise, the UK should always support it so as to prevent the compromise from being undermined – which indeed we did, even when this was contrary to the UK's interests in the particular issue at stake. The second was that the UK should never invoke the compromise itself, since it could not risk having it overridden a second time. When I discovered that the Foreign Office had developed this bizarre doctrine, and had persuaded Margaret that it was necessary if the compromise was to be preserved, I wrote to Geoffrey, with a copy to Margaret, pointing out that this more or less guaranteed that the compromise could be used only in a way that was harmful to the UK, which did not seem particularly sensible.

In fact, I had to write more than once to Geoffrey pointing out how unsatisfactory the current policy was, and that it clearly needed to be reviewed and changed. Eventually even the Foreign Office had to recognize elementary logic, and Geoffrey agreed that our policy towards the Luxembourg Compromise should be reviewed. The outcome of the review was still unclear at the time of my resignation in October 1989.

The third key provision of the Single European Act was what was clearly understood by both our major partners and the Commission to be a commitment to the achievement of Economic and Monetary Union (EMU). The preamble to the Act explicitly recalled the European Council's 1972 commitment to the objective of 'the progressive realization of Economic and Monetary Union'. This was a commitment which, over the intervening 13 years, had certainly fallen into desuetude and had arguably expired, since the 1972 commitment was to the final achievement of Economic and Monetary Union by 1980 – which made its revival in 1985 particularly significant. Moreover, the Act itself contained a chapter providing for closer economic and monetary co-operation in Europe – which would have been perfectly acceptable had it not been headed 'Co-operation in Economic and Monetary Policy (Economic and Monetary Union)'.

The Role of Jacques Delors

The plan to include in the Single European Act – which in effect created a new Treaty superseding the original Rome Treaty – a reference to EMU as an agreed objective had first surfaced early in November 1985, when Luxembourg, which at that time held the six-monthly rotating Community presidency, tabled a proposal to that end. They had been put up to it by Jacques Delors, who had become President of the European Commission in January 1984 – an event, incidentally, that should never have occurred. It had been agreed informally by all the member governments of the Community that when the Commission Presidency became vacant at the beginning of 1984, it was Germany's turn to fill it. Late in the day, however, Helmut Kohl, the Federal German Chancellor, pathetically announced that Germany could find no candidate of sufficient stature for the post, and that he had therefore agreed with President Mitterrand that it should go to France instead.

Until then, Delors had been my French opposite number as Mitterrand's first Finance Minister, so I had got to know him quite well. Slight, bespectacled, studious and unprepossessing in appearance, he was one of the cleverest men in Mitterrand's administration and one of the toughest, too. An intellectual, he compensated for not having made it to France's intellectual élite – he was not an *Énarque* or even a *Polytechnicien*, let alone an *Inspecteur des Finances* - by becoming a workaholic. Indeed, when I first came across him he had made himself ill by going without a holiday altogether, until he was forced to do so.

Like many intellectuals from a deeply Catholic background, he had a profound need to believe in some ideal. From an early age there had been two candidates for this role: socialism, reflecting to some extent his modest social origins, and Europe, where he had been inspired by working for Jean Monnet. His socialism had always been more social than economic in character; nevertheless the disaster over which he had to preside, and courageously steer a way out of, when the Mitterrand government entered office in 1981 committed to a socialist economic policy which proved so disastrous that it had to be completely abandoned within 18 months, undoubtedly took some of the bloom off his belief in socialism and made the European star shine brighter.

His other main characteristic was a single-minded appetite for power. I remember his telling me in the autumn of 1983 that Mitterrand had tried to persuade him to accept the job of Prime Minister, but that he had declined because under the French system, when the President was of the same Party, the Minister of Finance enjoyed more real power than the Prime Minister. Of course, all sensible politicians want power, since it is only through power that anything can be achieved; but with Delors this trait was particularly well developed. The trappings of power interested him not at all: it was power itself that mattered to him.

So when he agreed to leave the job of Finance Minister to become President of the Commission I was under no illusion as to how he was likely to behave. Indeed, it was a particularly happy niche for him; for it did not take a great deal of ingenuity to promote the notion that anyone who questioned the transfer of power to the Commission in Brussels was *ipso facto* a bad European. Regrettably, as he came to identify the sacred cause of Europe with himself, he became increasingly thin-skinned and intolerant of criticism.

My Opposition to Monetary Union

My own opposition to the idea of a single currency for Europe went back a long way. In June 1970, the Conservative Party, led by Ted Heath, took office and almost immediately embarked on negotiations to secure the UK's belated membership of the European Community, an objective I strongly supported. I had been a believer in closer European unity ever since my days as an undergraduate at Oxford in the early 1950s, well before the European Community had come into existence, when I had been President of the Strasbourg Club, a student society dedicated to that then unfashionable end. But my idea of Europe was that of de Gaulle's *Europe des patries*, a Europe of nation states, rather than the single federal superstate, or United States of Europe, which some espoused. Then, when the European Community came into being, and showed that it could work, I welcomed it as an inspired constitutional innovation far more intimate than any alliance, but less than a federation, providing a framework in which independent nation states could work together as never before.

Then, a few months after the Heath Government had opened negotiations for UK entry to the Community, the Werner Report on Economic and Monetary Union was published, recommending a common European currency. The implications appalled me, since it clearly implied doing away with the Community in favour of a single European superstate. As I wrote in *The Sunday Times* on 22 November 1970:

> . . . a national currency lies at the very heart of national sovereignty. A common currency is something that can only properly follow political union: it cannot precede it. It is significant that whereas the *Zollverein* or customs union paved the way to the German Federation a century ago, it was only after Prussia and Bismarck had achieved a political union, with blood and iron, that a common German currency could be born.

The heads of government of the Community member states, without any analysis of either the political or the economic consequences of what they were doing, and in most cases without the faintest understanding of what those consequences might be, duly committed their countries in 1972 to the goal of full Economic and Monetary Union by 1980, as the Werner Report had recommended; and promptly turned their minds to other things. When this sleeping dog was at last woken up by the Luxembourg proposal of early November 1985, I lost no time in minuting Margaret to warn her about it. On 14 November I wrote to her in these terms:

> The inclusion of EMU as a Treaty objective would be a political commitment going well beyond previous references to EMU, which have been non-binding European Council resolutions or solemn declarations. It would be perceived in political terms as a major change.

> Our objective in my view should be to avoid any amendment to Article 107 [this was the article in the Rome Treaty concerning exchange rates]. The Delors proposal is unacceptable both politically and in substance. So also is any reference to EMU.

Margaret took the point; but I remained concerned. At that time it was still the rule – as indeed it remained throughout my time as Chancellor – that, irrespective of the matters under discussion, Finance Ministers were not permitted to attend meetings of the European Council. The only colleagues the heads of government were able to take with them were their Foreign Ministers. This had originally been inspired by a patronizing pronouncement of the first President of the Commission, Walter Hallstein, that 'The business of the Community is politics, not business' – which, translated, meant that the European ideal must not be impeded or debased by contact with awkward realities – and had been perpetuated by the desire of Europe's Foreign Offices to protect their privileged position.

Yet despite the fact that when, in the 1970s, Giscard d'Estaing and Helmut Schmidt inaugurated the annual summits of the industrialized world, it was taken for granted that Prime Ministers would be flanked by their Finance Ministers as well as by their Foreign Ministers, the absurd and unhelpful exclusion of Finance Ministers from European Councils was something that Margaret never once challenged. Since I was not to be present at the Luxembourg Council, and the Foreign Office would inevitably be soft on the issue, I minuted Margaret again on Thursday, 28 November, 1985, just ahead of the Council which was due to start on the following Monday:

> Your line might be:

> 'There should be no reference in the Treaty to EMU, since this – which implies progress towards a common currency and a common Central Bank – would be no more credible to outside opinion than the commitments entered into in 1971 and 1972, and is in any case politically unacceptable to the UK.'

In the event, she was able, with German support, to get the Treaty reference to EMU watered down, but not removed altogether; and, preferring the on-the-spot advice of the Foreign Office, who told her that what remained was little more than hot air, to the counsel I had proffered in advance, she signed up. The great prize was allegedly the target of completing the single market by the end of 1992 and the facilitation of this by a large-scale move from unanimity to majority voting. I was sceptical about the wisdom of the deal she had struck. I felt that we had embarked on a dangerous slippery slope towards EMU; whereas the move to majority voting, which had been strongly urged by Delors as essential if Europe was to regain the momentum it had latterly lost, would have been agreed even without EMU.

The Road to 1992

Certainly, it was necessary to inject a new dynamic into the stalled progress towards the completion of the common or single market, and the 1992 deadline was to assume considerable importance both in maintaining the momentum and in changing for the better the perception of Europe overseas. Moreover, although the target was, in the event, not to be met, the progress made was impressive. But in achieving this, enshrining the 1992 target in a new Treaty was less important than two other factors that had already occurred. The first of these was the appointment, at the beginning of 1985, of Arthur Cockfield as the senior UK Commissioner and his securing of the internal market portfolio, as it was called. His formidable intellect, mastery of detail and above all his drive soon made a profound impression. He had published his seminal Community White Paper *Completing the Internal Market* which included the 1992 target date, early that year, and had had it endorsed at the June 1985 European Council in Milan; and having got his teeth into this bone he was not going to let go of it.

The second critical breakthrough which ended the log-jam, that had hitherto caused progress towards a genuine common market to grind to a halt was the acceptance by the Commission of the so-called passport principle established by the *Cassis de Dijon* case. Ever since its inception, the Commission had been busily trying to create the common or single market by the typically bureaucratic and absurd method known as 'harmonization': the process of imposing a common European standard for every conceivable product, satirized in the *Yes, Minister* episode about the Euro-sausage. Not surprisingly, progress became completely bogged down.

Then came the European Court's decision in the *Cassis de Dijon* case. This is an agreeable French blackcurrant liqueur, best added in very small quantities to chilled dry white wine to make the excellent summer drink, Kir. The import of this drink was banned in Germany because it did not conform to any of the German standards of alcoholic strength, and no common European standard had been agreed. The Court decided that since it was permissible under French standards, it must be accepted anywhere else in the Community. This was the great breakthrough: the recognition that harmonization was unnecessary for the completion of the single market. All that was needed was the principle that any product that conformed to the standards of one member state, must be free to compete throughout the Community. The only common European standards that needed to be established were those covering a limited number of matters such as safety, financial prudence, and some forms of pollution.

The Tax Approximation Row

In general, I had nothing but admiration for Arthur Cockfield's drive to complete the single market. Unfortunately, as a tax expert and former Inland Revenue man, he chose to concentrate most of his efforts on a fruitless and pointless effort to secure the harmonization or, in the post-harmonization jargon, 'approximation' of rates of indirect taxation throughout the Community. Arthur produced a plan according to which every member state would have to have two rates of VAT which could vary only within a range of between 4 and 9 per cent for 'essential' goods and between 14 and 20 per cent for the rest; and the same excise duties – the extra taxes which most countries levy on a limited range of products, notably petrol, alcoholic drinks and tobacco – which he suggested should be some sort of average of the existing range of duties, with only a very small variation indeed permitted.

Not only was this largely irrelevant to the single market – the United States is manifestly a single market, yet sales taxes vary from State to State – but there was never the remotest possibility of getting agreement on the excise duties, where the national variations were enormous. To take just one example, the Cockfield proposal for a uniform excise duty on spirits would have required Greece to increase its tax on ouzo by more than 2,000 per cent. The huge differences in excise duties derived partly from the fact that the Calvinist ethos of Protestant Europe tended to lead to higher taxes on alcohol (in particular) than those levied in Catholic and Orthodox Europe, but probably owed more to the secular consideration that those countries that were serious producers of, say, wine or tobacco tended to tax those products less heavily, if at all, than did those that were not. I remember being particularly moved by my Portuguese opposite number arguing that in his country home-produced brandy was the drink of the poor, and that to tax it at the average European rate would be socially and politically devastating.

Since the excise duty nut was impossible to crack, which should have led him to drop the whole idea in the first place, Arthur decided to start with VAT, where the most acute problem – but by no means the only one – was faced by the UK, with our politically sensitive zero rates; in particular for food. The initial Ecofin discussions, however, concerned not so much VAT rates – although the nature of the problem was exposed – as the complex issue of the VAT system, where Arthur tried long and hard, without success, to secure agreement to a highly bureaucratic 'clearing house' system which he had devised but which, to his disgust, found few friends.

It was not really until 1988 that the Ecofin Council returned to the question of tax rates, with a key discussion scheduled for the informal Ecofin to be held under the Greek presidency of the Community at the Astir Palace Hotel at Elounda in Crete – an agreeable place I happened to know well, since we had spent two family holidays there – over the weekend of 17 and 18 September 1988. I decided that Arthur Cockfield's paper ought not to be the only basis for the tax discussion, which was the main item on the Ecofin agenda, and circulated in advance, on 5 September, an alternative paper of my own. Headed 'Taxation in the Single Market – a market-based approach', the paper reiterated my thesis that tax approximation was unnecessary for the completion of the single market; but went on to argue that in any event the Cockfield proposals went far beyond what was necessary to achieve it.

What was essential, my paper argued, was to reduce frontier controls and allow a massive increase in the amount of goods travellers could bring back from other Community countries without attracting any further tax. Market forces would then ensure that a degree of approximation took place, since countries with high tax rates would tend to lose revenue as their nationals shopped in other Member States. The one exception I mentioned in the paper was that – on health grounds – it would be necessary *either* to maintain effective restrictions on the amounts of alcohol and tobacco people could take from one Member State to another without further tax *or* to set high minimum duty rates throughout the Community. This last point was somewhat disingenuous, since it was designed to protect the UK tax revenue. Finally, in so far as tax approximation was a means to an end, the so-called abolition of fiscal frontiers within Europe, this could readily be achieved by a system I sketched out which dispensed with VAT checks at national borders and confined the necessary controls to the traders' premises.

When we came to discuss the matter at the informal Ecofin, I pointed out that the Single European Act had explicitly preserved the unanimity rule for tax matters, that – irrespective of the merits of the issue – there had been a general election the previous year in which we had pledged that we would retain the VAT zero rate for food and a number of other items, and that there was no way in which we could break our solemn election pledge. I added that had we been starting from a *tabula rasa* I would have favoured a single positive rate for everything; but we were not. Arthur's response was to become abusive to the point where he ceased to amuse and started to embarrass my Community colleagues, and to brief the press that there was no way in which an allegedly isolated UK could halt the progress of Europe.

On the surface, my paper, and the case I made for it in Crete, did not appear to get very far. While my colleagues conceded that it was a serious contribution to the debate, when asked which of the two rival approaches they preferred, only Luxembourg supported the UK approach. Denmark abstained, and the other nine declared themselves in favour of continuing the discussions on the basis of the Commission's approach. One of their worries was that my proposal would lead to a Dutch auction in VAT rates, leading to an unacceptable loss of revenue. I replied that, although I was not advocating it – since I argued that it was not necessary – this concern could readily be met by extending my proposal of minimum duty rates for alcohol and tobacco to the other excise duties and indeed VAT itself.

Beneath the surface, it was clear the tide had turned. My opposite numbers' steadily diminishing enthusiasm for the Cockfield proposals, the more they studied them, was not confined to the political difficulties they saw in making sharp increases in some of their excise duties. Those whose indirect tax rates were well above average were equally concerned about the sizeable increase in direct tax that would be forced on them to make good the loss of revenue as they lowered their indirect taxes. All of them were uneasy that, with indirect tax rates rigidly fixed *à la* Cockfield, any increase they needed in their total tax revenues would have to be found overwhelmingly from higher income tax.

When the hitherto stern and unbending Arthur Cockfield came back to the subject, at the December 1988 Ecofin, he had abandoned the idea of a specified band for the main VAT rate, and proposed instead simply a minimum rate of 17 per cent. I welcomed what I called his 'death-bed flexibility'. Not that I was particularly concerned. The expression 'death-bed' referred to the fact that, to Arthur's fury, Margaret had decided to replace him with Leon Brittan when his first and last four-year term as UK Commissioner expired at the beginning of 1989 – his performance over the tax issue having been a major contributory factor to her decision. With Arthur's departure the various Commission portfolios were rearranged, and the poisoned chalice of tax approximation was given to a charming new French Commissioner, Christiane Scrivener.

After the wear and tear of dealing with a dogmatic Englishman, the pleasure of finding myself dealing with a pragmatic Frenchwoman was considerable. Christiane Scrivener wished to bring the whole issue to some sort of conclusion, and knew that the unanimity rule meant that she had to find a solution acceptable to the UK. She saw me privately at Number 11, and again privately over breakfast before the next Ecofin. At the second of these meetings, she agreed to bring forward a new proposal for VAT under which there would be a minimum standard rate of 12 per cent and the UK would retain all its zero rates. She also accepted that, if any arrangement could be agreed over the excise duties – which did not look likely, given the positions of the other member states – it would be on the basis of minimum rates. I warned her that I would have difficulty in getting Margaret to agree even to this; but assured her I would do my best.

I minuted Margaret on 6 February, 1989, seeking her endorsement of this provisional agreement, pointing out that, particularly after starting where we had with the Cockfield proposals, we could claim a major negotiating triumph for the Government, having fulfilled our election pledge to preserve the zero rates and beaten off for all time the Commission's challenge to them. I continued:

> We cannot expect to achieve progress towards practical solutions if we are not also prepared to play a reasonably constructive part in considering issues of real concern to other Member States . . . Moreover, we should lose the initiative which our determined stand in favour of market forces and realism has gained for us.

It was a waste of time. Margaret declared that she would not agree to any further European constraint on the UK's freedom of action to choose its own VAT rate, despite the fact that the idea of the Government wishing to reduce the standard rate of VAT to below 12 per cent was laughable. I was, of course, annoyed that what had undoubtedly been a negotiating success – the press, to a man, had predicted that I would be squashed flat by the Cockfield steamroller – could not see the light of day. But that was not my main concern at all.

Margaret Thatcher Unites Europe

Hitherto, I had frequently been embarrassed by the way Margaret conducted herself within the Community; but it was this episode that first fully opened my eyes to just how counter-productive and damaging to the UK's interests her tactics were. For her, unanimity meant she had a veto; and if you had a veto you used it. It was as simple as that. For everyone else, unanimity gave them a card that could from time to time be played to secure a national objective. Once the others realized that Margaret was playing by quite different rules, there ceased to be any reason, in any of the fields where unanimity prevailed – or in any other field for that matter – to make any concessions to the UK, since nothing could be secured in return.

Moreover, this, along with other aspects of her style and tone of voice, came to irk the others so much that they instinctively sank their differences and joined forces against her. Ironically, by 1989 she had become the Community's great unifying force – and the unity she had forged was a unity against the UK. Partly as a result of her undoubted triumph in the Community Budget negotiations of her early years as Prime Minister, she believed that only head-on confrontation yielded results in Europe; and she revelled in being one against eleven. But on most issues this approach was foolish and threw away many opportunities to build alliances and exploit differences among the others. In particular, we had major differences with our partners over both EMU and the so-called social charter. It was useless to expect any support from any of them over these major issues if we were never prepared to yield anything in return over matters which concerned us less. Yet another unhappy relic of her budget confrontation was a dangerous concentration on detail, at the expense of the underlying trend of events.

Had she proposed withdrawal from the Community altogether, at least there would have been some intellectual coherence. But she knew that was not possible: it would have provoked the biggest split in the Conservative Party since Tariff Reform, which had played a large part in the Party's crushing electoral defeat in 1906 and in keeping it in the wilderness until it was rescued by the need to form a coalition government during the First World War. So she pursued a policy which ensured that, while remaining in the Community, the UK's objectives were least likely to be secured.

In many ways my view of Europe was remarkably close to Margaret's. A great struggle was under way between two rival visions of Europe. As I was to put it in my Chatham House speech of 25 January, 1989, one vision was that of:

> . . . an over-regulated, bureaucratic, protectionist Europe, where uniform standards are enforced by new directives and new regulations from Brussels, where outsiders are excluded, and where competition is seen as a threat, rather than a challenge to greater efficiency; a Europe in which 'regulate and protect' might be the motto. On the other hand, there is the vision of a deregulated, free-market, open Europe; one where competition is seen as the key to improved economic performance; one driven by consumer choice, by transferring sovereignty not to Brussels but to the people.

EUROPE AND THE DAWN OF EMU

I was as determined as Margaret was that it should be that second vision that prevailed. Moreover, I shared her conviction that the political constitution of Europe must remain what it had so successfully become, a Community of nation states, rather than be transformed, contrary to the profoundest instincts of most of its people, into a single European state, albeit of a federal nature. But I departed from her not only in my judgement of tactics most likely to secure these ends and achieve Britain's objectives more generally. Our gut sentiments were just as far apart.

For Margaret, the special relationship with the United States was all-important, and she regarded the continental Europeans with distrust and, in private, with undisguised distaste and hostility. Germany, in particular, increasingly became the butt of the visceral sentiments she had developed during the war. I have no doubt that the reason why Nick Ridley felt it was safe to make the anti-German remarks in his *Spectator* interview, which were to lead to his enforced and reluctant resignation in 1990, was that he had many times heard Margaret utter precisely the same sentiments in private – as, indeed, had I. Margaret was, of course, at all times a politician; and I was never entirely sure how much the saloon-bar xenophobia of her later years represented her own uninhibited feelings and how far she saw it as a potential vote winner. Both elements were present.

But to return to the vexed question of tax approximation. My successor, John Major, discovering the deal that was there to be done on this issue, raised it very early on in his Chancellorship, only to have his head bitten off by Margaret. This so shook him that when, as Prime Minister in 1991, the deal was still on the table – although by then the minimum standard VAT rate had risen from 12 per cent to 15 per cent – it was not until the general election was out of the way and the UK had assumed the Community Presidency, that he eventually accepted it in July 1992. As a result of this long delay and evident reluctance, what was in fact a UK success was made to appear almost a capitulation.

But a success it was. The Community agreed to move to the elimination of VAT checks at national borders on 1 January 1993, a system of indirect tax approximation based on the setting of minimum rates only, at levels which cause no problems for the UK, the acceptance of the UK's zero rates of VAT, and an increase in travellers' allowances with a view to the eventual abolition of any limit at all by July 1999. These are more or less exactly the terms I had privately agreed with Christiane Scrivener and proposed to Margaret in February 1989, and involve no change whatever in any of the UK's indirect tax rates. Nor, indeed, do they prevent us from making any changes we are conceivably likely to wish to make. But all this was merely a prelude to the far greater problems we were to find ourselves in over the much more important issue of EMU.

CHAPTER 72

EMU MOVES TO CENTRE STAGE

Mixed Motives · Mishandling Hanover
France Agrees to Lift Exchange Controls · Bad Blood
The Delors Committee · My Chatham House Speech
EMU Facts and Fallacies · The Delors Report
Disaster with the Dutch

Mixed Motives

Having succeeded, at the Luxembourg European Council of December 1985, in getting the objective of EMU clearly written into the Community's constitution via the Single European Act, it was only a matter of time before those responsible for this coup would launch the process of achieving that objective. Its three main proponents formed a powerful trio, although their motives were rather different.

For Jacques Delors, the position was clear: EMU, and in particular monetary union, was the most promising route to the full European integration he had set as his goal. For François Mitterrand, the perspective was a different one. The political and intellectual leadership of Europe which France regarded as her birthright was threatened by the superior economic strength of Germany and in particular by the unquestioned dominance of Germany's central bank, the Bundesbank, in the crucial field of monetary policy. The only way the French could see of trumping the Bundesbank was to subsume it into a European central bank responsible for a single European currency. For Helmut Kohl, acting very much under the influence of his long-serving Foreign Minister, Hans-Dietrich Genscher, a strong Germany aroused too much fear for it to be able to exercise the political power and influence beyond its borders that its economic strength warranted. The solution was for it to allay that fear by exchanging its German clothing for European attire.

Nor was it hard for the big three to find allies – again, for different reasons. For example, of the other member states of the Community, leaving aside the UK, the largest – Italy – had been a nation state for little more than a hundred years. Indeed, my 1906 Harmsworth Encyclopaedia observes that, even then, 'the consolidation of Italy into one nation cannot be said to be yet complete'. Moreover, not only were the roots of its nationhood shallow, but despite its considerable success in a number of fields, it suffered from an underlying lack of confidence in its ability to govern itself. Handing over the task to some greater European entity, both politically and economically, might be a better bet.

What was most striking about the three main advocates was not only that their motives were different, and at least in the case of France and Germany to some extent conflicting, but that they had committed themselves to achieving this immensely ambitious, highly complex and historically unprecedented act of fusion without any serious attempt to analyse and assess the far-reaching political and economic consequences. It was an astonishingly rash and dangerous way to proceed.

Mishandling Hanover

The launch of the next step came with the assumption of the Community presidency by Germany on 1 January 1988. In the spring the Germans let it be known that their objective at the European Council to be held at Hanover on 27 and 28 June would be the setting up of a committee of experts to recommend the best way of creating a European Central Bank. Margaret had by then become worried at the genie she had allowed out of the bottle by agreeing to sign the Single European Act with its commitment to EMU; and was determined to block the German proposal. In front of the Luxembourg Council I had warned her about EMU, but she had chosen to accept the Foreign Office advice rather than mine. By the spring of 1988, however, as the reader will be aware, relations between us had sadly worsened, and in front of the Hanover Summit she did not even seek my advice, choosing to rely almost entirely on Charles Powell.

Between them they settled on a most extraordinary negotiating objective. Margaret realized that she would have to agree on some sort of study group. So she decided that her objective should be, first and foremost, to get any mention of a European Central Bank expunged from the terms of reference. Her secondary objective was to prevent the study group from being a committee of so-called experts. She always distrusted 'experts', whom she felt produced airy-fairy ideas unrelated to political realities; and believed that any post-Hanover study group should be composed of Central Bank Governors, who not only possessed the expertise required but could be relied upon to keep their feet on the ground. This would also mean that she had her own man on the group, in the shape of the Governor of the Bank of England, Robin Leigh-Pemberton.

The others, when they discovered where she stood at Hanover, must have been amazed at her innocence. At any rate, after a sufficiently long argument to enable her to feel that she had scored a signal success, they agreed that the study group should essentially be a committee of the Community's Central Bank Governors, albeit appointed in their personal capacity, but that the chairman should be, of all people, Jacques Delors – something that so far as I was aware had never even been canvassed prior to the Hanover Council itself: it may have been a Franco–German plot of which the Foreign Office had failed to get wind. Delors had just been given, exceptionally, a second term as Commission President. They also agreed that there should be no reference to a European Central Bank: instead, its terms of reference would be to 'study and propose concrete stages towards the progressive realization of Economic and Monetary Union (EMU)'.

The European Council had met, as usual, on the Monday and Tuesday. On the Wednesday, 29 June 1988, I had my regular weekly bilateral with Margaret. My tact extended to talking about other matters instead. But then she mentioned, as if it were some sort of triumph, her achievement in getting 'them' to drop all mention of a European Central Bank. 'Prime Minister,' I said, 'I'm afraid you've achieved nothing. There is no way that a committee with those terms of reference can possibly do anything else than recommend the setting up of a European Central Bank.' She abruptly changed the subject, no doubt feeling that I was being awkward yet again.

In fact, far from Hanover being a success, it was a disaster so far as anyone with her views or mine was concerned – and the irony is that this was an issue on which our views were very similar. Not that she had an easy task: having sold the pass over EMU and the Single European Act in 1985, the committee set up at Hanover could scarcely have had terms of reference that led to a different destination. But at least she could have avoided the disaster of having Jacques Delors as the committee's chairman, or even as one of its members. Any number of independent experts would have been better than that, and nothing could have been worse than that.

This was not simply because of his well-known dedication to EMU, the whole EMU, and nothing but EMU. It was rather that with the President of the Commission, newly renewed in office, as its chairman the committee's report would inevitably enjoy an authority within the Community that it could never otherwise have secured. At the same time, it was assured of securing the uncritical backing of the Commission to an extent that a report from a group chaired either by the chairman of the Community's long-established Committee of Central Bank Governors (at that time Karl Otto Pöhl), or even by a distinguished independent chairman, might well not have enjoyed.

I claim no great prescience in recognizing the reality of Hanover as I did. What amazed me was that Margaret, and those to whose advice she chose to listen, could have got it so wrong. It may be, I suppose, that she did not care because she was confident that, at the end of the day, nothing would come of it. That might have been a tenable position; but nothing she ever said to me suggested that she held it herself. On the contrary, she took the threat of EMU very seriously indeed. She simply failed to understand what she was about.

Her confusion became apparent when she made her Statement to the House the following day, 30 June. Having announced the formation of the committee, she said:

> The committee's task will be to study and propose concrete steps towards the progressive realization of Economic and Monetary Union. That goal was, of course, set out in the preamble to the Single European Act, which was approved by this House.

This was, incidentally, so far as I am aware, her first tacit admission that the pass had been sold in 1985. Kinnock then observed:

> It is well known that the Prime Minister . . . has said that a European Central Bank is 'not on the cards'. However . . . as it is obvious, as President Mitterrand has pointed out, that a central bank follows from monetary union, is it not clear that the Prime Minister is facing both ways?

To which she responded:

> With regard to the European Central Bank, we have taken part in the Single European Act, which went through the House and which said that we would make progressive steps to the realization of monetary union, and we have set up a group to consider that. Monetary union would be the first step, but progress towards it would not necessarily involve a single currency or a European Central Bank.

The last sentence was positively mind-boggling. Unlike economic union, monetary union had a clearly defined meaning, which had been established in the Community context by the Werner Report as far back as 1970, and which I had spelled out to her on the eve of the 1985 European Council. Now she appeared to be implying that it meant something completely different and relatively trifling, even though she had not the slightest idea of what that might be.

France Agrees to Lift Exchange Controls

Apart from the Hanover European Council, the German Presidency of the Community had been a satisfactory one from the UK's point of view. Within Ecofin in particular, we were able to secure, thanks to Stoltenberg's painstaking work as President, something that I had been urging for a considerable time: a commitment, by all those Community countries that still had them, to abolish exchange controls – for the most part by July 1990. With both Germany and the UK having long since abandoned exchange controls, the key member country whose traditional position had to be changed was France. It was a great help to Stoltenberg that the bulk of the negotiations took place during the brief period when France had a government of the Right and, in Edouard Balladur, a Finance Minister committed to deregulation: indeed, he had already embarked on the process of liberalizing capital movements.

Unfortunately, Stoltenberg was a little too patient in his negotiating tactics; and instead of forcing the matter to a conclusion before the French elections of May 1988, which he could have done, he delayed the final stage until the final Ecofin Council of the German Presidency, on 13 June. By that time the elections had been held, the Right had sadly been defeated, and in place of Balladur, Stoltenberg and I had to deal once again with our old Socialist friend, Pierre Bérégovoy.

The 13 June Ecofin was Bérégovoy's first since reassuming office, and he was extremely reluctant to sign up to the package that had been all but agreed by Balladur. In particular, he argued that the abolition of exchange controls would lead to a massive loss of tax revenues to France, as savings flooded overseas where the *fisc* could not get at them. There was no way, therefore, in which he could agree to abolish exchange controls unless we agreed to a Community requirement for every member country to have a 15 per cent withholding tax on savings income. I pointed out to him that, as he knew, tax matters required unanimity, and the UK for one could not agree to that. But of course, I added, there was nothing to stop France imposing a withholding tax of her own if she wished to do so.

Bérégovoy insisted that that would not do, since funds would leave France for the UK in order to avoid the withholding tax. I replied that even if all of us round the table were to agree, that would not stop funds leaving France for a non-Community country such as Switzerland to avoid the withholding tax. I offered, however, to send top officials from the Inland Revenue to France to explain how we in the UK dealt with the problem of tax evasion in the absence of exchange controls. He then sought to appeal to my sense of fair play, arguing that if France was prepared to help the UK by abandoning exchange controls, as

I had long been urging, I should in return help him by agreeing to his withholding tax proposal.

I explained that he had misunderstood my position. I had been urging the abolition of exchange controls not for the sake of the UK, but in the interest of the Community as a whole: this was a particularly important aspect of the single market to which we were all committed. From the narrow UK viewpoint, I explained, London would undoubtedly benefit competitively if Paris remained cocooned in exchange control regulations of one kind and another. This was something that had not occurred to him. After a long telephone call to the Elysée Palace he came back and announced that he would sign up provided that the rest of us agreed to look into the question of a withholding tax of the kind he had suggested as a matter of urgency. I said I could go along with that: I had no objection to a study of the matter, although I doubted if my views would change as a result. But it was just conceivable they might. With Bérégovoy signing up, there were few problems with the others.

I had, however, in one respect been economical with the truth. My desire to secure exchange control abolition throughout the Community was not solely because it was in the interests of the single market and of Europe as a whole. It was also because it satisfied one of Margaret's conditions for sterling's membership of the ERM. She had latterly taken up the position that, before the pound entered the ERM, the other Community countries would need to abolish their exchange controls, as the UK had done; imagining that they would refuse to meet this condition.

Honouring the undertaking to consider the French withholding tax plan, and reaching an Ecofin decision on it, proved to be a lengthy business, not least because the Commission took up the cause. Despite the fact that, as the argument developed, it became clear that it was not going to get anywhere – particularly after the replacement of Gerhard Stoltenberg by the strongly anti-withholding tax CSU leader Theo Waigel as Germany's Finance Minister in April 1989 – it was, ironically, not until the French presidency that Christiane Scrivener finally admitted at the informal Ecofin of September 1989 at Antibes that the proposal was dead. The French appear to have managed perfectly well without it.

Bad Blood

The Delors Committee began its deliberations in September 1988. Both Margaret and I saw the working papers which emerged from it on a *sub rosa* basis, and it soon became clear that the Delors Committee and the UK Government were set on a collision course. As if this were not troublesome enough, bad blood was being created in other ways, too. I doubt if Jacques Delors had deliberately set out to inflame

Margaret, but if he had he could not have done it better. He first boasted to the European Parliament that, in ten years time, 80 per cent of all the key economic and social decisions would be taken in Brussels rather than in the member States. Then, in September, he travelled to Britain to address the annual conference of the Trades Union Congress, where he said:

> It is impossible to build Europe only on deregulation . . . It is essential to strengthen our control of our economic and social development, of technology and our monetary capacity.

The theme of control rather than deregulation could not have been more clearly expressed, nor a more explicit rejection of the British Government's vision of Europe.

The idea for the Delors visit to the TUC had come from the Foreign Office, who thought it might help to make the unions and the Labour Party less hostile to the Community. So far as that was concerned it succeeded beyond their wildest dreams, and did more than anything else to bring about Labour's Damascene conversion over the European Community. But it was scarcely a triumph of diplomacy to have been instrumental in greatly widening the already dangerous rift between the British Prime Minister and the President of the European Commission.

Later that same month it was Margaret's turn to put the boot in, with her famous Bruges speech of 20 September 1988. In fact, in the form in which she delivered it, it said a number of things that needed to be said, in a perfectly reasonable manner. Her five main principles were a Europe of nations working closely together, without any concentration of centralized power in Brussels; a preference for the practical over the grandiose; an emphasis on deregulation and market economics; free trade; and a defence based on NATO. The best-known sentence in the speech, 'We have not successfully rolled back the frontiers of the State in Britain only to see them reimposed at the Community level,' also expressed a perfectly valid sentiment. But the newspaper reports, which reflected the gloss Bernard Ingham had given when briefing the press, few of whom bothered to read the text, were very different in tone and truer to her own feelings: intensely chauvinistic, and particularly hostile to the Community.

The Delors Committee

The practical question, however, was whether anything could be done, via Robin, to secure a report from the Delors Committee that the UK Government would not be obliged to repudiate out of hand. To this end, on 14 December, 1988, Margaret called the first of a series of meetings at Number 10 with Robin, Geoffrey and myself; with Charles Powell and usually Brian Griffiths in attendance. Robin told us that the report was likely to fall into three parts. The first would be a straightforward description of the current working of the ERM. The second would attempt to define economic and monetary union, and outline the institutional changes necessary to achieve it. The third section would examine the case for early constitutional change as a first step towards EMU. This last section, which was clearly crucial, had not yet been properly tackled by the Committee; and the greater part of our meeting was spent discussing the tactics that might be employed to make this section as modest and as tentative as possible.

We were agreed, so far as analysis was concerned, that the report ought to make it quite clear that a single currency was not essential for the completion of the Single Market. It was clear to us, too, that Robin's tactics should be to assemble the widest possible opposition within the Committee both to any early treaty amendment required to achieve the full EMU objective espoused by Delors, and to anything that smacked of a recommendation to take any particular course of action: the Committee's role should be confined to saying that *if* you wanted to achieve x, *then* you would need to do y. Robin was understandably anxious not to become isolated within the Committee, but at that stage he felt he could count on the support of Pöhl.

Pöhl, indeed, was the key. He was known to have doubts about EMU, nor did the Bundesbank relish its own extinction. Moreover, if Robin and Pöhl stood together, there was a good chance that some of the others would join them, notably the long-serving Governor of the Danish Central Bank, Erik Hofmeyr. This meant that any alternative ideas we put forward on this front should not be ones that might alienate Pöhl – for example, the idea, which I had for some time been urging, that European monetary co-operation could be improved by each country holding the currencies of the other Community countries in its reserves, something to which the Bundesbank, which held only dollars, was resolutely opposed. So while it was decided that we ought to prepare a contingency paper mentioning distinctively British proposals for improved monetary co-operation in Europe which would not involve any amendment of the treaty, it should for the time being be kept in reserve and not tabled.

But Pöhl proved a broken reed. Despite telling Robin privately about his grave doubts about EMU, and promising Robin his support in toning down the Committee's report, true to form he did not stand firm. He made a number of sceptical interventions in the Committee's deliberations, but he never really engaged himself; at the end of the day shrugging his shoulders and going along with Delors and de Larosière. This made a complete nonsense of the tactical plan we had evolved.

The draft of the Delors Committee report was circulated in February 1989. We discussed it at one of our Number 10 meetings. It was clear to both Margaret and myself that it was wholly unacceptable. It was equally clear that there was no possibility of Robin, on his own, securing a redraft that would be acceptable to the UK. I suggested to him that he might submit a free-standing statement of his own objections for inclusion in the final Report, emphasizing the need for practical co-operation between member States and stressing that the massive shift of political sovereignty implied by full EMU went far beyond the competence of a Committee of Central Bankers to pronounce upon. But at the end of the day he decided that he did not wish to be seen as a minority of one among his peers in any way, and contented himself with trying to get some of the wording in the draft Report toned down.

My Chatham House Speech

By the middle of January it was already plain that our plan to influence the Committee's conclusions from within had foundered on Pöhl's failure to live up to his promises to Robin, and I felt the time had come to speak out in public on the issue. The Royal Institute for International Affairs, better known as Chatham House, had long been asking me to address them; and this seemed the ideal forum for a pre-emptive strike against what the Delors Report was likely to recommend. I arranged to speak to them on 25 January, 1989.

I had three objectives in mind. First and foremost, it was time I set out exactly where I stood on an issue of the first importance that was likely to be at the forefront of the political debate for some years to come. Second, there was an outside chance that it might exercise some influence on the final draft of the Delors Committee's Report – and even if it did not, it would prepare the ground for what seemed Britain's inevitable rejection of the Report. And third, it would be a way of demonstrating to Margaret both the grounds on which EMU, as I saw it, *ought* to be rejected, and how this fundamentally differed from the ERM. Unlike most of my speeches, my Chatham House speech was subsequently published in pamphlet form, where I was able to add a foreword relating it more closely to the Delors Report, which by that time had been published.

The greater part of my Chatham House speech was devoted not to currency issues, but to the Single Market, and some of the problems we were then encountering, for instance in the banking and financial areas. Indeed I voiced the suspicion that:

> This divisive and intensely difficult new issue [EMU] has been propelled into the forefront of European debate at this time either

out of culpable carelessness, or as a smokescreen to obscure a lack of sufficient progress towards the Single Market – or, worse, as a means of running away from taking the practical but difficult steps the Single Market requires, running away from the challenge of freedom. [Even in 1992 the key decisions have not all been taken – still less implemented.] For it is an observable fact that those nations which are most vocal about their support for EMU now, tend to be those that are most assiduous in preserving barriers to free trade within the Community.

France was one country that sprang to mind in this context. As I have already indicated, one of my three key objectives at Chatham House was to distinguish between membership of the ERM and full-scale Monetary Union. It could not be more fundamental – a point echoed, incidentally, by the Delors Report itself. As I put it at Chatham House:

> The ERM is an agreement between independent sovereign states . . . Economic and Monetary Union by contrast, is incompatible with independent sovereign states with control over their own fiscal and monetary policies. It would be impossible, for example, to have irrevocably fixed exchange rates while individual countries retained independent monetary policies . . . Thus EMU inevitably implies a single European currency, with monetary decisions – the setting of monetary targets and of short-term interest rates – taken not by national Governments and/or central banks, but by a European Central Bank. Nor would individual countries be able to retain responsibility for fiscal policy. With a single European monetary policy there would need to be central control over the size of the budget deficits and, particularly, over their financing . . . What organization would really be the Government? It is clear that Economic and Monetary Union implies nothing less than a European Government – albeit a federal one – and political union: the United States of Europe. That is simply not on the agenda now, nor will it be for the foreseeable future.

EMU Facts and Fallacies

There were some, I knew, who disputed this, arguing that a single European currency was essentially no different from the classical gold standard, under which dollars, pounds and Reichsmarks were different names for an essentially metallic common currency. I pointed out, however, that the gold standard was far from a monetary union. 'Co-operation was informal and not institutionalized; and although countries could see advantages for themselves in maintaining their parities against gold, they were free to change if it seemed in their national interest to do so.'

The UK went off gold during the Napoleonic Wars, and then again in the First World War, not returning in the latter case until 1925. In addition, Peel's Bank Charter Act of 1844, which put convertibility into gold on a legal basis, could be temporarily suspended in a severe financial crisis – as indeed it was on three occasions in the seventy years between 1844 and 1914.

Yet none of this prevented the classical gold standard from providing an invaluable financial discipline; and it did not occur to those setting pay and prices in any major country in the half century and more before the First World War that a currency depreciation would bail them out if they went too far. By contrast, a full monetary union normally followed the establishment of a central political power. The German Customs Union or *Zollverein* of 1834 neither required nor led to monetary union. That did not come until more than forty years later, when Bismarck founded an all-German political union under Prussian hegemony.

I also voiced my suspicion of the structural and regional policies which the Delors Committee believed would be required once the poorer member countries had lost the right to devalue. This, I said, was 'quite simply a bid for ever larger awards of taxpayers' money to be placed in the hands of bureaucrats in Brussels, to be used for the sort of interventionist policies that failed [in the UK] so decisively in the 1970s.' Such policies were no more likely to be successful at the Community level: 'Subsidizing industry and subsidizing regions destroys their will to compete and their ability to compete.'

EMU was an issue of growing importance on which I had not previously pronounced – indeed, very few at that time had – and the views I expressed in my Chatham House speech of January 1989 I have seen little reason to change since. It was also worth drawing attention, in less strident terms than those that were later to be used by Margaret, to the major political implications of EMU, which were at that time underplayed, if not ignored, by those, especially in the City, who saw it in exclusively financial terms.

The City supporters of EMU could not be expected to understand the politics. It was the politicians whom I felt were particularly culpable. The blame attached not to those who openly sought a federal Europe, a perfectly reputable objective which I happened not to share; but rather to those who maintained that there was no real political issue at all, and that talk of sovereignty was simply a matter of semantics. It was hard not to conclude that the many politicians who fell into this camp were either deceiving themselves or, if not, deliberately deceiving the people.

I also felt it was worth trying to prevent the depressing polarization of opinion on Europe between, on the one hand, the chauvinistic anti-Europeans who opposed all forms of entanglement, and, on the other hand, the knee-jerk Eurofederalists who in practice believed in a strong concentration of power at the European centre. I was not worried that, as a result, the speech left me isolated from both the two warring camps. I am neither a Europhobe nor a Eurofanatic and have no wish to ingratiate myself with either group. Had my political standing not been damaged by the need to raise interest rates so much, my Chatham House speech might have come to be seen by the bulk of the Tory Party – and by many non-Tories too – as a standard around which to rally.

Although she did not relish my favourable mention of the ERM, Margaret was delighted with my Chatham House speech, citing it frequently and indeed remembering it long enough to refer to it in favourable terms in her very last and unforgettable speech as Prime Minister, in the House of Commons on 20 November 1990. But it was not her praise that I sought. What I needed from her was trust – or, at the very least, for her to refrain from undermining me.

The Delors Report

It was the custom to conduct the formal business at Ecofin Council meetings during the morning and afternoon sessions, leaving the trickier, more important, and more interesting matters for informal discussion over lunch, when no minutes were taken and to which no reference would normally be made afterwards, not least to the press. Thus it was over lunch at the April 1989 Ecofin Council at Luxembourg that Jacques Delors first unveiled his Committee's Report.

It mapped out the achievement of EMU in three stages. In essence, these were:

> Stage One: Completion of the financial aspects of the Single Market; all Community members to join the ERM within the narrow band; the development of the Ecu; and closer European monetary co-ordination.

> Stage Two: Rather vague, but essentially a transitional phase during which the new institutions required for Stage Three would be developed. In addition, ERM realignments would become few and far between, and it was implied that the various national central banks would become independent, as a prelude to their fusion into an independent European Central Bank in Stage Three.

> Stage Three: The Community's exchange rates would become irrevocably fixed. The European Central Bank would take over responsibility for monetary policy and eventually establish a single currency. The arrangement would be buttressed by binding conventions on

national Budget deficits and by enlarged subsidies to offset regional imbalances.

In the discussions Margaret, Geoffrey and I had had in London it had been agreed that we could accept Stage One, but that there was no way in which we could accept Stage Three. For myself, I saw no fundamental problems, and indeed some attractions, in Stage Two, particularly as it ultimately emerged from the subsequent intergovernmental negotiations, provided it could be changed from a transitional phase to a final destination. But Margaret was wholly opposed to Stage Two in any shape or form. Be that as it may, over lunch at Luxembourg Jacques Delors gave us a brief and lucid exposition of the merits of his Report, as he saw them; only to be followed by an awkward silence. It was clear that most of my colleagues did not see it as a matter for genuine debate, something that was to cause increasing problems as the saga unfolded over the years that lay ahead.

I brought the silence to an end by making it clear, after elaborate courtesies to Delors, complimenting him on the lucidity of the Report and so on, that the UK could not accept the massive transfer of sovereignty over fiscal and monetary policy implied by the Report. Pierre Bérégovoy then responded with a defence of Delors, arguing that for France sovereignty was a matter of having an independent defence capability, and was unaffected by the matters dealt with in the Delors Report. No-one else uttered a word. Bérégovoy subsequently told me that he had initially been very sceptical about EMU, but had been talked round to it by Jacques de Larosière, who as Governor of the Banque de France had been a key member of the Delors Committee.

Disaster with the Dutch

So far from causing the issue to go away, the Delors Report affected the question of sterling's membership of the ERM in two important if conflicting ways. On the one hand, it gave it a new lease of life, since the inclusion of all Community currencies in the ERM was an integral part of Stage One of the process outlined in the Report, which Britain was formally to accept. But it also fatally confused the essentially economic question of the ERM with the fundamentally political argument over EMU; and linked the hard-earned credibility of the ERM, which had by then been in existence for a decade, to the speculative and uncertain EMU.

Meanwhile, Geoffrey Howe had come to the conclusion that if anyone could persuade Margaret of the merits of the ERM, it would be the Dutch Prime Minister, Ruud Lubbers. Lubbers was a Conservative and the closest thing to an ally Margaret had within the Community. She was also attracted to his rugged good looks and personal charm. Despite the sharp contrast between his relaxed and benign style and her own strident and confrontational one, she undoubtedly had a soft spot for him. Geoffrey had therefore been trying for some time to persuade Margaret to hold what he called a mini-summit with the Dutch.

The UK had long held annual bilateral summits with the Germans, French and Italians. Having participated in these, and discovered that their only useful purpose was to provide attractive photo-opportunities for the host premier, I tried whenever I could to find a legitimate reason why I could not take part. Given that the dates were chosen to fit the diaries of the two Prime Ministers and Foreign Ministers, this was not usually too difficult. The idea of a mini-summit with the Dutch did, by contrast, have a real purpose; but I told Geoffrey it would never work, since Lubbers had nothing to gain from browbeating Margaret on the issue of the ERM. I had, in any case, sometime earlier had a private word with Lubbers myself, and he told me he regarded her as a lost cause on the ERM. Geoffrey was characteristically undeterred, and eventually found a good excuse to convene the mini-summit when Margaret wanted to secure Dutch support for the modernization of nuclear weaponry prior to an important NATO meeting.

Lubbers accordingly turned up at Chequers on Saturday, 29 April 1989, accompanied by his Foreign Minister, Hans van den Broek, and his Finance Minister, Onno Ruding. Margaret was accompanied by Geoffrey and myself, with Charles Powell as note-taker. I arrived, as requested, at four o'clock in the afternoon. It was only subsequently that I discovered that Margaret had met Lubbers privately in the morning and discussed EMU as well as the NATO summit with him. Lubbers apparently told Margaret that the Dutch had found membership of the ERM highly beneficial. He also endorsed the eventual goal of full monetary union. But he had serious misgivings about the passage in the Report that insisted that embarking on Stage One implied a commitment to the process as a whole. The Netherlands preferred, he said, to proceed step-by-step and gauge exactly what was needed at each stage rather than opt at the outset for amendments to the Treaty of Rome.

This was an obvious basis on which to build an Anglo–Dutch alliance against the Delors Report. But Margaret threw the opportunity away and instead told Lubbers that the UK's experience of stable exchange rates was much less happy than the Dutch one, and that it was in shadowing the Deutschmark that excessively loose monetary conditions had been allowed to develop. It was an unpromising curtain-raiser for the afternoon 'plenary' session.

Most of that session was taken up by Margaret berating the Dutch for not taking a sufficiently hard line over NATO modernization, at a time when the Germans had gone soft and even the Americans were wavering.

I found her manner distinctly embarrassing, and was surprised that the Dutch took it as well as they did. As the tirade went on, I began to suspect that she was deliberately postponing the EMU discussion because I had told her before the meeting that I would have to leave early to collect Thérèse from hospital, where she had undergone a minor operation. Unwilling to be outmanoeuvred quite so easily, I slipped out of the room to arrange for someone else to pick up Thérèse.

Eventually, and very belatedly, the discussion moved to the Delors Report. I said that the British Government was happy to discuss practical steps towards closer economic and monetary co-operation within the framework of the existing Treaty, but did not see any need for the Treaty to be amended. Ruding said that The Netherlands had an equally pragmatic outlook, and also preferred a step-by-step approach, even though the Dutch entirely accepted the eventual goal of full EMU. He added that the effectiveness of Britain's resistance to the recommendations of the Delors Report would be greatly enhanced by membership of the ERM.

The last point, although perfectly true, predictably aroused Margaret's wrath. She brusquely interjected that sterling differed from the guilder and that exchange rate stability was secondary to the defeat of inflation. For the first time she said to my face that it was shadowing the Deutschmark that had caused Britain's inflation to pick up again. I immediately intervened, saying that with hindsight it was arguable that the Mark should have been shadowed at a slightly higher rate; but that it was not the case that the shadowing itself had been inflationary. It was very embarrassing having to argue with Margaret in front of the Dutch, but I simply could not let the charge pass unchallenged.

Ruding then weighed in, saying that membership of the ERM would provide a stern anti-inflationary discipline if sterling entered at the right parity. He also suggested that, while the weakness of the British economy had made entry unthinkable when the system was first set up in 1979, the transformation of the supply side over the past ten years made it infinitely easier for the British authorities to sustain an exchange rate target. He then tried a different tack. He said that he was not advising Britain to join immediately but merely to give an undertaking to join on the completion of the Single Market by January 1993. Margaret was unpersuadable, claiming that membership of the ERM added nothing to monetary policy and took a great deal away. Ruding – with whom I had not had any prior discussions – re-emphasized his belief that it was only by joining the ERM that Britain could expect its objections to EMU to be taken seriously at the forthcoming European Council at Madrid.

It was at that point that Lubbers, who had received such a battering on the NATO issue, over which the Dutch had not in fact been at all 'wet', that he found it hard to summon much enthusiasm for the EMU discussion, made his only contribution to the argument. He said: 'Well, you can drive a car without a seat belt, but on the whole it is better to have one.' He warned that if Britain stayed out of the ERM, it would be much harder for Britain and The Netherlands to co-operate in a whole range of areas unconnected with EMU. With Margaret hectoring her Dutch guests and my contradicting her in mid-stream it was a ghastly and embarrassing occasion, and I was eventually glad to make my excuses and depart to see how Thérèse was, before the proceedings had formally ended.

CHAPTER 73

'I MUST PREVAIL'

A Battle of Wills · Margaret Tells the World . . .
. . . and Apologizes to Me · The Euro-Elections of June 1989
A Formula for Ripe Time · New Light on Monetary Union

A Battle of Wills

THE ANGLO–DUTCH mini-Summit had proved as useless for the purpose for which Geoffrey had intended it as I had warned him it would. Nevertheless, there was no point in pretending that it had not happened; and when I next saw Margaret in private, at my weekly bilateral the following Wednesday, 3 May 1989, I asked her how she thought it had gone.

She replied by saying what nonsense Ruding, the Dutch Finance Minister, had talked about the ERM. I said that, on the contrary, I thought the idea of setting a date by which we would enter the ERM had much to be said for it: it would establish the good faith of our repeated assurances that we would join when the time was right, which was beginning to be questioned. We had to keep our eye on the ball, and the ball, in this context, was the grave danger posed by the Delors Report and EMU. Our official position on that was that we could accept Stage One of the Report's recommendations, which involved sterling joining the ERM, within the standard narrow band, but that we could not accept Stages Two and Three. But this position, and our contention that the Community's monetary arrangements should remain the ERM, was unlikely to carry much conviction so long as we remained resolutely outside it.

Margaret would have none of it. Setting a deadline by which we would join the ERM would be 'particularly damaging'. Joining the ERM would in no way strengthen our hand against EMU. In any case it was shadowing the Deutschmark that had led to the resurgence of

917

UK inflation. We should never have 'given up control of monetary policy' by adopting a parallel objective of exchange rate stability. 'You cannot serve two masters,' she declared: what we had to do now was to concentrate on re-establishing our counter-inflationary credentials. I replied that it was not a question of serving two masters: downward pressure on inflation was obviously the paramount objective. However, there was a clear link between the internal and external value of a currency – something I could never get her to accept.

It was evident to both of us that the discussion was getting nowhere; but the terms in which she brought it to a close were particularly revealing. 'I do not want you to raise the subject ever again,' she said; 'I must prevail.' It was those last three words that said it all. The economic and political arguments had become an irrelevance. Joining the ERM, as she saw it, had become a battle of wills between her and me; and it had to be her will that prevailed. The humiliation, as she clearly saw it, of May 1988, when the press interpreted her prepared parliamentary answer on exchange rate policy – and, ironically, the half per cent base rate cut – as a defeat for her, still rankled.

Of course, she was quite right; in the sense that matters had now reached the pitch where there was a good chance that any decision to put sterling in the ERM would have been presented in the press as a victory for me and a defeat for her. That was one of the malign consequences of her habit of personalizing every issue and exposing every difference; but it was no basis on which to determine a matter of such importance to our country. I contented myself by saying that, while I would certainly cease discussing the subject then and there, I could give her no assurance that I would not come back to it again when it seemed right to do so. But it was the ominous 'I must prevail' that was still ringing in my ears as I left the room.

Margaret Tells the World . . .

It was clear to me that handling the EMU challenge was going to be far more difficult than Margaret apparently realized. The first substantive discussion of EMU was scheduled to take place later that month, on Saturday, 20 May 1989, at the informal Ecofin Council to be held under the first Spanish presidency of the European Community, at the coastal resort of S'Agaro.

Before then a number of events were held to mark the tenth anniversary of the formation of the first Thatcher Government in May 1979. One I particularly recall was a dinner Margaret gave at Number 10 on 4 May for Cabinet Ministers and their wives, marred in my case only by the fact that Thérèse could not be there as she was still recovering from her operation. Geoffrey Howe, as the senior of the few remaining survivors of Margaret's first Cabinet, spoke on behalf of us all; and in addition to an elegant tribute to Margaret he succeeded in evoking the camaraderie that had kept us going during those difficult early years. I could not help reflecting how much that spirit had changed. Elspeth Howe, sitting next to me, was quietly fuming throughout Geoffrey's well-judged speech. Evidently she felt that he was being a touch too fulsome to someone who treated him so badly.

The Press always love anniversaries: anything that can be portrayed as a major event and which can be prepared for well in advance is an obvious boon. The coverage of Margaret's tenth anniversary was therefore predictably lavish. Margaret herself, however, was shrewd enough to seek to play it down as much as she could. She recognized that, once it was over, the harsh realities of life would appear even harsher. It was a pity that she did not have the further insight to recognize that it was the ideal time for her to step down gracefully of her own free will.

I was in the car on the way to Northolt on Friday, 19 May, to catch the RAF plane to Spain for the informal Ecofin, accompanied by my G7 deputy, Nigel Wicks, when Thérèse rang through to ask me if I had heard what Margaret had said on the one o'clock news bulletin on BBC Radio. I told her I had not. To my horror, she told me that Margaret had given an interview in which she had blamed me for causing the upsurge in inflation. I thanked her for alerting me, and telephoned Alex at the Treasury, asking him to procure a transcript of the interview and fax it to me at the hotel I was heading for at S'Agaro, to await my arrival.

The fax was duly waiting for me at the hotel when I arrived, and I asked Nigel Wicks to come to my room so that he could read it, too. It was appalling. It turned out to be an extract from an interview she had originally given to the BBC World Service, in which she told the interviewer that we had 'picked up our inflation tendency' as a direct consequence of the intervention in which we had engaged in order to shadow the Deutschmark. The accusation was not, of course, new to me; but she had never before made it in public. What made it even more intolerable was that she chose to make what the BBC rightly interpreted as a personal attack on me just when I was on my way to represent Britain in a complex and difficult set of international negotiations on what was widely seen as a closely related issue. I told Nigel Wicks that I felt that this was the last straw, and that I would be telephoning Thérèse to discuss with her whether I should resign.

This was not a manoeuvre: I meant it and did indeed telephone Thérèse, who advised me to do nothing until I had got back to the UK. But Wicks was sufficiently alarmed to telephone Peter Middleton in London off his own bat, and Peter had evidently got straight on to Number 10 to ensure that Margaret was aware of my state of mind. Fortunately I was spared the attention of the UK press, who were at S'Agaro in force. So as to enable us to conduct our discussions in complete privacy Carlos Solchaga, the Spanish Finance Minister, had arranged for there to be a *cordon sanitaire* around the hotel where we were meeting and staying, which was very effectively policed; and there was to be no contact with the press until the meeting was over.

This also enabled me to refocus my mind on the agenda for the Council, of which the most important item was EMU. Given that I was in a minority of one over EMU, the meeting did not go too badly from the UK's point of view. The agreed communiqué issued by Solchaga at the end of the discussions, which had not been not easy, conspicuously stopped short of endorsing the Delors Report, stating merely that the Ecofin Council saw it as a 'valuable and comprehensive basis for further work'. I also succeeded in getting Stage One, which the UK could accept, detached from Stages Two and Three, which we could not. While, in my opinion, it was Stage Three, which created the single currency, which was wholly unacceptable, Margaret, as I have already mentioned, was not prepared to accept the somewhat nebulous Stage Two, either.

This separation was marked in the communiqué by the agreement that, while preparatory work for launching Stage One should be set in hand 'as a matter of urgency.' So far as Stages Two and Three were concerned, it was a matter of 'defining the operational elements' so that 'a decision can be taken in due course' on whether an intergovernmental conference should be called to consider amendments to the Treaty. Jacques Delors, who was, of course, an active participant at the meeting, made no secret of his displeasure with the outcome, and of his determination to secure a very different outcome from the European Council itself, which was due to discuss EMU at Madrid the following month. For my part, I felt that the outcome gave Margaret a useful foundation on which she might, with skilful handling, build at Madrid.

. . . and Apologizes to Me

The discussions had, in fact, only just begun when I was passed a telephone message asking me to ring Margaret in London. I waited until the coffee break and then did so. She was at her most emollient, apologizing profusely – a phenomenon so uncharacteristic as to have been almost unique – for the way her BBC interview had turned out. She had not intended any attack on me at all, she said, but had been provoked into saying what she did by the idiocy of the interviewer who had spoken as if joining the ERM were some magic solution to all our problems. I replied that it was clearly most unfortunate, but I was glad to hear her explanation. I then went on to let her know how the Ecofin meeting had begun.

When it had ended, and I crossed the *cordon sanitaire* to the hotel where the press were billeted, to give an *al fresco* press conference beside the swimming pool, all they were really interested in was, of course, Margaret's attack on me in her radio interview on the Friday. I told them that the Prime Minister had telephoned me to assure me that the interpretation that had been put on her words was incorrect. After establishing that the telephone call had been initiated by her and not by me, I was then asked whether she had rung up in order to apologize. I replied, rather stuffily, that it was a private telephone conversation and I did not propose to say anything further about it.

Whether the press simply put two and two together, or whether they had been told more by someone else, I do not know; but the story in the press on the Monday morning was of her having apologized to me – something which, although it happened to be true, she could not have relished. But, once again, she had brought it on herself. Presumably, the purpose of her call had been to prevent my resignation – not that either of us had so much as hinted at the possibility. In any event, by the time I landed at Northolt I had decided that, despite the problems I was having with Margaret, I would stick to my earlier resolve to soldier on. The fact that, as I recorded in Chapter 68, almost the first thing I had to do on my return was to raise interest rates a further point to 14 per cent, their highest level since the sterling crisis of January 1985, did not make life any easier.

The Euro-Elections of June 1989

The following month, June, was the scheduled date for the fixed-term four-yearly elections to the European Parliament. While of little importance except to the candidates themselves – the European Parliament was the least powerful of all the Community's institutions and the majority of the British electorate recognized this by not even bothering to vote – the political parties took them seriously as an indication of their general standing with public opinion. Moreover, with Europe having once again elbowed its way to the forefront of the political debate, there was rather more interest than usual in the 1989 elections.

Margaret opened the Conservative Party's campaign with a Euro-manifesto press conference on 22 May. Predictably, she was asked about the Government's attitude to the ERM, and lost no time in departing from the agreed compromise wording that we would not be joining until we had got inflation back under control, by adding 'and maybe not even then', followed by various gratuitous sidesweeps at fixed exchange rates in general and the ERM in particular – which, when all was said and done, it was the Government's official policy to join. The press inevitably interpreted this as yet another snub to me, and our back-benchers once again expressed concern at the re-emergence of a public split between the Prime Minister and the Chancellor. Walters' presence was clearly making itself felt.

But my concern was by no means confined to Margaret's attitude to the ERM. Under her instructions, the Conservative campaign for the Euro-elections was characterized by a crude and embarrassing anti-Europeanism which had never before played any part in the Party's stance on this constellation of issues. The new tone and nature was well encapsulated by the ubiquitous poster which simply asked 'Do you want to live on a diet of Brussels?'

Leaving aside the merits of the case, this seemed to me appallingly bad politics. One of the great strengths of the Thatcher Government had been that, unlike the case with many of its predecessors, whether you liked what it was saying and doing or not, at least you knew where it stood. This clarity had a considerable appeal. But over Europe, the public was totally confused. It had been the Conservatives under Macmillan that had first applied to join the Community, the Conservatives under Heath that had secured UK entry, and the Conservatives under Margaret Thatcher that had solved the problem of the budgetary injustice and, on that basis, reaffirmed the UK's position within the Community. Compared with the hesitancy and bitterly divided counsels of the Labour Party, it was the Conservatives who had always appeared as the Party of Europe. Yet suddenly the voters were presented with an election in which the Conservative Party appeared to be campaigning not against the Labour Party but against the European Community.

Needless to say, in addition to completely confusing the public, the Conservative campaign brought to the surface the conflicting views on Europe that had always existed in the Party but which had hitherto been largely quiescent. It was no surprise that the results of the elections, held on Thursday, 15 June, were an unmitigated disaster for the Government. While the unpopularity caused by the inexorable rise in interest rates had probably been the main factor, the nature of the Euro-campaign itself had clearly not helped.

Yet Margaret did not see it that way at all. I suddenly realized, with a shiver of apprehension, that she saw the Euro-campaign as a trial run for the next General Election campaign; and that, with the short-term economic outlook unpromising, she saw a crude populist anti-Europeanism as her winning strategy. It was a strategy that would undoubtedly have evoked a considerable response: xenophobia always does. But it would have been a disaster for the Party, splitting it from top to bottom and making no sense to the voters, who would not have understood what we stood for and, indeed, why we wished to remain within the Community at all if that was how we saw it.

I was, as I have said, never either a Eurofanatic or a Europhobe, and had become resigned to being caught in the crossfire between these passionate warring minorities within the Conservative Party, whose discordant and numbingly predictable views used to dominate every European debate in the House of Commons. It was always clear to me that the Conservative Party could be successfully led only by someone who took their stand in the centre of the spectrum on this issue, where the silent majority dwelt. Margaret's evident determination to lead the Party from one of the two extremes of that spectrum spelled nothing but trouble.

A Formula for Ripe Time

On Monday, 12 June, I was scheduled to appear before the House of Commons Select Committee on the Treasury, to give evidence to the Committee's inquiry into the Delors Report on EMU. I played to a full house, which must have stimulated the adrenalin. The meeting had to be shifted to the Grand Committee Room off Westminster Hall, the largest room the House could provide; and long before I arrived a queue of spectators had formed, consisting not only of journalists and curious members of the general public, but dozens of City analysts and a discreet sprinkling of more senior figures from Whitehall and the City.

The questioning inevitably covered the ERM as well as EMU. It is a tribute to the tradition of lively political debate in the UK that in no other European country could these subjects have had such appeal. The German press, for example, did not wake up to the threat to the Deutschmark implicit in EMU until after their Government had already signed the Maastricht treaty of December 1991.

I recalled Jacques Delors observing to me, when we were sitting together at an Ecofin lunch, that he received cuttings from all the European papers; and, although he did not welcome all he read in the UK press, he was impressed by the fact that there was more lively debate about European issues in the UK than in the rest of the Community put together. This *de facto* conspiracy of silence over Europe on the Continent is, I believe, storing up serious trouble for the future; and in this context the Danish people's rejection of the Maastricht treaty in a referendum in 1992 fired a healthy warning shot. But in the short term its main effect was to make the UK Government's task, particularly in relation to EMU, considerably harder.

As for the ERM, I put the case for it in a single sentence:

> It would reduce exchange rate fluctuations and we would be able to use it to assist us in our anti-inflationary policy.

I also dissented from the view that ERM members had to have identical interest rates. The market, I explained, had to take into account two currency risks: the possibility of a realignment and the scope for change within the existing bands. To achieve a successful domestic monetary policy, 'you have got to be prepared to make use of both elements of flexibility'.

But the most newsworthy item consisted of the essential conditions, which I specified for the first time, which needed to be satisfied before Britain could join the ERM. These were, first, a reduction in British inflation and, second, a lifting of exchange controls in the major Community countries, especially France and Italy. Community Finance Ministers had already agreed to do the latter by mid-1990 and, in fact, France was to move at the beginning of that year. Like the inflation condition, the exchange control condition was one on which I had reason to believe that Margaret and I would be able to agree.

It was the voicing of this condition which dominated the press headlines the next day, although there was less than complete agreement on quite how to interpret it. *The Times* had 'Lawson Gives Hint of Early British Move to Join EMS'; *The Financial Times* 'Lawson Signals 1990 as Probable Date for Full Entry into EMS'; and the *Independent* 'Lawson Calls for Truce in Row over EMS'. I certainly believed that this was a formula that might heal the rift in an acceptable way.

As for the inflation condition, the official published UK forecasts showed a strong decline in inflation throughout 1989 and onwards. This was indeed in the pipeline, despite the events which knocked the RPI off course and delayed the big reduction until 1991. (Despite my scepticism of official forecasts, I publicly supported the decision taken by my successor as Chancellor, John Major, to join at last in October 1990, when inflation was at a statistical peak, but clearly poised to fall dramatically.) As I said at the time, it was a far less favourable time than the opportunities I had been obliged to miss, notably in 1985; but there seemed nothing to be gained from waiting still longer.

New Light on Monetary Union

In some ways, what I said about European Monetary Union was more radical, if less newsworthy, than what I said about the ERM. At Chatham House I had followed Delors in accepting that Monetary Union required some central control over the size of fiscal deficits. But I had subsequently reflected on it further; and told the Committee, as I had told my opposite numbers at the S'Agaro informal Ecofin, that even a common currency did not in theory require either the control of the budgetary and fiscal policies of members, or a great enlargement of regional policy.

To make a monetary union work, I said, 'What you need is basically a simple rule that, if any member country gets itself excessively into debt, then there will be a clear understanding of no bailing out; but there is nothing further you need.'

I added that there was no federal system in the world, with the possible exception of Australia, where provincial government budgets were subject to the control of the federal government. 'There is no more reason for having central control of European deficits than there is to have central control of the borrowings of ICI.' I subsequently came to believe that both views on this tricky issue were probably correct: my second thoughts were certainly right in theory, but my first thoughts were probably closer to the mark in practice. As I was to put it in my 1990 Stamp Memorial Lecture:

> There is the minimalist position which holds that the market can be left to exercise a discipline on excessive borrowing by member states, just as it does on borrowing by individual companies within a single national currency area, provided there is a clear rule that no member country that gets into difficulties would be bailed out by the Community as a whole. Whether this would be enough would depend, *inter alia*, on whether such a rule could be made credible. The parallel is whether, say, if New York were once again to become bankrupt, it is credible that the US Federal Government would stand aside and allow it to default on its debts.

Continuing, in what was to be described in the press as an unscripted virtuoso performance, I described the Delors Report as 'totally flawed' in saying that there had to be 'a huge transfer of resources from the centre to the periphery . . . What you need for adjustment is flexibility of wage rates, of land prices, of the various factors of production . . . It is a complete illusion to suppose that if you devalue you are somehow gaining resources. You are not . . . There is no reason why you should be compensated for it [i.e. the inability to devalue].'

But even in a pure Monetary Union, without unnecessary paraphernalia, the crucial dimension of democratic accountability would still be missing. The Bundesbank itself was constitutionally subject to German law. To achieve accountability for a European Central Bank 'you would have to have a genuine European parliament'. National parliaments would become like county councils – a comparison which Norman Tebbit later took over. There would have to be a genuinely democratically elected European government to balance a European Central Bank. A small but crucial passage in my exchanges with the Treasury Committee concerned the relationship between ERM and EMU. I indicated the indirect linkage I had already raised with Margaret:

> Influence in these matters would be greater when the time has come that we are within the Exchange Rate Mechanism, or even if it were clear that we were going to be within the Exchange Rate Mechanism within a reasonable period of time. I think that would help us in the discussions that are to come on this matter. That cannot be decisive; but I think it is true.

Sadly, by joining the ERM as late as we did, the influence we secured, although by no means negligible, was far less than it could have been. Moreover, by the time we did join, a more direct and malign linkage had begun to emerge. For the first ten years of its existence, the ERM had stood on its own merits and had steadily gained in credibility as the years went by. But when EMU appeared on the horizon, and the ERM began to be seen as merely the first stage towards full Monetary Union, as soon as doubts about the prospects for EMU began to be widely entertained in 1992, the credibility of the ERM began to be questioned, too.

Throughout this period, sterling was being put under strain by the habit of financial analysts of treating Alan Walters' views, which had not only been widely publicized before his return but continued to be aired to groups of outsiders on both sides of the Atlantic at supposedly private gatherings, as representing the views of Margaret herself, and thus expecting that the pound would be allowed to sink freely without much preventive action. Paradoxically, Margaret's unwillingness to back me publicly on sterling added to the level of base rates required to maintain the pound at any particular level. During the first half of 1989, despite a further increase in base rates to 14 per cent, sterling had fallen by 6 per cent against the Mark and 7 per cent on the index. There was a real risk of a sterling crisis precipitating yet further increases in interest rates in late summer or autumn, particularly if Margaret mishandled negotiations at the Madrid summit later that June. The Walters problem was also starting to cause me – and the Government – considerable trouble in the House of Commons.

CHAPTER 74

———

THE ROCKY ROAD TO MADRID

To Resign or not to Resign? · Geoffrey Howe Enters the Picture
The First Thatcher/Howe/Lawson Meeting
The Second Thatcher/Howe/Lawson Meeting
Movement at Madrid ·· Geoffrey Howe Pays the Price

To Resign or not to Resign?

John Smith, my Labour opposite number, was an effective parliamentary debater with a particular talent for mockery. He was a likeable and successful Edinburgh advocate, one of the few Labour front-benchers who had the capacity to earn more outside Parliament than he did within it. Smith's jokes, which were often very successful – he has a good, dry, sense of timing – were invariably better than his speeches, which were entirely predictable. They were always about the importance of training and of manufacturing industry, accompanied by allegations of Government misuse of North Sea oil – to which, as a Scottish Member, he characteristically attached grossly exaggerated economic importance. After Labour's fourth successive election defeat in 1992, he was to succeed Neil Kinnock as his Party's leader.

Prior to Walters' reappearance in May 1989, Smith's poor understanding of economics and obvious reluctance to engage in serious economic argument had meant that I had very little difficulty dealing with him across the floor of the House. But once Walters was there Smith was able to ignore the economic policy issues with which he felt so uncomfortable and concentrate exclusively on the evident split between Margaret and myself, and in particular on Walters' role in this: a soft target which made the going very much more difficult. It was after a telling example of this in an Opposition Day debate in the House of Commons on 7 June that

·

I began to think once again that it might be better all round if I were to resign. Margaret would be having her annual reshuffle the following month, and if I were to go that would probably be the best time to do so. However, I needed to talk it over with someone first. I telephoned Willie Whitelaw at his home in Cumbria and asked him when he next planned to be in London, since I would value a private word with him. He said he would, of course, see me at any time, and we made a date for him to come to Number 11 at six o'clock on the evening of Tuesday, 13 June.

It so happened that I had agreed some time earlier to be interviewed about the economy by Jonathan Dimbleby on the BBC television programme *On The Record* on the previous Sunday, 11 June. As a result of my frame of mind, I was rather more relaxed than I might otherwise have been; although in any event the only way I could have avoided entering some very tricky territory indeed would have been to refuse all interviews without exception – an impossible position for any Chancellor. Inevitably, at the half-way mark the questioning turned to the contentious exchange rate issue. Dimbleby asked me whether I agreed with the Prime Minister that we had picked up inflation as a result of shadowing the Deutschmark. I replied, 'I think it's much more complex than that,' and cited 'the nature of the housing market in this country and the fact that we've deregulated our financial sector far more than any other country'.

Right at the end of the interview, I was asked whether, after six years as Chancellor, I wished to stay a further two years and become the longest-serving Chancellor since Gladstone. I replied, somewhat cryptically, 'I'm not interested in the record books. How long I'm there is a matter partly for the Prime Minister and partly for me. And it will be resolved in the fullness of time.'

When Willie Whitelaw came to have a drink with me on the Tuesday evening, I do not know whether he had seen the television interview or not. But he was well aware of the acute difficulty of the position I was in and clearly felt that Margaret had become impossible. I told him I was contemplating resignation. He was not surprised, saying that although he hoped I would not resign, it was clearly a matter for me and that he would fully understand it if I did. He repeated what he had told me on an earlier occasion, that although he had made clear that he was always available, Margaret never consulted him on anything. We talked for some time; and although it resolved nothing, I felt a little better to have got it all off my chest.

Geoffrey Howe Enters the Picture

My agonizing was to be overtaken by events. Despite the disastrous mini-summit with the Dutch on 29 April, Geoffrey was anxious to keep up the pressure, and suggested that we might send Margaret, jointly, an analysis of the economics and politics of the ERM, in the context of the new situation created by our need to respond to the threat of EMU. We had, of course, been working together on the EMU issue, under Margaret's chairmanship, since the previous December; but had clearly got nowhere. I was sceptical; but said that I was happy to have our respective officials work something up, to see what it looked like.

The putative joint paper went through a number of drafts, partly because Geoffrey and I started with different views as to how the situation might best be handled, and partly because I was doubtful of the utility of the exercise in the first place. Eventually, immediately following my exposition to the Treasury Select Committee on 12 June, described in the previous chapter, and reflecting some of the points I had made there, a joint draft was produced that was closer to what I felt might sensibly be sent to Margaret – if, and I was still by no means convinced, it was worth sending anything at all. Geoffrey and I agreed to meet at his room in the Foreign Office to discuss it after dinner on the evening of 13 June, the same day as my heart-to-heart talk with Willie.

Headed 'EC Issues and Madrid', the draft minute, which was of considerable length, argued that if we simply said 'no' to EMU at Madrid, the others would go ahead without us, creating a two-tier Europe, which would be very damaging for the UK in a number of specified ways. Our objective must therefore be to build on the S'Agaro formula of going ahead with Stage One of the Delors plan and postponing progress towards Stage Three until further work was done on what it really entailed, including notably its political implications; and there was some evidence that the Spanish presidency were prepared to work for an outcome along these lines (the Spanish Prime Minister, Felipe Gonzalez, subsequently confirmed this to Margaret when he saw her in London on 19 June). If it could be achieved, this would head off the intergovernmental conference and the subsequent amendment to the Treaty on which the French were so keen. But we could turn this trick only if we convinced a sufficient number of the others of our sincerity.

This was partly a matter of 'tone of voice', and partly of substance. The ERM issue, the paper argued, would inevitably arise at Madrid, given its central position in Stage One, and we would need to go beyond reiteration of the time-worn formula of entry when the time was right. It concluded that this should take the form of a 'non-legally binding' undertaking that sterling would join the ERM by the end of 1992 (the proposal that the Dutch Finance Minister, Ruding, had made at Chequers: a point the minute forebore to point out). Any such undertaking would be explicitly subject to the condition that all the major member states had abolished all exchange controls well before that date – as indeed the Community's Capital Liberalization Directive already required them to do – and an understanding that the pound could enter with the wider margins pioneered by the Italian lira and emulated by the Spanish peseta. As for UK inflation, that was a matter for us and not the Community, but we were, in any event, determined that it must be on the way down again well before the end of 1992. The minute concluded by asking for a meeting with Margaret to discuss all this.

Geoffrey explained that he was deeply concerned that Margaret would badly mishandle the Madrid European Council which was now less than a fortnight off. Her manner at these meetings had become increasingly strident and confrontational, something that was no longer bringing any useful results; and the issues at stake were, thanks to EMU, more important than ever. I replied that, while I did not go along with everything in the minute, I agreed with him about the dangers we faced at Madrid, the risk of Margaret mishandling the Council, and the desirability of underlining the genuineness of our commitment to join the ERM by giving a latest date by which we would enter the mechanism. But I had some doubts about the desirability of a joint minute, and its likely effectiveness. I said that I would sleep on it and let him know my verdict in the morning.

The First Thatcher/Howe/Lawson Meeting

When I got back to Number 11 I told Thérèse of this conversation. There was much about it that left me feeling uneasy. I had an innate distaste for cabals and plots, and had never been part of one; and while a minute to Margaret, drafted by senior Foreign Office and Treasury officials, and copied to the top officials in both Departments, could hardly be called a cabal or a plot simply because it was signed by two Ministers rather than one, her growing bunker mentality might make it seem to her that way.

On the other hand, although there was in fact a very considerable difference between my view of the Community and Geoffrey's, I shared his apprehension at Margaret's likely handling of the Madrid Council. Moreover, although my reasons may not have been exactly the same as his, I could hardly dissociate myself from a move designed to promote sterling's membership of the ERM. The notion of setting a self-imposed deadline was something I had warmed to, as Margaret knew, when Ruding had suggested it at Chequers the previous month; while the proposed conditions effectively reiterated the line I had taken with the Treasury Select Committee the previous day.

The next morning I telephoned Geoffrey and told him that I would sign the joint minute subject to a number of amendments, none of a fundamental nature, and to his agreeing that the minute was sent to Margaret on Foreign Office paper, since the nature and tone of the minute, even amended as I sought, made its origins blindingly obvious and it would be foolish to try and conceal this. Geoffrey agreed, accepting all my amendments – which, although they somewhat shortened the minute, still left it the best part of 12 pages long – and the paper was sent to Number 10 that evening, Wednesday, 14 June.

Margaret's reaction was extraordinary. I could not imagine any other Prime Minister considering it in any way objectionable to have a meeting with her Foreign Secretary and Chancellor before embarking on an international politico-economic negotiation of the first importance. Indeed, most would have taken the initiative themselves. Not only had Margaret not done so, but – so great had her hostility to ERM entry become, even when the suggestion was of a deadline more than three years off and well into the next Parliament – she was reluctant to hold a meeting even when her Foreign Secretary and Chancellor had sought one. Grudgingly, she agreed to see us at five o'clock in the afternoon the following Tuesday, almost a week ahead.

Geoffrey and I duly went to see her on the afternoon of 20 June. Geoffrey spoke to our joint paper, and she then waded in, saying that she disagreed completely with both our analysis and our conclusions. She was totally opposed to any commitment to join the ERM by any particular date, which would put an unwelcome constraint on economic and monetary policy as the date approached; it would in any case take no EMU tricks at all and we would simply have made a significant concession for no return; any departure from the 'when the time is right' formula, so soon after we had fought the Euro elections on that platform, would be seen by the Europeans as a sign of weakness; and the right course was not to decide any tactics now but for her to decide what to do when she was in Madrid and had heard what line the others were taking.

I argued that the EMU threat was very real indeed, and that, with such high stakes, simply playing it by ear was very dangerous; and that we were committed to joining the ERM – which I believed to be very much in our economic interest – anyway, so we had nothing to lose by playing that card at Madrid. Geoffrey came in again; but it was clear that we were getting nowhere, so I asked her not to close her mind but to reflect further on what we had written and said. She said she would, and trusted that we would reflect further on what she had said.

Her further reflection did not take nearly as long as she had taken to see us in the first place. Geoffrey telephoned me the following day, Thursday, 21 June, asking me if I could come across for a further word. When I arrived, he showed me a lengthy letter his office had received from Charles Powell, dated the previous evening. Purporting to be a note of our 20 June meeting, which for the most part it was, it also contained 'an alternative way of proceeding' to that which Geoffrey and I had suggested. Building on the approach I had taken with the Treasury

Select Committee of indicating the conditions that would need to be fulfilled for sterling to join the ERM, it added to the exchange control abolition and inflation improvement conditions which I had suggested, both the creation of a 'level playing field' in Europe on the monetary (*sic*) front and the final completion of the Single Market – both of which, moreover, would have to be in effect long enough for us to be able to judge that they were being genuinely implemented by all Member states.

This was palpably absurd. It had nothing whatever to do with securing an acceptable outcome from Madrid, and everything to do with postponing sterling's entry into the ERM as long as possible, if not indefinitely. The hand of Walters was all too visible.

The Second Thatcher/Howe/Lawson Meeting

Geoffrey understandably felt we could not leave the matter there, and that we should seek a further meeting. On the morning of Friday, 23 June, we sent Margaret a further joint minute, this time very much shorter. It gave a crisp restatement of the main thrust of the earlier minute, and responded to the 'alternative way of proceeding' by pointing out that this would take no tricks whatever at Madrid, which was the object of the exercise. Indeed, by inventing further, largely irrelevant, reasons to delay for a considerable number of years sterling's entry into the ERM, it would if anything be counter-productive. The minute concluded by asking Margaret for a further meeting before she and Geoffrey flew to Madrid on the Sunday evening, particularly since I would not be at Madrid myself.

After we had agreed the text of the minute, Geoffrey, who had clearly been thinking further about his future, told me that if the Powell letter really reflected Margaret's planned position at Madrid, and she was totally unwilling to make any forward move of the kind advocated in our original minute, then he would feel obliged to resign. This took me by surprise, as I had (wrongly as it eventually turned out) never thought of Geoffrey as the resigning type. But I told him that we were both in this together, and if he went, then clearly I would have to go, too.

Margaret was very angry indeed that we had returned to the charge. She first said she had no time to see us at all, as she would be working on the papers for Madrid. She then tried to fob us off by offering to talk to me on the telephone at midday on Sunday and to Geoffrey Howe afterwards on the flight to Madrid. This was a transparent divide-and-rule tactic, increasingly characteristic of her premiership. She had long believed that Geoffrey and I were plotting against her, but this was, in fact, the only instance in eight years as Cabinet colleagues when we combined to promote a particular course of action. Very grudgingly, she eventually agreed to a meeting at Number 10 at nine o'clock in the morning of Sunday, 25 June, a time which she knew would cause us both the maximum inconvenience. I was planning to go straight from Dorneywood to the Guards' Polo Club at Windsor, where Thérèse and I had been invited to watch the polo from the royal box. Geoffrey was, as usual, spending the weekend at Chevening, on the other side of London.

On the Sunday morning we left Dorneywood and Chevening respectively and met briefly at Number 11 before going next door to see Margaret. We made it clear that, this time, we wished to see her alone, with no official present. The atmosphere was unbelievably tense. As before, Geoffrey opened, and spoke briefly along the lines of the minute. Margaret was immovable. Geoffrey then said that if she had no time whatever for his advice, and was not prepared to make the sort of forward move at Madrid necessary to avoid the disastrous outcome he feared, then he would have no alternative but to resign. I then chipped in, briefly, to say 'You should know, Prime Minister, that if Geoffrey goes, I must go too'. There was an icy silence, and the meeting came to an abrupt end, with nothing resolved.

Movement at Madrid

On the aeroplane to Madrid that evening, Margaret refused to utter a single word to Geoffrey. When they arrived at the Ritz Hotel in Madrid, she immediately repaired to her room with Charles Powell to work out her line for the following day's meeting, ostentatiously excluding Geoffrey from the exercise. But in the short term it proved to be the storm before the calm. At the European Council meeting the next day the other heads of government, not to mention Geoffrey, were pleased and surprised to discover an apparently new Margaret Thatcher, and lost no time in informing the press. Where she had previously been strident she was now conciliatory. That was – to quote the Howe/Lawson minute – largely a matter of 'tone of voice'. But there was a change of content, too.

This concerned the sensitive issue of sterling and the ERM. In place of the hackneyed formula of joining 'when the time is right', she sought to spell out more precisely what this meant, in terms that were very much more forthcoming than those set out in the Walters-inspired 'alternative way of proceeding' contained in the Powell letter. She subsequently conveyed this to the House of Commons in an uncharacteristically obscure way. In her Statement to the House of 29 June on the outcome of the Madrid European Council she said:

> The Council agreed that the measures necessary to achieve the first stage of progressive realization of economic and monetary union will be implemented from 1 July 1990. These include completion of the

Single Market, abolition of all foreign exchange controls, a free market in financial services and strengthening of the Community's competition policy by reducing state aids . . . I reaffirmed our intention to join the ERM, but we must first get our inflation down. We shall look for satisfactory implementation of other aspects of the first phase of the Delors report, including free movement of capital and *(sic)* abolition of foreign exchange control.

It had been explained to the press that what this meant was that there were five so-called 'Madrid conditions': lower inflation and the abandonment of exchange control – the two conditions I had stipulated to the Treasury Select Committee – plus *further progress* towards completion of the Single Market, free competition in financial services, and the strengthening of European competition policy.

Irrelevant though these last three conditions were to the objective question of ERM membership, it was clear that they were as long as a piece of string: they could be interpreted as having been satisfied at any time. By contrast, the original Walters/Powell formulation had implied that there could be no ERM membership for some four years at the earliest – the single market was not due for final completion until the end of 1992, which meant that even in the unlikely event of everything going according to plan, it would have been well into 1993 before the monitoring period had been completed.

Margaret clearly felt that she had stood her ground. She had refused to give a deadline for ERM entry, and had produced a new formula which, although very different from the old one, would, she believed, give her almost as much freedom to decide that the time for entry had not yet come. She also believed Walters' assertion that the ERM would, in any event, collapse as a result of the removal of exchange controls. But despite all Ingham's efforts to sell the new formula as only a minor change, the press, perhaps influenced in part by her new tone of voice, universally interpreted it as a major new development and a big step towards ERM membership. And a particular interpretation of the Madrid conditions did indeed assist my successor, John Major, to persuade a Margaret Thatcher weakened by my resignation to assent to ERM membership some 16 months later. But that was not what she had in mind at the time.

Whether the original Howe/Lawson proposal would have succeeded in arresting the Treaty changes required to implement a single European currency managed by a single European central bank is something we shall never know. Certainly Margaret's contrary approach failed to do so. The Madrid Council went far beyond the S'Agaro Ecofin, agreeing to embark forthwith on the preparations for an Intergovernmental Conference to determine the Treaty changes required to implement Stages Two and Three of the Delors plan for a single currency, a process which was to culminate in the Maastricht Treaty of December 1991. Whether the single European currency ever comes about is a different matter altogether. The declared commitment on the part of the member governments is there, as are the necessary Treaty provisions. But it will be the political and economic realities on the ground that have the last word.

Geoffrey Howe Pays the Price

The Madrid Council ended on the afternoon of Tuesday, 27 June. I saw Geoffrey in his room at the House of Commons after the ten o'clock vote that evening, to discuss with him where we stood on the resignation question. The media, rightly or wrongly, were without exception hailing Madrid – which Margaret was felt to have handled with unaccustomed skill – as a major breakthrough on the ERM, and our back-benchers, particularly those in the pro-ERM camp, were echoing the chorus. He understandably felt that, although she had rejected our deadline proposal, a resignation in those circumstances would have been bizarre and incomprehensible. But the events that had preceded Madrid were a profound shock to Margaret, and relations between the three of us were never the same again. I have little doubt that, whether or not she was actually planning to do so, our joint resignation warning in June 1989 ensured that she removed Geoffrey from the job he loved above all others in her summer reshuffle the following month. No doubt she would have removed me, too, had she felt strong enough to do so.

Not that Geoffrey expected it. Right up to the last moment, David Waddington, the Chief Whip, was consulting him about the reshuffle, asking him whom he wished to have as his junior Foreign Office Ministers. It was in a state of considerable shock that he telephoned me at Number 11 on the morning of Monday, 24 July, to tell me that Margaret had told him that she was relieving him of the Foreign Office and that he could have the choice of being either Leader of the House or Home Secretary, a post then held by Douglas Hurd. If he chose the latter, Douglas would become Leader of the House. He said he would think about it and let her know later that day. He asked me what I thought he should do – he was clearly planning to consult a number of friends and colleagues – and told me he was thinking of accepting neither offer, and resigning.

I said that whether he resigned or not was a matter for him, on which I could not advise him. But if he chose not to resign, I had no doubt that he should choose the Home Office, which when all was said and done was a major Department of State and the only one of the 'big three' which he had not himself held, rather than be Leader of the House, which in my view was simply a second-rank job which provided no departmental power base at all. I also urged him, if he did want to stay, to insist on being nominated as Deputy Prime Minister. In the event, he did do the latter; but to my surprise opted for Leader of the House – a big mistake.

Later on he told me that he should have resigned. I was not surprised. Not only was his ministerial post a poor one, but Margaret went out of her way to humiliate him at every turn, berating him in front of colleagues and conspicuously excluding him from *ad hoc* meetings of senior Ministers. It was extraordinary conduct, since even if she had invited him – which she should have done, given his seniority and experience, leaving aside the empty title of Deputy Prime Minister she had reluctantly accorded him – she had no need to accept his advice. It was yet another example of her recklessness which one senior official, a particularly shrewd and close observer, described to me as the outstanding characteristic of her long-drawn-out final phase. She had become reckless over Europe, reckless over the Poll Tax, reckless over what she said in public, and reckless over her colleagues.

On the afternoon of the Cabinet reshuffle, after Geoffrey had decided he was not going to resign, Margaret asked to see me. She explained that Geoffrey would have to hand over the occupancy of Chevening to his successor as Foreign Secretary, my former number two, John Major, whom I had met emerging from her room in a daze as I arrived. John had of course expected promotion to a Department of his own, had always hoped to succeed me as Chancellor in due course, and had ultimate aspirations to Number 10; but never in his wildest dreams had he seen himself as Foreign Secretary.

Margaret told me that the reason why she wanted to see me was that, deprived of Chevening, Geoffrey would need to have Dorneywood instead. Did I mind handing it over to him? It was not, of course, a question, but an instruction. It was also a considerable, if not entirely unexpected, blow. We had grown to love Dorneywood; and it had been the tranquillity of that idyllic retreat, and the pampering I had enjoyed from its admirable staff, that had kept me going despite the stresses and strains of my problems with Margaret over the previous year and more. But Geoffrey was formally Deputy Prime Minister, and that was that. Margaret must have enjoyed the irony. I told her that we had planned to spend the children's summer holiday there, but that I would, of course, vacate it after that.

I happened to be in the Chamber when Geoffrey first rose to speak in his new capacity as Leader of the House. A loud and prolonged spontaneous cheer rose from the massed Conservative benches of a kind that is rarely heard. It was a tribute to the affection in which Geoffrey was held within the Party. But more than anything else, it was a clear warning to Margaret. No experienced Tory Member could have failed to get the message – except perhaps one: Margaret Hilda Thatcher.

CHAPTER 75

FROM MADRID TO WASHINGTON VIA ANTIBES

A Cabinet for the Election · Policy on the Hoof
Competing Currencies · Ecofin at Antibes
Posthumous Publication · My Last IMF Meeting
Eastern Europe Comes in from the Cold · White House Interlude

A Cabinet for the Election

MARGARET BEHAVED LITTLE BETTER to her colleagues after the July 1989 reshuffle than she had before. The press briefings by Ingham became ever more presidential and Margaret's trust in – and dependence upon – her kitchen cabinet ever more pronounced. Yet seeing her at close quarters it seemed clear to me that she had in fact been quite shaken by the turbulence created by the reshuffle. At the first subsequent Cabinet meeting she surprised us all by announcing, out of the blue, that she now had the Cabinet with which she planned to fight the next election, and that there would therefore be no further Cabinet changes for the remainder of that parliament. She had never before vouchsafed anything to Cabinet about her future reshuffle intentions: yet this statement was volunteered and clearly premeditated.

Meanwhile, after the drama of Madrid at the end of June, both Margaret and I began independently to start worrying about the domestic economy again. She asked for a meeting with me to discuss the situation, at which I was to bring along Peter Middleton and Terry Burns. This was fixed for 5 July. Two days earlier, I held a meeting of my own, to which I invited Robin Leigh-Pemberton and his senior colleagues from the Bank. I expressed concern at the slowness of bank lending and consumer credit, and the spending they were financing, to decelerate in response to the monetary squeeze. The narrow measure of money, MO, remained well above its target range. I was told that it was the considered view of the Bank that monetary policy should not be tightened further for the time being. So far as I was concerned, the operative words were 'for the time being'.

At Margaret's meeting of 5 July she expressed considerable concern at the outlook for inflation. The underlying rate of inflation, which in the first quarter of 1988 had still been well below 4 per cent, where it had stood for the previous two years, had since then risen steadily to within a whisker of 6 per cent. I told her I shared her concern, and felt that the time was fast approaching when we should raise interest rates by a further 1 per cent. Predictably, this did not attract her at all. Arguing that any further rise in interest rates would raise mortgage rates, and hence the headline RPI, which in turn would add to wage pressure and upset the financial markets, and might tip the economy into recession, she said she would rather see interest rates held at 14 per cent until the RPI started to fall, when they could be brought down again.

I gave a full warning of the risks in my annual 'end-of-term letter' to all Conservative MPs on 26 July 1989, when I said I would keep interest rates 'as high as is necessary for as long as is necessary', a formula I had been using for some time. As usual, I included a positive element, pointing out that business investment as a share of national income was higher than at any time since records began, and that the UK had moved from the bottom to the top of the European investment league. Not only had investment surged ahead, but its quality had improved out of recognition. Indeed despite the severity of the subsequent recession, investment remained much higher as a share of GDP than had occurred in previous downturns (see table in Annexe 7).

Policy on the Hoof

My other main preoccupation during the summer of 1989 was with developments on the EMU front. At her first pre-Madrid meeting with Geoffrey and me on 20 June 1989, Margaret had expressed the view that it would be more sensible to play the Summit by ear than to agree tactics in advance. This was of course a transparent device to explain her unwillingness to discuss tactics with either of us. But, amazingly, it was also how she did in part behave. In the middle of the discussions at Madrid she announced that the UK would be putting forward its own proposals for monetary union, as an alternative to the Delors plan which we rejected.

In itself there was much to be said for this sort of approach. It was clearly more positive than the 'No, no, no' which had hitherto been her preferred negotiating stance, and was more likely to bring out the underlying issues. But suddenly to announce this at a European Council without any prior discussion with her Chancellor, and without the faintest idea of what the UK alternative might be, was, to say the least, an unusual way of proceeding.

The first I and my senior officials knew of this proposal was a report on the radio from Madrid which stated that the Treasury was already working on alternatives to Delors. Peter Middleton subsequently told me that he heard the news when driving his car, and was so astonished that he nearly crashed into a tree. About twenty-four hours later came the request from Number 10 to validate the Prime Minister's promise. My officials gave me a submission setting out every possibility they could think of – there were not very many – including a return to the gold standard.

Competing Currencies

I soon decided that only one was really worth pursuing. The great economist and political philosopher, Friedrich Hayek, had some years previously come up with the idea of removing the monopoly of issuing currency from the Central Banks, privatizing it, and opening it up to competition. Hayek's idea was that as in other private markets, so with currencies: competition would ensure that the best currency – that which kept its value best, and was thus the most sought after – would steadily increase its share of the market.

I had long been interested in Hayek's analysis – and had, indeed, referred to it *en passant* in my IEA lecture the previous summer. I told Peter Middleton that the alternative form of monetary union we should propose should be based on the Hayekian idea of competing currencies, but with the fundamental difference that currency creation would remain in the hands of the national Central Banks, which in turn would act within the framework of the ERM. The element of competition would be achieved by removing all barriers to the use in any one Community country of the currencies of other member states, in the true spirit of the single market. With complete interchangeability and no legal impediments, good currencies would threaten gradually to drive out the bad, in a happy reversal of Gresham's law, until eventually Europe might theoretically find itself with a single currency, freely chosen by the people.

Certainly, Central Banks would have a clear incentive to compete, if only to collect the profit from the note issue, or seignorage as it is technically known, and if the competition failed to lead to a single currency – and competition does not normally lead to monopoly – that would be either because two or more currencies were considered more or less equally desirable, or simply because the people of Europe did not want a single currency. But even then the removal of all barriers between the different European moneys was something that could just about be considered a monetary union. But no new institutions, no treaty amendment, and no massive transfer of sovereignty would be required.

Peter then commissioned a Treasury paper along these lines, and I went off to enjoy my last summer holiday at Dorneywood with Thérèse and the children.

Ecofin at Antibes

When I returned in the latter part of August and found the paper waiting for me, it was clear that it would have to be completely redrafted. This was duly done, but the hiatus was sufficient to ensure that the paper could not be properly vetted by me and cleared with Margaret – who accepted the general idea, when I put it to her – in time for the informal Ecofin Council to be held on the French Riviera on 8 and 9 September at the Hôtel du Cap/Eden Roc at Cap d'Antibes.

This was one of the few informal Ecofins to which Thérèse decided to accompany me, and she certainly chose well. Only a Socialist government would have contemplated putting up twelve Finance Ministers and their wives, twelve Central Bank Governors and their wives, twelve 'deputies' and their wives, various European Commissioners and their wives, and assorted hangers-on, at a hotel whose cheapest room cost £800 a night   (our own suite was priced at £2,000 a night). If any hotel was worth that extraordinary price, however, that was: the setting, the comfort, the food – they produced what in my opinion was the best Mesclun salad in the world – the wines, the service and, so far as I had time to enjoy them, the facilities, were unbeatable.

When we got on to the subject of EMU and the Delors Report, I told my fellow Finance Ministers and the Central Bank Governors that we would soon be publishing the paper that Margaret had effectively promised at Madrid, and proceeded to give a resumé of its contents. Delors himself was, inevitably, extremely hostile, but few others were. The prevailing attitude was one of polite scepticism and of reserving final judgement until they had read the paper. I had no overt support, even though Karl-Otto Pöhl said to me, shortly after I had spoken, as he passed me on his way out of the room, 'I agreed with every word you said'. I was far too old a hand to believe that that would lead to anything: I was much more interested to discover the doubts that were beginning to dawn in the minds of my fellow Finance Ministers at the private discussion we had over lunch, and the strong desire of most of them to adopt a more cautious, step-by-step, approach than the Commission's.

Predictably, the British Press reported the UK proposal as having been greeted with total hostility and derision. During Margaret's time, the Brussels-based Press corps, who for the most part covered these events, had become accustomed to writing 'UK isolated' stories and could think in terms of little else. They had also got into the habit of taking their cue from the Commission, with whom they had a continuing close relationship. But I was myself remiss in not briefing selected journalists privately in advance. As it was, they had difficulty in understanding what the proposal meant, and scoffed at the idea of a tobacconist in Aberdeen being obliged to accept payment in Greek Drachmas. In fact, of course, he would have been no more obliged to take Greek Drachmas than he is to take credit cards – the true international money, in many ways, as it happens – since the idea was essentially permissive rather than mandatory.

Much, too, was made of the alleged problem of legal tender, which, admittedly, we had not then had time to explore properly. I suspected that it was a non-issue, a suspicion subsequently borne out by a study published in the *Treasury Bulletin* which concluded that 'Legal tender is a specialized legal concept with little practical significance for the acceptability of a currency'. The truth is that is an archaic concept which could readily be dispensed with altogether – despite the importance the Bundesbank attaches to it in connection with the proposed European Central Bank.

There is nothing bizarre in a choice of currencies, as anyone who visits frontier towns like Geneva well knows. The Treasury economists working on the scheme were, however, impressed by the persistence with which people hung on to familiar currencies except under Latin-American-type hyperinflation. The use of multiple currencies in border areas was, they believed, the exception. In presenting the scheme they therefore shifted the emphasis to competition in monetary policies. There were embarrassed smoke signals to the Press about this shift of emphasis. But I was fairly relaxed. The idea clearly had to be presented as a European currency proposal, in the context of an alternative to the Delors single currency proposal, and since it is monetary policy that chiefly determines the desirability of holding a particular currency, it was a distinction without a difference.

I suspect, too, that some Treasury officials were themselves confused, thinking (like the Press) of a currency in terms of physical notes and coins, rather than the much more important matter of the currency in which financial transactions are denominated. The key point in this context, which was to feature prominently in the paper, was that competition would, as Hayek had pointed out, ensure that only low-inflation currencies survived, at least on any significant scale, thus retaining the most important attribute of the ERM. The Delors approach had no such in-built anti-inflationary bias.

My proposals were, of course, disappointing to those who were interested in European money only as a means to political union. Some officials in the Foreign Office, Bank of England and even the Treasury were worried that the paper simply proposed an intensification of Stage One, and that no new international body was elaborated. That, however, was one of its great virtues.

In any event, I had no qualms about putting the emphasis on the twin pillars of a genuine single market and the fuller development of the ERM. It was not as if my proposals pointed to inaction. Even with the abolition of exchange controls there was a long way to go before currencies were freely interchangeable in the fullest sense. One example of the remaining restrictions related to the currency and geographical location of the assets of long-term savings institutions such as pension funds. Another was legal impediments to the simplification of international cheque-clearing systems. Some of these obstacles exist even in single currency areas such as the US, and are worth removing for their own sake.

Posthumous Publication

The press of events meant that it was not until October that the paper, which I called *An Evolutionary Approach to Economic and Monetary Union*, was in a final form with which I was content. It began by pointing out the flaws in the Delors approach, including *inter alia*, the fact that:

> By eliminating both competition and accountability . . . the Delors version risks producing a higher inflation rate in Europe. The administratively imposed changes that are required would inevitably fail to foresee future developments. And they involve major constitutional and institutional changes which are wholly unnecessary.

Its main argument was that the removal of exchange controls and the creation of a single financial area, together with the ERM, the possibility of currency substitution, and the influence of capital and labour mobility, would all exert a powerful influence towards stable prices and exchange rates. The emphasis was on the financial integration of Europe emerging from Stage One rather than from any new Brussels-type institutions. The currency basket known as the Ecu could come into wider use, first for financial, but perhaps eventually for everyday, purposes. The paper also suggested freezing the composition of the Ecu basket permanently – a step eventually incorporated into the Maastricht Treaty.

The evolutionary route to what might just be called a sort of monetary union was summarized in paragraph 23:

> Realignments would become rarer, fluctuations within the ERM band would become smaller, and the EMS could evolve into a system of more or less fixed exchange rates. Concurrently with minimal exchange rate uncertainty and reduced costs of switching between

currencies, all Community currencies would become effectively inter-changeable. In this way a practical monetary union would be achieved as a result of a gradual evolutionary process.

After I had sent the paper to Margaret, she decided that it would have to be formally cleared for publication by a small group consisting not merely of herself, myself and the Foreign Secretary, now John Major, as had been her practice on similar occasions hitherto, but also of Nick Ridley. Nick had become her strongest supporter over the ERM, and had already seen me privately to voice his disagreement with the policy I was pursuing.

Margaret of course well knew of Nick's views, and her inclusion of him in the meeting to clear the paper was not intended to make my task any easier. The meeting eventually took place on the afternoon of Wednesday, 25 October – ironically, the day before my resignation – and the paper was cleared for publication with only the most trivial of amendments. My officials, who had been apprehensive of Margaret's reaction to a paper whose proposals assumed sterling's membership of what would ultimately become an unequivocally 'hard' version of the ERM, felt that I had achieved something of a coup.

Certainly, it was never likely that the paper's proposals, particularly launched so late in the day, would deflect the rest of the Community's political leaders from the Delors path on which they had already embarked. Its long-term merit was that it set out a series of measures, desirable in themselves, to which the Community could return if and when the momentum for full-blooded monetary union faltered for other reasons. In the short term the paper's value was largely domestic. It contained, for the first time, a firm Government commitment that sterling would join the ERM when the Madrid conditions, which were clearly spelled out in a perfectly acceptable form, were satisfied. This definitive statement meant that, when Margaret subsequently sought to add further conditions as and when they entered her head, it was easier to ignore them as apocryphal.

My paper was eventually published, by my successor, John Major, on 2 November, the week after my resignation. Subsequently the Government shifted its allegiance to a new and much more complex alternative to Delors, the so-called 'hard Ecu' proposal. A highly ingenious but fundamentally unworkable proposal which included an unwise Euro-institutional component, it was understood by few and served chiefly as a talisman: for some time any Minister asked where the UK stood on EMU could reply, 'We favour the hard Ecu'. The scheme had been sold to Margaret by the irrepressible Michael Butler, a former UK Ambassador to the Community who, in 1979, had sold the previous Labour Government the idea of being in the EMS while outside the

ERM. Very few outside the UK showed the slightest interest in it, and John Major quite rightly abandoned it well ahead of the negotiations over the Maastricht Treaty.

My Last IMF Meeting

Meanwhile, in September, I had spent the customary week in Washington to attend what was to be my last annual meeting of the Fund and Bank as Chancellor of the Exchequer. The RAF flew me from Brize Norton to Dulles Airport on Friday, 22 September, in good time to prepare for the G7 meeting the following day. This proved to last an inordinate time – some seven hours in all – chiefly because Nick Brady was anxious for the rest of us to do more to persuade our commercial banks to co-operate in Brady plan schemes for various Latin American sovereign debtors. He clearly felt that persistence would wear down the resistance which some of us expressed, and was deeply disappointed when it did not.

The other main issue on the agenda which Brady, as Chairman, proposed to us was another old favourite, the current account imbalances and the exchange rate scene. On 15 September the dollar had risen above the DM2 level – putting it outside the Louvre range. It was always easier to reach agreement within the G7 when the dollar was high and the Deutschmark low than the other way about. The Americans, with their obsession about their current account deficit, did not want to see the dollar rise any further, and the Germans, always fearful of a resurgence of inflation, did not wish to see a low Deutschmark. There was therefore little difficulty in agreeing a passage in the G7 communiqué of which the main thrust was the standard asymmetrical formula:

> The Ministers and Governors considered the rise in recent months of the dollar inconsistent with longer run economic fundamentals. They agreed that a rise of the dollar above current levels or an excessive decline could adversely affect prospects for the world economy. In this context, they agreed to co-operate more closely in exchange markets.

The dollar duly obliged, and steadily retreated until, by the winter of 1990–91, it had fallen to below DM 1.50. But the September 1989 G7 was to prove the last brief flowering of Plaza-Louvre co-operation over exchange rates.

Eastern Europe Comes in from the Cold

However, by September 1989 my attention had been captured by the momentous events that were beginning to convulse the countries of

Central and Eastern Europe, freeing them from the grip of Communism and the Soviet Empire, and setting them on the difficult path to political and economic reform. It was still early days then: the Berlin Wall remained intact – it did not fall until the following November – and Czechoslovakia had not yet had its velvet revolution. But both Poland and Hungary had embarked on efforts to create a market economy, and I was astonished that Brady had included no reference to these events in the agenda he had proposed to us. Right at the start of the meeting I observed that we would be failing in our duty if we were not to discuss the situation in Central and Eastern Europe; and, with strong support from Germany, I was able to persuade Brady to add it to the agenda. This led to the G7 communiqué of 23 September stating that,

> The Ministers and Governors discussed the historic events now in progress in some of the countries of Eastern Europe, especially in Poland and Hungary, and expressed their strong support for plans to create more open and market-based economies.

The new non-Communist Polish Finance Minister, Leszek Balcerowicz, was in Washington for the annual meeting, and I took the opportunity to invite him and his team to see me. I was impressed by this lean, young, intense, bespectacled academic, with an excellent command of English, and equally impressed by the thoroughness of the reform plan he outlined to me in considerable detail, by his realistic assessment of the immense difficulties he was up against, and by his obvious intelligence and determination. It was a remarkable contrast to one of his Communist predecessors who had visited me about ten years previously, when I was Financial Secretary, seeking UK financial assistance, and had explained to me that there was nothing basically wrong with the Polish economy provided they had a normal harvest: it was just unfortunate that the harvest had been below normal for the past fifteen years.

The new Poles have shown considerable heroism in the way in which they have attempted the formidable and unprecedented task of adjustment from a Communist economy to a market economy. It is a great sadness that, in moving to democracy, they have saddled themselves with an electoral system – pure proportional representation – that makes it all but impossible for a strong government to be formed.

Meanwhile, at the Interim Committee meeting which followed the G7 I elaborated on the need for the West to rise to the challenge of the events in Central and Eastern Europe, arguing that for these countries a policy of gradualism would be self-defeating, and that the West should lift restrictions on Polish imports, reschedule Polish debts, and send management and financial experts to help the Poles make a success of their reform programme. Much of this has since become commonplace, and much has been done, but the severely limited nature of the European Community's concession to food, textile and steel imports from Central and Eastern Europe remains a disgrace.

When it came to my address to the annual Fund and Bank meeting itself, again I opened by talking about the importance of the reforms that were just beginning in Poland and Hungary. My main theme, however, in both the international and UK contexts, was the inevitability and normality of current account imbalances in a world of free and integrated capital markets. I was able to cite in support the latest IMF *Economic Outlook*, which marked a sharp change in tone from what it had said the previous year. The international imbalances, it remarked,

> . . .reflect in part the international implications of fundamental differences among countries in the balance between private saving and investment, resulting, *inter alia*, from different demographic or technological trends. In a world of highly integrated financial markets, these differences naturally give rise to capital movements in the direction of countries with relatively low savings rates and relatively high (risk adjusted) rates of return on capital.

I was not to escape altogether, however, from the malign tradition of trouble with the pound erupting during my annual week in Washington. An incorrect news agency report claimed that I, of all people, was unconcerned about a further fall in sterling. I hastily issued a statement that 'a firm exchange rate remains an essential plank of our policy', but not before sterling had plunged 2½ pfennigs and was once more down near the DM3 level.

White House Interlude

Nick Brady evidently felt that he had failed to secure an adequate response from his G7 colleagues on the only international subject in which he had any interest, that of Latin American sovereign debt, and that some more effective means of persuasion was required. As a result, we were all informed on the Monday that the President would like to see us at the White House early the following evening, Tuesday, 26 September.

I had already met George Bush at a very small dinner party Margaret had given for him at Number 10 a few months earlier, on 1 June. He was relaxed, friendly, unassuming and immensely likeable. He was almost as unlike his predecessor as it was possible to be. Reagan's style was that of the actor he once was. He knew his lines perfectly, and had rehearsed and polished them endlessly, with the result that everything, from the generalizations to the anecdotes, came across with impressive fluency, obvious sincerity, and complete command. But take him off the ground covered by his script, and he often had difficulty in grasping the point. Bush, by contrast, was conspicuously lacking in polish and fluency, but quick to grasp any point made to him.

It was clear, too, that the strong personal rapport Margaret had enjoyed with Reagan was not present in her relationship with Bush. It was in part this, I believe, that somewhat improbably led her to transfer her admiration and affection to the much more charismatic figure of Mikhail Gorbachev, whom she greatly overrated – an error which was partly responsible for her serious misreading of the tumultuous events in Central and Eastern Europe in the last year of her premiership, notably the question of German reunification, and which derailed British foreign policy as a result.

The Bushes were due to fly back to Washington the following morning. Normally, a Head of State would be seen off at the airport either by Margaret or – if she had some unbreakable engagement – by the Foreign Secretary. On this occasion, not only did she have an unbreakable appointment, but Geoffrey was abroad, as a result of which she asked Thérèse and me to see the Bushes off on her behalf. She would never have allowed Ronald Reagan to have been seen off by the Number Three in the Government's pecking order.

To return to the 1989 Fund and Bank annual meetings: I duly arrived at the White House at around half past five on 26 September, to be shown into a vast empty parquet-floored room, in one corner of which sat a Marine in full dress uniform playing light music on a piano. This turned out to be nothing more than a somewhat surreal prelude to the next large room, where the guests were assembling amid tables lavishly stocked with a hot and cold buffet, and a long bar. Not only were the full G7 cast present – Finance Ministers, their deputies and the Central Bank Governors – but also the Chairmen of all the leading commercial banks from the seven countries. This made it a double innovation: not only had there never before been a Presidential reception at the White House for the G7, but the private sector had never before been invited to any official G7 occasion. The Americans' desire to blur the public sector/private sector borderline on the debt issue could not have been more vividly demonstrated.

After what seemed an interminable wait, a lectern was erected at one end of the room and George and Barbara Bush entered. The President went up to the lectern, and read his script. It was mercifully brief and amounted to telling us that the Brady plan had the full backing of the President of the United States and, given the enormous importance of the issues involved, he hoped that we would all work together to ensure that it was a success. As he stood there, Barbara Bush was at his side, defiantly white-haired, proudly beaming, her robust and healthy physique emphasizing the apparent frailty of his. It was all a very soft sell indeed;

nor did the fact that he felt it necessary to read his lines enhance the impact. I found it difficult to imagine that a single G7 Finance Minister's stance on the issue was changed as a result of it.

The President concluded by saying that he and Barbara would like to meet us all, after which we were welcome to look around the White House picture collection in the next room. A line duly formed up, and we each had our handshake and few words before passing into the next room with the pictures.

Anxious to put this pointless, if harmless, occasion to good use, I took the opportunity to discuss the EMU issue with the Germans, whom I saw as the key. Hans Tietmeyer, the formidable, long-serving and likeable G7 Deputy, whom I had got to know pretty well over the years and who was about to join the Bundesbank as Vice-President, had suggested that I should have a word about it with Germany's relatively new Finance Minister, Theo Waigel. Waigel had succeeded Franz-Josef Strauss as Leader of the CDU's Bavarian sister party, the CSU, and as one of the party leaders in a three-party coalition government not only carried more political clout than his predecessor, Stoltenberg, ever did, but could take a more independent line. He was also no friend of the FDP's Hans-Dietrich Genscher, who was the principal enthusiast for EMU within the governing coalition.

Waigel, whom I had first met at the Paris Summit the previous July, when we had got on well together, made it clear to me that he had considerable reservations about the Delors Report, which Tietmeyer appeared to share, and he had been wondering how best to persuade Kohl to rethink the German stand. I said that there was much to be said for the two of us trying to reach a common position on the issue. He agreed, and invited me to Germany to discuss the matter privately between us both. I accepted, and it was agreed that a mutually convenient date should be sorted out between our respective offices. The date eventually fixed for our talks was 26 October. It was to prove a fateful date for a different reason.

CHAPTER 76

COUNTDOWN TO RESIGNATION

A Sticky Wicket · Bad Timing by the Bundesbank
15 Per Cent · The Siege of Stoney Stanton
Party Conference Success · The Iceberg and its Tip
The Die is Cast · On the Brink of Resignation

A Sticky Wicket

RETURNING TO LONDON FROM Washington on Thursday, 28 September, I had to turn my mind to my speech for the Party Conference, which was due to begin some twelve days later. The economic background had changed markedly for the worse since the previous year's Party Conference; but at least I could make something, if only as a peroration, of the remarkable events that were unfolding in Eastern Europe, with the collapse of Socialism and the first faltering moves towards a genuine market economy. The tide of ideas, which I had first invoked in my 1986 Party Conference speech, was flooding into areas that I had never then envisaged.

But there was no point in deluding myself that there was going to be an easy wicket on which to bat; and to add to the problem sterling was looking far from healthy. The big fall had been in the first half of the year, when the pound had dropped from DM3.21 at the start of 1989 to DM3.02 by the end of June, and from $1.81 to $1.55 over the same period. Then there had been a brief recovery in the course of July, but since then it had drifted down again to DM3.02 and $1.62. Market sentiment was not at all good, and in that context its proximity to the psychologically important DM3 level was particularly worrying. It was when sterling was weak that the Walters view, which was widely taken by the markets to be that of Margaret, too, that sterling should be free to 'find its own level', was most damaging. I set up a stocktaking meeting, with the usual cast, for the following Monday, 2 October.

Bad Timing by the Bundesbank

The news that Robin Leigh-Pemberton brought to the meeting could not have been more inconvenient. With the Party Conference due to start on Tuesday, 10 October, it appeared that there was a strong chance that the Bundesbank Council, at its regular fortnightly meeting on Thursday, 5 October, would raise German interest rates. I had believed for some time that a further one point rise in UK interest rates would probably be needed on purely domestic grounds. It was true that the underlying rate of inflation had fallen back slightly from the 6 per cent level reached in May, but the inflationary evidence that had worried me in the first week of July had in no way abated three months later. The timing, however, was diabolical: the last thing I wanted to do was to raise interest rates on the eve of the Party Conference. I asked Robin to find out more about the Bundesbank's intentions and to let me know.

On the Wednesday, 4 October, Robin informed me that the Bundesbank would definitely be raising their interest rates the following day. The only unresolved question was whether the increase would be half a point or a full point. I arranged to see Margaret at five o'clock that afternoon, to tell her the unpalatable news, and the consequences as I saw them. I told her that if the Germans moved by half a point, I was prepared to hold the line with the aid of large-scale intervention. But if they moved by a full point, then I saw no alternative but for us to follow, uncomfortable as it was on the eve of the Party Conference – and I was well aware of the sort of reception I could expect for my speech in the circumstances. Not to do so would be to risk a full-blown sterling crisis and the possibility of being forced to raise interest rates in the middle of the Conference itself.

Margaret very reluctantly agreed that following the Germans immediately, in the event of a full point increase, would in the circumstances probably be the lesser evil, but expressed the fervent hope that they would do only half a point.

I called a markets meeting, again with the usual cast, for half past eight the following morning, Thursday, 5 October. There was no dissent from my proposition that, if the Bundesbank moved a full point that day, we should follow. Not to do so would have sent a signal to the markets either that short-term political considerations now weighed more heavily than our anti-inflation resolve, or that we were no longer concerned about the level of sterling – or probably both. Even so, there was likely to be pressure on the pound and we agreed that we should not defend the

DM3 benchmark regardless of cost, but that it would be better if it were not breached. We then went on to discuss the nuts and bolts of the actions we might well have to make.

15 Per Cent

At lunchtime that day the Bundesbank announced that its interest rates would indeed be raised by a full point. We immediately followed, as did most other European countries, including a number of those, like us, outside the ERM. This meant base rates of 15 per cent, the highest they had been for very nearly eight years. I presented the move as part of an international attack on inflation, which had indeed been rising worldwide. In economic terms, I had no doubt that the move was correct; but the politics could not have been worse. It was clear to me that I would have to recast my Conference speech completely, taking the interest rate issue head on, and make a virtue of having put economic rectitude above short-term political advantage.

The Conservative Party Conference was, by tradition, held in the North of England and the South of England in alternate years. There were a number of different venues in the south, of which Brighton was the most popular; but in the north there was only one: Blackpool, a holiday resort unique in the world, which everyone should visit once in their lives, even if many may choose not to repeat the experience. In fact, the wonderfully old-fashioned gilt and plush interior of Blackpool's Winter Garden, where the Conference itself was held, made it my favourite venue, with an atmosphere no modern hall could match. It was Blackpool's turn in 1989, and I went home to Stoney Stanton on the Friday evening to start thinking about how I would rewrite my speech, as well as catching up on the rest of my workload, which was always particularly heavy at that time of year.

I was telephoned there on the Saturday evening and informed that the following day's *Sunday Times* was carrying a story that claimed that Walters had opposed the rise in interest rates, and that Margaret had 'reluctantly sided with her Chancellor.' The paper went on to describe this as 'another damaging disagreement on policy between Lawson and Walters', and the clear implication for the markets of Margaret's alleged 'reluctance' was that there would be no further increase in interest rates, whatever happened to the pound.

Through the good offices of the unfailingly cheerful and efficient Number 10 switchboard, I telephoned Walters at home, who professed complete mystification about the story, swearing that he had not spoken to anyone. But he refused to issue a denial. Similar suggestions had in fact appeared over the previous few days from some writers of City circulars and a group of journalists who considered themselves to be Margaret's praetorian guard;

but *The Sunday Times* story was by far the most serious one, as that paper has a wide circulation among the business community.

To this day, I do not know how the paper came by their story. Nor do I much care. The point was that Number 10 allowed *The Sunday Times* story to pass without an explicit denial: any dissociation was so feeble that the markets were left to draw their own conclusions. Not surprisingly, sterling, which had rallied at the end of the previous week following the base rate increase, plunged on the Monday morning, taking it below the DM 3 benchmark for the first time since the March 1988 uncapping.

The Siege of Stoney Stanton

One of the advantages of Stoney Stanton when the Party Conference was at Blackpool was its geographical location, almost exactly halfway between Blackpool and London. The Conference always started on the Tuesday, with my speech on the Thursday and Margaret's closing address on the Friday. It had been my custom to write my speech in the peace and quiet of the Old Rectory on the Monday and Tuesday, travelling to Blackpool in time for the Area receptions on the Tuesday evening, and remaining there for the rest of the Conference.

In 1989 I had to change my normal practice, since my excellent Constituency agent, Graham Smith, had been elected Chairman of the Society of Conservative Agents for that year. The high spot of the Society's year was a black-tie dinner given for the Prime Minister on the Monday evening before the Conference proper began. By tradition, there were four speeches at the dinner: one by the Prime Minister, one by the Party Chairman, one by the Chairman of the Society of Agents, and one by the Member for his Constituency. I accordingly arranged to travel to Blackpool on the afternoon of Monday, 9 October, in time to change and attend the Agents' dinner, after which I would be driven back to Stoney Stanton to give me all day Tuesday and the morning of Wednesday to concentrate on what was bound to be a particularly difficult speech, returning to Blackpool on the Wednesday afternoon.

I duly arrived at Blackpool on the Monday evening, and Margaret suggested that I call in at her suite in the Imperial Hotel *en route* to the dinner, so that we would be seen arriving at the dinner together as a show of solidarity. While the appearance was no substitute for the reality, I could see that the appearance was better than nothing, particularly so far as the media and the financial markets were concerned, and we were accordingly televised descending the staircase of the Imperial Hotel together, somewhat awkwardly, and to a distinctly sceptical massed Press. My speech to the Agents, which I delivered largely off the cuff, went down well: light-hearted enough for an after-dinner speech but with just enough content to boost confidence at a difficult time. As I left Blackpool for Stoney Stanton after the dinner, as planned, I had no inkling of the horrors in store.

The next morning, Tuesday, 10 October, I was assailed by the worst Press I encountered throughout the whole of my political career. Almost the whole of the front page of the *Daily Mail*, and much more, was devoted to a scurrilous personal attack on me, headlined 'This Bankrupt Chancellor' and accompanied by a large and grotesque cartoon. I was accused of betraying my party, my Prime Minister and the British people, and there was much else in a similar vein. Margaret telephoned me at home very early in the morning to tell me how horrified she had been to read it in her hotel suite at Blackpool – Party Conference week being one of the few occasions when she actually read the papers rather than Ingham's carefully drafted summaries.

But while that was the worst of the Tuesday Press, it was the rest which caused the greater problem. To my astonishment, the other papers were all running a cock-and-bull story that I had fled from Blackpool because I could not face the wrath of the Constituency representatives and that I might never return, resigning with my tail between my legs instead.

Before long, I found myself under siege. The garden of the Old Rectory was walled on three sides, with the fourth open to the old churchyard. Reporters, Press photographers and television cameramen turned up in the churchyard in large numbers, clambering over the graves to try and get a view of me inside the house – my study overlooked the garden – and to catch me should I venture outside. When a few tired of waiting in the churchyard and invaded the garden to try and get a better look through the window, and to ring the front doorbell in an attempt to get me outside, I was obliged to telephone the Leicestershire Special Branch, who looked after me splendidly whenever I was out and about in the county, to get them ejected. I had told the intrusive media people right at the start that I was working on my speech, that I would be returning to Blackpool the next day, and that I would appreciate it if they left me alone to get on with it. But they insisted on keeping a noisy vigil in the churchyard. The oasis of calm to which I thought I had repaired to write my speech turned out to be anything but that.

Party Conference Success

I returned to Blackpool the following afternoon, Wednesday, 11 October and walked into the Imperial Hotel to a battery of waiting television cameras and young girls holding out microphones, yelling at me, 'When are you going to resign Mr Lawson?' It was clearly even more important that my speech at the end of the economic debate went down well. Fortunately, it did, from the very beginning:

I warmly welcome this motion, with its emphasis on the paramount need to fight inflation. Indeed, that is why I raised interest rates to 15 per cent last week. It was not a decision I took lightly. But it had to be done. Of course, I knew it wouldn't be popular. But anyone who becomes Chancellor in order to be popular has chosen the wrong job. I have only one ambition in politics. That is the long-term well-being of the British people. There is no greater threat to that well-being than inflation.

Inevitably people ask whether there is an alternative to high interest rates at the present time. And whether they can be sure that the policy will work. Bluntly, the answer is that there is no alternative and the policy will work. I realize the problems high interest rates cause to homeowners, particularly those with large mortgages, and to many small businesses. But the damage caused by high inflation would be far, far worse.

This led to my message to the markets and to Margaret alike: 'Nor is there any salvation in the rake's progress of perpetual devaluation . . . The Conservative Party never has been, and never will be, the party of devaluation'; then to my reminder to the party that the Thatcher Government had faced economic problems in the past and surmounted them all; and financially to the 'Eastern Europe' peroration – almost all that remained of my original speech.

I was no doubt helped by a feeling amongst my traditionally loyalist audience that, whatever their own reservations about the level of interest rates, the *Daily Mail* had gone way over the top in its hatchet job on me, and that the party was not to be pushed around by the tabloid Press. At any rate, the speech, according to a somewhat nonplussed Press, was punctuated by more than thirty rounds of applause and greeted at the end by the longest and most enthusiastic standing ovation of any speech at that year's conference – apart, of course, from the ritual hysteria reserved for the Leader.

Indeed – something I would not have thought possible a week earlier – it turned out to be one of the few high spots of a generally lacklustre Conference. The theme of the Conference, too, was to prove ill-fated. Kenneth Baker, by then Party Chairman, and uncomfortably aware of Margaret's growing unpopularity in the country, decided to build on her post-reshuffle announcement to Cabinet that she had the Cabinet with which she planned to fight the next election, and make the Conference theme 'The Right Team', with omnipresent photographs of various members of what was by then for the most part a highly experienced Cabinet. Within little more than a year, one-third of 'The Right Team' – Geoffrey Howe, Norman Fowler, Peter Walker, Nicholas Ridley, Cecil Parkinson, Margaret Thatcher herself and, of course, myself – were, for one reason or another, no longer members of it.

There was no time, however, to savour my political success at Blackpool. The following Thursday, 19 October, I had to satisfy the financial markets at the annual banquet given by the Lord Mayor at the Mansion House. But before then, Margaret was off to Kuala Lumpur for the Annual Commonwealth Prime Ministers' meeting.

The Iceberg and its Tip

No sooner had Margaret left for Kuala Lumpur the following day than the Walters problem erupted once again. *The Financial Times* of Wednesday, 18 October carried extracts from an article by him scheduled to appear in due course in an obscure American academic journal. In it he reiterated his familiar view that the ERM was 'half-baked' and that the case for sterling joining the ERM had never 'attained even a minimum level of plausibility', adding that 'my advice has been for Britain to retain its system of flexible exchange rates and stay out . . . So far, Mrs Thatcher has concurred'.

So much, evidently, for the British Government's recently reaffirmed commitment to join, once a number of readily fulfillable conditions were met. Walters subsequently complained that he should not be criticized for an article he had written well before he returned to Number 10. That was disingenuous, to say the least. Certainly, the unpublished article had been written many months before. But it was well after he had been re-installed as Margaret's personal economic adviser that he had brought its existence to the attention of *The Financial Times* and sent them a copy with explicit permission to quote from it.

In fact, this particular Walters article was among the least serious of his hostile activities. As I was to remark in my resignation speech:

> It was of significance only inasmuch as it represented the tip of a singularly ill-concealed iceberg, with all the destructive potential that icebergs possess.

Walters' activities were well known on both sides of the Atlantic. To cite just one piece of evidence, Peter Riddell, then the highly respected American Editor of *The Financial Times*, wrote that:

> Alan Walters . . . has recently told US bankers and policy-makers that sterling needs to fall to avoid a severe recession in the UK . . . His comments concerned some of his American listeners, according to participants, who felt they contradicted the message from Mr Lawson about trying to secure a stable pound.

COUNTDOWN TO RESIGNATION

I received independent corroboration of this episode in a letter from an eminent British economist who happened to be present. Although the report appeared two days after my resignation, the event to which it referred occurred, of course, while I was still Chancellor and Walters was still personal economic adviser to the Prime Minister. It was the iceberg that concerned me; not the minor, if clearly visible, tip.

All the same the article was yet another gift to the Opposition, who made it the focus of their attack on the Government at Treasury questions the following day, Thursday, 19 October. I replied frostily that Walters' views on the ERM were 'clearly not the view of the Government'. Kinnock, too, made the apparent confirmation of the gulf between Margaret and myself contained in the Walters article the core of his assault at Prime Minister's questions, which immediately follow Treasury questions; to which Geoffrey Howe, deputizing for the absent Margaret Thatcher, responded almost as dismissively.

That evening I made what was to be my last Mansion House speech. I made the customary restatement of the Government's monetary policy, stressing the unavoidable reliance on interest rates and the spurious nature of the suggested alternatives, announced some minor technical improvements to funding policy, took the opportunity to reaffirm the Madrid formula for sterling's entry into the ERM in a positive light, and trailed my forthcoming paper on competing currencies as an 'evolutionary and market-based' route to a form of EMU, in preference to the Delors Report's 'centralist and bureaucratic agenda that poses grave threats to any known form of democratic accountability' – which, I added, if attempted, was likely to 'end in tears'. I concluded my last Mansion House speech with these words:

> In the perspective of history, what will stand out about this period is not the short-term vagaries of the economic cycle, which will always be with us, but the long-term improvement in the supply performance of the British economy. An improvement so clearly shown in the quantity and quality of business investment, and the greatly improved productivity and profitability of British industry. The people of Britain may have temporarily forgotten the habit of thrift. That is undoubtedly a short-term problem. But at the same time they have rediscovered the spirit of enterprise. And that is the greatest prize of all.

Some journalists read that as a valedictory: they were not entirely unperceptive. As to the people of Britain having temporarily forgotten the habit of thrift, which some had argued was not temporary at all but a permanent behavioural change, they were subsequently to return to it with a vengeance.

The Die is Cast

The next day, Friday, 20 October, I asked Mark Lennox-Boyd, Margaret's PPS, to come and see me at Number 11. I told him that Walters' activities had reached the point where they had become so damaging to the Government that I could tolerate them no longer, and that I felt he ought to know that straight away so that he could inform Margaret. I had never before spoken to him in these terms. Nor had I ever before asked him to see me at Number 11, rather than speak to him when we happened to bump into each other at the House.

Moreover this was against a background of growing concern among Conservative back-benchers about the political difficulties Walters was causing: both William Clark, then Chairman of the back-bench Finance Committee, and Cranley Onslow, then Chairman of the 1922 Committee of all Conservative back-benchers, had been to see Margaret about it; and the Whips, too, were inevitably well aware of the mood. Even most of those in the Party who disagreed with my policy felt Walters to be a troublemaker to whom Margaret would be well advised to bid a fond farewell.

Mark must have known the score and, having been for four years my own PPS, should have known me too. In particular, I assumed he would have realized that, in the normal course of events, I would have waited for Margaret's return from Kuala Lumpur the following week to say what I wanted to say to her face to face: the fact that I was asking him to pass the message to Margaret then and there showed that the situation had become ominous. Perhaps I should have been more explicit: in any event, Mark misread my message and state of mind, merely informing officials at Number 10 that I was irritated by Walters' latest intervention and ensuring that the full text of his American article was faxed to Margaret in Malaysia.

The problem, as I saw it, was not the difference between Margaret and myself over sterling's membership of the ERM. I had been living with that during most of my six years as Chancellor, and although it was far from ideal, I could have continued to do so.* What made my job impossible was Number 10 constantly giving the impression that it was indifferent to the depreciation of sterling. I cannot recall any precedent for a Chancellor being systematically undermined in this way.

This could be resolved, it seemed to me, in one of two ways. The first way would have been for sterling to join the ERM without further ado; but that was manifestly not on. The only other way was for Walters to go; quite apart from the fact that that was what, for sound political

---

*Hence my decision not to mention the ERM in my resignation letter: see next chapter.

reasons, the Party wanted, it would have been a clear sign to the market that the exchange rate policy with which he was so publicly associated had been unequivocally repudiated.

On the Brink of Resignation

My last speech as Chancellor outside the House of Commons was on Monday, 23 October at the Institute of Economic Affairs, which had decided to hold a dinner to celebrate the tenth anniversary of the abolition of exchange control. The two invited speakers were Geoffrey Howe and myself, the two Ministers who had been responsible for that historic step. I spoke off the cuff, and no record survives; but it was a happy, if piquant, occasion. Here were the two Ministers who, of all Margaret's Cabinet colleagues, had probably done most over the previous ten years to roll back the frontiers of Socialism, very often against Margaret's own cautious hesitation; yet we were now at the top of her blacklist. Earlier that day, at one o'clock, I had arranged for Geoffrey to see me briefly at Number 11, where I had told him that as things were I felt that there was no point in my continuing as Chancellor.

My last speech in the House of Commons as Chancellor was the following day, Tuesday, 24 October. Inevitably, the Labour Party, whose day it was, had chosen to hold a debate on the economy, and, equally predictably, the focus of their attack – for they could not have been given an easier target had we tried – was what John Smith, in a witty speech, described as 'the confusion and disarray in the formulation and explanation of Government economic policy', a charge backed by copious references to Walters. I replied that Walters was 'a part-time adviser and his views on the ERM are not the views of the Government' – adding, in a television interview later that afternoon, that 'I think it is right that advisers do not talk or write in public. It is a good convention that should be adhered to'. But, to repeat, the problem was not Walters as such; nor was it even the difference between Margaret and myself over the crucial question of exchange rate policy. It was her persistent public exposure of that difference, of which Walters was the most obvious outward and visible symbol.

Margaret returned from Kuala Lumpur at four o'clock in the morning of Wednesday, 25 October. I saw her for my usual bilateral at half past three that afternoon. I could see that she was absolutely exhausted. She had had only two or three hours sleep on the flight back and I felt it would have been unfair to tackle her in those circumstances. I gave her a run-down of the main economic and financial events while she had been away, and we had a brief discussion. As the meeting drew to a close, I simply said, 'I do not want to talk about Alan Walters now, but we must have a talk about him very soon. There is a problem there.' She replied that she saw no problem. I assured her that there was one, and that we would need to talk about it very soon. At that point John Major and Nick Ridley were shown in, and we embarked on the meeting that approved my competing currencies paper.

That evening I talked my position over with Thérèse and one or two close friends whom I could trust implicitly. I told them I felt that, unless she wished to get rid of Walters, which would transform the position in the financial markets, but which I was sure she would not be prepared to do, I had no real alternative but to resign. My position had become completely impossible. I had no wish to give up the Exchequer, and realized that, so far as my own reputation was concerned, I would be doing so at the worst possible time; but at least I could leave knowing that I had tightened monetary conditions sufficiently to bring inflation down again. One reason why, despite immense provocation, I had not resigned earlier, was that I wanted to do everything necessary to undo the inflationary surge over which, regrettably, I had presided, rather than leave any of that task to others. With the rise in interest rates to 15 per cent earlier that month, which I expected would be the peak – as, indeed, it proved to be – I felt confident that I had done what needed to be done and could resign with a clear conscience.

There was no dissent from the conclusion that I had, with much sadness, reached. Ministerial resignations on political grounds are few and far between, and I would be the first Chancellor to do so since Peter Thorneycroft in 1958. But I saw no other course that I could with integrity, and sensibly, pursue, much as I hated having to do it. I sat down to draft a resignation letter.

CHAPTER 77

'UNASSAILABLE'

26 October 1989: Resignation . . . · . . . and its Aftermath
Retrospect

26 October 1989: Resignation . . .

MY FIRST SCHEDULED MEETING on the morning of Thursday, 26 October, was at a quarter to ten, with Margaret, the Defence Secretary Tom King, and the industrialist Frank Tombs, with the Cabinet Secretary, Robin Butler, in attendance, to discuss the changes required at the Atomic Weapons Establishment at Aldermaston, where inefficiency had reached the point where it was causing serious problems. Early that morning I told John Gieve, my Principal Private Secretary, that it was essential I saw Margaret privately, before that, with no Private Secretary present, which of course made clear to her that it was a very serious matter I had to discuss. He got on the phone to Number 10, and came back with the message that she could see me at nine o'clock.

I went next door and up to the first floor study and came straight to the point. Reminding her of the fears I had expressed the previous year when I had first learned of her intention to bring Walters back to Number 10 as her personal economic adviser, I had to tell her that the reality had proved worse than my worst fears. His disagreement with Government policy and actions over a range of issues, in particular the highly market-sensitive question of the exchange rate, had been well known before his return; and despite everything possible being done to gag him, his views continued to seep out by one means or another, as indeed they were bound to do. Given his position as the Prime Minister's personal economic adviser, this made my job as Chancellor impossible. The markets heard two voices, and did not know which to believe.

Not only was this confusion giving aid and comfort to the Opposition, but it was doing great damage to the economy. It was impossible for any Chancellor to conduct economic policy successfully, unless he enjoyed authority in the eyes of the financial markets, and my authority was being almost daily undermined. I stressed that this was nothing to do with any personal desire on my part for unchallenged authority: any Chancellor would be in exactly the same position.

I had therefore come to the firm conclusion that, for the Government's sake, Walters would have to go. I realized, I said, that this would be difficult for her; for that reason I would understand if she did not want him to go immediately. It would be just about tolerable if he were to stay until the end of the year, and leave then, with whatever face-saving formula seemed appropriate. If not, my position as Chancellor would be untenable.

I spoke quietly and Margaret listened intently. When I had finished speaking, she said she had always thought I would want to stay and see the job through. Moreover, was I not close to becoming the longest-serving Chancellor of the twentieth century?* Did I not want to stay to achieve that record? As for my position, so far from being intolerable, it was very strong indeed. She then said something that I found more revealing than everything else taken together: 'If Alan were to go, that would destroy *my* authority.'

I told her that that was absurd: her authority owed nothing whatever to Walters. I reiterated my conclusion that, if she were not to get rid of Walters by the end of the year, I did not see how I could possibly remain as Chancellor, for the reasons I had already set out. She begged me not to go, and asked me to take no decision straight away but to reflect on what she had said. I said I would indeed reflect, and let her have my reply by two o'clock that afternoon; but warned her that it was most unlikely that I would change my mind. I added that, meanwhile, I very much hoped that she, for her part, would reflect on what I had said.

Before long I was back in that same study at Number 10 for the Aldermaston meeting. Neither of us betrayed a hint of what had passed between us. The industrialist, Frank Tombs, had been asked by the Government to take a good look at Aldermaston, and suggest a course of action to remedy the gross inefficiency of the place. The meeting was to discuss his report: hence his presence. What he proposed was rather too radical for Margaret: but I weighed in heavily on his side, on the merits

---

*The longest-serving twentieth-century Chancellor was David Lloyd George (1908–15), with a tenure of seven years and one month. When I resigned I had been Chancellor for six years and four months.

of the case, and she eventually agreed. From there it was straight into a rather dull Cabinet meeting, at which I brooded on my next meeting with Margaret and said not a word.

Back at Number 11, I found a glum and dejected Peter Middleton waiting for me. John Gieve was there too. He had clearly guessed what was afoot, and had alerted Peter. I told John that I had arranged to see Margaret again at two o'clock, and that in the meantime he had better stand down the RAF plane that was to have flown me to Germany – I was due to take off from Northolt at half past twelve – and telephone the office of the German Finance Minister, Waigel, to cancel the meeting we had planned for that afternoon, using any excuse he could think of. As soon as he had done that, I told him to get all Treasury Ministers and special advisers over to Number 11 for an important meeting.

I had gone to Margaret not to tell her I wished to resign, but to ask her to wave goodbye to Walters – making clear to her, however, what the consequences would be were she not to do so. She had made it clear she would not do so. There was really nothing for me to reflect on. Whether she actually wanted me to go, or was indifferent to whether I stayed or went, or whether she simply assumed that if she stood firm I would back down, was neither here nor there. I had issued no public ultimatum to her, and told none of my colleagues of my intention. Although, knowing her as I did, I never expected her to agree to get rid of Walters, I did everything I could to make it easy for her to do so. I wrote out, in longhand, a clean copy of my draft resignation letter.

By then it was time for me to inform my Treasury team of my imminent departure. We met for the last time in the room I used for meetings on the ground floor at Number 11. They urged me to change my mind. They said that what I was proposing to do would be bad for the Government, bad for the Party and bad for me. I thanked them for their kindness. But my mind was made up. Norman Lamont, then Chief Secretary and subsequently to be Chancellor himself in the Major Government, stayed behind afterwards to remonstrate with me in private but nothing he said raised any considerations that I had not already thought about. Shortly after he had left, a handwritten letter arrived from him, as a final attempt to get me to desist, before my two o'clock meeting with Margaret. In it he wrote:

> You have always been a very good friend to me over the years and often when I have least deserved it. My main concern in all this is for you. Leaving aside, for the moment, the effect on the Party and the Government, I am concerned that you would do yourself an immense injustice . . . Your position has in the past year certainly been made more difficult – and it should not have been allowed – but it has not become impossible. A resignation would be widely misunderstood and

no doubt unkindly it would be noted you had left when there were problems . . . I believe you would do yourself and your reputation harm . . . Lastly, I do beg of you to think of the blow it will be to the Party. No-one you say is irreplaceable. There are not many true believers left. It is not just your technical skill as Chancellor, it is the coherence, clarity and self-confidence you give us all. No-one else would do that. Please don't do it. It isn't necessary.

Norman was wrong about whether my position was impossible – something, I suspect, that his subsequent experience as Chancellor may have enabled him to understand more clearly than he could from the perspective of Chief Secretary – but he was of course right about my reputation. Once I had departed, it was inevitable that I should become the convenient scapegoat for every ill with which the economy was afflicted. I knew that it would be unpleasant for me; but although the experience was to prove even worse than I had expected – as is invariably the case – it would not have affected my decision had I fully realized what I was to endure.

When I returned to Margaret's first-floor study at Number 10 shortly after two o'clock, I told her straight away that I had reflected on our earlier discussion, and had not changed my mind. I handed her my resignation letter, telling her that I proposed to publish it as soon as practicable. At first she refused to take it; but then she took it and popped it into her handbag, unopened, saying that she did not wish to read it. She begged me not to resign, heaping extravagant praise and flattery on me. She reminded me of a private conversation we had had some two years earlier – she said she had 'squirrelled it away in her mind' – when she had asked me about the Governorship of the Bank of England when Robin Leigh-Pemberton's term came to an end, and I had told her that I would be interested in the job myself; to which she had responded favourably, without of course committing herself. Did I want to give that prospect up, too?

In fact, she said everything except the one thing that would have persuaded me to stay; namely, that she agreed that Walters should go. She then said that she had no time to discuss the matter any further as she had to prepare for Prime Minister's questions. She suggested we continued our discussion as soon as she returned from the House: her office would let me know when she was back at Number 10. I realized that my resignation, however welcome to her in many ways – despite what she had been saying to me – had come as a shock, and agreed.

Her return from the House was delayed, no doubt to enable her to confer briefly with her kitchen cabinet, but eventually, at about half past four, I went to see her for the third and last time that day. Once again, she begged me to stay, heaping praise on me, but this time she was simply going through the motions. She knew the die had been cast, and was already thinking of her next move. I agreed to defer the announcement of my resignation and the release of my letter until six o'clock, to enable her to announce my successor – and release her reply – at the same time. I was in any case anxious that the Treasury and Bank should have time to decide how to handle the likely effects on the financial markets. We had a short and civil discussion, during which she thanked me for all I had done, and asked me whom I would suggest as my successor. I told her that it was entirely a matter for her. She then said she would miss me, and we parted in an atmosphere of suppressed emotion.

The text of my resignation letter, and of her reply, read as follows:

Dear Margaret,

The successful conduct of economic policy is possible only if there is, *and is seen to be*, full agreement between the Prime Minister and the Chancellor of the Exchequer.

Recent events have confirmed that this essential requirement cannot be satisfied so long as Alan Walters remains your personal economic adviser.

I have therefore regretfully concluded that it is in the best interests of the Government for me to resign my office without further ado.

I am extremely grateful to you for the opportunity you have given me to serve in the Government, particularly over the past six and a half years as Chancellor; and I am proud of what we have achieved together.

I shall, of course, continue to support the Government from the back-benches.

Yours ever

Nigel

———————

Dear Nigel,

It is with the most profound regret that I received your letter. We have spoken since and, as you know, it was my most earnest hope that you would continue your outstanding stewardship as Chancellor of the Exchequer at least for the rest of this Parliament. There is no difference in our basic economic beliefs, and Britain's economy is vastly stronger as a result of the policies which you and I and the Government have planned and pursued together.

You took a key part in preparing our party for Government before 1979. Your work at the Treasury, as Financial Secretary, on the Medium Term Financial Strategy, and at the Department of Energy in overseeing the privatization of Britoil were landmarks in the Government's success. You have been responsible for possibly the most far-reaching reform of our tax structure this century, as well as for a period of unprecedented growth and prosperity. It is a matter of particular regret that you should decide to leave before your task is complete.

I know you will continue to support the Government vigorously from the back benches, but all in Cabinet will miss the great ability and breadth of understanding which you have brought to our deliberations.

Please thank Thérèse for her splendid support.

Yours ever

Margaret

While all this was happening, Thérèse was at Stoney Stanton with our two children, Tom, then thirteen and Emily, then eight. It was their half-term holiday. I had, of course, been on the telephone to Thérèse several times throughout the day, letting her know the state of play. She was half expecting Margaret to choose to keep me rather than Walters, and it was only when I telephoned her after my third and final meeting with Margaret, to tell her that my resignation would be announced on the six o'clock news, that she made arrangements to join me at Number 11. Telling them simply that she had to make an urgent trip to London, Thérèse left Emily with Jim Bradley, the local village newsagent, and his wife, Lilly, who had been such good friends to us over the years, and drove up to London with Tom.

They were still on the M1 when they heard the announcement on the six o'clock news, which revealed that my successor was John Major, with Douglas Hurd replacing him as Foreign Secretary – both of them thus acquiring the jobs they had always wanted – and David Waddington, surprisingly, becoming Home Secretary. Events then followed thick and fast. On the financial markets sterling plunged and gilts took a tumble. The pound fell two cents against the dollar in the first ten minutes, and was a further two cents down by the New York close. There was a similar dive against the Deutschmark, taking the pound once again through the DM 3 barrier, this time as far as DM 2.90. The collapse would have been considerably greater had there not been massive intervention by the Bank of England. The reserves I had accumulated were being put to good use.

That side of things, however, was no longer my responsibility; but other equally pressing matters were. I had to make plans to vacate Number 11 while requests for me to speak to the Press and television, not merely from the UK media but from all over the world it seemed, were flooding in. Resignation from high office, particularly in the sort of circumstances surrounding my departure, is a trauma unlike any other. Moving house can be surprisingly traumatic too. It is the misfortune of the tenant of a tied cottage to experience both at once. I telephoned Alex Allan, who had been my longest-serving Principal Private Secretary, and Robert Culpin, who had been my longest-serving Press Secretary, and asked them to come over to Number 11 to help me deal with everything.

Meanwhile, before the news broke at six o'clock, I had telephoned my Constituency Chairman, Ian McAlpine, and my agent, Graham Smith, to let them know of my impending resignation, and to ask them to handle the constituency end until I arrived. They were both shattered by the news, but rallied superbly. I always knew I had the best Chairman, the best agent and the most loyal Constituency Association any Member of Parliament could have wished for: the aftermath of my resignation proved it.

Without exception and without hesitation, they rallied to me at an exceptionally difficult time. Graham found himself in the unaccustomed position, for a young Constituency agent, of having the world's Press and television landing on his doorstep; and, despite a conspicuous lack of help or guidance from Conservative Central Office, handled them with a cheerful firmness and tact, as if he had been doing it all his life. Ian led the Association through the trauma superbly; and he and his wife, Caroline, very generously lent us their mews cottage in Pavilion Road as a London pied-à-terre and bolthole from the ever-intrusive media until we had time to find something more permanent. It was there that I composed my resignation speech.

Finding something more permanent was easier said than done: we had sold our London house when I became Chancellor in 1983, since when London property prices had rocketed. I had resigned with no other job lined up, and the only certainty was that my ministerial salary had disappeared overnight. We were rescued by the generosity of Angela and Richard Lascelles – Angela was one of Thérèse's oldest and closest friends – who were at the time trying to sell an empty house at the top of Camden Hill. With immense kindness, they took it off the market and rented it to us on favourable terms for several months until I was able to get myself sorted out.

But to return to that 26 October: before long Thérèse and Tom turned up at Number 11 – just in time before Downing Street was surrounded by the media hordes. So far as the media bids were concerned, I clearly had to state my case, but equally clearly had no wish to rock the Government's boat. I decided straight away that I would do nothing until I had explained my resignation to the House of Commons. Thereafter,

I would do one television programme and then hold my peace. It was not difficult to decide which television programme to accept. Margaret was due to be interviewed by Brian Walden, at that time probably the most formidable and serious political interviewer in the business, on the Sunday immediately following my resignation; and the *Walden Interview* people had offered me the same slot the subsequent Sunday. The programme with Margaret had, of course, been agreed well before I resigned; but it was bound to go into my resignation at some length, and I accepted the invitation to state my own case the following Sunday.

John Major telephoned me to say how bad he felt about inheriting my job in the circumstances in which it had come about, even though it was the job he had always wanted. I told him that there was no need for him to feel bad at all. It was my own decision, made in circumstances which he had had no hand in creating. I added that Thérèse and I proposed to vacate Number 11 that evening, and that I would remove all my private papers and other belongings from the official part of the building before doing so; but that we would need a few days to make the arrangements to move all our stuff from the private flat upstairs. This he readily accepted. The final move was heroically organized by Thérèse the following week, with the stalwart assistance of Penny Rankin, my super-efficient House of Commons secretary.

We had barely started on the process of sorting out and packing my private papers into assorted cardboard boxes, assisted by Alex and Robert, when the bittersweet news came through that Walters had been a casualty of the fall-out from the explosion caused by my resignation, and had resigned as Margaret's personal economic adviser. If she was to be believed, her object had been to keep both her Chancellor and her guru: yet she had chosen the one course of action that had caused her to lose both. I reflected that, however painful it was to me personally, I had performed a signal service to my successor and to the Government in general.

This seemed a good point to break for a bite to eat; and since there was nothing in the house, and a posse of Press waiting outside, Thérèse asked a tearful Marie Collier, the Number 11 doorkeeper (Arthur Woolley having retired not long before), to go out and get us all some fish and chips.

Alex discovered from the police that, by that time, the Press were keeping vigil outside the Old Rectory too, waiting for me to arrive there. He made arrangements for us to leave Number 11 via the basement that runs underneath both Number 11 and Number 10, into the Number 10 garden, and out through the garden gate into Horseguards Parade, where Thérèse's car would be waiting. The Leicestershire Police were informed of our estimated time of arrival at Stoney Stanton, and would ensure us trouble-free access to the Old Rectory. At about half past eleven on that very dark October evening we left Number 11, escorted by Alex, for the last time, and Thérèse drove us and Tom in her Metro back to Leicestershire. Two hours later, with the help of the Police, we drove into the Old Rectory without stopping, and locked the gates behind us.

. . . and its Aftermath

As usual, I slept well that night, but poor Thérèse could not sleep at all. I woke up to discover that the Old Rectory was once again under siege. Not surprisingly, the media men and women who had been waiting outside the house when we arrived in the small hours of Friday morning had not been all that numerous. By daybreak their numbers had swollen enormously, with the police patrolling the unwalled side of the garden to prevent access from the churchyard. I told the police I would make a brief statement to the Press and television people in the garden, after which they should leave. With Thérèse by my side, I walked out of the front door, stated my full and unqualified support for John Major, whom I regarded as a first-class choice as my successor, and declined to answer any questions. They then left the garden, but continued to lay siege to the property, back and front. Indeed, so far from going away, they erected tall gantries so that their television cameras, equipped with what looked like satellite dishes, could see over our high stone walls and through the upstairs windows – a fact that we discovered only when a friend telephoned to say she had just seen Thérèse, on television, in the bedroom.

The Press that day, Friday, 27 October, concentrated primarily on Margaret's position in the wake of my resignation, but there was inevitably comment on the resignation itself. The tabloids showed that Ingham's black propaganda machine was already fully cranked up, the most succinct example being, as ever, the *Sun*, with its simple headline, 'Good Riddance'. At the other end of the scale, the *Economist* a few days later came up with a different verdict, stating that I:

> was a main architect of the Thatcher Government's economic success; if there have been the beginnings of a British economic miracle they are in large measure Mr Lawson's. In his tax reforms he was the most radical Chancellor this century, if never as radical as his own instincts may have inclined him.

The article ended prophetically with the words:

> The day Nigel Lawson said 'enough' may be the day that Mrs Thatcher's term of office started to draw to its close.

Pretty soon, the letters started flooding in, in their hundreds, interspersed by a touching visit of support from Johnnie and Raine Spencer, friends of ours who had driven from Althorp, a good half hour away. The bulk of the letters came from ordinary members of the public, unknown to me. Although some were hostile, the overwhelming majority were supportive – and came predominantly from Conservative voters. There were also a huge number of letters from friends and colleagues, many of which greatly moved me, since they went far beyond the normal courtesies. They came from considerable numbers of Treasury officials – most of whom, in addition to paying generous tribute, stressed how much they had *enjoyed* working for me or with me, which pleased me. Other officials who wrote in more than merely conventional terms included ambassadors, executive directors of the Bank of England, and former officials of the Energy Department.

I was particularly touched by one very senior official, who wrote, 'It is harder for officials when they see ministers go whose judgement they admire than is sometimes realized.' They also came from Parliamentary colleagues, both back-benchers – even a small number from the Labour benches – and ministerial colleagues, past and present. Ian Gow wrote in characteristically generous terms, including the statement, 'The lady really did want to keep you – and so did I.' As for the first part of that statement, it seemed to me that Willie Whitelaw was, as usual, the most perceptive when he wrote, 'She could so easily have got rid of Walters, but increasingly I fear that she simply cannot bring herself to be on the losing side in any argument. That failing may ditch us all.'

There were also a large number of generous letters from abroad, particularly from fellow finance ministers and former finance ministers with whom I had worked. The French were particularly courteous; I received letters not only from Pierre Bérégovoy, the then Finance Minister, and his predecessor, Edouard Balladur, but also, in particularly generous and characteristically French terms, from Jean-Claude Trichet, the permanent head of the French Treasury, and Jacques de Larosière the Governor of the Banque de France.

Letters also flowed in from leading businessmen and various other quarters. I was greatly touched to receive a particularly kind note from Bob Runcie, then Archbishop of Canterbury, and not a close friend, although of course, we knew each other; while Peter Thorneycroft struck a chord when he wrote, 'I know from long ago what resignation involves and I have some understanding of your problems'. He added, 'The Conservative Party is faced with a very large problem in strategy and in some ways your resignation has brought [it] to a head.' Perhaps it had.

In an attempt to capitalize on the situation, the Labour Party had initiated an economic debate on Tuesday, 31 October, five days after my resignation. It was the obvious occasion on which to make my resignation speech to the Commons, and the Speaker called me, as is customary on these occasions, immediately after the two opening speeches – on this occasion, from John Smith and John Major, the latter's first as Chancellor. I knew exactly what I wanted to say, and kept it uncharacteristically brief, less than ten minutes. Speaking from the traditional place for such speeches – just below the gangway, one bench up from the front, the place normally occupied by the Father of the House – I made it clear that the 'cut and run' smears that were already being peddled by the black propaganda brigade were wholly untrue. My resignation, I pointed out,

> was not the outcome I sought. But it is one that I accept without rancour – despite what might be described as the hard landing involved.

The key economic issue I highlighted was whether the exchange rate was

> to be part of the maximum practicable market freedom or . . . a central part of the necessary financial discipline. I recognize that a case can be made for either approach. No case can be made for seeming confusion or for apparent vacillation between these two positions.

I went on to emphasize that systems such as the EMS were not 'panaceas or soft options. Tough decisions still have to be made.'

The speech was listened to with rapt attention and clearly went down well in the House. It received a better press than any I had made as Chancellor. It is reproduced in full in Annexe 4.

The previous Sunday, 29 October, I had watched with particular interest Margaret being interviewed by Brian Walden, knowing that I would be in her shoes a week later. It was not one of her better performances. Depressingly, she appeared to be adding to the Madrid conditions, unilaterally, as she went along. She insisted that 'Nigel was Chancellor, Nigel's position was unassailable, unassailable' – and altogether used the word 'unassailable' about me so many times that it acquired a new and ironic meaning in Westminster parliamentary discourse. But what made me almost fall off my chair was when, asked by Walden, 'Do you deny that Nigel would have stayed if you had sacked Professor Alan Walters?', she replied, 'I don't know, I don't know.' When Walden persisted, she stuck to the 'I don't know' line until, exasperated, she expostulated, 'I'm not going on with this.'

I had, of course, made it perfectly clear to her that in those circumstances I would have stayed, but she presumably realized that admitting it would have got her into even deeper trouble, particularly with Walters having departed too. My main concern for my own interview, the following Sunday, 5 November, was how to explain clearly, calmly and truthfully the reasons for my resignation, without appearing to brand Margaret a liar, which I had no wish to do, when Walden asked me about her extraordinary answer, as he was clearly likely to do. My interview with Walden had not been going long before he was asking why Margaret had said that she did not know why I had resigned – a slight variation on the same point. I gave the reply I had decided to use, 'The only conclusion I can come to is that she found it impossible to believe that I meant it . . . or she thought that I would back down.' The interview went well and I received another large mailbag of favourable letters; but I felt 'so what?'. The depression that inevitably follows a trauma of that kind was already beginning to set in.

Retrospect

There was some surprise that I could have resigned over, as some saw it, anything as minor as a part-time adviser to the Prime Minister. Indeed even some well-wishers felt that I had demeaned my high office by phrasing my resignation letter in the way that I did. It was quite true that Walters was in one sense simply a symptom of a growing rift between Margaret and myself, not just over the ERM, but over exchange rate policy more generally. But even that has to be set against the fact that over most other aspects of policy, I was, ironically, closer to her than was almost any other senior member of her Cabinet. What made it a resigning issue was the way in which she handled that difference of view over the exchange rate.

Essentially, the point is that Prime Ministers have an unfettered right to dismiss any Cabinet Minister, however senior – including the Chancellor – for whatever reason they like. That I always accepted. What is unacceptable conduct in a Prime Minister, however, is to recoil from sacking a Minister, and systematically to undermine him instead. Walters was a principal instrument of that undermining process, a process that made my job impossible.

The parting of the ways came over a genuine difference of opinion on exchange rate policy, which Margaret handled badly in personal as well as policy terms. It also arose from suspicions of me she began to harbour when I received much of the credit for the 1987 election result, and which did not diminish after my popularity began to wane. As to the substantive issue of policy, the plain fact is that no British Chancellor concerned with halting inflation has ever been able to turn a blind eye to the value of the pound on the foreign exchange markets. 'Benign neglect' may or may not be an option for a large continental power like the US – although I fear that even the US may still bear a heavy cost for neglecting the value of the dollar. But it is not an option for a British government; and all previous attempts to adopt it have ended in a humiliating U-turn and a screeching of the economic brakes. Sometimes nemesis arrives in a matter of weeks, sometimes after several years. But arrive it always does.

PART FIVE

———

The Abiding Legacy

CHAPTER 78

THE BALANCE SHEET

The Main Themes

LOOKING BACK ON MY decade in office from 1979 to 1989, two main themes emerge, one political and one economic.

The political theme is the remarkable success of Tory radicalism when the Conservative Party was led by a team of like-minded people, inspired by a coherent political and economic philosophy and the will to carry it through, and united under an outstanding leader; and how at the end it was undermined by that leader herself, who regarded her team as dispensable, and allowed the coherent philosophy to take second place to a cult of personality and personal infallibility.

The economic theme is that free-market Toryism proved both a success in the UK and a beacon to much of the rest of the world; and that my own stewardship, whatever its shortcomings, was an important part of that success. In the narrative chapters of this book I have inevitably been concerned with the squalls which blew up. But they need to be kept in perspective. Economic indicators, monetary aggregates, exchange rates and the like will always behave in unexpected ways. Far more important is a clear sense of direction and making progress in that direction over a reasonable period of time.

The international nature of the turn of the tide of ideas began to impress me particularly forcibly about halfway through my Chancellorship. When I was in Washington for the 1986 annual meetings of the IMF and

World Bank, what struck me most, as I subsequently told that year's Conservative Party Conference, was

> how, throughout the world, collectivism is in retreat and the forces of economic freedom are on the march. Privatization – deregulation – tax reduction: all have become part of the new world consensus. And we in Britain have been among the leaders in shaping that consensus.

Making all allowances for the conventions of conference hyperbole, I still believe that we were in many ways pioneering, and most certainly reinforcing, a trend which has swept the world, including the former Communist countries, and which had not run its course by the early 1990s.

A Look at the Numbers

How far do the statistics of Britain's economic performance during the 1980s bear out the thesis that a sea-change for the better took place? The most up-to-date and concise of the many assessments to have been published at the time of writing appeared in the summer 1992 *Treasury Bulletin*, and its conclusions are similar to my own. But it should be borne in mind that important but unquantifiable changes, such as the improvement in the quality of British management during the 1980s, can be expected to bring benefits to the measurable performance of the British economy gradually over a period of years, including years yet to come.

The chart in Chapter 69 showed the dramatic reduction in UK inflation in the 1980s, compared with the disastrous record of the 1970s, when the annual rate during the summer of 1975 reached a terrifying 27 per cent. The disappointment was, of course, the resurgence towards the end of the decade – although even this was markedly less severe than the rise associated with the two previous cyclical peaks of economic activity. I return to this blot on the Government's – and my own – economic record later in this chapter.

The most popular yardstick of economic performance over a run of years, however, is real economic growth. The official statistics of the UK's growth performance over the quarter of a century to 1989 are summarized in the table opposite, which is shown in terms of complete economic cycles, so that an entirely fair comparison can be made, undistorted by cyclical factors. I have also added a breakdown of the pre-1989 cycle into two periods broadly corresponding to the tenure as Chancellor of Geoffrey Howe and myself. It is far too soon to reach any conclusion about the post-1989 cycle, which has many more years to run.*

*The CSO dates the cyclical peaks at May 1979 and January 1989. By using 1989 rather than 1988 for the latter peak the table slightly understates the Conservative Government's record, given the marked growth slow-down in 1989.

Interpretation of the table is considerably affected by the treatment of North Sea oil and gas output. While its contribution to UK GDP is frequently exaggerated – even at its peak it accounted for little more than 5 per cent – its dramatic rise from virtually nothing, and its subsequent decline, make a considerable difference to the growth statistics. Oil was a big plus factor for Labour in 1973–79, and at best neutral for the Conservatives in 1979–89. The output of the North Sea is not to be sneezed at, but it is to a large extent a windfall, yielding a surplus well above production costs – a fact reflected in the special tax re-gime imposed to capture a large part of that windfall and described in Part Two of this book.* Excluding oil, growth was considerably faster in the Howe-Lawson cycle of 1979–89 than in the largely Labour cycle of 1973–79 which preceded it.

UK growth Per cent changes Annual average					
	1964-73	1973-79	1979-89	1979-83	1983-89
Real GDP*	3	$1^{1}/_{2}$	$2^{1}/_{4}$	$^{1}/_{4}$	$3^{1}/_{2}$
Non-oil real GDP	3	$^{3}/_{4}$	$2^{1}/_{4}$	$-^{1}/_{4}$	$3^{3}/_{4}$
Output per head:					
Manufacturing	$3^{3}/_{4}$	$^{3}/_{4}$	$4^{1}/_{4}$	$3^{1}/_{2}$	$4^{3}/_{4}$
Whole Economy	3	$1^{1}/_{4}$	$1^{3}/_{4}$	2	$1^{3}/_{4}$
Non North Sea Economy**	3	$^{3}/_{4}$	$1^{3}/_{4}$	$1^{3}/_{4}$	2
* Output measured as GDP (0)					
**)Treasury estimate					
Source: CSO, Treasury					

Any assessment of the growth record also needs to take account of the world slow-down which followed the first oil price explosion of 1973. The international data in the statistical Annexe shows that growth rates slowed down everywhere. In Japan, for example, they plunged from a remarkable annual average of 8 per cent to around 3 per cent. Against this background Britain's growth performance in the 1980s emerges quite creditably.

---

*The reason most commentators include oil is simply that CSO figures of GDP are all on an oil-inclusive basis. Non-oil GDP is a Treasury calculation published in the Budget Red Book, and even there not as a continuing year-by-year series.

THE BALANCE SHEET

Manufacturing and Other Myths

Looking at the productivity figures in the table, defined in terms of output per head, performance during the 1980s was also significantly better than it was in the previous cycle. Ironically, it was entirely due to the sparkling performance of manufacturing industry, whose productivity improved even faster than in the pre-1973 oil shock cycle – particularly during my own period as Chancellor. This was the sector of the economy of which the Conservatives in general, and I in particular, were regularly accused of at best neglecting, if not of subjecting to an actively anti-manufacturing policy. Once again, UK performance in the 1980s looks even better in the context of the overall world picture, since our competitors achieved no similar spectacular improvement.

Nor was this sharp improvement in manufacturing productivity achieved at the expense of a declining manufacturing base, as the Labour Party frequently alleged. Indeed, the boot was on the other foot. It is indeed true that, for some time, manufacturing in Britain has been declining as a proportion of total output – and even more as a proportion of employment – as indeed it has in almost all advanced industrialized countries. But in absolute terms, whereas manufacturing output fell by 5 per cent over the overwhelmingly Labour 1973–79 cycle, it rose by 12 per cent over the Conservative 1979–89 cycle – the entire rise occurring, again ironically, during my time as Chancellor. It is evident that manufacturing success depends on industry's own efforts and on the overall economic climate created by the Government, rather than on the frequency of political declarations of love and affection and similar emissions of ministerial hot air.

The big puzzle, at first sight, is why, by contrast, the recorded figures for productivity growth outside manufacturing, notably in the service sector, were so unimpressive during the 1979–89 cycle. There is, in fact, a simple explanation. The 1980s were characterized by a massive growth in part-time employment, almost exclusively in the fast-growing service sector, and largely composed of married women. Clearly a part-time worker cannot be expected to produce as much as a full-time worker. Thus the productivity record outside manufacturing, and hence also for the economy as a whole, would look considerably better in the 1980s were it not for the CSO's eccentric failure to distinguish between full-time and part-time workers. This also, incidentally, affects the international comparisons, since there was no comparable explosion of part-time employment among our major overseas competitors. In other words, the UK's record in the 1980s looked at in the world context would emerge even better were the CSO to calculate productivity on a less bizarre basis.*

The dramatic growth in part-time employment was, of course, well known at the time. Indeed, the Labour Opposition regularly claimed that it meant that the Government's employment figures were phoney, as if such workers should really have been counted as unemployed (or at least half unemployed) – despite the fact that official labour force surveys showed that in over 90 per cent of the cases part-time employment, which was particularly attractive to married women with children to look after, was a matter of choice and not forced on people by a lack of full-time work.† Yet the impact on the productivity figures was curiously overlooked.

In addition to neglecting manufacturing, the Government was widely accused of neglecting industrial investment. It is true that in my first Budget I reformed company taxation and removed the tax bias in favour of investment in industrial plant and equipment. But on the reasonable proposition that the proof of the pudding is in the eating, the latter charge of neglect is as much a myth as the former. As the table in the statistical Annexe shows, there was a dramatic acceleration in fixed investment in the 1980s compared with the lamentable performance over the 1973–79 cycle – indeed, investment grew significantly faster than consumption during the Conservative cycle.

This acceleration was particularly marked in non-housing investment. Business investment, which had risen by around 4 per cent a year over both the 1964–73 and 1973–79 cycles, increased by 6½ per cent a year over the 1979–89 cycle. During my own period as Chancellor – that is, for the most part, after my allegedly anti-investment Corporation Tax reform, it rose by 10½ per cent a year. A further irony, incidentally, is that the miserable overall investment performance during the predominantly Labour cycle of 1973–79 was largely due to a sharp decline in public sector non-housing investment – that is, schools, hospitals and the infrastructure – which was reversed by the Thatcher Government.‡

But it is probably at least as useful, if not more so, to look at the rate of return on capital, as at the sheer quantity of investment. The adjoining chart shows a marked improvement in the rate of return on capital employed in non-North Sea oil companies in the Howe-Lawson decade. Moreover, all the evidence suggests that UK companies, especially in

*The correct method would be to calculate productivity in terms of output per man-hour (or woman-hour); but a rough approximation could be achieved by counting part-time workers as half a person for productivity purposes.

†See Social Trends, HMSO, 1992, Chapter 4.

‡The public sector is here defined to exclude the nationalized industries, which are included in business investment so as to avoid privatization complications.

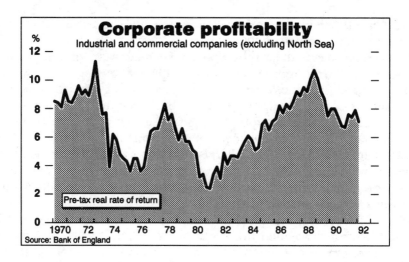

Corporate profitability
Industrial and commercial companies (excluding North Sea)

Pre-tax real rate of return

Source: Bank of England

manufacturing, are better poised to weather the problems of the 1990s and better placed to meet the challenge of recovery when it comes than for several decades past.

A Dash of Opportunism

The origins of the British productivity turn-round and the improvement in managerial performance go back to the traumatic first two years of the Thatcher Government, from 1979 to 1981. Superimposed on the pay explosion, following the collapse of the Labour Government's incomes policy, there was a sharp rise in sterling, reflecting notably both the oil and the 'Thatcher' factors, as recounted in Chapter 6. The result was a massive rise in the real exchange rate, which obliged management to re-assert its right to manage, leading to a blitz on overmanning and a related productivity spurt, which was to endure after the end of the recession.

It is quite true that the substantial appreciation of sterling in 1980, in par-ticular, was neither planned nor expected; but this does not mean that the Government's initial successes on the industrial and counterinflationary fronts were due, in some paradoxical sense, to errors in monetary policy, which was less gradualist than intended. I am not at all convinced that errors in monetary policy were the only or even the main reason for sterling's upward surge. The point, however, is that, whatever its cause, when the sharp rise in the exchange rate occurred, some of us deliberately and consciously exploited it to achieve our objectives, which were precisely those achievements the critics allege happened by accident. In fact it required considerable political resolve to act as we did.

In the real world the unexpected frequently happens, and a sensible government exploits opportunities when they arise. Inevitably Civil Servants tend to see things differently. Wishing to live an orderly existence in an orderly world, they dislike the unexpected and seek to undo or offset it. Ministers come from the entirely different culture of politics; and nothing could be more mistaken than to describe intelligent opportunism as a fortunate error. In any event, the exchange rate squeeze of 1980, although it provided the first impulse, was far from being the whole story. If it were, the industrial improvement would have come to an end as sterling eased back from its January 1981 peak. (By the time I became Chancellor in June 1983, the sterling index was back to where it had been when we first took office in May 1979.)

What happened was that the effect of the initial squeeze was powerfully reinforced by the Government's supply-side reforms. In the words of the 1992 *Treasury Bulletin*:

> Deregulation, measures to increase competition and encourage entrepreneurship, legislation to curb the powers of trade unions, privatization and tax cuts and reforms, helped to create the incentives and opportunities for British firms to emulate the methods practised by more efficient foreign competitors.

The abolition of exchange controls in 1979 coincided with the globalization and increased efficiency of financial markets. Both came together with the abolition of pay, price and dividend controls. The combined result was that it became impossible for firms to survive with a rate of return below the going international rate. As Douglas McWilliams, the chief economic adviser to the CBI, described the effect of the new economic climate:

> A consequence has been the growth in mergers, acquisitions, demergers, sell-offs, management buyouts and contracting out. Perhaps the most important of all has been the increase of self-confidence. There has been a pressure to improve and a massacre of 1970s excuses.

With no excuses left, management had to buckle down to it. Nor was it only a matter of large companies making themselves more efficient. For many years there was an average increase of 500 new firms a week – after deducting closures. There was a rise from little more than one million to over three million in the number of self-employed. The UK venture capital industry, which scarcely existed when we first took office, had by

1985 become twice as large as its counterparts in the rest of the European Community taken together.

Transforming the Supply-Side

A list of the achievements of a reforming Conservative Government cannot stop at the familiar economic indicators. Privatization, for example, which I discussed in Chapters 18–20, was an entirely new sphere in which Britain led the world and about which streams of overseas visitors came to London to learn and to provide useful business for the City. It was also an area where I was able to take something of a pioneering role, first as Financial Secretary and then as Energy Secretary, before becoming the chief orchestrator as Chancellor. At the beginning the idea was greeted with widespread scepticism, not least within sections of my own Party. Nevertheless, in the three Conservative Parliaments from 1979 to 1992, some three-fifths of state industry was successfully transferred to the private sector, and by the end of that period much of the remaining two-fifths was under consideration for privatization.

The amount of effort the Government in which I served, and indeed I myself, devoted to the nuts and bolts of supply-side measures required to improve the UK economy's long-term performance was prodigious, at least by the standards of previous UK governments. Perhaps inevitably, because it consists of a battery of detailed measures, rather than a small number of dramatic initiatives, and promises long-term amelioration rather than the illusion of short-term transformation, the importance of genuine supply-side improvements tends to be overlooked most of the time and regarded as particularly irrelevant during the depths of recession, when the clamour for a quick fix can become deafening. This is no doubt one of the reasons why previous governments had disregarded the supply-side in any serious sense and imagined that all our problems could be quickly solved by the manipulation of a small number of demand-side – and chiefly budgetary – levers. It would be disastrous if a combination of short-sightedness and impatience were to bring about a return to that approach, which did this country so much harm.

Even those who do recognize the importance of the Thatcher Government's supply-side achievements during the 1980s, however, and who acknowledge the transformation, albeit incomplete, that occurred in the country as a whole, became uneasy about the problem of the so-called underclass. Although an ill-defined concept, it reflects a reality that cannot be ignored. But just as hard cases make bad law, so it would be a grave mistake to allow the existence of an underclass to cause economic policy to be reshaped, or the values of self-reliance, self-respect, self-help and the enterprise culture more generally to be brought into question.

Indeed, the challenge to government and to society more widely is precisely to find a means of minimizing the size of the underclass and saving those on it from degradation, without in any way undermining either the policies or the values which the Government of which I was a member sought to pursue and instil during the 1980s.

A Dose of Competition

An important aspect of the supply-side revolution was the removal of barriers to competition. Although I would have liked to move further in the course of privatization, the Thatcher Government nevertheless succeeded in extending competition over a wide front. This included, for example, establishing the beginnings of effective rivalry in telecommunications and electricity generation, and extending it further in broadcasting. There are competitive bus services in many of our cities, and competitive tendering is now compulsory for many local authority services.

Britain has been in the lead in eliminating industrial subsidies, an area where public spending was cut drastically even in nominal terms. Nothing like it has been seen anywhere else in Europe, where vested interests have been allowed to prevail – even in Germany, with its pressing need to reduce its Budget deficit, swollen by the transfers to the East following unification.

A further area where Britain was unquestionably in the lead was in the freeing of capital markets. One of my earliest jobs as Financial Secretary was to lead the team set up by Geoffrey Howe to work on the abolition of exchange controls. This occurred in 1979 within a few months of our returning to office. On the home front, credit controls were swept away and arrangements like the building society cartel were allowed to wither under the competitive gale. Credit liberalization admittedly brought problems as well as benefits. Freedom always does, until people learn to use it properly.

Unlike the case in many other countries, not least the United States, the Government's economic policies and its firm rejection of protectionist sentiment in the 1980s, coupled with the common sense of the British people, created an unusually hospitable climate for inward investment. This is one reason why Britain has received the lion's share of Japan's European investment – the English language and the availability of golf courses being among the others.

So far as overseas trade was concerned, it was the UK which took the lead in the European Single Market programme. The Thatcher Government was able to steer the enterprise in a pro-competitive direction by putting its energies behind the main aim and refusing to be deflected by high-sounding projects such as tax approximation or – even more damaging – a 'European industrial policy'. None the less, the restrictive aspect of the European Community prevailed too much in trade relations with the rest of the world. In particular, we were handicapped by the Common Agricultural Policy, one of the greatest follies of our time. The CAP, together with the Community's import restrictions on sectors such as textiles, steel and coal, is a significant obstacle to the economic emergence of the former Communist states of Europe.

Labour Market Reforms

A further area where the UK was in the European lead during the 1980s was the liberalization of labour markets. While other countries – not to mention the Labour Opposition – were urging Social Charter type measures and controls, which could serve only to make the hire of workers more expensive, the Thatcher Government was greatly reducing the scope of Wages Councils – which I still hope will before too long be abolished altogether. Expensive obligations for employers under Labour's perversely named Employment Protection Act were greatly reduced.

The malign and coercive influence of trade union monopoly was reduced by a whole series of Acts, drastically limiting the closed shop, reducing intimidation by pickets, and lessening the legal immunities of trade unions and their officials. There was a steady fall in the proportion of employees who were trade union members and a marked shift from nationwide collective bargaining to bargaining by firm and by plant. The main redoubt of nationwide bargaining – as indeed of the unions themselves – is now the public sector. Even here some modest decentralization moves have been made.

The Government's role was not confined to the reform of trade union and labour market law. Crucially, it successfully stood up to the once legendary powers of intimidation of the National Union of Mineworkers, winning a year-long strike, and enabled the newspaper employers to break the power of the militants in the print unions.

Obviously the Chancellor is not the front-line Minister in labour market reforms. But not surprisingly, given their economic importance, I played my part in a number of them, as earlier chapters have recounted. Moreover, it should never be overlooked that it would not have been possible successfully to carry out the Thatcher Government's policies on the labour market front, and to secure what Len Murray, the General Secretary of the TUC, was to call 'the new realism' among trade union leaders, had it not been for the overall economic policy we pursued and the totally new climate that created.

The fact that unemployment should still be so high after all these measures is a disappointment, but not a failure. For one of the key messages of the Thatcher Government, and one which required greater political courage than previous governments had displayed, was the unpalatable truth that no government could guarantee full employment by the clever manipulation of a few financial levers, or by buying jobs in threatened industries or firms, irrespective of wage and price behaviour.

The 1.1 million unemployed which we inherited in 1979 is not a good benchmark for comparison, given the widely acknowledged extent of overmanning at that time. A good part of the subsequent increase consisted of people in effect moving from unemployment on the job to unemployment off it. During my time as Chancellor unemployment first rose from 2.8 million in 1983 to 3.1 million in 1986, before falling to 1.7 million by the time I resigned in 1989 and to a cyclical low point of 1.6 million in 1990. Given the still far from satisfactory state of the UK labour market – old rigidities tend to linger on, even when the factors that caused them have been removed – these lower numbers reflected unsustainable boom conditions, just as the subsequent gradual return to the 2.8 million mark by the summer of 1992 reflected a severe cyclical downturn in the economy rather than a new equilibrium.

It is a commonplace that if the performance of the economy is to fulfil its potential, there needs to be an improvement in the quantity and quality of industrial training in the UK. The main argument over this concerns the secondary but still important question of the extent to which this should be financed and run by the state, and the extent to which it should be financed and run by the employers themselves. The Conservative Government of the 1980s in fact substantially increased its spending on industrial training, and launched a number of new training initiatives, particularly during David Young's tenure at the Department of Employment. But I remain convinced that the bulk of the improved training should be left to employers to finance and organize – not least because they know best the sort of training required, and which of their employees can best benefit from it – and that government should concentrate its efforts on providing employers with a better educated workforce in the first place. Certainly, if one looks at how these matters are ordered in our most successful overseas competitors, that is broadly the pattern.

Spending and Taxation

Curbing the growth of public spending is one of the hardest tasks facing any government, since it affects services which people have come to consider as rights and involves taking on powerful public sector lobbies. The issue is – or should be – one that transcends party politics. It was not so long before we first took office that Roy Jenkins was speaking of the size and growth of public expenditure as a menace to freedom. It requires only a slight relaxation of vigilance over a few years to relapse into that position.

The table in Chapter 58, summarizes the record. The ratio of public spending to total national output rose remorselessly not only under the first Wilson Government of the 1960s, but also, regrettably, under the Heath Conservative Government. It then fell very slightly under the Wilson-Callaghan Labour Government of the 1970s under the *force majeure* of economic crisis and at the behest of the IMF. The big decline in the ratio occurred under the post-1979 Conservative Government, most of all during my own period as Chancellor. The achievement cannot be explained away as simply the effect of the business cycle. For if we move away from shares of GDP to the rate of increase in public spending in real terms, where the cyclical effect is much less pronounced, that too was easily lowest. Moreover, this degree of public spending control had not been achieved either in the UK in previous periods of cyclical upswing nor by other G7 countries over the same period.

The charge is sometimes made that public spending was controlled not by reducing the range of Government responsibilities for health, education, social security and so on, but by meanness and cheeseparing. In fact, by the standards of almost all other countries, the UK went further in the 1980s in trimming the range of state responsibilities, by concentrating services on those who needed them most and in charging for the business services that central and local government provide. But it would be wrong to sneer at tight-fistedness. In the absence of market disciplines it is usually the only practical substitute.

Because of the need to reduce substantially, and ideally to eliminate, the huge structural Budget deficit we inherited (equivalent to 5½ per cent of GDP in 1978–79, itself a boom year) it was not possible to reduce taxation as a proportion of total national income, which remained higher than it had been under Labour and indeed never moved far from 38 per cent while I was Chancellor. What I did manage to do, however, was to reduce marginal tax rates within an unchanged total burden. The basic rate taxpayer paid 39½ per cent on each pound of additional income in 1978–79 – 33 per cent in income tax and 6½ per cent in National Insurance contributions. By 1992–93 he paid 34 per cent – 25 per cent plus 9 per cent. Of this 5½ percentage points reduction, some 5 points occurred while I was Chancellor.

It was of course much less expensive to make large cuts in marginal tax rates at the very top, where the number of taxpayers is much smaller and where we inherited confiscatory rates, motivated by a desire to pander to envy rather than to raise revenue. Between 1979 and 1989 Geoffrey Howe and I between us reduced the top rate of tax on earned income from 83 to 40 per cent, and the top rate on savings income from an even more ludicrous figure of 98 per cent to 40 per cent. But in addition to cutting marginal rates, I was able, despite the political obstacles that lie in the reformer's path, to carry through an unusually far-reaching programme of tax reform based on the idea of lower tax rates and fewer tax breaks. I have described the key measures in previous chapters – and a summary of the tax reforms introduced by Geoffrey Howe and myself between 1979 and 1989 appears in Annexe 5 – so there is no need to repeat them here.

A Medium Term Framework

Leaving the supply-side, one achievement in which I take particular satisfaction is my part in putting in place a new orientation of macroeconomic policy, which has survived the inevitable mistakes of implementation and indeed has spread internationally. There were two aspects of this new approach, launched as the Medium Term Financial Strategy (MTFS) in 1980, when Geoffrey Howe was Chancellor and I was Financial Secretary. First, it was concerned with nominal magnitudes: that is, to curb inflation, but not to promote output and employment directly. The latter was to be nourished, as I have indicated, by supply-side reforms. Second, policy was to have a medium-term orientation, concentrating on setting a course and sticking to it, rather than on short-term fine tuning.

To the extent that similar sounding statements were made by Jim Callaghan and Denis Healey in 1976, these amounted to little more than lip service designed to attract international financial support, as both Alec Cairncross and Andrew Britton confirm in their studies of that period. The Labour Government, as our 1979 inheritance demonstrated, had turned recidivist well before it lost office, as soon as the pressures from the foreign exchange markets and the IMF had abated.

The main practical problem with the MTFS was that the domestic monetary guideline we inherited, known as Sterling M3, proved treacherous. There was no monetarist Golden Age (see Chapter 36). We did not abandon the monetarist guiding light. It was the light that abandoned us. Narrow money, M0, or in plain English, cash, surprisingly proved a better – although not infallible – indicator, but suffered from a lack of market credibility. I had long thought that membership of the ERM was the most satisfactory available alternative and I need not labour what prevented me from embracing it. So the Government had to depend more on judgement and discretion in steering the economy than I would have liked.

In this context, it is sometimes alleged that to rely on the ERM is a confession of failure: an admission that the Bundesbank is more capable of running an anti-inflationary monetary policy than the UK Government; indeed that the British Government is so hopeless that it has to have its hands tied by the Germans since it cannot be trusted to take the right decisions unbound. That is not how the French see their membership of the ERM, and with good reason; for the allegation is mistaken.

Certainly it is easier for an independent Central Bank, like the Bundesbank, to run a credible and successful monetary policy than for a Government – which is a major reason why I advocated and continue to favour independence for the Bank of England. But the key lies in the word 'credibility'. Success in monetary policy depends not only on the action the monetary authorities take, but also on the way in which private sector decision-makers react to the signals and measures of the monetary authorities. The credibility the Deutschmark has earned over the years as a currency that holds its value gives a very high level of anti-inflationary credibility to the decisions and actions of the Bundesbank, based on its track record as much as on its independence. Coupled with the simplicity of an exchange-rate discipline, as compared with the arcane complexity of the message of the monetary aggregates, it is not surprising that private sector decision-makers tend to react more swiftly and surely to this form of discipline.

The fact that the Germans manage to do without an exchange rate discipline – a requirement for the anchor currency in any such system – is itself largely a reflection of their long and impressive anti-inflationary track record.

Although I failed to persuade Margaret to agree to ERM entry during my time as Chancellor, I did at least put it firmly on the map in Britain, both within the Treasury and more widely, as an economic policy measure in its own right and not because it possessed a European label – and did so well before either the economic consequences of German reunification or the shadow of EMU complicated the issue. In retrospect, our failure to benefit from ERM membership before those complications struck was all the more costly.

In addition to its monetary core, the MTFS also of course had a fiscal component. This was fulfilled with outstanding success. Thanks to the unprecedently firm control of public spending to which I have already referred, and the prudent policy towards tax cuts, a PSBR or Budget deficit of 5½ per cent of GDP in 1978–79 was transformed into a Budget surplus – even excluding privatization proceeds – of 1½ per cent of GDP in 1988–89. Nor was this a cyclical phenomenon, as the choice of dates – from peak to peak – demonstrates. The fact that, by the end of the 1980s, the UK had the lowest ratio of public debt to GDP of all the G7 countries was a substantial achievement by any standards, and a valuable legacy for my successors.

My Share of Mistakes

In my resignation speech to the House of Commons, I conceded that 'I have no doubt that I have made my share of mistakes'. The reader who has read this far will know what I believe them to have been, and he will also know which charges I do not accept, such as the *canard* that the Conservative Government 'wasted' North Sea oil (dealt with in Chapter 17) or the complaint that I neglected the current account of the balance of payments (dealt with in Chapter 67).

At one level my central mistake was undoubtedly to underestimate the strength and duration of the boom of the late 1980s, and thus of the inflationary forces it unleashed. As the adjoining table shows, inflation during my time as Chancellor averaged under 5 per cent – the best performance since the 1960s, but not good enough. Moreover, during the last year and a half of my term of office it was on a rising trend, which continued for a further year after my resignation. At the start of that resurgence I described it on one occasion as a 'blip', an unfortunate expression in the circumstances and one which I was not allowed to forget. I was wrong in particular about the duration of the inflationary uptick. Yet in a longer-run sense, as the chart in Chapter 68 shows, it was a blip compared with the two previous cyclical peaks. Indeed, the chart exaggerates the underlying rate of inflation in 1990, when it appeared to reach its highest level since early 1982, since the headline rate was swollen not only by the mortgage interest rate distortion but also by both the effect of the Poll Tax and the short-lived impact of the Gulf War on the oil price. Allowing for these factors, the true peak was at most $7\frac{1}{2}$ per cent.

It is of course normal for inflation to rise during the final stage of an economic upswing, as it did throughout the seven major industrial nations that are represented at the annual Economic Summits. But our performance was worse than the others' in two key respects. First, although the underlying uptick was not significantly greater than that of our G7 partners, our starting point was too high: $3\frac{1}{2}$ per cent in 1986–87, compared with $2\frac{1}{2}$ per cent in France, 2 per cent for the G7 as a whole, and zero for Germany. Second, the extent of the true underlying rise in UK inflation understated the strength of the inflationary pressure, since a significant proportion of the excess demand was reflected not in higher prices but in a sharp rise in imports.

In itself, that is no bad thing. Taking the strain on the balance of payments does far less damage to inflationary expectations, and provides a safety valve and a breathing space while the necessary tightening of monetary policy has its effect. We have seen a similar phenomenon more recently in Germany, where the inflationary consequences of unification were reflected more in an upsurge of imports than they were in higher

	Inflation RPI ex mips	Inflation PPI	3-month interbank rate	Real interest rate in terms of RPI ex mips	Real interest rate in terms of PPI	Memo item: % change in ERI, yr on yr	Memo item: average G7 inflation	
1978	8.6	9.9	9.3	0.7	−0.6	− 0.2	7.3	1978
1979	12.5	10.8	13.7	1.2	2.9	+ 5.8	9.9	1979
1980	16.9	14.0	16.6	−0.3	2.6	+10.0	12.7	1980
1981	12.7	9.5	13.9	1.7	4.4	+ 1.2	10.2	1981
1982	8.5	7.7	12.3	3.8	4.6	− 4.5	7.1	1982
1983	5.2	5.4	10.1	4.9	4.7	− 7.4	4.6	1983
1984	4.4	5.7	10.0	5.6	4.3	− 4.5	4.6	1984
1985	5.2	5.3	12.2	7.0	6.9	− 0.6	3.9	1985
1986	3.6	4.3	11.0	6.4	6.7	− 8.4	2.1	1986
1987	3.7	3.9	9.7	6.0	5.8	− 1.6	2.9	1987
1988	4.6	4.5	10.3	5.7	5.8	+ 6.0	3.3	1988
1989	5.9	5.1	13.9	8.0	8.8	− 2.9	4.5	1989
1990	8.1	5.9	14.8	6.7	8.9	− 1.6	5.0	1990
1991	6.7	5.7	11.5	4.8	5.8	+ 0.5	4.3	1991
April 1992	5.7	3.8	10.4	4.7	6.6	− 0.4*	3.4	April 1992
Av 1978–79	10.6	10.4	11.5	0.9	1.2	+ 2.8	8.6	Av 1978–79
Av 1980–83	10.7	9.2	13.2	2.5	4.1	− 0.4	8.7	Av 1980–83
Av 1984–89	4.6	4.8	11.2	6.6	6.4	− 1.9	3.6	Av 1984–89
Av 1990–91	7.4	5.8	13.2	5.8	7.4	− 0.5	4.7	Av 1990–91

PPI = Producer (output) Prices Index; ERI = Sterling Exchange Rate Index; RPI ex mips = Retail Prices Index excluding mortgage interest payments.
*April 1992 on 1991 average

prices. But it is little more than a useful breathing space; and the monetary tightening required has to go further, and last longer, than the size of the inflationary upsurge might suggest.*

The table shows that monetary policy, judged by the conventional criteria, was unusually tight throughout my time as Chancellor. Real interest rates averaged 6½ per cent. But although monetary policy during my tenure of the Exchequer was tight, with the benefit of hindsight the conclusion can only be that it was not tight enough.

The Search for the Origins

Looking back, the inflationary boom of the late 1980s can be traced to four main influences:

First, the imprudent reaction of the lending institutions to financial deregulation, and the failure to foresee their folly. (See Chapter 50.)

Second, the sharp fall in the sterling exchange rate in 1986, which meant that – admittedly in the different and more difficult position of a major oil producer – we failed to gain as much advantage as our competitors did from the oil price collapse in the early part of that year. (See Chapter 52.)

Third, over-reaction to the 1987 Stock Market crash. (See Chapter 60.)

Fourth, a belated appreciation of the extent of overheating in 1988.

I have little doubt that the two key factors were the first and second. Stronger action to limit sterling's depreciation in 1986 – which would certainly have been necessary had we joined the ERM when I proposed it in November 1985 – would have reined back inflation in two ways. In the first place, there would have been a direct impact on the price level. Imports would have been cheaper, and, even more important, goods competing in international markets at home and abroad would not have been able to absorb excessive cost increases under the protection of sterling depreciation. In other words the UK would have been linked early on with low-inflation Germany.

Second, as the credibility of ERM membership would inevitably have

---

*There is, however, a risk of the Germans overdoing it. In 1988 the Bundesbank switched from its traditional composite target aggregate, so-called Central Bank Money, over half of which was cash (M0), to the broad money aggregate M3. There are signs that M3 may be giving the same misleading message in Germany in the early 1990s that it did in the UK in the early 1980s.

taken time to establish itself, we would have needed higher interest rates to sustain anything like the DM parity at which we might have joined the ERM at the end of 1985 or the beginning of 1986 (see Chapter 40). These higher interest rates would have exerted a direct squeeze on domestic spending much earlier on in the upturn. The lending institutions, too, might have been more circumspect in these conditions. The Thatcher Government would still have won the 1987 election, albeit probably with a smaller majority. The fall in unemployment would not have gone so far, but would have been more durable.

The third and fourth items, by contrast, simply occurred too late in the day to be plausible candidates for the main cause of the boom, which had by then already gathered considerable momentum. The worldwide interest rate cuts following the Wall Street crash did not occur until the fourth quarter of 1987, while the UK interest rate reductions which followed the uncapping of sterling in March 1988 had been fully reversed within three months. Moreover, as the chart in Chapter 67 shows, the brevity of the 1988 interest rate dip meant that there was only a minimal reduction in mortgage rates.

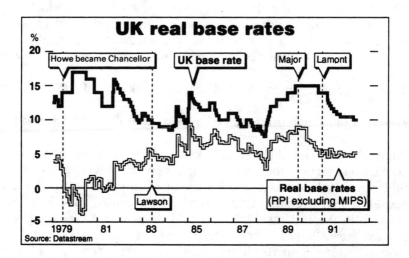

By June 1988, UK base rates were again on a sharply rising trend and, by the end of the year, real short-term interest rates had risen to levels not hitherto recorded. I find it hard to believe that quickly corrected errors over a short period at a late stage of the boom were nearly as important as the early mistakes which allowed the boom to gather momentum. There is of course a reason why some of my parochial monetarist critics fix on the end of 1987 and 1988 as the time of the key mistakes. That reason is their extreme distrust of any exchange rate objectives, which make them reluctant to attribute any errors to the·

period when sterling fell most. Moreover, they dislike admitting that we lacked domestic monetary indicators that gave us useful advance warning of changes in nominal spending.

As Chancellor during the period in question I must clearly take responsibility for any errors made. But what must be nailed very firmly is the myth that I disregarded cautionary advice in order to rush ahead in a pre- or post-election boom. On the contrary, I was if anything more inclined to raise interest rates than were most of my senior advisers. What made it difficult to act earlier and more drastically, as I should have done, was Margaret's detestation of high interest rates and her equal dislike of any clear policy towards sterling.

Moreover, if I am to take the blame for being slow to recognize the inflationary threat in the late 1980s, I can reasonably expect some credit for acting decisively once I realized it, at considerable cost to my own career and reputation. It would have been very easy to have reacted with a series of half-hearted or inadequate moves – or to have called off the struggle against inflation in 1989 by saying that enough had been done and allowing sterling to depreciate along the lines advocated by some prominent self-styled monetarists. It is largely because I did not hesitate to raise interest rates to the extremely unpopular level of 15 per cent, on the eve of the 1989 Party Conference, that the conditions for sustained low inflation were established.

A Worldwide Phenomenon

But it does not do to conclude this assessment on a parochial note. I mentioned earlier that the recrudescence of inflation in the late 1980s was not confined to the UK but was a worldwide phenomenon. In the United States, for example, it rose from just under 2 per cent in 1986 to 5½ per cent in 1990, in Japan from ½ per cent to 3 per cent, and in Germany from zero to 2¾ per cent. The mistakes for which I can most properly be held accountable are not those which led to the worldwide resurgence of inflationary pressure, but those which – after all appropriate adjustments have been made – allowed the resurgence of inflationary pressure in the UK to be somewhat greater than in most other countries.

The cause of the inflationary upsurge in the UK as in most other countries – including notably the United States, Japan and Canada among the G7, and Australia and Sweden outside it – was a credit binge associated with financial deregulation. Inevitably, whenever there is a credit binge there is a subsequent hangover, in the shape of recession, and the greater the binge the greater the hangover. None of this is intended to imply that the world recession somehow caused the UK recession, any more than that the UK recession caused the world recession. Nor is it intended to suggest that errors cease to be errors when they are committed by several others as well. But what it does mean is that the parochial search for some uniquely UK failing is largely misconceived.

Certainly, the chief characteristic of the UK recession of the early 1990s, its unusually long duration, was one shared by several other countries – most notably the United States, despite interest rates slashed to below 1 per cent in real terms. I have little doubt that the reason for this extended duration is that a recession created by the aftermath of a major credit binge – which itself, of course, prolonged the preceding upswing to an unusual extent – has to be cured by a debt work-out on the part of the economy's borrowers, both personal and corporate, and a rebuilding of balance sheets by the lending institutions, which is a more protracted business than that associated with recovery from a normal cyclical downturn in which debt plays a smaller role. None the less, once it is over it will be seen that the immense supply-side improvements to the UK economy achieved during the 1980s remain, to the lasting benefit of the British people.

In an earlier chapter I referred to a perceptive critic who claimed that my real mistake as Chancellor was to create a climate of optimism that, in the end, encouraged borrowers to borrow more than they should and lenders to lend more than they should. There is clearly a good deal in this. It may well be that optimism had become so unfamiliar to the British that they inevitably became intoxicated by it and threw prudence and caution to the winds. But I remain unrepentant in the belief that a climate of optimism was what Britain needed in the 1980s and what it continues to need today. The debilitating pall of defeatism which characterized the Britain we inherited in 1979 had to be swept aside. Not only was it infinitely depressing, but it had become self-fulfilling and made economic success impossible. For too long the British had been learning to live with decline and defeat. The unfamiliarity of optimism and success proved rather too heady an experience in the late 1980s. But it need not and must not do so in the future.

CHAPTER 79

EPILOGUE, 1989–92: 1. POLITICS

The Collapse of Communism · The Downfall of Margaret Thatcher
Why Margaret had to Go · The Election of John Major
The Demise of the Poll Tax · A Career Over and an Election Won

The Collapse of Communism

THIS BOOK IS ABOUT my own period in office, from May 1979 to October 1989, and a detailed story of subsequent events, however important, in which I played no part, has no place in it. But some of those events were so intimately connected with what went before that it would be incomplete without some account of them. They included sterling's belated entry into the ERM, the downfall of Margaret Thatcher, the demise of the Poll Tax, continuing problems over EMU, the Conservative Party's fourth successive general election victory, this time led by John Major, and, of course, the prolonged recession.

The most important political event of the period, however, was none of these, but the collapse first of the Soviet empire in Central and Eastern Europe and subsequently of the Soviet Union itself, these countries' abandonment of communism, and the end of the cold war. This historic process had, in fact, begun shortly before my resignation, but the dismantling of the Berlin Wall, the most dramatic of the events outside the former Soviet Union, occurred a fortnight after my departure, and the *bouleversement* within it later still.

One of the most striking aspects of this sequence of events was the way in which it took the West, governments and experts alike, by surprise. The cause of the relatively bloodless collapse of communist rule throughout the Eastern bloc was pre-eminently the abject failure of the command economy. This was so even when the proximate cause was political – for example Gorbachev's message to the unpopular rulers of the Soviet Union's Warsaw Pact partners that the Red Army would no longer be available to help them put down domestic unrest. For it was the catastrophic failure of the Soviet economy that obliged Moscow to retrench and to devote its inadequate resources to the massive problems within its own frontiers.

The reason why all this so palpably took the West by surprise was not that no-one knew about the mind-boggling scale of the economic failure of communism. Certainly, it was neither widely known nor widely reported, but the experts in the subject had a pretty good grasp of the situation. The point was rather that the experts on the Soviet and East European economies were a different group of people from the more numerous so-called experts on the political situation within the communist bloc. Thus the epoch-making political implications of economic catastrophe were scarcely addressed. This conspicuous failure of Western analysis applied not merely to the Western Press, but also to the marginally greater intelligence available to governments, and has obvious implications. It is a nice paradox that the events which finally and irrevocably demonstrated the bankruptcy of both Marxist economics and Marxist historicism at the same time conspicuously vindicated Marx's emphasis on the importance of economics in the understanding of history.

Taken by surprise, and disorientated by the collapse of the old certainties they had come to know and love so well, the leaders of the West were in general slow to come to terms with the changes that were taking place before their eyes. The most conspicuous exception to this was Germany's Chancellor Kohl, a leader with none of the qualities that made Margaret Thatcher at her best so impressive, but a politician with a formidable gut instinct none the less. Leaving his own foreign policy establishment gasping in his wake, he seized the chance to achieve the forty-five-year-old dream of German unification – thus securing a place in history that would in all probability otherwise have eluded him.

The economic consequences of unification, however, were another matter. Never something that was going to be easy to handle, in the event they were badly mismanaged. This was not a matter, as was frequently supposed, of the terms of the monetary unification of July 1990, when the East German currency, the Ostmark, was replaced by the Deutschmark, on an allegedly one-for-one basis. Absurdly favourable to the East Germans though this rate was, it applied only to a limited sum of savings deposits, and made no significant difference to monetary conditions in the new united Germany – of which the former East Germany comprised only one fifth in terms of population and very much less in terms of wealth.

996

The true mischief was quite different. Unlike the peoples of the rest of Central and Eastern Europe, who understood that their emergence from the disasters of central planning towards the potential of the market economy would be a long hard slog, the East Germans imagined that, despite their uneconomic industries and poor productivity, unification would bring them West German living standards overnight. The German trade unions, not wishing to see their existing members undercut by cheap labour from the Eastern provinces, sought to reinforce this impossible dream by a rapid extension of West German collective bargaining and wage levels to the workers of the East.

Left to itself, the result could only be a massive rise in unemployment in the East and a consequent highly unpopular mass exodus of Eastern workers to the West in search of jobs. In an attempt to prevent this, the Kohl Government compounded the underlying problem by a rapid extension of the high levels of West German social security provision to the impoverished East, and by subsidizing employment in the East on a vast scale. Unprepared to incur the unpopularity of financing this huge upsurge in Government spending on the East by cutting back public spending in the former West Germany (including West Berlin), for which there was ample scope, and increasing taxation, the German Government resorted to financing it by borrowing instead, allowing their Budget deficit to balloon to an unprecedented extent.

All these factors combined to produce a marked upsurge in inflationary pressure in Germany, to which an alarmed Bundesbank responded by a steady rise in interest rates to their highest levels for a decade. In fact, most of the strain of the inflationary pressure was taken on the balance of payments, with Germany's current account swinging violently from a surplus of $48 billion in 1990 to an unaccustomed deficit of $21 billion in 1991.* Recorded inflation, by contrast, rose only to 4½ per cent in the first half of 1992, which – albeit the highest for a decade – was likely to prove the peak: economic activity had already slowed down markedly during the course of 1991 and remained very subdued into 1992. But the Bundesbank was taking no chances; its inflationary worries reinforced by the persistent overshooting of the target for broad money growth to which it had switched, almost certainly unwisely, in 1988.

When the economy of the country that provides the anchor currency of an exchange rate system gets into difficulties, that inevitably presents problems for the other members of the system. So it was for the members of the ERM in 1991–92 – not least for the UK and sterling, the ERM's newest and thus least credible constituent. But the Kohl Government's mishandling of the economics of unification, and the Bundesbank's

*The figures are not entirely comparable, since those for the first half of 1990 relate to pre-unification West Germany. But they are the best available, and do not mislead.

largely necessary measures to neutralize this mishandling, were by no means the only factors causing problems for the ERM and the European economy more generally in 1992, as will become clear in the next chapter.

Compared to the continuing political and economic importance of the tumultuous events in Central and Eastern Europe, the Gulf War towards the end of 1990 was a relatively minor matter. Nevertheless, those who complain of the problems that it failed to solve, and of those that were created in its wake, should not forget the incomparably greater dangers to peace in the Middle East there would have been had Saddam Hussein's Iraq been allowed both to consolidate the annexation of oil-rich Kuwait and to retain its nuclear capability unimpaired.

The Downfall of Margaret Thatcher

In terms of domestic politics, the Gulf War was to have one particularly important consequence. When John Major became Prime Minister in November 1990, with at most roughly a year and a half to go before a general election, he was less well known to the average voter than any new Prime Minister this century. He had been in Cabinet for only three years, and for two of them he had not had a Department of his own, but had been my number two at the Treasury. But his constant exposure right at the start of his term of office as the leader of America's chief ally in the short and, on its own terms, very successful Gulf War not only enabled him to become a familiar figure far sooner than would otherwise have been the case. It also did so in the best possible context: as a national rather than a Party leader.

Far more surprising than the election of John Major was the departure of his predecessor, Margaret Thatcher. Much has been written about that extraordinary event, which was greeted around the world with disbelief, and which surprised not least the victim herself: the most readable account is to be found in Alan Watkins' book, *A Conservative Coup*. Inevitably, as in all such accounts, there is a great deal about who said what to whom, about whether there was a plot (there was not), and about how things might have gone had Margaret campaigned more vigorously on her own behalf, and much else in the same vein. However fascinating all this may be, it is essentially beside the point. No Conservative Prime Minister since Neville Chamberlain, in the very special circumstances of 1940, had left office other than at the behest of either the electorate or the doctors. How was it that the first to be obliged to do so was Margaret Thatcher, one of the most dominant Prime Ministers ever, in vigorous health, enjoying a huge majority in the House of Commons, and with a record of three election victories and no defeats? That is the real question.

It was quite clear that Margaret, whatever her occasional musings, firmly intended to 'go on and on and on', as she had once put it, so long as her health and the electorate permitted. Her premature removal would require her to be worsted in an election for the leadership; and the Party's constitution indeed provided for such an election each year, in November. But the only possible serious challenger was Michael Heseltine, who, since his resignation from the Cabinet in January 1986, had assiduously and with considerable skill – and showing a political maturity which he had not always evidenced in his previous ministerial career – built up a significant following both among Conservative back-benchers and the public at large. In the eyes of most Tory back-benchers, he had staked out a distinctive position on a sufficient number of issues, notably Europe, to make his implied challenge look like more than mere naked ambition, but not on so many as to appear disloyal; and Michael Heseltine had made it clear that he would not challenge Margaret – for the very cogent reason that he did not believe he could win. After an election, of course, if Margaret were to lose it, his hour might come. But not before.

Three closely connected events, in rapid succession, were to cause Michael to change his mind. The first and most important was the surprise resignation of Geoffrey Howe on 1 November 1990. I knew, of course, of Geoffrey's profound unhappiness, which had been greatly accentuated by his ejection from the Foreign Secretaryship in July 1989, over Margaret's increasing hostility to the European Community and all its works, and of his understandable resentment at the intolerable way in which she treated him. But the Madrid episode notwithstanding, I had never seen him as a resigner; and certainly he had not breathed a word of his intentions to me. Geoffrey's timing, almost exactly a year after my own resignation, was chiefly dictated by Margaret's notorious 'No. No. No.' assault on Jacques Delors and the European Commission in her report to the House of Commons, two days earlier, on the outcome of the Rome European Summit, where she had been voted down over a timetable for EMU. Its potency lay in the fact that it occured on the eve of the brief window of opportunity for a leadership election.

The second of the three events was the response of the Number 10 black propaganda machine. Margaret had come to detest Michael with an emotional intensity that not even Jacques Delors could evoke. When, in response to Geoffrey's resignation, Michael somewhat clumsily and opaquely stuck his head above the parapet, the Number 10 machine swung into action, telling the tabloids, who duly regurgitated the message, that he should 'put up or shut up'. Of all the nails that Ingham inadvertently hammered in his mistress's coffin, this was the most decisive. Anyone with a glimmering of understanding of the Tory Party, particularly at that time, would have recognized that the last thing that

Margaret wanted was a leadership challenge from Michael; and anyone who had the faintest understanding of Michael Heseltine would have known that, if publicly told to put up or shut up, the implication being that he was nothing more than a paper tiger, the chances of his mounting such a challenge were greatly increased.

The third and last in this sequence of events was Geoffrey Howe's resignation speech of 13 November 1990, a full ten days after the resignation itself. Always a deliberate man – one of his favourite sayings was that a government should proceed 'at all deliberate speed' – he had spent the intervening period agonizing and drafting and redrafting. By agreement, I sat by his side when he delivered it; but I was wholly unprepared for what he had to say. It was, quite simply, the most devastating speech I, or I suspect anyone else in the House that afternoon, had heard uttered in the House of Commons. He concluded with the words:

> The time has come for others to consider their own response to the tragic conflict of loyalties with which I have myself wrestled for perhaps too long.

It was all the more powerful because it was Geoffrey, that most moderate, long-suffering and patient of men, who was uttering it. The following day, just one day before the final date for nominations for the Tory leadership, Michael Heseltine, having considered *his* response, announced his candidature. In the first ballot, on 20 November, Margaret secured 204 votes to Michael's 152, with 16 abstentions – four votes short of the majority required, under the rules, for a first round victory. It was clear that her long premiership – the longest this century – had run its course; although she herself was not immediately persuaded of this.

Two days later, with reluctance and a commendable dignity she was later to find difficult to maintain, she announced that she would not, after all, contest the second ballot. This took place on 27 November, between Michael, John Major and Douglas Hurd, with John emerging a decisive winner. Despite all that had happened, it was impossible not to feel for Margaret in the hour of her downfall; even though, in the true classical tradition, it was she herself – not Geoffrey, not Michael, not me, and not a disloyal Cabinet – who was the author of her own misfortune.

Why Margaret Had to Go

If the Heseltine challenge might never have occurred, the outcome when it did occur was at once more surprising and less. It was unprecedented; yet there were good reasons why no fewer than 45 per cent of her parliamentary colleagues felt unable to support their leader of the previous fifteen years and more in the first ballot – and among the 55 per cent who did there were many, particularly among her ministerial colleagues, who had allowed their loyalty to get the better of their judgement in the first ballot but would not have done so in the second. Those reasons essentially boiled down to one: the conviction that Margaret had become an electoral liability, and that the Conservative Party could win the coming general election only under a new leader.

The problem, in electoral terms, was not to any great extent the economy. Not only did all the polls consistently show that, despite all the difficulties, the public continued to believe that the Conservative Party was more competent at managing the economy than Labour; but – more important – no Tory Member was under the illusion that a change of leader would make any difference. By contrast, where there would be a difference was over the hated Poll Tax, the greatest single political blunder of the Thatcher years. It was clear that so long as Margaret remained, so would the Poll Tax. By contrast, the one policy pledge that Michael Heseltine gave in his brief statement announcing his intention to stand against Margaret was that, if elected, he would institute 'an immediate and fundamental review of the Poll Tax'. As Michael had been a consistent opponent of the Poll Tax, both before and after his resignation over the Westland affair, this carried conviction – as well as the clear message that any fundamental review would lead to its replacement. Such was the support for this that, in the campaign for the second ballot, both John Major and Douglas Hurd felt obliged, under questioning, to match Michael's pledge.

Another, more elevated but less clear-cut, issue where it was felt that a new leader would make a change for the better was Europe – the issue over which Geoffrey had resigned. It was not that the Party as a whole shared Geoffrey's (or, for that matter, Michael's) Euro-enthusiasm, although some did. It was rather that they sensed that she was handling Europe badly, and feared that she would split the Party over it. But the issue which really vied with the Poll Tax, and where a change of leader clearly would make a difference, was Margaret Thatcher herself and her 'style'. Margaret had always been a leader who polarized opinion. Most people either admired, respected and even loved her, or they saw her as at best intolerable and at worst evil. Very few were indifferent to her. In the early years the votes gained by her strong personality clearly outweighed the votes lost by it. In her third term the balance began to switch. Conservative Members found that increasing numbers of their erstwhile supporters, let alone congenital floating voters, saw her as disagreeably strident, excessively authoritarian, and unbearably bossy.

To be fair, this marked change in the public's feelings towards her was not simply a reaction to the deterioration in her own manner and behaviour that had sadly occurred, particularly after Willie Whitelaw's enforced resignation at the end of 1987. It was also that, as the longest-serving Prime Minister of the twentieth century, she had outstayed her welcome. People had tired of her, and wanted a change, as they might have done whoever had been Prime Minister for that length of time. The sadness was that she failed to recognize this and to act on it at a time of her own choosing, most obviously on the occasion of the tenth anniversary of her premiership in May 1989.

Whatever the reason, the public clearly wanted a new Prime Minister; and, if the Conservative Party did not provide one, then the voters would have no alternative but to turn to Labour instead. Faced with this choice, Tory MPs knew which of the two they preferred. As one of the 152 who voted for Michael in the first ballot, my own reasons for doing so were much as I have ascribed, I believe accurately, to the majority of the other 151. Their number may well have been swollen by the opinion polls published on the weekend before the first ballot, all of which purported to show that, while Labour enjoyed a double-digit lead with Margaret leading the Conservative Party, with Michael as leader the Tories would actually be ahead of Labour.

The Election of John Major

After Margaret's departure I tried to persuade Geoffrey to stand in the second ballot, but he wisely declined, recognizing that it is the fate of the regicide never to become king. My support for him was based not simply on the comradeship that had existed for so long between us, but on my belief that what was needed, personal qualities apart, was what might be termed Thatcherism without Thatcher. As for the three candidates who did put their names forward, Michael Heseltine, Douglas Hurd and John Major, all were competent to do the job, and – while economic policy had been set on a course which I hoped would not be abandoned whomever was chosen – none of them was a Thatcherite. The fact that Margaret was under the impression that John was one, and backed him accordingly, merely underlined how out of touch she had become and the extent of the gulf she had allowed to arise between herself and her Cabinet colleagues.

Ironically, she had originally picked on John as her crown prince because, in addition to his undoubted ability and her mistaken belief that he was 'one of us', his relative youth and inexperience meant that he would not be ready to take over the reins for many years to come; something that fitted in well with the duration of her own planned tenure of office.

In purely personal terms, I was closest to Douglas and least close to Michael. I had little doubt, however, that John would win. Unlike Michael, he had very few enemies in the Party, and Margaret's active backing of him ensured him not merely the votes of her closest supporters: more important, it meant that all those who felt guilty at the brutal way in which Margaret had been ejected could expiate that guilt by voting for her chosen successor. Nevertheless, I decided to stay with Michael, while taking no part of any kind in the campaign. Having been a Cabinet colleague of his from 1981 to 1986, I suspect I knew his strengths and weaknesses rather better than did Margaret's last Cabinet, two thirds of whom had never sat round the Cabinet table with him at all, and of those who had only three had done so for more than a few months.

My silence was broken thanks to a telephone call from Geoffrey on the Saturday before the second ballot. He told me that he had promised Michael that he would declare himself that day in favour of Michael, as had Peter Carrington; and that Michael hoped that I would do the same. The purpose, of course, was to provide a story for the Sunday papers. I told Geoffrey that I would think about it, and telephoned Michael to ask him if he really felt that a declaration of support from me would be of any help to him. I myself doubted it. He claimed that it would be, and expressed the hope that I would give it. I told him I would. Had either John or Douglas also asked for my support I would have resolved the conflict of loyalties by keeping quiet and declaring for no-one, as had been my original intention; but neither of them did. I quickly drafted and gave the Press Association a statement which concluded:

> Above all, we have to ask ourselves who is most likely to lead the Conservative Party to victory in the next general election. For it is only by winning the next election that the immense achievements of the Thatcher years can be preserved. And let us not delude ourselves: despite the lack of public enthusiasm for Labour, for any Party to win an unprecedented fourth successive victory will not be easy. In my opinion it is Michael Heseltine who has the leadership qualities that will give the Conservative Party the best chance of achieving this vital objective.

This was an accurate representation of where I stood. On some policy issues – such as the Poll Tax and an independent Bank of England – Michael's views were the same as mine. On others – such as Europe and his predilection for a Japanese-style relationship between government and industry – they were not. But above all I had not worked long and hard for more than a decade to help rescue Britain and set the country on the right course only to see it all undone by Labour. Michael was, I believed, an election winner; Douglas, I feared, was not; while John, in this respect, was an unknown quantity.

The chief consequence of my public support for Michael was to incur the astonished wrath of the Major camp. I received a particularly intemperate telephone call from John's campaign manager and Chancellor-in-waiting, Norman Lamont – followed, I am glad to say, by a letter of apology once the dust had settled.

The Demise of the Poll Tax

Margaret's departure led, as I had hoped, to a dramatic improvement in the Government's support in the country at large. During the whole of Margaret's last year at Number 10 the Labour Party's lead in the opinion polls had been in double figures. As soon as John was there the polls showed a Conservative lead of around 5 per cent. The Labour Opposition had been completely wrong-footed. Never for a moment imagining that Margaret could be replaced, all their pre-election planning had been based on exploiting the anti-Thatcher mood in the country, in a highly personalized way. Now their fox had been shot.

But they still had the Poll Tax as a target. When he formed his first Government, John sensibly made Michael Environment Secretary – as, indeed, Margaret had done in 1979 – and charged him with lancing the Poll Tax boil. On 5 December 1990 Michael announced a thoroughgoing review of the structure, functions and finance of local government: a respectable if somewhat oversized cloak for covering what urgently needed to be done. He emphasized particularly strongly the consultative nature of the review. He announced to the House the outcome of this process on 21 March 1991:

> From the earliest possible moment the community charge will be replaced by a new system of local taxation . . . under which there will be a single bill for each household comprising two essential elements, the number of adults living there and the value of the property . . . I intend to publish a consultative document after the Easter recess setting out alternative approaches . . . we will conclude the period of consultation in the summer.

It was this pledge of yet further consultation that alarmed me. The issues were well known, as was the state of public opinion, and there was no chance of consultations producing a consensus in favour of any particular form of the new tax – in particular, over the crucial issue of the relative weights of the 'two essential elements', the Poll Tax and the property tax, of which it was to be comprised. Sooner or later the Government would have to grasp the nettle; and if it was not planning to make up its mind until after the summer, with a general election possible in the autumn, it was leaving things perilously late.

Speaking in the Budget debate four days later, I took the opportunity to air my concern. After discussing what I described as 'a very good Budget' at some length, I went on to explain the history of the problem of local government finance, concluding that the point had been reached where genuine local taxation financed such a small proportion of local spending that it might be simpler to abolish it altogether. Finally, in the last ninety seconds of a thirty-four-minute speech I turned to my worries about the delay in reaching a decision on the replacement of the Poll Tax, saying:

> The Government appears to be engaged in yet another consultative process . . . I have to say that the Government are in danger of giving consultation a bad name. Consultation as an aid to Government has an important place, but we are now in danger of seeing consultation as a substitute for Government . . . Consultation on the nature of the new local tax is nothing less than an infallible recipe for maximizing dissent.

This was emphatic enough, and I should have concluded there. Unfortunately, I rounded it off by saying:

> I think it was Pierre Mendès-France who said that to govern was to choose. I agree with that. To appear to be unable to choose is to appear to be unable to govern.

The television cameras had not entered the House of Commons by the time I resigned as Chancellor, so I had had no previous experience of the sound bite problem. Those of my colleagues who were in the Chamber, and heard my speech in its entirety – among them Norman Lamont – saw nothing to complain about (apart from its inordinate length). But in TV news bulletin after TV news bulletin that evening it was those last three short sentences alone that were shown; and instead of the thoughtful and analytical speech I thought I had made, I discovered from the media that I had launched a savage personal attack on John Major – a *canard* that some in the Cabinet were all too ready to believe and react to without bothering to read the speech. It was a waste of a good speech, and a careless mistake I was not to make a second time.

Fortunately – although I have no reason to believe it had anything whatever to do with my speech – the Government did not conduct its further consultations on the successor to the Poll Tax, nor did it wait until the summer before making up its mind. The following month, on 23 April 1991, Michael informed the House of what the new Council Tax would be. In all its principal features it was unmistakably a version of the property tax I had unsuccessfully urged on Margaret and my Cabinet Committee colleagues six years previously. I contented myself with congratulating the Government not merely on the property basis of the new tax – if there had to be one – but also on having 'had the courage and common sense to consign the Poll Tax to oblivion and [to] come to a firm decision as to the nature of its replacement'. The new tax could not be introduced until 1993, well after the election – which may have been just as well; since, despite its undoubted superiority, transitional problems can always be difficult. But the official demise of the Poll Tax had removed what had been the Labour Party's most rewarding target after Margaret Thatcher herself, with whom it was so closely identified.

A Career Over and an Election Won

For a time, after my resignation, I agonized over whether to leave the House of Commons altogether, or to remain on the back-benches. Leaving the Commons, however logical, is a wrench for anyone with an active mind and political instincts. Nor was I under any illusion that the Lords, whatever its attractions, could be a substitute. But as time passed, the thought of starting a new life began to seem more enticing than prolonging an old one for a further five years. Pressed by my Constituency Association to let them know whether I wished to stand again, on 23 October 1990, almost exactly a year after my resignation, I announced that I would not be doing so. As it happened, before too long Margaret was to reach a similar decision.

As for me, the hardest part had not been the trauma of my resignation, still less the extraordinary abuse which had rained upon me when I accepted a small number of part-time job offers. What I found unpleasant, if all too predictable, was the way in which I was made the scapegoat for all the ills with which the economy was afflicted. The campaign was launched, within minutes of my departure, by the Number 10 black propaganda machine; but many others found it equally convenient. Nevertheless, I felt it better to hold my peace, however frustrating, despite all the myths and half-truths that were propagated. Before the election my overriding concern was that the Government of which I had been a part for so long should win it. After the election, a measured and, so far as I was able to make it so, objective account of the 1980s as I saw them and of my part in the events of those years, the successes and failures alike, would, I felt, be of greater value than conducting a running media battle with those who found it expedient to rewrite history at my expense. But it was a distasteful experience.

The good news was that, although there were to be various alarms and excursions on the way, the Conservative Party, under a new leader and with the Poll Tax consigned to oblivion, was on track for the unprecedented and decisive fourth successive general election victory it was to win on 9 April 1992. It was, in general, an undistinguished campaign, in which the errors made by the Conservative Party managers were fortunately exceeded by the errors made by Labour. It was manifestly a personal triumph for John Major, whom the opinion polls had, without exception, written off. I have no doubt whatever that, had Margaret remained leader, the election would have been won by Labour. The trauma of 1990 demonstrated once again the Conservative Party's extraordinary instinct for survival and for office.

_____

CHAPTER 80

EPILOGUE, 1989–92: 2. THE ECONOMY

ERM Entry at Last · The Maastricht Treaty
Budgets and Public Spending · The Economy in Recession

ERM Entry at Last

I REFERRED IN AN EARLIER chapter to the run on the pound triggered by the announcement of my resignation as Chancellor. It was an unpleasant baptism for my successor, John Major; and although the immediate plunge was stemmed by large-scale intervention, sterling continued to drift downwards from a shade under DM 3 on the eve of my resignation on 26 October 1989 to a little over DM 2.70 by the end of the year, a level that was barely changed by the time of his first and only Budget the following March.

In addition to the initial sterling crisis, John also inherited from me a Treasury mandarinate which had been persuaded of the case for sterling's membership of the ERM. It was not long before he himself was convinced of the economic merits of joining. By the spring the news was mysteriously starting to percolate through to the foreign exchange markets, with increasing frequency as the months went by. Largely as a result, sterling started to edge up again. By the time John made his first serious attempt to persuade Margaret that the pound should enter the ERM without further ado, in July 1990, it was back within a whisker of DM 3. Although she rejected ERM entry then, it was the last time she was to do so.

In any event, Margaret was – and on this occasion rightly – becoming increasingly unhappy about the high level of interest rates. I had raised them to 15 per cent three weeks before my resignation, and John had subsequently held them there, arguing that any premature reduction would be very badly received on the foreign exchange markets and jeopardize the struggle to bring down inflation. When John went to see her shortly before the 1990 Party Conference, with Labour soaring in the polls, she could already see the attractions of combining the announcement of ERM entry the foreign exchange markets were looking for and by this time firmly expecting – the hints from the Treasury had become increasingly audible, and by the time of the annual Fund and Bank meetings in September the cat could already be seen poking its head out of the bag – with the interest rate cut for which she, and the Party, were becoming desperate. She persuaded herself that, with the wide 6 per cent margins, it was not really a serious commitment in any event; and on Friday, 5 October 1990 it was announced that sterling would be entering the ERM that weekend, at a central parity of DM 2.95, and that base rates would be reduced from 15 per cent to 14 per cent on the Monday – the day before the opening of the Party Conference.

Ironically, after five years spent resisting sterling's entry into the ERM, at great political and economic cost, Margaret was finally to accede to it only seven weeks before her involuntary loss of office. I warmly welcomed the decision; and in the subsequent debate in the House of Commons, on 23 October, added:

> The real tragedy is that we did not join the exchange rate mechanism of the EMS at least five years ago. That was not for of trying, as a number of my then Cabinet colleagues can testify . . . Not only would it have been economically beneficial, but had we joined five years ago there would have been no danger of confusing the ERM and the EMS with EMU.

Unfortunately, insistence on a full point interest rate cut at the moment of entry, without waiting to see whether the foreign exchange markets indicated it, created an unfortunate scepticism which the new Chancellor, Norman Lamont, was obliged to counter by delaying any further interest rate reduction far longer than would otherwise have been necessary, and for longer than was desirable. Interest rates remained at 14 per cent until February 1991, but it then proved possible to reduce them by a series of half point steps to 10 per cent by May 1992, all but extinguishing the customary difference between UK and German interest rates in the process.

But while the ERM decision had at last been taken, the argument over it continued, to an extent unknown in any other member country. This was in large part because Margaret's abuse of the forumla that sterling would enter the ERM when the time was right delayed its entry until

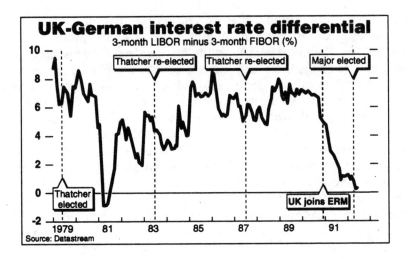

UK-German interest rate differential
3-month LIBOR minus 3-month FIBOR (%)

Thatcher re-elected

Thatcher re-elected

Major elected

Thatcher elected

UK joins ERM

1979 81 83 85 87 89 91

Source: Datastream

a time that could scarcely have been less right. Much of the world, including the UK, was in the early stages of a prolonged recession – a time when financial discipline is always particularly irksome and the perennial cry for lower interest rates particularly clamant.

At the same time, the system was under unusual strain for other reasons. I have already referred to the repercussions of the economic consequences of German unification. But that was not all. The United States, like the UK in the grip of a debt-ridden recession, sought to combat it by slashing interest rates to the point where, by the middle of 1992, they were below 4 per cent – and, in real terms, below 1 per cent. This caused the dollar to slide to hitherto unplumbed depths.

The flight from the dollar was exacerbated by the fact that German interest rates were rising, to combat the post-reunification inflationary pressures, as US rates were falling. Whereas, in 1989, US rates were some two points higher than German rates, not very different from the three-point differential that had been customary, by the middle of 1992 US rates were an unprecedented six points *lower* than German rates. A falling dollar had always put strains on the ERM, as nervous holders of dollars tend to look to the Deutschmark as the obvious alternative home, just as a rising dollar tends to bind the ERM currencies together; and the ERM in 1992 experienced a particularly virulent form of the former.

Moreover, there was yet another special factor creating difficulties for the ERM in the early 1990s. Whereas, throughout most of the 1980s, the ERM was seen as an exchange rate system in its own right, an important regional successor to the gold standard and the Bretton Woods dollar standard, by the end of the 1980s the Euro-politicians, with no thought for the consequences, were encouraging the markets to see it as nothing more than an unstable transitional stage towards EMU and a single European currency. This became particularly pronounced following the Maastricht Treaty of 10 December 1991. With the ink barely dry on the Maastricht Treaty, doubts about the misbegotten drive to a single currency, which had hitherto been voiced almost exclusively in the UK, began to emerge elsewhere in the Community. As a result, the whole foolish project appeared threatened, which led to an objectively unwarranted, but in the circumstances inevitable, weakening of confidence in the ERM.

All these factors made the task of the Major Government particularly difficult. They also played into the hands of those who, for various reasons, opposed ERM membership. In particular, an unprincipled alliance was formed between the 'expansionist' neo-Keynesians who had consistently been indifferent to inflation and averse to financial discipline of any serious kind; and those domestic monetarists whose commitment to floating exchange rates caused them to make common cause with the neo-Keynesians, arguing for a relaxation of monetary policy not to prevent prices from falling – of which there was not the least sign – but to boost real output.

These two groups were joined by two others. On the one hand there were those who – as I did – opposed EMU, but who unlike me swallowed the irresponsible and damaging Delors doctrine that the ERM was either the antechamber to EMU or it was nothing. On the other hand there were those who did not oppose ERM membership root and branch, but maintained that the rate at which the UK had joined, of DM 2.95 to the pound, was far too high. I could not help noticing that many of those who castigated John Major for having joined at the excessively high sterling rate of DM 2.95 to the pound were the same as those who had earlier castigated me for having shadowed the Deutschmark at the excessively low sterling rate of DM 3 to the pound.*

Had the UK joined the ERM when I made my most thoroughgoing attempt to achieve it in November 1985, there would have been no confusion with EMU – the Delors Report was not even commissioned until 1988 – and no worries that without EMU the system might founder, no complications from German unification and the historically high German interest rates that arose as a consequence, and no recession-induced disaffection. Of course, all these events – with the possible exception of EMU, which we would have been in a stronger position to head off – would still have occurred in due course. But by then we would have

---

*It will be argued that the correct comparison should be between the real, not the nominal, exchange rate at the time of uncapping in March 1988 and the real, not the nominal, exchange rate at the time of ERM entry in October 1990: that is to say, taking into account the difference between UK and German inflation over this period. But even on this basis, DM 2.95 in October 1990 was at most some 10 per cent higher than DM3 in March 1988. In short, there is no way in which it can seriously be maintained both that DM 3 was significantly too low in 1988 and DM2.95 significantly too high in 1990.

had several years of successful ERM membership under our belt, with all the credibility that would have brought – not to mention a lower rate of inflation and a less severe recession.

Indeed, it is likely that, by the time the strains emerged at the start of the 1990s, sterling's membership of the ERM would, as in other member countries, have become so much an integral part of the policy framework, so much a fact of life, that the argument over it would have long since been confined to the outer fringes of the public debate. As it was, however, we encountered the ERM's period of maximum strain during our running-in phase: the worst timing imaginable.

The nature and cause of the strains within the system made a strong case for a unilateral appreciation of the Deutschmark against all the other major currencies in the system, including the French franc, in order to help combat the exceptional circumstances of the inflationary consequences of German unification. There is an irony here. Most mainstream economists had tended to argue the case for a Deutschmark revaluation in order to rectify Germany's huge and seemingly endemic current account surplus. Yet, in line with my own balance of payments heresy (see Chapter 68), unification caused the German surplus, on which so much time had been wasted at international meetings during my time as Chancellor, to disappear overnight – not as a result of any Deutschmark revaluation, but because of a change in the balance of German savings and investment.

None the less, in its fight against inflation, the Bundesbank would have been happy to offer a post-unification Deutschmark revaluation at any time. The snag was the French, who had made the '*franc fort*' the cornerstone of their economic policy, with considerable anti-inflationary success, and were determined to maintain the French franc–Deutschmark parity come what may. However, others did not have to follow suit.

The Maastricht Treaty

On the wider European Community front, while half-hearted and highly tentative moves were made towards enlargement, in response to growing interest among the EFTA countries – Austria, Norway, Sweden and even Switzerland – for Community membership, the main focus of attention throughout the period from my resignation in 1989 to the general election of 1992 was the inexorable progress of the bandwagon towards EMU, to which a further vehicle, EPU (European Political Union) had become hitched. Although somewhat vaguer in content, this new development served further to underline the true political nature of the entire enterprise. At Margaret's last European Summit, at Rome towards the end of October 1990, it was agreed, to her intense displeasure, that the second stage of the route to monetary union should start in 1994 – a significant event, inasmuch as the first stage, to which the UK had agreed, did not require a new Treaty, whereas the subsequent stages did.

From then on it was full speed ahead to the new Treaty, to be agreed, under the Dutch presidency, at Maastricht in December 1991. This was an acutely difficult period for John Major, which he handled with considerable skill. Unlike the other member countries, Britain and the British Parliament were eccentric enough to wish to debate the momentous and difficult issues at stake before the Treaty was actually signed, and the Conservative Party was unsurprisingly divided on the matter. So, too, was Labour, but a split on the Government side of the House is always a greater problem than a split on the Opposition side. My own position was one of reasoned but unqualified opposition to the single currency and United States of Europe which lay at the heart of the EMU/EPU adventure, as indeed I made clear in the debates that were held on the issue – although in language distinctly more measured than that favoured by Margaret (which was not difficult).

John Major, for his part, predictably abandoned the confrontational and occasionally abusive style which had been among Margaret's contributions to European negotiations, and which had long since become counter-productive even on her own terms; and declared his wish to see Britain 'at the heart of Europe' – which, given that we were part of the Community and intended to remain so, could scarcely be contested. But none of this defined the sort of Europe of which we wished to be at the heart, or answered any of the critical and complex questions with which the UK, and indeed Europe as a whole, was faced.

John's overriding objective at that time was, rightly, to keep the Conservative Party together in the run-up to the election; and in this he succeeded admirably, passing the Maastricht test with flying colours. To Jacques Delors' annoyance, the twelve agreed that foreign affairs and defence should remain matters for intergovernmental decision, outside the framework of Community institutions: the foreign offices of Europe can be relied upon to attach more weight to their own departmental interests than to those matters which fall within the scope of other Departments, such as finance ministries. John also succeeded in securing special arrangements for the UK on the two issues which rightly caused greatest difficulty within the Party: we were able to remain untouched by the highly objectionable Social Charter, while as for participation in the proposed single currency, that would be for a future British Parliament to decide, if and when the occasion arose.

All this left Europe in the forefront of the political debate, with everything still to play for.

Budgets and Public Spending

Europe apart, the dominant issue of 1989–92 was, of course, the economy. The last three Budgets of the Parliament of 1987–92, introduced by my successors, for the most part built on the foundations which Geoffrey Howe and I had laid. The principal innovation in John Major's only Budget, the launch of TESSAs, has already been mentioned in a previous chapter. I was more doubtful of John's other reform, the abolition of the Composite Rate of Tax. The reader will recall that I had created a level playing field for banks and building societies in 1984 by bringing the banks into the Composite Rate of Tax system which had always applied to building societies. This was admittedly rough justice, but it produced a major simplification. John kept the level playing field but abolished the Composite Rate across the board. Although fairer, it has massively complicated the administration of the system for the taxpayer and the Revenue alike, at considerable expense. He evidently felt that the advent of independent taxation, involving millions of wives with small savings incomes, required strict fairness to prevail over all other considerations.

Norman Lamont's first Budget, in March 1991, after Margaret's resignation and her replacement by John Major, was dominated by the need to mitigate the effects of the Poll Tax. Hence the increase in VAT from 15 to 17½ per cent. As I made clear in my speech in the Budget debate, the mischief lay not in the choice of which central government tax to increase, but in the fact that the misbegotten Poll Tax had made a rise in central government taxation politically imperative – and the very small proportion of local government spending that remained financed by local taxation as a consequence.

The limiting of mortgage interest relief to the basic rate was a change I had long advocated, but so long as Margaret had been there it had been blocked. Given the weakness of the housing market, however, the timing was not ideal. The staged reduction in Corporation Tax from 35 per cent to 33 per cent was very much in line with my desire to reduce the gap between the rates of Corporation Tax and income tax. The increase in Profit Related Pay was welcome and I was happy with the further tightening up on company cars. The only really retrograde step in the 1991 Budget, which I tactfully forebore to mention in my speech at the time, was the decision, at John Major's insistence, to increase Child Benefit, which had been frozen for the previous four years, and to promise that it would henceforth be increased each year in line with inflation.

The fifth and final Budget of the 1987–92 Parliament was dictated entirely by its timing. With the general election scheduled for 9 April

1992, and thus the dissolution of Parliament for 16 March, a Budget on 10 March was bound to be as much the first chapter of the Conservative Election Manifesto as the last chapter of the old Parliament. Since a key theme of the election had to be the difference between the Parties over tax policy, Norman Lamont had no practical option but to underline this by presenting what would clearly be seen as a tax-cutting Budget.

The awkwardness lay in the fact that the PSBR for 1991–92 was officially estimated at £14 billion, or £22 billion excluding privatization proceeds, with a further massive rise, even without any tax cuts, to an estimated £26 billion, or £34 billion excluding privatization proceeds, equivalent to 5½ per cent of GDP, in 1992–93. This was a far cry from the Budget surplus I had secured, even excluding privatization proceeds, during my last two years as Chancellor, and difficult to reconcile with the rule of Budget balance over the economic cycle as a whole. In any case it was likely to be exceeded. For while it was true that the great bulk of the deterioration was purely cyclical, representing the automatic effects of recession, and as such acceptable; by no means all of it could be explained in this way. The prolonged pre-election period had seen a worrying discretionary relaxation of public spending control, of which the Child Benefit decision was the most conspicuous example.

The wisest path in these uncomfortable circumstances would have been to do the minimum required to reinforce the Conservative Government's tax-cutting credentials, and in particular the target I had set in 1988, subsequently reiterated by Norman Lamont and to feature prominently in the Party's 1992 Manifesto, of a basic rate of tax of 20 pence in the pound; while resolving to rein back public spending after the election. This pointed to the simple step, whose unrivalled political potency had been demonstrated in 1986, of cutting a penny off the basic rate, this time from 25 pence to 24 pence, and doing nothing else at all: indeed, there was a case for clawing back some of the cost elsewhere. Most unwisely, however – and quite unnecessarily in the light of the overall fiscal background – the Government allowed the prospect of a tax-cutting Budget to be widely trailed in advance; and the Labour Opposition conducted a sustained campaign to discredit the base rate income tax cut it feared so much.

Norman, none the less, should have carried on regardless. Instead, he chose to be clever and take the Opposition by surprise, introducing a reduced rate band of 20 pence in the pound on the first £2,000 of taxable income. It did indeed wrong-foot Labour, giving Norman a parliamentary triumph. Kinnock and Smith astonishingly failed to recognize that it was nothing more than the reintroduction of the reduced rate band that had been forced on a reluctant Denis Healey by the TUC in 1978, as part of the price for co-operating over incomes policy, and rightly abolished by Geoffrey in 1980, as a highly undesirable complication of the income tax system of no economic, fiscal, social or political merit. The idea behind its reappearance in 1992 – apart from that of surprise, which was a one-day wonder – was that, in the next Parliament, the Government could gradually extend the width of the reduced rate band until it encompassed the whole of the basic rate band, thus achieving the 20 pence basic rate target by easy and readily adjustable stages.

The political fallacy in this was inherent in the Government's boast that the reduced rate band had, at a stroke, given four million taxpayers a 20 per cent marginal rate – because their taxable earnings (that is, after deduction of all allowances) were no more than £2,000. This, however, was another way of saying that four million voters no longer had any interest in the Conservatives' 20 per cent target, since for them it had already been achieved. In other words, in terms of political reality, this 'innovation' made the 20 per cent target not more likely, but less likely, to be attained. The total cost of the tax reductions in the 1992 Budget, at some £2.6 billion in the first full year (1993–94) was rather greater than the cost of a penny off the basic rate.

Fortunately for the Government, however, its own tax error was eclipsed as an electoral factor by the far greater error made by Labour, on whose behalf John Smith presented a 'shadow Budget' of singular folly, which alienated millions of key voters, re-emphasized Labour as a high tax Party, and enabled the Conservatives to play the tax card to signal effect for the second successive general election.

As for public spending, the need to rein it back substantially after the election was encouragingly recognized by John's appointment of my one-time special adviser, Michael Portillo, a committed hawk, as Chief Secretary. By the summer of 1992 it emerged that Michael would be armed with a brand new technique. In place of the Star Chamber there would be a committee of senior Ministers chaired by the Chancellor; and there would be fixed cash sums available for a modified form of the old public expenditure planning total, in place of the slightly more flexible twin target of previous years (see Chapters 24 and 25). In fact, all this was very much less new than the Press imagined. A committee of senior Ministers chaired by Geoffrey as Chancellor, was what we had started with, before the Star Chamber under Willie Whitelaw was devised as an improvement. But without Willie, or someone of equal status, it might well be sensible to go back to the earlier system. Again, a fixed cash envelope was what we originally worked within during the early 1980s, and departed from for reasons I have described.

It was, however, tempting providence for the Government to promote, as it did, its 'new' system as a response to the alleged shortcomings of the system devised by Geoffrey and modified by me during Margaret's time. Certainly, in the unlikely event that, during the present cycle, the Government succeeds in confining the growth of total public spending to below the 1.3 per cent a year of the Howe/Lawson cycle, let alone the 0.6 per cent a year of my own years as Chancellor, I shall be the first to cheer. If it is to do so, it will depend more on the united will and determination of three people – the Chief Secretary, Chancellor and Prime Minister – than on any changes to the system.

The Economy in Recession

The recession that was the dominant economic phenomenon of the second half of the 1987–92 Parliament was surprisingly late in arriving, given the severe monetary tightening I had imposed as far back as the summer of 1988, when interest rates rose a full four points in twelve weeks, taking them to 7 per cent in real terms. The first indicator of the recession that lay ahead was house prices. These, which had been rising at a staggering annual rate of over 30 per cent at the end of 1988, had calmed down to a rather more sober 10 per cent by the time of my resignation, and by the spring of 1990 had ceased to rise at all. Bank and building society lending, which was still rising at 20 per cent a year as late as the first half of 1990, did not slow down significantly until the second half of that year, but thereafter decelerated sharply to little more than 5 per cent in the first half of 1992. This marked reduction in borrowing was reflected in a corresponding recovery in the personal savings ratio, which had fallen to a low of 5½ per cent in the boom of 1988: by the first quarter of 1992 it was more than twice that.

The swing in real output was particularly abrupt, with the turning point occurring in the middle of 1990. Real GDP was still growing at an annual rate of 2¼ per cent in the first half of 1990 as it had done in 1989 – not all that far below the trend rate. From then on it fell, at first sharply and then much more gently, right through to the first half of 1992. At the time of writing it is unclear whether the recession of the early 1990s will turn out to have been the deepest since the war but it will certainly prove to have been the most prolonged.

Not all the economic news was bad, although it may have felt like it: it always does in recessions. Underlying inflation, which did not peak until the autumn of 1990, thereafter fell fairly steadily to around 4 per cent by the summer of 1992. By then both factory gate prices and average earnings were rising more slowly than at any time in the 1980s.

There was even some consolation to be found in the behaviour of the 'real' economy. Manufacturing productivity began to improve quite early in the recession, despite the fact that there was not the overmanning to get rid of which had enabled manufacturing productivity to rise at a similar stage of the recession of the early 1980s. Business investment held up very much better than in the previous cycle, as did spending on both training and research and development.

What made it all seem worse than it was was the failure of the forecasters to predict the severity of the recession, and their subsequent predictions of a recovery which did not materialize – which led Norman Lamont to make his unfortunate 1991 reference to the 'green shoots of recovery'. Disappointed expectations inevitably intensify gloom, which can then all too easily become self-validating.

Despite the efforts of the incorrigibly parochial media, and the Government's assorted critics, it soon became clear that the recession was a worldwide phenomenon, differing in intensity from country to country, but remarkably similar in character. In the European Community as a whole, the downturn was remarkably similar in degree to that of the early 1980s, with real growth declining from 3½ per cent in 1989 to roughly zero in 1991, virtually identical to the experience of exactly a decade previously. With Germany, the largest economy in Europe and the fastest growing of all the major European economies in 1991, slowing down markedly towards the end of that year and into 1992, the recovery from the recession of the early 1990s looked as if it was going to be slower than the recovery a decade earlier.

The severity was greatest, however, in those countries – notably the English-speaking world – where the role of credit in the economy was greatest and the effect of financial deregulation most pronounced. Thus, of the seven Economic Summit nations, the three in which output actually fell in 1991 were the UK, Canada and the US – in the last of which the weakness of the banking and housing credit sectors was more acute than in the UK. There was a marked slowdown in Japan, too, again associated with the bursting of a financial bubble. This demonstrated, incidentally, the absurdity of simple-mindedly blaming either the severity or the duration of the recession solely on ERM membership.

In a sense, the primacy of the old stock or inventory cycle had been replaced, as techniques of stock control improved and credit expanded, by the reappearance of a pronounced credit cycle. This led to a number of new features. In the UK, one such, which in the past had been considered desirable but unattainable, proved more of a mixed blessing when it actually happened. This was the narrowing of regional differences, as the manufacturing-oriented North held up better than the financial services-oriented South, including London. Since it was here that the talking and writing classes were largely based, this led to the propagation of a greater sense of national malaise than might otherwise have occurred. Precisely the same phenomenon was observable in the United States.

Yet another aspect of the unwinding of a credit-based boom is that a large part of credit is associated with spending on expensive and readily postponable items. This alone is likely to make a credit cycle more pronounced. Again, in the UK the severity of the credit cycle is exacerbated by the nature of the housing sector, and the exceptionally high incidence of owner-occupation. The near-annihilation of the private rented sector, thanks to decades of rent control and other anti-landlord legislation, is something for which the UK has paid a heavy price.

Moreover the weakness of the banking sector, which had been a well-documented feature of the nineteenth-century economic cycle, but had been largely unknown in living memory until the debt recession of the early 1990s, contributed not only to the recession's duration but to its unfamiliarity and the sense of unease that unfamiliarity always breeds.

But it remained more likely that the basic principles of the sound conduct of economic policy, in the form that I have sought to describe in this book, were as valid as ever; and that impatience would prove the bad counsellor it always had been.

CHAPTER 81

IN PLACE OF CONCLUSIONS

A Classical Framework · Problems with Money
The Switch to the Exchange Rate · The Trauma of September 1992
Rules versus Discretion · An Independent Bank of England
A Deflationary Threat? · Europe: The Big Issue . . .
. . . and the Right Road · The True Challenge of the 1990s
Building on Sound Foundations

A Classical Framework

IT WILL BE FOR the historians of the future to draw their conclusions about that remarkable decade, the 1980s, during which I was in Government, and about the events described in this book. All I can hope to do is to draw a few threads together, and reflect on some of the main issues and themes, and their bearing on the future.

During the 1970s it had become clear that something had gone radically wrong with the world's economies. Throughout most of the industrialized world, inflation and unemployment alike were soaring to levels not known since the Second World War.

The root of the problem was that the formula on which the unprecedented growth in prosperity of the Western world over the hundred years from the middle of the nineteenth to the middle of the twentieth century had been based had been stood on its head. That formula was the development of free markets – both national and international – within the framework of an over-arching financial discipline. The classical expression of that discipline was, in turn, adherence to the gold standard coupled with the doctrine of the balanced budget. But in recent decades, what we had seen was increasing interference in the working of markets, coupled with a steady erosion of financial discipline.

Hence the deterioration in the world economic performance which had become so evident in the 1970s – and hence, too, the need to reverse this process and return to basics.

This was the origin of the economic policy approach of the new Government, in which I was to become the longest-serving Treasury Minister this century. On the one hand, impediments to market freedom were to be swept away. On the other hand, the Medium Term Financial Strategy was introduced, to provide the missing financial discipline. Like its classical counterpart, it had both a monetary and a fiscal component: in place of the gold standard, a steadily declining path for monetary growth; and in place of the balanced budget a similarly declining path for the public sector borrowing requirement – until, indeed, a balanced budget was once again secured.

This new approach represented a clear attempt to replace discretionary economic management by adherence to known rules. The potential advantages of rules were clear. Not only was financial discipline – as necessary for an economy as for an individual company – restored; but people, in particular businessmen, would know where they stood and could plan ahead accordingly, while the Government's actions would carry greater credibility in the financial markets.

On the fiscal side this presented relatively few problems of principle. Firm control of public spending, year in year out, enabled a balanced budget to be secured. The notion of fine-tuning tax changes for con-junctural reasons was abjured; instead, tax changes were to be seen in a medium-term structural context. In this way shocks to the system could be avoided, and a programme of tax reform designed to improve economic performance put in place. Within this context, it was the task of monetary policy to bring down inflation, by securing a reasonably steady reduction in the growth of GDP in money terms, gradually approaching the sustainable long-term rate of real growth.

Problems with Money

But it was here, in the conduct of monetary policy, that the problem of rules versus discretion became acute. If the rule was to be the growth of a monetary aggregate, which aggregate was it to be? For contrary to some expectations, the different aggregates began to exhibit widely divergent growth rates (see especially Chapter 36). The monetary squeeze of the early 1980s was clearly brought about by a sharp rise in the exchange rate, despite the chosen measure of money rising well above the growth target which had been set for it.

At a time when the monetary system was in a state of rapid evolution, not least because of the changed conditions brought about by our success in reducing inflation, the use of discretion was inescapable. Yet this clearly detracted from the market credibility that the strict observance of rules brought with it. How is the market to judge whether the exercise of judgement in departing from the rule is economically sound or merely politically expedient?

Moreover, there remains the question of what basis the monetary authorities should use for the exercise of discretionary action. If monetary policy is to be tightened or loosened – that is, if interest rates are to be raised or lowered – on any basis other than the observance of a monetary rule, it might seem obvious that this should be on the grounds of what is happening to demand within the economy, both actually and prospectively. Yet this is a good deal easier said than done. As the *National Institute Economic Review* recorded in 1990:

> The forecasters expected the growth rate of spending to *slow down* in 1987; in fact it accelerated. A similar mistake was made by the forecasters in March 1988; again they were misled about the recent rate of growth of spending; again they compounded the error by expecting a deceleration instead of even faster growth in the next year.

The same year, 1990, the Treasury's own *Bulletin* retrospectively sought to explain the problem:

> There are clearly some deep-seated problems with macroeconomic statistics. Revisions are frequent and substantial . . . Of course, unreliability of statistics has not been the only source of error . . . There were clearly structural changes going on which led to unprecedented and unpredictable shifts in personal and company behaviour.

Even after these words were written there were two further major errors: the failure to foresee the recession of the early 1990s, and the prediction of a recovery in the latter part of 1991, which conspicuously failed to arrive.

The Switch to the Exchange Rate

Long before this thick fog descended, however, I had come to the conclusion that the classical formula was in every respect the best rule, requiring the least exercise of fallible discretion. That is to say, not only was the balanced budget the most useful fiscal guide, but an external monetary discipline, such as the gold standard, was the best practicable monetary rule. In modern circumstances, this in practice meant adherence to the Deutschmark standard via membership of the Exchange Rate Mechanism of the EMS – which at long last, and at what proved to be the worst possible time, was secured.

The exchange rate, unlike the monetary aggregates, is clear and un-equivocal. It is both a symptom of inflationary pressures and a trans-mission mechanism through which inflation can be caused. It is a market price, and not a calculation subject to subsequent statistical revision. The discipline of a fixed exchange rate can be readily understood by employers and the general public alike – which is more than can be said for the monetary aggregates – and it can acquire considerable market credibility, provided the monetary authorities demonstrate a firm commitment to take whatever measures that may be needed to maintain it.

There are those who hanker after freely floating exchange rates, and ask why it is that, if freedom is best in other financial markets, it is not the case here too. I would answer in two parts. First, there is the greater gain to be had from using the exchange rate as the best avail-able anti-inflationary discipline. Second, in a twenty-four-hour global marketplace where capital flows, often of a speculative nature, rather than trade flows, dominate, the world's experience of freely floating exchange rates has not been a happy one. Massive gyrations can and do occur that have nothing to do with economic fundamentals, which are essentially slow-moving. These gyrations can damage growth in world trade. Businesses have to devote scarce management time and skills to coping with currency fluctuations, not least because of their huge potential impact on published profits, rather than improving company performance. Major uncertainties about exchange rate movements tend to inhibit risk-taking, and promote a frenetic switching of resources, as when the dollar first doubled in value and then returned to its original level in the early and mid-1980s.

It was this perception that led to the agreements at the Plaza and the Louvre of 1985 and 1987. Although international financial co-operation subsequently fell out of fashion, I have little doubt that, sooner or later, its desirability will once again be recognized. But whether that is so or not, one thing is clear. If the exchange rate is assigned the task of providing the essential financial discipline, it cannot also be assigned the task of securing equilibrium on the current account of the balance of payments. Nor, indeed, is there any reason why the current account *should* be in balance, except over the very long term.

For in a world of free capital movements, it is inevitable that there will be net capital flows between countries, depending on the distribution of savings habits and investment opportunities around the world. Just as there are bound to be countries that export capital and countries that import capital, it is inevitable – since the overall accounts must necess-arily be in balance – that the former will be in current account surplus and the latter in current account deficit. If the Government maintains a balanced budget over the business cycle and maintains the external value of sterling against a stable currency bloc, then there is no need for a balance of payments target or any of the other economic targets that have been proposed from time to time. Many of the problems of the past have arisen out of a confusing excess of official targets and objectives.

The Trauma of September 1992

The trauma of September 1992, which led to sterling's departure from the European Exchange Rate Mechanism, less than two years after it had joined, reflected credit on no-one. Not on the UK authorities; who demonstrated all too clearly that they were still wearing their ERM 'L' plates. Not on the German Government which so mishandled the economic consequences of unification that the Bundesbank was obliged to take extreme and destabilizing corrective action. Not on the Bundesbank; which was guilty not only of irresponsible talk but of a damaging reluctance to fulfil its intervention obligations – not merely under the Basle–Nyborg agreement but under the rules of the European Monetary System treaty itself.

Least of all did it reflect credit on the misguided architects of a United States of Europe; who were responsible for undermining the credibility of the ERM by vesting it with the incredibility of the federal vision of monetary union.

The events of September 1992 also demonstrated how much the UK suffered from failing to join the ERM in the relative calm of the expansionary mid 1980s, and waiting until the turmoil of the recessionary early 1990s instead. I had warned Margaret in my minute of November 1985 that 'not to join now would be a historic missed opportunity in the conduct of economic policy': so, alas, it proved – in every respect. The constant rubric of the Thatcher era had been that we would join when the time was right: it turned out to be a recipe for joining when the time was wrong.

No doubt, for a time, many in Britain will see this defeat as a deliverance. Certainly, there is a case for a floating pound, as I conceded in my resignation speech. But the lesson of economic history since the Second World War is that, in practice, the advantages are outweighed by the disadvantages. And whatever the case for a floating pound, there is no merit in a sinking pound.

Rules versus Discretion

The case for a balanced budget and an exchange rate anchor is an example of the more general case, which in fact transcends economic policy, for relying more on rules and less on discretion. Governments that believe in unfettered discretion are likely to be led astray by short-term pressures and the politically expedient. A government that simply reacts to the pressure of events is likely to make more mistakes than one constrained by rules embodying experience accumulated over a long period. There is a more fundamental point too. A government of rules is less intrusive and – in the long run – more acceptable to the public at large than a government of men. All politicians – and I do not exclude myself – have an urge to tinker, against which the need to follow prescribed rules is a useful check. The classical argument for rules can be found in Friedrich Hayek's *magnum opus*, *The Constitution of Liberty*.

The question of rules versus discretion, so central to the conduct of economic policy and of government more generally, must always be one of degree. All rules require interpretation and may need to be suspended in extreme situations – as the gold standard was in both the Napoleonic and the First World Wars (and, for very brief periods, in two or three financial crises in between). The practical question was whether the balance we inherited was right, or whether – as I believed – there was a need to shift more towards rules.

The balanced budget doctrine is an example of the interplay of rules and interpretation. There is the question of how to define the balance. An even bigger problem arises when, as in the UK, the rule is – for good reasons – restated in terms of balance over the economic cycle as a whole. When no-one knows how long a business cycle is going to be or how to distinguish, at the time, a temporary fluctuation from a shift in trend, it will frequently be possible to misuse the cyclical argument to justify almost any deficit.

Nor is this the only problem. In today's global financial markets, any one government may see the attractions of being a free rider so long as it can get away with it. That is to say, if the rest of the world were to maintain a balanced budget, it would be tempting for a maverick government to slash taxes and run a large budget deficit, since, in the short run, it would secure all the benefit of lower taxation for its own economy while the burden in terms of higher interest rates would be shared throughout the world. Such a situation would be unlikely to be stable. If a major nation is able to gain an advantage at the expense of the rest of the world by running a large Budget deficit, then others will sooner or later emulate it until no-one gets any advantage and all are worse off, through a form of Gresham's Law in which bad fiscal policies drive out good ones.

This struggle strongly suggests that international agreement on Budget deficit ceilings ought to be an aspect of international financial co-operation when such co-operation, which I believe to be desirable, comes back into fashion.

IN PLACE OF CONCLUSIONS

An Independent Bank of England

In the monetary field, insofar as the exercise of discretion is still required, as it manifestly is, it is likely to have far more credibility if it is exercised by an independent central bank rather than by politicians who, however austere they may be, are subject to electoral pressures which will be thought, rightly or wrongly, to affect their judgement. I have no doubt that, for this reason, the UK would benefit over the years from an independent Bank of England, provided it were given the right statutory framework.

There are those who claim that an independent central bank is undemocratic. That is clearly absurd. The Americans would rightly be more than a little astonished to learn that the independence of the Federal Reserve Board means that the United States is not a democracy. But what is true is that, in a democracy, an independent central bank has to be accountable. This is not, as some suppose, a contradiction in terms. The chairman of the US Federal Reserve Board is required regularly to testify to Congress, where he can be questioned on the Fed's policy, and where indeed he has the valuable opportunity to explain that policy and why it is being pursued. But that no more detracts from the Fed's independence than does, say, the fact that the German Finance Minister has the right to attend any meeting of the Bundesbank Council, and express his own views to that Council, in any way detract from the Bundesbank's independence.

The truth is that accountability should consist of a close working relationship between central bank and government and a statutory (but inevitably different) relationship between the central bank and the legislature; without in either case any sharing of ultimate central bank responsibility for monetary policy. Thus the legislation setting up an independent Bank of England might, as I originally suggested in 1988, oblige it, like the Bundesbank, to conduct monetary policy within the framework of the government's economic policy as a whole, *but only so far as that is consistent with the Bank's overriding responsibility for safeguarding the value of the currency*. Within this same context, there would be an obligation on the Governor of the Bank of England to appear regularly before the appropriate Parliamentary Select Committee, analogous to the arrangements in the United States.

A Deflationary Threat?

Much of this book has been about the need to use macroeconomic policy – that is, the financial levers under the control of the Treasury and Bank of England – to maintain reasonable price stability; while using microeconomic or supply-side measures – that is, policies to remove the impediments to improved personal and corporate performance – to facilitate the growth of output and employment. For almost the whole period since the Second World War most countries would have benefited from this policy assignment.

Is the world now, however, entering a new stage in which the main danger is that of depression due to inadequate demand? Such periods are historically the exception rather than the rule. Harold Macmillan was notoriously and damagingly soft on inflation because of his memories of Stockton-on-Tees in the 1930s and his misplaced fear that the great slump was about to recur. Nevertheless, the tendency to cry 'wolf' when there is no wolf does not mean that the animal is extinct. There is nothing in the foregoing pages to justify passivity in the face of genuine deflation or depression. The underlying argument, given more fully in Chapter 33, is for a *nominal framework*. This means that the ultimate aim of monetary policy is to sustain a moderate and stable growth of spending *in money terms*. Most of the time this has meant a struggle to stop spending from rising at an inflationary pace; and I have usually presented it in those terms.

But the same nominal framework is also relevant if there is a danger of too little demand. The question then is whether, should this threaten to get out of hand, nominal spending is best maintained by a Keynesian budget deficit policy or by cheap money. The first point to make is that, in the global economy of today, stimulatory action is most unlikely to be warranted unless the threat itself is worldwide – that is, if a global depression looms. If consumers and businessmen are reluctant to spend in one country alone, then export demand will fill the gap. The same applies if depression appears to be threatened by so-called debt-deflation, which is usually associated with a credit crunch and a generally debilitated banking sector. Again, if the banking sector in a single country alone is too weak to fulfil its role in the economy, strong banks from overseas will step in to fill the gap.

If, however, the threat really is of worldwide slump, then worldwide, and – if only to avert the serious threat of a relapse into autarky and protection – preferably co-ordinated, action would be warranted. As between the alternatives of a global expansion of budget deficits, or a worldwide reduction in interest rates, the latter is in my judgement to be preferred. It is more readily reversible – an important practical consideration – and less likely to lead governments into bad habits and to a bloated state sector.

The prejudice against this course stems from Keynes's famous aphorism that 'you cannot push on a piece of string'. Certainly, emerging from a worldwide slump is unlikely to be swift and easy whatever method is chosen. But the experience of the UK in the 1930s did not justify Keynes's dictum: quite the reverse. The UK economy recovered sharply from the slump of the 1930s and, contrary to popular myth, this was nothing to do with either the war or even rearmament, since it occurred before both of them. Between the depth of the slump in 1932 and 1937 the UK economy grew at an unprecedented rate of 4½ per cent a year.* The formula on which this was based was a balanced budget and cheap money. On the fiscal front, there would certainly be a strong case for accelerating infrastructure projects already approved as economically sound, but little more.

Europe: The Big Issue . . .

The two big issues facing the Conservative Government after the 1992 general election were the economy and Europe. Difficult though recessions are, they pass; and, in any event, the principles of the Government's economic policy had been hammered out in the 1980s, and it was essentially a matter of judging best how to implement them in the conditions of the time.

That is not, of course, to say that the conduct of economic policy would be easy: it never is. But Europe raised much more fundamental issues. The Government had been pitchforked into *terra incognita*, where passions ran high – not least because the very existence of the United Kingdom as an independent sovereign nation was at stake.

The European question has many facets, but at its core are two key issues: the proposal to move to a single European currency, and the centralizing drive of the Brussels Commission.

The single European currency, with its inescapable counterpart, the single European central bank, is, of course, what EMU is all about. It was originally presented, somewhat disingenuously, as an economic proposition, the argument being that it would eliminate both the transaction costs and exchange rate uncertainties inherent in having separate national currencies. In fact the savings in transaction costs are probably the least important of all the economic aspects of the single currency, and most of them could in any case be secured by improvements in bank transfer mechanisms within the context of the single market. As for exchange rate uncertainty within Europe, this had already been greatly reduced by the ERM (as it is known in the UK) or EMS (as it is universally known elsewhere). So far from being merely a stepping stone to EMU, the ERM is a different animal altogether, and one which – in defiance of academic warnings – was in existence and working increasingly well for a full decade until it was undermined by the Delors blueprint for monetary union in 1989.

---

*GDP had surpassed its 1929 peak level by 1934. Rearmament did not really start until 1936. (See A J P Taylor, *English History, 1914–1945*.)

If transaction costs and exchange rate uncertainties were the only matters at issue, the case for a single currency for the whole world – a horse that has never even come under starter's orders – would be still stronger. But in fact they are insignificant compared with the real economic and, still more, political issues at stake.

The economic issues include a whole raft of matters that were not even addressed in the Maastricht Treaty. These range from the national debt overhang of the various member states, to the method of operation of the European central bank and its relationship to the various national governments: a state of affairs without precedent. Perhaps these difficult and important issues *can* be satisfactorily resolved; but by the middle of 1992 there had still been no attempt to do so.

Where the economic consequences of EMU have been made clear, they are unequivocally damaging. One of these is regional policy. Logically, locking into a single currency, and thus depriving member states for all time of the possibility of adjustment through devaluation, should not require any growth of regional assistance whatever. For since devaluation does not create any new resources, there is no reason to compensate for the inability to devalue by the transfer of resources *via* an enlarged regional policy. But politically it is evident that the demands for increased regional assistance would be very strong indeed, as became clear from the increased programmes which the Commission put to the European Council as soon as the ink on the Maastricht Treaty was dry. We know from experience the massive economic distortions and inefficiencies that are inseparable from regional policy, both in the UK and in continental Europe, such as the subsidization of 'cathedrals in the desert' in southern Italy or the use of regional arguments to get round the Community rules on competition and state aids. Needless to say, a substantial enlargement of the Community's so-called regional policy also feeds the centralizing appetite of the European Commission.

Then there is the all-important question, on the economic front, of whether a single European currency managed by a single European central bank would provide an effective anti-inflationary regime. It may well not do so. Everything would depend on the way in which the central bank conducted itself – what rules it would steer by and how it would exercise such discretion as it felt was necessary. But the one incontrovertible fact is that, as a brand new institution, it inevitably would not possess the track record and the market credibility enjoyed by the Bundesbank – however unpopular that institution may be in the UK at the time of writing. Nor would it be able to count on the popular support for tough policies that a well-led and long-established national institution can evoke from the nation whose institution it is.

It is not, however, surprising that the economic consequences of a single European currency are almost certainly adverse. For the whole inspiration of EMU is not economic, but political. There is nothing reprehensible about this, provided it is avowed and not concealed; but it may well be mistaken. Sadly, I believe it is. The successful governance of a free society is possible only if the legitimacy of the government, and thus of the demands it makes of the people, is beyond reasonable doubt. This legitimacy has to rest on the principle of self-government in the only two senses possible for anything larger than a small city-state: the government has to be democratically elected, and it has to represent national self-determination.

A single European currency would offend against both these aspects of legitimacy, most notably the second. It offends against the democratic canon by entrusting monetary policy to an independent central bank unlike any in the world today. Independent *national* central banks – which I favour – are constitutionally acceptable because they satisfy two key requirements. First, they are accountable to the national parliament or congress; and second, subject to their overriding duty to suppress inflation, they are required to co-operate with the national finance ministry, headed by a finance minister who represents the democratically elected national government. But a European central bank would have no genuine European parliament for it to be accountable to, nor any European finance ministry for it to co-operate with.

Of course, those who wish to see the European Community become a United States of Europe, analogous to the United States of America, have a ready answer to this problem. For then there really would be a genuine European parliament or congress and a single European government with its single finance ministry and finance minister. But a move of this magnitude – the desire for which represents the true motivation of the architects of EMU – would serve only to make even more serious the breach with the second key aspect of legitimacy, the canon of national self-government. Indeed this breach is to some extent inherent in the creation of the European central bank itself.

You do not make a nation simply by decreeing it to be one. In general, the experience of multinational, multilingual federations is not a happy one. Whether the problems are faced in a civilized way, as in Canada, or a barbarous way, as in Yugoslavia, they are best avoided altogether. If a strong sense of national identity is denied the recognition of self-government, the ugliest manifestations of nationalism are likely to come to the fore, and political debate will degenerate into a sterile parade of national resentments, and desparate stratagems to contain them.

There is a parallel between self-interest and nationalism, the two strongest emotions with which politicians have to contend. Both can be unattractive and contemptuous of others. But just as self-interest, channelled through a well-ordered market economy and capitalist system can – as Adam Smith pointed out two centuries ago – confer benefits on all mankind; so nationalism, if channelled into loyalty to a liberal, democratic nation state, can equally be a force for good, and something to be cherished. By contrast, the politician who is foolish enough to ignore or deny either, does so at his very considerable peril.

. . . and the Right Road

I have been a committed supporter of closer European unity, with Britain playing a leading part in it, since I was president of the Strasbourg Club as an Oxford undergraduate. Although far from perfect in practice – nothing ever is – I saw the European Community as an inspired constitutional innovation; providing as it did for the most intimate form of co-operation between the various nation states of Europe, without becoming a federation: the United States of Europe. It got the balance right between the need for the closest possible co-operation and the retention of nation states. The latter is not only important historically, but profoundly important to the successful conduct of policy. The unpopular measures that from time to time are required in the interests of sound economic policy are politically possible in a democracy only if government and people are bound together by the cement of national solidarity.

It is the height of folly to seek to destroy this unique and careful balance between international co-operation and national sovereignty, instead of building on it by completing the single market (there is still much to be done) and entrusting the conduct of monetary policy to independent *national* central banks working closely together, ideally within the framework of the ERM.

This latter concept is, I believe, the European monetary evolution we should be seeking. Quite apart from the domestic case for an independent Bank of England, which I have already set out, it is clearly easier for independent central banks to co-operate effectively over monetary policy than it is for governments conscious of their immediate electoral pressures. Beyond that, the Community's monetary order should consist of the sweeping away of restrictions by individual member states over the use of other Community currencies, as proposed in the original UK Treasury paper of November 1989.

Since Maastricht, EMU has been severely damaged by the hostile Danish referendum, which the wafer-thin 'yes' majority in France has done little to remedy. It is true that, irrespective of these referenda, a case could be made for taking a more relaxed attitude towards EMU, confident that it will eventually collapse under the weight of its own absurdities and self-contradictions, and undermined by the unsustainable gulf it has demonstrated to exist between the leaders of Western Europe and many of their peoples. But such a course would be far too risky. It is hard to overstate the capacity of old men to become intoxicated by ideas whose consequences they will never live to see, or to exaggerate the folly that can be committed in the name of presumed historical inevitability.

Recent arguments over monetary – and still more political – union show the difficulty Britain has continued to find in coming to terms with continental aspirations for European unity. While there is undoubtedly a common European culture, with a heritage second to none in the world, there are also national cultural differences, and it is in the political culture that those differences are greatest. For a country with a deep belief in constitutional stability, the restless urge for constitutional change that characterizes our continental partners is unsettling.

Moreover, Britain is unused to coalition governments. The process of compromise, horsetrading, deals in smoke-filled rooms and the cultivation of *ad hoc* alliances that characterizes Community decision-making is unfamiliar to us. The British, who have grown up with the strong belief, well placed or not, in their ability to govern themselves, find the virtual absence of that belief among some of their partners distinctly alien. An Italian deputy in Tuscany, waxing eloquently in favour of the utmost degree of European federalism, was asked if he would really like to be governed by Brussels. Without a moment's hesitation he replied: 'It would be a good deal better than being governed from Rome.' The one country that used to share the British belief in governing itself, and was therefore closest to us in outlook, was France. But unfortunately the present French political leadership is obsessed by its fear of unified Germany. To the – much lesser – extent that this fear exists in Britain, different conclusions are drawn.

Yet despite these fundamental differences, we might have found the European question less difficult had we been more ready to launch initiatives – as we did so successfully, but uniquely, with the Single Market – that are in keeping with our own vision of Europe, rather than almost always leaving it to others to launch initiatives to which we then react with distinctly qualified enthusiasm. One such initiative might concern the important question of the constitution of Europe. The Brussels Commission has sought to meet the very real fears about its incorrigible centralizing ambitions by promulgating the so-called doctrine of 'subsidiarity', according to which decisions should be taken at the lowest effective level. But as it stands, the doctrine is virtually meaningless and wholly ineffective.

One of the main reasons why written constitutions have come into being around the world is the need to define, in a federal state, what lies within the responsibility of the federal centre and what remains the responsibility of its component parts.* A similar entrenched written

---

*It is only because the UK is not a federal state that we are able to dispense with a written constitution. Whether we gain from so doing is more doubtful.

constitution is required for the Community. 'Subsidiarity' will have real meaning only when there is such a constitution, clearly defining what lies within the writ of the Community as such, with everything else remaining with the member states. The Treaty is no substitute. Not only is it silent on some of the key issues, while containing a great deal that is far too detailed for a constitutional document: it can also be amended far too easily – as we have seen with two fundamental changes, the Single European Act and the Maastricht Treaty, in six years, with yet a further change scheduled for 1996. Not only is a stable constitutional framework, rather than a constitution permanently on the move, necessary for any successful society, but with each change that occurs there is pressure for yet more power to be given to the centre.

The True Challenge of the 1990s

There was something almost indecent in the obsession of the Community's leading politicians and bureaucrats with pressing ahead with the construction of a United States of Western Europe, at a time when the countries of Central and Eastern Europe were suffering the pain and travails of making the transition, never before achieved, from the disasters of communism and the command economy to the complexities of capitalism and the market economy. Making a success of this, and not 'deepening' the Community, is the great European challenge of the 1990s. Moreover, it is particularly important that one of the former Soviet bloc countries – it matters not which – should achieve this transition at a relatively early date, as a demonstration to others that it can indeed be done.

While it is on the peoples and governments of these countries themselves that success or failure will ultimately depend, the Community can do a great deal to help. Most important, it needs to open up its markets to agricultural produce, steel, and textiles from Central and Eastern Europe – something that requires a calibre of political leadership that has yet to appear.

It is also clear that these countries badly need Western investment. This is not simply, or even mainly, a matter of the capital that Western investment brings with it. Even more important, at this stage, are the know-how, the training, the management and marketing skills, and the practical example of capitalism at work, that only Western private investment can provide. While the decision of whether or not to invest in Central and Eastern Europe is a matter for Western businesses to decide for themselves, and not a matter for government, there can be no doubt that such investment will be more readily forthcoming, particularly at the start when local purchasing power is relatively modest, if companies operating there are assured of open access to the markets of Western Europe. Moreover, the crusade that the European Community should be spearheading, to secure access for exports from Central and Eastern Europe to the markets of the rest of the world as a whole, not least the United States and Japan, cannot even begin so long as the Community itself is unwilling to open its doors more than a crack.

No doubt it is politically safer to make the political gesture of sending an embarrassingly futile European peace mission to the Balkans than to risk alienating European farmers. But Western Europe not only has a wider duty to the other half of the continent we all inhabit: it also has a narrower political interest. For keeping its doors closed to their produce risks precipitating the far more embarrassing problem of would-be emigrants from Central and Eastern Europe banging on those same doors. Despite their dismal inheritance and the immense problems – political, economic, psychological and cultural – of making the transition to democracy and the market economy, the peoples of Central and Eastern Europe have the skills and the determination to succeed. Time is short, and without adequate signs of progress the hopes of the heady winter of 1989 could give way to cynicism and despair.

There is an understandable tendency, particularly in the television age, for the attention of the West to be directed to those parts of Europe where the problems are the greatest – usually where ancient ethnic enmities erupt into seemingly uncontrollable violence. The overriding need is to assist those who are doing most to overcome their own problems to achieve the functioning market economy they seek. For the success of one will be a beacon to the others.

Building on Sound Foundations

If constitutional stability is important for Europe, so it is for Britain. That does not mean that there should never be any change at all: I have already indicated my advocacy of an independent Bank of England, which may be said to fall into the category of constitutional change. But this is the exception; and I have little sympathy with the rush of constitutional reforms that were being peddled in the early 1990s. Our first-past-the-post electoral system, for example, came in for another of the bouts of abuse it has received intermittently over the years.

Views on this are likely to differ, particularly when one Party has been in office for a considerable period of time, depending on whether one is a supporter or opponent of that Party. But what is plainly a myth is the suggestion that our electoral system is some curious national eccentricity of ours, responsible for whatever are believed to be our national failings. In fact, of the seven major industrial nations that attend the annual Economic Summit, five – the UK, the US, Japan, France and Canada – all employ some variant of first-past-the-post, while only two

– Germany and Italy – employ proportional representation. Moreover, in the case of Italy, this is widely believed within Italy itself to be a major reason why, of all the G7 countries, it is the only one on the edge of ungovernability.

The history of the UK in the 1980s demonstrates that our constitutional framework was no impediment to the successful prosecution of a thoroughgoing programme of radical change, of a kind that had hitherto been considered politically impossible. Indeed, it may even have succeeded in changing the Labour Party, the most backward-looking institution of all.

There were, of course, disappointments in the 1980s, quite apart from the excesses of the post-deregulation credit boom, which I have discussed at some length. Some were purely ephemeral, such as the unattractive vulgarity associated with the height of the 'yuppy' phenomenon, which was simply a product of the financial services bubble and which disappeared when that bubble burst, as bubbles always do. Others were more deep-seated. 'Short-termism', which had long been a characteristic of the UK business scene, and which I criticized in my 1986 Mansion House speech, became slightly less pronounced. But despite the election of a government explicitly committed to abjuring short-term expedients and taking the long view, the difference between the normal business time-horizon in the UK and that in Germany, for example, was still too great. As I saw it, it was associated, *inter alia*, with the nature and behaviour of the UK pension funds and their domination of the stock market. This was one reason why I sought to promote wider share ownership and to reduce the tax privileges of the pension funds. Again, although the enterprise culture was put firmly on the map in the 1980s, and the stigma attached to business success removed, the decade ended with that culture still not as deeply rooted as it needs to be.

But the successes were sufficient to make it clear, as indeed the electorate sensed in April 1992, that there was no case for a change of direction. The notion that was briefly in vogue at the turn of the decade, that the policies of the 1980s needed to be replaced by different policies for the 1990s, attached a political significance to the decimal system that was difficult to comprehend. What was called for was essentially more of the same. More privatization, more tax reform, and a firm grip on public spending. As I have indicated earlier, I hope, too, that the Major Government will grasp some of the nettles that were too radical for Margaret, such as the raising of the state pension age, and a much-needed improvement in the working of the labour market by the introduction of a nationwide 'workfare scheme'.

No doubt in an ideal world a Government would always persuade the people of a wisdom of a policy before implementing it. In practice, however, that is often not possible, and becomes simply a recipe for inaction. A sensible Government does what it believes to be right, explains why it is doing it, and stands to be judged by the results. It dare not succumb to the familiar fallacy, beloved by the mandarinate and *bien-pensant* commentators alike, of so-called consensus politics – certainly if that consensus is meant to be sought between the two major parties. In Britain, at any rate, the sole consensus possible is around the *status quo*. It is only by abjuring consensus politics that a new *status quo* can be secured around with a new consensus can develop. Britain in 1979 was a country where change was badly needed. In many ways, it still is. Looking back, I have no doubt that the substantial achievements of the Thatcher era will survive its sad and messy disintegration – and indeed, in the perspective of history, will become even more apparent.

It was a great adventure on which we embarked in 1979; an adventure to rescue Britain from economic and political decline of a kind that is now barely remembered, but which stank to high heaven at the time; the adventure of charting a radically new way forward and – despite universal doubt and cynicism – seeing it through. It could not have been done without Margaret Thatcher, who will go down in history as one of the greatest Prime Ministers this country has known. But equally, Margaret could not have done it without her core team, who translated her strong will, courage and conviction – wayward and self-contradictory though it could be – into a coherent and consistent course of action. This book is an account of the stewardship of one who was fortunate enough to be a member of that core team.

PART SIX

———

Annexes

THE NEW CONSERVATISM
(1980)

The advent of the Thatcher Government in 1979, with its radical 'new'
approach to economic policy, aroused considerable interest in many
countries overseas. One such country was Sweden, which was beginning
to entertain doubts about the Social Democratic consensus that had
enjoyed decades of uninterrupted sway. Geoffrey Howe was accordingly
invited to address the Socio-Economic Council of the Skandinaviska
Enskilda Bank in Stockholm in May 1980, but was unable to accept and
I arranged to go in his place. Just as I was about to leave, a general strike
in Sweden grounded all aircraft and the occasion had to be called off. Not
wanting to waste the work I had put into my talk, I arranged to give it to
a meeting organized by the Bow Group in London in August of that year.
In September the Stockholm invitation was reinstated, so I delivered it
a second time there. Fortunately, there was no overlap beween the two
audiences. The text of my talk was published later the same year by the
Centre for Policy Studies, as a pamphlet, which is now out of print. The
following is the full text, as originally delivered.

It is now a little more than a year since the first woman ever to lead
a British political party led the Conservatives to a remarkable election
victory, becoming in the process the first woman Prime Minister of any
western democracy.

   Until the general election of 3 May 1979 the Conservative party had been going through a lean patch during the 'sixties and 'seventies, losing four out of the previous five general elections, while the Government formed after the one election it did win had been brought to a premature end in circumstances which had led many to write off Conservative government for good: the trade union movement, it was argued, possessed an irrefragable power of veto.

Yet in the event the result recorded in 1979 was the most decisive secured by any party since the Labour landslide of 1945 – and in the process the Conservatives secured the support of more trade unionists than at any time in the party's history.

Even so, the election of 1979 might have been little more than a psephological curiosity had it not been for something far more important than the statistical outcome. For the fact is that the Conservative party had been swept into office on a programme which seemed to mark a conscious change of direction, not merely from that charted by its political opponents, but from that followed by all British Governments since the war, including its own Conservative predecessors. Hence the seemingly self-contradictory notion of 'The New Conservatism'.

But the truth of the matter is that the new Conservatism which the present British Government has been putting into practice for the past year and more is very much in the broad historic tradition of Conservatism.

That tradition has been well summed up by Lord Blake in the opening paragraph of the Epilogue to his book *The Conservative Party from Peel to Churchill.* 'Vast changes took place in Britain during the 125 years covered by this book' he wrote:

> Yet the person who was a Conservative of the thoughtful sort in Peel's day, his outlook, prejudices and passions, would have been quite recognizable to his counterpart who voted for Winston Churchill in the 1950s. There was a similar belief that Britain, especially England, was usually in the right. There was a similar faith in the value of diversity, of independent institutions, of the rights of property; a similar distrust of centralizing officialdom, of the efficacy of government (except in the preservation of order and national defence), of Utopian panaceas and of 'doctrinaire' intellectuals; a similar dislike of abstract ideas, high philosophical principles and sweeping generalizations. There was a similar readiness to accept cautious empirical piecemeal reform, if a Conservative government said it was needed. There was a similar reluctance to look far ahead or worry too much about the future; a similar scepticism about human nature; a similar belief in original sin, and in the limitations of political and social amelioration; a similar scepticism about the notion of 'equality'.

But during the 25 years that followed Churchill it was a very different outlook that gained the intellectual ascendancy: the philosophy of social democracy, with its profound faith in the efficacy of government action, particularly in the economic sphere, and its deep commitment to the notion of 'equality'. To a greater or lesser extent, the Conservative party embraced both these delusions, the latter with some misgivings but fundamentally with a sense of resignation in the face of seeming historical inevitability, the former with little short of enthusiasm – based (in the economic sphere at least) in equal parts on a misreading of the economic lessons of the inter-war years and a misunderstanding of Keynes.

The distinctive feature of the new Conservatism is its rejection of these false trails and its return to the mainstream. Old lessons have had to be painfully relearned. The old consensus is in the process of being re-established. To the extent that new Conservatives turn to new sages – such as Hayek and Friedman – that is partly because what those writers are doing is avowedly reinterpreting the traditional political and economic wisdom of Hume, Burke and Adam Smith in terms of the conditions of today; and partly because, as specialists in economics (although Hayek in particular is a great deal more than that) they are of particular interest in an age in which, for better or worse, economic policy has achieved a centrality in the political debate which it never enjoyed in, say, the golden age of Disraeli and Gladstone. I shall have more to say about this later. But the essential point is that what we are witnessing is the reversion to an older tradition in the light of the failure of what might be termed the new enlightenment. This is important, politically, not in the sense of some kind of appeal to ancestor-worship or to the legitimacy of scriptural authority: it is important because these traditions are, even today, more deeply rooted in the hearts and minds of ordinary people than is the conventional wisdom of the recent past.

I mentioned a moment ago that economic policy tends to be at the heart of politics in a modern democracy in time of peace, and there is no doubt that the new Conservatism sprang from a growing awareness of the palpable failure of the conventional wisdom to deal with the worsening problems of the British economy. To describe the new Conservatism purely in terms of an approach to economic policy would be manifestly inadequate – it goes a great deal wider than that, as I shall hope to show. But it is the obvious place to begin.

The economic policy of the new Conservatism has two basic strands. At the macroeconomic level, our approach is what has come to be known as monetarism, in contradistinction to what has come to be known as Keynesianism, although the latter doctrine is a perversion of what Keynes actually preached himself. At the microeconomic level, our emphasis is on the free market, in contradistinction to state intervention and central planning. While these two strands fit easily and harmoniously together, so much so that they are frequently confused, they are in fact distinct. It is quite possible to be a monetarist and a central planner. Equally, Keynes was not a central planner, and his great objective was to find a means of influencing the level of economic activity *without* resort to direct intervention in markets. Indeed, it might well be argued that one of the early signs of the failure of Keynesianism in Britain was the increasing resort of those who espoused it to planning and interventionism.

I take the monetarist dimension first – the macroeconomic policy of the new Conservatism.

In essence, monetarism is simply a new name for an old maxim, formerly known as the quantity theory of money. So far from being the controversial brainchild of an eccentric American professor, it was – in one form or another – the common belief and shared assumption of politicians and administrators of all political parties throughout the industrialized world for the century and more that preceded the Second World War.

It consists of two basic propositions. The first is that changes in the quantity of money determine, at the end of the day, changes in the general price level; the second is that government is able to determine the quantity of money. In practical terms, this was translated into the twin axioms of the pre-Keynesian consensus: that the primary economic duty of government was to maintain the value of the currency, and that this was to be achieved by not increasing its supply – a constraint which operated quasi-automatically for a country on the gold standard, as Britain was for most of the pre-Keynesian period.

Today, the intolerable social consequences of the present high levels of inflation, and the still greater dangers to the fabric of society that would stem from any further acceleration, have combined with the economic dislocation caused by inflation to reinstate the old conviction that the prime economic duty of government is to maintain the value of the currency.

There is, perhaps, rather less agreement on the means to this end. Our conviction that the means themselves must be monetary in no way denies the existence of a political dimension to inflation. After all, the proposition that Governments have permitted inflation to occur – indeed ensured that it will occur – by printing too much money, leaves open the question of *why* they have behaved in this way, and it may well be that political forces have played a prominent part in this. And insofar as they have, it is legitimate to strive politically to weaken those forces. But that in no way derogates from the crucial economic role of monetary policy.

I shall return in due course to a brief history of the evolution of economic policy in Britain since the war, since it is the experiences we have undergone which – far more than any abstract theory – explain and justify the course on which we have now embarked. Suffice it to say at this stage that we are committed to a steady reduction in the rate of growth in the money supply for the foreseeable future, and that we have published – for the first time ever – a quantified medium-term financial strategy setting out a gradualist path to a monetary growth target of around 6 per cent in 1983–4 and committing us to a fiscal policy compatible with this path: that is to say, a marked decline in total government borrowing as a proportion of gross domestic product, which we have suggested might fall from the estimated 1979–80 Public Sector Borrowing Requirement outturn of some 5 per cent of GDP (and the 5½ per cent we inherited from our predecessors in 1978–9) to some 1½ per cent in 1983–84. After initial difficulty in bringing monetary growth under control, which necessitated raising the Bank of England's minimum lending rate to a record 17 per cent last November, we are reasonably well on course on the monetary front. And, following the usual time lag, from now on we can expect the trend of inflation to be downward.

Meanwhile, at the microeconomic level, we have made considerable progress during our first year of office towards our parallel aim of rolling back the frontiers of the State and improving the functioning of the market economy.

We have abolished completely all forms of pay controls, price controls, dividend controls and exchange controls. The first three of these had been in operation, under governments of both parties, almost continuously throughout the past decade: the fourth, exchange controls, had been in force for over forty years.

Government spending, which had been planned to rise steadily over the coming years – as it has done under successive governments for the past quarter of a century, has been cut substantially and is now planned to fall, in real terms, in each of the next four years. Given the requirement to increase defence expenditure in an increasingly dangerous world, and the need (to take a very different example) to finance a growing pensioner population, whose state retirement pensions are price-protected, this has meant some very difficult decisions elsewhere in order to achieve a reduction in Government spending overall – although the successful negotiation of a substantial reduction in the UK's net contribution to the EEC Budget has undoubtedly helped. But those decisions have been taken.

As part of this, we have embarked on a steady reduction in the size of the ever-growing Civil Service. This is already some 25,000 smaller than when we took office, and a further substantial reduction is planned.

We have also embarked on a major programme of 'privatization' of the state-owned industries, of which British Aerospace and British Airways will be among the first candidates. While the extent of private ownership will vary from case to case, it should always be enough to shift the weight substantially from state control to the disciplines of the market. Meanwhile, various state holdings in private companies (including a reduction in the Government stake in British Petroleum from 51 per cent to 46 per cent) have already been sold. Throughout this exercise we are anxious to see the widest possible spread of private shareholding – so that the so-called public sector industries really do belong to the public – including in particular employee shareholding.

Despite the cuts in government spending, the overriding need to reduce government borrowing, to which I have already referred, has so far prevented us from reducing the overall burden of taxation – although that remains our long-term objective. But we have at least been able to introduce a major switch from taxes on earnings to taxes on spending, with the result that income tax has been cut all round, with the top marginal rate on earned income coming down from 83 per cent to 60 per cent. This is absolutely essential to restore personal incentives.

Even so, at the lower end of the scale, the incentive to work has been severely blunted by the fact that, whereas earnings are taxed, unemployment benefit is tax-free. As soon as administratively practicable, we shall be rectifying this anomaly: in the meantime, legislation has been enacted to ensure that this year, for the first time, unemployment benefit is increased by a lesser amount than the rise in prices. We have not shrunk from controversial measures: what is perhaps interesting is that this one, which was announced in this year's Budget, appears (like the planned restriction on the payment of Supplementary Benefit to strikers, from which previous administrations had also recoiled) to enjoy substantial popular support.

Other measures which have become law during the current session of Parliament include the Employment Act, which will improve the working of the labour market by providing redress against a limited number of the worst abuses of trade union power, and the Housing Act, which will improve the working of the housing market and further the traditional Conservative aim of the property-owning democracy by giving local authority tenants the right to buy – on attractive terms – the homes in which they live. Meanwhile, a whole host of Government controls in the field of business and industry have been swept aside, unnecessary government-sponsored bodies abolished, and a package of measures introduced (in this year's Budget) to provide a more encouraging fiscal climate for that most market-orientated sector of the economy, small businesses. But perhaps the most imaginative measure in the 1980 Budget was the proposal to set up, in the heart of half-a-dozen of our most derelict industrial areas, so-called 'Enterprise Zones', where the burden of corporate taxation, regulation, and form-filling will be reduced still further.

I have given you this somewhat breathless account of what we have actually done over the past year or so, not in order to boast of success: it is far too soon for that. The proof of the pudding is in the eating. But I did think it worth taking a little time to establish two basic propositions. First, that there is a great deal more to the new Conservatism than control of the money supply; and second, that there is a practical reality (and I have sought to give the flavour of that reality) behind the rhetoric of the new Conservatism.

To describe what we are engaged in as a peaceful counter-revolution would be somewhat fanciful. Whatever else they may be, Conservatives are not revolutionaries. But there is no doubt that our chosen course does represent a distinct and self-conscious break from the predominantly social democratic assumptions that have hitherto underlain policy in post-war Britain. Yet, looked at dispassionately, the steady trend towards ever more governmental interference with the free and vigorous working of the market that has characterized every western economy in recent decades seems distinctly perverse.

After all, it was the market economy that created the prosperity of the West in the first place – and even today, over-regulated and constrained as it is, it continues to outperform the state-controlled command economies of the communist bloc. Moreover, if there is one value that we in the West claim to elevate above all others it is freedom; yet those who claim to be its most dedicated standard-bearers in every other sphere have no time for it in the economic sphere: as Nozick has wryly observed, 'In the United States today, the law insists that an 18-year-old girl has the right to fornicate publicly in a pornographic movie – but only if she is paid the minimum wage'.

But in fact this perversity is readily explained. There is a widespread delusion that the economic case for the market economy is based on a theory of perfect competition that has no relevance whatever to the real world, and that merely to identify the manifest imperfections that characterize markets in the real world is to justify state intervention.

This is mistaken on at least two counts. In the first place, as Hayek has cogently pointed out in his essay on 'The Use of Knowledge in Society', individual agents acting on imperfect information can operate a market economy quite successfully. An effective price system does not require the chimera of 'perfect competition': prices are still the most efficient signals we have for transmitting the minimum necessary information about consumer wants and investment opportunities. If not enough shoes are being produced, citizens do not have to sign petitions or lobby Parliament, nor do bureaucrats have to go out into the streets to conduct surveys of need. Instead, a businessman will discover he can sell his stock for a higher price and will order more from his suppliers. The point is as important as it is elementary.

In the second place, while markets are undoubtedly imperfect, so is the State. Market imperfection can be held to justify state intervention only if the State – which means the Civil Servants and Government Ministers – have somehow been spared the frailties and imperfections that mar the rest of the human race. Not only is it unclear why this should be so, but there are very real reasons why the imperfections of State intervention in the economic field are likely to be not merely equal to, but greater than, the imperfections of the market. One is that, however genuine the desire of Government to arrive at an objective judgement, its decisions will not only be subject to all the inherent uncertainties of economic life, they will also, inevitably, be politically skewed. It is no use complaining about this: we live in a democracy, and the decisions that politicians take will inevitably be coloured by the sorts of phrases that sound well in speeches and the harvests of votes they might be expected to gather.

Nor is it only the politicians whose motives may be less than perfect. We are all imperfect – even the most high-minded civil servant. Academic work is still in its infancy on the economics of bureaucracy; but it is already clear that it promises to be a fruitful field. For civil servants and middle class welfare administrators are far from the selfless Platonic guardians of paternalist mythology: they are a major and powerful interest group in their own right. But there is this important distinction. While in the private sector persistence in failure is likely to lead eventually to bankruptcy or at least severe financial loss, the incentive for self-correction on the part of the State is very much weaker: indeed, nothing is harder than the admission of failure in the political arena.

Thus it is that we are driven to the very practical – and I would say very Conservative – conclusion that, so far from ever more State intervention being justified by virtue of the admitted imperfections of the market, a greater reliance on markets is justified by virtue of the practical imperfections of State intervention.

Burke used a particularly good metaphor which illuminates this point, when he compared State action to light rays approaching the prism of society – they would be bent and refracted on meeting the glass of social relations. It is a particularly Conservative point – for if socialism is the creed of utopianism and the perfectibility of man, Conservatism is the creed of original sin and the politics of imperfection – that the bad in society is so intimately and unknowably linked with the rest that an intention to deal with one specific and agreed evil may well do more harm than good.

One of the most crucial of all markets, of course, is the labour market; and here one of the more important contributions of the new Conservatism has been to show the damage that wages policies do.

While monetarism might demonstrate why it is that you cannot use a wages policy to control inflation on its own, it still leaves it open to more sophisticated advocates to claim that a wages policy is nevertheless a desirable, if not essential, adjunct of monetary policy since it alone can ease and make politically acceptable the transitional costs of monetary restraint by forcing workers to respond more rapidly to the changed monetary conditions, thus reducing (if not actually preventing) any rise in unemployment.

Practical experience of wages policies has given the lie to this thesis; but the explanation of why this is so lies in the economics of markets. Despite the manifest imperfections of the labour market in a unionized economy, it remains true that the price of labour is one which balances supply and demand, and that the price which the employer of labour can afford to pay reflects the productivity of labour. If wages are controlled then imbalances arise with shortages of labour in some areas and excess supply – that is, unemployment – in others, and there is no way in which labour can be attracted to profitable firms.

The loss is far more than merely economic. The ultimate connection between the productivity of a man's labour and his wage is lost, and he regards his pay as being determined by government rather than by his own output and efforts. The harmful economic, social and political consequences of the growing politicization of the labour market can scarcely be exaggerated.

So far, since the collapse of the previous Government's wages policy and its formal abandonment by the present Government, wage settlements have been running at a higher level than is sensibly compatible with the Government's monetary framework, with unhappy consequences for the level of unemployment. But it is at least thoroughly healthy that there has been a much wider range of settlements: the market is once more beginning to fulfil its function, as workers are encouraged to move to jobs where their contribution to the general welfare is greatest.

If, as I firmly believe, the traditional Conservative scepticism of State power and State intervention – except, as Lord Blake rightly identified, in the context of the preservation of order and national defence – is firmly echoed in the instinctive beliefs of the British people in general, and of the working classes in particular, it is worth asking why it is that it has taken so long for that prejudice to be reflected in the election of a like-minded government. No doubt there are many reasons. But one which has, I believe, particular force, is the experience of the Second World War. This, for a whole generation, was Britain's finest hour: it was also a time when the State was seen to arrogate to itself, in a cause whose rightness was not open to question, all the apparatus of central planning and direction of labour. In fact what is sensible in war, when there is a unique unity of national purpose and when a simple test can be applied to all economic activities (namely whether or not they further the success of the war effort), is wholly inappropriate in time of peace, when what is needed is a system that brings harmoniously together a diversity of individual purposes of which the State need not even be aware. Nevertheless, the apparent beneficence, rationality and justice of central planning cast a spell that long outlived the wartime world to which it belonged.

The Federal Republic of Germany provides the perfect counterpoint to this. There, too, State power was associated with war. But there it was associated not with the benevolent despotism of a Churchill, but with the evil tyranny of a Hitler. As a consequence, the economic lesson the German people learned from the war was of the evil of State power rather than the benevolence of State power; the German trade union movement was imbued with a hostility to State intervention (which had been used to suppress free trade unionism altogether) in contrast to the British trade union movement's delusion that its objectives can most effectively be secured through the agency of State intervention; and even the social democrats were driven to embrace the principles and practice of the market economy.

That is, of course, by no means the only explanation of the different post-war economic performances of Britain and Germany, but I am convinced that it has played an important part.

And now, as the false lessons taught by the war have begun to be unlearned, the new Conservatism has another historical obstacle to overcome: the immense vested interests created by the growth of State power and State patronage, by State employment and State subsidies. But if these great vested interests (on which, nowadays, social democracy, barren of ideas, wholly depends) are an effective practical barrier to radical or revolutionary change, there is no reason to suppose that they need prevent gradual and evolutionary change. And this, after all, is the Conservative way. But it emphasizes just how long the task will take. Nor is it only the existence of vested interests in the material sense which counsel patience: those liberated from the dungeons of State control are often at first blinded and bewildered by the bright sunlight of freedom.

On the macroeconomic front, too, there is a sense in which the monetarist policies espoused by the new Conservatism represent a belated unlearning of what were mistakenly believed to be the lessons of the war.

In the first place, the war bred a desire to make a clean break from the orthodox monetary policies which were wrongly believed to have been responsible for the depression of the 'twenties and 'thirties. In fact, of course, dispassionate analysis of this period if anything underlines the explanatory power of monetary theory. In the United States, as Friedman's researches have shown, the authorities permitted a quite inordinate reduction of one third in the supply of money between 1929 and 1933, while in the United Kingdom Churchill's misconceived decision in 1925 to return to the gold standard led to severe monetary contraction. In both countries, a marked departure (in a contractionary direction) from the orthodox canons of monetary policy, which inevitably had a severely disruptive effect on the real economy, were wrongly interpreted as proof that the orthodoxy itself was mistaken.

In the second place, the historical accident that Keynesian policies in practice emerged from the war years, when a whole variety of wartime devices such as wage and price controls were in force, and the functions of markets and of money temporarily suspended, led to an association between Keynesianism and interventionism that is wholly alien to the thinking Keynes himself – as indeed is the so-called Keynesians' dismissal of money. But it was this false interpretation of the events of the 'twenties and 'thirties, coupled with this equally perverse interpretation of Keynesian economics, which ostensibly held that money didn't matter, that was to hold the field for the next quarter of a century and which eventually collapsed under the weight of its own inflationary excesses in the 'seventies.

In reality, the Keynesians attributed much greater power to money than monetarists do. Although they did not express it in these terms, the essence of their belief was that an increase in the supply of money via a budget deficit would have a sustained and indeed predictable expansionary impact on real things such as output and employment. By contrast, monetarists hold that, at the end of the day, what a Government does to the supply of money will produce purely money effects – although there may well be brief interludes during which monetary policies produce real effects. As David Hume pointed out as long ago as 1752 in his essay, 'Of Money':

> Though the high price of commodities be a necessary consequence of the increase of gold and silver, yet it follows not immediately upon that increase; but some time is required before the money circulates through the whole state, and makes its effects be felt on all ranks of people. At first, no alteration is perceived; by degrees the price rises, first of one commodity, then of another, then of another; till the whole at last reaches a just proportion with the new quantity of specie which is in the kingdom. In my opinion, it is only in this interval or intermediate situation, between the acquisition of money and rise of prices, that the increasing quantity of gold and silver is favourable to industry.

Monetarists also believe that excesses in monetary policy – whether in the direction of an expansion or a contraction in the supply of money – will cause a greater or lesser degree of economic collapse and large-scale unemployment. A modern economy simply cannot function without reasonable stability of money.

Initially, the excesses of the Keynesian delusion – and I do not attribute this delusion to Keynes himself – were held in check by two factors: the existence of a fixed exchange rate system and the fact that the numeraire of that system, the dollar, was managed by a country which itself pursued broadly non-inflationary policies. During this period foreign exchange crises served as a proxy for monetary disciplines and, coupled with the persistence of what has come to be known as money illusion – the belief by economic agents, and in particular wage bargainers, that the currency will hold its value – this enabled a form of monetarist policy to be pursued in a Keynesian guise, with an initially significant but gradually declining degree of success, as the fact of inflation steadily eroded money illusion.

But it was not until the late 1960s and early 1970s that what has come to be known as Keynesianism entered its terminal phase. The inflationary financing of the Vietnam war undermined the whole basis of the dollar standard – while the necessary transition from a fixed to a floating rate regime removed the only existing proxy for overt monetary restraint.

In Britain, certainly, there seemed to be no awareness that the new conditions made explicit control of the money supply essential. Instead, money supply was allowed to expand without restraint, and the symptoms were treated by a fruitless intensification of controls – wage controls, price controls, dividend controls, tighter exchange controls – and intervention to 'support' industry, to the point where industrialists found it more rewarding to tramp the corridors of Whitehall in search of subsidies and grants than to remain in their factories actually trying to generate profits. In the event, industrial performance merely deteriorated further, inflation rocketed, the external value of the pound collapsed, and after a short spell of hothouse growth output and employment fell back sharply. By 1976 the British economy was in intense crisis and the IMF had to be called in, humiliatingly, to bale us out and impose its *de facto* monetarist terms.

It was this experience that, more than any other, at last shifted the economic consensus which the new Conservatism had earlier influenced and has now inherited. Like all great political changes, this one preceded the election of the Government that was destined to inherit it. Thus it was Mr James Callaghan, addressing the Labour Party Conference, who, in September 1976, said this:

> We used to think that you could just spend your way out of a recession and increase employment by cutting taxes and boosting Government expenditure. I tell you, in all candour, that that option no longer exists and, insofar as it ever did exist, it only worked by injecting a bigger dose of inflation into the economy followed by a higher level of unemployment. That is the history of the last 20 years.

And two months later his Chancellor of the Exchequer, Mr Denis Healey, wrote this in his Letter of Intent to the Director-General of the International Monetary Fund:

> an essential element of the Government's strategy will be a continuing and substantial reduction in the share of resources required for the public sector. It is also essential to reduce the PSBR in order to create monetary conditions which will encourage investment and secure sustained growth and the control of inflation.

Regrettably, the commitment of the Labour Government to the new consensus was, perhaps inevitably, somewhat half-hearted. The jibe once made at Roosevelt – that he was for sound money and plenty of it – seemed increasingly apt, and the old Adam reasserted itself. But in all the confusion it had now been demonstrated that there was no coherent Keynesian alternative to monetarism. And the only alternative economic theory now in the ring is such a bastard form of Keynesianism, with its addition of import controls to all the other controls tested to destruction in the 'seventies, that it is really closer to central planning and the command economy, and is scarcely recognizable as a variant of Keynesianism at all.

But if the social democrat alternative is in confusion and disarray, it is only fair to acknowledge that among some Conservatives, too, there are doubts about the new Conservatism.

Is it really Conservatism at all, or is it some alien creed masquerading as Conservatism? I can only say that, as a Conservative, it feels pretty Conservative to me.

There is, of course, no clearly defined political litmus test which proves whether a policy is true blue, but perhaps as good a description of Conservatism as any – at least in its British context – is Anthony Quinton's phrase 'the politics of imperfection'. That is to say, Conservatism is founded on the basic acceptance of the ineradicable imperfection of human nature. This general proposition has a number of very clear practical consequences.

First, it means that a great deal of weight is attached to tradition, for the very good reason that none of us alive today can possibly know better than what has emerged through trial and error over the generations. Second, there is, running through Conservatism, and deriving directly from the imperfection, both moral and intellectual, of man, a profound scepticism: scepticism about the likely results of State intervention in every aspect of our lives; scepticism about radical new plans of any kind.

And third – and of course all three are intimately connected – there is what might be termed a generally conservative disposition: a preference for gradualism in politics; a conviction that whatever needs to be done should be done in a conservative way.

The economic approach of the new Conservatism, with its scepticism of Keynesian fine-tuning and State intervention in the economy seems plainly to fall within this tradition, as it does within Robert

Blake's characterization of the practical Conservative approach which I quoted at the start of this talk.

It reinforces the Conservative reluctance to bring all social and economic relationships within the political realm. It stresses the vital importance of stability in society, which requires as its economic underpinning a stable currency. It implies a government that is strong, rather than weak, by the very virtue of its own restraint; since it seeks to preserve its authority by sticking to those tasks which are properly the responsibility of government and which it can hope to execute effectively, rather than try and do too much and end up achieving nothing. It accepts a duty for the State to relieve poverty, but rejects the idea that it is the function of the State to create (let alone to destroy) wealth.

Above all, the hallmark of the new Conservatism is a new (in post-war terms) and healthy humility about the scope for Government action to improve the economy. The distinctive feature of our medium-term financial strategy, which differentiates it from the so-called national plans of other times and other places, is that it is confined to charting a course for those variables – notably the quantity of money – which are and must be within the power of government to control. By contrast, governments cannot create economic growth. All the instruments which were supposed to do this have succeeded only in damaging the economy and have ultimately broken in the hands of the governments that sought to use them. All we can do is something more modest: to try and prevent the occurrence of conditions inimical to growth – and the most inimical of all, as well as being an evil in itself, is inflation. When governments have tried to do more than this they have ended up achieving far less than this.

Those Conservatives who none the less feel ill at ease with the new Conservatism are inclined to suggest that it smacks far too much of classical liberalism. The charge is a strange one. Nineteenth-century politics was about wholly different issues. There was, behind the rhetoric, a fundamental consensus on economic policy. Disraeli may have used the Corn Laws and protection to secure the leadership of the Conservative party, but in practice he was operating in precisely the same world of non-intervention in industry, adherence to the gold standard (and thus to stable money) and free trade as was Gladstone. They had their differences outside the field of economic policy, but what matters to us today is what they had in common – which is scarcely surprising given that Gladstone himself was a Conservative Cabinet Minister before becoming the embodiment of Liberalism. Of all forms of heresy-hunting, this variety seems particularly futile.

But perhaps the 'alien creed' school of Conservative critics of the new Conservatism are concerned less with its affinity to classical liberalism and rather more with a feeling that it is somehow too theoretical (and therefore allegedly extremist, although this identity is never satisfactorily demonstrated) and not pragmatic enough.

I have to concede that there is something in this. There *is* a difference – but it is a necessary one. In the nineteenth century Conservatives could afford to disavow theory and affect a disdain for abstract ideas and general principles, for the simple reason that the theories, ideas and principles on which Conservatism rests were the unchallenged common currency of British politics. The rise of social democracy has changed all that. Conservatives have a need, as they did not have in the nineteenth century, to fight the battle of ideas.

When Conservative critics of the new Conservatism propound the paradox that the traditional thinking of Conservative theory is that there is no theory and that the only political rule is that there are no political rules, I assume that the underlying message is that problems should be judged on their merits. But this doesn't help us to decide what their merits are – instead, it leaves it to other political creeds to determine them. To this it might be replied that the Conservative can exercise his own judgement and be a force for moderation; but this won't do. In the first place, while denying ideology, it is in fact itself profoundly ideological, since it implicitly accepts the concept (wholly alien to the Conservative tradition and to the true nature of politics alike) of a simple linear left–right spectrum, along which a suitably moderate position can be judiciously selected. (Not that the adoption of a particular point on an ideological scale is any less an ideological act by virtue of being nearer the middle than the end of the scale.)

But, second and more important, the only characteristic of a point in the middle of an ideological spectrum is that it is determined, not by the person or party ostensibly choosing that point, but by the position of the two extremes. As Keith Joseph has pointed out, if Conservatives are always to split the difference between their former position and that of the Socialists, not only will they be dragged along by the Socialists, but they will actually provide them with an incentive to be more extreme. Thus the pursuit of moderation necessarily becomes self-defeating.

Moreover, it is far from clear where the voter comes in all this. Those who are unhappy with the new Conservatism automatically assume that, by having an identifiable view, it will frighten off the electorate. The result of the election which swept the present Conservative Government into office should surely have put paid to that particular charge, at any rate. Nor is it surprising that people might actually want to vote for a Party that appears to share their views. The notion that Conservatism is nothing more than a technique of governing is altogether too pallid and bloodless an account of the role of a major political Party.

What, then, really is new about the new Conservatism? In economic terms, as I have tried to show, very little. But equally important, it has a robust common sense quality that is wholly in harmony with the everyday experience of the ordinary family.

Monetarism, after all, is really rather obvious: if you produce too much of something, its value falls. If you borrow too much, you're likely to get into trouble. It is Keynesianism, which seems to stand everything on its head, which is the difficult and esoteric doctrine.

Nor is distrust of Government and what it can do new either: the novelty is, if anything, the surprising degree of trust and confidence in big Government which so many British citizens displayed for so long after the war.

All that is new is that the new Conservatism has embarked on the task – it is not an easy one: nothing worthwhile in politics is; but at least it runs with, rather than against, the grain of human nature – of re-educating people in some old truths. They are no less true for being old.

THE EUROPEAN MONETARY SYSTEM (1985)

The following is the full text of my minute to the Prime Minister of 11 November 1985.

ON ANY OBJECTIVE TEST the British economy is doing well. For over four years now it has grown at a steady 3 per cent a year, and we have the prospect of this continuing in the period ahead. We are achieving the steady growth which Governments have sought in vain for many years.

But we cannot take this for granted. The only way we can keep growth going (and with it any prospect of a fall in unemployment), in the world in which we live, is to keep inflation coming down – *and* convince people that it will continue to come down and stay down. The main threat to steady growth is the fear that inflation will re-emerge and that measures which the Government would then take to combat it would thrust the economy into recession and a further rise in unemployment.

Given our record since 1979 it is fair to ask why these fears about inflation persist. The answer is history. Low inflation is a relatively recent phenomenon. In the eyes of the world's financial markets, and this includes our own, British Governments remain suspect. There is still a nagging fear that sooner or later we will succumb to the temptation of going for an easy inflationary option. The only means of countering this fear has been explicitly to constrain our own freedom of action by setting targets for monetary growth, and supporting this by a tight fiscal policy. This was the thinking that lay behind the publication of the MTFS. The conduct of economic policy must always be guided by a mixture of rules and discretion. Since the collapse of Bretton Woods in 1971, policy in the UK seemed to rely wholly on discretion and not all on rules – and we were simply not trusted to use our discretion in a consistently non-inflationary way. So we had to make a fresh commitment to a new set of anti-inflationary rules, the MTFS.

This commitment has served us well, but it is running out of steam. First, as a matter of substance, the measures of money, including in particular sterling M3, are going through a prolonged period of instability. They are doing so for the best of reasons. The liberalization of the economy, which is an essential element in our overall strategy, includes financial liberalization, which is progressing apace. But the fact remains that the money numbers cannot be taken at their face value when the institutional structure is in a state of flux. The rules based on them have inevitably lost much of their original clarity, and to carry conviction in the markets we have needed to buttress them by adopting a visibly cautious approach to setting interest rates, certainly since last January.

Second, it is most unusual for a British Government to maintain the same policy for as long as we have done. This carries with it great advantages, but it does give us a growing problem of presentation. After a period of some years there is a need for a shot in the arm – a touch of imagination and freshness – to help the explanation, and to ensure that our policies continue to carry conviction.

After grappling with these problems as Chancellor for over two years now, I have come firmly to the conclusion that joining the Exchange Rate Mechanism of the EMS would deal with both the issue of substance and the issue of presentation, and is the only practicable means of doing so. The exchange rate is more readily comprehensible than monetary targets, and we are already relying on it to a major extent as an indicator. To join the EMS would reinforce the discipline and commitment inherent to the MTFS, and be seen to do so. The interested public seem ready for it. Industry certainly is.

We should respond to a general yearning for a greater degree of exchange rate stability, and we could give policy the new impetus we need to carry us up to the election and beyond.

The public stance of the Government has consistently been that sterling would join the Exchange Rate Mechanism when the time was right. Answering Dr Owen on 31 January this year in the House of Commons, the Prime Minister said:

> We have always said that we shall join the Exchange Rate Mechanism when we believe that the time is appropriate. It is kept under review from time to time, but I must make one thing clear. Joining the EMS would not obviate increases in interest rates. It would not obviate the need for financial discipline, and indeed it might increase it.

I am convinced that the time is now right. The economy is strong. Inflation is coming down, and the exchange rate is not under threat. Over the past three years now, (see Chart 1), the sterling/Deutschmark exchange rate has bobbed about within a range of broadly 3.60 to 4.00 Deutschmarks to the pound. We are now in the lower half of that range, at a little over Deutschmarks 3.70 and we should take the opportunity to join at around this rate. On the other hand, if we defer the decision much longer, we will simply run out of time. We clearly could not join too close to the Election, and I have in any case to recast the presentation of policy fundamentally between now and the Budget following the patching up job I did at the Mansion House. I believe that we should seize the initiative and join now.

Of course there are risks. But the balance of argument is now very different from what it was two or three years ago. We are not now in a state of general crisis with Europe over our Budgetary contribution. We do not have an inflation rate which is out of line with the EMS countries in general. The petro-currency problem – the tendency of sterling alone among European currencies to move in line with the price of oil – is a shadow of its former self (see Chart 2). And the main currency concern – the dollar (and to some extent the yen) – is one which we share with the other EMS currencies.

The main risk that remains is one which will be with us indefinitely – that sterling will be subject to excessive fluctuations because of the openness of our markets and the fact that ours is such a widely held currency. The plain fact is that if a bout of exchange rate pressure were to arise on this account, we should be bound in practice to adjust our interest rates accordingly whether or not we were in the EMS, as the experience of this January clearly showed.

We must recognize this reality. If interest rates are going to change anyway in response to the exchange rate, we should be foolhardy to forgo the advantages of an explicit exchange rate policy which, through its effect on expectations, would have a beneficial long-term influence on interest rates. And the only possible explicit policy we could have is to join the ERM.

The state of affairs I have just described is indeed likely to become progressively more pronounced. Now that we are disabled from steering by sterling M3, although of course we continue to watch it closely, and are obliged to place greater weight on the exchange rate, markets will increasingly come to wonder why it is that we are *not* joining the EMS. And the only conclusion they can reach, aided and abetted by periodic moans from industry, is that we may wish to see the exchange rate lower, if not now then before too long. Thus the gap between the level of interest rates needed to maintain the sterling parity within the EMS, and the higher level of interest rates needed to maintain roughly the same parity outside the EMS, already evident today, will steadily widen.

The reference to industry deserves some elaboration. We all know that the most intractable economic problem apart from unemployment itself, and with which indeed it is closely linked, is the persistent tendency of British industry to allow its labour costs per unit of output to rise faster than its competitors do. This can be resolved only in one of two ways: a falling exchange rate to accommodate steadily rising costs, or industry controlling its costs better. Industry is far more likely to buckle down to the latter, which is the infinitely preferable course, if it knows that the former has been rendered unlikely by virtue of our joining the exchange rate mechanism of the EMS – a step, incidentally, which, for reasons of exchange rate stability, they themselves have called for.

There is however one further risk which cannot be left out. Whether or not we are in the EMS, it must be quite likely that the outcome of the next General Election will not be a foregone conclusion in advance, and thus there will, before polling day, be a precautionary flight from sterling which could well be of considerable dimensions. In or out of the EMS we will wish to turn this to our political advantage by pointing out that if the mere prospect of a Labour Government causes such alarm, it is not difficult to imagine how much worse the reality would be. But in or out of the EMS, this would still leave us with a nasty financial crisis to handle.

In my judgement it would be marginally easier to handle if we were inside rather than outside the EMS. This is because inside the EMS the flight would be likely to arise at a much later stage, and thus last much less long, and could be pinned much more convincingly on the political threat rather than being seen as a lack of confidence in our own economic management. Indeed if we were in the EMS at the time, we would almost certainly wish to take temporary leave of absence to deal with what would clearly be a temporary political phenomenon.

But well before then we would, if we were to join the EMS now, have established our fundamental credibility as a member of the system. Indeed for the reasons set out in the earlier parts of the paper, I am forced to the conclusion that not to join now would be a historic missed opportunity in the conduct of economic policy, which we would before very long come bitterly to regret.

One last point. My judgement is that the advantages of joining now outweigh the risks. This is shared not only by the Governor of the Bank of England, but also by senior officials in both the Treasury and the Bank. They all believe that it makes operational sense to join, and that we can now deliver our policy objectives more effectively in the EMS than if we remain outside it.

AN INDEPENDENT CENTRAL BANK (1988)

*The following is the full text of my minute to the
Prime Minister of 25 November 1988.*

ONE OF THE MOST important achievements of this Government has been to place the defeat of inflation at the very heart of our economic policy. Although we are still only part of the way there, we have unequivocally reversed the rake's progress of the 'seventies and brought about a major cultural change.

I have been giving a great deal of thought to how we can best entrench that hard-won change, and make it a permanent feature of UK economic policy, while at the same time assisting us in the completion of our present task. I have reached the view that the best way to do this would be to give statutory independence to the Bank of England, charging it with the statutory duty to preserve the value of the currency, along the lines already in place and of proven effectiveness for the US Federal Reserve, the National Bank of Switzerland, and the Bundesbank.

Such a move would enhance the market credibility of our anti-inflationary stance, both nationally and internationally. It would make it absolutely clear that the fight against inflation remains our top priority; it would do something to help de-politicize interest rate changes – though that can never be completely achieved; above all there would be the longer-term advantage that we would be seen to be locking a permanent anti-inflationary force into the system, as a counter-weight to the strong inflationary pressures which are always lurking.

It would also, incidentally, make clear that we see a very different role for the Bank of England than absorption into some European central banking federation.

Clearly, since we have no written constitution, it would in theory be open for any future Government to repeal the legislation. But in practice there would be a powerful market sanction against that: the mere announcement of the intention to do so would in itself be so damaging to market confidence that any Government would be extremely reluctant to attempt it. And of course the longer the independent central bank had been in place, the more effective that sanction would be.

I have had some work done on this proposal by a very small, high-level group in the Treasury (I have *not* mentioned any of this to the Bank of England at this stage). It is clear that the move would be perfectly feasible. The heart of the scheme would consist of the following division of responsibilities:

(a) The Bank would assume sole responsibility for the operation of monetary policy, with a statutory duty to protect and maintain the value of the currency. It would thus be responsible for setting short term interest rates and monetary targets.

(b) The Government would remain responsible for determining the exchange rate framework – for example, whether we were part of any international agreement, of whatever kind, formal or informal. The Bank would then be responsible for the conduct of exchange rate policy within that framework.

I have set out in an annexe a number of other points which would probably be necessary to define the new arrangement and ensure it worked successfully.

While there was of course a time, in the era of the gold standard, when the Bank of England possessed more independence than it enjoys today, there is no doubt that what I am proposing would constitute a radical change. But I believe it has substantial merit: it would provide a beneficial jolt to inflationary expectations and would help to lock into the body politic of this country a permanent anti-inflationary force. If you are content, the next step would be to bring the Bank of England into this discussion. My plan would be to publish a White Paper on Budget Day, with the necessary legislation introduced in November 1989.

I should be happy to discuss this when we next meet.

Annexe: Further characteristics of an independent Bank of England

(i)   The Bank would be obliged, as is the Bundesbank, to conduct monetary policy within the framework of the Government's economic policy as a whole, but only so far as that is consistent with its primary function of safeguarding the currency. There would also, and within this context, be a joint obligation on the Government and the Bank to work closely together in the conduct of economic policy.

(ii)   The Treasury would be responsible for funding the Government's borrowing requirement (or for buying in debt when the Government was in surplus). But it would not be permitted to do this in a way which added to money or liquidity – i.e. it would have to sell longer-term instruments. This is the arrangement followed in Germany.

(iii)   A portion of the reserves would be available to the Bank for use in intervention, but the Government would be able to set limits on total intervention (in either direction) and the Bank would have to obtain the Government's agreement before those limits were exceeded.

(iv)   The Bank would, at least for the time being, retain responsibility for supervising the banking system and the wholesale and gilt-edged markets. It would, of course, continue to discharge traditional central bank functions such as issuing notes and acting as the bankers' bank.

(v)   We should probably need to make the Bank of England answerable to Parliament in the sense that the Governor would appear regularly before a suitable Select Committee. But we would want this to be set up in a way which did not subject the Bank to unwarranted Parliamentary pressure.

(vi)   The Court would be made up, as now, of a Governor, Deputy Governor, Executive Directors and non-Executive Directors. They would be appointed by the Government, though there might well be a case for making the appointments of all but the Governor himself subject to the approval of the Select Committee. Members of the Court would be appointed for a long period, to ensure their independence – probably for a term of 8 years. The appointments could be arranged so that one new non-Executive member came up for appointment each year.

(vii)   We should also take the opportunity of a new Bank of England Act to put the Bank's finances on a proper statutory footing.

———

RESIGNATION SPEECH
(1989)

The following is the full text of my speech in the House of Commons on 31 October 1989, following my resignation as Chancellor of the Exchequer five days earlier.

I AM OLD FASHIONED enough to believe that my first comment on recent events should be made to this House. This is not an easy speech for me to make, and I am sure that the House will understand that. I shall do my best to be brief, and I hope that the House will assist me in this.

I am most grateful for what my right honourable Friend the new Chancellor of the Exchequer has said about me, and I wish to take this further opportunity to wish him every success in the task that lies ahead of him. As he reminded the House, we worked closely together for just over two years, and he has my full and unstinting support.

As for my own record, I have no doubt that I have made my share of mistakes; but I am content to be judged when the passage of time has provided a greater sense of perspective than is possible today.

No-one, however long he has held the post, lightly gives up the great office of Chancellor of the Exchequer. Certainly, I did not. As the resignation letter that I wrote to my right honourable Friend the Prime Minister clearly implies, it was not the outcome I sought. But it is one that I accept without rancour – despite what might be described as the hard landing involved. I would only add that the article written by my right honourable Friend's former economic adviser was of significance only inasmuch as it represented the tip of a singularly ill-concealed iceberg, with all the destrucive potential that icebergs possess.

I have long been convinced that the only successful basis for the conduct of economic policy is to seek the greatest practicable degree of market freedom within an over-arching framework of financial discipline to bear down on inflation. That being so, a key question is where the exchange rate fits in. Is it to be part of the maximum practicable market freedom, or is it to be part – indeed, a central part – of the necessary financial discipline?

I recognize that a case can be made for either approach. No case can be made for seeming confusion or for apparent vacillation between these two positions. Moreover, for our system of Cabinet government to work effectively, the Prime Minister of the day must appoint Ministers whom he or she trusts and then leave them to carry out the policy. When differences of view emerge, as they are bound to do from time to time, they should be resolved privately and, whenever appropriate, collectively.

But to return to the exchange rate. Faced with the question that I posed a moment ago, my answer is, unhesitatingly, that it should be seen as an essential element of financial discipline, with the rider, incidentally, that exchange rate stability is itself an economic benefit.

There is nothing novel, of course, in any of this. The House will recall the classical period of the gold standard, before the First World War; the Bretton Woods system after the Second World War; and, of course, over the past ten years, within the European context, the EMS.

None of these systems were or are panaceas or soft options. Tough decisions still have to be made. None of them were or are without difficulties. But those difficulties, in my judgement, are very much less than the practical difficulties and disadvantages which the world has experienced during periods of freely floating exchange rates. Nor, incidentally, can there be any doubt that the less credible the exchange rate discipline is, the greater the weight that interest rates will have to bear, and the higher they need to be to maintain the necessary anti-inflationary pressure.

Full United Kingdom membership of the EMS – I was glad to hear much of what my right honourable Friend the Chancellor said – to which, again, as my right honourable Friend the Prime Minister made clear at Madrid, this Government are committed, would signally enhance the credibility of our anti-inflationary resolve in general and the role of the exchange rate discipline in particular, and thus underpin the medium-term financial strategy. Indeed, given the existence of the EMS, our continuing non-participation in the exchange rate mechanism cannot fail to cast practical doubt on that resolve, however ill-founded such doubt may be.

There is, I believe, one other way in which anti-inflationary credibility might be enhanced in the eyes of the market. That is why, a year ago, I proposed to my right honourable Friend the Prime Minister a fully worked-out scheme for the independence of the Bank of England. But that would be a buttress; it would not be a substitute for what I was saying earlier.

But if full United Kingdom membership of the EMS, although not indispensable, would facilitate the conduct of economic policy in general and the battle against inflation in particular, as those already participating have demonstrated, there is also a vital political dimension.

As my right honourable Friend the Prime Minister made clear in her Bruges speech, Britain's destiny lies in Europe as a member of the European Community – and let me be clear that I am speaking, as she speaks, of a Europe of nation states. Within that context, it is vital that we maximize Britain's influence in the Community so as to ensure that it becomes the liberal free-market Europe in which we on the Conservative Benches so firmly believe. I have little doubt that we will not be able to exert that influence effectively, and successfully provide the leadership, as long as we remain largely outside the EMS. So, for economic and political reasons alike, it is important that we seek the earliest practicable time to join, rather than the latest for which a colourable case can be made.

Finally, a word about the short-term prospects for the British economy. There always has been, and there always will be, an economic cycle. During our period of office so far, we experienced a sharp downturn between 1979 and 1981, followed by a remarkably vigorous and prolonged upswing which lasted from 1981 right through to 1988. We are now once again on the downswing, and I see no need for a further policy tightening. While this downswing will not be as sharp as the previous downturn, not least given the very much lower level of inflation that we now have, a dull 1989 is bound to be followed by a difficult 1990.

But from then on, I have every confidence that, with the policies that the Government have been pursuing and will continue to pursue, as we heard from the Chancellor today, the long-term upswing will continue, based on lower inflation and on the unprecedented underlying strength that the British economy now possesses.

I have every confidence, too, that this will lead at the end of the day to a fourth election victory under the leadership of my right honourable Friend the Prime Minister, whose outstanding contribution to the renaissance of Britain over these past ten years I am proud to have been able to assist.

THE HOWE–LAWSON TAX REFORMS (1979–89)

1. Main Reforms, Tax by Tax

Income Tax

Basic rate reduced in stages from 33p in the pound to 25p in the pound.

New objective of 20p in the pound set in 1988 Budget.

Personal allowances up by more than 25 per cent in real terms.

Top rate of tax reduced from 83 per cent to 40 per cent. All other higher rates of tax (there were nine in 1978–79) abolished.

Starting point for higher rate tax up by more than 15 per cent in real terms.

Investment income surcharge abolished in 1984.

Independent taxation of husband and wife implemented in 1990 (legislation in 1988 Finance Bill, following two Green Papers).

Other tax penalties on marriage abolished in 1988.

Capital Gains Tax

Indexation introduced in 1982, and extended in 1985: in 1988, all gains rebased to 1982, so no taxation of 'paper' gains.

Rates aligned with income tax in 1988.

Inheritance Tax/Capital Transfer Tax

Tax abolished on lifetime gifts made more than seven years before death in 1986.

Threshold more than doubled in real terms.

Top rate of tax of 75 per cent reduced to 60 per cent in 1984 and 40 per cent in 1988. All other rates (there were thirteen in 1979) abolished.

Business and agricultural reliefs improved.

Corporation Tax

Major restructuring in 1984:

– main rate reduced in stages from 52 per cent to 35 per cent;

– small companies rate reduced from 42 per cent to basic rate of income tax (25 per cent by 1988);

– most 100 per cent first-year capital allowances phased out;

– stock relief withdrawn.

Special arrangements for short-life assets introduced in 1985.

Companies, too, benefit from rebasing of capital gains to 1982, and indexation of gains since then; as for individuals, capital gains taxed at same rate as income (profits).

Value-added Tax

Dual rate of VAT replaced by single 15 per cent rate in 1979.

Base broadened, to include hot take-away food and building alterations in 1984, advertising in newspapers and periodicals in 1985, non-domestic construction (European Court ruling) in 1989.

Option introduced in 1987 for small businesses to move to cash accounting to ease cash flow problems, and (starting in 1988) to annual accounting to ease compliance burden.

Excise Duties

Tax bias in favour of unleaded petrol introduced in 1987 and further increased in both 1988 and 1989.

Stamp Duties

Rate on shares halved to 1 per cent in 1984, and again to ½ per cent in 1986.

Maximum rate on land, houses and other buildings halved to 1 per cent in 1984, and threshold raised.

Capital duty and unit trust instrument duty abolished in 1988.

Several minor duties abolished in 1985.

Development Land Tax

Abolished in 1985.

Taxation of North Sea Oil

Reformed and burden reduced in 1982.

Oil royalties abolished in 1983.

National Insurance

Surcharge abolished in 1984.

Contributions reformed in 1985 and 1989.

2. Other Reforms, grouped by Themes and Objectives

Promoting Enterprise, Participation and Saving

Business Expansion Scheme introduced (as Business Start-up Scheme in 1981 and enlarged into BES in 1983). Subsequently revised to improve targeting – notably limitation to £500,000 raised per company per year in 1988.

ANNEXE 5

New all-employee share scheme introduced in 1980; successive improvements to both that and 1978 employee share legislation in subsequent Budgets.

Employee share option scheme introduced in 1984.

Personal Equity Plans introduced in 1986 and improved in subsequent Budgets.

Tax relief introduced for Profit-Related Pay in 1987 and improved in 1988.

Tax relief extended to new personal pensions in 1987, also to free-standing additional voluntary contributions (AVCs).

Pensioners' earnings rule abolished in 1989.

Helping Charities

Improvements in tax regime for charitable giving and charities in successive Budgets, including:

– reduction in minimum period of charitable covenants from 7 to 4 years in 1980;

– gifts to charity exempted from stamp duty in 1982 and CTT/inheritance tax in 1983;

– employers given tax relief on salary costs of employees seconded to charities in 1983;

– new Payroll Giving Scheme, to enable individuals to give regularly to charity with tax relief, in 1986;

– abolition of limit on higher rate relief for covenanted donations by individuals, in 1986;

– extension of certain VAT concessions for charities, especially for the disabled, in 1986;

– tax relief for one-off company donations in 1986.

Reducing Tax Reliefs and Tax Breaks

Life assurance premium relief abolished for new policies in 1984.

Premium relief for pre-1984 life policies reduced in line with basic rate of income tax.

Tax on company cars trebled in real terms.

Commercial woodland taken out of income and corporation tax in 1988, ending notorious abuse.

Mortgage interest relief withdrawn from home improvement loans and multiple mortgage interest relief ended in 1988.

Tax relief abolished for new covenants, except to charity, in 1988.

New rules introduced in 1986 to limit surpluses that can be built up in pension funds free of tax.

Limit introduced on size of tax-free lump sum pensions, and on tax relief for fast-accrual pensions, in 1987.

Tax relief for pensions capped in 1989.

Simplifying system and improving administration

PAYE computerized, to be followed by computerization of taxation of the self-employed.

Administration simplified in a number of ways, e.g. giving mortgage interest relief at source (MIRAS), extending composite rate of tax to the banks, and taking maintenance payments (like non-charitable covenants – see above) out of tax.

Close company apportionment rules abolished in 1989.

Keith Committee set up to investigate enforcement powers of the Revenue departments; gradually implementing recommendations.

Planning for the 1990s: legislated for 'pay and file' system for corporation tax, to be implemented when new computer system is operational.

Countering Tax Avoidance

Tax charged on profits of investment in certain offshore funds in 1984.

Tax charged on certain controlled foreign companies in 1984.

Tax advantage in bond washing (conversion of income into capital) eliminated in 1985.

Restriction on use of losses by dual resident companies in 1987.

Tax provisions affecting acquisition of shares by employees in unapproved share schemes simplified and retargeted in 1988.

ABBREVIATIONS AND A FEW DEFINITIONS

What follows makes no claims to be a full glossary of economic and financial terms. It is first and foremost a guide to the abbreviations found in this book. Second, it is a selective guide to a few of the more technical expressions unavoidably used in this text. It should be used in conjunction with the Table of Contents and Index.

For fuller information the reader should consult a volume such as The Pocket Economist *by Rupert Pennant-Rea and Bill Emmott (The* Economist/*Basil Blackwell, 1987).*

APRT	Advance Petroleum Revenue Tax. See Chapter 17.
AGR	Advanced Gas-cooled Reactor.
Balance of payments	Record of a country's transactions in goods, services and money with other countries and with international institutions. Has two accounts, current and capital. If there is a surplus on one there is a deficit on the other; by definition the two must balance. **Current Account:** the current account of the balance of payments on which appear exports and imports; invisible trade; private transfers and official transfers. **Capital Account:** long-term and short-term capital flows.

ANNEXE 6

Bank of England	Founded 1694. It has five main functions:
	1 As the Government's bank manager, taking in taxes, making payments, and managing the National debt. It floats new loans for the Government and lends money directly to the Government.
	2 In consultation with the Treasury, the bank carries out the monetary policy of the Government. The bank issues all bank notes and coins; it keeps the country's foreign reserves; it influences the money market by changes in the interest rates at which it deals with the City and by sales or purchases of gilt-edged stock and commercial bills.
	3 As the bankers' bank, holding on deposit some of the commercial bank's reserves, and acting as lender of last resort to the financial system.
	4 As supervisor, of banks and some financial institutions.
	5 As a representative and spokesman of City views.
Big Bang	Name for changes in the City which occurred on 27 October 1986. Signified the breaking-down of barriers between different types of financial institutions.
Bretton Woods	The agreement set up in 1944 that shaped the International Monetary until 1971, and which set up the IMF and the World Bank. See Annexe 1 and Index.
BGC	British Gas Corporation.
BNOC	British National Oil Corporation.
BT	British Telecom.
BSA	Building Societies' Association.
Bundesbank	West Germany's Central Bank.
BES	Business Expansion Scheme.
Central Bank	Organization analogous to the Bank of England which implements monetary policy, assists in the finance of Government and in some countries, supervises financial institutions.
CPRS	Central Policy Review Staff. Founded by the Heath Government (1970–74) to assist Cabinet and strategic thinking.
CSO	Central Statistical Office.
CPS	Centre for Policy Studies.
CAP	Common Agricultural Policy.
CBI	Confederation of British Industry.

1072

CRS	Conservative Research Department.
Corporation Tax	Tax on company profits.
'Corset'	Bank of England's 'supplementary special deposits scheme' introduced as an instrument of monetary control in December 1973, and finally abolished in June 1980. See Chapters 7 and 8.
Deflation	A prolonged and continuing fall in the general price level. It is sometimes more loosely and controversially used for policies to bring down inflation and for a slowdown or fall in output and employment believed to emanate from tight financial policies.
Demand	Total level of spending or attempted spending in economy. Sometimes known as 'aggregate demand'.
Deregulation	A reduction or elimination of official restrictions and prohibitions, allowing competitive commercial behaviour.
Devaluation	Reduction of exchange rate, making it worth less in terms of other currencies.
Dow Jones	Widely used index of New York Stock Exchange Industrial Average prices.
Dry	Opposite of wet
Ecofin	Regular meeting of European Community Finance Ministers.
EETPU	Electrical and Electronic Telecommunications and Plumbing Union
EPEA	Electrical Power Engineers' Association
ECU	European Currency Unit. Basket of currencies used by the European Monetary System to set values for its central exchange rates and for some central bank transactions.
EC	European Economic Community founded 25 March 1957 under the Treaty of Rome (British membership 1973). A customs union with elaborate rules, which has gradually extended its scope and ambitions.
EMS	European Monetary System. March 1979. A mechanism linking the exchange rates of EC currencies.
Exchange Rate	The rate at which one currency exchanges for another, e.g. the number of dollars or Deutschmarks obtained for one pound sterling.

ERM	Exchange Rate Mechanism. The operating arm of the EMS.
EFL	External Financing Limits. Maximum Government credit for British nationalized industries.
Federal Reserve System	The United States central bank, popularly known as the Fed.
Fiscal Policy	Government use of tax and spending powers, to influence aggregate demand, maintain public sector solvency or influence national savings. Fashions in its use have changed.
FRNs	Floating Rate Notes.
GGE	General Government Expenditure.
Gilt-edged stock	All British marketable government securities except Treasury Bills are known as gilts and have guaranteed interest levels and redemption values.
Goodhart's Law	Any statistical measure will start behaving differently the moment it becomes an official target.
GDP	Gross Domestic Product. A country's annual output of goods and services.
GNP	Gross National Product. GDP plus residents' income from economic activity abroad and property held abroad, minus the corresponding income of non-residents in the country. For many countries the trend of GDP and GNP are similar and used interchangeably, depending on availability of figures.
Group of Five	The five largest capitalist economies: USA, Japan, West Germany, France and Britain. Their governments met informally at various levels.
Group of Seven	Group of Five plus Italy and Canada. Heads of Government meet annually at economic summits and Finance Ministers more frequently.
Group of Ten	Ten leading capitalist countries: G5+ Belgium, Holland, Italy, Sweden and Canada plus honourary 11th member Switzerland. Forum for discussing international monetary arrangements. Now less frequently used.
Hot Money	Cash that is held in one currency, but is liable to switch to another at a moment's notice.

Incomes Policy	Legal or voluntary restrictions on pay and sometimes prices. Meant to aid policy against inflation.
Inflation	A continuing rise in the general level of prices.
IDA	International Development Agency.
IPCS	Institution of Professional Civil Servants.
IMF	International Monetary Fund. The Fund was set up at Bretton Woods in 1944 with the aim of establishing a financial basis of free trade at stable exchange rates.
Louvre Accord	Attempt by Group of Seven meeting in Paris in February 1987 to stabilize exchange rates.
Macroeconomic policy	Policies such as fiscal, monetary and exchange rate policy designed to influence the level of spending (demand) in the economy (see Chapter 33).
MTFS	Medium Term Financial Strategy. See Chapter 7.
Microeconomic policy	Policies Designed to influence behaviour of individuals, households and firms by affecting incentives.
MLR	Minimum Lending Rate. 1973 October–August 1981. Minimum rate at which Bank of England would lend money to discount houses. Used to set level of short-term rates in economy. Occasionally revived.
Money	Monetary Base M0: the narrowest measure of money supply: just currency in circulation, bank's deposits at Bank of England and holdings of notes and coins.
	M1: total of cash and current account deposits at any given time.
	M3: M1 plus other types of bank accounts.
	Sterling M3: M3 excluding foreign currency accounts.
	M4: equals M3 plus building society accounts.
	M5: equals M4 plus money market instruments such as Treasury Bills.
	See Chapter 8.
Monetary Base Control	Attempt to regulate M0 directly without interest rate target. See Chapter 9.
National Debt	Government's total outstanding debt.
National Economic Development Council	Known as Neddy. Britain's tripartite forum (Government, employers, unions) for considering economic issues. Abolished 1992.

NICs	National Insurance Contributions
NIS	National Insurance Surcharge.
NUM	National Union of Miners.
NAIRU	Non-Accelerating Inflation Rate of Unemployment
NIBM1	Non-interest bearing M1.
NATO	North Atlantic Treaty Organization
OECD	Organization for Economic Co-operation & Development. Twenty-four advanced industrial countries based in Paris. A forum for countries to discuss economic issues of mutual interest.
OfGas	Office of Gas Supply. Regulatory group.
OfTel	Office of Telecommunications. Regulatory group.
OfWat	Office of Water Supplies. Regulatory group.
OPA	Oil and Pipeline Agency. Regulatory group.
OPEC	Organization of Petroleum Exporting Countries. Established in 1960 to try to co-ordinate production among the main oil exporters. Has attempted to regulate level of oil prices.
PAYE	Pay-as-you-earn. The automatic deduction of Income Tax from the weekly or monthly pay packet of employees.
PAC	Public Accounts Committee.
PEP	Personal Equity Plans.
PRT	Petroleum Revenue Tax. See Chapter 17.
Plaza Accord	22 September 1985. Statement of Finance Ministers and Central Bank Governors from G5 announced that the dollar exchange rate should be brought down, if necessary by intervention. See Chapter 43.
PWR	Pressurized Water Reactors.
Price Controls	Government attempts to counter inflation by regulating prices directly. Sometimes used for specific industries for particular purposes.
PRP	Profit-Related Pay.
PESC	Public Expenditure Survey Committee. See Chapter 24.
PSBR	Public Sector Borrowing Requirement. Shortfall between spending by the public sector and revenues, financed by borrowing.
RSG	Rate Support Grant.

Red Book	Popular name of Financial Statement and Budget Report published every year with UK Budget.
RPI	Retail Prices Index. Reflects the prices of a basket of goods and services weighted according to the spending patterns of a 'typical' family. Most common measure of inflation in Britain.
Rooker-Wise Amendment	1977 amendment to Finance Bill requiring the Government in its Spring Budget to raise the tax-free threshold for all personal income tax by the percentage increase in retail prices in the previous year.
Stagflation	Combination of low growth and high inflation.
SGHWRs	Steam Generated Heavy Water Reactors.
SPD	Supplementary Petroleum Duty. See Chapter 17.
Supply-side	Policies designed to influence grass roots performance in contrast to overall demand. See microeconomic policy and Chapter 33. In the USA has special reference to tax reduction.
TPI	Tax and Prices Index. See Chapter 5.
TESSAs	Tax Exempt Special Savings Accounts.
TINA	'There is no alternative'. Slogan ascribed to Margaret Thatcher. (See Chapter 10.)
TSRB	Top Salaries Review Body.
Treasury Bills	Short-term borrowing instruments issued by Government which typically carry a three-month maturity and a fixed rate of interest. Used for meeting the residual financing needs of Governments during periods when revenues and receipts may be low. All held by institutions.
TSB	Trustees Savings Bank.
VAT	Value Added Tax.
Wet	Tories who had no stomach for the fight ahead. Term coined by Margaret Thatcher. See Dry
World Bank	Alternative name for the International Bank for Reconstruction and Development (IBRD) established at Bretton Woods.

ADDITIONAL SELECTED STATISTICS

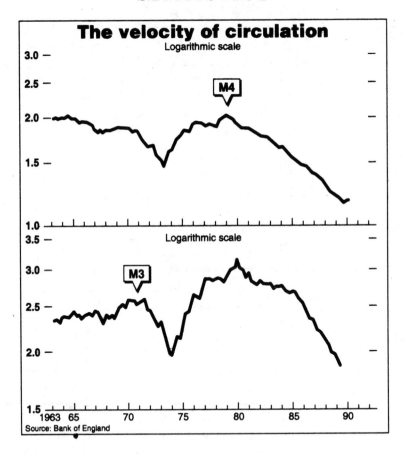

Source: Bank of England

MONETARY TARGETS AND OUTCOMES

Year Targeted	Year of publication of FSBR (March) percentage increases								Outcome
	1979	1980	1981	1982	1983	1984	1985	1986	
£M3									
1978–79	8–12								
1979–80	·7–11								16.2
1980–81		7–11							18.4
1981–82		6–10	6–10						12.8
1982–83		5–9	5–9	8–12					11.1
1983–84		4–8	4–8	7–11	7–11				9.5
1984–85				6–10	6–10	6–10			11.9
1985–86					5–9	5–9	5–9		16.3
1986–87						4–8	4–8	11–15	18.7
1987–88						3–7	3–7		
1988–89						2–6	2–6		

MO	1984	1985	1986	1987	1988	1989	1990		
1984–85	4–8								5.4
1985–86	3–7·	3–7							4.1
1986–87	2–6	2–6	2·6						3.5
1987–88	1–5	1–5	2–6	2–6					6.4
1988–89	0–4	0–4	1–5	1–5			6.8		
1989–90			1–5	1–5	1–5	1–5			5.0
1990–91				0–4	0–4	0–4	1–5		3.1
1991–92					0–4	0–4	0–4		2.3

Source: Treasury

MEDIUM TERM FINANCIAL STRATEGY

Nominal GDP growth (% change on previous financial year)

Year of projection	78–79	79–80	80–81	81–82	82–83	83–84	84–85	85–86	86–87	87–88	88–89	89–90	90–91	91–92	92–93	93–94	94–95
'80–81 (1)			15.25	11.50	9.50	10.25											
'82–82 (1)		13.00	10.50	9.75	9.75	10.00											
'82–83				10.50	9.75	9.75	9.50										
*'83–84					8.25	7.75	8.75	7.50									
'84–85						8.25	8.00	6.75	6.00	5.00							
'85–86						7.75	6.75 (8.25)	8.50 (7.00)	6.50	5.75	5.00						
'86–87								9.50 (8.25)	6.75	6.50	6.00	5.50					
'87–88									6.00	7.50	6.50	6.00	5.50				
'88–89										9.75	7.50	6.50	6.00	5.50			
'89–90											11.00	7.75	6.00	6.00	5.50		
'90–91 (2)												8.50 (8.50)	5.75 (7.50)	6.75	6.25	5.75	
'91–92													7.25	6.00	7.50	7.00	6.25
Outturn		20.00	14.00	9.75	9.50	8.50	7.25 (5.25)	9.25 (10.25)	7.75	10.75	11.25	8.25	5.75				

(1) Figures in brackets are adjusted for the miners' strike
(2) Figures in brackets adjust for the distortion arising from the abolition of domestic rates

Source: Treasury

NON-NORTH SEA TAXES, SOCIAL SECURITY CONTRIBUTIONS AND THE COMMUNITY CHARGE AS A PERCENT OF NON-NORTH SEA MONEY GDP

29½	1963–64	36¾	1975–76	38¼	1987–88
30	1964–64	36½	1976–77	37¾	1988–89
31¾	1965–66	35½	1977–78	37¾	1989–90
32½	1966–67	34¾	1978–79	37¼	1990–91
38	1967–68	35½	1979–80	36¾	1991–92
35¾	1968–69	36¾	1980–81	35¾	1992–93
37½	1969–70	39¼	1981–82	36	1993–94
37	1970–71	38¾	1982–83	36¾	1994–95
35¼	1971–72	38¼	1983–84	37¼	1995–96
33	1972–73	38½	1984–85	38	1996–97
33¾	1973–74	37½	1985–86		
36¼	1974–75	38	1986–87		

1. 1992–93 onwards: MTFS projections.
2. Based on non-North Sea money GDP figures adjusted for the years before 1990–91 to remove the distortion caused by the abolition of domestic rate.
3. Including the council tax from 1993–94, when it will replace the community charge.

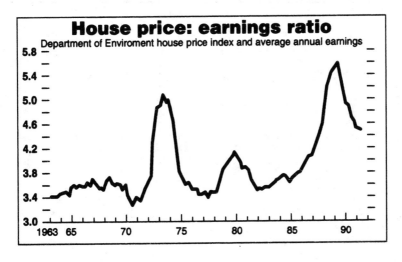

House price: earnings ratio
Department of Enviroment house price index and average annual earnings

INDICES OF REAL GDP PER WORKER UK 1979 – 100

	UK	USA	JAPAN	GERMANY	FRANCE
1963	70	126	35	68	69
1979	100	156	91	113	121
1983	100	152	100	113	122
1988	118	180	117	125	130

Source: Summers, R. and Heston, A. 'The Penn World Table: An expanded set of International Comparisons, 1950–1988' The Quarterly Journal of Economics, May, pp.327–368.

INDICES OF MANUFACTURING OUTPUT PER HOUR UK 1979 – 100

	UK	USA	JAPAN	GERMANY	FRANCE
1965	54	131	27	64	56
1979	100	214	133	173	166
1983	120	236	166	191	189
1988	151	289	207	214	217

Source: Hooper, P. and Larin, K. A. (1989), 'International Comparisons of Labour costs in Manufacturing', The Review of Income and Wealth, Series 35, No.4.

Annual percentage changes in real GDP per capita				
	OECD Europe	US	Japan	UK
1964-73	3.6	2.6	8.0	2.6
1973-79	1.9	1.4	2.5	1.4
1979-89	1.7	1.8	3.5	2.0

Source: OECD

THE COMPONENTS OF UK GDP

	GDP	Consumer Exp	GOV Consumption	Total Consumption	Gross Domestic Fixed Capital Information	GDFC in Dwelling	GDFC excluding Dwelling	Private GDFC excluding dwelling	Public GDFC excluding dwelling
Total Growth (%)									
64–73	31.6	30.2	24.9	28.8	37.5	28.3	40.7	34.2	59.1
73–79	9.3	8.2	11.8	9.1	1.1	−1.1	1.8	20.5	−55.8
79–89	25.1	38.3	10.6	31.0	45.0	9.0	56.1	58.2	38.0
79–83	1.8	5.8	4.7	5.5	−5.3	−8.4	−4.3	−2.8	−17.9
83–89	22.9	30.8	5.6	24.2	53.0	18.9	63.2	62.8	68.1
Average Growth (%PA)									
64–73	3.5	3.4	2.8	3.2	4.2	3.1	4.5	3.8	6.6
73–79	1.9	1.6	2.4	1.8	0.2	−0.2	0.4	4.1	−11.2
79–89	2.8	4.3	1.2	3.4	5.0	1.0	6.2	6.5	4.2
79–83	3.8	5.1	0.9	4.0	8.8	3.2	10.5	10.5	11.3

Source: CSO

UK BALANCE OF PAYMENTS (£bn)

	Oil	Non-Oil	Visibles	Invisibles	Current Account	Balancing Item
1978	−2.0	0.4	2.7	−1.6	1.1	1.7
1979	−0.7	−2.6	2.9	−3.3	−0.5	1.0
1980	0.3	1.0	1.5	1.4	2.8	0.9
1981	3.1	0.1	3.5	3.3	6.7	0.5
1982	4.6	−2.7	2.7	1.9	4.6	−2.1
1983	7.0	−8.5	5.3	−1.5	3.8	0.8
1984	6.9	−12.3	7.1	−5.3	1.8	6.0
1985	8.1	−11.4	6.2	−3.3	2.9	1.2
1986	4.1	−13.6	9.7	−9.6	0.2	7.0
1987	4.2	−15.7	7.4	−11.6	−4.2	−1.7
1988	2.8	−24.4	6.1	−21.6	−15.5	5.9
1989	1.3	−25.9	4.2	−24.6	−20.4	7.5
1990	1.6	−20.2	2.7	−18.6	−15.9	1.6
1991	1.2	−11.3	4.9	−10.1	−5.2	−3.7

Source: CSO

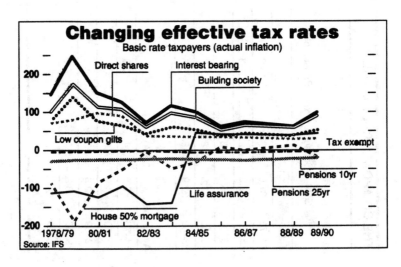

Changing effective tax rates
Basic rate taxpayers (actual inflation)

Direct shares
Interest bearing
Building society
Low coupon gilts
Tax exempt
Pensions 10yr
Life assurance
Pensions 25yr
House 50% mortgage

Source: IFS

CHANGE IN MAIN TAX RATES SINCE 1979

	1978–79	1979	1980	1981	1982	1983	1984	1985	1986	1987	1988	1989	1990	1991–2
						Budgets								
Income tax:														
– top rate on 'unearned' income	98	75	75	75	75	75	60	60	60	60	40	40	40	40
– top rate on earnings	83	60	60	60	60	60	60	60	60	60	40	40	40	40
– basic rate	33	30	30	30	30	30	30	30	29	27	25	25	25	25
– starting rate	25	25	30	30	30	30	30	30	29	27	25	25	25	25
National insurance contributions														
– employers 1/	10	10	10.2	10.2	10.2	10.4	10.4	10.4	10.4	10.4	10.4	10.4	10.4	10.45
– employees	6½	6.75	7.75	8.75	9	9	9	9	9	9	9	9	9	9
Value added tax														
– standard rate	8	15	15	15	15	15	15	15	15	15	15	15	15	17½
– higher rate	12½	–	–	–	–	–	–	–	–	–	–	–	–	–
Corporation tax														
– main rate	52	52	52	52	52	52	45	40	35	35	35	35	35	33
– small companies rate	42	42	40	40	40	38	30	30	29	27	25	25	25	25
National insurance surcharge	3½	3½	3½	3½	3½	2	1	–	–	–	–	–	–	–
Capital gains tax														
– higher rate	30	30	30	30	30	30	30	30	30	30	40	40	40	40
– lower rate	15	15	15	15	15	15	15	15	15	15	25	25	25	25
Inheritance tax														
– top rate	75	75	75	75	75	75	60	60	60	60	40	40	40	40
Car tax	10	10	10	10	10	10	10	10	10	10	10	10	10	10
Stamp duty on property	2	2	2	2	2	2	1	1	1	1	1	1	1	1
Stamp duty on shares	2	2	2	2	2	2	1	1	½	½	½	½	½	½

1/ rate from 83 Budget = 10.45

ANNEXE 7

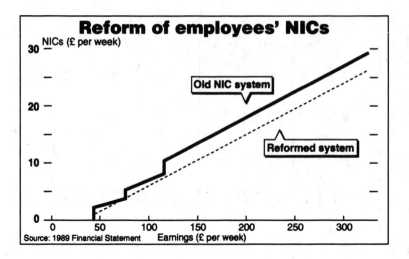

Reform of employees' NICs

NICs (£ per week)

Old NIC system

Reformed system

Source: 1989 Financial Statement   Earnings (£ per week)

1086

LIST OF WORKS CITED

Chapter 1

Daniel Bell, *The Cultural Contradictions of Capitalism*, Heinemann, 1979

Edmund Burke, Speech on arrival at Bristol, 13 October 1774
The Works of Edmund Burke, Vol II, Little Brown, 1894

Rudyard Kipling, *A Choice of Kipling's Verse*, (ed. T.S. Eliot), Faber & Faber, 1941

Irving Kristol, *Two Cheers for Capitalism*, Basic Books, New York, 1978

Nigel Lawson, 'Principle in Opposition', third and final article of series 'A Tract for Tories', *Spectator*, 3 March 1967

Anthony Quinton, *The Politics of Imperfection*, Faber & Faber, 1978

Joseph Schumpeter, *Capitalism, Socialism and Democracy* Fourth Edition, Allen & Unwin, 1952

Chapter 2

James Callaghan, *Time and Chance*, Collins, 1987

Bernard Donoughue, *Prime Minister: The Conduct of Policy under Harold Wilson and James Callaghan*, Jonathan Cape, 1987

LIST OF WORKS CITED

Chapter 3

Dean Acheson, *Present at the Creation: My Year at the State Department*, Hamish Hamilton, 1970

William Keegan, *Mr Lawson's Gamble*, Hodder & Stoughton, 1989

Leo Pliatzky, *Getting and Spending: Public Expenditure, Employment and Inflation,* Basil Blackwell, 1982

Kathleen Burk and Alec Cairncross, *'Goodbye, Great Britain': the 1976 IMF Crisis*, Yale University Press, 1992

Chapter 4

Joel Barnett, *Inside the Treasury*, André Deutsch, 1982

Denis Healey, *The Time of My Life*, Michael Joseph, 1989

Sir Geoffrey Howe, Lecture to Institute of Fiscal Studies, 1991

OECD, *Economic Outlook*, No 25, London, HMSO, July 1979. Special Section: 'The Oil Situation'

Chapter 5

Alan Budd, 'Disarming the Treasury' in *The Taming of Government*, Institute of Economic Affairs, 1977

Alan Budd and Terence Burns, *London Business School Economic Outlook*, October 1971

Conservative Party, *The Right Approach to the Economy*, Conservative Central Office, 1977

Garret Fitzgerald, *All in a Life*, Macmillan, 1991

David Hume, 'Of Money', reprinted in *Essays; Moral, Political and Literary.* 1777. Mod. edn. Liberty Press, Indianapolis, 1985

Institute for Fiscal Studies, *Budgetary Reform* ('The Armstrong Report'), 1980

HM Treasury, *Budgetary Reform* (Cm 1867), HMSO, 1992

Alan Walters, *The Economic Adviser's Role*, Centre for Political Studies, 1981

Chapter 6

Denis Healey, *The Time of My Life*, Michael Joseph, 1989

Nigel Lawson, *Thatcherism in Practice*, Conservative Political Centre, January 1981

Geoffrey Maynard, *The Economy under Mrs Thatcher*, Basil Blackwell, 1988

Chapter 7

C. Allsopp, T. Jenkins and Derek Morris, 'The Assessment: Macro-economic Policy' in *Oxford Review of Economic Policy*, Vol 7, No 3, Oxford, Autumn 1991

Terence Burns, 'The UK Government's Financial Strategy', Chapter 20 of *Keynes and Economic Policy* (ed. W. Eltis and P. Sinclair), Macmillan, 1988

Nigel Lawson, *The New Conservatism*, Centre for Policy Studies, 1980

Geoffrey Howe, 'The 364 Economists: Ten Years On', *Fiscal Studies*, Autumn 1991

Chapter 8

David Llewellyn and M. Holmes, *Competition or Credit Controls?* Institute of Economic Affairs, 1991

Treasury, *Monetary Control*, Cmnd 7858, March 1980

Milton Friedman, *The Optimum Quantity of Money*, Aldine Publishing, 1969

Gordon Pepper, *Money Credit and Inflation*, Institute of Economic Affairs, 1990

Chapter 10

House of Commons, Treasury Select Committee, 1980 Reports

Nigel Lawson, Speech to Lombard Association, 16 April 1986 (Obtainable from HM Treasury)

Leo Pliatzky, *The Treasury under Mrs Thatcher*, Basil Blackwell, 1989

James Prior, *A Bid for Power*, Hamish Hamilton, 1986

Chapter 14

M. Adeney and J. Lloyd, *The Miners' Strike 1984–85*, Routledge, pbk edn, 1988

Samuel Brittan, *A Restatement of Economic Liberalism*, Macmillan, 1988

Chapter 15

W.S. Jevons, *The Coal Question, 1865*. Reprinted, Augustus Kelly, 1965

Chapter 16

Jack Wiseman, *Cost, Choice and Political Economy*, Edward Elgar, 1989

LIST OF WORKS CITED

Chapter 17

House of Commons Select Committee on Energy, *Report on North Sea Oil Depletion*, Parliamentary Papers, 1981–2, Vol 337

Chapter 18

Peter Riddell, *The Thatcher Decade*, Basil Blackwell, 1989; pbk edn, 1991

Richard Pryke, *Public Enterprise in Practice*, MacGibbon & Kee, 1973

Richard Pryke, *The Nationalised Industries, Policies and Performance since 1968*, MacGibbon & Kee, 1981

Richard Pryke, *The Comparative Performance of Public and Private Enterprise*, Fiscal Studies 1982, Vol 3, No 2

Chapter 19

Peter Walker, *Staying Power*, Bloomsbury, 1991

Samuel Brittan and Barry Riley, *A People's Stake in North Sea Oil*, Lloyds Bank Review, April 1978. Reprinted in *Privatisation and Ownership* (ed. Christopher Johnson), Pinter Publishers, 1988

Thomas Paine, *The Rights of Man*, 1791–2

Chapter 20

M. Bishop and J. Kay, *Does Privatisation Work?*, London Business School, 1988

J. Kay and D.J. Thompson, *Privatisation: A Policy in Search of a Rationale*, Economic Journal, Vol 96, 1986

Nigel Lawson, *The Frontiers of Privatisation*, Adam Smith Institute, 1988

Peter Lilley, *Privatisation and Regulation*, in Eamon Butler (ed.), *Privatisation, East and West*, Adam Smith Institute, 1991

John Moore, *Privatisation Everywhere*, Centre for Policy Studies, London, 1992

Leo Pliatzky, *The Treasury under Mrs Thatcher*, Basil Blackwell, 1989

Chapter 21

Kenneth Harris, 'The Making of a Chancellor', *Observer*, 3 and 10 March 1985

Edward Pearce, *The Senate of Lilliput*, Faber & Faber, 1983

Edward Pearce, *Hummingbirds and Hyenas*, Faber & Faber, 1985

Hugo Young, *One of Us*, rev. edn, Pan Books, 1990

Chapter 24

S.T. Bindoff, *Tudor England*, Penguin, 1950

Herbert Brittain, *The British Budgetary Mechanism*, Allen and Unwin, 1959

David Kynaston, *The Chancellor of the Exchequer*, Terence Dalton, 1980

Erskine May, *Parliamentary Practices*, 1844, revised periodically

Leo Pliatzky, *Getting and Spending*, Basil Blackwell, 1982

Leo Pliatzky, *The Treasury under Mrs Thatcher*, Basil Blackwell, 1989

HM Treasury, *The Next Ten Years*: *Public Expenditure and Taxation in the 1990s*. Cmnd 9189, HMSO, 1984

HM Treasury, Autumn Statement Supplements, annually

Chapter 25

Leo Pliatzky, *The Treasury under Mrs Thatcher*, Basil Blackwell, 1989

William Whitelaw, *The Whitelaw Memoirs*, Headline Press, 1990

Chapter 26

Samuel Brittan, *Steering the Economy: The Role of the Treasury*, Penguin, 1971

Chapter 27

Nigel Lawson, *Tax Reform*, Conservative Political Centre, 1988

James Meade et al, *The Reform of Taxation*, Institute of Fiscal Studies, 1978

A.C. Pigou, *The Economics of Welfare*, Macmillan, 1960

Norman Tebbit, *Upwardly Mobile*, Futura, 1988

Chapter 30

Department of Social Security, *Households Below Average Income (HBAI)*, 1990

Institute for Fiscal Studies, *Green Budget*, 1991

Mervyn King, *On Policies Towards Saving*, Bank of England, 1991

Bill Robinson, *How Should Savings be Taxed?*, National Westminster Bank Quarterly Review, November 1990

Chapter 31

Leo Pliatzky, *The Treasury Under Mrs Thatcher*, Basil Blackwell, 1989

Robert Blake, *Disraeli*, Eyre & Spottiswoode, 1966

Diana Goldsworthy, *Setting Up Next Steps*, HMSO, 1991

LIST OF WORKS CITED

Peter Hennessy, *Whitehall*, Fontana, 1991

Chapter 32

The Collected Works of Walter Bagehot, volumes 9-11 (The Economic Essays), edited by Norman St John-Stevas, *The Economist*, 1978
Banking Supervision (Cmnd 9695), HMSO, 1985
  Bank of England Annual Report, 1985
Report of the Committee Set up to Consider the System of Banking Supervision (Cmnd 9550), HMSO, 1985
Stephen Fay, *Portrait of an Old Lady*, Penguin, 1988
L.C.B. Gower (Chairman) *Review of Investment Protection* (Cmnd 9125) HMSO, 1984–85
Lord Roskill (Chairman), *Fraud Trials Committee Report*, HMSO, 1986

Chapter 33

Samuel Brittan, *How to End the Monetarist Controversy*, Institute of Economic Affairs, 1981
Nigel Lawson, *The British Experiment* (The Mais Lecture), City University London, 1984

Chapter 34

Samuel Brittan, *The Role and Limits of Government*, Temple Smith, 1973
Christopher Johnson, *The Economy Under Mrs Thatcher*, Penguin, 1991
Richard Layard et al, *Unemployment: Macroeconomic Performance of the Labour Market*, Oxford, 1991
P. Minford et al, *Unemployment Cause and Cure*, Martin Robertson, 1983
Francis Pym, *The Politics of Consent*, Macmillan, 1984
David Young, *The Enterprise Years*, Headline Press, 1989
Martin Weitzman, *The Share Economy*, Harvard University Press, 1984
Report from the Select Committee on Overseas Trade, House of Lords, 30 July 1985 (238-I)

Chapter 35

Christopher Johnson, *The Economy Under Mrs Thatcher*, Penguin, 1991
Martin Weitzman, *The Share Economy*, Harvard University Press, 1984

Chapter 36

T. Burns, 'The UK Government's Financial Strategy' in *Keynes and Economic Policy* (ed. W. Eltis and P. Sinclair), Macmillan, 1988

Financial Statement and Budget Report, (the annual 'Red Book'), HMSO, 1982 and 1983

Chapter 37

Robert Harris, *Good and Faithful Servant*, Faber & Faber, 1990
Bernard Ingham, *Kill the Messenger*, HarperCollins, 1991

Chapter 38

Centre for Policy Studies, *Whither Monetarism? The Chancellor's Mansion House Speech, with comments by Three Wise Men*, 1985
Alan Walters, *Sterling in Danger*, Fontana, 1990

Chapter 39

Andrew Britton, *Macroeconomic Policy in Britain 1974–1987*, Cambridge University Press, 1991

Chapter 40

Alan Walters, *Britain's Economic Renaissance*, Oxford University Press, 1986
Alan Walters, *Sterling in Danger*, Fontana, 1990

Chapter 41

Samuel Brittan, *The Role and Limits of Government*, 1983; 2nd edn, Wildwood House, 1987

Chapter 42

Yoichi Funabashi, *Managing the Dollar: From The Plaza to the Louvre*, Institute for International Economics, Washington, 1988
E.A. George, *Some Influences on Bank Behaviour*, TSB Forum Lecture, Reprinted in the *Bank of England Bulletin*, May 1992
Donald T. Regan, *For the Record: From Wall Street to Washington*, Harcourt Brace Jovanovich, 1988

Chapter 43

I.M. Destler and C. Randall Henning, *Dollar Politics: Exchange Rate Policy-Making in the United States*, Institute for International Economics, Washington, 1989
Yoichi Funabashi, *Managing the Dollar: From the Plaza to the Louvre*, Institute for International Economics, Washington, 1988

LIST OF WORKS CITED

Chapter 44

Instituto Bancario San Parlo di Torino, *Economic Summits 1975–86*, Turin, 1987 (in English)

Paul Volcker and Toyoo Gyohten, *Changing Fortunes: The World's Money and the Decline of American Supremacy*, Times Books, 1992

Report of the Working Group on Exchange Market Intervention (Chairman Philippe Jurgensen), 1983, obtainable from HM Treasury

Chapter 45

Green Paper, *Alternatives to Domestic Rates*, (Cmnd 8449), December 1981

Peter Riddell, *The Thatcher Decade*, Basil Blackwell, 1989

Chapter 46

Green Paper, *Paying for Local Government*, (Cmnd 9714), January 1986

John Muellbauer, *The Great British Housing Disaster and Economic Policy*, Institute of Public Policy Research, 1990

Nicholas Ridley, *My Style of Government*, Hutchinson, 1991

Chapter 47

Samuel Brittan and Stephen Webb, *Beyond the Welfare State*, Aberdeen University Press, 1990

Norman Fowler, *Ministers Decide*, Chapmans, 1991

HM Government Green Paper, *Reform of Social Security* (Cmnd 9517/8), HMSO, 1985

HM Government White Paper, *Reform of Social Security* (Cmnd 9691), HMSO, 1985

HM Government Green Paper, *The Reform of Personal Taxation* (Cmnd 9756), HMSO, 1986

Chapter 48

Corelli Barnett, *The Audit of War*, Macmillan, 1986

Chapter 49

DHSS, *Working for Patients*, (Cmnd 553), HMSO, 1989

Lord Chancellor's Department, *The Work and Organisation of the Legal Profession*, (Cmnd 570), HMSO, 1989

Lord Chancellor's Department, *Conveyancing by Authorised Practitioners*, (Cmnd 572), HMSO, 1989

Lord Chancellor's Department, *Contingency Fees*, (Cmnd 571), HMSO 1989

Quintin Hailsham, *A Sparrow's Flight*, Collins, 1990

Lord Chancellor's Department, *Legal Services: A Framework for the Future*, (Cmnd 740), HMSO,1989

Chapter 50

Central Statistical Office, *Economic Trends,* January 1991

Milton Friedman, *The Optimum Quantity of Money and Other Essays,* Aldine Publishing, 1969

Milton Friedman, *A Theory of the Consumption Function*, Princeton University, 1959

Robin Leigh-Pemberton, 'Financial Change and Broad Money', *Bank of England Quarterly Bulletin*, December 1986

Mervyn King, *On Policies Towards Savings*, Keynote Address to SUERF Colloquium, Bank of England, 1991

John Muellbauer, *The Great British Housing Disaster and Economic Policy*, Nuffield College, Oxford, 1990

J. R. Sargent, *Debt, Regulation and Downturn in the UK Economy*, National Institute Review, August 1991

Chapter 51

'The Treasury's Forecasting Performance', *Treasury Bulletin*, HMSO, Autumn 1990

Chapter 54

Fourth Report from the Defence Committee, House of Commons, 1986

Magnus Linklater and David Leigh, 'Not With Honour', *Observer*, 1988

Chapter 55

C.V. Brown et al, *Taxation and Family Labour and Supply in Great Britain*, University of Stirling, 1986

C.V. Brown and C. Sandford, *Taxes and Incentives: The Effects of the 1988 Cuts*, Institute of Public Policy Research, 1990

Chapter 56

Colin Hughes and Patrick Wintour, *Labour Rebuilt*, Fourth Estate, 1991

LIST OF WORKS CITED

Nigel Lawson, *The New Britain: the tide of ideas from Attlee to Thatcher*, Centre for Policy Studies, 1988
Norman Tebbit, *Upwardly Mobile*, Weidenfeld & Nicolson, 1988
David Young, *The Enterprise Years*, Headline Press, 1990

Chapter 60

I. M. Destler and C. Randall Henning, *Dollar Politics: Exchange Rate Policymaking in the United States*, Institute of International Economics, Washington, 1989
William Keegan, *Mr Lawson's Gamble*, Hodder and Stoughton, 1989

Chapter 62

Monopolies and Mergers Commission, *The Government of Kuwait and the British Petroleum Company*, (Cmnd 477) HMSO,1988
David Young, *The Enterprise Years*, Headline, 1990

Chapter 64

Paul Volcker and Toyoo Gyohten, *Changing Fortunes: The World's Money and the Decline of American Supremacy*, Times Books, 1992
Report of the Working Group on Exchange Market Intervention (Chairman Philippe Jurgensen), March 1983, obtainable from HM Treasury

Chapter 68

Nigel Lawson, *The State of the Market*, Institute of Economic Affairs, 1988

Chapter 69

John Fforde, *The Bank of England and Public Policy 1941–1958*, Cambridge University Press, 1991
Geoffrey Howe, Keith Joseph, James Prior and David Howell, *The Right Approach to the Economy*, Conservative Central Office, 1977

Chapter 70

The Taxation of Husband and Wife (Cmnd 8093), HMSO, 1980
The Reform of Personal Taxation, (Cmnd 9756), HMSO, 1986

Chapter 72

Nigel Lawson, *What Sort of Europe?*, Conservative Political Centre, 1989

Ronald McKinnon, *Towards a Common Monetary Standard*, Economics Department, Stanford University, 1989

Chapter 73

Nigel Lawson, *Rules versus Discretion in the Conduct of Economic Policy* (Stamp Memorial Lecture), University of London, 1990

Chapter 78

Samuel Brittan, 'The Thatcher Government's Economic Policy' in *The Thatcher Factor* (eds. D. Kavanagh and A. Seldon), Oxford University Press, 1989

Andrew Britton, *Macroeconomic Policy in Britain*, 1974–87, Cambridge University Press, 1991

Kathleen Burt and Alec Cairncross, *'Goodbye Great Britain' – The 1976 IMF Crisis*, Yale University Press, 1992

'Cyclical Indicators', latest version monthly in *Economic Trends*, CSO

D. Henderson, 'Perestroika in the West' in John Niewenhuysen (ed.) *Towards Free Trade Between Nations*, Oxford University Press, 1989

Nigel Lawson, *British Capitalism Resurgent*, Stock Exchange, 1985

Geoffrey Maynard, *The Economy under Mrs Thatcher*, Basil Blackwell, 1989

P.E. Middleton 'Economic Policy in the Treasury in the Post-War Period', *National Institute Economic Review*, February 1989

D. McWilliams, Inaugural Lecture, Kingston Business School, 1988

Social Trends, CSO, 1992

HM Treasury, *Supply-side Performance in the 1980s*, Treasury Bulletin, Summer, 1992

Chapter 79

Alan Watkins, *A Conservative Coup: The Fall of Margaret Thatcher*, Duckworth, 1991

Chapter 80

Institute for Fiscal Studies, Green Budget, 1991

Oxford Economic Forecasting, *UK Economic Prospects*, April 1992, Templeton College, Oxford

INDEX

INDEX

INDEX

INDEX

INDEX

1110

INDEX

INDEX

1117